COUNTERPOINT

COUNTERPOINT
Perspectives on Asian America

Editor
Emma Gee

Associate Editors
Bruce Iwasaki
Mike Murase
Megumi Dick Osumi
Jesse Quinsaat

Assistant Editor
June Okida Kuramoto

Art Directors
Dean S. Toji
Glen Iwasaki

Asian American Studies Center
University of California
Los Angeles

ACKNOWLEDGEMENTS AND COPYRIGHT NOTICES

Grateful acknowledgement is made to:

University of California Press for permission to reprint, with changes, the "Introduction" by Yuji Ichioka from *A Buried Past: An Annotated Bibliography of the Japanese American Research Project Collection* by Yuji Ichioka, Yasuo Sakata, Nobuya Tsuchida, and Eri Yasuhara. Copyright © 1974 by The Regents of the University of California. This is an updated version of the original essay.

Raymond Okamura for permission to print "The Concentration Camp Experience from a Japanese American Perspective: A Bibliographical Essay and Review of Michi Weglyn's *Years of Infamy*." Copyright © 1976 by Raymond Y. Okamura.

The Journal of Ethnic Studies for permission to reprint a book review on Ivan Light's *Ethnic Enterprise in America* by L. Ling-chi Wang. Copyright © 1974 by the College of Ethnic Studies, Western Washington State College.

Amerasia Journal for permission to reprint, with changes, "A Buried Past: Early Issei Socialists and the Japanese Community" by Yuji Ichioka. Copyright © 1971 by Yale Asian American Students Association.

Bulletin of Concerned Asian Scholars for permission to reprint, with changes, "A Historical Survey of Organizations of the Left Among the Chinese in America" by H. Mark Lai. Copyright © 1972 by Bulletin of Concerned Asian Scholars. This is an expanded version of the original article and appears here under the title of "A Historical Survey of the Chinese Left in America."

Studies in Race and Nations for permission to reprint material from "In Search of a New Paradigm: Minorities in the Context of International Politics" by Don T. Nakanishi. Copyright © 1975 by (Colorado Seminary) University of Denver. The excerpts from pages 1-7, 21-25 appear here under the title "Minorities & International Politics."

Raymond Okamura for permission to print "Iva Ikuko Toguri: Victim of an American Fantasy." Copyright © 1976 by Raymond Y. Okamura.

Bridge for permission to reprint "The Vietnam Evacuees... What Now?" by Le Anh Tu. Copyright © 1975 by Basement Workshop, Inc.

Philippine News and Alex A. Esclamado for permission to reprint "The Story of the Marcos Coercion." Copyright © 1975 by Philippine News.

The New Korea and Woon-Ha Kim for permission to reprint "KCIA Agents All Out to Get *New Korea*," copyright © 1975 by The New Korea, and to use his congressional statement of 17 March 1976, "The Activities of the South Korean Central Intelligence Agency in the United States."

Bridge for permission to reprint "The Kuomintang in Chinatown" by [Brett de Bary and] Victor Nee. Copyright © 1972 by Basement Workshop, Inc.

University of California Press for permission to reprint material from *The Indispensable Enemy: Labor and the Anti-Chinese Movement in California* by Alexander Saxton. Copyright © 1971 by The Regents of the University of California.

University of the Philippines Press for permission to reprint material from *Carlos Bulosan and the Imagination of the Class Struggle* by E. San Juan, Jr. Copyright © 1972 by the University of the Philippines Press.

Yuji Ichioka for permission to print "The 1921 Turlock Incident: Forceful Expulsion of Japanese Laborers." Copyright © 1976 by Yuji Ichioka.

CONTENTS

PART II: CONTEMPORARY ISSUES

EDUCATION

COMMUNICATIONS AND MASS MEDIA

x

Preface

The tumultuous events of the sixties and seventies dramatized the existing fissures in our nation, belying the smug self-image of America as a harmonious, democratic, and open society. The struggles of Afro-Americans to achieve equality revealed how racism is still deeply embedded in national attitudes and established institutions. The brutal intervention in Southeast Asia raised disturbing questions about our foreign policy and its relationship to domestic politics permeated by that racism. In the late 1960s, following the example of Afro-Americans, other racial minorities (and even some white ethnic groups) began to reassess their past experience in America and to reaffirm their ethnic identities, which had survived despite overwhelming pressures to obliterate them.

All these events influenced Asian Americans. They too turned to reexamine their own histories, experiencing mixed emotions of anger at past injustices, of pride in their own distinctive ethnic identities and cultures, and of hope in solving present problems. In short, they deepened their understanding of their own past and present political, economic, and social position in American society. Concurrent with and inseparable from this richer understanding was the emergence of Asian American studies in many colleges and universities. A pioneering venture, the scope and direction of Asian American studies have yet to be defined clearly, but certain lines of development can be discerned. The purpose of this anthology is to present works which reflect some of the current trends.

Realizing that no one anthology can be comprehensive, we have selected works which explore racial and economic conflicts and analyze the impact of international politics. These forces of conflict substantially shaped, and continue to shape, the experience of Asian Americans. Although the selections take different approaches, with few exceptions they share a common thread. They view Asian Americans as active participants in the making of history. From the standpoint of various Asian American groups, each with their own distinctive identity and history, these works examine their diverse responses to these dynamic forces within the larger American socio-economic context.

The anthology is divided into three major parts: I) Critical Perspectives, II) Contemporary Issues, and III) Literature. Parts I and III had separate editors who provide their own introductions. Part II is subdivided into four sections; each section had separate editors who also have written their own introductions. The two appendices, one on statistical highlights of the 1970 census and the other on bibliographical sources, are designed as aids to the readers for further study. Half of the selections appear in print for the first time; the remainder are expanded, revised, or unrevised reprints with deletions from the originals indicated by ellipses. In contemporary articles, instead of "Filipino" we have used "Pilipino," the preferred designation of many members of the Pilipino American community; in reprinted articles, we have retained the original spelling of the authors.

Specifically, Part I offers bibliographical essays and book reviews which critique the conventional approaches of past works and suggest new ones for future studies. Recent studies interpreting the Asian American experience within a national and international context follow as concrete examples of new approaches. Central to this part is the notion that the implicit or explicit conceptual framework of the author determines her or his findings.

Part II covers some of the major present concerns of Asian Americans. The first section, Education, has essays on ethnic studies and higher education, community educational projects, quality bilingual and bicultural education, and personal accounts of teaching classes on ethnic studies and Asian American women. The next section, Communications and Mass Media, traces the invidious influences, both historic and contemporary, of the communications and media industry in portraying Asian Americans as less than human. It also reveals Asian Americans have been creating their own forms of communications to express their concerns and distinct ways of living. The third section, Land, Labor, and Capital, discusses the nature of economic exploitation and racial oppression in relation to Asian Americans. Finally, the last section, Recent Immigration, contains essays on the much neglected Asian Americans and Pacific peoples—Koreans, Pilipinos, East Indians, and Samoans.

Part III is devoted entirely to literature. Asian Americans are now discovering their literary past and present. It is no accident that some of the most powerful creative stories by Asian American writers center on the daily lives of Asian immigrants, be they the strong but tragic Issei women of Hisaye Yamamoto and Wakako Yamauchi, the manongs and migrant workers of Bienvenido Santos and Carlos Bulosan, or the aged Chinatown bachelors and fathers of Louis Chu and Frank Chin. The writings here exemplify the literary creativity of Asian American writers whose works communicate a vision, a vision rooted in the social realities of Asian America.

A cooperative undertaking, this book rests on the labors of others. We are indebted to so many persons and groups that we despair of acknowledging all we owe. If we are remiss in acknowledging our indebtedness in a particular case, we ask indulgence. Without the experience, assistance, and advice of many members of our communities, this anthology could not have been undertaken. In particular, our gratitude to those who originally saw the pressing need for a new volume on Asian Americans and provided the initial impetus. To all those who submitted their works for our perusal, we thank them for teaching us about the many facets of the Asian American experience. Any failings in understanding, of course, are ours. We regret we were forced to omit many interesting works owing to the intractable problem of space, time, and cost. For generously allowing us to use their photographs and laboratory facilities, our thanks to Visual Communications, a creative group of Asian American filmmakers. We, to say the least, owe an enormous debt to our contributors—the authors, illustrators, and photographers. Without them there would have been no anthology.

We thank the former and present members of the UCLA Asian American Studies Center for recognizing the need for this work and for supporting our project this past year. We are indebted especially to Michiko Takahashi for her critical comments and proofreading skills, and for saving us from many mistakes. For assistance in the production work, our gratitude to Aleen Holly for enthusiastically doing more than her share of the laborious typesetting and for returning to help us in the final, nerve-wracking stage; to Carol K. Ng for aiding us in proofreading the voluminous galleys; and to Alan Takemoto for his illustrations and suggestions that reflect his imaginative spirit. The thanks we owe to Carolyn Yee and Ron Hirano cannot be easily rendered. Despite their many responsibilities at the Center, they suffered through our countless meetings and worked with us, a motley and cantankerous group. Their encouragement, interest, and sense of humor kept us going. Putting their special knowledge, editorial skills, and critical judgment at our disposal, they gave liberally of their time and wit.

It is only fair to say this volume contains ideas with which many of us, including the staff, may disagree. That is its intent. The selections are intended to be suggestive rather than definitive. We present this book with a heavy load of gratitude and with the hope that it is kept alive by criticism. The dialectical process, after all, shapes our Asian American experience with all its anguish, its delights, its diversity, and its hopes.

—**Emma Gee**
Editor

CRITICAL PERSPECTIVES

WE WISH TO LIVE
LIKE AMERICANS-
BUT IMPOSSIBLE
77¢ A DAY

Introduction

No matter what the subject may be, all inquiries start out with questions which embody assumptions. In the words of Susanne K. Langer, "questions make the framework in which its picture of facts is plotted . . .; they give the angle of perspective."[1] Why did God create the universe is a question, for example, which assumes that God exists, that the universe was created, and that it is causally intelligible. The question rules out the contrary propositions that God does not exist, that the universe was not created, and that it is unintelligible. Thus the way the question is formulated defines the perspective within which it will be answered and limits the possible answers to it. This holds true for any questions posed about Asian Americans.

Asian Americans have been studied with specific questions which have defined perspectives and limited answers. This section consists of critiques of past and recent studies and essays on special topics suggesting alternative perspectives. Some are polemical; others are preliminary probings to chart new terrains. All are here to aid in the search to uncover the wrong questions divorced from social reality and to raise new questions rooted in it.

Two diametrically opposing explanations of the Chinese exclusion movement illustrate the vital importance of perspectives in studying Asian Americans. Gunther Barth, an American historian, attributes the causes of the movement to the Chinese laborers themselves. Assuming assimilation as desirable and the willingness of white America to accept the Chinese as equals, he concludes that the failure of the Chinese to take the opportunity to assimilate aroused the animosity of white Americans who then excluded them.[2] On the other hand, Liu Ta-nien, a Chinese historian, ascribes the causes to the American capitalist class. Assuming class struggle as the primal force in history and the common class interests of Chinese and white workers, he asserts that the capitalist class misled the white workers, who were in the forefront of the movement, to believe falsely that the Chinese were responsible for their unemployment.[3] This difference of interpretation is not one of facts. Rather it is explained by the different questions, embodying divergent assumptions, which the two historians raised about the exclusion movement. In short, they had different perspectives.

CRITIQUES

The emergence of Asian American studies marks a shift away from old perspectives. To critique past and present ones, the section begins with three bibliographical essays. In the first essay, Yuji Ichioka surveys the English-language secondary literature on

CRITICAL PERSPECTIVES

the history of the Japanese in America prior to World War II. The literature has severe limitations because it is preoccupied with the origins, causes, and development of the Japanese exclusion movement and the effects it had on U.S.-Japan relations. Since immigrant-language sources rarely have been studied, the literature offers nothing in the way of analyzing how the Japanese immigrants, the excluded, reacted to being excluded, and little about the origins and development of Japanese immigrant society. The use of immigrant-language sources has been a long accepted requirement in the study of European immigration to America. Future studies on the Japanese, Ichioka concludes, must research Japanese-language sources and raise questions about the immigrants themselves, a conclusion which applies equally to other Asian immigrant groups.

Reviewing the literature on the World War II internment of Japanese Americans, Raymond Okamura reaches a similar conclusion in the third bibliographical essay. Based for the most part on War Relocation Authority records and data collected by WRA-affiliated persons, most works on this topic, wittingly or unwittingly, adopt the point of view of the WRA. Accepting the argument that internment was a "military necessity" and for the "safety" of the Japanese themselves, they justify it, interpret it as

having been beneficial to the prisoners, and present camp life as having been harmonious. Michi Weglyn, *Years of Infamy*, a recent publication, exemplifies how old interpretations can be debunked, according to Okamura. Using hitherto untapped sources, the book contests past causal explanations, proving the culpability of the American government and placing the responsibility for internment on the highest civilian authorities. Okamura believes that more analytical works in the light of additional sources and new questions should be written by Japanese Americans to present the internment experience from their own perspective.

Past studies of Asian Americans have been dominated overwhelmingly by questions relating to their so-called assimilability into American society. These questions were posed within the framework of various theories of assimilation, and though the theories differed, they shared three essential assumptions. These were 1) the willingness of the dominant political and economic classes to accept racial minorities as full and equal members of society; 2) the superiority of urban, middle-class, and predominantly Anglo-Saxon Protestant values; and 3) the necessity of racial minorities to discard conflicting values, derived from their own ethnic heritage, as the price of acceptance. Sympathetic as well as unsympathetic writers, both of European and Asian origins, have spent an inordinate amount of time, energy, and money to prove or disprove the assimilability of Asian Americans within the framework of these assumptions. Will they assimilate, can they assimilate, and, more recently, how have they assimilated?—these questions literally fill tens of thousands of pages in academic journals and books, political tracts, church and newspaper accounts, government studies, and popular literature.

In the second bibliographical essay, Lucie Cheng Hirata surveys the sociological works on the Chinese, most of which are written within an assimilationist framework. She argues that past sociological models applied to them upheld the maintenance of the status quo in the larger society because they placed the burden of social change on the Chinese themselves. Tracing the responses of sociologists to the events of the 1960s, she then examines alternative theories to explain the sociological position of racial minorities. Specifically, they are the theories of cultural pluralism, the culture of poverty, institutional racism, internal colonialism, and Marxism. Since the first two alternatives still do not challenge the status quo, the last three alone offer meaningful interpretations, for they recognize the need for fundamental structural changes in American society. As a step in the right direction, Hirata recommends that future studies on the Chinese, and by extension on other Asian American groups, should be conducted accordingly.

Four separate reviews of specific books follow the foregoing bibliographical essays. Before World War II, Asian Americans were attacked for having certain cultural traits which allegedly hindered their assimilation. Now they find themselves praised for "unique" cultural traits in order to explain their current "success." Jerry Surh reviews Harry H. L. Kitano, *The Japanese Americans: The Evolution of a Sub-Culture*, and William Petersen, *Japanese Americans: Oppression and Success*, while L. Ling-chi Wang reviews Ivan H. Light, *Ethnic Enterprise in America: Business and Welfare Among Chinese, Japanese, and Blacks*. All three studies attempt to interpret the postwar "success" of the Japanese and Chinese in cultural terms. Both reviewers take the authors to task for their cold statistical definition of success.[4] They also fault them for their woefully inadequate historical and sociological knowledge of the Japanese and Chinese. For Surh, Kitano's study has the one redeeming value of being a personal account, albeit it unconscious, of a middle-class Nisei who is not yet ready to dismiss racism towards Asian Americans as a relic of the past. Finally, both reviewers are dismayed at the implication of the studies, especially Petersen's and Light's. Attributing the success or failure of racial minorities to factors within the groups, they invidiously compare them and absolve the larger society of any responsibility. Such a comparative cultural approach "pits one minority group against another," as Wang states, "and instills hatred among minority groups," and moreover, as Surh declares, glosses over "the whole ugly history of white domination of political, social, and economic power in the United States and the use of it to subordinate colored and other minorities to the sway of white money and property."

Linda P. Shin reviews three studies of Chinese Americans: Gunther Barth, *Bitter Strength: A History of the Chinese in the United States, 1850-1870*, Betty Lee Sung, *The Story of the Chinese in America* (published first under the title, *Mountain of Gold*), and Stanford M. Lyman, *Chinese Americans*. Reviewing the first two studies, Shin regards them as examples of the pitfalls awaiting historians who blindly accept assumptions and values. She contends that Barth neither questioned the value judgements and assumptions of the nineteenth century English-language sources on which he entirely based his study, nor those of his own times. The result is his book in which he depicts the Chinese in highly negative, if not downright insulting, terms, adhering to a chauvinistic white interpretation of the Chinese and perpetuating the myth of American goodness. Though not as sanguine about America as Barth, Betty Lee Sung reveals herself as a Chinese American who also fails to question American society. Still feeling the need to prove the assimilability of the Chinese, according to Shin, she chronicles the achievements of successful persons and attributes to individual shortcomings social problems encountered by the Chinese. Shin considers Stanford M. Lyman's study the most informative of the three. Critical of assimilationist views and sensitive to the racism faced by Chinese Americans, Lyman, though, does not adequately correlate the social problems of the Chinese to the larger American social structure in Shin's opinion.

As the final review, Don T. Nakanishi reviews Roger Daniels and Harry H. L. Kitano, *American Racism: Exploration of the Nature of Prejudice*. Though this study combines history and modern social science, he believes that it offers a much too simple interpretation of the nature of American racism. Viewing California society as divided along a color line in a paternalistic two-category system, the authors' analysis, argues Nakanishi, is disjointed and fuzzy, and does not provide any deeper insights into the dynamics of racism.

From these bibliographical essays and reviews, it should be apparent that the Asian American experience, in all its diversity and richness, has never been fully studied either on its own terms or as an integral part of American history and America's relation to

Asia. We know much about what has been done to Asian Americans, but principally through the parochial and distorted perspectives of whites. General histories, not to mention specific community histories, of the various Asian American groups remain to be written. Forced by the tumultuous events of the sixties and seventies, some scholars belatedly began to recognize the centrality of racism in American society. Acknowledging no more than its existence, their analyses still do not delve into the deep roots of racism, which continue to have a powerful and dynamic impact. Riddled with wrong questions and dubious value judgements, the perspectives of the past clearly are inappropriate for the present. At best they form a useful point of departure to develop more promising approaches to understand the Asian American experience, and by extension, America.

RECENT PERSPECTIVES

The selections which follow are examples of newer perspectives. They dig down into that experience, offer new ways of understanding the forces which shaped the present, and raise new questions for more improved research in areas which have yet to be mined. Each article treats its subject from a particular perspective, but all of them generally attempt to interpret their topics within a broader national or international context.

The first two historical essays are unique in that they rely primarily on immigrant-language sources and uncover in detail a little-known radical tradition among the Japanese and Chinese in the United States. Yuji Ichioka studies Issei socialists and anarchists in the first decade of the twentieth century, adopting the perspective that they can be understood only by examining the impact modern Japanese political history had on them within the larger context of American history. Within his broad framework, he demonstrates how the immigrant leftists were influenced by socialist leaders from Japan and events there, why they became disillusioned with American socialists, how they tried to organize Issei migrant laborers into an agricultural labor union, and how the 1911 Bakersfield lese majesty incident was related to the activities of Issei socialists as well as to anti-Christian ideas originating in Japan. H. Mark Lai, on the other hand, traces the organizations and activities of the Chinese left in America from the eve of World War I through the McCarthy era of the 1950s. He approaches his subject by delineating the intimate connection between the experiences of Chinese immigrants and the political developments both in China and America. Central to his study is his thesis that Chinese American leftists were influenced significantly by three interrelated factors: the discrimination and exploitation faced by the Chinese in America, their desire for a strong, independent China free from foreign imperialism, and the intellectual attraction to modern political ideologies of nationalism, democracy, and socialism. Hence Lai too places his study in a broad perspective similar to Ichioka's. Both essays suggest that other facets of Asian American history might be fruitfully studied in like manner.

Minorities and International Politics

The third essay is a theoretical piece by Don T. Nakanishi who proposes new abstract, conceptual tools to study minority groups. Seeing minorities as both victims and beneficiaries of international politics, Nakanishi advocates a multidisciplinary approach within an international context. To support his contention that many wide-ranging topics can be explored with his approach, he presents eighteen of them matched by empirical examples. His perspective rests on several assumptions which he discusses in his piece.

The next eight articles cover the past and present consequences of foreign relations on Asian Americans and their responses to them. Like Ichioka and Lai, each author places his or her topic in the context of the triangular, interacting relationships between Asian immigrants and their descendants, the Asian emigrant countries, and the United States. The mass imprisonment of Japanese Americans during World War II is, of course, the starkest instance of how the advent of a war led to the brutal treatment of a racial minority by the American government. Raymond Okamura's essay on Iva Ikuko Toguri, popularly but erroneously known as "Tokyo Rose," documents in an extreme form how a Japanese American, to paraphrase Ohiye Mori, was a clay pigeon perched on the electric wire of national and international hate once war broke out between America and Japan. Focusing on her plight, he shows how the dynamite mixture of militarism, racism, and sexism caught her in an incredible Kafkaesque web of circumstances from which she still is not completely free, even after an ordeal lasting thirty-five years.

Pilipino stewards in the U.S. Navy and recent Vietnamese refugees constitute the next topics. Sangley Point in Manila Bay, the rent-free headquarters of the U.S. naval forces in the Philippines and the chief support base of the Seventh Fleet, has a special meaning for Pilipino Americans. In 1973 U.S. Navy statistics recorded 9,000 Pilipinos out of a total of 11,000 stewards in the navy. Beginning with their recruitment in the Philippines at Sangley Point, Jesse Quinsaat examines the background and lives of the Pilipino stewards. U.S. naval vessels with such stewards, in his judgement, are "floating plantations" which hark back to the colonial era in Philippine history and result from the unequal "special relations" that the Philippines has with the United States. The American effort to impose its will upon the people of Indochina met a stunning defeat in 1975. With the total collapse of the Thieu regime in April, the American government spread unsubstantiated reports of an impending "communist bloodbath" and undertook a sudden, massive evacuation of certain Vietnamese to America. Le Anh Tu analyzes the immediate and future human consequences of this evacuation for the Vietnamese in America.

Supported by the U.S. government, the Philippines, South Korea, and Taiwan all have dictatorial regimes which are opposed by sizable segments among various Asian American groups. Confronted by the opposition in America, as they have done domestically, these governments have tried to stifle it through unlawful and coercive means. Pilipino Americans, for example, have protested against the Marcos government. One of the most vocal critics is Alejandro A. Esclamado, publisher and editor-in-chief of the *Philippine News,* the largest circulating ethnic newspaper among Pilipino Americans. Reprinted here is an affidavit signed by Esclamado which catalogues the "harassment and blackmail" to which his newspaper, staff, and family have been subjected by the Marcos government and its agents in America.[5]

The effort of the Park Chung-hee government of South Korea to silence the opposition of Korean Americans is notorious. Through the widespread activities of the South Korean Central Intelligence Agency (KCIA), it has resorted to countless forms of pressures, threats, and ill-concealed bribes. Two former high officials of the State Department confirmed these illegal and repressive activities in testimonies on 17 March 1976 before the House Subcommittee on International Organizations investigating KCIA activities in the United States. Gregory Henderson, the erstwhile cultural attache and political officer of the American Embassy in Seoul from 1958-1963, described the KCIA as

> a state within a state—a vast, shadowy world of an estimated 100,000-300,000 bureaucrats, intellectuals, agents and thugs often the real substance of South Korean rule for which . . . the Korean Government Ministries and Parties are frequently a slightly more respectable facade.

Shielded by diplomatic titles and operating out of the Korean embassy and consulates, according to Henderson, KCIA agents with the aid of informers and contacts try to control the Korean communities in America.[6] Responsible for the formulation of U.S. policy towards South Korea, Donald L. Ranard, the Director of the Office of Korean Affairs in the State Department from 1970 to the end of 1974, also testified on the extensive KCIA efforts in the United States to ensure continued American military and economic support of the Park government. According to Ranard's testimony, the KCIA has interfered with the rights of Korean Americans to meet and express freely their views on Korean affairs, has organized pro-Park demonstrations and attempted to break up opposing groups, has supported pro-Park Korean newspapers and journalists, and has made offers of financial support to candidates for political office in the United States.[7]

A staunch and courageous opponent of the Park government is Woon-Ha Kim of Los Angeles who has been subjected to the harsh intimidations of the KCIA. He is the publisher and editor of *The New Korea,* the oldest Korean-language newspaper on the continental United States, founded in 1905. An editorial from the newspaper published on 27 November 1975 and his testimony before the same congressional committee on 17 March 1976 follow as the next selection. The editorial is an indictment of the Park dictatorship, while his testimony vividly describes the many threats upon his person, his staff, and family made by the KCIA in an effort to force him into silence and to shut down his newspaper.

The past actions of the Taiwan government are strikingly parallel to those of the Marcos and Park governments. In a reprinted news article, Brett de Bary Nee and Victor Nee write about the past activities of the Chinese Nationalist Party (KMT) in America. In 1949 the KMT suffered a resounding defeat in China and fled to the province of Taiwan. To insure the survival of its government-in-exile, the KMT mustered anti-communist support and suppressed opposition in the Chinese American communities. Through the so-called China Lobby, it also influenced American public opinion as well as the American government.[8] The Nees trace the connections between the Taiwan consulate and the Chinese Benevolent Association of San Francisco, a KMT-dominated organization of well-to-do merchants, and their mutual efforts to control Chinatown politically. The authors believe that the KMT was successful in controlling Chinatown over the years, but that new forces have emerged to challenge that control.

Regardless of national origins, all immigrant groups retained an interest and involvement in the political affairs of their native countries, at least through the first generation. More than other immigrants, however, the Chinese in America sustained their interest in China and involvement in her political fortunes for over a century. In his original essay, H. Mark Lai explains why. He attributes this prolonged, often passionate participation to two crucial factors. On the one hand, the exclusion of and discrimination against the Chinese in America fostered a sense of rejection, causing them to look to China as their sole homeland where they would be able to enjoy a better life. On the other hand, China was the victim of western imperialism, which reinforced and heightened their identification, propelling them to participate in political movements to establish a strong, modern, and independent China. With events in America and China as the background, Lai examines the origins, composition, and development of three major sociopolitical organizations, their fierce battles with each other, and the impact they had on the Chinese communities from the nineteenth century down to the post-World War II period. Because of the sustained interest in China, Chinese Americans participated in the vortex of Chinese politics through these organizations which originated in the mother country.

Like the Chinese, Korean immigrants in America were deeply committed to the establishment of an independent and modern nation free from foreign domination in their native country. Excerpts from a lengthy manuscript written in 1950 by Kingsley Kyungsang Lyu detail Korean nationalist activities in America from 1901-1945. Based on extensive interviews with Korean immigrants who participated in these political activities and his own experience and observations, Lyu attributes the activities to the colonization of Korea by Japan from 1905 to 1945 and to their keen sense of ethnic consciousness. His study suggests conflict rather than harmony characterized the highly politicized Korean communities in America during that period.

Internal Colonialism

Departing from the perspectives of the preceding essays, John Liu places racial minorities within the national context of America in his essay on internal colonialism. To characterize race relations and highlight institutional racism, Black Power advocates first used the colonial analogy in the 1960s. The position of Blacks in America, they asserted, was analogous to colonized peoples. Other racial minorities then adopted it to describe their own position in society. Soon the term "Third World" emerged in the late 1960s, signifying the common position and interest of racial minorities, the common bonds with the Third World, and the belief that classical colonialism and white racism had the same roots in Western imperialism. Though the colonial analogy was never defined clearly, it implied that just as an irreconcilable conflict existed between colonizers and the colonized, so, too, were racial minorities in conflict with whites.[9] When Black social theorists such as Harold Cruse and Kenneth Clark employed the analogy, they used it mainly for descriptive purposes. It was not until the publication of *Black Power: The Politics of Liberation in America* by Stokely Carmichael and Charles Hamilton in 1967, in which they refined the analogy into a theory, that it came into vogue as a serious concept in social analysis. Thereafter other scholars and political activists followed suit and formulated their own versions of it. John Liu reviews the considerable literature on this topic. Comparing internal colonialism to classical colonialism, he examines the assumptions and political implications of the internal colonial model.

Class and Race

Modern ideas of class, race, and nation are inventions of the West in the nineteenth century. Reinforced by evolutionary doctrines justifying ruthless competition and exploitation, they had profound influences on Western societies which developed into capitalist social orders marked by the appearance of distinctive class relations. As industrialization proceeded, accompanied by an increasing disparity of wealth and power endemic to the capitalist system, all western societies experienced deep class conflicts. Parallel to and inseparable from this industrialization was the onslaught of Western imperialism on non-European peoples. To sanction the ensuing colonialism, racial ideas were honed attributing superiority to the white ruling race and imposed upon subject colored races.[10] With few exceptions, American scholars have failed to dissect and analyze the interrelationship of class and race in America. Concentrating on either class or race exclusively—admittedly the latter much more than the former—they have not explored the dynamic interplay of class and racial conflicts in the development of America. The remaining four selections assess the interaction of the two as they affected Asian Americans.

In the excerpt from his book, *The Indispensable Enemy,* Alexander Saxton reinterprets the relationship between the anti-Chinese and labor movements in the post-civil war period. Postbellum America underwent rapid industrial growth characterized by great concentrations of wealth and severe periodic depressions, both of which sharpened class conflicts. Placing the anti-Chinese movement within this national economic setting, Saxton challenges the long-held view that the movement was unique to the west coast and that economic competition between Chinese and white workers explains it. Given the sharpening class conflicts and preexisting racist ideas, white workers were pulled in two directions. They were attracted simultaneously to ideas of class consciousness and of white racial exclusivity, but in Saxton's words "racial identification cut at right angles to class consciousness." Foregoing class solidarity, they opted for Chinese exclusion and racial exclusivity. Saxon argues that the white hostility towards the Chinese was an extension of preceding national patterns of racial hatred of Indians and Blacks and antedated the appearance of economic competition. He concludes that the Chinese served as the "indispensable enemy" to unite heterogeneous whites into a racially exclusive white labor movement and helped further the dominance of the skilled trades in organized labor, the effects of which still exist today.

From the nineteenth century, Hawaiian haole sugar planters imported many laborers of diverse ethnic origins to Hawaii to meet their labor demands. Failing to recruit white laborers and fearing the predominance of any one non-white group, they preferred a mixed labor force divided along ethnic lines. At the turn of the century, however, Japanese laborers comprised the majority of plantation workers. In 1909 and 1920 these Japanese laborers instigated two major strikes which, in contrast to earlier spontaneous and isolated strikes, were well-organized, protracted, and widespread. In addition to Japanese laborers, Pilipino workers also participated in the 1920 one. To crush the strikes, especially in 1920, the white planters obscured the class issues raised by the strikers, accusing the Japanese workers of nationalism and unassimilability and depicting the Pilipinos as puppets of Japanese agitators. Alan Moriyama examines the responses of the Japanese strikers to these accusations, and concludes his essay on the implications of class and race in multiethnic coalitions in labor conflicts.

A Pilipino laborer, labor organizer, and talented writer, Carlos Bulosan wrote about Pilipino peasants and immigrants with whom he shared a common experience in both the Philippines and America. The excerpt here is from *Carlos Bulosan and the Imagination of the Class Struggle,* a literary critique of his extensive writings by E. San Juan, Jr., another Pilipino American writer (excerpts from Bulosan's writings appear in other sections of this anthology). Capturing the racism, exploitation, and poverty suffered by Pilipino immigrants, in San Juan's opinion, Bulosan's artistry was combined with his perception of a class-divided Philippines and America. He fused "life and art," merged his private self into the collective identity of the exploited, which San Juan attributes to his deep sense of roots in peasant origins. Sustain-

ing him through periods of bitterness and despair, Bulosan had faith in the unlimited potential of the exploited as a class, regardless of race or national origins, to change its human condition and to be in turn changed.

Finally, Yuji Ichioka writes about the 1921 Turlock incident in the last essay. Involving the forceful expulsion of Japanese agricultural laborers from the town of Turlock, his original study shows how class and racial factors were both causes of the incident. Though economic competition existed between Japanese and white laborers, it was not the only cause. The expulsion was planned by leading citizens of the town, sanctioned by the majority of the townspeople, and executed by white laborers. Occurring when the Japanese exclusion movement was reaching its peak, class and racial factors were so intermeshed that, at least in this instance, it is impossible to separate them in the author's view.

CONCLUSION

The selections in this section barely scratch the surface of the Asian experience in America. Offering glimpses into the past history and present status of Asian Americans, they suggest the need for much more in-depth research. Because past researchers have failed to examine immigrant-language sources, there are no adequate general histories of any Asian American group, making history the field where research is most sorely required. For every Asian American group, major historical topics still await full treatment. The origins and causes of emigration, the birth and development of immigrant communities, the social, political, economic, cultural, and religious aspects of immigrant life, and biographies of eminent and ordinary immigrants—these and other topics all require monographic study based on immigrant-language sources. In sum, many historical monographs must be undertaken to gain the necessary historical knowledge upon which future general histories, and indeed future sociological works, can and must rest.

Apart from the need for historical studies, the importance of perspectives cannot be overemphasized. The mere study of immigrant-language sources does not automatically preclude narrow or distorted interpretations. By immersing themselves in such sources, researchers can easily fall prey to the pitfall of treating Asian Americans in total isolation without any relationship to forces outside them. To be truly meaningful, future studies must place Asian Americans in a wider context, whether that be American society, the emigrant nation, the dialectical interplay between both,[11] or broad theories derived from the social sciences. Ideally, questions should be so formulated that answers to them will increase understanding not only of Asian Americans but also of the larger forces that have influenced them, and that they in turn have influenced. The articles in this section exemplify perspectives which place the study of Asian Americans in a wider context. By no means exhausting the possibilities, they are presented as tentative examples. To contribute to the further understanding of the diversity and richness of the Asian experience in America, it is hoped that future studies will refine and expand them.

—Emma Gee

Notes

1. Susanne K. Langer, *Philosophy in a New Key: A Study in the Symbolism of Reason, Rite, and Art* (Cambridge, 1951), 4.

2. Gunther Barth, *Bitter Strength: A History of the Chinese in the United States, 1850-1870* (Cambridge, 1964). For a more detailed discussion of Barth's book, see the book review of Linda P. Shin in this section.

3. Liu Ta-nien, *Meiguo Chinhua Shi* (A History of American Aggression against China) (Peking, 1951), 56-68.

4. We should be wary of statistical definitions of success. Like any fact, statistics themselves have no meaning — they must be interpreted. I would like to comment briefly on two statistical indices used by scholars who support the contention that the Chinese and Japanese Americans have been "successful." The first index is that of education based on the 1970 census. Relative to the total population, Chinese and Japanese, 25 years and over, have a slightly higher level of educational attainment. The national median is 12.1 years, the Chinese 12.4, and the Japanese 12.5. But Chinese and Japanese incomes, on the other hand, are not commensurate with their educational levels relative to the total population (see Table 11 in the appendix). If we break down the figures and compare, say, whites and Chinese who have the same educational level and personal income of $10,000 or more, the disparity between education and income is stark. In 1969, of male college graduates, 59.6% whites and 38.3% Chinese earned $10,000 or more, a disparity of 21.3%, despite the fact that twice as many Chinese males have college degrees as compared to whites (Betty Lee Sung, *Chinese American Manpower and Employment* [New York, 1975], Tables 24 and 20 on pp. 94 and 80).

This discrepancy holds true for Asian Americans employed by the so-called most liberal of institutions — colleges and universities. Measured by the criteria set by academia, the American Council of Education in a survey of over 50,000 academics reported that faculty of Asian descent in 1972-1973 earned less than white or black faculty, though better qualified than either, and that they were substantially underpaid relative to others with the identical qualifications in the same fields (Thomas Sowell, " 'Affirmative Action' Reconsidered," *The Public Interest*, 42 [Winter 1976], 52 and 62). Moreover, the least qualified whites were paid more than the least qualified minorities. Despite their concentration in the high-paying natural sciences and with more Ph.D.'s from higher-ranked departments, according to Sowell, Asian American faculty "are almost invariably the lowest paid, by two or three thousand dollars per year in every field for any given level of degree and any given number of articles published" (*ibid.*, 62). In short, the disparity in education and income, reflected in even

institutions of higher learning, means that the educational level of Asian Americans divorced from income is a questionable measure of success. Education no doubt has been a prime means of upward economic mobility for a good number of Asian Americans since World War II, but that mobility is still limited. Rather than proving their "success," the disparity raises the question of why they are doing so poorly relative to whites.

The second statistical index is that of national median family income. Family income statistics are also very misleading unless they are related to other factors. It makes a significant difference, for example, if a given family income is earned by a single breadwinner, or by two or more persons. According to the 1970 census, Asian Americans have a much higher percentage of families with more than one earner (51% of all U.S. families compared to 60% of Chinese and Japanese families, and 61% of Pilipinos; see also census highlights on incomes in the appendix). To cite a specific example, of all Chinese families in the $10,000 to $14,999 income bracket, 56.9% had more than one earner, of whom 9.4% had five (Sung, 204). If we add unpaid Asian American family workers commonly found in small business, who are not counted by the Census, the percentage would be even higher. The point is simple. Family income alone does not mean much either without correlating it to the number of earners families have. If it takes one breadwinner to earn $10,000 in one family and two or more in another to make the same income, the two families cannot be judged equally "successful."

Family income should also be correlated to the national distribution of income. While real income in general has risen since World War II, the national distribution has been constant. Notwithstanding the economic growth in the postwar period, the gross inequalities in income distribution have not been reduced. In 1972 the bottom 20% of families received 5% of the total income whereas the top 20% earned an astounding 43% — figures hardly at variance with those of the late 1940s (Alice M. Rivlin, "Income Distribution — Can Economists Help?" *The American Economic Review*, 65:2 [May 1975], 4). The absolute gap between the relatively rich and relatively poor and between the poor and median families indeed have widened, according to Rivlin (*ibid.*, 1-4; U.S. Census reports for 1974 and 1975 confirm this growing gap between the rich and the poor). The family incomes of Asian Americans take on meaning only when they are placed within the context of this national distribution of income.

Finally, the national distribution of wealth (wealth defined as the value of an individual's property and possessions) offers the best gauge to interpret family income statistics. The top 20% of all families, who earned 43% of the total income in 1972, had close to 80% of the total wealth in the country. The findings of a M.I.T. economist more glaringly reveal the extreme concentration of private ownership of wealth. According to Lester C. Thurow, "those with wealth of more than $5 million (the top 0.008% of the population) own as many assets as the bottom half of all families" ("Tax Wealth, Not Income," *The New York Times Magazine,* 11 April 1976, p. 32). Within the context of the national distribution of wealth, the income of Asian Americans — and the vast majority of all Americans — pales into insignificance, making any statistical definition of success based upon census median income figures rather ludicrous.

5. For other articles on the intimidation of Pilipino Americans, see various issues of the *Philippine News.*

6. In his testimony, Henderson, professor in the humanities at Case Western Reserve University (Cleveland), described the eight bureaus of the KCIA and its multifarious activities at home and abroad. See Gregory Henderson, "The Activities of the Korean Central Intelligence Agency," testimony given before 94th Congress, 2d sess., House, Committee of International Relations, Subcommittee on International Organizations, hearing on 17 March 1976, fourteen-page mimeo.

7. In his testimony before the House, Ranard came right to the point. The present KCIA, "as its name alone connotes, was established with the technical advice and financial assistance of our government" immediately following the military coup of Park Chung-hee in 1961. He also testified that in mid-1973 he had called for an FBI investigation of the KCIA in the United States, but it never "got off the ground." He surmised that "the FBI, or those above it in authority, had no inclination to follow through on an investigation which could wind up embarrassing an ally." See Donald L. Ranard, "The Activities of the Korean Central Intelligence Agency in the United States," statement before the House subcommittee on International Organizations . . . , eleven-page mimeo.

8. See Ross Y. Koen, *The China Lobby in American Politics* (New York, 1960); recently reissued by Harper & Row in 1974, ed. and with an introduction by Richard C. Kagan. This influential coalition of Chinese Nationalist officials and right-wing American supporters successfully pressured MacMillan, the first publisher, to take the book off the market as soon as it appeared in 1960. Enjoined from distributing it, the publisher destroyed over 4,000 copies according to Richard C. Kagan.

9. These ideas, directly or indirectly, influenced such diverse political movements as cultural nationalism, separatism, national liberation struggles, ethnic studies, community control, and other revolutionary programs among various racial minorities.

10. The political history of the twentieth century is in large measure one of chickens coming home to roost. Tenets of nationalism, race consciousness, and class doctrines are now used by Third World countries to ward off the power and influence of the West.

11. One possible study which comes to mind is the relationship of industrial development in nineteenth-century America to American imperialism in China and Chinese immigration to America. To be more precise, in view of the high demand for capital and labor in railroad construction, how were the lucrative China trade, the investments in railroad building, and the importation of Chinese immigrant labor interconnected? As a distinct capitalist class, many linked by kinship ties, Boston merchants engaged in the China trade, some of whom were American merchant-consuls stationed in Chinese treaty ports. Arthur M. Johnson and Barry E. Supple, *Boston Capitalists and Western Railroads: A Study in Nineteenth Century Investment Process* (Cambridge, 1967), shows that the huge profits from the early China trade, consisting of opium, silk, and tea, were invested in railroads built from the eastern seaboard westward from 1830-1890. Other studies demonstrate clearly the crucial role of Chinese labor in railroad construction in the American West. (For example, see Ira B. Cross, *A History of the Labor Movement in California* [Berkeley, 1935]; Ping Chiu, *Chinese Labor in California: An Economic Study* [Madison, 1967]; and Alexander Saxton, *The Indispensable Enemy: Labor and the Anti-Chinese Movement in California* [Berkeley, 1971].) No study has yet explored the role of Boston merchants and American shipping companies in the contracting and transporting of Chinese laborers to America, nor their connections with Chinese merchants on both sides of the Pacific specifically in this regard. Nor has any study tried to link up, directly or indirectly, the Chinese merchants to railroad and other investors in the American West. To explore fully all of these likely interrelationships, the study which I have in mind would cut across the separate fields of Sino-American relations, Asian American studies, and American labor and economic history. Only by undertaking studies within a broad perspective can we hope to understand the degree to which the industrial development of nineteenth-century America was based on the exploitation of Chinese in China and America, and the manner in which China, indirectly or directly, provided both capital and labor to America's economic growth.

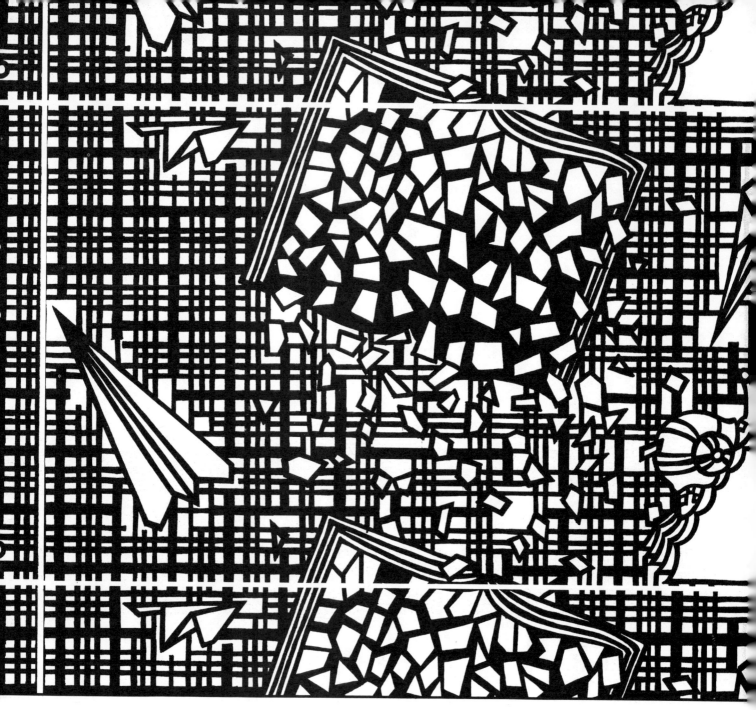

In recent years an intense interest in the experience of minority groups has emerged, not only among minority groups themselves but also in segments of the larger society. The flood of new publications on and by minorities reflects this interest. Ideally it should entail a search for a meaningful historical past—the debunking of old distortions and myths, the uncovering of hitherto neglected or unknown facts, and the construction of a new interpretation of that past. Interest in Japanese-Americans is no exception to the general trend. Absorbed as they are in the question of their ethnic identity, Japanese-Americans too are looking at their past. Rather than reexamining their entire history, however, they (and others) have tended to highlight the World War II internment ordeal. Reflecting this preoccupation, various works on Japanese-Americans—some of dubious value—have been published in the last several years.

Most of these publications fall into two major categories. First, there are sociological works written within a specific theoretical framework. Depending heavily on secondary historical works, they do not break new ground in historical knowledge of the Japanese immigrants and their descendants but rather rearrange established facts into a modified interpretative order. The best example is the recent book by William Petersen, *Japanese Americans* (New York, 1971). Similar works are Harry L. Kitano, *Japanese Americans: The Evolution of a Subculture* (Englewood Cliffs, N.J., 1969); Stanford M. Lyman, *The Asian in the West* (Reno, 1970); and Ivan H. Light, *Ethnic Enterprise in America: Business and Welfare among Chinese, Japanese, and Blacks* (Berkeley and Los Angeles, 1972). Secondly, there are works specifically devoted to some aspect of the wartime internment

A Buried Past

A Survey
of English-language works
on
Japanese American History

BY YUJI ICHIOKA

experience—these are the most numerous and of very uneven quality. They are Edward H. Spicer et al., *Impounded People: Japanese-Americans in the Relocation Centers* (Tucson, 1969); Audrie Girdner and Ann Loftis, *The Great Betrayal* (New York, 1969); Anthony L. Lehman, *Birthright of Barbed Wire: The Santa Anita Assembly Center for the Japanese* (Los Angeles, 1970); Dillon S. Myer, *Uprooted Americans: The Japanese Americans and the War Relocation Authority during World War II* (Tucson, 1971); Paul Bailey, *City in the Sun: The Japanese Concentration Camp at Poston, Arizona* (Los Angeles, 1971); Roger Daniels, *Concentration Camps USA: Japanese Americans and World War II* (New York, 1971); John Modell (ed.), *The Kikuchi Diary* (Urbana, 1973); Jeanne Wakatsuki Houston and James D. Houston, *Farewell to Manzanar* (Boston, 1973); Arthur A. Hansen et al., *Voices Long Silent:*

An Oral Inquiry into the Japanese American Evacuation (Fullerton, 1974); Gary Y. Okihiro, "Resistance in America's Concentration Camps: A Re-Evaluation," *Amerasia Journal*, 2:1 (Fall, 1973); and Arthur A. Hansen and David A. Hacker, "The Manzanar Riot: An Ethnic Perspective," *Amerasia Journal*, 2:2 (Fall, 1974). Past studies of Japanese-Americans have overwhelmingly concentrated on what happened to them. For example, we know a great deal about the Japanese exclusion movement that predated the internment camps. But we know very little about how the Japanese immigrants, the excluded, felt and thought about being excluded. In this sense, the recent books on internment are an extension of past historiography. Once again books on what happened to the Japanese have rolled off the presses. That the internment experience deserves serious study is beyond dispute. But the history of

illustration by DEAN S. TOJI

the Japanese in America dates back to the 19th century, and if the current interest remains predominantly restricted to that experience it can lead only to a myopic view of Japanese-American history.

A few publications fit into neither of the foregoing categories. William K. Hosokawa, *Nisei: The Quiet Americans* (New York, 1969), is a popular personalized narrative about the leaders and activities of the Japanese American Citizens League, the national organization of the second generation. Dennis Ogawa, *From Japs to Japanese: The Evolution of Japanese-American Stereotypes* (Berkeley, 1971), is a brief, superficial treatment of the stereotypic images of Japanese-Americans. Frank Chin et al. (eds.), *Aiiieeeee!* (Washington, D.C., 1974), is an anthology of Asian-American writings, including Nisei authors. Minako K. Maykovich, *Japanese-American Identity Dilemma* (Tokyo, 1972), is a shallow study of the self-identity problems of the third generation. Out of all the recent books, only three have the merit of contributing to our historical knowledge of the Japanese before World War II: Hilary Conroy and T. Scott Miyakawa (eds.), *East across the Pacific* (Santa Barbara, 1972), a collection of historical and sociological essays on Japanese-Americans; Akira Iriye, *Pacific Estrangement: Japanese and American Expansion, 1897-1911* (Cambridge, 1972), a study of Japanese and American ideas and attitudes relating to expansion into the Pacific; and Kazuo Ito, *Issei: A History of Japanese Immigrants in North America* (Seattle, 1973), a compilation of Issei reminiscences of immigrant life in the Pacific Northwest, originally published in Japanese under the title, *Hoku-Bei Hyakunen Sakura* (Seattle, 1969), and translated by Shinichiro Nakamura and Jean S. Gerard.

A Survey of the Historical Literature

A broad survey of the English-language secondary historical literature preceding these recent publications points to the need to shift our attention to the Japanese immigrants before World War II. Practically the entire corpus of the historical literature on Japanese-Americans (excluding those in Hawaii) is tied directly or indirectly to the past exclusion movement. Some works concentrate on the exclusion movement. Among these are such scholarly studies as Raymond L. Buell, "The Development of the Anti-Japanese Agitation in the United States," *Political Science Quarterly,* 37:4 (December, 1922) and 38:1 (March, 1923); Jacobus tenBroek et al., "Genesis," *Prejudice, War and the Constitution,* part I (Berkeley and Los Angeles, 1954); and Roger Daniels, *The Politics of Prejudice* (Berkeley and Los Angeles, 1962). These studies set out to explain the origins, causes, and development of the exclusion movement.

Others restrict themselves to one aspect of the movement. For example, there are specialized studies of the California land tenure controversy, such as Thomas A. Bailey, "California, Japan, and the Alien Land Legislation of 1913," *Pacific Historical Review,* 1:1 (March, 1932); Spencer C. Olin, Jr., "European Immigrant and Oriental Alien: Acceptance and Rejection by the California Legislature of 1913," *Pacific Historical Review,* 35:3 (August, 1966); Paolo E. Coletta, "'The Most Thankless Task': Bryan and the California Alien Land Legislation," *Pacific Historical Review,* 36:2 (May, 1967); and Dudley O. McGovney, "The Anti-Japanese Land Laws of California and Ten Other States," and Edwin E. Ferguson, "The California Alien Land Law and the 14th Amendment," *California Law Review,* 35:1 (March, 1947). Though perfectly valid studies, all of these—and others like them—tell us nothing about Japanese immigrants except that they were objects of the exclusion movement.

Another set of works adds an international relations context to the study of the exclusion movement. Perhaps the best example is Thomas A. Bailey, *Theodore Roosevelt and the Japanese-American Crisis* (Stanford, 1934), in which the 1906 San Francisco school question is placed within the context of U.S.-Japan relations. Examining additional sources, Raymond A. Esthus, *Theodore Roosevelt and Japan* (Seattle, 1966), and Charles E. Neu, *An Uncertain Friendship: Theodore Roosevelt and Japan, 1906-1909* (Cambridge, 1967), do the same thing for this and other topics. Other studies along this line are Raymond L. Buell, *Japanese Immigration* (Boston, 1924), and Eleanor Tupper and George E. McReynolds, *Japan in American Public Opinion* (New York, 1937). Diplomatic histories, such as A. Whitney Griswold, *The Far Eastern Policy of the United States* (New York, 1939), Hikomatsu Kamikawa (ed.), *Japanese-American Diplomatic Relations in the Meiji-Taisho Era* (Tokyo, 1958), and Akira Iriye, *Across the Pacific: An Inner History of American—East Asian Relations* (New York, 1967), also discuss the Japanese immigration question. These works examine the exclusion movement in order to explain the frictions between Japan and America. Thus, they too do not tell us much about Japanese immigrants, except that they had something to do with the discord between the two nations.

There are innumerable works written during and after the exclusion movement that take sides on the controversy. Whether they are for or against Japanese immigration, certain questions recur in them again and again: Are the Japanese assimilable? What happens when racial intermarriage (amalgamation, as it was called) occurs? Is the picture-bride practice moral or immoral, legal or illegal? What is the Japanese birthrate? What are the purposes of Japanese language schools, and what is their influence on the second generation? Should the Japanese be granted naturalization rights? Is there economic competition between Japanese and white laborers? If so, how does it affect the standard of living of both? Are the alien land laws constitutional? Do they violate the international treaty between Japan and America? Is the Gentleman's Agreement of 1907-1908 satisfactory? If not, what kind of immigration restriction is necessary? The answers to these questions comprise the content of the works in this category.

A few white American writers defended the Japanese within this framework. For example, Sidney L. Gulick's first book, *The American Japanese Problem* (New York, 1914), is a refutation of charges advanced by the proponents of exclusion, and a proposal of both naturalization rights for the Japanese and nondiscriminatory immigration restrictions. *American Democracy and Asiatic Citizenship* (New York, 1918), his subsequent work, which includes the Chinese, elaborates on this theme. Harry A. Millis wrote from the same perspective in *The Japanese Problem in the United States* (New York, 1915), which was based on the United States Immigration Commission, *Reports of the Immigration Commission,* part 25 (Washington, D.C., 1911).

White American writers also wrote from the opposite viewpoint, of course. Apart from the countless anti-Japanese tracts, a good example is Montaville Flowers, *The Japanese Conquest of American Opinion* (New York, 1917), which attacks the views and proposals of Gulick, Millis, and Japanese such as Karl K. Kawakami. Still others conclude that no Japanese immigration problem exists. Manchester E. Boddy, *Japanese in America* Los Angeles, 1921), finds that the Japanese question is a manufactured one with no basis in fact, and Jean Pajus' later study, *The Real Japanese California* (Berkeley, 1937), arrives at an identical conclusion.

To counter the exclusionists, the Japanese themselves wrote many books. The most prolific author was Karl K. Kawakami. In the section devoted to Japanese immigration in his earliest work, *American-Japanese Relations* (New York, 1912), he argues for naturalization rights. His second book, *Asia at the Door* (New York, 1914), responds to the charge of nonassimilability and economic competition, while recording the achievements of prominent Japanese and discussing the 1913 California Alien Land Law. His next work, *The Real Japanese Question* (New York, 1921), takes up where the second left off and comprehensively covers all the questions.

Many other books were written by the Japanese, but none compares in importance to Yamato Ichihashi, *Japanese in the United States* (Stanford, 1932), because it is still the accepted standard work on the Japanese immigrants. Starting as a pamphlet in 1913, it was submitted in an expanded form as a doctoral dissertation at Harvard University in 1914 and then published the following year under the title *Japanese*

Immigration: Its Status in California (San Francisco, 1915). This early version was designed to present facts on the Japanese in California as a retort to the exclusionists, relying heavily on the *Reports of the Immigration Commission,* Gulick's *American Japanese Problem,* and Millis' *Japanese Problem in the United States.* The 1932 edition is expanded and updated in many ways, with new chapters on the character and causes of Japanese emigration and the second generation, but it still retains the original purpose. Like all the other works cited, it tells us more about the exclusion movement than about the Japanese immigrant and his soceity. While Ichihashi did use some Japanese-language sources, these were very restricted, which further limits the value of the book. But for all its shortcomings, it remains the standard work incorporated into general histories of American immigration. Maldwyn A. Jones, *American Immigration* (Chicago, 1960), and Carl Wittke, *We Who Built America,* rev. ed. (Cleveland, 1967), for example, both depend heavily on it for their treatment of Japanese immigration.

In addition to the above studies, there are more specialized ones related to the exclusion movement. Roderick D. McKenzie, *Oriental Exclusion* (Chicago, 1928), and Eliot G. Mears, *Resident Orientals on the Pacific Coast* (Chicago, 1928), analyze the effect on the Chinese and Japanese of the 1924 Immigration Act and regulations and judicial decisions under it. Jesse F. Steiner, *The Japanese Invasion* (Chicago, 1917), studies the Japanese immigration question in terms of the physical features and skin pigmentation of the Japanese. And Milton R. Konvitz, *The Alien and the Asiatic in American Law* (Ithaca, 1946), treats the Asian immigrants' relation to immigration laws, citizenship, and other legal questions.

In the 1930s a number of studies were produced on the second generation. Departing somewhat from the previous framework, they explore the "problems" of the Nisei,[1] seeking answers to questions connected with their adjustment and assimilation into American society. Stanford University produced four such works. Based on interviews with approximately 10 percent of the Japanese population in California, the first volume, by Edward K. Strong, *Vocational Aptitudes of Second-Generation Japanese in the United States* (Stanford, 1933), compares the second generation to whites in terms of psychological tests, delinquency, and ability to use the English language. The second, also by Strong, *Japanese in California* (Stanford, 1933), provides data on the birthplace, age, sex, size of family, birth and death, education, occupation, and religious affiliation of the Japanese. The third, by Reginald Bell, *Public School Education of Second-Generation Japanese in California* (Stanford, 1935), compares Japanese and white students in public schools. The last, by Strong, *The Second-Generation Japanese Problem* (Stanford, 1934), summarizes the first three. Two points should be noted about these studies: 1) they are based on interviews, not on research into new historical sources; and 2) they are an extension of preceding studies, for they simply reexamine the Japanese question emphasizing the problems of the second generation. William C. Smith, *Americans in Process: A Study of Our Citizens of Oriental Ancestry* (Ann Arbor, 1937) and Forrest E. La Violette, *Americans of Japanese Ancestry* (Toronto, 1946), likewise study the problems of the second generation.

The remaining secondary works indicate the paucity of the historical literature. Our knowledge of the origins and causes of Japanese emigration consists of a ten-page article by Yosaburo Yoshida, "Sources and Causes of Japanese Emigration," *Annals of the American Academy of Political and Social Science,* 34:2 (September, 1909), and "Causes of Japanese Immigration," chapter 6 in Ichihashi's book, both of which provide merely superficial generalizations. The most solid (yet again incomplete) study on this topic with reference to Japanese emigration to Hawaii is Hilary Conroy, *The Japanese Frontier in Hawaii, 1868-1898* (Berkeley and Los Angeles, 1953). Hardly anything has been written on the origins of Japanese immigrant society. Inasmuch as the overwhelming emphasis has been on the exclusion movement, which began at the turn of the century, it is not suprising to find this void. The exceptions are Henry Taketa, "1969, the Centennial Year," *Pacific Historian,* 13:1 (Winter, 1969), a brief essay on the 1869 Wakamatsu Tea Colony; Robert E. Park, *The Immigrant Press and Its Control* (New York, 1922), which has a short treatment of the early Japanese immigrant press in San Francisco; and the United States Immigration Commission, *Reports of the Immigration Commission,* part 25 (Washington, D.C., 1911), which has already been cited. There are no serious studies of the early Christian institutions of Japanese immigrant society, of the Gospel Society founded in 1877 from which the others originated, of the first *dekasegi-shosei* who laid much of the foundation of immigrant society, or of the crucial transmigration of laborers from Hawaii to the continental United States. In short, the origins and development of Japanese immigrant society are unknown.

To see Japanese immigrants as live participants in history, biographies and autobiographies of eminent and ordinary Issei are required. But what exists? The answer is: Very little. Aside from Karl K. Kawakami, *Jokichi Takamine: A Record of His American Achievements* (New York, 1928), and Gustav Eckstein, *Noguchi* (New York, 1931), two biographies of eminent Issei scientists; Kiyoko T. Kurosawa, "Seito Saibara's Diary of Planting a Japanese Colony in Texas," *Hitotsubashi Journal of Social Studies,* 2:1 (August, 1964), a sketch of the founder of the Japanese rice colony outside Houston; Eleanor Hull, *Suddenly the Sun* (New York, 1957), a

biography of Shizuko Takahashi; and Tohru Morita, "The Story of a Japanese Emigrant: The Life of Domoto Takanoshin," *The East,* 5 (March/April, 1969), there are no biographical studies of Issei. The only autobiographies that come to mind are Haru Matsui, *Restless Wave* (New York, 1940); Etsu Inagaki Sugimoto, *A Daughter of the Samurai* (New York, 1929); Toru Matsumoto and Marion Olive Lerrigo, *A Brother Is a Stranger* (New York, 1947); and Taro Yashima, *The New Sun* (New York, 1943) and *Horizon Is Calling* (New York, 1947) (these last two are more an autobiography through drawings). The literature on the second generation is no better. Besides the frequently cited autobiography by Monica Sone, *Nisei Daughter* (Boston, 1953), there are some autobiographical sketches in Fisk University, Social Science Institute, *Orientals and Their Cultural Adjustment* (Nashville, 1946), and Dorothy S. Thomas, *The Salvage* (Berkeley and Los Angeles, 1952). The most recent autobiographies are Daniel I. Okimoto, *American in Disguise* (New York, 1971), and Jim Yoshida, *The Two Worlds of Jim Yoshida* (New York, 1972). Biographical studies of Nisei simply do not exist, save for Ralph G. Martin, *Boy from Nebraska* (New York, 1946), an account of the life of Ben Kuroki and his World War II exploits.

A number of other works of uneven historical value complete this broad survey. The often cited reference to the Japanese Associations, the most important Issei political organization, is a superficial eight-page article by Michinari Fujita, "The Japanese Associations in America," *Sociology and Social Research,* 13:3 (January/February, 1929). The only study of the eta or pariah caste is Hiroshi Ito, "Japan's Outcastes in the United States," in George De Vos and Hiroshi Wagatsuma, *Japan's Invisible Race* (Berkeley and Los Angeles, 1966). Masakazu Iwata, "The Japanese Immigrants in California Agriculture," *Agricultural History,* 36:1 (January, 1962), is a historical essay on the Japanese contributions to California agriculture; Teruko Kachi, "Notes on the Japanese in California Agriculture, 1900-1910," *Tsudajuku Daigaku Kiyo,* No. 4 (1972), and Charles Wollenberg, "Race and Class in Rural California: The El Monte Berry Strike of 1933," *California Historical Quarterly,* 51:2 (Summer, 1972), are two recent articles on the Japanese in agriculture, the former on the 1910 MacKenzie Report of the California State Bureau of Labor and the latter on the 1933 El Monte berry strike involving Mexican farm workers and Japanese farmers. Yuji Ichioka, "A Buried Past: Early Issei Socialists and the Japanese Community," *Amerasia Journal,* 1:2 (July, 1971), is a recent study of early Issei socialists and anarchists. As for local or regional studies, there are Frank S. Miyamoto, "Social Solidarity among the Japanese in Seattle," *University of Washington Publications in the Social Sciences,* 11:2 (December, 1939); his later essay, "The Japanese Minority in the

Pacific Northwest," *Pacific Northwest Quarterly,* 54:4 (October, 1963); Marvin G. Pursinger, "The Japanese Settle in Oregon, 1880-1920," *Journal of the West,* 5:2 (April, 1966); Marjorie R. Stearns, *A History of the Japanese People in Oregon* (Eugene, 1939), yet another example of the exclusion-oriented studies; William M. Mason et al., *The Japanese of Los Angeles* (Contribution in History No. 1, Los Angeles County Museum of Natural History, 1969); and Susie Sato, "Before Pearl Harbor: Early Japanese Settlers in Arizona," *Journal of Arizona History,* 14 (1973). John Modell, a new student of Japanese-American history, has written "Class or Ethnic Solidarity: The Japanese American Company Union," *Pacific Historical Review,* 38:2 (May, 1969), and "Tradition and Opportunity: The Japanese Immigrants in America," *Pacific Historical Review,* 40:2 (May, 1971), the latter almost exclusively relying on survey data. Harry H. L. Kitano, "Japanese-Americans: The Development of a Middleman Minority," *Pacific Historical Review,* 43:4 (November, 1974), is a recent sociological essay analyzing the past and present social position of Japanese-Americans. Roger Daniels, "Westerners from the East: Oriental Immigrants Reappraised," *Pacific Historical Review,* 35:4 (November, 1966), is a review of the historiography of Chinese and Japanese immigrants; and his most recent essay, "American Historians and East Asian Immigrants," *Pacific Historical Review,* 43:4 (November, 1974), updates this review. The latest summary of historical and sociological studies of Japanese immigrants in America and other countries is John B. Cornell and Robert J. Smith, "Japanese Immigrants Abroad," *Rice University Studies,* 56:4 (Fall, 1970). Ernest R. May and James C. Thomson, Jr. (eds.), *American-East Asian Relations: A Survey* (Cambridge, 1972), is a valuable review of the literature on American-East Asian relations, including the Japanese immigration question.

While not comprehensive, this broad survey should make evident that the history of Japanese immigrants remains to be written.[2] In the judgment of one historian, "although some studies of Asiatic emigration were made during the period of the immigration restriction controversy, we still lack adequate histories of Chinese, Japanese, and other Far Eastern emigration. Indeed this vast field of investigation is untouched."[3] The sparse literature that is unrelated to the exclusion movement is so limited that it only touches the surface. The real need is to refocus our attention on the Japanese immigrants themselves, which requires the examination of Japanese-language source materials. Except for Ichihashi, Conroy, Iriye, Ichioka, and Miyamoto, past and present researchers have ignored these materials. On the one hand, they have not been equipped to handle the language, and, on the other hand, they have adhered to the myth that no such sources exist. Marcus L. Hansen, the pioneer in European immigration history, long ago called attention to the necessity of studying immigrant language materials and the intimate connection between the emigrant nation and the immigrant land.[4] Yet his elementary maxim has not been heeded in the study of Japanese immigrants. To delve below the surface and uncover the history of Japanese immigrants, future studies must be based on Japanese-immigrant-language source materials. ★

November, 1975

Notes

1. The term *Issei* and *Nisei* refer to the immigrant generation and the American-born second generation respectively. *Kibei* denotes Nisei who were entirely or partially educated in Japan. For additional Japanese words employed in the bibliography, see the Glossary of Japanese Terms. Throughout the bibliography we have used *Japanese immigrants, Japanese-Americans,* and *Japanese in America* interchangeably. In discussing the 19th century, it is impossible to make the distinction between Japanese immigrants and other Japanese in America. Many *dekasegi-shosei,* for example, though they eventually returned to Japan, laid the foundations of Japanese immigrant society. For the 20th century, however, when the term *Japanese in America* is used, we do not have in mind Japanese diplomats, businessmen, students, and other transient individuals.

2. For socio-psychological studies, wartime internment literature, and other works, see the following bibliographies of English-language materials: Edward N. Barnhart, *Japanese American Evacuation and Resettlement* (Berkeley: University of California, General Library, 1958); Orpha Cummings and Helen E. Hennefrund, *Bibliography on the Japanese in American Agriculture* (Washington, D.C.: U.S. Government Printing Office, 1943) (U.S.D.A. Biblio. Bul. no. 3); Isao Fujimoto et al., *Asians in America: A Selected Bibliography* (Davis: University of California, 1971) (Asian American Research Project, Working Pub. no. 5); Harry L. Kitano et al., *Asian Americans: An Annotated Bibliography* (Los Angeles: University of California, Asian American Studies Center, 1971); William W. Lum, *Asians in America: A Bibliography* (Davis: University of California, 1969); William W. Lum, *Asians in America: A Bibliography of Master's Theses and Dissertations* (Davis: University of California, 1970) (Asian American Research Project, Working Pub. no. 2); U.S. Library of Congress, General Reference and Bibliography Division, *Japanese in the United States: A Selected List of References* (Washington, D.C.: U.S. Government Printing Office, 1946); U.S. National Archives, *Preliminary Inventories, No. 77: Records of the War Relocation Authority* (Washington, D.C.: U.S. Government Printing Office, 1955); U.S. War Relocation Authority, *Bibliography of Japanese in America,* 3 vols. (Washington, D.C.: U.S. War Relocation Authority, 1942-1943); U.S. War Relocation Authority, *Bibliography on War Relocation Authority: Japanese and Japanese-Americans* (Washington, D.C.: U.S. War Relocation Authority, 1945).

3. Carlton C. Qualey, "Prospects for Materials in Immigration Studies," in Henry S. Commager (ed.), *Immigration and American History* (Minneapolis: University of Minnesota Press, 1961), p. 132.

4. Marcus L. Hansen, "The History of American Immigration as a Field for Research," *American Historical Review,* 32:3 (April, 1927), pp. 500-518.

The Civil Rights Movement and the Third World Student Strikes in the 1960's have led to a re-examination of many social science professions. Sociology, a discipline which has pioneered the study of race relations, is perhaps most influenced by this widespread social movement. Events in the past decade have forced sociologists to reevaluate their studies on race relations, in particular their theories, methodologies, and most importantly the implicit underlying assumptions of their works. This essay will discuss the major perspectives as represented in studies about Chinese Americans published in the four oldest and most widely read sociological journals: *American Sociological Review, American Journal of Sociology, Social Forces,* and *Sociology and Social Research* (formerly, *Journal of Applied Sociology*). Other studies considered important by sociologists but published elsewhere will also be discussed.

Major Perspectives

Continuing in the tradition of Weber and Mills who maintained that theories of social behavior reflect the social experiences and social motives of

Part of this essay was prepared at the request of NIMH for presentation at the American Sociological Association Annual Convention, August 27-30, 1973, New York City. I am grateful to the staff of the Asian American Studies Center at UCLA for their suggestions and comments.

20   illustration by KAREN AKAMINE

The Chinese American in Sociology

By Lucie Cheng Hirata

the theorists, Horton argues that American sociology has been dominated by the "order perspective," which assumes that consensus is at the base of society:

> Order theories have in common an image of society as a system of action unified at the most general level of shared culture, by agreement on values (or at least on modes) of communication and political organization.[1]

Minority problems are thus seen as deviations from the accepted norm, and are to be solved through socialization and social control.

An examination of sociological studies on the Chinese American supports Horton's observation. From the earliest writings appearing in the *Journal of Applied Sociology* down to studies published in the 1960's, there is a series of variations on the same theme, sometimes not even variations but simply refrains. The melody goes like this: there is the American cultural system, and there is the Chinese cultural system. Some of the elements in the latter are consistent with the American ones, and some are not. If the Chinese would give up the ones that are not consistent with ours, then everyone will be happy. The question is, can they and will they give them up?

This theme is a step forward from the previous theme that the Chinese were an inferior race sung by scientists and laymen alike. Perhaps as a reaction to Social Darwinism from which this theme derived its scientific justification, social scientists in the 1920's attempted to show that the Chinese, although possessing certain undesirable traits and strange customs, could be assimilated if they were helped along by white Americans.[2] The assimilation proponents assumed the superiority of white culture to which minorities should adapt themselves. The change in perspective was not the elimination of the "white supremacy" assumption but rather from white *racial* supremacy to white *cultural* superiority.

Some sociologists were not optimistic about the assimilability of the first-generation Chinese, but held great hopes for the second generation. Hayner and Reynolds went even further to claim that there was no basic difference between the American-born Chinese and the American-born European, both could be Americanized.[3] However, they acknowledged that due to racial-cultural barriers which prevented the Chinese Americans from full membership in American society, their Americanization was left incomplete. A series of articles in the '30's and early '40's discussed the problems of the second-generation Chinese and proposed programs for their solutions. Although the problems remained the same—conflict between American values transmitted through schools and Chinese values clung to by parents—the proposed solution sometimes differed. Some social scientists emphasized retaining certain aspects of Chinese culture as the solution,[4] others proposed complete acculturation.[5] In any case, if some form of accommodation was not achieved, the Chinese American was seen as maladjusted.[6]

Prejudice and discrimination against the Chinese were from the beginning topics for social scientists who considered them as the barriers toward assimilation.[7] Not viewing anti-Chinese sentiments as indicative of structural problems of American society, the policy implications of these studies were hinged on the assumption that contact, communication and education would eventually eliminate these barriers and allow the Chinese to complete their process of assimilation. Although white prejudice and discrimination per se were denounced by many social scientists writing since the '20's, the causes of this phenomenon were often attributed to the Chinese themselves. After saying that the American-born Chinese were unadjusted or maladjusted, a writer continued:

> If the American-born Chinese will prove to America that they have developed a personality of which both America and China may be proud, and that they have contributed to the world by interpreting the East to the West and the West to the East, the social distance between them and the Americans, and between the younger and older generation Chinese will be bridged, and consequently the door of equal opportunity to achieve higher social and economic status will be gradually opened to them, on the basis of merit.[8]

The efforts to explain (or explain away) prejudice and discrimination usually follow one of two lines:

1) The Chinese brought it upon themselves by having undesirable traits or behavioral patterns. Nora Sterry in 1922 and James Loewen (*The Mississippi Chinese*) in 1971 regarded the "clannishness" of the Chinese as at least partially responsible for white prejudice and discrimination. A more sophisticated version of this self-inflicted victimization thesis stemmed from the notion of the "sojourner," popularized by Paul Siu, Rose Hum Lee, and many others. Since the Chinese were merely sojourners, so the argument went, they tried to make the most money within the shortest time. This money-grabbing behavior caused resentment among the whites, therefore resulted in their prejudice and discrimination against the Chinese. This thesis has caught the fancy of American sociologists to such an extent that the majority of writings since 1948 have included this concept. It has been used to explain not only white prejudice and discrimination but also Chinese American institutional forms and personality. Although historically many early Chinese immigrants did not intend to settle in America, how long this sojourner attitude lasted is still debatable. In addition, it is more probable that an interrelationship existed between white hostility and Chinese sojourning psychology, rather than a one way causal relationship which has been assumed. To say that the sojourner's behavior led to white antagonism is to blame the victims for their victimization.

2) Another common explanation is the use of an economic model that does not specifically identify the sojourner's role, but considers economic competition to be the cause of anti-Chinese persecution. The Chinese was seen either directly involved as one of the competing groups or indirectly involved as a scapegoat.[9] While the importance of economic competition in shaping race relations cannot be denied, the emphasis placed on it has subsequently led to the view that if we can do away with current economic inequality, racial oppression will *naturally*

disappear. Such a view, as pointed out by Blauner,[10] ignores the endemic nature of racism in American society. I am not suggesting that there is something magical that makes America naturally racist. But the doctrine of white supremacy, the colonization of Africa and Asia by the white people, the history of international relations between the racial groups, though they may be rooted in perceived or actual economic competition, have made racism a part of the American tradition and exploitation along color lines possible. Stuart Miller observed that a negative attitude toward Asia existed before any Asian immigrants ever stepped on American soil.[11]

Other less popular lines of reasoning include the "psychopathological" and the "altruistic" theses.[12] The former regards anti-Chinese persecution mainly as the aberrations of a small number of sick people or people who had a history of prejudice against other colored people,[13] and the latter altruistic hypothesis assigns the white Americans the role of the gallant knight who came to the rescue of Chinese laborers from the hands of their own clansmen.[14]

To counter white prejudice and discrimination, a few social scientists sought to mollify the whites by stressing what they assumed to be the "positive" traits of the Chinese. Three types of studies may be discerned.

The first developed a stereotype of the Chinese that explicitly or implicitly reinforced the status quo. An article in defense of Bret Harte talked about what a great service Harte had done for the Chinese American by pointing out that their most adorable trait was that they were loyal to white children.[15] In other words, the Chinese would make good servants for any white family.

Along this line of reasoning, a more subtle treatment is reflected in those studies that emphasize occupational and economic achievements of the Chinese Americans.[16] This emphasis on their rise to middle-class status in the United States resulted in the much hailed "model minority" image of the Chinese, hardworking, taking care of themselves, and most importantly, silent and unobtrusive. Reacting strongly against this image, Nishio suggested that Asian Americans were considered models only if they remained as middleman minorities, not in control of American social institutions, and yet occupying a middle economic and social position which can serve as examples of "success," and thereby performing a buffer function.[17]

The second type of study is largely the creation of the educated Chinese, most of whom were born in China and received higher education in the United States. These writers attribute white prejudice and discrimination against the Chinese to whites' confusing the two classes of Chinese immigrants: the lowly laborer and the refined gentleman. Thus Tow considered it unfortunate that the laborers came to America and embarrassed the other classes of Chinese immigrants;[18] and Lee, Kung, Sung and Hsu emphasized the outstanding achievements of the educated Chinese and their distinguished place in American society.[19]

The third type of study deals with the individual and social pathology of the Chinese. While writers before the 1920's tended to emphasize the tong wars, the opium addicts, the illegal activities, and the diseases among Chinese Americans to show why they would not be desirable Americans, later writings emphasized the decline of these pathologies to counter the argument and to demonstrate that the Chinese were getting themselves ready to be acculturated. After discussing the effects of tong wars in slowing down the process of assimilation, Reynolds considered the passing of the fighting tong a shot in the arm toward that process, now that "the Chinese invader had learned his place and was keeping in it."[20] Ball and Lau, in their discussion of the Chinese narcotic addict in the United States, attributed the high incidence of drug addiction among the Chinese Americans during the first half of this century to the Chinese culture.[21] According to them, drug use, being a part of contemporary Chinese culture, has been transmitted from generation to generation. And the virtual termination of drug addiction by the 1960's was due to the modernization of Chinatown and the severance of cultural ties with the homeland. In this connection, it is particularly interesting to recall Rose Hum Lee and later on Kenneth and Elizabeth Abbott's articles on the rise of juvenile delinquency in the Chinese American community of San Francisco.[22] Both writers attribute the increase to the breakdown of traditional Chinese family structure and solidarity resulting from the "Americanization" process. One gets the impression that even in the area of social pathology, the Chinese Americans have proved themselves true Americans by substituting Chinese forms of deviance, such as tong wars and drug use, to the American form of deviance such as juvenile delinquency. The change from one form of deviance to another is reflective of the earlier concern over American-born Chinese: to acculturate or not to acculturate, that is the question.

While social scientists were busy demonstrating that indeed the Chinese can and will assimilate, or have already been assimilated, they were really missing the central point. White America was really not interested in their assimilation. While assimilation was held to be the ideal outcome of European immigrants, it was really never the ideal for colored people. Yet, social scientists fell into the same conceptual net and spent their energies debating over a false question. Stanford Lyman observed:

> If American racism may be defined as the attempt to impose White Anglo-Saxon culture on the inhabitants of a continent, then two epochs may be distinguished. The first, that of total exclusion for non-whites and imposed acculturation on continental Europeans, may be said to have begun in 1607 and ended in the twentieth century. Characteristic of the exclusionist mechanisms of this first period were total institutionalization of the non-white population on plantations and reservations. The second epoch continues the cultural imposition of Anglo-Saxon norms on Europeans, but substitutes segmented, partial, institutionalized racism in a wide variety of arenas of action for the abandoned and moribund method of total incarceration. The pivotal group for the study of this transition from total to partial institutionalized racism is the Asian and especially the Chinese.[23]

While Robert Park must be considered the sociologist who charted the course of race relations studies, Milton Gordon has to be credited with keeping the order perspective alive. Park's influence, which has lasted through the fifties, is perhaps best illustrated by the fact that the majority of writings on Chinese Americans cited his work or assumed assimilation to be the final outcome. Rose Hum Lee, the most productive Chinese American sociologist, wrote in this tradition and her work is cited in almost every subsequent study on the subject.

Milton Gordon's refinement of the assimilation concept caught on quickly and became the inspiration of many studies on the Chinese and Japanese Americans in the 60's. Cultural pluralism, instead of assimilation, is now seen as a desirable goal, and sociologists work hard to show that pluralism is good for America, given that many racial minority groups have not assimilated anyway.[24] Adherents of the pluralism perspective seek only to legitimize the maintenance of minority cultures and institutions, and do not challenge the fundamental structure of American society.

In short, the order perspectives, thus far, have dominated the sociological studies on Chinese Americans in general. They, moreover, have strongly influenced studies of the Chinese American communities.

Community Studies

Social scientists have long engaged in community studies. The target of investigations ranges from the fairly isolated and enclosed rural communities to the loosely defined urban areas. The changing conceptions of "community" reflect the changing patterns of life in industrializing and industrialized societies.

The various sociological approaches to the community focus on spatial relationships, people, shared institutions and values, interaction, a distribution of power, and the social system.[25] These approaches, singly or in combination, have been used by social scientists to study communities as divergent as Jonesville,[26] Levittown,[27] and the "enduring ghetto."[28]

Harlem, Watts, and other ethnic communities

have all been the objects of many sociological investigations. Regardless of the specific approach that is adopted, the overwhelming majority of these studies have focused on the social pathology of the ethnic communities. The culture of poverty, institutional racism, internal colonialism and Marxian perspectives emerged as competing explanations of the ghetto problem. Each, of course, has its political implications.

The culture of poverty thesis is the one that has provoked the strongest reaction from scholars and minority political leaders, largely for its implications for social action. The issue is not that there exist distinct cultural patterns in American society, but that if the culture of poverty is presumed to cause poverty, then to eliminate the problem, the behavior patterns of the impoverished people must be changed—perhaps through various means of resocialization.[29] Replying to the Moynihan report which suggests that the Black family structure is responsible for the conditions of Black America, James Farmer writes:

> By laying the primary blame for present-day inequalities on the pathological condition of the Negro family and community, Moynihan has provided a massive academic cop-out for the white conscience and clearly implied that Negroes in this nation will never secure a substantial measure of freedom until we learn to behave ourselves and stop buying Cadillacs instead of bread.[30]

An alternative explanation of the ghetto problem is the thesis that minorities have been kept out of the channels of social mobility due to racial discrimination in our social institutions. The obvious solution for those who adopt this perspective of institutional racism is to win equal opportunities for oppressed peoples in employment, housing, education, and other areas of our society. The Civil Rights Movement in the early sixties especially attempted to employ this solution with only limited success.

The publication of *Dark Ghetto*[31] and *Black Power*[32] in the mid-sixties introduced a new model to the analysis of Black communities. The central theme of internal colonialism is that the ghetto is a colony within the boundaries of America, and that the white-black relationship is characterized by the relationship between the colonizer and the colonized. According to Tabb, "There are two key relationships which must be proved to exist before the colonial analogy can be accepted: (1) economic control and exploitation, and (2) political dependence and subjugation. Both necessitate separation and inferior status."[33] He then proceeds to demonstrate that the experience of Blacks in America fulfills both requirements. Recognizing the limitations of the internal colonial model and yet realizing its potential in understanding race relations in America, Blauner refined the model and applied it to his study of ghetto revolts.[34] Blauner maintains

that there are five basic components of the colonization complex: (1) forced, involuntary entry, (2) cultural destruction or transformation, (3) political and legal manipulation by representatives of the dominant power, (4) racism, and (5) the separation in labor status between the colonized and the colonizers.[35] The internal colonial model is not used solely to describe the Black ghetto. Scholars have also applied it to the study of Chicano communities.[36] Viewing the ethnic community as a colony within and the minority peoples as oppressed nationalities leads to movements of separatism, cultural nationalism and struggles of national liberation as forms of political action. While the model has definite revolutionary implications, the emphasis is on racism, and the proposed solution is to organize primarily along racial lines to combat economic, political and cultural oppression. This perspective differs from the "institutional racism" model in that it does not end with institutional reform, but pushes toward a more fundamental change of the social system which will allow for the self-determination of minority peoples.

The internal colony conception of the ghetto has met with criticism not only from the liberals but also from some sectors of the left.[37] Marxian writers have directed their criticism against the emphasis on racism, maintaining that such an emphasis masks the nature of capitalism which exploits all working people, Black and White, and tends to confuse the real issue of class conflicts. These writers have tried to develop an explanation of the ghetto problem by focusing on the development of the capitalist relations of production in the United States and treating the race issue as a by-product, though a significant one.[38] Adopting this perspective, minority struggles cease to be mainly struggles for national liberation but become merged into a general class struggle. While the internal colonial model leaves the character of the revolution an open question, the class model is insistent on a socialist revolution as the only way to Black liberation.

In contrast to the culture of poverty theme, the institutional racism, internal colonialism and Marxian perspectives all share in common the notion that the American social structure is the major source of the ghetto problem. Although these are not mutually exclusive concepts, the adoption of one or the other will lead to different strategies of community organizing and political action.

Chinatown Studies

Both the cultural and structural interpretations are reflected in the studies of American Chinatowns.[39] The majority of these studies, particularly those published before the mid-sixties, have adopted a primarily cultural explanation of the emergence and maintenance of Chinatown as an ethnic community. One difference between the Black ghetto studies and the Chinatown studies is that while the Black culture has almost always been seen as negative, the Chinese culture has been treated with mixed feelings. For example, the Chinese family structure is seen as the stabilizing mechanism in the community which has depressed juvenile delinquency in Chinatown.[40] Yet, the same familial structure is also seen as producing cliquishness which has prevented the Chinese from being fully assimilated into the American society.[41] The former became a cause for praise, the latter, regret. Light and Wong recently concluded that the cultural interpretation was overdrawn, and instead suggested that the peculiar industrial division of labor found in Chinatown could account for its conditions: ". . . [Chinatown's] lopsided dependency upon tourism, a hyper-vulnerable industry set up a mono-lithic unity of interest which outsiders too facilely attributed to Chinese culture."[42]

A large number of Chinatown studies utilize the institutional racism perspective. Various investigations have shown that discrimination in the legal system not only has prevented the development of a stable family life in Chinatown in the early immigration days, but persists to this day to the disadvantage of the Chinese American.[43] Discrimination in housing to a certain extent forced the Chinese to segregate them-selves;[44] the absence of bilingual education and the prevalence of unfair employment practices limited the degree and channels of social mobility;[45] and stereotypes in the mass media created and perpetu-ated a negative or one-dimensional image of the Chinese American.[46] One after another, American institutions were exposed for their discrimination against the Chinese. Consequently, social activism was directed toward eliminating these practices and furthering civil rights for Chinese Americans.

In comparison to studies on the Black and the Chicano communities, the relative absence of China-town studies that draw upon the internal colonialism analogy is rather conspicuous.[47] Also, although some writers have attempted to analyze the class structure of Chinatown, these studies are usually very prelimin-ary and typically do not discuss the basis for the particular class analysis. For example, in *Longtime Californ'*, perhaps the best work on San Francisco Chinatown, the authors state that there are the following social classes in Chinatown: old bachelors, immigrant workers, American Chinese workers, small shopkeepers, merchant-businessmen, professionals, and white collar workers. While they gave descriptive profiles of each of these categories, they do not tell us why these groups form classes.[48] A few progressive Chinese American political organizations have issued position papers on the Asian American national ques-tion or reports on their community work in which Chinatown is discussed from a loosely formulated Marxist perspective. However, they are usually too brief or too fragmented to allow a clear understanding of the political economy of Chinese America.[49] How-

ever, in spite of these weaknesses, they constitute a step in the right direction for they view root causes of racial problems to lie in the basic structure of Ameri-can society.

In contrast, assimilation and pluralism, both based on an order perspective because they seek acceptance into the existing American structure, ignore the central fact that racism is an integral part of the American social system, and no amount of contact, communication and education is going to rid America of its racism without a simultaneous radical transformation of the economic and political arrangements of the society.

More and more social scientists are asking the question, research for what and for whom? As a sociologist and an Asian American, my answer is that research must not be conducted to support the status quo, to find markets for the "Welfare State,"[50] but to serve the people by "performing the necessary intel-lectual task of defining problems, seeking solutions and providing concrete ideas from which a future may be constructed." In Richard Flacks' words, "to join in an effort to help people realize that funda-mental social alternatives are not only needed, but possible."[51] ★

Notes

1. John Horton, "Order and Conflict Theories of Social Problems as Competing Ideologies," *American Journal of Sociology,* 71 (May 1966), 703.

2. Nora Sterry, "Housing Conditions in Chinatown, Los Angeles," *Journal of Applied Sociology,* 7 (Nov.-Dec. 1922), 70-75; and Nora Sterry, "Social Attitudes of Chinese Immigrants," *Journal of Applied Sociology,* 7 (July-Aug. 1923), 325-333.

3. Norman S. Hayner and Charles N. Reynolds, "The Chinese Family Life in America," *American Sociological Review,* 2:5 (October 1937), 630-37.

4. K. F. Tom, "Function of the Chinese Language School," *Sociology and Social Research,* 25 (July 1941), 557-66.

5. Kit King Louis, "Problems of Second-Generation Chin-ese," *Sociology and Social Research,* 16 (January-February 1932), 250-58; and Kit King Louis, "Program for Second-Generation Chinese," *Sociology and Social Research,* 16 (May-June 1932), 455-62. See also Francis Y. Chang, "An Accommodation Program of Second-Generation Chinese," *Sociology and Social Research,* 18 (July-August 1934), 541.

6. Louis, "Program for Second-Generation Chinese," 455-62.

7. Robert Lee, "Acculturation of Chinese Americans," *Sociology and Social Research,* 36 (May 1952), 319-21; Robert Lee, "Community Exclusion: A Case Study," *Phylon,* 15:2 (1954), 202-05; and Mary Elizabeth B.S. Coolidge, *Chinese Immigration* (New York: Holt and Company, 1909).

8. Louis, "Program for Second-Generation Chinese," 462.

9. Stanford Lyman, *The Asian in the West* (Reno and Las Vegas: University of Nevada Press, 1971); Alexander Saxton, *The Indispensable Enemy* (Berkeley: University of California Press, 1971); Betty Lee Sung, *Mountain of*

Gold: *The Story of the Chinese in America* (New York: Macmillan Company, 1967); and Ping Chiu, *Chinese Labor in California, 1850-1880: An Economic Study* (Madison: State Historical Society of Wisconsin, 1963).

10. Robert Blauner, *Racial Oppression in America* (New York: Harper and Row, 1972).

11. Stuart C. Miller, *The Unwelcome Immigrant: The American Image of the Chinese, 1785-1882* (Berkeley: University of California Press, 1969).

12. Ben Tong, "The Ghetto of the Mind: Notes on the Historical Psychology of Chinese America," *Amerasia Journal,* 1:3 (November 1971), 1-31.

13. Rose Hum Lee, "A Century of Chinese and American Relations," *Phylon,* 11:3 (1950), 240-45.

14. Gunther Barth, *Bitter Strength: A History of the Chinese in the United States, 1850-1870* (Cambridge: Harvard University, 1964).

15. M. L. Keim, "The Chinese as Portrayed in the Works of Bret Harte: A Study of Race Relations," *Sociology and Social Research,* 25 (May 1941). 441-50.

16. Beulah Kwoh, "The Occupational Status of American-born Chinese Male College Graduates," *American Journal of Sociology,* 53 (1948), 192-200; and D. Y. Yuan, "Chinatown and Beyond: The Chinese Population in Metropolitan New York," *Phylon,* 27:4 (1966), 321-332.

17. Alan Nishio, "The Oriental as a Middleman Minority," *Gidra,* May 1969.

18. J. S. Tow, *The Real Chinese in America* (New York: Academy Press, 1923, Reprinted by R and E Research Associates, San Francisco, 1970).

19. Rose Hum Lee, "The Chinese Abroad," *Phylon,* 17:3 (1956), 257-70; Shien-woo Kung, *Chinese in American Life: Some Aspects of Their History, Status, Problems and Contributions* (Seattle: University of Washington, 1962); Francis L.K. Hsu, *The Challenge of the American Dream: The Chinese in the United States* (Belmont, California: Wadsworth Publishing Company, 1971); and Sung.

20. Charles N. Reynolds, "The Chinese Tongs," *American Journal of Sociology,* 40 (March 1935), 612-23.

21. John C. Ball and M.P. Lau, "The Chinese Narcotic Addict in the U.S.," *Social Forces,* 45 (Sept. 1966), 68-72.

22. Rose Hum Lee, "Delinquent, Neglected, and Dependent Chinese Boys and Girls of the San Francisco Bay Region," *Journal of Social Psychology,* 36:1 (Aug. 1952), 15-34; and Kenneth A. Abbott and Elizabeth L. Abbott, "Juvenile Delinquency in San Francisco's Chinese-American Community: 1961-66," *Journal of Sociology,* (National Taiwan University) No. 4 (April 1968), 45-56.

23. Lyman.

24. Chia-ling Kuo, "The Chinese on Long Island—A Pilot Study," *Phylon,* 31 (Fall 1970), 280-89.

25. Roland L. Warren, *The Community in AMERICA* (New York, 1973), 21-51.

26. W. Lloyd Warner and associates, *Democracy in Jonesville* (New York, 1964).

27. Herbert J. Gans, *The Levittowners: Ways of Life and Politics in a New Suburban Community* (New York, 1967).

28. David R. Goldfield (ed.), *The Enduring Ghetto* (Philadelphia, 1973).

29. Warren, 20.

30. Quoted in *The Black Ghetto: Promised Land or Colony?* ed., R. J. Meister (Lexington, Mass. 1972), xiii.

31. Kenneth Clark, *Dark Ghetto* (New York, 1965).

32. Stokely Carmichael and Charles V. Hamilton, *Black Power* (New York, 1967).

33. William Tabb, *The Political Economy of the Black Ghetto* (New York, 1970).

34. Robert Blauner, *Racial Oppression in America* (New York, 1972), 82-110.

35. Blauner, 84.

36. Tomas Almaguer, "Toward the Study of Chicano Colonialism," *Aztlan,* 2:1, 7-21.

37. For example: Donald Harris, "The Black Ghetto as Colony: A Theoretical Critique and Alternative Formulation," *Review of Black Political Economy,* 2:4 (Summer 1972), 3-33; also reply by William Tabb, "Marxian Exploitation and Domestic Colonialism: A Reply to Donald J. Harris," *Review of Black Political Economy,* 4:4 (Summer 1974), 69-91; and Christopher Lasch, *The Agony of the American Left* (New York, 1966).

38. For example, see Harris; Paul Baran and Paul Sweezy, *Monopoly Capital* (New York, 1966); James Boggs, *Racism and the Class Struggle* (New York, 1970). This paper will not deal with the differences among the Left.

39. Ivan Light and Charles C. Wong, "Protest or Work: Dilemmas of the Tourist Industry in American Chinatowns," *American Journal of Sociology,* 80:6, (May 1975), 1342-68.

40. N.S. Hayner, "Social Factors in Oriental Crime," *American Journal of Sociology,* 43 (May 1930), 908-911.

41. Rose Hum Lee, "The Chinese Abroad," *Phylon,* 17:3 (Autumn 1956), 257-70.

42. Light and Wong, 1364.

43. Stanford Lyman, "Marriage and the Family Among Chinese Immigrants to America, 1850-1960," *Phylon,* 29:4 (Winter 1968), 321-30; Asian Law Collective, "Past and Present: Asian Law Collective," *Amerasia Journal,* 2:2 (Fall 1974), 1-15.

44. D. Y. Yuan, "Voluntary Segregation: A Study of New York Chinatown," *Phylon,* 24:3 (Fall 1963), 255-65.

45. Cheng-tsu Wu, ed. *"Chink!"* (New York, 1972), 214-15, 227-47; and Ling-chi Wang, "Lau v. Nichols: The Right of Limited English-Speaking Students," *Amerasia Journal,* 2:2 (Fall 1974), 16-45; and R. Takashi Yanagida, "The AAFEE Story: Asian Americans for Equal Employment," *Bridge,* 3:4 (Feb. 1975), 47-51.

46. Michio Kaku, "Racism in the Comics," *Bridge,* 3:1 (Feb. 1974), 25-29; Benjamin Liu, "Adhesive Tape Orientals," *Bridge,* 2:3 (Feb. 1973), 7-10.

47. Some unpublished attempts include Isao Fujimoto: "The Legacy of Internal Colonialism and Its Impact on Asians in America," and John Liu, "The Internal Colonial Model and the Asian American."

48. Victor Nee and Brett De Bary Nee, *Longtime Californ'* (New York, 1972).

49. Some widely circulated writings include *IWK Journal,* (Aug. 1974); "The Asian American National Question" issued by a group in New York; and Wei Min She pamphlet (Sept. 1974).

50. Alvin W. Gouldner, "Toward the Radical Reconstruction of Sociology," *Social Policy,* 1 (May-June 1970).

51. Richard Flacks, "Notes on the Crisis of Sociology," *Social Policy,* 2 (March-April 1972) 4, 6-12.

THE CONCENTRATION CAMP EXPERIENCE FROM A JAPANESE AMERICAN PERSPECTIVE:

A BIBLIOGRAPHICAL ESSAY AND REVIEW OF MICHI WEGLYN'S YEARS OF INFAMY

By Raymond Okamura

At first glance, the sub-title of Michi Weglyn's *Years of Infamy: The Untold Story of America's Concentration Camps* (New York: William Morrow, 1976) might seem presumptuous. The concentration camp experience is undoubtedly the most written about aspect of Japanese American history: over fifty books on the subject have been published earlier. But a careful review of previously published works indicates the sub-title is fully justified.

Most prior books were reiterations of the War Relocation Authority (WRA) conceptual framework, i.e., the camps made the best of a bad situation. Such a pervasive influence by the WRA might be expected since they controlled the written record within the camps, and WRA-affiliated scholars gathered the basic data which formed the basis for all subsequent works. This author disagrees with Howard H. Sugimoto's "Bibliographical Essay on the Wartime Evacuation of Japanese from the West Coast Area" in *East Across the Pacific: Historical and Sociological Studies of Japanese Immigration and Assimilation* (Santa Barbara: American Bibliographical Center/Clio Press, 1972), and the following analysis is presented as an alternative.

There was a dearth of white liberals who protested the mass incarceration. About the only person of national stature to do so at the time was Norman Thomas in *Democracy and Japanese Americans* (New York: Post War World Council, 1942). Carey McWilliams initially applauded the forced removal, but after he observed the camps first-hand, he

changed his mind in *Prejudice: Japanese Americans: Symbol of Racial Intolerance* (Boston: Little, Brown, 1944).

Numerous white sociologists and anthropologists were attracted to the camps: with a captive community, they were textbook settings for conducting social research. Whether employed directly by the WRA or not, all social scientists adhered to WRA policies and regulations. No matter how well intentioned, the presence of non-prisoner scholars in a prison camp environment conjured tacky questions about the purposes for the research.

Dorothy Swaine Thomas and Richard S. Nishimoto in *The Spoilage* (Berkeley: University of California Press, 1946) acknowledged that "research" often meant "inquisition," and an "informant" was indistinguishable from an "informer." Thomas and Nishimoto chronicled the stormy history of Tule Lake and clearly delineated the separate and distinct phases of evacuation, detention, and relocation. (Other authors erroneously referred to the entire episode as "evacuation" or "relocation.")

Morton M. Grodzins' *Americans Betrayed: Politics and the Japanese Evacuation* (Chicago: University of Chicago Press, 1949) offered a compelling and detailed documentary on the organized campaign by West Coast pressure groups to get rid of the Japanese Americans. Jacobus tenBroek, Edward N. Barnhart, and Floyd W. Matson in *Prejudice, War and the Constitution* (Berkeley: University of California Press, 1954) disagreed with Grodzins' conclusions and

provided an even more comprehensive background by going back into the century of anti-Asian prejudice. TenBroek, Barnhart, and Matson more squarely blamed the federal government and presented an unsurpassed discussion of the constitutional issues.

Alexander H. Leighton's *The Governing of Men: General Principles and Recommendations Based on Experience at a Japanese Relocation Camp* (Princeton: Princeton University Press, 1945) contained useful historical information on the Poston strike, but the recommendations made this work into an administrator's guide on the control of prison populations. Leonard Broom and Ruth Riemer's *Removal and Return: the Socio-Economic Effects of the War on Japanese Americans* (Berkeley: University of California Press, 1949) might have served some useful purpose in obtaining redress for losses, but it did not. Working for the Office of War Information, Ruth Benedict also conducted social research in the camps, and while her *The Chrysanthemum and the Sword:*

Patterns of Japanese Culture (Boston: Houghton Mifflin, 1946) failed in its purpose to describe the contemporary Japanese in Japan, it did provide a record of Japanese immigrants' perceptions of Japanese culture.

The government presented its side with numerous official publications. The forced removal was justified in U.S. War Department, *Final Report: Japanese Evacuation from the West Coast, 1942* (Washington, D.C.: U.S. Government Printing Office, 1943). The camps themselves were rationalized in 12 volumes published by the U.S. Department of the Interior, *War Relocation Authority Books* (Washington, D.C.: U.S. Government Printing Office, 1946). Two of the WRA volumes were later reissued: Dillon S. Myer, *Uprooted Americans: The Japanese Americans and the War Relocation Authority During World War II* (Tucson: University of Arizona Press, 1971); and Edward H. Spicer, Asael T. Hansen, Katherine Luomala, Marvin K. Opler, *Impounded People:*

illustrations by MINE OKUBO

Japanese Americans in the Relocation Centers (Tucson: University of Arizona Press, 1969). Whether written by administrators or sociologists, the common theme was explicitly expressed in one title: *WRA: A Story of Human Conservation* (Washington, D.C.: U.S. Government Printing Office, 1946).

After the camps were closed, Louis Obed Renne wrote his reminiscences of Japanese American friends in *Our Day of Empire: War and Exile of Japanese Americans* (Glasgow, Scotland: Strickland Press, 1954). Morton M. Grodzins' *The Loyal and the Disloyal: Social Boundaries of Patriotism and Treason* (Chicago: University of Chicago Press, 1956) examined the McCarthy era obsession with loyalty oaths in light of the Japanese American precedent. Scholarly interest continued with Leonard J. Arrington's *The Price of Prejudice: The Japanese American Relocation Center in Utah in World War II* (Logan: Utah State University Press, 1962). Anne Reeploeg Fisher's *Exile of a Race* (Seattle: F & T Publishers, 1965) was one of the first to suggest Japanese Americans were the scapegoats for cover-ups and blunders of high government officials.

Sparked by the fear of revived concentration camps in the late 1960s, the Japanese American experience was exhumed in popular books: Allan R. Bosworth, *America's Concentration Camps* (New York: W. W. Norton, 1967); and Roger Daniels, *Concentration Camps USA: Japanese Americans and World War II* (New York: Holt, Rinehart, Winston, 1972). In order to fully appreciate Daniels' book, the reader should consult his background works: *The Politics of Prejudice: The Anti-Japanese Movement in California and the Struggle for Japanese Exclusion* (Berkeley: University of California Press, 1962) and *The Decision to Relocate the Japanese Americans* (Philadelphia: J. B. Lippincott, 1975). Charles R. Allen, Jr. visited the remnants of Tule Lake and discussed the new potential dangers in *Concentration Camps USA* (New York: Marzani and Munsell, 1966).

Audrie Girdner and Anne Loftis wrote a comprehensive and well-documented history in *The Great Betrayal: The Evacuation of the Japanese Americans During World War II* (New York: Macmillan, 1969), but much of their information was gleaned from secondary sources. Two sympathetic, but curiously insensitive, books were printed: Anthony L. Lehman, *Birthright of Barbed Wire: The Santa Anita Assembly Center for the Japanese* (Los Angeles: Westernlore Press, 1970); and Paul Bailey, *City in the Sun: The Japanese Concentration Camp at Poston, Arizona* (Los Angeles: Westernlore Press, 1971).

The first pilgrimage to a former concentration camp site was sponsored by the Manzanar Committee in 1969, and Japanese Americans started to openly discuss their camp experiences for the first time. A chronology of the internment years was prepared by Sue Kunitomi Embrey in *The Lost Years: 1942-1946* (Los Angeles: Manzanar Project/Moonlight Publica-

tions, 1972). On the other side of the coin, books like William Petersen's *Japanese Americans: Oppression and Success* (New York: Random House, 1971), and Bill Hosokawa's *Nisei: The Quiet Americans: The Story of a People* (New York: William Morrow, 1969) glorified submissive behavior and promoted the "success story" myth. Two children's books likewise emphasized the "success story" theme: Japanese American Curriculum Project, *Japanese Americans: The Untold Story* (New York: Holt, Rinehart and Winston, 1971); and Jennifer Cross, *Justice Denied: A History of the Japanese in the United States* (New York: Firebird/Scholastic, 1974). The "success story" books were a disservice to the aspirations of other minorities.

Each personal statement represented the perception of one person only, but the totality of such views gave a good idea of what camp life was like. Dorothy Swaine Thomas' *The Salvage* (Berkeley: University of California Press, 1952) and Leonard Broom and John I. Kitsuse's *The Managed Casualty: The Japanese American Family in World War II* (Berkeley: University of California Press, 1956) recorded a multitude of case histories. Two Christian ministers presented their opinions: Toru Matsumoto, *Beyond Prejudice: A Story of the Church and Japanese Americans* (New York: Friendship Press, 1946); and Daisuke Kitagawa, *Issei and Nisei: The Internment Years* (New York: Seabury Press, 1967). Charles Kikuchi's observations at Tanforan are recorded in John Modell, *The Kikuchi Diary: Chronicles from an American Concentration Camp* (Urbana: University of Illinois Press, 1973). Daniel I. Okimoto's essay *American in Disguise* (New York: Walker/Weatherhill, 1971) revealed how the camps affected his later thinking.

In recent years, more reliance was placed in oral histories: Arthur A. Hansen and Betty E. Mitson, *Voices Long Silent: An Oral Inquiry into the Japanese American Evacuation* (Fullerton: California State University, 1974); and Betty E. Mitson, *Looking Back in Anguish: Oral History and Japanese American Evacuation* (New York: Oral History Association, 1974). Such personal recollections by-passed the dependence on WRA documents.

Photographs and drawings also represented personal statements. Ansel E. Adams' portraits in *Born Free and Equal: Photographs of the Loyal Japanese Americans at Manzanar Relocation Center* (New York: U.S. Camera, 1944) were strong and determined. On the other hand, Maisie and Richard Conrat's *Executive Order 9066: The Internment of 110,000 Japanese Americans* (San Francisco: California Historical Society, 1972) used the forlorn and helpless figures of photographer Dorothea Lange. Allen H. Eaton photographed the arts and crafts in *Beauty Behind Barbed Wire: The Arts of the Japanese in Our War Relocation Camps* (New York: Harper, 1952). Estelle Ishigo's drawings in *Lone*

Heart Mountain (Los Angeles: Anderson, Ritchie & Simon, 1972) were refined and gentle; while Jack Matsuoka's Camp II, Block 211: Daily Life in an Internment Camp (San Francisco: Japan Publications, 1974) and Mine Okubo's Citizen 13660 (New York: Columbia University Press, 1946) were poignant, ironic, and bitter. Mine Okubo's retrospective work Mine Okubo: An American Experience (Oakland: Oakland Museum, 1972) indicated she had mellowed with time.

Novels and biographies about the camps, or its lingering aftereffects, include: Jacqueline Briskin, California Generation (Philadelphia: Lippincott, 1970); Jerome Charyn, American Scrapbook (New York: Viking Press, 1969); James Edmiston, Home Again (Garden City: Doubleday, 1955); Jeanne Wakatsuki and James D. Houston, Farewell to Manzanar (Boston: Houghton Mifflin, 1973); Karen Kehoe, City in the Sun (New York: Dodd, Mead, 1946); Florence Crannell Means, The Moved Outers (Boston: Houghton Mifflin, 1945); John Okada, No-No Boy (Rutland: Charles E. Tuttle, 1957); Monica Sone, Nisei Daughter (Boston: Little, Brown, 1953); Yoshiko Uchida, Journey to Topaz: A Story of the Japanese American Evacuation (New York: Charles Scribner's Sons, 1971). For a discussion on works of literature the reader is referred to two excellent reviews: Bruce Iwasaki, "Response and Change for the Asian in America: A Survey of Asian American Literature," Roots: An Asian American Reader (Los Angeles: University of California Asian American Studies Center, 1971); and Frank Chin, Jeffery Paul Chan, Lawson Fusao Inada, Shawn Hsu Wong, "An Introduction to Chinese and Japanese American Literature," Aiiieeeee!: An Anthology of Asian American Writers (Washington, D.C.: Howard University Press, 1974).

After all that has been written, one may wonder what more can be said. Yet, Michi Weglyn discarded preconceptions, went back to primary sources, and re-wrote the camp experience from a Japanese American frame of reference. Years of Infamy contains an astonishing number of facts previously de-emphasized, ignored, or censored. She sets the tone for her book with rarely published photographs of WRA brutality, coupled with the Japanese American response of defiance and resistance. The opening photographs shatter the previous image of WRA benevolence-inmate cooperation.

Years of Infamy first discusses the secret investigations conducted on the Japanese American communities on the West Coast and Hawaii several months before Pearl Harbor. The snooping was undertaken because high government officials were aware of the imminent danger of war and the likelihood of Pearl Harbor as the first target. A report by Special Investigator Curtis Munson, backed by decades of Federal Bureau of Investigation and Navy Intelligence files, unequivocally certified that the Japanese and Japanese Americans were of no menace. High government and military leaders were fully cognizant of Munson's findings, but they kept it a secret and callously promulgated public policy contradictory to what they knew. The Munson Report was declassified in 1946, but no other author picked up on this crucial piece of information which totally debunks the military necessity theory.

Another little known facet was the hemispheric conspiracy to hold all persons of Japanese ancestry as a "barter reserve" for prisoner exchanges with Japan, and as a "reprisal reserve" to insure the safety of American prisoners in Japanese hands. Not satisfied with just Japanese American hostages, the U.S. State Department pressured Central and South American nations into arresting and shipping their Japanese populations to the United States for internment. Shocking discussions were held with Canada about the possibility of deporting all persons of Japanese ancestry, regardless of citizenship, from North America. Michi Weglyn carefully documents these sinister plans and destroys any illusions about the camps being safe havens for the duration.

Government and military officials were acutely aware of the conflicts with the U.S. Constitution and Geneva Convention. Executive Order 9066 made no mention of the Japanese, but everyone knew it applied to the Japanese alone. Highly imaginative euphemisms were coined to obscure the facts: "non-alien" for American citizen, "evacuation" for forced removal, "relocation" for imprisonment, "reception center" or "assembly center" for interim detention camp, "relocation center" for concentration camp, "evacuee" for prisoner. (Ironically, Japan retaliated by calling their prison camps in China "assembly centers.") As a testament to the original propagandists, these euphemisms survive in usage to this day.

Years of Infamy is the first book since The Spoilage to adequately cover the protest movement within the camps, and the issues generated by the loyalty oath. Michi Weglyn adds a new dimension to the understanding of Tule Lake with information from the files of Wayne M. Collins. Collins labored some 25 years, mostly without fee, to correct the injustices perpetrated against the resisters, renunciants, expatriates, and the hostages from Peru. Several other authors have claimed "democracy corrects its own mistakes," but Years of Infamy proves such ideas to be naive. The victims had to wage a long and bitter struggle against an unyielding government, and Wayne Collins, more than any other single individual, was the agent for justice.

In sum, Years of Infamy represents a major breakthrough for the telling of Japanese American history from a Japanese American perspective. A history of the concentration camp experience has finally been written from the viewpoint of an outraged victim. This author hopes many more will follow. ★

BOOK REVIEWS

Japanese Americans: The Evolution of a Subculture. By Harry H.L. Kitano. (Englewood Cliffs, N. J. : Prentice-Hall, 1970)

Japanese Americans: Oppression and Success. By William Petersen. (New York: Random House, 1971)

Reviewed by JERRY SURH

Both of these books address themselves to the same problem: explaining the "success" of Japanese Americans during the postwar period, expressed in high income and educational levels and low rates of "deviance" (crime, juvenile delinquency, mental illness), despite racial oppression before the war and imprisonment during it. Moreover, both books cite the same general explanation, the support given individuals by a strong community and sense of identity; they both stress the cohesiveness and viability of the Japanese American community as a defining characteristic of the group. Finally, both books confine their definitions of "success" to those things which can be easily measured for the group as a whole, like median income and mental hospital admission rates. This tends to reduce the actual, living people they have studied to a social quantity, whose individual and subjective experience, had it been consulted, might not justify the term at all. This results in a massive insensitivity to the human dimension of the phrase "Japanese Americans," a kind of sociological amnesia as to the inner reflection of their sacrifices and successes as well as to the binds, tensions, and conflicts of identity and self-worth implicit in the lives of a non-white minority in a racist society.

The distinguishing feature of Kitano's account of the Japanese Americans is his reliance on Japanese cultural norms to explain their behavior. He uses this quaint relic of a bygone era in the social sciences without apology or explanation as to what it could mean. The fact that he gives the norms their Japanese names only adds to the mystery: "*on* (ascribed obligation); *giri* (contractual obligation); *chu* (loyalty

to one's superior); *ninjo* (humane sensibility); and *enryo* (modesty in the presence of one's superior)" (p. 102). These norms are most marked in the *issei* generation, but are passed down, Kitano does not explain how, to the *nisei* and *sansei* as well. In particular, he does not explain how he can speak of second- and third-generation Japanese Americans, who, by his own definition, differ from the *issei* chiefly in culture and behavior, as bearing Japanese characteristics at all. Kitano's application of these ahistorical cultural norms conflicts with his use of the generational terms to signify anything but the most ephemeral differences. The norms mystify the nature of cultural change among the Japanese Americans and make it seem peculiarly static and essentially impervious to non-Japanese influence.

An illustration of how Kitano uses these norms will be helpful. In his chapter on the wartime internment, he writes, "The evacuation was rapid, smooth, and efficient, *primarily* because of the cooperativeness of the Japanese population. . . . The manner in which the Japanese *obediently marched* to the trains and buses hauling them to camp presaged a conflict-free camp life" (p. 33. Emphasis added.). Of course, camp life was *not* "conflict-free," but this untruth seems an appropriate complement to the vicious half-truths preceding it. Later, he poses the question of "why the Japanese did not resist" and finds "social-psychological explanations" to be the most convincing: "The emphasis on norms—the 'how to behave in situations' direction of the Japanese culture also contributed to their docility. Norms and values emphasizing conformity and obedience meant that those in power (e.g., the U.S. Army) were able to use this position to gain the cooperation of the evacuated population" (p. 45). Kitano writes as if the Japanese Americans were the first group in history to fail to resist military power! He seems angry that they did not put up more resistance, and this feeling at least shows that inwardly he has not excused them from some share of the responsibility for their fate. Outwardly, however, he does excuse them by citing a special Japanese docility as the reason for non-resistance. Any even-tempered consideration of the political situation prevailing at the time would certainly show that we do not have to resort to cultural arguments to explain Japanese compliance. Kitano is insistent, however, and repeats the point on

illustration by ANTHONY COX

the next page (pp. 44-46).

Kitano follows Milton M. Gordon's classification of assimilation processes into acculturation, structural assimilation (crossing ethnic lines in primary group relations), and marital assimilation.[1] Kitano maintains that Japanese American assimilation has been confined to acculturation (adoption of cultural and behavioral norms) and that the Japanese have kept their souls by continuing to socialize and marry among themselves. However, he admits some slippage in the third generation: "Sansei college students now sometimes join non-Japanese fraternities and sororities, and inter-marriage is increasing, although the preference of most remains to marry within the group" (p. 142). The actual situation at the time he wrote these words was less reassuring. In 1973, Kitano and others published figures showing that the rate of out-marriage among Japanese Americans rose strikingly to around 50%, beginning in the mid-1960s.[2] This would seem to destroy a large part of Kitano's intellectual scaffolding in the book under discussion, although he did not admit this in the later article. The figures show that Kitano misjudged the Japanese-American community's opposition to out-marriage and misunderstood *sansei* assimilation.

Although he pays lip service to it, Kitano fails to follow through with Gordon's method on a key point. Gordon maintains that ethnic groups are internally stratified and segmented according to social class and geography. Yet Kitano does not present Japanese Americans as internally differentiated to any significant degree. Despite occasional mention of lower class Japanese and isolated references to Japanese in other areas and states, Kitano's study confines itself to middle-class Japanese Americans in the Los Angeles area. On the question of social class, Kitano plays both sides of the court: at one point, he says that the Japanese like other immigrant groups have differentiated along social class lines from the original immigrant base, which was more homogeneous in occupation, education, and income (p. 58); later, he says class distinctions among *nisei* are still negligible, adding that "The gardener, the CPA, and the doctor may make up a threesome at golf" (p. 141). His discussion of social class unfortunately does not rise above that level. Very little about the social structure of the Japanese-American community can be established from this book. In neither the text nor the 22 pages of statistical tables appended to it is there a reference to income distribution among Japanese Americans. From Kitano's account it is impossible to learn that Japanese Americans in Hawaii, Washington, and rural areas differ from those in Los Angeles, let alone what those differences are. The reader is given no choice but to think of the community solely in terms of generation and Kitano's woolly cultural categories.

The book is further marred by what can only be called poor scholarship. Kitano cites a number of studies of Japanese Americans by other scholars, but in such a brief and breezy manner that only vague impressions are communicated. For instance, he reports that studies by Fenz and Arkoff have "noted that Sansei males expressed high need for deference, abasement, nurturance, affiliation, order, and exuberance, and a correspondingly reduced need for dominance, aggression, autonomy, exhibition, and heterosexuality when compared to Caucasian males" (p. 111). One can only wonder at Kitano's reasons for citing this article with such mysterious brevity, not discussing its import or even indicating what he thinks the statement means. The result of such lightning squibs is to confuse and mislead.

On other occasions, Kitano claims he is demonstrating something specific to Japanese Americans because the evidence originated among them, while in fact it could apply to any ethnic group. For instance, he cites the following statement by a *nisei* woman in order to illustrate some unique quality of the "Japanese-American family":

> I don't know whether you would call it guilt or shame but I felt that my parents or others were looking over my shoulder all of the time. Whether I went out on a date or whether I was studying at school I knew I couldn't let them down. I know it inhibited me in the sexual area and helped me study hard at school (p. 68).

In fact, the statement could easily have been made by a middle-class person of WASP or Jewish or almost any other extraction.

The burden of Kitano's ahistorical argument is that the strength of the family, the community, and behavioral norms drawn from Meiji Japan explain the success and stability of Japanese Americans as a whole. He does not discuss the price they have paid for this success. He does mention, in passing, a "permanent psychological damage" the Japanese Americans have suffered and compares their behavior to that of Memmi's colonized, but he does nothing to integrate such observations with his main argument, and it is impossible to treat them as more than fleeting remarks. The reader is thus unprepared for and somewhat surprised by the following passage, encountered at the very end of the book:

> . . .the judgment of Japanese Americans as the 'model American minority' is made from a strictly majority point of view. Japanese Americans are good because they conform—they don't 'make waves'—they work hard and are quiet and docile. As in a colonial situation, there tends to be one set of prescriptions for those in power and another for the subject people. But, ideally, members of the ethnic community should share in any evaluation of the efficacy of their adjustment. For if the goals of the American society include freeing an individual for self-expression and creativity, and if social maturity includes originality, participation,

and the opportunity for individuals to function at their highest levels, then certain questions may be asked about the Japanese (p. 146).

Yet Kitano himself has made a case for viewing Japanese Americans as a "model minority." He seems to be playing both sides of the court again. The disorienting feeling that Kitano dissents from the very views he has presented is strengthened when we read on the previous page, "This writer feels that social interaction based primarily on interest and achievement is healthier than one based on ethnicity." One wonders why we did not read this earlier in the book, where he gave the impression that Japanese American avoidance of structural assimilation (and therefore of "interaction based primarily on interest and achievement") constituted the strength of the community and family and was therefore a key to their "success." Still, one must be grateful that he registered his recognition that Japanese-American "success" has not been unmixed, even if such recognition has been ineffective.

It appears that Kitano's closeness to his subject matter has been more of a drawback than an advantage. He seems not to have removed himself sufficiently from his own commitments to the subject, and the book can too easily be read as an embodiment of middle-class *nisei* views, values, and conflicts, barely concealed behind a facade of sociological jargon and "models." This view of it would explain the bland and politically chaste tone; the stiff avoidance of the full consequences for the Japanese of white racism (being still too emotionally charged an issue); the failure to consider conflicts and controversy within the Japanese-American family and community or the effects of the internment on Japanese-American psychology and behavior; the reverent and respectful treatment of the *issei* and the slightly disbelieving and mildly disapproving attitude toward the *sansei*. The book does center itself on *nisei* achievements; it displays less empathy for the first generation and has little to say about the future and direction of Japanese Americans. It thus has some value as an unwitting statement of a *nisei* outlook; but as an account of Japanese Americans it leaves almost all the hardest and most interesting questions unasked and unanswered.

William Petersen's book is a different story. Although it gives the same general answer to the same question as Kitano's book, it does so with altogether more self assurance and professional polish. It is also much more sharply aware of the conservative political interpretation of Japanese-American "success" and does not hesitate to align itself with that interpretation. For a book which seeks to explain the behavior of the Japanese minority in the U.S., it devotes a disproportionately large amount of time to discussing Japanese society and culture.

In contrast to Kitano, Petersen does not have

any use for Japanese behavior norms or traits of national character in accounting for Japanese American behavior. He writes:

> Even a sympathetic observer of the psychological analysis of national character. . .cannot characterize this subdiscipline as well-grounded in conceptual clarity and empirical fact, and Americans' analyses of the national character of the Japanese are not the best examples of the genre (p. 160).

He has in mind naive and dated works like Benedict's *The Chrysanthemum and the Sword*, which Kitano, by contrast, cites with approval (p. 102).

Petersen has fewer illusions and certainly no axes to grind with respect to the Japanese-American community's response to the internment. His chapter on the subject confines itself to describing life in the camps, the court fights against internment, and the unanimity with which public opinion lined up against the Japanese, especially among liberals, whose behavior Petersen analyzes with particular interest and attention. His judgment that the "infestation" of liberal organizations by Communists was the main factor behind their failure to aid the Japanese Americans rather too easily exonerates liberals from any share in the racist hysteria; this is not to deny, of course, that the Communist Party had immense influence on the Left or that its support of the internment was a repulsive and hypocritical act.

Petersen's book represents no original research, but it does examine a great deal of secondary literature with a critical eye. Although he focuses his attention on the Japanese sources of Japanese American behavior, his knowledge of and interest in Japanese history and traditions does not lead him to exaggerate their influence. Successive chapters on "The Country of Emigration," "Religion," and the "Family" all basically reject the notion that there was any simple and direct relation between Japanese traditions, values, and institutions, on one side, and Japanese-American "success" on the other. In particular, Petersen admits (in refreshing contrast to Kitano, who repeatedly blurs this point) that "the discrepancy is enormous between Japanese Americans of the first and second generations—in age, in culture, in occupational level, in social roles. . . . Whatever made this second generation different, whatever gave the Nisei the strength to thrive on adversity, it was more than the continuity from the culture of Meiji Japan that their family and religion effected" (p. 210).

Unfortunately, this critical attitude does not last throughout the book. In the last chapter, entitled "Subnation," he abandons scholarly restraint and gives us his answer to the question of Japanese-American "success," at the same time delivering an unwanted and superfluous message on race relations. Partly reversing himself on the importance of the legacy from Japan in making it possible to adapt "successfully," Petersen reminds the reader "that the boundaries Japanese draw in their institutional controls very often include the whole of the ethnic community.... Even old-fashioned parents are relatively indifferent to an interfaith marriage of their son or daughter, while even thoroughly Americanized Sansei typically avoid one that crosses racial lines" (p. 214). Without ever uttering the word, Petersen thus suggests that the Japanese adapted "successfully" to racist oppression by themselves becoming racists. He observes that the Japanese "truly believe (as do Jews) that they are innately superior, that others are inferior" (p. 225). He reminds us that "Long before they had any contact with either Caucasians or Africans, the Japanese valued 'white' skin as beautiful and deprecated 'black' skin as ugly," (p. 227) and that Japanese Americans still seem to ostracize the Eta or outcast peoples of Japan (pp. 228-229). Petersen compares the Japanese Americans favorably with American Blacks, arguing that unlike the Japanese, "a Negro can name no other homeland, he has no refuge when the United States rejects him." Has he forgotten that the U.S. is more the homeland of the Blacks than it is of most whites? One wonders what he would say about the condition of American Indians. This kind of distorting and ignoring the plain facts of the historical record is worthier of a race ideologist than of a serious and critical sociologist. Petersen goes on to quote the words of a conservative editor of a Japanese-American newspaper admonishing the Black community for failing to take responsibility for their unhappy lot, implying that the editor somehow speaks for all Japanese Americans.

Not finding an answer to the question of Japanese-American "success" through careful and critical inquiry, Petersen resorts to artifice, inventing the concept of "subnation" on the basis of information about a single group, and quite incomplete information at that. Using the concept as a prop in a rather sophomoric polemic against Marxists and assimilationists (pp. 215-220), he makes a straw man out of R.E. Park's assimilation cycle, reducing it to mean "that all races are essentially the same and that any initial differences would inevitably disappear in a predestined, four-stage succession" (p. 232). The alternative Petersen holds out to this oversimplified version of assimilation is the equally simplified notion of the subnation, which may be said to mean that all races are essentially different, and that despite superficial assimilation, the differences are predestined to remain. Of course, neither proposition adequately represents the aspirations or behavior of any ethnic or racial group, except perhaps whites of the same religious persuasion.[3]

Petersen's "subnation" and Kitano's less ideologically aggressive "subculture" both rest on a falsification of the record. This is not the place to take up the question in a comprehensive manner, but there is abundant evidence that the Japanese were far more willing to acculturate and assimilate than white America was ever willing to tolerate; and that, consequently, affirmation of the Japanese heritage was, from the beginning, a mixture of the voluntary and the involuntary. This was true not only for the *nisei*, whose marginality has been extensively discussed, but for the *issei* as well.[4] Petersen and Kitano suppress or minimize this aspect of Japanese-American experience, consoling themselves with the happy thought that it has not resulted in extensive deviant behavior (they might have turned out like the Blacks!), while ignoring the fact that racism and the response to it, even by "successful" minorities, lead lively existences today.

Like Kitano, Petersen leaves out of account the rates of Japanese-American outmarriage prevailing since the 1960s; he cites only evidence about the third generation that strengthens his case. The quickened interest among *sansei* in Japanese culture which he notes (pp. 208-209) does represent an actual trend, but its meaning changes when one adds the fact that this same generation is simultaneously outmarrying at a dramatically increased rate. Neither author understands the *sansei* generation very well, and neither devotes much attention to it. Both insist on defining a single trend for the whole Japanese-American group, and although this practice has a limited usefulness, it leads to ignoring a group's heterogeneity, idiosyncracies and internal conflicts or to reducing them to a single formula. With the passing of arranged marriages and the power of parental consent, marriage has become a more purely personal matter for Japanese Americans, as it is and has been for most Americans. This change has not simply added another factor to the authority of the group in marriage decisions; it specifically *denies* the authority of the group over this kind of decision and represents, to some degree, the individuation and liberation of its members from its hold.

While outmarriage does not necessarily signify the disappearance of the ethnic group, it does indicate a change of self-conception and group boundaries, hardly an appropriate juncture at which to describe the group as a "subnation." One can only speculate as to Petersen's reasons for doing so. At the same time, it is difficult not to observe that his subnation concept can serve as a soothing balm for those who are wearied and distraught by two decades of racial revolution in this country. It argues that the effects of white racism have not been so debilitating that they cannot be overcome by a stiff dose of ethnic parochialism; while the rigid racial boundaries most whites observe seem no worse than those the Japanese have allegedly drawn round themselves. If one defines ethnocentricity and feelings of racial superiority as normal and proper to subnations, how can the same feelings logically be denied to whites? The subnation concept thus implicitly rationalizes white rejection of blacks and other racial minorities.

In addition, the concept holds every ethnic group solely responsible for its own fate, so that praise for Japanese "success" implies censure for Black "failure," as Petersen has made explicit. The whole ugly history of white domination of political, social, and economic power in the United States and the use of it to subordinate colored and other minorities to the sway of white money and property is thereby plastered over and made to seem simply a matter of competing ethnicities and lost cultural heritages.

January 1976

Notes

1. *Assimilation in American Life: The Role of Race, Religion and National Origins* (New York, 1964).

2. H. Kitano and Akemi Kikumura, "Interracial Marriage: A Picture of the Japanese Americans," *Journal of Social Issues,* 29:2 (1973), pp. 67-81. For additional figures and more interesting interpretive remarks, see John N. Tinker, "Intermarriage and Ethnic Boundaries: The Japanese American Case," Ibid., pp. 49-66.

3. See Gordon, *Assimilation in American Life,* pp. 122-124.

4. E.g., see Daisuke Kitagawa, *Issei and Nisei: The Internment Years* (New York, 1967) pp. 9-12.

Bitter Strength: A History of the Chinese in the United States, 1850-1870.
By Gunther Barth. (Cambridge: Harvard University Press, 1964)

The Story of the Chinese in America.
By Betty Lee Sung. (New York: Collier, 1967)

Chinese Americans. By Stanford M. Lyman. (New York: Random House, 1974)

Reviewed by LINDA P. SHIN

In spite of the great interest that has developed over the last decade in the history of the Chinese people in the United States, there are still very few books on the subject. The books under review are widely used today in the mid-1970s. As a group, they reveal great changes in styles of historical writing over the past 25 years, illustrating the way that historians respond to the events of their day and reflect social trends within their own society.

Bitter Strength by Gunther Barth is a history of the interaction between Chinese and white Californians from 1850-1870. Barth analyzes Chinese society of the Canton delta area in the 1840s and 1850s, the structure of Chinese emigration to Southeast Asia and the Americas, the structure of Chinese society in California, and the rise of the anti-Chinese movement. A product of lengthy historical research in English-language primary materials, *Bitter Strength* nonetheless presents a biased and distorted picture of the Chinese in America. The distortion is largely due to Barth's shallow knowledge of Chinese society in the mid-nineteenth century. This leads him to rely upon misleading analyses of Chinese society as well as upon sources laden with notions of white racial supremacy. The second source of the distortion is Barth's unexamined assumptions and value judgements about mid-nineteenth century America, amounting to a form of unreflective patriotism.

Barth's thesis is that the Chinese migrants themselves caused the torrent of hostility that marked their stay in the United States up to 1870. According to Barth, white Californians wanted a free, democratic society, and "unfree" peoples like the Chinese threatened their goal (p. 2). In an approach that sees the acculturation of the Chinese as the only desirable goal of the early interaction with Americans, Barth charges that the structure of Chinese migration prevented them from acculturating and thereby accepting American ideas of democracy and equality. Without examining the fact that this "dream" reflected white supremacist notions, Barth asserts that the Chinese and other non-whites were obstacles for reasons other than race.

According to Barth, because the Chinese were

"sojourners," whose goals in the United States were "limited" to that of earning money, they were unresponsive to the "universal message of the American democratic creed" (p. 157). Moreover, Barth asserts that the Chinese migrants functioned under an alien system of repression and control administered by other Chinese and existed apart from white society. White Californians could not tolerate an enclave of unfree persons in their midst, so the argument goes, and reacted violently against the Chinese.

The idea that the Chinese alone came to the United States to earn money and return home, in contrast to European migrants, does not stand up to historical reality. The gold rush in California brought sojourners from many nations hoping to strike it rich: the Chinese were certainly not unique.

Barth's assertion that the Chinese functioned under an alien system of repressive control rests upon two arguments: 1) the pattern of overseas migration was unfree; and 2) the organization of the "work camp" in California was unfree. Let us examine these two areas and see what proof Barth brings forth to prove his assertions:

1) Overseas Migration: Much Chinese emigration to the United States was in the form of the credit-ticket system, in which a merchant advanced the migrant the passage money. The migrant then agreed to pay him back on a yearly or monthly basis until the debt was paid off. Barth charges that this system constituted "in part" a "disguised slave trade" (p. 67) creating a system of debt bondage for Chinese "indentured emigrants," who were forced by their merchant creditors to accept low-paying jobs under regimented, slave-like conditions. These conditions enabled the creditors to control a tight system of supervision. From this Barth concludes that Chinese society in the United States constituted a closed structure in which exploiter and exploited were locked in a "vertical" relationship that existed apart from its surroundings.

While there was certainly exploitation of Chinese workers under the credit-ticket system, Barth does not prove that it constituted a "slave trade" of regimented slave-like workers. Barth's main evidence that the system was a "slave trade" is based upon the anti-slavery and "anti-coolie" writers of the 1850s such as Persia Campbell, where anti-slavery and anti-Chinese attitudes blended to form a biased picture. In contrast to the situation among contract laborers in Latin America, the Caribbean and Southeast Asia, there is little evidence to suggest that Chinese migrants in the United States were subject to the same strict supervision and control by their creditors.

Why does Barth so readily assert that the Chinese were indentured bond slaves? Perhaps the reason is that the white Californians in the 1850s and 1860s perceived them as unfree, and Barth uncritically accepted that judgement. But the white Californians'

ideas of China and the Chinese were conditioned by a century of contacts between the United States and China, marked by the development of many unfavorable stereotypes of China, as amply shown by Stuart Creighton Miller in his *The Unwelcome Immigrant: The American Image of the Chinese, 1785-1882* (Berkeley, 1969). By assuming that his sources were unbiased, Barth fell into a trap that historians should try to avoid.

2) Regimented Work: In his treatment of the "work camp," Barth says that "an invisible control system based on district loyalty, filial piety, and fear circumscribed the realm of Chinese California and re-enforced the basic allegiances of traders and miners in isolated mountain camps," where they labored under "the chains of daily drudgery" (p. 109). Barth's evidence for these loaded assertions consists of: (1) two accounts showing that the Chinese miners lived in crowded conditions; (2) one contemporary opinion that the Chinese miners got less pay than whites; (3) one description of a Chinese workteam with a foreman or "boss," and (4) one instance of a Chinese thief being harshly punished by other Chinese for a crime (pp. 144 ff.).

This is far from conclusive evidence for such loaded assertions. Crowded quarters may also suggest the need for self-defense in a hostile environment or companionship. Lower pay and a Chinese supervisor— or someone a white passerby thought was a supervisor—are too intangible to suggest a structure of regimented work gangs. Indeed, as Alexander Saxton shows in his book, *The Indispensable Enemy: Labor and the Anti-Chinese Movement in California* (Berkeley, 1971), many Chinese miners worked for themselves and not for a "boss." When historians make strong charges using loaded terminology, as Barth has, they have to come up with stronger proof than *Bitter Strength* does.

This example illustrates a common pitfall for historians: failure to subject their sources to the kind of rigorous cross-examination that is commonplace in courts of law. How good is this witness? How accurate is her memory? Were his views clouded by gross prejudice or bias? Does she have a vested interest in the case? Trial lawyers and judges must consider these issues, and so must historians. When there is any question about the reliability of the sources, they must be used with considerable caution.

Barth's work is largely based upon contemporary newspapers, memoirs and documents written by white Americans, many of whom had virulently anti-Chinese attitudes and ideas of white racial supremacy. The only Chinese-language material used is Liang Ch'i-ch'ao's journal of his trip to America written around the turn of the century and cited in two footnotes in inconclusive fashion. With this exception, all of Barth's sources are English-language materials that provide not even the slightest clue to the inner life, ideas and experiences of the Chinese migrants. Scarce wonder that they appear to him as a silent mass of "inscrutable" Asians! Barth did not tap the rich store of materials dealing with the life of the Cantonese in the mid-nineteenth century that exists in Chinese. Because he did not use Chinese materials, Barth was forced to rely upon English and German sources for his analysis of Chinese society in China and the United States, leaving him with a fragmentary picture which reinforces his own point of view.

Since Barth is a highly trained historian and his books has been published by Harvard University Press, some people may wonder how Barth, his teachers and his publishers could have been so careless. This book was researched and written in the late 1950s, when because of the lingering effects of McCarthyism, scholars often feared being labelled un-American. Or worse, many scholars did not challenge the patriotic image of American history as a panorama of freedom-loving people living out a democratic creed of liberty and equality. Themes of conflict, racism and imperialist expansion were often ignored or interpreted in less "controversial" ways. Barth's portrayal of the white Californians as solely inspired by democratic values and humanitarianism and his ignoring of more negative qualities are characteristic of American historical writing during the 1950s.

Likewise, the anti-Chinese bias of the book seems to reflect the American public's perception of China as a regimented, totalitarian society, in which docile peasants were ruled by power-hungry bosses and bureaucrats. In the 1950s the press and media commonly used such value-loaded terminology in reporting events from China, and Barth unquestioningly applied the same loaded terminology in writing his book. These phrases from the first eight pages of *Bitter Strength* are illustrative of the loaded terminology found throughout the book: "tidal wave," "flood" and "hordes" of Chinese; "docile subjects of bosses," laboring under a "control system" of "regimented labor," with a "machinery of control and work" or "supervision and drudgery" and living in "teeming blocks." This is certainly the way that Americans and Europeans perceived of China in the mid-nineteenth century, but it also sounds much like the American press reports of the establishment of the people's communes in 1957-1958! Barth's views of the Chinese fit well with contemporary anti-communist ideas of China and patriotic notions of American history, perhaps because he could not avail himself of Chinese-language materials nor through his own research in primary materials develop an analysis of Chinese society of the mid-nineteenth century.

Thus *Bitter Strength* shows the pitfalls that await the historian who approaches a subject with unexamined value judgements and biases, who is inadequately prepared to deal with important facets of his topic, and who misuses his sources as a result.

Written for adolescents but of interest to adults as well, Betty Lee Sung's *The Story of the Chinese in America* is a useful survey of the history of the Chinese in America up through the 1950s. In sharp contrast to the faceless, regimented "hordes" of Barth's book, Sung shows us the Chinese as people with dignity, pride, humor and feelings. The utility of the book is enhanced by the fact that Sung has included material on subjects not readily available elsewhere, such as the chapter on Christian churches in Chinese communities, and the sections dealing with population and intermarriage. For these reasons, the book is certainly an advance over writings such as Barth's.

Still, this book has many limitations. The author states that she does not intend to "whitewash" or do a "P.R." job on behalf of the Chinese (p. 8) but there are times when major areas of difficulty are glossed over. For example, while the chapter on the Chinese family presents a balanced account of the traditional family, elsewhere the traditional family and the Confucian doctrines that maintained it are presented in a highly romanticized way (e.g., pp. 18-19, 95). As an extreme example of this tendency to gloss over difficulties, even the economic problems of immigrant garment workers in Chinatown sweatshops are dismissed (p. 146)!

Sung also presents a highly rosy picture of American society. While not so dogmatic on the matter as Barth, Sung still believes that racial discrimination is not a significant issue for Chinese and that any Chinese with initiative can become a success (e.g., pp. 89-90, 143). If a Chinese has a problem "making it," that is his or her individual problem of "adjustment" and not a problem for the social structure at large. In the author's words, "For minority groups, it is always more convenient to shout discrimination" (p. 125).

Sung drives this point home by concluding her books with biographies of twelve famous Chinese in America. The message is clear: the United States is the land of opportunity, and if you haven't become a millionaire or great success, you have nobody to blame but yourself. Thus the burden of accommodation falls upon individual Chinese, obviating the need to examine the socio-political structure of the United States.

Yet Sung's biographies suggest an entirely different interpretation. Of the twelve famous persons she discusses, ten were born in China, and two in America. The two born in the United States are U.S. Senator Hiram Fong, born in Hawaii, and Dong Kingman, educated in China. What Sung's biographies suggest is that persons of privileged social background in China found it easier to translate their social status and superior education into a privileged American sector than have Chinese born in the United States, who are rarely from elite social backgrounds and who have been handicapped economically and educationally in America.

For all her assertions that anti-Chinese sentiments

are no longer significant in American life, Sung tacitly acknowledges that they do indeed exist. Again, however, the onus falls upon the Chinese to accommodate themselves to the situation rather than try to change it. For example, recognizing that the Chinese form a "visible" minority by virtue of race, Sung advises them to avoid clustering in large cities or certain regions for fear of incurring hostility from whites (p. 91)! In the section on intermarriage, Sung goes so far as to suggest that intermarriage (presumably with whites) may ultimately "solve" the problem of visibility. If a white person were to suggest this sort of "final solution" to the "Chinese problem," it would be clearly seen for the racist notion it is. For a Chinese American to suggest it constitutes an unconscious acceptance of the values and standards of a white-dominated society. This is perhaps the logical outcome of the kind of "survival" mentality forced upon minority peoples in the United States.

This "survival" mentality is also shown in the veiled slurs against other minority groups, as for example in the condemnation of Chicano migrant farm workers for constituting an unstable and marginal social group in California (pp. 70-71) and in praising the Chinese for their "healthy" attitude towards prejudice—by trying to ignore it—in implied contrast to other minority groups who are perceived as "belligerent or pushy" or else as "submissive and servile" (pp. 261, 252).

The same mentality is also seen in the persistent assurances to the reader that the Chinese in America are strong anti-communists and firmly loyal to American principles. Since the option of returning to China now no longer exists, Sung says, the Chinese in America have been forced to seek a "new niche" (p. 20). Perhaps the recent thaw in relations between the United States and the People's Republic of China will reduce the need for American Chinese to make testimonials of this sort.

From today's vantage point, Sung's book seems dated. Late recognition of Chinatowns as urban ghettoes exacerbated by the influx of immigrants since 1965, the rise in militancy of many minority peoples in the 1960s, and the demands of Chinese and other people for a more even shake make Sung's optimism seem anachronistic.

Published in 1974, *Chinese Americans* by Stanford M. Lyman is the most up-to-date of the books under discussion. Covering much the same ground as Sung's book, Lyman gives the reader a survey of the history of Chinese in America and then looks at contemporary trends. While Lyman, like Barth, uses no Chinese-language sources, he has been able to draw upon a greater range of scholarly work on China and the United States than was Barth. Written by a professional academic sociologist, *Chinese Americans* is an attempt to provide a balanced portrait of Chinese in America by presenting a

number of viewpoints in a manner that aims at "objectivity." Lyman's discussions of nineteenth-century Chinese in America, with sections on Chinese village structure, community organization in the United States, the anti-Chinese movement and the "institutional racism" of the twentieth century, are on the whole accurate and concise. Herein lies the book's greatest strength.

The later chapters dealing with events of the 1950s and 1960s are less satisfying. Chapter 6 (The Beginnings of a Chinese American Middle Class) and Chapter 7 (Social Problems and Community Cooperatives) have a good deal of valuable information but are marred by the author's tendency to avoid linking problems faced by Chinese to a more general critique of American society.

In the section on "vexing social problems," for example, Lyman focuses on the problems of the "bachelor society" of older men without families, who usually live in crowded conditions and in great poverty, sometimes solving their problems through drug abuse or suicide. The implication is that most of the social problems for Chinese in America are linked to the ghetto and generationally to the elderly, who will eventually die off, thereby eliminating the source of the problem. Lyman implies that although Chinese who leave the ghetto and move to surburbia may experience a spiritual loss by being cut off from the familiar environment, this is a relatively small price to pay for the advantages of moving into the mainstream of American life.

Indirectly, this analysis reflects the perspectives of the majority society in dealing with minority groups. In spite of the numerous problems linked to ghetto conditions, such as poverty and poor housing, ghettoes also give minority peoples the basis to wield political power through the greater concentration of numbers. Chinese isolated in surburbia cease to be a problem for the majority society, because their isolation leads to a loss of political power. Yet the problems of surburban life for Chinese and indeed for Americans of all races are not raised.

Lyman's discussion of the exploitation of garment workers shows a similar reluctance to link their problems to the larger society. Properly noting the problems of immigrant Chinese women who need to work close to home and in a Chinese-speaking environment, as well as the issue of racism in the American labor movement, Lyman does not sufficiently explore the fact that minority business-men generally operate with highly limited capital and a low profit margin. Community cooperatives for garment workers, the solution discussed in the book, are largely recognized now as an inadequate solution to the problem of exploitation of immigrant Chinese women. The problems faced are not those of the Chinese community alone but are shared by many small businesses in an economy dominated by corporate giants. By focusing on this issue in isolation as a Chinese community problem, Lyman avoids raising it as a problem that affects many other Americans as well.

Lyman's treatment of trends of the 1960s (Chapter 8: Alienation, Rebellion, and the New Consciousness) poses even greater problems. In this chapter Lyman deals with "youthful rebellion," Asian-American studies, problems in defining the term "Asian," what he terms "the dilemma of Chinese American constituencies," and "The Two Chinas and Chinese Americans." In general, this chapter suffers from less thorough research than that which characterizes the earlier historical sections. Some parts of the chapter are quite good, as for example, the section "The Two Chinas and Chinese Americans." Likewise, the section on "youthful rebellion" has some good insights into the rise of juvenile gangs in the larger Chinese communities. Yet as in the cases cited previously, Lyman does not attempt to discuss the problem of Chinese juvenile delinquency within the overall context of American society, but instead sees gangs as "pre-political" rebels as suggested by E. J. Hobsbawn in an entirely different historical context. This unwillingness to discuss the problem within the context of American life constitutes a most glaring omission in the area of a social problem that has generated a substantial body of social science literature.

The sections dealing with Asian American studies and the definition of the term "Asian" are even less satisfactory. Lyman asserts that Asian American studies programs on college campuses are in a period of transition in which the immediate goals of the late 1960s, such as reform of textbooks, have been accomplished (so he says) but no new goals have yet been formulated.

There is still much work to be done in genuinely integrating ethnic studies into American history and studies in the humanities and social sciences. Unless faced with constant pressure from inside and outside the college campus, traditional academic departments are unwilling to engage in basic research in subjects they still feel are "unacademic," i.e., non-traditional subjects that still have not been accepted as valid areas of inquiry. This, rather than an internal shifting of goals, is the major problem faced by Asian-American studies in the mid-1970s. As to Lyman's problem with the term "Asian," most persons involved with Asian-American studies will view this as a spurious issue, without great relevance.

Somewhat disturbing is Lyman's tendency to treat Chinese social problems in a sensationalist way. For example, his discussion of Chinese criminal organizations of the 1920s and 1930s is handled in an exaggerated way and without reference to the flourishing of large-scale criminal syndicates throughout American society during the same period— remember Al Capone?

In summary, Lyman's work is very useful for its analysis of Chinese American social structure in the nineteenth and early twentieth centuries, but far less successful in dealing with contemporary events.

The author's quest for "objectivity" leads to a number of interesting ramifications. On the one hand, it leads Lyman to attempt to "be fair," that is, to mention alternate theories, to present a "balanced" picture of a situation, to take everything into account. The result of this effort is often a "buckshot" approach with pellets scattered far and wide but lacking a coherent analysis. No one can truly avoid a viewpoint, if that is how "objectivity" is defined. As we have seen Lyman's "objectivity" sometimes masks an unexamined assimilationist approach to the study of Chinese in America.

These three works illustrate the ways that historical writing reflects the preoccupations and social interests of the researcher and his or her historical period. In Barth's book we see anti-Chinese perceptions of China and the Chinese coupled with a view of American society so rosy that it borders on chauvinism. In Sung's book we see the beginnings of self-assertion by the Chinese in America but within a framework that accepts the basic premises of American society and politics and calls upon the Chinese to accommodate themselves to the system rather than press for social change in the majority society. In Lyman's work we see the way that the social movements of the 1960s have brought forth responses from academia attempting to incorporate the new critiques of American history and society, but as yet inadequately.

These works show the strength of the assimilationist framework for the analysis of Chinese and other minority peoples in America, a framework that dominated writings on the subject by whites and non-whites alike for many years. In Barth and Sung there are unexamined assimilationist views and assumptions that provide the framework of their analyses. While Lyman is highly critical of assimilationist views in sociological theory—and the racism that lies beneath them—he too has perhaps unconsciously reflected them while striving for "objectivity."

A key point for us to learn from these works is that all historical writing has a viewpoint. It is impossible to avoid having one and still have anything to say. The very choice of subject matter and questions asked reflect viewpoints. If one cannot be "objective" in writing history, what use is it? Simply because "objectivity" is impossible, it doesn't mean that there are no standards towards which historians strive. Historians should try to examine their values and assumptions in the light of their research and should constantly examine their approaches to their subjects in an attempt to avoid misrepresenting what happened in the past. Honesty, intelligence and *commitment* are the hallmark of good historians, who contribute to the world around them through their humanity, not in spite of it.

Ethnic Enterprise in America: Business and Welfare Among Chinese, Japanese and Blacks. By Ivan H. Light. (Berkeley and Los Angeles: University of California Press, 1972)

Reviewed by L. LING-CHI WANG

Why have the Chinese and Japanese been so success-ful in developing small businesses in their own communities while the retail trade in Black communi-ties across the U.S. have been dominated by White merchants? Why is it that Asians in America have rarely been found on public welfare rolls while impoverished Blacks have regularly turned to public agencies for relief? Or more dramatically speaking, why did race riots occur in Watts, Detroit, Newark, etc., and not in Chinatowns and Japantowns in American cities? In other words, given similar historical experiences—racial discrimination and economic exploitation—why can't the Black be like the Asian in America? These essentially are the major questions Ivan H. Light, through a research grant from the Manpower Administration, U.S. Department of Labor, seeks to answer in his recent book, *Ethnic Enterprise in America.* This review will focus primarily on Light's thesis, how he develops it and what's wrong with it. Through this process, the reviewer hopes to expose the author's bias and errors. No attempt will be made to correct the factual errors on the Chinese in the U.S. in this book.

To answer the above questions, Light first dismisses a number of previous answers as unsatis-factory. He describes the "consumer-demands" theory advanced by R. H. Kinzer and E. Sagarin as "correct, but inadequate." According to this explana-tion, the special demands of ethnic consumers or the so-called "culturally derived consumer preferences" (e.g., lasagna, kosher pickles, won-ton or sukiyaki) created protected markets for ethnic retailers. Black retail tradesmen, on the other hand, are subjected to competitive and inhibiting White retailers. Unfortun-ately, this explanation, according to Light, could not

account for the disproportional over-representation of Asian retailers and their substantial non-Asian clientele. Moreover, the explanation assumes no "cul-turally-derived differences" in the economic behavior and organization of foreign-born Asians and native-born Blacks.

Light next dismisses a two-hundred-year-old explanation that blames the Black under-representa-tion in small business on the difficulty of Blacks in securing business loans from institutional lenders. Citing conclusions from a few studies on small businessmen, he contends that loans from institutions have been "relatively insignificant among the finan-cial resources actually employed by proprietors in the capitalization of small firms"; besides, the Chinese and Japanese would have suffered the same discrimin-ation in lending. Instead of relying on lending institu-tions, heavy reliance on personal resources, especially personal savings and loans from kin and friends, has been found to be the case, according to Light. He makes no mention of the close connections between banking and industrial complexes and their common interests in exploiting the cheap labor source of the minorities and the poor in the U.S.

Light also sees no merit in E. Foley's explana-tion: lack of business success symbols. He describes it as "flimsy and probably incorrect." However, he finds E. Franklin Frazier's theory "relevant." Frazier placed the blame for the lack of business success on the lack of traditions among the Blacks in the field of business enterprise, that is, experience in buying and selling. But, according to Light, Frazier "failed to follow up lines of inquiry suggested by his own conclusion," meaning that he should have examined the cultural traditions relevant to the capitalization of small business.

With these criticisms as background, Light proceeds to do a lengthy search for those relevant traditions or what he calls "the culturally preferred style of economic organization" among the Asian in America. In brief, he finds the most important single cultural tradition relevant to the financing of small business enterprises among the Asian to be the tradition of "informal financial cooperation" or what anthropologists call "the rotating credit associa-tion." He accepts Shirley Ardener's definition of this type of cooperative financial institution as "an association formed upon a core of participants who agree to make regular contributions to a fund which is given, in whole or in part, to each contributor in rotation." This system is embodied in the concept of *hui* or *ko* among the Chinese in China and in the U.S., *tanomoshi* or *mujin* among the Japanese and *esusu* among the Blacks in Africa, Britain and parts of the Americas, notably the West Indies. Since Asian and Black-owned banks in the past ended usually in dismal failure, which Light blames on such administrative problems as incompetence, mismanagement and official venality, they provided no viable financial resources for small business development. In fact, their failure heightened the importance of the Asian rotating credit association as a viable alternative not available to the Black whose African *esusu* tradition was totally eradicated under the American slavery regime. Thus, Light concludes, "what was remarkable about the Negro's efforts to finance himself was not the systematic bank failures which frustrated his efforts, but the lack of a traditional alternative."

In addition, Light attributes the success of the *hui* and *ko* to "the strong, informal, and moralistic social relations of lenders and borrowers," which could only be sustained by what he calls "a continuous attention to the punctilio of decorum, honor, and especially of family reputation." From this, he plunges into a long discourse on the various well-publicized Asian community organizations commonly known as family and district or regional associations. According to him, the Japanese *kenjin* and the Chinese family and district associations were "ascriptively defined, mutually supportive moral sub-communities," set up to promote regional and clan solidarity and to look after the social and economic welfare of their sojourning members. These organizations were bound by a strong sense of ethnic, clan and territorial honor, and they provided an extensive spontaneous social trust and intensive internal solidarity, which according to Light, facilitated the commercially necessary and useful rotating credit associations. The same community structure accounts for the widespread Chinese preference for partnership over solo proprietorship. It is this same sense of ethnic honor, says Light, that accounted for the "very favorable popular image of Oriental honesty" and for the "extraordinary success" of Asian school children.

In marked contrast to the Asian, urban Black communities had to depend on *voluntary* organizations as the foundation of their social structure, because, according to Light, "Old World ties of region, tribe, and extended kinship had been torn up by slavery and had not been subsequently regenerated on a new basis." In other words, the southern-born Blacks "lacked a highly evaluated past which would stimulate the establishment of organizations based on regional loyalties," meaning, they had no worthy cultural traditions. Worse yet, lower class Blacks

adopted "the perspective of unenlightened whites" which regarded Africa as "a region of steaming jungles, naked savages, blood-thirsty cannibals, and idolatrous religious beliefs." The image, according to Light, was hardly conducive to personal identification with Africa or to social organization on the basis of African origins, meaning, Blacks must adopt the dominant White culture and traditions. Moreover, caste subordination of Negroes deprived Negroes of any valued ethnic identity or honor. As a result, "Blacks were free to act as individuals quite apart from group approval of the impact of their actions on Black honor. The rampant individualism contributed to the disorganization of social life in the slums."

Light identifies four basic types of voluntary organizations in the Black community: business development organizations (e.g., the National Negro Business League), social welfare organizations (e.g., National Urban League), churches and fraternal orders. He finds members of both the Business League and Urban League, unlike the Chinese and Japanese regional and clan associations, lacking in "migrant solidarity," and the people both organizations served were "not subordered into ascriptively bounded moral communities as were Chinese and Japanese." Thus, the Urban League was elitist, condescending and professionalistic while the Business League was bourgeois, selfish, profit-motivated, individualistic and therefore counter-productive. The failure of these two types of Black organizations, according to Light, could be attributed to the Black community's inability to suborder into kinship, tribal, or locality groups like the Chinese and Japanese.

Churches and fraternal orders, on the other hand, are the only primary social institutions able to enlist the voluntary participation of broad masses of Black people. They are institutionalized moral communities like the regional and kinship associations of the Chinese and Japanese. However, they failed to attain the intensity of internal social solidarity characteristic of the Chinese *fong* and Japanese *kenjinkai* because they were voluntary and their membership, drawn from "a culturally undifferentiated mass," was "ascriptively unrelated." Proliferation of churches and fraternal orders created theological rivalry, competition for membership, overlapping membership, skepticism, sectarianism and disloyalty, all of which were absent in Asian organizations. Only Father Divine's movement, as a successful but transitory effort to develop Black-owned businesses and to eliminate welfare dependency among the Blacks during the Great Depression, was able to achieve internal solidarity and cooperation comparable to the Asian.

Therefore, Light's answer to the questions posed at the beginning of this review is simple: Asians were successful in the small business world in comparison with Blacks in America because Asians had inherent and relevant cultural traditions such as the rotating credit association, tightly controlled family and district associations, ethnic solidarity and honor while Blacks had none. For the same reason, Asians needed no public assistance while there was an extensive dependency on welfare by the Blacks.

This line of thinking is of course not original. Public media have been propounding it since World War II when Asians were first allowed to enter selected technical occupations in war-related industries, essentially jobs non-competitive with Whites. Popular racist myths and stereotypes about Asians describe Light's thesis in plainer language: "the quiet Americans," "the silent minority," "they pull themselves up by their bootstraps," "they take care of their own kind," "they have no problems," "the successful minority," "they are too proud to go on welfare," "why can't they [Blacks] be like the Asians," etc. The presumption of Light's thesis and these popular myths is that Asians were economically successful ("the model minority") in spite of adversities and that they did not have social and economic problems as a result of being victims of racism. The solid proof of this thesis is their fine cultural traditions and the high percentages of self-employed Chinese and Japanese in the U.S. by 1920 and the high median family income in the last two decades.

I do not want to engage in a lengthy discussion of the social and economic problems among the Asians except to say that they did and still do exist. I do want to make a few points in connection with the development of the Chinese business class in America since this is the focus of the book. Light does not differentiate between the business and labor classes in the Chinese community nor does he make a distinction between the treatment accorded to both classes by the U.S. government and White businessmen. All existing available historical documents point to the existence of the Chinese business class prior to the major influx of Chinese laborers in 1852 (Frazier's theory is relevant here). This same business community maintained a non-Chinese clientele and established close contact with not only white businessmen but also the rising Chinese capitalists in the treaty ports in China. The famous China trade figured prominently in this joint venture on both sides of the Pacific.

During the Gold Rush period, some of them were instrumental in providing logistic supplies and vital services for the White miners, and many through the district associations played key roles in eventually recruiting and supplying cheap labor for the flourishing mining, railroad, agricultural and manufacturing industries in the West and in providing goods and services for the Chinese in the U.S. This same class, unlike the great majority of Chinese working people, was exempt from the famous Chinese Exclusion Act of 1882 and given special treament by the U.S. government and big business. The exploitation of the Chinese laboring class by these businessmen, both Chinese and Whites, was not only tolerated but legitimized by the government. In short, the existence of the Chinese business class in America is not simply the result of some unique cultural traditions, as alleged by Light. It antedated the massive arrival of Chinese laborers, and it expanded with this arrival and was accorded special privileges and protection because of American interests in maintaining good trading relations with China. The development of Chinese business therefore hardly needed the help of the rotating credit system, even though it was undoubtedly used. This helps to explain Light's difficulty in substantiating both his claim of widespread use of the system and his main thesis.

The preceding paragraph amply illustrates three major issues confronting Asian American scholarship today. First, sources and authorities currently used by many historians and scholars, Light included, are both inadequate and biased; they are almost exclusively English sources. This may mean that they do not read nor have access to Chinese sources. Hence the findings of these writers are highly questionable. Second, most scholars treat the Chinese community as if it were monolithic and they are unable to deal with the internal contradictions and developments of the Chinese community. The parallel development of the merchant and laboring classes is an excellent example which Light fails to recognize. Third, almost without exception, they ignore the important role of U.S.-China relations on the development of the Chinese community. The China trade and American interests in the treaty ports and throughout China have definite direct effects on the Chinese in the U.S. By relying on inadequate and unreliable scholarship, Light was uninformed about many aspects of the Chinese American community.

Even though Light acknowledges the historical and destructive role of racial discrimination and economic exploitation on the development of both the Black and Asian American communities, his thesis clearly undermines, if not actually negates, the role of racism and monopolistic capitalism in oppressing the Third World and poor people. By attributing the Black's failure in small business development to alleged lack of cultural traditions, Light diverts attention from these important issues and factors. Similarly, he posits that Asians became successful in spite of oppression and exploitation. Light in this respect must be considered as trying to justify and legitimize the above-mentioned popular, racist beliefs, that every minority group should be able "to pull itself up by the bootstraps" and that the Blacks should be more like the Asians, even with a different culture and historical experience. His logic renders him an apologist for racism and economic exploitation. Light's use of some supposed Asian cultural values as the criteria for analyzing and judging the historical experience and performance of the Black community raises two serious questions. First, from the comparative methodological point of view, these criteria are not only inapplicable but improper. Such strenuous imposition of one set of cultural values on another culture and community is just as erroneous and unjustifiable as injecting White middle-class values into any studies on minorities in the U.S. In this regard, the method must be considered racist.

Second, the thesis, in the present political and racist context, is extremely divisive. It pits one minority group against another and instills hatred among minority groups. If one of the purposes of this study is to draw attention from the real problems arising from racism and social injustice, it has outdone itself. From the tactical point of view, this is the familiar divide-and-conquer tactic.

American Racism: Exploration of the Nature of Prejudice. By Roger Daniels and Harry H.L. Kitano. (Englewood Cliffs, N. J. : Prentice-Hall , 1970)

Reviewed by DON T. NAKANISHI

If you think about a "big" social problem in great detail, there is a tendency either to become hopelessly entangled in its complexity or to anchor it to a simple explanation.[1] Racism in American society is one such problem, which has generated its share of knotty commentaries and simple generalizations. It is a problem in which actions probably speak louder than words, but instead words have been copiously used to describe the actions. Real solutions have been as difficult to locate as the Loch Ness monster. And like the search for the monster, many people believe that solutions can be found if we keep wading through the murky, and sometimes turbulent, water.

American Racism by Roger Daniels, a historian, and Harry Kitano, a social psychologist, is one of many attempts to isolate and tie-down the beast of racism and race relations in American society. It is a book which is not intended to be definitive, but nonetheless has all the ingredients for being an ingenious contribution to the understanding of the subject. It uses, for instance, the oft-praised multi-disciplinary approach by combining historical analysis with a social science framework to compare an array of minority groups—Blacks, Chicanos, Native Americans, Japanese Americans, Chinese Americans, and Pilipino Americans. It gives an analysis of how

so-called "ordinary solutions" to problems of race relations such as prejudice, discrimination, and segregation can lead to "extraordinary solutions" such as apartheid, concentration camps, expulsion, and extermination. And it focuses on California where the center stage of racial strife and controversy was occupied, until quite recently, by groups other than American Blacks. But all these ingredients do not necessarily stir up good food for thought, especially when the ingredients have a tendency of working against each other. This is the case with *American Racism,* which provides not only a fleeting but also an unsystematic and contradictory account of the nature of racism in American society. The beast, as many of us have come to know it, remains elusive and untied.

American Racism attempts to follow the ancient adage that a work of composition must have a beginning, middle, and end. This is what Aristotle identified as the order of a tragedy. The book begins with a presentation of a perspective on race relations, which rests on a two-category system. "By 'two-category'," write Daniels and Kitano, "we mean a system of stratification that is divided into two broad categories: the white and nonwhite. . . . a paternalistic structure—that is, one group presumes superiority over the other. . . . Physical visibility, based primarily on skin color, means that a quick differentiation can be established." (p. 5) They hypothesize that attempts will be made to develop and maintain boundaries between the races,[2] and that this process of racial separation evolves around four basic stages of ordinary and extraordinary solutions. Ordinary solutions such as prejudice, discrimination, and segregation are the first three stages and "do not appear to be unusual responses to the racial problem in American life." (p. 11) Extraordinary solutions, on the other hand, represent the fourth stage and are employed when the first three stages have failed. Apartheid, concentration camps, expulsion, and extermination are examples of extraordinary solutions and require "triggering mechanisms" which "may be external to the group (e.g., wartime evacuation of the Japanese), or it may arise from within the group (e.g., the Watts riot of 1965)." (p. 12) The term "nonwhite," as Daniels and Kitano use it, refers to groups which are commonly identified as racial minorities such as Black and Asian Americans. The term "white," though, refers "primarily to the white Anglo-Saxon Protestant (WASP). He is our 'national type' as represented by the *Mayflower*, George Washington, Davy Crockett, and Abraham Lincoln." (p. 13)

The middle section of *American Racism,* which approximates the beginning and end in length, provides a historical analysis of racism in California from 1769 to 1942, and from 1942 to the present. The aim of this rapid march through history is to demonstrate "that a two-category model is, in fact, the most suitable." (p. 87) The historical experiences of California's racial minorities are presented one after another, with emphasis placed on major events such as the campaign to end Chinese immigration, World War II evacuation of Japanese Americans, Zoot Suit Riots, Sleepy Lagoon case, and the Watts Riot. No attempt is made to systematically compare the experiences of the different racial groups with a set of hypotheses or variables, and the two-category model is simply ignored because of its inability to provide anything more than the broadest possible outlines for explaining the richness of the historical information. Economic competition, party politics, and international relations, for instance, are three of a number of different factors which are used in an ad-hoc fashion in the historical narrative and are absent from the two-category framework. What the commentary does suggest is a constantly changing pecking order of racial abuse with each racial minority becoming the primary victim of some form of racism at different periods in California's history. No group was spared, but the particular configuration of actors and factors which was responsible for making a specific group the target of such abuse was not always the same.

The ending to *American Racism* is potentially its most insightful section, and yet it becomes its most confusing one. Both confusion and insight result from the two-category stratification model, which assumes as many appearances as a chameleon can change its color. Daniels and Kitano, for instance, begin this section with the following remarks:

> We began by assuming a simple two-category stratification system which, like most ideal models, violates somewhat issues which are infinitely complex; nevertheless, the historical data suggest that a two-category model is, in fact, the most suitable. Two simple categories, white and non-white seem to dominate the social structure, and the color barrier seems to have been the single most important factor in determining white and nonwhite relationships. (p. 87)

Beginning with this statement, Daniels and Kitano proceed to amplify on the features of the two-category model by first identifying the variables which account for the permeability of the color barrier by certain racial minorities (e.g., Japanese and Chinese).[3] Then they advance some "hypotheses" (awkwardly defined, "in the sense of summarizing and guiding our thinking, rather than using it in the sense of final empirical verification" p. 98) on the experience of California's minorities. They go on to explore the nature of extraordinary solutions by posing the question, "Can It Happen Again?" referring to the World War II evacuation and the Watts Riot. Finally, they conclude with a discussion of the so-called "ethnic crisis of our time," which they feel consists "of simply this: for the first time in our history almost all submerged groups in our country—groups that Gunnar Myrdal styles the 'underclass'—are demanding entrance into the major institutions of our society (especially in the areas of education, jobs, and housing). . . . on their own terms." (p. 98) In the process of discussing these topics, the two-category model or system is said to be, as the above passage argues, an "ideal model," and yet the "most suitable" in the light of historical evidence: "in actual practice. . . impossible to enforce" (p. 98) but "in some form or other, is likely to be with us for some time" (p. 124) and "increasing[ly] recogni[zed] by more and more members of the black community of at least [its] relative permanence." (p. 121) At the same time, the so-called color barrier is seen as "the single most important factor in determining white and nonwhite relationships" which is "neither rigid nor impermeable" (p. 89) and as both a real and artificial boundary between the groups. The difficulty in pin-pointing the nature of these oft-used terms—as conceptual schemes, perspectives, actual state of affairs, or personal beliefs—makes the ending of *American Racism* extremely unwielding and vague. Despite this sloppiness, this section presents some insightful comments about the mood of racial relations in the late 1960s.

American Racism, though, simply does not hang together. It lacks a basic unity and satisfies Aristotle's ancient notion of order in form rather than substance. In many respects, this is a case where two heads were not better than one. Both Daniels and Kitano are capable of excellent and insightful scholarship, but both sacrificed their talents and knowledge in producing this work: Daniels had to fight his data with an inadequate explanatory model, and Kitano had to fight his model with an overwhelmingly complex empirical foundation. Both assert that the historical information supports the conceptual scheme, but this must be assumed at face value because a systematic analysis never takes place. The book reads like two separate essays, one historical and the other conceptual. And it should be read in that manner.

It provides very few, if any, timeless contributions to the understanding of race relations in American. The historical analysis of California's racial minorities does not necessarily present any new evidence or explanations, and the two-category model is not new.[4] It is similar to other "paternalistic" (vs. "competitive") models of race relations.[5] It is far from being a theoretical work, if theoretical means "a logically interrelated system of general propositions that are close enough to the operational level to be directly or indirectly testable."[6] And it is not a scientific one, if scientific at least means to operationalize variables, consider alternative hypotheses, and to make an effort to test one's own hypothesis with rival ones. *American Racism* could have, for instance, made a real contribution if it had attempted to assess the explanatory value of both paternalistic and competitive conceptions of race relations for specific historical periods in California's experience with nonwhite groups. It could have also benefited from making the implicit notion of some form of shifting pecking order of racial minorities a more explicit framework of analysis.

American Racism might not offer timeless contributions, but, I think, it was a timely work. It was written in the late 1960s, when American society was faced with the "big" problem of racism and the "big" problem of Vietnam. Both problems generated controversy and violence, and had a polarizing effect on the country. It was a time when it seemed like you were either *this* or *that*: a hawk or dove, WASP or Third World, pig or part of the people. It was also a time when it seemed like all American institutions were under attack, and long-cherished American values and conceptions were being questioned, if not simply ignored. In the mid-1970s, these battle lines seem somewhat blurred and simplistic, and even though racism is still a "big" problem, Vietnam is not. *American Racism* may strike most readers as being outdated for the simple reason that it is. For instance, Daniels and Kitano write about the racist campaign that Sam Yorty waged against Tom Bradley in the 1969 Los Angeles mayoral race. They say that "the election demonstrated clearly the racist nature of the electorate. Despite disillusionment with Yorty, the real choice of only a quarter of the voters (in the primary), a majority was willing to continue him (or

probably any white man) in office rather than try a black man." (p. 123) Such an observation, of course, gives us no guidance for understanding why Bradley was later elected. The same could be said for the McCarran Act of 1950 and its Title II provisions, which they say makes the possibility of internment for other racial groups aside from the Japanese Americans so much greater. Again, we cannot really assess why it was repealed. And finally, the observation that "certain lifestyles usually attributable to lower social classes (inability to take financial risks, a fate orientation, conformity, and distrust of politicians) are probably also related to nonwhite status" (p. 100) may seem almost true for all Americans in the 1970s, no matter what social class or race, following Watergate and during a period of economic recession. Daniels and Kitano were not the only ones who accepted the rudimentary features of the prevailing dichotomous perspective of the late 1960s, and due credit should be given to their attempt to capture it.

American Racism, though, should be seen as an attempt to lasso the beast of racism in American society with a simple explanation. But like many other attempts, Daniel and Kitano might have thought that they had captured it all, when, in fact, they had caught nothing.

Notes

1. I am extremely indebted to Marsha Nakanishi for her many substantive and editorial suggestions.

2. Daniels and Kitano refer to "boundary maintenance" or "the set of beliefs, attitudes, organizations, structures, institutions, and mechanisms which support the distinction between races." p. 7

3. Ibid., pp. 89-95. It should be observed that the notion of permeability is not the same as the idea of pecking orders. The analysis which is given here is not dynamic and cannot account for the change of position of California's racial minorities in an evolutionary social ladder.

4. See, for instance, Gunnar Myrdal, *An American Dilemma* (New York: Harper and Row, 1972), pp. 690-693; and W. Lloyd Warner, *American Life: Dream and Reality* (Chicago: University of Chicago Press, 1953), pp. 66-72. Examine their diagrams and commentary with that of Daniels and Kitano, especially pp. 95-96.

5. See Pierre L. Van den Berghe, "Paternalistic Versus Competitive Race Relations: An Ideal-Type Approach," in Bernard Segal (ed.), *Racial And Ethnic Relations: Selected Readings* (NY: Thomas Crowell Company, 1966), pp. 53-69 for a comparative analysis of the two models of race relations.

6. Hubert M. Blalock, *Toward a Theory of Minority-Group Relations* (New York: Capricorn Books, 1970), p. 1.

EARLY ISSEI SOCIALISTS AND THE JAPANESE COMMUNITY

BY YUJI ICHIOKA

The Japanese government "is not by the people, of the people, for the people. It is the government of the few, of the nobles, of the titles, and above all, of the figurehead—the Mikado."

—Kaneko Kiichi, May, 1905.

INTRODUCTION

Much of Japanese-American history remains unwritten in English, not because of any conscious efforts by past historians to ignore it, but due to a particular preoccupation they have had.* On the whole historians have only been interested in Japanese-Americans as "objects" of the prewar exclusion movement or have focused upon the "excluders" with the former then studied only in relation to the latter. Secondary reasons, in either case, account for their studies which has led one historian to say "other immigrant groups were celebrated for what they had accomplished; Orientals were important for what was done to them."[1] The results of this preoccupation are apparent. Whether we speak of general political, social, economic or cultural histories, or specific community histories, or biographies, there is an appalling dearth, if not an absolute void, of historical studies on Japanese-Americans in English. As an illustration of what can be uncovered in what, in the opinion of the writer, is a rich and varied history which still remains essentially buried, this essay will examine the early Issei socialists and anarchists in the San Francisco Bay Area and Fresno and a related lèse-majesté affair which occurred in Bakersfield in 1911.

---

* All Japanese names are in Japanese order, last name first and without commas, except for Japanese authors of English works, who are listed with last names second in the notes.

THE MEIJI BACKGROUND

As with other aspects of the Japanese immigrant and his society, an understanding of the Meiji background is essential. The modern labor and socialist movements in Japan developed after the Sino-Japanese War of 1894-95. And, curiously enough, in the case of the labor movement itself, it had immediate roots in the incipient Japanese immigrant society in California. The first organized group to investigate the possibility of forming industrial trade-unions was formed in Tokyo in April, 1897. Called the Shokko Giyukai (Friends of Labor), this group, under the influence of the American Federation of Labor, was initially formed in San Francisco in 1890 by Takano Fusataro, Sawada Hannosuke, Jo Tsunetaro, and others to study labor problems. Upon their return to Japan, they reconstituted it in 1897 out of which two other organizations developed.[2] In July, 1897 the Rodo Kumiai Kiseikai (Society for the Promotion of Trade-Unions) was created with a wider membership than the Shokko Giyukai, including the later renown communist, Katayama Sen.[3] Like its forerunner, it was a study society intent upon examining labor problems and solutions. In December, 1897 the first industrial trade-union, the Tekko Kumiai (Iron Workers' Union), was successfully organized in the Tokyo-Yokohama area, and simultaneously the *Rodo Sekai* (Labor World), the first labor journal, was launched under the editorship of Katayama Sen.[4]

Socialist Movement

The beginning of the socialist movement can be

Katayama Sen at age 25   Kotoku Shusui, 1871-1911

traced to the formation of the Shakaishugi Kenkyukai (Society for the Study of Socialism) in October, 1898.[5] As its name implies, it was a study group whose aim was "to examine the principles of socialism and determine whether or not they are applicable to Japan."[6] Most of the original twelve members were Christians; three were Christians who had studied in America. And five members played some kind of role in the activities of the Issei socialists and anarchists in America. These five were: Kawakami Kiyoshi, Katayama Sen, Abe Isoo, Kaneko Kiichi, and Kotoku Shusui. This group later established the first socialist political party in Japan on May 20, 1901, the Shakai Minshuto (Social Democratic Party), whose existence was short-lived. As soon as the party published its proclamation and platform, the Meiji government declared it illegal and ordered it to disband. Confronted by a repressive government, the members of the party had no choice but to reorganize themselves, this time into an "educational" organization called the Shakaishugi Kyokai (Socialist Association), with Abe Isoo as its head, which conducted public lectures on socialism and labor problems in various parts of Japan. It dared not step directly into the political arena, however, for the Public Peace Preservation Law of 1900 strictly prohibited labor agitation designed to form labor unions to fight for higher wages and better working conditions.

The Russo-Japanese War of 1904-05 had far-reaching effects on the socialist movement. As with the war in Vietnam, anti-war voices emerged, especially from socialist and Christian quarters. Chief among the socialist dissenters was Kotoku Shusui. In November, 1903, just at the time when war with Czarist Russia appeared imminent, Kotoku and Sakai Toshihiko formed the Heiminsha (Commoners' Society). From the very first issue of its journal, the *Heimin Shimbun,* published on November 15th, this society started an anti-war campaign which became more and more strident as hostilities opened and the war continued. In November, 1904 Kotoku was arrested for violating the National Press Law, tried and found guilty, and sentenced to five months imprisonment.[7]

Upon the conclusion of the war and the inauguration of the new Saionji Cabinet in January, 1906, the Meiji government adopted a less repressive policy towards the socialist movement. Under this circumstance, the second socialist political party, the Nihon Shakaito (Japan Socialist Party), was launched in February, 1906. Emphasizing parliamentary tactics aimed at securing universal suffrage and electing candidates sympathetic to or actually drawn from the working class, its constitution incorporated the key phrase "we advocate socialism within the limits of the law." But within a year these tactics came under heavy criticism at the party's first anniversary conference in 1907. The main critic was Kotoku who, in its stead, advocated what he called "direct-

Kotoku Shusui at the San Francisco Pier

action."[8] By direct-action Kotoku meant the use of massive general strikes, interpreting them as the only real means by which the working class could secure power. Over this issue a heated debate took place between Christian socialists and anarcho-syndicalists, and when the party adopted a compromised position which nonetheless deleted the key constitutional phrase "within the limits of the law," the government immediately suppressed it. This party hence suffered the same fate as its abortive predecessor, and the socialist movement split into a number of factions until the celebrated "High Treason Affair" of 1910.

This event involved the wholesale arrest of leading anarchists and socialists, beginning in May, 1910, with the disclosure of a "plot" to assassinate the Meiji Emperor.[9] The controversial trial which ensued was conducted in secrecy, and despite the fact that no conclusive evidence was presented—except that four individuals, excluding Kotoku Shusui, had some kind of preliminary plan to manufacture bombs—26 persons were found guilty. Twelve persons, including Kotoku, were executed in January, 1911, twelve others were sentenced to life imprisonment, and the two remaining defendants were sentenced to serve definite terms in the military. Of the effects of this event on the socialist movement, Katayama Sen wrote: "All books on socialism were confiscated and all public libraries were ordered to withdraw socialist books and papers. Even moderate papers like ours

Picture taken when Kotoku departed for Japan in June, 1906. The banner reads Shakai Kakumeito (Social Revolutionary Party). Members of the Party sending him off are from left to right: 1. & 2. listed as spies 3. Hasegawa Ichimatsu 4. Yamagata Bakuetsu 5. Nishizawa Yaeko (wife of Yamauchi Gonjiro) 6. Ogawa Kinji 7. Oka Shigeki 8. Albert Johnson 9. Sagitani Nankyo 10. Kotoku Shusui 11. Nakayama Kyuichi 12. Takeuchi Tetsugoro and 13. Kotoku Koei (Kotoku Shusui's nephew).

were severely censured and a few months after the said trial it was practically suppressed by the authorities."[10] Japanese historians call the year 1911 the start of the "cold, wintry period" for socialists, for they were subsequently driven into hibernation until after World War I when they emerged again under the influence of the Russian Revolution.

SAN FRANCISCO BAY AREA

Issei socialists came from the foregoing Meiji background. Since the socialist movement began after the Sino-Japanese War of 1894-95, one would not expect any immigrant socialists before this period.[11] Immigrant socialists indeed do not appear until after the turn of the century, and among those who do many are Christians and, not too surprisingly, much of their activities centered in a Christian organization, the Fukuinkai or Gospel Society, in San Francisco.[12] By the beginning of 1904, there were two socialist groups, akin to discussion-study societies, one located in San Francisco and the other in Oakland, which were influenced by the arrival of certain socialist leaders from Japan.

Both Katayama Sen and Abe Isoo came to the Bay Area. Katayama arrived in January, 1904 to attend the National Convention of the American Socialist Party in Chicago in May and then to proceed to Amsterdam for the Sixth Congress of the Second International. Landing first in the Pacific Northwest, he, assisted by Kawakami Kiyoshi, spoke on socialism in Seattle on January 19, before a Japanese audience in a talk sponsored by the Japanese Association.[13] Upon his arrival in the Bay Area, he also spoke before Japanese groups, and on February 3 he formed the Soko Nihonjin Shakaito (San Francisco Japanese Socialist Party).[14] According to Iwasa Sakutaro, one of its founding members and at that time the manager of the Gospel Society, this organization dissolved as suddenly as it was formed. Though entrusted with the responsibility of drafting up the party constitution and governing rules, Iwasa confesses that he never got around to this task. "Our minds had not progressed to the thought of starting a movement," he stated, and the 38 original members drifted away.[15] Yet they did undertake one activity: an anti-war meeting in San Francisco. Under the influence of Kotoku Shusui's anti-war campaign in Japan, they held their meeting in the San Francisco Japanese Methodist Episcopal Church in March, with the support of the Oakland group led by Uyeyama Jitaro and Takeuchi Tetsugoro, amid accusations of being "traitors" and "disloyal Japanese subjects."[16] Following the heels of Katayama, Abe Isoo visited the San Francisco area in the spring of 1905 leading the Waseda University baseball team. During the interval between Katayama's departure and Abe's arrival, very little occurred aside from occasional meetings of the immigrant socialists. Abe, too, addressed different groups and met with immigrant socialists, but his moderate brand of Christian socialism did not appeal to them.[17] The decisive influence had to await the arrival of Kotoku Shusui.

Kotoku Shusui in America

Upon his release from Sugamo Prison, Kotoku decided to come to America to regain his health and to observe at first-hand the socialist movement in this country. To Albert Johnson, a veteran anarchist in California with whom he had corresponded before his imprisonment, he wrote that he had entered Sugamo "as a Marxian Socialist and returned as a radical Anarchist" and that he wished to criticize Japan from "where the pernicious hand of 'His Majesty' cannot reach."[18] In addition, he had in mind the possibility of making San Francisco a "logistical base of operation" for the Japanese socialist movement as well as a "sanctuary for the persecuted" such as Switzerland had become for Russian revolutionaries.[19] On December 5, 1905 he arrived in San Francisco from Seattle. Besides Albert Johnson, among the welcoming party there was Oka Shigeki, a former newspaper associate. Much to his delight and satisfaction, he was quickly whisked off to the San Francisco branch of the Heiminsha, established earlier in the year by Oka and 10 others.[20]

Thus Kotoku's sojourn in the San Francisco area started, a sojourn that lasted six months, and during which he undertook many activities both within and without the Japanese immigrant community. At the invitation of Sagitani Seiichi, a reporter for the *Nichibei Shimbun*, he contributed a number of articles to his newspaper, written primarily for immigrant readers, on the need for socialism.[21] He attended the weekly Sunday night meetings of the Heiminsha, and he joined the American Socialist Party. He conducted study sessions on socialism at the Gospel Society; after the Great Earthquake of April 18th, 1906, he moved to Oakland and led similar sessions there. He also spoke before special gatherings and rallies and met a wide variety of people, including members of the Industrial Workers of the World, and lamented that "the majority of Japanese workers, not only are ignorant of socialism, but also do not know of the existence of the I.W.W."[22] Most historians consider Kotoku's sojourn as the period in which he finally shifted from Marxist socialism to anarcho-syndicalism. While here he is even reported to have stated:

> . . . in order to introduce new social ideas into Japan it would be necessary to destroy the traditional belief in the divinity of the Emperor and that the most effective method would be to assassinate him and thus demonstrate that he was mortal.[23]

Regarding the two immigrant socialist groups on either side of the bay, he wrote: "Among the Japanese in Oakland there are new knowledgeable students and socialist thought is very prevalent. In the future, if the comrades here and in Oakland join hands and work together, I believe their influence will be great."[24]

Social Revolutionary Party

The main product of his sojourn was the formation of the Shakai Kakumeito (Social

50

Revolutionary Party) in the East Bay. Officially launched on June 1, 1906, just before his return to Japan, it brought together certain members of both groups for political action. Its general aims were spelled out as follows:

> 1) We will abolish the current system of industrial and economic competition, making all land and capital the common property of the people, thereby rooting out the causes of poverty;
>
> 2) We will reform the traditional, superstitious class system and guarantee equal rights to all;
>
> 3) We will eliminate national and racial prejudices and work for true brotherhood and international peace; and
>
> 4) To accomplish the above stated purposes, we recognize the need to unite with the comrades of the world to carry out a great social revolution.[25]

Though the party's original membership is counted at 52 members, many of them were listed as living outside of the Bay Area (some outside the State of California and one in France). Among those outside the Bay Area, only two played a role in party activities: Kaneko Kiichi, one of the founders of the Society for the Study of Socialism, in Chicago where he was active in the American Socialist Party, and Saijo Toru who was in Iowa but later came to Oakland.[26] Even among those who were listed as original members in the Bay Area—the majority of the membership—most of them played no role in the party—some like Takeshita Shizuma, for example, never participated in any manner; others like Oka Shigeki were not present in the early period of the party; and still others like Iwasa Sakutaro were erroneously listed as original members.[27] The actual number of members in the Bay Area therefore probably never exceeded more than 15 individuals, and the active core consisted of Takeuchi Tetsugoro, Konarita Tsunero, Kuramochi Zensaburo, Hasegawa Ichimatsu, Uyeyama Jitaro, Ogawa Kinji, and Iwasa Sakutaro (who later joined).[28]

The Social Revolutionary Party appeared in public almost immediately after its establishment. On the evening of June 10, 1906, on the corner of 8th and Franklin Streets in Oakland, it attempted to hold a street rally. Several hundred persons had congregated at this site in the heart of the Japanese and Chinese settlement, and the party made its grand entrance with red flags inscribed with the Chinese characters in black "Shakai Kakumeito." No permit had been secured. The police prohibited the rally and arrested two party members.[29] Subsequent to this rather inauspicious debut, the party supported in mid-June the International Seamen's Union of the Pacific which had gone on strike for higher wages. Since shipping companies sought Japanese workers as scab seamen through Japanese employment agencies in San Francisco, the party issued two separate leaflets exhorting the Japanese not to become scabs in the name of the international unity and brotherhood of workers. Party members went to the docks

to dissuade Japanese workers who went to sign-up or had actually done so.[30]

The party's support of the Seamen's Union was ironic. The party was established, it must be remembered, at the time when the anti-Japanese exclusion movement was gaining momentum.[31] The San Francisco *Chronicle,* on February 23, 1905, had begun its anti-Japanese crusade with a front-page editorial headlined: "The Japanese Invasion, The Problem of the Hour." The Japanese and Korean Exclusion League (later called the Asiatic Exclusion League) had been organized in May, 1905. After the disastrous earthquake in April, 1906, there occurred many anti-Japanese outbursts in San Francisco. The major event in 1906, however, was the San Francisco School Board's resolution to segregate Asian students in October which caused an international crisis. The Seamen's Union, along with other labor groups, played a prominent role in this movement; and its leader, Andrew Furuseth, a man who had definite prejudices against Asians, consistently favored exclusion.[32]

This irony points to the dilemma faced by the Japanese immigrant socialists, for there was a basic contradiction in the American socialist position. On the one hand, American socialists were proclaiming the international solidarity of workers and, on the other hand, supporting the call for the restriction of Asiatic laborers. At its annual convention in September, 1906 the California Socialist Party adopted a resolution favoring restriction.[33] The National Executive Committee of the American Socialist Party adopted a similar resolution in March, 1907.[34] Some American socialists used economic reasons to rationalize their position on this matter, while others like Ernest Untermann bluntly stated: "I am determined that my race shall be supreme in this country and in the world."[35] Others justified exclusion with tortuous, theoretical subterfuges:

> . . . the rational Japanese socialist of the Japanese labor movement will certainly see that if the capitalists in Japan can ship their surplus millions to America, the Japanese labor movement, if it depends, as those who favor unlimited immigration into this country assert, on the 'philosophy of misery,' will be injured by this deportation of the very element that tends to make the misery in Japan sufficiently keen to breed revolution.[36]

Designed to conceal the racial motive, this line of reasoning concluded with the statement: "the working class of each nation owes its first duty to itself." The working class of America by definition meant the *white* working class!

The racial motive behind the growing clamor for exclusion never escaped the attention of Japanese socialists. In 1905 Abe Isoo observed that "it is rooted in racial prejudice," and went on to comment that, though those who favor exlusion can use the 'labor problem' as the surface reason..., they cannot use the racial reason in public. The United States is known as a Christian nation. But if she will not accept the yellow race because we are not to her liking, then she no longer has any justifications for sending Christian missionaries to Japan and China.[37]

In January, 1907 the Japan Socialist Party sent an open letter to American socialists on this exclusion question signed by Kotoku Shusui, Sakai Toshihiko, and Nishikawa Kojiro. This letter read:

> Comrades: We believe that the expulsion question of the Japanese laborers in California is much due to racial prejudice. The Japanese Socialist Party, therefore, hopes that the American Socialist Party will endeavor to bring the question to a satisfactory issue in accordance with the spirit of international unity among workingmen. We also ask the American Socialist Party to acquaint us with its opinion as to this question.[38]

No reply was ever given to this open letter.[39] Kaneko Kiichi, through whom the letter was distributed, perhaps best pinpointed the problem when he asked "whether or not American socialists are going to be true to the exhortation of Marx—'Workingmen of all countries, Unite'—or whether they are to encourage contention and division on the ground of race prejudice."[40] As a Japanese socialist, the dilemma was perfectly clear to him, and his indignant disappointment stemmed from the clarity of his perception:

> I was really disappointed to have found that the Socialists in this country are not altogether good fighters . . . . Not only have they been silent in this matter but they have vainly tried to narrow their socialism by joining with the cheap political grafters and so-called labor leaders in the disapprobation of Japanese immigration. So far as I know, not a single Socialist paper in this country spoke out plainly on this Japanese question without showing race prejudice.[41]

In short, the Social Revolutionary Party emerged in the midst of the exclusion movement, and Japanese socialists, immigrant or otherwise, were aware that American socialists, too, were very much a part of it.

THE REVOLUTION

Kakumei (Revolution)

Two subsequent events brought the Social Revolutionary Party into sensational light: the first

issue of its official journal, the *Kakumei* (Revolution), and an "Open Letter" addressed to the Meiji Emperor. Primarily in Japanese but with some English, the first of only three issues of the *Kakumei* appeared on December 20, 1906.[42] It was published out of the party headquarter, a lodginghouse operated by Uyeyama Jitaro located at 2459 Parker Street in Berkeley and dubbed the "Red House" because it was painted red. Somehow a copy of the first issue found its way into the hands of the Secretary of the San Francisco School Board who passed it on to the newspapers. The immediate cause for the ensuing controversy was an English passage which read: "Our policy is toward the overthrow of Mikado, King, President [sic] as representing the Capitalist Class as soon as possible, and we do not hesitate as to means." All the Bay Area newspapers carried sensational stories. The San Francisco *Chronicle,* on December 30, 1906, headlined its story "Secret Service Men on the Trail of Japanese Publishers—Japs Favor Killing of President Roosevelt." The San Francisco *Examiner* echoed the *Chronicle:* "Japanese Anarchists Publish Paper Urging President's Death." The San Francisco *Call* had an almost identical tone: "Japanese Socialists Threaten Roosevelt—Violent Pronouncement Is Issued." And the Berkeley *Daily Gazette* voiced its own alarm: "Hotbed of Japanese Anarchists Located Here—the Yellow Peril."[43] In each instance the central focus was placed on the implied threat to assassinate President Theodore Roosevelt. The local Japanese-language paper, the *Shin Sekai,* carried its story under the title "Rantings of Socialism."[44]

The authorities began an investigation and the question of responsibility became crucial. The Japanese Consul explored the possibility with U.S. Immigration officials and the U.S. Attorney General of having the responsible individuals deported. Ultimately the matter came before a Special Board of Inquiry of the San Francisco Immigration Commission, and Takeuchi Tetsugoro, who had assumed responsibility for publishing the first issue, was ordered to appear before it for deportation hearings. Takeuchi appeared on January 3, 1907 with Austin Lewis, a lawyer and one-time socialist candidate for the governor of California. To exonerate himself, he pleaded his knowledge of English was so insufficient that he even made the error between "evolution" and "revolution" in the title of the journal, accounting for the unfelicitous English passage. According to the existing law relating to anarchists, Takeuchi could not be deported. To do so, the government had to prove that he had been an anarchist at the time of his entry or that he had been in the country less than three full years and had committed an overt act of anarchism. Takeuchi had come to America in 1903 and had only expressed anarchistic thoughts.

The content of the first issue—and indeed of the

later two issues—definitely was anarchistic, particularly the Japanese section which was written with a good deal of youthful gusto. In the first issue, for example, an article on the development of socialism put forth the view that the revolutionary tide had made parliamentary tactics passé and ended with the exhortation: "People, wake up! And arise! Arise and seize your freedom! Seize your happiness! Destroy evil governments, the enemies of freedom, with bombs!"[45]   Another article stated the message more clearly:

> The only revolutionary means is the bomb. The bomb is also the means to harvest the revolution. The bomb is also the means to destroy the bourgeoisie. Today, with the mergers of capital and the rapid increase of the poor, the different policies of reform and parliamentarianism are equivalent to a child squirting his water pistol into a conflagration.[46]

An anti-Emperor system current also ran through the pages of the *Kakumei*. Labelling the Meiji shibboleth "Chukun Aikoku" (Loyalty to the Emperor, Love of the Nation) as a "slave morality," it expressed contempt for the institution as a tool of the ruling class, a denial of scientific knowledge, and a vestige of superstitious belief. The third issue reprinted Kotoku Shusui's speech on "direct-action" which he had delivered in February, 1907 before the first anniversary conference of the Japan Socialist Party.

Open Letter to the Emperor

The next incident spelled the end of the party. During most of the course of 1907, besides publishing the second and third issues of the *Kakumei*, the party continued to conduct indoor meetings in a quiet manner. But on November 3, 1907—the Meiji Emperor's birthday—it again came to public attention by causing an uproar in the Japanese community. On the morning of that day, certain members of the party—generally conceded to be Takeuchi, Konarita, Iwasa, and Kuramochi—tacked on the entrance to the Japanese Consulate a mimeographed "Open Letter to Mutsuhito Emperor of Japan" and distributed copies throughout the community. This open letter declared that the Emperor and the writers had evolved from "monkeys" and hence were "peers"; that the Emperor is responsible for the poverty and suffering of the poor; that he is "vanity" personified if he believes the "fabrications" scholars relate about his origins. And it concluded with the following remarks:

> When spring arrives, flowers bloom; when summer comes, fruits ripen; this is the power of nature. When a revolution arises, it is not because someone brings it about; it arises naturally. And

our terrorism is what comes at the end of this process.
> Don't mistake this for an empty, armchair theory. Terrorism is now succeeding in both Russia and France. Our terrorism will come into being based upon detailed studies of the successes and failures of terrorism in these advanced nations. Mutsuhito, pitiful Mutsuhito, your life will not be long. There will be a bomb planted beside you which will soon explode. And then![47]

This open letter was signed: "Anarchist-Assassin." The local community response was adverse to say the least, for the Emperor's birthday was one of the most important Japanese national holidays which it commemorated with nationalistic reverence. The Japanese Consul again tried unsuccessfully to have the responsible party members deported.[48] In the end a split occurred within the party because a few members had drafted up the open letter without consulting everyone. So what began as a small, youthful group of Issei socialists and anarchists organized for political action for all intents and purposes came to an abrupt end, and members eventually started either to return to Japan or to disperse to regions outside the Bay Area.

FRESNO AND JAPANESE AGRICULTURAL WORKERS

During this period, as it still is today, the Fresno area was a major grape-growing region, and Japanese agricultural laborers then comprised 60% of the grape-picking labor force. In 1908 upwards of 4000-5000 Japanese workers migrated into this area for the picking season which ran from mid-August through the fall months.[49] Labor conditions were far from ideal, especially with the common outbreak of malaria and typhoid; from 1898-1907, 182 Japanese laborers had died, and out of this total 40 had passed away in 1907 alone.[50] In mid-1905 a socialist study group in Fresno similar to the earlier Bay Area groups had formed.[51] The arrival of a key member of the Social Revolutionary Party led to the establishment of a much bigger organization than either this group or the party itself which tried to cope with the basic problems of Japanese agricultural laborers in this area.

Fresno Labor League

This organization was the Fresno Rodo Domeikai (Fresno Labor League) organized on August 20, 1908. The central figure was none other than Takeuchi Tetsugoro. After the split in the party, he first went to Vacaville and worked as an agricultural laborer. From there he proceeded to Fresno to organize Japanese agricultural laborers. His efforts resulted in the formation of the Labor League which became an incipient agricultural labor union with a sizable membership of about 2000 workers.[52] Its aims were outlined as:

1) To prevent the lowering of wages and to secure the highest possible;
2) To vigorously attack the **unfair** competition of corrupt labor contractors; and
3) To unify members to take concerted action to elevate the status of workers and to gain the confidence of grape-growers.[53]

Neither anarchistic in tone nor in fact, these aims addressed themselves to the concrete problems facing agricultural laborers.

In the 1908 picking season there were many problems in the Fresno area. One of these was the competition among Japanese labor contractors. To prevent harmful competition, 53 Japanese contractors met on June 7, 1908 in Fresno. They organized themselves into the Central California Contractors' Association and agreed upon $1.65 per ton as the set rate to contract with the growers in the coming season.[54] To punish violators, or "corrupt bosses" as they were called, the Association members resolved to request the San Francisco Consulate not to have any dealings with such contractors, to report their "immoral" activities to their hometowns in Japan, to inform other Japanese organizations in other areas of these individuals, and to sever all personal relations with them. The Association anticipated some difficulties in contracting with one of the biggest vineyards in the area, the 900-acre Tarpey Ranch, because of similar troubles in the previous season. In early August, contrary to the agreed upon rate and to the dismay of the Association, three renegade Japanese contractors from Kings County contracted with this vineyard for $1.25 per ton.

The news of this event brought an instantaneous response from the Japanese community. The Contractors' Association appealed to Japanese laborers not to work for these "corrupt" contractors. Issuing a circular couched in nationalistic language, it asserted that Japanese laborers should "make as much money as possible and send remissions to Japan" to make her a big power and that the contractors in question were only interested in enriching themselves. The circular ended with the assurance that, as far as the Contractors' Association was concerned, it would continue to insist upon the $1.65 per ton rate.[55] The contractors secured the support of the Japanese Association of America whose Secretary, Kuma Toshiyasu, attempted to persuade the three renegade contractors to break their contract with the Tarpey Ranch but to no avail. As additional pressure two of the renegade contractors, who were members of the Hanford Japanese Association, were officially expelled on August 31, 1908 from that organization. The *Shin Sekai* lined up behind the Contractors' Association.

Reviewing the arguments for exclusion in a major editorial on August 13, 1908, it noted the three contractors lent substance to the charge that Japanese laborers worked for lower wages—Japanese laborers, in its view, should be demanding the same wages as white laborers. And in sharp terms it condemned the three contractors as "one type of traitors."

In California agriculture, beginning with Chinese laborers in the nineteenth century, a system of labor contractors had been established as the principal mechanism by which a migratory labor force was organized.[56] Within this system the labor contractor was more than a labor boss or agent of the employer, for he occupied an intermediate position between the employer and his labor gang. On the one hand, his role as a contractor depended on his ability to meet the labor demands of the employer by supplying a required number of workers for a specific period to do a designated task. But since he was not paid by the employer for this service, his own income came from the wages of his workers through a flat commission, and sometimes additional kickbacks. In the case of a contractor who was in the retail merchandising business—such as Kamikawa Riichi in Fresno at this time—his income came from his exclusive right to supply provisions to his workers, usually on credit. In either case the contractor had to offer sufficient wages to attract and maintain his workers, and in this limited sense, he had to represent their interests. Hence, whenever Japanese contractors resorted to short strikes before the harvest season, refused to scab against other Japanese, regulated the supply of labor to seek higher wages, defined territorial rights, and even boycotted certain growers, they were functioning as quasi-labor leaders. And precisely because of this intermediate position, it was crucial for the contractor to eliminate competition. If competition existed, he could be underbid by another contractor or deserted by his workers for better wages offered by his competitor which would threaten his own livelihood. The Central California Contractors' Association was organized to prevent this kind of competition to protect the contractors themselves.

The three aims of the Fresno Labor League were formulated directly out of the controversy generated by the three renegade contractors who had defied the Contractors' Association. The $1.25 per ton rate inevitably meant lower wages for Japanese laborers. Takeuchi and others actively opposed them, going out to Fowler and other places to obstruct their attempts to recruit Japanese workers. The members of the Labor League were so successful that no Japanese would work for the three contractors, forcing them to hire Mexican, Indian, and Korean laborers to fulfill their contract with the Tarpey Ranch. The U.S. Immigration Commission surveyed the Japanese population in the Fresno area in 1908. Emphasizing the significance of the Contractors' Association's role in controlling contract prices and wages, its report stated: "When the dependence of the vineyardists upon the Japanese is considered, the importance of this organization will be realized."[57] If the word "Japanese" is changed to "Japanese contractors," then another important dimension comes into focus in connection with the Labor League. In 1903, in one of the earliest attempts of its kind, 1000 Japanese and Mexican sugar beet workers in Oxnard, California went on strike to eliminate labor contractors and to secure the right to bargain directly with the grower.[58] Though there is no record of the Labor League contracting with any grape-grower, Takeuchi did go to the Tarpey Ranch, trying to get the contract for his own organization, and the Labor League did oppose the Contractors' Association. To this extent the Labor League can be interpreted as an effort to organize Japanese agricultural laborers free from Japanese contractors into an agricultural labor union.

In addition to the competition of contractors, there were other problems in the Fresno area in 1908. Two problems in particular stood out: Chinese gambling houses and Japanese prostitution. In an editorial "Debauchery and Gambling—What Did You Come to America For?," June 12, 1908, the *Shin Sekai* decried the prevalence of these two "vices" among the Japanese throughout the State of California. In Fresno Christian and Buddhist ministers banded together in the spring into a Kyofukai or Moral Reform Association which initiated a drive to close down Chinese gambling houses.[59] According to the Congregational minister, Fukunaga Kumazo, there were 19 such establishments in operation which took approximately $200,000 from Japanese laborers who patronized them during the previous season.[60] One of the biggest houses, operated by a Lee Troy, supplied free wine, beer, and tea and had a moving picture display that changed once a week to attract customers. Through the summer and fall of 1908, the Association carried out a crusade against them, usually with limited success, and the Labor League joined in.[61] But the Association's anti-prostitution campaign was a different matter. Not only did the Labor League disagree with such a campaign, it also criticized the ministers. Estimates vary as to the exact number, but it is safe to say that there were between 20-40 Japanese prostitutes in Fresno during the picking season.[62] The Association had a number of these women arrested in October and undertook a concerted campaign against them in 1909.[63] The Labor League pointed out, rather bitterly, that the zealous ministers already had wives and that, until the laborers had the opportunity to lead stable family lives, prostitution was an evil but unavoidable necessity. But more important, since prostitution from the Labor League perspective was a product of a capitalistic system, to chase the prostitutes out of Fresno, as the ministers tried, did not solve this social problem. The problems of labor and prostitution were interrelated and could

be solved only by fundamental changes in society, not by a moral crusade.

Rodo (Labor)

The official organ of the Labor League, *Rodo* (Labor), was published from November 20, 1908 to Setpember 14, 1909.[64] Its editorial staff consisted of Takeuchi Tetsugoro and Matsushita Zenpei in Fresno and Iwasa, Konarita, Kuramochi, and Ogawa in San Francisco, members of the Social Revolutionary Party who had remained in the Bay Area. From the few extant issues of the *Rodo*, it is possible to get an idea of its content. Articles which attacked the Emperor system, the capitalist class, and militarism were prominent along with the constant appeal to workers to unite:

> According to recent statistics, out of 1000 persons 343 ruling class members live to the age of 60-years old but only 256 members of the working class. Why is this so? We workers die early from physical ailments caused by excessive labor, by working in dangerous factories or in mines with inadequate facilities. Or by working long hours with an injury, by unsanitary living conditions injurious to health, and by mental disorders stemming from living in perpetual poverty.
>
> But no matter how dangerous the work may be, no matter how long the working hours may be, we workers have no right to voice our grievances. For if we express our likes and dislikes, we will never be able to secure work, and will pitifully starve to death.
>
> If one thinks in these terms, what difference is there between workers today and the slaves of old? . . . ,
>
> Today the workers of the world are awakening to how wretched their conditions are. The workers in Japan are also awakening. This is natural. Thus we workers also must unite.[65]

Other articles went further and advocated the public ownership of land and the means of production, stating that unions (such as the Labor League)

> cannnot take effective measures to cope with the evils which come from the private property system and laissez-faire economic competition, nor with unemployment and dips in wages which accompany economic depressions . . . .
>
> Thus if we workers are to seek our own welfare, we must not stop at denouncing exploiting employers, shady merchants, and corrupt bosses. We must also go one more step forward and destroy

the private property system which continually spawns unemployment and poverty. We workers must make all land and the means of production public property for society as a whole and eliminate laissez-faire competition . . . . [66]

In the year 1909 the Labor League participated in two major activities. First, on August 25, 1909, it convened a labor convention of Japanese workers in Fresno timed to coincide with the beginning of the picking season. Representatives from Sacramento, Los Angeles, Fresno, and San Francisco addressed an audience of 300 workers, and the convention passed four resolutions to further the labor movement among Japanese workers which stated:

> 1) that the welfare of workers cannot depend upon ministers, community leaders, or newspaper reporters—the slavish jesters of the capitalist class—it can be secured only by resorting to the principle of justice and the power of worker unity; and resolved:
> 2) to affiliate with labor groups in other areas and to establish branches of the Labor League in other areas to further the labor movement;
> 3) to publish an English monthly to educate and inform ignorant anti-Japanese elements; and
> 4) to affiliate with other labor groups in other areas to ban Chinese gambling. [67]

Second, on September 19, 1909, the Labor League held a joint rally with the Fresno branch of the Industrial Workers of the World in Japanese-town. Besides the Fresno I.W.W. head, Mexican and Italian I.W.W. speakers also spoke, and Takeuchi himself talked on the international brotherhood of workers and on the necessity of workers to unite irrespective of nationality or color.

Despite the resolutions passed by the labor convention, the Labor League did not expand its activities—it neither established branches in other locales nor published an English monthly. Indeed it ceased publishing its official journal on September 14, 1909, forecasting the eventual demise of the organization in the following year. One explanation for this setback is the lack of funds; litigation costs to defend Takeuchi in a court case drained the Labor League's limited financial resources. Japanese-language newspapers had not been sympathetic to the Labor League, and one in particular, the *Soko Shimbun,* carried caustic articles by Otsuka Zenjiro which attacked the Labor League as an anarchist organization. Incensed by these articles, Takeuchi and another member of the Labor League had gone to San Francisco in November, 1908 ostensibly to challenge him to a public debate. On November 30, 1908, however, a knife fight between Takeuchi and Otsuka occurred in which both were badly lacerated, resulting in costly expenses to defend Takeuchi in the court case that ensued. [68]

Yet in a more basic sense the cessation of the journal, when coupled with the Labor League's failure to expand its activities as outlined by the labor

convention, was a symptom of a larger problem. For the Labor League undoubtedly experienced the inherent difficulties of organizing a migratory agricultural labor force. The very fact that Japanese laborers, for the most part, did not remain in the Fresno area except for the duration of a picking season—a short 2½ months — made it difficult, if not impossible, to maintain an ongoing, cohesive organization. The composition of the labor force moreover underwent seasonal changes with some workers migrating to other areas like Southern California while others moved on to become farm operators. In addition to a hostile Japanese-language press, the Labor League also met local community opposition. The Japanese Association of Fresno refused to recognize it as a legitimate organization, obstructed its activities, and labelled it as a group with anarchist elements. And when news of the High Treason Affair in Japan came into this already trying situation in the summer of 1910, it made it next to impossible for anyone associated with Kotoku Shusui, as Takeuchi and other immigrant socialists were, to function in any Japanese community. [69] Finally, Takeuchi, the founder and principal leader of the Labor League, departed from the Fresno area sometime in 1910, marking the end of this organization which was an unsuccessful but significant attempt to organize Japanese laborers into an agricultural labor union.

THE 1911 BAKERSFIELD LÈSE-MAJESTÉ AFFAIR

On November 3, 1911, less than 10 months after Kotoku's execution, the small Bakersfield Japanese community, like all the other Japanese communities in California and elsewhere, came together to commemorate the Meiji Emperor's birthday. The event was held at the Bakersfield Buddhist Hall with representatives from various local groups participating in the program; Takeda Shojiro represented the Bakersfield Japanese Methodist Mission. At this local commemoration, Takeda reportedly paid no respect to the Emperor's portrait, an important ritual in this event, and went further in his "disrespect" by asserting, two days later at a meeting in the Methodist Mission, that such a practice was a form of "idolatry" which Christians should not follow. [70] As a local cause célèbre, Takeda was accused of being a "traitor" for these assertions. What started as a local incident developed into an unprecedented lèse-majesté affair which was related in a significant way to the previous activities of the Issei socialists and anarchists.

At the heart of this lèse-majesté affair was Kitazawa Tetsuji, the pastor of the Fresno Japanese Methodist Episcopal Church. Because of the unfavorable newspaper coverage of Takeda's remarks, as the minister responsible for supervising the Methodist Mission, Reverend Kitazawa went to

Bakersfield two weeks later. While there, on November 17, 1911, he presented a talk entitled: "The Christian Viewpoint on the Emperor's Portrait."[71] In this talk he made the distinction between the act of showing respect and its meaning. Though the outward act appeared uniform for all people, the inner meaning differed and could be categorized into those who respect the Emperor in Japan through the portrait, those who respect the portrait as a portrait and nothing more, and those who respect the portrait as the embodiment of some transcendental value. Christians, he insisted, look upon the portrait and pay respect only in the second sense. In addition, he defined the difference between "respect" and "worship." The former was a secular term used to denote human relationships based upon ceremonial propriety; the latter was a religious term used exclusively to designate man's relationship to God. Hence, while Christians should "respect" the Emperor's portrait in the second sense, they should never "worship" it. The newspaper described his talk as "pouring oil into a small fire," for Reverend Kitazawa "justified" Takeda's conduct by saying "to show respect or not is an individual choice" and not to do so "did not violate any law."[72]

The furor quickly spread to Fresno. Besides being the pastor of the Fresno Japanese Methodist Episcopal Church, Reverend Kitazawa was also at the time the President of the Japanese Association of Fresno. Due to the discrepancy between the public explanation of his talk and the earlier newspaper coverage of it, a dissident group, led by Taira Chizan, Yoshii Setsunan, and Ito Bansho, met in Fresno on November 27, 1911 and decided to send a delegation to Bakersfield to investigate exactly what had occurred in that city. In spite of this initial uproar, the Board of the Fresno Japanese Association, in an emergency session on December 5, 1911, gave Reverend Kitazawa a vote of confidence, rejected his resignation, and declared the matter closed. On the next day a public hearing was convened at which the Fresno delegation to Bakersfield presented its report, and 302 individuals present adopted a resolution which labelled him a "fukeikan" or disrespectful turncoat and "called upon the Fresno Japanese Association to take punitive measures."[73] Upon being presented with this resolution, the Board refused to alter its position, and most of its members then resigned from their posts. As the last but most significant act of the year, on December 27, 1911, at a specially called membership-wide meeting of the Fresno Japanese Association, a similar resolution was overwhelmingly endorsed. It read:

> The head of our Association, Kitazawa Tetsuji, cannot be forgiven, for he is a person who has disloyal and disrespectful ideas and moreover has publicly expressed them. Because he is a 'fukeikan,' we relieve him of his post and expel him forthwith.
>
> The above action will be reported to the San Francisco Japanese Consulate General, the Japanese Association of America, and all local Japanese Associations, and a public notice of expulsion will be published in all newspapers.[74]

Since most of the officers had already resigned, the execution of this resolution had to be postponed until the election of new officers in January.

This action was the harbinger of a prolonged, bitter conflict which divided the Fresno Japanese community into two hostile camps. The regular annual membership meeting took place on January 7, 1912, and the newly elected officers decided to execute the resolution. The first public notice of expulsion appeared on February 14, 1912. The Japanese Association of America in San Francisco, to which local associations were affiliated, on the same day, responded by withdrawing the "endorsement right" from the Fresno Japanese Association on the ground that "under present circumstances" it "could not advance the welfare of the Japanese," and severed its ties with it.[75] In the meantime the former members of the Fresno Japanese Association who had disagreed with the action against Reverend Kitazawa organized another association which was officially inaugurated on March 10, 1912 as the Fresno County Japanese Association. Efforts by the older association to regain the endorsement right—through negotiation with San Francisco, by direct appeals to Consul General Nagai, and even through a mediator—all proved fruitless. Thus two associations came to exist, one old and one new, each claiming to represent the Fresno Japanese community.

This unprecedented situation was not settled until 1914. To worsen the problem, the Japanese Association of America recognized the new association on April 3, 1912 and bestowed upon it the endorsement right. Throughout the rest of the year there were many unsuccessful attempts at mediation with this act being one of the main sources of contention. To exacerbate matters even more, on March 11, 1913, a group of men from the old association, led by Taira Chizan again, invaded the office of the Fresno Japanese-language newspaper, assaulted the reporter, and left the place in a shamble in response to a series of vituperative articles in this newspaper which called the old association a "total fraud."[76] And again, under the influence of this latest development, renewed efforts at mediation took place. But the final reconciliation did not occur until January, 1914 at which time by common consent both the old and new associations formally dissolved themselves and then came together to form another new organization.

Here the significance of this strife is neither in the details nor the underlying causes, but in the anti-Christian nature of the action against Reverend Kitazawa. Since 1891 Christians had aroused suspicions and enmity in Japan when the noted Christian, Uchimura Kanzo, had refused to pay his respect to the Emperor's portrait.[77] This most celebrated lèse-majesté affair led to the acrimonious debate between the critics of Christianity and its

Christian defenders during the 1890s. Led by Inoue Tetsujiro the critics attacked Christian teachings as incompatible with the Meiji state: because Christianity stressed the equality of all men, they first asserted, it made no basic distinction between different races and nations so central to the Meiji Constitution and the Imperial Rescript on Education which defined the uniqueness of the Japanese people; because it taught universal love and charity, it transcended the limited ideals of the state; because it emphasized salvation in another world, it was antithetical to the secular orientation of the state; and lastly—and here the critics were the harshest—because Christianity did not teach filial piety, it did not inculcate loyalty to the Emperor. Indeed, Christians recognized a higher authority in God! These criticisms of Christianity were reenforced by the Christian participation in and leadership of the socialist movement in the succeeding decade. During the Russo-Japanese War certain Christians like Uchimura Kanzo and Kinoshita Naoe added their voices to the anti-war campaign begun by Kotoku Shusui, providing additional substantiation to the charge that they were disloyal subjects.[78] And the later public association of Christians with anarchists, especially after the disclosure of the High Treason Affair, was an extension of their involvement in the socialist movement that made them more suspect.

The Bakersfield lèse-majesté affair was a reflection of this anti-Christian bias. Reverend Kitazawa was labelled a "disloyal" Japanese with "subversive ideas" for expressing his "Christian Viewpoint on the Emperor's Portrait" by the anti-Kitazawa forces who defined themselves as "patriots." On March 31, 1912, the leaders of the old Fresno Japanese Association, in cooperation with Soejima Hachiro and others in the Bay Area, convened a conference of "Imperial Subjects" in Oakland.[79] Soejima was the founder and one-time publisher of the *Shin Sekai* and a recognized community leader. Naming the Bakersfield event another "Uchimura Kanzo Fukei Jiken," the conference participants denounced the Japanese Association of America, the Fresno County Japanese Association, and even the Consul General for their failure to take action against Reverend Kitazawa. As the head of the conference, Soejima Hachiro stated that "Consul General Nagai" and "the Japanese Association of America . . . were protecting a 'fukeikan'" and had subversive ideas."[80] And in the attack upon Consul General Nagai, it was no accident that he was referred to as a "Christian." The logic in its crudest form ran:

> Persons who protect traitors are traitors. Kitazawa Tetsuji is a traitor. Nagai Matsuzo, the Executive Council of the Japanese Association of America, and the Fresno County Japanese Association are protecting Kitazawa. Therefore, the Consul General, the members of the Executive Council of the Japanese Association of America, and the Fresno County Japanese Association are traitors.[81]

Since Japanese-language newspapers refused editorially to condemn Reverend Kitazawa, they too came under fire. Of all the newspapers the *Nichibei Shimbun* was the object of the heaviest criticism, for the anti-Kitazawa forces linked it to Kotoku Shusui and the Social Revolutionary Party, implying that the publisher, Abiko Kyutaro, had socialistic leanings. Abiko, too, was a Christian who had been the head of the Gospel Society. They accused him of having assisted the socialists by permitting them to reside in the Gospel Society, by allowing Kotoku to conduct meetings there, and by letting him become a guest contributor to his newspaper. To insinuate Abiko had more than sympathy with the socialists, they noted he had had Sagitani Seiichi on his staff, an individual who was identified with the Social Revolutionary Party. Associating him in this manner with Kotoku, the anti-Kitazawa forces hoped to discredit the Executive Council of the Japanese Association of America as well because Abiko was also a member of it. Their dissatisfaction with the newspapers was so great that they even initiated their own newspaper called the *Kokumin Shimbun*.[82]

That the local Bakersfield incident mushroomed into this type of lèse-majesté affair is not surprising. Subsequent to the High Treason Affair, the Japanese community became extra-sensitive to instances of "disrespect" to the Emperor and prepared to take action against them (the death of the Meiji Emperor in the summer of 1912 no doubt reenforced this sensitivity). Coming as it did less than 10 months after the execution of Kotoku and others, all socialists and anarchists by definition were "treasonous" individuals, whether in Japan or America. In America the words and deeds of the members of the Social Revolutionary Party and the Fresno Labor League, both of which could be traced to Kotoku, provided tangible evidence for this judgement. And their protest activities in response to the High Treason Affair left no room for any doubt. From November, 1910 through February, 1911 Issei socialists and anarchists issued open letters of protest to the Japanese government and held rallies in San Francisco and Oakland in conjunction with American socialists, including the noted writer, Jack London. On the evening of January 25, 1911, the day after the execution of Kotoku and others, 19 individuals conducted an all-night vigil in San Francisco, declaring that "the deranged Japanese government, heedless of the protest movement throughout the world, murdered the warriors of humanism and the forerunners of the Japanese revolution" and "designated January 24, 1911 as a commemoration day of the Japanese Revolution."[83] Christians to be sure were not *ipso facto* "disloyal" Japanese subjects. Yet with the antecedent historical bias against them, strong suspicions lurked. In San Francisco back in 1902, well before the socialists and anarchists had arrived on the scene, an instance of Christian "disrespect" had taken place which had confirmed these suspicions. In that year Sakon Yoshisuke had written articles critical of the Meiji Emperor in the monthly publication of the San Francisco Japanese Methodist Episcopal Church. He had to resign his job as its editor and his position as the English instructor in the church because of the community response.[84] In the patriots' mind Reverend Kitazawa gave further confirmation of these suspicions. Given the activities of the socialists and anarchists in the intervening time and the public tendency to associate all Christians with them, his behavior called for prompt, unequivocal condemnation in the name of the Meiji shibboleth "Chukun, Aikoku"—Loyalty to the Emperor, Love of the Nation.[85] ★

Conclusion

It might be worthwhile to dwell upon the meaning of the early Issei socialists and anarchists and the Bakersfield lèse-majesté affair of 1911 to conclude this essay. The most obvious point is that there were Issei socialists and anarchists in the early inchoate stage of the Japanese community. Admittedly the Social Revolutionary Party consisted of only a handful of individuals, but it did have an impact upon the community, brief though it may have been, and the Fresno Labor League which developed from the party was a significant attempt to organize Japanese laborers into an agricultural labor union. And all their combined activities did reenforce the historical, anti-Chrisitan bias as evidenced by the Bakersfield lèse-majesté affair, suggesting conflict rather than unity may have been more characteristic of the Japanese community, at least during this period.

But beyond this there is a deeper meaning. Marcus L. Hansen, a past historian of European immigration to America, indicated long ago the intimate relationship between emigration and imigration, between the emigrant nation and the immigrant land, demonstrating the need to study both.[86] The two subjects of this essay exemplify his dictum: neither the Issei socialists and anarchists nor the Bakersfield lèse-majesté affair can be separated from Japan—they can be fully understood only by reference to events in late Meiji times. By extension other aspects of Japanese-American history such as Japanese language schools or the entire 1930 period cannot be understood without reference to modern Japanese history. To insist Japanese-American history must be studied alongside the history of modern Japan, however, does not mean the two are synonymous. Japanese-American history after all is an integral part of American history, the essential larger context from which its basic meaning derives.

But to the extent modern Japanese history influenced it, it cannot be ignored. In sum, Japanese-American history must be studied with reference to the influence of modern Japanese history within the larger context of American history to be fully understood. From this perspective Japanese-American history remains essentially a buried past.

Notes

1. Roger Daniels, "Westerners from the East: Oriental Immigrants Reappraised," *Pacific Historical Review*, 35:4 (November, 1966), p. 375.

2. Hyman Kublin, "Takano Fusataro: A Study in Early Japanese Trade-Unionism," American Philosophical Society, *Proceedings*, 103:4 (August 15, 1959), p. 573 and p. 577. The purposes of the Shokko Giyukai in San Francisco were stated as "to study the labor problems in Western countries and to apply the knowledge to solutions to labor problems in Japan in the future." Quoted in Katayama Sen and Nishikawa Kojiro, *Nihon no Rodo Undo*, reprinted in *Meiji Bunka Zenshu*, Shakai-hen (Tokyo, 1929), p. 169.

3. Hyman Kublin, pp. 578-580.

4. *Ibid.*, pp. 580-582. Except for a short three-week period in which the *Rodo Sekai* became a daily under the title *Naigai Shimpo* in January, 1902, it continued until March, 1903 when its title changed to *Shakaishugi*. See Watanabe Yoshimichi and Shiota Shobei, *Nihon Shakaishugi Bunken Kaisetsu* (Tokyo, 1958), pp. 48-49. In 1902 Katayama Sen formed the Tobei Kyokai (Association for the (America-bound) whose aim was to encourage Japanese to come to America and used the *Rodo Sekai* and its successors as its official organ to disseminate information about America, attempting to combine such information with knowledge about labor problems and socialism. In January, 1905 the *Shakaishugi* changed to the *Tobei Zasshi* (America-bound Magazine) which then focused exclusively on the procedures for coming to America and news about it. See Sumiya Mikio, *Katayama Sen—Kindai Nihon no Shisoka* (Tokyo, 1960), pp. 136-143. Some Issei came to America through the help of Katayama's Tobei Kyokai.

5. Hyman Kublin, "The Origins of Japanese Socialist Tradition," *Journal of Politics*, 14:2 (May, 1952), p. 261.

6. Quoted in *ibid.*, p. 262.

7. Hyman Kublin, "The Japanese Socialists and the Russo-Japanese War," *Journal of Modern History*, 22:4 (December, 1950), pp. 322-339. Before Kotoku and Sakai formed the Heiminsha, they worked as reporters for the *Yorozu Choho*, one of the leading Tokyo dailies. In early October, 1903 the publisher adopted a jingoistic, pro-war stance, and so both individuals resigned at once.

8. Nobutake Ike, "Kotoku Denjiro: Advocate of Direct Action," *Far Eastern Quarterly*, 3:3 (May, 1944), pp. 222-235.

9. For details of the High Treason Affair, see Itoya Toshio, *Daigyaku Jiken* (Tokyo, 1970).

10. Sen Katayama, *The Labor Movement in Japan* (Chicago, 1918), p. 140. The newspaper he refers to is the *Shakai Shimbun* which he edited.

11. The major source for this portion of this essay is the special report compiled by the Ministry of Home Affairs of the Japanese government entitled *Beikoku ni Okeru*

Nihonjin Shakaishugisha Museifushugisha Enkaku which has been reproduced in Shakai Bunko, *Zaibei Shakaishugisha Museifushugisha*, v. 1 (Tokyo, 1964), pp. 34-455. This report will hereafter be cited as B.S.M.E. The Japanese government began secret surveillance of socialists during the Russo-Japanese War and in July, 1908 compiled its first secret report under the title *Shakaishugisha Enkaku*. Report no. 2 followed in July, 1909, no. 3 in July, 1911. This special report on the Japanese socialists and anarchists in America was compiled from portions of no. 1 and no. 2 in July, 1911 and covers the period from December, 1903 to June, 1911. See Ohara Kei, "Zaibei Nihonjin Shakaishugisha Museifushugisha no 'Kotoku Jiken' ni Oyoboshita Eikyo," *Tokyo Keidai Gakkaishi*, no. 26 (January, 1960), pp. 157-169. Japanese historians have studied the early Issei socialists and anarchists mainly in terms of their influence upon the socialist movement in Japan. The best summary of their activities is Matsuo Shoichi, "Meiji Makki in Okeru Nihonjin Shakaishugi Museifushugi Undo Shoshi," in Shakai Bunko, pp. 17-29, which I have used freely. Other works are cited in subsequent notes.

12. The Fukuinkai was the first Japanese-American organization formed in America. Established in October, 1877, it started out as a bible-study group under the direction of Rev. Otis Gibson, the Superintendent of the Chinese Methodist Episcopal Mission, and met on Saturday evenings in the basement of the Mission headquarter located at 916 Washington St. Out of this modest beginning, the first Japanese Presbyterian Church and the Japanese Methodist Episcopal Church of San Francisco developed in the mid-1880s. By the time of the Russo-Japanese War, it had evolved into an independent residence for young men and a center for social and other activities located at 725 Geary St. See Zaibei Nihonjinkai, *Zaibei Nihonjinshi* (San Francisco, 1940), pp. 340-346.

13. On the same program, according to Katayama, a member of the Seattle Socialist Party spoke who urged the Japanese to form a socialist group with which he promised to cooperate. Before the end of this meeting, Katayama, Kawakami, and 7 others organized the Seattle Japanese Socialist Party. See Katayama Sen, "Beikoku Tayori," nos. 2-4, *Shakaishugi*, February 18, 1904 and March 3, 1904. Before coming to America, Kawakami Kiyoshi had worked on the *Yorozu Choho*, along with Kotoku Shusui and others, and he was one of the founders, as noted already, of the short-lived Social Democratic Party. Less than three months later, in August of that year, he came to America and studied at the University of Iowa where he took his master's degree in political science. See Kawakami Kiyoshi, *Bei-So Tatakawaba* (Tokyo, 1949), especially pp. 213-215 in which he recollects about his motives for coming to America. In 1903 the University of Iowa published his thesis, written in 1902, entitled *The Political Ideas of Modern Japan* (Iowa City, 1903) in which he discussed the fate of the Social Democratic Party. At the time of Katayama Sen's visit to Seattle, he was working as a reporter for the *Shin Nihon*, a Seattle Japanese-language newspaper. Later he became a prolific journalist who wrote on Japanese-American relations in English as well as in Japanese. See Fujioka Shiro, *Ayumi no Ato* (Los Angeles, 1957), pp. 42-48.

14. Katayama Sen, "Beikoku Tayori," no. 7, *Shakaishugi*, April 3, 1904. Enroute to San Francisco, he also gave talks in Portland and Sacramento.

15. Iwasa Sakutaro, "Zaibei Undoshi Banashi," in Shakai Bunko, pp. 425-525. A native of Chiba Prefecture, Iwasa was a graduate of Tokyo Hogakuin (later Chuo Daigaku) who arrived in 1901 to study law through the assistance

of Katayama's Tobei Kyokai. See *ibid.*, p. 523, and Shakai Bunko, *Shakaishugisha Museifushugisha Jimbutsu Kenkyu Shiryo*, v. 7 (Tokyo, 1964), p. 43.

16. B.S.M.E., pp. 44-46, and Iwasa Sakutaro, in Shakai Bunko, pp. 525-526. Uyeyama Jitaro, a Christian, was a native of Oita Prefecture who arrived in 1902. One of the few early married Issei, he later operated a small lodginghouse in Berkeley where many of the socialists would gather. See Shakai Bunko, v. 7, pp. 157-158. Takeuchi Tetsugoro was a native of Iwate Prefecture who came to America in 1903 (reportedly as a draft dodger) who later became a key leader. See *ibid.*, pp. 136-137.

17. Iwasa Sakutaro, "Hokubei Soko Yori," *Chokugen*, May 28, 1905. Iwasa records that Abe was invited to speak in Oakland on April 30th for the International Workers' Day, but he declined the invitation. See also B.S.M.E., p. 48, and Otsuka Zenjiro, *Hishakaishugi* (Tokyo, 1911), pp. 146-147.

18. Hippolyte Havel (ed.), "Kotoku's Correspondence with Albert Johnson," *Mother Earth*, 6:6 (August, 1911), pp. 182-183.

19. Shiota Shobei, *Kotoku Shusui no Nikki to Shokan* (Tokyo, 1965), p. 216. Kotoku's correspondence and diary while in America have been reprinted in this volume. For the diary, see pp. 129-146.

20. Like Kotoku Shusui, Oka Shigeki was a native of Kochi Prefecture who came to America in the spring of 1902. Before leaving Japan, he too had worked for the *Yorozu Choho*, and hence personally knew Kotoku. His brother writes that Oka came here because he had had a fight with one of the staff members of the newspaper and had been asked to resign. See Oka Naoki, *Sokoku wo Teki to Shite* (Tokyo, 1965), pp. 7-8. The members of the Heiminsha were Oka and his wife, Toshiko, Kuramochi Zensaburo, Ogawa Kinji, Hasegawa Ichimatsu, Yamauchi Gonjiro, Ichikawa Toichi, Ashida Tsunejiro, and Nobeoka Tsunetaro, and it was located at Oka's home at 680 Hayes St. See *ibid.*, p. 9, and B.S.M.E., p. 59. No precise date for its establishment is given in either source.

21. Kotoku wrote three articles: "Nichi-Bei Kankei no Shorai," January 21, 1906, in which he predicted a future war between Japan and America over economic issues; "Nihon Imin to Beikoku," February 20, 1906, in which he blamed the Japanese government for the wretched plight of the Japanese people which forced them to emigrate and argued for the return of political and economic power to the common people; and "Zaibei Doho wa Kofuku Nariya," February 25, 1906, in which he argued for a socialist society which would not force people to emigrate to a foreign land and be homesick for their native place. These articles have been reprinted in *Kotoku Shusui Zenshu*, v. 6 (Tokyo, 1968), pp. 43-52, 53-57 and 57-61 respectively.

22. Shiota Shobei, p. 228.

23. Quoted in Nobutake Ike, p. 225. These remarks were made to Oka Shigeki.

24. Shiota Shobei, p. 223.

25. B.S.M.E., pp. 104-107.

26. Kaneko Kiichi, a native of Kanagawa Prefecture, came to America in 1901 and studied at Harvard University. While here he became active in the American Socialist Party in Chicago. In 1908 he married Josephine Conger, an American woman who edited the *Appeal to Reason* and *Socialist Woman*. He returned to Japan and died in October, 1909 of consumption. See Kindai Nihon Shiryo Kenkyukai, *Shakaishugisha Enkaku*, v. 1 (Tokyo, 1956),

pp. 312-313, and Kaneko Kiichi, "Tsushin," *Kumamoto Hyoron*, August 20, 1908. Saijo Toru, a Christian and a native of Kumamoto Prefecture, came to America in 1899. See Shakai Bunko, v. 7, pp. 225-226.

27. Interview, Takeshita Shizuma, November 10, 1970. Takeshita states he was a close friend of Uyeyama Jitaro which may account for his name appearing on the list of original members. An active Christian, he was the Oakland correspondent of the *Nichibei Shimbun* at the time. Oka returned with Kotoku to Japan in early June, 1906 to purchase Japanese type. See Oka Naoki, p. 10. Iwasa recalls he was away when the party was organized. See Iwasa Sakutaro, "Zaibei Undoshi Banashi," p. 529.

28. Konarita Tsunero, a native of Iwate Prefecture, came to America in 1902. See Shakai Bunko, v. 7, pp. 90-91. A native of Ibaragi Prefecture, Kuramochi Zensaburo arrived in 1904. See *ibid.*, pp. 167-168. Hasegawa Ichimatsu, a native of Nagasaki Prefecture, arrived in 1904. See *ibid.*, p. 53.

29. Iwasa Sakutaro, "Beikoku Yori," *Hikari*, August 5, 1906, and Oakland *Socialist Voice*, June 16, 1906. Takeuchi Tetsugoro and Saijo Toru were arrested, but Austin Lewis, a socialist lawyer, got the charges dropped.

30. Kuramochi Zensaburo, "Shakai Kakumeito Okoru," *Hikari*, July 20, 1906. Despite the help rendered by the Social Revolutionary Party, there is no mention of it in the Seamen's Union official journal, the *Seamen's Journal*. For details of the 1906 strike, see Hyman Weintraub, *Andrew Furuseth: Emancipator of the Seamen* (Berkeley and Los Angeles, 1959), pp. 74-78.

31. Roger Daniels, *The Politics of Prejudice* (New York, 1968), pp. 24-45.

32. Hyman Weintraub, pp. 112-113.

33. Oakland *Socialist Voice*, December 8, 1906. This issue was devoted to what was entitled "Oriental Exclusion Symposium."

34. Ira Kipnis, *The American Socialist Movement, 1897-1912* (New York, 1952), p. 277.

35. Quoted in *ibid.*, p. 280.

36. Oakland *Socialist Voice*, December 8, 1906.

37. Abe Isoo, *Hokubei no Shin Nihon* (Tokyo, 1905), pp. 76-77.

38. Oakland *Socialist Voice*, January 19, 1907. Kaneko Kiichi distributed this open letter to all socialist newspapers in America.

39. Ira Kipnis, p. 277.

40. Oakland *Socialist Voice*, January 19, 1907.

41. *Ibid.*, March 16, 1907.

42. The three issues appeared on December 20, 1906, February 10, and April 1, 1907. They are reproduced in Shakai Bunko, v. 1, pp. 461-485.

43. San Francisco *Examiner*, December 30, 1906; San Francisco *Call*, December 30, 1906; and Berkeley *Daily Gazette*, December 31, 1906.

44. *Shin Sekai*, December 30, 1906. Unfortunately the two other Japanese-language newspapers of San Francisco, the *Nichibei Shimbun* and *Soko Shimbun*, have not been preserved.

45. Shakai Bunko, v. 1, p. 466.

46. *Ibid.*, p. 467.

47. The complete text of this open letter is in B.S.M.E., pp. 178-189.

48. The San Francisco Consulate reported to the Foreign Ministry that Uyeyama Jitaro, Iwasa Sakutaro, Takeuchi Tetsugoro, Konarita Tsunero, Kuramochi Zensaburo, Ogawa Kinji, Hasegawa Ichimatsu, and a few others were behind this incident. Believing that they required careful watching, it employed two agents to spy on their activities. See wires from San Francisco Charge D'affaires to Foreign Minister, November 4, 1907 and November 15, 1907, in *Meiji Bunka Zenshu*, v. 6 (Tokyo, 1955), pp. 578-581. Japanese historians have related this incident and the other activities of the Social Revolutionary Party with efforts by the genro, Yamagata Aritomo, to topple the Saionji Cabinet for being too lenient on political radicals. See Kanzaki Kiyoshi, *Kakumei Densetsu: Tenno Ansatsu no Kan* (Tokyo, 1960), pp. 91-110; Ohara Kei, "Takahashi Sakue Kyoju Ate Koike Chozo Tatsumi Tetsuo no Tegami," *Tokyo Keidai Gakkaishi*, no. 29/30 (October, 1960), pp. 395-424; and Ohara Kei, "Genro Yamagata Aritomo e no Shokan," *Tokyo Keidai Gakkaishi*, no. 39 (June, 1963), pp. 157-197. This incident was also brought out in the High Treason Affair secret trial to connect Kotoku Shusui with it. See Itoya Toshio, pp. 53-62.

49. U.S. Immigration Commission, *Reports of the Immigration Commission, Immigrants in Industries*, Part 25 (Washington, D.C., 1911), p. 577.

50. Fujioka Shiro, p. 425. These figures were compiled by the Fresno Japanese Association and published in the *Shin Sekai*, September 1, 1908.

51. "Hokubei Furesuno Shakaishugi Kenkyukai," *Chokugen*, August 27, 1905.

52. It is difficult to determine the exact membership. To begin with there are conflicting figures ranging from 2000 to 4000 members. See B.S.M.E., p. 217 where the figure 2000 is given and p. 237 and p. 251 where the figure is stated at 4000. One could account for the discrepancy by showing that the smaller number is for 1908 while the larger one is for 1909. Another source hostile to the Labor League places the membership at 1000. See Ito Bansho, *Fukei Jiken no Shinso* (Fresno, 1912), p. 126. Because of the migratory nature of Japanese laborers in Fresno, it is hard to believe 4000 laborers out of an approximate labor force of 4000-5000 could be organized in one short picking season. Moreover, membership was simply determined by an annual $1.00 due paid by workers, and so figures by themselves do not mean much. I have elected to take the lower figure of 2000.

53. B.S.M.E., p. 213.

54. *Shin Sekai*, June 9, 1908.

55. The circular was printed in full in the *Shin Sekai*, August 22, 1908. An English version of it appeared in the Fresno *Morning Republican*, August 31, 1908.

56. For the following analysis, see Chapter 2, "History of Contract Labor in California Agriculture," in Lloyd H. Fisher, *The Harvest Labor Market in California* (Cambridge, 1953), pp. 20-41.

57. U.S. Immigration Commission, p. 592.

58. Stuart M. Jamieson, "Labor Unionism in American Agriculture," v. 1 (Ph.D. Dissertation, University of California, Berkeley, 1943), p. 140.

59. *Shin Sekai*, May 25, 31, 1908. Japanese laborers were single men in their twenties and thirties. Recreational outlets were few and far between, and gambling provided a release from the dull monotony of grapepicking. Chinese gambling houses were so numerous throughout California and the Japanese losses so great that there was the exag-

gerated story about the Japanese having financed the 1911 Chinese Revolution. See Karl K. Kawakami, *Asia at the Door* (New York, 1914), p. 116.

60. Fresno *Morning Republican,* June 10, 1908.

61. The Moral Reform Association issued circulars, held public meetings, monitored the gambling houses, and tried to organize boycotts. It also submitted a formal petition to the Mayor and sought the cooperation of the local Chief of Police. See Fresno *Morning Republican,* June 9, 11, 1908, and *Shin Sekai,* June 11, 1908.

62. *Shin Sekai,* October 23, 1908, cited a figure of 40. During the 1909 picking season, the Moral Reform Association submitted a formal petition to the Fresno City Council asking for the elimination of "ill-fame houses" with "20 women." See Fresno *Morning Republican,* July 1, 1909.

63. In 1909 Rev. Kitazawa Tetsuji, the Methodist minister, took the lead and filed formal complaints in August and September against the prostitutes and Iwata Hidekuni, the prostitution ringleader, and had them arrested a number of times for vagrancy. See Fresno *Morning Republican,* August 5, 7, 29, and September 15, 1909.

64. At first the *Rodo* was a bi-weekly published from November 20, 1908 to April 20, 1909. It became a weekly, *Shukan Rodo,* on August 5, 1909 and lasted until September 4, 1909. Its lowest press run is reported to have been 2500; its average between 4000-5000. See Ohara Kei, "Furesuno Rodo Domeikai ni Tsuite," in *Fujibayashi Keizo Hakase Kanreki Kinen Ronbunshu* (Tokyo, 1960), pp. 36-37. Only four issues have been preserved (August 5, 14, 21, and 28, 1909), and they are reproduced in Shakai Bunko, v. 1, pp. 489-505.

65. B.S.M.E., pp. 230-231.

66. *Ibid.,* pp. 233-234.

67. *Ibid.,* pp. 248-254.

68. Otsuka Zenjiro worked for the *Soko Shimbun.* A bitter foe of socialists, he felt that they were "disloyal Japanese" and that loyal subjects, like himself, "felt the natural urge to kill them," Otsuka Zenjiro, p. 164. For details of the knifing incident, see *ibid.,* pp. 161-182; B.S.M.E., pp. 263-269; *Shin Sekai,* December 1, 4, 1908; and Ohara Kei, "Furesuno Rodo Domeikai ni Tsuite," pp. 42-45.

69. The first mention of the mass arrests appeared on June 4, 1910 in the *Shin Sekai* under the caption "Great Plot of the Socialist Party." Thereafter, whenever news of the High Treason Affair appeared, Kotoku Shusui was always referred to as a "traitor" (gyakuto). See the last section of this essay.

70. *Shin Sekai,* November 12, 19, 1911.

71. Because of the uproar caused by his talk, Rev. Kitazawa prepared a written statement on it. It was printed in the *Shin Sekai* on November 25, 1911.

72. *Ibid.,* November 21, 1911.

73. *Ibid.,* December 8, 1911.

74. *Ibid.,* December 29, 1911.

75. *Ibid.,* February 15, 16, 1912. Effective January, 1909 the Japanese Foreign Ministry delegated the "endorsement right" to local Japanese Associations through the Consulate General and the Japanese Association of America in San Francisco. The right was tied to certain certificates issued by the local Consulate in connection with the Gentlemen's Agreement and Japanese laws. To secure any certificate, Japanese immigrants had to apply at the local association within whose jurisdiction they resided. Based on the authority of the endorsement right, local associations performed the bureaucratic job of "endorsing" or verifying certificate applications to see that applicants in fact were bonafide residents within their jurisdiction and that the socio-economic data in applications were accurate. The Japanese Association of America, the central body to which local associations were affiliated, retained the power to withdraw the endorsement right from any local association.

76. *Shin Sekai,* March 13, 14, 1913. This newspaper was the *Chuka Jiho* published by Doi Uchizo. Unfortunately no copies of this paper have been preserved. The reporter was Wakao Kyonan. Out of this incident 7 persons, including Taira Chizan, were arrested and charged with assault and battery, and 32 individuals were charged with disturbing the peace. See *ibid.,* March 17, 1913, and Fresno *Morning Republican,* March 15, 1913.

77. Kuyama Yasushi, *Kindai Nihon to Kirisutokyo,* Meiji-hen (Tokyo, 1962), pp. 201-204.

78. *Ibid.,* pp. 270-275.

79. *Shin Sekai,* April 1, 2, 1912. The conference was officially called "Conference of Imperial Subjects in the East Bay."

80. *Ibid.,* April 2, 1912.

81. Ito Bansho, p. 87.

82. Soejima Hachiro, Ikeda Kando, and Taira Chizan started this newspaper in 1912. As with other newspapers, as far as the writer knows, no copies have been preserved.

83. B.S.M.E., pp. 311-384, and Ohara Kei, "'Daigyaku Jiken' no Kokusaiteki Eikyo," *Shiso,* no. 471 (September, 1963), pp. 62-73.

84. Toga Yoichi, *Nichi-Bei Kankei Zai-Beikoku Nihonjin Hatten Shiyo,* (Oakland, 1927), p. 102. The monthly was entitled *Yorokobi no Otozure* (Glad Tidings) and had been published since 1894. No copies are available. Interesting enough, Sakon had sympathized with the people near the Ashio Copper Mines in Tochigi Prefecture who had suffered over the years from the sulfuric gas discharged by the mines. Just two months prior to his first controversial article which appeared in February, 1902, an incident relating to the mines had occurred. In an unheard of manner, Tanaka Shozo, in December, 1901, had unsuccessfully attempted to directly present a petition, drafted up by Kotoku Shusui, to the Emperor to bring the plight of the people to his attention. See Itoya Toshio, *Kotoku Shusui Kenkyu* (Tokyo, 1967), pp. 143-149, for further details of this event.

85. After his November 25, 1911 public statement, Rev. Kitazawa never expressed his opinion in print again. Instead he quietly returned to Japan in June, 1912. Different underlying causes can be given for this lèse-majesté affair. On the simplest level it might have been a personality clash between Kitazawa and those opposed to him. As a part of this explanation, it is said that certain persons resented his anti-prostitution campaigns and were out to discredit him at the first opportunity. Secondly, it might have been—as it was suggested by the *Shin Sekai*—an internal factional strife over the position of Secretary of the Fresno Japanese Association. Since the position of President, which Kitazawa occupied, was largely honorary, he was not the central issue, the real fight having been the Secretary's position which administered the endorsement right and in which power and influence hence rested. Takeda Shojiro, the initial focus of the controversy, returned to Japan in 1912 and died enroute.

86. Marcus L. Hansen, "The History of American Immigration as a Field for Research," *American Historical Review,* 32 (April, 1927), pp. 500-518.

A Historical Survey of
the Chinese Left in America
By H. Mark Lai

Introduction

The history of the left among the Chinese in America is a neglected chapter in the history of the Chinese community. This is a preliminary survey of the left movements until the end of the 1950's; most of the emphasis in the present essay is on activities in the San Francisco Bay Area. It is the author's hope that this initial sketch, superficial as it may be, will inspire others to probe to greater depths into this

little investigated but significant phase in the history of the Chinese in this country.

Two main factors were largely responsible for the development of left-wing activities among the Chinese in America in roughly the first half of the twentieth century. Members of the Chinese left in

Above - During its 1938 strike, the first Chinese Ladies' Garment Workers' Union, Local 341 of the ILGWU, picketed the National Dollar Stores, owner of the largest garment factory in San Francisco's Chinatown at that time.

America were inspired by the quest for China's national salvation under the leadership of Sun Yat-sen's revolutionary nationalist party (the Kuomintang before 1927) and subsequently of the Chinese Communist Party. They at the same time were also motivated by the desire for a vast improvement of their own situation in America due to their experience of exploitation and discrimination here. These two factors were present throughout the history of the left among the Chinese in America, though one or the other predominated at different times.

The Introduction of Socialist Doctrines to the Chinese

The latter half of the 19th Century was a time of travail for the Chinese people. After the bayonets and cannons of the West had battered down China's wall of isolation, the ancient empire found herself unable to cope with the aggressive Westerners as her traditional social structure and self-sufficient economy crumbled before their thrusts, and territories and concessions were yielded to the pugnacious occidentals. Toward the end of the century, the partitioning of China by the powers and submittal to colonial status appeared inevitable.

This was a time of peril for the nation. Concerned Chinese began quests for ways toward national salvation. Among these were a number of intellectuals who examined and accepted socialism as the goal toward the eventual regeneration of the Chinese nation.

At the turn of the century, China was greatly dependent upon Japanese sources for information on Western culture, and the introduction of socialism was no exception.[1] It was through Japanese writings that Chinese students and intellectuals were first exposed to the doctrines of Marx, Engels, and others. Beginning in 1903, books, pamphlets and articles on socialism also were published in Chinese. Many articles on this subject appeared in the newspapers and periodicals established at the time by both the Chinese Empire Reform Association (Zhongguo Weixinhui) led by Kang Youwei and Liang Qichao, and the revolutionary Zhongguo Tongmenghui, led by Sun Yat-sen. Drawing much of their support from overseas Chinese, both organizations' publications had broad reading audiences in the overseas Chinese communities, and as a result had wide circulation abroad. Certainly, in an age when most Chinese readers were not familiar with Western languages, these publications were important sources for those Chinese interested in socialist doctrines.

Initially the brand of socialism from the West espoused by the Chinese writers was generally that advocated by social-democrats of the Second International. Ideological limitations of most of these intellectual socialists, derived as they were mainly from the gentry classes, led to great hostility toward violent revolutionary methods. Paralleling this development, however, was a growing interest in anarchism and nihilism among some of the younger revolutionaries.[2]

By mid-decade, articles advocating anarchism as the guide for revolution began to predominate in Chinese socialist writings. The doctrines of Proudhon, Bakunin and Kropotkin became the fad in Chinese revolutionary circles. Many young, impatient, romantic petit bourgeois intellectuals became attracted to the simple solution of committing individual heroic acts of terrorism to pull down and destroy the old order as represented by the Manchu dynasty.

The Russian Revolution of 1905 gave further impetus to the growth of popularity of anarchism, and by 1907 anarchist groups formed among students in Japan and France. Within a short time the doctrine spread to China and to the overseas Chinese.[3]

The American Milieu and Development of the Left among the Chinese in America

Chinese peasants emigrating to America had hoped to find a better life. Instead, in the land of liberty they found not freedom and prosperity, but discrimination and intolerance. They then suffered the dubious distinction of being the first ethnic group to be singled out for exclusion from the U.S. in 1882. The great majority of Chinese who lived and worked in America were exploited by employers, merchants and labor contractors both within and without their own community. Although Chinese labor had been characterized as being docile and tractable, the not so infrequent strikes and sometimes violent reactions of Chinese laborers to exploitation showed that they did not take their miserable lot as passively and fatalistically as some Western historians had put it. Contemporary accounts show that they fought back when given the proper leadership and organization.[4] Socialist doctrines pointing the way towards a better world would strike sympathetic chords among at least some of the Chinese in America.

At this time, many members of the American working class were strongly influenced by the socialist doctrines. Worker solidarity was one of the basic tenets of socialism, whether Marxist or Anarchist. However, during the early years of the 20th Century, this was a myth as far as Chinese workers were concerned, because the American labor movement in general was extremely hostile to Chinese labor. Even the so-called Marxist Socialists, in spite of their professed belief in the brotherhood of the working man, supported the "unconditional exclusion of Chinese, Japanese, Koreans, and Hindus. . . ." from this country.[5] Only the anarcho-syndicalist Industrial Workers of the World (IWW) held true to the belief that fraternal bonds existed among all wage earners regardless of racial lines, and tried to enroll Asian workers, including Chinese, into the unions on an equal basis with workers of other racial groups. The I.W.W. was never too successful in their recruiting campaign. But at least some Asians were won over to their cause. During this period at least two Chinese were translating I.W.W. literature into Chinese in San Francisco.[6]

At this time, the Chinese in America were excluded from large scale modern industries, thus they lacked the discipline that workers in large industries acquired. Moreover, stimulated on the one hand by anarchist writings from China, and on the other by the fraternal hand extended to them by the I.W.W. it was natural for some early Chinese radicals to lean toward syndicalist ideas.

As early as 1914, a small group of socialists had formed a Chinese Socialist Club in San Francisco.[7] A few years later the *Chinese World* of August 18, 1918 reported the organization of Meidong Huaren Gongwuhui (Chinese Labor Affairs Association of the eastern part of the U.S.) in Boston. One of its objectives was to promote socialism.

By the end of World War I, small groups of anarcho-syndicalists were active in the major Chinese communities of New York and San Francisco. In 1919, the Unionist Guild or Sanfanshi Gongyi Tongmeng Zonghui (Workers' League of San Francisco) was formed in San Francisco[8] which at that time had the highest concentration of Chinese workers, many of whom labored under inhumane conditions.

The Unionist Guild aimed its first action at Chinese shirt manufacturing factories in San Francisco and Oakland. On May 18, 1919, the new workers' organization presented nine demands to the factory owners.[9] After strike threats and several negotiating sessions at the Young Wo Association in San Francisco, they finally signed agreements with 32 factories.

Following this initial success the league soon created two additional departments: one for agriculture and one for miscellaneous occupations. In September, 1919 a branch was established among Chinese agricultural workers in Suisun, California. The Unionist Guild then changed its Chinese name to Meizhou Gongyi Tongmeng Zonghui (Workers' League of America) to suit the new situation.

In the meantime, the owners had organized to counter-attack. During the next few years, by presenting a united front against the workers, the employers defeated several strikes led by the Guild. Unable to rally broad workers' support, the Guild's fortunes declined. It disappeared from the Chinatown scene around 1927.

At its height the Unionist Guild claimed a nominal membership of about a thousand. It was the high point of anarcho-syndicalist activity among Chinese workers in America. This peak was never to be approached again. The demise of the Guild, how-

courtsey of H. MARK LAI

The first issue of the *Kung Sing,* the organ of the Workers' League of America, published 1 March 1924 in San Francisco, which contains the proclamation of the organization.

ever, demonstrated the difficulty Chinese workers would have in achieving lasting gains in a situation where they were going it alone without much fraternal support from workers in the larger society.

Following the disappearance of the Unionist Guild, the anarchist movement in San Francisco's Chinese community was sustained by the Ping Sheh (Equality Society), a political club. Occasional police harassment[10] and lack of community support made it difficult for this small group to accomplish much except to publish pamphlets and a monthly magazine *Pingdeng (Equality)* from 1926 to around 1931,[11] and infrequently to distribute leaflets in support of workers' struggles in Chinatown.[12] In 1934 another group of anarchists organized the Wuzhengfu Gongchangzhuyizhe Lianmeng (Alliance of Anarcho-Communists) and issued another monthly publication, the *Wuzhengfu Gongchan Yuekan (Anarcho-Communist Monthly).*[13] But this, however, represented the efforts of only a few zealots without much mass following.

Times continued to be difficult for the anarchists in the midst of the Great Depression of the 1930's. By this time Marxism had become dominant in the socialist movement. However, the Equality Society managed to survive until the eve of World War II.

The Chinese anarcho-syndicalist movement of the 1920's and 1930's was not limited only to the San Francisco Bay Area. The Chinese Labor Association (Huaren Gonghui) founded in Vancouver, B.C., during the mid-1920's to struggle against labor contractors, had an anarchist leadership.[14] And during the late 1920's, there was a Hei She (Black Society) in Mexico, a Jue She (Awakeness Society) in New York City, and a Ren She (Benevolence Society) in Los Angeles.[15]

By the end of the 1930's, however, the anarchist movement had run its course. The cause of its decline among the Chinese in America was directly connected with its decline in America as a whole. The growth of mass unions and large complex industries was contradictory to anarcho-syndicalist concepts of decentalization and anti-leadership. Bigness engendered a need for disciplined mass action which was contrary to the syndicalists' ideas of spontaneity. Their extreme left wing tactics, such as standing aloof from conservative trade unions, isolated them from the mass of workers. Moreover, following the Russian Revolution, the better-organized Marxist communists attracted many elements from the syndicalist organizations, thus sounding their death knell.[16] As syndicalism withered to a mere splinter on the left anarchists tended to become anti-capitalist, anti-soviet and anti-communist (Marxist).

The anarcho-syndicalists formed one of the earliest radical socialist organizations among the Chinese in America. But just as the Neanderthal Man was an early branch which deviated from the main line of development leading to *homo sapiens,* the anarchist movement in Chinatown was an early development of the Chinese left which led into a blind alley. Today its effects upon the Chinese community can hardly be detected.

The Communist-Kuomintang Alliance in China and its Effects

It is not known when the Chinese in America first became interested in Marxism. Undoubtedly there were already some who received a smattering of the socialist doctrines during the 1900's. The October Revolution was the stimulus spurring more Chinese in China as well as Chinese in this country to study the Marxist doctrines. For instance, in December 1919 there was already a group calling themselves Xin Shehui (New Society) formed in San Jose, California, "to study capitalism and communism and the radical politics of the New Russia."[17] However Marxism was not influential among the Chinese left in America

until after the Canton Revolutionary Government led by Sun Yat-sen made an alliance with the USSR and admitted Communists to the Kuomintang. Because of this alliance, Marxists among the Chinese in America were very active in support of the Chinese Revolution. They were found in many Kuomintang organizations.

Given the discriminatory conditions under which the Chinese in America lived, and the hope for the creation of a strong independent China by the successful completion of the Chinese Revolution led by the Revolutionary Government of Sun Yat-sen, it was not surprising that Marxism augmented its influence in the Chinese community at this time. This period saw the first political involvement of many who were to continue to participate in activities of the Chinese left in America during the next three decades. And it was probably during these years that the first Chinese in the U.S. joined the American Communist Party. By the late 1920's, a Chinatown branch of the party had been established in San Francisco, where it was active until around the beginning of the Korean War. However, it was the popularly-based organizations of the left which had the greatest effect on the Chinese community. And in these organizations, Marxists, liberals, nationalists and others worked together to promote certain economic and political programs as reflected by the needs of the times.

One of the earliest such groups was the Sanminzhuyi Yanjiushe (Association for the Study of the Three Principles of the People). It was formed in 1926 by young militant Chinese workers in San Francisco to support the Chinese revolution and was alleged to be the first Chinatown organization to display openly the Kuomintang national flag.[18] A year after, the Kuomintang-Communist split in China sent repercussions into Chinese communities all over the world. The remaining years of the 1920's saw many organizational changes as supporters of the right and left fought in the Chinese communities. The political situation became extremely complex and confusing.

Shortly after the suppression of the Canton Commune in China, the Sanminzhuyi Yanjiushe changed into the Kung Yu Club (Gongyu Quluobu) in 1927. In an attempt to widen its base among Chinatown workers, the club in 1928 was reorganized into the Huaren Gongrenhui (Chinese Workers' Club). This was a significant milestone, for it marked the reorientation towards the labor movement of many in the Chinatown left who had outgrown their student careers.

It was not long before disagreements on policies and tactics split the organization. One faction, calling itself the Huaqiao Gonghui (Overseas Chinese Club) abandoned militant tactics and acted as a center for job placement. It became pro-Kuomintang. The left-wing faction, in the meantime, apparently resumed the name Kung Yu Club and continued to work together with progressive elements in the American labor movement.[19]

Another organization supporting the Chinese Revolution during this period of the Kuomintang-Communist Alliance was the Chinese Students' Club (Zhongguo Xueshenghui), composed of Chinese students of various political beliefs all over the U.S. interested in the building of a China free from foreign domination. The San Francisco chapter included university and high school students, mostly from China, but also some American-born. It was formed in 1927 and was known as the Sanfanshi Zhongguo Xueshenghui (San Francisco Chinese Students' Club). Following Chiang Kai-shek's coup in Shanghai in 1927, many of the more conservative students in the Chinese Students Club turned their backs on the Revolution. The San Francisco Chinese Students' Club, however, continued its staunch support of the Chinese Revolution.

In the same period, left elements withdrew from the KMT and formed another group, the Zhongguo Gong-Nong Geming Datongmen (Grand Revolutionary Alliance of Chinese Workers and Peasants, ACWP) to oppose the KMT right-wing in San Francisco's Chinatown. The ACWP also published a weekly newspaper, *Xianfeng Zhoukan (The Vanguard)* to air their support of the Chinese Revolution.[20] In the community feelings ran high as the left and right denounced each other. Political street meetings frequently broke up as hecklers from the opposition engaged in fights with the participants.[21]

On the Eastern seaboard, left elements opposing the Kuomintang right-wing also were active as early as their compatriots on the Pacific Coast. A branch of the ACWP also existed in Philadelphia as early as 1928. By 1930 the Chinese Anti-Imperialist Alliance of America (Meizhou Huaqiao Fandi Datongmeng), a successor organization to the ACWP, established the *Chinese Vanguard (Xianfeng Bao),* as a monthly in Philadelphia.[22] Later it was moved to New York City and published as a weekly. After its demise during the mid-1930's, another weekly of similar editorial views, *National Salvation(Jiuguo Shibao),* was transferred from Paris to commence publication in New York City.[23] However, the masses in Chinatown then were not in a revolutionary mood and the circulations of these papers remained small; their effects on the Chinese community were limited. However, these publications marked the beginnings of the press of the Marxist left among the Chinese in America.

Besides hostility from the right in the Chinese community, the left also received much harassment from the police. For example in 1929 the San Francisco police, perhaps egged on by the KMT right-wing, raided the headquarters of the San Francisco Chinese Students club and closed it for alleged communist activities.[24, 25]

By the end of the decade, overt activities in support of the Chinese Revolution had ebbed among the Chinese in America. The Kuomintang right, in collaboration with the police and supported by the conservative merchants, gained control in the community.

The new alignment of forces in Chinatown saw increased contacts between the Chinese and American left. It was undoubtedly through such collaborative efforts that a delegate of the militant Chinese Laundry Workers Union (Xifutang) was asked to attend a San Francisco Labor Council meeting in 1929 to report on their victory in a week-long strike against Chinese laundries in the San Francisco Bay Area.[26] This was the first time a Chinese organization was invited and marked the small beginnings which led to a fuller participation of Chinese workers in the American labor movement. (Earlier in 1925 the Unionist Guild had appealed to American labor unions for donations and support for Chinese striking in protest against Japanese and British brutality in Shanghai; however, this was not followed up by further efforts at closer collaboration.)[27]

The Chinese Workers' Mutual Aid Association

The 1930's were hard times for the American working class, as industry stagnated during the Great Depression. The labor-management struggle in America became acute as labor fought for better working conditions. In Chinatown the Chinese left worked actively with the American Marxist left.

In 1930, led by the Kung Yu Club, Chinese workers formed an unemployment council in San Francisco's Chinatown and led unemployed Chinese on a march to the Chinese Six Companies,[28] the nominal spokesman for the Chinese in America, to ask for relief. The Chinatown marchers later joined a demonstration of the unemployed on Market Street to mark one of the earliest instances of American Chinese participating in such action outside the Chinese community.[29] Soon afterward the same group organized the Chinese Workers Center (Huagong Zhongxin, CWC) to help Chinese workers find employment, and to call upon them to unite and support the Chinese Revolution. However, after a brief career, the headquarters of the CWC was demolished by the San Francisco Police around the time of the San Francisco General Strike of 1934.[30]

The following years saw increasing collaboration between the Chinese left and left-wing elements in the American labor movement. The experience gained by these Chinese militants led to an increasing awareness among Chinese that cooperation with groups outside the Chinese community was essential to help effect changes in Chinatown and to improve workers' conditions.

In the 1930's, in cooperation with American progressive elements, the Chinese left in San Francisco undertook an abortive attempt to unionize the garment industry by establishing an independent Chinese Lady Garment Workers' Union. (The more

CHINESE WORKING PEOPLE IN AMERICA.

A storefront with signs announcing the fourth anniversary of the Chinese Workers' Mutual Aid Association commemorated on 5 October 1941 in San Francisco.

conservative, well-established, and wealthier Ladies Garment Workers' Union was more successful in their rival attempt.)[31]

In another try, which was more successful, Chinese left elements worked with American labor to attack the notorious Chinese contract system existing in the Alaskan salmon canneries and to demand collective bargaining rights. In 1936, picket lines were set up at the docks to halt the loading of ships of the Alaskan Packers' Association. (However, because of intimidation and threats by the Chinese contractors, the Chinese only worked behind the scene and did not appear on the picket lines.) The association capitulated and the workers, which included many racial groups, gained the right to unionize. The contract system was finally abolished.[32] As an aftermath of the victory, a group of Chinese workers on a ship returning from a canning season in Alaska developed

the idea of forming a Chinese workers' association.[33] The Chinese Workers' Mutual Aid Association (CWMAA, Jiasheng Huagong Hezuohui) was officially established in September 1937. Its aim was to unite Chinese workers and through the cooperation and exchange of experiences, to raise the status of Chinese workers in the labor unions and improve their working conditions.[34] Profiting from experience, its formation was a manifestation of a more mature stage in the development of the Chinese left movement.

Starting as a center for channeling information on employment in the canneries and as a gathering place for returned cannery workers, the CWMAA went on to broaden the scope of its functions to encourage Chinese workers to join the trade unions and to recognize the value of working collectively to better the working man's condition. The CWMAA filled a need in the community, for soon after its formation there were 400 to 500 members on its membership rolls.[35]

The CWMAA was the first Chinese workers' organization to work actively with people in the American labor movement to achieve a common goal. Their many links with CIO and AF of L unions, such as the International Longshoremen's Union, the Cannery Workers' Union and Miscellaneous Workers Union, etc., were extremely useful in introducing Chinese to employment in the larger society. However, it was true that the contacts of the CWMAA with the larger community were hampered somewhat by the fact that many members lacked facility in the use of English. But the basic philosophy of identity of interests among members of the working class regardless of ethnic background was accepted. Much of the association's strength and success was based on the demonstration of this concept.

The Chinese Hand Laundry Alliance[36]

There was no catalyst leading toward the formation of a Chinese workers' association in New York City, because of the greater dispersal of Chinese workers in the Eastern part of the country. Instead, the great number of laundries, many with common problems and grievances, served as the nucleus for the formation of a popularly based organization of the left.

By the 1930's, Chinese exclusion had been in effect half a century. Those "fortunate" enough to be able to reside in the land of liberty experienced discrimination as part of daily life. Economically the Chinese were systematically excluded from many industries and relegated to the least sought after areas of occupations, such as the laundry business. But even in these areas generally despised by most whites, the ugly head of racist discrimination reared itself.

A systematic campaign was directed against Chinese laundrymen in the eastern U.S. In 1933 an ordinance was proposed in N.Y.C. to charge a license fee of $25 per year on all public laundries plus a security bond of $1,000. This was designed to discriminate against small laundries, many of which were run with marginal profits by Chinese who could ill afford exorbitant fees. The traditional Chinese organizations, especially the Chinese Benevolent Association (Zhonghui Gongso),[37] handled the issue ineptly. As a result, a coalition of dissatisfied radical and liberal Chinese, with the support of the *Chinese Journal,* a New York City paper, organized the Chinese Hand Laundry Alliance (Huaqiao Yiguan Lianhehui, CHLA) in 1933 to oppose the bill. After much maneuvering the ordinance was passed, but the license fee was reduced to $10 and the security bond to $100. The CHLA received the major credit for these reductions.

After this initial success the Alliance won a large following. New York City laundrymen who joined were organized into districts each with their own representatives to the CHLA council. It raised small amounts of revenue by serving as witness to the sale of laundries, a function which formerly was the prerogative claimed by the Chinese Benevolent Association, the nominal leader of the New York Chinese community. It also provided help for its members to fill out tax forms and license applications. It became the first successful Chinese organization to work outside the framework of the traditional Chinese establishment.

The CHLA's outlook on Chinese relations with the greater community was far more progressive than most other Chinese groups. During the depths of the depression, for example, more than 500 Chinese laundrymen from the Alliance marched in the NRA (National Recovery Act) parade. This was a high water mark for the participation of a Chinese organization in the East in American national affairs.

The traditional Chinese power structure was unwilling to let the Alliance's challenge to their authority go by without reaction. One year after the formation of the CHLA, a conservative faction within it was induced to split away and form the Chinese Hand Laundry Association (Huaqiao Yiguan Tongye Zonghui). Most of the members remained loyal to the CHLA, however, and in 1934 it still enjoyed an active membership of over 3,200.

The CHLA considered itself a new type of Chinese organization. It put itself on record against what it considered to be outmoded ideas and feudal customs in Chinese society. Many members had little to do with traditional Chinese organizations.[38] Some members of this organization helped to establish and support the first Chinese daily paper of the left in America—the *Chinese Daily News,* which succeeded the *National Salvation Weekly* in 1940.[39]

The CHLA was never more than an alliance of small proprietors. Its importance lay in the demonstration of the value of collective strength. For years it was a staunch supporter of the Chinese Revolution within the New York Chinese Community, the largest in the eastern part of America.

The War Against Fascism

The CWMAA and the CHLA were both born during troubled times for the peoples of the world. Beside the economic disaster of the Great Depression, the 1930's saw the marching armies of the axis powers—Germany, Japan and Italy—menacing the world. By the end of the decade, internal contradictions, especially between labor and capital, had to be temporarily shelved as both turned to concentrate on defeating the common enemy. For the Chinese community this had added meaning. Their motherland, China, was fighting for survival against Japanese

WORLD EMBARGO AGAIST JAPAN

BARGO AGAINST JAPAN

Following the Japanese invasion of China in 1937, Chinese American women and their supporters protest the sale of scrap iron to Japan by the United States.

aggression. One of the major programs of the CWMAA was to rally support among Chinese workers to oppose the Japanese aggression in China. At this time, the Communists and the Kuomintang had effected a truce in China. Similarly, both the left and right in the Chinese community called a temporary halt to their quarrels to unite against Japanese militarism. The Association became very active in the United China War Relief Society (Lu Mei Huaqiao Tongyi Yijuan Jiuguozonghui), the overall organization coordinating war relief fund drives and other activities in the U.S. Chinese community.

Before the Pearl Harbor attack, some profit-hungry American businessmen were still selling material to the Japanese war machine. However, an increasing sector of U.S. public opinion, in which the left and the liberals figured prominently, opposed this short-sighted policy. One of the most visible targets for the protesters was the sale of scrap iron to Japan,

and during the closing years of the decade, picket lines were often seen at various U.S. ports to protest against loading scrap iron on ships headed for the Land of the Rising Sun.

In San Francisco, this protest was expressed particularly vehemently in December 1938 when the Greek freighter *Spyros* began loading scrap iron destined for Japan. The CWMAA received news of the intended shipment from friends in the American labor movement. While its members hastily manned picket lines at the pier, the organization called on the rest of the community to join them. A few days later students, workers, merchants, housewives and others from Chinatown, as well as many sympathizers, converged upon the waterfront to register their disapproval. The longshoremen refused to cross the picket lines. By the time the action ended, the number of pickets had swelled to 3,000. Even though the freighter finally did load its holds with the scrap metal, this dramatic exhibition of unity by the Chinese impressed many Americans and led to renewed calls to ban the sale of scrap iron to Japan. During the succeeding months the CWMAA continued to play a prominent role in picketing other ships loading scrap iron.

The CWMAA also held weekly public meetings at which guest speakers representing different political opinions were invited to air their views on subjects ranging from support for the war effort to union activities.[40] However, the new left-right alliance among the Chinese was built on shaky grounds and lasted only a few years. When the New 4th Army Incident of 1940 disrupted the Communist-Kuomintang truce in China,[41] the CWMAA withdrew from further active participation in the Kuomintang-dominated United China War Relief Society in San Francisco's Chinatown.

In the Eastern part of the country the CHLA also took part in similar war activities as the CWMAA. These two organizations raised large sums of money to support China's war effort. But it was the youth organizations who were most active and conspicuous in the cultural aspects of propaganda work required to further this effort. The rise of such organizations can be attributed to the Japanese invasion of China.

During the late 1930's many Chinese refugees of the Sino-Japanese War emigrated to the U.S. They included a number of young people and intellectuals who had been exposed to two decades of new ideas and changes in China and whose style and thinking differed significantly from that of established Chinese groups in the U.S. Their ideologies included nationalism, liberalism, and socialism. Many had participated in anti-Japanese war propaganda work in China. It was natural for these young people of kindred interest to seek each other out in the new environment. Some of them became active in an Overseas Chinese Literary Movement (Huaqiao Wenyi) that lasted into the 1950's, in which budding Chinese-American authors sought to create a literature based on the daily life of the Chinese in America. Even more joined or helped to establish social clubs which sprang up in many Chinese communities. These organizations often organized cultural activities, such as stage dramas, choral singing, and music, which appealed to young people and intellectuals and also played important supportive roles in war propaganda work. These events had a vitalizing influence in the American Chinatowns as new cultural forms and ideas were popularized. The left played a prominent role in these activities, especially in major communities such as New York and San Francisco. Owing to their dedicated leadership and organizational skills, they were much more successful in attracting youths than their rivals in the Kuomintang camp.

One of the earliest youth groups was the Niuyue Huaqiao Qingnian Jiuguotuan (familiarly known as Qing-Jiu, Chinese Youth Club) founded in New York

City in 1938. The club not only participated in anti-Japanese war work within the Chinese community but also was active in the broader U.S. youth movement, participating in events such as May First Labor Day parades.[42]

In San Francisco, the Chick Char Musical Club was established in 1937 with the encouragement of Chinese educator Tao Xingzhi.[43] This club had a generally liberal outlook and often took part in cultural programs at war rallies. By 1941, however, it had lost much of its initial momentum and another group, the New Chinese Alphabetized Language Study Society (NCALSS, Sanfanshi Xinwenzi Yanjiuhui), arose to play a more prominent role.

The NCALSS was originally organized to push the alphabetic spelling of Chinese words and to do away with Chinese characters, as a means of eradicating illiteracy. It grew out of a mass movement in China during the 1930's which had similar aims.[44] By 1936 news of the movement had spread to the Chinese in Hawaii,[45] and in 1940 the Society was formed in San Francisco.[46] In addition to promoting language reform, younger members of the society began to organize activities such as harmonica playing, choral singing, drama, etc. Within 3 months the activities of the organization were vastly expanded, and the membership increased to approximately 30, most of whom were recent immigrants in their late teens and early twenties, all fired with the enthusiasm and idealism of youth. The club rented a headquarters in a basement at 812 Stockton Street a few buildings from the headquarters of the local KMT. For almost 20 years this was to be the center of progressive youth activities in San Francisco's Chinatown. The NCALSS soon became the most active youth group in the community.[47]

In 1942, a coalition called the Lianhe Jiuguo Xuanchuan Tuan (United National Salvation Propaganda League), comprising the NCALSS and two other local Chinese youth clubs, presented a drama, whose proceeds went toward the purchase of gifts for Chinese serving in the U.S. armed forces. This organizational structure proved to be unsuitable for recruiting new members, however, and early in 1943, the Propaganda League was reorganized as the Jiasheng Huaqiao Qingnian Jiuguotuan (familiarly known as Qing-Jui, Chinese Youth League). Cultural activities were diversified and vastly expanded. Funds were raised to buy gifts for servicemen and to send them publications and letters. This organization, because of its superior organization and esprit de corps, remained throughout the war the most active among Chinatown youth groups. Excellent liaison was maintained with other Chinatown youth clubs and with left and liberal groups outside the Chinese community.[48]

Maximum CYL membership was about a hundred, but their programs, which included music and drama of modern China, reached a public many times this number. Like the CWMAA, the Chinese Youth League was also significant as a pioneer Chinese group that reached out to groups outside the Chinese community.

Between Hot and Cold Wars

During the years immediately following the end of World War II, the Chinese Hand Laundry Alliance (CHLA) in the East, the Chinese Workers' Mutual Aid Association (CWMAA) and the Chinese Youth League (CYL) in the West all were strong vocally in their support of the Chinese Revolution. In New York City the *China Daily News* continued to speak out as the news organ of the left among Chinese in America. As civil war between the KMT and the Communists seemed increasingly likely, several members of the CWMAA in San Francisco organized the Co-operative Publishers (Hezuo Chubanshe) for the purpose of printing, in Chinese, several classics of Chinese communism, thus for the first time offering to U.S. Chinese the opportunity to acquaint themselves with the program of the Chinese Revolution.[49]

During and immediately after the war some erosion in the mass base of the left organizations in the Chinese community occurred. On the Pacific Coast the Alaska Packers' Association moved its headquarters to Seattle upon the outbreak of hostilities between the U.S. and Japan and no longer recruited workers in San Francisco. As a result, the membership of the CWMAA—a large number had been cannery workers—began to dwindle.[50] The end of the war saw the wilting of the Chinatown youth movement. Many erstwhile youths acquired family responsibilities; others lost the idealism and fire of youth. There no longer appeared to be any urgent task to unify youths. The Chinese Youth League was one group that survived although with reduced membership rolls. It established links with groups outside the Chinese community such as the American Youth for Democracy. In 1946 it changed its name to Chinese American Democratic Youth League of San Francisco (CADYL, Sanfanshi Minzhu Qingniantuan, familiarly known as Min-Qing).[51]

The CADYL was active politically, giving support to candidates of the Progressive Party in local and national election campaigns. However its effectiveness in the politically apathetic Chinese community was limited.

The post-war period also saw the formation of other short-lived organizations of the left among the Chinese in America. The Overseas Chinese League for Peace and Democracy in China (Lu Mei Zhongguo Heping Minzhu Lianmeng, OCLPDC) was founded in New York City in November 1947 by Gen. Feng Yuxiang who at that time was in exile in the U.S. The proclaimed aim of the organization, which had chapters in New York, Washington, D.C., Minnesota and San Francisco, was to urge a stop to American interference in Chinese internal affairs, especially in the civil war. Members of the group, which at its height totalled more than 200, were mostly businessmen and intellectuals.[52] Later as the Chinese Revolution drew to a successful conclusion, organizations also appeared among Chinese university students which advocated returning to the homeland to join in the construction of a new China.[53] Among these was the nation-wide Alliance of Chinese Scientific and Technical Workers (Liu Mei Kexue Gongzuozhe Xiehui).

This was indeed a most favorable period for the left in the Chinese community. And on May 4, 1949 the *China Weekly (Jinmen Qiao Bao),* some of whose backers were members of the CWMAA, began publishing in San Francisco, joining the *China Daily News* as news organs in the U.S. Chinese community supporting the New China. It would seem that slowly but surely, the forces supporting the Chinese Revolution were gaining ground among the Chinese in America. Fate was to prove treacherous, however.

On the evening of Oct. 9, 1949, at the 12th anniversary celebration of the Chinese Workers' Mutual Aid Association held at Chinese American Citizens' Alliance Hall in San Francisco's Chinatown, a celebration of the recent founding of the People's Republic of China was in progress. The five-starred red flag of China was prominently displayed. The meeting had hardly commenced when KMT-hired hoodlums invaded the premises, seized the flag, beat up some participants and dashed blue dye all over the clothing of members of the audience. The next day, KMT elements passed out leaflets marking 15 individuals for eradication from the Chinese community.[54] This show of the mailed fist by the KMT was a blunt warning to U.S. Chinese not to display their sympathy for the Chinese Revolution too openly.

For a time, however, the forces supporting New China appeared to have recovered. *The China Weekly* and the *China Daily News* continued to publish. Later in 1949 another group of businessmen, some of whom were members of the OCPDC, purchased the right-wing *Chung Sai Yat Po* and changed to an editorial policy favorable to People's China. However, the Korean War soon brought an end to this era.

The Right-wing Reaction

The 1950's signaled hard times for the left in the U.S. as the forces of reaction launched a full-scale attack upon them. Left organizations either dissolved or suffered drastic declines in membership. The Chinese organizations were no different; in fact, they suffered attacks from both the American right and the KMT.

The cold war had already begun as the U.S. and the U.S.S.R. confronted each other in Europe. In June 1950, war broke out in Korea. Later that year, when Gen. MacArthur's armies threatened China's frontier, Chinese troops crossed the Yalu River. Many Chinese in this country became fearful that they would be put in concentration camps just as the Japanese were during World War II. Increased activity by F.B.I. agents and immigration officials in the Chinese community added to this apprehension and succeeded in intimidating many. The first victim among the left Chinese newspapers was the *China Weekly*. It ceased publication when the Chinese firm printing the paper refused to service it after Chinese troops entered the Korean War. Next was the *Chung Sai Yat Po* which folded in Jan. 1951 due to declining circulation as frightened readers cancelled their subscriptions. The U.S. government then moved against the *China Daily News,* accusing it of traffic with the enemy because of its advertisements for the Bank of China. In 1955 the paper was found guilty, fined and its manager jailed.[55] The paper's circulation dropped precipitously due to harassment of subscribers. Today it struggles along, publishing twice weekly with a small circulation of about 1200, and exists by relying on donations from its few remaining loyal supporters.

Among the left-wing Chinese organizations, membership declined during the 1950's as apprehensive Chinese ceased to attend meetings and stayed away from social functions. In San Francisco, the CWMAA finally closed its doors in 1954 after the membership dwindled to about 20. In New York the Chinese Youth Club also was dissolved at about the same time.

The Chinese Hand Laundry Alliance nearly suffered the same fate. When Chinese armed forces entered the Korean War the CHLA refused to join the anti-communist campaign launched by the Chinese Benevolent Association (CBA) of New York City. For this heresy the CHLA was expelled from the CBA.[56] During the 1950's, immigration authorities and F.B.I. agents continually harassed CHLA members, and its membership declined sharply. Today the organization exists only as a pale shadow of its former self.

The only group which managed to maintain a fairly extensive program during this era was the Chinese-American Democratic Youth League of San Francisco (the name was later changed to Chinese-American Youth Club, but it was still known familiarly in Chinese as Min-Qing). During the late 1940's, many members had dropped out because of family or business responsibilities, and it looked as if Min-Qing was a dying institution. However, in 1949 and for a few years afterward, a number of newly arrived young immigrants from China joined the club and infused new life. In spite of this revitalization, the cold war, the Korean War, and the assault against liberals and the left during the McCarthy era, all severely curbed the club's scope of activities. There began a period of harassment of individual members by governmental investigation agents. Practically every

member was questioned by the F.B.I. as the federal agents sought a non-existent link with the Chinese People's Republic. Members who were in the armed forces were barred from sensitive positions, and attempts were made to give several of them undesirable discharges. However, in this the government was unsuccessful as it was unable to establish its charges of subversion. In spite of these unfavorable circumstances Min-Qing managed to keep a fairly constant membership of about 40 for almost a decade, and was the most active independent youth group in Chinatown.

During this difficult period the club concentrated heavily on educational and social activities. A counseling, tutorial and remedial program was initiated in 1952 for the benefit of members and friends, most of them new immigrants. Members were encouraged to learn some skills in order to become more useful members of society. The club presented cultural programs at its headquarters at 812 Stockton St. two or three times per year. The performances included plays, songs and other representative aspects of the new Chinese culture. Min-Qing was one of the first organizations in the San Francisco Chinese community to present Chinese folk dances as well as the famous *Yellow River Cantata (Huanghe Dahechang)* of Xian Xinghai. In addition to this a biweekly mimeographed publication in the Chinese language, *Min-Qing,* gave friends and members opportunity to express their views. It is worth noting that this publication was probably the first in this country to use the simplified characters promulgated by the Chinese government in 1956. The club also pioneered the use of the Hanzi Pinyin spelling to teach Mandarin to members and friends. The club provided a social gathering place for members and friends. Through emphasis on mutual aid, group guidance and wholesome collective activities, Min-Qing was able to achieve for its members things which each individual could not have done.

The success of Min-Qing from start to finish was limited by the difficulty of instilling and maintaining a truly collective spirit within a larger society which encourages individualism. As long as the club held together with an active, ongoing program the basic guiding principles of collectivism worked well. But whenever activities declined or when the organization was temporarily broken up, members tended to become more concerned with personal career and family. Youth organizations are notoriously ephemeral in nature. Min-Qing through its various metamorphoses from the New Chinese Alphabetized Language Study Society to the Chinese Youth Club survived almost two decades wherein it witnessed the rise and fall of many other short-lived youth clubs. Few independent youth organizations in the Chinese community of America can match this longevity record.

In 1959 Min-Qing lost its headquarters and disbanded. Some members attempted to form another organization called the Haiyan Club, but this club never regained the momentum of Min-Qing. However, even if the club had not disbanded, it probably would have been drastically affected by the immigration investigations during the late 1950's, for during the Chinese exclusion era, many Chinese, including some of those who subsequently became active on the left, had entered this country by fraudulent claims of citizenship. The immigration authorities were well aware of this, and by threats, coaxing, and other means they induced or forced many Chinese to confess their fraudulent citizenship status. Members of the left were special targets as they and their relatives were systematically harassed. Many, including most of the members of Min-Qing, were stripped of their "citizenships." Some were prosecuted for defrauding the government so as to warn others to be more cooperative. Others were not given the right of permanent residence in this country, thus having the threat of deportation hovering over their heads indefinitely. In this manner the left and their sympathizers were put on the defensive and their effectiveness in the community was curbed drastically.

Some Concluding Words

For almost half a century from the eve of World War I to the dying years of the McCarthy era, there was nearly always some organization representing some type of socialism within the Chinese community in America. In the past these groups were always a minority in the community, but in spite of this they made a significant impact. This was especially true of the groups springing up after the late 1930's.

The Chinese left faced many obstacles. They were often subjected to acts of harassment by government officials. Raids by the San Francisco Police upon the Ping Sheh and the Sanfanshi Zhongguo Xueshenghui in the late 1920's were clear examples of this. Moreover, the Chinese exclusion acts over the years had led to numerous illegal and fraudulent entries among Chinese immigrants. Thus many Chinese have questionable immigration status. American authorities were not oblivious to this and for years they have used this as a weapon to crack down on politically active Chinese. Thus the threat of deportation and prosecution on criminal charges were always hanging over the heads of these political nonconformists. For example, Xavier Dea, (Xie Cang), one of the activists in the Sanfanshi Zhongguo Xueshenghui, was deported to the U.S.S.R.[57] Even during the 1960's, deportation was still the favorite weapon of the U.S. government against the Chinese left. As late as 1965 an official of the Chinese Hand Laundry Alliance, Louie Pon, was charged with fraudulent entry and threatened with deportation by the Justice Department. One of the counts against him was that he was affiliated with the *China Daily News*.[58] Another

weapon often resorted to by the authorities was to prosecute members of the left for fraudulent entry, as was the fate of four members of Min-Qing during the late 1950's and early 1960's.[59] The effect of actions such as these has generally been to cow the Chinese population into silence, and to intimidate the Chinese with sympathies for the left.

For the most part of the first half of this century China was convulsed in struggle as the Chinese people sought the road to national rebirth while at the same time fighting for national survival against Japanese aggression. Since most members of the Chinese left in America at this time were China-born, it was natural that they reacted strongly to events across the Pacific. Concern for support of the Chinese revolution and for resistance to Japanese aggression dominated their activities. In this area they were able to render valuable service by informing and educating the larger society as well as the U.S. Chinese community.

The organizations of the left also were interested in effecting certain domestic programs aiming toward change in the community. In this regard they encountered obstacles which were difficult to surmount. Successful implementation of their programs, of course, ultimately rested upon the support of the people within the Chinese community. However, since the Chinese were but a small minority in this country, radical change in the Chinese community could not be fully effected independently of the situation in the larger society. The anarchists of the 1920's were at first successful in bringing some improvement to workers' conditions in the Chinese community, but ultimately failed because the conservative forces in the Chinese community were too strong for them to tackle alone without some support from the larger society. The Marxists of the late 1930's and 1940's were able to achieve a somewhat greater degree of success because they could draw upon the backing of friendly American progressive forces. On the negative side, when the anti-communist hysteria swept the larger society during the 1950's, the Chinese left in America was among its victims.

The popular organizations formed by Marxists in alliance with liberals during the 1930's displayed some promise of growth into strong organizations counter-acting the conservative Chinatown establishment and providing leadership for the forces desiring a change from the status quo, for the groups were originally organized around popular economic issues which had great appeal. However after a promising start, the coming of World War II curbed their development as the American people were asked to make sacrifices in order to win the war against Fascism. Other objective factors such as wartime "prosperity," as well as the factors previously mentioned, all worked to prevent the Chinese left from maintaining and augmenting its popular base in the community, thus hampering the carrying out and expanding of any programs for change. After the hot war, the cold war hysteria put the brakes on the resumption of such activities. Thus even though the situation in Chinatown called for drastic change, the KMT conservative merchant coalition, in collaboration with U.S. governmental authorities, was able to sustain an atmosphere discouraging any challenge to the established order.

In view of their limited mass support, their continual harassment and other handicaps, it is surprising that these groups have been able to accomplish as much as they have. They have for years brought idealism, zeal, and a sense of direction into Chinatown's atmosphere of materialist mediocrity and political apathy. They have been the vanguard presenting new ideas and concepts and representative samples of the new Chinese culture. They have been pioneers in recognizing that the Chinese in America must work across racial lines in order to achieve change. More than a decade has elapsed since the last of the "old" left organizations of Chinatown has faded into the past. Other groups representing the "new" left have appeared in the Chinese community, their ideologies varying from left-liberal to Marxist. In conjunction with the larger society, much of the new movement has taken off from the momentum generated by the civil rights, Black power, and the Third World movements of the 1960's, and was reinforced by an identification with the positive image generated by a victorious Revolutionary New China.

The ties between the "new" and "old" left groups are few since the decade that elapsed between disappearance of the one and appearance of the other was an effective divide. However the "old" and the "new" left share common goals in striving for a better community and a better world.

Three significant characteristics distinguish the "new" left from the "old" left: First, the new activists are predominantly native-born. Their appearance represents a new stage in the historical development of the Chinese community, a stage in which the Chinese of America have completed the transformation from sojourners to permanent residents. Second, the "new" left consists largely of students, professionals and intellectuals; so far few workers have participated in the movement. Third, although the "new" left organizations are still interested in the Chinese Revolution, the movement exhibits much greater concern in community problems such as housing, employment, racism, etc., and participates to a greater extent in the politics of the larger society.

Today these groups still have only limited support in the Chinese community and they are split into several factions. Most of the Chinese in America are still barely affected by their activities. However, the rise of these groups after two decades of total domination of the Chinese community by the KMT, is a sign that the forces for change are again stirring. Judging by their activities, a new stage has been reached in the development of the Chinese left in America. With proper implementation of programs administering to the aspirations of the people of the Chinese community, this "new" Chinese left can grow to become a significant force. However, the full story of the "new" Chinese left is outside the scope of this essay and will have to be the subject of another paper. ★

Notes

1. An account of the introduction of socialist doctrines into China may be found in "The Triumph of Anarchism over Marxism, 1906-1907," by Martin Bernal in *China in Revolution: The First Phase 1900-1913,* edited by M.C. Wright (New Haven: Yale University Press, 1968), pp. 97-142.

   The organs of the Chinese Empire Reform Association were the first to introduce socialist writings to China. In 1903, the Guangzhi Shuju (Broadening of Knowledge Book Co.), founded in Shanghai in 1902 by reformist Liang Qichao and his supporters, published three surveys on socialism translated from the Japanese. That same year two other books on socialism were issued by other publishers in Shanghai. From 1903 on many articles on socialism appeared in *Xinmin Congbao (New People's Miscellany),* a Yokohama periodical also founded by Liang's supporters in 1902. Sun Yat-sen and some members of the revolutionary Tongmenghui were also influenced by western socialism.

2. An account of the development of anarchism in China may be found in *The Chinese Anarchist Movement,* by Robert A. Scalapino and George T. Yu (Berkeley: Center for Chinese Studies, 1961).

3. One of the first to bring the anarchist doctrines to Chinese soil was a student revolutionary, Liu Sifu, better known as Liu Shifu, a native of Xiangshan (now Zhongshan) district in the Pearl River delta near Canton. The relation of Liu Shifu to the anarchist movement among the Chinese in America is not clear at present but it is worthy of note that his native district of Xiangshan was the region of origin for many Chinese in America. And certainly, at least in the San Francisco Bay Area, Xiangshan (Zhongshan) people were prominent in the anarchist movement. According to Wending, "The Biography of Mr. Shifu," in *The Collected Works of Shifu* (Shanghai, 1928), Liu Shifu went to study in Japan in 1904. In the following year he took an active role in the formation of the Tongmenghui in Tokyo. Liu left Japan in 1906 and for the next few years engaged in revolutionary activities in the Hong Kong area. After the revolution he and his followers founded the Huiming Xueshe (Society of Cocks Crowing in the Dark) in Canton in 1912. The object was to propagate anarchism to the masses.

   In 1913 reflecting his disgust with his former comrades of the Tongmenghui who now seemed only to be concerned with advancing their personal interests, Liu helped to organize the Xin She (Heart Society) which was intended to be a preliminary to a nation-wide anarchist movement. However, Liu died in 1915 of tuberculosis. He was only 31 at the time.

4. Chinese strikes for better working conditions were not rare. The first recorded instance occurred on June 8, 1852 when Chinese construction laborers working on the Parrott building in San Francisco went on strike for more wages (*Chinese Historical Society Bulletin,* San Francisco, Vol. 2, No. 5, May 1967). Other instances occurred

among the railroad workers, the most famous strike was in June 1867 when some 2,000 Chinese in the Sierra Nevadas walked off their jobs on the construction site of the Central Pacific (*Sacramento Union,* July 1 and 3, 1867).

Violence also accompanied some of the Chinese labor disputes. For instance the San Francisco *Call* on Aug. 17, 1896 reported attempted arson by members of the Garment Workers Guild against a factory owner who was reluctant to come to terms with the guild.

5. Isabella Black, "American Labour and Chinese Immigration" *Past and Present,* No. 25 (July 1963), pp. 59-76, quoting from *The International Socialist Review,* Vol. 10 (1910), p. 1121.

6. Philip S. Foner, *History of the Labor Movement in the U.S.* (New York: International Publishers, 1947), Vol. 4, p. 82.

7. A pamphlet, *China and the Social Revolution,* was published by Kiang Kang-hu, care of the Chinese Socialist Club, 1045 Stockton St., San Francisco, Calif. The preface of this pamphlet, written by Kiang himself in California, was dated June 25, 1914. The club may have been the Pingmin Shu-Baoshe formed by Kiang Kang-hu (See Feng Ziyou *Shehuizhuyi yu Zhongguo* [Hong Kong, 1920]).

8. The *Young China* of January 19, 1919 reported a police raid on IWW headquarters in N.Y. Chinatown. *Kung Sing,* No. 1 (Mar. 1, 1924) and No. 2 (April 1, 1924), included a detailed account of the history of the Workers' League of America up to 1924. The publication is the monthly magazine issued by the WLA.

9. The nine demands were as follow:
(1) The work day is to be limited to 9 hours.
(2) The employers are to guarantee that in the future wages are to increase and not decrease.
(3) Time and a half is to be paid for work over 9 hours.
(4) Double time is to be paid for Sunday work.
(5) Paid time off is to be given for American holidays.
(6) The employers are to pay medical bills for injuries incurred during performance of work on the factory's premises.
(7) The term of apprenticeship shall be set at two months, during which time the apprentice is to be allowed weekly expense money of $1.00.
(8) In case of a fire if a worker lives on the premises of his employer, the employer shall recompense him $50.00 to pay for losses incurred.
(9) Workers not obeying the above regulations are subject to discharge by the League.
All but the ninth demand were eventually accepted by the factory owners.

10. *Chung Sai Yat Po* (San Francisco), March 23, 1928 gave an account of a raid by San Francisco plain-clothes police officers on the Ping Sheh, where two members were arrested for preaching anarchism. This was typical of the general police attitude toward radical groups in the 1920's.

11. The Ping Sheh advertised free copies of various pamphlets in *Chung Sai Yat Po,* Nov. 29, 1926. The first issue of *Equality* was published July 1, 1927, according to an advertisement in *Chung Sai Yat Po,* June 24, 1927.

12. The author possesses copies of leaflets issued by the Ping Sheh in support of the Laundry Workers' strike of 1929 and the garment workers' strike against the Chinatown factory of the National Dollar Stores in 1938.

13. The first issue was published June 1, 1934. Communications were to be addressed to Ray Jones (Liu Zhongshi).

14. Ping Sheh, *May Day Special Issue,* May 1, 1927.

15. *Equality,* Vol. 1, No. 1 (July 1, 1927).

16. William Z. Foster, *Outline Political History of the Americas* (New York: International Publishers, 1951), pp. 391-2.

17. *Chung Sai Yat Po,* Dec. 4, 1919.

18. *Chung Sai Yat Po,* April 8, 13, 1927.

19. Huo, "Meiguo Sanfanshi Huaqiao Ge'ming Douzhengshi Pianduan," *Wei Min,* April-May, 1975. Also an interview with a former member of the San Francisco Chinese Students' Club. The paucity of documentation on changes in the names of the various workers' organizations during this period makes it very difficult to ascertain historical facts. But one can perceive some of the struggles going on by reading between the lines of advertisements and news items of the various groups; see *Chung Sai Yat Po,* June 25, July 27, 1928; March 30, May 29, 1929.

20. *Minutes of the Second Convention of the Kuomintang in San Francisco* (Zhongguo Guomindang Zhu Sanfanshi Zongzhibu Di'erci Daibiao Dahui Shimoji), 1928, p. 163. *The Xianfeng (Vanguard)* may have been the precursor of the publication of the same name published in Philadelphia in 1930.

21. See Note 18.

22. Leong Gor Yun, *Chinatown Inside Out* (New York: Barrows, 1936), pp. 143, 154, 156.

23. Interview with former worker at the *China Daily News* (New York).

24. See Note 18.

25. *Chung Sai Yat Po,* Jan. 14, 28, 30, 1929.

26. Philip Taft, *Labor Politics American Style, The California State Federation of Labor* (Cambridge: Harvard Univ. Press, 1968), p. 175, quoting from the *Proceedings of the 34th Annual Convention of the California Federation of Labor,* 1929, p. 29.

27. *Chung Sai Yat Po,* 1925, June 10, 11; July 1, 6, 10, 13, 15, 16, 20, 22, 24; August 17, 1930. The occasion was the celebrated "May 30th Incident" in Shanghai.

28. The Chinese Six Companies or the Chinese Consolidated Benevolent Associaton of the U.S.A. is the organization claiming to be the spokesman for all the Chinese in America. It is at the apex of the pyramid formed by Chinese organizations in the community and is formed by the seven major district associations in San Francisco: Ning Yung, Sam Yup, Kong Chow, Young Wo, Shew Hing, Hop Wo and Yan Wo Associations.

29. Interview with former member of CWMAA. Also Huo: *op. cited.*

30. Interview with former member of CWMAA.

31. See Note 30.

32. L. W. Casaday, *Labor Unrest and the Labor Movement in the Salmon Industry of the Pacific Coast* (unpublished Ph. D. thesis, Univ. of Calif. Berkeley, 1938), pp. 387-97. Also see "Yushiye Jianshi" (Alaska Cannery Workers), *Getting Together (Tuanjie Bao),* (San Francisco). Mar. 18-21, 1972.

In the Chinese contract system the cannery owner made agreements with contractors to can the salmon at certain fixed price per case during the canning season. The contractor then hired the workers. During the 19th Century practically all the labor at the canneries were Chinese. Later Chinese, Filipinos, Japanese, Mexicans, etc. were hired. Under this system, the workers were under the control of the contractors. They were frequently provided poor food, charged exorbitant prices for goods, and provided inadequate and unsanitary quarters. Thus it became one of the most hated features of cannery work.

33. Interview with Willie Fong, one of the founders of the CWMAA. Two Chinese most active in the founding were Willie Fong and Sam Young.

34. Jianfu, "Shi'ernianlai di Gongzuo Guocheng ji Jinhou di Renwu" (A Review of Work of the Past 12 Years and the Task for Now and the Future), *China Weekly*, Oct. 8, 1949. Lin Jianfu (Happy Lin) was secretary of the CWMAA and also one of the founders of the NCALSS.

35. See Note 32.

36. Leong Gor Yun. Chapter 5 gives a good account of the early history of the Chinese Hand Laundry Alliance.

37. The Chinese Benevolent Association or Zhonghua Gongso of New York City is an organization similar to the Chinese Six Companies (See Note 30), and claims to speak for the Chinese in New York City.

38. Virginia Heyer, *Patterns of Social Organization in New York City's Chinatown* (unpublished Ph.D. thesis, Columbia University, 1953), Chapter 8.

39. Liu Boqi, "Meiguo Huaqiao Baoye Fazhanshilue" (Brief History of the Development of Newspapers of the Chinese in America) in *Wenyi Fuxing Yuekan (Literary Renaissance Monthly)* Taiwan, No. 19, pp. 49-56. Also verified by verbal information from a former worker at *China Daily News*.

40. For example there were meeting announcements in the *Chung Sai Yat Po*, Mar. 4, 12, 1938, May 15, 22, 1938, etc.

41. During the Sino-Japanese War the Communist New 4th Army operated in the lower Yangtze Valley near Shanghai. The Nationalists felt it to be a threat to what they considered to be their territory, even though at that time it was held by the Japanese. In 1940 the KMT government ordered the New 4th Army to withdraw north of the Yangtze. While the army was withdrawing, protesting the KMT order, the Nationalists attacked the New 4th Army Headquarters Unit and accompanying rear guard, and inflicted several thousand casualties. Many overseas Chinese protested this action, pointing out that the most important task should be to unite to fight the common enemy, Japan.

42. *The Chinese Youth (Huaqiao Qingnian)*, published by the Chinese Youth Club, N.Y.C. Special Issue, No. 3 (Oct. 1940), pp. 7-11.

43. Interview with a former member of the NCALSS.

44. Ni Haishu, *Zhongguo Pinyinwenziyundong Shi Jianbian* (Shanghai, 1948), Chapter 6.

45. Chen Qiao, "Guanyu Yatgo Gaoyuk Daijong Muntai ge Hinyi" (On a Proposal with Regards to the Problem of Mass Education) in *25th Anniversary Commemorative Album of the Mun Lun School, Honolulu* (1936).

46. *Yuwen Yanjiu (Ymen Ingau) (Language Study)* published by the New Chinese Alphabetized Language Study Society (Apr. 1942).

47. See Note 46.

48. Rucong, "Xiaoxiao Shinian" (A Brief History of 10 Years) in *Min-Qing Tuanbao*, New Series No. 1, (Dec. 1, 1949). This is a mimeographed publication issued biweekly by the Chinese-American Democratic Youth League. The development and activities during the period 1940 to 1949 is covered in this article. Zhu Rucong (James Young) was one of the founders of the NCALSS.

49. The publications were:
(1) *New Democracy*, by Mao Tse-tung
(2) *The Truth about the Liberated Areas*, by Dong Biwu
(3) *On Coalition Government*, by Mao Tse-tung
(4) *Critique of "China's Destiny,"* by Chen Boda

50. See Note 33.

51. The aims of the CADYL as stated in its constitution were as follows:
(1) To unite Chinese and American youths to study and work together for the interest of young people.
(2) In cooperation with all Chinese here and abroad to fight for the establishment of a free, peace-loving, democratic, united, independent, wealthy and strong new China.
(3) In cooperation with Chinese and non-Chinese liberals and progressives to work toward freedom and equality for all mankind and world peace.
(4) In cooperation with other progressive organizations, to undertake educational programs, protect the public interest, and establish a democratic way of life.
(5) Through collective strength, to advocate ways of serving society, to strengthen the membership's belief in service to society, and to increase the usefulness of the membership in serving society.

52. James E. Sheridan, *Chinese Warlord, The Career of Feng Yu-hsiang* (Stanford: Stanford Univ. Press, 1966), pp. 279-280. Also, *Feng Yuxiang Jiangjun Ji'niance* (Album in Memory of Gen. Feng Yuxiang) (Hong Kong, 1948), pp. 114-115.

53. *Liu-Mei Xuesheng Tongxin*, Nov. 26, 1949; Jan. 21, Feb. 4, 1950.

54. *San Francisco Chronicle*, Oct. 10, 1949.

55. *China Daily News*, editorial July 4, 1970.

56. Heyer, p. 94.

57. Interview with a former member of the San Francisco Chinese Student's Club.

58. *Annual Report of the Immigration and Naturalization Service, 1965*, p. 11.

59. These were the cases of Jackson Chan, Maurice Chuck, Kai Dere and Wing Joe.

GLOSSARY OF ORGANIZATIONS OF THE CHINESE LEFT IN AMERICA

By H. M. Lai

Note: The Hanzi Pinyin system is used for transliterating Chinese words except for those spellings used officially by persons or organizations concerned, or commonly used and accepted in English-language publications (e.g., Canton, Mao Tse-tung).

Organizations & Institutions

Chick Char Musical Club (Qicha Yinyueshe)
叱咤 音 樂 社

Guangzhi Shuju
廣 智 書 局

Haiyan Club
海燕社

Hei She
黑社

Hezuo Chubanshe
合作出版社

Huiming Xueshe
晦鳴學社

Huagong Zhongxin
華工中心

Huaqiao Gonghui
華僑工會

Huaqiao Yiguan Lianhehui
華僑衣館聯合會

Huaqiao Yiguan Tongye Zonghui
華僑衣館同業總會

Hua-Qing
華青

Huaren Gonghui
華人工會

Huaren Gongren Hui
華人工人會

Jiasheng Huagong Hezuohui
加省華工合作會

Jiasheng Huaqiao Qingnian Jiuguotuan
加省華僑青年救國團

Jue She
覺社

Kung Yu Club (Gongyu Quluobu)
工餘俱樂部

Kuomintang (Guomindang)
國民黨

Lianhe Jiuguo Suanchuantuan
聯合救國宣傳團

Lian-Hui
聯會

Liu Mei Kexue Gongzuozhe Xiehui
留美科學工作者協會

Lu Mei Huaqiao Tongyi Yijuan Jiuguozonghui
旅美華僑統一義捐救國總會

Lu Mei Zhongguo Heping Minzhu Lianmeng
旅美中國和平民主聯盟

Meidong Huaren Gongwuhui
美東華人工務會

Meizhou Gongyi Tongmeng Zonghui
美洲工藝同盟總會

Meizhou Huaqiao Fandi Datongmeng
美洲華僑反帝大同盟

Min-Qing
民青

Mun Lun School (Minglun Xuexiao)
明倫學校

Niuyue Huaqiao Qingnian Jiuguotuan
紐約華僑青年救國團

Pingmin Shu-Baoshe
平民書報社

Ping Sheh (Ping She)
平社

Qing-Jiu
青救

Ren She
仁社

Sanfanshi Gongyi Tongmeng Zonghui
三藩市工藝同盟總會

Sanfanshi Minzhu Qingniantuan
三藩市民主青年團

Sanfanshi Xinwenzi Yanjiuhui
三藩市新文字研究會

Sanfanshi Zhongguo Xueshenghui
三藩市中國學生會

Sanminzhuyi Yanjiushe
三民主義研究社

Tung Sen Association (Tongshantang)
同善堂

Wuzhengfu Gongchanzhuyizhe Lianmeng
無政府共產主義聯盟

Xifutang
西福堂

Xin She
心社

78

Xin Shehui
新社會

Young Wo Association (Yanghe Huiguan)
陽和會館

Zhonghua Gongso
中華公所

Zhonghua Zonghuiguan
中華總會館

Zhongguo Gong-Nong Geming Datongmeng
中國工農革命大同盟

Zhongguo Guomindang
中國國民黨

Zhongguo Tongmenghui
中國同盟會

Zhongguo Weixinhui
中國維新會

Zhongguo Xueshenghui
中國學生會

Geographical Terms

Bolo
博羅

Canton (Guangzhou)
廣州

Dongguan
東莞

Hong Kong (Xianggang)
香港

Kwangtung (Guangdong)
廣東

Long Du
隆都

Shekki (Shiqi)
石岐

Xiangshan
香山

Zengcheng
增城

Zhongshan
中山

People

Chen Boda
陳伯達

Chen Qiao
陳巧

Chiang Kai-shek (Jiang Jieshi)
蔣介石

Dong Biwu
董必武

Feng Yuxiang
馮玉祥

Feng Ziyou
馮自由

Huo
活

Jianfu
堅夫

Kang Youwei
康有爲

Kiang Kang-Hu (Jiang Kanghu)
江亢虎

Liang Qichao
梁啓超

Liu Boqi
劉伯驥

Liu Shifu (pseudonym for Liu Sifu)
劉師復（劉思復）

Liu Zhongshi (Also Ray Jones)
劉中時

Mao Tse-tung (Mao Zedong)
毛澤東

Ni Haishu
倪海曙

Rucong
汝聰

Sun Yat-sen (Sun Yixian, also Sun Zhongshan)
孫逸仙（孫中山）

Tao Xingzhi
陶行知

Wending
文定

Xavier Dea (Xie Cang)
謝創

Xian Xinghai
冼星海

Publications & Published Works

Chinese World
世界日報

Chung Sai Yat Po (Zhongxi Ribao)
中西日報

Feng Yuxiang Jiangjun Jiniance
馮玉祥將軍紀念册

Guanyu Yatgo Gaoyuk Daijong Muntaige Hinyi
  (Guanyu Yige Jiaoyu Dazhong Wenti di Xianyi)
關於一個教育大衆問題嘅獻議

Hezuo
合作

Huanghe Dahechang
黃河大合唱

Huaqiao Qingnian
華僑青年

Huaqiao Wenyi
華僑文藝

Jinmen Qiao Bao
金門僑報

Jiuguo Shibao
救國時報

Kung Sing (Gongsheng)
工聲

Liu Mei Xuesheng Tongxin
留美學生通訊

Meiguo Huaqiao Baoye Fanzhan-shilue
美國華僑報業發展史略

Meiguo Sanfanshi Huaqiao Ge'ming Douzhengshi di
  Pian duan
美國三藩市華僑革命鬥爭史的片段

Meizhou Huaqiao Ribao
美洲華僑日報

Min-Qing Tuanbao
民青團體

Pingdeng
平等

Shehuizhuyi yu Zhongguo
社會主義與中國

Shi'ernianlai di Gongzuo Guocheng ji Jinhou di
  Renwu
十二年來的工作過程及今後的任務

Shifu Xiansheng Zhuan
師復先生傳

Tuanjie Bao
團結報

Wei Min Bao
爲民報

Wenyi Fuxing Yuekan
文藝復興月刊

Wuzhengfu Gongchan Yuekan
無政府共產月刊

Xianfeng Bao
先鋒報

Xianfeng Zhoukan
先鋒週刊

Xiaoxiao Shinian
小小十年

Xinmin Congbao
新民叢報

Ymen Ingau (Yuwen Yanjiu)
語文研究

Young China
少年中國晨報

Yushiye Jianshi
漁濕業簡史

Zhongguo Guomindang Zhu Sanfanshi Zongzhibu
  Di'erci Daibiao Dahui Shi-mo Ji
中國國民黨駐三藩市總支部
第二次代表大會始末記

Zhongguo Pinyinwenziyundong Shi Jianbian
中國拼音文字運動史簡編

Minorities
and
International Politics

By Don T. Nakanishi

"Japanese Americans"

Behold
We are clay pigeons traveling swiftly and aimlessly
On the electric wire of international hate
Helpless targets in the shooting gallery of political discord
Dulled by the clattering shells
That rip toward us from both sides.
Perhaps we are merely incidental to the gunplay,
Irrevocably set in the dizzy pace of whining bullets,
Forced to travel up and down an uncertain line
The hesitating border of two countries.[1]

Ohiye Mori

I must be honest. Negroes—Afro-Americans—showed no inclination to rush to the United Nations and demand justice for themselves here in America. I really had known in advance that they wouldn't. The American white man has so thoroughly brainwashed the black man to see himself as only a domestic 'civil rights' problem that it will probably take longer than I live before the Negro sees that the struggle of the American black man is international.[2]

Malcolm X

An African proverb states that "when two elephants fight, it is the grass that suffers." A less cited Burmese proverb says that "when lightning strikes the log, the chameleon is also destroyed." Both proverbs serve to highlight one aspect of the general topic of minorities in the context of international politics, *viz.*, when minority groups become victims of the global arena. The evacuation of Japanese Americans during World War II, the extermination of Jews during the Holocaust, the precarious position that the Kazakhs occupy in the borderland disputes between the USSR and the People's Republic of China are but a few of the many cases that might be cited.[3]

But to simply assert that minority groups have been the only victims of international politics would be an overstatement. It does not take a scholar of global affairs such as the late Arnold Wolfers to convince most people that the "common man" wherever and whoever he might have been "has traditionally been more the victim than the beneficiary of international politics."[4] A popular truism, of course, goes directly to the heart of the matter when it argues that in times of war there are no winners, only losers.[5]

Just as it would be an overstatement to claim that minorities are the only victims of world politics, it would be an understatement to say that they have nothing to gain from the global arena. A previous study demonstrated that some *Nisei* (second generation Japanese American) leaders in Los Angeles believe that the increasing acceptance of Japanese manufactured goods by American society is invaluable in their efforts to change the misconceptions and prejudices that Americans have towards Japanese Americans and Japan.[6] In the case of many American immigrant and minority groups, the positive identification with and purposeful political actions towards their homelands (at times with the goal of assisting in the founding of a nation-state) have served as important focal points from which collective activities and the collective pursuit of a group identity could be launched and sustained.[7] But there are additional ways in which minorities have benefited from the international arena. The granting of political self-determination to national minorities in East-Central Europe after World War I by the League of Nations is matched by the more recent example of the East Bengali in founding the new state of Bangladesh.[8] And only time will tell if the efforts of the Irish Catholics in Northern Ireland, Soviet Jews, Palestinian refugees, Basques, and Native Americans in seeking international support and action for their domestic plights meet a success similar to that of the East Bengali or the failure of the Biafrans.

The general topic of Minorities in the Context of International Politics deals with these and other phenomena (see Table I), which many of us have heard or read about but have not seriously considered as important or legitimate topics for teaching and research. It also deals with a number of questions about these phenomena, in which the two most fundamental ones are as follows: first, *in what ways, under what conditions, and to what extent does international politics affect minority groups?* and second, *in what ways, under what conditions, and to what extent do minority groups transcend domestic political systems and venture into nondomestic (i.e., transnational or international) ones?*[9] The answers to

these questions have implications for governmental decision-making and minority actions. They also have particular relevance to the stability and instability of the world arena as the recent events in Cyprus, the Middle East, and other areas illustrate.

Minorities in the Context of International Politics deals with phenomena and substantive questions which are potentially *inclusive,* and yet presently *exclusive* of the paradigmatic boundaries which guide research (and instruction) in the fields of international politics, minority-majority relations, and transnational politics. The topic can be inclusive because it considers the processes of interaction among similar actors such as nation-states and minorities and can benefit from and contribute to the theoretical and empirical developments in these areas. At present, though, the topic is quite exclusive of these established boundaries of inquiry, and much of this can be attributed to what James N. Rosenau calls "conceptual jails" which separate the practitioners of these fields and thwart all attempts towards a needed synthesis.[10] The result of these conceptual jails is that the fields remain isolated from each other and the general topic, for the most part, remains neglected by all of them.

The task of synthesizing these fields for the purpose of understanding and analyzing the questions and phenomena encompassed by this general topic necessitates the initial acceptance of a specific perspective. This perspective may appear to be at odds with the generally accepted paradigms of these three fields, but as Table 1 illustrates it can be justified by a number of empirical examples to warrant serious consideration. Quite succinctly, this perspective contains the following assumptions:

1. It assumes that the status and experience of minority groups cannot be explained or understood by focusing solely on the domestic relationship between minority groups and majorities. This assumption goes against the dominant view in minority-majority relations research by claiming that nondomestic factors and actors ofttimes have an influence on what minorities do, how majorities act toward and perceive minorities, and how the relationship develops between them.[11]

2. It assumes that international politics is not confined solely to the actions and processes of interaction involving nation-states but also includes other actors, their actions, and processes of interaction. This assumption goes against the prevailing view in international politics research by claiming that nation-statehood (or sovereignty) cannot be the sole criterion for an international actor.[12] Minority groups are an example of these other actors which do not meet the test of nation-statehood but are nonetheless engaged in international politics.

3. It assumes that transnational relations is not confined solely to those actors which are engaged in a "significant" (however defined) transaction of

TABLE 1

PHENOMENA DEALING WITH MINORITIES IN THE CONTEXT OF INTERNATIONAL POLITICS

General Phenomenon	Empirical Examples
1. Secessionist movement involving a minority, a majority, and outside interventionists	Biafra Bangladesh
2. Minority identification with homeland	"Hansen effect" witnessed in some American minorities
3. Influencing the foreign policy of a nation-state by a minority	Efforts by Irish, Eastern European, and Jewish Americans in influencing American foreign policy; Zionists and British foreign policy
4. Going to international organizations or bodies for assistance	European national minorities at the League of Nations and United Nations; Native Americans, Black Americans, and the Palestinian Liberation Organization (PLO) at the United Nations
5. Being entrapped or victimized by international events	The Jewish Holocaust; Japanese Americans and World War II; Kazakhs between the USSR-People's Republic of China border
6. Sending goods, money, and other resources to homelands or other states	Chinese Americans supporting the efforts of Sun Yat-Sen; Japanese Americans sending funds to Japan during the Manchurian Crisis; and American Jews and Israel
7. Seeking or attaining homeland/nondomestic support for a minority's domestic plight	Japan's intervention in the San Francisco School Board incident; minorities in the Balkans; Palestinian refugees
8. Serving as a fifth column force or advance guard	Serbian nationals during World War I; the Deutschtum of Nazi Germany
9. Advancing a claim for the historical possession of land	European minorities, especially in the controversies surrounding Alsace-Lorraine; Chicanos and Aztlan
10. A Return to the Homeland Movement	Garveyism; Jewish concept of *Aliyah*
11. Assisting in the founding of a nation-state by members of that nation, who reside in another State	Irish Americans and Ireland; Zionists and Israel; Czech and Slovak Americans and Czechoslovakia
12. Pan-ism movements and linkages involving nongovernmental, minority groups	Pan-Slavism; Pan-Africanism; Pan-Zionism; Pan-Aryanism
13. Transfer of minority populations and deportations	Asians in Uganda; Greeks and Turks; Chicanos
14. Irredentist policies and actions involving a minority, its homeland, and its host state	Balkans-Macedonia; Aryanism
15. Seeking recognition and benefits from participating in a host society's war efforts	Chicano G.I. Forum; 442nd Regimental Unit of Nisei
16. Serving as a cultural bridge between countries	American immigrant groups and their efforts to introduce their homelands' cultures to America and vice-versa
17. Serving as economic middlemen between countries	Chinese minorities in Southeast Asia
18. Minority questions becoming "issue areas" for bargaining and contention between states	Soviet Jewry issue; Cyprus situation; Gentlemen's Agreement between Japan and America

values across state boundaries but includes all actors which are engaged in transactions across such boundaries.[13] This assumption says that actors such as minority groups might not engage in the types of activities which are considered "significant" from the standpoint of transnational actors such as multinational corporations but are nonetheless involved in transnational relations when they conduct activities with nondomestic actors.

4. It assumes that minority groups have and will continue to engage in actions which transcend domestic political systems and thereby enter nondomestic ones. This assumption goes against the claim that minority groups have and will continue to conduct activities which are exclusively domestic-oriented. The assumption, though, makes no normative claim about the legitimacy or soundness of these actions but merely argues that they have and will probably continue to be undertaken.

These assumptions run counter to the prevailing paradigms which guide research (and instruction) in these fields. Their intent, though, is to break through the admittedly necessary, but somewhat artificial, barriers which separate these fields from an initial multidisciplinary assault on the topic of minorities in the context of international politics. A multidisciplinary approach does not imply a synthesis of fields, but rather a recognition of the mutual contributions that the fields can make to the topic. The thrust of this perspective, therefore, does not lie with its believability but with its present (and hopefully future) usefulness.

Multidisciplinary approaches have been used to examine a number of different social phenomena, but what this means for the present analysis and teaching of this topic can be stated quite simply: most phenomena which deal with minorities in the context of international politics can and should be approached at different levels of analysis and with the use of theories, explanations, and methods derived from the fields of international politics, minority-majority relations, and transnational politics.[14] A multidisciplinary approach suggests a continuum of possible research and teaching strategies. One pole of this continuum would be strategies that accept the above assumptions and proceed with an *a priori* justification for a suitable level of analysis (e.g., the individual) and a single theory of explanation derived from one of these three fields (e.g., misperceptions in international politics).[15] The opposite pole would be strategies that accept the assumptions and proceed at multiple levels of analysis and with the use of explanations or theories derived from all three fields.[16] For example, suppose we were interested in knowing why American Jews maintain such active and seemingly all-encompassing transnational relations with its affiliated nation-state of Israel, while a group like the Japanese Americans does not exhibit similar relations with Japan. The question deals with the transnational relations and activities that minorities maintain with nondomestic actors. It also has some relevance to the two broad questions which were presented at the outset. The comparison is necessary in order to avoid the manifold problems associated with case studies and to increase the internal and external validity of the analysis.[17] At the same time, the comparison is desirable because it can be used to exploit and check our hunches about the uniqueness of the groups.[18] A multidisciplinary approach to the question suggests that explanations potentially can be nested in different levels of analysis and can be derived from all three fields. As we will see later, there are at least eleven different explanations which can account for this difference in transnational interaction. Some of them focus on the differences in status and experience of the two groups in America; others on the differences between Israel and Japan; and still others on the perceptual readiness and political efficacious orientation of individual members in undertaking these activities.[19] The eleven explanations form a typology of different perspectives, which are pitted at multiple levels of analysis and have their origin in all three fields. The selection of one or a combination of explanations from this typology may be a matter of personal choice, but the choice has particular implications for the manner in which research and instruction are conducted. Implicit in one's decision are assessments of the relative importance not only of different levels of analysis but also the theoretical and empirical considerations of the three fields.[20] This example is indicative of other phenomena encompassed by the topic of minorities in the context of international politics. Whether we are looking at transnational relations or the efforts of international organizations in resolving minority issues, a multidisciplinary approach is possible and desirable. Such an approach can assist in the future synthesis of these fields in examining this long-neglected topic. ★

Notes

1. O'Brien, Robert W., *The College Nisei* (Palo Alto: Pacific Books, 1949), pp. 16-17.

2. Little, Malcolm, *The Autobiography of Malcolm X* (New York: Grove Press), p. 364. Also see Patterson, William L. (ed.), *We Charge Genocide* (New York: International Publishers, 1971).

3. For the Japanese American evacuation during World War II, see Girdner, Audrie and Anne Loftis, *The Great Betrayal* (New York: The McMillan Company, 1969); Bosworth, Allan P., *America's Concentration Camps* (New York: W.W. Norton and Company, 1967); Grodzins, Morton, *Americans Betrayed* (Chicago: University of Chicago Press, 1949); Kitagawa, Daisuke, *Issei and Nisei: The Internment Years* (New York: Seabury Press, 1967); and tenBroek, Jacobus, et al., *Prejudice, War, and Constitution* (Berkeley: University of California Press, 1968). For the Holocaust, see Schoenberger, Gerhard, *The Yellow Star* (New York: Bantam Books, 1973); Reitinger, Gerald, *The Final Solution* (New York: Barnes, 1961); and Hilberg, Raoul, *The Destruction of the European Jews* (Chicago: Quadrangle Books, 1967). For an evaluation of the Kazakhs, see Moseley, George, *A Sino-Soviet Cultural Frontier: The Ili Kazakhs Autonomous Chou* (Cambridge: East Asian Research Center, Harvard University Press, 1966). See also Nakanishi, Don T., "Can It Happen Again? The Impact of the Evacuation and the Holocaust on the Political Behavior of Japanese American and American Jewish Leadership," Ph.D. dissertation, Harvard University, 1975.

4. Wolfers, Arnold, *Discord and Collaboration* (Baltimore: The Johns Hopkins Press, 1962), p. 5.

5. This truism, like other truism, is either believable or not. It depends, in large measure, on the perspective that one uses.

6. Nakanishi, Don T., "The Visual Panacea: Japanese Americans in the City of Smog," in Akira Iriye, *Mutual Images between Japan and the United States* (Cambridge: Harvard University Press, 1975).

7. Stevens, Richard P., *American Zionism and U.S. Foreign Policy*, 1942-47 (New York: Pageant Press, 1962); Lopata, Helena Znaniecki, "The Function of Voluntary Associations in an Ethnic Community: 'Polonia,'" in Burgess, Ernest W., and Donald J. Bogue, *Urban Sociology* (Chicago: University of Chicago Press, 1967), pp. 117-137; Fagan, Richard R., et al. *Cubans in Exile: Disaffection and the Revolution* (Stanford: Stanford University Press, 1968); Fuchs, Lawrence H., *American Ethnic Politics* (New York: Harper and Row Publishers, 1968); Sykrin, Marie, "How Israel Affects American Jews," *Midstream*, Vol. XIX (May 1974), p. 28; Gerson, Louis L., *The Hyphenate in Recent American Politics and Diplomacy* (Lawrence: University of Kansas Press, 1964); Isaacs, Harold R., *The New World of Negro Americans* (New

York: The John Day Company, 1963); Smith, Arthur L., Jr., *The Deutschtum of Nazi Germany and the United States* (The Hague: Martinus Nijhoff, 1965); Garvey, Amy Jacques, *Philosophy and Opinions of Marcus Garvey* (New York: Antheneum Press, 1969); and Keohane, Robert C., "The Big Influence of Small Allies," *Foreign Policy,* No. 2 (1971), pp. 161-182.

8. See Claude, Inis L., *National Minorities: An International Problem* (Cambridge: Harvard University Press, 1955): Deutsch, Karl W., "Problems of Justice in International Territorial Disputes," paper presented at the 6th Symposium, Conference on Science, Philosophy, and Religion; Friedrich, Carl J., "Intranational Politics and Foreign Policy in Developed (Western) Systems," in Farrell, Robert B., pp. 97-109; Hammond, Thomas T. "Nationalism and National Minorities in Eastern Europe," *Journal of International Affairs,* Vol. 20, No. 1 (1966), pp. 9-31; Janowsky, Oscar, *Nationalities and National Minorities* (New York: The Macmillan Company, 1945); Junghann, Otto, *National Minorities in Europe* (New York: Covici-Friede Publisher, 1932); Mayer, Kurt B., "Migration, Cultural Tensions, and Foreign Policy: Switzerland," *Journal of Conflict Resolution,* Vol. XI (1967), pp. 139-152; Vali, Ferene A., "Transylvania and the Hungarian Minority," *Journal of International Affairs,* Vol. 20, No. 1 (1966), pp. 32-44; and Wolfe, Henry C., *Human Dynamite* (New York: The Foreign Policy Association, 1939).

9. Wirth defines a minority as:

A group of people who, because of their physical or cultural characteristics, are singled out from the others in the society in which they live for differential and unequal treatment, and who therefore regard themselves as objects of collective discrimination. The existence of a minority in a society implies the existence of a corresponding dominant group enjoying higher social status and greater privileges. Minority status carried with it the exclusion from full participation in the life of the society. Though not necessarily an alien group the minority is treated and regards itself as a people apart.

This definition of a minority group is used in this discussion. See Wirth, Louis, "The Problem of Minority Groups," in Linton, Ralph (ed.), *The Science of Man in the World Crisis* (New York: Columbia University Press, 1945), p. 347.

10. Rosenau, James N., *The Scientific Study of Foreign Policy* (New York: The Free Press, 1971), p. 314.

11. See Gordon, Milton, *Assimilation in American Life* (Englewood Cliffs, N.J.: Prentice-Hall, Inc., 1964); Myrdal, Gunnar, *An American Dilemma* (New York: Harper and Row, 1944); Schermerhorn, R.A., *Comparative Ethnic Relations* (New York: Random House, 1970); Deutsch, Karl W., *Nationalism and Social Communications* (Cambridge: The MIT Press, 1953); Van den Berghe, Pierre L., *Race and Racism* (New York: John Wiley and Sons, 1967); Kitano, Harry and Roger Daniels, *American Racism* (Englewood Cliffs, N.J.: Prentice-Hall, 1970); Blauner, Robert, *Racial Oppression in America* (New York: Harper and Row, 1972); Blalock, Hubert M., *Toward a Theory of Minority-Group Relations* (New York: Capricorn Books, 1970); and Rabushka, Alvin and Kenneth A. Shepsle, *Politics in Plural Societies* (Columbus, Ohio: Charles E. Merrill Company, 1972).

12. See Morganthau, Hans, *Politics among Nations* (New York: Alfred A. Knopf, 1967); Kaplan, Morton, *Systems and Process in International Politics* (New York: John Wiley and Sons, Inc., 1967); Allison, Graham, *Essence of Decision* (Boston: Little, Brown, and Company, 1971); Wolfers, Arnold, *Discord and Collaboration* (Baltimore: The Johns Hopkins Press, 1962); Deutsch, Karl W. and J. David Singer, "Multipolar Power Systems and Inter-national Stability," *World Politics,* Vol. 16 (1964), pp. 390-406; Schelling, Thomas C., *Arms and Influence* (New Haven: Yale University Press, 1966); Rosecrance, Richard, *Action and Reaction in World Politics* (Boston: Little, Brown, and Company, 1963); Haas, Ernst, *Beyond the Nation-State* (Stanford: Stanford University Press, 1964); Claude, Inis, *Power and International Relations* (New York: Random House, 1969).

13. See Nye, Joseph S. and Robert O. Keohane, *Transnational Relations and World Politics* (Cambridge: Harvard University Press, 1971); Huntington, Samuel P., "Transnational Organizations in World Politics," *World Politics,* Vol. 25 (1973), pp. 333-368; and Hernes, Helga, "The Visible Hand of the Multinational Corporation: A Review," *European Journal of Political Research,* Vol. 1 (1973), pp. 265-292.

14. See Singer, J. David, "The Level-of-Analysis Problem in International Relations," in Klaus, Knorr and Sidney Verba (eds.), *The International System* (Princeton: Princeton University Press, 1961), pp. 77-92; Wolfers, *op. cit.;* Allison, *op. cit.;* Rosenau, James N., "Pre-Theories and Theories of Foreign Policies," in Farrell, Robert B. (ed.), *Approaches to Comparative and International Politics* (Evanston, Ill.: Northwestern University Press, 1966), pp. 27-92; and Waltz, Kenneth, *Man, the State, and War* (New York: Columbia University Press, 1965).

15. Jervis, Robert, "Hypotheses on Misperceptions," *World Politics,* Vol. XX (1968), pp. 454-479.

16. See Eulau, Heinz, *Micro-Macro Political Analysis* (Chicago: Aldine Publishing Company, 1969); Verba, Sidney, "The Use of Survey Research in the Study of Comparative Politics: Issues and Strategies," in Rokkan, Stein, et al. (eds.), *Comparative Survey Analysis* (The Hague: Monton and Company, 1969), pp. 56-107; and Price, Douglas, "Micro and Macro-politics: Notes on Research Strategy," in Oliver Garceau (ed.), *Political Research and Political Theory* (Cambridge: Harvard University Press, 1968), pp. 102-142.

17. Campbell, Donald T. and Julian C. Stanley, *Experimental and Quasi-Experimental Design for Research* (Chicago: Rand McNally and Company, 1972).

18. We know, for instance, that American Jews did not have a "homeland" in the same sense that Japanese Americans and other immigrant groups had a "homeland." We also know that Japanese Americans were the only group collectively interned when its "homeland" and the United States engaged in war. But instead of accepting these assertions as untested and common sensical truisms, efforts could and should be made to use them as possible explanations and to disentangle them in the search for additional variables. This not only enlarges the pool of possible explanations but also impels us to analyze the various factors which surround seemingly unique aspects of a minority group's experience.

19. Jerome Bruner defines perceptual readiness as:

The relative accessibility of categories to afferent stimulus inputs. The more accessible a category, the less the stimulus input required for it to be sorted in terms of the category, given a degree of match between the characteristics of the input and the specifications of the category.

Bruner, Jerome S., "On Perceptual Readiness," in Robert J.C. Harper, et al. *The Cognitive Processes: Readings* (Englewood Cliffs, N.J.: Prentice-Hall, Inc., 1964), p. 251. This concept has been explored by Robert Jervis in his attempt to see what decision-makers learn from history. See Jervis, Robert, "How Decision-Makers Learn from History," unpublished manuscript, 1975.

20. See Singer, "Level-of-Analysis," and f.n. 18.

IVA
IKUKO
TOGURI:

VICTIM
OF AN
AMERICAN FANTASY

by Raymond Okamura

This article is a modified and updated version of a pamphlet titled *Iva Toguri (d'Aquino): Victim of a Legend* published by the Japanese American Citizens League National Committee for Iva Toguri in September 1975. The author is deeply indebted to Clifford Uyeda and Isami Waugh for providing most of the research materials, and to Masayo Duus and Bill Hosokawa for making substantial corrections of factual errors.

Introduction

The treason trial of Iva Ikuko Toguri in 1949 was probably the most publicized case in history involving a Japanese American woman. The tragic story of Iva Toguri represents one example of how an individual can be victimized by international affairs and domestic racial fantasies. Trapped in Japan during World War II as a young American woman, she survived harassment by the Japanese government only to face 30 years of persecution by the United States government. The cumulative effect of over 100 years of anti-Asian prejudices and stereotypes was so pervasive, it was impossible for her to receive a fair verdict from an all-white jury. Even after serving her prison sentence, she was threatened with deportation and property confiscation. The United States government did not relent until 1975 when the last bit of retribution was collected.

Iva Ikuko Toguri

Iva Ikuko Toguri was born on July 4, 1916 in Los Angeles, California, the second child of Jun and Fumi Toguri.[1] Her father was a British subject from Canada and her mother a citizen of Japan. The United States prohibited all persons of Asian ancestry from becoming naturalized, so neither parent had an opportunity to gain American citizenship.[2] Two months after her birth, her father entered her name in the genealogical registry at the family's ancestral village in Japan. This procedure was customary at the time, and it would have given her *jus sanguinis* rights in Japan, but her father cancelled the registration in 1932. Her father did not register her with the Canadian government, so she lost any eligibility for citizenship rights in Canada. Thus, by the time she was 16 years of age, Iva Toguri was a citizen only of the United States.

The Toguri family lived in predominantly white neighborhoods in various parts of Southern California: Los Angeles, Calexico, San Diego, and Compton. She had an older brother, Fred, and two younger sisters, June and Inez. English was the primary language spoken at home, the family belonged to the Methodist

Church, and Iva Toguri's friends were mostly white. She attended public schools, music and business schools, and Compton Junior College. She became an accomplished pianist and graduated from UCLA with a bachelor's degree in zoology in June 1941. During her childhood and student years, she had very little contact with Japanese culture. She had many talents, but her all-American upbringing ill-prepared her for the unexpected ordeal ahead.

Soon after her college graduation, her family learned her maternal aunt in Japan was stricken with diabetes and high blood pressure and possibly on the verge of death. Since her mother also was bed-ridden with the same ailments, Iva Toguri was selected as the family's representative to go to Japan to help care for her aunt. Because the matter seemed urgent, she could not wait for an official passport (which took at least a month to obtain), so she settled for a notarized State Department Certificate of Identification as her travel document. The only mode of transportation available was by ship (airline passenger service was not inaugurated until 1947). She hurriedly sailed for Japan on July 5, 1941, one day after her 25th birthday, and arrived in Yokohama on July 24th with just enough money to buy a ticket back to the United

States and with practically no knowledge of the Japanese language or customs. Her uncle, Hajime Hattori, met her at the pier and took her to his home. After several weeks of getting acquainted with relatives she had never met before, she applied in August for an American passport at the United States Consulate in Tokyo. She presented her birth certificate and State Department Certificate of Identification, but persons of Asian ancestry claiming American citizenship faced considerable difficulties because this was during the period of prohibiting Asian immigration under the provisions of the Immigration Act of 1924.

When she did not receive her passport by October (she later learned her application was ignored), she became alarmed over the increasing war rumors in Japan. She contacted her father to ask if she should return, but her father reassured her and told her to stay longer for the sake of her sick aunt. Like most other Americans, her father underestimated the ominous war signs during 1940-41.[3] Finally recognizing the danger, her father sent an urgent cable on December 1st instructing her to board a ship leaving for the United States the next day. She frantically tried to get aboard, but Japanese authorities refused port clearance because she did not have a passport. It actually made no difference because that Japanese-owned ship was in mid-Pacific when Admiral Chuichi Nagumo's Task Force attacked Hawaii, and was ordered to return to Japan.

One day after the outbreak of hostilities, the Japanese Army Thought Control Police (Kempeitai) interrogated Iva Toguri and demanded she renounce her American citizenship and apply for Japanese citizenship or else life in Japan would be difficult. She flatly refused, stating she was raised as an American and could never become a Japanese citizen. She soon learned the meaning of the Kempeitai's threats: she was classified as an enemy alien, her movements were restricted, she was denied food rations, and was constantly harassed by the Internal Security Police and Kempeitai. Ironically, if she had succeeded in returning to the United States, she would not have been much better off. She would have shared the fate of her fellow Japanese Americans who were classified as the "enemy race," restricted by racial curfews and prohibited zones, intimidated by the police and federal agents, and eventually imprisoned en masse. Iva Toguri's own family was incarcerated at the Gila River, Arizona, Concentration Camp.

In February 1942, Iva Toguri learned the neutral Swiss legation representing the United States was accepting applications from American citizens who wished to repatriate. She applied to the Swiss legation, but without a passport she was informed her U.S. citizenship must be confirmed by the American consulate. On April 4, 1942, the American consular staff, themselves awaiting repatriation, belatedly processed her August 1941 passport application by attaching the notation that her U.S. citizenship was "not proved." Again, the lack of passport thwarted her attempt to leave.

Owing to her outspoken support for the United States, inability to speak Japanese well, and frequent visits from the Kempeitai, neighbors taunted her aunt and uncle for harboring an enemy. Life became so intolerable that in June 1942, the Hattoris told Iva Toguri to move out. From that time on, she was on her own. Wandering the streets of Tokyo, she quickly used up what little money she had. Without an income or food ration card, she faced the probability of starvation. She asked Japanese authorities to imprison her with other American nationals, but was refused. Job hunting was difficult because the only marketable skills she possessed were her abilities in the English language. First, she worked for a pittance ($5 per month) at the Matsumiya Language and Culture School. Later that June, she found a part-time job typing and monitoring English language shortwave broadcasts at the Domei News Agency. Felipe J. d'Aquino was a fellow monitor at Domei and they became good friends. D'Aquino, a Portuguese citizen of Japanese ancestry, later became a linotypist at Domei.

In September 1942, she received a notice from the Swiss legation announcing a second and final repatriation ship. Since most of the diplomats and other supposedly important (i.e. white) Americans had already left on the first ship, her chances of getting aboard were good if she could raise the necessary $425 passage. Unfortunately, she had no savings (her $20 per month salary at Domei was spent for bare survival), was repudiated by her relatives in Japan, and had no means of contacting her parents in America. Lacking the passage money, she was forced to cancel her application.

Unable to purchase much food on her low wages, she was suffering from malnutrition and beriberi by June 1943. Nursed back to health by her friend d'Aquino, she regained enough strength by August to take a second part-time job as a typist in the business office of Radio Tokyo. There she met three prisoners of war (POWs): Major Charles Cousens, an Australian captured in Singapore; Captain Wallace Ince, an American captured in Corregidor; and Lieutenant Norman Reyes, a Pilipino captured in Bataan. Assigned to work on the English language "Zero Hour" since March of that year, the three men were experienced radio broadcasters prior to their capture. She befriended the POW broadcasters, and at considerable risk to herself, secretly provided food, clothing, blankets, tobacco, vitamins, and medicines for the POW broadcasters and other prisoners at the Bunka POW Camp in Tokyo.

In November, Japanese officials decided to add a female voice to the "Zero Hour" program. The POWs persuaded the Japanese to select Iva Toguri because they needed a trustworthy companion to join them: they were covertly subverting the Japanese propaganda intent through skillful burlesque. Since the Japanese were not well versed in the nuances of the English language, they did not catch on to the charade. When informed of her new duties, Iva Toguri refused. She was then ordered to broadcast by Japanese officials and was reminded she had "no choice" in the matter since she was an enemy alien without any rights. Refusing a direct order in militaristic war-time Japan usually resulted in severe consequences, including beatings, starvation, and execution. She was well aware that others who refused direct orders were taken away by the Kempeitai and never heard from again. Major Cousens took her aside, confided their scheme, and assured her that she would not harm, and might possibly help the American war effort. Cousens' confidence won her over. She read her first POW-written script over the air on November 10 or 11, 1943.

In December 1943, she was forced to quit her other part-time job at Domei because of constant arguments with other employees over her pro-American statements, and because her friend d'Aquino got into a fist-fight defending her position.

Initially, she called herself "Ann" (short for

announcer) on the air, but later switched to "Orphan Ann" because she identified with the comic strip character "Little Orphan Annie." It was a bitter-sweet, self-mocking name for the young woman who felt lonely and forsaken, but also thought she was resisting the enemy while waiting to be rescued from her predicament. In January 1944, she went to work as a full-time typist at the Danish legation, and on most evenings reported to Radio Tokyo to host a program of music, humor, nostalgia, and news. She read the scripts exactly as written by her POW compatriots, and her program was always aired from 6 to 7 p.m. Tokyo time. However, the female voice on "Zero Hour" was not always that of Iva Toguri: she refused to work on Sundays and American holidays, and took frequent sick leaves. During her absences, she was replaced by one of the 13 other English-speaking women announcers employed by Radio Tokyo: six Japanese Americans, one white American, one Japanese Canadian, one Japanese Briton, one Swiss, one Japanese, one with a Japanese surname of unknown nationality, and one with a European surname of unknown nationality. Radio Tokyo had many other English-language programs broadcast at different hours of the day, and each program had its own staff.

On April 19, 1945, she married Felipe J. d'Aquino and converted to Catholicism. She became eligible for Portuguese citizenship under the laws of Portugal, but she chose to retain her American citizenship under the laws of the United States. The Cable Act, as amended in 1931, nullified the discriminatory provision that any American female citizen who marries an "alien ineligible to citizenship" (i.e., Asian) would lose her U.S. citizenship.

During the war years, Iva Toguri's problems were similar to an estimated 10,000 other young Japanese American men and women stranded in Japan. Some, like her, were in Japan to visit relatives, but most were there to attend school or work. Due to severe employment discrimination in the United States, it was not unusual for parents to insure an alternative means of livelihood for their children by sending them to Japan for part of their education.[4] Most Japanese American college graduates found that the only means of gaining employment commensurate with their education was to work in Japan. All Japanese Americans were placed under intense pressure to change citizenship; young men were drafted into the military; others were forced to work for the government or war industries.[5] With only partial education in Japan, Japanese Americans could not compete with the natives for regular jobs and had to resort to their English-language skills as a means of survival.

When the war ended, the U.S. State Department proclaimed any Japanese American who served in the Japanese military, worked for the Japanese govern-ment, or voted in a Japanese election had automatically lost their American citizenship in accordance with the Nationality Act of 1940. If this was true, Iva Toguri was no longer a citizen of the United States, and not subject to the charge of treason. (Later in the 1950s, court decisions restored citizenship to approximately 5,000 Japanese Americans affected by this ruling.)

The Legend of "Tokyo Rose"

Unknown to Iva Toguri, or anyone else in Japan, American soldiers invented the name "Tokyo Rose" and applied it to any and all female broadcasters heard on Japanese radio. "Tokyo Rose" was used as early as December 1941, and part of the experience of fighting in Asia and the Pacific Islands consisted of listening to a woman with a seductive voice who played the latest popular American music, announced American troop movements, and read the latest war news. The soldiers knew the programs were supposed to be propaganda, but they felt compelled to tune in anyway and spread the word about the broadcasts. They laughed at the obvious propaganda ploys and enjoyed the recently released American records which they could not hear on American shortwave broadcasts. Some listeners said she spoke with a British accent; others attributed a Japanese or Asian accent; while still others insisted she had an American accent and used American slang. The listeners even differed on the languages used: some said English was the only language spoken, but others claimed Japanese, Chinese, and other Asian languages were mixed in.

The lonely soldiers undoubtedly internalized and romanticized what they actually heard, and there was considerable speculation about her physical appearance. "Tokyo Rose" existed more in the imagination than in fact, and the image was not entirely unpleasant. In 1944, the Alaskan Defense Command issued a bulletin instructing officers to urge their men to listen to "Tokyo Rose" broadcasts because they were free from propaganda and were "the strongest factor for building morale of our troops in the Alaskan Chain."[6] Just before the war ended, the Director of Welfare for the United States Navy issued a citation to "Tokyo Rose" for "meritorious service contributing greatly to the morale of U.S. armed forces in the Pacific . . . by persistently entertaining them during those long nights in fox holes and on aboard ship by bringing them excellent state-side music, laughter, and news about home."[7] The citation was made in jest, but it also reflected the fact American soldiers enjoyed the broadcasts. Also, a survey conducted in 1968 found that 93 percent of veterans of the Pacific War thought the "Tokyo Rose" programs did not have a demoralizing effect, and 84 percent considered the programs to be successful as entertainment.[8]

Historic stereotypes about Japanese Americans

in general,[9] and Asian women specifically, created an atmosphere whereby war-weary soldiers and civilians could easily transfer their racial fantasies and hostilities to a real person. Negative images of Japanese Americans originated in the 1890s when the first sizable number of immigrants from Japan arrived in the United States and became targets for the anti-Asian prejudice directed previously against the Chinese pioneers. The anti-Japanese feelings were fueled by Japan's empire building in Asia, and West Coast newspapers were full of stories implying Japanese Americans were the outpost for an ever expanding Japanese empire. Newspaper commentary depicted Japanese Americans as being unassimilable and incapable of loyalty to the United States because somehow their ancestral ties to Japan would predominate. This theme was memorably expressed later by Lt. General John L. DeWitt, military chief of the Western Defense Command: "A Jap's a Jap. It makes no difference whether the Jap is a citizen or not. He's still a Jap and can't change."[10] Numerous state and federal laws were passed discriminating against Japanese and Japanese Americans, and by 1942 the negative stereotypes were so well implanted in the public's consciousness that there was practically no protest over the mass incarceration of American citizens based solely on a presumption of disloyalty.

The image of the seductive and sinister Asian woman emerged during the height of anti-Chinese agitations during the 1880s, and became particularly prominent when Japan became a military power in the 1930s. Hollywood movies and newspaper cartoons confused and combined Chinese and Japanese images into a general "oriental" stereotype, and Asian women were portrayed as exotic, sexy, and determined to corrupt the morals of white American men. San Francisco newspapers promoted such racism and sexism with provocative headlines: "Japanese Women a Menace to American Women."[11]

Public distrust of Japanese Americans did not subside after the end of the war.[12] The well-published sacrifices of Japanese American soldiers on the European Front (442nd Regimental Combat Team) did little to ameliorate prejudices. In fact, more violence was committed against Japanese Americans returning to California in 1945-46 than during the aftermath of Pearl Harbor in 1941-42. In August 1946, the National Opinion Research Center reported two-thirds of all Americans still believed Japanese Americans had spied for Japan, and only 13 percent believed they had no part in espionage activities for Japan. Newspapers continued to reinforce distorted images of Asian women through comic strips, such as "Steve Canyon" and "Terry and the Pirates." "Dragon Lady" became the indulgence of immature white males.

Immigrant Japanese were still prohibited from becoming citizens, owning land, and engaging in occupations requiring licenses. New immigration from Japan was banned, and 4,724 persons of Japanese ancestry were deported during 1945-46. Bitter over being locked up in a concentration camp, 5,766 Japanese Americans renounced their American citizenship as an act of protest, but nearly all filed lawsuits in 1945 to regain their birthright. (It took until 1968 for all renunciants, including those who expatriated, to regain their citizenship through the courts.) American citizens of Japanese ancestry were still prevented from owning homes by restrictive covenants, denied employment in most fields, hindered in social mobility by anti-miscegenation laws; and even dead soldiers were refused burial in hometown cemeteries.

Japanese Americans embarked on a campaign to overcome these injustices, but the struggle was hard and long: every issue created a prolonged court battle, bitter legislative campaign, or heated public debate. All branches of the government were unyielding, and the white racists had not lost any of their vigor. The resolution of these issues during 1945-49 carried great import for the well-being of every Japanese American, and in particular for Iva Toguri, who was in Japan and unaware of the circumstances closing in around her.

Tyranny of a Legend[13]

By the end of the war, the legend of "Tokyo Rose" had become so exaggerated that "Tokyo Rose" was probably the third best known Japanese name to Americans (after Emperor Hirohito and Prime Minister Tojo). American journalists landed in Japan a few days before the formal surrender was signed and began a frantic and competitive search for the legendary "Tokyo Rose." Two particularly aggressive and unscrupulous newsmen were Harry Brundidge of *Cosmopolitan* Magazine and Clark Lee of International News Service (both Hearst publications). They contacted Leslie Nakashima, a Domei News Agency writer whom they knew before the war, but Nakashima told the Americans that no one broadcasted as "Tokyo Rose" and there were five or six women at Radio Tokyo who might fit their description. But the legend could not be deflated so easily. Undaunted, Brundidge and Lee asked Nakashima to locate any "Tokyo Rose," and Nakashima, who had a prewar obligation to repay, accommodated by introducing Iva Toguri.

Brundidge and Lee, in army uniforms and armed, met Iva Toguri on September 1, 1945 and offered her $2,000 for an exclusive story to be published in *Cosmopolitan*. That sum was a fortune for anyone who survived the war years in Japan, and she agreed to their interview. However, when Brundidge cabled *Cosmopolitan* editors about his "scoop," the editors rejected his article stating they would not glorify a traitor and refused to pay the $2,000. Meanwhile, other correspondents were filing stories implicating numerous other women, and it soon became obvious no single individual was "Tokyo Rose." But during this hectic and confusing period, Iva Toguri gained the unfortunate distinction of receiving the most publicity. She considered herself a patriot and heroine, and had no reluctance about granting interviews and signing autographs.

Her triumph was quickly shattered for she alone became the scapegoat. A few days after the Brundidge-Lee interview, she was arrested but released the next day. She was rearrested on October 17th and held at a Yokohama prison for one month; then she was transferred to Sugamo Prison in Tokyo, where she remained incarcerated for another eleven months. (Sugamo was the prison for Japanese leaders accused of war crimes. Prime Minister Tojo and six other high officials were executed there in 1948.) During her twelve-month imprisonment, she was never informed of the charges against her, was denied legal counsel, and was denied speedy trial.[14] Prohibited from sending or receiving mail, she was held totally incommunicado for over two months until a Christmas visit from her husband was allowed. Thereafter, the only person permitted to visit was her husband—for only one twenty-minute session per month. After an exhaustive investigation by the Army and Federal Bureau of Investigation (FBI), the Justice Department concluded there was insufficient evidence to bring charges and ordered her release on October 25, 1946. Government agents promptly lost or destroyed their phonograph records and written transcripts of the alleged "Tokyo Rose" broadcasts, and the case appeared closed. Her life temporarily returned to normal. She settled in Tokyo with her husband and became pregnant in 1947.

Iva Toguri learned that her mother died in 1942 at the Tulare, California, Interim Concentration Camp, and that her father, brother, and sisters had moved to Chicago. She desperately wanted her child to be born in the United States as the only sure way of conferring American citizenship,[15] and she had a great desire to see her family. She applied once again for that long-elusive passport, and she became one of the thousands of Japanese Americans stranded in Japan who sought to return home. Ignoring the amended Cable Act, American consular officials told her she was "stateless" due to her marriage to a Portuguese citizen, but that she could apply to re-establish her American citizenship.

The State Department was caught in a bind: if she was permitted to return, there surely would be a public uproar; but there was no legal means to prevent her return because she was native-born and cleared by the Army and FBI. Moreover, the Justice Department was in the embarrassing position of having destroyed or lost the evidence which originally cleared her. Hence, the government issued a statement to the press that "Tokyo Rose" had applied to return to the United States and the government was powerless to stop her. The expected public outcry was immediate and impassioned. Radio commentator Walter Winchell, joined by singer Kate Smith, vociferously campaigned against her return; and radio at that time was a powerful medium. The American Legion and Native Sons and Daughters of the Golden West, both with long histories of anti-Asian sentiments, issued strong protests. The Los Angeles City Council adopted a resolution opposing her return on the curious basis that she might adversely affect "loyal" Japanese Americans. Probably because white Americans could not envision her as an American, no one particularly demanded the prosecution of Iva Toguri for treason. The traditional goals of anti-Japanese racists were removal and exclusion, not prosecution under due process. The protests delayed her return, and in January 1948, her baby died at birth.

Many newspapers published an appeal from the FBI for anyone able to identify Iva Toguri as "Tokyo Rose" to report to that agency. Brundidge called his friend, FBI Director J. Edgar Hoover, and boasted he possessed a "confession," i.e., the notes taken by Clark Lee at the 1945 interview. But Attorney General Tom Clark said those unsigned interview notes do not constitute proper evidence. Infuriated, Brundidge demanded and received a government-paid trip to Japan to get Lee's notes signed by Iva Toguri. The U.S. Occupation Army summoned Iva Toguri to a meeting in Tokyo with Brundidge and John B. Hogan, a Justice Department attorney. She had been reading the American newspapers and was aware of the controversy surrounding her application to return. She was tired of the uncertainty, and had come to the conclusion if a trial was the only means to clear herself once and for all, she wanted to get on with it. Without legal advice at this critical moment, she willingly signed the notes.

Presumably on the basis of the signed notes, Iva Toguri was arrested once again on August 26, 1948 in Tokyo and charged with treason. While the government denied her citizenship before, they now used the same birth certificate in her passport application as proof of her citizenship and eligibility for the treason charge. According to law, when an alleged treason takes place abroad, the trial must take place at the first location where the accused is returned to American territory. Attorney General Clark publicly admitted she could not receive a fair trial in California. On the other hand, Hawaii might be too fair, so Clark initially announced she would be brought directly to the East Coast. For an unexplained reason, Clark changed his mind and ordered her brought to San Francisco—a city with a long tradition of anti-Japanese prejudice. The ship carrying Iva Toguri purposely by-passed Hawaii and docked in San Francisco on September 25, 1948.

Escorted off the ship by numerous big FBI men, she was taken before Federal Commissioner St. J.

Fox, who read a complaint charging her with treason. She was then taken to the old county jail near Chinatown's Portsmouth Square where she saw her family for the first time since 1941. She was finally home in America, albeit behind bars. The Toguri family searched for a lawyer to defend her, but the family was financially impoverished and unable to pay much. After several lawyers refused to take her case, Attorney Wayne M. Collins volunteered to represent her without fee. Collins, a strong advocate of civil liberties, also was a non-paid volunteer attorney for Fred T. Korematsu's constitutional challenge to the wartime incarceration, for the renunciants' fight to regain American citizenship, and for the Japanese Peruvians' battle to prevent deportation to Japan. Collins took these unpopular and controversial cases when the National American Civil Liberties Union and National Japanese American Citizens League refused to help.

A federal grand jury was convened in San Francisco in October 1948 to determine if there was probable cause for the treason charges. After reviewing the evidence, the grand jury refused to indict Iva Toguri unless the other American citizens involved at Radio Tokyo were similarly charged. The jurors were especially insistent that Captain Ince be charged. When prosecutors claimed Ince was still in the army and outside of their jurisdiction, the grand jury adjourned without an indictment and announced they would hold no further sessions until prosecutors prepared charges against Ince. Harried prosecutors then promised Ince would be charged before an army court martial. Based on that explicit promise, the grand jury issued an eight count indictment against Iva Toguri.[16] In retrospect, the eight "Overt Acts" charged were vague and inconsequential. Also, Ince was never charged by the army—instead, he was promoted to major.

Following the indictment, Collins made a motion for bail, but Federal Judge Louis B. Goodman ordered her confined without bail. She was in prison for nearly two years (counting her imprisonment in Japan) before her trial started the next year.

The Trial

At the arraignment before Federal District Judge Michael J. Roche[17] on January 4, 1949, Iva Toguri pled innocent to all charges. Two other lawyers, Theodore Tamba and George Olshausen, volunteered their services and joined Collins at the defense table. In preparation for the trial, defense lawyers petitioned the court to subpoena witnesses from Occupied Japan. Although the U.S. Occupation Army could have ordered any Japanese to appear, Judge Roche denied her right to summon witnesses in her favor.[18] Meanwhile, prosecutors teletyped the names and addresses of potential defense witnesses to the

FBI office in Tokyo, and FBI Agent Frederick Tillman, accompanied by armed American soldiers, called on the Japanese witnesses and intimidated them. Later, the judge allowed expenses for one defense lawyer and one translator to travel to Japan and obtain written depositions, but most witnesses were too frightened by then to cooperate. The prosecution did not have such handicaps. Realizing that in-person testimony is more effective than a piece of paper, prosecutors used government funds to bring 19 Japanese prosecution witnesses from Occupied Japan, paid the Japanese witnesses $10 per day, and gave them a free sightseeing tour of California.

The trial began on July 5, 1949 in the Federal District Court in San Francisco,[19] with Judge Roche presiding. Jury selection proceeded with unexpected speed and was completed within two hours. Eight non-whites (six Black Americans, two Asian Americans) were on the first jury list, but prosecutors used peremptory challenges to remove all eight. As soon as the panel was all-white, prosecutors announced acceptance.[20] Inexplicably, defense lawyers also promptly accepted the all-white jury of six men and six women without protest.

The principal prosecutors were: Frank J. Hennessy, head of the Justice Department's Northern California office; Thomas DeWolfe, a specialist in treason trials who had earlier convicted Robert H. Best and Douglas Chandler for broadcasting from Radio Berlin; John B. Hogan, the same Justice Department attorney who accompanied Brundidge to Japan. The prosecution was required to prove Iva Toguri committed treason as defined in the Constitution: "Treason against the United States shall consist only in levying war against them, or adhering to their enemies, giving them aid and comfort. No person shall be convicted of treason unless on the testimony of two witnesses to the same overt act. . ."[21]

Clark Lee, a well-known writer, took the witness stand, but he could only testify as to what Iva Toguri allegedly told him at that single interview and had no direct knowledge of what went on at Radio Tokyo. Co-accuser Harry Brundidge was present in San Francisco during the trial, but strangely enough, the prosecution did not call Brundidge to the witness stand. The reason became obvious when FBI Agent Frederick Tillman testified he knew that a key witness before the grand jury, Hiromi Yagi, was bribed by Brundidge with clothing, whisky and a vacation in the United States to falsely say he saw and heard Iva Toguri broadcasting as charged.[22] Brundidge was never allowed to testify—apparently because the prosecutors, defense lawyers, and the judge all agreed Brundidge was an unreliable witness.

Numerous former soldiers testified they heard "Tokyo Rose" while stationed in the Pacific Theater, but they contradicted each other on the announcer's voice, accent, theme song, language, and time of broadcast. The inconsistency was due to the fact the soldiers actually heard different women, on different programs, at different times, on different stations. The ex-soldiers were identifying the legend of "Tokyo Rose," not the person on trial. None of the prosecution's American witnesses saw Iva Toguri commit the overt acts charged. Also the prosecution was unable to present any recordings or scripts linking the defendant to the charges.

Thus, the prosecution's case depended on the testimony of officials present at Radio Tokyo during the war. Shigetsugu Tsuneishi, former Lt. Colonel in the Japanese army and chief of propaganda broadcasting, testified "Zero Hour" was eventually supposed to contain propaganda, but since the Americans won every battle after "Zero Hour" was inaugurated, it never got beyond building listener interest with appealing music. He observed that propaganda messages from the losing side of a battle were rather ineffectual. Tsuneishi testified English-speaking women announcers were recruited from the native populations and used on 12 Japanese-operated radio stations outside Japan: at Bandung, Bangkok, Hsinking, Korea, Manila, Nanking, Rangoon, Saigon, Shanghai, Singapore, Soerabaja, Taiwan (the specific locations in Korea and Taiwan were not identified). Also, he said English-language programs were broadcasted from Arai in Western Japan.

The critical witnesses for satisfying the constitutional requirement for two observers of the same act were two Japanese Americans. One was George Mitsushio, who was born in San Francisco and educated at the University of California at Berkeley and Columbia University, but left for Japan in 1940 and was the civilian chief of the "Zero Hour" program. The other was Kenkichi Oki, who was born in Sacramento and educated at St. Mary's College in Moraga and New York University, but left for Japan in 1939 and was the production supervisor at Radio Tokyo. Both men claimed they changed nationality by signing their names in the Japanese family registry. Under the *jus sanguinis* laws of Japan, this action made them Japanese citizens, but they did not legally renounce their American citizenship before the U.S. Consul. They were thus citizens of both nations, and technically subject to treason charges by the United States. Newspaper commentary focused on the irony of Iva Toguri being charged with treason because she retained her American citizenship while the key witnesses against her were "turncoats."

The main defense witnesses were the three former POWs who worked on the "Zero Hour" program. Charles Cousens, who was previously cleared by an Australian civil court, came from Australia to testify. Upon arrival at the San Francisco airport, Cousens was secretly detained and intimidated by FBI agents, but Collins found out about it and burst into the interrogation room to demand prompt release. Cousens testified he personally recruited Iva

Toguri for the broadcasting job because he trusted her and because she had a raspy, non-seductive voice. He recalled he talked her into broadcasting by assuring her that the programs were purely entertainment and that his scripts were covertly designed to be morale-boosting. Cousens said he wrote in the British idiom, so Iva Toguri could not have spoken with the alleged American slang.

Major Wallace Ince, who was cleared by the U.S. Army and stationed at the Presidio of San Francisco, confirmed Cousens' testimony. But Ince was a cautious witness because of the grand jury's demand for his prosecution, and he added a self-serving claim that Iva Toguri's friendliness with the POWs actually made him suspicious. Norman Reyes, who likewise was cleared by the Philippine government, came from Tennessee where he was attending Vanderbilt University. Reyes testified he was so sure of Iva Toguri's loyalty he would have trusted her with his life. When prosecutors produced a statement signed by Reyes in 1948 which was inconsistent with his courtroom testimony, Reyes explained the FBI intimidated him into signing a fabricated statement at a frightening 20-hour interrogation in Occupied Japan. But Judge Roche ruled Reyes to be an unreliable witness and disqualified everything said by Reyes.

Defense lawyers argued that numerous other American citizens were involved in broadcast work at Radio Tokyo, but no one else was charged with treason. Other Americans named included: John D. Provoo, an army sergeant captured in Corregidor; Mark Streeter, a civilian construction worker captured on Wake Island; Genevieve Fayville Topping, a missionary living in Japan; and six Japanese American women stranded by the war.

As the final defense witness, Iva Toguri told her own story to the court. She emphasized she had no intent to betray the United States and believed she was only entertaining American troops. She said she took great pride in her American citizenship and remained loyal throughout the difficult war years. She was a sympathetic and convincing figure for the courtroom audience. The trial started out in the expected anti-Japanese mode (selection of an all-white jury, disparaging use of "Jap," and segregation of Japanese and white witnesses into separate waiting rooms), but by the time the trial was nearing conclusion, courtroom spectators and newspaper reporters were nearly unanimously sympathetic to the defendant. In a straw vote, the usually anti-Japanese San Francisco press corps voted 9 to 1 for acquittal on all counts. This remarkable transformation was brought about solely through the persuasiveness of the defendant's case. In contrast to the present day political trials where defense support groups help in raising pertinent issues, there were no defense committees for Iva Toguri in 1949.

The trial lasted 56 days and cost the government

over $500,000. It was the longest and most expensive trial on record at the time. In the early ballots, the jury stood 10 to 2 for acquittal on all counts, but after 20 hours of debate they came to a 6 to 6 deadlock and relayed a message to the judge they were unable to reach a verdict. Judge Roche called the court into session at 10:15 p.m., declined to rule a hung-jury, and admonished the jurors until midnight, reminding them how long and expensive the trial had been for the government. He also appealed to their sense of patriotic duty. The jury deliberated two more days and announced their verdict on September 29, 1949: innocent on seven counts; guilty on one count. Iva Toguri was convicted for "Overt Act VI," i.e. "on the day during October 1944, the exact date being to the Grand Jurors unknown, defendant in the offices of the Broadcasting Corporation of Japan did speak into a microphone concerning the loss of ships." The broadcast in question was allegedly aired shortly after the resounding American victory at the Battle of Leyte Gulf, and the exact words found treasonable were: "Orphans of the Pacific. You really are orphans now. How will you get home, now that all your ships are sunk?" It is difficult to imagine how the victorious American troops could have been demoralized by such words—if anything, it must have sounded like hilarious comedy.

On October 7th, Judge Roche sentenced Iva Toguri to 10 years in prison and a $10,000 fine. Loss of American citizenship was automatic under provisions of the Nationality Act of 1940.[23] Thus, at age 33, she lost the citizenship she so tenaciously preserved and the citizenship which caused her to be convicted of treason. Defense motions for mistrial, arrest of judgement, clemency, and bail pending appeal were all denied by Judge Roche. Supreme Court Justice William O. Douglas later granted bail for $50,000 but there was no way such a sum could be raised. She said a final goodby to her husband who was in San Francisco for her trial, and was taken to Alderson Federal Reformatory for Women in West Virginia. Felipe d'Aquino was forced to sign a statement he would never enter the United States again and was taken back to Occupied Japan. Attorney Marvel Shore joined Collins, Tamba, and Olshausen for the appellate phase, but their appeals based on denial of legal counsel, unlawful detention, denial of speedy trial, destruction of evidence, perjured testimony before the grand jury, denial of defense witnesses, misconduct by prosecutors, prejudicial instructions by the judge were all denied by the Ninth Circuit Court of Appeals.[24] The Supreme Court rejected appeals for review three times in the next three years.

Continued Persecution

Iva Toguri was released from prison in January 1956, after serving six years and two months, with reduced time for good behavior.[25] She was reported to have been a model prisoner. She went to live with her family in Chicago, but her struggle was not over. The Immigration and Naturalization Service promptly began deportation proceedings, claiming she was an "undesirable alien" and deportable under provisions of the McCarran-Walter Immigration and Naturalization Act of 1952. She had presumably paid her debt to society by serving her sentence, exile was not part of her sentence, and the 1952 law was *ex post facto,* nonetheless, the government gave her 30 days to leave the United States or be forcibly expelled.[26] She moved back to San Francisco to defend herself in the deportation hearings and lived with the Collins family. In 1958, the Immigration and Naturalization Service cancelled her deportation order, meekly explaining they had nowhere to deport her since she held neither Japanese nor Portuguese citizenship. She returned to Chicago to live with her father and work in the family store. Reunion with her husband was not possible: the United States refused to grant d'Aquino an entrance visa, and if she left the country as a stateless person, she could not expect to return. Despite these barriers, they have not divorced in deference to their Catholic religion. (In 1975, Felipe d'Aquino was reported to be back working in Tokyo.)

In 1968, the Justice Department demanded payment of the $10,000 fine, but she was without assets and worked only for subsistence in the family store. A Federal District Court in Chicago ordered her to surrender the cash value of two life insurance policies. The Chicago Japanese Civic Association Credit Union granted a loan equal to the cash value of $4,745 and the fine was partially satisfied. In 1971, the Justice Department again summoned her into court to demand payment of the balance of $5,255.[27] Attorney Jiro Yamaguchi represented her in the Chicago proceedings, but Collins remained as associate counsel and Collins blasted the government for capricious harassment. Collins charged the government has billions of dollars in fines which they never try to collect. In November 1972, the Seventh United States District Court of Appeals denied her a hearing to show cause why she should not be made to pay the remaining fine.

Theodore Tamba filed a petition on her behalf for executive clemency (pardon) on June 7, 1954 with President Dwight D. Eisenhower, but the petition was not answered. Wayne Collins filed a second petition requesting her pardon on November 4, 1968 with President Lyndon B. Johnson (Richard M. Nixon was elected one day later), but the second petition was not answered either. A petition for presidential pardon can be filed only once during a six-year period.

Iva Toguri's father died in 1972 and left a will stipulating the remaining fine be paid from his estate. On August 15, 1975, the government collected the last cent of the fine from her inheritance and closed her case. She took over as the manager of the family imported goods store, but she was handicapped by her stateless status and inability to travel abroad. Her long ordeal was not over: she could not shed the "Tokyo Rose" label, and she was plagued with continual abusive and threatening letters and telephone calls.

Epilogue

The legend of "Tokyo Rose" was imperishable, but Iva Toguri outlived her human antagonists: Journalist Clark Lee died in 1953; Prosecutor Thomas DeWolf in 1959; Journalist Harry Brundidge in 1961; Judge Michael Roche in 1964; Prosecutors Frank Hennessy and John Hogan in 1968. But her most loyal advocates did not live to see her redemption either: Theodore Tamba died in 1973; and Wayne Collins in 1974. (George Olshausen is living in Europe.)

One might wonder why the Japanese American community did not support Iva Toguri during her trial. At that time, the position of Japanese Americans was very tenuous and under attack; and most Japanese Americans were horrified and fearful about the effect of her trial on their own lives. Larry Tajiri, editor of the Japanese American Citizens League newspaper, had no sympathy for Tomoya Kawakita and Iva Toguri: "Both are in direct contradiction of the stories of Nisei loyalty which have come out of World War II and which have played such an important part in the reacceptance of the Nisei . . . the principals have played fast and loose with the well-being of Americans of Japanese ancestry."[28] But as their struggle to gain fundamental rights progressed and Japanese Americans felt more secure, they slowly warmed up to the idea of helping Iva Toguri. In 1957, Bill Hosokawa suggested in the same JACL newspaper: "Perhaps it is time to acknowledge that she does indeed exist, and say firmly that we are interested in seeing that she gains justice."[29] Yet it took 17 excruciating years before such ideas were accepted by the JACL. Several proposals during 1969-71 were defeated or ignored, but finally in 1974, the National JACL passed a resolution offering assistance.[30]

One might wonder, too, about the white liberals and radicals who were mute during her trial. A repressive period (later known as the McCarthy era) was dawning in 1949: congressional committees were investigating alleged communists in government and the movie industry, and loyalty oaths were imposed on college professors. Yet, some liberals and radicals had the courage to speak out on the Judith Coplon espionage trial and Alger Hiss perjury trial which were going on at the same time (Hiss was readmitted to the practice of law in August 1975 even though his original conviction stands), and the Julius and Ethel Rosenberg sabotage trial two years later at the height of McCarthyism. Whites were generally disinterested in the plight of a lone Japanese American woman.[31] But during her deportation hearings in 1956-57, white liberals and radicals awakened to the possible repercussions if the government succeeded in deporting a native-born person for being "undesirable." A small left-wing support committee was formed in San Francisco in 1956, but they were unable to gain wide public support.[32]

When Wayne M. Collins, Sr. died, his son Wayne M. Collins, Jr., also an attorney, took over as Iva Toguri's lawyer. Collins, Jr. has lived with the Toguri case since childhood. He decided to carry on family tradition by representing her without fee. He is planning to file another petition for presidential pardon in mid-1976, and the JACL is supporting Collins' petition through public education and political lobbying. A pardon can restore Iva Toguri's American citizenship and redeem her name. By early 1976, there was a growing public awareness of the injustices perpetrated against Iva Toguri,[33] but as of this writing (February 1976) it is not known if the pardon campaign will be successful. Iva Toguri was to observe her 60th birthday on the same day the United States of America celebrates its 200th birthday. The final chapter to the story of Iva Ikuko Toguri has not been written. ★

Notes

1. For biographical information see the newspaper coverage of the trial: Stanton Delaplane, *San Francisco Chronicle,* July 5 through October 7, 1949; Francis B. O'Gara, *San Francisco Examiner,* July 5 through October 7, 1949; Marion Tajiri, *Pacific Citizen,* July 9 through October 15, 1949, reprinted December 21-28, 1973.

2. Jun Toguri was born in Japan and naturalized in Canada in 1906. Canada called their citizens "British Subjects" until 1947 when "Canadian Citizen" came into official usage. The United States Naturalization Act of 1870 extended naturalization rights previously limited to "free white persons," to aliens of African nativity and persons of African descent. In *Takao Ozawa v. United States* in 1922, the Supreme Court ruled Japanese are "ineligible for citizenship" along with other Asians. This prohibition for Japanese was not lifted until the Immigration and Naturalization Act of 1952.

3. John K. Fairbank, Edwin O. Reischauer, Albert M. Craig, "Imperial Japan: From Triumph to Tragedy," *East Asia: The Modern Transformation* (Boston: Houghton Mifflin, 1965), pp. 606-612.

4. See Richard T. Kenmotsu, "The Forgotten Nisei," *Pacific Citizen,* December 19-26, 1975, pp. A1-A8; and Jim Yoshida and Bill Hosokawa, *The Two Worlds of Jim Yoshida* (New York: William Morrow, 1972).

5. The only other Japanese American convicted of treason was Tomoya Kawakita, who was drafted to work as an interpreter at a nickel mine using POW laborers. Kawakita was sentenced to death, but he was granted commutation in exchange for exile to Japan. See *Pacific Citizen,* June 19 through October 9, 1948.

6. Testimony of Warrant Officer Kamini Kant Gupta at the trial.

7. Captain T. J. O'Brien, as quoted in the *New York Times*, August 8, 1945, p. 11.

8. Rose Maria Fazio, "The Effects of the Broadcasts of 'Tokyo Rose' During World War II," M.A. Thesis, Pennsylvania State University, 1968.

9. See Roger Daniels, *The Politics of Prejudice: The Anti-Japanese Movement in California and Struggle for Japanese Exclusion* (New York: Atheneum, 1967); Robert F. Heizer and Alan J. Almquist, "Words and Acts Against the Japanese," *The Other Californians* (Berkeley: University of California Press, 1971); Dennis M. Ogawa, *From Japs to Japanese: An Evolution of Japanese-American Stereotypes* (Berkeley: McCutchan, 1971); Jacobus tenBroek, Edward N. Barnhart, Floyd W. Matson, "The Anti-Japanese Heritage" and "The Activation of the Stereotype," *Prejudice, War and the Constitution* (Berkeley: University of California Press, 1954).

10. Testimony before the United States House of Representatives Subcommittee on Naval Affairs, San Francisco, California, April 13, 1943.

11. Paul Jacobs and Saul Landau with Eve Pell, *To Serve the Devil: Volume 2: Colonials and Sojourners* (New York: Vintage Books, 1971), p. 176. Also see: Michio Kaku, "Media: Racism in the Comics," *Bridge*, 3:1 (February 1974), p. 25; Irvin Paik, "That Oriental Feeling: A Look at the Caricatures of the Asians as Sketched by American Movies," *Roots: An Asian American Reader* (Los Angeles: University of California, 1971), p. 30; Evelyn Yoshimura, "G. I.'s and Asian Women," *Roots: An Asian American Reader* (Los Angeles: University of California, 1971), p. 27.

12. Problems of the post war period are discussed in nearly every issue of *Pacific Citizen*, January 1946 through December 1950.

13. Phrase used by Larry Tajiri in a *Pacific Citizen* editorial, July 2, 1949. The best documentation for this period may be found in James J. Martin, "The Framing of 'Tokyo Rose,' " *Reason*, 7:10 (February 1976), p. 6; David A. Ward, "The Unending War of Iva Ikuko Toguri d'Aquino," *Amerasia Journal*, 1:2 (July 1971), p. 26; Isami Arifuku Waugh, "The Trial of 'Tokyo Rose,' " *Bridge*, 3:1 (February 1974), p. 5.

14. In violation of the United States Constitution, Amendment 6.

15. Since her own citizenship was under question, there was no guarantee her child could be registered as a derivative citizen; and naturalization for persons of Japanese ancestry was still prohibited in the United States.

16. According to Harry T. Brundidge, "America's First Woman Traitor," *American Mercury*, January 1954. Also see John Hada, "The Indictment and Trial of Iva Ikuko d'Aquino—'Tokyo Rose,' " M.A. Thesis, University of San Francisco, 1973.

17. Judge Roche denied a petition for *writ of habeas corpus* from Mitsuye Endo in July 1943. *Ex Parte Endo* was a challenge to the confinement of Japanese Americans in concentration camps, and the Supreme Court reversed Roche's decision in December 1944. See Audrie Girdner and Anne Loftis, *The Great Betrayal: The Evacuation of Japanese-Americans During World War II* (New York: McMillan, 1969), p. 373.

18. In violation of the United States Constitution, Amendment 6.

19. See trial transcript: *United States of America, Plaintiffs, v. Iva Ikuko Toguri d'Aquino, Defendant*, District Court of the United States for the Northern District of California, Southern Division, Case No. 31,712-R, Federal Archives and Records Center, San Bruno, California.

20. Special prosecutor Thomas DeWolf was an observer at the 1948 treason trial of Tomoya Kawakita in Los Angeles. See Note No. 5. The three jurors who held out longest against conviction were reported to be minority persons: a black American, a Japanese American, and a Jewish American.

21. United States Constitution, Article 3, Section 3.

22. See Theodore Tamba, "An Example of U.S. Justice: More Revealing Sidelights on Tribulations of 'Tokyo Rose,' " *Hokubei Mainichi*, May 14, 1973; George Olshausen, " 'Tokyo Rose'—Folklore and Justice," *City Lights*, July 1952, p. 19. Also see two other installments of Theodore Tamba's memoirs in *Hokubei Mainichi*, May 1 and June 18, 1973.

23. *United States Statutes at Large*, Volume 54, Part I, page 1169, section 401(h); *United States Code (1970)*, Title 8, page 1222, section 1841(a-9).

24. See briefs for the appellant and appellee: *Iva Ikuko Toguri d'Aquino, Appellant v. United States of America, Appellee*, United States Court of Appeals for the Ninth Circuit, Case No. 12,383, Law Library, City and County of San Francisco, California.

25. An interesting controversy on the loyalty of Japanese Americans erupted on the occasion of her release from prison. See *Congressional Record*, Volume 102, Part 3, page 2851, February 20, 1956.

26. The government's position is given in *Congressional Record*, Volume 102, Part 2, page 1683, January 31, 1956.

27. *United States of America, Plaintiffs, v. Iva Ikuko Toguri d'Aquino, Defendant*, District Court of the United States for the Northern District of Illinois, Eastern Division, Case No. 66-C-1136, Federal Archives and Records Center, Chicago, Illinois.

28. Larry Tajiri, "Nisei USA: Kawakita and 'Tokyo Rose,' " *Pacific Citizen*, June 19, 1948, p. 4.

29. Bill Hosokawa, "From the Frying Pan: The Disgraced Sister," *Pacific Citizen*, February 15, 1957, p. 2.

30. The JACL offered "Iva Toguri and her family its belated apology for long silence and inaction" in the resolution adopted by the National Council on July 27, 1974 at the 23rd Biennial National Convention in Portland, Oregon.

31. An exception was Rex Gunn, "Dear Enemy: The Story of 'Tokyo Rose,' " unpublished manuscript, Hoover Institution on War, Revolution, and Peace Archives, Stanford University, Stanford, California.

32. Steve Murdock, "The 'Tokio [sic] Rose' Case—A Menacing Precedent," *People's World*, August 9, 1956. Also see William Reuben, "The Strange Case of 'Tokyo Rose,' " *Frontier*, 8 (February 1957), p. 10.

33. Jerry Carroll and Keith Power, "Was 'Tokyo Rose' Really a Patriot?," *San Francisco Chronicle*, February 4-6, 1976; Masayo Umezawa Duus, *The Orphan of the Pacific*, manuscript submitted for publication in Japan; David Holmstrom, "Was 'Tokyo Rose' Really a Traitor?," *Christian Science Monitor*, August 18, 1973; Phil Jordan, "Interest in Case Looms as Matter of Justice," *Pacific Citizen*, December 21-28, 1973; Paine Knickerbocker, " 'Tokyo Rose': The Prevalence of a Legend," *Nichi Bei Times*, December 6-11, 1973; Dean Lipton, "Did We Convict the Wrong 'Tokyo Rose'?," *Nexus*, 1:5 (Spring 1964), p. 51; Betty Segal, "Justice for Japanese?: 'Tokyo Rose' Racism," *Berkeley Barb*, January 9-15, 1976.

An Exercise on How to Join the Navy . . .

Sangley Point, 1965—A U.S. Naval base in the Philippines across the bay from Manila.

Lying at the tip of a peninsula known as Cavite, Sangley Point is in a strategic position at the mouth of an immense bay. Early Spanish colonialists must have had this in mind when they built the 100 foot-tall, now crumbling towers which dot the Cavite landscape. Designed, so legend says, to help spot Moro warriors coming from the islands to the south, they proved to be of little value in stopping the onslaught of the American Navy, which slipped quietly into the bay in 1899. Admiral Dewey, of "you may fire when ready" fame decimated the Spanish fleet off this very peninsula.

The wreckage from that lopsided battle is still at the bottom of the bay. And now, over 65 years later, the Americans are still here—as so-called "lease-holders" of Sangley Point.

Pilipinos who immigrated to the United States as a result of their service in various military branches form a distinct segment of the Pilipino community. To learn their unique history, a group of UCLA Pilipino students during the early months of 1974 interviewed a total of 15 Pilipinos who had been involved with the U.S. military at one time or another. What follows is an introductory report on the U.S. Navy and the relationship it has had with Pilipinos.

The interviews were performed by Joaquin Geaga, Sheila Tabag, Henry Empeno, Juliet Masculino, Jennifer Masculino, Norma Bautista, Paul Fernandez, Casimiro Tolentino and Jesse Quinsaat with research assistance by Dorothy Hannah. . . .

For a very brief period after Dewey won his much hallowed encounter, the land which is now Sangley Point belonged neither to Spaniards nor Americans. It belonged to Pilipinos. It was from here that Emilio Aguinaldo directed a successful but incomplete indigenous campaign which liberated nearly all of the Philippines from Spanish control. The Spanish capital, Manila, remained under the colonialists' control. American troops, with Spanish capitulation, entered the city in 1900 and then proceeded to wage a long and brutal war against the same Pilipinos who had helped to defeat the Spanish army. The result was the transformation of the Philippines into the first and only American colony in Asia.

Excepting a three-year period during World War II when the Japanese were the occupying imperial force, Sangley Point remained under American control until 1945, when the Philippine Independence was declared. In 1947, as a parcel in a series of treaties which assured that the Philippines would essentially continue its prior relationship with the United States, Sangley Point was leased to Americans, along with 22 other sites in the Philippines, for 99 years. The particular treaty which accomplished this arrangement was termed The Military Bases Agreement. One other aspect of the Bases Agreement allows the United States to recruit Pilipinos into its navy.

Sangley Point is where this recruitment is carried on. Aside from this function it also serves as the headquarters of the U.S. Naval Forces in the

illustration by DEAN S. TOJI

and Still Not See the World
by Jesse Quinsaat

Philippines. The base is physically small, as U.S. Navy bases go, roughly occupying about six square miles of the Cavite peninsula. Nevertheless it has some strategic value; from here, American aircraft fly reconnaissance missions to Viet Nam. Other than the small airstrip, the naval base carries few of the trappings which mark a military installation which is at war. In fact, most of the base is made up of housing and living facilities for the base personnel.

The biggest housing space is taken up by the home of the admiral, who is the Commander of U.S. Naval Forces in the Philippines. It is a huge, two-story, white-washed structure surrounded by stately palms and finely trimmed shrubbery. A driveway curves around to the front door, where one is usually greeted by one of the Admiral's Navy Pilipino stewards. There are usually two or three of these stewards at the house kept busy by the admiral or his wife, especially when they entertain some high ranking official or dignitary. Then the stewards can be seen serving drinks or cleaning up after these affairs. With its manicured lawns, shaded portals and ubiquitous dark skinned servants dressed in white smocks, the whole scene is mindful of some antebellum southern plantation.

Surrounding the admiral's home are houses of lesser ranking officers. Although they are not nearly as imposing as the admiral's home, many of these houses are also white-washed. Pilipino gardeners recruited from the outlying town of Cavite keep the surrounding yards neat and trim while Pilipina maids tapped from the same city, clean the homes and take care of their employer's children.

A smooth concrete road winds around the entire base and leads to an air-conditioned shopping center, an olympic-size swimming pool and even a recreation center for the sons and daughters of the navy families. Almost all of these facilities are staffed by Pilipinos. Since one American dollar can buy four Philippine pesos on the foreign exchange, and the wages paid on the base are high when compared to those paid in Philippine society, getting labor is cheap and easy.

At 5 p.m., the Pilipino workers will walk along the smooth concrete road and file out a narrow opening known as "The Main Gate." After this mass exodus, Sangley Point resembles some small quiet town in the United States. In the late evening, when a tank truck will circulate the base spraying insecticide in the incessant war against the ubiquitous mosquitos, one is once more reminded that this is not America.

Some other reminders are the miles of barbed wire and fence which separate Sangley Point from Cavite city, a barrier interspersed with signs marked "BAWAL PUMASOK" (DO NOT ENTER). "The Main Gate" is the only break in the self-imposed wire wall. There, an armed marine guard checks identification before allowing anyone to enter or leave. The human traffic flowing through "The Main Gate" is always orderly. The guard has been known to reach for his .45 pistol all too quickly. Exactly at "The Main Gate" the smooth concrete road of Sangley ends and is replaced by the Cavite city road, a rough asphalt strip full of potholes. It is the rainy season so there are more holes than usual. Rain collects here and mosquitos breed by the millions, flying undeterred past the marine guard at "The Main Gate." Once in a while, a few Cavite city workers will come along and fill up the holes, but by the next rain, the holes and the mosquitos will re-appear. The standing joke, a traditional cynical jibe at the efficiency of Philippine government is that the city won't undertake the work to re-surface the entire road because it will result in a loss of jobs to the hole fillers. When the typhoon season is on and the road becomes filled with giant craters, no one laughs.

Following this asphalt road beyond "The Main Gate" one runs immediately into an area which the sailors of Sangley Point disaffectionately call "The Beach." It is a two-block stretch of bars, discotheques and tourist shops. During the hot day, it sits in quiet repose, but come evening it is humming with activity. Then, swarms of hustlers hang about on street corners promising to sell anything imaginable to the unwary. Raggedly dressed, scruffy looking children will cling to sailors as soon as they walk out "The Main Gate" crying, "Hey, Joe" and offering cheap shoe shines. Loud music blares from inside the bars and prostitutes with make-up piled high onto weary looking faces mill about inside, their bright dresses glittering in the flashing lights. A sailor back from an evening on "The Beach" can often be heard to proclaim that he's been cheated, taken or swindled by one of those "gooks" or "Huks" or less commonly, "Filipinos."

Past "The Beach" the potholed road winds into the city and out to the provinces which make up the Philippines. This is where the "gooks" live, a land of great physical beauty matched only by the depth of the poverty of its people. Here the hard rains beat down on tin corrugated roofs sitting atop dilapidated shacks put together from odd pieces of lumber, loose cardboard boxes and pieces of tin, some of them marked "U.S. Aid." These homes are not whitewashed; no amount of make-up can hide the misery within.

Today standing outside "The Main Gate" at Sangley Point are two groups of men. One is a nervous-looking collection of about 30 young men, most who appear to be in their early 20's. They are dressed neatly in white shirts with dark shoes and slacks. The other group is a much older set of about 10 men who look like they are in their 50's and 60's. Dressed casually in shorts and rubber slippers, nearly all carry umbrellas or plastic raincoats—in anticipation of the always-impending rain.

The young men have come from all over the Philippines, some hailing from as far south as the island of Mindanao and many from the Ilocos region several hundred miles north of Sangley. They are nervous because in a few minutes they will be allowed to enter "The Main Gate" to take a series of tests which will determine whether or not they can join

the United States Navy. One or two of these 30 men will make it with the desperate hope of avoiding that sense of hopelessness which marks life in the Philippines.

The old men are conspicuously unmindful of the young. They have gone through a similar experience once before. Twenty or thirty years ago they joined the navy and became stewards, an occupation devoted to dishwashing, cleaning and similar menial chores. Now they have returned to the Philippines to spend their lives in retirement. On a designated day of the week they come to Sangley Point to exercise the few "privileges" which they have earned at great cost by serving in the U.S. Navy for so long. One of these "privileges" is shopping at a special base commissary meant expressly for retired Navy personnel. It is a small store where coffee, cigarettes and other dry goods are sold. Retired Navy men can only make a limited number of purchases here, a policy which supposedly prevents "black marketing" (the sale of cheaper-priced U.S. goods on the Philippine market, where they fetch high prices). Although the policy discriminates against the old Pilipinos since it does not apply equally to the Navy personnel who live on the base, these men seem to bear the humiliation for they are rarely heard complaining. One gripe they do often make, though, is that the goods sold in the store are either spoiled or rejects.

Soon, the young Pilipino men are led through "The Main Gate" by a white man in a white sailor suit. They pass through in single file and are marched about a quarter of a mile past the white-washed houses and manicured lawns to a two-story white building where they will be given a battery of mental and physical exams. This procedure will go on for a period of several weeks to similar groups of 30 or 40 similar young men. Eventually, a small company of about 20 Pilipino sailors will be formed. They will be drilled in basic military discipline before they are sent to mainland America. Once there, they will learn less spartan skills, such as how to set dinner tables for Navy officers.

As light rain begins to fall, the potholes in the asphalt road fill up with mud and the old men still waiting outside pull out umbrellas or put on their raincoats. At the same time, some of the young men, who were eliminated by the exams, now walk back from the testing areas to "The Main Gate." Since they did not prepare themselves for the rain, their clothes are soaking wet, belying their deep dejection. Just as they go past the gate, the old men enter and there is a sudden confusing mass of people at that borderline. Then the old men are off to do their shopping and the young men are out onto the crude asphalt road, walking past "The Beach" into buses which will take them back to their respective provinces. As they pass one street corner, one of "The Beach" hustlers, chancing to see them thrust a cigarette into a mud-filled pothole, chortles, "Ay, Bagsak!"

Sangley has since become Philippine property but the American foreign policy which helped to create the above scenario continues to this very day. This year, as it has been for the last 30 years, approximately 100,000 young Pilipino men will come to the vast U.S. Subic Bay Naval Station on the outskirts of Olangapo City of Zambales province in the Philippines. Each man carries with him the slim hope that he will be one of those selected to join the U.S. Navy. Hopes are slim because the competition to join is severe; perhaps 2000 or less will ultimately be chosen. Those few who are picked will most likely follow a life routine which by now has become the pattern for Pilipinos who join the U.S. Navy. Spending long 20 to 30 year terms in the service, most will acquire U.S. citizenship along the way and eventually settle in the United States.

The upshot of this practice is the current growth of large Pilipino communities made up largely of Pilipino navy men and their families who can be found living in cities throughout the United States where there is a sizeable military concentration. In San Diego, for example, the site for a number of Navy installations, Pilipino community organizers claim that roughly half of the estimated Pilipino population of 15,629 have some association with the Navy.[1] Similar large communities exist in Long Beach and in the San Francisco Bay Area as well as in cities on the East Coast which have Navy facilities.

Such communities will normally be composed of the whole range of generations of Pilipinos who made, are making or will make a Navy career their livelihood. The first and oldest of these generations are Navy retirees who finished 20 to 30 years of service and have settled in these cities because they like being near a Navy installation where they can have access to the retirement benefits they earned by serving in the navy for so long. These include shopping at military commissaries or utilizing military hospitals and other health care facilities. Additionally, they like living close to old Navy comrades with whom they spent a great deal of time while in the service. The other Navy Pilipinos in these communities are those who are in the process of serving their terms and are in these cities not specifically by choice but by government orders. In cities such as San Diego, which has a training center for Navy recruits, this group will include young Pilipino men just recently arrived from the Philippines undergoing indoctrination and training.

While these generations span the whole history of Pilipino participation in the U.S. Navy, they nearly all can claim one common experience: as a condition of their enlistment they had to join the Navy as stewards. In the Navy, stewards are responsible to

officers for serving them their food, washing their dishes, cleaning their living quarters and caring for their uniforms. Unofficially, as stewards will tell you themselves, they are often ordered to do chores like walking officers' dogs or acting as general servants for their wives. It is obviously not the case that Pilipinos are inherently suited to do this kind of work nor do they particularly enjoy doing it. The Navy, however, until recent years restricted Pilipinos to this single job category as the price for entering the service.

As a rule, the United States does not make it a practice to recruit foreign nationals to become stewards in their navy. Pilipinos, however, can join the U.S. Navy because of the Military Bases Agreement, which was signed by the United States and the Philppines in 1947. The relevant provision of this agreement, Article 27, reads as follows:

> "It is mutually agreed that the United States shall have the right to recruit citizens of the Philippines for voluntary enlistment into the United States Armed Forces for a fixed term of years, and to train them and to exercise the same degree of control and discipline over them as is exercised in the case of other members of the United States Armed Forces. The number of such enlistments to be accepted by the armed forces of the United States may from time to time be limited by the two governments."[2]

Nowhere is it stated in this article or anywhere else in the Agreement that Pilipinos would be expressly recruited to be stewards.

Most Pilipinos who joined the Navy and became stewards were unaware that Article 27 did not have this qualifying provision. In fact, most Pilipinos have never even heard of the Military Bases Agreement, and it would no doubt come as an ironic surprise to them that the U.S. Naval stations in the Philippines where they were initially recruited exist by virtue of the same treaty. Nonetheless, the hiring policy of the Navy has been a matter of common knowledge to Pilipinos, and despite the awareness of the humble quality of a steward's tasks, there has been no lack of applicants. Throughout the years, the competition to join the Navy has been so marked that one of the favorite topics of conversation among Navy Pilipinos is relating how tough it was to get in. Often, these talks are punctuated with allusions to falsified birth certificates and Philippine pesos dropped in proper palms in order to speed up applications in the recruitment procedure.

Joining the Navy, even as a steward, has been a traditional response to the lack of economic mobility in the Philippines. Favorable monetary conversion rates between the American dollar and the Philippine peso enable a Pilipino steward in the U.S. Navy to make more money than an officer in the Philippine Navy. In addition, Pilipinos who join the Navy have a relatively easier time becoming U.S. citizens. The Nationality Act of 1940 and its later amendments, give aliens who have served three or more years in the

U.S. Armed Forces the opportunity to become U.S. citizens without their having to meet normal requirements, such as residence. To Pilipinos in the Philippines, U.S. citizenship is the springboard of escape from poverty.

That there is a great deal of difference in the potential that life in the U.S. Navy offers, even as a steward compared to the prospects offered by remaining in the Philippines cannot be denied. This explanation, so often cited as the classic rationale for immigration, however, cannot adequately account for why there are so many Pilipino navymen living in the United States today, let alone why they all had to become stewards for that to occur. Indonesia, Brazil, Great Britain, to name a few, are countries which like the Philippines, cannot match the kinds of economic opportunities which the United States can offer to laborers. Yet, Britons, Brazilians and Indonesians are not found in the U.S. Navy to the same extent that Pilipinos are found. Indeed, Pilipinos seem to be the special case, with over 22,000 joining the Navy between 1944 and 1973.[3]

The reason citizens of countries like Brazil or Indonesia are not in the Navy in the same degree as citizens of the Philippines is because these countries do not have the same kind of "Special Relations" that exist between the Philippines and the United States. "Special Relations" is a term which diplomats euphemistically use to describe the kinds of treaties and agreements which were entered into between the United States and the Philippines at the end of World War II, when the Philippines was granted its Independence.

Once a former colony, the Philippines suddenly emerged as an ostensible new U.S. ally and a supposedly old friend. Based on these newly developed "Special Relations" the United States could effectuate such agreements as the Bell Trade Act with the Philippines, a treaty which gave U.S. citizens the right to equal ownership of Philipppine soil as well as extending favorable economic trade arrangements to the United States. U.S. diplomats call this arrangement "mutually beneficial."[4]

Such an expression grates on the ears of nationalistic Pilipinos, who have had to live with the ring of President McKinley's "benevolent assimilation" call, the popular euphemism for justifying the Philippine-American War and a saying which could not quite drone out the roar of unkindly American bullets. These Pilipino nationalists have pointed out that such treaties as the Bell Trade Act (and its later substitutes, including the Laurel-Langley Agreement) are largely responsible for the economic retardation of the Philippines and its existence as a semi-colony of the U.S. Until martial law was declared in 1973, they were quite outspoken in their demands for the end of "Special Relations."[5]

Signed in 1947, the Military Bases Agreement is one of these "Special Relations" treaties and has also been referred to as "mutually beneficial." Along with the Article 27 provision giving the U.S. the right to recruit Pilipino citizens into the Navy (a kind of agreement it does not share with any other country in the world), the U.S. was granted the right to lease 23 sites in the Philippines, including the giant Subic Bay Naval Station from which Pilipinos may apply to join the navy.

The bases supposedly exist to provide the United States and the Philippines with mutual security and defense capabilities in Southeast Asia. However, like the ubiquitous presence of American corporations which resulted from the "mutually beneficial" Bell Trade Act, the existence of these bases has been a constant physical reminder to Pilipinos that the independent Philippines may not in fact be so independent.

Ever since the 1947 agreement gave them official sanction, the bases have been a continual source of conflict between Pilipinos and Americans. One smouldering issue has been the question of jurisdiction, or from the Pilipino point of view, the lack of it. Americans have the right to try crimes committed by American servicemen on the bases. Thirty-seven Pilipinos have been killed by Americans on the bases and thus far, not a single American has been convicted. In one exemplary incident, one Pilipino was shot by a Navy guard who mistook him for a "wild boar."[6]

Pilipinos have pointed out that there are obvious, not so "mutually beneficial" features to these bases, such as the exposure of the Philippines to any aggression primarily directed at the United States by other countries. Furthermore, the overall strategic value of the bases in a nuclear age has been questioned, leading some to believe that the bases are in the Philippines not to insure the security of the Philippines and the United States, but to protect and maintain American interests in the Philippines. As Renato Constantino, one nationalistic Pilipino put it, "The bases are the dagger at the throat of our sovereignty."[7]

If the presence of U.S. military bases in the Philippines, as mandated by the Bases Agreement, are overtones of a time when Philippine autonomy was subservient to American policy in Asia, the practice of recruiting Pilipinos to serve as stewards, a product of the very *same* agreement, is a direct throwback to the colonial era. When the Philippines became an American "protectorate" as a result of the Philippine-American war at the turn of the century, the Navy began to utilize Pilipinos as stewards in its fleet without any particular legal mandate. When the Philippines was granted Independence, in 1946, recruitment could no longer be unilaterally authorized since Pilipinos had become citizens of their own country.

Owing to "Special Relations" the Navy practice was maintained and sanctioned by Article 27 of the Bases Agreement, albeit without the mention of the singularly assigned role of Pilipinos. A telling feature of the nature of these "Special Relations" is that the two provisions of the Bases Agreement (one giving the right to Americans to establish bases in the Philippines and the other allowing the Navy to recruit Pilipinos) are mutually independent. That is, military bases are not necessarily required to recruit stewards, nor do Pilipino stewards have to be recruited for the bases to exist. Such a curious circumstance found in the treaty can probably only be explained in terms of a colonial appetite that not only takes away the cake and eats it too, but has the insistent demand of being served on a platter as well.

The practice of employing Pilipinos as stewards was probably originally one of those fruits of imperialism transferred from one colonizer to the next. Spain was the first to use Pilipino seamen, impressing them into service for the Galleon trade. As early as the 18th century, Pilipino fugitives escaping from Spanish ships established some of the first Pilipino communities of North America in what is now Louisiana.[8] During the early 1900s when American power had asserted itself in the Philippines, Pilipino seamen began to appear in the merchant marine and the U.S. Navy. In 1903, the Navy already had 9 Pilipinos in its ranks, and by 1905, that figure had jumped to 178.[9]

Since then Pilipino stewards have been a constant feature of the U.S. Navy personnel system and have accounted for roughly 4.5% of the total Navy manpower throughout the years. Despite their numerical significance, very little has been written or reported about these men. In an effort to learn more about the experiences of Pilipinos in the Navy, as well as other ocean-going services such as the U.S. Coast Guard and the merchant marine (which have been similar vehicles of immigration) a group of students at UCLA conducted a series of interviews with Pilipinos who have made the sea life their careers. What follows are some highlights from those conversations.

Interviews

Pilipinos will often say that the reason they took to the seas was for the thrill of experiencing new places. One of the oldest Pilipinos we talked to was Jack S. who at age 80 still possesses that spirit of adventure. Jack was a sailor with the merchant marine. A stowaway at age 15, in 1910 he arrived in San Francisco in what he describes as "the Barbary Coast thing—a rough situation." Jack still practices the art of escrima (Philippine knife handling) and told us about his first use of this skill with Pilipino gangs in the Bay Area. At the time he describes, there were about 300 Pilipinos in the general area, most of them sailors in the merchant marine or the Navy.

Q: You had a Filipino gang, didn't you?
S: Yeah, Kearney gang. . . . all Pilipinos, about a hundred of us. Sometimes when we make a big

raid, we ask the boys that work on board on different transports to help us. Ten or fifteen of us were escrimadors. We always get in front. You see, I always pick out 10 or 15 boys right in front in case of knife-wielding opponents. We shouldered the shock first, then the rest comes in. When we escrimadors start, then the others come in.
Q: Why did you raid other gangs?
S: In retaliation for the insults, for everything that happened to the Filipinos. On Market Street, I tell you, you can't even walk with your girl friend there if she's an American. So we retaliated until they were crippled up.

Dangerous and glamorous as Jack's street life was, his daily work routine proved quite the opposite. At this time, the American tradition of using Pilipinos in the more subservient tasks of shipboard life began to develop.

Q: What kind of work did you do in the merchant marine?
S: Oh, waiter, you know.
Q: They wouldn't allow you to work at other positions?
S: Not the merchant marine, but on the government transport—the Thomas, Sherman, Sheridan, and others—the deck hands that work are mostly Filipino boys, about 75% are Filipinos—but the merchant marine, no there are hardly any Filipinos except in the steward department. The steward department is ahhh . . . if it's a passenger ship they assign you as roomboys. See, when the guys get up, they fix up the bed and clean up the room. Then about lunch time or supper time, you serve in the dining room.

The Navy duplicated this merchant marine policy, recruiting men such as Jack to serve exclusively as stewards in the fleet. By 1917, 2000 Pilipinos were in the navy, where they joined black sailors who were similarly denied the opportunity to work anywhere on board ships except the galleys and messhalls. During World War I, enlistment of Pilipinos increased dramatically and by 1919, 6000 were serving. Eventually, they displaced blacks, who were prevented altogether from joining the navy after World War I.[10] So ubiquitous had Pilipinos become along sea routes that Jack was led to comment:

When I went to South America, Chile, anywhere, there are Filipinos there. They are just like me—work on board ship in the steward department. In every port you see Filipinos. And Chinese, too. It's two kinds of people you can always see around the world—Chinese and Filipinos.

After World War I, the number of Pilipinos in the navy remained constant at roughly 4000. This figure represented about 4.5% of the total population of men in the navy at the time. Along with the adventurous life that induced men like Jack S. to join, more material factors could be considered for explaining the presence of all these Pilipinos. The average pay of a steward in the navy at that time was about $67.50 a month.[11] If he served 16 years, he could earn over $105 a month—a substantial amount when measured against the Philippine peso. A Navy steward serving this much time could lump his retirement pay and savings together and live relatively handsomely in his home town. Those who chose this route emerged as symbolic representations of what a navy life could offer—probably one reason why, even now, the Navy has not had to bother with extensive advertising in the Philippines to fill their annual quotas.

During World War II, Japanese forces occupied the Philippines and there was no enlistment of Pilipino sailors. However, Pilipinos who had migrated to the United States before the war were given the chance to join the U.S. Army or the Navy. Those who signed with the latter disappointingly learned that the discrimination they had long suffered while in America was not yet over—Pilipinos in America were only also allowed to become stewards.[12]

With Allied landings in the Philippines in 1944, recruitment again resumed, with Pilipinos joining the Navy as soon as naval bases were secured from the Japanese. Since the Philippines had not yet been granted independence no formal agreement was necessary. Between 1944-46 about 2000 Pilipinos enlisted. The servicemen joining in this era constituted the source for the majority of interviews conducted by the UCLA student group. When the interviews were conducted, most had already retired from the Navy after serving between 20-30 years.

In our conversations with them most stated that they joined the navy not out of any particular patriotic duty to the United States but to escape the poverty of the Philippines. Many talked about the devastation of World War II and its attendant sense of despair. Joining the Navy was an inviting alternative or, as some stated, it was the only alternative. In addition, some of the interviewees, such as Jorge M., a 20-year veteran, came from towns in which joining the Navy had become a tradition:

> J: I joined the Navy on account of the social economic standing of retired ex-navy men from our town in Nabua.
> Q: Were there a number of Navy personnel who came back?
> J: There were several of them, you know. Nabua is, you know, a navy town. It used to be a farming town but now it's famous for its retired sailors. A lot of young Nabuans look up at the life of the retired sailors in our town because they lead a nice social and economic life. And the only people who could ever get out of Nabua were the navy men and teachers . . . So it made a trend for young boys who weren't going to go to college or who weren't going to get anything from their parents; so they try to join the navy because of the retired navy men and they say 'I'll be like them.' So for that reason, a lot of young Nabuans went to Manila, went to Subic Bay, right after the Americans landed at Leyte Gulf and joined the navy right away.

As is the present case, the number of Pilipinos wanting to enlist in the Navy far out-numbered those who were eventually accepted. Our interviewees described the conditions around recruitment centers as generally chaotic, with thousands of Pilipinos standing in long lines hoping to join. Mr. F. R., who joined the navy in 1944, described to us this somewhat extreme effort to get into the service:

> One of the requirements for joining the Navy back then was that you had to weigh at least a hundred pounds. Well, when I went to join, I only weighed 90 pounds. I couldn't qualify for that first physical they give you. I really wanted to join the Navy really bad at that time so what I did was to go across the street from the recruiting station to this market place where they were selling bananas. And you know what I did? That's right. I ate 10 pounds of bananas! I went right back in the line, and this time I qualified.

Even though most realized they would be assigned to do the most menial chores while in the service, Navy men now consider themselves "lucky" to have been selected. Thus, for 20-30 years, most spent the majority of their time washing dishes, shining officers' shoes and generally doing cleaning and kitchen duties. They regard this circumstance with a kind of philosophic hindsight—"you're a Pilipino, you'll always be washing dishes . . . you might as well wash dishes where no one can see you," but some balked when ordered to do work by wives of officers:

> I could never understand why I had to take orders from an officer's wife, even when she was the admiral's wife. She's still a civilian you know . . . There would be times when they would order you to move furniture around their houses but what could you do, say 'I refuse to take orders from you because you're a civilian?' You just couldn't do that.

In addition to the discrimination of having to become stewards in order to enter the Navy, our interviewees had to bear the common prejudices of officers who thought of Pilipinos as their virtual servants:

> Yeah, they called you 'boy.' That was a common expression with Americans. Some of us were adults and resented name-calling and stuff like that but in the military you cannot object everytime you hear the word or else the relation between you and your superior officer will start to get more delicate.

As citizens of a foreign country, Pilipinos had little recourse to make formal protests and the Navy men we talked to brushed aside the option as one of utter futility. They did, however, exert their own kind of pressure:

> The officers, some of them from the South were

really very nasty, they thought you were a man-servant through an act of Congress, that you were inducted to be their personal servant. Well, some of them learned the hard way. They didn't know what was going on in the kitchen. Yeah, that's right, they didn't know how their coffee was made—with our socks that we had worn for a week. And that some of their food had Filipino saliva in it. Sometimes it took a while until some-one told them that the worst enemy you could have was your steward.

While Pilipinos did engage in these kinds of "silent protests" against their superiors, they could do very little to change their basic lot. Transfer to any other of the many ratings that an enlisted man can hold in the navy, such as fireman, electrician, corpsman or storekeeper was described to us as an exceedingly difficult course of action for a Pilipino. Even passage of the relevant qualifying examinations did not mean that a steward would be allowed to transfer to another position. Of the Pilipinos we talked to, the few who were lucky enough to do so told us about extremely fortuitous circumstances, such as being the personal favorite of the admiral or similar high-ranking official who could "pull strings."

Still, this situation was not always a guarantee because officers often developed attachments to their stewards and were reluctant to let them transfer to a rating where they could not enjoy the good services of the Pilipino. As one retired navy man told us, "I made his coffee just the way he wanted it, the right amount of sugar and the right amount of coffee and he wouldn't let me go." An increased manpower demand for navy typists gave several navymen we talked to the opportunity to become yeoman (administrative clerks) while one interviewee told us that he became the ship's barber when he kept breaking plates in the galley.

Since 1944, the Philippines has served as a pool of labor from which the Navy has chosen to draw whenever it felt the need. From 1947-52 no Pilipinos were enlisted but with the onset of the Korean conflict in 1952, recruitment again became desirable. Over 5000 Pilipinos joined the Navy between 1953-58. By 1970, over 22,000 Pilipinos had entered the Navy since recruitment began during World War II.

Their existence became particularly noticeable in Washington, D.C., where over 150 stewards served high-ranking brass at the Pentagon and the President. This brown skinned servant force caught the attention of Timothy Ingram who wrote an article entitled "The Floating Plantation" in *The Washington Monthly*. Ingram pointed out some hitherto unpublicized facts: Of the 16,669 Pilipinos in the navy at that time 80 per cent were stewards. A steward was assigned to officers on the basis of their rank—one for captains and three for admirals. "In this way," Ingram wrote caustically, "officers can continue to live out the lazy slob syndrome, which gets them fattened and paralyzed into easy chairs as they become more and more important."[13]

Ingram's article was followed by a similar article in *Time* magazine and Senator William Proxmire later conducted a full-fledged investigation on the use of stewards in the military as well as on the President's staff.

Since these events, the Navy policy towards Pilipinos has relaxed somewhat. According to the Navy, Pilipinos are now recruited without any restrictions in the rating to which they may enter but they cannot take positions which require a security clearance. Whether or not the Navy is following this policy in good faith is another matter. In 1973, according to statistics released by the Dept. of the Navy, over 9000 of the 11,000 stewards serving in the Navy were Pilipinos. These "Malaysians," as the statistics refer to them, could be found in the next greatest numbers as storekeepers and seamen and less frequently in the more skilled positions, such as corpsman and radar-man.[14]

Whether or not the Navy's "liberalization" trend will continue will probably be less dependent on bad publicity and senatorial investigations but more contingent on changes in the basic relationship of the Philippines and the United States. Certainly, the Navy's "equal opportunity" switch in policy has not contemplated a fully equalized program, such as a recruiting arrangement with Philippine colleges, similar to the ROTC programs in the U.S. At the very least, this would require some alteration in the original bases agreement. With the re-alignment of power in southeast Asia following the defeat of the United States in Viet Nam, the existence of the bases may come under closer scrutiny by the Philippine govern-ment.[15] Hence, if a truly "mutually benefitting" treaty were to be re-negotiated there could exist the possibility that Pilipinos might be recruited into the Navy on more equal footing. Still, such a move would seem highly unlikely, given the kind of attachment the Navy has with "tradition." Furthermore, the prospect of having increasing numbers of Pilipinos in the American Navy has questionable merit, if only from the standpoint that it would more glaringly reflect economic disparity between the two nations.

At any rate the Pilipinos who have made the Navy their career are now a significant portion of the Pilipino community in the United States. Most have chosen to settle permanently in this country. The standard practice for the men to whom we spoke was to return to the Philippines to marry after about four years of service and to immigrate with their families shortly thereafter to the United States. In general, Pilipinos who came to the United States after World War II had a much easier time than the early Pilipino farmworkers in establishing a normal homelife. With the repeal of such racist legislation as the specific prohibition against Pilipinos owning property and the relaxation of constraints on citizenship for military Pilipinos, a more secure life was possible.

On the whole the men we interviewed cite that they are "much better off" than they would have been had they remained in the Philippines. Most say that they are reluctant to return home, often pointing to the material gains they have accumulated here or their desire for their children to get a "good education in the United States."

It seems highly out-of-tune, though, in these modern times that Pilipinos have had to serve exclusively subservient roles in order to achieve a relative degree of material comfort. So long as serving in the U.S. Navy remains one of the few outlets for Pilipino males to get "much better off," it will continue to point to the fact that the historical inequitable relationship between the two countries is still to be redressed. As this relationship remains unchanged, Pilipinos will also continue to experience its effects personally. Almost all of the Pilipinos we spoke to expressed the desire to eventually "go back home." However, they were discouraged from doing so by the ill treatment that retired navy men receive in the Philippines by the Navy.

> There's a 'retired's commissary' at Subic Bay, right there next to the main gate. I saw it when I was stationed back there. They make the retired Navy guys wait for certain days to shop at this place. And there's not much of a selection of things to buy in that store, you know, and you can't buy all you want. This is what you deserve after serving all those years?! It's humiliating. Not for me. I won't go home for that. ★

Notes

1. Grace Blaskowski, of the Asian American Affairs Office, San Diego Human Relations Commission, stated to the California Advisory Committee to the U.S. Commission on Civil Rights that 80 per cent of the Pilipino labor force in San Diego was employed by the U.S. Navy. (See a report of the California Advisory Committee to the U.S. Commission on Civil Rights, *Asian Americans and Pacific Peoples: A Case of Mistaken Identity*, February 1975, page 51.) The population of 15,629 is cited in the U.S. Bureau of the Census, U.S. Dept. of Commerce Publication PC(2)-1G, *Subject Reports. Japanese, Chinese and Filipinos in the United States*, July 1973. Organizers of Project Samahan, the umbrella organization for Pilipino service and community groups in San Diego, claim that this figure is grossly deflated and estimate that as many as 50,000 Pilipinos live in San Diego.

2. U.S. Treaties and Agreements, 22 U.S. Treaties 1469.

3. *Report to the Congress by the Comptroller General of the United States.* "Enlisted Aide Program of the Military Service," B 177S16, 1973, p. 55.

4. One particularly bitter feature of "Special Relations" to Pilipinos was that in order for war reparations to be paid to the Philippines, the Bell Trade Act had to be agreed to by the Philippine Government. For an American diplomat's view of these relations see *The United States and the Philippines: Problems of Partnership,* George Taylor, New York, Frederick Praeger Publishers, 1964. For a more critical look at "special relations" see William

Pomeroy, "The Philippines—A Case History of Neo-Colonialism," in *Remaking Asia,* edited by Mark Selden, New York, Pantheon Books, 1974.

5. See for example, "The Lichauco Paper," *Monthly Review Press,* July-August 1973, a copy of the address delivered by Alejandro Lichauco to the Philippine Constitutional Convention of 1971. Lichauco, a prominent lawyer, businessmen and delegate to the Convention describes the deeply rooted nature of American imperialism in the Philippines and analyzes the instruments which it uses to maintain itself. He was arrested after declaration of martial law by President Marcos in September 1972 and released after a prison term, but later placed under house arrest in January 1973.

6. *Makibaka, Huwag Matakot,* a publication of the Committee of Returned Volunteers, 840 W. Oakdale Ave., Chicago, Illinois 60657. *Makibaka* is a collection of materials describing protests opposing U.S. presence in the Philippines. The pamphlet includes clippings from various Philippine newspapers. See in particular "Moomey is the Root of All Evil" on page 12. Moomey is the serviceman who mistook a Pilipino for a wild boar and shot him while at Subic Bay Naval Base. Moomey was found not guilty by a U.S. Military Court and allowed to return to the United States.

For the most detailed treatment of the military bases in the Philippines see an essay by Enrique Voltaire Garcia in *The Journal of East Asiatic Studies,* Vol. II, September 1967, entitled "U.S. Military Bases." The essay is an in-depth analysis of the many colonial-like features of the presence of bases. Voltaire describes the entire history leading to the institution of the Military Bases Agreement in 1947 and discusses the sovereignty aspect as well as the extended leasing arrangements granted to the United States. The Bases Agreement is reproduced in full with comments by Voltaire on the articles. As to the Article 27 agreement which gives the U.S. the right to recruit Pilipinos into the Navy, he notes sardonically, "The agreement was not reciprocal."

7. "The Lichuaco Paper," p. 159.

8. Marina K. Espina, "Filipinos in New Orleans," *Proceedings of the Louisiana Academy of Sciences,* Vol. 37, Dec. 1974, pp. 117-121.

9. *U.S. Navy Reports,* 1925.

10. Lee Nichols, *Breakthrough on the Color Front,* New York, Random House, 1954, p. 39.

11. Bruno Lasker, *Filipino Immigration,* New York, Arno Press, 1969, pp. 61-64.

12. Bienvenido Santos, "Filipinos at War," *Far Eastern Review,* Vol. 11, November 30, 1942, pp. 249-250.

13. Timothy Ingram, "The Floating Plantation," *Washington Monthly,* Oct. 1970, pp. 17-20.

14. Statistics from the Department of the Navy for 1973, BUPERS, NMIS, Report 5310-0371-00 N21. The designation "Malaysians" is misleading and was questioned by Proxmire in the GAO report. A Pilipino joining the U.S. Navy in the Philippines as a Pilipino citizen cannot become an officer even though there are some "Malaysian" officers reported in the Navy. These officers must either be U.S.-born Pilipinos or from another "Malaysian" ethnic group which is not Pilipino.

15. Reuters News Service reports in the *Philippine News,* August 16-22, 1975, p. 2, that President Marcos is re-examining the Bases question and is already considering steps to change the jurisdictional status of the Philippines with respect to crimes committed by U.S. servicemen.

KOREAN NATIONALIST ACTIVITIES IN HAWAII AND AMERICA 1901-1945

by

Kingsley K. Lyu

[Editor's note: This is a detailed account of Korean nationalist activities in Hawaii and the continental United States from 1901-1945 by a participant, Kingsley K. Lyu. For his original study done in 1950, the author interviewed many Korean immigrants who were involved in the Korean independence movement. For these reasons, we have included here excerpts from his valuable work in order to make the fruits of his research more widely available to the public. Owing to limited space, we regret we are unable to print his entire manuscript of 153 pages. Deletions from the original are indicated by ellipses. We have retained his romanization and western word order of Korean names. We have not changed his personal style of footnoting nor his bibliography except for renumbering the footnotes for the sake of continuity, so as to remain faithful to the original. Only minor editing for technical consistency has been done; additions by the editor are marked in brackets except for the subheads. (For additional bibliographical information, see Kingsley K. Lyu, Korean Nationalist Activities in the United States and Hawaii, 1900-1945, University of Washington, Seattle, 1947 [a collection of documents and clippings in Korean and English, available through the Library of Congress]; and Arthur L. Gardner, The Koreans in Hawaii: An Annotated Bibliography [Honolulu, 1971].) We acknowledge our indebtedness to the author for contributing to the historical knowledge of Koreans in America, an area in which there is an appalling dearth of information. To Mrs. Kingsley K. Lyu and Seung-Kwon Lyu, we extend a special note of thanks for granting us permission to print excerpts from the manuscript of the late author.]

The history of Koreans in the United States is in part the history of their political activities for the restoration of their national independence. The first arrival of Koreans in this country was the Korean Diplomatic Mission, headed by Young-ik Min, the cousin of Queen Min of Korea, which arrived in September of 1883. . . . to strengthen Korean independence against outside forces with the help of the American government.[1] . . .

Korean immigrants did not come in large numbers to the Hawaiian sugar plantations until the latter part of 1902. Korean men and women numbering 102 aboard the *S. S. Gaelic* at Yokohama on December 22, 1902 arrived at Honolulu on January 12, 1903. The destination of this group was to be the Mokuleia Sugar Plantation on Oahu. There are still about a half dozen of those [who were] aboard the Gaelic. . ., namely, Mrs. Chi-woon Kim, Yi-che Kim, Chan-che Kim, Dashin Whang, Kisun Whang, and Taishin Park, living in Honolulu.[2] . . . From May 20, 1898 to December 31, 1905, then, 7,866 Koreans including 677 women and 465 children immigrated to Hawaii, and for the same period a total of 721 Koreans including 40 women and 28 children, left the territory.[3] This last group, although mostly recruited for the sugar plantations, later left for the continental United States and settled themselves in the coastal states. . . .

In order to stabilize them as a labor force the introduction of "picture brides," brought from

106

Koondan Military Drill

Korea, was permitted and, at times, encouraged, even after emigration from Korea was forbidden in 1905. Wives and relatives were to form the bulk of Korean immigration to this country after the summer of 1905.

The origin of "picture brides" to Hawaii is said to be three-fold: the contact of the families at home with their relatives in Hawaii, the returnees' contact with their friends in Hawaii, and the contact of "picture brides" with their friends in Korea. . . . [In] July, 1924 . . . the newly passed Immigration Laws finally closed the door for all Oriental "picture brides" entering the United States territory. The exact number of "picture brides" to Hawaii and the United States is not certain, but it may be assumed that there were more than 300 "picture brides" from 1910 to 1924.[4] . . .

Of the 7,395 adult Korean immigrants to Hawaii a minority had already become members of Protestant churches in Korea. They were either Presbyterians or Methodists, since other denominations were not yet known to the Koreans, and all opened their mission work later, except for the Catholics. Many of these Korean Christians were encouraged to emigrate to Hawaii by their American missionary friends. . . . The majority of the Korean emigrants who had already become Christians came to Hawaii with their families to settle down. They were looking forward to better living conditions than they had had in Korea. These families did not come to Hawaii as did the unmarried Koreans simply to

acquire a fortune and return, but rather they came to this country to live. In other words, these Korean Christian emigrants to Hawaii became the backbone of Korean colonies and mainspring of Korean nationalism in America. . . .

Nearly all of these men and women knew how to read and write the Korean language, because they had been taught the Korean written language before they were taken into the membership in a church. Some were even versed in the Chinese Classics. Naturally they tended to become leaders in their communities on the sugar plantations, educationally and socially as well as politically. Some of these Christian Koreans were soon elected by plantation managers and by the superintendent of the Methodist Missions in Hawaii to serve as pastors for the Korean congregations on each sugar plantation.[5] . . . This also led to the importation of trained Korean ministers from Korea, starting as early as 1906.

These trained pastors were soon joined by Korean-language school teachers and Korean students. Some of the American-educated Koreans chose to remain in Hawaii and the United States before and after the annexation of Korea by Japan in 1910. Chang-ho Ahn, Yong-man Park, Henry Chung, Syngman Rhee and others were some of the Korean students who chose to remain in this country.

Chang-ho Ahn, who was a patriot, educator, and popular speaker in Korea, was taken to the United States by an American missionary in 1897 or 1898 to study. When he returned to Korea, Ahn founded the

Daisung Middle School in Pyungyang, north Korea in 1905 or 1906.[6] However, he was soon forced to take refuge in the United States via Siberia in 1907 because of his antagonism to Japanese encroachment upon the sovereignty of Korea. In that year Ahn organized the Korean National Association in America and became its first president. The primary purpose of the Association was to secure collective security for the Koreans abroad and to engage in Korean nationalist activities. In 1908, he formed a secret organization called the Heungsa Dan, or the Militant Spirit Arousing Corps. The main objectives of this organization were to carry out Korean nationalist movement in secrecy, to strengthen his political position in the Korean National Association through the well-trained leadership of the Heungsa Dan members.

Yong-man Park came to the United States in 1904. He had already had some youthful experience of political activities in Korea. While he was studying at the Hastings. Military Academy, Nebraska, Park established the Young Korean Military School there and taught military science to Korean youth.[7] It was about 1908. Upon his graduation from the University of Nebraska in 1912,[8] he was appointed editor of the *New Korea*, the official organ of the Central Korean National Association at San Francisco and held the position until he was invited to Hawaii by the Hawaii Korean National Association in the latter part of the same year. Park became the editor of the *Korean National Herald*, the official organ of the Hawaii Korean National Association and took the reins of the Association.

Syngman Rhee landed in the United States to study in January of 1905, his youthful efforts in patriotic activities having resulted in failure.[9] He studied at George Washington University, Harvard University, and Princeton University, receiving a Ph.D. degree from the latter in June, 1910. Rhee returned to Korea to become General Secretary of the Korean Young Men's Christian Association in 1911. Because of Japanese censorship over Korean nationalism, however, he left Korea for Hawaii to become superintendent of the Methodist Mission's educational work for Koreans. He arrived in Honolulu sometime in April, 1913.

American-educated Koreans soon assumed leadership of their countrymen in Hawaii and the mainland United States. For some time there was a constant series of conflicts between the new and old leadership of Koreans. Some welcomed the new American-educated leadership, while others continued to follow the hand-picked leadership from the sugar cane fields. These Korean leaders held important positions in Korean organizations in America and in Hawaii. Some of them became the presidents of Korean societies, and still others held the editorships of the existing newspapers such as the *Korean National Herald* and the *Korean Pacific*

Weekly. These intellectual Koreans had become not only the source of strength in Korean nationalist activities, but also the storm center of political factionalism in Hawaii and the continental United States for over four decades.

MOTIVES FOR KOREAN IMMIGRATION TO HAWAII

There were various factors that motivated the Korean immigrants to come to Hawaii in the early 1900s. They were not imported as contract laborers. Unlike the other Oriental immigrants they emigrated to Hawaii as free laborers. Furthermore, the period of their emigration to Hawaii was very short — shorter than that for any other Oriental immigrants. The major Korean immigration lasted but four years from 1901 to April 1905.

However, there were certain pertinent factors in leading the 7,866 Koreans to immigrate to Hawaii and the United States. In the first place, there were apparent efforts of the Korean government to export the Koreans abroad. In the second place, there were the activities of the Korean Kaibal Hoisa or the Overseas Development Company. Thirdly, there was an American in the person of David W. Deshler whose main business was to make money through the Korean immigration to Hawaii. Lastly, there were undeniable influences of American missionaries upon the Korean Christians to emigrate to Hawaii. These factors will be discussed in detail in the following sections.

The Korean Government Efforts

Korean immigration to Hawaii was sponsored by the Korean government when the Korean laborers began to emigrate to Hawaii at the turn of the 20th century. According to the old laws of Korea, all Koreans were prohibited from emigrating to foreign countries. The Korean official position in regard to emigration, however, was changed when famine visited severely all over Korea in 1901. The Korean government was more than willing to change its official position regarding emigration. In fact the government actually established a new department to handle the emigration and encourage the people to emigrate abroad. This new department was called the Yumin Won or the Department of Immigration.[10]

According to the Korean immigrants here, the Korean government posted its proclamations for emigration to Hawaii in market places all over Korea. The official proclamations listed the conditions for laborers on the Hawaiian sugar plantations. The government also issued questions and answers for those applicants who wished to go to Hawaii to work. The questions and answers listed the following:

Yong-man Park (Pak Yong-man)
1881-1928

Syngman Rhee (Yi Sung-man)
1875-1965

Chang-ho Ahn (An Ch'ang-ho)
1878-1938

What is your name? My name is so and so. Where are you going? I am going to Hawaii. What is the purpose of your trip to Hawaii? I am going to work on sugar plantations. How much money do you have with you? I have $300, and etc.

When the applicants passed the examinations, they were given passports issued by the Department of Immigration of the Korean government. They were then led to living quarters nearby the Kaibal Hoisa local offices until they proceeded to Kobe, Japan in groups. The Korean Department of Immigration thus coordinated the emigration of Koreans to Hawaii, while the Kaibal Hoisa acted as recruiting agents for the Korean Department of Immigration. There were local field offices of the Department of Immigration in Chemulpo, Seoul, Inchun, Kunsan, Mokpo, Taiku, and Pusan, and these immigration local offices were authorized to issue passports. . . .

The Activities of the Kaibal Hoisa or the Overseas Development Companies

Since the Kaibal Hoisa had been acting as one of the recruiting agents that recruited Korean immigrants for Hawaii, many Koreans were unable to distinguish the work of the Korean Department of Immigration from that of the Kaibal Hoisa. The function of the Kaibal Hoisa was to recruit Korean laborers and send them to the Hawaiian Islands. There were clerks and interpreters at all the field offices of the Kaibal Hoisa who were cooperating with the local offices of the Department of Immigration and were authorized to even issue Korean passports to those recruits. The Kaibal Hoisa furnished the transportation for the labor recruits from the local office to Kobe, Japan, and then the field office of the Kaibal Hoisa at Kobe took care of their transportation to Hawaii, when they passed their physical examinations.

There was apparently more than one Kaibal Hoisa. . . . all recruiting Korean immigrants.[11]

The activities of the Kaibal Hoisa were to recruit Korean laborers for the Hawaiian sugar plantation companies, by the promise of high wages and other advantages such as school education for those willing to study in the evening schools and free education for children and etc. Besides, the free transportation to Hawaii had attracted wandering young peddlers, gold diggers, some 300 ex-soldiers of the Korean Army, and the poverty-stricken poor people, who had suffered most from the oppression of Korean officials and the rich class of people.

As to the free transportation for the Korean labor recruits for Hawaii, there are differences of opinions on the part of the Korean immigrants here. Some say that they were shipped over to Hawaii free of charge. Others say that they had borrowed $50

from the Kaibal Hoisa and paid it back to the agent of the Kaibal Hoisa at the Honolulu Immigration Station when they passed the question put to them by immigration officials. Still others state that they were given a check for $150 by the local recruiting office of the Kaibal Hoisa, and when they landed in Honolulu they were asked to give it back to the Kaibal Hoisa agent whose name was Yoonsup Park at the Honolulu Immigration Station. Still others claim that they were not given any money or check by the Kaibal Hoisa. They refused to pay their transportation expenses amounting to $150, when David W. Deshler and Chungsoo Ahn and others made a trip to Hawaii in 1905 to collect the money.

According to the letter of the American Minister at Seoul, [Horace N.] Allen, . . . "The Koreans are so poor that not many of them have the necessary funds without borrowing, for the purpose of emigrating with their families, but I am not at all inclined to think that this Government has any intention of assisting its people to emigrate by advancing the necessary funds."[12] It seems that up to the time of Allen's letter to Governor Dole there was apparently no agreement yet between the Kaibal Hoisa and the Hawaii Sugar planters on who was going to pay the Korean immigrants' transportation and other expenses.

It is, however, probable that the Kaibal Hoisa was assisted or subsidized by the Hawaii Sugar Planters Association in early 1900s. According to a "Letter of Transmission" (First Report of the Board of Immigration, January 31, 1907), . . . the Korean immigrants were one of many nationalities that had been subsidized.[13] The Report said in part: "The exact number of these immigrants is not certain, but there have been approximately 180,000 brought to this country, and a conservative estimate of the cost of bringing them here is approximately $9,000,000.00."[14]

Furthermore, according to the Commissioner of Labor's Report on Hawaii, 1905, there is evidence that emigration companies were subsidized to ease the labor situation for the planters. It said, in part,

. . . While the time for extending absolute exclusion to nationalities not at present so treated has passed, there is no probability that any relaxation in existing laws applying to the entire Union will benefit the employing interests of Hawaiian Islands, while any session of Congress may see legislation enacted that will make it illegal to subsidize emigration companies in other countries or to extend assistance to immigrant labor through Korean banks.[15]

Another factor that motivated the Korean immigration to the Hawaiian Islands in the early 1900s was the desire of the sugar planters in Hawaii to ease the labor situation. Many Japanese laborers left the Islands, when they had made enough money to live in Japan in a comparatively comfortable way. Furthermore, the Chinese were excluded from entering the United States territory by the Chinese Exclusion Act of 1882 as laborers. The Governor's Report for 1901 explains this fact plainly:

> An increased immigration of Japanese would not entirely relieve the situation, for as they now constitute the great majority of laborers on the plantations, it would seem to be a sounder policy to augment the Japanese immigration with some other nationality.[16]

This other nationality was apparently to be meant for Koreans, since "Japanese and Koreans are the only two classes of aliens who present themselves for admission in any great numbers."[17]

The planters were reluctant to bring more Japanese laborers to the Hawaiian Islands, for they feared the solidarity of the Japanese and rather desired to break it up. The Report of the Commissioner of Labor, 1905, clearly shows this fact, and it said in part:

> ... the table of immigration shows the arrival of 7,394 Koreans from July 1, 1900 to December 31, 1905 ... If the immigration of Koreans continues at the same rate, the planters will have succeeded before long to a considerable extent in breaking up the solidarity of the plantation labor force and the consequent economic control now held by the Japanese on the plantations.[18]

... The Korean emigration to Hawaii was apparently stopped by the Japanese pressure upon the Korean officials. ... Korea was placed under the protectorate of Japan formally in 1905. Korea had to follow the suit of Japan, when the Root-Takahira Agreement of 1908 had caused Japan to cease the Japanese [labor] emigration to Hawaii and the United States voluntarily.

Rise of Korean Nationalism from 1903 to 1910

When the immigrant Koreans began to work in the same cane fields with the Japanese, Chinese, Portuguese, Hawaiians and other races the sense of nationality grew stronger than ever before. ... This racial self-consciousness on the part of the Korean immigrants became a factor of Korean nationalism in Hawaii.

From the need of defending and protecting their fellow countrymen from other nationalities there came into existence two movements, namely, the local societies of Koreans for mutual benefit, and the sworn brotherhood among the plantation working Koreans. These two things did much for the arousing of Korean nationalism, on the one hand, and for the creation of Korean factionalism in the later years, on the other. For example, many local Korean societies later forgot their primary objectives of protecting the mutual interests of their fellow countrymen, because they could not transcend the narrow scope of localism. Those from the same localities in Korea cliqued together and became a source of weakness for Korean societies in the later years.

Furthermore, the sworn brotherhood among the Korean immigrants also had merits as well as demerits because of its scope. ... Some Koreans had 50 or 60 sworn brothers in the hope that they might be well protected. ...[19] If any of the sworn brothers had quarrels with any foreigners, all the brothers became one in unity to help him. If any of their number were sick, he was assisted financially, morally, and otherwise. The scope of these sworn brotherhoods included merely mutual protection from foreigners, at first, but later on the scope was further extended to resistance to all those not belonging to their own brotherhood. By tatooing on the arms sworn brothers were identified.

Furthermore, Korean colonies in Hawaii were organized wherever there were Koreans with their families on the sugar plantations. There were more than 600 Korean families in the Hawaiian Islands by December, 1905, for there had arrived already some 677 adult Korean women out of the 7,860 [sic] Korean immigrants from 1901 to 1905. These families did not live at one place, but were scattered on different plantations. And yet, these families played a major role in the Korean Societies; they ... became the backbone and mainspring in the nationalist activities of Koreans in this country. Most of these families were running the kitchens called the *Koksang* for single Koreans. More than 6,000 single and unmarried Koreans got their board chiefly through the Korean families, though they lived in their separate quarters. Korean womenfolks, naturally, were cooking and laundering for most of the single and unmarried Koreans in order to help their family finance.[20] ...

The Establishment of Korean Language Schools in Hawaii

When 7,860 Korean immigrants arrived in Hawaii from 1901 to 1905, there were 465 children under 14 years of age.[21] Although some of these children were too young to go to schools, most of them were sent to public schools. All the Korean families keenly felt the need of teaching their children their mother tongue. In the first place, by teaching the Korean language to their children, who were going to the English-speaking schools, these children could act as their interpreters. In the second place, they wanted to bring up their children as Koreans. . . .

. . . There was, however, a tendency on the part of the public as well as the authorities of the Territory to suppress foreign language schools. The result was the foreign language school legislation, enacted as Act 30 of the Legislature in special session, November 1920.[22] . . . This suppression [of] foreign language schools made all nationalism in foreign language schools go underground.

It was quite natural for the immigrant Koreans to continue their nationalistic ties with their old country. It was more so when they had left behind a fatherland which was being exploited by Japanese and Russian imperialists. . . . This sentiment led to the formation of Korean patriotic societies in the United States and Hawaii.[23]

Korean Patriotic Societies Abroad

According to one of the Korean leaders in Hawaii, Hongki Lee, who participated in the major Korean nationalist activities, the first Korean society in Hawaii was formed at Kapaa, Kauai, in December 1904. . . . the Shinmin Hoi or the New People's Society. The aim of this society was to rebuild Korea with regenerated people at home and abroad. Many Koreans who did not belong to the Shinmin Hoi did not like the radical ideas of its members and dubbed it the Yerkchuk Hoi or the Traitor's Society.[24]

The next Korean society was formed in October, 1905 at Hanapepe, Kauai as the Hawaii branch of the Chakang Hoi or the Self-strengthening Society of Seoul, Korea. . . . to reform Korea from inward and self-efforts, and not from outside aid by some other nation's efforts.[25] . . .

By 1906 on every large island there were Korean organizations for the protection of Korean interests at home and abroad. It was felt, however, that there was need of a united society for all Koreans in the Territory of Hawaii. Local Korean societies were not enough to meet the needs of all Koreans in Hawaii and many Korean leaders came to an agreement to [form] a united society for all the Koreans on the Hawaiian plantations. The Hapsung Hoi, or the United Society for Hawaii was formed thus in the latter part of 1906.[26] . . .

In the mainland United States, the Kookmin Hoi or the Korean National Association was organized under the leadership of Chang-ho Ahn in 1907. The purpose of the Association was to represent the Korean interests in the United States. It was the primary objective of the Association to protect Korean nationals economically and politically in this country. Although the charter of the Association described it as a non-political, non-profit, eleemosynary corporation, in practice it was nothing but a political organization. The president of the Associa-

tion acted as if he were a consul-general, the presidents of its local chapters as consuls in those localities, and the *Kyung-chal Puchang* as the chief of police. The mainland headquarters of the Korean National Association had at one time complete charge over the Hawaii headquarters of the Korean National Association at Honolulu, almost as if it were the Korean Embassy in the United States. The Hawaii Korean National Association annually sent delegates to the mainland headquarters at San Francisco for the annual convention.[27]

The Hapsung Hoi of Hawaii, or the United Society was changed in name to the Hawaii Korean National Association. The purpose of changing the name in 1909 was apparently motivated by the desire to unite its strength with the mainland Korean National Association. Korea was about to be annexed, and all patriotic societies needed a united front in America. Chang-ho Ahn was elected president of the Choong-ang Chong-hoi, or the Central Headquarters of all Korean National Associations in the United States. Ahn as the president of the Central Headquarters of the Korean National Association was to supervise all Korean nationalist activities in this country, including Hawaii. His leadership was unfortunately soon to be challenged by rivals, namely Yong-man Park and Syngman Rhee, as shall be seen in the following chapters. . . .

THE CRUSADING ACTIVITIES OF KOREAN NATIONALISTS IN THE UNITED STATES AND HAWAII FROM 1910 TO 1919

As the result of the Protectorate of Korea by Japan created in 1905, the Korean government became merely a Japanese puppet, and it was only a matter of time for Korea to be annexed by Japan finally in 1910. The processes of the Japanese annexation of Korea by means of the Protectorate treaties were opposed by the Koreans sporadically. They employed the technique of guerilla warfare against the Japanese regime in Korea all through these years. The organized guerilla war was started in July, 1907 and continued to harass the Japanese police and gendarmerie in Korea from the rugged mountains until 1912. After 1913 this organized guerilla force called the Righteous Army, and many Korean patriots took refuge in Manchuria, and Siberia as well as China. . . .[28]

In the meantime, the Japanese regime in Korea had taken very militaristic, stern measures to blot out the awakening spirit of Korean nationalism by setting up a thorough-going military rule. Many patriots were put to death and other suspected patriots were put in jails. Many nationalist activities in Korea began to be carried out in the underground. For this reason, many Korean patriots were forced to get out of Korea into exile. . . .

112

Furthermore, the period in question was politically very important in that all the Korean nationalist activities at home and abroad were centered in one direction and that was the establishment of a provisional Korean government. Up to this time the Korean independence movement had been rather disconcerted, but from now on it became unified under the leadership of the Korean Provisional Government-in-exile. In other words, all Koreans at home and abroad looked up to the provisional government as the symbol of their hope for the restoration of Korean independence. They believed that some day the Japanese regime would surely be succeeded by this provisional government-in-exile. . . .

As soon as their political activities were unified in the name of the Korean Provisional Government in Shanghai, Korean political leaders abroad commenced another epoch-making step in their independence movement by establishing a diplomatic agency in Washington. The agency called the Korean Commission was set up in April, 1919, when the peaceful revolution of the preceding month in Korea startled the world.[29] The following section will be devoted to the preparatory activities of two leading patriots in Hawaii, whose policies on the restoration of Korean independence were diametrically different from one another. They were Yong-man Park and Syngman Rhee.

POLITICAL RIVALRY BETWEEN YONG-MAN PARK AND SYNGMAN RHEE

As has been observed in the preceding chapters, some 300 ex-soldiers of the Korean army were recruited among the 7,860 Korean immigrants to the Hawaiian Islands. The average age of these ex-soldiers was about 25. . . . They were largely discharged by the Japanese army advisers for their loyalty to their country and patriotic activities.[30] They emigrated to the Hawaiian plantations. . . .

When they arrived in the Islands, they began to practice military drill whenever they found convenient time. Almost all the Korean camps on the plantations witnessed the practice of military drills of young Koreans together with some former Korean soldiers for some time. According to the interviews of the writer with some former Korean soldiers, some plantation managers disliked the military drills and ordered the practices stopped. . . but the Koreans on the plantations on Kauai and at Kahuku continued their weekly drills until their recruitment in the Korean Military Academy under Yong-man Park.[31]

Born in the Yangban class, or gentry of Korea, Yong-man Park was early associated with many patriotic activities there. As a youth of 14 Park became a sworn brother of Syngman Rhee and Soo-man Chung [and their] nationalist activities

against Japan had put them in jail even before the Russo-Japanese War [1904-1905]. As soon as he broke prison, Park [hid] . . . among the students of the Paichai Mission School, who were at that time just going on an excursion to Inchun, or Chemulpo. He was immediately taken abroad a steamer with the help of an American missionary and the Rev. Dukki Chun. It was early 1904 when he arrived in the United States.

After working as a laborer on the transcontinental railroads for some time, he was admitted to the Hastings Military Academy, Nebraska. While a student there, Park himself established a military school for Korean youth.[32] . . .

Upon his graduation from the University of Nebraska in June, 1912, Park accepted an invitation from the Central Board of the Korean National Association [of North America] at San Francisco to be the editor of its official organ, *The New Korea* [Sin-Han Minbo] and remained there until the later part of the year. . . . When Park was urged to accept the post of editor of the *Korean National Herald* by Sang-ha Park and other officials of the Korean National Association of Hawaii, he decided to accept it in December of 1912. His decision to remain in Hawaii. . . usher [ed] in a new era for Korean nationalist movement here.[33] . . .

[Syngman] Rhee came to Honolulu [in April 1913] to become the principal of the Choong-ang Hakwon known as the Korean Compound. He was given control over Korean educational work in the Hawaii Methodist Missions. . . .

According to Moonsur Yang, when Yong-man Park arrived in Hawaii he had already collected some funds for establishing a Korean language high school. Hongki Lee confirms this story. . . . What Park had in mind was to make the Korean high school an Officers' candidate school. . . . This ambition of Park soon materialized when he and Rhee and others held an organizational meeting. . . in December of 1913. . . [and] decided to open the military school in the following April.[34]

When the military school, or the Koondan, literally meaning military corps, was opened in April, 1914, there were about 80 students, most of them from the rank and file of the former Korean army. Yong-man Park became the principal of the Military Academy and the commandant of the Koondan. . . . The first building of the Koondan was erected with contributions from among the Koreans. The dedication ceremony was held in August, 1915. . . . at Ahemanu, Koolau District; there were about 800 Koreans present. . . .

The spirit of militarism was then high among the Koreans in Hawaii. But the zeal for military activities of the Koondan was soon to die out in the following years. There were several factors that led to the disbandment of the Koondan. Some alleged that the jealousy of Rhee over the popularity of Yong-man

Park was the cause of its dissolution. Others admitted the jealousy of the lower ranks toward those who had held higher ranks. Still others charged swindling of the Koondan finance by those who were in charge of it.[35] Park continued to act as editor of the *Korean National Herald* until 1917 and held an important place in the policy-making body of the Korean National Association of Hawaii. . . .

However, the seed of disputes among the Korean societies in Hawaii began to grow rapidly, because it was planted in the fertile soil of rival leadership between Syngman Rhee and Yong-man Park. . . . Those siding with Rhee lavishly denounced Park as a traitor to the cause of Korean independence. Sukchoo Ko and Yongwhan Seung put out weekly propaganda materials against Park as being a drunkard and indulging in extravagant parties with beautiful ladies etc. They employed high-handed methods to win opponents over to their side. . . .[36]

Moonsur Yang asserts that Rhee carried out his anti-Yong-man Park propaganda through his lieutenants from early 1916 on, both by writings and by speeches. Rhee himself went to outer Islands often to seek support from the Koreans there. Sang-ha Park states that Rhee became jealous of Park (Yong-man) because of the large crowd of supporters for the Koondan. Taikyun Park asserts that about 90 percent of the Koreans in Hawaii supported and followed the leadership of Yong-man Park then. All those men charged that Rhee, even though he would lose his supporters to Park, came out gradually to oppose and undermine the activities of the Koondan. . . .

In time the Koondan supporters were won over to the educational activities of Syngman Rhee gradually and the Military Academy faced increasing financial difficulties. The members of the Koondan had been engaged in raising pineapples and the profits therefrom were to be used for the support of the school. . . . Indeed, contributions from the Koreans dwindled away considerably and the pineapple raising brought forth little profits, if any. The Koondan had to give up the academy at Ahemanu, Koolau district and moved to Kahuku plantation by early 1917. There it continued until the late autumn of the same year.

In 1917, Rhee wrote an article in his *Korean Pacific Magazine* criticizing Park's Koondan activities. Many of the Koondan members naturally were

Kungmin Koondan (Korean National Military Corps) in Hawaii

114

enraged against Rhee and wanted to kill him. But Park blocked the scheme and admonished them not to do so. . . .

And those who sided with Park in the Korean National Association of Hawaii left no stone unturned in finding fault with the administration that had been under the influence of Rhee. Disputes over the matter of the finance of the Society went from bad to worse. . . .

In other words, there were now two factions formed in the Korean National Association of Hawaii: the one supporting Rhee, and the other following Park. The pro-Park faction charged that Chipum Hong, Hansik Hong, Chungsoo Ahn, and Hyunkyung Ahn, in cooperation with Rhee, [were] attempting to make the Association nothing more than a Rhee club. The Rhee faction was enraged by the charge and came out to brand the pro-Park group as traitors to the cause of Korea. Some 100 persons were so branded by Rhee and his followers.[37]

However, Yong-man Park tried to heal up the wounds of the fractionalism [sic] among the Koreans in Hawaii and attempted to reunite the two factions. Park published the Lyunhap Kongpo, or the United Official News in the hope that it might create a harmonious spirit among the members of the Association. It was, however, fruitless and the Park faction held together firmly from 1917 on, and finally, on March 3, 1919, the Toklip Dan, or the League of Independence was formally organized.[38] The Korean Pacific Times, or the Taipyeng-yang Shisa was published on the linotype as the organ of the Toklip Dan by Sukcho Lee and Yong Hur from 1919.

. . . Park was recruited by the United States Siberian Expeditionary Forces to act as an intelligence officer and went to the Far East on a United States transport in May, 1919.[39] When the American Expeditionary Forces withdrew from maritime Siberia, Park decided to remain in China to become the Foreign Minister of the Provisional Korean Government-in-exile at Shanghai, China.[40] During this period he became acquainted with the scholar-general P'ei-fu Wu, who later held the reins of government at Peking for sometime. Park and General Wu agreed to set up a Korean military headquarters in North China from which Koreans could cooperate with China to regain their national independence. . . .

Yong-man Park returned to Hawaii about May, 1925.[41] Upon his return, the first thing he did was to see Rhee. However, the followers of Syngman Rhee branded him as a Bolshevik. Some Koreans who did not like Park petitioned the Immigration Service to deport him on the ground that he was a Communist. The pro-Park faction charged that it was done by Rhee himself. Strange enough the Immigration Service notified Park to leave Hawaii by the Asama Maru next day. After many hectic experiences, finally Park was granted freedom to stay in the United States. . . .[42]

When Park received a letter from General Wu requesting him to return to China for the contemplated plan for a military school, he went back to China in early 1927. . . . He trained some 300 Chinese and Korean soldiers for six months period. . . .[43]

Assassination of Yong-man Park

However, a tragic incident for the Korean nationalist movement occurred there in China, when Yong-man Park was assassinated by a Korean fanatic, on October 17, 1928. He could do much more for the cause of Korean nationalist activities if there was no such tragedy. The militant spirit of Park sadly died out with his last breath at the hands of the assassin. Only the patriotic songs which he wrote for the Koreans in Hawaii still are sung by the living Koreans, recalling his militant spirit.[44] . . .

It was . . . impossible for Korean educators and patriots to train the young Koreans in Korea proper, because of the Japanese regimentation of Korean institutions after 1910. No subjects that might arouse Korean nationalism were permitted to be taught in schools, and Korean history and language were naturally included in the list of the prohibition. For this reason, many patriots were either driven out of the country or put themselves into voluntary exiles abroad. Some went to Siberia, others escaped to China and Manchuria, and still others came to the United States in the hope that they might here be engaged in Korean independence movement.[45]

The appearance of Syngman Rhee on the scene of the communities in Hawaii was also motivated by his desire to be engaged in Korean nationalist activities,[46] . . . he had been very active in patriotic and reform movement while he was still in his teen-age. For his patriotic activities he had been jailed for some years in Seoul Prison before his arrival in the United States in the early part of 1905. . . . He then went to Washington to study at the George Washington University. Later he enrolled at Princeton University, majoring in political science under President Woodrow Wilson, and was awarded a Ph.D. degree in 1912.[47]

Being the first holder of a Ph.D. degree among Koreans from an American university, the arrival of Syngman Rhee in Hawaii increased the prestige of the Korean community in the Islands considerably. All the Koreans here began to look up at him as a leader when he was installed as the principal of the Choong-ang Hakwon, or the Korean Boarding School in Honolulu, in June, 1913. . . . in charge of Korean educational work in Hawaii . . . . He could thus easily carry out his leadership training program for the young Koreans in the Territory. . . .

As we have seen, however, there was already another Korean leader who had held a position of importance in the Korean community here prior to the arrival of Rhee. . . . Park was a firm believer in democracy as the *Constitutions of the Korean National Association of Hawaii* and the *League of Korean Independence,* which he wrote for them, remind [us] of his democratic spirit clearly. . . . What Park wanted to do was to teach the democratic way of life to the Koreans in Hawaii. Furthermore, believing in democracy, he advocated that the business of the Association should be conducted in accordance with the rules and by-laws provided for in the constitutions.

On the other hand, Syngman Rhee felt that the mass of ignorant Koreans should be directed toward what democracy is. He felt that majority rule for ignorant people could be a dangerous obstacle to any democratic institutions. When a majority decision by the mass of ignorant people seems to hurt their cause and their general welfare, someone who knows better should tell them to stop it. In other words, the people must be educated, and for the duration of their education they must be wisely directed by educated leaders. It is not strange to see why he was so anxious to become the power behind the throne for the Korean societies in the Territory. It is alleged that Rhee often told the Koreans, "If you want Korean independence, raise the Independence fund; if you have $5, bring it to me; if you have $10, also bring it to me; the more the Independence funds you raise for me, the quicker I will restore Korean Independence to you!"[48]

Yong-man Park and Syngman Rhee soon agreed that the spheres of their activities should be divided. The training of the Koreans in military science and guerilla warfare was placed in the hands of Park while educational and diplomatic activities of the Koreans were entrusted with Rhee.[49]

The first school Rhee established was the Korean Girls' Seminary in Honolulu. . . . Rhee was the principal of the seminary as well as of the Choong-ang Hakwon.

At this junction, a word or two must be said in order to explain the relationship between Rhee and Superintendent [Wm. Henry] Fry. . . . appointed as superintendent of the Hawaiian Methodist Mission in January of 1914. . . . [Fry] was ambitious to supervise every detail of the Mission, and he made no exception to the rule for the school administration of the Korean Compound. Especially, he wanted to know every detail of the financial matters of the school. Moreover, Fry objected to the use of the school as a training ground of politicians or for political activities.[50] . . .

Rhee wanted to teach Korean nationalism and train Korean political leaders. He would not take the orders from Superintendent Fry, for, he declared, the Korean Compound was built for the Koreans and not for the Americans. Besides, Rhee asserted that since the Korean Methodist Church and the Korean Boys'

School have been supported almost entirely with the money contributed by the Koreans in Hawaii, self-government for these institutions should be granted to the Koreans. . . . This demand was flatly refused by Superintendent Fry, and the result was that Rhee and Fry became enemies and there were divisions in the Korean Methodist Church and the Korean Compound from 1916 on.[51] . . .

The progress of self-rule for Koreans would have been far better accomplished and it would have been better for the administration of his churches, if Rhee had told his followers to strictly observe the constitution and the by-laws of the church, which he wrote. Of many characteristics he has a peculiar propensity for the fear of losing his supporters.[52] Another characteristic of his is to demand from his followers a slavish obedience.[53] . . . Many life-long and faithful supporters were cast aside because they dared to raise questions about his directives. Since this was the case, many of his ignorant followers knowingly or unknowingly hurt the cause of his work. They could make an ardent supporter appear treacherous by just accusing him of being a doubter or critic.[54]

So far as the training program for Korean leaders was concerned, Syngman Rhee pioneered many things in Hawaii. The first thing was the establishment of the Korean Girls' Seminary, and then the Korean Christian Institute. The next was the formation of the Dongji Hoi and the Dongji Investment Company. The last and not the least was the separation of his group in the Korean Methodist Church and [the founding of] the Korean Christian Churches in Hawaii. These pioneering projects became the monuments for his life-time work in Hawaii, though some of them turned out to be in failure.

DECLARATION OF INDEPENDENCE OF KOREA, MARCH 1, 1919

Many of the Korean people did not understand the true meaning of the annexation of Korea by Japan in 1910, until some striking changes took place in their daily life. This history of Korea was banned from the schools, the Japanese language replaced Korean, and the government officials were gradually replaced by the Japanese. Whenever there were disputes between Japanese residents in Korea and the Koreans, always the Japanese were right, and the Koreans were wrong. Korean children were forced to serve the Japanese sometimes, because of the foreclosure of the property of their family by the Japanese usurers or by the Oriental Development Company. They had no place to appeal because they had lost their independence to Japan.

The gospel of the self-determination for small nations was timely rung into the ears of the Koreans

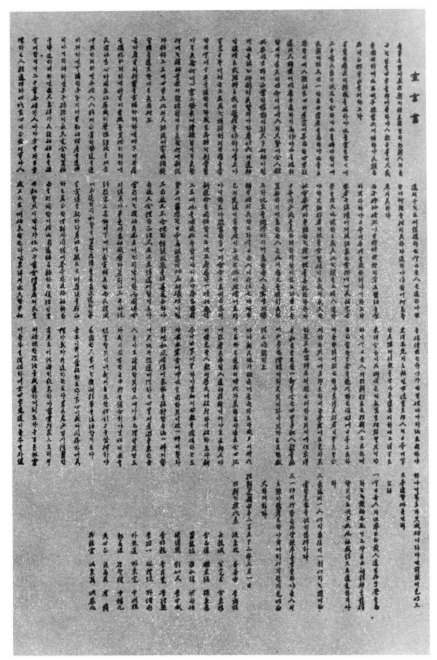

The Korean Declaration of Independence, 1 March 1919

when President Wilson advocated the rights of small nations in his famous Fourteen Points. He explained that the purpose of the League of Nations was "to provide for the freedom of small nations by big ones." Furthermore, the principle of self-determination of the peoples of the world gave the Korean people great courage to rise up against the swords and machine guns of Japanese military might with bare fists.

On March 1, 1919, the Declaration of Independence of Korea was signed by 33 Korean patriots and read to the Korean people. An organized passive revolution broke out throughout the whole country and continued throughout April. On April 16, representatives from the 13 provinces assembled in Seoul and constituted themselves a National Council and proceeded to formulate a constitution. They elected officers of the new Republic of Korea, and Syngman Rhee was chosen as Chief Executive, or the *Chipchungkwan Chong chai.*

However, the newly formed Republic was without its territory, because Korea was still occupied by the armies of Japan then. When the first cabinet meeting [of] the new government-in-exile was held in the early summer of 1919 in Shanghai, China, President Rhee was absent in the United States. Other cabinet members consisted of leaders who had escaped from Korea: Premier Dong Whi Lee; Minister of Foreign Affairs, Yong-man Park; Minister of Interior, Dong Yung Lee; Minister of War, Paiklin Lo; Minister of Finance, Si Young Lee; Minister of Law, Kiu Sik Shin; Minister of Education, Kiusic Kimm;

Minister of Communications, Chang Pum Moon; Director of Bureau of Labor, Chang-ho Ahn; Chief of Staff, Tong Yul Lew; Cive [sic] Chiefs of Staff, Sei Yung Lee and Nam Soo Hahn.[55]

Even before the news about the Korean independence revolution of March 1, 1919 had reached Rhee and the Koreans in Hawaii, he hurried to Washington, D.C., in the preceding January. Some two scores of leading Korean patriots met in Independence Hall, Philadelphia, and read the Declaration of Korean Independence and held a Liberty Conference there. Among them were the venerable patriots Philip Jaisohn, Syngman Rhee, Henry Chung, Hugh Cynn and others present. In consultation with other compatriots, Rhee established the Korean Commission at Washington, D.C. and appointed Kiusic Kimm as its first chairman. The purpose of the commission was to act as the diplomatic agency for the Korean Provisional Government-in-exile at Shanghai. The staff of the Korean Commission consisted of Soon Hyun as treasurer, [and] Henry Chung as secretary when it was officially opened in April, 1919.[56] The first official effort of the Commission was to get the Korean Provisional Government-in-exile recognized by the Government of the United States. The next was to attend the Peace Conference at Paris. Third effort was to raise funds to carry on the Korean nationalist activities by issuing the bonds for the new Republic, as is shown in the Certificate of Indebtedness.[57] . . .

SPLITS WITHIN THE KOREAN INDEPENDENCE MOVEMENT IN HAWAII

As has been noted above already, there had been a division in the Korean National Association of Hawaii from 1915. From 1918 there were divisions even in the Rhee group in the Korean National Association. . . .

Up to this time [1920], the Korean National Association of Hawaii had given financial support to him but it was not as full a support as he desired. There had always been some bickering about its financial reports, for the power behind the throne, i.e., Rhee, as the unofficial adviser, refused to make reports to the Korean National Association meetings. The reason for that was that he believed he was above any Korean societies. His followers insisted that it would be an insult to him if he were so required to make reports to the meeting concerning any money raised for him. On the other hand, some members of the Association wanted to know where he spent its money.[58]

Since that was the case, Syngman Rhee wanted to have his own society, which would finance him unconditionally and wholeheartedly. He wanted to form a large political party whose membership could

embrace one million, and whose finance could become the backbone of the whole national economy. These ideas were expressed in the "Three Great Principles" of the Korean Dongji Hoi,[59] which he and his followers organized. . . .

Formation of Dongji Hoi by Rhee

The aim of the Dongji Hoi then was to uphold the spirit of Korean independence which manifested in the March First peaceful revolution of 1919, and to recruit millions of Koreans into the membership of the Dongji Hoi, or the Like-minded People's Society. . . . Ostensibly, the Dongji Hoi was a part of the Korean National Association of Hawaii until its separation from the Association in 1929.

The organization of the Dongji Hoi was criticized by opponents as something similar to a benevolent monarchy. Syngman Rhee as the founder held the title of Chongchai, or advising director, for life. . . . In other words, Rhee as Chongchai was above all the laws provided for in the constitution.

Many ardent supporters and followers of Syngman Rhee tried to correct the arbitrary organization of the Dongji Hoi, and many were expelled by him for such appeal to him. . . . He lost many of [his] faithful followers in the Democratization Revolt of Henry Cu Kim, 1929 to 1931. Some of them rejoined the Korean Methodist Church, and others joined the Toklin Dan, or League of Korean Independence. Still others formed their own organizations. Since this revolt against Rhee, the Dongji Hoi has been completely at odds, the avowed enemy of the Korean National Association. This split of the Korean nationalists in Hawaii greatly weakened the cause of their independence movement in succeeding years. . . .

Sensing the approach of 2nd World War not too far away, Syngman Rhee determined to carry on the Korean independence movement at Washington and left Honolulu with his wife.[60] He then reopened the Korean Commission in the later fall of 1939 and resumed its chairmanship.[61] The reopening of the Korean Commission was for the third time since its establishment in April, 1919! The Dongji Hoi decided to send him $1000 a month. Syngwoon Sohn became the president of the Dongji Hoi and faithfully carried out its pledges until 1946. Rhee then went back to Korea.

The Japanese attack on Pearl Harbor came on December 7, 1941. The Koreans abroad . . . now had the most powerful country in the world as an ally. They were more than glad to do their small part in winning the war against their arch enemy – Japan. The political and diplomatic activities of Syngman Rhee and the Korean Commission were injected with a sudden boom. Many Koreans in the United States and Hawaii began to campaign for the purchase of

War Bonds. Young Koreans volunteered to join the United States Armed Forces. Almost all the Korean students in this country were recruited to serve as interpreters and translators for the Army and Navy. Some Koreans enlisted in the Marine Corps as interpreters and risked their lives in the Solomons and New Guinea jungles.[62]

... Many Koreans contributed their small part to the winning of the war by giving as much as they could. In Hawaii alone, a total of $26,000 was raised from among the Koreans, and was donated to the Commanding General, Lt. General Richardson, as a token of their willingness in defeating Japan.[63] Dongji Hoi alone raised some $36,000 in support of the Korean Commission and the Korean Provisional Government-in-exile at Chungking, China from October, 1944 to 1945.[64] It would have been impossible for Syngman Rhee to return to Seoul in October, 1945 if Dongji Hoi had not advanced him a sum of $10,000.

Formation of Kyomin Dan by Rhee in 1921

The Korean nationalist activities in America were centered in the two cities, namely, San Francisco and Honolulu, from early 1910s, because the headquarters of the Korean National Association [was] there. These two headquarters of the Korean National Association were able to control all political activities of the Koreans in this country, because all local Korean societies had been then united into this Association. The objectives of the Korean National Association were to promote and protect the mutual interests of Koreans in America and Hawaii, and to carry out their political activities effectively and collectively....

The name of the Korean National Association of Hawaii, however, was changed to the Kyomin Dan, or the Korean Residents Association, by the order of Syngman Rhee, when he came back from the first cabinet meeting of the Korean Provisional Government at Shanghai, in 1921.[65] There were several reasons for this move. In the first place, President Rhee was desirous of strengthening his position in America by this action. He said that the objectives of the Korean National Association had been fulfilled by the establishment of the Korean Provisional Government-in-exile. All the political and other nationalist activities should be carried on by this Provisional Government, of which he had been elected president by the Provisional National Council headed by Yee Man Jik, on April 16, 1919.[66] The functions of the Kyomin Dan then would be to carry out the orders of the Provisional Government, to promote friendly relations for resident Koreans and to carry on social functions for local Koreans.

By this order, President Syngman Rhee placed all Korean societies on an equal footing. The Kyomin Dan, the Toklin Dan, the Dongji Hoi, and the Korean Women's Relief Society all recognized the authority of the Korean Provisional Government and supported it financially. This meant to Rhee and his followers nothing less than the recognition of the authority of President Syngman Rhee. Whatever he said and did carried more weight than any other persons. He was in such a powerful position that he could even influence some federal and local government agencies in this country, as many Korean leaders later asserted.[67] ...

Another factor for the move was that Syngman Rhee wanted to test his strength on this side of the world. .... It is said that Rhee had had a difficult time at the first cabinet meeting at Shanghai, when almost all of his cabinet members and other leaders of the Provisional Government questioned and condemned the proposed mandate of the League of Nations over Korea. According to a public statement condemning Syngman Rhee and Henry Chung, Rhee and Chung had submitted such a petition to the League through the Department of State of the United States in 1920.[68] Kiusic Kimm, a special envoy of the Korean Provisional Government to the Paris Peace Conference, upon returning, stated that such a petition for a Mandate for Korea had come to the notice of the League of Nations. Korean leaders and revolutionists had been outraged by Rhee's action, and he was actually obliged to flee from Shanghai, for his life, in 1921.

Democratization Revolt, 1929-1931

Then the so-called Democratization Revolt against Syngman Rhee broke out in 1929 and continued until 1931 under the leadership of his long trusted associate, Henry Cu Kim. According to Duk-yin Shon, who was elected president of the Kyomin Dan for 1929-30, Henry Kim had been treasurer of the Kyomin Dan and the editor of the *Korean National Herald.* The trouble started when officers of the Kyomin Dan refused to mortgage its property for Rhee, when he wanted to reorganize the Dongji Investment Company which faced bankruptcy then. This refusal enraged Rhee and consequently he demanded Henry Kim to resign the position of the treasurer of the Kyomin Dan....

Moreover, Rhee declared that the Annual Delegates Conference of the Dongji Hoi in 1930 passed a resolution to the effect that all political activities of the Koreans in America should be carried out under a unified command. It would be a good thing and welcome news to all Koreans if a united front for the Korean nationalists could be achieved, as the resolution proposed.[69]

Henry Cu Kim, however, was opposed to the unification movement, because he said that it would dissolve all existing Korean societies if there were just to be one society. Furthermore, Kim asserted that the Korean independence movement in this country had been the work of the Korean National Association and the present Kyomin Dan. Now Rhee had taken away all the political functions from the Kyomin Dan and gave them to his Dongji Hoi. Since the chief functions of the Kyomin Dan, namely, political activities, were taken away and since there is nothing important to be done by the Kyomin Dan, it would naturally die out if the political activities of the Kyomin were not restored to it.

All Korean societies in Hawaii held their allegiance to the Korean Provisional Government-in-exile in China. Taking advantage of his position as president of the Korean Provisional Government, Syngman Rhee was in a privileged position in which he could unify all Korean nationalist activities under the Provisional Government and under his leadership. But his attempt to do so was soon challenged by some Korean leaders, because he wanted to make the Dongji Hoi the strongest and leading organization among all Korean societies. His policy was to absorb all existing local Korean societies into the Dongji Hoi by permitting members of other societies to hold offices in the Dongji Hoi. For this reason, the Kyomin Dan, Toklin Dan, and Dongji Hoi members could hold offices in [more than one] . . . of the societies.[70] Through this interfusion of the membership in the Korean societies, Rhee wanted to influence and control their activities directly or indirectly.

Naturally, members of the oldest organization, the Kyomin Dan, or the Korean National Association [in Hawaii], were sensitive concerning the activities of the other societies. This sensitivity helped to stimulate rivalry and jealousy of the Kyomin Dan and the other two organizations. The result was that the Dongji Hoi and Kyomin Dan were entangled in the legal suits numbering 89 since the Democratization Revolt broke out in 1929.[71] . . .

As the result of the *Minchoong Wha,* or Democratization Revolt against the leadership of Syngman Rhee, the name of the Kyomin Dan was restored to the Korean National Association of Hawaii. The reason for the restoration of the former name was to mean the restoration of the political functions of the Kyomin Dan, which had been taken by Rhee. . . .

It must be said that the *Minchoong Wha* against the leadership of Syngman Rhee had many unfortunate effects upon the Korean nationalist movement abroad. The factional wounds suffered then have never since been healed. Very few Korean societies in Hawaii ever paid any attention to the support of the Korean Provisional Government-in-exile then, because they had been lost in the heated factional disputes for some years. The *Minchoong Wha* disputes caused a great financial loss to the Koreans in Hawaii, but the greater loss to the

Koreans here had been the indelible spiritual loss.

Dan Hap Hoi, or the United Society of Kauai, 1930

Appealing to Koreans abroad for unity and financial assistance, Koo Kim, then Minister of Home Affairs and Minister of War, in the Provisional Government of the Republic of Korea-in-exile at Shanghai, had been writing letters to many Korean leaders in America as well as Hawaii. . . .

To support the Provisional Government effectively, the Korean residents on Kauai agreed to form a United Society, or Dan Hap Hoi, on the occasion of celebrating the 12th anniversary of the Korean Declaration of Independence, on March 1, 1930. They decided to lay aside all their petty differences and renewed their pledge to support the Provisional Government. They began to collect funds, called the Korean Independence Fund, to support their compatriots in the Korean Provisional Government. . . .

In 1931, Koo Kim asked the Kauai Dan Hap Hoi for a large sum of money. He said he would like to use it for his contemplated trip to Moscow to see Stalin and other Soviet leaders. . . . But the number of Koreans living in Kauai was not large, only about 200. . . . They started an earnest campaign for the Independence Fund drive, as soon as Kim's letter was received. $1,000 was raised from among them, of which $500 was contributed by the treasurer, Sang-ho Kim.[72]

The money sent to Koo Kim was not, however, used for his contemplated trip to Moscow, as he later revealed in his letter to the Dan Hap Hoi. It was used for his startling plots for the assassination of Japanese military leaders in China. He personally supervised the funds for manufacturing bombs with which Bongchang Lee, a member of his "suicide squad" of the Provisional Government Army, was sent to Tokyo in an attempt to kill the *Mikado,* on January 8, 1932, as well observed by Robert T. Oliver. Lee threw a bomb into the midst of an imperial procession, but, due to a change in plans at the last minute, Hirohito was in a different car than expected and thus saved his life. A number of high Japanese officials in the procession, however, were killed or wounded. Oliver continued:

> In April 29, 1932, many prominent Japanese generals and government officials held a meeting in the Honkew Park in Shanghai to celebrate the conquest of Manchuria. Another of the Provisional Government's "suicide squad," Pong Kil Yun, . . . was able to get close enough to throw a powerful grenade onto the receiving platform. The Japanese Commander-in-Chief, Sirakawa, and General Kawahara were killed; Admiral Nomura, Ambassador to the United States at the time of Pearl

Harbor attack, was wounded and lost the sight of one eye; and nearly a dozen other high Japanese officials were injured.[73]

Once this incident at Shanghai startled the world, the Korean Provisional Government drew the attention of Chinese leaders. The Chinese government began to give some financial assistance to the Provisional Government of Korea. This cordial relation between the two governments politically and financially continued from 1932 through the 2nd world war. Generalissimo Chiang Kai-shek began to develop his admiration for the Korean patriotism and bravery, and became a close friend of Koo Kim.

The effect of the bombing by Pong Kil Yun was very great on the Koreans abroad. Koreans in this country began to renew their pledges of allegiance to the Provisional Government after the patriotic example of the Kauai Dan Hap Hoi. The Korean National Association and other local Korean societies began to collect Independence Funds and occasional financial assistance was given to the Provisional Government in China. The Dan Hap Hoi alone sent several thousand dollars to the Provisional Government until the mail service to China ceased in 1938 on account of the undeclared war of Japan with China.[74] . . .

The Korean National Army Service of Kauai in 1943

The Koreans on the Island of Kauai were well known to the Korean communities in Hawaii for their patriotic activities ever since they immigrated there. They were much dissatisfied with the activities of the United Korean Committee in America [headquarters in Honolulu and Los Angeles], which had been supposedly formed to support the Korean Commission and the Korean Provisional Government on April 1, 1941. The officers of the United Korean Committee tried to send some of its members to Chungking, where the Provisional Government had gone with the Chinese Nationalist Government. . . .

When the contemplated trip to Chungking could not be realized, Ho Kim, Jacob Kyungmu Dunn, Shidai Hahn, and other officials began to attack the supposedly ineffective work of the Korean Commission under Syngman Rhee. Ho Kim started a campaign for the removal of Rhee from the chairmanship by making speeches before Korean communities from Washington, D.C., to California. He attacked the manner of conducting the Korean Commission affairs by Rhee as outmoded, ineffective and undemocratic.[75] Through his influence on the United Korean Committee, that body decided to demand that the Provisional Government at Chungking, of which Koo Kim was chairman, recall Syngman Rhee from the chairmanship of the Korean Commission.

When the demand was refused by the Provisional

Government in the early fall of 1942 the United Korean Committee in America declared its financial support suspended. . . .

Knowing the urgent need of supporting the Korean Provisional Government at this opportune time for the restoration of their independence, the Korean compatriots on the Island of Kauai, for example, agreed unanimously to form a society to raise funds to support its activities. All the Korean residents of Kauai decided to withdraw their membership in the United Korean Committee, and they formed an organization called the Limsi Chungpu Koonsa Whowon Hoi, or Korean National Army Service of Kauai in December 1943, under the leadership of Kingsley K. Lyu, who had been working with the Office of War Information, Pacific Division, at San Francisco. The officers of the newly formed organization were as follows:

Kyungsur Lee, president; Kunsil Park, vice-president; Kingsley K. Lyu, secretary-treasurer; Chisam Cho, Mrs. So Yun Chun Kim, Hoyoung Chung, and Mrs. Mary Hahn Woo, committee members.[76]

News of the formation of the Korean National Army Service of Kauai was sent to the Korean Provisional Government at Chungking through Koo Kim in January, 1944. . . .

The Provisional Government in Chungking faced a serious predicament on account of lack of funds and of the "Nine Conditions" imposed upon it by the Chinese Government and military authorities about this time. The "Nine Conditions," demanded of the Provisional Korean Government, were, in short, to put the Korean National Army under the command of the Chinese Military Committee even after the war. The Chinese Military Committee would direct all activities of the Korean National Army and even the Korean Provisional Government would have no authority over its own army. Otherwise the Chinese Government would not give financial assistance to the Korean army as well as to the [Provisional] Government. . . .

Upon learning these conditions imposed upon the Korean Provisional Government by the Chinese military authorities, in the winter of 1942, the Korean compatriots on Kauai came out wholeheartedly in support of the Provisional Government. Within a few months, a few thousand dollars were collected from among the Koreans there. . . .

The patriotic activities of the Koreans on Kauai in supporting the Korean Provisional Government in China were not without some effects upon Korean societies in the Territory. In the winter of 1944, the Dongji Hoi and the Korean National Association of Hawaii began to collect military funds for the Provisional Government. The Dongji Hoi members subscribed to the Military Funds amounting to about $500, but the fund was never sent to the Provisional Government. The Korean National Association of

Hawaii collected more than $30,000 for the military activities of the Provisional Government, but not a penny was remitted to the fighting compatriots in Chungking. The money was later divided among the ten men and women of the Association, who went to the Korean capitol for "reconstruction" work in the summer of 1946.[77]

UNITED KOREAN COMMITTEE IN AMERICA, 1941

There had been a lack of unity among Korean societies in America as well as in Hawaii. Many Korean leaders continued to feel that they should be united in their efforts to regain their lost independence. Ideas were exchanged among Korean leaders in Hawaii and those on the mainland about ways and means to realize this unity. These leaders came to agree on the formation of an all-inclusive society for the great cause of Korean independence.

A half dozen Korean leaders arrived in Hawaii in early April of 1941. They represented the Korean societies of all shades in the mainland United States. Some of their names were as follows: Ho Kim, Shidai Hahn, Chong-ik Song, Pyung-yun Kim, and others. These representatives began to meet with the leaders of local Korean societies formally and informally. The result of their discussions was the organization of the United Korean Committee in America.[78]

The form of the newly born organization, however, was somewhat weak and ineffective. The reason was that all the existing Korean organizations were allowed to retain their old names and carry on their activities as before. But the functions of all organizations other than social and friendly were taken over by the new United Korean Committee in America. All political and diplomatic activities of the Koreans in this country were to be handled by and through this Committee.[79]

To carry on these political and diplomatic activities, all members of organizations were obligated to pay monthly dues, called the *Toklip Keum,* or Independence Funds, to the United Korean Committee in America. The Committee had two separate head offices, in Honolulu and Los Angeles. The Honolulu Headquarters of the United Korean Committee was given the legislative functions while the Los Angeles Head Office was to exercise the executive functions. The officers were to be chosen from the member organizations in proportion to their membership and were to serve on the Committee for one year. From these representatives of member societies one chairman, a vice-chairman, secretary, and treasurer were respectively elected. However, there were two treasurers, representing the two large Korean societies, namely Dongji Hoi and the Korean National Association of Hawaii.

There were 15 member organizations when the United Korean committee in America was formed. Of the 15 organizations, 4 represented the Korean Societies on the mainland, while all [others] were from the Hawaii Korean communities. [80] ...

Splits, 1943

... The Korean Students' Federation in North America joined the United Korean Committee in America in October, 1944, while the Dongji Hoi both in Hawaii and in America and the Korean Women's Relief Society withdrew their membership in December, 1943 from the Committee.

As has already been observed, the objective of the United Korean Committee in America was to unify all Korean nationalist activities under one single organization, so that the desired Korean independence movement might be effectively carried out. The *Toklip Keum,* or independence funds, the *Inkoo Seh,* or poll tax, the *Koonsa Keum,* or military funds, and other funds were collected from each member organization and sent in to the United Korean Committee in Los Angeles. Out of these funds, mainly from the Independence Fund, two-thirds were transmitted to the Korean Provisional Government in China while one-third was sent to the Korean Commission in Washington.[81]

An unfortunate dispute, however, started in the fall of 1942 between Syngman Rhee and the United Korean Committee in America, when Ho Kim began to attack Rhee and attempted to oust him from the chairmanship of the Korean Commission by appealing to the Provisional Government for his removal from the office. Prior to the dispute, Ho Kim, Henry Chung, and Wonsoon Lee had been appointed to serve as members of the Korean Commission by the United Korean Committee Executive Division meeting in June, 1942. They went to Washington, D.C., to serve in that capacity shortly after their appointment....

When Ho Kim and Jacob Dunn of the United Korean Committee learned that Syngman Rhee did not welcome Chung and Ho Kim as Commission members, and ... that the Provisional Government would not remove Syngman Rhee from the chairmanship of the Commission, they demanded that the Korean Commission be reorganized with Rhee as adviser. Rhee and his followers regarded this move of the United Korean Committee as an insult to Syngman Rhee. The pro-Rhee groups in California held several Korean mass meetings, or *Michoong Daihoi* in Los Angeles and Central California from the late fall of 1942 to the spring of 1943 to criticize the attitude of the United Korean Committee in Los Angeles, on the one hand, and to raise funds for the Korean Commission and the Provisional Government.

In the meantime, the Provisional Government tried to pacify the United Korean Committee leaders and Rhee for about two years. But when the Provisional Government officials came to know that their efforts were in vain, Koo Kim instructed Rhee and the United Korean Committee leaders to reorganize the Korean Commission in early 1944. He suggested that the leaders of all Korean societies in this country should gather together with Rhee and reorganize the Commission.[82] When such conference would not be realized soon, the United Korean Committee set up its own diplomatic mission in Washington, D.C. in the spring of 1944, with Jacob Dunn and Won-yong Kim as its representatives.

There are now at least four separate Korean Diplomatic agencies, each claiming to represent the people of Korea, at Washington. These were the 1) Korean Commission, 2) the Sino-Korean League Office, with Kilsoo Hahn as its spokesman, 3) the Korean Affairs Institute under the sponsorship of the Korean National Association in America with Yong-jung Kim as its director since 1944, and 4) the Washington Office of the United Korean Committee in America. . . .

. . . When the proposed reorganization of the Commission was not carried out soon, President Koo Kim appointed a committee of seven to reorganize the Commission, in the early summer of 1944. They were, besides Rhee, Henry Chung, Wonsoon Lee, Sareum C. Lee, Hearnju Song, Peongkoo Yoon, and one other. When the United Korean Committee in America held the All Korean Leaders' Conference in October of 1944 at Los Angeles, the Korean Commission Chairman, Syngman Rhee, was ousted, at least in name, and in his place Wonyong Kim was chosen, along with 14 other Commission members including Jacob K. Dunn, Kilsoo Han, Shidai Hahn, Henry Cu Kim, Ho Kim, Edward Pai, Arthur Yong-sung Kim, and others. . . .

When the United Korean Committee attempted to force the Provisional Government to its demands by refusing its financial support, many of the Korean National Association members in America deserted the Association and joined the Dongji Hoi. . . .

The Dongji Hoi Annual Delegates' Conference held in December, 1943, decided resolutely to withdraw its partnership in the United Korean Committee in America and renewed its pledge to support the Korean Provisional Government and the Korean Commission.[83] . . . Thus unity among Korean societies in Hawaii and the United States was shattered when the unfortunate dissension arose between the leaders of the Korean National Association and the Dongji Hoi. From January, 1944, on, the Korean Provisional Government at Chungking and Korean Commission had been supported solely by the Korean National Army Service of Kauai and the Dongji Hoi, until Syngman Rhee and the Provisional Government officials were invited to return to Korea by the Commanding General of the United States Army Forces in Korea in the fall of 1945.

When the Dongji Hoi separated from the United Korean Committee in America, it was attacked by many Koreans as well as American opponents of Rhee for breaking the united front of Koreans in this country. They all doubted the ability of the Dongji Hoi and its leaders to carry on its patriotic program for the Provisional Government. . . .

> . . . The United Korean Committee now embraces all former parties except one, the Dongji Hoi. . . . The number not accepting Dr. Rhee's leadership is now greater than that of his followers and includes the United Korean Committee.[84]

The Dongji Hoi leaders, however, did their best in support of the Provisional Government morally and financially. The first thing they started to do was to publish their own weekly, called the *Korean Pacific Weekly,* to counter-attack the undermining activities of the Korean National Association through the *Korean National Herald.* Furthermore, they came to know the urgent need of arousing patriotism of all Koreans in Hawaii and the Continental United States. They were badly in need of someone who could do the job. . . .

. . . Knowing fully well that all Korean compatriots must support the Provisional Government and its official agency, the Korean Commission, as their patriotic duty, [this] writer accepted the Dongji Hoi invitation and became the editor of the re-born *Korean Pacific Weekly,* upon obtaining the permit for publication from the Military Governor [of Hawaii] on February 12, 1944. . . .

Since the primary objectives of the Dongji Hoi were to support the Korean Provisional Government and the Korean Commission, the first thing for the editor to do was to emphasize the need for united efforts in the cause of Korean independence. His effort was not in vain, for many non-members of the Dongji Hoi began to join the Dongji in support of the united front movement. . . .

> To include all partisan groups in a Korean Delegation corps to any International Conference is not a simple matter, . . . [Rhee] appointed four Delegation members from Korean National Association, one of the groups which opposes him, two from Korean Revolutionary Party, two from Dongji Hoi, and lastly two from other minority groups.[85]

All seemed to be in unison as far as the Korean Delegation to the San Francisco United Nations Conference Organization was concerned.[86] . . .

However, [in a] last minute change of stand, the Korean National Association of Hawaii refused its cooperation with Syngman Rhee. Those who refused to cooperate with him formed their own *Minchoong Dairyo Dan,* or Korean People's Delegation to the San Francisco United Nations Conference and began to campaign against Rhee. The Korean People's Delegation consisted of the three partisan groups, namely, the Korean National Association, the Sino-Korean League, and the Korean Revolutionary Party. The Government Delegation was reorganized with the approval of the Provisional Government at Chungking, when the above groups, influenced by the United Korean Committee, withdrew their membership in the Government Delegation.[87] ...

All through the United Nations Conference at San Francisco, the Korean People's Delegation, under the influence of the United Korean Committee in America, opposed the Government Delegation by claiming that it truly and only represented the Korean people. Many public statements of the Korean Delegation such as the one on the Yalta Agreement were challenged not by the Department of State or the Russian Delegation, but by the Korean People's Delegation itself by attacking Syngman Rhee as hurting the feelings of the Russian and American people, and etc. The Korean Delegation, however tried to do its best for the cause of the Korean Provisional Republic at the United Nations Conference until the end of June.[88]

SUMMARY

... Korean nationalist activities may be divided into three periods, namely, from 1903 to 1910, from 1910 to 1919, and from 1920 to 1945. The first period may be called the rise of Korean nationalism in Hawaii and in the mainland United States. In this period, many Korean societies were organized among the plantation-working Koreans in the Hawaiian Islands, for the protection and mutual benefit of their fellow countrymen.... Furthermore, it was quite natural for the immigrant Koreans to continue their nationalistic ties with their old country. For this reason, they began to organize Korean patriotic societies.... These Korean societies were united in the latter part of 1905 under the name of the Hapsung Hoi, or United Society of Hawaii.... [and] changed to the Kookmin Hoi, or Korean National Association of Hawaii, in February, 1909.

The period from 1910 to 1919 may be called the crusading period of Korean nationalist activities in Hawaii. The Korean immigrants in this country especially resented the annexation of Korea by Japan in 1910. They were more than eager to do something for the restoration of their national independence.... They all supported political activities of leading Koreans in Hawaii, morally and financially.

Two American-educated Korean leaders arrived in Honolulu soon after Japan set up a military regime in Korea. Yong-man Park was the first of the two, and Syngman Rhee was the other. These two had already had bitter experiences in their youthful political activities in Korea in the early 1900s. They sharpened their patriotism while studying in Ameri-

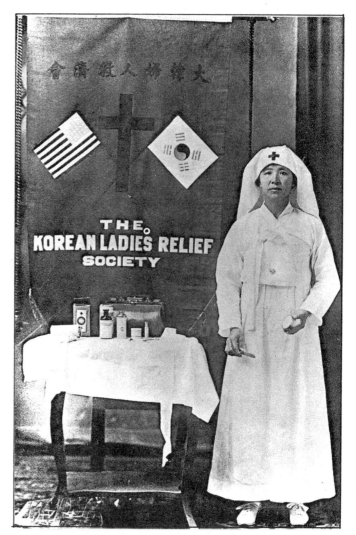

The Korean Ladies' Relief Society of Hawaii formed in 1919 supported the Korean Provisional Government-in-exile.

can universities. And yet they differed [a] great deal in their views as to how to restore Korean independence. Park wanted to regain Korean independence by military action while Rhee insisted that it should be done by training Korean leaders and by diplomatic activities.

The different views held by the two powerful leaders in Hawaii led their followers to disputes in their communities. The first dispute started in 1915 in the Korean National Association between the followers of the two leaders. Park's followers came out for the establishment of the Koondan, or Korean Military Academy, in the district of Koolau, Oahu, in 1914, while those supporting Rhee founded the Korean Girls' Seminary in Honolulu, in 1913. The disputes went from bad to worse, and the result was the formation of the Toklip Dan, or the League of Korean Independence, in 1919 by the followers of Yong-man Park. Rhee's followers lost no time in founding the Korean Christian Church in 1917, and the Korean Christian Institute in 1918.... When the Korean Provisional Government was established in Shanghai, in April, 1919, all Korean societies in Hawaii as well as in the [continental] United States pledged their allegiance to the Government-in-exile. Major Korean societies such as the Dongji Hoi and the Korean National Association as well as the Toklip Dan and the Korean Women's Relief Society of Hawaii worked harmoniously in support of the Korean Provisional Government, headed by Rhee himself in Hawaii, until the *Minchoong Wha,* or Democratization Revolt against Syngman Rhee broke out in 1929 and continued until 1931.

During this period from 1920 to 1931, Korean societies, both large and small, in Hawaii came to forget their patriotic duties to support the Provisional Government in Shanghai morally and financially. They were blinded by heated controversies over the leadership of Rhee. Koo Kim, Minister of Home Affairs of the Provisional Government, appealed to the Koreans in Hawaii for unity and financial assistance to the Government-in-exile. Most of the Korean societies in this country were deafened to Kim's appeal.

There were, however, a few Korean societies in the Hawaiian Islands that had been moved by the earnest appeal of Koo Kim. The result was the formation of the Dan Hap Hoi, or United Korean Society of Kauai, on March 1, 1930. . . .

Syngman Rhee, in the meantime, was busily engaged in diplomatic activities in America during this period. He established the Korean Commission in Washington in April, 1919, in cooperation with other Korean compatriots such as Philip Jaisohn, Kiusic Kimm, and Henry Chung. The Commission represented the Korean Provisional Government abroad. When the Washington Conference on Limitation of Armament convened in the American capitol, Syngman Rhee hurried to the mainland. Philip Jaisohn, as chairman of the Korean Commission, Henry Chung as its secretary, and Rhee as member, presented the case of Korea before the Washington Conference. When the Manchurian Incident was taken up by the League of Nations, he went to Geneva to present the Korean problems in connection with Manchuria. When he saw the second World War approaching rapidly, Syngman Rhee hurried back to Washington to reopen the Korean Commission in the winter of 1939.

For about two years Korean nationalists in America and Hawaii came to be united into a single organization, called the United Korean Committee in America, from April of 1941. The United Korean Committee for the first time in history succeeded in coordinating all political activities of Koreans living abroad in support of the Korean Provisional Government-in-exile. The chief objectives of the Committee were to collect the Korean Independence and Military Funds for the Korean Commission and the Provisional Government, at Chungking, China.

The united front of the Korean nationalists in America came to grief, however, when the leaders of the United Korean Committee in America, under Ho Kim and others, refused to support the Korean Commission after their unsuccessful attempt to take over the Commission administration in the fall of 1942. Ho Kim and Jacob K. Dunn urged the Koreans in California to oust Syngman Rhee from the chairmanship of the Korean Commission. Many Koreans, both members of Dongji Hoi and non-members, came out in support of Rhee and criticized illegal action taken by the Executive Division of the United Korean Committee in Los Angeles. . . .

The United Korean Committee in America set up its own diplomatic agency in Washington, D.C., with Jacob K. Dunn and Wonyong Kim as its chief and treasurer respectively, in the winter of 1943. The Dongji Hoi then separated itself from the United Korean Committee because of the anti-Rhee policy advocated by the Committee. From the early part of 1944, the Dongji Hoi began to publish the *Korean Pacific Weekly* separately from the *Korean National Herald* for the two papers had been published jointly by the United Korean Committee from 1941.

When the United Korean Committee in America stopped the financial and moral support to the Provisional Government from 1943, Korean patriots on the Island of Kauai organized the Korean National Army Service of Kauai in the winter of 1943. The chief objective of the Army Service was to collect military funds in support of the Korean Provisional Government and its army. Several thousand dollars were raised and sent to President Koo Kim until he and his cabinet members were invited to return to Korea by Lt. General John R. Hodge in the early winter of 1945.

The leaders of the United Korean Committee in America never gave up their antagonism to the leadership of Syngman Rhee until he returned to Seoul in October, 1945. They came to San Francisco in April, 1945, when the United Nations Conference on International Organization was in session in an attempt to embarrass the Provisional Korean Government Delegation, headed by Rhee. They claimed before the public that they, and not the Government Delegation, truly represented the will of the people in Korea. When the leaders of [the] world witnessed the Korean house divided into factions, both Korean delegations were denied a hearing before the conference.

From what has been observed in this study one may justly conclude that Hawaii became the pivot of Korean nationalist activities in America. . . . [and] raised more independence funds and in other funds for the cause of Korean independence than those living in any other places. From this point of view, the Korean immigrants in Hawaii may be called the crusaders for Korean nationalism and the architects of Korean independence.

Furthermore, this study is of significance toward the understanding of Korean problems, because the newly established Republic of Korea has been built largely by the same Syngman Rhee whose experience in Korean politics in Hawaii has a great bearing upon the present-day politics in Korea. For this reason, the writer has attempted to systematize Korean nationalist activities in Hawaii and America in the hope that it might give a clear picture of Korean independence movement abroad. The written and unwritten materials for this study are of no small importance, since they are either original documents, or first-hand informations from those Korean leaders who were actually engaged in Korean politics in Hawaii. To know Korean political activities in America is, therefore, to know Korean politics in Korea. Thus it may be concluded that the history of Korean immigrants in Hawaii is, in large part, the history of their national independence movement. ★

Notes

1. Syngman Rhee, *The Spirit of Independence*, Honolulu, Korean Pacific Magazine Co., 1917, p. 127.
2. The writer's personal interview with Mrs. Chi-woon Kim.
3. *Third Report of the Commissioner of Labor in Hawaii, 1905*, p. 15.
4. *First Report of the Board of Immigration to the Governor of the Territory of Hawaii*, April 29, 1905/January 31, 1907, Honolulu, 1908, pp. 18-24.
5. *Statement by William H. Fry of July 27, 1915 to Governor Pinkham* stated the Methodist mission had charge of Koreans.
6. The writer's personal interviews with Mr. Duk Yin Shon who knew Mr. Ahn personally in north Korea.
7. The picture of the Young Korean Military School faculty and student body taken about 1908 [showed] its enrollment was not too large.
8. Syngman Rhee, *The Spirit of Independence*, Honolulu, Korean Pacific Magazine Co., 1917, p. 214 stated the University of Nebraska, not Lincoln University as some assumed it. Yong-man Park, America Hyukmyong, Honolulu, Korean National Herald, 1915, p. 2 confirmed the writer's statement.
9. Robert T. Oliver, *Korea, Forgotten Nation*, Washington, American Pacific Council, 1944, p. 49.
10. The passport issued to Hong Pok Kim on February 9, 1902 was signed by President of the Department of Immigration, Young Whan Min.
11. Deshler's letter to Huntington Wilson [Charge d'Affaires, American Legation, Tokyo] of January 27, 1906. The writer's personal interview with Messrs. Sang-ha Park and Duk-yin Shon, who went to Mexico in 1905.
12. Horace N. Allen to Governor Dole, December 10, 1902.
13. *Letter of Transmission* is kept in the Hawaii Public Archives.
14. *Ibid.*
15. *Third Report of the Commissioner of Labor on Hawaii, 1905*, Washington, Government Printing Office, 1906, p. 74.
16. *Report of the Governor of the Territory of Hawaii to Secretary of Interior*, 1901, p. 63.
17. *The Governor's Report for 1905*, p. 76.
18. Commissioner of Labor, *op. cit.* p. 44.
19. The writer's personal interviews with Pong-sun Kwon.
20. The writer's personal interviews with Mrs. Mary Kong, Mrs. Mary Hahn Woo, and Messrs. Sang-eui Kim and

Sang-ha Park who had experiences of running the kitchens.
21. *Third Report of the Commissioner of Labor on Hawaii, 1905*. Washington, Government Printing Office, 1906, p. 14.
22. *Reports of the Governor of Territory of Hawaii, 1921-25*, Honolulu, 1926, p. 11.
23. The writer's personal interviews with Hongki Lee and Kyungsur Lee, who participated in Korean nationalist activities.
24. The writer's personal interviews with Mr. Hongki Lee.
25. *Ibid.*, and with Chancho Nahm.
26. The writer's personal interviews with Mr. Hongki Lee. .
27. [This footnote is illegible. For another version of the organization of the Korean National Association of North America, see Kim Won-yong (Warren Y.), *Chae Mi Hanin Oshimnyon Sa* (Fifty Year History of Koreans in America) (Reedley, Ca., 1959). For additional information on Ahn Chang-ho, see Linda Shin, "Koreans in America, 1903-1945," in *Roots: An Asian American Reader*, ed. Amy Tachiki et al. (Los Angeles, 1971), 201-207; and Lee and Chang-su Houchins, "The Korean Experience in America, 1903-1924," *Pacific Historical Review*, 43:4 (Nov. 1974), 548-576.]
28. *Annual Report on Administration of Chosen 1935-36*, Keijo, p. 172.
29. Oliver, *op. cit.*, p. 100.
30. James H. R. Cromwell, *Why Isn't Korea Recognized?* Washington, Korean American Council, 1942, p. 9. See also Government-General of Chosen, *op. cit.* p. 172.
31. The writer's personal interviews with ex-soldiers Chinok Choo, Kunsil Park, Taikyun Park, Moonsur Yang, Pyung-yo Cho, etc.
32. The writer's personal interviews with Moonsur Yang.
33. The writer's personal interviews with Sang-ha Park.
34. Cromwell, *op. cit.* p. 9 says that Dr. Rhee founded the military school. Sang-ha Park said it was opened in June, 1914.
35. Hankyung Kim, Taikyun Park, Kunsil Park, Sang-ha Park, and added that the price for pineapples was too cheap to be of any help.
36. The writer's personal interviews with Hongki Lee.
37. Those so branded by Dr. Rhee as traitors or Landang later became charter members of the Toklip Dan when founded in 1919.
38. Its charter was granted by the Governor of Hawaii, May 4, 1921.
39. Inyong Chi and Pongchoon Lim drove him in a car to the ship. Chancho Nahm, Taikyun Park and Moonsur Yang confirmed it.
40. Oliver, *op. cit.*, p. 46.
41. Moonsur Yang puts it at 1926, while Chancho Nahm and Taikyun Park said it was in 1925 when Park returned to Hawaii.
42. The writer's personal interviews with Moonsur Yang. It might be quite possible that some Koreans did petition the Immigration authorities. [The rest of the footnote is illegible.]
43. *Ibid.*
44. The song of the *Daidong Pardoka* and others are still sung by those who even opposed Mr. Park, on patriotic occasions.
45. Oliver, *Korea, Forgotten Nation*, p. 62.
46. Cromwell, *op. cit.*, p. 9.
47. Syngman Rhee, *op. cit.* front pages put the date as 1912.
48. Pyung-yo Cho, Hongki Lee, Kyungsur Lee, Sang-eui Kim, Kunsil Park, and the Rev. Noah K. Cho heard Dr. Rhee say so.
49. Cromwell, *op. cit.*, p. 9.
50. The writer's personal interviews with Sang-ha Park and Nodie Kimhaikim Sohn confirmed this view.

51. Dr. Rhee and Dr. Fry admitted freely they were enemies. The writer's personal interviews with Mr. Nodie K. Sohn.
52. *Sasil Sulmyung* [A statement of fact] admitted Dr. Rhee feared losing his followers.
53. 2nd Principle of Dongji Hoi demands absolute obedience.
54. The writer's personal interviews with Sang-eui Kim and Sang-ha Park, who were supporters of Dr. Rhee for many years.
55. Oliver, *op. cit.*, p. 45-46.
56. *Korean Pacific Weekly*, Honolulu, vol. 15, no. 511, March 25, 1944, p. 2.
57. The certificate promised the redemption of the bonds within one year after the recognition of Korea by the U.S.
58. The writer's personal interviews with Hongki Lee and Kunsil Park and Mrs. Yousil Lee, who belonged to both anti-Rhee and pro-Rhee factions for long time.
59. These principles have been printed on the cover of the *Korean Pacific Weekly* ever since its first publication.
60. Rhee married an Austrian woman while staying in Geneva, 1933.
61. It is based on Dr. Rhee's own statement of July 9, 1942 as a part of the financial report of the Korean Commission.
62. The *Korean Students Directory of 1940* listed some 70 students.
63. *Paradise of the Pacific*, Honolulu, December, 1944, p. 82.
64. The writer's personal interviews with Mrs. Yousil Lee, who was the treasurer of the Dongji Hoi of Hawaii, from 1939-1946.
65. The writer's personal interviews with Pongkil Kim, Duk-yin Shon, Sang-eui Kim, and others. However, Mrs. Yongwhan Moon asserts that she heard the name of Kyomin Dan when she arrived in Honolulu in May, 1920.
66. Oliver, *op. cit.*
67. Duk-yin Shon stated that Chang-ho Ahn's landing in Honolulu was prevented by Immigration Service in 1923 through the influence of Dr. Rhee.
68. The *Sungto Moon*, or the Public Condemnation Statement was signed by 54 prominent Korean nationalists such as Chaiho Shin, Kirk-lo Lee, Kunsang Chang, Pyungshik Kim, and others. The statement was published on April 19, 1921.
69. *Sasil Sulmyung*, p. 2, 4.
70. *Ibid.*, p. 5.
71. The writer's personal interviews with Duk-yin Shon.
72. The writer's personal interviews with Hongki Lee and Mrs. So Yun Chun Kim.
73. Oliver, *op. cit.*, pp. 52-53.
74. The writer's personal interviews with Hoyong Chung, Mrs. Kim So Yun Chun, and Hongki Lee.
75. The writer's interviews with Sayong Whang, Kilsoo Han, Ben C. Limb, and Jacob K. Dunn, who [were] involved in the affair. The writer personally heard Ho Kim speaking thus at San Francisco in the winter of 1942.
76. The writer's personal recollection and the *Minutebook of Army Service*.
77. The "Reconstruction Party" of the Korean National Association consisted of the following: Jacob K. Dunn, Wonyong Kim, Chang-ho Ahn, Jay-un Cho, Chungsong Ahn, Do-ok Chung, Doo Ok Choy, Keumwoo Park, Chinho Tough and one other.
78. Dr. Rhee's Statement on the Commission Finance, July 9, 1942.
79. The Minutes of the United Korean Committee in America, 1944, p. 15.
80. The Minutes of the United Korean Committee in America, October 28-November 5, 1944, p. 1.
81. Dr. Rhee's statement on the Korean Commission Finance, July 9, 1942. It tells about the formation of the United Korean Committee in America in 1941. Also, see *Korean North American Monthly*, February, 1943, vol.1, no. 6, p. 7.
82. *Korean North American Monthly, op. cit.,* p. 1, 7.
83. Oliver, *op. cit.*, p. 130.
84. Alice R. Appenzeller, "Koreans in a Generation in Hawaii," *Paradise of the Pacific*, Honolulu, December 1944, p. 83.
85. The *Korean Pacific Weekly*, vol.16, no. 563, March 31, 1945, p. 1.
86. The writer acting as member of the Government Delegation and its treasurer gathered all financial reports while in San Francisco from April 22-June 30, 1945.
87. Members were Shidai Hahn, Ho Kim, Jacob Dunn, Chinsuk Youth from Korean National Association, Kilsoo Han and Sayong Whang from Korean Revolutionary Party. [The rest of the footnote is illegible.]
88. The Government Delegation work was entrusted to Dr. Henry Chung and the writer, who had been an accredited correspondent to the United Nations Conference; when Dr. Rhee and six other members, Sareum Lee, Sayong Whang, Peongkoo Yoon, Hearnju Song, and Ben Limb went home on May 23, 1945.

A Select List of Persons Interviewed by the Writer

Chang-ho Ahn, pastor of Korean Methodist Church, Honolulu, Territory of Hawaii.

Chang, Peter, pastor of Korean Community Church, Honolulu.

Cho, Chisam, Anahola, Kauai.

Cho, Noah K., former pastor of St. Luke's Mission, Honolulu.

Cho, Pyung-yo, former president of Korean National Association of Hawaii, Honolulu.

Chung, Agnes Park, first graduate of Korean Girls' Seminary, Honolulu.

Chung, Hoyoung, former president of Dan Hap Hoi of Kauai.

Dunn, Jacob Kyangmu, formerly of Honolulu.

Choo, Chinok, Honolulu.

Han, Kilsoo, formerly of Honolulu, now in San Francisco.

Kim, Hong pok, formerly of Hilo, Hawaii.

Kim, Hankyung, Honolulu.

Kim, Mrs. Chiwon, Honolulu.

Kim, Pongkil, Honolulu.

Kim, Sang-eui, Honolulu.

Kim, Mrs. So Yun Chun, formerly of Kauai.

Kim, Sungwha, formerly of Kona, Hawaii.

Ko, Pongchoo, formerly of Waialua, Oahu.

Kong, Mrs. Mary Shin, formerly of Kauai.

Kwon, Pongsun, formerly of Kauai, and now in Honolulu.

Kwon, Sungchai, Honolulu.

Lee, Chaiyun, charter member of Korean Christian Church.

Lee, Hongki, former president of Dan Hap Hoi and of Korean National Association of Kauai.

Lee, Mrs. Kyungsil, wife of the manager of Dongji Store, Hilo.

Lee, Kyungsur, former president of Korean National Association of Kekaha, and of Korean National Army service of Kauai.

Lee, Soonpo, caretaker of the Dongji Village in 1931.

Lim, Yilkwang, former student of Choong-ang Hakwon, Honolulu.

Lim, Neisoo Kang, first president of Kauai Puin Hapsung Hoi.

Lee, Kyungsik, former Sachal of Makaweli Dong-hoi.

Lee, Yousil, charter member of Korean Christian Church and sometime treasurer of Dongji Hoi.

Limb, Ben C., former secretary of Korean Commission.

Liu, Mrs. Hannah Kim, charter member of Korean Christian Church and one of the leaders against Yongjik Lee.

Moon, Yongwhan, Honolulu.

Moon, Mrs. Yongwhan, who came to Honolulu, in May, 1920.

Lyum, Tuksoon, former student at Choong-ang Hakwon, Honolulu.

Nahm, Mr. and Mrs. Chancho, formerly Makaweli, Kauai.

Park, Mrs. Annie, former student of Korean Christian Institute.

Part, Kunsil, former president of Korean National Army Service, and charter member of Toklip Dan and Koondan.

Park, Sang-ha, former president of Korean National Association of Hawaii.

Park, Sungum, first graduate of Korean Girls' Seminary.

Park, Taikyun, charter member of Koondan, and of the Toklip Dan, Honolulu.

Park, Mr. and Mrs. Laisun, charter member of Korean Christian Church and of Dongji Hoi, and faithful followers of Dr. Syngman Rhee, Honolulu.

Shon, Duk-yin, former president of the Kyomin Dan, and one of the leaders in the Democratization movement.

Shon, Mrs. Maria, formerly one of the Korean immigrants to Mexico, and first president of Korean Women Relief Society, Honolulu.

Sohn, Mrs. Nodie Kimhaikim, sometime superintendent of the Korean Christian Institute and an ardent supporter of Dr. Syngman Rhee, Honolulu.

Sohn, Syungwoon, wartime president of Dongji Hoi, Honolulu.

Sur, Haksur, former resident on Hawaii.

Sur, Chungyil, key-figure in the 1946 Dongji Hoi and Korean Christian Church controversies, Honolulu.

Whang, Sayong, member of Heungsa Dan, tried to get a visa from State Department and approval from Chinese Embassy and from Dr. Rhee.

Yang, Moonsur, charter member of Toklip Dan, and first student at the Koondan, Honolulu.

You, David Chinsuk, former student at Choong-ang Hakwon.

Woo, Mrs. Mary Hahn, of Kauai and longtime operator of Korean kitchen or *koksang*.

Bibliography

Board of Immigration, Territory of Hawaii. *Report of the Board of Immigration to the Governor of the Territory of Hawaii.* Honolulu: Star Bulletin Printing, 1905-1926 (in separate volumes).

Board of Immigration, Territory of Hawaii. *Letter of Transmission,* January 31, 1907.

Board of Immigration, Labor and Statistics, Territory of Hawaii. *Annual Report to the Governor of the Territory of Hawaii.* Honolulu: Star Bulletin Printing, 1905-1925 (in separate volumes).

Cannon, James. *History Southern Methodist Missions.* Nashville, Tenn.: Cokesbury Press, 1926.

Commissioner of Labor. *Third Report of the Commissioner of Labor on Hawaii.* Washington, D.C.: Government Printing Office, 1906.

Cromwell, James H. R. *Why Isn't Korea Recognized?* Washington, D.C.: Korean-American Council, 1942.

Governor of Hawaii. *Annual Report of the Governor of the Territory of Hawaii to the Secretary of the Interior.* Washington, D.C.: Government Printing Office, 1901-1940 (in separate volumes).

Department of Public Instruction. *Annual Report of Superintendent of Public Instruction to Governor of Hawaii.* Honolulu: Star Bulletin Printing, 1904-1940 (in separate volumes).

Government-General of Chosen [Korea], *Annual Report on the Administration of Chosen, 1936.* Keijo [Seoul], 1937.

Hawaiian Almanac and Annual. Honolulu: Thos. G. Thrum, 1904-1931 (in separate volumes).

Hawaiian Japanese Annual and Directory 1937-38. Honolulu: The Nippu Jiji Co., 1938.

Korean Christian Church Constitution and By-laws. Honolulu: Korean Pacific Weekly, 1937.

Korean Students' Directory. New York: Korean Students' Christian Association, 1940.

Korean Women Relief Society By-laws. Honolulu: Korean Women Relief Society, 1940.

Korean Christian Missions Minutebook. Honolulu, 1940.

League of Korean Independence, Constitution. Honolulu: Korean Pacific Times, 1919.

Oliver, Robert T. *Korea, Forgotten Nation.* Washington, D.C.: American Council on Public Affairs, 1944.

Grajdanzey, Andrew J. *Korea Looks Ahead.* New York: American Council, Institute of Pacific Relations, 1944.

Park Yong-man. *American Hyokmyung.* Honolulu: Korean National Herald, 1915.

Park Yong-man. *Koonin Soochi* (Soldiers' manual). San Francisco: The New Korea, 1911.

Rhee, Syngman. *Toklip Chungshin* (Spirit of Korean Independence). Honolulu: Korean Pacific Magazine Co., 1917.

United Korean Committee in America Convention Minutes October 28-November 5, 1944. Los Angeles: United Korean Committee, 1944.

Periodicals

Korean Pacific Weekly, Honolulu, vols. 15-18, nos. 506-563 (1944 February-November 1947).

Korean National Herald, Honolulu, December numbers, 1943.

Korean North American Monthly, February 1943. New York: Dongji Hoi, 1943.

Korean Commission News, No. 94, March 1, 1944.

Korean Christian Church Decision, Honolulu, September 27, 1930.

Paradise of the Pacific, Honolulu, December 1944 and 1945.

Honolulu Advertiser, July 3, 1915.

Korean National Army Service of Kauai Minutes, 1944.

Letters and Statements

Passenger Statements 1898-1900. Honolulu, Public Archive.

Sungto Moon (Public Condemnation Statement on Dr. Rhee). Shanghai, April 19, 1921.

Certificate of Indebtedness. Washington, D.C., Korean Commission, 1919 (Government bond).

Certificate of Share of Dongji Investment Company. 1926, Honolulu.

Nine Conditions of the Chinese Military Committee on Korean National Army. December 1942, Chungking.

Rhee, Syngman. *Sasil Sulmyung* [Statement of Fact]. September 24, 1930, Honolulu.

Rhee, Syngman. *On Korean Commission Financial Situation.* July 9, 1942, Washington, D.C.

Japanese Consulate Registration Book 1895-1925. Honolulu.

Acting Governor Atkinson's Letter to Acting Secretary Robert Bacon. March 10, 1906.

Deshler, David W. *Letter to Huntington Wilson.* January 27, 1906.

Fry, William H. *Statement to Governor Pinkham.* July 27, 1915, Honolulu.

Limb, Ben C. *Letter to Kingsley K. Lyu.* December 10, 1942, Washington, D.C.

Governor Lucius Pinkham's Letter to Acting Secretary of Interior Jones. July 27, 1915, Honolulu.

Wadman, John W. *Statement to Governor Pinkham.* July 27, 1915, Honolulu.

Rhee, Syngman. *Letter to Kingsley K. Lyu.* July 1, 1943, Washington, D.C.

Wilson, Huntington. *Letter to Secretary of State Elihu Root.* January 27, 1906, Tokyo.

Williams, E. T. *Memorandum for Secretary of State Lansing.* July 26, 1915, Washington, D.C.

Rhee, Syngman. *Radiogram.* November 10, 1947, Seoul.

Allen, Horace N. *Letter to Governor Dole.* December 10, 1902, Seoul.

THE VIETNAM EVACUEES...
WHAT NOW?

BY LE ANH TU

Camp Pendleton, 1975.

The American war effort ended as it began: with the massive relocation of refugees. In 1954 and 1955, amid rumors of communist bloodletting and fears of a U.S. atomic attack, some 900,000 Vietnamese moved to the South. The U.S. government supplied units of the Seventh Fleet to transport the refugees south and provided $93 million to finance the relocation program.

Years later, it became publicly known that the refugee flight was, according to historian Bernard Fall, "the result of an extremely intensive, well-conducted, and in terms of its objective, very successful American psychological warfare operation." The mastermind of this operation, CIA Colonel Edward Lansdale, filed a report describing how he trained Vietnamese army units and the Saigon Ministry of Information to spread scare stories. "The first rumor campaign was to be a carefully planted story of a Chinese Communist regiment in Tonkin [North Vietnam] taking reprisals against a Vietminh village whose girls the Chinese had raped," Lansdale wrote. "Weeks later, Tonkinese told an excited story of the misbehavior of a Chinese Communist regiment in Vietminh territory. Investigated, it turned out to be the old rumor campaign, with Vietnamese embellishments." Lansdale told how his teams had engineered a number of "black psywar strikes" (his own words), including the forging of leaflets signed by the Vietminh outlining the measures they would take after coming into power. "The day following the distribution of these leaflets, refugee registration tripled," Lansdale crowed.

The generating of refugees became a standard feature of American policy in Indochina. By the end of the war, the U.S. Senate Subcommittee on Refugees reported that over 11 million Vietnamese had been driven from their homes, mostly as a result of the saturation bombing. The U.S. government's interpretation which was generally accepted by the American media, however, was that the refugees were "fleeing from communism." High officials were especially fond of citing the first mass exodus of people to the South as proof that they were "voting with their feet." Thus, they argued, Americans had a moral obligation to come to the rescue of those who clearly wanted to be saved from the totalitarian clutches of communism.

In April 1975, another massive evacuation took place as whole divisions of General Thieu's army disintegrated, often without a fight, before the approach of the revolutionary armed forces. It began with the collapse of the Thieu administration, first in the Central Highlands, then in the coastal provinces from Quang Tri to Khanh Hoa. Generals and high government officials were the first to flee, followed by lower-echelon officers and bureaucrats, businessmen, and well-to-do landowners, creating a panic that engulfed shopkeepers, schoolteachers, and ordinary farmers.

For some, flight seemed preferable to living under a new revolutionary administration which they considered to be an unknown, if not fearful, quantity, but for many others, it was simply to avoid being caught in the middle of a cross-fire. Panic engendered more panic, and many fled because others were fleeing. People swarmed into the coastal cities of Danang and Nhatrang in desperate search of transportation to a safe haven.

Ironically, there was hardly any fighting except at Xuan Loc. Whole cities surrendered to the Provisional Revolutionary Government with scarcely a shot fired. But the refugee exodus created a mood of panic, fear and uncertainty that pervaded throughout the last days of the regime. To make matters worse, the U.S. Embassy in Saigon stepped up its campaign to convince the Vietnamese public that a communist bloodbath was underway. Unsubstantiated stories of atrocities and executions churned out by the U.S. Embassy and repeated in Saigon government television broadcasts and newspaper articles intensified the mood of fear and apprehension.

With the realization that the collapse of the regime was inevitable, U.S. officials finally gave the go-ahead to plans for massive evacuation. In the last weeks before the war ended, a flotilla of airplanes,

helicopters and ships carried some 131,000 Vietnamese and Cambodians from their homeland. President Ford's plan, announced to Congress, was to evacuate those "who would be most endangered under a communist regime." It soon became clear that others targeted for evacuation included those who could play an important role in Vietnam's reconstruction. For example, two weeks before the regime's demise the United States helped evacuate the employees of corporations involved in off-shore oil explorations, and U.S. Embassy personnel were boasting openly of their role in persuading most of the professors in the Saigon University's Faculty of Medicine to evacuate. But their objectives were never fully realized. According to a Senate study mission report, "whatever plan existed was implemented badly, plagued with disorganization," and "events in the field rapidly overtook whatever decisions our national leadership was making."

"Half the Vietnamese we intended to get out did not get out—and half who did get out, should not have," high U.S. officials in Guam told Senate investigators. Almost the entire Vietnamese CIA apparatus was left behind, while some 69,000 farmers, fishermen, students, street vendors, shopkeepers, local policemen, common soldiers and prostitutes found their way to U.S. reception centers in Guam and elsewhere.

As was the case throughout the war, corruption was endemic. One Illinois congressman was shocked to read in a Chicago newspaper an article quoting Americans who were signing signature affidavits for $3000 each, enabling certain Vietnamese to be listed as relatives of American citizens for evacuation purposes. Another reporter from the *Los Angeles Times* learned that one "nightclub sharpie" had made $100,000 by acting as a conduit for bribes to evacuate bargirls.

By then, the Ford Administration was exploiting to the hilt the propaganda value of thousands of refugees "fleeing from Communist rule." It was the final psychological consolation. Having failed to Americanize Vietnam, at least it could bring as many Vietnamese as it could to America. The Administration's tactic was to divert public attention from events in Vietnam, and, according to journalist Frances Fitzgerald, succeeded in persuading the press "to serve as a platform for a propaganda spectacular designed to . . . show the triumph of American virtue over the savagery of the Vietnamese. . . . The 150,000 refugees in the United States received five or ten times the attention given to the 18 million people in the throes of one of the most dramatic political changes in the past two or three decades."

In opting for the short-term political pay-off, the Administration gave little consideration to the human consequences of its decision. The sudden evacuation of thousands of refugees, without foresight or pre-planning, without determining the needs of those evacuated, without considering the ill effects of bringing large numbers of people into a totally alien culture, and without consulting the American people, has created a traumatic situation for these refugees. The public welcome accorded to the new immigrants was at best lukewarm and at worst callously racist. "They say it's a lot colder here than in Vietnam," one resident near Fort Chaffee was overheard saying. "With a little luck, maybe all these Vienamese will take pneumonia and die." In Florida, high school students talked about organizing a "gook klux klan." A public opinion poll found that 66 percent of the American people wanted to have the refugees resettled in Asian countries.

The government's own refugee program left much to be desired, according to the findings of a Senate study mission. "From the start, the Task Force has been characterized by a failure of leadership, poor organization, inadequate planning, and belated decision making," the report observed. The Administration's attitude, while encouraging the mass evacuation, was to leave it to the private voluntary agencies to take care of resettling the refugees. And many of the agencies accepted this responsibility without question. To date, ten relief organizations, the U.S. Catholic Conference, American Fund for Czechoslovak Refugees, Church World Service, Lutheran Immigration and Refugee Service, United HIAS Service, International Rescue Committee, American Council for Nationalities Service, Travelers Aid, the American Red Cross and the Tolstoy Foundation, have programs for refugee resettlement.

As of August 21, some 46,703 refugees remain in four military camps: Fort Chaffee in Arkansas, Camp Pendleton in California, Eglin Air Force Base in Florida, and Fort Indiantown Gap in Pennsylvania. While the atmosphere varies somewhat at each camp, the physical facilities are on the whole adequate. The refugees are confined to living quarters and recreation areas set aside for them, and are discouraged from entering the visitors' center or the offices of voluntary agencies unless specifically invited. In Indiantown Gap long white cloths mark out the living and recreation areas of the refugees, as well as the paths they can walk on to go from one barrack area to the next. Visitors to the camp may not enter the refugee areas marked by the white cloth, and refugees cannot pass this boundary without permission from camp authorities. The inmates have virtually no contact with the outside world, and have very little knowledge of what life is actually like in the United States.

Many of the camp refugees are under severe emotional strain. They cannot cope with their sudden transplantation into an alien culture which they find incomprehensible. They feel homesick but are convinced that they will never again see their native land. "Every night I cry," an old woman at Indiantown Gap told this writer, "it is the worse thing that has happened in my life. Everything is left behind, my

house, my friends, there is no more future for me." Many of the camp refugees have relatives remaining in Vietnam and they are anxious to have some contact. But they hear from rumors that cablegrams sent to Vietnam would endanger their family members. They are afraid to make the first move.

All the Vietnamese at Indiantown Gap interviewed by this writer said that they had no news about the current situation in their homeland. The camp newspapers offer little information, and independent Vietnamese-language newspapers, such as *Doi Dien Hai Ngoai* (published by the Vietnamese community in the United States), which do contain extensive news on recent developments, are not allowed to be distributed within the camps. The camp commander at Indiantown Gap, who has authority to determine what written materials can be brought into the camp, argues that the refugees need to be protected from "left-wing" and "right-wing" propaganda. Others, such as William Thoma of the Tolstoy Foundation, regard the activities of outside Vietnamese residents to provide news to camp inmates as an important threat. He told the House Subcommittee on Immigration, "Another problem as been posed by attempts of rump leftist organizations and native Indochinese provocateurs to subvert the morale of the refugees at several of the camps."

In the meantime, rumors about "terrible atrocities in Vietnam" abound. One common rumor is that all Northerners are being forcibly returned to North Vietnam. Another, broadcasted through loudspeakers in Camp Pendleton, claims that the "Viet-Cong" murdered 15,000 of 40,000 refugees on Phu Quoc island. Refugees also repeat to each other scare stories they heard before leaving Vietnam: girls will be forced to marry wounded soldiers, children will be separated from their parents who will be forced to work in state industries far away, sons will be urged to denounce their mothers, spies will hover everywhere, people will be required to report on the attitudes and habits of their friends and neighbors, and so on.

Camp officials, because of their anticommunist attitudes, reinforce the fears of the refugees. One State Department official at Indiantown Gap discounted the validity of reports from Westerners in Vietnam that no bloodbath has occurred, saying, "We know that executions are going on regularly, and that people are being forced into the countryside." He said that some refugees had made tentative inquiries about the possibilities of repatriation, including an airforce pilot whom he was not "encouraging." At Fort Chaffee, visitors found that most of the Task Force employees believed that anyone returning to Vietnam would be immediately killed. This attitude was conveyed to the refugees who were considering repatriation. One camp official observed that the building handling repatriation requests was "hard to find," since it was off the main road. "It's a good thing they don't find it," he added, "cause then they won't want to go back. They're better off here."

Peer pressure also plays an important role in discouraging those who wish to return home. Visitors to Fort Chaffee talked to a young woman who had worked for the U.S. Defense Attache Office in Saigon. She claimed that a bloodbath was taking place in Vietnam. The communists are not beheading or shooting enemies, she said, but rather they were drawing out all their blood so that their enemies would die. She recounted her dinner conversation with a very upset woman who wanted to return home. She told the woman that the communists would kill her. The woman broke into tears, wept, and said she would remain in America. On another occasion, visitors at Camp Pendleton reported having their conversation with a 16 year-old boy about repatriation interrupted by a former ARVN pilot who declared that it would be smarter to jump in the mouth of a whale than to return to Vietnam.

Ignorant of the real situation in their home country, the refugees are more prone to believe wild rumors of bloodbath and mass executions. The decision of the camp commanders, however well-intentioned, to deny the refugees access to a wide range of information about postwar Indochina has created serious emotional hardships for the camp inhabitants. Freedom of information is a fundamental right, and in the case of the refugees, it is also an urgent human need. At this most difficult time in their life, they must have adequate information about the situation both in the United States and in Vietnam in order to know what options are available to them.

The primary concern of Task Force officials and camp personnel is to find sponsors for the refugees. Success is measured by how fast the camps can be emptied out. Voluntary agency personnel, who are under intense pressure by the Task Force to hurry refugees through the sponsorship program, become influenced to think mainly in terms of finding sponsors. Even those who are generally sympathetic to the needs of the refugees succumb to this pressure, and display impatience when the refugees express their reluctance to resettle in "cold-weather" states.

Task Force officers are critical of voluntary agencies for being slow and inflexible in their screening of would-be sponsors. "One example cited," according to a *New York Times* article on 18 June 1975, "was the reported unwillingness of the agencies to work with the list of thousands of persons who called the task force on a toll-free line to offer some form of sponsorship, on the grounds that most of the offers came from persons who simply wanted cheap labor."

But some, like Gaetana Enders, do not share the scruples of the voluntary agencies. A former member of the President's Advisory Committee on Refugees and wife of Assistant Secretary of State Tom Enders,

Mrs. Enders is considered to be one of the most energetic people in Washington in finding sponsors for the refugees. "My big thing, darling," she told *Washington Post* reporter Sally Quinn, "is to make it kind of chic to have a family of refugees for a couple of months." The problem, she acknowledged, is that most people want servants, not families. "I don't think it would be too bad to be a domestic for a while," she said, "but it would be too bad if the intellectuals had to do it." Besides, she added, "they don't know how to work the appliances and they break them." Mrs. Enders claims credit for placing nearly 400 refugees, though acquaintances complain of being harassed by her inquiries on their "servant situation."

Reverend Carl McIntire, the fundamentalist preacher, has other ideas about how the refugees could be of use. He owns about 300 acres of land in Cape Canaveral, Florida, which he intends to transform into a "Viet habitat" complete with paddy fields, irrigation dikes, water buffalo, cows, chickens, ducks, palm trees and banana trees. In one area will be an "authentic" Vietnamese village "like our boys went into during the war," McIntire told visiting *Newsweek* reporters, and adjoining the village will be a mock Special Forces camp. Some 40 Vietnamese in native dress will "inhabit" the village and behave in an exotic manner. The Special Forces camp will have trenches, mortar bunkers, sandbags and sham machine guns. "Outside those bulwarks will be crisscrossing barbed wire, punji stakes, and fake Claymore mines, then a moat, more punji stakes, more barbed wire and, at the edge, another sandbag wall," *Newsweek* reported on 8 September 1975. McIntire's plan is to open this "Vietnamese Disneyland," which he calls the "New Vietnam," in time for the winter tourist season. "After a tour gets inside the camp, we'll have a recording broadcast a fire fight, mortars exploding, bullets flying, Vietnamese screaming," an associate of McIntire said. According to *Newsweek*, "While an air raid siren shrieks, Floridians outfitted as G.I.'s will fire blanks at an unseen enemy and tourists who get into the spirit can take shelter in the barracks." "Tourists are going to love this," McIntire declared, "and every penny will go back to the Vietnamese. The Bible says love your neighbor. We're taking them in our arms and giving them our love."

In California, an evangelist got together with an Air Force veteran who flew some 300 bombing missions over Vietnam to establish "Hope Village," a reception center to help refugees find homes and jobs. When the refugees—assisted by Hope Village—were given jobs at Egg City, said to be the world's largest egg production facility, they found themselves being used as pawns in a labor dispute. They had been hired to replace striking workers allied with the United Farm Workers. "The problem with the Vietnamese is that they're a captive labor force," a UFW organizer said. They can be manipulated by the Egg

City bosses, he explained, because "they've just been through a traumatic experience and are very insecure . . .they have no place to go."

The Pentagon is interested in scooping up certain refugees, *Air Force Times* on 9 July 1975 reported. Enlistment preference will be given to some 8000 Vietnamese and Cambodians who previously had been trained by the U.S. Armed Forces. Defense officials emphasize the economic advantages, noting that the program would enable the military services to "acquire trained individuals at minimum costs."

The careless attitude of the Task Force towards refugee sponsorship, in their frantic rush to get the camps emptied out, has created additional hardships. Problems are multiplying between Vietnamese released from the camps and their American sponsors. "At this point, there appears to be a very alarming rate of breakdown," said Dale DeHaan, of the Senate Refugee Subcommittee. "We're getting scores of phone calls from refugees and sponsors who have nowhere to turn. . .In all my 12 years in refugee placement I've never seen a breakdown rate like this." Much of the blame, in the view of private agency officials, rests on the "direct release" program run by the Task Force. They contend that the breakdown rates between refugees and their sponsors have increased rapidly to the point where it "may now slow down the entire resettlement program—already lagging far behind schedule—and add unexpected extra costs." (*Washington Post*, 9 July 1975). Although the Task Force claims that their sponsorship program is going on well, DeHaan reported that in fact the rate of refugee releases from the camps have fallen off sharply, from the goal of 1,000 a day to between 400 and 800 daily.

It is difficult to estimate how many refugees would wish to return home if they were given reliable information about current conditions in Vietnam. Many have been deterred by the bloodbath rumors they hear in the camps. Thus far, some 2,000 Vietnamese have formally declared their intention to repatriate, and the Provisional Revolutionary Government (PRG) of South Vietnam has expressed its willingness to accept those who wish to return. In late May 1975, the PRG formally asked the U.N. High Commissioner for Refugees to take the necessary steps to begin the repatriation effort. Refuting earlier reports that the U.S. government was the initiator, a U.N. spokesman stated: "They [the PRG] said they wanted to allow refugees who wanted to return home a chance to come back to their native land. It's not a matter of forcing them to do it as some have suggested. They came to us first and asked us to help return refugees who wanted to return to Vietnam."

Many of those seeking repatriation say that they were forced to leave Vietnam or that they fled in panic. Among them are members of a group of 65 Vietnamese airmen who were flown to Guam against their will. Thirteen of the group charged—and the

U.S. Air Force has admitted—that they were forcibly drugged and knocked unconscious with sodium pentathol and thorazine and then abducted to Guam. Several of the group revealed that they had left South Vietnam by commandeered aircraft on the last day of the war. They had disagreed with their commander's orders to fight the PRG, and became frightened when military police shot and killed several would-be deserters.

The official U.S. position is that the refugees are free to return to Vietnam if they wish. In actuality, State Department officials have been anything but helpful on the matter of repatriation. Despite its role in transporting thousands of Vietnamese from their homeland, the Ford Administration has refused to contact the PRG directly on repatriation questions. Moreover, high U.S. officials have made false charges about the PRG's attitude. For example, L. Dean Brown, former head of the Task Force, told Congress on May 22 that the return of the Vietnamese was hampered by the "obstreperous attitude" of the PRG. He also implied that there was a delay in repatriation because the UNHCR was waiting for assurances that the returned Vietnamese would not be punished. The following day, a UNHCR spokesman disputed Brown's assertion, noting that their relations with the PRG have been "positive" and that the PRG was "cooperating" with his agency. The spokesman also said that the question of punishment had never arisen since "there have been no reprisal actions taken against refugees repatriated by this office." On another occasion, UNHCR officials were obligated to refute U.S. government charges of deliberate foot-dragging on the part of the PRG. As one U.N. source put it, the PRG "is in the process of reorganizing their country, and this may not be their number one priority. So I don't consider it an abnormally long time, given that the two countries were more or less at a state of war some months ago."

But the underlying reasons for the false U.S. charges are that, having brought the Vietnamese here originally presumably to "save them from communism," it would be both embarrassing and counter-productive to the Ford Administration if they were allowed to return to their homeland. A superpower should never admit when it is wrong, as Kissinger has been fond of saying. Throughout the history of the war, the U.S. government has ignored the basic needs of the Vietnamese people in trying to establish an American model of democracy in Southeast Asia. Although the American war effort in Vietnam has essentially ended, the U.S. government continues to ignore the basic needs of the Vietnamese people, especially those who have been brought here. What kind of life lies ahead for these isolated Vietnamese? When will the U.S. government realize that Vietnam and the Vietnamese are not America or Americans and cannot necessarily be forced to follow such a pattern? ★

*from the **Philippine News*** *Week of October 4-10, 1975*

The story of the Marcos coercion

Following is an affidavit executed by Alex A. Esclamado, publisher and editor-in-chief of *Philippine
News,* detailing the harassment and blackmail campaign launched by President Marcos against *Philippine
News.*

UNITED STATES OF AMERICA
STATE OF CALIFORNIA
CITY & COUNTY OF SAN FRANCISCO

AFFIDAVIT

I, ALEJANDRO A. ESCLAMADO, of legal age,
married to LOURDES MITRA-ESCLAMADO, resident of San Francisco, California, after being sworn
to in accordance with law, hereby depose and say:

1. That my wife and I and our seven children
are all citizens of the United States of America;

2. That I am the Publisher and Editor-in-Chief
of the PHILIPPINE NEWS (formerly the MANILA
CHRONICLE, U.S. EDITION), a weekly newspaper
published in San Francisco, California, and of general
circulation primarily within the Filipino community
in the United States and Canada, since August 30,
1961; that the PHILIPPINE NEWS is my sole proprietorship; that I have not received any financial
support for its operation from anyone other than
from members of my family and that of my wife;
and, that the PHILIPPINE NEWS does not serve as a
mouthpiece for any particular vested interest anywhere whatsoever;

3. That the editorial policy of the PHILIPPINE
NEWS is against the continuation of martial law in
the Philippines and for the restoration of American-
style democracy in that country, which we believe is
what the greatest majority of the people of the Philippines want if given their full and free choice;

4. That in pursuance of this editorial policy, the
PHILIPPINE NEWS has been publishing events and
news items which are critical of Philippine President

Ferdinand E. Marcos and his martial law regime,
materials which do not find print in the controlled
press in the Philippines;

5. That the latest expose, which we have carried
in the front pages of the PHILIPPINE NEWS and
continues to be the dominant item of news at this
time, is the now well-publicized MIJARES-MARCOS
bribery affair which was originally reported by Washington Columnist Jack Anderson in his internationally syndicated column of July 2, 1975, (Annex "A,"
"A-1," "A-2"), a matter which is now of record in
the Subcommittee on International Organizations of
the Committee on International Relations of the U.S.
House of Representatives and the subject of a current
investigation by the U.S. Department of Justice,
particularly, the F.B.I.;

6. That in retaliation to the extensive PHILIP-
PINE NEWS coverage of the MIJARES bribery
scandal and its persistent anti-martial law editorial
policy which have obviously become prejudicial to
the efforts of the Philippine government in creating
for itself a positive image upon the minds of the
Filipinos in the United States and the American
people, especially Official Washington, so that U.S.
military and economic assistance to his government
shall continue to flow, President Marcos has now
launched in the United States a campaign of harrassment and blackmail against PHILIPPINE NEWS by
virtually coercing its advertisers to withdraw their
advertisements from the PHILIPPINE NEWS;

7. That while the formal means used in such
subtle coercion are so-called "requests" for cooperation, these "requests" are actually coupled with
unwritten and veiled threats to the effect that failure
on the part of advertisers to comply with the government's "requests" would result in great prejudice to
their business operations because privileges formerly
accorded by the Philippine government to these busi-

[Editor's note: Owing to space consideration, the Annexes
referred to in this article have not been reprinted. Please see
Philippine News, October 4-10, 1975.]

*In retaliation for the anti-martial law
editorial policy of the Philippine News
and its extensive coverage of the bribery scandal,
Marcos has now launched in the US a campaign
of harassment and blackmail against the newspaper
by pressuring advertisers to boycott the paper.*

nesses dealing with the Philippine Consulates and dealing with other Philippine governmental agencies, like the tourism, customs and immigration officers, will be withdrawn, in some form or another;

8. That the businesses which have now succumbed to the campaign of coercion are travel agencies, which constitute the biggest PHILIPPINE NEWS advertisers; that these travel agencies have no choice but to grant the so-called "requests" because substantial documentation is being handled by the Philippine Consulate offices in the United States and facilitation of which would be made difficult; that Filipino tourists fares of visiting the Philippines are partly subsidized by the government under what is called a "Balikbayan" program and such subsidy is being controlled by the Philippine Consular establishments; that tourists who arrive in the Philippines are accorded certain privileges such as free customs inspection and other courtesies of the port. Those courtesies could be withdrawn from passengers or clients of travel agencies which do not comply with the "requests" of the Philippine government; that the Philippine government, through other indirect means, can make it difficult for business dealing with the Philippines to transact their usual business in the Philippines once they are blacklisted by the Marcos regime as being "uncooperative";

9. That the individual and officials used by Marcos in carrying out his plans of harrassment of our advertisers are: The Secretary of Tourism, Jose D. Aspiras, who was the former press secretary to President Marcos, and a close confidant; The Consul General of the Philippines in San Francisco, Trinidad Q. Alconcel, who was the principal figure in the Mijares bribery attempt; Presidential Assistant Guillermo De Vega, the other co-principal in the Mijares bribery scandal; The Director of Tourism, Jose Clemente, Jr., recently elected president of East Asia Travel Association; Mr. Jose O. Cobarrubias, a top tourism industry official, Owner of the Filipinas Hotel; De. Leonilo Malabed, a San Francisco physi-

cian, who claims to be a townmate of President Marcos and his "eyes and ears" within the Filipino-American community in the area and a very close associate and adviser to Consul General Alconcel; and other minor officials;

10. That the details of the harrassment and coercion activities are as follows:

(a) As to PHIL-AM TRAVEL AGENCY: Mr. Emile Heredia, President and Owner of the agency, was in Manila during the third week of August, 1975. While there, Consul General Alconcel brought him to Malacanang Palace wherein Presidential Assistant Guillermo De Vega, in concert with Alconcel, strongly urged Heredia to withdraw the advertising of PHIL-AM TRAVEL AGENCY from PHILIPPINE NEWS. Mr. Heredia informed me that he resisted the requests by explaining to both officials that it would be bad public relations for the government if the plans they had would be carried out. Heredia also informed me that he told De Vega and Alconcel that PHIL-AM TRAVEL has a five year advertising contract and that PHIL-AM TRAVEL has paid for the advertising insertions one year in advance. Heredia intimated to me that the two officials told him flatly that the contract was immaterial to them and that he should really withdraw completely from patronage of PHILIPPINE NEWS.

Sometime thereafter, on or about August 20, 1975, Heredia was again approached by Jose O. Cobarrubias, a top travel industry official, that Secretary of Tourism Jose D. Aspiras has requested him to convey Aspiras' request that PHIL-AM TRAVEL withdraw its advertising in the PHILIPPINE NEWS. According to Heredia, he wanted Mr. Cobarrubias to make the request in behalf of Aspiras in writing so that he could have something to hold on to or with which to explain to me in case I would inquire about the reason for the breach of our contractual relations. Consequently, Mr. Cobarrubias made the formal letter, ANNEX "B-1";

When Mr. Heredia arrived in San Francisco he

called me up at my home on Sunday, August 24, and requested that we talk about [our] advertising contract. My wife and I went to see him in his office at 210 Post Street, San Francisco on that day. During our meeting, Mr. Heredia explained to us in detail what had transpired in Manila, particularly, the requests of Malacanang officials and Alconcel to have PHIL-AM TRAVEL withdraw its advertising program notwithstanding our existing advertising contract. Heredia related to us how he tried to explain that it would be a mistake for the government to proceed with its intended course of action because the advertising program was helping the Philippine government promote tours to the Philippines, at the travel agencies' expense. However, Heredia sounded worried and did not know what to do at that time because he was seriously concerned of what the Marcos government would do against his business and family interests. He also told us that he would have a conference with Dr. Leonilo Malabed the following day, Monday, August 25th, after which conference he would let us know his decision.

After their conference with Dr. Malabed, Mr. & Mrs. Emile Heredia talked to my wife and myself. Both sounded very much alarmed. Mr. Heredia said that Dr. Malabed told him, in so many words, that (Malabed) had received a call from Malacanang and that the government is unhappy about Heredia's "uncooperative" remarks before Presidential Assistant Guillermo De Vega and Alconcel. Heredia then proceeded to explain to us how vulnerable his travel agency would be because of the tremendous volume of tourists which go to the Philippines and that documentation of their passengers in San Francisco could be delayed or made difficult and that their passengers in San Francisco could be delayed or made difficult and that their passengers could be harassed in the Philippines in some form or another. During our conversation, I tried to convince the Heredias that all of the things being done were actually just coercion and blackmail but that the Marcos government would not dare do the obviously discriminatory acts which Heredia feared would be done to his passengers and to his business. However, our reassurances did not work, as the Heredias remain visibly concerned about the continuing pressures made to bear upon them by the Marcos government, through Dr. Malabed. Mr. Heredia then informed us that he had a scheduled conference with a visiting official from Manila, The Director of Tourism, Mr. Jose Clemente, Jr. He told us that he would then let me know their decision, on or about August 26, 1975.

Immediately after the conference with Director Clemente, Heredia informed me that he informed Mr. Clemente of his stand that it would be a mistake to withdraw advertising from PHILIPPINE NEWS exactly on the same points which he mentioned to Presidential Assistant De Vega and Consul General Alconcel in Manila. He told me that Director Clemente was going to call Manila and propose some kind of a compromise. According to Heredia, the compromise proposed was to reduce the advertising of PHIL-AM TRAVEL in the PHILIPPINE NEWS by one half its current volume and not withdraw it completely. However, Heredia informed me later that Director Clemente, had informed him that Malacanang did not want any "half measures" and that the advertising must be completely withdrawn.

On the basis of Director Clemente's information, PHIL-AM TRAVEL AGENCY had no choice but to decide to completely withdraw its advertising from the PHILIPPINE NEWS, consisting of one (1) full page in every weekly issue. A copy of the formal letter of cancellation, dated August 27, 1975, is hereto attached as ANNEX "C";

PHIL-AM TRAVEL AGENCY has been our consistent advertiser for over ten (10) years.

(b) As to GEM TRAVEL SERVICE: Also during the third week of August, 1975, Mr. Joseph A. Libunao, a top executive of GEM TRAVEL SERVICE, was in Manila. Like Heredia, he was also approached by the same Marcos government officials and was likewise "requested" to withdraw his agency's advertising from PHILIPPINE NEWS.

The impact of Malacanang's approach hit Mr. Libunao with such intensity that he immediately sent a panicky telex to his main office announcing his arrival and requesting for an immediate "executive meeting" of the top officials of the company the day following his arrival. In Libunao's words: "WE ARE INVOLVED NOW WITH THE CONSULATE SCANDAL (referring to the Marcos-De Vega-Alconcel bribery attempt on Mijares) . . . . I AND HEREDIA WAS REQUESTED BY ASPIRAS TO COOPERATE WITH MALACANANG TO HELP THEM WITH THE SCANDAL . . . . WILL EXPLAIN IN DETAILS AT THE MEETING" . . . . "Please refer to copy of a telex received in San Francisco through Telex machine EVERTEX67697, on or about August 21, 1975, and attached hereto as ANNEX "D";

One can only figure out what transpired during the executive meeting of GEM TRAVEL SERVICE. In my various conversations with Mr. Larry Marquez, the company's President, and other top GEM executives, I was informed of the same pressures made to bear upon them as outlined earlier, in detail, in the case of PHIL-AM TRAVEL AGENCY. Mr. Marquez and some of his top associates, apologetically told me that even if their company needed the advertising exposure in the PHILIPPINE NEWS which, they admitted, was producing tremendous results, they have to cooperate with President Marcos' government. Like the Heredias, they fear that their business operations would suffer harassment and discrimination, in many ways, at the all-powerful hands of the Philippine government, if they fail to cooperate.

Then, GEM TRAVEL SERVICE was furnished a

The Conjugal Dictatorship of Ferdinand and Imelda

copy of the formal letter of request written by Jose Cobarrubias to Heredia in behalf of Aspiras, earlier referred to as ANNEX "B-1." The corresponding letter of transmittal addressed to Mr. Larry Marquez, is attached hereto as ANNEX "B."

Like PHIL-AM TRAVEL AGENCY, the advertising contract of GEM TRAVEL SERVICE with PHILIPPINE NEWS is also a five-year agreement, with a prepayment of one year. Ironically, GEM TRAVEL SERVICE had just increased its advertising insertion from one-half (½) page to one (1) full page, effective June 19, 1975. The increased advertising insertions are fully paid in advance until December 31, 1975. Like PHIL-AM TRAVEL AGENCY, it has been our consistent advertiser for many years.

Notwithstanding the foregoing factors, GEM TRAVEL SERVICE had to accede to the Marcos' demands, apparently against its will. The company's letter of cancellation of August 28, 1975, is attached hereto as ANNEX "E."

(c) As to JOANN'S TRAVEL AGENCY: On or about August 18, 1975, I went to see Mrs. Annie Abenojar, sole proprietress of JOANN'S TRAVEL SERVICE. At that time, we made an accounting on our past advertising contract and agreed on a one (1)

year renewal. Mrs. Abenojar paid PHILIPPINE NEWS the sum of ONE HUNDRED EIGHTY DOLLARS ($180.00), as initial payment, in advance, for the small advertising program to be carried out in September, 1975. During my conversation with Mrs. Abenojar, she informed me that she was approached by Consul General Alconcel, Dr. Leonilo Malabed and other Philippine Consulate officials in San Francisco, requesting her to withdraw her agency's advertising from PHILIPPINE NEWS and transfer the same to a newly-published weekly newspaper in San Francisco reportedly owned by the Marcos family. Mrs. Abenojar informed me that she refused the request and that she would advertise only in the PHIL-LIPPINE NEWS.

On or about Tuesday, August 26, 1975, Mrs. Abenojar and her assistant, a certain Mr. Vince Flores, called up our office and informed our Advertising Department that JOANN'S TRAVEL SERVICE was cancelling its advertising from PHILIPPINE NEWS effective immediately. When asked why, they informed PHILIPPINE NEWS, in so many words, that they received a call from Manila requesting that the ads be withdrawn immediately. Mrs. Abenojar prides herself in referring to Secretary of Tourism Jose

Aspiras as a "relative." Attached is a copy of the letter of cancellation of JOANN'S TRAVEL SERVICE, dated August 27, 1975, as ANNEX "F";

(d) As to ORIENTEX TRAVEL: I was informed by Mr. Primo Quesada, President of ORIENTEX TRAVEL, that he was also approached by Director of Tourism Jose Clemente, Jr., during the same period (August 25-28, 1975), requesting for the same favor of withdrawing its advertising from PHILIPPINE NEWS in the interest of the Philippine government. Mr. Quesada informed me that he politely listened to the official's message but that he has not decided to accede to the request. He is maintaining a "wait-and-see" attitude and is expecting that some form of harassment will be done to his business very soon. Like PHIL-AM TRAVEL and GEM TRAVEL SERVICE, Mr. Quesada's ORIENTEX TRAVEL has a substantial advertising program in PHILIPPINE NEWS and is also paid in advance.

11. That in all my various conversations with the executives of the travel agencies mentioned above, it was very clear to me that they are all afraid of displeasing the government of President Marcos even if they believe that what is being done to them and the PHILIPPINE NEWS constitutes a serious infringement upon the fundamental rights of free American businessmen.

12. That in connection with the present campaign of harassment upon PHILIPPINE NEWS and its advertisers, Alconcel, Malabed and Aspiras have reportedly assured President Marcos that PHILIPPINE NEWS "WILL CLOSE DOWN WITHIN SIX (6) months and that the Esclamado family will start starving," or assurances to that effect;

13. That prior to the present economic pressures being exerted upon the PHILIPPINE NEWS through the use of coercion on its advertisers, the PHILIPPINE NEWS, its staff and my family were subjected to various forms of harassment, intimidation, coercion and blackmail, as follows:

(a) THE PHILIPPINE NEWS STAFF WAS BLACKLISTED AND THREATENED WITH DEPORTATION — Upon the declaration of martial law on September 21, 1972, and during the few months thereafter, PHILIPPINE NEWS did not take a stand on the martial law question because it gave the benefit of the doubt to President Marcos, who was then serving a legal tenure of office under the old Philippine Constitution. The declared noble objectives of Marcos' "emergency" authoritarian rule were worthy of commendation although they could have been done during his long democratic tenure as a Philippine political leader.

After six months of martial law, however, the pressing reasons for its declaration had become non-existent. For instance, peace and order was completely restored, the alleged communist rebellion was fully controlled and the life of the people had returned to normal. Then another set of reasons for

its continuance was pronounced, i.e., the reformation of the Old Society into a New Society where there would be a redistribution of wealth so that the gap between the rich and the poor would be narrowed down, corruption would be completely abolished and the Philippines will be ushered into a new era of progress and social justice.

Unfortunately, as time went by, it was becoming clear that Marcos had really in mind ruling the Philippines permanently as a dictator. The redistribution of wealth policy became merely the transfer of ownership of properties and businesses from Marcos' enemies to his family, friends and cronies. The gap between the rich and the poor has widened significantly. As time went by, the regime became more and more oppressive and corrupt. Marcos has abolished Congress and popular elections. He has corrupted all other established democratic institutions in the country to serve his personal interest and ambitions. He ruled by decrees, as a dictator, and desired to "own" the country and its patrimony for as long as he can manage it.

PHILIPPINE NEWS, therefore, in April, 1973, started to take a strong stand against President Marcos and his martial law regime. It started advocating a return to democracy in the Philippines. It started the exposing the evils of the regime.

As Marcos' immediate response, he ordered the cancellation of the passports of several hundred persons known to have taken a stand against the continuation of martial law through a cabled order by his Secretary of Foreign Affairs Carlos P. Romulo. The PHILIPPINE NEWS staff and the Publisher were among those blacklisted on a ridiculous basis. Attached are copies of two cablegrams sent to the Ambassador of the Philippines in Washington, D.C., by Secretary Romulo enumerating the persons being blacklisted. They are submitted, herewith, as ANNEX "G" and ANNEX "G-1."

The strategy of Marcos was that once the passports were cancelled, the U.S. Immigration & Naturalization Service would be forced to deport the individuals concerned for lack of valid papers.

In order to escape from the Marcos deportation move, all the staff members of the PHILIPPINE NEWS who were affected filed for political asylum. Luckily, my wife, myself, and my children had already acquired permanent residence status at the time and were beyond the control of the Philippine government, to a degree. Later on, my family was able to acquire American citizenship, thus becoming beyond the jurisdiction of the Marcos government. However, some of my staff members remain under political asylum status.

(b) COERCIVE PRESSURES EXERTED ON ME THROUGH MR. EUGENIO LOPEZ TO ENABLE MARCOS TO ACQUIRE OWNERSHIP OF PHILIPPINE NEWS — The late Mr. Eugenio Lopez was under pressure to transfer his giant industrial empire (The MANILA ELECTRIC COMPANY, the biggest private corporation in the Philippines, etc.) to the control of the Marcos family and associates for practically NO JUST CONSIDERATION. As exposed in the world press, he submitted to the demands of Marcos in order to secure the release of his son, Eugenio Lopez, Jr., who has been a Marcos prisoner for almost three years now. During the time of the Marcos-Lopez negotiations, Marcos tried to include the PHILIPPINE NEWS as part of the infamous transaction. (The U.S. Congress, the American people and press organizations throughout the world are familiar with the Marcos-Lopez extortion affair. PARADE MAGAZINE published a substantial coverage on the subject.)

My wife and I resisted the blackmail and coercion tactics of Marcos and his agents exerted through Mr. Eugenio Lopez, by completely dissociating ourselves from Mr. Lopez with whom [we] were closely associated for many years.

Attached, hereto, is a copy of my letter of dissociation from Mr. Lopez, dated October 16, 1973, and marked as ANNEX "H." The term "Joey" in the letter was the nickname we called each other in private. Attached, also, is a copy of my telex to the Chairman of the Board of the Manila Electric Company, marked as ANNEX "H-1." The story behind that telex, was one of fierce resistance on the part of my wife and myself to the tremendous pressures of coercion, harassment and blackmail which is too long to include in this Affidavit.

(c) HARASSMENT ON MEMBERS OF MY FAMILY – During the period of my dissociation from Don Eugenio Lopez, my father-in-law, Hon. Ramon P. Mitra, became seriously ill in Manila. He had to come to the United States to seek medical attention at the University of California Hospital where in 1966 he was operated on for carcinoma of the prostate. The Philippine government doctors had properly certified to his need for treatment and recommended that he be allowed to travel to the United States. Please see attached medical Certification marked as ANNEX "J" and ANNEX "J-1."

Because of the stand taken by my wife and myself in resisting the purchase of PHILIPPINE NEWS by Marcos, (through his brother-in-law, Kokoy Romualdez) my father-in-law was not permitted to leave the Philippines unless he gave assurances that he would "work on" my wife and myself to change the editorial policy of PHILIPPINE NEWS in favor of the martial law regime. My father-in-law was too honorable to be used for Marcos' purposes. He preferred to remain in the Philippines and face the dire consequences of his illness. (He was a former member of the Philippine Congress for twenty-four years and at one time, concurrent Chairman of the House Appropriations Committee and the House Foreign Relations Committee. He was also consistently selected as one of the First Ten Most Outstanding Congressmen.)

Without his knowledge, therefore, I sought the intervention of the good offices of San Francisco Congressman Philip Burton and of the State Department so that he was finally able to leave the Philippines. Please refer to the attached copy of a letter I sent to Mr. Joseph A. O'Connell of Congressman Burton's office which is marked as ANNEX "K" and ANNEX "K-1"; a copy of Congressman Burton's letter to Hon. Linwood Holton of the Department of State, marked ANNEX "K-2"; and, a copy of a cablegram by Secretary Kissinger to the U.S. Embassy in Manila, as ANNEX "K-3."

As a result of the representation made by the Office of Congressman Burton and by the State Department, my father-in-law arrived in the United States on December 6, 1974 and he was able to get the desired medical treatment.

It may be mentioned, in this connection, that during this process of harassment by Marcos, I was made to understand that my father-in-law would be allowed to leave the Philippines if my wife would fetch him from Manila. It was suggested that my wife could arrive in Manila on a Saturday; and the following day, Sunday, both my wife and my father-in-law could leave the Philippines together. The suggestion was clearly an attempt to have my wife within the physical jurisdiction of the Marcos government so that she could be held as hostage for as long as the PHILIPPINE NEWS remained anti-Marcos and anti-martial law. The regime could have devised some kind of criminal excuse to imprison my wife even if she were a U.S. citizen.

14. That there were other incidents of harassment, intimidation and blackmail which PHILIPPINE NEWS and my family have been subjected to which are too long to mention in this document;

15. That this AFFIDAVIT is executed for the purpose of documenting the positive acts of President Marcos and his agents in extending the reign of fear, under martial law, to the territorial limits of the United States, especially, within the Filipino-American community; and,

16. That no amount of harassment, coercion and blackmail can make us change our editorial stand against the illegal and oppressive dictatorial and "conjugal" rule of Mr. and Mrs. Ferdinand E. Marcos; that PHILIPPINE NEWS shall continue to publish events and news materials about the truth of the repressive martial law regime, so that the American people may realize that the 43 million Filipinos need to be helped in their desire to be, once again, free.

IN WITNESS WHEREOF, I have hereunto signed this AFFIDAVIT, this 9th Day of September, 1975, with all ANNEXES made as integral parts thereof, in the City and County of San Francisco, State of California, U.S.A.

(Sgd.) ALEJANDRO A. ESCLAMADO
Affiant ★

The New Korea Editorial

KCIA Agents All Out to Get New Korea

To Our Readers and Concerned Citizens;

South Korean dictator President Park Chung-hee's acts of violence and repression of human rights aren't limited to Korea. Having succeeded at last in silencing the last bastion of the free press in South Korea by applying pressures to the advertisers to cancel their contracts with the *Dong-A Ilbo,* the largest and the only outspoken daily in Korea, Park regime is now applying the same tactics to the American citizens of Korean extraction and Koreans living in the United States.

In flagrant violation of the sovereignty of the United States, consulate officials and agents of the South Korean government in Los Angeles have been abusing consular privileges and have brought pressures upon Korean-Americans and Korean residents in California to mute their criticisms of Park regime.

Through seduction, open intimidation, and actual threat, those South Korean officials are illegally engaged in clandestine operations to control and manipulate life of the Korean-Americans.

First, in recent months my paper, *The New Korea,* which is the only independent Korean community newspaper in Los Angeles since 1905, was an object of the Korean consul general's subtle but brutal retaliation. Young Park, South Korean consulate general in Los Angeles, and the operatives of the

(continued on page 142)

[Editor's note: This editorial originally appeared on 27 November 1975 in *The New Korea,* a Korean-English language newspaper of Los Angeles. The oldest Korean publication in the United States, it was founded in 1905 by An Ch'ang-ho, one of the key leaders of the Korean independence movement in the United States. The following editorial by Editor-Publisher Woon-Ha Kim charges South Korean consular officials and agents of attempting to silence *The New Korea* for its open criticism of the Park Chung-hee government.]

Editor-Publisher Testifies

The South Korea in the

Statement by Woon-Ha Kim

Mr. Chairman and distinguished members of the committee:

To begin with, I wish to express my appreciation to you for your initiative in holding hearings on abusive and illicit activities of the Korean CIA in the U.S. This will be very beneficial to both Koreans and U.S. citizens.

Indeed, Korean CIA agents in the United States have committed many brutal deeds. The effect of these deeds is increasing. This causes concern on the part of the U.S. government and its citizens, so the importance of this hearing should be emphasized. First, Korean CIA agents who have taken freedom and human rights from people in Korea and demoted Koreans to the level of domestic animals, are now manipulating and intimidating Koreans in the U.S. by using clandestine means. They are creating a prison type atmosphere for many Koreans living in the U.S. just as they have done in Korea. These Korean-Americans are losing freedoms guaranteed under the U.S. Constitution just as their relatives in Korea have lost their freedom. They cannot express their feelings in public assemblies and are losing their human rights here; these Korean-Americans feel great pain from this kind of bondage.

The Korean community in Los Angeles where I live is the biggest in the United States. Because of abusive KCIA activities, the Korean-American residents of this area, call Los Angeles the second Seoul;

[Editor's note: This is the original unedited statement of Woon-Ha Kim, editor-publisher of *The New Korea,* before the House Subcommittee on International Organizations of the Committee on International Relations on 17 March 1976. Chaired by Congressman Donald M. Fraser of Minnesota, the subcommittee held hearings on the activities of the South Korean Central Intelligence Agency in the United States. The hearing will be published in late 1976.]

Activities of the Central Intelligence Agency United States

and they call the Korean Consul General a generalissimo, emergency decree commander, and a KCIA Los Angeles chief. Los Angeles is not U.S. territory to Korean-Americans; it has become rather a territory of South Korea. To these Koreans, the mayor of Los Angeles is not Tom Bradley but the Korean Consul General.

I would like to speak about how the KCIA is influencing Korean-Americans and Americans in the Los Angeles area. First, I would like to describe my own situation. I am publisher and editor of the weekly *The New Korea,* the oldest Korean language newspaper. My newspaper was established in 1905 in San Francisco. Until the 1960s, it was the only newspaper for the Korean community in the U.S. Before I came to the United States, I worked for *Chosun Ilbo* which is the oldest newspaper in Korea and very influential. I was associate city editor for ten years.

From 1969 to 1970, I served the Korean Journalists Association as chairman of the Committee on Freedom of the Press. From March to December, 1971, during the Korean presidential campaign between Kim Dae-jung and Park Chung-hee, I was first vice-president and acting president of the Korean Journalist Association; I headed the first movement for freedom of the press. My colleagues and I organized a nationwide resistance against Korean government and KCIA pressures on the press. At that time, the KCIA had many agents in press rooms and were trying to increase the intervention by preventing truth, real events and criticism of the government from being printed. They increased arrests and torture of journalists. We could not endure it any longer; therefore, we protested and resisted nationwide by calling for the withdrawal of KCIA agents from our companies. Because of this resistance, my colleagues and I of the Korean Journalist Association were summoned several times by the KCIA. I underwent inquisitions and intimidation. They came to my house

several times frightening my wife and children. The leaders of this resistance were fired and replaced. At that time, the president of the association resigned because of KCIA pressure. I took over the presidency but was also forced to resign. Immediately after that a Presidential Emergency was announced. I could do nothing in Korea. Therefore, in June, 1972, I came to the United States as a special correspondent for the *Chosun Ilbo* in Los Angeles. In August, 1973, I decided to take up residence in the United States and moved to the Los Angeles bureau of *Tonga Ilbo*.

In my new position, I was once again surprised because Korean-American journalism in the U.S. suffered conditions similar to those in Korea. This was true in the United States which guarantees freedom of the press! At that time, *Hankook Ilbo, Tonga Ilbo, Miju Shinmun, The New Korea* and the Korean Television Broadcasting Company had offices in Los Angeles. There were two KCIA agents who also held the titles of Consul and Vice Consul. They directly controlled the news media. They controlled news and advertising. When reporters did not obey their instructions, they intimidated them; and additional intimidation came from newspaper headquarters in Seoul at the direction of KCIA-Seoul. Their methods of intimidation included threats of losing jobs, refusing extension of passports and other red-tape, pressuring newspaper companies to recall the Los Angeles-based journalists and sometimes physical threats were used. I was also intimidated and experienced direct intervention from the KCIA for about one year. In July, 1974, I made up my mind to resign as editor-in-chief of the *Oriental Daily News*.

In August of that year, I took over *The New Korea* and announced a policy in that paper of protecting human rights of Korean-Americans, of protecting their well-being, of promoting the general

(continued on page 143)

KCIA Agents All Out to Get New Korea

(continued from page 140)

notorious Korean Central Intelligence Agency (KCIA) under the disguise of consulate staff in the city, have brought pressures on Korean Air Lines (KAL) Los Angeles office, Ms. Sonia S. Suk's real estate company, and other major advertisers to cancel their contracts with my paper.

My paper had concluded a contract with the Korean Air Lines last July 31 to run the airlines advertisements for 26 consecutive weeks starting the same month for $1,430. However, a few weeks later an ad manager of the airlines dropped by my office and asked me to discontinue running the ads saying that he was instructed to do so from his head office in Seoul. We did as we were told by the airlines.

As I understand, the KAL had taken a policy of so-called separation of business and politics and decided to do business with us because they knew *The New Korea* was the only Korean community newspaper that can speak out against corrupt and lawless Korean government and its agents in Los Angeles thus getting ever popular among the Korean residents in the United States.

Pressed to explain why the airlines decided to halt the ad abruptly, the embarrassed KAL officer said, "I am sorry I cannot explain the reason for the cancellation. But without saying, everybody knows why it is."

In the case of Ms. Sonia Suk, a local realtor, she asked to take out her ads from my paper saying, "I really cannot stand their (the consulate officials') pressures to refrain from helping *The New Korea*. Let me protect my business interests."

As the result of the consulate's pressures, one ad sponsor after another followed suit leaving some of the ad columns blank. And this series of unbelievable acts on the part of the advertisers resulted in [the] most peculiar and interesting ad columns a newspaper can have. Our readers are beginning to fill in the blank ad spaces with their statements of encouragement for us.

A young woman who identified herself only as Sunie asked in the ad, "*The New Korea,* Where am I supposed to emigrate for the second time when you tumble down?" She said she came to the U.S. in disappointment after the *Dong-A Ilbo* was knocked out by the government forces. A second middle-aged amateur advertiser said, "How come you keep chasing and suffocating me?"

Second, the Korean government agents have issued stern orders to the local Korean shopowners not to display books and booklets published by my paper. The Olympic Market and the Somun-nan-jip beef dealer in Los Angeles returned the "Kim Dae-jung Essays" and "Kim Chi-ha Poems" to us saying,

"We cannot sell them in my shop because the consulate officials ordered not to."

Third, Park Young, the consul general, told the organizers of the annual Korean Festival last September not to let *The New Korea* sponsor the "Little Princess and Prince Contest" in his move to discourage promotion of the paper during the Festival period.

The consul general is also coercing board members of *The New Korea* to quit their positions. He has used Mr. Kim Si-myun and Prof. Kim Hyong-il, both board members of my paper, to buy off the publisher of *The New Korea* in the favor of the Korean government.

Fourth, as the publisher of the paper persists in his independent editorial policy despite the Korean government's cunning maneuvers to win over him, the consul general is trying to discredit him as a Communist. According to the Rev. Kwon Hi-sang, the consul general described *The New Korea* as "Communist" last September.

The South Korean government's persecution of the Korean news media in the United States knows no bounds.

On October 5, 1975, the Korean Television Broadcasting Co. of Los Angeles which airs Korean-language program on weekends on Channel 22 made a public statement through its own program that the press attache of the Korean consulate general in Los Angeles has "attempted to annihilate this broadcasting."

In the statement, Pai Ham-duk, president of the Korean television, charged, among other things, that the press attache has frequently demanded in threatening manner that the company air certain materials the Korean government source supplied, and that he also pressured advertisers to withdraw their advertisements from this television company in an attempt to bring it under the sway of the Park Chung-hee government.

These incredible activities of the Korean officials are in clear violation of the First Amendment and other U.S. laws. Besides, these are most unfriendly, unorthodox, unforgivable, and very hostile acts of a foreign government in violation of the sovereignty of the United States.

To uphold the ideals and principles set forth in the Constitution of the United States, and to maintain this great country as a free, democratic, peaceful and safe society to live in, I respectfully demand that the people and government of the United States take effective measures to put an end to all such illegal activities of Park Chung-hee government in this country, and expel its officials responsible for these activities from the United States so that people could live free of such fear from Park's spooks. ★

(continued from page 141)

welfare of the Korean-American community, and of upholding the tenets and spirit of democracy. This is not Korea; this is America. Korean-Americans in this country are not people of South Korea; they are U.S. citizens or in the process of becoming U.S. citizens. Most Korean immigrants dislike dictators. They immigrated here in search of freedom and human dignity. Why should they suffer at the hands of a dictator here? Why should they accept the intrusion on their freedom and human rights? Reflecting on this, I decided to work for the restoration of human rights and to work for social justice for my motherland. This decision and determination were immediately reflected in *The New Korea*.

Korean residents overwhelmingly welcomed this kind of determination. My newspaper became a gospel of democracy, an advocate of human rights for the Korean people, and it enjoyed the reputation of fighting for these things. As a result, the Korean Consul General and the KCIA tried to influence me to become pro-Park. In September, 1974, Mr. Young Park, the Korean Consul General in Los Angeles, recommended that the Korean government invite me to Korea at government expense. They gave me several round trip tickets to Korea and said if I went to Seoul, the Korean government would treat me very well. I rejected the offer and returned the tickets. The press attache of the Korean Consul General in Los Angeles invited me to lunch and dinner several times. He asked me not to criticize the Korean government's pressure on Koreans and the illicit acts of Korean government agents. I ignored his request.

I cannot remember the exact day, but I think it was in March, 1974 that the KCIA agents, who were also the Consul and Vice Consul, invited me to Pear Garden, a Korean restaurant in Los Angeles. They intimidated me by saying that I would experience retaliation if I continued to criticize the inhuman activities of the Korean government and to publish activities of anti-Park resistors. As I rejected their requests repeatedly, Consul General Young Park, the KCIA station chief, and the press attaché invited me to luncheon at the Grand Garden Restaurant of Los Angeles. They emphasized their request again. They especially asked me not to criticize President Park directly. They pressured me to publish false stories slandering Admiral Young-woon Lee who was the former Chief of Staff for the Korean Navy. He is a leader in the movement for democracy and is Vice Chairman of the Korean Congress for Democracy and Unification. Mr. Chairman, I would like to submit that false story for the record. This story was handed to me already printed. I would like to submit this as real evidence of KCIA tactics.

In spite of this kind of request and intimidation, I did not obey their instructions, and they then applied very subtle and brutal pressures on my newspaper. They pressured advertisers not to support my paper. They invited Korean businessmen to golf clubs and private parties and then asked them not to help *The New Korea* and to cancel their advertising contracts with me and not to give my paper any new business. Mr. Young Park also organized a Korean information committee which consisted of representatives from the Korean government, Korean institutes and big Korean businessmen. He became chairman of the committee, then he asked each member not to help my paper and not to give me advertisements. Under these circumstances, Korean Air Lines cancelled their advertising contracts with me. Korean Air Lines had signed a contract with me on July 31, 1975. They wanted to run their ads for 26 weeks at a total price of $1,430, but after a few weeks, the ad manager and one of his aides came to my office and appealed to me to cancel their ads. The manager said instruction came from Seoul headquarters. He said he was sorry that he could not give the exact reason for the cancellation, but that I could guess the reason for the ad contract's cancellation. He said I should be able to guess who brought the pressure. "If you report this cancellation in your newspaper," he said, "I will be fired." Thus, he wanted me to remain silent. To compensate me for the cancellation, he gave me $300. He was innocent of any wrong-doing, so I could not report this immediately. That I should be able to guess where pressure came from is easily understood among Koreans. It goes without saying among Koreans that the reference is to the KCIA.

The KCIA regularly reports news media activities to headquarters. If they have trouble which cannot be handled here, they ask Seoul headquarters to handle it directly. Mr. Chairman, I'd like to submit the Korean Air Lines ad contract for the record. Other major advertisers also cancelled their ad contracts; still others reduced the amount of their ads. The thing of greatest importance here is that new advertisers could not submit ads to my paper for fear of KCIA retaliation, though they did advertise in other papers. They told me they knew I was all right and wanted to give me ads, but they couldn't give me ads because they wanted to protect their lives and business interests. They told me they were sorry.

The case of one realtor is also relevant here. She said she tried to ignore KCIA pressures, but finally she said she could not endure it any longer. So, she asked me to withdraw her ad from my paper. She said if she didn't withdraw her ad, her business would be damaged. Thus, my advertising revenue began to decrease.

The KCIA also ordered restaurant and grocery owners not to display in their shops the books I published. One of the books was Kim Dae-jung's essays, the other the poems of Kim Chi-ha. After issuing this kind of stern order, one of the grocery owners returned those books. Other owners put them in the corners of their stores, where they were not easily seen. Some restaurant owners bought all of them and gave them in bulk to their close friends.

Another instance. Since two years ago, Korea Town Development Company has held an annual Korean festival. *The New Korea* has sponsored the "Little Princess and Prince Contest" for this Korean festival during the past two years. The KCIA pressured the Korean Festival Executive Committee to discontinue the sponsorship of the contest by *The New Korea*; and they pressured Korean residents not to join in the various activities of *The New Korea*. They wanted to minimize the influence of *The New Korea*'s activities.

The KCIA began to distribute very vicious slander and false propaganda about my newspaper throughout the Korean community. In August, 1975, I can't recall the exact date, Korean National Assemblyman Kee Chun-kang, who was formerly chief commander of the Korean Marine Corps, visited me and said he was meeting me on behalf of the director of the KCIA, Mr. Shin Jik-soo, and Minister of Culture and Information Lee Won-kyung. At that time he offered me a deal: if I stopped criticizing the Korean government, the Korean government could give me a special fund through direct and indirect channels. The amount would be considerable. He said this was the final offer. "If you reject this," he said, "you will face retaliation." I flatly rejected his offer. Right after his return to Korea, the Los Angeles KCIA sent one guy to me who has a close connection with the KCIA and is known as an underground KCIA agent. That guy invited me to lunch at Kyung Hae Rhy, a Korean restaurant. At that time he said he brought the final notice from the KCIA which he said came from Seoul headquarters and was confirmed by the Los Angeles KCIA. He asked me to choose from among three alternatives: one was to stop criticizing the Korean government and receive a newspaper fund or a government position if I wanted it. The second was to sell the newspaper or close it down. The third was to face retaliation. I asked him what kind of retaliation there would be. He said they would begin to isolate me from the Korean community as a first step. I rejected all three alternatives.

Immediately after this, KCIA agents including Young Park, Korean Consul General, distributed vicious slander to discredit me by calling me a communist. Among Koreans, being called a communist means very serious damage. The KCIA told Korean organizations, institutions and readers that to continue to have a close relationship with *The New Korea* would discredit them as communists. With this kind of slander and false stories, they brought me great damage and discredited my newspaper. They created a fearful atmosphere around me. Many friends of mine and supporters began to worry about their relationship with me. Two of my staff resigned. I put want ads in my paper to recruit reporters and an

ad manager. I carried this ad for one month. There were no applicants because of the fearful atmosphere created by the KCIA. Now, I am publishing my newspaper with the aid of my wife. I have spent several nights without sleeping at all.

Besides my own case, I would like to speak of the plight of another newspaper. Since the criminal code which prohibits criticizing Korean institutes and government to foreigners was promulgated with the issuance of Presidential Emergency Decree #9, the KCIA has given warning to publishers, editors, and reporters. If they reported any anti-government news openly, and if publishers, editors, and reporters received more warnings than permitted, they would be punished. A new KCIA agent in charge of the press came to Los Angeles. He had been a correspondent in Japan for the Korean Broadcasting Company and became a KCIA agent. He has control of all pro-government news media. Many of my Korean friends who are reporters in Los Angeles told me about this man and KCIA control of the press, but they did not want to speak out publicly as eyewitnesses for fear of retaliation from the KCIA. This is a matter of great importance which I hope to impress upon you.

The KCIA is following tactics to control the Korean community by intimidating all kinds of organizations. Those under the influence of the KCIA and the underground KCIA are organizing all kinds of groups to control anti-Park Chung-hee people so that they cannot join in the Korean community. In this way, the community is controlled. The KCIA is also trying to manipulate organizations which have already been formed and to bring these organizations under their influence.

For example, Mr. Young Park, the Los Angeles Consul General, pressured the Korean League of Southern California to come under his influence. In pressuring this organization, he became a permanent member of the Board of Trustees for the Korean Center which was purchased by the Korean League of Southern California. The Korean League of Southern California raised funds from Korean residents in the area so that it could purchase the Korean Center. The Korean government donated $150,000 which was half the amount needed for the Korean Center. Because of this government donation, Young Park insisted that he must be elected a member of the Board of Trustees. Many Korean residents want to be free politically, physically, and mentally from the Park Chung-hee government, so many Korean residents opposed the Consul General's bid to become a member of the Board of Trustees. Because he was involved in the purchase of the Korean Center, it was inevitable that the Korean Center would be under the influence of the Consul General. Therefore, the Korean Center will not be for all Korean residents of Southern California. Many think it belongs only to the pro-Park regime residents. In connection with the dispute over this Korean Center, a local Korean businessman who donated $20,000 filed a law suit but he dropped his suit because of pressure from the Consul General. With the Consul General honored as a member of the Board of Trustees, I worry that the Korean Center which should receive the love of all Korean residents of Southern California will remain under the influence of a brutal, dictatorial and foreign regime. Mr. Chairman, I'd like to submit newspaper articles from my paper which dealt with this Korean Center issue.

Furthermore, the Korean CIA is trying to intrude into American society and trying to manipulate members of that society. For example, the so-called "Friends of U.S. Senator Tunney" planned to hold a fund-raising dinner party for U.S. Senator John V. Tunney last September 12 at the Ambassador Hotel in Los Angeles. Two people who were invited to this fund raising party came to me and revealed that the KCIA was trying to raise money to give to Senator Tunney and thus encourage him to be pro-Park. One plate at that dinner party cost $100. They asked Korean local businessmen to join in at that party. If some businessmen didn't have enough money to attend, the KCIA promised to give it to them. Those relating this showed me the invitation card which they received on which the name of Young Park, the Consul General, appeared as a distinguished guest. We confirmed this story through some businessmen, and we informed Senator Tunney's Los Angeles and Washington, D.C. offices about this. Senator Tunney's office in Washington sent word to a good acquaintance of mine: Senator Tunney would not attend that fund raising dinner party. The party did not take place. Immediately after this news was published in my newspaper and the *Oriental Daily News,* the man who made the reservations for the party room went to the hotel and removed his signature as securer of the room.

The KCIA invited influential American journalists of the Los Angeles area to Korea. Of course, the KCIA gave them free round trip tickets and offered to wine and dine them. They tried to gain the sympathies of journalists in the Southern California area which is home of the largest Korean American community in America. They are continuing to invite influential American figures of this area to Korea.

Mr. Chairman, when I received retaliation from the KCIA, I felt very angry but I could not speak out and expose this kind of story because I was afraid of brutal retaliation. The KCIA's brutality is very well known. When somebody becomes their target, he can lose his life, so I could not speak out. The Korean CIA kidnapped about thirty Koreans from West Germany and England in 1967. I am well aware of these cases because I traveled in these very countries immediately after these kidnappings. They also kidnapped Kim Dae-jung from Tokyo, Japan in August, 1973, and put him in jail on the 11th of this month. They

killed by torture Prof. Chung-kil Choi who was educated at Harvard University Law School and who was a professor at Seoul National University. They also executed eight innocent men charging them with being communist accomplices in a plot to overthrow the government.

The Korean CIA sent their aides to me several times and intimidated me. Actually, Korean Air Lines which lands and takes off in Los Angeles on trips between Seoul and Los Angeles carries one or two KCIA agents on every flight. These agents' presence on the planes is a threat to Korean-Americans who fear being kidnapped. The KCIA also can retaliate against me through my parents and children in Korea, so I could not say anything at first, but I cannot endure any longer. I have reached a limit that I cannot accept. I know from my own personal experience that many Korean immigrants cannot speak out to relate their own stories because of fear of retaliation from the KCIA.

It is necessary that some courageous people appear in the Korean communities of the United States and that the KCIA's brutal activities be exposed and their agents be expelled from this country. I prayed and asked for courage from God, then decided to expose KCIA activities and to fight their illicit acts. I decided to do my best to realize freedom and security for the Korean community in this country. Mr. Chairman, I should like to submit newspaper articles of mine which dealt with exposure of KCIA activities. Mr. Chairman, I have a deep appreciation for your committee because of your accomplishments in the field of human rights. Your committee can accomplish great things through this series of hearings.

Mr. Chairman, my grandfather was interpreter for the first Korean residents who came to Hawaii in 1903. Since then, for 73 years he has lived in this country and I am taking care of him now. My uncle is a U.S. citizen and a professor of theology at the University of Oregon. My younger brother is a U.S. citizen and architect. My younger sister is also a U.S. citizen and her husband works for the Department of Transportation here in Washington. I am a lawful permanent resident of the U.S. Today, many Korean-Americans including me are suffering from oppression by officials of another government in this country. I come here on behalf of weak, pitiful, fearful, and good Korean-American citizens in this country. Mr. Chairman, to uphold the ideals and spirit of freedom and human rights in the Constitution and to maintain a free democratic, peaceful, and safe country, I respectfully demand that the U.S. government and citizens take the necessary steps to end all kinds of illicit activities on the part of the Korean government agents, and I'd like to demand the expulsion of those who are in charge of this kind of illicit activity.

Mr. Chairman, I truly appreciate your giving me this opportunity to speak before you. ★

The KUOMINTANG in CHINATOWN

By Brett de Bary and Victor Nee

In 1952, a Washington reporter, Max Ascoli, observed that a small group of lobbyists and zealots had "jammed the rudder" of America's China policy in the single direction of support for the Government of Chiang Kai-shek. The Chinese Nationalist Government, Mr. Ascoli quipped, was in fact little more than this lobby, "not a great nation, but a regime playing at being a great power."

Exiled to the island of Taiwan and lacking a real constituency among even the people on Taiwan, it counted mainly on its "American constituency," which forwarded yearly stipends from Washington.

For the next 20 years this "American constituency," better known as the China Lobby, derived its impressive influence in American politics from three main bases: wealthy relatives and former Kuomintang, or Nationalist party, officials residing in the United States; the handful of American politicians, businessmen and publicity agents enlisted in the cause of Nationalist China, and hundreds of thousands of Chinese in the United States who, through their "highest representative body," the Chinese Consolidated Benevolent Association, proclaimed publicly each year that they were among "21 million overseas Chinese loyally in support of the Republic of China."

Two decades later, a beleaguered Republic of China is looking to American Chinatowns as the last stronghold of its American constituency. Death and old age have bereaved it of former spokesmen for the Kuomintang elite, while political necessity, or, according to some, opportunism, has caused such one-time friends as Richard Nixon to declare that a Nationalist seat on the United Nations Security Council "no longer reflects the realities of the situation."

In spite of the official shift in United States policy, an advertisement sponsored by the various Chinese Benevolent Associations in the United States appeared in *The New York Times* last fall. It said: "We represent the ethnic Chinese of all Chinatowns and all walks of life in the United States. We appeal . . .to delegates who are now in New York attending the U.N. General Assembly to prevent Communist China from shooting her way into the U.N."

In further testimony to Kuomintang strength, when the United Nations General Assembly session opened on Sept. 22, several thousand Chinese, including some from Canada and the Midwest, demonstrated their support for the Republic of China on Hammarskjold Plaza in front of the United Nations. They faced a smaller, pro-Peking group of several hundred.

On the same evening, there was a parallel demonstration in San Francisco. Twelve hundred people paraded through Chinatown to emphasize the nationwide solidarity of Chinese-Americans who backed the CBA appeal.

A week before these developments, an official of the Republic of China's consulate in San Francisco, asked how recent international developments had affected political attitudes in the Chinese community, replied: "I believe they are loyal. I can say that definitely."

He called attention to the community's successful boycott of integrated school busing. "This just proves how conservative the Chinese people are," he said. "The family is still the most important thing to them, and their Family Associations are very strong. Communism will never penetrate." He deplored what he termed President Nixon's hypocrisy and crass political stuntsmanship that motivated his

146

Nationalist flag carried by 100 women in New York Chinatown in 1938

plan to visit Peking. Asked what the precise relationship was between the Republic of China and Chinatown, he said: "We support them. We support them as long as they are loyal."

"I don't want to deny that the leaders of the Consolidated Benevolent Association have contact with the Chinese government," he went on. "Before, there was a gap between the government and the overseas Chinese because the people here speak their own Cantonese dialect. But since World War II, China has become one of the big powers. Naturally, as overseas Chinese leaders saw China growing stronger than ever before, they were proud to learn some Mandarin. So many Mandarin-speaking officials began coming to this country they [overseas Chinese] wanted to learn Mandarin to communicate with them. You know, Chinese in America don't have much contact with the American Government. But if a Chinese official is invited by Gov. [Ronald] Reagan, the Chinatown people have a contact with the Governor through this visiting official. We always invite the Chinatown

leaders when we have a dinner party or a big cocktail party because they have close relations with our Chinese officials."

"Besides," the consulate aide added, "the situation of the Government of China [in Taipei] is worse than before. We need more support than ever before. We ask them if there is anything they can do diplomatically, through their own Government, to help us," he continued. "We make it possible for Chinatown leaders to come to Taiwan to see what the motherland is doing. This year they are all coming to Taipei to celebrate the 60th anniversary of the Republic of China. During the summer, we had 500 American-Chinese youngsters visiting in Taiwan for free."

If, indeed, the Republic of China can claim to "have" San Francisco's Chinatown, it is because of the loyalty of a small band of businessmen and community leaders who are frequently in contact with its nearby consulate and its more distant center in Taipei. Ironically while J. Edgar Hoover annually

photo courtesy of BRIDGE/AARC

147

warns that Chinese-American communities have been infiltrated by foreign agents of Communist China, San Francisco's Chinatown has long harbored the headquarters of the "American" Nationalist party, registered with the Department of Justice as a foreign agent whose purpose is "to secure and maintain the interest of Chinese residents of the United States to aid and further the aims of the Central Executive Committee of the Kuomintang."

Traditionally, the consulate has avoided betraying its extensive involvement in Chinatown affairs to the American press. Chinatown newspapers, however, are liberally sprinkled with photographs of the Consul General—gracing the opening of a new restaurant with the current president of the CBA, celebrating the completion of Chinatown's first high-rise building, the Mandarin Tower; attending the spring banquet of the Chinese Chamber of Commerce with the year's Miss Chinatown at his side.

Physical proximity and strong economic bonds to the Chinese community enhance the consulate's political influence there. Numerous import-export dealers, merchandising Taiwanese goods, all get their invoices from the consulate. It has granted the highest-ranking local member of the Kuomintang, Wong Yen Doon, exclusive rights to import Taiwan black mushrooms into this country, at a commission of one dollar per box.

One insurance agent who is an active member of the KMT boasted openly of the close cooperation between the Consul General and the CBA. "Sure, we met him just last night," he said one day. "The CBA is planning a nationwide protest movement against Red China." (Later, it was reported that Wong Yen Doon had received $20,000 of Republic of China "support" to launch the protest movement.)

The insurance agent denied that the Kuomintang following in Chinatown had been affected by recent events. "We're still the majority by far," he said. "The Kuomintang has 300 members in all the important organizations in the community. You know, if Chiang Kai-shek were to invade the mainland tomorrow, the Kuomintang could collect a million dollars from the community in a month. No other group could do that."

The CBA can claim a prodigious record in raising funds from Chinese in the United States. In 1937, during the anti-Japanese war, the CBA raised $30,000 of war relief in Chinatown within one week. The September 1937 *Chinese Digest* observed: "Of all overseas Chinese, none consider themselves more patriotic than the 75,000 Chinese who live in the U.S. today. Too far away from the motherland to offer their services or their lives for the building of a new China, they invariably do the next best thing. They send home their hard-earned cash."

Throughout the late thirties and World War II, while the startling generosity of Chinatown's resi-dents elicited paternalistic sighs of awe from fellow San Franciscans, the CBA carefully kept its actual fund-raising methods a community secret. The *Chinese Digest* relates the information tersely: A war relief quota for San Francisco's Chinatown was sent from Nanking to the Chinese consulate. The consulate relayed the quota to the CBA which became responsible for soliciting contributions.

The *Digest* reported: "The largest individual contribution came from Joe Shoong, head of the National Dollar Store, his employees, numbering several hundred, each pledged one month's salary as their contribution. Many employees in Chinatown stores did likewise.... In Fresno, the CBA considered deducting 10 percent of the wages paid all Chinese employees of Chinese business houses represented by the CBA."

Besides receiving contributions from workers at their place of employment, the CBA regularly sponsored fund-raising parades in Chinatown throughout the forties. A huge flag of the Republic of China was carried through the streets and unfurled to receive bills and coins from the people it passed. "We never knew where all that money went," is a frequent joke of Chinatown's residents when they reminisce about the period.

Despite Richard Nixon's view of the "realities of the situation" in 1971, the dream of recapturing the mainland does live on with the KMT. On New Year's day 1971, Chiang Kai-shek hailed the decade of the '70s as "an era which could only lead to a mainland repetition of the 1911 revolution."

A few months earlier, looking forward to the 60th anniversary of that revolution, he predicted that "no matter how desperately Mao and his followers try to struggle before their death throes," Chinese people would move "with singleness of purpose and spirit" towards national recovery and the final defeat of Communism.

This speech was attended by the numerous overseas Chinese leaders who had been flown to Taipei for the event, and Chiang's vision was carried home by them to inspire other KMT members abroad. Thus the editor of Chinatown's *Young China Daily*, insisting that "the concern of the Republic of China for overseas Chinese is greater than you can imagine," explained: "You know that the first revolution in China was mainly achieved through the efforts of overseas Chinese. Overseas Chinese have a strong sense of patriotism towards the motherland."

It would seem there is more to the CBA's dedication to the cause of Nationalist China than first meets the eye. This is not to imply that a deep sense of loyalty to China would be unnatural in Chinese in this country. Everything in their experience here has encouraged this feeling. Nearly a century of legislative racism between 1850 and 1943 denied Chinese immigrants the right to American citizenship and full participation in American society.

In 1943, when the right of citizenship was finally granted, the number of Chinese permitted to enter this country was still held to a bare minimum of 105 per year, compared with smaller countries such as Britain and Germany that had large, unfilled quotas. Confined to America's first racial ghettos, Chinese had no right to testify in courts, were prohibited by law from entering white public schools, and vengefully excluded from the 19th century unionization movement. The hostility of white labor led to repeated demands for legislation that would completely bar Chinese from the country.

Within their isolation the Chinese quickly developed a social structure to meet the demands of the new environment.

The strongest and most basic units of organization were extended family or clan groups known as Family Associations. Family Associations were merged on a higher level into District Associations, defined according to the district of an immigrant's origin in Kwangtung Province. At the pinnacle of this three-tiered structure stood the highest organ of community control, a board of directors composed of representatives from each district association.

This body, popularly known as the Six Companies, represented Chinese to American society under the title of Chinese Consolidated Benevolent Association. Its leaders were invariably those men with the highest status in the community, the well-to-do merchants who negotiated the contract of Chinese laborers to American employers.

During the 19th century, the merchant elite of the CBA sporadically attempted to better the lot of Chinese in America. However, like the national bourgeoisie of pre-revolutionary China, its overriding interest was in enhancing its own position of wealth and power. This position was dependent on continuing Chinatown's historic isolation, without which the merchants could not enforce the system of exploitation of Chinatown workers.

The merchants of the CBA gradually found that loyalty to Chiang Kai-shek could be wielded as a tool to consolidate their ruling position. Two particular developments in international history made this possible: the first was a concerted attempt, by the Republic of China in the late 1930s, to cement ties with overseas Chinese; the second was the wave of American anti-Communist hysteria, following the Communist victory in China, which came to envision all ethnic Chinese as a potential fifth column of Mao Tse-tung.

By the culmination of this process in 1954, the fortunes of Chinatown's leaders were firmly bound to the destiny of Nationalist China. The largest Chinese community outside of Asia lay hidden behind an impenetrable facade of loyalty to Chiang Kai-shek, which was one and the same as loyalty to its local leaders in the CBA.

In 1923, during the period of the first united front between the KMT and the Chinese Communist Party, Comintern representative Michael Borodin was sent to reorganize the Kuomintang along the lines of the Bolshevik Party. In the late thirties, the reoganized KMT sent agents to the far-flung overseas Chinese communities to strengthen the party branches established by Sun Yat-sen and to put them under the direct control of Generalissimo Chiang. It was the task of these reorganized branches in turn to mobilize their own communities in support of Republican China.

In the fashion of the Soviet Communist Party, after which it was molded, the Kuomintang implemented a policy of control from above by a dual strategy of recruiting local leaders, and by placing agents sent out by the Central Executive Committee in key positions within the community.

The success of this campaign is visible in the careers of any number of leaders in Chinatown today. Take, for example, the man identified in a recent *East/West* report as a "72-year-old retired political scientist" who was a principal speaker at the CBA's September protest against Communist China's admission to the United Nations. Two years earlier, the same man, Dr. Kalfred Dip Lum, appeared at a meeting of the San Francisco Board of Education. Dr. Lum announced the Chinese community's firm opposition to the integrated busing plan as a spokesman for the CBA, which he called "the highest organization of Chinese in America."

The real beginning of his career as a Chinatown "leader" is revealed in the *Chinese Digest* of January 1938, which said: "Dr. Kalfred Dip Lum, special envoy from China...went to Chinatown in September 1937 with full authority to adjust Kuomintang affairs in this country."

It was in 1937, when Dr. Lum entered Chinatown, that the Chinese Nationalist Government carried out its first attempt to make the KMT synonymous with the local elite. At the time there was tremendous political ferment in Chinatown because of the war with Japan. Dr. Lum's task was to unite "the three factions of the Kuomintang in Chinatown ...Right, Left and Center," none of which was solidly in support of Chiang Kai-shek.

To consolidate the new base of support, Dr. Lum set up a completely new KMT headquarters and appointed six special commissioners. Among them he carefully included the most prestigious leaders in Chinatown.

His key appointment was one man who had obtained the most extensive control in Chinatown by capturing leadership of both the CBA and the Chinatown underworld. This man, Wong Goon Dick, was a leading member of the largest (Wong) family association and the largest (Ning Yeung) district association, and therefore the most influential director of the CBA. He was also president of a powerful secret society in Chinatown's underworld, the Bing Kung

Tong. Mr. Wong's bond to the Republic of China was further reinforced by his being granted the title of Adviser to the Chinese Consulate, a position calculated to bring him even greater prestige within the community. When Wong Goon Dick died, the Chinese Nationalist Government, by then in its insecure retreat in Taiwan, went to even greater lengths to ensure the loyalty of his successor. It made him a member of the government of Nationalist China.

This man, Wong Yen Doon, is still the most powerful leader in Chinatown today, bearing the title National Policy Advisor to Chiang Kai-shek. (Former U.S. Attorney James Schnake, who handled Chinese immigration cases in the 1950s once commented: "If an effort had been made to dig up the evidence, Mr. Wong would have to be denaturalized on the basis of his official position in a foreign government.")

From this point on the destiny of the KMT was fused with that of the CBA leadership in Chinatown. Through its party headquarters in San Francisco, the KMT's Central Executive Committee had a system of direct communication to Chintown. Party members included the leaders of key institutions in the community, from the CBA to the powerful tongs of the underworld.

Yet the KMT could not claim complete control of Chinatown until another turn in international history brought a second dimension to the meaning and practice of loyalty in Chinatown. In 1949, the unexpected victory of Chinese Communist forces on the mainland and a resulting wave of hysteria in the United States focused a new spotlight on Chinese-Americans.

As the United States confronted Chinese Communist forces in Korea, and Joe McCarthy (with the encouragement of the China Lobby) began the search for "Communist traitors" in the high levels of government, loyalty for Chinese-Americans took on a new requirement: anti-Communism. The theme was ripe for the CBA to destroy its opposition in Chinatown by accusing it of treason not only to China, but to the United States.

In 1954, when Chinatown businessmen found themselves objects of the jibe, "You Chinese are killing our boys in Korea," the CBA publicly announced the birth of a new community organization, the Anti-Communist League, whose stated purpose was "to let the American people know that the Chinese are not Communists, and to rally all overseas Chinese people against Communism and to the support of the Republic of China."

The Anti-Communist League wrote letters to American politicians urging them not to recognize the Communist Government in China, sponsored a yearly memorial service for "compatriots killed by Communists on the mainland," and, as one Chinatown newspaper editor recalls, "succeeded in convincing the American public that Chinatown was 100 percent in support of Chiang Kai-shek."

What the Anti-Communist League did not tell the American public was that it had been organized by Liu Pei-chi, a KMT agent, and that it had enlisted the strong-arm support of the Bing Kung and Hop Sing tongs in the Chinatown underworld. The league was able to parade Chinatown's unanimous support for Chiang Kai-shek only through the most vicious suppression of the Chinatown Left. Liu Pei-chi, who is now retired and living in Chinatown, was sent by the KMT's Central Executive Committee in 1940 to organize the *Chinese Nationalist Daily*.

"After the Chinese crossed the Yalu River, I could see the Communists were coming up, even the American people began to be afraid," Mr. Liu recalled. "There was a lot of trouble in Chinatown with people looking for Communists among us. Some people stopped coming to Chinese restaurants. The CBA was searching for a way to prove that the Chinese were not all Communists. I saw a good chance to organize. Do you know Mr. Doon Wong? He was a member of the CBA, a big member. I suggested to him that we should set up an Anti-Communist League in Chinatown to prove to the American people that we are against Communism."

Mr. Liu recalled that in 1949 "the Chinese Communist supporters here were very happy. On Oct. 9, they rented a hall to hold the celebration of Communist victory. But some of our people went inside and beat them up."

Out of Chinatown's political ferment in the late thirties and forties, three leftist organizations had appeared and attracted considerable popular support. The most powerful of these was the militant left-wing Chinese Worker's Mutual Aid Association. Originally organized during the CIO campaign to unionize Chinese cannery workers in Alaska in the 1930's, it established itself in Chinatown in the early forties to promote the cause of unionism. Another group, the Chinese Youth for Democracy (Min Ching), sponsored study groups in Chinese history and developed an intense interest in the Chinese revolution and Maoist theory. The third and least known group was the League for Peace and Democracy. This was composed of progressive businessmen, organized by the famous Christian General Feng Yu-hsiang on a tour of the United States.

On Oct. 9, 1949 a coalition of these groups organized a celebration of the founding of the Chinese People's Republic in a large Chinatown auditorium. Members of the groups prepared speeches, and vases of flowers were placed around the hall. A large red flag was hung in the front of the room.

The celebration attracted 800 people, including a sprinkling of white dock workers. Jerry Ja, one of the speakers, remembers: "The ceremony had gone on for about forty minutes. It was my turn to give a speech. As I was standing behind the podium, the door opened and I saw about twenty men come in. Several rushed up to the front hall, and tore down the flag that was hanging on the stage, and knocked away the vase of flowers that was in front of me on the podium. They began to hit and kick people in the audience and throw blue dye on their clothes. An older graduate student in the audience was hospitalized. After twenty minutes the meeting was completely disrupted." The following day a black list was issued citing the names of 15 leftists and offering a $5,000 reward for the death of anyone on the list.

Over the next few years economic sanctions (such as cancellations of the lease for the Min Ching headquarters), and constant harassment from FBI and Immigration officers alerted by the KMT, slowly wore down the leftist groups. For fifteen years there was no public expression of radical sentiment in Chinatown. Only in the last two years has an openly pro-mainland newspaper, the Chinese Voice, been able to attract a substantial following in the community.

In the three decades that the Kuomintang has quietly ruled in Chinatown, what has it done? True to its interest as a merchant elite, the KMT-dominated Chinese Benevolent Association has used its prestige as "representative of Chinese in America" to completely and successfully fight every attempt that has been made to raise the wage levels of Chinatown workers. In 1967 it fought off an AFL-CIO attempt to unionize Chinatown restaurant workers who were earning $180 per month for a 60 to 70 hour work week (excluding tips). In 1969 it ground to a halt the bitter ILGWU struggle to unionize 3,000 Chinatown seamstresses who produce 75 percent of San Francisco's garments. These seamstresses, working through Chinese contractors for white manufacturers, earn an average wage of $1 per hour.

A fact-finding committee in 1969 estimated that 40 percent of Chinatown's population was below the Federal poverty level. The number of Chinese who made their way through the English-speaking bureaucracy to San Francisco's welfare rolls was the lowest in the city. In 1965, however, when the Federal anti-poverty program tried to make an inroad into Chinatown, it was rebuffed by the CBA. Suburban-bred Chinese social workers who staffed the program were branded as "Communists" in the influential Chinese-language newspapers controlled by the CBA.

When it gradually became clear that the anti-poverty program had the economic backing to persist in Chinatown and threaten CBA power, the CBA launched a fierce campaign to seize control. It called a community forum, the third in its 100-year history, where a Taiwan tea-importer, Foo Hum, charged that the liberal anti-poverty board was "not up to par." He asked for more seats to be added to the board "because we represent the poor."

While a reporter from the San Francisco Chronicle caustically noted that the protesting contingent "looked like merchants in flannel suits," persistent CBA pressure finally forced the anti-poverty board to enlarge itself by seven seats. These were promptly filled with men from the KMT stronghold, representatives of the seven largest Family Associations. Pointing out that the family associations owned $35 million worth of property in San Francisco, an East/West editorial asked, "Is this the poor?" And what is the CBA's record in fighting for the poor?

In December, 1969, a San Francisco government agency commissioned an independent evaluation of the Chinatown program. The report stated: "The immediate phasing out of this program will not affect the community in any way except for the approximately 25 staff members who will be unemployed."

As a spin-off from the anti-poverty shake-up, a new liberal element still remains active in Chinatown. Through its participation in citywide campaigns for minority rights to employment, education and political participation, this articulate group has gained some attention in the arena of city politics.

However, the fact that it is merely a gnat-like minority gnawing at the iron-bar of the KMT power structure has been dramatically revealed by the success of Chinatown's school busing boycott. Again sensing a threat to its power in the breakdown of Chinatown's isolation, the CBA began its campaign against integrated school busing as early as 1967, when it was contacted by representatives from Mothers Support Neighborhood Schools, a white racist group.

Newspapers such as the KMT mouthpiece, Young China Daily, produced a steady flow of propaganda that stirred up parental fear of outside schools. Chinatown's Kuomintang offered its own building for use as a "freedom school" and sponsored a benefit performance at the Sun Sing Theatre.

In the spring of 1972, while the KMT has had its back turned, busily shoring up its walls in Chinatown, the historical dialectic that played into its hands is swinging in another direction.

Years of disillusionment with the tragic result of America's Asia policy have shattered the simplistic anti-Communist world view projected two decades ago by the China Lobby. Movements for social justice and equality spawned by the black struggle of the sixties have brought a new generation of Chinese Americans back to the borders of Chinatown.

Here they have set up the camps of a new Left dedicated to radical transformation of the community and its status in American society. At the same time a spectacular rise in prestige of the People's Republic of China has led even the United States to abandon its unswerving support of Chiang Kai-shek.

With the convergence of these forces, Chinatown's Kuomintang is caught in a death vise. Yet the KMT's loyal members will have no choice but to continue their public relations campaign for the Republic of China. Without it, they, too, would collapse. ★

CHINA POLITICS and the U.S. CHINESE COMMUNITIES

By H. MARK LAI

When immigrants settle in a foreign land, it is natural for them to retain interest in events occurring in the country of their birth, often to the point of actively participating in the politics of their native land. Usually as they sink roots into their new home this interest will gradually be overshadowed by new interests developed in the new environment. If, however, other factors intervene, interest in the politics of the motherland may be sustained for a lengthy period.

Such was the case with the Chinese in America. They encountered white racism soon after they arrived in California in large numbers during the mid-nineteenth century. In 1882 Chinese labor was excluded and for the next half century the Chinese were continually subjected to prejudice and discrimination. Feeling that they had a limited future in this country, many Chinese continued to be oriented toward China and often participated in China's domestic politics even though they had lived in America for decades. The purpose of this essay is to trace the development of three major immigrant social-political organizations involved in the politics of China. Their involvement demonstrates that China's domestic and international politics exerted a strong influence on Chinese communities in the U.S. for many years. This was the situation in the past and, to a lesser degree, it is still true today.

Before the 1911 Revolution

During the middle of the nineteenth century, modern political parties were non-existent in China under the autocratic rule of the imperial Ching (Manchu) government (1644-1911). To express mass dissatisfactions, groups organized clandestinely and led insurrections. Two such groups were the Taipings and the Triads. The Taipings, a massive popular movement, launched a great uprising in 1851 in South China that expanded into a fourteen-year civil war throughout most of the empire. The Triads, the largest secret society in South China, advocated the overthrow of the Manchus (non-Han Chinese people) and restoration of the Ming Dynasty (1368-1644). This latter organization was widespread in Southeast

[Editor's note: All Chinese names are in Chinese order, last name first and without commas.]

China, where in the mid-1850s members of the society also instigated a number of uprisings in Kwangtung and Fukien Provinces.

The Taiping Rebellion (1850-1864) and the Triad uprisings failed. As a result, thousands of their adherents fled overseas to avoid persecution and execution, joining some of their compatriots who had preceded them. Triad members settling in the U.S. established numerous lodges. They formed a loose organizational network among the Chinese communities all over America, known later as the Chee Kung Tong. Triad membership in the U.S. was drawn mainly from the middle and lower strata of society, such as small shopkeepers, laborers, labor contractors, and others alienated from the conservative mercantile power structure of Chinatown.

During this period, the Chinese empire suffered the encroachments of the West. China's traditional society with its self-sufficient economy was collapsing rapidly under these pressures. Toward the last decades of the nineteenth century, as China appeared to be heading toward dismemberment by the major powers, enlightened members of the gentry and the budding bourgeoisie began to see that solving China's problems required the reform of traditional Chinese society.

A demonstration in San Francisco Chinatown celebrating the 1911 Chinese Revolution. The banners read "Success to the Revolution" and "Long Live the Chinese Republic" in both Chinese and English.

Because of their own relatively privileged positions within Chinese society, they saw reform attainable within the framework of the established system. The reformers wished to save China from foreign domination. Correspondingly, they viewed reform as a means to remove obstacles to the development of capitalism in China, a desirable road in their eyes to building a wealthy and powerful country.

By 1898, the reformers had gathered enough support to gain the confidence of the young Guangxu Emperor (1871-1908), who reigned from 1875-1908. They issued numerous reform decrees in the Emperor's name. But 100 days later, the ultraconservatives under the leadership of the Empress Dowager (1835-1908), recognizing a threat to their power, launched a coup d'etat and imprisoned the Emperor. Many reformers were captured and executed; others fled China with prices on their heads.

In America, meanwhile, a class of entrepreneurs was also forming among the Chinese. Some of those starting as merchants in the 1850s spread into fields such as labor contracting, agriculture, and light manufacturing. By the 1880s factories of 30-50 employees were established in San Francisco. There was even one shoe manufacturer with 300 employees.[1] However

the expansion of Chinese business ventures in this country was hampered by a strong American bourgeoisie and the prevailing, hostile anti-Chinese climate. If Chinese businessmen turned to their motherland as an outlet for their capital, the way was blocked by feudalism and imperialism. Therefore this small but growing Chinese bourgeoisie in the U.S. had a strong interest in a China freed from the domination of feudalism and imperialism and offering opportunities to those who favored the development of a modern capitalist society.

Thus, when the leader of the reform movement, Kang Youwei (1858-1927), came to Victoria, B.C. in 1899, he found that many leading Chinese merchants were ready to support his cause. On July 20, 1899, the Chinese Reform Association (also called Protect the Emperor Association in Chinese) was established as the first organized political party among the Chinese in America.[2]

Subsequently, Reform Party leaders visited Chinese communities all over Canada, the United States, Mexico, and Hawaii, and found sympathetic ears. By 1904 the Reform Association had spread all over the Americas, establishing 103 branches and claiming a membership of 10,000.[3] The leadership included many affluent merchants of the Chinatown mercantile elite.

By the end of the first decade of the twentieth century, the Reformers had established newspapers in the large Chinese communities of San Francisco, Honolulu, New York and Vancouver.[4] Under the supervision of Homer Lea and other American mercenaries, military schools were organized in many Chinatowns to train young Chinese to return to China and restore the emperor.[5] The Chinese Reform Association also made many investments, especially in Mexico, to finance their political activities. In Mexico their undertakings included a bank, land speculation, and a streetcar line franchise in Torreon.[6]

During this period the Reform Association was a major political force in American Chinatowns. They claimed credit for promoting the 1905 anti-U.S. boycott to protest the Chinese exclusion laws.[7] When Manchu envoys visited the U.S. in 1910, members of the Association in various cities led moves to present petitions calling for the convening of a parliament in China.[8]

Toward the end of the first decade of the twentieth century, however, internal problems racked the organization.[9] The Reform Movement's program of change from within was not achieving the desired results.

Meanwhile, a revolutionary movement was developing parallel to the Reform Movement. Among the overseas Chinese this movement was personified by Sun Yat-sen (1866-1925), who started his first revolutionary organization, the Xingzhong Hui (Society to Revive China), in 1894 in Honolulu to work for the overthrow of the Manchu empire and establishment of a republic.[10]

Sun visited the U.S. mainland for the first time in 1896.[11] He found only a few sympathizers, mainly among small merchants, young intellectuals, and some workers. He especially gained the attention of members of the Chinese Christian community who were influenced strongly by the ideas of western republicanism and by middle-class values.

In a second trip in 1904 Sun also won over the leadership of the Chee Kung Tong (Triads) in San Francisco and converted its news organ, *The Chinese Free Press,* from a pro-reform to a pro-revolution line.[12] At that time however, many Chee Kung Tong members in other lodges were also members of the Reform Association, and Sun found it a slow process to win over the Chinatown populace to his radical philosophy.

The revolutionaries gradually gained support for their political program. In 1905 Sun Yat-sen and various Chinese revolutionary groups met in Japan to form a coalition, the Tongmenghui (The United Covenanters Society), to pursue more effectively the objectives of restoration of Han-Chinese rule by overthrowing the Manchu monarchy and establishing a republic in China. Agents were sent among the Chinese abroad to preach the doctrine of revolution.

For example, Lee See Nam, a Chinese American, was given the task of organizing young people in the U.S. He formed the Young China Association in San Francisco as a front for revolutionary activities.[13] Its influence, though, was limited.

In 1910 Sun arrived again in the U.S. and started chapters of the Tongmenghui. He also ordered Tongmenghui members in the Americas to join the Chee Kung Tong so as to widen the revolutionaries' base of support and to gain access to an extensive organizational network useful for raising funds. Actually, aside from a common desire to overthrow the Manchus and to restore Han-Chinese rule, the two groups had little else in common. Members of the Tongmenghui were influenced strongly by Western bourgeois republicanism. Others were supporters of socialist or anarchist doctrines. On the other hand, although the Chee Kung Tong was nationalistic, its political program was only vaguely defined. Many of its conservative members were steeped in the beliefs of feudal China.

Notwithstanding its weaknesses, the alliance emerged as a significant political force in Chinese communities in the U.S. and Canada. It became increasingly active in raising funds for the revolution and bolder in its attacks on the imperial system.

Within Chinatown society, initially a coalition led by small businessmen, students, and intellectuals opposed the affluent conservative merchants controlling the Chinese associations and professing loyalty to the Emperor. Much of the struggle between these groups consisted of editorial debates published in the newspaper organs supporting each side. Sometimes there was physical violence as hecklers and partisans engaged in fisticuffs at street corner rallies.[14] But by around 1910, affluent merchants as well as many members of the Reform Party had become discouraged with the decaying government since the situation in China had not improved. Few regretted the overthrow of the Manchus sparked by the 1911 uprising at Wuchang.

1912-1927

The continued hostile climate toward Chinese in the U.S. led many to conclude that their future lay in an industrialized China. After the 1911 Republican Revolution, the Chinese in this country entertained great expectations. Businessmen anticipated opportunities for investments; intellectuals and students looked forward to better chances for upward mobility. Their pro-republican and nationalist sentiments reflected their expectations. Many invested in enterprises in the motherland.[15] Others returned to join in the building of the Republic. However, a succession of corrupt, ineffective regimes and China's lapse into civil war and political chaos soon dashed their hopes.

At this time, the main political groups in the

Left - A banner in San Francisco Chinatown expressing opposition to the martial arts troupe from the People's Republic of China which toured the United States in 1974. *Right* - a banner also in San Francisco Chinatown welcoming the same troupe.

overseas Chinese communities supported the concept of a republic, but each for its own reasons. The Constitutionalist Party (the former Reform Party) [16] was the most conservative politically. Having connections with the landlord class and local warlords as well as the upper echelons of the Chinese bourgeoisie in China, it supported the Peking government. It even supported efforts to push Confucianism as a state religion.

The Chee Kung Tong (Triads) [17] was also basically conservative in its political leanings. It too supported the Peking regimes and maintained links with secret societies as well as local warlords in China. The funds advanced by the Chee Kung Tong for revolutionary activities before the 1911 Revolution were never repaid by the Tongmenghui, nor its successor organization, the Kuomintang (Nationalist Party). After the 1911 Revolution, it was not permitted by Sun Yat-sen's lieutenant, Hu Han-min, to register as a political party in Kwangtung Province. These factors led to cool relations between the Chee Kung Tong and the Kuomintang (KMT).

The third group was the Tongmenghui, led by Sun Yat-sen and supported by elements of the national bourgeoisie. After the 1911 Wuchang uprising, the Tongmenghui leadership, feeling too weak to gain political dominance on its own, reached a compromise with Yuan Shi-kai in Peking. Yuan, formerly a viceroy of the imperial Manchu government, was elected provisional President of the Republic in February 1912, while the Tongmenghui united with four other political groups to form the Kuomintang (KMT) in China. It became one of the major political parties and soon became involved in a power struggle with President Yuan, who suppressed the party in 1913. The KMT again had to operate outside China. It considered Yuan and his successors, the northern warlord governments, as usurpers of the Republic and became their bitter foes.

At this point the KMT was the most militant group in the Chinatowns. Its members were in the forefront of the anti-Yuan, anti-Peking warlord government demonstrations. They raised funds and recruited Chinese in America to support their cause. They sometimes would use vigilante tactics to press their points. For example, in the midst of a discussion by the Chinese Consolidated Benevolent Association in 1914 to decide whether to welcome the impending arrival of a Yuan envoy, a phalanx of KMT youth charged in to tear down Yuan's picture and broke up the meeting. [18] In the winter of 1915, KMT assassins in San Francisco shot Huang Yuanyong, a visitor alleged to be a Yuan supporter. [19]

On the other hand, the two conservative organizations, the Constitutionalists and Chee Kung Tong, sharing some similar interests and with ties to the warlord regime in Peking, began to work cooperatively. Together the two groups controlled the major part of the conservative establishment in the Chinese communities. In addition, they had the support of many of the heads of the Chinatown secret societies or tongs. In this manner they tried to thwart KMT efforts to push the national revolution in China forward, and to lay claim to a larger share of the

photos by H. MARK LAI

155

Chinatown power structure in America.

In 1920 the pro-KMT military forces in China captured Canton, and in 1921 a military regime was established there in opposition to the Peking authorities. Preparations were made for a northern expedition to unify China. Meanwhile, the Constitutionalists and Chee Kung Tong in America continued to support the northern government and provided covert financial and logistical support to anti-KMT forces in Kwangtung to try to subvert and overthrow the Canton regime.

During this whole period the KMT appeared as the vanguard in the Chinese communities in America. They advocated the abolition of many ideas they regarded as backward, such as Chinese New Year. Members established the Morning Bell School, the first modern school in the San Francisco Chinese community to allow coeducation and to present regular stage dramas.[20] The KMT party newspapers, the *Young China* in San Francisco and the *Mun Hey* in New York were popular among many of the young.

As the revolution in China progressed and the KMT became even more militant, the more conservative Chinese merchants in the U.S. became estranged from the KMT. When the KMT Canton government attempted to seize control of the Sunning Railroad in the Toishan District the party became very unpopular among the Chinese in the U.S. who had invested in the railroad.[21] The breach between the conservatives and militants widened when the KMT formulated its alliance with the USSR and accepted communists into its party after the 1924 KMT party congress in China.

It was during this period of KMT militancy that organizations of the left started in the Chinese communities in the U.S. In 1919 syndicalist elements founded the Unionist Guild;[22] many members were sympathizers of the KMT. Others were attracted by the promise of the 1917 October Revolution in Russia. A few years after the 1924 KMT party congress, a Chinatown section of the U.S. Communist Party was established in San Francisco, location of the most populous Chinese community in the U.S. Communists joined the U.S. KMT. Many were workers and students. They flaunted the KMT flag, and frequently gave street corner speeches supporting the national revolution and denouncing imperialism.

By this time many businessmen members in the KMT had become alarmed due to the radical direction taken by the KMT in China and the U.S., coming as it did in the anti-communist atmosphere in this country. In 1925 the General Branch of the KMT in San Francisco openly joined with the right-wing faction of the party in China to denounce communism.[23] (This was before the Chiang Kai-shek anti-communist coup d'etat of 1927.) However, other U.S. branches refused to follow this line.

Subsequently, the KMT split into hostile right and left factions with separate headquarters and party news organs. But after the establishment of the Chiang Kai-shek government in Nanking in 1927, the right-wing faction had a political advantage and became the stronger group. The party schism continued until the Sino-Japanese War in 1937, when the factions combined again to unite against the common enemy.

During these years the interest in China politics still remained strong among Chinese in America. The failure of major U.S. Chinese enterprises, such as the China Mail Steamship Company, the Canton Bank and the Pacific Canning Company, served only to strengthen the beliefs of many that their destinies were tied with China.

1927-1949

After the Communist-KMT split in China in 1927, the Marxist left in the U.S. branch of the KMT was expelled from both right and left factions of the party. The conservatives now controlled the KMT. As for the Marxist left, it began to link up more and more with American national left-wing politics. In the late 1920s and early 1930s it became active in the American trade union movement to encourage Chinese workers to join labor unions and improve workers' conditions. This was the beginning of a break from an exclusive focus on Chinese politics. But in a period when Chinese labor was still excluded and suspected radicals were subject to deportation, the left's effectiveness was limited.

For the KMT, due to the establishment of a KMT national government, the conditions were favorable for it to extend its political domination over the Chinese community in the U.S. The first order of business of the right-wing faction was to eliminate its political rivals. It provided the Nanking government with information so that members of the opposition returning to the motherland were marked for harassment or arrest.[24] Opposition publications were barred from China.[25] The party even tried to engineer the deportation of opposition spokesmen to muzzle their criticism of the KMT regime here.[26] As for the Chee Kung Tong and the Constitutionalists, they had lost their political allies in China and rapidly lost much of their support in the Chinatown establishment to the KMT.

After the KMT government at Nanking was established in 1927, the Japanese military launched its attempt to conquer China, seizing Manchuria in 1931, attacking Shanghai in 1932, and invading the region north of the Great Wall in 1933. In 1937 general war with Japan broke out in China. Soon afterwards, China War Relief Associations sprang up in the Chinatowns to raise funds supporting the war effort. As quasi-official representatives of the Chinese government, the KMT and their supporters held key positions in these Chinatown groups. With the

The Chinese Workers' Mutual Aid Association on 9 October 1949 in San Francisco Chinatown celebrating the founding of the People's Republic of China.

motherland facing this threat to her existence, patriotic fervor was high as Chinese workers and merchants donated about $56 million to support China's war effort.[27]

The war gave the KMT an excellent opportunity to expand its influence into all areas; its political rivals could do little to stop it. Taking advantage of nationalist feelings, the KMT recruited numerous ambitious and opportunistic people into the party, including many key community leaders from district and clan associations and secret societies. Many of these soon became part of the local party leadership as well as members of its U.S. Central Committee. The party's interests became intimately and firmly intertwined with that of the Chinatown establishment. By the time the war ended in 1945 the KMT had become solidly entrenched in a politically dominant position in the Chinatowns. Neither the Chee Kung Tong nor the Constitutionalists were effective opponents any longer.

The triumphant KMT, however, bore little resemblance to the party of the 1920s. Gone were many of the idealistic intellectuals and young people who comprised its corps of cadres. Instead the party supported the status quo and relied on support from the conservative Chinatown mercantile power structure. The workers no longer played a significant part in the party's program in the U.S.

During the war, the left was also very active mobilizing people to promote support for the war effort. After a brief period of working with the KMT, they began to work through other channels, and were especially active among the workers and the youth.[28] They remained, however, a small group compared to the KMT.

World War II with China as an American ally brought about the repeal of Chinese exclusion and greater opportunities for Chinese Americans. It created favorable conditions for the growth of a Chinese American middle-class rooted in this country. Members of this class formed the beginnings of a liberal group in the Chinese community.

After the war, the KMT in China ended the tutelage period in China and set up a facade of democratic government. Attempts were made to draw in other parties. However, KMT corruption and oppressive rule in China caused disenchantment among the U.S. Chinese. In the postwar years as inflation and corruption mounted in China and civil war erupted between the KMT and the communists, both the left and the liberals as well as remnants of the old opposition to the KMT in the Chinatowns criticized KMT misrule in China. The KMT responded by strengthening their propaganda machine and by recruiting more conservative leaders from the Chinatowns to enlarge and strengthen their base of support.

After 1949

After KMT rule in China collapsed in the face of the advancing People's Liberation Armies, the KMT regime fled to the island of Taiwan, and the People's Republic of China (PRC) was established in Peking in 1949. Some of the left envisioned a change of alle-

157

giance by the Chinatown establishment similar to that which took place after the 1911 Revolution and after the establishment of the KMT national government in 1927. This time, though, the KMT was in firm control of the Chinatown establishment unlike the other two occasions when no single political group was in a dominant position.

In 1949 the left-wing Chinese Workers' Mutual Aid Association celebrated the founding of the People's Republic. The meeting was broken up by KMT-hired tongmen.[29] Subsequently, other critics were threatened with harassment and death. Editor Dai Ming Lee of the *Chinese World,* the Constitutionalist Party organ opposing the KMT, had to call for police protection.

Opposition to the KMT would have been stronger were it not for the reluctant entrance of Chinese troops into the Korean War in 1950. Many Chinese Americans feared that they might suffer the fate of the Japanese Americans during World War II, i.e., massive incarceration in American concentration camps. The Cold War and the anti-communist hysteria in the country helped the pro-KMT China Lobby to push for a U.S. government policy hostile to the PRC and allied with Taiwan to ensure the continued existence of the exiled KMT regime. Under these conditions critics were silenced and the KMT managed political opinion in the Chinatowns for the next two decades. The U.S. government also cooperated by harassing liberals and applying pressure on the Chinese left. To cite one example, in 1952 the New York organ of the Chinese left, the *China Daily News,* was indicted for violation of the Trading with the Enemy Act.[30]

Taking advantage of these conditions, Taiwan ordered the formation of Anti-Communist Leagues in the U.S. in 1954. Cultural and trade ties with Taiwan were established with local school and merchants to ensure KMT influence.[31] The activities of the KMT Overseas Chinese Affairs Commission were stepped up to check on the loyalty of local Chinese to Taiwan. Loyal followers in the Chinatowns were appointed as advisors to the commission.

In the meantime, as a result of the conditions caused by the world-wide struggle against colonialism and imperialism, and the struggle for democratic rights in this country, many discriminatory laws were repealed. Overt discrimination decreased and better opportunities became available to the American-born Chinese Americans. The Chinese American middle-class grew in number and strength, benefiting from America's cold war prosperity and civil rights movement. Their economic roots were in America, and they generally did not have many interests with either the KMT or the old Chinatown mercantile power structure. Also, during the mid-1960s the left in America and in Chinatown again became active, with most of its adherents being students and intellectuals on the campuses.

Influenced by the activism sparked by the civil rights movement, Johnson's Great Society Program, and the anti-Vietnam war movement, the new left and the new middle-class began actively demanding change in Chinatown. But they also challenged the KMT policy of slavish allegiance to Taiwan, as open support for the PRC and against Taiwan found expression. A certain polarization again occurred, now with the KMT and the traditional establishment on one side, and members of the new Chinese American middle-class and young Chinese Americans on the other.

Today, however, the situation in the Chinatowns is different from the past. During much of the period before World War II, the Chinese had been a rejected minority in this country. Many were forced to pin much of their hope for betterment of their status on an improvement in China's situation. Hence many Chinese in America felt it to be in their interests to participate actively in the politics of China.

This participation, however zealously expressed, had always been in an ancillary and supportive position, mainly in the areas of logistics, finances and propaganda. The Chinese abroad were too few in number, dispersed geographically, and far away from China to play a leading role in guiding the political destiny of the motherland.

But because of common class interests, numerous political, economic and cultural links had been forged over the years between the overseas Chinese and members of the various political factions in China. Thus, it was not surprising that for many decades, China politics continued to be a significant factor in shaping the lives of many Chinese Americans and exerted a strong influence on community attitudes as well as on individual behavior. Recently, different circumstances have been affecting the Chinese in the U.S. and the people in China. The two have been developing in different directions. In recent years a new generation of Chinese Americans has arisen with interests firmly rooted in American society, with few interests identifiable with the motherland.

The PRC was established as a result of a revolution based on the workers and peasants, with little reliance on assistance from the overseas Chinese. Thus it was a revolution in which the Chinese in America played only a minor, insignificant role, compared to their earlier participation in the Republican Revolution, the KMT and the struggles of other political factions in previous years. Although the PRC welcomes the support of the overseas Chinese, the socialist society established in China obviates the necessity of participation in her politics by Chinese living abroad, except perhaps for propaganda activities on her behalf. Moreover, the policy of the PRC has been increasingly clear in recent years that it discourages the "sojourner" mentality and encourages the overseas Chinese to identify with and to seek their destinies in the countries where they live.

On the other hand, although the KMT regime still actively seeks to retain support of the overseas Chinese, its exile status on Taiwan inspires neither confidence nor support.

Many American Chinese still take political sides, but the reasons for partisanship today are different from the past. Some support the PRC or Taiwan because of economic ties or nationalist feelings. Others are partial to the PRC because of a desire to promote friendly U.S.-China relations or because of a recognition of political realities. A few may still be loyal to Taiwan because of ideological ties. Likewise, others may favor the PRC because they regard her as a model for the socialist movement. But there is little motivation to go to China or Taiwan to serve in a spirit of patriotism as in the past.

Today we witness the ending of an era. At present China politics are still influential in community politics, but the role has greatly diminished. We can expect it will continue to fade as the Chinese in America became increasingly involved in the struggles in American society and participate more and more in American politics. U.S. Chinese may still be interested in events in China, but it is unlikely that they will view China politics with the same perspectives as in the past. ★

Notes

1. San Francisco Board of Supervisors, *San Francisco Municipal Reports 1884-1885* (San Francisco, 1885), pp. 215-219.

2. Wu Xianzi, *Zhongguo Minzhu Xianzhengdan Dangshi* (History of the Democratic Constitutionalist Party of China), p. 25.

3. Ibid., pp. 26-27.

4. Ibid., p. 41.

5. Carl Glick, *Double Ten* (London, 1945); Lo Jung-pang, *Kang Yu-wei Biography and Symposium* (Tucson, 1967), p. 271 (note 33).

6. Lo, pp. 201-203 and p. 275 (note 49).

7. Wu, p. 42.

8. For example, see *Chinese World,* Apr. 25, 26; May 2, 18, 19, 28, 31; Oct. 17, 22, 24; Nov. 7, 1910.

9. The panic of 1907 led to financial reverses. Additional losses were caused by mismanagement of funds by various individuals. Party leaders in Mexico fought each other for control of part of the financial empire. Finally in 1910 the Mexico revolutionaries confiscated the holdings of the Reform Party in Mexico and gave it a staggering blow.

10. Luo Gang, *Zhonghua Minguo Guofu Shilu Chugao* (A Draft of the Veritable Record of the Father of the Republic of China) (Taipei, 1965), p. 159-167.

11. Luo, pp. 192-193.

12. Fung Chi You, "Sun Zongli Kui'mou You Mei Bu Shu" (Additional Details on Dr. Sun Yat-sen's Travels in the U.S. in 1904) in *Ge'ming Yishi* (Reminiscences of the Revolution), Vol. 2 (Chungking, 1943), pp. 110-119.

13. Fung Chi You, "Xin Xiaosheng Lee See Nam" (The New Opera Actor Lee See Nam) in *Ge'ming Yishi,* Vol. 2 (Chungking, 1943), pp. 272-275.

14. Mei Qiaolin and Li Yi'an, "Kaiguo Qian Meizhou Huaqiao Ge'ming Shilue" (Short History of the Revolutionary Activities among the Chinese in the Americas before the Establishment of the Republic), in *Jianguo Yuekan* (National Construction Monthly) (Nanking, April 1932), pp. 7-20.

15. Chinese newspapers in America during this period frequently ran advertisements calling for investment in enterprises in China. These advertisements often appealed to nationalist sentiments, using such slogans as "helping to build a strong wealthy nation" and "preventing rights and profits from being lost to outsiders."

16. Wu, p. 46. The Chinese Reform Association changed its name to the Constitutionalist Party in 1906.

17. Wang Sam Ark, *Hongmen Ge'ming Shi* (Revolutionary History of the Triads) (San Francisco? 1936), pp. 23-25.

18. *Chinese World,* July 25, 1914.

19. *Young China,* Dec. 26, 1915.

20. The stage drama using dialogues spoken in the vernacular was then widely regarded by many progressive elements as an excellent vehicle for disseminating political propaganda and new ideas.

21. *Chung Sai Yat Po,* Aug. 4, Sept. 24, Oct. 6 and 15, 1923.

22. *Kung Sing* (Workers' Voice), No. 1, Mar. 1, 1924; No. 2 Apr. 1, 1924.

23. Ma Dianru, "Zhongguo Kuomintang Zhu'mei Zhongzhibu Chengli Jingguo" (The History of the Formation of the U.S. General Branch of the Kuomintang of China) in *Meizhou Kuo Min Yat Po Diliu Zhou'nian Ji'nian Tekan* (Special Album commemorating the 6th Anniversary of the Chinese Nationalist Daily of America) (San Francisco, 1934), p. 26-27.

24. Hu Shuying, editor of the *Mun Hey Daily* of New York, was accused of supporting the left faction of the KMT. On a visit to China in July 1927, he was arrested and shot as being anti-party and anti-government.

25. Uncataloged KMT documents at the University of California at Davis Library included such a list, probably dating from the early 1930s.

26. An attempt was made to deport Wu Xianzi, editor of the Constitutionalist *Chinese World.* See "China Wants Editor Back," *New York Times,* June 23, 1929.

27. Huang Zhenwu, "Huaqiao yu Zhongguo Ge'ming" (The Overseas Chinese and the Chinese Revolution) in *Zhonghua Minguo Kaiguo Wushi Nian Shilunji* (Collection of Historical Essays on the 50th Anniversary of the Establishment of the Republic of China), Vol. I, (Taipei 1964), p. 373.

28. See H. M. Lai, "A Historical Survey of the Chinese Left in America" in the Critical Perspectives section of this book.

29. Ibid.

30. The Committee to Support the *China Daily News, The China Daily News Case* (New York 1952?).

31. Section 3 of the Kuomintang, *Kuomintang zai Haiwai,* (The Kuomintang Overseas), Vol. 1 (Taipei, 1961), pp. 242-243.

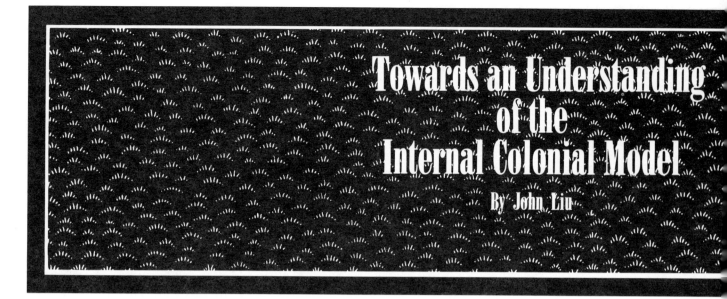

Towards an Understanding of the Internal Colonial Model

By John Liu

The civil rights movement, the outbreak of racial violence, and the growth of nationalist and separatist movements among America's racial minorities during the sixties were events social scientists failed to foresee. This was because the dominant model in the area of race relations up to this time was the assimilation/integration model, which was based on the proposition that America was willing to extend to her racial minorities the same rights and privileges enjoyed by white Americans. Within the framework of this model, social scientists focused on the barriers to assimilation and proposed strategies nonwhite minorities could adopt in order to facilitate their transition to full political and social equality.[1] The subsequent events of the sixties, however, forced social scientists to reassess this basic proposition.

From this reassessment, a new model in the field of race/ethnic relations emerged. Advanced by both social scientists and political activists, it is referred to as the internal colonial model. Those who advocate it assert that American society has never been willing to incorporate her racial minorities as equals. They contend, on the contrary, that racial minorities in America have been relegated to a position of underdevelopment and dependency in a socio-economic structure similar to that of a classical colony. Based on this contention, they assert that the situation of America's racial minorities is essentially that of an internal colony and that this approach in marked contrast to the assimilation one leads to a better understanding of race relations in America.

The purpose of this essay is to discuss the various interpretations of the internal colonial model as presented by its proponents. Since they base their analysis on the similarities between classical colonialism and internal colonialism, I will first discuss their views on the similarities. Then I will analyze important differences between the two.

In this essay, colonialism refers to the process by which Europeans established their dominance over nonwhite people during the past three hundred years. The basic characteristics of the colonial process are: (1) the forced entry of nonwhite populations into the colonizer's society; (2) the creation of a dual labor market economy; (3) the sharing of a single polity by the colonizer and the colonized in which the former is totally dominant; and (4) racial and cultural oppression, leading to the development of racist rules or norms. These characteristics form the framework in which the following examination of the similarities between classical and internal colonialism will proceed.[2]

CLASSICAL AND INTERNAL COLONIALISM — A COMPARISON

Forced Entry

Writers using the internal colonial approach argue that the development of internal colonialism in the U.S. is directly linked to the colonization of North America by the European colonists. This colonization not only involved the subjugation of the indigenous population but also the importation of slaves via the trade triangle, namely, the movement of commodities between the colonial powers, Africa and the colonies in the New World. The colonial powers provided the exports and the ships, Africa, the manpower (i.e., the slaves), and the colonies, the raw materials. Finished products were exported to Africa in exchange for slaves who, in turn, were shipped to the colonies and exchanged for raw materials such as sugar, tobacco, and cotton. These raw materials were then sent back to the "mother countries" to be made into finished products, thus completing the triangle. This trade triangle was one of the bases of capital accumulation in both the colonies and the mother country.[3] Even after American independence, this triangle continued for another sixty years, except

160

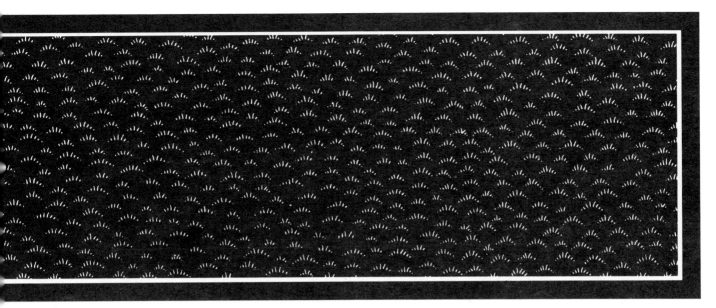

that the New England states now provided the ships and exports instead of the mother country while the Southern states continued to supply the raw materials.

The continuance of the trade triangle after American independence, according to this view, provides a linkage between internal and classical colonialism. As Casanova contends: "It is well known that upon reaching independence, the old colonies' international and internal social structure does not suddenly change."[4] In other words, the policies and structures which arise in the classical colonial situation continue to exist in an internal colonial situation.[5] After 1776, the continuance of slavery and the slave trade as well as the retention of a genocidal policy towards Native Americans are other examples of this linkage. Moreover, the continuity of social and economic structures of former colonies further demonstrates that the political separation between a colony and its mother country is not the essential feature in understanding colonialism.

> A people may be colonized on the very territory which they have lived for generations or they may be forcibly uprooted by the colonial power from their traditional territory and colonized in a new territorial environment so that the very environment itself is 'alien' to them. *In defining the colonial problem it is the role of the institutional mechanisms of colonial domination which are decisive.* Territory is merely the stage upon which these historically developed mechanisms of super exploitation are organized into a system of oppression. (Emphasis added.)[6]

Blauner contends one of the processes common to both the internal and classical colonial situation is the forced entry of the colonized people. Just as classical colonies were forcibly established by the colonialists through conquest, so the entry of racial minorities into American society has also been accompanied by some degree of coercion exerted by

the host society.[7] Schermerhorn also argues that the continued existence of ethnic and racial minorities has been dependent upon the degree of coercion exerted by the receiving society. He presents a sequence of migration which reflects a descending order of coercion on the part of the receiving society: (1) slave transfers to a receiving society; (2) movements of forced labor from one area of the host society to another; (3) contract labor transfers including the so-called "coolie trade."[8]

Applying Schermerhorn's construct, it can be seen that racial minorities have entered under some degree of coercion on the part of American society. Blacks experienced both slave transfers and the forced movement of slaves from one area of the host society to another. An example of the latter is the mass movement of slaves from the tobacco-producing border states of Kentucky, Virginia, Tennessee and Maryland to the cotton-producing states of the Deep South. Asians entered the U.S. as contract laborers, particularly those who went to Hawaii.[9]

In addition to this migration sequence, Schermerhorn suggests that the experience of Chicanos offers a fourth type of forced entry. Although Chicanos have recently entered this country as contract laborers, their initial entry was through annexation of the Southwest. Schermerhorn distinguishes annexation from colonization as being contiguous vs. noncontiguous domination, but he recognizes that both processes result in relatively identical relations of subordination. This is especially true in instances where annexation is historically preceded by an experience of colonization, as in the case of the U.S. annexation of the Southwest from Mexico. In these situations, the subsequent racial and cultural gaps that developed closely resemble the barriers that emerge in a colonial situation.[10]

Under conditions of forced entry, two options available to voluntary immigrants but denied to the colonized are: (1) free geographical and status mobility within the host society; and (2) the chance to develop mutually reciprocal ties with the host population.[11] The relative absence of these two options in the U.S. is reflected by the continued concentration of homogenous racial groups within certain urban areas (ghettos, barrios, and Chinatowns) as well as in certain geographical regions (e.g., Chicanos in the Southwest).

Economic Dependency — Dual Labor Market

A second common feature of both classical and internal colonial situations is the development of a split-labor or dual labor market economy. In both situations, there is a primary market "offering relatively high-paying wages, stable employment, with good working conditions, chances of advancement and equitable administration of work rules" for members of the dominant group (the colonizers).[12] However, for the colonized, those people who experienced a forced entry, there is a secondary market where wages, employment, working conditions and chances for advancement are well below those available to the colonizing population.[13] Some writers have argued that a dual labor market creates a condition in which the colonized are "super-exploited." As Harris states:

> One way of putting the idea of an internal colony would be to argue that the rate of exploitation is higher for black labor than for white labor or that, in other words, there is 'super-exploitation' of black labor . . . The question to be asked is whether there is a systematic pattern of underpayment of black labor relative to whites *for the same task, same level of skill, and same level of productivity.*[14]

Bonacich's definition of a split labor market also implies super-exploitation. According to her, a split labor market "must contain at least two groups of workers whose price of labor *differs for the same work, or would differ if they did the same work.*" (Emphasis added.)[15] While these writers have defined a dual labor market in terms of super-exploitation, it is suggested here that a clearer indicator of a split labor market can be seen in the existence of *task segregation* which tends to minimize the actual competition between white and colonized labor. Task segregation is apparent in the persistent overrepresentation of minorities in the semi-skilled occupations and their corresponding underrepresentation in the professional occupational categories. A pattern of task segregation can also be historically demonstrated. Although the classical example is the sole use of black slaves in growing cotton, task segregation occurred with other racial minorities as well. In California during the second half of the 19th century:

> There were several labor markets co-existing in time and space. Each was relatively insulated from the income and job competition of the others. The Chinese labor was concentrated in the low-priced, low-wage fields, primarily in agriculture and import-competing industries. The majority of the white workers were in the high-priced, high-wage fields and in non-competing industries.[16]

The Japanese and Pilipino workers in Hawaii developed the sugar industry, an occupation which attracted few white laborers. Mexican labor provided between 65% to 85% of the common labor used to develop the Southwest's agriculture between 1900 and 1929, which in that year produced 40% of the nation's supply of vegetables, fruit, and truck crops.[17]

Using either super-exploitation or task segregation to define a split labor market does not change what Blauner has referred to as the "colonial labor principle," i.e., the use of colonized labor solely to advance the development of the colonizer's economy. In the classical colonial situation, the cheap labor force provided by the colonized and the exploitation of the colony's natural resources are regulated by the colonizer for the purpose of maintaining the hegemony of the mother country — not only in relation to the colonized but also with regards to competing international rivals. As Maunier notes, colonial possession functions to guarantee the economic and political autonomy of the mother country by providing the latter with an uncontested market for finished products as well as a readily available source of raw materials.[18] Similarly, in the internal colonial situation, colonized labor has frequently been engaged in one sector of the economy in order to produce a single commodity (e.g., gold, silver, tobacco or cotton).[19] Blauner asserts that:

> Like European overseas colonialism, America has used African, Asian, Mexican and to a lesser degree, Indian workers for the most unskilled jobs, in the least advanced sectors of the economy, in the most industrially backward regions of the nation. In a historical sense, people of color provided much of the hard labor (and the technical skills) that built up the agricultural base and the mineral-transport-communication infrastructure necessary for industrialization and modernization, whereas the Europeans worked primarily within the industrialized, modern sector.[20]

As a general rule, the colonized labor force has been typically concentrated in those areas where labor has been most needed.[21] In contemporary times, this has meant an increasing urbanization of racial minorities and their concentration in the service sectors of the economy. Although the geographical setting has changed, the economic development of the ghettos and barrios is still tied to the decisions made in the white community and continues to reflect the pattern of white economic dominance.[22]

Expansion into the petty bourgeois market by the corporate sector is limited since few business ventures within the ghetto can generate enough profits to sustain an extended period of corporate growth. Furthermore, the cost of training labor and innovating technical procedures may be prohibitive in many areas. But most important, corporate expansion into ghetto markets is inherently unstable, following the ineluctable pattern of boom and recession that characterizes the international market.[23]

This economic dependency is experienced by other racial minorities as well. Almaguer notes that Chicanos have been affected by the decreasing number of unskilled jobs in the private sector of the economy. This decrease has resulted in the need to train a new educated work force. But because Chicanos in general are excluded from higher levels of education, they have continued to remain dependent upon unskilled jobs.[24] Dean Lan, in his study of San Francisco Chinatown's sweatshops, also demonstrates how garment factory employment in the Chinese-American ghetto is directly tied to the economic fluctuations in the white economy.[25]

In addition to economic dependency in the labor market, the dependency of racial minorities as well as their supporting role within the colonizer's economy can also be seen in the function that welfare fulfills. Because the income of many racial minorities are below the poverty levels, they receive welfare payments to help them survive. However, these payments also play a significant role in maintaining the circulation of commodities for the benefit of the dominant white economy:

> Government spending in poor communities is as transient as water in a dishrag. No sooner is money poured into them then private entrepreneurs wring it out again ... The people we call welfare recipients are, in fact, *conduits*. They *conduct* money from one sector of the economy (the public treasury) to another (into the hands or private entrepreneurs). The *real* welfare recipients are those people who prey on the conduits every welfare check day.[26]

Political Dependency

The maintenance and perpetuation of this economic dependency point to a third dimension shared by both the internal and classical colonial situations: the fostering of political arrangements which institutionalize the inequities between the dominant society and her racial minorities. In the classical colonial situation, political dependency is maintained by keeping the colonized people in a separate and subordinate legal category. In an internal colonial situation, political dependency persists in spite of the legal equality between the colonizer and colonized.Viewing the barrio as an internal colony, Barrera outlines several mechanisms that have been employed to perpetuate political dependency among Chicanos.[27]

1. The most obvious and direct mechanisms are those involving force and intimidation. Notable examples are the actions taken by the Texas rangers

to prevent Chicanos from politically organizing and the violence encountered by civil rights marchers in Selma, Alabama.

2. Disenfranchisement measures such as poll taxes, English literacy tests and grandfather clauses.

3. Gerrymandering of voting districts to dilute the voting strength of racial minorities. Thus, while the Mexican community in East Los Angeles is the largest outside of Mexico City, Chicanos have been able to elect only one Congressman (Roybal), one State Assemblyman (Alatorre) and no city councilperson.

4. Setting candidacy requirements which hinder the participation of racial minorities in the electoral process.

5. Co-opting selected individuals which serves not only to deprive the community of potential leadership but also provides the colonizer with tokens to be displayed. "Tokenism," according to Flores, perpetuates the system in two ways because:

> (1) it offers a member of the nonwhite community as success symbols for each group and thus makes a truly closed system appear open through selective social mobility, and (2) it provides the system with apologists of individualism.[28]

Another means of maintaining political dependency is to grant a limited amount of local or community autonomy while remaining in control of the local tax base. Without control of the local tax base, communities cannot sustain or carry out any programs without prior approval from the white political structure.[29] In short, racial minorities do not control either the institutions which affect their immediate lives or those institutions which could effect meaningful change.

Racial and Cultural Oppression

One final feature shared by classical and internal colonialism is the use of racial and cultural oppression in maintaining social order. Unlike previous race models, the colonial theory asserts that racism is not merely an ideology but an integral part of the social structure. Balandier's comment on the importance of race and culture in the classical colonial situation could also apply to internal colonialism: "The colonized society is different from the colonial society by race and culture. In these respects, the antinomy appears absolute: it was expressed in the language by the opposition of 'primitive' and civilized, pagan and Christian, technical culture and 'backward cultures.' "[30] This polarization of the dominant and the subordinates is essential for the maintenance of colonial society. As Memmi states:

> The colonizer-colonized, people to people relationship within nations can, in fact, remind one of the bourgeoisie-proletariat relationship within a nation. But the almost airtight colonial groupings must also be mentioned. All the efforts of the

colonialist are directed toward maintaining this social immobility and racism is the surest weapon for this aim. In effect, change becomes impossible.[31]

Racism allows the colonialist to exert economic and political domination and is crucial to perpetuating the system. By destroying any unique sense of history or humanity that the colonized may entertain, racism and cultural oppression perpetuates the system which nurtures it. Malcolm X points to some of the mechanisms involved in this destruction. One means is to destroy a people's tongue, through which their history and ways of living are transmitted from generation to generation. Thus slaves were forbidden to speak in their native tongues.[32] But specific sanctions against the colonized using their native tongue may not be necessary. The fact that economic and political transactions are conducted in the language of the colonizer dictates the learning of that language. As Memmi eloquently shows, this dependency on the language of the colonizer leads eventually to a cultural dependency. The colonized must not only rely on the colonizer's language to conduct daily affairs but also to express their sentiments (e.g., in petitions of grievance), even if this means using terms which rob the colonized of their historical identity.[33] Malcolm X notes that when Blacks accept the designation "Negro," nothing is revealed of their past, their native tongue, or even their color.[34]

In lieu of the colonized's displaced culture, the culture of the colonizer is set as the standard. This culture socializes both the colonized and the colonizer to the "rule of the game." These rules, in turn, serve three functions: first, they legitimize the system of stratification based on the colonizer's presumed racial and cultural superiority as well as their actual monopoly of power; second, they instruct both the colonized and the colonizer as to how they should socially interact with each other; and third, they direct economic behavior. Fanon comments on one such rule:

> The native intellectual had learnt from his masters that the individual ought to express himself fully. The colonialist bourgeoisie had hammered into the native's mind the idea of a society of individuals where each person shuts himself up in his own subjectivity, and whose only wealth is individual thought.[35]

Applied to the political realm, this means that the colonized are socialized to present any grievance on an individual rather than collective basis. In fact, the rules define any collective action not only as illegitimate but also as an admission of the individual's weakness to stand up and fend for him/herself. The colonizers, on the other hand, are socialized into a paternal role of treating grievances as evidence of the colonized's inability to understand their obligations. The colonizers often view the demands of the colonized as equivalent to the tantrums of small children, who, because of their immaturity, are unable to see that the actions of the parents are in the best interests of the children. These rules of behavior are not only crucial in providing a rationale for the current state of affairs but instrumental in socializing each new generation to its proper role in society. The social structure of a colonial society is erected so as to reinforce the illusion that the existing inequitable social relations are immutable.

In sum, according to the internal colonial approach, internal and classical colonialism share a common social structure, characterized by an inequitable dual labor market, based on the forced entry or participation of colonial labor, and fostered by a political system which seeks to perpetuate these inequalities through the socialization and institutionalization of racial and cultural oppression. Now let us turn to the differences between classical and internal colonialism.

CLASSICAL AND INTERNAL COLONIALISM – A CONTRAST

The literature dealing with the internal colonial model has mainly been concerned with drawing parallels between the classical and internal colonial situations. As yet there has been no systematic attempt to analyze the differences. This section will contrast these two situations by focusing on three areas: (1) the legal status of the colonized; (2) the colonizer/colonized population ratio; and (3) the nature of decolonization.

Legal Status

One of the basic differences between the two situations is that the classical colonial model considers the colonized legally subordinate while the internal colonial model considers them legally equal.[36] Although the presence or absence of formally equal legal status may seem trivial on its face, the consequences of *de jure* equality are important. First, the granting of the rights of citizenship to the colonized tends to obscure their condition from the outside world. Thus, while the U.S. has been criticized for its treatment of her racial minorities, this criticism has never approached the gravity of criticism that has been leveled against either Rhodesia or the Union of South Africa, where the Africans are legally kept in an inferior position. Nor has there ever been any type of official sanction placed against the U.S. such as the official U.N. embargo against Rhodesia. While it may be argued that such criticism and sanctions are by and large ineffectual, such actions nonetheless affect the exercise of power by these countries both in terms of international and domestic politics.

Secondly, critics argue that the granting of *de jure* rights to racial minorities in the U.S. also has a bearing on the goals of their political movements.

164

Because of the existence of equal rights, the direction of their political movements has tended to be channeled towards the exercise of these rights rather than towards the fundamental reconstruction of society. According to O'Dell, the civil rights movement has primarily been directed against the ideology of white supremacy rather than against the institutional basis of that power.[37]

Population Ratio

A second difference between classical and internal colonialism can be seen in the colonizer/colonized population ratio. In classical colonialism, the colonizers are numerically the minority while the colonized are the numerical majority.[38] In the internal colonial situation, the colonizer/colonized population ratio favors the colonizer either because of: (1) massive settlement; (2) intermarriage; (3) genocide of the indigenous population; (4) immigration restrictions; or (5) a combination of these four courses of action. This situation has ramifications.

First, a principal reason as to why the colonizers in an internal colonial situation can grant *de jure* equality to the colonized is simply due to the fact that the latter does not constitute a numerical threat to the political and economic hegemony of the colonizer.[39] To grant such equality in the classical colonial situation would be tantamount to being expelled. This is precisely why Rhodesia cannot allow Black majority rule. In the U.S., statehood was not granted to New Mexico and Arizona until sixty years after the signing of the Guadalupe-Hidalgo Treaty, even though one of the provisions of the Treaty called for the granting of early statehood to the territories of the Southwest.[40] A prominent factor in this delay was that New Mexico alone, at the conclusion of the Mexican-American War, had over 50,000 Mexican inhabitants who would have been eligible for immediate citizenship.[41] McWilliams, observing this point, suggests that "when one compares the celerity with which California and Nevada were admitted to the Union with the prolonged struggle for statehood in New Mexico, it is readily apparent that forces were at work, both within and without the states, to delay admission until an Anglo-American majority had been established."[42] For the U.S. to have granted New Mexico statehood immediately after the Mexican-American War would have meant giving political control to the majority Mexican population. In short, the numerical strength of the colonizers generally allows them to grant *de jure* rights without affecting their political, economic, and cultural dominance.

A second ramification of this ratio is its effect on political strategies. In the classical colonial situation, strategies of the colonized leaders are centered on winning the majority's participation in a national liberation movement to counterbalance the colonizer's technological and military superiority. The determination of political strategy in an internal colo-

nial situation would be more complex. As mentioned earlier, the existence of *de jure* rights has tended to channel political movements in the direction of political reform. Yet, being a numerical minority prevents their effecting any of these reforms. Hechter observes that "this often results in politics of 'stable unrepresentation.' "[43] The size of the colonized population also would greatly reduce the possibility of successful armed rebellion on the basis of their strength alone. In either case, their population size necessitates establishing broader support by forming coalitions or alliances with other minorities or with members of the larger society, or with both. Such a strategy offers a wide range of possible outcomes, depending on the resolution of two problems: (1) with whom to form coalitions (e.g., white liberals, the working class, students); and (2) what the basis of these alliances are to be (e.g., the pooling of legal resources, acceptance of a revolutionary program, third world coalitions).

Nature of Decolonization

The third area — and the most controversial — in which internal and classical colonialism differs centers around the nature of decolonization. Classical colonialism is usually thought of as involving a process which includes the conquest of an overseas territory and the establishment of an administration to run the political and economic affairs of that territory by a colonial power.[44] Casanova states that the term "colony" has come to be understood "in both official circles and in common language, as possession of a territory in which European emigrants dominated indigenous people."[45] Given this usurpation of territory and of political and economic administration, national liberation movements have fought not only for political independence but also for the immediate return of their land and control of its administration. Decolonization in this situation involves the *simultaneous* and inseparable demands for political autonomy and for nationhood with the returning of native land.

In the internal colonial situation, there are two different positions concerning the nature of decolonization. One position agrees with the classical demand for both political independence and territory. However, given the circumstances of an internal colonial situation, this position contends that the two demands should be separated for strategic reasons. Eldridge Cleaver in discussing the black power movement contended in 1968 that:

> Black power as a slogan does not attempt to answer the land question. It does not deny the existence of the question, but rather frankly states that at the present moment the land question cannot be dealt with, the *black people must put things first, that there are a few things that must be done before we can deal with the land question. We must first get some power so that we will be in*

a position to force a settlement of the land question. (Emphasis added.)[46]

Following a similar line of reasoning, Earl Ofari argues that one of the things that needs to be accomplished is the establishment of an economic base capable of supporting an independent black nation. According to his observation:

> Simple ownership [of land] means little. Blacks must have complete collective control over the means of production. If this is not the case then the land is either rendered useless and nonproductive or becomes prey for neo-colonialism.[47]

People who support this position contend that internally colonized people have neither the political nor economic resources to immediately establish an independent nation. This lack of resources dictates the separation of political independence from its territorial aspects. Decolonization, according to this position, means that these goals are *sequential* rather than simultaneous as in the case of classical colonialism.

Critics of advocates for the establishment of a separate nation represent a second position. They view the demand both for political independence and for a separate territory as unrealistic. These critics argue that while racial minorities in America have suffered many of the same grievances that other colonized people in the Third World have undergone, their strategies and goals cannot be similar because the establishment of an independent nation is no longer a viable option. While assessing the Chicano experience as internal colonization, Almaguer concludes:

> Unlike his brother in the Third World, the Chicano because of his internal colonization, no longer holds the classical option of national independence.[48]

Concerned about the possible implications of depicting the situation of blacks in America as an internal colony, William Tabb writes:

> The colony analogy becomes misleading when it is used to suggest the possibility of meaningful black independence within the context of American society.[49]

Writing from a Marxian perspective, James Boggs' comments catch the essence of this second position. He remarks:

> In developing a revolutionary ideology for the U.S., it is necessary to be very scientific about the difference between the role that black people have played in the development of this country and the role that colonized people play in the development of the imperialist country which exploits them. In relation to U.S. capitalism, blacks have played a role which is both like and unlike that of colonial peoples, but they have also played an integral part in the internal development of this country from its very beginning. *This country has no history separate and apart from the history of black people inside it. By the same token, the history of*

black Americans can't be separated from their history in the development of this country. Therefore, nationalism can't possibly have the same meaning as nationalism in countries like Kenya, or Ethiopia or Ghana. (Emphasis added.)[50]

The source of disagreement between both these positions, as Boggs suggests, revolves around the issue of whether or not the colonized have an extant history and culture independent from that of the colonizer's. For those who answer in the affirmative, the demand for independence and nationhood is a reaffirmation of the colonized's distinct identity. For those who answer in the negative, the absence of a distinct history and culture removes any objective basis for creating a separate nation. Thus, they believe the efforts of America's racial minorities during the decolonization stage could be directed toward reconstructing the society of which they are an integral part.

In summary, the essence of both classical and internal colonialism is the colonizer's monopoly of political, economic and military power. In both situations, racism provides the rationale for the colonizer's dominance. It is reflected both in the split labor market based upon the forced participation of the colonized and in the development of a political system designed to maintain the colonizer's privileged position.

The differences between internal and classical colonialism result from the manner in which political dominance is exercised. In the classical colonial situation, because the colonized are the numerical majority, the colonizer is prevented from granting the former rights of citizenship. While the size of the colonized population inhibits obtaining *de jure* equality, it does provide a basis for the establishment of an independent nation. In the internal colonial situation, the colonized have *de jure* as distinguished from *de facto* legal rights principally because they are in the numerical minority and therefore are not in a position to effectively use the colonizer's political system to their advantage. These legal rights in no ways change the colonized's economic and political dependency upon the colonizer but instead tend to obscure the latter's monopoly of power. The size of the colonized population also makes the attainment of independence and nationhood more problematic than is the case in classical colonialism.

CONCLUSION

This essay has presented some of the defining characteristics of the internal colonial model by examining the similarities and the differences between the classical and internal colonial situations. In discussing these characteristics, at least two major discrepancies between the internal colonial and the assimilation/integration models appear. First, the assimilationist model approaches the problem of race relations in terms of nonwhite *adaptation* to the dominant white society. This follows from their assumption that America is an open society for anyone willing to adopt the dominant group's values and norms. In contrast, the internal colonial model emphasizes the political and economic struggles that occur between the colonizer and the colonized. From this perspective, racial minorities are not passive actors merely adopting the standards of the dominant society but rather are active participants in *conflict* with the dominant group over differing conceptions of self-interest.

Second, the assimilationist model tends to analyze race relations in terms of class — as defined by income, occupation, consumption patterns and self-perception — rather than race. In simplified form, its supporters contend that racial minorities are at the base of the social hierarchy not because of race per se but because they possess lower class characteristics (e.g., present as opposed to future time orientation, large families, lack of education). These theorists argue that once racial minorities acquire middle class habits and orientations, they like previous immigrant groups will be upwardly mobile. On the other hand, race or more specifically racism, plays a crucial role in the internal colonial mode. Unlike assimilation theorists, advocates of the internal colonial model do not conceive of racism only in terms of attitudes. On the contrary, they assert that racism is built into the very social fabric of society, to such an extent that explicit racist attitudes are no longer needed to maintain the super-subordinate relationship between the colonizer and the colonized. They contend that racism has been institutionalized and therefore will continue to exert an influence on social interaction relatively independent of class and status criteria.

These contrasts between the assimilation/ integration and internal colonial models indicate that the latter in challenging the status quo raises different questions. For instance, because a racial minority in an internal colonial situation is a numerical minority, if any particular minority wants to effectively challenge the colonizer's authority, political coalitions would be needed. Chinese, Japanese, Pilipinos, and Koreans are all racial minorities. But what is the nature of social interaction among these various groups? If these groups form alliances with each other, will the basis strictly be political or will cultural elements be involved? If Asian Americans decide to act as a bloc, what will their relationship be to other minorities in America such as Blacks and Chicanos? When the model is applied to these various racial minorities, will the model be equally applicable to the experiences of each of the nonwhite minorities in American society?[51] Only by answering these types of questions, will we be able to determine to what extent the internal colonial model contributes to our understanding of race/ethnic relations in American society?

In writing this essay, I have tried to present the internal colonial argument as concisely as possible. I did so not in the belief that the model is necessarily valid. On the contrary, the internal colonial and the assimilation models share one glaring deficiency, the inability to state succinctly the relationship between race and class. Any model that is valid will need to handle this complex relationship. However, while the model is not necessarily *valid*, this in no way means that the model is not *significant*. A model can be wrong or poorly constructed yet still provide valuable insights. The internal colonial model falls into this category.

As the previous paragraph suggests, the internal colonial model directs attention toward areas which by and large have been ignored by previous race/ ethnic models. For instance, the internal colonial model raises the whole problem of the relationship among the various racial minorities in American society. Obviously, there can be no theory which ignores this problem. Yet, besides the internal colonial model, no other perspective has explicitly examined this question. Because the internal colonial model raises many important unexplored questions, the model should be further explicated. The tentative answers it provides may be of value in the development of a valid and comprehensive theory of race/ ethnic relations in American society. ★

Notes

1. For a prime example of this approach, see Nathan Glazer's "America's Race Paradox" in Peter I. Rose, ed., *Nation of Nations: the Ethnic Experience and the Racial Crisis* (New York: Random House, 1972), pp. 165-180.

2. The approach used here is largely adapted from Robert Blauner's work. See his *Racial Oppression in America* (New York: Harper and Row, 1972). This essay, however, will be based on the proposition that internal colonialism is one possible outcome of the colonial process. Neo-colonialism represents an alternative outcome. Since both situations are possibilities, the variables which differentiate internal from classical colonialism should also explain some of the differences between internal and neo-colonialism.

3. Ronald Bailey, "Economic Aspects of the Black Internal Colony" in Frank Bonilla and Robert Girling, eds., *Structures of Dependency* (n.p., 1973), pp. 164-165.

4. Pablo Gonzalez Casanova, "Internal Colonialism and National Development," *Studies in Comparative International Development,* 1:4 (1965), p. 32.

5. *Ibid,* p. 32.

6. J. H. O'Dell, "A Special Variety of Colonialism," *Freedomways,* 7:1 (Winter, 1967), p. 8. See also William K. Tabb, "Race Relations Models and Social Change," *Social Problems,* 18:4 (1965), p. 32.

7. Blauner, pp. 53-54.

8. R. A. Schermerhorn, *Comparative Ethnic Relations: A Framework for Theory and Research* (New York: Random House, 1970), p. 98.

9. While "contract labor" does not imply coercion per se,

conditions, such as the credit ticket system, under which the Chinese, for example, were brought to the U.S. constituted a form of economic coercion.

10. Schermerhorn, pp. 96-97.

11. Blauner, p. 56.

12. Michael J. Piore, "Public and Private Responsibility in On-the-Job Training of Disadvantaged Workers" (Cambridge: M.I.T., Dept. of Economics, Working Paper, no. 23, June, 1968), cited by Tabb, p. 439. See also Harold M. Baron, "Black Powerlessness in Chicago" in Norman R. Yetman and C. Hoy Steele, *Majority & Minority: the Dynamics of Racial and Ethnic Relations* (Boston: Allyn & Bacon, 1972), pp. 391-400.

13. Tabb, p. 439.

14. Donald J. Harris, "The Black Ghetto as Colony: A Theoretical Critique and Alternative Formulation," *The Review of Black Political Economy,* 2:4 (1972), pp. 10-11.

15. Edna Bonacich, "A Theory of Ethnic Antagonisms: the Split Labor Market," *American Sociological Review,* 37:10 (October, 1972). p. 549.

16. Ping Chiu, *Chinese Labor in California, 1850-1880: An Economic Study* (Madison: State Historical Society of Wisconsin, for the Dept. of History, University of Wisconsin, 1963), p. xi.

17. Tomas Almaguer, "Toward the Study of Chicano Colonialism," *Aztlan,* 2:1 (Spring, 1971), p. 12.

18. Renee Maunier, *Sociology of Colonies,* trans. E. O. Lorimer (London: Routledge, 1949).

19. Casanova, p. 30.

20. Blauner, p. 62.

21. Bailey in Bonilla, p. 170.

22. Tabb, p. 436.

23. Harris, pp. 19-25.

24. Almaguer, pp. 16-17.

25. See Dean Lan, "The Chinatown Sweatshops: Oppression and an Alternative," *Amerasia Journal,* 1:3 (Nov., 1971), pp. 40-57.

26. Quote by Charles V. Hamilton, cited by Bailey in Bonilla, p. 178.

27. Manuel Barrera et al., "The Barrio as an Internal Ghetto" in Harland Hahn, ed., *Urban Affairs Annual Review,* 6 (1972), pp. 488-490.

28. Guillermo V. Flores, "Race and Culture in the Internal Colony: Keeping the Chicano in His Place" in Bonilla, p. 214.

29. Almaguer, pp. 18-19 and Tabb, p. 436.

30. George Balandier, "The Colonial Situation" in Pierre L. van den Berghe, ed., *Africa: Social Problems of Change and Conflict* (San Francisco: Chandler, 1965), p. 43.

31. Albert Memmi, *The Colonizer and the Colonized* (Boston: Beacon Press, 1972), p. 74.

32. *Malcolm X on Afro-American History* (New York: Pathfinder Press, 1970), p. 36.

33. Memmi, pp. 108-109.

34. Malcolm X, pp. 31-37.

35. Frantz Fanon, *The Wretched of the Earth* (New York: Garden Grove Press, 1968), p. 47.

36. "The crucial distinguishing characteristic between internal and external colonialism does not appear to be so much the existence of separate territories corresponding to metropolis and colony, but the legal status of the colonized. According to our usage, a colony can be considered 'internal' if the colonized population has the same formal legal status as any other group of citizens, and 'external' if it is placed in a separate legal category." Barrera, p. 483.

37. J. H. O'Dell, "Colonialism and the Negro American Experience," *Freedomways,* 6:4 (Fall, 1966), pp. 296-297.

38. "The important fact is that this dominant society (i.e., the society of the colonizer) remains a very small minority: there is a great disequilibrium between the colonials and the mass of the colonized. The colonials fear, more or less consciously, that group size alone will become the criterion of hierarchy." Balandier in van den Berghe, p. 39.

39. In calculating the colonizer/colonized population ratio, the numerator refers to the total colonizing population. However, in geographical regions which are isolated in terms of communication and transportation and not yet under the effective economic and political control of the colonizer, the numerator is determined by the number of colonizers in that region. When these regions are populated primarily by colonized people, they are unlikely to be granted citizenship rights until the region achieves a population ratio in favor of the colonizer; or the region becomes integrated into the colonizer's political-economic-communication infrastructure. The experience of Mexicans between 1848-1900 exemplifies the first case while Asian Americans in Hawaii exemplify the second. Mexicans did not receive citizenship until an Anglo majority was achieved in the Southwestern states. On the other hand, when Hawaii was admitted to the Union, Asian Americans still constituted the majority population. However, because Hawaii was already effectively integrated into the U.S.'s economic and political system, their numbers no longer constituted a threat to the overall system.

40. Almaguer, p. 17.

41. Joan W. Moore, "Colonialism: the Case of the Mexican-American," *Social Problems,* 17:4 (Spring, 1970), p. 465. Moore also notes that the Spanish population of this area was politically organized. Even today, political participation of Mexican-Americans is higher in this state than in any other.

42. Quoted in Almaguer, p. 17.

43. Michael Hechter, *Internal Colonialism: the Celtic Fringe in British National Development, 1536-1966* (Berkeley: University of California Press, 1975), p. 40.

44. O'Dell, A Special Variety . . ., p. 8.

45. Casanova, p. 29.

46. Eldridge Cleaver, "The Land Question," *Ramparts,* 6:9/10 (May, 1968), p. 52.

47. Earl Ofari, "Marxism, Nationalism and Black Liberation," *Monthly Review,* 22:10 (March, 1971), p. 32.

48. Almaguer, p. 18.

49. Tabb, p. 442.

50. James Boggs, "Beyond Nationalism," *Monthly Reivew,* 25:8 (January, 1974), p. 42.

51. Barrera cautions users of the internal colonial model that "the general concept appears to apply to a number of cases and is valuable in emphasizing the structural similarities and common historical origins of the positions of Third World peoples inside and outside the U.S. However, it should not be used to obscure variations in individual cases." p. 467.

The 1909 and 1920 Strikes of Japanese Sugar Plantation Workers in Hawaii

By Alan Moriyama

The history of Asians in the United States has always been affected by racial and economic factors.[1] Much of the writing in this field has dealt with the issue of race, particularly as it affected inter-group conflict,[2] though the history of Asians in this country has equally been influenced by economic considerations. From the very beginning of Asian immigration these considerations were present. To help develop the western part of the United States, Asians were brought to this country, specifically to work in mines, on railroads, and on agricultural plantations. Many Asians themselves wanting to

create better lives for themselves came to this country to seek their fortunes.

A number of writers have attributed the basis of conflict between Asian workers and their employers to be economic. Others stress the labor conflicts in America between the Chinese, Japanese, and Pilipinos on the one hand and the white working class on the other. In fact, one of the major theories about the existence of prejudice and discrimination among white Americans toward these Asian groups maintains that the roots of the conflict can be found in the economic competition between white workers and

Asian workers.[3] To substantiate this thesis, writers point to the agitation against the different Asian groups in this country, in particular movements begun by groups of white workers and subsequently perpetuated by organized labor groups that resulted in Asian exclusion laws.[4]

Neglected in the history of Asians in this country is a serious examination of the interrelationship between the three different groups involved in these conflicts—the Asian workers, the white workers, and the owners of the businesses, farms, and plantations who hired the workers. Such an approach would enable us to better understand the different kinds of interactions that existed between these groups and, more importantly, to discover the fundamental reasons for these conflicts. Using this approach, my study will deal with two major labor strikes of Japanese sugar plantation workers in Hawaii, the first in 1909 and the second in 1920.

Operating under the assumption that Hawaii because of unique economic and social characteristics is the "great exception,"[5] most of the studies on the experience of Asians in America view the situation of Asians in Hawaii as vastly different from that of Asians on the continental United States. These studies contend that general lessons about ethnic group relations cannot be derived from the situation of Hawaii because of its history of colonization by British and Americans, its large percentage of Chinese, Japanese, and Pilipinos in the population, and the way class lines were drawn in that society.

This is not only much too narrow an interpretation but also a misreading of the complex situation in Hawaii. There were differences between the situation in Hawaii and the rest of the United States. Yet, as will be seen by this paper, these differences make the understanding of the internal social contradictions and the relationships between different ethnic groups in Hawaii easier to reach.

While the history of the Hawaiian islands prior to 1900 is beyond the scope of this study, there are several characteristics of pre-1900 Hawaii that need to be mentioned in order to understand events in the twentieth century. Since 1798, with the coming of the British and American explorers, traders, and missionaries, the number of native Hawaiians had decreased rapidly, mainly due to a number of deadly western diseases including measles, chicken pox, and syphilis. In 1832, there were about 130,000 native Hawaiians in Hawaii.[5] This number decreased to 67,000 in 1860, to 29,000 by the turn of the century, and to 23,000 by 1920.[6] This decrease in the native population was highly significant. For the native Hawaiians, it revealed the lethal consequences of colonization. For the plantation owners, it meant a severe shortage of laborers because native Hawaiians constituted the bulk of the work force on the early sugar plantations.

While the number of workers decreased, Hawaii was simultaneously undergoing a period of economic expansion. The descendants of the early missionary families expanded from one sugar plantation in 1835 into an entire industry. In 1876, 13,000 tons of sugar were produced in Hawaii. This increased to 87,490 tons by 1891, to 360,039 tons in 1901, and over 425,000 tons by 1906.[7] Sugar was "king" and all of Hawaii was dependent on this one crop. In 1915, sugar constituted nine-tenths the value of all the agricultural produce in Hawaii, and more than one-fifth of the entire population in the islands worked in some way on a sugar plantation.[8] The nature of the planting of sugar cane required a large number of unskilled laborers. All of the work in the fields including the harvest was done by hand. When the cane was ready to be harvested, it had to be done in a matter of days or the sugar was lost. This required a large, dependable supply of workers.

From the very beginning of the establishment of large-scale agricultural plantations, the *haole* missionary families, together with their business partners, faced the classic dilemma in a colony.[9] They had the option of keeping Hawaii essentially a white territory dominated by a small group of influential families, which meant little hope of economic expansion *or* bringing non-white workers into Hawaii to work on the plantations, and thus increasing the economic prosperity for the islands as well as for those who controlled her economy. However, for these white families, the undesirable consequences of the latter choice might be whites would no longer dominate Hawaii in the future. In the end, the plantation owners took the risk of the latter choice, and decided to expand their plantations by systematically bringing new, non-white workers to Hawaii. This is not to say that the planters did not try to recruit white workers to work at low wages in Hawaii. The planters made it clear that they would hire all the white workers the government could bring to Hawaii at wages one-third higher than that of the non-white workers.[10] Since wages were higher in Australia and the United States, the planters were never able to attract a sufficient number of white workers.

In 1850 the first organized group, the Royal Hawaiian Agricultural Society, was formed for the purpose of recruiting laborers to Hawaii.[11] In 1864, the Planters' Society was formed to send recruiters and agents abroad to actively seek workers.[12] In 1882, the most important of these groups was founded, known at that time as the Planters Labor and Supply Company.[13] In 1895, it became known as the Hawaiian Sugar Planters' Association (hereafter HSPA), a group which not only recruited the laborers but also represented the different sugar plantations in subsequent negotiations with labor groups.[14] The most important government agency working with the plantations and the workers was the Bureau of Immigration. Established in 1864, it oversaw the importation of workers and, theoretically, was responsible for their well-being once they got to Hawaii.[15] Both the private companies and the government agency spent a great deal of money in their recruitment efforts. From 1864 to 1886 the planters spent over $850,000 and the government over $1,000,000 to promote immigration to Hawaii.[16] As a result Hawaii became a multi-ethnic, multi-racial society. The inability of the planters to attract white laborers to Hawaii meant the population of whites in Hawaii during this period remained very small. In 1900, whites made up but one in every fifty members of the population, and in 1910 and 1920, no more than one in every thirteen persons was white.[17] The result was that unlike the situation in California facing Asian workers, there was no large white working class who competed with Asians for jobs.

The usual way of characterizing the early years of Japanese settlement in Hawaii has been to describe plantation life among workers, the way in which the Japanese moved off the plantations, and the general processes of assimilation and acculturation that the Japanese underwent.[18] The emphasis has been on the ways in which these Japanese adjusted to Hawaiian society and adopted its values.

One point ignored in these writings has been labor conflicts that existed from the earliest days the Japanese were working on the plantations. In fact, there were several strikes by Japanese workers before the turn of the century. Several strikes took place in 1885.[19] These were followed by strikes in 1890, 1891, 1892, and 1894.[20] There is also ample evidence of many other smaller strikes and walkouts. In several cases acts of violence took place. For example, during a strike in 1905 on a Lahaina, Maui plantation, one worker was killed and three others wounded.[21] All of these strikes were inspired either by grievances over wages, working hours, working conditions, or mistreatment by *lunas* (foremen). None of them was organized, none involved more than one plantation, and in all cases the workers went back to work after a quick settlement or a compromise. The following is a summary of the recorded plantation strikes by Japanese in the 1900-1920 period:[22]

Year	Number	Estimated Workers Involved
1900	20	8,000
1901-1902	2	Not available
1903-1905	12	10,165
1906	1	1,700
1909	1	7,000
1920	2	15,000 (including Pilipinos)

The first major strike by Japanese laborers took place in 1909. The significance of that sugar plantation strike lies first in the fact that it was not a spontaneous walkout. The decision to strike was made after more than eight months of discussion and preparation.[23] After a series of articles describing the low wages on the plantation appeared in the *Nippu Jiji,* a Japanese language newspaper, a number of public meetings were held in Honolulu. Out of these meetings, the Higher Wages Association (*Zokyu Kisei Kai*) was formed in December of 1908 to help articulate the demands of the workers and to serve as an informal support group in the event of a strike.[24] The meetings in Honolulu served another purpose. They functioned as the mechanism through which representatives of workers from a number of different plantations could meet in order to present some semblance of a "united front." Previous attempts at labor walkouts had resulted in disturbances only on one plantation at a time. In 1909, however, all of the larger plantations on the island of Oahu participated in the strike. The main issue throughout the conflict was that of wages and profits. The first three newspaper articles by Motoyuki Negoro pointed out that since the plantations' profits had risen twenty percent in the previous year workers deserved a similar twenty percent raise in their wages.

The HSPA refused to recognize the legitimacy of the Higher Wages Association, and after another series of public meetings and more demands, the walkout began on May 8th.[25] Although six of the eleven Japanese-language newspapers, originally viewed as "conservative," cautioned the workers about walking off the plantations, once the strike began, all but one paper supported the strikers.[26] Besides the issue of higher wages, one of the major grievances of the Japanese was the wage differential between workers of other ethnic groups and themselves. Japanese workers were paid the least though they performed the same work as other workers. According to the Bureau of Immigration the plantation wage averages for the 1888-1890 years for contract laborers were as follows:[27]

Portuguese	$19.53 per month
Hawaiian	18.58
Chinese	17.61
South Sea Islanders	15.81
Japanese	15.58

The situation did not change after the turn of the century. In 1902, the daily income of the average laborer worked out this way:[28]

Caucasian	$4.22
Hawaiian	1.80
Portuguese	1.69
Chinese	1.22
Japanese	1.06

For the Japanese who had traveled thousands of miles across the ocean seeking a better life, this was a bitter pill to swallow. In a pamphlet put out during the strike entitled *The Higher Wages Question* the laborers pleaded their cause:

> If a laborer comes from Japan, and he performs [the] same quantity of work of [the] same quality within the same period of time as those who hail from [the] opposite side of the world, what good reason is there to discriminate one as against the other. It is not the color of the skin or hair, or the language that he speaks, or manner or custom, that grow cane in the field. It is labor that grows cane, and the more efficient the labor, the better crop the cane field will bring.[29]

When the HSPA realized that this was not the usual walkout but an organized strike, they ordered the strikers to evacuate their homes which were on plantation-owned property. This eviction placed an additional burden on the workers who not only lost their source of income but had to gather their belongings and move—all in a matter of days. Many of them turned to their labor leaders for help. The strike headquarters in Honolulu housed up to 5,000 people at a time. Other families were taken in by Japanese families in Honolulu for the duration of the strike.

Besides evicting them from their homes, the HSPA struck back at the Japanese workers in other ways. They began to hire strikebreakers. Bused daily to plantations needing workers, Chinese, Hawaiians, Portuguese, and Korean workers were hired at $1.50 a day.[30] Although almost 7,000 Japanese workers were off their jobs at the height of the strike, enough strikebreakers were hired by the plantations to keep their losses to $2,000,000 over the four-month period ending August 6th.[31]

As the strike dragged on into June, the plantations resorted to legal means to end the strike. On June 10th, eleven of the Japanese strike leaders were arrested for disorderly conduct and conspiracy.[32] On June 18th, the investigating grand jury returned a total of fifty-five indictments against the defendants.[33] In the middle of the trial, an attempt was made by one of the strikers on the life of the editor of the *Hawaii Shimpo*, Sometaro Shiba, who had argued against the strike. The next day the *Pacific Commercial Advertiser's* headline read: "Higher Wage Fanatic Attacks and Stabs Editor of Shimpo."[34] The arrests of the Japanese leaders and the stabbing ended, for all practical purposes, the strike. The strikers had counted on a united Japanese community for support and, at least, neutrality from the rest of Hawaiian society. The strike leaders and thus the entire strike suffered the stigma of guilt because of the arrests. Their credibility with the public gone, the strikers slowly began returning to work. At the end of the trial in August, the defendants were found guilty of third degree conspiracy charges, fined $300 and sentenced to ten months in jail.[35]

One sidelight of this strike was revealed in 1912, when it was learned that two of the Japanese newspapers, the *Hawaii Shimpo* and the *Hawaii Nichi Nichi,* had received monthly subsidies of $100 from the HSPA since 1908. In addition, the papers received special subsidies totaling $11,700.[36] In 1909, these two conservative papers had argued that the Japanese workers should not go out on strike.[37]

In 1909, the leaders of the strike gave a number of reasons for the failure of the strike. They felt that there had not been enough cooperation among the strike leaders and that the workers had been too weak financially to withstand a long walkout. They also felt that the Japanese people had no real political power which could have been used in the struggle. The leaders also agreed that the strike had been conducted along national lines and thus had failed to generate enough support from members of other ethnic groups. Finally, they agreed that the strike had dragged on for too long a period.[38]

During the 1909 strike Japanese dominated groups such as the Honolulu Retail Merchants Association, the Public Bath Operators Association, the Carpenters Association, the Japanese Hotel and Inn Association, the Barbers Association and other groups, made public their support of the strike.[39] There was also considerable support from the sugar plantations on the outer islands that did not go on strike. For example, on the island of Kauai, strike supporters adopted a resolution to raise $70,000 by assessing each of the Japanese workers $20.00—a remarkable sum considering their daily wages.[40] The image of a unified Japanese community willing to support financially and spiritually their workers was impressed upon them by unsympathetic observers. It was also felt that the Japanese workers were willing to band together because of their racial ties. This became a fear in the minds of the HSPA. In 1905, the Commissioner of Labor in Hawaii referred to it as "blood unionism":

> While no distinctly [sic] labor organizations could be found among the laborers on the plantations, the blood unionism of the Japanese has shown itself even a stronger bond than the trade unionism of American and European workmen.[41]

In later struggles of the Japanese laborer, the support of the Japanese community would again be seen. The HSPA would characterize this support as the threat of a monolithic Japanese community supporting these workers.

Throughout the 1909 strike the Japanese felt that morally and logically they had a good case in demanding a raise in their wages. They felt that this, together with the support of the Japanese community, would be enough to win the struggle. They failed to take into consideration the vast resources at the disposal of the HSPA as well as the ways in which the planters would respond: bringing in strikebreakers, using eviction and arrests. In the end, the "failure" of this strike might be attributed to the weaknesses of the workers as well as their inability to recognize the strength of their enemy.

Months after the strike several concessions were made to the workers. The planters agreed to pay workers according to individual ability, rather than nationality. However, the HSPA never recognized the legitimacy of the Higher Wages Association. They also claimed these concessions were not a result of the strike. From a traditional point of view, this was not a strike won by the laborers. In the end, they had to return to the plantations with no promise of concessions. The rejection of the Higher Wages Association meant the HSPA was not willing to concede the right of the laborers to collective bargaining. Nevertheless, another view of this strike must be considered. Although concessions were late in coming, clearly it was not a coincidence that several concessions sought by the laborers were finally granted, though after a period of time. The "success" of the 1909 strike was in terms of its long-term significance. The Japanese workers experienced their first attempt in an organized labor strike. The 1909 pattern of seeking community assistance, of setting up support committees, of trying to hold the labor group together for the duration of the strike would be repeated again and again. Similarly, the planters who felt the might of organized labor for the first time would in the future use charges of nationalism, of the danger labor presented to Hawaiian society, and would use legal means to prevent the labor movement from spreading. The 1909 strike set the pattern of future strikes in Hawaii.

From 1910-1920 there were no major strikes. The attention of the Japanese workers was directed toward getting back their jobs on the plantations and, for some of them, moving off the plantations into urban areas of Hawaii. Others moved to the mainland United States. There were numerous attempts to organize workers in Hawaiian society at this time. For example, in 1915, the American Federation of Labor had only five union locals, but by 1920 there were at least eighteen locals with about 1500 members.[42]

The attention of the HSPA was directed towards the problem of finding more workers for the plantations. Labor recruitment had always been a problem, and during this period further expansion of the sugar industry continued. The strike in 1909 also caused great concern about the reliability of the Japanese workers. Once again, the planters tried to recruit white workers for Hawaii. According to one historian:

> Following the strike of 1909 this policy of inducing Europeans was renewed with increasing enthusiasm and the planters were willing, without reserve, to employ all the Caucasians the government could bring to the Islands. . . .[43]

Once again this attempt failed. From 1910 to 1920, the population of whites in Hawaii increased from 14,867 to only 19,708.[44] The workers that did come

to Hawaii continued to come from Asia. The Japanese population during this same ten year period increased by 30,000 and the Pilipino population by almost 20,000.[45]

Like the 1909 strike the 1920 strike centered around the issue of wages and profits. In the post-World War I period, the Hawaiian economy experienced a period of inflation and prices rose rapidly. The cost of a hundred-pound bag of rice cost $10.00, about half the basic monthly pay for plantation laborers.[46] In late 1919, this economic pressure manifested itself in a series of local meetings held on different plantations on the island of Oahu among young Japanese workers. In the beginning, these meetings were called by Buddhist organizations, as the Young Buddhist Association and the Young Men's Association.[47] Meetings were also held on the outer islands.[48] On December 1, representatives of a number of plantation groups met in Honolulu to form the Japanese Federation of Labor.[49] Significantly, they decided for the first time that all requests and grievances would be handled by this one central organization who in turn would negotiate with the HSPA representatives. Also organized at that time was the Plantation Laborers Supporters Association, which attempted to formalize and organize the kind of community support the striking Japanese workers received in 1909.[50] On December 6, the Federation submitted a request for higher wages to the HSPA representatives. Their basic request was for a wage increase to $1.25 for men and $.95 for women per day.[51] In addition to the wage increase, the Federation asked for a change in the bonus system, a reduction in the number of work hours in a day to eight, paid leave for women workers for childbirth, double time for overtime, and more money for cane-growing contractors. There was also a request to improve health conditions in the plantation camps. The following are excerpts from the letter presented to the planters:

> . . .do [people] know that there are thousands of laborers who are suffering under the heat of the equatorial sun, in field and in factory, and who are weeping with ten hours of hard labor and with a scanty pay of 77 cents a day? . . .The War is over, and our plight has increased. The sugar industry has prospered. . . . We fully realize that capital is entitled to a fair return. On the other hand, we feel that it would be only fair and just that workers' economic plight be recognized and consideration be given to increasing their wages.[52]

The HSPA denied all requests. A strike was inevitable. However, there were complications which resulted in two strikes being called, one called off and then called on again. There were charges of bribery by plantation representatives and of labor leaders betraying the workers. One reason for these complications may be seen in the ethnic makeup of the plantation force in 1920:[53]

173

Another "Strike" About Due

STRIKE

SUGAR PLANTERS

LABOR FEDERATION

From the *Pacific Commercial Advertiser,* editorial cartoons: *left* - 1 February 1920, *opposite page* - 15 February 1920.

Laborers Employed on Sugar Plantations, 1920

Hawaiian	1,322
Caucasian	893
Portuguese	3,086
Porto Rican[sic]	1,422
Chinese	2,378
Japanese	19,474
Korean	1,982
Filipino	13,061

The significant difference from 1909 was the large number of Pilipino workers on the plantations. From 1910-20, their population increased in Hawaii from 2,361 to 21,032.[54] Most of them were plantation workers replacing those workers who were moving off the plantations. The Pilipino workers also felt their wages should be raised.

The problem was that the labor unions established on the plantations were based on racial or ethnic lines. Thus, the Japanese Federation dealt with the concerns of the Japanese workers while its counterpart among the Pilipinos, the Pilipino Labor Union, dealt with the problems the Pilipinos faced. There was also the problem of different levels of organization. The Japanese organizing had started on the local level with meetings of small groups of workers. The Japanese workers also received a lot of support from their families and from the Japanese community. The power in the Japanese Federation lay with the local groups that made up the Federation. The Pilipinos, on the other hand, did not have

local community organizations as the basis of their power.[55] Theirs was a centralized labor union with power concentrated in the hands of one man—Pablo Manlapit. The question was one of coordination. Would both groups of workers go on strike at the same time? They also discussed who would present the demands and how the larger Japanese Federation would support the Pilipinos. Evidence now seems to point to a growing desire on the part of the Japanese leaders as well as the Pilipinos to form a coalition. The original request by the Federation to the HSPA was refused, but negotiations continued, and the Federation waited for a final response to their demands before it decided whether to strike. Then the Pilipino workers led by Manlapit walked off their jobs on January 19. Although the walkout was called by the Pilipino Labor Union, a number of Spaniards, Portuguese, Chinese, and Koreans also joined them.[56] In addition, a number of Japanese sympathizers, instead of waiting for word from the Japanese Federation, walked off with the Pilipinos.

Finally, on January 26, the Japanese Federation decided to call for a strike beginning February 1. On February 8, Manlapit announced that the Pilipinos had decided to call off their strike. This caught the Pilipinos, to say nothing about the Japanese Federation and the Japanese workers, by surprise. In his statement to the press announcing the end of the strike, Manlapit echoed the propaganda of the planters and the English-language newspapers:

The Kind That Doesn't Strike

> I now believe that instead of being an industrial strike for the purpose of raising wages, that the real object of the Japanese in declaring a strike is to cripple the industries of the Territory of Hawaii in the hope that they may be taken over by an unscrupulous alien race.[57]

Some of the Pilipinos started back to work. Apparently, Manlapit made the decision independently, and a large number of Pilipinos stayed off their jobs with the Japanese workers.[58] On February 14, Manlapit re-issued the strike order. Certainly, this confusion at the very beginning of the strike, when morale should have been at its highest, hurt the Pilipino and Japanese workers.

Another problem arose when it was revealed by one of the Japanese newspapers that Manlapit had been approached by the HSPA to call off the strike. Manlapit maintained that he received an offer of $25,000 from Frank Thompson, the attorney for the HSPA, to call off the strike and leave Hawaii.[59] Manlapit claimed he had asked for $50,000, but that he would have turned it over to his union strike fund and continued the strike.[60] Thompson claimed Manlapit approached him with an offer to call off the strike for $25,000.[61] Needless to say, this confusing episode raised doubts in the public's mind about the character of the union leadership as well as the motives for calling the strike.

Eighteen days after the Japanese struck, the plantations once again responded with eviction notices to the strikers. This time the workers and their families were given forty-eight hours to leave. It is estimated that over 12,000 workers and their families were evicted and had to move elsewhere. To make matters worse, an influenza epidemic hit Honolulu in the midst of the moving, and over 1,000 people were afflicted with the flu.[62]

The HSPA also brought in about 2,200 strikebreakers to work on the plantations. Portuguese and Hawaiians were hired at $4.00 a day, and Chinese and Korean workers at $3.00 a day.[63] This was two or three times more than the wage demands of the Japanese workers. Although the Pilipino Labor Union was on strike, the planters were able to attract many Pilipino strikebreakers. In fact, after the strike there were 1,000 more Pilipinos on the plantation than before the strike. The practice of using strikebreakers proved so successful that as early as April 1 the HSPA claimed the strike, from their point of view, was over![64]

The HSPA also had at its disposal two Honolulu newspapers, the *Honolulu Star-Bulletin* and the *Pacific Commercial Advertiser,* to present their views. Newspaper stories and editorials asserted that Hawaii faced both an economic and political crisis. While their main target of attack was the Japanese, they portrayed the Pilipinos as puppets of the Japanese leaders as seen in the following editorial from the January 27 issue of the *Advertiser:*

As regards the Filipinos, there is good reason to think they are mere catspaws, used by wily agitators to further the interests of the subjects of the Mikado, and particularly the interests of the agitators. If there shall be violence and lawlessness in connection with the strike, it is a safe prediction that the ignorant Filipinos—leaderless except for an unscrupulous agitator—will be the goats.[65]

These newspapers were used in other ways. The HSPA through these two newspapers brought up the issues of racial differences, of nationalism, and of radicalism. Their argument was not only that the Japanese were using the Pilipinos, but that the Japanese were seeking economic and political domination of Hawaii. The issue of the relationship between Japanese workers and the nation of Japan was also brought up. Finally, even the issue of political radicalism emerged. In the February 12 issue of the *Advertiser,* the editors managed to bring up all of these issues in their report of a speech made by one of the Japanese leaders:

Following exactly the program of the I.W.W. [Industrial Workers of the World] T. Tsutsumi, Japanese strike leader, is reported to have stated during a speech he recently made in Waialua that "when the weeds grow up in the cane fields beyond control and the planters give up the plantations we will go in and take possession of same and will conduct the plantations ourselves." Tsutsumi is recorded to have stated during the course of his speech in Ewa, "Don't worry. A Japanese cruiser is coming to take you home. Why deny that the Japanese Government is back of the labor question. Don't deny it. It will surely scare the Americans!"[66]

The element of Japanese nationalism and of the inability of the Japanese workers to assimilate into Hawaiian society was continually brought up. In an analysis done of the 1920 coverage of the strike by these two newspapers, one writer wrote:

Scarcely a week passed without an attack upon some aspect or other of local Japanese life: the language press, the language schools, Buddhism and Shintoism, picture brides, dual citizenship of the Hawaii born, the distressing fact that so many thousand Japanese children were attending school whilst their parents paid no taxes. . .[67]

On February 14, the Reverend Palmer of the Central Union Church in Honolulu offered a plan which he felt would solve the problem for both sides. Under the so-called "Palmer Plan" the Japanese workers would first return to work. Then, on each plantation, committees would be set up by secret ballot elections which would then work out problems of wages and living conditions with the management of each plantation. Finally, each of these committees would be multi-racial in composition. In effect, this would have set up multi-racial company unions on

each plantation. A number of religious and community leaders came out in support of this plan. After initial hesitation, the Japanese Federation came out in favor of the plan. The HSPA understood that this meant collective bargaining on all plantations with coalitions of ethnic groups and rejected the plan.

As the strike dragged on into April the strike leaders decided to dramatize the plight of the workers by having a parade in downtown Honolulu. Over 3,000 Japanese and Pilipino workers and their families participated in this demonstration which was called "The 77 cents Parade." Men, women, and children marched and carried American flags, portraits of Abraham Lincoln, and signs. Some of their signs read:[68]

THE PLANTATIONS WILL STILL MAKE ENOUGH MONEY EVEN IF THEY ACCEPT OUR DEMANDS.

WE PLEDGE TO GOD THAT WE ARE NOT RADICALS.

WE DEEPLY DESIRE PROSPERITY FOR HAWAII.

GOD HAS CREATED US EQUAL.

WE ARE NOT REDS; GOD FORBID. BUT ARE BROWN WORKERS WHO PRODUCE WHITE SUGAR.

Once again a trial played an important role in ending the strike. A Japanese man who was opposed to the strike on the island of Hawaii had his house bombed, and fifteen members of the local labor association were arrested. Though the strike was held the following year, the arrests lent credence to the idea that these workers were out to destroy Hawaii and might resort to violence. The strike was finally called off on July 1. It was estimated that the strike cost the Japanese community about $300,000 and the planters about $12,000,000.[69]

Once again, after the strike was over and after the HSPA had proven its strength, it made certain concessions to the workers, particularly in terms of housing and living conditions. There were no increases in wages or formal recognition of the Federation.

This last point of the recognition of the Federation was an important one. Throughout this strike there was an underlying issue, recognized by the leaders on both sides, which had to do with the right of the plantation workers to organize and bargain collectively. In terms of the labor disputes which had taken place previously, and with the growing economic strength of the Japanese and the Pilipinos, it had become obvious to the planters that to allow organized labor on the plantations would have meant a revolution—not only economically but socially as well. It would have meant a change in the power structure of that society. Thus, the planters refused to acknowledge this, and dealt with other, more emotional issues. One historian characterized this strategy in the following manner:

...to make no concessions, absolutely to refuse to bargain, to minimize discussion of the economic issues, virtually to ignore the Filipino Union in propaganda, and to concentrate upon attacking the alleged instigators of the Japanese union movement.[70]

In some respects this strike may be seen as a "failure" for the workers. Certainly, the HSPA did not give in to the demands of the workers. They retaliated using eviction measures, hiring strikebreakers, and using the newspapers at their disposal. In the end it was labor that gave in. Still, this is too simple an explanation for a series of such complex events, events which continue to puzzle us today when we look back on them. No previous strike had been so well organized, had involved so many workers on so many plantations, had caused such a disruption of the Hawaiian economy, and perhaps most important of all, had involved two major ethnic groups—the Japanese and the Pilipinos.

The point of inter-ethnic cooperation is of particular importance when we consider it within the context of inter-group relations in Hawaii. Even in California, it had been difficult for different minority ethnic groups to band together in time of economic or political crisis. Coalitions between Blacks and Chinese or Chicanos and Japanese have been the exception rather than the rule. There have always been problems in terms of old antagonisms arising, of seeking different goals, and of a strong sense of ethnocentrism. However, in 1920, the first serious attempt at a class coalition between the Japanese and the Pilipinos on the sugar plantations took place. It began with talks between the Japanese Federation and the Filipino Labor Union. There had been an agreement between the two groups that both had sought the same goals. Evidence shows that Japanese workers on Pilipino-dominated plantations walked off their jobs with the Pilipinos when the latter went out on strike. Furthermore, most Pilipino workers did not go back to work when Manlapit called off the strike but instead stayed off their jobs with the Japanese workers. In the end, both groups did strike around similar demands, and this strike did pave the way for later multi-racial, industry-wide unions which brought about a social revolution in Hawaii.

Throughout this strike, the Japanese Federation, in their speeches, in their pamphlets, and in the press argued that their cause was just. To do so, they relied on the argument that this was essentially a class conflict. Takashi Tsutsumi, the secretary to the Hawaii Laborers Association (Japanese Federation), wrote a history of the labor movement in Hawaii in 1921. In it, he recounted the events of the 1920 strike. He argued in his writing that this conflict was essentially an economic one:[71]

> ...capitalists must be made to recognize the laborer's personality. Hitherto capitalists have regarded laborers as a sort of machinery....

> ...theirs was a movement of self conscious and awakened laborers....
>
> In spite of the fact that recent movement was purely a movement of laborers and was not prompted by either racial or international motive, and since by mere coincidence the capitalists were haoles and the laborers, Japanese and Filipinos, Hawaiian Sugar Planters Association deliberately propagated that the movement is a racial controversy between the yellow and the white people....
>
> There are ample reasons for laborers to move and act in solid body. Direct causes of recent labor movement were: capitalistic tyranny over industry, general awakening of labor throughout the world, and high cost of living....

In early 1920, before the beginning of the strike, the Japanese Federation changed its name to the Hawaii Laborers' Association in order to counter the argument that this was essentially a Japanese strike. Its members were sensitive to the racial and national issues that were brought up. Throughout the strike, the Japanese tried to emphasize the American basis for their struggle and the American ties they had. In their "77 cents Parade" they held up signs which read, "WE WANT TO LIVE LIKE AMERICANS," and "HOW CAN WE LIVE LIKE AMERICANS ON 77 CENTS."[72]

The planters, on the other hand, did not answer these charges. The HSPA refused to get involved in a labor vs. capital argument. They always reverted to charges that the Japanese were operating along racial lines and were seeking to dominate Hawaiian society. The workers themselves, in a pamphlet published in July of that year, *Facts About the Strike on Sugar Plantations in Hawaii,* argued the following:

> When we submitted our demands for increased wages the public sympathized with the laborers and considered our requests reasonable. But the local English papers which have always tried to create an anti-Japanese feeling...have skillfully transformed this purely economic matter into one of racial antagonism...this is not a Japanese nationalistic movement based on political considerations.[73]

Despite its success in preventing the Japanese and Pilipinos from winning the strike, the HSPA saw the beginning of change on the plantations. The planters had recruited a number of different racial and ethnic groups to work on the plantations based on their assumption that the easiest way to maintain their dominant position in Hawaiian society was to "balance" out the rest of the society with a number of racial and ethnic groups. They feared the possibility that one ethnic group would numerically dominate Hawaiian society and would eventually usurp the power of the planters. HSPA agents were sent to such diverse places as Siberia, Mongolia, the Azores, Austria, Poland, Malaysia, and the East Indies.[74] There was even an attempt to recruit American Blacks to work in Hawaii. The major immigrant arrivals to Hawaii between the years 1852 and 1931 were as follows:[75]

Group	Number	Years of Arrival
Chinese	46,000	1852-85, 1895-97
Portuguese	17,500	1878-86, 1906-13
South Sea Islanders	2,500	1878-85
Japanese	180,000	1885-1907
Norwegians	600	1881
Germans	1,300	1882-85
Puerto Ricans	6,000	1901
American Blacks	200	1901-02
Koreans	8,000	1904-05
Spanish	8,000	1906-13
Pilipinos	120,000	1907-31
Hindus	650	1908-09
Russians	2,500	1910

By 1920, the Japanese had established themselves as the major labor group in Hawaii. In their eagerness to maintain a large, cheap labor supply on the plantations, the planters had permitted, from their point of view, too many Japanese into Hawaii. The Japanese through their numbers and aggressive union activities had become a threat. There was also the fear that the Japanese born in Hawaii would become eligible for citizenship and thus, a political threat to the rulers of Hawaii. Finally, there were certain personality characteristics attributed to the Japanese by the planters, so that the Japanese would be perceived as a source of potential problems on the plantations. They were throught to be aggressive, clannish, stubborn, and "more difficult to manage than the Chinese."[76]

The planters made an attempt in 1921 to solve this problem. They offered to the U.S. Congress a plan which they hoped would insure adequate labor for the plantations without further disrupting the ethnic balance in Hawaii. Under this plan, they proposed that workers from China be allowed to come to Hawaii but only for a period of five years. After the work period, the workers would be returned to China. They included a provision which would have forced those workers who would have left the plantations to return to China. Although this plan did not receive Congressional approval, it gives us an indication of the way in which the planters viewed their workers. These immigrants were brought only for laboring purposes, not to live in Hawaii and become members of Hawaiian society.

The events during this period raise questions about the role of race and class considerations in the labor conflicts which took place. During 1900-1920, both the factors of race and class were important and present as causes of the different labor disputes. Although the 1909 strike might be termed a "Japanese strike," that is clearly not the case with the strike in 1920. From the Japanese point of view, the

argument in 1920 was one of class struggle. They saw themselves representing labor and the planters representing the interest of the capitalists. While it is clear that certain economic considerations did shape the attitudes and actions of the planters, their public response to the strike was solely in terms of the racial danger presented by the Japanese. Whether, in fact, the planters felt the racial danger to be primary or whether the issue was raised to work against the possibility of a multi-ethnic coalition is difficult to tell from the sources available today.

If there is anything we can learn from these two strikes, it is that both race and class considerations can be present in a labor conflict. They may be manifest in different ways and articulated differently by various groups. It seems that in a conflict involving several racial groups, the question of race will arise, and inevitably emphasized by those who can profit by the subsequent antagonisms. In the same way, we may have to re-examine group conflicts where causes have been attributed to racial and ethnic antagonisms. A study of these two strikes indicates first, that economic factors, or class antagonisms if you will, play a vital role in creating the conditions which lead to inter-group conflict. What is more important, and perhaps more frightening, is the way in which this economic conflict can be hidden under the guise of more emotional issues which are readily seen—issues like nationalism and race.

Although both strikes in 1909 and 1920 might be seen as "failures" for the Japanese plantation workers, it must be remembered that they progressed from an "ethnic" strike in 1909 to a strike in 1920 which involved a coalition with another ethnic group and which managed to bring forward fundamental questions involving the economic relationships in Hawaiian society. There is another measure of "success." The 1909-1920 period in Hawaii for Japanese sugar plantation workers was a time of economic struggle. They actively took steps to remedy their situation. They were willing to engage in several of the longest, most bitter labor struggles in Hawaiian history. In doing so, they laid the groundwork for the later activities of the trade union movement in Hawaii. The success of organized labor in the late 1940's was directly tied to this early heritage of strikes and ethnic coalition building. ★

Notes

1. This paper was originally written for a seminar class on U.S. labor history taught by Professor Alexander Saxton. The research for this paper could not have been done without the help of John Moriyama. I want to thank particularly Professor Saxton and Don Nakanishi for helping me revise my original paper.

2. See for example, Roger Daniels and Harry Kitano, *American Racism* (Englewood Cliffs, N.J.: Prentice Hall, 1970) or the sections on the Chinese and the Japanese in

Paul Jacobs, Saul Landau, with Eve Pell, *To Serve the Devil*, Volume 2 (New York: Random House, 1971).

3. Edna Bonacich, "A Theory of Ethnic Antagonism: The Split Labor Market," *American Sociological Review*, 37 (October, 1972), 547-559. See also her article, "A Theory of Middlemen Minorities," *American Sociological Review*, 38 (October, 1973), pp. 583-594.

4. The role of white workers and unions in this anti-Asian agitation has been covered in Alexander Saxton, *The Indispensable Enemy* (Berkeley and Los Angeles: University of California Press, 1971) which deals with the Chinese experience and Roger Daniels, *The Politics of Prejudice* (New York: Atheneum, 1972) which deals with the Japanese exclusion movement. See also Elmer Sandmeyer, *The Anti-Chinese Movement in California* (Urbana: University of Illinois Press, 1973) and Morton Grodzins, *Americans Betrayed* (Chicago: University of Chicago Press, 1949) the latter deals with a much later period. A different view is given by Karl Yoneda, "100 Years of Japanese Labor History in the USA," in *Roots: An Asian American Reader*, ed. by Amy Tachiki, Eddie Wong, Franklin Odo with Buck Wong (Los Angeles: UCLA Asian American Studies Center, 1971), pp. 150-158.

5. James H. Okahata, Chairman of the Publication Committee, ed., *A History of the Japanese in Hawaii* (Honolulu: The United Japanese Society of Hawaii, 1971), p. 277.

6. Ibid.

7. Takashi Tsutsumi, "History of Hawaiian Laborers' Movement," trans. Umetaro Okumura, typewritten (Honolulu, 1921), p. 35.

8. U.S. Congress, House, *Labor Conditions in Hawaii: Letter from the Secretary of Labor Transmitting the Fifth Annual Report of the Commissioner of Labor, Statistics on Labor Conditions in the Territory of Hawaii for the Year 1915*, 64th Congress, 1st session, 1916, p. 11.

9. The word "haole" is usually used to refer to whites in Hawaii.

10. Ernest Wakukawa, *A History of the Japanese People in Hawaii* (Honolulu: The Toyo Shoin, 1938), p. 187.

11. Take and Allan Beekman, "Hawaii's Great Japanese Strike," *Pacific Citizen*, December 23, 1960, p. 72. This article along with several others were reproduced with special permission in a packet of material for an Ethnic Studies class at the University of Hawaii. Thus, the page numbers refer to the packet itself. Individual page numbers for each of the articles were deleted.

12. Wakukawa, *Japanese People in Hawaii*, p. 16.

13. Beekman, "Hawaii's Strike," p. 72.

14. Ibid.

15. Wakukawa, *Japanese People in Hawaii*, p. 16.

16. Andrew Lind, "Economic Succession and Racial Invasion in Hawaii" (Ph.D. dissertation, University of Chicago, 1931), p. 268. While this work has not been published in this form it is the basis of Lind's *Modern Hawaii* (Honolulu: University of Hawaii Press, 1967) as well as his earlier *Hawaii's People* (Honolulu: University of Hawaii Press, 1955). The interesting thing to note is the way in which Lind's ideas, particularly in terms of the role and importance of the plantations have changed since 1931.

17. Okahata, *Japanese in Hawaii*, p. 277.

18. See the above cited books by Lind, Kitano, Hosokawa, as well as any introductory work on Hawaii.

19. Yayoi Kurita, "Labor Movements Among the Japanese Plantation Workers in Hawaii," typewritten (Honolulu: University of Hawaii, 1952), p. 11. See also Karl Yoneda, "A Brief History of Japanese Labor in Hawaii," *Hawaii Pono Journal*, 1 (October 1971), pp. 55-63.

20. Ibid.

21. Ibid.

22. Edward Johannesson, *The Hawaiian Labor Movement, A Brief History* (Boston: Bruce Hunphier, Inc., 1956), p. 74.

23. Wakukawa, *Japanese People in Hawaii*, p. 169.

24. Okahata, *Japanese in Hawaii*, p. 174.

25. Ibid., p. 177.

26. The reference to "conservative" newspapers and "radical" newspapers is from Kurita, "Labor Movements," p. 11. Her analysis shows that of the five radical papers, three were from Oahu and the other two from the island of Hawaii. Of the conservatives, two were from Oahu, two from the island of Hawaii, and one each from Kauai and Maui. The paper which backed the strike most strongly was the *Nippu Jiji* which had printed the original articles on wages and profits. The two leading papers which argued that the workers should not strike were the *Hawaii Shimpo* and the *Hawaii Nichi Nichi*. While it seems that both papers opposed the strikes, Wakukawa argues that only one newspaper, probably the *Kauai Shimpo*, failed to support the strike.

27. Katherine Comen, *The History of Contract Labor in the Hawaiian Islands* (American Economic Association publication, 1903), p. 23.

28. Francine Du Plessix Gray, "The Sugar Coated Fortress," *The New Yorker*, March 4, 1972, p. 72.

29. Wakukawa, *Japanese People in Hawaii*, p. 176. The reference here is to Puerto Ricans and Portuguese people. In the writings during this period, people from Puerto Rico are referred to as "Porto Ricans." I will use the more commonly accepted spelling.

30. Kurita, "Labor Movements," p. 11. See also, Okahata, *Japanese in Hawaii*, p. 177. This $1.50 was $.85 more per day than the Japanese had been earning.

31. Ibid.

32. Ibid. See also Okahata, *Japanese in Hawaii*, p. 179. The importance of the Japanese ethnic press in this labor struggle is apparent in that six of the eleven men had some connection with the *Nippu Jiji*.

33. Ibid.

34. Beekman, "Hawaii's Strike," p. 92.

35. Kurita, "Labor Movements," p. 11. See also Okahata, *Japanese in Hawaii*, p. 180. Eventually the defendants served about four months in jail. The original sentence had been appealed, and even though the appeal failed, the Acting Governor of Hawaii pardoned the strike leaders on July 4, 1910.

36. Okahata, *Japanese in Hawaii*, p. 181.

37. See footnote 26.

38. Wakukawa, *Japanese People in Hawaii*, pp. 182-183.

39. Okahata, *Japanese in Hawaii*, p. 175.

40. Ibid., p. 179.

41. Johannesson, *Hawaiian Labor Movement*, p. 63.

42. John Reinecke, "The Sugar Strike of 1920: Catalyst," typewritten, p. 98. This article was reproduced and included in the University of Hawaii packet.

43. Wakukawa, *Japanese People in Hawaii*, p. 187.

44. Okahata, *Japanese in Hawaii*, p. 277.

45. Ibid.

46. Ibid., pp. 186-187.

47. Herbert Probasco, "Japanese and Filipino Labor Unions and the 1920 Plantation Strike in Hawaii," typewritten, n.p., 1966, p. 2.

48. Okahata, *Japanese in Hawaii*, p. 187.

49. Ibid. While Okahata refers to this organization as the Japanese Federation of Labor in Hawaii, some of the organization's pamphlets in 1920 listed The Federation of Japanese Labor in Hawaii. Kurita claims the group's name was the Federated Association of Japanese Labor in Hawaii. There was added confusion when in 1920 the name was changed to the Hawaii Laborers Association although Okahata refers to them as the Hawaii Japanese Laborers Association. I will refer to this group simply as the Japanese Federation. By this, I mean that group founded in the first week of December 1919, which changed its name in April of 1920.

50. Kurita, "Labor Movements," p. 14.

51. Okahata, *Japanese in Hawaii*, p. 187.

52. Ibid., p. 188.

53. Ibid., p. 185 and Lind, "Economic Succession," p. 344. Although both authors have substantially the same figures, they differ on their count of the Hawaiians on the plantations. Okahata claims 1,322 Hawaiians while Lind claims 4,408 Hawaiians and part-Hawaiians.

54. Ibid., p. 277.

55. Fuchs, *Hawaii Pono*, p. 220.

56. Hawaii Laborers' Association, *Facts About the Strike on Sugar Plantations in Hawaii* (Honolulu, 1920), pp. 11-12.

57. Reinecke, "Catalyst," p. 104. See also Fuchs, *Hawaii Pono*, pp. 214-218 and Wakukawa, *Japanese People in Hawaii*, p. 250. William Abbott in "Filipino Labor Struggles in the Islands," *Hawaii Pono Journal*, Vol. 1, No. 3, July 1971, deals with what he terms the "ordeal of Pablo Manlapit." He particularly examines the 1924 strike and the trial of Manlapit. In terms of the 1920 strike Abbott states that Manlapit "struck a low blow at the Japanese unionists in 1920 by denouncing them as un-American aliens who were trying to take over the country. . ." (p. 67).

58. Wakukawa, *Japanese People in Hawaii*, p. 250.

59. Probasco, "Japanese and Filipino Labor Unions," p. 29. Thompson claims to have had a stenographer at the meeting but those notes have never been published. See also Fuchs, *Hawaii Pono*, p. 218.

60. Ibid.

61. Fuchs' figure is $50,000. See Fuchs, *Hawaii Pono*, p. 218.

62. The influenza epidemic has been a source of confusion with a number of writers. Okahata, *Japanese in Hawaii*, writes that sixteen people died (p. 191), but Johannesson, *Hawaiian Labor Movement*, insists that during this epidemic about 1200 Japanese from the plantations died (p. 68). Harriet Bouslog, "Memorandum on History of Labor and the Law in the Territory of Hawaii" (University of Hawaii Ethnic Studies Packet, pp. 30-48) also maintains that the figure was 1200 (p. 34). Reinecke, "Catalyst," claims 1056 illnesses and 55 deaths among the Japanese and 1440 illnesses and 95 deaths among the Pilipinos (p. 105). Fuchs, *Hawaii Pono*, claims 1200 illnesses. While the estimate of 1200 deaths seems too high, we do know that the Acting Governor of the Territory of Hawaii and the President of the Board of Health at the time pleaded with the planters to allow the families of the workers to remain in their homes until the epidemic was over. The planters refused.

63. Probasco, "Japanese and Filipino Labor Unions," p. 32.

64. Reinecke, "Catalyst," p. 107.

65. John Reinecke, "The Big Lie of 1920" (unpublished manuscript for the *Honolulu Record*, 1958), Installment 3, p. 1. Reinecke wrote this series of articles in 1958 in anticipation of another sugar strike. He felt that in 1920, the HSPA, through the newspapers, lied about the racial and national issues involved. The manuscript is divided into a number of installments. Because there was no strike in 1958, the series of articles was not published.

66. Ibid., Installment 17, p. 1. According to Reinecke, "Catalyst," Tsutsumi insisted he said, "We will not give up until we win our demands, even if Oahu becomes a grassy meadow or a guava-covered plain" (p. 114).

67. Ibid., Installment 18, pp. 1-2.

68. Okahata, *Japanese in Hawaii*, p. 192.

69. Ibid. At least one writer, Kurita, believed the cost to the strikers to be much higher, in the neighborhood of $4,000,000.

70. Reinecke, "Catalyst," p. 100.

71. Tsutsumi, *Hawaii Laborer's Movement*, p. 5, 8, 11, 54.

72. Okahata, *Japanese in Hawaii*, p. 192.

73. Hawaii Laborers' Association, *Facts About the Strike*, pp. 19-20.

74. Aller, "The Evolution," p. 134 refers to attempts to import Malayans, East Indians, and Blacks. Comen, *The History of Contract Labor*, refers to plans to get workers from the Azores as well as the Canary and Cape Verde Islands (p. 24). Theodore Morgan, *Hawaii: A Century of Economic Change, 1778-1876.* (Cambridge: Harvard University Press, Harvard Economic Studies, Vol. 83, 1948) mentions recruiting attempts in Siberia, Austria, and Poland (p. 188).

75. This is a combination of several sources. Richard Liebes, "Labor Organization in Hawaii: A Study of the Efforts of Labor to Obtain Security Through Organization (M.A. thesis, University of Hawaii, 1938), on page 11, uses a fairly complete chart. However, he maintains that Chinese immigrants arrived beginning in 1876, when they actually began coming in 1852, and he does not include any figures for American Blacks. Johannesson, *Hawaiian Labor Movement*, has a chart (p. 28) but since his figures go up to 1945, it is difficult to decipher the figures for the period in question. Most of his figures match those of Liebes, except Liebes claims a figure of 2000 for Russian immigrants.

76. This particular point has been made by a number of writers. Curtis Aller, "The Evolution of Hawaiian Labor Relations: From Benevolent Paternalism to Mature Collective Bargaining" (Ph.D. dissertation, University of Hawaii, 1958) maintains that planters saw the Japanese as being more difficult to manage than the Chinese (p. 136). Comen, *The History of Contract Labor*, uses the terms "difficult to deal with," "restless," "self-assertive," and "remarkably clannish" in describing the Japanese (pp. 45-46). In U.S. Congress, House, *Labor Problems in Hawaii, Hearings Before the Committee on Immigration and Naturalization*, 1921, Governor-elect Walter Farrington testified about the "solidarity" of the Japanese (p. 236).

from
THE INDISPENSABLE ENEMY:
Labor and
the Anti-Chinese Movement
in California

By Alexander Saxton

Having broken from the old circumference in search of new territory, European explorers and entrepreneurs found themselves involved in a quest for labor to work the lands they had laid open. A large segment of the history of the Americas could be bracketed within this context.

The first effort at labor recruitment was the impressment of Indians, an attempt generally unsuccessful north of the Rio Grande. The second effort was the importation of African slaves. The third, beginning as the slave trade tapered off, was the coolie traffic from South China. Out of that hungry and overpopulated region, Chinese laborers were carried to the ocean islands, reached the Pacific coasts of North and South America, and passed on across the Isthmus to the sugar plantations of the Caribbean. The Chinese were followed—briefly and in much smaller numbers—by Japanese, Hindus, and Filipinos. Immigration of Chinese to the United States, then, from its earliest beginnings during the Gold Rush through flood tide in the early eighties and rapid decline thereafter, formed only one phase of a more extended historical episode.

In another respect also the half century of Chinese labor in the West was contained within a larger historical context. North Americans of European background have experienced three great racial confrontations: with the Indian, with the African, and with the Oriental. Central to each transaction has been a totally one-sided preponderance of power, exerted for the exploitation of nonwhites by the dominant white society. In each case (but especially in the two that began with systems of enforced labor), white workingmen have played a crucial, yet ambivalent, role. They have been both exploited and exploiters. On the one hand, thrown into competition with nonwhites as enslaved or "cheap" labor, they suffered economically; on the other hand, being white, they benefited by that very exploitation which

was compelling the nonwhites to work for low wages or for nothing. Ideologically they were drawn in opposite directions. Racial identification cut at right angles to class consciousness.

Clearly, the importation of indentured workers from an area of relatively depressed living standards constituted a menace to a society developing, at least after 1865, on the basis of free wage labor. This will be taken for granted. Yet America's hostile reception of Chinese cannot be explained solely by the "cheap" labor argument, although many historians have endeavored to do so. The dominant society responded differently to Irish or Slavic than to Oriental cheap workers, not so much for economic as for ideological and psychological reasons. What happened to Orientals in America, while similar in many ways to what happened to other immigrants, is generally more like what happened to blacks, who were certainly not immigrants in the usual meaning of the term.

The purpose of this study is to examine the Chinese confrontation on the Pacific Coast, as it was experienced and rationalized by the white majority....

A Brief Recapitulation

From the time of the gold rush, California's labor force was divided between Chinese and non-Chinese contingents. During the seventies and early eighties, Chinese comprised one-quarter to one-fifth of those working for wages. Lines of division were sharply drawn. Throughout the state Chinese dominated the menial service trades. In rural areas they worked in mining, heavy construction, and agriculture, for the most part at tasks of low skill and minimal prestige. In the city, aside from menial trades (domestic and laundry), they worked at the manufacture of goods subject to national market competition. Their social organization was vertical from the indentured laborer to the importer-padrone. Pressure from outside tended to strengthen the cohesiveness of this nonclass structure.

The remaining three quarters of the labor force was of diverse origin. Native and immigrant, comprising many different language and cultural backgrounds, they included groups which had elsewhere been in sharp conflict. In California, however, the divergent elements were drawn together by a sense of frustration and dispossession that was common to all. Despite their own differences, they believed that a greater difference separated them from the Chinese. These two psychological factors—frustration and consciousness of non-Chineseness—welded the non-Chinese labor force into a bloc that would deeply modify the politics and social relationships of the Far West. Here, by contrast, the organizational pattern was horizontal: the workers, the producers, the dispossessed joined in self-defense against non-producers, exploiters, monopolists. And since these producers viewed the Chinese as tools of monopoly, they considered themselves under attack on two fronts, or more aptly from above and below. But when they struck back, they generally struck at the Chinese. The result was a crusade initiated by the non-Chinese sector of the labor force, in which groups outside the labor force acquiesced or participated.

The anti-Chinese impulse has generally been presented as economic in origin and unique to the West Coast. The assertion of economic origin is probably correct, that of uniqueness probably not. First of all it is clear that the main carriers of the movement were those who came in competition with Chinese or feared possible exposure to such competition. These fears, based on the low living standard of imported Cantonese laborers and on the contract system of their importation, were by no means imaginary. A more or less free labor force was being pressed into competition with indentured labor. On the other hand, the main defenders of Chinese importation were to be found among those who benefited from the employment of contract gang labor. To this point, the division was quite simply economic. The economic division, however, coincided with a pre-existing dichotomy of ideological and organizational patterns that stemmed from Jacksonian politics of the antebellum East.

For the Democratic party especially, the defense of slavery had become a condition of political survival. Essential to the defense was an assertion of black inferiority. This in turn required the denial, or at least neutralization, of the concept of the equal rights of man upon which the intellectual system of the Democracy was premised. Ideological inconsistency tended to rub smooth with time and usage; moreover, the racist addendum was constantly reinforced by social and economic insecurity among eastern workingmen, especially among Irish immigrants. And during these same years in which the Democratic party was adjusting itself to the defense of slavery, its entire structure was being infused with the emotional tones of romantic nationalism. All this was part of the manifest destiny that moved westward with the ox teams and wagons.

Hostility to slavery, on the other hand, had thrown up its barricades largely within the old Whig party. The slavery issue tore the Whigs apart. In the course of the ensuing realignment, antislavery became associated not only with the emergent Republican cause, but with the opening of western lands for settlement and finally with preservation of the Union itself. The Democrats, stripped of their nationalistic mantle, were in turn divided. Their proslavery elements were separated by secession while the antislavery and nationalistic components were drawn into coalition, for the sake of saving the Union, with the Republicans.

There had been from the beginning within the antislavery movement a dynamic but always minority phalanx of true believers: the abolitionists. Since the early thirties they had denounced slavery for its violation of those twin mandates of equality premised rationally in the Declaration of Independence and to faith revealed by the word of God. This, because of its inner cohesiveness, proved an almost indestructible line. Through crises of war and through all the political exigencies of Reconstruction (when Republican dominance seemingly depended on extension of the franchise to Negro freedmen), the abolitionist ideology had frequently seemed to be that of the Union-Republican coalition.

After Appomattox, what remained of the Democracy set about mending its shattered image. Issues which came readily to hand were restoration of the Union through quick readmission of the seceded states and maintenance of white supremacy by the restriction of blacks to a lower caste role. Both issues held powerful voter appeal; yet both had been tainted by secession as had the party itself. The problem was how to split former Democrats away from the Union-Republican coalition without at the same time giving fatal ammunition to the enemy. This required adroit tactics; and so long as the abolitionist line remained dominant within the Republican coalition, not much maneuvering ground was left open.

One of the first Democratic breakthroughs occurred on the Pacific Coast. In California, aside from European immigrants, the bulk of the citizenry were men from the Midwest and from the central and north Atlantic regions. Before the war a majority had been Democrats. Their typical thought pattern, the Jacksonian persuasion with its romantic nationalism and foreshortened egalitarianism, had become characteristic of the new state. Few blacks were to be found then in California; but there were plenty of Chinese— a people of different color and strange ways, who

illustration by BETTY CHEN

while not exactly slaves were not quite free either. The Chinese fitted readily enough into that mental compartment which in the East had been reserved for blacks. Already in the mines and at railroad construction camps there had been collisions of Chinese and non-Chinese; and now, during the years following the war, intense conflict was developing in the new urban areas.

But while Chinese had been identified with Negroes, hostility to Negroes was not identical with anti-Chineseness. This was of key importance; for one was tainted politically, the other was not. In 1867 California Democrats launched their offensive against the Chinese. The result, as earlier noted, was a bonanza. The party laid hands on an issue of enormous potential in its own right—a new issue, uncontaminated by the sad history of civil war, yet evocative of that entire syndrome of hatreds and loyalties which still could not quite openly be declared.

As to the Republicans, given the northern whiggish origins of their movement and the fact that war had vastly stimulated Yankee enterprise in the West, it is scarcely surprising that California's new Republican elite should largely have coincided with the users of Chinese labor. Defense of the Chinese on economic grounds (though certainly the Republicans mounted such a defense) held the disadvantage of exposing their own interest. And here it was not so much a matter of concealment, for they believed their interest legitimate; it was rather that of seeking some higher ground than private profit. Under pressure of the Democratic attack, they turned (as had their colleagues in national leadership at each crisis of war and Reconstruction) to the abolitionists' twin mandates, the Declaration and the Bible.

It is clear that, while the economic circumstances which gave rise both to the importation of Chinese and to the crusade against the Chinese were unique to the Far West, the ideological and organizational patterns within which pro- and anti-Chinese interests found expression were of much older origin. In a sense these two causative sequences ran parallel. It would be possible to define, and derive, the sides of the debate either in economic or in ideological terms, although in actuality the sequences intermeshed and continually modified each other. At all events, in 1867 the Democrats swept California. One outcome of their victory was nationalization of the Chinese question, an issue which worked strongly for the Democrats by threatening to split their opponents. That most advanced (and ideologically formidable) contingent of the Republican coalition, the abolitionist phalanx, stood upon positions from which no retreat was permissible; but the main forces gave ground, and this withdrawal foreshadowed—in a sense justified and helped bring about—later evacuation of the entire southern salient which they had held since the Emancipation Proclamation.

Entanglement of an economic conflict over contract labor with older ideological and organizational cleavages precluded any single or simple solution. The racist assault on importation of Chinese guaranteed a rebuttal in abolitionist terms; and the converse also held true. Thus the abolitionist line at its latter end became tied to an economic position soon to be abandoned as indefensible; while the inevitable restriction on foreign indentured labor was achieved in purely racist terms—and carried with it a specific reaffirmation of the old racial denial of citizenship. Within the Republican and Democratic traditions what resulted was an ever more rapid erosion of the twin mandates, rational and revealed, upon which both traditions were based.

Meanwhile, the non-Chinese workingmen of California and their leaders were discovering in the anti-Chinese crusade a powerful organizing tool. Politically this had been evident since the gubernatorial campaign of 1867 when trade unions and anti-coolie clubs had joined with the Democrats to upset Republican control of the state. It was displayed even more dramatically in the challenge posed by the Workingmen's party to the bipartisan establishment. Afterward the trade unionists, alarmed at the implications of Kearney's and Gannon's appeals to the unskilled and unemployed, had separated themselves from mass politics. They determined to make the most of such bargaining advantages as their skills imparted to them. The result was a focus on economic or "pure" trade unionism, comparable to the impulse in the East and Midwest which during those same years was bringing national craft unions to ascendancy within the labor movement. California, however, remained semicolonial. Craft unions, isolated from their national centers, were at best only meagerly self-sufficient. If they were to exercise any influence in California, it must still be done as it had been done earlier through the medium of the labor force as a whole. Thus, while their eastern counterparts built up centralized national unions and established the American Federation of Labor, skilled tradesmen on the West Coast were endeavoring simply to sustain (under their own leadership if possible) a regional labor center.

Pure trade unionism proved inadequate as a unifying appeal to segments of California's labor force outside the skilled trades. Unionists were therefore obliged to compete with the labor politicians, whom they had so recently brushed off, for leadership in the anti-Chinese cause. Both the Trades Assembly and the League of Deliverance represented efforts, though unsuccessful, toward impounding the anti-Chinese dynamic as an aid to trade union recruitment. Founders of the Federated Trades had better luck in this regard; for many years the council they set up managed to direct some of the fire and steam of anti-Orientalism to its own organizatonal purposes. A summary of the several attempts to establish an effective regional labor center in California brings these connections sharply into focus:

(1) The first such effort developed during the flush times of the Civil War. As boom conditions subsequently slacked off, the new council ventured into politics with the aim of protecting through state legislation the favorable conditions recently gained by skilled tradesmen of San Francisco. The necessary bid for mass support was made on the basis of anticoolie-ism, and on this same basis the council allied itself with the Democratic party in the campaign of 1867. During the ten-year postwar depression which followed, the gains of the unionists were lost and the council itself went out of existence.

(2) The second attempt, the San Francisco Trades Assembly, grew directly out of the sandlot agitation of 1877 and the Workingmen's party. This was the point at which the trade unionists, failing to win leadership of the party, began to preach the gospel of no politics. Their assembly barely survived the depressed seventies. It flouished briefly as conditions improved in 1881-82, then wilted again with the return of slack times. Trade union leaders in 1882 endeavored to recoup the assembly's fortunes through sponsorship of the League of Deliverance. But the league failed because passage of the Exclusion Act in that year cut the ground from under it. The assembly disintegrated soon afterward.

(3) In 1885, spurred by the expulsions of Chinese from small towns up and down the Pacific Coast, San Francisco labor organizations summoned a coastwide anti-Chinese congress. The congress founded the Trades and Labor Federation of the Pacific Coast (Federated Trades), which, afterward reorganized as the San Francisco Labor Council, has enjoyed a continuous existence ever since.

(4) The crusade against Chinese terminated in 1902 with permanent exclusion. Its place was taken by the anti-Japanese campaign in large part initiated and led by trade unions through their Asiatic Exclusion League. The league served as a unifying center during the early years of the century for the rapidly growing trade union movement; and when the first political expression of that growth, the Union Labor party, faced disaster in the San Francisco graft prosecutions, its chief riposte was to provoke an international crisis over Japanese school children. Subsequently, a more enduring expression of labor's new strength took the form of alliance with the Progressive reformers—an alliance based in part on agreement as to certain legislative goals and in part on the reciprocal exploitation of anti-Oriental rhetoric.

Throughout this entire discussion, a question which keeps recurring in different contexts is that of the relation between Chinese labor and the skilled trades. The presence of Chinese in the Far West served generally to strengthen the position of white craftsmen. This was so for several closely interrelated reasons, which can most conveniently be summarized under the headings of economic, organizational, and political.

Control by craftsmen over entry into their various fields—the key to their advantaged economic position—was enhanced by racial division within the remainder of the labor force. The Chinese, always available for unskilled tasks, were excluded from entry, either as competitors or as strikebreakers, into skilled occupations. At the same time their presence inhibited immigration to California of young and aggressive unskilled workingmen. White workers actually forced into competition with Chinese in the construction gangs, harvest fields, or sweatshops, were for the most part those who were no longer capable (if they ever had been) of bidding for jobs against skilled white tradesmen.

As an organizational tool, anti-Orientalism was limited to certain users. It could serve the needs of political organizers or of craft union leaders who wished to secure the support of unskilled working-men without assuming trade union responsibilities to them. Even under the most favorable circumstances, the unionization of unskilled or semi-skilled was difficult enough in nineteenth-century America; it remained virtually impossible so long as a large group among the unskilled were relegated to an untouchable and therefore unorganizable caste. Gains of any kind were foreclosed for all the rest. When Roney and Haskell with their socialist academy colleagues launched the League of Deliverance in 1882, they had apparently hoped for miraculous results, that the inspirational effects of the anti-Chinese slogan would transcend the boundaries of craft interest and enable them to unionize the army of the unskilled. No such miracle occurred. By 1885 Roney seems to have reconciled himself to a craft horizon; and when in that crucial year he took charge of the Federated Trades Council, he exploited the Chinese issue in a calculated and successful effort to establish skilled trades' dominance.

Beyond these economic and organization aspects, the Chinese issue tended to reinforce the position of craft unionism through its working in mass politics. Its result, as Henry George had pointed out after the constitutional convention of 1879, was to short-circuit pressure for radical reform. On the one hand it provided a suitable instrument for labor politicians intent on doing business within the System, while on the other it freed craft unionists to exploit their advantaged position to the maximum without interference from the nonskilled and the unemployed. Though George might denounce the duplicity of anti-Chinese politicians even as Roney was futilely kicking against the harness of craft unionism, there were a host of others who would neither kick nor denounce. These were content to take things as they found them in both fields of endeavor. The Chinese question became for them an indispensable professional asset. The only real danger was that the Chinese might finally leave or die out; but happily the Exclusion Act had been written only against Chinese, and there remained a parade of Asian menaces—Hindoos, Filipinos, Japanese—waiting in the wings to provide employment for subsequent generations of craft union officials and labor politicians.

All the while, of course, the trade unionists were decrying partisanship and warning against the dangers of involvement in mass politics. Yet a kind of symbiotic relationship bound them to the labor politicians. The gist of it was that a clear field would be left the politicans to push their stock of proletarian, racist, and religious motifs in working class districts as long as their activities kept the unorganized and unemployed off the backs of union officials. When pressure for radical reform became powerful enough to upset the labor constituencies, this partnership was likely to break down. Union leaders would then be forced into mass politics in opposition to the discredited politicans. This roughly was what occurred in 1894 during the Populist insurgency, and again even more precisely in 1911 when the ascendant wing of the trade union apparatus swung labor's vote to the Progressives.

The 1911 alliance between Progressive reformers and leaders of the San Francisco Labor Council and State Federation acknowledged the power and cohesiveness achieved by the labor force in California. Throughout more than half a century labor had played a major role in state politics; and for more than ten years the metropolis of the Pacific Coast had been famed as a *union* town—the archetype of skilled trade dominance. To this result, as the foregoing pages have endeavored to show, the presence of Chinese had substantially contributed. Here one comes up against the logical impossibility of asserting that any particular situation existed because of some antecedent situation. Yet perhaps without overtaxing the argument it may be suggested that the Chinese, and the factor of anti-Orientalism which their presence occasioned, furthered the dominance of the skilled trades by enabling those trades to control and direct the energies of the entire white labor force.

Erosion of the Producer Ethic

From the foregoing it seems clear that, by the mid-eighties at least, the institutionalization of anti-Orientalism was firmly established. What did this involve in terms of thought patterns within the labor force? First of all, the long erosion in the Republican and Democratic traditions of the twin mandates of equality had been deeply influential. Experiences and responses of California workingmen had intensified this process; and to the extent that they were Republicans or Democrats, they had been in turn affected by the outcome. Beyond these two major traditions, common to the entire population, the pattern most characteristic of the labor force was the one which stemmed from the producer ethic of the Jacksonian era. Productive workers of all sorts, according to this view, regardless of whether industrial or agricultural, wage workers or self-employed, together comprised the honorable and creative elements of society. These were the value carriers; and it therefore became the mission of the labor movement, as perceived by many advocates of labor organization both before and after the Civil War, to unite them against the ever encroaching conspiracy of privilege and monopoly. Here, explicitly, was the credo of the Knights of Labor; and during the eighties trade unionism along with labor activity of all sorts was being justified largely within this framework. In the East, however, laboring men had sanctioned the exclusion of blacks from the ranks of acceptable value carriers; and in the West a similar reservation had been placed against Chinese.

The majority of American workingmen, doubtless, did not lead intense ideological lives. They were accustomed to inconsistencies in their patterns of thought and seem to have accepted without much discomfort a producer ethic from which one-tenth to one-fourth of all producers had been proscribed. Yet there were certain ideologically conscious minorities which resisted racial proscriptions. Such were the "political" labor unionists exemplified by William Sylvis and A.C. Cameron who, immediately after the Civil War, had argued for inclusion of Negroes in the National Labor Union.[1] The controversy over Negro membership in the NLU raised scarcely an echo in the Far West. But as to the exclusion of Chinese, there were some, especially European immigrants of republican revolutionary background, who held grave doubts. Most of these, probably, like Frank Roney, found their way into the socialist movement. At all events it was the socialists alone in the California labor force who mounted any criticism of the anti-Chinese crusade. Socialists took their ideology seriously; and few though they were in number, they played a crucially important role in West Coast labor. Consistently with their general view, they endeavored to redefine the producer ethic—which they considered fuzzy, agrarian, and petty bourgeois—into a wage earner ethic. But within this redefinition, any exclusion of wage earners (and who could deny that Chinese in the West, like black laborers in the East, were wage earners?) confronted the socialists with a theoretical and moral dilemma. They strained mightily over the problem and ended by agreeing, with Roney, to "sail under the flag" of anticoolieism. This was to serve merely as a tactic, a means of uniting and educating the working class.

Tactics, however, have a way of becoming habits; and so at the turning point in 1885 when, conceivably, there was a chance to have hauled down the tactical flag and raised in its stead a strategic flag of working class unity, the socialists could summon little more than a gesture. It is scarcely possible, now, to read the statement made on their behalf at the first convention of the Federated Trades by Sigismund Danielewicz, the San Francisco barber turned seamen's organizer, without believing that Danielewicz was indeed, as Roney described him, "ardent" —and totally sincere. Yet Danielewicz must have known beforehand that his comrades would permit him to be guffawed and howled and booed from the podium. Haskell the firebrand, Roney the labor statesman, who both were present, said nothing in his defense.

Perhaps one reason for this passivity was that many socialists rejected, really, what Danielewicz was saying. Haskell, for one, had found his way to labor's cause through the anti-Chinese crusade. Only three months after the Federated Trades convention, W.C. Owen, another ardent socialist and a long-time colleague of Haskell and Roney in the socialist academy, wrote an article for the Denver *Labor Enquirer* (which had inherited the readership of Haskell's short-lived *Truth*) titled "The Coast Crisis: An Argument Justifying Socialists' Anti-Chinese Agitation."[2] Owen began by quoting Victor Hugo on the crusades. "It was a mighty popular movement, and all such, be the cause and design what they may, ever unchain the spirit of freedom." He proceeded then to an analogy between the crusades and the anti-Chinese agitation. Yet, as he regretfully noted, some of the "best and purest minded comrades" were standing aloof from this cause because it did not "square with their preconceived theory of fraternity." Also, and apparently for the same reason, many socialists still looked askance at the "trades union movement."

In both instances, the *Enquirer's* correspondent continued, their reluctance stemmed from failure to understand the processes of evolution. Change came only through struggle. It was therefore the duty of socialists to aid the people in acquiring habits of struggle; the goals toward which struggle might be directed were of less importance than the fact of struggle itself:

> I regard it as the adding of a fresh ring to the tree of solidarity whenever men are roused to the self-sacrifice of putting aside their selfish private interests for the sake of a common cause. The workingman may not be able to explain his motives with scientific precision, but when he beats a scab, I believe that if we could see into his mind, we should discover that he is prompted to his action by an instinctive sense that the scab is false to the cause of labor, that he is a traitor to the principle of solidarity by which alone the proletariat can hope to win. So it is with the anti-Chinese crusade; a great part of the repugnance felt to them upon this coast is that they do not act as citizens, that they have no concern in the solidarity of the nation. A precisely similar sentiment has dictated the persecutions of the Jews in Germany, Austria and Russia, persecutions which have been justified precisely on this ground....It

is, in short, but the public method of voicing the sentiment, "no rights without duties," or, as Comte puts it, "Man has no rights except to fulfill his duties."

> In a word, I believe that we ought to welcome every opportunity which presents itself to the proletariat of developing itself in the only way, as evolution proves conclusively, in which anything ever did develop itself since the beginning of the world—that is to say, by struggle.

It would be pleasant to suppose that this argument, drawn up fifty-five years before Belsen and Auschwitz, had been naively or innocently conceived. The circumstances of its presentation scarcely permit such a supposition. During the latter part of 1885 and the early months of 1886 came that series of pogroms which resulted in the dispossession and murder of Chinese and the leveling of small town ghettoes from San Diego to Seattle. The plan of abatement by violence advocated by Kearney and Kalloch—and by Roney and Haskell—was at last being tried out in action.

The silencing of the "best and purest minded comrades" on this issue was comparable to the disintegration of the abolitionist line within the Republican coalition. General retreat followed, bringing with it a continuing restriction of the producer ethic. Just as in the major political traditions, the ideological heart of the old structure was being gnawed away. These events within the labor force of the Far West fed back to the larger national context, and especially so through their impact on the developing ideology of national craft unionism.

Race and the House of Labor

When the National Labor Union at the close of the Civil War had debated the question of black membership, speakers on both sides respected in principle that declaration of labor unity which had been set before the public in the official NLU Address: "we are of the opinion that the interests of the labor cause demand that all workingmen be included within its ranks, without regard to race or nationality."[3] As noted earlier, this was an expression of the Jacksonian producer ethic adjusted to the postwar situation in which black slaves were seemingly being transformed by Reconstruction into citizens, voters, independent economic agents. To press a contrary view too diligently in 1868 might have suggested a taint of secessionist sympathies. Moreover, since the labor force had no other ideology at its disposal, groups within the labor force had little alternative but to rationalize their divergent viewpoints with reference to the producer ethic. Thus the NLU, while proclaiming the unity of labor, ended in practice by accepting exclusion of blacks at the local level.

Craft unionism, then in its infancy but at the

threshold of rapid growth, exhibited a similar ambivalence. Economically rather than politically oriented, the craft unionists and their leaders sought to maximize bargaining power through union control over competition for skilled jobs. To this purpose they strove to define the limits of each craft, to restrict entry by means of rigorous apprenticeship, and to establish union supervision over apprenticeship and hiring. The type of organization dictated by the craft concept was necessarily *exclusive*: optimum membership for each craft would be that which took in all trained practitioners of the craft, excluding all others. Since the recently emancipated black contingent of the labor force remained unskilled and inexperienced at industrial occupations, it was certain to fall largely within the excluded portion. Regardless of ideology, the logic which flowed from the practice of craft unionism tended to prohibit entry of blacks.[4]

Indeed, the preeminence of practice over ideological principle would soon become one of the seminal ideas of craft unionism. Selig Perlman, in the massive *History of Labour in the United States* on which he and John R. Commons collaborated at the University of Wisconsin, wrote that, having freed themselves of the old faith in "cooperation, social reform and politics," the craft unionists turned instead to the "wage consciousness of Marx and the International, purged of its socialist ingredients."[5] Having thus shuffled off both the producer ethic and the proletarian mission, these unions were ready to accept the industrial apparatus as they found it and do what they could for themselves. A recent study of American labor organization by the economist Lloyd Ulman has taken the drive of skilled workingmen to improve their collective bargaining potential as the chief dynamic factor in the growth of national unions. This was the decisive factor, Ulman argues, in the drawing of boundaries around particular skills. And given the mobility of American society, it was this same factor which impelled craftsmen, grasping for some means of control over entry into the various trades, to unite their separate locals into national organizations, then to permit the transfer of effective power to the national level. The result was that surge of organization and consolidation described in the previous chapter. The number of trade unions increased during the eighties by 169 percent and again the following decade by 52 percent. Membership more than quadrupled. And as indicated by the statistics referred to earlier, the new unions were now equipped with treasuries, with rather stable strike and benefit funds, and with the beginnings of full-time professional leadership.[6] And they were almost totally white.[7]

Capstone to this structure of national craft unionism was the American Federation of Labor, founded in 1881, which provided an annual convention and an executive to speak for, and serve, its affiliated organizations.[8] The Federation, whose officers liked to speak of it as the "House of Labor" and of themselves as representative of the entire American labor force, could not so conveniently disregard ideology as could the affiliated unions. What developed, therefore, was a right hand-left hand arrangement by which the national unions made their practical decisions in the field, while the Federation, created by the nationals but lacking any coercive power over them, continued to speak of (and to) Negroes in the old egalitarian language of the producer ethic. At its convention of 1894—to select one example among many—the Federation proclaimed its devotion to working class unity "irrespective of creed, color, sex, nationality or politics."[9] Samuel Gompers, president of the Federation for all but one of its first forty-three years, regularly denounced racial exclusiveness. Labor could never achieve its goals, he asserted, unless it struggled to "eliminate the consideration of a color line. . . ." "If we fail to make friends of [black workers], the employing class won't be so short sighted. . . . If common humanity will not prompt us to have their cooperation, an enlightened self-interest should."[10] In the early nineties, the AFL executive board refused to charter several applicant groups which insisted upon explicit antiblack clauses in their constitutions. The real point in dispute, however, was not acceptance of Negroes into these organizations (which simply transferred the discriminatory rule to the local initiation ritual) but the overt expression of exclusionary policy in a union constitution. After these semantic deviations had been corrected, the applicants soon won admission to the House of Labor.[11]

No such inhibition even at the semantic level applied in the case of Chinese. Throughout the nineties and on into the twentieth century, the Federation kept up a barrage, in openly racist terms, against Chinese and other Orientals. Thus, one year before the apostrophe to working class unity cited above, an AFL convention resolved that Chinese brought with them "nothing but filth, vice and disease"; that "all efforts to elevate them to a higher standard have proven futile"; and that the Chinese were to blame for degrading "a part of our people on the Pacific Coast to such a degree that could it be published in detail the American people would in their just and righteous anger sweep them from the face of the earth." Samuel Gompers, in his presidential report, informed the convention of 1901 that "every incoming coolie means. . .so much more vice and immorality injected into our social life."[12] That same year in a pamphlet published by the Federation for mass distribution, Gompers and Herman Guttstadt, a West Coast official of the Cigar Makers' Union, quoted with approval a memorial sent to Congress by citizens of San Francisco in which they warned the lawmakers to beware especially of the offspring of miscegenation between Americans and Asiatics, for these proved "invariably degenerate."[13]

188

It is hardly necessary to extend this recitation in order to make the point that the Oriental issue seems to have served trade unionists—much as it had earlier served Democratic and Republican politicans during Reconstruction—for a language of double meaning. The language justified not only what was being done to Orientals but to Negroes; and its constant repetition paved the way for a more explicit advocacy. By the late nineties the Federation was making no fuss with its affiliates over exclusionary practices, verbal or substantive.[14] In a report prepared for Atlanta University in 1902, W.E.B. DuBois estimated that some 40,000 Negroes belonged to unions affiliated to the AFL; but 75 percent of these were in three organizations of heavy black membership and semiskilled status. That left approximately 10,000 black craftsmen forming a modest 3 percent of the remaining AFL membership. The bulk of these were in the South, in segregated locals, often receiving lower rates of pay than whites doing the same work. As of 1900 the United States Bureau of Labor Statistics listed 82 unions affiliated to the AFL. DuBois reported that 39 of these had no black members and another 27 only a scattering. Gompers and his AFL colleagues—still advocating unity of all workingmen—gave their approval to special segregated locals which controlled the competition of blacks and collected their dues money while denying them any effective voice in union policy.[15]

Exclusion now came to be blamed on the blacks themselves on the assumption that their readiness to be used as strikebreakers lay at the root of the matter. In 1898 an article featured in the *Federationist,* official organ of the AFL, explained that Negroes were not suitable for trade unionism because they were "of abandoned and reckless disposition" and lacked "those peculiarities of temperament such as patriotism, sympathy, sacrifice, etc., which are peculiar to most of the Caucasian race." The best solution would be to export them to Liberia or Cuba.[16] Gompers himself completed the circle of identification: "But the caucasians," he told a presumably Caucasian audience at St. Paul, Minnesota, in 1905, "are not going to let their standard of living be destroyed by negroes, Chinamen, Japs, or any others."[17] ★

Notes

1. The National Labor Union was established in 1866 as an annual convention of labor and reform organizations. [Editor's note: See also author's original work from which this article is reprinted: *The Indispensable Enemy: Labor and the Anti-Chinese Movement in California* (Berkeley and Los Angeles: University of California Press, 1971), 40-44.]

2. W.C. Owen in a letter dated San Francisco, February 23, 1886, printed in the Denver *Labor Enquirer,* March 6, 1886. (Cross Collection Newspapers on Microfilm, Bancroft Library.) On Owen, see Frank Roney, *Frank Roney: Irish Rebel and California Labor Leader* (Berkeley,

1931), 437, 473. On Haskell's connection with the Denver *Labor Enquirer,* see Ira B. Cross, *A History of the Labor Movement in California* (Berkeley, 1935), 158.

3. Cameron, *Address* (Chicago, 1867), quoted in John R. Commons et al., *A Documentary History of American Industrial Society,* 10 vols. (New York, 1958), IX, 158-160.

4. Alexander Saxton, "Race and the House of Labor," in Gary Nash and Richard Weiss, eds., *Race in the Mind of America* (New York, 1970).

5. John R. Commons et al., *History of Labour in the United States,* 4 vols. (New York, 1918), II, 354.

6. Lloyd Ulman, *The Rise of the National Trade Union* (Cambridge, Mass., 1955), 49-152, and tables on 4, 19. See above, pp. 238-241.

7. Ray Marshall, *The Negro and Organized Labor* (New York, 1965), 14-20; Charles H. Wesley, *Negro Labor in the United States, 1850-1925* (New York, 1927); Marc Karson and Ronald Radosh, "The American Federation of Labor and the Negro Worker, 1894-1949," in Julius Jacobson, ed., *The Negro and the Labor Movement* (Garden City, N.Y., 1968).

8. Philip Taft, *Organized Labor in American History* (New York, 1964), 92-96, 110-122. Slightly remodeled in 1886, the American Federation of Labor adopted its present name.

9. American Federation of Labor, *Proceedings of the 14th Annual Convention* (1894), 25.

10. Samuel Gompers to James H. White, September 14, 1889, and to H. M. Ives, November 10, 1892, as cited in Philip S. Foner, *History of the Labor Movement in the United States,* 4 vols. (New York, 1947), II, 196.

11. Bernard Mandel, "Samuel Gompers and the Negro Workers, 1886-1914," *Journal of Negro History,* XL (January, 1955), 34-60; Arthur Mann, "Gompers and the Irony of Racism," *Antioch Review,* XIII (Summer, 1953), 203-214; Herbert Hill, "The Racial Practices of Organized Labor: The Contemporary Record," in Jacobson, ed., *The Negro and the Labor Movement,* 286-287.

12. AFL, *Proceedings* (1893), 73; (1961), 22.

13. AFL, *Some Reasons for Chinese Exclusion. Meat vs. Rice. American Manhood Against Asiatic Coolieism. Which Shall Survive?* (Washington,1901), 34. (Also published as U.S. Senate Document 137 (Washington, 1902). With minor revisions, this pamphlet was reissued in 1908 by the Asiatic Exclusion League, San Francisco. The 1908 title page ascribes authorship to Samuel Gompers and Herman Guttstadt.

14. Karson and Radosh in Jacobson, ed., *The Negro and the Labor Movement,* 156-158; Marshall, *The Negro and Organized Labor,* 15-18.

15. W. E. B. DuBois, ed., *The Negro Artisan: Report of a Social Study Made Under the Direction of Atlanta University* (Atlanta, Ga., 1902), 8-10, 157-177. U.S. Bureau of the Census, *Historical Statistics of the United States, Colonial Times to 1957* (Washington, D.C., 1960), 67. DuBois actually listed 43 unions with total exclusion of blacks, but four of these were railroad brotherhoods not affiliated with the AFL.

16. Will H. Winn, "The Negro: His Relation to Southern Industry," *American Federationist,* IV (February, 1898), 269-271.

17. *American Federationist,* XII (September, 1905), 636-637, quoting a report of a speech by Gompers from St. Paul *Union Advocate.*

from

CARLOS BULOSAN
and the
Imagination
of the
Class Struggle

By E. SAN JUAN, JR.

Man and Masks

Bulosan acquired a passionate and searching comprehension of actually existing tendencies in society by consistently identifying himself with the victims, outcasts, the insulted and injured. In doing so he transformed the exploited class from its condition of being simply a static category into a dynamic agency for its liberation, from a class-in-itself to a class-for-itself. One can observe the growth of this consciousness in the transaction of "I" and "We," the private and the collective, in this meditative sequence:

> I was very young when I landed, [in Seattle on 22 July 1930] and the savage impact of a machine country only splintered the frail vestiges of the civilization of which I was born. I arrived here at a time when the crisis was at its height, and there were suicides everywhere among the "important" and "rich" men who were "touched" by the economic concentration. But I am wondering to this day why there were no suicides among the very poor, the very miserable and homeless, those who really were good to die. And I found out that the bond between the poor is tighter than that between the rich and important. Of course this is not to be found in books or in any history, because the poor man does not write books; he is too busy looking for something to fill his stomach. And when he comes to, his mind is too weak, his recollection too short, his imagination too blurred, etc. Thus the history is not yet written.

Pain and isolation compelled Bulosan to change himself. He read continually in libraries, "wherever there is a chance—in bed, at work, in street-cars, in toilet rooms," in theatre lobbies, bus stations, restaurants. This "savage instinct to read" became an obsession which deflected his mind from self-pity and physical torment. Though weakened by the Depression, Bulosan always tried to maintain a historical viewpoint by constantly renewing his attachment to the people:

> There were days, and even now, when I do not eat at all; but I only laugh and say this is nothing because I am used to it.
> The McDuffie-Tydings Law has affected us so much. It has thrown us into dungeons; it violated our rights and civil liberties. It is savager than the Platt Amendment of Cuba. Life for us here in California is very hard, and I wonder if the people in the East realize this fact. . . .
> I am still living in Los Angeles, out of work, living a hand-to-mouth existence, looking at the angry American sun.

If you read the official histories and biographies of the politicians lauded for the Tydings-McDuffie law, you would not find a single mention of "dungeons" or violation of rights. On the contrary, you would be overwhelmed by the sheer hypocritical praise and apotheosis of the elite who, in retrospect, have plundered the country of its wealth and persecuted its toiling citizens.

Anger impregnated and enriched Bulosan's life from the time when at the age of seventeen he first set foot on American soil up to the time he died in 1956.

What has surprised many philistines is the fact that the experiences of being tortured by racist violence, insult and hunger in the West Coast as a casual laborer and crop-follower did not permanently embitter Bulosan's sensitive and honest mind. This is because he had incorporated in his deepest self the images of his father ploughing his land, his mother selling salted fish in Binalonan, his brothers arduously trying to escape the cruel fate of wage slavery in Pangasinan. His brothers became failures with a vengeance—they personified the immorality of exploitation in a class-divided society. Macario, the older son, was being supported by the father to be a full-fledged teacher; but when the usurers seized the farm, Macario's future declined to that of a busboy in the United States.

Bulosan completed only three years of schooling, though friends claim that he was able to attend the Pangasinan Provincial High School. At twelve he was employed in a bakery shop, at fourteen in an ice factory. In his first day in Seattle, he was shanghaied by a hotel proprietor who sold him for five dollars to an Alaskan fish cannery where he was paid thirteen dollars for a season's work. For months he picked apples in the Yakima valley and received—nothing. As told in *America Is In The Heart,* this episode ended in the white vigilantes' burning of the workers' bunkhouse and Bulosan's fight in a box car to California. Carlos P. Romulo is alleged to have commented on this incident in the New York *Times:*

> It was the beginning of his long flight against fear. It carried him into years of bitterness, degradation, hunger, open revolt, and even crime. The poolrooms and gambling houses, dance halls and brothels, were the only places he knew. They were the only places a Filipino could know.

This is flagrantly short-sighted and prejudicial. Ignorant of Bulosan's other writings, Romulo isolated one aspect and labeled it the distinguishing characteristic of Bulosan's life, whereas the really significant content of the autobiography lies in the protagonist's ability to transcend the limitations of his environment by a profound grasp of the socio-historical process.

From the time he learned to read from books in the children's section of the Los Angeles Public Library to his busy years of writing from 1936 to 1946 when *America Is In The Heart* was published, Bulosan reversed the "flight from fear" to an embrace of the causes of fear as part of a wide-ranging and accurate vision of the world. So that to detach the initial stages from the totality of Bulosan's development as an artist, is to distort the whole picture and sanction a fraud.

Bulosan aligned himself with the fiery labor movement of the time, organizing migrant workers into unions and shouldering the consequences: he was lynched and insulted by outrageous racist intolerance. His sufferings culminated in a two-year sojourn at the Los Angeles County Hospital where after thirteen operations he lost the ribs of one side of his body and the use of one lung and was left with a shorter foot and a limp. One cannot ignore in this period Bulosan's anxious self-education and apprenticeship when as a TB patient he devoted his energies absorbing "the best that has been thought and said in the world," to use Matthew Arnold's phrase.

During the years of global chaos and disaster, Bulosan reconstituted his past and, in *America Is In The Heart,* re-animated the ethos of a society that included the dead, the living and the unborn. If his mode of transcribing his experiences suffered from being stereotyped or histrionic, he was never insensibly complacent or smug about it. He always desired to choke "sudden tears of regret" and to jolt himself out of being arrested by "the crystalline purity of childhood tears." He perpetually craved for order, combating a lingering sense of defeat, inquiring about life's pilgrimage: "Is it planned or purposeless? . . . Is it not only sex and alcohol and hot air? . . . The exacting demands of sudden manhood, the cruel responsibilities of manhood: these are the forces that have confronted our youth in America" (27 December 1946).

While protesting against the "pain in the mind," the betrayal and conspiracies of Filipinos, Bulosan always nourished his need for happiness. He gave the title *Joy to Every Man* to a manuscript burdened with loneliness, privations and other mental aberrations. While celebrating the virtues of the common man, he despised the "abysmal ignorance" of the American masses. These hesitations, ambivalence and reservations did not become a liability. For Bulosan was equipped with what Keats called "negative capability," the capacity to negate one's limited ego to permit the imagination to exhaust the plenitude of the material and spiritual world.

Bulosan's cosmos was pervaded with a chiaroscuro of moods, an atmosphere of instability and precarious zigzagging that paradoxically gave him a steady grip on the tragicomedy of existence. He dissected his misgivings and guilt feelings as myths, allowing history to render the final verdict. Bewailing his lack of formal education because of the "atrocious barbarity" of the times, Bulosan displayed a sincerity and courage that salvaged the wreck of his body from anonymity. With desperate pride and monkish determination, he sustained his critical distance. Yet he was too honest not to admit distress:

> I am trying to write every day in the midst of utter misery and starvation. I locked myself in the

room, plugged the phone, pulled down the shades and shut out the whole damned world. I know enough of it to carry me for a lifetime of writing. . . . Writing is a pleasure and a passion to me—I seem to be babbling with multitudinous ideas, but the body is tired and weak. (*4 and 6 May 1949*)

The Economy of the Spirit

Bulosan died in 1956, a casualty of his accumulated sufferings in the West Coast. The letters he wrote in the Fifties express both anguished withdrawal and resolute foresight caused by his illness, his disappointment with the Filipino intelligentsia, his lacerated conscience. As the logic of his attitudes entailed, he plunged into intense labor-union activity, becoming secretary of a confederation of labor unions. But somehow he felt moorless, a schism of the soul forcing him to revaluate his convictions to make it so utopian that he eventually yielded to unwarranted futurism and retroactive despair:

We have reached the stage of civilization at last, where everything has petrified, including man's anatomy; but those who have social responsibilities (which means, too, in endeavors toward moral cogencies) accept without a tint of pessimism or cynicism death's inevitable ambuscade. For we are ambushed by death in every corner of life; one little mistake and we are stricken down with impunity. Death like old age is a shocking reality. But humanity has always suffered; there was not a time in man's history when the mundane paradise which we are all seeking actually existed. Perhaps this is why in our panoramic ideals, we sacrifice our individual ambitions for what we believe to be glorifying—the universal happiness of mankind. Luckily, we cerebral animals have a tremendous conscience; otherwise, the world as we know it, besieged by immoralities, would become an anarchy of irresponsiblity. (*24 April 1953*)

Despite his "endeavors toward moral cogencies" and because of the lack of any historical orientation to his thoughts, Bulosan for the moment lost hold of perspective and of the future in the process of emer-

193

gence. He succumbed to agnostic relativism and narrow empiricism:

> I have seen, and often, the insensibility of men and women lacerating the lives of others with their talons of hate, greed and fear, and I wonder, now, if I have showered the comforting perfume of my love in the wrong places. I have a tremendous passion to make others happy. So daily I have to fortify my heart against assaults, abuses, inconsiderations of people around me, close to me, dear to me.

In the next month, however, Bulosan recovered his composure and with it the horizon of hope via self-knowledge. He declared that he had regained his faith in his fellowmen:

> Human life could truly be a paradise, in many respects, if the money spent for destruction were used for the elimination of disease, schools propagating tolerance, factories for necessary consumer goods, and research centers, clinics, hospitals, maternity wards, etc. In fact, we should have a Department of Peace in the cabinet, instead of a Department of War. Hate, greed, selfishness—these are not human nature. These are weapons of destruction, evolved by generations of experimenters in the service of ruling groups, be it a tribe, a clan, a prince, a king, a democracy. These destructive elements have finally become so subtle, so intricate, so deeply rooted in man's minds in our time, the era of international finance, that many people sincerely, though ignorantly, believe them to be the guiding forces of nature. Love, kindness, pity, tolerance, happiness, beauty, truth—these are the *real* human nature from which a galaxy of other relevant virtues spring, take root and flourish in manifold form; in what we call brotherhood or common humanity, as the ideal of honest men in the world.
>
> And because of this cultivated ability, plus my enduring fidelity to enduring human virtues and their amplitudes in our everyday life, I can clearly see my place in the vast panorama of human struggle.

In Bulosan as in every man, there exists the interpenetration of opposites in terms of values or emotions which impel him to action. These two phases of subjectivist despair and forward-looking humanism comprise the converging motions of the dialectic in Bulosan's psyche. They infuse his writings with scrupulous rigor and relevance.

On 2 June 1953, Bulosan wrote about the American minority, the informed vanguard, which is "illuminating our democratic heritage." But he also warned of the calamitous effect of living only with professionals insulated from the masses by their wealth: "the two classes" of the have-nots and the affluent few "cannot compromise on a lasting allegiance."

What is important in these last letters is the coalescence of the two faces of Bulosan: first, the delicate introspective poet of the idyllic homeland who wrestles with nightmarish nostalgia and a Quixotic code of honor; second, the prophetic radical whose moral poise depends on his love of man's spiritual heritage and his unlimited potentiality for improving the conditions of life. Each side reinforces the other. Thus we cannot legitimately split Bulosan's sensibility into the categorical sectors of the vulgar and the refined. For his sensibility articulates itself in a totalizing insight into the fusion of life and art, ideal and fact, consciousness and matter:

> To listen to a Scarlatti's violin solo, remembering a lost mountain village is a beautiful and tear-provoking experience: to watch hundreds of workers building the towering scaffolding of a new bridge—well, that is breath-taking and tear-provoking, too. But it would be tears of joy, seeing the magnificence of man's collective labor.

"The magnificence of man's collective labor" can be used to designate the prime object of Bulosan's ardor, the target of his homiletic technique and his self-sacrificing decorum in art.

The son who registered the laughter of his father in the forgotten barrio of Pangasinan in the Twenties never ceased hearing it and proclaiming it amidst hardships, futile renunciations and denials. Without this affection for his birthplace and his role as member of a revolting class in the Philippines and in America, Bulosan could not have produced the stories, poems and epic chronicles filled with so much poignant intimacy and plastic spaciousness. His manner afforded a penetrating insight into objective possibilities, into the immanent power emerging from the matrix of everyday appearance:

> Once when I was a little boy in that village where I had been born, I dreamed that we could remake this world into a paradise. In such a world there would be no darkness, no ignorance, no brutality to man by another man. In such a world there would be no deception, no ugliness, no terror. In such a world there would be mutual assistance, mutual cooperation, mutual love. This is the dream which has sustained me down the terrible years, and it is with me still; only it is more lucid now, more terrifying in its vastness.

It is the peculiarity of Bulosan's discriminating rhetoric that he always projects a vision of the future from the solid groundwork of the concrete possibilities implicit in the actuality of changing life. And this faith in a progressive unfolding of the world stems from his origin. The genesis of the future is in the collective past, for it posits a commitment to the task of liberation:

> Everywhere I roam I listen for [my native language] with a crying heart because it means my roots in this far-away soil; it means my only communication with the living and those who died without a gift of expression. My dear brother, I remember the song of the birds in the morning, the boundless hills of home, the sound of the language.... ★

THE 1921 TURLOCK INCIDENT:
FORCEFUL EXPULSION OF JAPANESE LABORERS
BY YUJI ICHIOKA

"Akusen kuto" is a phrase which often appears in the writings of Issei to describe their immigrant experience in America. Literally meaning "difficult battles, bitter struggles," it tersely expresses the Issei's continuous fight against the mistreatment of Japanese immigrants from at least the turn of the century, culminating in the World War II internment ordeal. Much has been written on anti-Japanese legislation and sensational incidents, not to mention the wartime internment. But very little has been produced on the many extra-legal acts which the Issei had to endure prior to the war. While admittedly not as sensational, these acts nonetheless constitute an important part of the Issei experience lying behind the usage of the phrase. One such incident occurred in the town of Turlock in Stanislaus County, California, in 1921 that involved the forceful expulsion of Japanese agricultural laborers. Today Turlock still has an old sign which reads "Water, Wealth, Contentment, and Health" marking the entrance to the commercial center of the town; in 1921 the sign should have had the added condition "except for Japanese laborers." A small agricultural community with a population of 3,394 in 1920, Turlock was known as a cantaloupe-producing area.[1] From mid-July Japanese migratory laborers, expected to reach an estimated number of 200-300, started to enter the town to toil in the surrounding fields. In 1920 there were only 478 Japanese residents in the county.[2] Undistinguished by any special characteristics, the few settled Japanese in Turlock itself had lived in peaceful isolation. Once the expulsion took place, however, the town and the Japanese residing in it attracted the attention of the people of California, the national press, and even the governments of Japan and the United States. Because of wide press coverage, the event created a minor turmoil. From today's vantage point, the incident is noteworthy as an example of extra-legal acts suffered by the Issei.

The facts are fairly clear.[3] On the night of July 19, 1921, shortly after midnight, approximately 50-60 white men, armed with clubs, some with firearms, surrounded the Iwata Store in town where 18 Japanese workers were sleeping. The cantaloupe-picking season had just commenced, and these workers had migrated to the town to harvest the crop. The white men first knocked on the door, but the Japanese refused to open it. Whereupon the white men forced themselves in. After rousing all 18 laborers, the armed white men ordered them outside. Placing 8 of the laborers on a Japanese-operated truck parked nearby, they commanded the Japanese driver, who had been sleeping in the truck, to take them to Stockton and not to return. The remaining 10 workers were loaded on another waiting truck and driven to Keyes, an adjacent town five miles north of Turlock. There the white men transferred them to a railroad freight car and warned them never to come back to Turlock at the risk of being lynched.

This event was repeated twice in the course of the night. The white men returned to Turlock and raided another Japanese bunkhouse in which other Japanese laborers were quartered temporarily. They rounded up an additional 20 laborers in like manner and again dumped them off at Keyes. Meanwhile, another group of 50-60 white men went to three Japanese farms on the outskirts of the town from which they dragged out 20 more laborers who had been hired by the Japanese farmers, and they too were taken to Keyes and warned never to return. According to all accounts, the unarmed Japanese offered no resistance. This incident followed a similar one in Livingston, a neighboring town to the south, which had occurred just a week before on July 13th. Ten Japanese laborers had been expelled from that town by white men wearing masks.

As soon as he heard of the expulsion, the Japanese Consul of San Francisco, Yada Shichitaro, quickly acted.[4] The evening newspaper, the San Francisco *Bulletin*, on July 20th, carried a front-page story under the caption, "700 JAPS FLEEING TURLOCK MOB—150 ORIENTALS DRIVEN FROM CITY DURING NIGHT." On that evening, Consul Yada dispatched a wire to Governor William D. Stephens requesting an investigation. "I respectfully urge an immediate investigation by the proper state authorities," his telegram in part read, "and ask that the results of such inquiries be communicated to this Consulate."[5] Fearful less he worsen the situation, he decided not to send a Consular staff member to look into the matter. Instead he arranged to have two representatives of the Japanese Association of America, one a Japanese and the other a white American, to go to Turlock to ascertain exactly what had happened. Two days later, in a formal letter to the Governor, Yada conveyed his hopes that measures would be taken "to prevent any recurrence of irregularities and that the interested authorities in question will find it possible to fully protect Japanese subjects in this State in the exercise of their clearly defined treaty rights."[6]

Ever since the 1906 San Francisco school crisis, the Japanese government had consistently protested anti-Japanese legislation and acts as violations of the rights guaranteed by the existing commercial treaty between Japan and America. The Treaty of 1894 was invoked in 1906 and its revised version of 1911 was applied in the Turlock affair. The salient portion of Article I of the 1911 Treaty read:

> The subjects or citizens of each of the high contracting parties shall receive, in the territories of the other, the most constant protection and security for their persons and property and shall enjoy in this respect the same rights and privileges as are or may be granted to native subjects or citizens, on their submitting themselves to the conditions imposed upon the native subjects and citizens.[7]

The meaning was unequivocal. Despite the fact that Japanese were aliens in America, as long as they abided by the law, they had in theory the same civil rights as ordinary American citizens, except those rights which inhered in citizenship itself such as that of voting. To be run out of Turlock by force in the middle of the night obviously violated the terms of the treaty. Consul Yada's letter to Governor Stephens was based on this fact.

Economic competition between Japanese and white farm laborers unquestionably existed. A few days prior to the expulsion, white workers had circulated a petition among growers which attributed white unemployment to the presence of Japanese laborers. The petition called for the discharge of Japanese laborers and the employment of only white laborers, and also demanded a wage-scale of 25 cents

illustration by DEAN S. TOJI

per crate for picking which was 3 cents higher than the previous season. In his formal report on the incident, Mitoma Shigeru, sent to investigate it by the Japanese Association of America, indicated that a few Japanese laborers worked for as little as 16 cents per crate and that most worked for 18 cents or more, with the average in the neighborhood of 20 cents.[8] Newspapers also reported similar wage-scale disparities.[9]

But economic competition was not the only causal factor. To begin with some 70-80 local merchants and businessmen had endorsed the white workers' petition. Their own preamble to the petition stated:

> We, the undersigned merchants and business men of Turlock, protest against the annual influx of Japanese into this community and, believing that it is the birthright of American citizens to fill all available jobs, we call upon the growers and farmers of this district to employ *white* labor exclusively. We call upon the packers and distributors to handle only such fruits and produce as has been produced by American labor exclusively. As evidence of our good faith, we pledge our hearty and unqualified support to the accomplishment of this purpose. (Italics mine.)[10]

On July 18th, just a day preceding the incident, this petition was submitted to the Turlock Chamber of Commerce. W.C. Cook, a local attorney and member of the American Legion, made the presentation on behalf of the white workers. The members of the Chamber of Commerce passed a resolution deploring the practice of hiring Japanese and urged all growers to employ white workers. The key section of the resolution read:

> Whereas, the Chamber of Commerce has heretofore taken the stand that this district should be a district for *white* people and American citizens, now therefore
> Be it resolved that we condemn the practice of giving employment to Asiatics when there are white workers available to do the work and that they further call upon the employers of labor to give preference to white help on account of the greater efficiency obtained. (Italics mine.)[11]

As to the white workers' higher wage demand, the Chamber of Commerce[12] did not endorse it. Class interest no doubt lay behind its refusal. Yet the adoption of the resolution indicated that the members of this body fully shared the anti-Japanese sentiments of the white workers. The local chapter of the American Legion likewise passed a similar resolution. All of the foregoing actions transpired before the incident and were taken by the leading citizens of the town. Taken together, they suggest that the conflict between Japanese and white laborers entailed more than economic competition.

A thorough sifting of other evidence confirms this suggestion. When the armed white men first knocked on the door of the Iwata Store, one of the Japanese swiftly telephoned the head of the local Japanese Association who lived a few doors down the street. He in turn promptly called the local police station for assistance. Two officers were supposed to be on duty that night. No one was there to answer the call. Later investigation revealed that both officers had been informed of the impending expulsion and had conveniently absented themselves from the station. Four or five trucks and at least five automobiles were used in the raids. William Ryder, the American representative of the Japanese Association of America, noted that white migratory workers did not have enough money either to hire or own vehicles. So they had to have had the cooperation of vehicle owners to use them that night. Moreover, the raids were carried out in a co-ordinated and disciplined manner. None of the small Japanese shopkeepers or their families was molested, nor were the three Japanese farmers on the outskirts of Turlock harmed. Only Japanese laborers had been picked out for the forceful expulsion. Based on conversations with the local white citizens, Ryder wrote that "when I arrived in Turlock, I believe that the general sentiment was in condonement, if not in open approval of the raid," and concluded that it "had been planned and managed by certain of the townspeople of Turlock who believed that public sentiment would approve their action."[13] According to the San Francisco *Chronicle,* a Turlock Citizens Committee, composed of approximately 150 persons, half of whom were residents of the town, had planned the entire affair. Six men were eventually arrested. Having been assured by their leaders that the American Legion, businessmen, and the Chamber of Commerce supported the expulsion, they confessed that they had been induced to participate.[14] In short, the Turlock incident was more than an act committed by a group of disgruntled white laborers because of economic competition—it was planned by the local populace, sanctioned by local leaders, and executed by white laborers.

Subsequent events substantiate this judgement. On the morning of July 20th, Furukawa Yoshikazu, head of the local Japanese Association, went to Modesto and reported the incident to the County District Attorney's office. Ten Modesto police officers were summarily dispatched to Turlock to prevent any possible recurrence. On the following day Governor Stephens supplemented this force by adding state law enforcement officers. The federal government acted by sending Edward P. Morse, a special agent of the U.S. Department of Justice, to investigate the incident.[15] After the initial news of the explusion broke, newspaper reporters converged on Turlock, and the press on the whole had harsh words to print about the town. In the end, a general public outcry against the town developed.

Admonitory words even came from unlikely sources. Governor William D. Stephens, himself a proponent of Japanese exclusion, on July 21st, declared:

> California is the leader among the States in the movement that is now nation-wide for the complete cessation of immigration of all peoples ineligible to citizenship. Rapid progress is being made, but every happening such as that at Livingston or Turlock materially injures our cause and sets us back tremendously.[16]

The leaders of the Japanese Exclusion League, J.M. Inman and John S. Chambers, released a public statement on the same day employing the identical line of reasoning:

> The Turlock incident is deeply deprecated, not only as injustice to the Japanese, but because it is an injury to the cause of exclusion. A campaign of education is being conducted throughout the East by the Exclusion League and any acts of violence against the persons or property of the Japanese in this State will inevitably prejudice our cause and destroy some effects of that educational work.[17]

The views of the Governor and the Japanese Exclusion League were the same. They both feared the exclusion movement would be discredited, especially on the East Coast, by Turlock-like incidents associated in the public mind with ignorant mobs. The New York *Times* indeed confirmed their fear. Editorially denouncing the people of Turlock, it asserted, in a sarcastic tone, that they were in favor of "deportations."[18] The exclusionists themselves condemned the Turlock incident, not because of basic moral scruples, but rather because they were afraid that it would jeopardize their twin goals of seeking national legislation to curtail all Japanese immigration and to deprive the American-born Nisei of their American citizenship.

Faced with the sudden unexpected public indignation—and no less than from exclusion leaders—the citizenry of Turlock had to find a scapegoat upon whom to displace the blame. They sought it in the Industrial Workers of the World.[19] Before World War I when it had considerable membership and support, I.W.W. had been the most militant segment of the labor movement. Unlike the general labor movement, the I.W.W. did not discriminate against any group, did not make any distinction between so-called American versus alien laborers, and even had attempted to organize agricultural laborers. Thus the finger pointing of the people of Turlock was patently absurd, an obvious ploy to shift the blame by playing on the image of I.W.W. members as Bolshevik monsters. The San Francisco *Chronicle* reflected the anti-I.W.W. feelings of the press which Turlock hoped to manipulate to its advantage. "It is said that the mob was composed mainly of Industrial Workers of the World," the newspaper stated editorially. "Very likely. We do not know. If so, it may be said that as between the Japanese and the I.W.W. our choice would be the Japanese."[20]

The legal proceedings which ensued concluded the Turlock affair. The six arrested suspects—out of an estimated 100 or more participants—were all Turlock residents, young men who had been participants but not the main instigators. The preliminary hearing was held in the Modesto Court of Justice on August 5th. Two Japanese witnesses testified with Miss Nobuko Wakimoto, a Nisei and recent graduate of Modesto High School, acting as their interpreter. At this hearing an instance of intimidation occurred which augured what the final outcome of the incident would be. While waiting outside the courtroom to testify, a Japanese witness was threatened by white men. Requesting that a police officer be assigned in the hallway, the Deputy District Attorney stated to the judge:

> I have been informed that some people in the hall . . . started some kind of a demonstration against one of the Japanese witnesses here, with the words that they were going to knock him down and drag him out and a few other things.[21]

In addition, the Deputy District Attorney lamented the fact that he had only two witnesses. Referring to another possible witness by the name of Hoshizaki Yusaburo, identified as a victim of the expulsion, he asserted that the person "is apparently so scared of his life that he will not return to the County of Stanislaus and I don't know where he is."[22] Constable A.M. Stahl, however, testified that all six suspects had confessed to their participation in the incident, and so the judge ruled that there was sufficient evidence and set the trial date for November 29th on the charge of kidnapping.

The prosecution experienced difficulties from the outset. All the Japanese victims had been migratory farm workers who had no settled domicile. They moved from crop to crop, from place to place, and then temporarily settled down during the off-season, usually in an urban area. By the time of the scheduled trial, they were no longer present in the Turlock area. Already encountered at the preliminary hearing, the lack of witnesses became so pressing that special ads had to be placed in the Japanese-language newspapers which urged them to come forward. Those Japanese living in Turlock who had witnessed the expulsion were themselves reluctant to testify, fearful of reprisals from the people of the town. Inasmuch as no bloodshed had occurred and the Japanese laborers had been permitted to return and work, so they reasoned, they felt no need for legal action.[23] On November 29th, the first scheduled trial date, the prosecutor had to ask the court to issue special subpoenas in order to summon desired witnesses underscoring the problem. And precisely because of the lack of witnesses, the trial was postponed until January 31, 1922, only to be continued again until April for the same reason.

The trial officially began on April 26th. The prosecution had only 8 Japanese witnesses, and

198

among them only one who was able to identify positively one of the six defendants. That witness was Hoshizaki Yusaburo. The jury was composed of 8 men and 4 women who were all white. After deliberating for a mere 10 minutes, on May 5th, they delivered a verdict of acquittal for all six defendants. According to the Japanese-language newspapers, which sent reporters to cover the court proceedings, the trial was conducted in a hostile atmosphere.[24]   To sway the jury in favor of the defendants, the defense attorneys resorted to emotional and racial arguments, harping on the prevalent theme of the "little brown men" and the perils of Japanese immigration. To attack the credibility of the testimony of Hoshizaki, they played on the prevalent image of the racial untrustworthiness of the Japanese, of the sly and sneaky Jap. Coupled with the ruling that the confessions of the six defendants were inadmissible as evidence, it is not surprising the jury reached the verdict of not guilty. Looking back at the history of the incident, it appears to have been an almost foregone conclusion.

Conclusion

The Turlock incident is an example of the extra-legal acts experienced by the Issei. Economic competition between Japanese and white laborers was a factor, but it was not the only one. The expulsion actually involved, if not the entire populace of the town, at least a good percent of the citizens. The incident was neither exclusively the result of economic competition nor racism; the two factors were so interwoven that it is impossible to isolate one from the other. The Japanese Consul was ineffective in pressuring the authorities to safeguard the rights of Japanese immigrants; he did no more than protest formally. Fear without any doubt determined the small number of Japanese witnesses at the trial, and the defense attorneys successfully influenced the jurors by racial arguments. Rendered as it was when the exclusion movement was gaining national momentum, the final verdict reflected the prevailing anti-Japanese prejudice of the time. Similar extra-legal incidents took place in other locales in the 1920s—in Delano in 1922, Los Angeles in 1922 and 1924, Porterville in 1922, Hopland in 1924, and Woodlake in 1926.[25]   The phrase "akusen kuto" frequently appears in the writings of Issei to describe their immigrant experience in America. When used, the Issei have in mind not only legal discrimination but also the Turlock incident and similar extra-legal acts they had to suffer prior to World War II. ★

Notes

1. U.S. Bureau of Census, *Fourteenth Census of the United States*, v. 1, *Population, 1920*, Washington, D.C., 1922, p. 185.

2. *Ibid.*, v. 3, p. 110.

3. The only account of this incident heretofore has been the brief reference to it in Raymond L. Buell, "The Development of the Anti-Japanese Agitation in the United States," Part II, *Political Science Quarterly*, 38:1 (March, 1923), p. 73. Buell inaccurately dates the incident as occurring on July 18th. My account is drawn from the sources cited below.

4. Yada to Uchida, Telegram, July 22, 1921, in Japanese American Reserach Project Collection, Japanese Foreign Ministry Archival Documents, Reel no. 33. Hereafter cited as JARP, JFMAD, Reel no. 33.

5. *Ibid.*

6. *Ibid.*

7. Relevant extracts of the 1911 Treaty can be found in H.A. Millis, *The Japanese Problem in the United States*, New York: The MacMillan Co., 1915, Appendix A., pp. 313-315.

8. Mitoma Shigeru, "Tarakku Jiken Chosa Hokokusho," July 23, 1921, in JARP, JFMAD, Reel no. 33.

9. For example, see San Francisco *Chronicle*, July 21, 1921.

10. Turlock *Daily Journal*, July 18, 1921.

11. *Ibid.*, July 19, 1921.

12. Unfortunately I do not know the exact composition of the Chamber of Commerce.

13. W[illiam] R[yder] to Takimoto [Tamezo], Letter, July 25, 1921, in JARP, JFMAD, Reel no. 33.

14. San Francisco *Chronicle*, July 24, 1921, and Turlock *Daily Journal*, July 23, 1921.

15. Ambassador Shidehara discussed the incident with the U.S. Department of State on July 27, 1921. See Shidehara to Uchida, Telegram, July 31, 1921, in JARP, JFMAD, Reel no. 33. Feeling that local authorities appeared to be conducting an adequate investigation, Shidehara did not file a formal protest note. The fact that the federal government had already dispatched Edward P. Morse reenforced the Ambassador's opinion.

16. San Francisco *Chronicle*, July 22, 1921.

17. *Ibid.*

18. New York *Times*, Editorial, July 22, 1921.

19. W[illiam] R[yder] to Takimoto [Tamezo].

20. San Francisco *Chronicle*, Editorial, July 22, 1921.

21. Transcript, August 5, 1921, Preliminary Hearing, Superior Court, Stanislaus County, Modesto, California.

22. *Ibid.*

23. Yada to Uchida, Telegram, December 8, 1921, in JARP, JFMAD, Reel no. 33.

24. See *Nichibei Shimbun*, May 7, 1922, in JARP, JFMAD, Reel no. 33, and *Shin Sekai*, April 26, 27, and May 7, 1922. See also Turlock *Daily Journal*, May 6, 1922. Unfortunately the trial transcript is unavailable. Since the verdict was never appealed, no transcript was made.

25. Shishimoto Hachiro, *Nichi-Bei wa Do Naru ka*, Tokyo: Jitsugyo no Nihonsha, 1934, pp. 113-115. Such incidents of course were not restricted to California. One occurred in Toledo, Oregon in 1925. Nor were they limited to the 1920s. The most noted one in the 1930s took place in Arizona in the summer of 1934.

CONTEMPORARY ISSUES

Introduction

In the past decade or so, with the resurgence of community and political struggles and the development of ethnic studies programs, many people have become interested in the history of Asian immigration and the Asian American experience. For many students, ethnic studies provided the first opportunity to examine their histories and current conditions. Asian Americans have faced oppression, exploitation and racial hostilities in America; one further example of the Asian American experience is the denial of their *own* history.

From personal experience Asian Americans also know that they still face discrimination in employment and housing (See Labor & Capital Section), and stereotyping in the media and in various forms of social interaction (See Media Section). There are many problems that confront Asian American people in urban ethnic communities: unemployment and poverty; substandard housing and overcrowdedness; inadequacy or total lack of human services such as childcare, health care and welfare assistance programs; high prices and low wages; and high crime rates and inadequate police protection with instances of police harassment and brutality.

But when it comes to education, many people—Asian and non-Asian alike—still believe that Asian Americans, as well as others, have an equal chance, and that through hard work and diligence Asian Americans and other minorities can overcome past discriminatory practices. Some even believe that for Asian Americans problems related to education are negligible or non-existent.

Many parents work hard all their lives in menial or unfulfilling jobs, believing that their children, at least, will have a chance to "make a decent life" for themselves, if only they get a good education. In some instances, formal educational attainment has been singlemindedly thought of as *the* way for Asian Americans to "make it" in America. And making it usually means both achieving economic security and gaining acceptance from the rest of society.

Statistical data that, *on the average,* Asian Americans have achieved their goal of obtaining formal education, are often cited as evidence of successful assimilation into the American Way of Life. (See Census Highlights, Chart 1 and Table 5 in the appendix.) While the census figures are signficant, the numbers fail to reveal some very important facts: (1) Biases inherent in the census are that the non-English-speaking, the poor and less educated, and the transient or migrant working people are not represented in the same proportion as those with a more stable community life. (2) Although the *average* of the total sample may be relatively high, one cannot assume that the combined figures make a perfect bell-shaped curve. The opposite may be true. For example, for Chinese Americans, significant numbers are clustered at the extreme ends of the scale, and

202

EDUCATION

those at the upper end have incomes which do not reflect their educational attainment. (3) Through stereotyping and "tracking," Asian Americans were encouraged (or forced) to pursue majors and occupations in narrowly defined areas where verbal skills, creativity, judgment and discretion are not required. (4) Finally, the numbers do not reveal the extent Asian Americans have had to sacrifice materially, or how much they have had to reject their own cultures and backgrounds in order to adapt themselves to classrooms where Anglo-American, Judeo-Christian, male-dominated and capitalist values are prevalent.

The articles in this section are self-limiting in several ways. First, they deal specifically with only one aspect of American life and deal directly with one institution—the educational system. While a comprehensive analysis of the dynamic relationship between the educational system and the whole of society is necessary to place the role of education in its proper context, it is also important to focus on this one aspect because it plays a crucial role in the socialization and stratification of society. As one of the key mediating institutions in the superstructure of the capitalist system, the school system mirrors the goals and priorities of the economic base of this country. A second limit is that the articles focus on Asian Americans. Many of the issues raised in this section are applicable to other minorities, and some are even more striking for Blacks, Chicanos, Puerto

Ricans, and Native Americans. Thirdly, the articles may reflect a West Coast or Mainland bias. Many Asian Americans in other parts of the country, most notably in Hawaii and the East Coast, are engaged in similar struggles from which vital lessons can be learned.

The Education Section consists of five articles that reflect the authors' views of the role of knowledge and education. All of the articles in this section are written by Asian Americans who have participated—both as students and as teachers—in the American educational system, and have taken part in various struggles related to educational issues. Each is a description and analysis of a learning process, not only in classrooms, but more importantly, in the process of participating in efforts to bring about change in the communities. Each article describes the process of gaining knowledge which is meaningful and relevant to the people, and one in which people take that knowledge and in turn, *use* that knowledge to make changes. The articles also capture the continuing nature of the process of learning (education), of using what is learned to make changes (application in practical work), and of learning again.

The first article by Mike Murase retraces the long and at times violent campus struggles of the late 1960's to establish ethnic studies programs in American colleges and universities. The author attempts to place these struggles into a larger historical context by examining the development of educational institutions in the United States. While not comprehensive, the article provides an analysis of some of the goals and priorities of the American educational system.

Discussing the difficulties of "working within the university and yet being inherently anti-establishment," May Ying Chen taught the Asian Women in America course at UCLA with a group of women in 1972-1973. The course—a combination of women's and Asian American studies—raised the issues of race, class and sex, examined materials of the women's liberation movement, and encouraged direct community involvement. Like other authors in this section, Chen concludes that there is still a need for "a sound and unified analysis and strategy" for Asian American Studies.

The next article is written by Linda Wing who taught the first Asian American Studies course at Berkeley High School. She describes the bureaucratic processes involved in her hiring as the instructor and the role that community interest and involvement played; she also discusses the insensitivity and reluctance of the Berkeley Unified School District in approving the course, and later, in accepting it as part of the educational program. Wing also relates the growing awareness among her students who later played a leadership role in developing the content of the courses, and ultimately began taking part in projects involving the community.

Because many of the Asian American Studies courses are designed to be relevant and practical, many students invariably turn to the questions of what and how they can take an active part in changing the conditions in our communities.

Many members of the Chinatown Education Project (CEP), who wrote the fourth article, have their roots in Asian American Studies programs and the student movement. One of them recalls, "...the Asian Women course started me thinking, and got me interested in working in the community." For another student who joined the Chinatown Education Project, it was the Chinese in America course that "made me aware that I'm Chinese and that it means something." After these courses, some students participated in Asian American Tutorial Project, the film series, childcare, Creative Play and the Neighborhood Youth Corps programs in Los Angeles Chinatown, and eventually formed the Chinatown Education Project, thus translating awareness and knowledge to action and involvement.

The CEP article is an account of various struggles and learning experiences within the community in the process of effecting change, first through the creation of alternative programs to meet the immediate needs of limited-English-speaking children, then of growing political awareness and realization that "it is the school system's responsibility to educate children, not CEP's responsibility." The Chinatown Educational Project represents one of many community groups who are concerned with the future of their children and are taking active steps to deal with it.

While CEP immersed themselves in alternative services and political struggles, another group in San Francisco used a legal challenge in the case of *Lau v. Nichols.* The inherent inequalities that existed in the San Francisco Unified School District for the limited-English-speaking students are amply documented by L. Ling-chi Wang who was an active participant in the struggle for the development of bilingual-bicultural educational programs. The U.S. Supreme Court handed down a favorable decision in January, 1974, but the implementation of that decision has been impeded by the stubborn opposition of the school board. Wang details the problems faced by community groups in the struggle for equal and quality education. He sums up the lessons learned from his personal involvements by noting that: (1) there are dangers in relying solely on legal remedies and that a coordinated and persistent political and community action is necessary to bring about meaningful and systematic change; (2) a sound strategy for institutional change comes only out of a thorough and correct analysis of the forces involved in the situation; (3) the needs of the poor, the non-English-speaking and non-white people are secondary, if not negligible, to the rulers of American society; and (4) short term gains in the long struggle for quality and equality in education should not be mistaken for a lasting victory.

Needless to say, these articles are neither comprehensive nor complete because the struggles themselves are far from over. For example, since the development of college ethnic studies programs in the late 60's, most of them have faced financial limitations and opposition from administrators and faculty, who see ethnic studies as basically experimental "fringe" programs. With the recent economic crisis, many of the programs face cut-backs and extinction. In order to maintain and expand these programs, the lessons learned from past struggles must be summed up and translated into coordinated action.

Aside from the external threat, there is also a great need to develop a common understanding about the ultimate goals of ethnic studies and to formulate a direction consistent with those aims. Currently, various trends and directions manifest in different programs. Some programs emphasize classroom instruction and curriculum, while others emphasize community involvement and political struggles, and still others focus on research and social investigation. All of these trends must be directed toward a common goal. The definite priority for the coming period is the concrete analysis of all the forces at play and the method for achieving goals that are in the interest of all the people.

Thus the process of learning continues.

—Mike Murase

Ethnic Studies and Higher Education for Asian Americans

BY MIKE MURASE

One approach to understanding the experience of Asians in America is a study of the history of ethnic studies and the context of the system of higher education in which it arose. It is a good point of departure for several reasons. First, the history of development of ethnic studies is in itself a significant part of Asian American history. It marks the first organized effort within the context of the formal educational system to reinterpret the history of Third World peoples in this country to accurately reflect our perspectives: as an ideal it represents an honest attempt—through rigorous research and investigation, through critical analysis of ourselves and of the social institutions in our society, through dynamic and innovative approaches in instruction and sharing, and through bold new attempts to actively *apply* what is learned to reshape our society—to disseminate the life stories of millions of non-white people in America.

Secondly, a study of ethnic studies raises the question of why ethnic studies was necessary and why its maintenance and growth seem so tenuous. It presents an opportunity to delve into deeper questions of why the resistance to ethnic studies is so strong. The examination leads to the conclusion that the priority within the system of higher education in the United States has been and will continue to be the maintenance and transmission of class privileges.

Thirdly, such a study leads to an examination of the process by which ethnic studies came about—the struggles that were necessary to overcome serious and determined resistance on the part of powerful institutions. It is an account of a historic event that was created by a peculiar mix of objective social conditions and the subjective will and determination of many people working together to make knowledge more relevant to themselves and more useful to society in general.

The first Asian American studies courses were initiated seven years ago in 1969. Programs were established at San Francisco State College (now California State University at San Francisco) and at the University of California at Berkeley only after the most prolonged and violent campus struggles in this country's history.

The immediate origins of the struggle may be traced to the fall of 1966. In the wake of the civil rights movement that had grown for a century after the Civil War and had flared in the late 1950s and early 1960s, Black and other Third World students presented a proposal to the administration of San Francisco State College for the admission of more Third World and other economically and culturally disadvantaged students, and for a Black-controlled Black Studies Department.

Students had been taught that all groups who had serious grievances got a fair hearing and that in order to make changes, they must make use of the "proper channels." So the students exhausted every possible avenue in the bureaucratic maze. They wrote proposal after proposal to deans and presidents. They wrote letters and appeals to campus and community newspapers. They met for endless hours and days with various administrators. They negotiated with the authorities at the school. For *sixteen months,* they negotiated and waited patiently:

> Although Black and other Third World peoples have been waiting hundreds of years for justice in America, still they were patient. . . But how could they "negotiate," after all, when the administrators had all the power? But the students had power, too, if they had the courage to use it together. They had the power to stop the school from operating. And that's what they did. They were through with brainwashing.[1]

By fall of 1968, the students had tried every "reasonable" way to raise the issues of ethnic studies, lack of student control, and easier access to higher education for minority peoples. Yet they received no indication that there would be recognition and rectification of injustices deeply rooted in the system of education. On November 6, 1968, a general student strike was called by the Third World Liberation Front (TWLF), "a coalition based on the operative and substantive principle of self-determination for each of its constituent organizations as representatives of their *communities* within the context of the academic setting."[2]

The students who spearheaded the strike were Blacks, Chicanos, Native Americans and Asian Americans. As minority group members in a system of higher education that had systematically excluded them, they had a special awareness of the depth of American racism. They were keenly aware of the way public schools had robbed them of their true heritage. They were among children of all races who went through school learning and relearning "American" history. . . . three, four and even five times—at least once each in elementary, junior high and high schools, and for those who were admitted to college, yet another course in "American" history. At each level of schooling, students were taught the same one-sided and distorted history of "our (European) forefathers" who settled along the Atlantic seaboard, and of the "pioneers in their covered wagons" who journeyed westward "to tame the wilderness."

The long and rich history of several million native Americans who lived for centuries in North America before the first white ever set foot on this land was ignored or distorted. American "Indians" were presented most often as troublesome savages who impeded the fulfillment of the European settlers' "divine right" of Manifest Destiny.

Black children were taught that their ancestors were slaves who were "emancipated" through the benevolence of white men in the North. Blacks were also portrayed most often as primitive savages who had to be "domesticated." But no mention was made of the fact that white men hunted down 100 million Blacks in the interior of Africa to sell them as slaves, and that during a 400-year period, five Africans were killed for every one that made it to the "New" World.[3]

Chicano children were taught—in English—stories about "illegal" immigration of wetbacks despite the fact that parts of California and all of the Southwest once belonged to Mexico, and that Spanish was widely spoken. The massive influx of white settlers into Mexican territory was inspired by (1) the discovery of gold in California and other rich minerals in the Southwest, (2) the completion of the transcontinental railroad by Chinese and other immigrant workers, and (3) the development of large cattle and sheep ranches, all of which took place only in the last half of the nineteenth century.

It was during this period in which the first Asians arrived in significant numbers. Yet, for the most part, the Asian American experience was omitted from the educational curriculum or has received only token mention. A sentence or two on Pearl Harbor and a line about Chinese "coolies" was the sum total of our history. Asians were depicted as oxen-like creatures who performed menial tasks, as the following example from Mark Twain's writing illustrates:

> They are a harmless race when white men either let them alone or treat them no worse than dogs; in fact, they are almost entirely harmless anyhow, for they seldom think of resenting the vilest insults or the cruelest injuries. They are quiet, tractable, free from drunkenness, and they are as industrious as the day is long. A disorderly Chinaman is rare, and a lazy one does not exist. . . He always manages to find something to do.[4]

In each of these cases, Third World people have been portrayed as faceless, dumb creatures upon which some external actor (white man) had done something to them, rather than actors and doers in and of themselves who have played vital roles in shaping the course of American history. Asian Americans had no sense of our roles, contributions and struggles in this country because we were not taught about ourselves.

So then, it was not surprising that Third World students played the leading role in the struggles for ethnic studies and for a more flexible admissions policy which would better meet their educational needs. But the San Francisco State strike involved not only the students from that campus, but it also mobilized thousands of other students, people from Third World communities all over the state, rank-and-file members of unions, an overwhelming majority of the faculty, and ultimately, the whole political apparatus of the state of California.

A comprehensive account of the five-month-long strike would be too lengthy to be repeated here. Yet a brief recapitulation of the progression and scope of activities during the strike is necessary to approximate the sense of commitment and deepening frustration felt by Third World students.

The Strike

In the fall of 1968, despite the fact that 70% of all public school students in San Francisco were Third World,[5] they represented only 16% of the entire student body at San Francisco State College.[6] At the same time, the administration announced that 47 full-time teaching positions were unfilled, but Black Studies courses were to receive only 1.2 teaching positions of the 47 available.[7] Yet, the authorities at the college continued to insist that they were doing everything possible to facilitate the demands of the Black Students Union (BSU) and other Third World organizations.

Finally, after two years of "negotiations," the Trustees moved to have a Black instructor, George Murray, fired; and the BSU called for a student strike to begin on November 6, 1968. The Third World Liberation Front quickly came into being and was composed of Latin American Student Organization, Intercollegiate Chinese for Action, Pilipino American Collegiate Endeavor, and Asian American Political Alliance. By the first day of the strike, the Third World Liberation Front was well organized; the Students for a Democratic Society (SDS) and other unaffiliated white students began to mobilize for the strike. The strike leaders picketed buildings on campus and took up the chant which was to be echoed on campuses across the country, "On strike, shut it down! On strike, shut it down!" A set of demands was formulated. The demands revolved around the establishment of a School of Ethnic Studies, student control, faculty for the program, minority admissions and the specific case of George Murray.

They held a rally culminating in a march to the office of President Smith. The strikers also marched around the campus, closing down classes one by one. Smith responded by calling the San Francisco Police Tactical Squad, a special unit within the police department trained for smashing campus unrest and urban ghetto rebellions.

The student strike picked up momentum and spread. By the third day of the strike, most departments reported attendance below 50%. "On strike, shut it down!" The rhythmic chanting of a thousand voices reverberated throughout the campus. The first arrests came the following week when two students discovered the Tactical Squad occupying the boiler room and tried to alert other students. The presence of armed police on campus created an atmosphere of uneasiness and tension. With uniformed men marching around the plaza and walkways, students began to understand the extent to which the administration was threatened by their demands and their ultimate power.

> They discovered that brainwashing in the classroom wasn't the only weapon in the establishment's arsenal. When brainwashing failed, the authorities turned to headbusting. American education is a system of social control . . . but education is not the only means. When everyday mechanisms of control break down, then the Trustees and administrators resort to extraordinary means.[8]

On November 13, during the noon hour, the Tactical Squad appeared in front of the BSU office, standing in formation and intimidating students. The presence of police attracted more students. Some began shouting, "Pigs off campus! Pigs off campus!" Others hailed them with dirt clods and food. Then, in an instant, the police broke formation and began chasing and clubbing students indiscriminately. Students became outraged. The Tactical Squad, with their guns drawn, was forced off campus by some 2000 strikers who fought back. "Pigs off campus! Pigs off campus!" President Smith was forced to close down the campus indefinitely.

Throughout the month of November, students formed discussion groups to talk about the issues involved. At the suggestion of a faculty, a "crisis" convocation was called to "resolve the issues." BSU-TWLF agreed to participate in the convocation as an educational tactic, but when President Smith tried to resume classes, the striking students walked out of the convocation. All the while, 200 plainclothes police occupied the college. In the signal word of the day, the campus was definitely "polarized."

Meanwhile, the faculty played a mediating role by first suggesting department meetings and suspension of classes, and later, the resumption of classes and withdrawal of police from campus. The Student Strike Committee responded in a leaflet issued on November 25 entitled, "Rely on the People—Build the Strike:"

> . . .
> The faculty has played a dual role in this strike. On one hand, many members took a positive step by going out on strike and trying to win other faculty members to join them. But, on the other hand, the faculty has seen itself as a buffer zone between the administration, its cops, and striking students. We see this as an untenable position. In this stike one must clearly take either the administration side or the side of Third World liberation. . .

> By supporting Smith's plan to resume classes on December 2, whether or not the demands are met, the faculty is taking a strike-breaking position.

The BSU-TWLF made their position clear with respect to division of labor and on the question of leadership within the strike:

> Certain segments of the faculty have tried to impress on students that the faculty will resolve the issues of the strike. This says that the faculty has the power to resolve the conflict, and they see themselves in the leadership position. Both of these hypotheses are wrong.

They explained further:

> Students should realize that their power flows from the strength of the people involved in the struggle. It is this attitude, relying on ourselves, that will win. Winning will not come from relying on the faculty or the administration. The faculty must be won to the idea that they must unite with white students supporting the Third World demands. Also, the idea that some faculty members believe they are in a position to lead students in this fight must be defeated. *The BSU-TWLF are in the leadership of this struggle.* The position for the faculty and other white students is to support the demands. They, along with white students, must take the offensive in fighting racism among other white faculty, white students and in the white community.[9]

On Tuesday, November 26, the BSU-TWLF called an end to the convocation when the administration acted in breach of good faith by singling out some striking students for suspension. Unable to pacify students and restore order to the San Francisco campus, President Smith submitted his resignation at a meeting of the Trustees in Los Angeles that afternoon. A half hour later, the Trustees appointed linguistics expert S. I. Hayakawa as president.

Hayakawa, who was in agreement with the political philosophy dominant among the Trustees and Governor Reagan, served well as the middle-man minority with his hardline "state of emergency" tactics and 650 policemen. On the Monday after Thanksgiving, Hayakawa reopened the campus and called for the resumption of regular classes. When he saw that students were not responding to his call, he marched off campus to a sound-truck rented by the Strike Committee, climbed on it and tore loose the speaker wires from the sound system. When he was reminded that he was violating the students' right of free speech, he retorted, "Don't touch me, I'm the president of the college."[10]

The next morning, on December 3, a picket line formed by thirty students at a classroom building was routed by forty club-swinging Tactical Squad men. The picketers were chased into the student Commons where all students were indiscriminately hassled and clubbed. Following a noon rally where Third World community leaders spoke in support of the strike, a march on classroom buildings was met with 650 police. A bloody two-hour battle ensued between thousands of students and police. Hayakawa summed up the day by saying that it was his "most exciting day since I rode a roller coaster on my tenth birthday."[11]

In the days and weeks that followed, support for the demands of the Third World Liberation Front and the strike continued to mount. Community people picketed the San Francisco City Hall and the Hall of Justice to protest the presence of armed police on campus. They marched through downtown to the San Francisco *Chronicle* and *Examiner* buildings to protest racist, one-sided media coverage of the strike.

On campus, confrontations between students and police became a daily occurence. By the third month of the strike, 300 professors (members of AFT Local 1352) and the Teaching Assistants' Union (AFT Local 1928) struck in support of TWLF demands, and classroom count showed the strike to be 85% effective.[12] The entire campus was paralyzed for the remainder of that semester as clerical and library staff workers joined the strike. Other union workers chose to honor the picket lines and stopped deliveries to the college and dormitories. Supplies were cut off and garbage began to pile up all over the campus. Police on horseback chased students, using mace and billy-clubs on them. Strikers retaliated by throwing stink bombs in order to clear the classrooms. They clogged up toilets all over the campus. Striking teachers refused to give final exams, refused to turn in grades. The campus was immobilized.

During the period between December 2, 1968 and January 30, 1969, 600 striking students and bystanders were arrested. According to statistics gathered by doctors on injuries to those arrested, 56 suffered head injuries including two fractured skulls and one fractured eye orbit.[13] Other arrestees sustained a variety of injuries from police clubbing and macing: ruptured spleens, fractured ribs, broken hands, arms and legs, and welts and burns to stomach and groin areas.[14]

Rather than break the strike as the administration had hoped for, the mass arrests gave the students increased determination to fight against and defeat those who would go to any lengths to maintain a system based on racism and class biases. In its fourth month, the TWLF-called strike continued to build and grow.

The San Francisco State strike engulfed the whole state and captured the attention of the entire country. Students at other colleges began organizing and made similar demands for an equitable admissions policy and for relevant, truthful education.

Across the Bay, at the University of California at Berkeley, students followed the events of San Francisco State attentively. Students from the Afro-American Students Union, Mexican American Student Confederation and the Asian American Political Alliance, which made up the Third World Liberation Front, had gone through similar experiences in "negotiating" with Chancellor Roger Heyns during the academic year 1967-68. On January 21, 1969, the Third World Liberation Front called for a general strike "for the betterment of conditions of Third World students."[15] Principal among the demands was the establishment of a free and independent Third World College. They explained the global context from which their aspiration flowed; their protests were not limited to institutions of higher learning:

> Rather, they were part of a larger Third World movement representing the growing awareness of Third World people throughout the world of their common experiences under colonial domination, within and without the continent of the United States. The Third World movement was and continues to be a demand of colonized peoples for freedom and self-determination—for the right to control and develop their own economic, political, and social institutions.[16]

The strike at Berkeley involved thousands of students and community people, and lasted for more than forty days. One hundred and fourteen students were arrested, 155 students faced university disciplinary measures, and countless others were beaten and and harassed by the police. During the strike, a number of meetings took place where issues of ethnic studies and open admissions were discussed. At one meeting of the Berkeley Division of the Academic Senate on March 4, 1969, the faculty voted in support of ethnic studies by a margin of 550 to 4:

> It is the sense of the Berkeley Division of the Academic Senate that it favors the establishment of an Ethnic Studies Department.... Its structure should be of sufficient flexibility to permit evolution into a College.[17]

The Third World Liberation Front strike came to a close on April 7, 1969 when Chancellor Heyns announced that President Hitch had authorized the establishment of an independent Department of Ethnic Studies.

Relative calm was restored to the two campuses, but it was clear that the issues raised by the strikes—ethnic studies, student control, and access to education by children of Third World and working people—were dramatized, but not solved, by the strikes.

At UCLA, the emergence of ethnic studies took a different course which reflected the differing conditions on that campus. In the fall of 1968, a new team of administrators headed by Chancellor Charles Young took over for the retired Chancellor Franklin Murphy. Chancellor Young was well aware of the "basic inequities in our social system which have mitigated against full and equal participation in that system by members of certain ethnic groups."[18] The administration was also aware that many Third World students had begun to organize and had attempted to initiate meetings with the administration to discuss the possibility of establishing ethnic studies and increasing minority student enrollment.

The school year began after a summer of social upheaval which included the Democratic Convention in Chicago and ghetto rebellions, but because UCLA had a reputation for being a school with relatively few instances of student "unrest" and social protest, Chancellor Young was anxious to maintain the image of UCLA as a peaceful campus.

Young explained his perception of his role as an administrator in an interview with the campus newspaper:

> I am going to have to devote a part of my time to what is really a basic public relations—political kind of effort. . . . I'm going to try to prevent having any (demonstrations.)[19]

In his letter to the Academic Senate, Young reiterated that tension will exist between those who seek change and those who oppose it, and that "our task is to keep that tension at an absolute minimum."[20]

By January, the administration had designed a conciliatory measure dictated by fear: the "American Cultures Project." Under this plan, the Black, Chicano, Asian American and Native American components were organized as research units called Centers which were to take into account "the uniqueness of each individual group,"[21] and "determine a need, mount data through research, perceive goals and directions, and *solve problems through direct action.*" (Emphasis added.)[22] These ethnic studies centers did not have the authority to offer courses.[23] Initial courses in ethnic studies were offered through the much less "permanent" Council on Educational Development, another new program whose charge was to encourage innovative and experimental courses. Thus, the mechanisms for a modified version of ethnic studies were set up according to the administration's plan. Although the program was born in the absence of a campus-wide strike, the struggle for ethnic studies was not without its violence. On January 17, 1969, Black Panthers John Huggins and Alprentice "Bunchy" Carter were shot to death immediately following a meeting of the Black Students Union in Campbell Hall on the UCLA campus. It was reported at the time that disagreements about prospective candidates for the directorship of the Afro-American Studies Center led to the shootings of the Black Panthers by an opposing faction of "Black militants."[24]   Reports of the Senate Intelligence Committee in 1976 recently revealed that the FBI undertook a two-year (1969-1971), nation-wide program to discredit the Black Panther Party by such illegal means as provoking hostilities between the Panthers and rival groups. The FBI's covert involvement in activities of various colleges and universities has also been recently disclosed.

In the succeeding years, many Asian American studies courses have been introduced into the curricula of colleges and universities throughout the country, often in response to pressures from Asian American student organizations. In every case, these campus struggles represent long hours spent by many dedicated students to establish these programs. Many of the ethnic studies programs began as experimental courses taught by existing faculty members or by specially appointed instructors. A few of the campuses were able to develop reasonably autonomous and permanent programs. Numerous state-wide and national conferences on ethnic studies were held, and a number of journals, periodicals and bibliographies were produced to supplement curriculum materials.

Programs, however, continued to be limited by the small number of courses offered, and the temporary and experimental nature of the courses. There were also "internal" problems that arose in some of the budding programs:

> Faculty and students, sometimes, did not agree on program objectives, courses, and means of implementation, leading to major conflicts or disillusionment by one or both parties. The early absence of qualified instructors on many campuses and the dearth of curriculum materials also created difficulties.[25]

In the brief period of seven years or so, the Asian American programs have made great contributions in an effort to grasp concrete knowledge of the history of Third World peoples and to redirect that knowledge to the practice of changing social conditions in our society, but they have also continued to suffer from growing pains. Some of the difficulties can be attributed to . . .

> . . . a decline in student interest. Part of this can be traced to the graduation of the initial group of student participants who helped to establish these programs, and the absence of committed replacements. Part is due to discouragement because of intraprogram conflicts, the constant struggle for recognition and funding, or the development of highly conventional academic programs with little concern for contemporary community problems. . . [S]ome of the decline in interest might be related to the general slackening of student concern with activism and social problems, including those in the area of race and ethnic relations.[26]

But in the final analysis, it has been the lack of commitment to ethnic studies on the part of the governing bodies of the schools, and the subsequent lack of resources, that have placed severe limitations on the programs.

With the general economic crisis beginning in 1973, there has been a persistent effort by school authorities to chip away at the concessions that were made during the height of campus struggles. Budget cuts in higher education and social services began with ethnic studies courses, minority admissions and scholarship programs for Third World students, as administrators became increasingly reluctant to "expand or even continue what they see as basically innovative and experimental 'fringe' programs."[27] Thus, Third World students were hardest hit by recent cutbacks.

> The most striking example of a pattern of racism in cutbacks is the drop in the number of minority students enrolled in college. . . . Minority enrollments had been steadily rising since 1968, due to a mass upsurge of Third World students and their allies in the 1960's. . . . But in the last two years, those hard-won gains have come under sharp attack. A University of Michigan official summed up the general policy of college administrators on the cutbacks, asserting that "nonessential programs," which included third world studies programs, would be the first to be cut.[28]

When the actual attempts at financial cutbacks and diminution of autonomy were made by school authorities, they were met by a new "generation" of students who rallied to the defense of programs from which they had benefited.

Student dissatisfaction surfaced again on the campus of the University of California at Berkeley when, in 1974, the administration moved to integrate the independent Ethnic Studies Department into the larger College of Letters and Science.[29] An Ethnic Studies Defense Committee was formed to oppose the integration of ethnic studies into a larger curriculum and to demand the establishment of the College of Third World Studies as originally contemplated. The student resistance to the erosion of hard-fought gains has not been entirely successful. Some financial aid admissions programs have been cut back or eliminated. Student groups acknowledged and reasserted their role in bringing about progressive change.

A similar group called the Student Support Committee for Ethnic Studies was organized at UCLA in 1974 when a faculty committee denied proposals for several ethnic studies courses. The student group continued to meet with administration representatives until early 1975, when the administration released a Five Year Review of the ethnic studies centers, in which the administration-appointed review committee recommended the implementation of an umbrella-type structure over the centers to exercise more authority over them. Students organized a series of rallies and demonstrations to communicate their grievances and mistrust of the university.[30]

At still another University of California campus, at Santa Barbara, a week of protest and marches against minority cutbacks culminated in "a tense three-hour occupation of the North Hall Computer Center by seventeen members of the Students for Collective Action" on May 4, 1975.[31]

As the cutbacks were announced on campuses through the country, there was also a nationwide response from Third World student activists. On the West Coast, campus mobilization took place on virtually every campus of the University of California system as well as California State University at Los Angeles, Loyola, Claremont and Pepperdine. On the East Coast, forty members of the Third World Coalition staged a take-over of the administration building. At Brandeis University, students occupied the sociology building from April 29 to May 5, 1975 to protest a cutback totalling $2.2 million in their educational budget.

In New York City, several hundred Hunter College students occupied the dean's office and about 1500 students and faculty of the City University of New York demonstrated outside the Board of Higher Education to protest Mayor Beame's $69.7 million cut from the university's budget that would have effectively dissolved the SEEK (Search for Education, Elevation and Knowledge) program whose constituency was mainly Third World.[32]

Institutional responses to the need for ethnic studies, and for overall *quality* and *equality* in the educational process, mirror the racial discrimination of an entire society. Asian Americans and other Third World peoples have been confronted with the stubborn remnants of over a century of racism.

The history of Third World peoples in this country has been one of resistance and struggle in a hostile environment. Oppressed and exploited, Asian immigrants were forced to accept verbal and physical abuse at times, but they also waged an unyielding struggle against the unjust treatment they faced in every sphere of their lives: employment discrimination and exclusion, prohibition against land ownership, antimiscegenation laws, disproportionate taxes, disenfranchisement and lack of citizenship rights, and social discrimination.

In the field of education, as in other areas, efforts were made to win basic democratic rights. Sometimes, the courts were used to seek judicial remedies; most often, various ethnic groups struggled in isolation from one another and tried to win concessions only for themselves. Recently, Asian American students have united with other ethnic groups and progressive people to change the educational system.

Viewed in this light, the struggles of Asian American students for a just system of higher education is a significant chapter in Asian American and American history—one that is certain to continue as Asian American students continue their efforts to gain for themselves and others, equal education that is both high in quality and relevant. In this sense, their search for their past leads Third World students to participate in the very process of making history.

The Historical Development of Higher Education in the U.S.

In the preceding section, an attempt was made

to provide a description of what took place in the struggles for ethnic studies and for the admission of more minority students. But what of the causes? The history of ethnic studies and admission policies reveals the defects in our educational system. But what of the whole society? It is not enough to describe the events, but we must also analyze and place them in their historical context. The brief seven-year history recaptures, in many ways, the effects of long-standing inequities in the colleges and universities. In order to put a *part* into its proper context, we must also understand the *whole*.

In the United States today, about three out of ten persons are direct participants in the educational process. Out of a population of nearly 214 million, over 58.9 million students go to public and private schools at all levels, from kindergarten through graduate school. About 3.1 million persons are employed as classroom teachers, and an additional 300,000 are working as principals, supervisors, counselors and instructional staff members.[33]

Most of us are required by law to attend schools from ages five to sixteen; many of us spend twelve to sixteen or more years as students. No one can deny the enormous influence that the system of education has on all of us in shaping our patterns of behavior, morality, aspirations, political outlook . . . and the very way in which we think. We become adept at following instructions, learning by rote and memorizing data. We learn that there are no rewards for raising questions about the prevailing assumptions of the society in which we live.

The issues highlighted during the struggles of the late 60s raised a fundamental question about the very nature of the system of higher education: What are the implicit goals of the universities, and whom do they serve? Questions relevant to this inquiry are: What purposes do colleges and universities, and the educational system as a whole serve in America? What are the means by which control is accomplished? How have minority peoples in general, and Asian Americans in particular, been affected by this sytem?

Historically, colleges and universities in America did not always have the prominence that they are accorded in modern society. They neither existed in great numbers nor had a direct effect on the lives of most. The development and proliferation of institutions of higher learning paralleled the growth and expansion of Industrial America. The structure and goals of universities were adapted to suit the changing needs of the captains of industry.

Before the middle of the nineteenth century, most colleges were controlled by the religious denominations which founded them. Harvard College was founded 1637 to avoid "an illiterate ministry. . ."[34] The state of Massachusetts provided for the establishment of reading schools because illiteracy was "one chief project of that old deluder, Satan, to keep men from knowledge of the Scriptures."[35] Students were invariably the children of wealthy landowners and merchants who were preparing themselves for positions of power and prestige in the young and developing country. The curriculum included the arts, the classics and theology.

For the overwhelming majority of the people, formal education was limited to basic reading skills. The average worker required little technical expertise. Skills were learned at home or as apprentices. Thus, institutions of higher learning played a well-defined role, educating only a handful of ministers, doctors, lawyers and children of the elite.

This pattern continued until the industrial revolution. With the development of a northern-based textile industry in the 1840s, and the end of the Civil War, America entered a new era in which northern capitalists won complete hegemony in the economic and political spheres of American life. Robber barons like John D. Rockefeller, Andrew Carnegie, and Commodore Vanderbilt amassed large fortunes and consolidated their power; they built their empires in the steel, oil, and railroad industries, often at the expense of the native Americans whose lands they seized, Chinese and other immigrant workers whose labor they exploited, and weaker competitors whose aspirations they crushed.

Sweeping changes took place in the industrial and political life of the country. The tempo of technological development accelerated and business organization became increasingly complex. The capitalists began to reinvest some of their huge stockpiles of profits into higher education to insure a supply of skilled labor necessary for their industry.

> At the same time that colleges and universities were springing up at practically every crossroads, a reorientation of their purpose gradually took place under the impact of demands for a more practical education. . . . With the force of big money behind them, scientific, technological, and commercial instruction chipped substantial niches in the standard course of study.[36]

Colleges shifted their focus from an intellectual, "impractical" education to an education designed to meet the practical needs of industry.

The impact of business on the educational system was swift and massive. The need to train technicians and workers can best be seen by the size of the investment made by the robber barons.[37] From 1902 to 1938, the leading foundations, Carnegie and Rockefeller, spent a total of $680 million on colleges and universities to ensure the training of technical, scientific and administrative workers for their companies.[38] The classical colleges that were superfluous to business and industry became obsolete, or even permanently transformed into institutions for the training of workers in business and industry. This shift affected not only the class backgrounds of the student population, but also its numbers. In 1850, only 120 colleges existed;[39] but in the fifty years following the

Civil War, 453 colleges were founded.[40] In 1870, only 67,350 students were enrolled in colleges; by 1890 this figure had reached a total of 156,756 students, and by 1910, it had surpassed 355,000.[41] Not only the magnitude but the character of higher education was influenced. To better suit specialization and departmentalization of the labor force, colleges developed a structural device' to fragment the curriculum which came to be known as the elective system.

Post-graduate education was also expanded to accommodate further stratification and to train students for new "problems of internal personnel management, marketing, salesmanship, research, efficiency engineering, and public relations" as well as problems created by "the emergence of a stable and effective trade union movement."[42]

A necessary consequence of the rapid expansion of colleges and universities was the corresponding emergence and growth of the public high school. As a response to the needs of mushrooming business enterprises, the high school became the screening mechanism for universities as well as the institution for the effective socialization and pacification of the emerging working class movement, and one of the justifications for a stratified workforce based on class distinctions. Those in power reasoned that

> . . . the extension of the high school (to the children of working people) would provide the more intelligent son of the worker with an education that would enable him to find an honorable and profitable place within the existing industrial system, and prevent him from becoming an agitator.[43]

Secondary education thus became the primary institution through which *skilled* and *passive* workers could be created.

With more high schools than ever before, the need for qualified teachers to socialize the students became acute; teacher-training programs quickly and for the first time integrated large numbers of women into the system of higher education.[44]

At the turn of the century, most of the endowments were concentrated in a few colleges that were most responsive to the needs of the corporations. Rockefeller invested over $128 million in the General Education Board which he set up in 1902 to coordinate his philanthropy.[45] The trustees of the Board had within their power the ability. . .

> . . . to determine whether or not an institution would continue to exist. Coercion may not have been overt, but in making grants the board naturally selected those institutions whose policies and programs they approved. As a result these practices became unofficial standards for many other colleges.[46]

The recipients of the huge sums of money from companies like Standard Oil, DuPont, General Electric and Shell Petroleum were colleges that could adapt themselves best to the needs of the emerging chemical and electrical industries, as well as to the increasingly sophisticated needs of the steel and oil industries.

As the dependency of corporations on universities increased, so did their control of them. Grateful college administrators "drafted men of money into the service of collegiate direction until at the end of the (nineteenth) century the roster of American trustees of higher learning read like a corporation directory."[47] Leading capitalists had become firmly entrenched in positions of power with the university structure through appointments on various boards of trustees. By 1917, the rich and powerful had a firm grip on the reigns of the educational system.

> [C]ollege and university boards are almost completely dominated by merchants, manufacturers, capitalists, corporation officers, bankers, doctors, lawyers, educators and ministers. The nine occupations contain nearly four-fifths of the total number of trustees.[48]

According to a survey conducted in 1924, the average annual income for 734 trustees included in the survey was $35,000, during a time when the average worker was paid $1,563.[49] Furthermore, during the Great Depression of the Thirties, the average income of the trustees was over $61,000, a full sixty times the income of the average worker.[50]

Corporate control of the educational system has continued uninterrupted to the present. Rosters of most boards of trustees and regents still read like corporation directories. A cursory examination of the Board of Regents for the University of California shows California to be no exception.[51]

With the advent of World War II, state and federal governments have played key roles in supporting the military-industrial complex's educational objectives. Universities were a vital source of military personnel. The Reserve Officers Training Corp (ROTC) usually supplied 45% of all Army officers on active duty; 65% of all first lieutenants and 85% of all second lieutenants are graduates of the ROTC program.[52]

In the years following World War II, as America and the world entered the period of the Cold War, the federal government poured more money and resources into weapon development and space exploration programs. The Korean War and the conflict in Indochina led to the augmentation of budgets in every sphere of military spending. In this effort, every Presidential administration took an active part in beefing up war-oriented educational programs. Truman appointed a Commission on Higher Education in 1946 for the purpose of conducting an intensive reexamination of the university system and its function in national defense. The National Science Foundation was founded in 1950 to promote engineering and scientific research for the armed forces. In 1956, President Eisenhower appointed the second Commission on Higher Education, and two years later, the National Defense Education Act (NDEA) was passed as a governmental response to the technological advances made by the Soviet Union as evidenced by the launching of the Sputnik satellite. The United States became panic-stricken: tens of billions of dollars were allocated for the massive NDEA scholarship and assistance programs with the rationale that,

> . . . the present educational emergency requires additional effort at all levels of government. It is therefore the purpose of this Act to provide substantial assistance in various forms to individuals, and to states and their subdivisions, in order to insure trained manpower of sufficient quality and quantity to meet the national defense needs of the United States.[53]

The Kennedy Administration forcefully backed state investment in educational matters. The Manpower Development and Training Act of 1962 and subsequent bills helped to keep the rising unemployment level in check and swelled the ranks of highly skilled workers.

An additional $1.2 billion was allocated for the Higher Education Facilities Act, which was signed into law by President Johnson the following year. A number of other bills and laws, including the Higher Education Act of 1965 and the Elementary and Secondary Education Act of 1965 were passed throughout the 1960s. Undergraduate students—especially Third World students and economically disadvantaged students—benefited very little from the government spending since most of the funds were ear-marked for various weapon-development centers within the university-military-industrial complex.

The University of California system and a number of other prestigious institutions around the country are involved in numerous other research endeavors financed by the U.S. government. In the academic year 1967-68, UCLA had no less than 79 research projects that were financed by the Department of Defense.[54] Additionally, names of some courses offered by the UCLA Extension Program suggest further complicity of the university with the military: "The Guidance and Control of Tactical Missiles," "Integrated Logistic Support," and "Advanced Missile Flight Dynamics," to name a few.[55] And perhaps not as striking, but nevertheless concrete evidence of the role of the university in the military-industrial complex is a project officially known as the Academic Advisory Council on Thailand (AACT, popular name of Thailand Project), which is funded by the State Department and its Agency for International Development (AID). The role of the Thailand Project is to "organize, coordinate and conduct investigations, seminars or conferences, under AACT auspices dealing with development and counterinsurgency problems, issues, and activities, including research, relating to AID operations in Thailand."[56] Professors from various departments,

including Political Science and Anthropology, were employed in this project.

Finally, the link between the university and the military is made through mutual cooperation in recruitment efforts. At UCLA, the Placement Center participates in the recruitment of Central Intelligence Agency (CIA) personnel. The National Security Agency (NSA) sends recruiters to various departments and ethnic studies programs to recruit individuals to study foreign countries in depth and gather intelligence data on customs, lifestyles, and social and political institutions. Certain "trouble spots" like the Middle East, Chile, the Philippines, and Africa have been its recent focus.

As corporate and federal involvement in higher education increased, the goals of the universities were reevaluated by the authorities to attract more corporate investment and federal "assistance." In a survey conducted by sociologist Edward Gross in 1964, 7,000 administrators and faculty members from 68 major universities were questioned. The respondents were asked to place in rank-order a list of 47 goals of the university. Out of the top 12 goals, only the sixth mentioned "students," and even that was in connection with scientific research. Ranking first was the goal of protecting the faculty's right to academic freedom. Goals No. 2 through No. 12 were all related to research and/or to the maintenance of a good image of the university. In contrast, the bottom 12 goals were predominantly concerned with the welfare of students.[57]

So the system of education, which has become largely state-supported (taxpayer-supported), continued to maintain the illusion that it was indeed responsive to the aspirations of people and that it created maximal opportunities for everyone. Yet in reality, the mass education system has had quite different goals and has had quite the opposite result— that of fulfilling the needs of war-oriented capitalist economy.

The Impact on Asian Americans

Throughout the period of industrial growth and stratification of the workforce, Third World peoples were systematically excluded from even the lowest rungs of the educational ladder. Native Americans were forced onto reservations where they received little or no formal education as a colonized people. In many states in the South, it was illegal to conduct classes for Black children. The non-English speaking Chicanos and Asian immigrants were effectively left out of the developing educational system.

In September of 1859, a segregated day school for Chinese was opened in the basement of the Chinese Chapel in San Francisco, but it was closed within ten months because of the lack of interest on the part of the Chinese (government perspective), and of the lack of meaningful and relevant curriculum (Chinese American perspective). In an 1859 report concerning this school, Superintendent Denman of the San Francisco Board of Education stated:

> The teacher has been faithful and energetic in the discharge of his difficult duty but the prejudices of caste and religious idolatry are so indelibly stamped upon their [Chinese] character and existence that his task of education seems almost hopeless. According to our laws, the Mongolians can never be elevated to an equality with the Anglo-Saxons and receive the title and immunities of American citizens. They, therefore, take but little interest in adopting our habits or learning our language and institutions.[58]

In many cases, instruction in any language other than English was forbidden. For example, in one state, a law was passed in 1919 which provided that:

> [No] person shall in any private, public, denominational, or parochial school teach any subject to any person in the first eight grades in any language other than the English language.[59]

It was argued that the purpose of the act was "to protect the child's health by limiting his mental activities," and that the enforcement of this law will "promote civic development by inhibiting training of the immature in foreign tongues before they could learn English."[60]

In 1925, the legislature of Hawaii and the department of public instruction adopted regulations which provided as follows:

> No foreign language (meaning any school but a Sabbath school conducted in any language other than the English or Hawaiian languages) shall be conducted without a written permit from the department and unless a fee of one dollar per pupil will have been paid. . . . No pupil was to attend a foreign-language school for more than one hour each day nor for more than six hours per week. . . . The department had the power to appoint inspectors for these schools. Violation of a provision was a misdemeanor.[61]

Over 200,000 pupils and 300 teachers of various Asian ancestries were affected by this legislation. Had it not been struck down by the courts a year later, this would have meant that $200,000 (a dollar per pupil) would have been paid although none of the foreign-language schools received any public funds, and all of the children also attended public schools taught in English.

While foreign-language schools were prohibited or discouraged, at the same time, most of the public and private schools taught in English were limited to white children only. The segregation of Asian children continued in California into the twentieth century, and followed the general patterns of segregation found in other parts of the country with respect to Blacks. The segregation led to an international

crisis in the early 1900s.

In 1905, the San Francisco School Board relied on an 1870 California law and ordered Asian children to attend a separate, all-Asian school. This law, which remained on the books formally until 1946, read in part as follows:

> . . . trustees shall have the power to exclude children of filthy and vicious habits, or children suffering from contagious or infectious diseases, and also to establish separate schools for Indian children and for children of Mongolian or Chinese descent.

The following autumn, the Board passed a second resolution which was implemented immediately:

> . . . principals are hereby directed to send all Chinese, Japanese or Korean children to the Oriental public school [located near the earthquake-devastated Chinatown] on and after Monday, October 15, 1906.[63]

Agitation against Japanese became blatant and intense in labor-dominated San Francisco as many called for the complete exclusion of Japanese as they had done to Chinese in 1882. Candidates of all major parties stood on platforms to exclude Asians.[64] The San Francisco School Board made clear their intentions for setting up separate schools:

> . . . not only for the purpose of relieving the congestion at present prevailing in our schools, but also for the higher end that our children should not be placed in any position where their youthful impressions may be affected by association with pupils of the Mongolian race.[65]

Newspapers also got embroiled in the anti-Asian campaign and employed various scare tactics. The San Francisco *Chronicle* disseminated hatred of Asians, explaining that:

> . . . whatever the status of the Japanese children while still young and uncontaminated, as they grow older they acquire the distinctive character, habits and moral standards of their race, which are abhorrent to our people. We object to them in the familiar intercourse of common school life as we would object to any other moral poison.[66]

Other stories contended that many Japanese adults had infiltrated the classrooms:

> It is difficult to tell the age of a Japanese boy or man, and we have learned from experience that we could not take their word for it. The parents of white children—especially of girls in the adolescent period—began to feel that these men should be excluded from the public schools altogether. . . .[67]

The racism against Japanese and other Asians did not end with words as attacks on Japanese grew more frequent: people were stoned by ruffians, businesses were wrecked and children were bullied.

News of the mistreatment of Japanese citizens in California soon travelled to Japan. The San Francisco

School Board incident became an international concern as Japanese authorities reminded the American government of a treaty which was in effect at the time, which read in part as follows:

> Article I: . . . The citizens or subjects of each High Contracting Power (Japan and the United States) shall . . . in all . . . matters connected with the administration of justice . . . enjoy all the rights and privileges enjoyed by native citizens or subjects. . . .[68]

Other appeals were made by concerned Japanese educators, expressing indignation and hope. The Dean of the University of Tokyo wrote to President Jordan of Stanford University in California:

> . . . to pass a law condemning the Japanese wholesale, for no other reason than that they are Japanese, would be striking Japan in her most sensitive point. An open declaration of war would not be resented so much. The reason is not far to seek. Japan has had a long struggle in recovering her rights as an independent state. . . . If . . . her old friend . . . should turn her back on her and she would no longer associate with her on even terms, the resentment must necessarily be very bitter.[69]

President Theodore Roosevelt's private response was that he was "more concerned over the Japanese situation than almost any other. Thank Heaven we have the navy in good shape."[70] Still, uncertain about the military strength of Japan, Roosevelt played the mediating role between racist Californians on the one hand and Japan and the Japanese community in San Francisco on the other.

Attacks against the Japanese in California continued, and they were accused of "imperiousness, impudence, of taking honors away from white children."[71] White citizens argued that California was making a gift to the Japanese by setting up separate schools, and that therefore the Japanese should be grateful with the privilege, and not demand equal treatment.

> It is the height of Oriental conceit to demand more. It is the climax of Japanese swell-headedness to persist in their demands. This insistence in demanding that they be allowed to attend white schools proves their unfitness to enjoy such a privilege. The sons of Nippon should be made to understand that . . . they cannot compel the Young Giant of the West to abrogate her laws or destroy her customs simply to meet the Japanese caprice or tickle Japanese fancy.[72]

President Roosevelt wanted to avoid war with Japan if it were at all possible, because the Japanese military was at full force following a victory over Russia. Californians, on the other hand, insisted on separate educational facilities for white and Third World children, and eventual exclusion altogether of the Japanese, "whether the putting out of the way involves the U.S. in war (or not.)"[73] A delegation of civic leaders and government officials from California went to Washington, D.C. to negotiate with the federal government. In 1907, a compromise was reached wherein

> . . . the Californians got what they most wanted—assurances that the influx of coolies would be stopped; the federal administration got what it most wanted—a promised repeal of the school order. The San Francisco delegation, fully aware that a surrender on the school issue would cause a storm of protest in their city, were [sic] reluctantly brought around to Roosevelt's point of view. . . .

The Yellow Peril scare was created more in the minds of men than in reality as there were only 93 Japanese children, one-third of them American-born, in the San Francisco school system at the time. Additionally, the census of 1910 listed a total of 41,346 Japanese in the whole state, of which 4,518 lived in San Francisco, less than two percent of the population of that city.[74]

The school order as it applied to Japanese was rescinded, and the "Gentlemen's Agreement" limiting Japanese immigration to the United States was concluded. The children of Chinese immigrants were still excluded from regular schools, as were the relatively few Korean children living in San Francisco. The San Francisco School Board incident was officially closed, but Roosevelt spent the next two years building up the navy, and in San Francisco, mobs renewed their attacks on the Japanese community.

American (white) courts had consistently upheld segregationist legislation passed by various (white) legislatures that separated Black and white children into different, unequal schools. The laws were made by white persons to . . .

> . . . protect themselves against the infusion of blood of other races, on the assumption that if the children of different races associate daily in school rooms, the races will at last intermarry, and so the purity of each race is jeopardized by the mingling of children in school rooms.[75]

In the case of *Gong Lum v. Rice*,[76] decided in 1927, the state court and the Supreme Court held unanimously that it was not a denial of equal protection to classify a Chinese as "colored." Martha Lum, an American-born Chinese, applied for admission to a school that was open to white children only. There were no "Negro" schools in her district. Martha's father was a taxpayer in the school district and the county. Yet the trustees of the high school district and the State Superintendent of Education denied her admission to the school. The state court held that the law required a separation of pupils into a *white group,* on the one hand, and a *group consisting of all other races,* on the other. The Supreme Court upheld, in this case and in dozens of others like it, the racist rule of "separate but equal" facilities for white and for Third World children.

Objective conditions in schools throughout the country showed that the doctrine of "separate but equal" was nothing more than legal fiction. Yet it was not until 1954 that this rule was overturned by the Supreme Court in the case of *Brown v. Board of Education of Topeka.*[78] In spite of the court ruling, practices have proved to be less than ideal. In the twenty years following the *Brown* decision, the inner-city schools remained virtually unaffected as they continued to be segregated and of low quality.

The educational system has become the major mechanism through which a neatly stratified work-force is created. Schools at all levels have become the training ground for workers who are socialized to be obedient in whatever roles they are assigned.

> The key thing about work under capitalism is that the vast majority of jobs are oppressive, dehumanizing, unsatisfying and require ideally (for the boss) a high degree of obedience to supervisors. Schools work to provide workers who are suitable for this kind of work.[79]

Much as we like to believe that schools teach children important cognitive skills and standards of morality, the one thing that schools do best is teach obedience in school and later in work. Students are taught to do and accept repetitive and meaningless work, day after day, year after year. Thus the schools serve as the prototype of the work experience. Students learn to do repetitive and meaningless tasks, to take orders and to compete. In the end they are essentially taught to conform.

Moreover, schools indoctrinate students that non-conformity to societal norms is an individual problem of a particular student. They teach that in society, there must necessarily be important, powerful and prestigious positions, and that those who fill those positions have earned them by virtue of some special talent, intelligence, or through diligent work. Thus class differences are legitimized. What is disguised ever so subtly is that the standards for measuring qualities like intelligence and behavior by the schools are designed to replicate or reveal the socio-economic status of parents or the cultural and racial background of children. Put another way, a child who has visited Valley Forge on his family vacation is more likely to know that George Washington slept there, and a child who received a set of ABC blocks for Christmas is more likely to remember configurations of the alphabet.

Questions that are most familiar to the middle-class, white, suburban child with a Christian back-ground are most often included in the IQ tests, while questions more familiar to poor and Third World children are systematically omitted. Consider, for example, the Wechsler Test. Some questions are:

1. Who wrote *Hamlet?*
2. Who wrote the *Iliad?*
3. Where was Christ born?
4. What does *audacious* mean?
5. What does *plagiarize* mean?[80]

If the Wechsler Scales were translated into Spanish, Swahili and Chinese and given to every ten-year-old in Latin America, East Africa or China, the majority would obtain IQ scores in the mentally retarded range because *they have not been exposed to the information requested.* It seems intuitively incorrect (and absurd) to conclude that all the children of the world except middle-class America and possibly Europe are retarded.[81]

Other tests have been developed in the twentieth century beginning with the College Entrance Examination Board in 1900 and the Scholastic Aptitude Test in 1920. Today, the tests that by far affect students at all levels are administered by the Educational Testing Service (ETS). In the fall of 1974, 2.5 million Americans took one of these ETS-administered tests:

16,000 in order to qualify for prestigious "pre-secondary" schools;

20,000 in order to qualify for exclusive secondary schools;

1,800,000 high school juniors and seniors and graduates who want to go to college;

100,000 more who want a head start in college by getting advanced placement or by becoming National Merit Scholars;

300,000 college seniors and graduates who want to go on to graduate schools;

74,000 college students who want to go to business schools; and

120,000 aspiring law students.[82]

All of the tests that decided or played a significant role in shaping the lives of 2.5 million students in one year are

> . . . written by 58 people who work for a private untaxed, unregulated corporation called the Educational Testing Service. They are backed by a staff of 3,000, most of whom work at the head-quarters located on the secluded 400-acre Princeton "campus" that has its own hotel, lake, and flock of ducks, golf course, tennis courts and swimming pool.[83]

Since 1948, ETS has doubled its size and profits every five years. Their gross annual receipts were reported at a staggering $53 million tax-free. ETS has a near-monopoly status, and test questions reflect the same cultural, racial and class biases as those of the IQ tests discussed above. Additionally, even if we assume the negligibility of those biases, the reliability in determining the lives of so many must be put in question:

> Even ETS admits that aptitude and achievement cannot be measured in terms nearly as specific as the score that is recorded. If, for example, among possible scores ranging from 200 to 800 you get a 600 on your SAT, this only means that there is a two-in-three chance that your "true" score—the score you would receive if all external factors, like

luck in guessing, could be eliminated—would fall somewhere between 570 and 630. There is also a one-in-three chance that your true score will fall somewhere below 570 or above 630.[84]

This one-dimensional way of testing does not test for creativity, stamina, motivation or ethics. But it doesn't much matter to ETS or to the university system which *individuals* are hampered or aided by this testing method, as long as the general pattern of social stratification according to class and race and its legitimization is maintained.

> An ETS study reveals that there is a direct, continuous correlation between family income and SAT scores; the correlations is, in fact, consistent for seven different categories of income. Other ETS data show that males do better than females. Probably the most significant difference is associated with skin color: non-whites have much lower median scores than whites.[85]

The tests are designed so that those test-*takers* who are made in the image of the test-*writers*—that is, white, middle and upper class males—have the greatest chance of success.

For poor and Third World students who "pass" the first hurdle, there are more stumbling blocks in the educational obstacle course. Equally frustrating are the preconceived, stereotypic notions of school personnel, and the demeaning depictions of themselves which minority students find in a racist curriculum. Counselors and advisors perform the task of assigning students to particular courses of study and majors. In this process, students are again confronted with a situation in which their values and aspirations are often placed at odds with the values and assumptions of the counselor. For Asian American students, cultural patterns of interaction with authority figures, adopted through a century of oppression, come into play. Even with such a vast difference in the frame of reference and perspective, counselors often direct students to classes that *the counselors* feel are best suited for students despite contrary views or reluctance expressed by students. The Black student who aspires to become a lawyer is encouraged to take wood shop; the Asian student who has hopes of becoming a novelist is exhorted to take chemistry; the woman who wishes to become a doctor is told to major in elementary education.

When students enter the classroom, they are faced with racist textbooks and teachers who know nothing about what students do with their lives outside the classroom. They are taught to take orders and to compete. Grades are substituted for test scores as the single one-dimensional measure of students. In this system, some are supposed to succeed and others are supposed to fail. It can be no other way as long as the function of schools is to stratify the workforce.

The competitive system affects all children, but there were other biases that have had particular effects on generations of Asian American and Third World children. There is no question that the frame of reference affects perspective. In a course inappropriately titled "World History," students were taught that significant developments in human history occurred in Europe and later in the United States. Such courses are invariably textbook-centered and followed a chronological arrangement. The emphasis was on political history—dates and men, wars and governments. Little attention was given to other considerations, such as how people lived, what they created, how they viewed themselves and others.

> The study of areas beyond Europe entered this version of world history only peripherally, mainly when these areas were "discovered" by Europeans and later by Americans during periods of overseas exploration and colonization. In one major textbook published in the 1940's, fifty important dates in world history were listed and the only one which referred to Asia was the notation of Japan having been "opened" by Commodore Perry.[86]

Consider the way in which students study countries in Asia. Because the major motivation for studying other cultures is related to current events and narrowly conceived national self-interests, the treatment reflects this narrow concern. Of the eleven study-guide questions used in this course, eight mention the United States by name: "Why is Southeast Asia important to the U.S.? What is the nature of Chinese Communist threat to the U.S.? What are the 'trouble spots' in Asia, and how do they affect the U.S.?..." The connotation of words such as "threat" or "trouble spots" is clear.

> Consider, too, the invidious words which are used consistently to characterize the peoples and cultures of "non-Western" countries—words such as "backward," "underdeveloped," or "emerging." To refer to contemporary India as "emerging" is especially ironic when we recall that it was India and the "Far East" which Columbus was eagerly seeking when he discovered the "New World" (which, of course, was "new" only from the European viewpoint). This designation, however, encouraged the explorers to claim lands as if they were uninhabited and *really* new.[87]

The distorted perceptions and American biases found in international studies can also be found in textbooks and courses about Asian *Americans*. In a study of 300 social studies textbooks currently available for elementary and secondary schools, there was a consistent pattern of neglect and stereotyping with regard to China and Chinese Americans.

> About 75% of the 300 texts made no mention of Chinese at all. Of the remaining seventy-six, fifty-three (17% overall) gave a token representation with a picture of an Asian, often in an interracial group of Americans, and/or one or two lines mentioning the existence of urban Chinatowns (e.g. "San Francisco's Chinatown is a must stop for visitors to the lovely city of the Golden Gates."), several lines about Chinese railroad

workers, the laundry and culinary skills of Chinese people, or their relation to China where their ancestors first developed silk.[88]

In a similar study of textbooks with regard to Japanese Americans, researchers rated the books for accuracy of content. Not surprisingly, nine out of ten books examined were evaluated at an *average* rating of "zero" on a scale of zero to five.[89] Omissions and distortions are more blatant with respect to Pilipinos, Koreans, Southeast Asians and Pacific Islanders. The general neglect of the Asian American is not a phenomenon limited to school teachers, but manifests itself at the highest levels of American society. On May 10, 1969, 20,000 people, many of them Chinese Americans, gathered at Promontory Point, Utah, for the centennial celebration of the completion of the transcontinental railroad. The main speaker was Transportation Secretary John Volpe, who extolled those who labored on the railroad with a series of rhetorical questions:

> Who else but *Americans* could drill ten tunnels in mountains thirty feet deep in snow? Who else but *Americans* could chisel through miles of solid granite? Who else but *Americans* could have laid ten miles of tracks in twelve hours?[90]

The Chinese delegation sat silent, stunned by the total omission of their ancestors who played *the* key role in building the Central Pacific line over the Sierra Nevadas. No mention at all of 12,000 Chinese "coolies." More often than not, the initial reaction to such slights was to dismiss them as individual "identity" problems. But as people came together to confront the ever-present racism and lack of respect for Third World peoples, a demand to have themselves depicted accurately and from their perspective developed. These attempts to challenge even seemingly harmless omissions and distortions have sometime led them into courtrooms.

In March, 1972, Raquel Gutierrez, Ron Hirano, Kay Gurule and Rudy Salinas sued the California Board of Education to prevent the latter from using certain textbooks in the California schools *(Gutierrez v. State Board of Education)*. Their contentions were based on a newly adopted California law, which reads in part:

> The [School] Board shall, when adopting textbooks and teacher's manuals for use in elementary schools for the teaching of courses in civics and history of the United States and the State of California, include only such textbooks which correctly portray the role and contribution of the American Negro and members of other ethnic groups and the role and contributions of the entrepreneur and labor in the total development of the United States and of the State of California.[91]

Franklin Odo, an instructor in Asian American Studies at California State University at Long Beach and a member of the Ethnic Studies Task Force appointed by the State Board of Education, characterized the portrayal of Asian Americans and Asians in twelve basic social science textbooks adopted by the Board as "grossly inadequate and manifestly demeaning."[92]

In a written statement to the court, Odo provided some examples of omissions and distortions found in textbooks:

> *Social Sciences: Concepts and Values* (Harcourt, Brace, Jovanovich, 1970). Chinese Americans were mentioned superficially on one page out of 366 pages, this textbook entirely omitted mention of Japanese, Pilipinos, Koreans and Samoans.
> *Social Studies and Our Country: Concepts in Social Sciences* (Laidlaw Brothers, 1970). There were only two pictures of Asians out of a total of 136, both of them in a "passive" pose.
> *The Human Adventure* (Field Educational Publications, 1970). The following passage illustrates the biases found in this book: "The East (Asia) was tied to the past in ways that prevented change and future growth. The West (America), though primitive and barbaric, would be able to grow without being held back by past traditions." This passage implicitly states that Asians are incapable of change and progress, and that Native Americans are "primitive and barbaric" people who would not hold back Westerners from expansion.[93]

These are examples of the treatment Asian Americans have received in textbooks used in classrooms throughout the state of California. Omissions and distortions of the histories of other nationalities are no less pervasive and are in many ways more offensive.

In addition to class and race biased testing mechanisms, ignorant and indifferent counselors and advisors, and ethnocentric textbooks, Third World students also suffer from patterns of racial and economic segregation in schools reflecting the segregated character of neighborhoods and the unequal distribution of wealth. These factors continue to manifest themselves in unequal educational facilities between Third World and low-income area schools, on the one hand, and suburban white middle-class schools on the other. The net effect of such a system is that it necessarily reproduces the hierarchical division of labor. Both the quantity and quality of one's education correlate with the social position and wealth of parents and family. Among those who graduate from high school, children of families earning over $15,000 are over six times more likely to attend college as are the children of families earning less than $3,000 per year.[94] Further stratification takes place among junior colleges, state colleges and the Universities as figures for 1964 illustrate below:[95]

Annual Family Income and Access to Higher Education in California, 1964

Annual Family Income	All Families	Familes w/o Children in California Public Higher Education	Families with Children in California Public Higher Education		
			Junior College	State College	University of California
Less than $6,000	30.9%	31.9%	24.0%	14.3%	12.5%
$6,000–$9,999	37.0%	37.3%	36.5%	34.2%	24.2%
$10,000–$13,999	19.8%	19.4%	21.6%	30.7%	24.6%
$14,000 and over	12.3%	11.4%	17.9%	20.8%	38.7%
Median Income	$8,000	$7,900	$8,800	$10,000	$12,000

A more recent survey conducted in 1975 among Los Angeles city high school graduates indicated that of those from low-income areas eligible to enroll at the University of California or other similar institutions, only 60% did. By contrast, 80% of the UC-eligible graduates from high-income areas entered four-year colleges.[96] According to a report issued by the Assembly Permanent Subcommittee on Post-secondary Education, lack of money remained a major reason why scholastically eligible low-income students—who are usually Third World students—failed to go to college.[97] Many Third World students are denied admission to universities because the lack of prerequisites which sometimes results from unavailability of the required courses in their high school curriculum or from lack of adequate counseling.

Unequal schooling manifests itself in more than differences in years of schooling attained by students from different social classes and nationalities. Differences in dress codes, rules of conduct, opportunities for choices and the overall campus atmosphere are all reflections of social class positions of the various student bodies. In the inner-city schools attended by mostly Third World and working class children, authoritarian methods of disciplining students are favored by administrators, teachers and parents alike. That the working class parents often seem to prefer more authoritarian educational methods is perhaps a reflection of their own experiences, which have demonstrated that submission to authority is an essential ingredient in one's ability to get and hold a steady job.[98]

The inequalities in the educational system that affect Third World children are not accidental. They have been long recognized and discussed in numerous volumes. No one can deny that the effects have been devastating on Black and Chicano children. But what of the Asian American?

Many questions have been raised recently—especially in the context of special minority admissions programs for professional and graduate schools—about the status of Asian Americans as economically and culturally disadvantaged: Have they been able to achieve "successes" in the educational system? Have they been able to escape the deteriorated conditions of ghetto schools? Should they really be considered "minorities"?

An examination of Asian Americans in public schools provide some clues. Public schools that service recognized Asian American neighborhoods such as Chinatowns, Little Tokyos, and Manilatowns are in need of upgrading. Most Asian American students living outside those areas also attend secondary schools where they are likely to be stifled in their educational development—schools that have all the earmarks of sub-standard inner-city schools. Most Asian Americans in Los Angeles schools attend working-class schools with other Third World and working class children. In 1975, 63.3% of Asian students attended high schools where more than half of the student body was comprised of Third World students. In contrast, only 20.4% of the Asian students in Los Angeles high schools attended schools with two-thirds white student population. To further illustrate the difficulty of entering colleges faced by Third World students, 81.6% of Black students in Los Angeles schools attend high schools where the average drop-out rate is 33.2%, and 85.7% of Asian Americans attend schools with an average drop-out rate of 25.5%. These figures contrast unfavorably with 78% of white students who attend schools with a drop-out rate of 17.9%.[99]

Even within the schools themselves, students from different classes and nationalities are given different educations. "Tracking" (the practice of placing students in either college prepatory or vocational curriculum) was systematized by the California Master Plan for Higher Education which was passed into law by the state legislature in 1960. The effect of the Master Plan was to systematize and legitimize all the preexisting inequalities in the school system by standarized testing and tracking of students according to so-called "objective" standards. Not only did this Plan coordinate the stratification and facilitate the inequalities in primary and secondary schools, it also served to create a class stratification within higher education by creating and expanding the junior college system to "cool out" working class children who aspired to go to four-year colleges. The Master Plan outlined the official policy of class and race discrimination that determined who attended college. Drastic changes took place in California higher education: In 1960, for example, 12 percent of the students at San Francisco State College were Black; in less than a decade, by 1968, Black student population at that school dropped to three percent.[100]

The handful of Third World students who were able to make it through the maze of obstacles before them, and enroll in colleges found themselves isolated from their families and communities. Many of them struggled all of their lives for a chance to get a "decent" education they needed for a "good job." Yet many were faced with the most blatant contradictions in the system of higher education. On the brink of "success" they discovered that "making it" in American education really meant only individual success which required that they divest themselves of all remnants of their cultural backgrounds.

The "successful" Asian American student might become a scholar in one of our universities—and learn to speak a Chinese dialect that 90 percent of the Chinese in this country do not understand—while Chinatown ghettos continue to exist in San Francisco, New York, Los Angeles and elsewhere with the country's highest tuberculosis and suicide rates, sweatshops and overcrowding.

The "successful" Asian American might become an engineer or an agency bureaucrat who plays an active part in the destruction of Little Tokyos, Manilatowns and Chinatowns under the guise of urban renewal, leaving residents and small businesses in those communities with no place to go, as high-rise tourist hotels, banks and corporations take over.

The "successful" Black college student can "make it" by becoming a public school teacher—and watch his Black students become numbed to an environment that is totally unsuitable for learning. Or he can become a social worker and hand out subsistence monies and false promises to fellow human beings.

A "successful" Chicano can make it by joining a big corporation—perhaps the Safeway Stores which will pay him $12,000 a year to be their public relations man while Safeway sells inferior food to Chicanos in the barrios at exorbitant prices, and sells Gallo wines and grapes to undermine unionizing efforts of Chicano and Pilipino farmworkers.

For the Third World student to be a "success" meant that he or she faces the very real possibility of turning his/her back on the community from which he/she came and become oblivious to its problems.[101] Many Third World students at colleges across the country decided in the 60s that they could not live that kind of life. They rejected the individual, competitive values of American education, and its definition of success, and they demanded instead an education that is relevant to their lives in their communities.

Those students who participated in the struggles for more relevant education and open admissions understood well the obstacles they faced. They came to learn through their struggles,

> . . . the fundamentally conservative functions of the institutions, namely, the reproduction of the social class system from generation to generation, and the legitimization of the resulting inequalities in higher education. Acquiescence to class stratification is encouraged by maintaining the illusion that social mobility and personal betterment are possible through open access to higher education.[102]

The struggles that led to ethnic studies and minority admissions challenged "the hierarchy of credibility associated with academic work and the nature of biases existing in knowledge, [and provided] an alternative approach to gaining new explanations" for the problems currently faced by Third World people in America, albeit within the framework of the existing system of higher education.[103]

In the 1960s, Third World students recognized the ever-increasing need to challenge and reshape higher education to meet the needs of their communities, and engaged in prolonged struggles to win those demands. In the era of the 1970s, with the economic crisis facing American society, government and school officials are making renewed efforts to cut back and phase out ethnic studies and other progressive programs. These conditions call for demands to be raised again to maintain the hard-fought gains made in progressive, relevant educational programs. Students of ethnic studies need to reexamine the goals of the university and our social system as a whole, and reassess our personal and individual educational and occupational goals. Then we must *understand* the needs of our communities, and of the whole society. But the educational process cannot stop there:

> . . . the most important problem does not lie in understanding the laws of the objective world and thus being able to explain it, but in *applying* the knowledge of these laws actively to change the world.[104]

Theory—the intellectual understanding of how social systems function, and for what ends—is important precisely and only because it can be a guide to our actions and behavior. What we learn must be put to practical use for the good of society. Finally, because the resistance to change—ethnic studies, and other programs that emphasize equality, quality and relevance—is so great, the task of making these changes calls for scientific collective action in which people come together to do practical work in a coordinated way. ★

Notes

1. Research Organizing Cooperative of San Francisco, "Strike At Frisco State: The Story Behind It," pamphlet, n.d., pp. 21-22.

2. Penny Nakatsu, keynote address at the National Asian American Studies Conference II, held at California State University at San Jose, July 6-8, 1973.

3. Shih Chun, "Why It Is Necessary to Study World History," *Peking Review*, No. 21, May 26, 1972, p. 3.

4. Samuel Clemens (Mark Twain), *Roughing It* (Hartford: American Publishing, 1880), p. 391.

5. Loren Baritz, *The American Left: Radical Political Thought in the Twentieth Century* (New York: Basic Books, Inc., 1971), p. 453.

6. Nakatsu, loc. cit.

7. Black Students Union, "Black Students Union Demands and Explanations," mimeograph, n.d.

8. Research Organizing Cooperative of San Francisco, p. 22.

9. San Francisco State Strike Committee, "On Strike—Shut It Down," 1969, p. 4.

10. Baritz, p. 461.

11. San Francisco *Chronicle,* December 4, 1968.

12. Baritz, p. 463.

13. These statistics do not include injuries sustained before December 2, injuries not reported, and injuries to people who were not arrested. In many police sweeps, no arrests took place but demonstrators were beaten.

14. Research Organizing Cooperative of San Francisco, p. 31.

15. University of California, Berkeley, Ethnic Studies Committee of the Department of Ethnic Studies, "A Proposal for the Establishment of the College of Third World Studies," unpublished manuscript, dated September 18, 1974, p. 3.

16. Ibid., p. 2.

17. Ibid., p. 1.

18. *Daily Bruin,* November 14, 1968, p. 1.

19. *Daily Bruin,* September 30, 1968, p. 15.

20. *Daily Bruin,* November 14, 1968, p. 1.

21. Quote by Vice-Chancellor Paul Proehl (University Relations), January 20, 1969.

22. Quote by Joaquin Acosta, who was the assistant to Vice-Chancellor Proehl and administration's liaison with Third World student organizations. *Daily Bruin,* January 20, 1969, p. 1.

23. Technical requirements in the university permit only "departments" to offer courses, but "centers" cannot offer courses.

24. For details on Black Panther shooting and FBI involvement, see various issues of *Daily Bruin,* January, 1969.

25. Russell Endo, "White Ethnic Studies: A Reexamination of Some Issues," *Asian Americans: Psychological Perspectives* (Palo Alto, Calif.: Science and Behavior Books, Inc., 1973), edited by Stanley Sue and Nathaniel N. Wagner, p. 282.

26. Ibid.

27. Ibid., p. 283.

28. *Guardian,* May 7, 1975, p. 6.

29. *The Asian Student,* newsletter of Asian Students Union of UC Berkeley, Vol. 3, no. 1 (November 1974), p. 10.

30. *Rafu Shimpo,* May 17, 1975. p. 1.

31. *Daily Nexus,* University of California at Santa Barbara, Vol. 55, no. 123, May 5, 1975, p. 1.

32. *Guardian,* May 14, 1975, p. 5.

33. Statistics are from U.S. Department of Health, Education and Welfare, *HEW News,* bulletin no. HEW-F67, 1975.

34. Walter Lunden, *The Dynamics of Higher Education* (Pittsburg: Pittsburg Printing Company, 1939), p. 188. Also cited in David N. Smith, *Who Rules the Universities?* (New York: Monthly Review Press, 1974).

35. Edmund Morgan, *The Puritan Family* (New York: Harper and Row, 1966), p. 26.

36. Merle Curti and Roderick Nash, *Philanthropy in the Shaping of American Higher Education* (New Brunswick: Rutgers University Press, 1965), p. 60.

37. Lunden, p. 177. Between 1878 and 1898 alone, $140 million was poured into the system of higher education. According to Curti and Nash, pp. 78-79, many of the technical and scientific schools designed solely for industrial research purposes profited the most. Illinois Institute of Technology, for example, received a $20 million contribution from photography magnate George

Eastman.

38. Ernest V. Hollis, *Philanthropic Foundations and Higher Education* (New York: Columbia University Press, 1938), p. 283.

39. John S. Brubacher and Willis Rudy, *Higher Education in Transition: An American History* (New York: Harper, 1958), pp. 62-63.

40. Lunden, p. 175.

41. Richard Hofstadter and C. Dewitt Hardy, *The Development and Scope of Higher Education in the United States* (New York: Columbia University Press, 1952), p. 31.

42. Ibid., p. 93. In 1850, there were only eight graduate schools in the country, but the numbers soared rapidly to 198 within eleven years, and to 2,382 by 1890, and finally rose to 5,668 by the beginning of the twentieth century. According to Elbert Vaugh Wills, *The Growth of American Higher Education* (Philadelphia: Dorrance & Company, 1936), p. 99, also cited in David N. Smith, p. 183, schools of business administration were established between 1881, when Wharton School of Finance and Commerce opened, and 1925.

43. Merle Curti, *The Social Ideas of American Educators* (Patterson, N.J.: Pageant Books, 1935), p. 220.

44. The 11,000 women enrolled in colleges in 1870 comprised only one-fifth of all college students. Mabel Newcomer, *A Century of Higher Education for American Women* (New York: Harper, 1959), p. 19. By 1900, women had become forty percent of the college population, according to Laurence R. Veysey, *The Emergence of the American University, 1865-1910* (Chicago: University of Chicago Press, 1965), p. 1. Moreover, according to Newcomer, p. 91, 43,000 of the 61,000 women enrolled in coeducational colleges in 1900 were in teacher training courses.

45. From 1902 to 1934, only 20 institutions received more than 73 percent of the funds disbursed. See Hollis, p. 285. According to Curti and Nash, p. 222, between 1923 and 1929, over $88.5 million out of a total of $103 million donated by the largest foundations went to 36 colleges and universities out of the more than a thousand institutions in the country at the time.

46. Curti and Nash, pp. 216-17.

47. Charles and Mary Beard, *The Rise of American Civilization* (New York: MacMillan, 1936), Vol. 2, p. 470.

48. A survey of Scott Nearing, cited in David N. Smith, p. 38.

49. A survey by Hubart Park Beck, cited in David N. Smith, p. 40.

50. Troy Duster, "The Aims of Higher Learning and the Control of Universities" (University of California at Berkeley, n.d.), cited in David N. Smith, p. 40.

51. For examples, listed below are four of the Regents and their "affiliations" past and present:

Edward W. Carter - President of Broadway-Hale Stores; director of AT&T; Southern California Edison; director of Del Monte Corporation; Irvine Ranch; director of Pacific Mutual Life Insurance Company; United California Bank; director of Northrop Corporation; Pacific Telephone and Telegraph Company; Western Bancorporation.

Frederick G. Dutton - Former Assistant U.S. Secretary of State; director of Irvine Foundation; Southern Counties Gas Company; attorney.

William Matson Roth - Director of Pacific Intermountain Express Company; Atheneum Publishers; Mandell Industries; U.S. Leasing Corporation; Matson Navigation Company; Crocker Citizens National Bank; Crown-Zellerbach Corporation.

William French Smith - Attorney for Ronald Reagan; director of Pacific Lighting Corporation; director of Pacific Telephone and Telegraph Company; director of Mutual Life Insurance Company; director of Crocker Bank.

52. UCLA Strike Committee, "The Three Wars," pamphlet, n.d., n.p.

53. Homer Babbidge and Robert Rosenzweig, *The Federal Interest in Higher Education* (New York: McGraw Hill, 1962), pp. 50-51.

54. UCLA Strike Committee pamphlet. The UCLA Medical School, Baylor University, the University of Texas, Stanford Research Institute and Cornell Aeronautical Laboratory all collaborated with the Army Chemical Center in testing and developing various chemical and biological weapons. See Sidney Lens, *The Military-Industrial Complex*. Between 1960 and 1969, $2.5 billion were spent on deadly gases and germs; some 5,000 technicians and scientists were engaged in developing "poison chemicals ranging from the 'mild' CS (gas) used in Vietnam to GA, GB and V nerve agents that are odorless, tasteless, invisible, and can kill a human being in a matter of seconds." Chicago *Daily News,* August 12, 1969.

55. UCLA Strike Committee.

56. Amendment III, paragraph B-6 of *Contract,* cited in UCLA Strike Committee.

57. The top twelve goals of university officials are: (1) Protect the faculty's right to academic freedom; (2) Increase or maintain the *prestige* of the university; (3) Maintain top quality in important programs; (4) Ensure the *confidence of contributors;* (5) Keep up to date; (6) Train students for *scientific research;* (7) Carry on *pure research;* (8) Maintain quality in all programs; (9) Ensure the *favorable appraisal* of validating bodies (government agencies, foundations, etc.); (10) Ensure efficient goal attainment; (11) Disseminate new ideas; and (12) Carry on *applied research.* In contrast, the bottom twelve goals (out of forty-seven) dealt more directly with students: (47) Elevate the *student* culturally and make a person who is able to think for himself; (46) Preserve the character of the school; (45) Involve *students* in the administration of the school; (44) Emphasize *undergraduate instruction;* (43) Keep interdepartment harmony; (42) Develop faculty interest in university rather than to their own jobs or professional concerns; (41) Protect and facilitate the *students' right* to advocate direct action on social and political concerns; (40) Accommodate *students* of high potential; (39) Educate *every high school graduate* to his utmost capacities; (38) Develop the inner character of *students* so that they can make sound, correct moral choices; (37) Provide special training to part-time and adult *students,* and (36) Make sure that the faculty is heard on all important issues. Compiled from Edward Gross and Paul V. Grambsch, *University Goals and Academic Power* (Washington, D.C.: American Council on Education, 1968).

58. Cited in "Education of Children in Chinatown," *Gidra,* Vol. III, No. 12 (December 1971).

59. Milton R. Konvitz, *The Alien and the Asiatic in American Law* (Ithaca, N.Y.: Cornell University Press, 1946), p. 220.

60. Ibid., p. 221.

61. Ibid., p. 222. See also *Farrington v. Tokushige,* 273 U.S. 284 (1926).

62. Quoted and discussed in William Thomas, "San Francisco and the Japanese," *World Today,* Vol. II (December, 1906), p. 1310. Cited in David Brudnoy, "Race and the San Francisco School Board Incident: Contemporary Evaluations," *California Historical Quarterly,* Vol. 50 (1971), p. 76.

63. Quoted in the Metcalf Report, "Final Report on the Situation Affecting the Japanese in the City of San Francisco, California," message from the President of the United States to Congress (December 18, 1907), p. 3.

64. Brudnoy, p. 79.

65. John P. Young, "The Support of the Anti-Oriental Movement," *Annals of the American Academy of Political and Social Science,* Vol. 34 (September, 1909), p. 236.

66. San Francisco *Chronicle,* November 6, 1906.

67. Cited in Brudnoy, p. 302.

68. Discussed in part in *The Japanese School Segregation Case, No. 4754, in the Supreme Court of the State of California, Keikichi Aoki v. M. A. Deane* (March, 1907). Cited in Brudnoy, p. 76.

69. Quoted in *World Today,* Vol. II (December, 1906), pp. 1312-13.

70. H. F. Pringle, *Theodore Roosevelt: A Biography* (New York, 1931), p. 407.

71. Brudnoy, p. 85.

72. Quoted in Brudnoy, p. 305.

73. Ibid.

74. Thomas Bailey, *Theodore Roosevelt and the Japanese American Crises* (Palo Alto, Calif.: Stanford University Press, 1934), p. 134.

75. Brudnoy, p. 83.

76. Konvitz, p. 228.

77. 275 U.S. 78 (1927). Cf. 163 U.S. 537; 211 U.S. 45; 332 U.S. 631.

78. 347 U.S. 483; 74 S. Ct. 686; 98 L. Ed. 873 (1954).

79. David Finkelhor, "Education Under Capitalism," *Up Against the American Myth,* edited by Tom Christoffel, David Finkelhor and Dan Gilbarg (New York: Holt-Rinehart-Winston, 1970), p. 321.

80. Jerome Kagan, "The I.Q. Puzzle: What Are we Measuring?" *Inequality in Education* (Center for Law and Education, Harvard University, July 1973. How would middle-class white children fare against urban Black youths if the questions asked were, for example: Who is the leader of the "Miracles?" What does "greez" mean? What are "chitterlings?" And what if Asian Americans were asked: What is "Manzanar?" What is a "wok?" Consider also, the children of blue-collar workers or welfare mothers: What are "the projects?" What is a food stamp? What is "chump change?"

81. Ibid.

82. Steven Brill, "College Entrance Exams: How Valid?" Los Angeles *Times,* October 13, 1974.

83. Ibid.

84. Ibid.

85. An additional note on ETS is that, in conformity with university and government functions, the ETS does much more than merely test and classify students. Potential CIA agents are sorted out by the ETS as are would-be medical specialists, finance managers, stockbrokers, foreign service officers and law enforcement officers. Students who need financial assistance must have their "need" verified by ETS. Ibid.

86. Seymour H. Fersh, "Studying Other Cultures: Looking Outward Is 'In,' " reprinted by The Asia Society from National Council for Social Studies, Washington, D.C., 1968 Yearbook, Chapter 8, p. 1.

87. Ibid., p. 7.

88. Albert H. Yee, "Myopic Perceptions and Textbooks: Chinese Americans' Search for Identity," *Journal of Social Issues,* Vol. 29, number 2 (1973), p. 107.

89. The textbooks were rated according to the following criteria:
- Does content reflect true history and contributions of Japanese Americans?
- Are ethnocentric views worked against, while encouraging a postive self-image?
- Are serious "sins of omission" successfully avoided?
- Are social group differences presented in ways that will cause students to look at the multi-racial character of our country?
- Does the text seek to motivate students to examine their own attitudes and behaviors and to comprehend their duties and responsibilities?
From Carol Hatanaka and Naomi Katayama, "The Treatment of Japanese Americans in Elementary Social Studies Textbooks in Los Angeles City Schools" (Unpublished thesis, 1974).

90. Yee, loc. cit.

91. California Education Code, section 9305.

92. Franklin Odo, a Declaration submitted to the court in the case of *Gutierrez v. State Board of Education.*

93. Ibid.

94. For recent evidence of these points, see U.S. Bureau of Census, *Current Population Reports.*

95. Bowles, p. 223.

96. Jack McCurdy, "Many of Poor Eligible for UC Fail to Enroll," Los Angeles *Times,* November 12, 1975.

97. Ibid.

98. Bowles, p. 224.

99. Figures computed from abstracts published by the Los Angeles City Schools District, 1974-75.

100. Research Organizing Cooperative, p. 2.

101. It should be noted here that most University of California campuses are located in "prime" areas of the state, far removed from and least accessible to Third World and working class communities. The Berkeley campus is set on a sprawling hillside overlooking the San Francisco Bay; UCLA is in suburban Westwood, adjacent to exclusive Bel Air residences; and Santa Cruz, San Diego, Irvine and Santa Barbara campuses are in secluded areas overlooking the Pacific.

102. Bowles, "Contradictions in U.S. Higher Education," *Political Economy: Radical versus Orthodox Approaches,* edited by James Weaver, 1971, p. 494.

103. George Kagiwada and Isao Fujimoto, "Asian American Studies: Implications for Education," *Personnel and Guidance Journal,* Vol. 51, No. 6 (February 1973), p. 402.

104. Mao Tse-tung, "On Practice," July 1937.

ASIAN AMERICAN STUDIES AT
Berkeley High

by Linda Wing

Part One: ROOTS

"Hello, Linda? This is Jim Louie. Can you come to a meeting for a few minutes? Nothing important. The Asian Task Force wants to meet you."

I drove immediately over to the meeting. The building was located in an area where numerous Japanese American families had lived until Topaz, Utah had abruptly changed its population patterns.

Upon entering the room, I was directed to the only seat available. It was at the front of the room, facing some forty people who were eyeing me curiously. Within a few minutes, I found that "nothing important" was instead the last and most important of a series of interviews that I was to complete before obtaining a job teaching Asian American studies at Berkeley High School.

I was questioned and observed by a community group of Asian parents, students and teachers.

My first interview had been with Astor Mizuhara, a member of the Asian Task Force and the school district's liaison with the group. He questioned me for two hours about my political

views, my experiences with students, my ideas about teaching Asian American studies, and a wide range of other topics. Later, Astor and Jim Louie (a parent and chairman of the Task Force) were to be instrumental in convincing the school board of the necessity of hiring an Asian American studies teacher.

In 1969, both men had been among a small group of people who began questioning the school district's education of Asian children. It was noted, for example, that in establishing ethnic ratios for each school when mandatory busing was instituted in 1968, the district had not taken into account the Asian American children who made up seven or eight percent of the school district's population. Similarly, there was a heavy emphasis on Black studies with no attention given to the needs of other racial groups.

Small neighborhood meetings blossomed into a large public meeting of several hundred people who presented their concerns and recommendations to the superintendent. Not only did the people want

change in the school system, they also realized that they had to take an *active role* in this change. Shortly afterwards, the school board recognized a group of thirty Asian teachers, parents and students as the official body responsible for recommending and implementing new school programs.

After countless discussions about what must be done, a summer workshop was planned; parents, teachers and students were to write Asian American studies curriculum for every grade level, kindergarten through twelfth grade. A complete high school course was developed.

At the community meeting, I was given a short introduction by Jim. Then a series of questions were directed at me from various parts of the room. It was soon clear that a wide variety of opinions about me existed, including skepticism among some about my age and lack of professional teaching experience. I was a University of California Urban Task Force teaching intern and had only just begun my

credential program. If they were going to hire me, it would be a gamble.

The second interview had taken place at UC's Ho Chi Minh Hall. The bombing raids on Cambodia the previous spring had sparked the formation of picket lines marching around Sproul Plaza. While Alameda County Sheriff's Department deputies—blue-suited, helmeted, rifle-toting men—patrolled every corner of the campus, Berkeley Police in unmarked cars travelled the streets, metal pipes stuck out of their windows spewing out pepper gas. Sounds of tear gas cannisters being fired were heard everywhere, occasionally being drowned out by the cacophony of the helicopters overhead. A year later, Ho Chi Minh Hall, a green building located on a side street near campus, remained a symbol of the Asian student movement.

Steve Hayashi, who was in charge of interviewing students for summer workshop positions,

illustrations by KEN MINAMIJI

met me in a small room on the second floor. A sophomore at UC, he had graduated from Berkeley High School. Both of his parents, Fumi and Tad Hayashi, were among the founders of the Task Force. He filled me in on the details of the workshop organization: the people involved, the salary, and so on. I found that with the exception of myself, all the student workers were either currently students at the high school or recent graduates. This same policy of giving priority to students who have been most directly influenced by the Berkeley public schools was established early in the history of Asian American studies and has been followed ever since.

"We need new blood," commented one of the students at the meeting. Her comment set off a barage of statements about my qualifications, perspectives and goals as compared with those of the only other applicant, a man who had taught in the district at the elementary level for a number of years.

"I think it would be best if both applicants left the room," someone said loudly. "Then we can express our opinions about them freely."

This process of selection was unique not only for me but for everyone involved. It was unusual enough for a community group to provide input to school boards regarding policy, but for a community group to be able to make the decision on hiring of an instructor was unprecedented.

My third and fourth interviews took place at 1414 Walnut Street, the site of the school administration and school board meeting rooms. Arriving for the first of my two "legitimate" job interviews, I was ushered into an air conditioned office to meet the personnel director.

I emerged after a brief meeting; the interview included a few questions about classroom management ("Can you control a classroom of rowdy high school students?"), passing of the buck ("My hands are tied. The board has frozen the budget, and there are no new 'hires.' "), and finally evidence that the Task Force had applied some pressure ("I want you to know that I've hired Asian teachers for the district; I've gone on recruitment trips to Hawaii!") The interview was far from conclusive.

A few days later, I met with the superintendent. Since this was strictly a courtesy meeting requested by Jim Louie, the superintendent spent most of the time leisurely explaining what the "Anglos" must do in the schools to eliminate racism. He was a man whose talent at public relations nearly masked his message that the only means by which I, or any other Asian American studies teacher, could be hired was through steady and intense pressure from the Asian American community.

The closed door session was over. I was called back into the room. It had been decided that I was to be recommended to the board for hiring.

Two months later, the board capitulated on this demand, not only finding funds for my salary but for an Asian American studies budget, an Asian American studies

coordinator, and a teacher for English as a Second Language (ESL).

These events took place four years ago. My memories of that time are tangled with images of other meetings, classes, crises and faces. But the beginning must be recalled if any of us who were involved at that time are to retain a clear understanding of what we have done, why, and what significance Asian American studies in the Berkeley public schools has for us in this city and for other Asian American communities throughout the country. In Berkeley, many Asian people are involved in a dynamic struggle with the politics, economics and racism of the school system. It is out of this struggle that the Asian youth have begun to shape their own destinies. It is out of this struggle, along with many other struggles, that the future of Asian American people in the United States will be determined.

Part Two: BROTHERS AND SISTERS

Although Berkeley has only one high school, the board decision to fund a program and hire a staff came too late in the summer to implement a full-fledged course for the high school. However, six weeks after the fall semester began, a special short seminar was organized. Since it was available only to students who were willing to sacrifice their lunch periods in order to add an extra class to their schedules, we were concerned about how other students not enrolled in the class would be able to participate in Asian American studies.

The idea of a retreat was developed.

The theme chosen for the retreat was Asian Identity and Awareness. By now this phrase has become rather hackneyed, but at that time, it was a new concept to most students. The students in the class, mostly juniors who had worked at the summer workshop, selected a remote mountain camp as the site. Our intent was to have a retreat in an isolated setting where there would be no distractions typically found in the city. The students pointed out that during the school day there was no time or place to meet or to talk about being Asian. The Asian students at Berkeley High School were and still are only a small minority of about two hundred students, engulfed by the school population of nearly fifteen hundred Black and an equal number of white students.

At the retreat we tried to define ourselves in positive ways. Freed from the pressures imposed by other racial groups, from school hassles, and class-room boredom, we would either "make it" together as Asians on our own terms or be stranded high in the Napa Mountains for three days trying. And most of the people who went succeeded in this purpose, much of it through the revelation of many painful truths.

The camp bunks were filled with people, legs
dangling over the edges of the thin mattresses.
For hours, the discussion/work group stayed
together, talking quietly:

Language changes people.
People pass through varied experiences by
    language.
When I came to Berkeley, I didn't know the
    meaning of language.
Since I was speaking in Japanese
    unintentionally,
I didn't realize language was so important.
I experienced solitude.
I understood what it means to be alone.
I experienced loneliness by language.
Loneliness is solitary and empty.
Loneliness can't trust anybody.
Everybody looks like an enemy.
Because at that time I can't understand the
    language,
I would shout in a loud voice:
Bakayaro.
But nobody cared,
I'd shout often and make myself look stupid.
I don't like to think about these things
    everyday.
I want to run away from this.
But if I run away from here now
will I lose myself?
I don't want to lose myself.

* * *

If I could only see the world that I hold
    in my hand,
A world so beautiful, so alive and full of magic.
I look in the picture books and see it all there,
but I can't seem to find it out here.

I hold out my hand and reach and stretch
    to grasp it or touch it,
if only for a moment.
But it is only air that seems to fill my hand.

I can smell life in this world, I can smell
    the scent,
so strong and vibrant.
Ohhh.... I love it, I want it, I need it.
But the winds keep blowing it away,
So far, far away.

The truth is coming my way.
The sound is pulsating and the vibrations
    are strong.
They say to know the truth is to know life.
Let it sink into my brain, let me absorb it

all please.
But no, my mind is someone else's.

I am in a wall of silence,
I cannot hear the world that is passing by me
    so quickly and fiercely.
If only I could hear what life is about.
To hear the sounds of laughter and love
But there is a wall of silence which surrounds
    me.

I want to say my thoughts and feelings,
To tell the world that I am here, alive,
    surviving, and whole,
But someone has put tape over my mouth.

I sit here, alone, blind, deaf, and dumb,
Motionless, dying slowly,
Crying, crying because I know I am not alone.

* * *

I am an Asian
who people
don't see.

I am a person
who people
ignore.

I am an Asian?
I am a person?
I am an Asian person...

* * *

Stereotypes of Asians in the minds and
institutions of the American people are indeed
insulting, but for many Asian youth they are also
debilitating, separating and isolating. Institutionalized racism in the educational system has denied the
history and culture of Asian people in America but
for some Asian youth, it has also denied them self-
confidence in the validity of their very existence.
Feelings about parents, friendship, jobs, school, as
well as many fears and hopes were surfaced and
shared among small groups at that first retreat and at
the four which followed it during the next three
years.
    The results are seen in this account:

    This past weekend I had a very interesting
    experience. I went on my first retreat. There
    were quite a few instances that shook me up but I
    think in all it made me open my eyes to people
    and who they really are, not just people-people,
    but Asians.

227

In my discussion/work group I got to know and understand the foreign-borns and their feelings about living in the US. Even though there was a communication problem in trying to understand their broken English, the feeling of what they were trying to express was all there. And they too tried to comprehend words that may have seemed to them to be going fifty miles per hour. After that, I took a long walk and got my head together. Wow! Who'd think that I'd be laughing, sharing, and eating with Asians, Asians that I never thought I'd get to know! But that was one of my purposes for going and it was fulfilled.

I'm glad that I went and am proud to know that I opened doors in my life that I left locked to other Asians that I had ridiculed. I opened my eyes and saw visions of me relating and not criticizing first.

The concrete ways in which this commitment manifested itself at the retreat were seen in the ways the students learned an amazing number of skills and organized simple but practical work relationships and creative programs, all in a tremendous, ever-expanding spirit of collectivity.

At the earlier retreats, we relied totally upon speakers from outside Berkeley to provide us with ideas through speeches and to work with us as discussion and workshop leaders, but more recently there has been more emphasis on self-reliance and self-development. While it has always been the case that Saturday nights were devoted to skits performed and created by each work/discussion group, it was not until the last retreat that the program became almost completely a product of student thought, creativity, and experiences such as Pham Thanh's account of his life in war-torn Vietnam. A segment of the program focused on Eddie Mapanao bringing his slide and film presentation to a climax with a dazzling burst of *tinikling*, a Pilipino bamboo dance, which he taught to everyone. At the last retreat Julie Wong, Herminia Banez and Dorise Yee performed a skit about Asian women, and Lesli-Jo Morizono read several poems. Nearly every hour was filled with similar presentations by students.

None of what I have just described was accomplished without struggles and conflicts. During the last retreat, a mass meeting that lasted for six hours resulted when a few students exploded in frustration over their observations of cliques, the lack of work being shared, the hedonistic attitudes exhibited by many in using the retreat for their own pleasures. Harsh statements were made; angry recriminations were yelled out. Minds were dazed, feelings were tense until finally the tirade subsided into quiet, serious discussion about how this crisis came about and what must be done if it was to be overcome. One student wrote later:

The next day was the test, a test to see if the point of the whole retreat was known to those who came. And it was better, everyone partici-

pating, enjoying each other's company. Sure there were minute problems but nothing like that could break the togetherness that filled the air.

The fact that Asian students can shape their lives for one three-day weekend is an important first step towards the realization that Asians can control their lives on a daily basis, particularly at school.

Part Three: THE SYSTEM

The task of taking back with us into our classroom the things we had learned at the retreat—the working relationship, the creativity, and the sense of collective responsibility—has been impeded by a formidable opponent: the school system itself.

Although Berkeley has experienced busing for six years and Third World people have been on the school board, there are very few teachers in the district who recognize and acknowledge the existence of institutionalized racism in the schools and its impact on their attitudes. In a supposedly enlightened and progressive school system, one all too frequently hears comments such as:

Integration is what we had before organizations such as Raza Educators were formed.

Black studies preaches violence and is directly responsible for school vandalism, extortion and theft.

The English Department teaches literature of value. If there were any Asian American literature of value, we would already have it in our curriculum.

School board members sanction this type of attitude among school personnel by consistently and vigorously impelling policies which benefit interest groups rather than the education of Asian, Black and Chicano children who are a majority of the school district's population.

Additionally, youth in general are not accorded the dignity and respect to which they are entitled. They are effectively barred from functioning in useful roles in society; instead they are relegated to being students in school systems where they receive inadequate education and where inequality between them and adults are sharply delineated. Asian students in particular feel victimized by this situation. The students believe that some teachers assume that Asians are least likely to resist poor teaching and abuse of authority, and that they are treated in accordance with such stereotypes by school teachers and administrators.

In the early period of our development, the influence of the repressive atmosphere of the school setting was felt and reflected. The Asian American studies classes fluctuated wildly from days when everyone worked hard on many projects—teaching children Asian American studies at Washington Primary School and putting together the book *Sojourner*—to days when the students lapsed into more ordinary patterns seen in school: sitting like robots or jiving around.

One notable example, however, of the rising level of expectations that the students have of the school and of themselves while at school, is the existence of the English course, Asian Writers' Project. While the first Asian American studies class, a history course entitled the *Asian American Experience*, became a reality at the school through the efforts of parents, teachers and students in the Asian Task Force, this second course was the product of student leadership alone.

Two years ago, fifty Asian American students and I decided to participate in an alternative school located on campus at Berkeley High School. The alternative school was a program funded by the federal government; there were no limitations on the development and offering of new courses. Consequently, we were able to experiment with an English class, and the Asian Writers' Project was initiated.

Serious problems developed because of staff turnovers. Students proposed the incorporation of the class into the regular Berkeley High School curriculum. Our investigation into how this could be done involved daily discussions during class and meetings with the principal, vice-principal and the English department chairman. Finally, the students presented the proposed course to the English department staff. The students began with a history of institutionalized racism, pointing out its relationship to the lack of Asian American material in any of the English department courses.

"This is the English department, not the history department," interrupted one of the teachers, who began to contest the students' statements, engaging the students in debate. Offended, the students reacted strongly. Soon the meeting had disintegrated into a heated confrontation, ending in a stalemate.

The students made an appeal to the principal, an Asian. Dubious about the credibility of Asian American studies when it first began, he had gradually become one of our strongest supporters. With his help, the students struck a compromise with the English department. The Asian Writers' Project was not accepted as an alternative to the required American Literature class, but it became an English department elective. Top priority was given to the acquisition of ethnic literature for the department's required World Literature and American Literature courses. Finally the students were exempted from the normal sequence of English classes into which other students were required to enroll, thus enabling them to remain in Asian Writers' Project for its first semester as a fully recognized class at the high school.

Part Four: CHALLENGE

Unfortunately, struggles similar to ours in Berkeley do not seem to be taking place in other communities. And in those cities where Asian American studies programs of some kind exist, only a handful of them have their roots in the communities among the people.

There are programs which include Asian American studies within a multi-cultural curriculum. Ironically, many programs of this type are located in school districts where the Third World population is minute. In other cities, the Asian professional staff has attempted to institute educational change without the involvement of Asian American students and parents. Still other programs, which were developed because of the availability of funds from the federal government or the mandates of state laws, involved many Third World people in high-paying, prestigious jobs but have notoriously little or no impact on the people, the funds or law are purported to serve.

In Berkeley, different community groups have assumed leadership at different times and have involved different issues. The students, the Task Force, the Asian Alliance, and Concerned Filipinos have all played key roles. Despite some internal struggles, new faces and new directions, Asian American studies has rarely wavered from its basic principle: the fulfillment of the needs and interests of the Asian American community in this city, and the involvement of the widest possible segment of its people.

A revolution has taken place among us. In the past, it was the norm for Asian American people to assume that the schools could do no wrong; it is now common for an Asian parent to examine the schools critically, to expect that his or her opinion and recommendations will be heard by the school administration and staff. The community was successful in electing an Asian American to the school board itself.

In the past, it was not unusual for Asian American students to either tolerate school or to view education in narrow academic terms. It is now the case that the students—not only in high school but those at every grade level—shape the schools to be vital parts of their lives. It is this wide impact on the lifestyle, goals and concerns of the Asian American residents in this city that gives Asian American studies in the public schools its basic strength, its life-giving blood, and which is a challenge to Asian Americans everywhere. ★

Writings and poems by students
Charlie Sakamoto, Janet Shimoko,
Donna Chan and Lesli-Jo Morizono.

An Experience in Community Work

by
The Chinatown Education Project

Some of us live in Chinatown; some of us work here. Some of us are students who work in community projects. We are all interested in improving the education of children in Chinatown. We have been involved in the Chinatown Education Project because we feel that we can work effectively in the area of education. We are beginning to see that our work in this area has broader implications. Not only must we work with children, we must also work with their parents and with groups in other communities if we are to make significant changes in education. We see that these changes must be made along with changes in the social system. In the long run, that is the only way we can improve education.

We came together in the fall of 1972 bringing a variety of experiences from participating in community children's programs, such as the Asian-American Tutorial Project (tutoring elementary school children on Saturday mornings), film series childcare (supervising children while their parents attended community showings of films from China), and Creative Play (a daily elementary school age children's workshop run by volunteer supervisors and teenagers from the 1972 Summer Neighborhood Youth Corps program). Many of us felt, however, that the Chinatown community needed programs with longer-range effects on the education of its children.

Our experiences centered around Castelar School, which is located in Chinatown and serves almost all of the children in this community. Castelar has an enrollment of around 800, of which 75% are Chinese and 24% Chicano. When we began working with the school, few teachers were Chinese and fewer were Chinese-speaking. Los Angeles Chinatown has a large and growing immigrant population, and these children enter Castelar with little or no knowledge of English. They were receiving only 30 minutes of English as a Second Language instruction daily, if any. This, plus a small and deteriorated physical plant, had contributed to a repressive atmosphere in the school.

Outside of school, the situation is worse. The Chinatown community is a working class community in downtown Los Angeles. In most cases, both parents must work long hours to support the family. They have little time to supervise and teach their children, let alone play with them or give them the enriching experiences of trips to the museum or park.

The Chinatown Education Project, when it began, planned Dai Jung (Community) school to meet this need. Fifty children, ages five to twelve, were enrolled in the first session of the Saturday afternoon program which featured arts and crafts activities, recreation, music, cooking, and field trips. The program's underlying objectives were: to build the self-image and self-reliance of the children, to create a sense of open-mindedness and critical thinking, to bring about cooperation and sharing within the group, to expand the children's environment to include experiences outside of Chinatown, and to increase their awareness and understanding of people of other cultures.

Dai Jung started its third year of operation in the fall of 1974, having run on Saturdays during the school year and four days a week in the summers. Some structural changes have been made in the program to reflect our increased awareness of the needs of the children and appropriate teaching methods, but the basic objectives and content still remain the same.

Until the spring of 1973, all the efforts of every member of CEP went into running Dai Jung. Then, some members questioned the effectiveness of a two and one half hour a week program in dealing with the extensive language problem at Castelar, which had been one of our initial concerns. After investigation that included studying ESL materials and methods for children from an Asian language background, and visiting model ESL programs in the San Francisco Bay area, CEP launched the two hours a day, five days a week Transition ESL class at Castelar. It was begun as an experiment with the objective of convincing the principal to institute this as a regular school program.

Initially, eight CEP members planned, wrote, and taught with English lesson materials based on social studies themes relevant to a Chinatown child, such as the geography of Chinatown, or shopping at a department store downtown. In its second year, the program was run by CEP volunteers and an ESL teacher at Castelar, a slight acknowledgement by the school of its language problem. In the program's third year, after a demand was made to the principal, two paid aides worked with an ESL teacher to run the Transition Class. In the coming year, Transition will be phased out as a CEP service project with the intent that the school will institute it as a regular program. If this takes place, the school will have been made to respond, in a limited way, to the needs of the students and community.

Low-cost, full-time childcare is a desperate need in Los Angeles Chinatown. Only 21 pre-schoolers receive full-time care at the Castelar Children's Center, which is run by the Los Angeles School District, and they have a waiting list of over 200. Several smaller programs exist, but even all these programs together are insignificant when compared to the great number of children who do not receive childcare services. In this low-income community, mothers must work to insure that the family has an adequate income, but they cannot do so unless low-cost childcare services for pre-school children are available to them. For these reasons, two CEP members and some community mothers began Little Friends Community Playgroup in the spring of 1973. It began as a two days a week program because it was and still is difficult to find a suitable building in Chinatown.

In the summer of 1974, Little Friends started a full-time childcare service in an apartment in Chinatown for up to 15 children. One problem that has to be worked out is how to keep tuition low enough so that low-income families can afford to send their children, and at the same time meet the expenses for a quality program.

One of CEP's goals is to involve parents in the education of their children. To get to know the parents better and to let them know more about our programs, we visited the homes of each of the children that we worked with. From our talks with the parents, we found out that many parents needed practical information about social services available to them. We thought that a newsletter would be a good way of letting parents know about these things, and about school and education news. It would also inform the parents about our programs and increase our communication with them. The newsletter is tri-lingual. We personally deliver it to over 100 families a month.

CEP has grown since the beginning, but the growth has not all been smooth. New members have joined the project, and others of us have left. We have struggled over our personal priorities and time commitments, over philosophies and goals, and we have grown through this struggle. Our project, and any other community project, is made up of strong individuals who bring into the project diverse backgrounds and unique personal histories. Many of us came originally from student backgrounds, and for us there is the problem of correcting our approach to working in the community and integrating ourselves into the community. We are struggling with ourselves to make a longer-range commitment to working in the community, to see problems and solutions in a broader perspective, and to learn from the community. In attempting this, some of us who do not speak Chinese face a major obstacle.

We would like to share three different people's stories and the experiences they have brought to CEP, and their thoughts about the project in the spring of 1974. These people worked with CEP at the beginning and have influenced each other and influenced the group's development. CEP members have all grown personally, and the group's growth can be seen as a reflection of individual growth.

****

I grew up in Los Angeles Chinatown. There are not many people like me in Chinatown because other people who grew up here have moved away and have gone on to "bigger" things. No one wants to stay here. I was more Americanized than most teenagers here; I read a lot and had good teachers.

I've seen the community change. Programs like NYC didn't exist at first. When they got started, I knew about them, but I didn't investigate them. I don't know how the process of becoming critical, analytical, really begins. How does it happen? It might be because of the people you associate with. For me, it was when I was pushed into another culture. I went to Taiwan for a summer to study Chinese. There I got for the first time a perspective on the things that the United States government does. I saw US oppression of the people in Taiwan. There were US army camps all over Taiwan, and racist army officers. I heard one US colonel say that all the street names should be in English so that he could understand them.

When I got back, the Asian Women's course was offered at UCLA, where I was a student. The course started me thinking, and got me interested in working in the community. My work with CEP started with the Creative Play workshop. After that summer a group of us that had been working with children in Chinatown decided to continue meeting, and that's how CEP started.

CEP is one of the things I feel good about in my life. I feel like I helped start it, but I can't pin down the beginning to just two or three people. A whole lot of us struggled together. Since I helped start it, I feel a responsibility to the project. That's why I worry about the new people. They don't have this historical experience. What will make the new people want to stay? What will there be for them to do that will make them want to stay? CEP's development has been a reflection of people's personal development, so we should reach out to new people. They come in because they know something is wrong and they want to help, but they don't know what to do. Talking to people and making personal contacts with them is important. People stay because their political attitudes change. They can develop an awareness of what's happening in this country through working in the community.

****

My past is not typical of most people working in Chinatown. I grew up in East Los Angeles, but I feel my cultural identity with Chinatown. When I was growing up I had very strict discipline at home. I had to rebel, so I got into conflicts with teachers and other authority figures. For a while I dropped out of society and got into drugs. Then I got drafted, and that really freaked out my mind. I couldn't handle the oppression of military life, and I built up a lot of hate. In growing up I had more than my share of racism from the white community, but it really came down the hardest when I was drafted.

When I got out, I got into an Asian-American student group, and there I worked out the hate in a constructive way. It was an alternative to being strung out. I got into society again. But this did not satisfy me at the gut level, so I decided that I wanted to work with children and I joined Tutorial. Then I wanted to get more into community work, so in the summer of 1972 I worked in the Creative Play work-shop. This led me to being in CEP. My first experiences in Chinatown weren't all happy, though. The first time I came to Chinatown just to check it out, somebody ripped off my car.

Since I got into CEP my attitudes have really changed. I still have conflicts about my past, and sometimes I think maybe I belong somewhere else,

but I am trying to do what I believe in. I am worried that this year CEP as a group is not as solid as last year. There is not enough unity between the old members and new members, and between the projects. We do not have enough people to support all the projects. We are branching out a lot, but skinny branches break.

****

I didn't grow up in Chinatown. I grew up in Inglewood and went to UCLA and majored in psychology. I knew I was Chinese, but I didn't really think anything of it. Lowell Chun-Hoon's course on the Chinese in America was what made me aware that I'm Chinese and that it means something. Lowell convinced me to get involved in Chinatown. When I came down to see what it was all about, I was trapped into working here. I went to a meeting for the summer NYC program, and Susie asked me, "What kind of car do you have?" I said, "A station wagon," and she said, "Oh, good. You're signed up for our workshop," which was Creative Play.

I'm finding better reasons for working here as I go along. On a lower level, it's meeting people, making friends. I don't want to downplay that aspect of working in CEP. The way I think about society has changed a lot since I've been working here. As a student, I was kind of aware that the world is a messed up place. Students tend to see the problems, but not do anything about them. I think now that it's a contradiction if you don't, so I have become more politically active. When I first became involved, I really got into it. I loved going to three or four meetings a day. I felt like I was really doing something. After a while, the enthusiasm wore off. Now I think that doing something means more than just going to meetings.

My views are very different now from what they were before I joined the project. Now I am much more aware. When I used to see Charlie Chan and karate movies, for example, I didn't see anything wrong with them. Now I am conscious of the racism in those movies. My goals in life are very different now. I am getting my teaching credential. Having worked two years in this community now, I would not ever forget it or leave it. I hope to move in here when I get through with school.

****

Now CEP is going through the long process of redefining its philosophy and goals, evaluating, assessing our political growth, and gearing our work accordingly. We feel that the best way to present CEP is not as a group with no problems, but one that is questioning and struggling to find direction. Over the years, through our work and the work of other people in Chinatown, we have begun to see that this cannot be done in isolation. The limitations of alternative programs are becoming more apparent.

What real changes have we made in education in Chinatown? What and how much effect have we had?

We came together originally because we wanted to make changes in education in this community. Our goal was always more than ineffectual, band-aid programs, or we wouldn't have struggled with the project as long as we have. Now we realize that changes can be made only by linking our work with other political struggles. This is because the education system is part of the American social, political, and economic system. Education is used by powerful business interests, who have political ties with the government, to maintain a social system that benefits the rich at the expense of the poor.

Therefore, we must place alternative programs in perspective. Reforms are needed to better people's living conditions, so we are not saying they shouldn't exist. But we should not stop there. We will only be able to effect the changes we want if we link up with other work in Chinatown and work in other areas as part of a greater political movement. Yet, because of the particular nature of the problems here, we still need to concentrate our work within the community.

Not everyone in the project develops his or her ideas in the same way or at the same rate. This has been the cause of some conflict in Dai Jung between those who are satisfied with the project as it exists and those who want to push it ahead with some political direction. In the newsletter, our growth has been reflected in the change from seeing it as a social service to using it to tell the community our views on educational issues. In our articles, we have been more critical of the school and the educational system in the United States. Our future format, whether it is a newsletter, pamphlet series, or some other form, will depend on what will be the most effective way of getting our ideas across to the community. Little Friends is now looking into the possibility of government funding and trying to make more contacts with people in other areas working with childcare.

Some of us are seeing the importance of directly confronting the educational system to make changes. A few of us are working at Castelar School as teachers' aides and others have gotten or are getting teaching credentials and hope to get jobs in the schools in this area. Some of us have been working with parents in the Castelar Community Advisory Council to make it a stronger body, able to represent the parents' concerns to the school. In our jobs and as we work with the parents, we will have opportunities to point out contradictions that exist in the school system. We also see the need to do more investigation at the junior high and high school levels.

****

This is where CEP stands in the spring of 1975—

a community project that wants to bring about changes in the educational system. By the time this article is published, there will undoubtedly have been many more changes in the project. We realize we don't have all the answers yet. We must always try to increase our understanding of the relationship of education to the social system, and bring our community work in line with our understanding. ★

Note: The authors of this article are a few of us who worked with the Chinatown Education Project (CEP) since the beginning, but the article does not represent the thinking of everybody who worked with the project.

This article was originally written in the spring of 1974 and revised and updated at the end of 1974. Since then, CEP has undergone many changes. Many of the projects do not exist anymore. The work has either continued in other forms, or has taken on a broader political direction. For most of us, CEP has been a valuable experience, but it has become important for people to go beyond the scope of the project.

For example, the Little Friends Playgroup (one part of the project) is no longer limited to providing alternative childcare services; the people working with the Playgroup are taking up the broader struggle for childcare as a democratic right in our society. This involves: (a) helping to organize mass support within the community so that people will struggle for their own needs, (b) conducting political education to make people aware that we live under a capitalist, profit-oriented system in which the needs of a few rich take priority over the needs of the vast majority of the people, such as childcare, and (c) working with other communities and groups that fight for childcare and issues such as housing, health, employment, and education to build a broad struggle against the problems engendered by the present social system.

Through political study and analysis of our work, we began to see the limitations of alternative educational programs such as tutorial classes and creative arts workshops. It is the school system's responsibility to educate children, not CEP's responsibility. For this reason, we terminated our alternative programs, but people still work in the interest of educational needs. This can take many different forms, including: (a) working with parents in the community in order to join with them to fight for quality education, (b) maintaining contact through the school and school district to better understand the contradictions of educational system and to raise people's awareness of this situation, and (c) uniting with other groups, communities, and individuals whenever possible to fight for the highest quality of education for children and to struggle against a system which continues to deny equal education to all people.

These changes in CEP have been a part of a necessary and good developmental process. For some of us, the changes in CEP have mirrored our deepening understanding of the educational system. The programs and goals that we had set up earlier did not challenge the root of the problems. We tended to look at education apart from the other aspects of the society. We did not understand that unequal education is a consequence of the capitalist system that operates for the benefit of the wealthy at the expense of the majority of working people. While we should always fight to improve education in every way possible, we should not suffer under any illusions. Complete equal education is not possible under the present system and can only come under a system where exploitation by a wealthy elite no longer exists. Political work in education must be done with this larger goal in mind. CEP, as it was, could not fulfill that purpose.

Teaching a Course on Asian American Women

by May Ying Chen

In many ways, the university educational system represents the highest form of "bourgeois ideology." This means that a great deal of emphasis is placed on individual expertise, elitism, and just plain "boss mentality." It is still generally accepted that the university is the training ground for the future leaders and defenders of today's society. In spite of cynicism and unemployment statistics, the college degree is considered a ticket to success—a pass to a white collar job and a stable position in the middle class.

Until recently, most minorities and women were never able to avail themselves of a college education, and until a few years ago, the college curriculum consisted almost exclusively of rich, Anglo-American male perspectives, culture and values. Working within the university, and yet being inherently anti-establishment, Asian American Studies courses and programs face the difficult task of promoting and

popularizing new information and new ways of thinking and acting. The dominance of traditional or "establishment" ways of thinking has made the development of new consciousness difficult. Yet, the past three to five years have seen tremendous development of consciousness among Asian American men and women that has brought forth new sources of energy to help sustain and shape Asian American Studies programs and a large number of community efforts as well. Valuable experience has been gained in these struggles, but the Asian Woman course as well as other Asian American Studies courses continually encounter difficulties in trying to develop a coherent and consistent analysis that goes beyond mere perceptions or "gut feelings" of oppression that Asian women face. The information in this paper remains primarily description of the perceptual knowledge gained through teaching the Asian Woman

234

course at UCLA. Hopefully, the analysis here can provide some data for the much needed theoretical approach to Asian American Studies.

CONSCIOUSNESS RAISING

Teachers of the Asian Woman courses have been able to identify several key contradictions facing Asian women by looking over personal histories, examining the situation of women in Asian communities, and analyzing various descriptive and theoretical readings about women. Historically, the roots of women's oppression can be traced to the period immediately preceding slave society. The development of surplus wealth, the transfer from matriarchy to patriarchy, and the introduction of monogamy to assure that the woman bear one man's heirs signalled the beginnings of confining women within the home and establishing their dependence on men. This period also marked the beginnings of class society, where a relationship of exploitation and oppression existed between the owners of the wealth of society and the majority of other people who did most of the work for society. From class society eventually developed conditions of racial discrimination and the subjugation and oppression of different nationalities.

For Asian women today, the most critical day-to-day problems revolve around issues of race, sex and class. In U.S. society, there are sharp contradictions between being an Asian woman and being a white woman; between being a liberated woman and living up to traditional ideals of femininity; between being a working class woman and living up to a capitalist economy's symbols of status and prestige. In every case, the aspect of being a white American, adopting traditional standards of femininity, and being swept unquestioningly into a competitive and exploitative economic way of life maintains strong domination in many minds, thoughts and values.

As a women's group, the teaching collective for the Asian Woman course began its work with a struggle against the traditional limits of stereotyped "femininity." Instructors found the experience of lecturing and speaking out, reading in an analytical and critical way, and assuming responsibilities independently was new and bewildering. The group rebelled against individualistic, authoritarian, self-centered approaches to teaching and consciously looked for other alternatives. The writings of white middle-class women on "women's lib" helped, but in general, failed to speak relevantly to Asian American women. Many Asian women faced discrimination not only as women, but also on the basis of race, cultural background or low socio-economic status. We discovered that issues of race and class were inextricably bound up with the questions of female roles and identity. With this in mind, we set out

collectively to strengthen the presently weaker, though rising, aspects of the above contradiction—the aspects of being Asian women, being liberated women, and being working class women—struggling for a better society.

Following this analysis came the question of how to develop these issues and share them with students. An understanding of the students needed to be developed—what kinds of backgrounds did they come from? What are their main concerns? What experiences or attitudes can be drawn out? How were they affected by the three key contradictions posed in the course?

For most students, the main contradiction clarified by their participation in class was a new awareness of themselves as distinctly Asian, rather than "melting pot" American, and a realization of the tension and struggle of Asian Americans in racist U.S. society.

Initially, many students had to struggle against their own colonized ideas of what being Asian was like. In one of the first Asian Woman courses at UCLA, some students seemed uncomfortable sitting among such a large group of Asians. Many were caught up in labelling and stereotyping each other, while claiming themselves to be unique or more assimilated, or just different. The early class meetings were actually tense and awkward, as students were hesitant to speak out or to interact with each other. But over the three months of the class—through lectures on racial stereotypes and Asian women's history, discussions on the socialization process in the Asian family, group projects and community experience—many students increased their understanding about "being Asian," with a better understanding of both the conflicts and the contributions of Asian Americans in U.S. society.

The Asian women students, those who sensed the difference between their own situation and those described by white women, could understand the need to unite as Asians first, and not to separate themselves from Asian men. Many women related incidents of sexist racism directed at them by non-Asian men who viewed them only in terms of the stereotypes—Suzy Wong, dragon lady, geisha girl, etc. They felt the need for Asian women and men working together to protest racist media images and the stereotyping of sexy Asian women and sexless Asian men. They also began to reject the divisiveness and self-hatred created by such images. In this and other ways, the aspect of being colonized Asians wishing to be invisible or white-washed yielded a bit to a rising aspect of being strong and aware Asian Americans. This type of consciousness is exemplified in a student evaluation:

I learned quite a bit about myself as an Asian in America, as an individual in America. It has helped me tremendously

235

in understanding and becoming closer to my Asian sisters and brothers. It made me see that many of my problems are common problems among Asians in America, that I am not weird, peculiar and strange because I have these feelings and conflicts whereas my Caucasian friends do not. I learned much about racism and stereotypes in America. This course has helped me understand more about how and why I feel about things and about people, both Asians and others. I have learned more about myself in this course than I have at any one time throughout my entire life. This course has really provided me with a lot of different views and a lot of information.

For other students in the course, the contradiction of being a woman seeking liberation from the sexism in society was a key issue. Many women in the class, both Asian and non-Asian, had already felt very keenly the discrimination against women—the sexist remarks and attitudes, the limited job opportunities, the exploitation of the poor working woman, the plight of the welfare mother. As women, many students felt the restraints of their own socialization—fears of speaking out and of appearing aggressive, dependence on men for approval, and the frustration of habitually falling into roles which now were uncomfortable. Some women brought with them frustrations about Asian men and the Asian family with its authoritarian, male-centered bias. Others had questions about women's working rights, health and child care. Some of the men had questions about male roles in a sexist society. The course aimed to provide opportunities for airing these questions and to facilitate research into these areas. The course gave support to men and women who were becoming conscious of the need to create changes in these areas, to fight back instead of submitting to traditional standards of femininity and masculinity. Readings from women's liberation materials were assigned, and all the lectures, readings, films and discussions in class centered on women and women's issues in Asia and the United States.

While the social position of Asian women was quite clear in the students' experiences, information on her economic status was relatively new, since most of the class had not entered the work force full time. Thus, only a few students felt strongly from direct experience the contradiction between working class women and the prevailing economic system. Still, many students could see manifestations of this contradiction in their parents' struggles to make ends meet, in the plight of immigrant women or warbrides working long hours at menial wages. Students who had worked in service or blue collar jobs understood the feeling of exploitation, and

students who grew up in low-income communities saw the discrimination against working class people—the lack of equitable educational institutions, medical services, fringe benefits, etc. In order to raise consciousness in this area, the course attempted to tie these student experiences into a larger context. U.S. immigration and foreign policies, especially towards early immigrants from Asia, were exposed for their exploitation of foreign resources and cheap labor. The women's role and movement in various developing Asian countries were studied. And of course, the bread-and-butter issues confronting women in Asian American communities were discussed along with the need for organized efforts to effect change.

In grappling with these contradictions, most students recognized and accepted the idea that incidents of racism, sexism, and economic exploitation were larger than the individuals who practiced them, and that these were societal problems requiring collective as well as individual solutions. Thus, it became clear that the enemy was much larger than just one "male chauvinist pig" (though he might be part of it); in fact, it was the whole economic and social system and its ruling class. Arriving at this type of understanding is the basic aim of consciousness-raising, that is, the awareness to distinguish enemies from friends, to identify institutionalized forms of oppression, and to attack and act for change. The role of the Asian Woman course has been to facilitate this awareness, and where possible, to suggest concrete avenues for action and change.

COMMUNITY INVOLVEMENT

Community involvement follows logically from consciousness-raising, since it is in the communities that the questions of race, sex and class are the clearest, and since community involvement presents a starting point for action and change. Different Asian Woman classes have varied in the nature and extent of community efforts, depending on the proximity and familiarity between campus and community. At UCLA, the nature of involvement differed each time the course was offered. At both Berkeley and UCLA, entire discussion sections have concentrated on studying women in the community and involving students directly in community activities, while other sections studied such areas as education, media, roles and relationships, etc. In the first course at UCLA, credit was given to students for attending meetings and helping to plan the annual community pilgrimage to Manzanar, a World War II relocation camp. In the Bay Area, Berkeley students participated in the planning of an International Women's Day celebration in San Francisco's Chinatown. Entire classes have travelled to Delano, California, to work on Agbayani Village, a retirement housing project of the United Farmworkers Union.

There, students met and talked with many of the Pilipino farmworkers who were among the original grape strikers in 1965. As a classroom community, some classes have organized letter-writing campaigns, for example, to protest racist television commercials involving Asian women and men. Support from classes has also been organized to increase the participation of Asian students in campus government or organizations, or to build Asian students' groups and projects.

At UCLA, organized attempts to bring the whole class into various Asian American communities have been made, by publicizing community programs and activities, by encouraging volunteer work, and by organizing trips and visits. One successful total class effort was a series of film showings and forums held at different centers around the Chinese, Japanese and Pilipino communities during the Spring 1973 quarter. The purpose was to physically move the class into the community by holding weekly meetings at different community agencies or centers. Panels of speakers discussed topics such as Nisei Women, Asian Men's Perspectives on Women's Liberation, Asian Women Leaders, Young Asian Women and Drug Abuse, etc. Non-students who attended these forums were also able to learn from the discussions and exchanges that took place.

NISEI WOMEN'S FORUM

The most outstanding of these forums was the first panel, consisting of five Nisei women discussing their own childhoods, the camp experience, their families and children, and their perspectives on Asian women. The meeting was held at the Senshin Buddhist Church in Los Angeles, an important community center for many Japanese American families. Students brought friends to the meeting and some even came with their mothers. The panel was convened by a Nisei staff member of the Asian American Studies Center at UCLA, who invited her friends and acquaintances to speak about their own concerns in their own ways. All the women were very active and articulate, even though they had never spoken in this type of forum on these issues before.

The women had very different childhood experiences. One described growing up in a rather traditional Japanese household. Being highly educated and cultured, her parents insisted on maintaining many old customs, including the sharp differentiation of male and female roles. Brothers got most of the privileges, while the girls, particularly the eldest sister, were trained in household chores and responsibilities. As the youngest child, this speaker remarked that she was very pampered and got her way quite a lot more than her older sister. One area of equality was education, and this speaker had the opportunity to go to college with the help and encouragement of her family.

In contrast, another panelist described the strenuous effort by all her family members to send just one son to college. Such an honor was simply not considered for a daughter, even though she was the eldest child. It was understood that the college-educated man would have a much better chance of success and a higher earning power than the woman. Saving money to send a son to college was sensible and more realistic. Eventually, this woman worked her own way through college. A third speaker had a totally different childhood, born and raised in rural Colorado with a great deal of freedom to run around, roam and explore without adult supervision.

One woman spoke about an incident of open racism that occurred in her early school years. An active and enthusiastic member of various school clubs, this panelist felt at the time that her participation in school and extracurricular activities was on an equal par with others, regardless of race. This record was marred by an incident in the period just before World War II when anti-Japanese sentiment was mounting. It happened in her home-making class, when the teacher appointed her to be a team captain for cooking. When she asked a girl in her group to do something, the girl retorted, "I won't take orders from a Jap!" A quarrel and fight resulted in the speaker's suspension from school. Several years later, the principal apologized for the severe punishment; he explained that at the time of the incident he was hiding the fact that he was Jewish in order to keep his job, and that he understood the anger and humiliation of this racial incident.

The camp experience caught most of these women in their adolescent years, a sudden jolt from childhood into a rather different style of life. While the experiences of humiliation and imprisonment have created bitterness and a strong desire among Nisei to forget the war years, the camps provided a sense of isolation and shelter from the outside world. Teenagers who previously were not allowed to go out on a date found a new social life where romances and growing pains were allowed to take place, though subject to heavy gossip and the close scrutiny of parents and friends. For some of these Nisei women, the camp years created a sense of crisis in the Japanese American family. With the family imprisoned together, with parents unemployed and dispossessed, the traditional feelings of respect and authority broke down.

In most cases, the return to normal life after the camps was a shock. One woman recounted an unforgettable incident in a servicemen's club in Minneapolis after the war. She and some friends decided to take some disabled Nisei veterans, just back from serving in the armed forces in Europe in the famous "442," to this service club. As they tried to enter, the owner turned them away, kicking them out because they were Japanese. For these Nisei with such a strong sense of patriotism and proven loyalty to the United States, this incident came as a shock and humiliation. The angry young people actually picked up some rocks and thew them at the building.

The women were unanimous in feeling that young Asian American women today have a great deal more freedom and many more career and educational alternatives than they had. They all felt they made conscious efforts to bring up their own daughters with a greater sense of independence and equality.

This panel was significant in several ways. First, it provided a sense of historical perspective on Asian women. Second, it raised the voices of an often-neglected yet extremely important group in the Asian communities—the women who indirectly through their husbands and children as well as through their own involvement in clubs, community organizations and work, are a great influence. Many insights, both familiar and surprising, were brought out to clarify and strengthen the position of these women in the minds of all who participated.

PANEL ON MEN'S PERSPECTIVE

Probably the most anxiously awaited of the community forums was the Men's Panel. The question of men's role and participation in issues concerning Asian women has undergone many changes in response to the growing Asian women's movement. In the early stage of women getting together, while men were laughing at the very idea and women angrily lashed out at every "MCP" (male chauvinist pig) in sight, women seriously questioned whether men should participate at all. On several campuses, women's groups debated whether or not to allow or encourage men to enroll in the Asian Woman class. For these women, the struggle against sexism seemed to require at least a temporary separation so that sisters could feel totally free to speak out and "get their heads together" without any kind of influence, help or hindrance from men. In some places, men also felt the need to meet and discuss and understand the women's struggle and its implications for themselves and other men.

As the Asian women's movement has grown and gained more depth, awareness and confidence, and especially as more and more Asian women have assumed positions of more importance and leadership in community activities, the desire to discuss issues related to sexism openly and rationally among both women and men has gained strength. Community groups began to hold meetings on sexism, and various study groups were formed. Meanwhile, even more women were encouraged and recruited into active community involvement.

Set against this background, the men's forum had an important impact. Speaking to an audience of women and men with a broad range of attitudes and ideas was a panel of young Asian American men explaining their reasons to support the liberation of Asian women and some of the personal conflicts this entailed. The moderator from the Asian American Studies Center introduced the purpose of the program: "In this presentation, we hope to raise certain fundamental questions about men's relationship with women, about chauvinism, and about men's attitudes toward such things as relationships, marriage and bringing up children."

The program included one skit, three short talks, and small discussion groups involving the entire audience. A feeling of tenseness seemed to fill parts of the presentation, as one speaker introduced his talk as "True Confessions, Number Three," and another remarked on the difficulties men faced in reversing their socialization:

> I just want to say that there are these definite problems that men have to deal with and whereas this may sound like some kind of rationalization rap where I'm saying that men are the way we are because that's the way we were brought up, that's true. But first we have to recognize that there are no inherent dominant forces in men. In other societies, there are men that play different roles and women have different roles. The training institutions are where these role differentiations really develop. So recognize the problems and struggle for more equality and more egalitarian relationships.

In general, the evening brought out some insights which were made even more important by the fact that they were presented by men. Here are some selected quotes from the panel:

On Changes: The mood of the country reflects a consciousness of the right of everyone to enjoy democratic freedoms, not from the standpoint of everyone being able to do his or her own thing to the detriment of someone else, but from the standpoint of the fact that outmoded social pressures shouldn't dictate the kind of role a person plays in society or a person's free access to the benefits of the society.

On "Sexploitation": In our society, we have this money exchange or barter system where you put a value on everything. When we find ourselves in that situation, sooner or later someone's going to put a price on physical characteristics and then you come down to sexploitation. And this works both ways. I think that the man in

238

Harris and Frank suit is the same image as the woman in the whatever Paris fashion. You concentrate on physical characteristics and things like that and get hung up on looking good rather than being something—like yourself.

On Male Chauvinism: In this sense, women have become sort of a commodity, sort of like a car. Like when the cat buys a car, he says, "Wow, I've got this car now, and it's looking good, and I run it into the ground or I do what I want with it, 'cause it's my car." And the same sort of thing happens with women, I think (now remember, guys, this is all general), in the sense that personal relationships tend to become dehumanized. Even movement men whom we can all count on to just mimic the demands that are made by the women's liberation struggles, are guilty of not practising what they preach. So in a way, this kind of makes them a little more insidious, definitely hypocrites, because you never know where they stand. To press for the democratic rights of women on the one hand and then turn around and say that you can only relate to really fine-looking sisters is really a contradiction.

On Mother: My mother always wanted to do just about everything for me; like when I was a junior applying to colleges, she wanted to type my applications. She wanted to read them and proofread them. Or even when I was going to college, she wanted to pack my bags for me, and she'd say, "Here, why don't you take these with you?" One thing I always kind of objected to about that was it didn't allow me to develop as a person and kind of make my own mistakes—like maybe buy really bad clothes and then learn from that; I just felt as an individual I would have had more opportunity to learn and experiment and to learn by making mistakes if my mother hadn't been so conscious about wanting everything to be perfect or wanting everything to be just right. And finally, I just asked myself, "Why does she behave that way?" I came to the conclusion that her children were really the most important thing in her life, that this was the whole way she affirmed her life as a person—this was meaning in life for her. She saw her son go out and do this and this and this, and she'd say, "Did you hear about my son?" This was what was important for her in life. Probably this was the only

outlet she had for expressing her personality. I see the liberation of women as being a good thing, allowing women other ways of fulfilling themselves.

On Liberated Marriage: So what do I mean by "liberated marriage?" To put it succinctly, I think it means a relationship based on shared responsibilities and the recognition of a relationship based on equality. Because of the disadvantageous position of women in the traditional marriage relationship, they are the most aware of the changes that are necessary towards a liberated marriage and will be the ones that will consistently demand these changes. On the other hand, because men enjoy the benefits of a traditional relationship much more than women, their consciousness tends to be pretty low and they're the ones that have to be educated to this new concept.

SUMMING UP

The Asian Woman course and the Asian American Studies curriculum and program in general must struggle to see themselves within the larger framework of the university and society. The Asian Woman course in particular has emerged out of a history of struggle against the tendency to react to or rebel against the most immediate sources of oppression; that is, "getting down" on every sexist man to the exclusion of study and understanding of the broad situation. This type of mistake has led to seeing men as the main enemy, or as in some Asian American Studies courses, seeing white people as the main enemy.

In the coming years, the struggles to deepen the roots of Asian American Studies in an increasingly hostile university environment will continue to sharpen and grow. Asian Woman courses and instructors have been criticized as "unqualified" or "not up to standard." Courses are being cut or remolded to the more traditional "establishment" forms. Increased communications and exchanges among Asian Woman course instructors on different campuses have attempted to improve the direction and content of the courses. Much of these efforts, however, have been more descriptive than analytical, more mechanical than political. In order to sustain the political impact of the Asian Woman course and the Asian American Studies program in the years to come, a great deal of conscious study and theoretical work remains to be done—through reading, investigation, and summarizing the work of recent years. Developing a sound and unified analysis and strategy that extends beyond "reacting and rebelling" is the clear priority of the coming period of time. ★

LAU v. NICHOLS:
History of a Struggle for Equal and Quality Education

BY L. LING-CHI WANG

On January 21, 1974, the Supreme Court of the United States decided in the case of *Lau v. Nichols* that the failure of the San Francisco Unified School District (SFUSD) to provide special assistance to nearly 2,000 Chinese American students who do not speak English denies them "a meaningful opportunity to participate in the public educational program" and thus violates regulations and guidelines issued by the Secretary of Health, Education and Welfare (HEW) pursuant to Section 601 of the Civil Rights Act of 1964.[1] Recognizing the special educational needs and rights of limited English-speaking students for the first time in the history of the United States, the Supreme Court held that:

> ...there is no equality of treatment merely by providing students with the same facilities, text-books, teachers, and curriculum; for students who do not understand English are effectively fore-closed from any meaningful education.

To expect limited English-speaking students to know English before they can effectively participate in the educational program, the Court declared, "is to make a mockery of public education." Addressing itself directly to the plight confronting non-English-speaking students, the Supreme Court Justices unanimously concluded, "We know that those who do not understand English are certain to find their classroom experience wholly incomprehensible and in no way meaningful." The Supreme Court sent the case back to the U.S. District Court in San Francisco

with an order that "appropriate relief" be fashioned by the SFUSD and that it be subject to the approval of the court.

The purposes of this article are to trace briefly the history and issues leading to the Supreme Court victory, and the ensuing community struggle first, for the right to fashion the "appropriate relief" mandated by the Supreme Court and secondly, for the right to have quality bilingual-bicultural education for students of all language and cultural backgrounds.[2] The long stuggle for the right to an equal and quality education and for community control of the school provides valuable insight and understanding into the nature and working of American legal and educational institutions and gives clues to future strategies for bringing about institutional and systemic changes in America.

HISTORY OF LAU V. NICHOLS

On March 25, 1970, Kinney Kinmon Lau and 12 non-English-speaking Chinese American students, over half of them American-born, filed suit in Federal District Court in San Francisco against Alan Nichols, president of the San Francisco Board of Education on behalf of nearly 3,000 Chinese-speaking students.[3] Their class action suit alleged that Chinese-speaking children were not receiving the kind of education to which they are entitled in the SFUSD because they needed special help in English. The denial of such an education, according to their parents, "doomed them to become dropouts and to join the rolls of the unemployed."[4] The plaintiffs asked the Federal District Court to order the Board of Education to provide special English language classes with bilingual teachers, asserting that laws enacted by both Congress and the California State Legislature demonstrated the need for bilingual teachers. Without bilingual teachers, the plaintiffs contended that even special instruction in English would be a fruitless gesture: students would merely parrot teachers rather than learn English.

The suit was not developed in a vacuum; it was the last resort after all known channels for seeking equal educational opportunity had been exhausted. For a number of years, the Chinese American community had tried innumerable meetings, heated negotiations, documented studies, peaceful and violent demonstrations, and concrete proposals to rectify the educational deprivation suffered by the limited English-speaking Chinese American students.[5] While the number of new immigrants entering the school system continued to escalate each year by leaps and bounds since 1962, these good faith efforts of the Chinese American community resulted invariably in token gestures. For example, no formal special language program existed in the elementary and secondary schools before 1966. In that year, the first pilot program of teaching English as a Second Language (ESL) was established. The program provided 40 minutes of ESL class each day for *some* of the limited English-speaking Chinese students. For the remainder of the day, they were required to attend regular classes taught only in English and compete helplessly and hopelessly with their English-speaking peers in all subject areas.[6] In San Francisco, this approach is known as the "ESL-pullout" or "one-a-day ESL bitter pill."

In the following year, the school district identified 2,456 limited English-speaking Chinese students and appropriated $88,016 to establish hastily a Chinese ESL Program, misnamed the Chinese Bilingual Education Program, staffed mostly by non-bilingual ESL teachers. Again, many Chinese-speaking students did not even get the minimal benefit of one ESL class a day. In 1968-69, the budget for the program was increased to $280,469, but the on-going ESL program was found to be "woefully inadequate" according to SFUSD's own report which was issued in February 1969. That report with the pretentious title of *The Education Equality/Quality Report* indicated that the program lacked ESL teachers (only 14 full-time teachers in elementary schools and four in junior high), an inadequate in-service teachers training program and a "language specialist on the administrative level to design an effective program that can be implemented in an orderly manner throughout all grade levels." The report also noted that ESL materials were "virtually non-existent beyond the beginning level" and that there was no personnel assigned to develop materials and curriculum. In spite of such mild self-indictment, the report dealt exclusively with ESL classes: it made no reference to the use of Chinese language as a medium of instruction and the need for the Chinese-speaking students at all grade levels to learn and progress academically in other subject areas in a language they understood while they were in the process of acquiring English-language proficiency. Worse yet, the ESL program is always seen as an added program to the existing, regular school curricula, hence an added burden.

Illustrative of the indifferent attitude in San Francisco was the school district's acknowledgement of the following facts found by the Federal Court on May 28, 1970:[7]

1. 2,856 Chinese-speaking students in SFUSD needed special instruction in English.
2. Of these, 1,790 received no special help or instruction at all, not even the 40-minute ESL a day.
3. Of the remaining 1,066 who did receive some help, 623 received help on a part-time basis and 433 on a full-time basis.
4. Only 260 of the 1,066 receiving special instruction in English were taught by bilingual teachers.

Only one-fourth of the limited English-speaking Chinese students were getting help in English, most by non-bilingual teachers, and little or no help in other subject matters. Students were placed arbitrarily into classrooms by ages, irrespective of English-language proficiency and achievement in subject areas. The negative and demoralizing effects of this repressive approach was fully recognized by the school district. In a report issued in 1969, the school district freely admitted:

> When these (Chinese-speaking) youngsters are placed in grade levels according to their ages and are expected to compete with their English-speaking peers, they are frustrated by their inability to understand the regular work....For these children, the lack of English means poor performance in school. The secondary student is almost inevitably doomed to be a dropout and another unemployable in the ghetto.[8]

Paralleling the deteriorating situation in the school district was the accelerating juvenile delinquency rates in the 1960's in the Chinese community. According to data released by the San Francisco Police Department, the juvenile delinquency rate for Chinese between 1964 and 1969 rose by 600%.[9] The school data admitted openly in the Federal Court and the police records clearly and directly related to the plight of these students.

During the District Court hearing on *Lau v. Nichols,* the school district acknowledged the grave needs of these children to receive special instruction, but vigorously contended that such needs did not constitute legal rights because they were provided the same educational setting offered to other children throughout the district. A bilingual education program, according to the attorney representing the school district, would be offered only "gratuitously," as personnel permitted, rather than as a matter of right and duty.

In its decision, the Federal District Court agreed with the school district and denied the limited English-speaking Chinese students any relief.[10] The Court expressed sympathy for the Chinese American students, but concluded that their rights to an education and to equal educational opportunities had been satisfied as "they received the same education made available on the same terms and conditions to the other tens of thousands of students in the SFUSD." It is important to point out that, though the Chinese American students contended that the "surface equality" of identical textbooks, teachers and classrooms afforded no education to non-English-speaking children, the Federal District Court ruled that the school district had no legal duty to rectify this situation.

The Chinese-speaking students appealed the decision to the U.S. Court of Appeals for the Ninth Circuit.[11] Their contention that the lower court decision should be reversed was supported by the United States Government, which filed an *amicus curie* (friend of the court) brief. However, a three-judge panel, in a two to one decision, affirmed the lower court order on January 8, 1973 and accepted the school district's argument that its responsibility to non-English-speaking children "extends no further than to provide them with the same facilities, textbooks, teachers and curriculum as is provided to other children in the district."[12] The panel further observed that the problems suffered by the Chinese American children were "not the result of law enacted by the state....but the result of deficiency created by (the children) themselves in failing to learn the English language."

The implications of the appellate court decision are devastating: "surface equality" was ruled adequate and legal and the language deficiency of the non-English-speakers, as if they knew *no* language at all and possessed neither culture nor knowledge, was self-created and self-imposed. In other words, if they happened to be Native Americans, Chicanos, or immigrants from non-English-speaking countries, they were entitled to attend schools, but they had no right to expect the same educational benefits as the English speakers.

Faced with this disastrous decision, the Chinese American students petitioned the U.S. Supreme Court to take their case and reverse the appellate decision. On June 12, 1973, the Supreme Court granted the petition to hear the case and oral arguments were heard on December 10, 1973, again with the support of the U.S. Government and a number of national organizations representing educators and ethnic communities.[13]

Finally, on January 21, 1974, after nearly four long years of litigation, the U.S. Supreme Court delivered its *unanimous* decision which directly refuted both the position and language of the lower courts:

> ...There is no equality of treatment merely by providing students with the same facilities, textbooks, teachers and curriculum; for students who do not understand English are effectively foreclosed from any meaningful education.

The limited English-speaking students, according to the Supreme Court decision, must be able to participate effectively in the classroom and they must receive an education that is both "meaningful" and "comprehensible." This could be achieved only through bilingual-bicultural education.

The significance of the *Lau v. Nichols* decision nation-wide was immediately felt.[14] Not since the *Brown v. Board of Education* decision in 1954 which outlawed school segregation was there such an important decision on education handed down by the Supreme Court. There are, according to the U.S. Office of Education, approximately five million school children in the United States covered by the decision.[15] Congress immediately amended in August 1974 the bilingual education law by expanding Federal involvement in bilingual education[16] and the U.S. Department of H.E.W. announced in January 1975 its plan to conduct *Lau* enforcement activities nation-wide to assure equal educational opportunity for the limited English-speaking students.[17] Nine "*Lau* Centers" were established under Title IV of the Civil Rights Act of 1964 to assist school districts across the United States to develop bilingual educational programs to meet the *Lau* mandate.[18] To help identify the precise number of children of limited English-speaking ability, H.E.W. initiated a project in June 1975 to develop language survey instruments.[19] States such as Massachusetts, Illinois, Texas, New Jersey and Colorado now have state laws mandating bilingual education for students of limited English-speaking ability.[20] To date, all court decisions which have applied and interpreted *Lau v. Nichols* have all concluded that *Lau* requires bilingual-bicultural education to overcome the deprivations suffered by the limited English-speaking children.[21] Similarly, in a first nation-wide report on bilingual-bicultural education, the U.S. Commission on Civil Rights urged on May 13, 1975 that bilingual-bicultural education be provided for students of limited English-speaking ability.[22]

Beyond the impact on public education, the *Lau* decision has long-range legal implications on both the effectiveness and quality of government-sponsored social and legal services now provided to non-English-speakers across the nation. For example, the new Voters Rights Act of 1975 cited *Lau v. Nichols* as one of the bases for extending voting rights to non-English-speaking citizens.[23] Other issues will undoubtedly follow in the near future.

With a decision as far-reaching and significant as *Lau v. Nichols* on the future of education for limited English-speaking children, one naturally expected the SFUSD, the defendant in the case, to respond promptly and creatively to the educational needs of children from various language and cultural backgrounds, especially when the school district now had a chance to reorder its priorities and develop a meaningful educational plan in response to the Supreme Court mandate. As mentioned above, the Court remanded the case back to the Federal District Court in San Francisco and the SFUSD was expected to submit an "appropriate" educational plan for court approval. Unfortunately, the SFUSD acted as if it were under no court order for a long time. When confronted by communities in San Francisco to respond, it reacted with arrogance and contempt. It is to this phase of community struggle that we now turn.

COMMUNITY STRUGGLE FOR THE RIGHT TO FASHION REMEDY

Perhaps the most important educational and political development in San Francisco after the Supreme Court remanded the case back to the Federal District Court was the long struggle between the entrenched and unyielding school administration and the increasingly politicized minority communities over initially, *who* should be responsible for drawing up the "appropriate relief" plan mandated by the Court and subsequently, *what* is educationally and legally "appropriate" and "effective." The stuggle was predicated on the desire of the communities to have some control over the education of their children and a prevailing distrust of the school administration and Federal District Court's ability to define what was educationally important to their children. On the one hand, the school administration wanted to provide only the minimum required, meaning least costly, and above all, no parental and community input or interference if possible. On the other hand, the minority language communities in San Francisco, long alienated by a white-dominated political process and an irresponsive school bureaucracy, had no confidence in the school administration's competence and willingness to formulate an effective plan that would meet the educational and cultural needs of their children. What follows therefore is a sketch of how San Francisco community organizations and parents fought the school administration by forming a strong coalition of minority communities and won the right to fashion a city-wide master plan for the education of the students from different language and cultural backgrounds, what they eventually defined as the most appropriate and effective response to the *Lau* mandate, and how they collectively won what was generally conceded to be a political impossibility for any minority group in San Francisco, the approval of the master plan by the Board of Education, the governing body long plagued by factionalism, indecisiveness and ineffectiveness.

In order to understand the gradual unfolding of the remedy phase of the *Lau v. Nichols* decision, it is essential to begin with a brief description of the San Francisco situation in terms of its diverse but declining population, overall language needs of its school population and the school administration's response prior to the *Lau* decision.

A. School Population Characteristics

San Francisco as a city has long been known to be cosmopolitan. In addition to her Italian and Irish populations which long dominated San Francisco politics, there are numerous white ethnic groups and a rapidly increasing minority population. Like many old cities in the U.S., the population of San Francisco has been decreasing since 1950. Population figures of the city for the last three decades are: 775,357 in 1950, 740,310 in 1960 and 715,674 in 1970. Paralleling the population decline has been the rapid disappearance of manufacturing industries and sharp increases in white collar and service occupations, reflecting the new role of San Francisco as a headquarter for large corporations and a tourist/convention favorite.[24] According to one estimate, San Francisco had a population of 681,200 in 1973. The ethnic composition in that year is as follows:[25]

Ethnic Composition of the City of San Francisco, 1973

	Number	% of Total
White	361,300	53.0%
Asian American	117,500	17.2
Chinese	64,800	9.5
Filipino	38,000	5.6
Japanese	11,800	1.7
Korean	2,900	0.4
Black	99,000	14.5
Spanish surname	90,400	13.3
Other non-white	9,900	1.5
Native American	3,100	0.5

In absolute numbers and percentages, the white population has been declining rapidly while the opposite trend prevails for the minority groups, especially the Asian groups. In spite of these trends, the white population continues to have almost full control of the city's elected offices, appointed positions, and bureaucracies.[26]

A look at the school population reveals the same trends. In the 1973-1974 school years, the year of the Supreme Court decision, the SFUSD had a total student enrollment of 78,023, kindergarten through twelfth grade, and its racial distribution was as follows:[27]

Ethnic Composition of the San Francisco Unified School District, 1973-74

	Number	% of Total
White	21,001	26.9%
Asian American	19,728	25.3
Chinese	12,315	15.8
Filipino	5,715	7.3
Japanese	1,304	1.7
Korean	394	0.5
Black	23,794	30.5
Spanish surname	11,131	14.3
Other non-white	2,103	2.7
Native American	266	0.3

Among the "Other non-whites" are Samoans, Arabs, Hindi, Burmese, Vietnamese, Pacific Islanders and others. This means that 73.1% of the students in the school district are from minority backgrounds, as compared to five years ago when the school district had only 58.9% minorities. In spite of such high percentage of minority school population, the administration of the SFUSD continues to be totally controlled by whites. Of the seven persons on the Board of Education, only two are from minority backgrounds, one Black and one Spanish-surname. This political reality of course has a tremendous bearing on the struggle for equal and quality education for students of limited English-speaking ability, as we shall soon see.

B. Limited English-speaking Students in SFUSD

The dramatic decline of white student population and sharp increase of minority students, due largely to Chinese, Filipino and Korean immigration, account for the changing student composition. In fact, court records on *Lau v. Nichols* showed an average net gain of 80 limited English-speaking students per month or 960 a year in 1969-1970. In

1969, the school district reported 5,269 limited English-speaking children. The number increased to 9,084 in 1973, or an increase of 72.4% in four years. Among these 9,084, 3,457 are Chinese, 2,980 Spanish-speaking, 1,519 Filipino, 202 Japanese, 179 Samoans, and 747 other languages.[28] Both immigration policy and government statistics to date point to a continuation of the patterns established since 1965.[29] In other words, the school district must reasonably expect the number of limited English-speaking children to increase steadily at approximately the same rate as in the past ten years.

In spite of this well-established trend, the school district reported a total of 6,511 limited English-speaking students in April 1974, an unexpected and unexplained drop of 29% in one year.[30] According to school data, 2,330 Chinese, 1,860 Spanish-speaking, 1,076 Filipino, 187 Koreans, 151 Samoans, 124 Japanese and 782 other languages made up the 6,511 figure. Subsequently, in a testimony before the Ways and Means Committee of the California State Assembly on December 10, 1974, Raymond del Portillo, Director of Bilingual Education Division of the SFUSD, gave new data which further reduced the 6,511 total to 4,911 limited English-speaking students, representing a net reduction of almost 100% between 1973 and 1974.[31] The unexplained reduction from 9,084 in 1973 cast serious doubts on both the results and methods of the annual state-mandated survey of students of limited English-speaking ability and raised questions on the intention and political implications of the reduction.[32] A closer examination of the raw data indicated that the initial computation in May 1974 yielded a figure slightly above 9,000—a figure more consistent with the well-established trend of the previous few years.

The conflicting figures underscore the importance of developing a more objective, reliable yardstick to conduct the annual census. For the time being, the method and figures are highly suspect. A check on the enumeration methods revealed that figures were arrived at by totalling the subjective judgment of some 2,500 classroom teachers, a method of questionable standardized character and scientific value. A culturally unbiased and linguistically sound device for detecting language proficiency must be developed to assess those students and to make precise determination of student placement and to devise the appropriate educational program best suited to their needs. If such a standardized device or test could not be formulated for each of the language groups in the near future, the increasingly favored method, and recently incorporated into the new Federal law on bilingual education, ought to be utilized. Instead of relying solely on individual teachers' impressions as has been done in San Francisco and elsewhere, a series of simple questions on each child's home language is used to provide the preliminary identification of his or her language

proficiency.[33] A more thorough linguistic and academic assessment then follows. This method, in fact, was used by the SFUSD in 1972 and the outcome showed that there were 20,000 students whose primary languages were other than English.[34]

C. District Efforts to Meet the Needs in 1974

What was the SFUSD's response to the needs identified prior to the development of a new remedy as a result of Lau? In this section, these efforts will be examined in terms of the educational programs set up, the allocation of district funds for these programs, and the hiring of qualified bilingual personnel.

Regarding the educational programs available to limited English-speaking students, the Spring 1974 survey indicated the following:[35]

Table 3

	ESL	BBE*	No Help	Total
Chinese	1,138	193	1,000	2,331
Spanish-speaking	604	454	802	1,860
Pilipino	524	49	503	1,076
Japanese	70	4	50	124
Korean	144	2	41	187
Samoan	50	2	98	150
Other Languages	423	0	359	782
Total	2,953	704	2,853	6,510

*Bilingual-Bicultural Education

Of the 6,510 limited English-speaking students in 1974, 2,953 were getting the 40-minute ESL Pullout classes a day, and 2,853 were getting no assistance at all. Therefore, of the conservatively estimated 6,510 in 1974, only 704 were getting the full benefit of bilingual-bicultural education programs; the rest were getting either minimal or no benefit whatsoever.

As for the cost of providing these ESL programs for the limited English-speaking students, the following data comes from the Division of Research in March 1974:

Table 4

Administration of Bilingual Office	$ 50,688
Chinese Program	975,122
Spanish Program	948,414
Pilipino Program	283,282
Japanese Program (Bilingual)	40,290
ESL Program at McAteer High	140,338
Total: District Programs	2,438,134
Total: Federal & State Funded Programs	982,391
GRAND TOTAL [All Programs]	$3,420,525

The SFUSD figures on the surface show a substantial increase of expenditures towards the special education of the limited English-speaking students, from $809,168 in 1968-1969 to $2.4 million in 1973-1974, excluding the $982,390 from various State and Federal sources. To the school district, the $2.4 million was an additional cost beyond the funds already allocated for the education of the 6,510 limited English-speaking students. In other words, as long as the 6,510 students were occupying classrooms bodily everyday during school hours, the district was required to provide full-time teachers and other costs for these classrooms regardless of their ability to communicate with and provide an education for these students. Since almost all the teachers present in these classrooms were non-bilingual, it would not be difficult to understand why the U.S. Supreme Court found such classroom experience "wholly incomprehensible and in no way meaningful." In other words, funds were being spent on these students and in these classrooms, but no benefit was being derived from such expenditures.

The $2.4 million spent on hiring administrators and ESL teachers was considered by the school district as *additional costs* or burden, an argument soundly rejected by the Supreme Court. A closer examination of how the district channeled its funds into the various programs reveals that only a small portion of this $2.4 million was spent in support of some of the State and Federally funded bilingual program and the rest was used for hiring of teachers for the ESL Pullout and the ESL-oriented newcomers programs.[36] Such additional ESL teachers were necessary because the regular classroom teachers for the 6,510 students did not know how to teach English as a second language. Simple logic requires us to draw the conclusion that, if the classrooms occupied by the 6,510 limited English-speaking students were assigned bilingual teachers, the Supreme Court would not have found the school district in violation of the rights of these students and there would have been no need to have the floating ESL teachers creating an additional financial burden on the school district.

Whatever funds made available to start any bilingual program in the SFUSD, therefore, have consistently come from non-district sources, as the data from the Division of Research in March 1974 clearly show. For example, the district operated four bilingual-bicultural programs in that year:[37]

Chinese Bilingual Program (1-6): Federal
Chinese Bilingual Program (7-9): State
Spanish Bilingual Program (K-6): Federal
Japanese Bilingual Program (K-3): Fed. & District

The district's contribution to these bilingual programs was limited to one teacher, not necessarily with

bilingual competency, for each Federally or State-funded bilingual class.

It is clear from the above analysis that the SFUSD has no commitment to provide bilingual-bicultural education for students of limited English-speaking ability.[38] The District would set up a bilingual program only on the condition that either the State or the Federal government provides the necessary funds. As a result of such policy, programs are set up not on the basis of needs and sound planning; they are established because certain Federal or State funds for various purposes happen to be available.[39] Programs, therefore, proliferate as funds flow in from different and varying sources and for assorted purposes, and programs may be abruptly terminated if their funding sources dry up.

Closely related to the effectiveness of any program designed for students of limited English-speaking ability is the availability of teachers who can communicate with students in languages they understand. That of course is the heart of education. The need for bilingual/bicultural teachers is self-evident. In 1974, the SFUSD employed more than 10,000 persons, serving its 73,040 students. Five years before that, it had 6,206 employees, serving 93,204 students. Of the 1974 employees, 4,572 are teachers, reflecting a net gain of 174 teachers, from 4,398 in 1969-1970 school year.[40] In terms of teacher-student ratio, this meant one teacher for every 24.5 students, or a drop from 25.4 five years before. As for the ethnic composition of the teaching staff, a recent survey shows the following: 73% White, 11% Black, 5% Spanish-surname, 6% Chinese, 2% Japanese, 2% Filipino and 1% Native American—a completely reverse proportion to the ethnic composition of the student population.

On account of the declining student enrollment in recent years, virtually no new teachers were hired in the past few years, except those hired with funds from Federal and State sources. Herein lies the difficulty of recruiting and hiring qualified bilingual teachers desperately needed to provide the kind of education needed by students of limited English-speaking ability. With most school districts in the nation facing virtual bankruptcy and being forced to lay off teachers, San Francisco is no exception; most of the minority teachers recruited in the past few years undoubtedly will be the first to be let go. This will have adverse effects on the few bilingual programs now operating in the SFUSD. It would indeed be a tragedy if teachers were to be pitted against minority teachers and communities.

This sketchy program and budget analysis demonstrates clearly a serious contradiction between district policy and action. On March 16, 1972, the Board of Education committed itself to provide bilingual-bicultural education to students of limited English-speaking ability.[41] The above review indicates that less than 10% of such students are receiving bilingual-bicultural education, over 30% are getting no help at all, and the remainder (55.3%) are deriving only minimal benefit, one out of six classes a day, through the ESL Pullout program.

Furthermore, the Board, through its budgetary decisions, has consistently failed to commit district funds for bilingual-bicultural education. Instead, it has allowed bilingual-bicultural programs to exist mostly on Federal and State funds. In 1974, the school district contributed less than 3% of its own $148 million budget toward bilingual-bicultural programs. Faced with these glaring contradictions, we must inevitably conclude that the district has thus far assigned a very low priority to the educational needs of children of limited English-speaking ability.

Perhaps the most disturbing part of this analysis is the indifference shown in the budget decisions. The school enrollment dropped 21.6% in the five year period before 1974. However, there was no comparable decline in the number of students of limited English-speaking ability; in fact, that number increased over the same period. Within this same period, the district budget increased from $120 million to $148 million a year, or the cost per student rose a spectacular 58%, from $1,286 to $2,035. If we use a rough estimate of 10,000 limited English-speaking students in the district, the amount of money appropriated for meaningful bilingual education programs in 1974 should have been at least $20 million instead of the $2.4 million cited above. If the students of limited English-speaking ability are not getting the full benefit of public education, as the Supreme Court ruled, then it is clearly the responsibility of the Board to make sure that they do, and to see that district funds are used properly to achieve the kind of educational results expected by the Court.

D. Creation of the Citizens Task Force

With these kinds of political and educational conditions existing in San Francisco, it was not surprising that the communities with most to gain—the Chinese, Filipino, Japanese, Korean and Spanish-speaking communities—greeted the Supreme Court decision with jubilation and great expectation while the San Francisco Board of Education reacted with a typical evasive, non-commital statement and inaction.

In a press statement issued on February 5, 1974, Eugene Hopp, President of the Board of Education, expressed "hope" to work with the community on a program to be submitted for approval to the Federal District Court. He said that the Board "will probably propose a Committee of the Whole hearing to provide a means of communication for the parents." The district staff, according to Hopp, was directed to proceed with "a study of the problem along with an inventory of the present program and then develop a program to present to court." The hearing did not

take place until January 28, 1975, a year later; even then, it was used as a parliamentary maneuver to delay a decision on the master plan submitted to the Board on January 7, 1975 by the Citizens Task Force on Bilingual Education. However, the study and program mentioned in the press release was initiated immediately under strict secrecy and revealed on April 15, 1974 at a meeting of a group of 44 parents and citizens called in by Raymond Del Portillo, Director of Bilingual Education, to rubber stamp the proposed program by the district staff. Needless to say, no community group, parents or teachers were consulted in the formulation of the program. In fact, the school administration ignored any community offers of assistance or input. To make the situation worse and more divisive, someone was spreading a rumor that the Chinese community was trying to use the court decision to seize control of the district's bilingual funds and programs.[42] The rumor greatly incited fear among the Spanish-speaking parents active in the cause of bilingual education and effectively frustrated various ethnic groups from working together for a common cause.[43]

The first community organization to take an active part in leading the fight for full community control of the formulation of the plan was Chinese for Affirmative Action (CAA), a community-based civil rights organization with extensive experience in dealing with education and employment problems facing the Chinese in San Francisco.[44] Through a series of consultations and meetings within the Chinese community, a two-page position paper was developed by early February 1974 and formally transmitted to the Board of Education on February 15.[45] The position paper contained a list of concrete school problems related to the *Lau v. Nichols* decision and a series of recommendations to the Board of Education for consideration. Essentially, the heart of these recommendations was a proposal that the Board apppoint a Citizens Task Force on Bilingual Education "to develop a city-wide master plan for bilingual education for the purposes of (a) complying with the order of the U.S. Supreme Court, (b) submitting it to the U.S. District Court for approval and (c) meeting the educational needs of *all* limited English-speaking students otherwise not covered by the original order."[46] According to the proposal, the Task Force would not be made up of just Chinese Americans, but representatives from the various languages in San Francisco. The position paper further outlined the responsibilities of the Citizens Task Force.

The Board of Education, not surprisingly, ignored the letter. On March 19, 1974, another letter was sent to the Board of Education, reiterating the recommendations and at the same time requesting information on "the specific steps the Board planned to take to implement the Supreme Court mandate."[47] Again the letter was ignored.[48] This perhaps is the most arrogant expression of the Board's utter contempt of community organizations.

It is important to point out here that CAA did not work in isolation. Over a thousand copies of the position paper were sent to individuals and community organizations throughout the city for support and endorsement. In addition, CAA also sent letters to both state and Federal government officials, urging their support and intervention to assure community participation in the planning process and quality education in the final plan. By early May, or three months after the *Lau* decision, many community organizations and civic leaders had endorsed the recommendations and sent letters to the Board of Education urging the same. Among them were: the San Francisco Human Rights Commission, Coalition for Effective Schools, Asian Education Caucus and some school district bilingual education advisory committees. In addition, almost all of the state and federal elected officials representing San Francisco and many television and radio stations joined in a concerted effort to urge the Board to set up the Citizens Task Force. The only opposition came from a very small handful of high-level school administrators who stubbornly hung on to the secret plan then under way and flatly refused to deal with the broadly supported community proposal.

The demand of parents and community organizations received unexpected, indirect support from the California State Superintendent of Public Instruction, Dr. Wilson Riles, who told the press in Washington, D.C., that the performance of the San Francisco school system was "an embarrassment" to him as the head of the California school system.[49] Riles was referring to the fact that the San Francisco school district spent more money per capita than most school districts in California, but its reading and achievement levels were consistently the lowest in the state.[50] His remark received extensive headline coverage in San Francisco for a few days and generated public outcries for improvement of the school system.[51] The bad publicity lent credence to the community demand for the creation of a Citizens Task Force and for some voice in the future of the children in San Francisco.

As outside and city-wide pressures mounted rapidly and the administration tried frantically to complete its secret plan, the April 15 meeting was suddenly called by Del Portillo. Forty-four parents and citizens known to be interested in bilingual education were asked to "advise" the district on "the overall planning and coordination of the programs that (would) serve the needs of non-English-speaking and limited English-speaking students in San Francisco."[52] At that meeting, the invited citizens, already angry about the poor performance of their schools and the Board's indifference and arrogance, were told that they constituted the "Special Advisory Committee on *Lau v. Nichols*" and were presented a 53-page "preliminary Report to Dr. Lane DeLara on Bilingual/ESL/Newcomer Staff Response to Implications of *Lau v. Nichols*," dated April 3, 1974.[53] The report, prepared by an Anglo administrator, included a narrow interpretation of the Supreme Court decision, descriptions and costs of some 15 existing ESL/Bilingual programs, a series of recommendations, and a timeline which anticipated the presentation of a final plan to the Board of Education on May 14, 1974—29 days after the April 15 meeting!—for adoption. The plan, put together in utmost secrecy, essentially called for the maintenance and slight expansion of the *status quo* to meet the *Lau* mandate. According to the timeline, the Director of Bilingual Education was to submit the whole package to the Superintendent Steven Morena on April 26, eleven days after the April 15 meeting. In other words, the parents and citizens were invited that night to rubber-stamp the plan prepared in secret by a white school administrator. It soon became clear to most of those present at the meeting that the complete silence that greeted the community proposal was part of an overall school strategy to keep parents and communities affected by the *Lau* decision out of the planning process. In fact, according to reliable sources inside the school administration, the strategy further called for the same delaying tactics so effectively employed by segregated school districts across the nation in their response to the *Brown v. Board of Education* decision of 1954. The 44 parents and citizens were called in to legitimatize the proposed plan. Many felt insulted by the treatment accorded them by the school administration.[54]

After a long discussion and some serious conflicts among the various language groups, the majority of those invited eventually decided to reject the responsibility assigned the group by the school administration and demanded instead that the Board of Education reconstitute the multilingual-multiracial group into a viable Citizens Task Force charged with the responsibility of developing a master plan to respond to the *Lau* decision.

Because of the Board's failure to respond to the community proposal, a coalition of community organizations, prior to the April 15 meeting, arranged a press conference for April 16 to publicly protest the Board's continuing disregard of the educational needs of at least 10,000 students of limited English-speaking ability and to reiterate the demand for a Citizens Task Force to develop the master plan. During the press conference, CAA specifically made the following charges against the Board of Education:[55]

1. The Board has taken no action and made no plan to effectively meet the mandate of the Supreme Court.
2. The Board, to date, has made no attempt on its own to solicit ideas and inputs from parents and concerned citizens as to how the

Board could best meet the mandate of the Court.

3. The Board has so far ignored innovative ideas and concrete proposals from concerned citizens and parents groups.

4. The Board has been deliberately kept ignorant on what its own staff is doing or not doing and has been effectively shut off from activities at State and Federal levels relative to the *Lau* decision.[56]

5. The Board has even failed to comply with a simple State Education Code, requiring the District to conduct annual census of students of limited and non-English-speaking background by April 1 each year.[57]

6. The Board's inaction already has caused the school system to lose a rare opportunity to seek available Federal funds for bilingual education and has placed the District in a position most vulnerable to lose all its existing Federally funded programs due to non-compliance with Title VI of the Civil Rights Act of 1964 and the order of the U.S. Supreme Court.[58]

CAA further warned that it might seek a contempt citation against the Board of Education and/or sue the School District for damage. The press conference was covered extensively by local media.

On April 22, the Clerk of Federal Judge Lloyd Burke unexpectedly phoned the Board of Education and conveyed the judge's intention to have a court hearing on June 28 on *Lau v. Nichols*. In addition, the judge asked that any plans for complying with the Supreme Court order be filed with the Clerk of the District Court "no later than 10 days prior to the date of the Court hearing," namely June 18, 1974. The surprise phone call led George Kreuger, representing the School Board, to demand that "whatever plan is to be presented to the Court" be submitted to his office no later than June 3. This meant that the school district had only a few weeks to complete, review and adopt a plan before June 3. The task became particularly difficult when the citizens group put together by Del Portillo on April 15 refused to be used by the school district and demanded full participation in the formulation of the master plan.

As pressure continued to build from all sides, the U.S. Department of Health, Education and Welfare on April 9 asked the U.S. Department of Justice to represent the U.S. Government to intervene as a party plaintiff in Burke's Court in San Francisco on the ground that the outcome of the San Francisco case would have national implications. A motion to intervene was filed in May and Judge Burke promptly scheduled a hearing on the motion for May 17, creating a crisis situation for the school administration.[59] Furthermore, the school district needed to have some kind of response to the motion before the Court by May 17 instead of the originally scheduled June 28 hearing.

It was largely due to these pressures that the Board finally allowed a resolution creating a Citizens Task Force to appear on its agenda and reluctantly approved it on May 14, 1974. According to the resolution, the Citizens Task Force on Bilingual Education was to develop "a master plan for bilingual education with special emphasis being given to designing a program in response to the *Lau v. Nichols* decision."[60] The resolution specifically called for cooperative effort between the Task Force and the Office of the Superintendent in the development of the master plan. As we shall see later, the Superintendent misguided the Task Force, his staff, and the attorneys representing the Board, the U.S. Government and the plaintiffs by rewarding their good faith and hard work with contempt and insults.

At the same Board meeting on May 14, the Board also authorized $15,000 to retain the Center for Applied Lingustics "to provide technical assistance in the preparation of a master plan to be presented to the Board and the Court in the case of the *Lau v. Nichols* decision."[61]

The two resolutions adopted by the Board proved to be a life-saver for the school district in the May 17 hearing before Judge Burke. During the May 17 hearing, the Judge granted the Government's motion to intervene and approved an agreement reached by the attorneys representing all parties that the Board-created Citizens Task Force would develop the master plan cooperatively with the Superintendent's Office, Center for Applied Lingusitics, plaintiffs and the U.S. Government. The Judge further cancelled the June 28 court date indefinitely as long as all parties were working cooperatively in good faith.[62] Another court date would be set when the master plan was ready for court review.

The four-month struggle for control over the development of the master plan finally came to an end with a victory for the communities and parents in San Francisco. That of course was just the beginning of an uphill battle. For the next eight months, the Citizens Task Force on Bilingual Education worked hard and cooperatively with the staff of the Superintendent and the Center for Applied Linguistics to come up with a 700-page master plan for bilingual-bicultural education, as mandated by the Board resolution and approved by the District Court. When the plan was completed and transmitted to the Superintendent, he first publicly disclaimed any responsibility to the formulation of the plan and then attempted to prevent the approval of the plan by the Board. When that became impossible, he altered and mutilated the plan to the point of totally destroying it. Once again, the parents and communities found themselves in a fight against the Superintendent and the Board to restore the full master plan. Finally, a compromised version of the master plan was approved by the Board on March 25, 1975 and its implementation was set for September 1975.

In the next two sections, we shall describe first the work of the Citizens Task Force and then the struggle with the Superintendent and his deputy, Lane De Lara.

E. Work of the Citizens Task Force

Following the decision of the Board of Education, the Superintendent appointed fifty parents and citizens from the entire cross-section of the San Francisco community to the Task Force. Not only were the Chinese, Filipino, Japanese and Spanish-speaking communities significantly represented, the white and black communities were also included among the appointees. In addition, to assure continuous input from the Board of Education, each Board member named a personal representative to the Task Force, pursuant to the same resolution establishing the Task Force.

With the consent of the Superintendent's Office, the Task Force decided in June to reconstitute itself to increase its effectiveness and efficiency and to assure fair and adequate representation by all parties and communities concerned with the plight of the students from different language and cultural backgrounds. The reorganization called for five representatives from each of the Chinese, Filipino, Japanese and Spanish-speaking communities and provisions for five additional seats for representatives of other language groups, such as Samoan, Korean, Hindi, etc., not included among the original fifty approved by the Superintendent.[62] Of the five from each language group, two were to be parents with children in existing bilingual programs, one parent with a child in the SFUSD and two representatives of the language community at large. Unfortunately, despite active solicitation by the Task Force, only one of the five vacant seats for other languages was filled. Also, only six of the seven Board members appointed their representatives to the Task Force. Each Task Force member was allowed to designate an alternate. The Task Force also elected Richard Cerbatos, a Filipino American parent, to be its chairman.

The Task Force, therefore, had a total membership of twenty-seven. Even though the Task Force was created to address itself solely to the needs of limited English-speaking students in the SFUSD as required by the U.S. Supreme Court, the composition of the Task Force reflected in fact the ethnic composition of the total enrollment and displayed a kind of sensitivity normally not shared by the dominant white society.[63]

Two types of committees were formed within the Task Force. First, there were ethnic or language caucuses designed to deal with the particular needs and interests of each language or cultural group and to facilitate a direct link between the Task Force and each of the language communities. These caucuses held neighborhood public meetings to assess educational needs of their communities and to establish goals and objectives within each language community.[64] These meetings conducted by the caucuses became a vital means of community education and mobilization, both indispensable for the successful struggle for bilingual-bicultural education against the school administration.

The second type of committee on the Task Force performed many concrete tasks throughout the planning process. For example, each report or document prepared for the Task Force by the Center for Applied Linguistics was first scrutinized by such a committee and then brought before the Task Force with recommendations for further scrutiny and approval. Sometimes, the Task Force approved somthing in principle and authorized one of these committees to work out the details. Without exception, each of these committees was represented by at least one person from each language caucus. The task-oriented committee eventually became an effective tool of the Task Force for dealing with specific problems related to the master plan, such as school integration, facility utilization, school personnel, budget, etc.[65]

Besides the four language caucuses and the task-oriented committees, a Steering Committee, also consisting of one representative from each caucus, was set up to provide planning directions and strategies, to represent the Task Force in various capacities, including public relations, to develop preliminary policy recommendations and to carry out the mandates of the Task Force. Without exception, all decisions of the Steering Committee were subject to the final approval of the full Task Force.

Even though all meetings were conducted publicly, the Task Force was particularly concerned about the input of teachers who eventually would have the sole responsibility of implementation of the master plan within each classroom. A Teachers Advisory Committee to the Task Force was set up to promote a formal and continuous basis for active participation of classroom teachers. Many of the active teachers were members of minority teacher organizations and of either the American Federation of Teachers (AFT) or California Teachers Association (CTA). The advisory committee had access to all documents of the Task Force. Teachers were also urged to attend all meetings of the Task Force: a number did with considerable regularity. The full Task Force met regularly once every two weeks with caucus and committee meetings between regular Task Force meetings. Minutes of all meetings were kept and all full Task Force meetings were taped.[66]

The Task Force, of course, had many problems to overcome. To begin with, it was the first time that such a coalition of minority communities had come together to work on a common cause. Prior to this, communities were separated and preoccupied by the school administration through a continuous proliferation of powerless community advisory committees for every little project or program in the school district. The scheme instilled mutual suspicion among minority communities and forced each committee to be protective of its own project or program. It was therefore rather difficult, especially at the beginning, for the Task Force with all major language communities represented to work together without factionalism and suspicion. On numerous occasions, the Task Force almost became another victim of the divide-and-conquer strategy of the school administration. Fortunately, a desire to work for the common good of all facilitated considerable give and take among Task Force members and solidified the coalition as work progressed from month to month. The strong coalition became the most important single factor in the Task Force's subsequent struggle against both the school administration and the Board. Secondly, it took months for the professional staff of the Center for Applied Linguistics and the Citizens Task Force to arrive at a good working relation because of different interests and conflicting expectation.[67] For example, the Center understood its contractual requirement to extend no further than a description of *how* to devise a master plan, while the Task Force expected the consultants to deliver a master plan with specific data on student assignments, teacher and budgetary allocation, curriculum and facilities needed. Thirdly, the district staff assigned to work with the Task Force was never given clear directions, full authority and sufficient resources by the Superintendent. This often created tension between the Task Force and the staff, especially with regard to access to district data considered to be either confidential or controversial.

These were some of the major problems with which the Task Force had to reckon in almost every meeting. But, in the final analysis, the Task Force did succeed in forming a viable coalition of minority communities and managed to work cooperatively with the Center and the Superintendent's staff in completing the master plan for bilingual-bicultural education. The question now is: Will the Superintendent and the Board of Education approve the master plan fashioned by the Task Force with the assistance of the Center and the district staff? Before we answer this question, it is necessary to mention a few words about the substance of the master plan itself.

F. Master Plan for Bilingual-Bicultural Education

In early December 1974, as the planning process was coming to an end, the Task Force, based on the working papers of the Center and projected work to be completed by both the Task Force and the staff of the Superintendent, decided that the master plan would consist of three components:

Component 1: an "Abstract" of the master plan to include not only a detailed summary of the entire master plan, but also the following documents: (a) Description of the work of the Task Force, (b) History and interpretations of the *Lau v. Nichols* decision, (c) Needs assessment and District 68 efforts to date, and (d) Rationale of the master plan.

Component 2: the master plan consists of documents prepared by the Center for Applied Linguistics and revised and approved by the Task Force.[69]

Component 3: implementation or administrative details of the master plan to be completed by the Task Force and the Superintendent's staff before February 25, 1975.[70]

What follows is a concise summary of the master plan without the details of Component 3.

Essentially, the master plan criticizes the existing approaches of the district as "totally inadequate and ineffective" and calls for a comprehensive, full-time bilingual-bicultural education program of the maintenance type for *all* children of limited English-speaking ability.[71] The plan also invites active participation of English-dominant and English-monolingual students to achieve real integration and to promote peer learning in a truly multilingual and multi-cultural setting.[72] The master plan or Component 2, in four volumes, but summarized in 55 pages in the "Abstract," includes chapters on the system, the student, staff training, curriculum and materials, counseling and assessment, community, management, and research and evaluation.[73]

Bilingual-bicultural education is defined as a full-time program of instruction in which two languages, one of which must be English, are used as media of instruction with full appreciation of the history and cultural heritage of these children.[74] The program is also designed to develop and reinforce their self-esteem and to foster a legitimate pride in and development and maintenance of both languages and cultures.[75] Furthermore, the master plan recommends that as many bilingual schools at the elementary and secondary levels as needed for each of the major language groups in San Francisco—Chinese, Filipino, Japanese and Spanish—be established to provide full bilingual-bicultural programming, and to serve as assessment, resource, and training centers for satellite bilingual-bicultural classes in other schools throughout the city. For language groups with small numbers of limited English-speaking students, the master plan recommends that they be provided bilingual support wherever they are enrolled.

This, in essence, is the master plan.

COMMUNITY STRUGGLE FOR APPROVAL OF THE MASTER PLAN

As mentioned above, Component 2 of the master plan prepared by the Center for Applied Linguistics provides only the necessary steps to be taken by the school district to implement a bilingual-bicultural education program: it does not provide details such as prospective time lines for attainment of measurable goals in the development of curriculum, the employment of objective test instruments, the assignment of students, and the full utilization of district bilingual teachers. Obviously no plan is complete without these details; hence Component 3 is necessary. By November 1974, the Task Force recognized that such data must be included in the final plan and must be supplied by the Task Force with fullest cooperation of the Superintendent's top aides. Moreover, in order to achieve implementation of the master plan by fall 1975, it was necessary for the Task Force to have all the details in the plan no later than the end of February 1975 when the budgetary, personnel and programmatic planning process for the following academic year was to begin by the Board of Education.

It was largely due to this dilemma that the Task Force decided in November 1974 that the following steps would be taken to complete the master plan and to have it included in the budgetary deliberation of the Board scheduled in February:[76]

1. Submit the "Abstract" of the master plan or Component 1 to the Superintendent and the Board in early January so that the school district can mobilize its staff to supply the necessary details for the implementation of the plan, and so that additional technical details could be secured for inclusion in Component 3, scheduled to be completed by February 24, 1975.
2. As soon as the Board approved the master plan in principle, the Center for Applied Linguistics would complete the revisions of the working papers and the Task Force would work closely with the Superintendent's top aides to fill in the details of the master plan.
3. The Board of Education to submit the final master plan to the Federal District Court for further scrutiny. (The schedule allowed plenty of time for the Court to examine the plan and to call in expert witnesses to validate the appropriateness of the plan).
4. Upon the approval of the plan by the Board and the District Court, the Task Force would work with district staff to begin preparation for the fall and would conduct extensive community education and preparation to assure parental awareness and participation. (During this time, the monolingual English-speaking students would be actively recruited to participate in the bilingual-bicultural education program).

The above four steps and schedule were considered by the Task Force and the district staff assigned to work with the Task Force to be realistic and workable. When the attorneys for the school district, plaintiffs and the U.S. Government met on December 17, 1974, they too agreed to these same steps subsequently confirmed in a December 31 letter from the U.S. Department of Justice to the school district attorney.[77] Since Del Portillo was designated by the Superintendent to be his personal representative to work with the Task Force and every recommendation, including the above steps, developed by the Task Force met his approval, it was natural for the Task Force to expect no difficulty in following the four steps and meeting the schedule outlined above. That turned out to be a false assumption on the part of the Task Force. In fact, it required even more time, energy, manpower and community pressure to just achieve the first step than the creation of the Task Force. As a result, the Task Force was unable to adhere to the original schedule. What follows is a brief sketch of the struggle that took place after January 9, 1975 when Component 1, an 80-page document, entitled, "Response to the Mandate of *Lau v. Nichols* by the San Francisco Unified School District: An Abstract of the Master Plan for Bilingual-Bicultural Education," was transmitted to both the Superintendent and the Board.

Shortly before the completion of the "Abstract," the Task Force decided that it would be useful to have a preliminary meeting with the Superintendent himself to brief him directly on what to expect from the Task Force and to get his suggestions on how to get the Abstract approved by the Board as fast as possible and how the second step could be best carried out administratively. The meeting took place on January 7 in the Superintendent's Office. It was a friendly meeting and the Superintendent was very pleased with the progress made by the Task Force and his representative, Del Portillo. As for the content of the master plan, he said that as long as Del Portillo had no problem with it, he would have none either. When asked how to best seek the approval of the master plan in principle by the Board, he suggested that the Task Force should include a draft of the resolution it wanted at the time of official delivery of the "Abstract." On the question of getting a headstart on the second step to be taken, the Superintendent volunteered to make arrangements personally for the Task Force: appointments were made for the Task Force to meet with Margerie Levy, Director of Desegregation and Integration, on

January 9, Milton Reiterman, Associate Superintendent of Administration, on January 10 and 14, Lyle Eckert, Director of Budget on January 17 and Fred Kennedy, Director of Personnel on January 22. The Superintendent further agreed to present the "Abstract" to the Board on January 21, the first anniversary of the *Lau v. Nichols* decision and to set February 25 for the completion of the final master plan with all the necessary implementation details to be supplied by those persons with whom he made appointments for the Task Force. As far as the Task Force was concerned, the meeting with the Superintendent was a complete success.

In accordance with the instruction of the Superintendent, the Task Force officially transmitted the "Abstract" of the master plan together with the requested draft of a resolution approving the master plan in principle on January 9 to the Superintendent and the seven members of the Board of Education. The "letter of transmittal" called the master plan "realistic and necessary" and commended "the cooperation and expert assistance rendered by both the staff of the Center for Applied Linguistics and of the Superintendent's Office." The Task Force promised a detailed implementation plan "no later than February 24, 1975" and requested the Superintendent to provide "technical information and clerical support" to complete the planning process on time.

On January 13, the Task Force met again with the Superintendent to discuss the "Abstract" and to work out the procedures and strategy for the Board's approval of the draft resolution prepared by the Task Force and Del Portillo. At this meeting, the Superintendent brought with him his deputy, Lane DeLara. Essentially, the resolution called for the Board to approve the basic concepts embodied in the master plan with the understanding that the detailed master plan would be forthcoming "no later than Feb. 24, 1975." The resolution would also direct the Superintendent "to commit all such departments as will be necessary to work in cooperation with the Bilingual Department to complete the implementation of the master plan." Again, the Superintendent was very pleased with the work of the Task Force and promised the Task Force that he would present the proposed resolution to the Board on January 21 for the first reading and the final reading on January 28.[78] The Task Force told the Superintendent that the communities would turn out en masse on January 28 to support the approval of the resolution. He again repeated his commitment to assist the Task Force in getting the necessary data between then and February 24.

Something drastic, however, happened soon after the January 13 meeting and led the Superintendent to reverse his earlier cooperative posture: he abruptly and unilaterally decided not to present the "Abstract" and the resolution on the January 21 meeting of the Board, even though he repeatedly had promised the Task Force that he would do so. Moreover, he did not even inform the Task Force of his decision. A subsequent telephone conversation with his secretary and a newspaper article in the San Francisco *Examiner* on January 20 indicated that nothing on the master plan would be on the Board's agenda and no plan was underway to present the "Abstract" and the resolution in future Board meetings. Just as peculiar and abrupt was the complete inaccessibility of the Superintendent. It was as if an iron curtain had descended between the Task Force and the Superintendent. Lane DeLara, the Deputy Superintendent, a hardline, anti-bilingual education administrator, became the stone wall separating the Task Force from the Superintendent and from the Board.[79] Del Portillo, now working directly under DeLara, suddenly lost his enthusiasm and effectiveness and became rather inaccessible and uncooperative. There was no mistake that DeLara was very much in charge of the school administration. He was determined not to let the master plan go before the Board and not allow any staff member to render any assistance to the Task Force without his authorization.[80]

Faced with this unexpected and insurmountable barrier erected by DeLara, the Steering Committee met hastily on January 18 to develop an alternative way to present both the "Abstract" and the resolution to the Board and to devise a plan to mobilize the communities to begin to exert pressure on the Board. It was decided at the meeting that the Task Force would flood the Office of the Superintendent with phone calls on January 20 and 21 to remind him of his earlier promise of cooperation. If that failed, at least one Board member would be asked to introduced the resolution as the first reading on January 21. John Kidder, one of the seven Board members, was asked to introduce the resolution over the objection of DeLara and apparently some Board members as well.

Through parliamentary maneuvers, the resolution was unexpectedly referred to a Committee of the Whole Board for public hearings on January 28, meaning no action could be taken by the Board on that date. About 500 persons from the various communities turned out as planned in January to urge prompt approval of the proposed resolution. The Task Force further sought and received letters of support from numerous civic organizations throughout the city and elected officials at all levels. The two State Senators representing San Francisco made personal appearances to express their support of the master plan. From the questions raised by Board members and the Superintendent, it appeared that none had read the "Abstract" and most reacted with total indifference and distrust; in fact, the Superintendent surprised the Task Force and some Board members by publicly disassociating himself completely from the proposed master plan and the work of his personal representative, Del Portillo, on the Task Force. Before the long and frustrating night was over, an amendment by Sam Martinez to delay the second reading of the resolution until February 25 and two substitute resolutions by Eugene Hopp and Zuretti Goosby were introduced; the former would have watered down the original resolution to such generalities that it could hardly have been implemented, while the latter would have had the effect of burying the entire master plan.[81] The way the discussion took place between the Superintendent and the Board that night, the U.S. Supreme Court decision, the work of the Task Force, the meetings with the Superintendent on January 7 and 13 and the agreement among the attorneys of the three parties involved could just as well have not existed!

Precisely what led the Board members to do what they did is still unknown. DeLara, a staunch opponent to bilingual education and ethnic studies, clearly had a hand in it. One thing that was clear, the Board could not possibly have come to an agreement in its next meeting on February 4 with four out of the seven Board members locked in three conflicting resolutions and a disruptive amendment. Given this situation, DeLara could have effectively blocked the Task Force from moving forward and could have easily controlled the divided Board. It was equally clear that the Task Force and community organizations had to adopt one single strategy and lobby each Board member separately before the February 4 meeting. The Task Force met on January 30 to assess the situation and decided not to push for the original resolution introduced by Kidder because the four votes needed could not be firmly secured. Besides, Kidder himself was having doubts about the resolution.[82] Instead, the Task Force decided to concentrate its effort on putting some teeth into the Hopp substitute resolution. The plan therefore called for some modification of the Hopp resolution and intensive lobbying of the other six Board members.

On February 3, Hopp accepted some of the modifications proposed by the Task Force. At the Board meeting on February 4, the Board unanimously adopted the modified Hopp resolution, over the strong protest of a small handful of white mothers representing the P. T. A.[83] The resolution approved the concept of bilingual-bicultural education for children of limited English-speaking ability, imposed a February 25 deadline for "the entire report" on the master plan and authorized the Superintendent "to commit the staff needed for implementation no later than September 1975."[84] Even though the language of the resolution was vague, both the Task Force and the U.S. Department of Justice independently arrived at the same interpretation: the Superintendent was required by the Board to complete the details of the master plan by February 25, and to implement it by September 1975.[85]

On February 5, 6 and 7, the Task Force repeatedly called the Superintendent to set up a meeting to delineate the specific tasks to be completed before the February 25 deadline mandated now by the Board and to work out a time-line for the completion of the final master plan. These phone calls, however, failed to reach the Superintendent. So, on February 7, a registered letter was sent to the Superintendent, requesting a meeting with the Task Force on February 10. To make sure that the Board was fully aware of what was happening to its own resolution, the Task Force sent a letter to all the Board members on February 6, reiterated the importance of completing the master plan on schedule and indicated the difficulty it was having in getting an appointment with the Superintendent. On February 10, the Task Force was told by the Superintendent's secretary that he would be out of town that day. Another letter was sent to reiterate the importance of having the meeting if the Task Force was to complete the master plan by February 25 as the Board resolution called for. The letter requested a meeting the following day. On February 11, the chairman of the Task Force personally went to the Superintendent's Office at 8:30 a.m. to see if he could catch the Superintendent on his way to his office and get an appointment to see him on February 12. He was allowed only to talk with his secretary who relayed the following message: the Superintendent would meet with the Task Force on February 13 at 8 a.m., he considered the February 4 resolution to be a request for a "final report" on February 25, *not* the final master plan, and he understood "the final report" of the Task Force to be the basis for him to draw up his own master plan.[86] In short, the Task Force did its work for nothing: the Superintendent would devise his own master plan! To make the situation even more incredible was the sudden and unexpected departure of Del Portillo for an indefinite period of vacation!

When the meeting took place on February 13, the Task Force submitted two supplementary documents, entitled, "Models for Bilingual-Bicultural Education Schools" and "Recommendations for Elementary Bilingual Classroom Models," both designed to assist district staff in filling in facts and figures necessary for completion of the master plan. The Superintendent and his deputy, DeLara, however, reiterated his interpretation of the February 4 resolution. When Task Force members told him to stop playing games, he "angrily stomped out of the meeting without a word" barely ten minutes into the meeting. The meeting ended soon after.

On the next day, the Task Force sent the Superintendent a letter, accusing him of "using the unprofessional-like and insulting walk-out tactic" and of unilaterally undoing "ten months of intensive study and planning conducted by the Board-created, Board-appointed Task Force, by Board-hired outside consultants, and by his own personal representatives." The

Task Force said, "Our goodwill and strict compliance with Board resolutions apparently was naivete on our part; our good faith effort was rewarded with insult and rejection. The Superintendent clearly abused our trust...and was in violation of the Federal Court approved agreement on May 16, 1974." The Task Force told the Superintendent that it would not allow "one man's defiance and obstruction to prevent it from fulfilling its mandates from the Board and the Supreme Court.... The Task Force intends to proceed with the limited and incomplete data it has accumulated to date and to work with whoever on his staff is willing to cooperate with us." That same day, the Superintendent called the chairman of the Task Force to apologize for his behavior a day before, but there was no change in his position regarding cooperation with the Task Force.

By then, the Task Force only had ten days left to prepare the final master plan without the assistance of vacationing Del Portillo. On February 20, the Task Force wrote the President of the Board and informed her that the Task Force was getting "neither oral nor written communication from the Superintendent or his staff." However, the Task Force would make every effort to submit the final master plan on February 25. No staff person was willing to help without an authorization from the Superintendent or his deputy.[87] Even though the Task Force kept the Board fully informed of all its frustrating attempts to work with the Superintendent, not once did any member of the ineffective and incompetent Board offer to bring the Superintendent and the Task Force together to carry out the mandate of the Board.

When the Board actually met on February 25, it was not surprising that the Task Force was unable to submit the final master plan, Component 3. The school administrators made sure that the Task Force had no access to the data needed to complete the plan. Instead, only Component 2, as revised by the Task Force, was submitted. As pointed out earlier, Component 2 was summarized in the "Abstract." It contained only the framework of the master plan.

The failure of the Task Force of course was a victory for the Morena-DeLara clique. The originally planned timetable for completion of the planning process was completely upset. Worse yet, the commitment and ability of the Board to implement the master plan by fall 1975 became increasingly uncertain as the Morena-DeLara delaying tactic became more effective. The Task Force was exhausted and demoralized. Fortunately, the Task Force, having gone that far, was determined not to let two indifferent and irresponsible school administrators block its mandate from the Supreme Court and its commitment to fight for equal educational opportunity for thousands of children in San Francisco. Moreover, the U.S. Department of Justice began to realize that its agreement on the timetable with the district staff was not being met. On February 12, the Justice Department wrote the school district, "A timetable is necessary so that the plaintiffs can insure appropriate review in time for implementation for the Fall 1975 semester. We are concerned that any further delay in the presentation of the master plan will jeopardize implementation for this Fall." The letter concluded with a demand for a new timetable for the presentation of the master plan to the U.S. Government. When it became obvious that the Board was not going to abide by its earlier commitment on a February 25 deadline, the Justice Department telephoned on February 21 and 24 and wrote on February 25, requesting a new timetable again.

By the end of February, two possible courses of action emerged from the Task Force. On the one hand, the Task Force would bypass the Superintendent and continue to press the Board of Education for the approval of the master plan and its February 4 commitment to implement the plan by September 1975. On the other hand, the Task Force would seek possible legal action to remove the stalemate. Once again, task-oriented committees of the Task Force were formed to work on the two areas. Board members were contacted and resolutions were drafted for Board members.

On March 4, 1975, Board member Sam Martinez introduced a new resolution "to accept the full master plan with the understanding that it is subject to further revision and final approval of the Board" and to set the March 25 date for the final approval of the master plan. The resolution was approved on March 11 in time for the meeting with the frustrated attorney of the Justice Department on March 13. At that meeting, the Board and staff agreed that "to be properly evaluated the master plan must include sufficient detail such as student and teacher assignment, and timeline projections" and that "this information and the master plan with all modifications would be available on March 25, 1975."[88]

The deadline required by the March 11 resolution and agreed upon by both DeLara and the Justice Department's representative on March 13 was ignored again for the third time. Instead of completing the entire master plan with "sufficient detail" by March 25 as promised, DeLara, acting in behalf of the Superintendent, introduced unexpectedly on March 18 another resolution that presumed to approve the master plan and commit the school district to the maintenance of the *status quo,* the very conditions that led the Supreme Court to find the San Francisco school system "a mockery of public education." The resolution called for the approval of the master plan without the necessary data, and under the following major conditions: (1) "top priority" be given to instruction of English using the bilingual-bicultural techniques, (2) all recommendations for administrative changes be deleted (meaning, maintenance of existing structure), (3) community council's role be "advisory in nature " (meaning, no power of decision), (4) recommended expansion of staff "be held in abeyance" (meaning, no staff increase), (5) recommended bilingual schools to be given "additional study" (meaning, no bilingual schools), (6) existing methods of instruction be continued for another year (meaning, continue the sink-or-swim and ESL Pullout approaches), and (7) bilingual education be considered a "compensatory education program."[89]

The resolution was promptly and soundly denounced by a chorus of community spokesmen as "deceptive, insulting and arrogant" and branded as "an irresponsible product of a lame-duck superintendent."[90] Some wanted the resolution rejected, others demanded summary removal of the Superintendent, and none spoke in support of the resolution. By the end of the Board meeting, the Superintendent's resolution was dead.

Capitalizing on the unpopular sentiment against the Superintendent's ill-conceived and ill-intended resolution, the Task Force and community organizations once again organized its multi-ethnic, task-oriented committees to mount yet another intensive campaign for the approval of the master plan. Up until then, the Board had made only the following decisions: approval of the concept of bilingual-bicultural education and commitment to implementation of a master plan by September 1975 on February 4, 1975 and acknowledgement of the reciept of the "Abstract" on March 11. In other words, the Board had yet to approve the master plan, with or without the details required. Instead of introducing a substitute resolution, the Task Force and community organizations decided to work with Board members on a major revision of the Superintendent's resolution.[91] After intensive lobbying between March 18 and 25 and the editorial support of the San Francisco *Examiner* on March 24, the Board finally agreed on March 25 to a series of amendments which deleted highly objectionable clauses 5, 6, and 7, substantially modified clauses 2, 4 and 6 of the Superintendent's resolution, and added the following provisions: "the plan for implementation shall include prospective time lines for attainment of measurable goals in the development of curriculum, the employment of objective test instruments, the assignment of students, and the full utilization of District bilingual teachers. That on or before May 15, 1975, the Superintendent shall provide the Board with necessary data to implement the Master Plan by September 1975." The amended resolution, however, still changed considerably the master plan submitted by the Citizens Task Force and the Center for Applied Linguistics. However, it retained the bilingual-bicultural education of the maintenance type,[92] mandated extensive reassignment of administrative responsibilities beyond the existing Bilingual Education Department, allowed expansion of staff, required existing ESL and Newcomer programs to be modified to comply with the master plan, called for aggressive pursuit of state and federal funds "to supplement the District's effort," and included all provisions in the master plan not mentioned or unaltered by the resolution.

The approval of the master plan of course did not mean that its implementation would be guaranteed in September 1975. The Board's inability to make its staff carry out its policy decision is a rule rather than exception;[93] the Superintendent's ability to withhold vital information from the Board and to prevent the Board from making sound decisions and long-range plans is obvious. The distrust and division among Board members render the Board ineffective and vulnerable to staff manipulation. The reality of the situation in the San Francisco school district therefore requires laborious and independent monitoring of the implementation of the master plan, to see to it that all provisions are carried out faithfully.

Returning to the mandate of the March 25 resolution, the Superintendent once again ignored the May 15 deadline.[94] Actually, the data requested by the Board was submitted to DeLara, but it was withheld from the Board as of this writing.[95] This is another example of the defiance of the Superintendent and his deputy and the Board's inability to do anything about it. The administration's tactic has been to do the minimal and to delay the transmittal of the master plan to the Federal Court until it could no longer be carried out in September 1975.

Fortunately, the U.S. Department of Justice took the necessary step toward the implementation of the approved master plan. As if he knew that the May 15 deadline would again be ignored by the Superintendent, J. Stanley Pottinger, Assistant U.S. Attorney General, filed pleadings on April 29 at the Federal District Court seeking "the information that is necessary for the plan's implementation."[96] He reminded the school district that the questions in the interrogatories were "similar to those I presented in my letter of October 16, 1974, which have not been fully answered."[97] The school district was given 30 days to answer 23 very extensive questions. If these questions were answered adequately, they would have provided the very information the Task Force had tried in vain to obtain since January 1975. The Justice Department further expressed its desire to meet with both the plaintiffs' attorney and the attorney representing the school district to evaluate the master plan and the answers to the interrogatories.

Between November 1974 and April 1975, the U.S. Department of Justice was repeatedly given false promises and misinformation. Numerous attempts were made in February and March 1975 to either kill the master plan or significantly modify it into either an ESL plan or an ethnic studies program. It was not until March 25, 1975 that the Board reluctantly approved the master plan with some minor modification. It was the result of months of intensive lobbying and pressures from all sides. The resolution approving the master plan also called for its implementation by September 1975.

The master plan was subsequently submitted to the Federal Court for further scrutiny and approval. No decision to date has been reached by the Court, and in the meantime, the school administration failed to carry out the Board resolution, calling for the implementation of the master plan in September last year. According to the 1975 figures released by the school district, only 931 out of 5,258 limited English-speaking students at the elementary level were receiving BBE called for by the master plan, 2,820 were getting the inappropriate, inadequate ESL program and 1,507 getting nothing. No figures were available for the secondary students. There is no way to ascertain the quality and effectiveness of these programs now in operation.

In terms of district funds committed to meet the needs of the limited English-speaking students, there was budget increase from $2.4 million in 1974 to $2.5 million in 1975. The $2.5 million represents about 2% of the total district budget; the meager increase was not even sufficient to cover the cost of living increase. However, Federal and state funds for BBE increased sharply from $982,000 to about $2 million between 1974 and 1975.

It is clear that the district is still not putting its own resources into BBE programs and is depending almost solely on Federal and State hand-outs to support BBE now mandated by the Supreme Court. The school administration continues to ignore the Supreme Court decision, H.E.W. guidelines and the master plan approved by the Board of Education.

CONCLUSIONS

The struggle of the Chinese American students and parents in San Francisco, as lengthy and oftentimes as hopeless as it may seem, points to the importance of fighting for the legal right of equal and quality education on all fronts and at various levels. We are just beginning to understand the full legal and educational ramifications of the *Lau v. Nichols* decision nation-wide. Socially and politically, the decision should begin to alter public sentiment against non-English languages and non-WASP cultures in American society on the one hand and to instill pride, instead of shame and self-hatred, in one's own language and culture on the other hand. But no significant change of public attitude will take place unless established institutions and policies are continuously pressured by community groups to meaningful and systemic changes. This means coordinated and persistent, rather than isolated, efforts in the struggle to achieve equal rights. The experience of the Chinese American indicates the limitations of relying solely on legal remedy: political and legislative actions at the local, state and Federal levels must go hand in

hand with litigation. In fact, well planned political and community actions are most crucial in times of legal setback and bureacratic resistance.

Secondly, sound strategy for institutional changes could only come out of thorough and correct analysis of a situation. The decision to avoid seeking the "appropriate remedy" through litigation in the Federal Court and to have the master plan fashioned solely by parents is basically sound because Federal Court and the ineffective and irresponsive Board of Education should not be placed in a position of determining what type of education could best benefit students of limited English-speaking ability and because the divided and powerless minority communities had a rare opportunity to be united as a political force in San Francisco through working on a common cause. The many months spent mobilizing the communities and fighting for the right to develop the master plan and to have bilingual-bicultural education are in fact vital to raising the political and legal consciousness of the communities and to forming a solid political coalition never before existing in San Francisco. Instead of being divided and working against each other, the strategy brought the communities together to work for their common interests.

Thirdly, the difficulties and barriers the parents in San Francisco had to go through to secure what they are legally entitled to demonstrated clearly whose interests are being best served by the public school system in the U.S. Throughout the struggle, the school administration displayed arrogantly not the slightest interest in responding to the educational needs and legal rights of students from different language and cultural backgrounds. In fact, legal and political pressures failed to persuade the school administration to modify its posture. Morena, DeLara and company could care less that a substantial portion of students was receiving no education, inferior education or dropping out of schools and turning the school system into a "mockery of public education" and a national disgrace. The school administration sees itself protecting and serving the interests and needs of those who are white and those who come from an upper socio-economic background. To the administrators, the interests and needs of the poor, the non-English-speaking and non-white are secondary, if not negligible. Moreover, the political and administrative structure of the school system is set up to facilitate maximum participation and reinforce the interests of the rich and the powerful and to prevent and frustrate effective minority participation. The ability of Morena and DeLara to stall and ignore community pressure single-handedly is a perfect example of the biased nature of the structure of our public educational system.

Finally, the short-term, small gains in the long struggle for bilingual-bicultural education made by the Task Force and the minority communities in San Francisco should not be construed as a lasting victory. Even as this article is being completed, there are indications everywhere that the master plan will be largely ignored or deliberately destroyed through faulty implementation and uncooperative administration. Therefore, to assure lasting equality of educational opportunity, the class bias in public educational services and decision-making processes must be removed. As long as there is no fundamental change in the existing political structure, the distribution of power and resources, and educational priorities, the problems encountered in this study will continue to exist and inequality and exploitation of the poor and the minorities will not only be tolerated but pursued with vigor. Similarly, bilingual-bicultural education as effective and appropriate as it may be, will be rendered useless and given no chance to survive in an environment that is both intolerant and hostile to the needs and interests of the students of different language and cultural backgrounds.

The *Lau* decision has made important contributions toward recognizing the rights of non-English-speaking Americans and has helped put together a strong coalition of minority communities in San Francisco, California and nation-wide to fight for meaningful change in our social institutions. However, like *Brown v. Board of Education*, these changes will not come easy and fast. Persistence and unity among the ignored and oppressed thus far seem to be the key to any successful struggle. ★

January 1976

Notes

1. Supreme Court of the United States, Slip Op. No. 72-6520. The full text of the Supreme Court opinion is reprinted in *A Better Chance to Learn: Bilingual-Bicultural Education,* pp. 207-212, published by the U.S. Commission on Civil Rights, Clearinghouse Publication No. 51, May 1975; also in *A Synthesis of Theories and Research on the Effects of Teaching in First and Second Languages: Implications for Bilingual Education.* Austin, Texas: National Educational Laboratory Publishers, June 1974. Title VI of the Civil Rights Acts of 1964 provides: "No person in the United States shall, on the ground of race, color, or national origin be excluded from participation in, be denied the benefits of, or be subjected to discrimination under any program or activity receiving Federal financial assistance." (42 U.S.C. 2000 d). The regulations promulgated by the Secretary of HEW under this statute include 45 C.F.R. 80.3(b)(1). The specific passage cited by the Supreme Court opinion is: "Where inability to speak and understand the English language excludes national origin-minority group children from effective participation in the educational program offered by a school district, the district must take affirmative steps to rectify the language deficiency in order to open its instructional program to these students." (35 *Fed. Reg.* 11595; July 10, 1970; popularly known as the "May 25, 1970 Memo"). For the full text of this important memo, see the Commission on Civil Rights' report, pp. 204-206.

2. A small section of this paper is based on this writer's article in *Amerasia Journal,* Vol. 2:2 (Fall 1974), pp. 16-45. Another section of this paper is based on the writer's contribution to the "Abstract" of the San Fran-

cisco Unified School District's master plan, to be discussed later in this paper. I am indebted to Edward Steinman, attorney for *Lau* plaintiffs, for his assistance in the legal section of this paper.

3. For significant papers in *Lau v. Nichols,* see *Equal Educational Opportunity: Hearings before the Select Committee on Equal Educational Opportunity, the U.S. Senate,* Part 9B, pp. 4715-4754. 92nd Congress, 1st Session, 1971.

4. Press Statement of the Plaintiffs, March 25, 1970.

5. Many community committees and school-appointed committees worked diligently for years to rectify the situation, but very little was accomplished. Among the committees actively working for better education for the Chinese prior to the lawsuit were: Education Committee of the Chinatown-North Beach District Council, Chinese Bilingual Education Advisory Committee, Title VII Chinese Bilingual Education Advisory Committee, Board-appointed Bilingual Advisory Committee and the Rosenberg Education Committee. The complaints and aspirations of the Chinese community are best represented in a statement distributed during a rain-soaked demonstration on February 14, 1969 in front of the school board headquarters at 135 Van Ness Avenue. (Paul Jacobs and Others, *To Serve the Devil,* Vol. 2, pp. 158-160. New York: Random House, 1971). The most violent outburst of student and parental anger and frustration erupted on February 27, 1969 in an open confrontation with Superintendent Robert Jenkins in a jam-packed auditorium of the Commodore Stockton Elementary School in Chinatown. (See *East-West Chinese American Weekly,* March 5, 1969 and the *San Francisco Chronicle,* February 28, 1969). The distrust and frustration culminated in the long school boycott and protest in 1971-72 when a city-wide school busing program was initiated. Needless to say, the SFUSD offered the Chinese community no educational programs relevant to her needs. Min S. Yee, "Busing Comes to Chinatown," in *Chinese-Americans: School and Community Problems,* pp. 69-74. Chicago: Integrated Education Associates, 1972.

6. SFUSD had never undertaken any planning study on the educational needs of limited English-speaking students in the district, even though it always had a sizeable non-English-speaking population. All the classes set up for immigrant children were remedial in nature and had the sole objective of Americanization. The *Lau* decision and the push of the parents and communities forced the SFUSD to conduct its first comprehensive planning on the problem.

7. It is important to point out that the data was collected by the school district in December 1969, and no objective standards were developed to collect the data. The subjective judgment of individual classroom teachers was the basis of the survey. Moreover, placement of these students into the few special English classes was generally arbitrary and was not based on specially designed testing procedures or ascertainable standards. Outside of these special English classes, most of the Chinese-speaking students, who needed help in English, were placed in regular classes that were taught only in English. They could not adequately compete with their peers, and this led to eventual frustration, discouragement, resentment, truancy, delinquency and dropout. For some of the educational problems of the Chinese students in San Francisco, see the writer's testimony in *Equal Educational Opportunity: Hearings before the Select Committee on Equal Education Opportunity of the U.S. Senate,* Part 9A, pp. 4229-4235. 92nd Congress, 1st Session, 1971.

8. SFUSD, *Pilot Program: Chinese Bilingual,* p. 3A, May 5, 1969.

9. For some data and brief discussion on education and delinquency among the Chinese students in San Francisco, see reference in footnote 7.

10. U.S. District Court for the Northern District of California, Civil No. C-70 627 LHB Order, May 26, 1970. An important passage of the order reads as follows: "This Court fully recognizes that the Chinese-speaking students involved in this action have special needs, specifically the need to have special instruction in English. To provide such special instruction would be a desirable and commendable approach to take. Yet, this Court cannot say that such an approach is legally required. On the contrary, plaintiffs herein seek relief for a special need—which they allege is necessary if their rights to an education and equal educational opportunities are to be received—that does not constitute a rights which would create a duty on defendants' part to act. These Chinese-speaking students—by receiving the same education made available on the same terms and conditions to the other tens of thousands of students in the San Francisco Unified School District—are legally receiving all their rights to an education and to equal educational opportunities. Their special needs, however acute, do not accord them special rights above those granted other students. Although this Court and both parties recognize that a bilingual approach to educating Chinese-speaking students is both a desirable and effective method, though not the only one, plaintiffs have no right to a bilingual education. Again, this Court is in no position to mandate that such instruction must be given by bilingual Chinese-speaking teachers; though desirable, there is no legal basis to require it."

11. For relevant legal papers for the appeal, see Note 3.

12. *Ibid.* The appellate court further observed that the problems suffered by the children were "not the result of law enacted by the state. . .but the result of deficiencies created by the (children) themselves in failing to learn the English language." As Edward Steinman, attorney for the plaintiffs, correctly pointed out, "Such a statement. . .not only suggests that the 'sins' of the fathers be visited upon the children; it further labels the child 'sinful' for not absorbing on his own, the language of the society into which he has been cast." He called such legal opinion "incredible." "Testimony of Edward Steinman before the Committee on Ways and Means of the California State Assembly," December 10, 1974.

13. For the legal brief of the United States before the Supreme Court in the *Lau* case, see *Bilingual Education Act: Hearings before the General Subcommittee on Education of the Committee on Education and Labor, U.S. House of Representatives,* pp. 10-19. 93rd Congress, 2nd Session, 1974. Other national organizations are: Childhood and Government Project, National Educational Association, California Teachers Association, San Francisco Lawyers' Committee for Urban Affairs, Center for Law and Education of Harvard University, Efrain Tostado, Mexican American Legal and Educational Fund, American G.I. Forum, League of United Latin American Citizens, Association of Mexican American Educators, Puerto Rican Legal Defense and Educational Fund, and ten Chinese American community organizations in San Francisco: among them is Chinese for Affirmative Action, which played an active part in the case.

14. The national significance of the *Lau* decision is attested by the prompt decision by Congress to conduct a series of public hearings, from March 12 to May 10, 1974 on the effects of that decision on local school districts and the states. For the record of the hearings, see *Ibid.* The decision was cited among the bases for a new bilingual

education legislation by both houses of Congress. See *Education Amendments of 1974: Report. . .of the Committee on Labor and Public Welfare, U.S. Senate,* pp. 44-49. 93rd Congress, 2nd Session, Report No. 93-763, March 29, 1974; *Elementary and Secondary Education Amendments of 1974: Report. . .of the Committee on Education and Labor, U.S. House of Representatives,* p. 69. 93rd Congress, 2nd Session, Report No. 93-805, February 21, 1974; *Education Amendments of 1974: Conference Report,* pp. 147-154. 93rd Congress, 2nd Session, Report No. 93-1026, July 22, 1974.

15. Testimony of Frank Carlucci, Under Secretary of HEW, on March 28, 1974 before the General Subcommittee on Education of the Committee on Education and Labor. *Op. cit.*

16. Public Law 93-380. For the new regulations on Title VII of ESEA, see *Federal Register,* 40:49, March 12, 1975.

17. Chief State School Officers in 26 states were asked by the Office for Civil Rights (OCR) of HEW to help assure that some 333 school districts are providing equal educational opportunity to national origin minority students. This is a follow-up effort of a policy established in the "May 25, 1970 Memo," requiring school districts receiving Federal funds "to rectify the language deficiency and open instructional programs" to national origin minority students who face language barriers. Of the 333 districts, 157 are in California. These school districts were to complete an HEW Form OS 53-74 or the "*Lau* Form," within 45 days. Compliance review is now underway. For a criticism of this latest OCR effort, see a paper by this writer delivered at the 4th International Conference on Bilingual-Bicultural Education, Palmer House, Chicago, May 22, 1975, entitled, "Federal Response to the *Lau v. Nichols* Decision: A Critical Assessment of HEW's Policies and Actions."

18. The *Lau* centers are now being set up pursuant to Section 503 of the *Education Amendments of 1972* (Public Law 92-318) and pursuant to the authority contained in Title IV of the Civil Rights Act of 1964, 78 Stat. 246, as amended (42 U.S.C. 2000 c–2000c–9). For a description of the regulations and guidelines for the *Lau* centers, see *Federal Register,* 40:52 (March 17, 1975), pp. 12244-12250. These are centers designed to assist local school districts in meeting the requirements of *Lau.* A total of nine centers would be established with a total funding of $3.7 million for fiscal year 1975. See *East-West Chinese American Weekly,* April 9, 1975.

19. A preliminary study is being conducted by the Center for Applied Lingusitics through a contract with the National Center for Educational Statistics of HEW.

20. The Massachusetts, Texas and Illinois bilingual education laws could be found in *A Better Chance to Learn,* pp. 217-244. In 1973, the National Advisory Council on the Education of Disadvantaged Children conducted a nationwide survey on state legislation on bilingual education. The result of the survey could be found in *Education Legislation, 1973: Hearings before the Subcommittee on Education of the Committee on Labor and Public Welfare, U.S. Senate,* Part 7, pp. 2578-2584. 93rd Congress, 1st Session, October 31, 1973. The California Legislature is considering similar legislation. The most important bill is SB 7, sponsored by Senator George Moscone of San Francisco. The bill passed the Senate on June 26, 1975 and was referred to the Assembly for further deliberation. Meanwhile, the California Advisory Committee of the U.S. Commission on Civil Rights held a two-day hearing on bilingual education in Sacramento on June 26 and 27, 1975. The Committee is expected to issue a report with

recommendations soon.

21. *Serna v. Portales New Mexico School District:* The U.S. Court of Appeals for the Tenth Circuit ruled on July 19, 1974 that bilingual-bicultural education is the only appropriate remedy under the *Lau* decision. In *Aspira v. Board of Education of the City of New York,* the Federal District Court on August 29, 1974 relied on the *Lau* decision in sanctioning the immediate implementation of a complete bilingual-bicultural education program for nearly 200,000 Spanish-speaking Puerto Rican children in New York City. Similarly, the *Keyes v. Denver Unified School District* case held on April 9, 1974 that bilingual-bicultural education is required by *Lau.* The Federal Court in *Keyes* held the *Lau* decision demonstrates that it is ineffective to require non-English-speaking children to learn a language with which they are unfamiliar, and at the same time acquire normal basic learning skills which are taught through the medium of that unfamiliar language. For the Denver plan for remedy, see Jose A. Cardenas, *An Education Plan for the Denver Public Schools.* National Education Task Force de La Raza, San Antonio, Texas, January 21, 1974; also by the same author, *Addendum to the Intervenor's Education Plan for the Denver Public Schools.* Congress of Hispanic Educators, February 1974. It is important to point out also that in the 20 educational plans negotiated by the OCR in its enforcement effort of the May 25 Memo, all required bilingual-bicultural education. For a detailed description of one of these compliance reviews of HEW, see the example of the Beeville Independent School District in Texas. *Education of the Spanish-Speaking: Hearings before the Civil Rights Oversight Subcommittee of the Committee on the Judiciary, U.S. House of Representatives,* pp. 41-67. 92nd Congress, 2nd Session, June 1972.

22. U.S. Commission on Civil Rights, *A Better Chance to Learn.* See also, Illinois Advisory Committee to the U.S. Commission on Civil Rights, *Bilingual-Bicultural Education—A Privilege or a Right?,* May 1974. The Commission report attracted national attention, e.g., *S.F. Examiner,* May 13, 1975 ran a long report by the Associated Press; *Washington Post,* May 14, 1975.

23. *Voting Rights Act Extension: Report of the Committee on the Judiciary,* pp. 20-21. 94th Congress, 1st Session, House Report No. 94-196, May 8, 1975. The pending legislation on bilingual court systems in the U.S. (S. 1724 and H.R. 7728) is probably going to be the next major reform based on *Lau v. Nichols.*

24. In 1953, San Francisco had 158,817 or 40.8% of the San Francisco Bay Area's 230,186 industrial jobs. But in 1975, it has 140,002 or 24.96% of the 420,764 industrial jobs in the Bay area. However, the city's white-collar jobs in areas such as banking, insurance, general administration and retailing increased substantially as were the jobs related to tourism and convention business. See San Francisco Department of City Planning, *Commerce and Industry: Industrial Trends: Report Containing Background Infromation for the Commerce and Industry Element of the Comprehensive Plan of San Francisco,* May 1975. For earlier trends, see *San Francisco Industrial Trends* by the City Planning Department, October 1968. See also, *Yerba Buena: Land Grab and Community Resistance in San Francisco* by Chester W. Hartman, pp. 158-183. San Francisco: Glide Publications, 1974. For a discussion on the tourist-convention industry in San Francisco, see *San Francisco Convention and Visitor Study,* Parts 1 and 2 by Herbert H. Oestreich and Dirk J. Wassenaar, Institute for Business and Economic Research, School of Business, San Jose State College, San Jose, California, May 1971 and August 1972.

25. State of California, Employment Development Department, Northern California Employment Data and Research, "Ethnic Groups, Veterans and the Handicapped in San Francisco," June 1974.

26. For data on the under-representation of minorities in city government, see "Survey of San Francisco Commissions, Agencies and Boards" in Minutes of the San Francisco Human Rights Commission meeting on January 23, 1975. On minority participation in educational institutions, see forthcoming "Study of Employment Discrimination against Asian Americans in the San Francisco-Oakland SMSA: Educational Institutions" by Asian, Inc., San Francisco. On the politics of San Francisco, see Chester Hartman, *op. cit.,* pp. 28-89 and Frederick M. Wirt, *Power in the City: Decision Making in San Francisco.* Berkeley and Los Angeles: University of California Press, 1974.

27. San Francisco Unified School District, "Selected Data for Study in the Challenge to Effect a Better Racial Balance in the San Francisco Public Schools, 1973-1974." This report is issued every year. The changing composition of enrollment discussed in this section is based on data accumulated in the last six years.

28. San Francisco Human Rights Commission, "Status Report: Bilingual Education in the San Francisco Public Schools, 1973-74 Academic Year," November 7, 1974. See also, *English Programs for Speakers of Other Languages* by Frances Noronha, Program Evaluator, Division of Research, SFUSD, July 1974.

29. *Annual Reports* of the Immigration and Naturalization Service, U.S. Department of Justice, 1960-1974. Also, U.S. Department of HEW. Office of Special Concerns. *A Study of Selected Socio-Economic Characteristics of Ethnic Minorities Based on the 1970 Census;* Vol. II, "Asian Americans." HEW Publication No. (OS) 75-121, July 1974. For the impact of Chinese immigration on San Francisco, see San Francisco Bay Area Social Planning Council, *Working Papers of Background Information on the Study of San Francisco's Chinese Newcomers,* San Francisco, June 1970.

30. Percentage derived by comparing the data in the Human Rights Commission reports for 1973 and 1974. See Note 28.

31. Del Portillo, Raymond, Director of Bilingual Education, SFUSD, "Testimony Given at the Ways and Means Committee, California Legislature," December 10, 1974.

32. *San Francisco Examiner,* January 9, 1975. The number of limited English-speaking students in a school district is now a politically and legally sensitive issue since the *Lau* decision. School districts are required by the California law to conduct such a census at the beginning of each year. To avoid embarrassment and being cited for non-compliance, many school districts in California have been using highly questionable methods of conducting the annual survey and vastly reduced the actual numbers of limited English-speaking students to the minimal.

33. According to the definition of "limited English-speaking student" in the new Title VII law, self-identification method could be used initially to identify the students. The preliminary survey could then be refined and collaborated by more sophisticated instruments, teacher assessment and direct observations.

34. Data supplied by Del Portillo. The 20,000 figure is of course quite different from the official 6,611 figure given by the district. It is understandable that school districts prefer not to use this method of survey.

35. See Note 28.

36. Both Federal and state guidelines require that classroom teachers in any Federal or state-supported bilingual program be paid by the local district. Under these guidelines, SFUSD had to hire bilingual teachers for the few bilingual programs funded by the state and Federal government. Otherwise, most of the teachers are non-bilingual. For an example of violation of this Federal guideline, see "$3.5-million Shocker at School Board," *San Francisco Chronicle*, June 25, 1975.

37. SFUSD, "Preliminary Report to Dr. Lane DeLara on Bilingual/ESL/Newcomer Staff Response to Implications of *Lau v. Nichols*," April 3, 1974.

38. There were actually 1,454 students enrolled in the various bilingual-bicultural programs in the SFUSD. Of these, 704 were limited English-speaking, the remainder was made up of mostly black and white students. Such mixture in bilingual programs is required by state and Federal guidelines to achieve school integration. Both Title VII of ESEA and AB 2284 prohibit linguistic and racial isolation. For problems involving bilingual education and school integration, see *San Francisco Examiner*, May 11, 1974; "Board of Education Exempts Many Bilingual Students from School Bus Program," *San Francisco Examiner*, June 12, 1974.

39. In 1974-75, Federal sources for bilingual education are: $631,994 from ESAA Bilingual Set-aside, $198,056 from ESAA, $493,608 from Title VII of ESEA, $275,000 from CETA. State sources are: $187,946 from AB 2284 and $72,036 from AB 116.

40. "School Costs Rose As Enrollment Fell," *San Francisco Chronicle*, November 22, 1974. Cf. "San Francisco Staff Still Outnumbers Teachers," *San Francisco Chronicle*, March 16, 1972.

41. Board Resolution No. 23-16-Sg 5. The resolution was recommended by a Board appointed Bilingual Advisory Committee following a massive protest by Chinese parents and students from the Marina Junior High School. Unfortunately, adoption of a good policy statement means very little in San Francisco.

42. The unfounded rumor was probably based on a well-established practice of the school district: yield only to pressure. The Supreme Court decision obviously was presumed to be a major pressure on the Board and would make the Chinese needs appear more urgent and visible. Also, the attempt to organize a Citizens Task Force made up of all ethnic groups happened to have come out of the Chinese American community first. This may have been presumed as a threat. Individuals and organizations with vested interests in the *status quo* naturally saw the formation of a citizens task force a threat as well.

43. The SFUSD responded only to community pressure. For example, in 1966-67, the district appropriated $190,000 to the Chinese only. In 1967-68, when the Spanish-speaking community put pressure on the Board, $61,132 was given to a Spanish ESL program. It was not until 1971-72 when the Filipino community first received $145,651 for its ESL program. Under pressure in 1972-73, the Board allocated $41,000 to start a Japanese bilingual program. S.F. Human Rights Commission, *op. cit.*

44. CAA has long been active in the field of education and employment. Many members of CAA too have long advocated bilingual-bicultural education of both Chinese immigrants and Chinese Americans.

45. The position consisted of two parts: description of current problems and recommendations to the Board.

46. For details of this recommendation, see the position paper.

47. Letter of CAA to Board of Education, March 19, 1974.

48. In a letter, dated February 27, 1974, to J. Stanley Pottinger, Assistant Attorney General of the U.S., CAA recommended four specific courses of action to be undertaken by the government. The fourth recommendation sought Federal intervention in San Francisco. Also on February 27, 1974, CAA requested Dr. Wilson Riles, State Superintendent of Public Instruction, to assist San Francisco parents in their effort to come up with solutions to school problems related to *Lau*.

49. "San Francisco Schools Are Bad, Riles Says," *San Francisco Chronicle*, March 20, 1974; "Riles Indicts San Francisco Schools," *San Francisco Examiner*, March 20, 1974.

50. *Ibid.*

51. "Angry San Francisco Parents Ask State for Help," *S.F. Chronicle*, March 23, 1974; "Angry Board Members Talk: Why Schools Don't Improve," *S.F. Examiner*, March 21, 1974. After months of public outcries and intensive, behind-the-scene maneuvers, the Board finally accepted the recommendation of Riles early this year which called for the appointment of a blue-ribbon commission to see what could be done to improve the school system from the management point of view. The appointment of the commission is like declaring the school district a disaster area, in need of outside and state assistance.

52. Letter of Del Portillo to Advisory Committee members, April 5, 1974.

53. Actually, the first draft of this plan was completed in total secrecy as early as February 15, 1974. The draft, entitled, "Bilingual/ESL/Newcomer Staff Response to Implementation of *Lau v. Nichols*," was apparently prepared under Lane DeLara's direct supervision, following Hopp's press statement of February 4. However, most Board members were unaware of the existence of this report until they were told of it in mid-April 1974.

54. Most of the parents and citizens had had considerable experience in dealing with the school bureaucracy. Most knew immediately what the district staff was up to. But there were a few defenders of the district staff as expected. *S.F. Examiner*, April 16, 1974 and *S.F. Chronicle*, April 17, 1974.

55. *S.F. Examiner*, April 16, 1974; *S.F. Chronicle*, April 17, 1974. Prior to the press conference, the *S.F. Examiner* gave a special coverage on the problems of getting a public response to *Lau* from the school district: "Schools Dragging Bilingual Feet," *S.F. Examiner*, April 15, 1974.

56. For example, the Board of Education was not informed by the Superintendent of a letter, dated March 11, 1974, from Edward Aguirre, Regional Commissioner of the U.S. Office of Education, informing the SFUSD that it was "ineligible for funding under the Emergency School Aid Act" because of the Supreme Court decision on *Lau*. In fact, DeLara transmitted a request for a waiver of the ineligibility to the Office for Civil Rights on March 20, again without the Board's knowledge. Another example is the Board's total ignorance of Federal funds available for Chinese bilingual education curriculum development. The SFUSD was asked to submit a proposal, but no such proposal was submitted. Funds for this project are now awarded to the Berkeley Unified School District for Asian bilingual curriculum. Still another example is the Board's unawareness of the decision by the U.S. Department of Justice to intervene in the *Lau* case at the U.S. District Court when it considers remedies for *Lau*. The school district eventually was granted a waiver on the ground that a plan was being developed. *S.F. Chronicle*, May 2, 1974.

57. *California Education Code,* Section 5761.3.

58. See Note 56.

59. Three documents were filed by the Department of Justice: "U.S.'s Notice of Motion and Motion for Leave to Intervene as Party Plaintiff," "U.S.'s Memorandum of Points and Authorities in Support of Motion for Leave to Intervene," and "Complaint in Intervention." John B. Rhinelander, General Counsel of U.S. Department of HEW to J. Stanley Pottinger, Assistant Attorney General, April 9, 1974 letter included among these legal documents.

60. Board Resolution No. 44-23A5, May 14, 1974.

61. Board Resolution No. 44-9A2, May 1974.

62. "*Lau v. Nichols:* the Legal Struggle for Bilingual Education," *S.F. Examiner,* May 27, 1974. For an excellent series of nine articles on bilingual education in San Francisco, see *S.F. Examiner,* May 27-31, 1974. For a rare and sympathetic coverage on bilingual education by the *S.F. Chronicle,* see "Learning Barrier in San Francisco Schools," *S.F. Chronicle,* August 19, 1974. Since the *Lau* decision, the *Examiner* has done no less than thirty articles related to the case and to bilingual education. *Chronicle,* on the other hand, has done about four or five articles.

63. Exclusion of minority participation is a long established tradition in San Francisco. As a result of the civil rights movement of the 1960's, token minority representation is sometimes tolerated. See Note 24. Allegations that the Task Force had no white respresentatives were totally false and hypocritical.

64. There are four ethnic or linguistic caucuses: Chinese, Filipino, Japanese and Latino. As a rule, each caucus invited community participation beyond the members of the Task Force. It organized and took part in numerous community events dealing with education and bilingual education.

65. In 1971, in the case of *Lee v. Johnson,* the SFUSD was ordered by the Federal District Court to integrate through an extensive busing program based solely on race, rather than socio-economic backgrounds and educational and language needs. If the master plan was to be implemented, it must conform with the integration order. The Task Force, therefore, had to meet with the staff of the Office of Desegregation and Integration (D & I). Similarly, the forced closing of many schools under the Field Act requirements (earthquake safety measures) necessitated relocation of thousands of students and programs. Again, the Task Force had to meet with the staff dealing with facility utilization, Office of Association Superintendent of Administration.

66. Minutes and tapes of Task Force meetings are kept in Del Portillo's office.

67. Center for Applied Linguistics, an internationally renowned center for linguistic research, is located in Arlington, Viginia. The Task Force was to provide input to the Center and working papers prepared by the Center. Unfortunately, because of the distance between San Francisco and Washington, it was difficult for Center staff to be present in all meetings of the Task Force. Moreover, messages and recommendations of the Task Force had to be relayed through the Superintendent's staff to the Center. Oftentimes the Task Force asked that the tapes of meetings be sent to the Center; but apparently none had been sent. Communication, therefore, was one of the major problems.

68. This component was officially transmitted to the Superintendent and all members of the Board on January 9, 1975. Acknowledgement of the receipt of this component was not made by the Board officially until March 11, 1975 in a resolution No. 53-4A6. See *Minutes of Regular Meeting of Board of Education,* March 11, 1975, pp. 17-19.

69. This component, as presented to the Board, is not the totality of the master plan. The background papers in Component 1 are not included. A number of working papers, documents and recommendations from the Center were included in the master plan, but not fully explained. Also, the details in Component 3 were absent in Component 2. The Board of Education officially accepted this component with Component 1 in Board Resolution No. 53-4A6 on March 11, 1975.

70. The Task Force, district staff, Center for Applied Linguistics and U.S. Department of Justice all agreed that the master plan could not be carried out without Component 3. Yet this is one component that the Superintendent most stubbornly refused to cooperate and complete. In spite of repeated demands by the Board in resolutions adopted on February 4, March 11 and 25, the Superintendent ignored the demand for this component. As of this writing, June 15, the Superintendent has yet to comply.

71. Unlike the transitional bilingual-bicultural education program, the master plan calls for a program which utilizes the student's native language and culture in instructing, maintaining and developing all the necessary skills in the second language and culture. The end result is a student who can function, totally, in both languages and cultures. For extensive discussion on various types of bilingual education program, see William F. Mackey, "A Typology of Bilingual Education," in *Bilingual Education in a Binational School,* pp. 149-171. Rowley, Mass.: Newbury House Publishers, 1972; Valencia, Atilano, *Bilingual-Bicultural Education: A Perspective Model in Multicultural America.* Albuquerque, N.M.: Southwestern Cooperative Educational Laboratory Inc., April 1969; Fishman, Joshua and John Lavas, "Bilingual Education in Socio-linguistic Perspective," *TESL Quarterly,* IV:3 (Sept. 3, 1970), pp.215-22; Cornejo, Ricardo J., *op. cit.,* pp. 31-38; Kjolseth, Rolf, "Bilingual Education Programs in the U.S.: For Assimilation or Pluralism?" in *The Language Education of Minority Children: Selected Readings,* pp. 94-121, edited by Bernard Spolsky. Rowley, Mass.: Newbury House Publishers, 1972; Troike, M. and R., *A Handbook on Bilingual Education* (Revised Edition), pp. 24-31. Washington, D.C.: Teachers of English to Speakers of Other Languages, 1971.

72. See Note 38 on integration requirements and also Note 65.

73. SFUSD, Center for Applied Lingusitics and Citizens Task Force on Bilingual Education, "A Master Plan for Bilingual-Bicultural Education in the SFUSD in Response to the Supreme Court Decision in the Case of *Lau v. Nichols,*" February 25, 1975.

74. This definition is consistent with both state and Federal laws' definition. See Component 1, pp. 18 and 19.

75. For a detailed discussion on this point, see U.S. Commission on Civil Rights, *A Better Chance to Learn,* pp. 30-47.

76. "No Bilingual Student Aid Plan," *S.F. Examiner,* August 8, 1974. This article explains also why the Task Force could not possibly complete an implementable plan for September 1974.

77. Letter of J. Stanley Pottinger to the SFUSD, December 31, 1974.

78. The Superintendent's promise again was very firm. DeLara sat through the meeting without saying much. The only assurance the Superintendent wanted from the Task Force

was that the Board be given a chance to review the plan without debates in news media. The Task Force agreed fully and subsequently refused to speak with reporters about the substance of the plan. However, the *S.F. Examiner* managed to secure a copy through district sources and reported about the master plan on January 20, 1975.

79. DeLara's reputation as a hard-line anti-bilingual administrator was well known. On May 31, 1974, he was quoted in the *S.F. Examiner* as admitting frankly he preferred instruction in English "pure and simple" as a way to satisfy the high court's demand to provide a "meaningful education" to non-English-speaking youngsters. He said, "If the primary objective is to teach the youngster English and get him into the mainstream, then I think ESL is a much more effective and efficient way to do it." He also claimed that bilingual education was too costly to the district.

80. Reliable district sources told this writer. In spite of U.S. Government's request, no action was taken to complete the plan. "Bilingual Plan Asked," *S.F. Examiner,* January 27, 1975.

81. Kidder Resolution No. 51-21A12 of January 21. See *Minutes of Regular Meeting of the Board of Education, January 21, 1975,* pp. 18-19; Martinez Resolution No. 51-21A13 of January 21. See *Minutes,* p. 20; Hopp Resolution No. 52-4A11 of January 21; and Goosby Resolution No. ? of January 21, 1975. Even though circulated copies of Hopp and Goosby resolutions were dated January 21, official minutes of the Board indicated no such motions were made. Moreover, the same official minutes did not show that the Kidder resoltuion was referred to the Committee of the Whole. In fact, the minutes of January 21 reads as follow: "Commissioner Kidder moved adoption of the following resolution which was seconded by Commissioner Dr. Goosby and held over to the next Board meeting pursuant to Paragraph 15.4 of Board Policy P120." (p. 18). The Martinez resolution too was held over to the next meeting which was January 28, 1975. It is interesting to note that the beginning statement in the official minutes of January 28 reads: "President Mrs. Abrahamson stated that the Board convened at the regularly scheduled hour of 7:00 p.m., and will adjourn at 8:00 p.m., in order to convene as a Committee of the Whole for the purpose of discussion of the Abstract of the Proposed Master Plan for Bilingual Education." (p. 1). Obviously, the resolutions of Hopp and Goosby were not introduced on January 21 and the resolutions of Kidder and Martinez were not referred to the Committee of the Whole as claimed by the President.

82. Kidder was under pressure from advocates of integration who presumed that the bilingual education plan would undermine the already defunct integration program and set up a separate bilingual school system with the SFUSD.

83. The small handful of white parents wanted to have a chance to address the board, but they were cut off abruptly. From private conversations and public statements of this small, but extremely active group of PTA mothers, one could easily identify their major concerns: preservation of what was left of the integration program, fear of a potential separate bilingual school system, presumed high cost of the master plan, and fear that approval of the master plan would mean reallocation of school priorities which gave top priority to their children. Their concerns were brought out and debated publicly in a series of confrontations with minority communities at the meetings of the San Francisco Human Rights Commission, dating back to Nov. 1974. See minutes of the Commission in January, February and March 1975.

84. Board Resolution No. 52-4A11, Feb. 4, 1975: "Resolved, that the Board of Education approves the concept of Bilingual/Bicultural education; further be it resolved, that the Board requests the Superintendent to commit the staff needed for implementation no later than September, 1975; further be it resolved, that the final plans or whenever options are arrived at, be presented to the Board for public appraisal and Board approval; further be it resolved, that the *entire report* be provided the Board no later than February 25, 1975."

85. Task Force letter to the Board, February 6, 1975 and Justice Department's letter to the SFUSD, February 12, 1975.

86. Citizens Task Force for Bilingual Education, "Report by the Steering Committee," February 12, 1975, p. 2.

87. Note 80.

88. Board Resolution No. 53-4A6. *Minutes of Regular Meeting of Board of Education, March 11, 1975,* pp. 17 and 18.

89. Board Resolution No. 53-18S-p. 1.

90. "Morena v. Task Force on Bilingual Education," *S.F. Chronicle,* March 19, 1975; "Citizens Task Force's Attack: Bilingual Program Denounced," *Examiner,* March 19, 1975.

91. This decision was based on a realistic understanding of the relations between the Board and the Superintendent, and between the Superintendent and the communities. Actually, a substitute resolution was going to be prepared. But it was decided that such a resolution could not bring in the necessary four votes on the Board. Amendments to the Superintendent's resolution were proposed. However, the Board accepted some and rejected some.

92. Martinez amendments No. 53-25A6. *Minutes of Regular Meeting of the Board on March 25, 1975,* pp. 21-22. Goosby's attempt to further water down the amendments was defeated. (Resolution No. 53-25A7). *S.F. Examiner,* March 26, 1975. *Chronicle* reporter was apparently not present or unaware of what resolution was passed because it came out with this headline, "Bilingual Policy Unchanged," a reference to the Superintendent's original resolution. (*S.F. Chronicle,* March 26, 1975).

93. The Board has been accused repeatedly for interfering with the school administration. Morena in particular made this accusation. The accusation was supported by the commission set up by Riles to improve the San Francisco school system. There is some truth to this accusation. However, the cause of Board interference is probably due to the Board's inability to force the Superintendent to carry out its policies. As a result, Board members find themselves intervening in many administrative matters and repeatedly bargaining with the Superintendent on just about anything. Often time, the Superintendent successfully divides the Board by trading favors with Board members and helping the pet projects of each member.

94. This is just another example of the inability of the Board to make its Superintendent comply with its policy decision!

95. Sources from within the school administration informed this writer that the data was indeed submitted to the Deputy Superintendent.

96. The relevant legal documents are: "Plaintiff-intervenor's Request to Defendants for Admissions," and "Interrogatories of Plaintiff-intervenor to Defendants."

97. Letter of Justice Department to the SFUSD, April 29, 1975.

Introduction
ASIANS IN THE MEDIA: The Shadows in the Spotlight

In the years to come, the broad subject area described as "communications and media" will be a topic of increasing import for Asian Americans. In a land where optimum value is placed on "freedom of expression" and where "freedom of the press" is constitutionally protected, it is not easily apparent why Asian Americans should be especially concerned. But in this country, the so-called "freedoms of speech" are largely circumscribed by another dominant principle: private ownership of property. Thus, the capacity not only to speak freely, but meaningfully, is a function of who has the means to speak.

Newspapers, television and radio, which are the most powerful means available to exercise these freedoms, are actually businesses, just like any other industry in America. As such, they are parts of an economic order which is based on a structure of corporations. Large businesses are usually incorporated, and in turn, can be owned by parent corporations. This pattern is generally followed in the media industry. RCA Corporation, for example, owns NBC. Time Inc. owns cable television stations.[1] The Los Angeles Times Syndicate owns other newspapers.[2] Essentially, who controls the media is who has controlling interest in the parent corporations.

Asian Americans, even in an aggregate sense, do not have controlling interest in these corporations. The very few individuals who do possess enormous power. They can manipulate public opinion on important issues or dictate patterns of consumption of goods. Moreover, they can ultimately determine how Asian Americans will be seen and whether or not they will be heard.

Since media and communications in the United States are part of the system of private enterprise, these determinations are not made on the basis of "public interest" as might be generally believed but by considering economic outcomes. Thus, "serving the public interest," a claim often made by networks and newspapers, literally translates into catering to the segments of the population which have the greatest capability to affect the ability of the media industries to make profits.

Hence, for Asian Americans, a numerically small minority in the United States, the "public interest" often means no interest. As a rule, sensitivity towards the needs and concerns of Asian Americans has never been a feature of media policy in America, and the best that Asians have come to expect from the major news dailies, television and radio stations is neglect. In fact, as a matter of history, the past treatment of Asians by the media is more accurately described in terms of outright hostility. As early as 1853, when the first arriving Chinese came to America, the editors of the *Daily Alta,* a San Francisco newspaper, had this comment:

COMMUNICATIONS AND MASS MEDIA

We have a class here, however, who have most of the vices and few of the virtues of the Africans. We allude to the Chinese. Every reason that exists against the toleration of free blacks in Illinois may be argued against that of the Chinese here.[3]

By 1882, with the avid support of the press, Chinese were barred from immigrating to the United States. During the 1900s, the press began aiming its exclusionary efforts at Japanese in America. William Randolph Hearst, founder of the powerful media empire which bears his name, gave meaning to the phrase "yellow journalism" with a sustained series of vicious and inflammatory attacks on Japanese immigrants. Although Hearst's weapons were mostly his newspapers, in 1916 he produced and distributed a film which nearly scored an ironic bulls-eye in current headlines. Entitled, *Patria,* it was a movie about a group of fanatical Japanese who invade the United States and attempt to rape a white heroine.[4]

When Japanese were excluded in 1924, the press then turned its attention to Pilipinos. In 1930, V.S. McClatchey, former owner of the influential Sacramento *Bee,* testified personally in Congressional hearings to exclude Pilipinos:

We had first the invasion by the Chinese, next the invasion by the Japanese, then by the Hindus and now we are called upon to resist the invasion of the Filipinos.[5]

Clearly, the press was acting not merely as a mirror of public hostility towards Asians, but was itself an instigator of racial antagonism, building the false allegations and the deprecatory images which contributed to the exclusion of every Asian group which ever came to America in large numbers.

Hostile treatment of Asians by the press did not stop with the respective legal exclusion of each ethnic group. The press vigorously campaigned for anti-alien land laws, anti-miscegenation laws and even "repatriation." Most notorious was its behavior with regard to the incarceration of Japanese in 1942.[6]

One fact which should give Asian Americans at least some cause for concern is that the same press which held intolerant attitudes still exists today in even more influential capacities. Hearst press is one obvious holdover. Aside from the implications of this continuity, those distortions of facts and events first initiated by the press have been transmitted as "popular" history. The extent to which this distorted "popular" history has permeated American culture is revealed in the first article in this section, "Ambush at Kamikaze Pass," by Tom Engelhardt. Engelhardt, a free lance writer, describes how Asians are seen by the movie industry as inhuman invaders, ripe for extermination. This cinematic perspective, characteristically reserved for the Native American, was also Hollywood's view of Asians in films made from the 1930s to the 1960s. While thematically concerned about Asians as subjects of a "Far East" which had become discomfortingly close, these films obviously have some relevance for any Asian American who has ever experienced being called a "foreigner."

In its most current offering, the movie industry has finally arrived at the idea that Asians were victims in America. In March, 1976 NBC aired *Farewell to Manzanar,* a dramatic film version ostensibly of the Japanese American concentration camp experience. Ray Okamura reviews this movie in "Farewell to Manzanar: A Case of Subliminal Racism," a craftly manipulative motion picture. The review shows clearly that the movie industry's current perception of Asians as victims, while novel, is tainted with historical inaccuracies.

Furthermore, this kind of outlook is at best only a limited perspective. The history of Asians in America is certainly one which can be characterized as the oppression of a minority group, but it is also a story of a people with their own unique life styles and institutions. Asian Americans created their own forms of communications, wrote their own literature,[7] involved themselves in internal and international politics[8] and generally lived a brand of cultural pluralism long before the term had become a model of attainment in ethno-sociology.

A complete picture of Asians in America as full human beings is one that has never been developed by the communications and media industry. In fact, the "entertainment" media has cultivated quite the opposite characterizations by traditionally depicting Asians as degrading stereotypes. Even as early as 1858, Chinese "stock" characters (of the "no tickee, no washee" variation) were introduced in the theatre of melodrama to provide "comic relief."[9] During the 1900s pulp novels and serials popularized the fiction of "the yellow peril." When film arrived as a new medium, Asians were depicted either as exterminable creatures, as Engelhardt describes in his article, or were sheer fabrications created by the industry to capitalize on public interest in things which were "foreign," or pseudonymously "oriental."

In the 1920s, Chinatown-born Wong Liu Tsong, later to be known as Anna May Wong, broke into films by starring in a series of typecast roles which were a depressing omen of the price Asians had to pay for acceptance. In "Anna May Wong," Judy Chu narrates the tragic story of an early Chinese American actress by using largely the clippings from movie magazines which helped to create her image.

From the 1860s until the present, stereotyping of Asians has been a constant feature in nearly all forms of entertainment media. As such, it can be a fascinating way to examine the social history of Asian Americans.[10] Some stereotypes, introduced seemingly out of harmless intent, nevertheless had damaging effects. For instance, in 1941 writer John Fante, friend of worker/writer Carlos Bulosan, wrote a dramatic short story about Pilipinos for the *Saturday Evening Post.* The story, entitled "Helen, Thy Beauty Is to Me" described the infatuation of a young Pilipino for a blonde taxi-dance hall dancer. It touched off the ire of another Pilipino writer, Manuel Buaken and 300 "others." Not all Pilipinos chased women that lustily, protested Buaken, and the story presented an unfair image.[11]

On the whole, the possible harmful effects of constant sterotyping of Asian Americans has rarely been considered by the entertainment media industry. Caricatures like the bumbling Charlie Chan and the diabolical Fu Manchu, who were bred in the early 1900s, have consistently appeared in books, on stage, in the movies, on television and currently in the comics.[12] These characterizations developed a kind of "marquee value," which really meant they held a market value which could be exploited.

In the early 1970s, the latest presentation of "oriental" exotica was Kwang Chang Caine, otherwise known as the star of the television series, "Kung Fu." Caine, played by the white actor, David Carradine, was a non-violent, mystical Shaolin monk who managed to punch somebody senseless in every episode, notwithstanding his peaceful predilections. The producers of "Kung Fu" were interviewed by Irvin Paik, who worked on the production crew of the show. Paik's interview, entitled "Kung Fu Fan Klub" demonstrates that the industry still has little awareness of the concerns and needs of Asian Americans or the possible detrimental effects of shows like "Kung Fu."

At the same time that Caine was barefooting it through the West, leaving behind a trail of broken bones and dropping off bits of philosophy by blurbing incoherent one-word aphorisms, the first of the Hong Kong produced Gung Fu films were shown in the United States. These films starred a real Gung Fu expert, Bruce Lee. Lee was the antithesis of Caine—he never turned down a fight and he was an Asian in real life. Enormously popular internationally, the films drew mixed reactions from Asian American communities. To some, Lee, like Caine was a corrupter of the pure art of Gung Fu. To others, he was admittedly an unreal character, but at least, a positive switch from unheroic and unmasculine Asian caricatures like Fu Manchu and Charlie Chan.

Still, even if Lee did manage to chop up those old molds which made it impossible to cut the Asian as a "macho" figure, the Gung Fu films had another stereotypic effect—every Asian automatically became a martial arts freak! In February, 1974, Vons Inc., a food chain enterprise in Southern California sponsored a television commercial which depicted a leaping, yelping Asian dressed in a karate gi slashing food prices.

The commercial provoked the outrage of a number of Asian Americans in the Los Angeles area. Protesting publicly, they eventually forced the removal of the offensive commercial. The group banded together permanently to form the organization, AAFM, or Asian Americans for a Fair Media. Its primary goals were to educate the public about the abuses of media and to serve as an organization which could relay the concerns of Asian Americans to the industry. AAFM had counterpart organizations in New York (also called AAFM) and San Francisco (Chinese Media Committee or CMC) which had been formed previously in response to offenses by the media in their respective communities.

While the Chinese Media Committee also has branched into the area of media production, AAFM in Los Angeles has devoted most of its efforts to informing the public about the particularly harmful practices of the media industry and its general policies. The group has held a series of forums for the Asian American community. These have included slide shows giving graphic examples of Asian stereotyping and panel discussions with spokesmen of various media industry and Asian Americans involved in the industry AAFM also distributes a handbook which instructs citizens on how to protest media practices effectively. In 1974, AAFM in conjunction with CMC protested CBS' resurrection of Charlie Chan in the series "Khan!" It was shelved after two episodes. The result was a revealing demonstration of an informed and vocal minority group's capacity to affect media policies which have national implications. Asian Americans are congregated in New York, San Francisco and Los Angeles—cities which happen to be centers for the media industry. Thus, organized Asian Americans, while numerically small in relation to the national population, have the power to influence media which is greater than often realized.

Asian American responses to degrading stereotyping and exclusionary media policies have taken on other forms besides direct protest. In 1965 the East/West theatre group was organized in Los Angeles as an alternative for the many Asian Americans who were prevented by racism in the arts from ever developing or displaying their talents. Known initially as a workshop, East/West has since become a reknowned theatrical group which has been a show case for a culture that is distinctly Asian American, devoid of degrading stereotypes. Plays written by Asian American writers are often premiered by East/West.[13]

Live theatre was also the medium employed in the 1970s by KDP (Katipunan Ang Demokratikong Pilipino), a political organization with a socialist outlook and a strong anti-Marcos stance. KDP's plays were performed by the members of their organization and their contents were visibly political. While lacking the experience and sophistication of a true theatre ensemble, the organization has reached a wide audience by taking their plays and skits directly to the people. They perform at colleges, high schools and community gatherings.

Other modes of response were developed along "counter-cultural" lines. There was Asian American art, dance and music. Asian American bands, who once were identified as whoever played at the infamous Asian American dances, created new forms of communication. In Los Angeles, "Hiroshima," the oldest and most popular of these groups, has evolved into a polished professional unit displaying a wide repertoire which reflects not only its talents but its roots and politics.

Also in Los Angeles, a group was initiated in 1970 which managed to surmount the tremendous economic and institutional barriers to becoming an independent film and communications unit. Calling themselves "Visual Communications" or VC, they produced films, slide shows, and other educational materials on the Asian American experience. Ron Hirano, a former staff member of the organization, writes about its history, the methods it used to overcome certain hurdles and the constraints imposed on it by external conditions in "Media Guerrillas."

But by far the most popular and prolific form of alternative media engaged in by Asian Americans was printed communications. Literally dozens of newspapers and magazines were produced in the late 1960s and 1970s. The literature presented in these publications included Asian American perspectives on the news, history and politics. In addition, they often contained creative writings. Rocky Chin, a member of the organization which produced *Bridge,* a national Asian American magazine, describes other publications which survived this era and some which did not in "Getting Beyond Vol. 1. No. 1."

The appearance of these publications in the late 1960s and the early 1970s was linked directly to the emergence of what is now referred to as the Asian American Movement. While traditional ethnic press at that time was an influential tool in Asian American communities, its lack of response or cautious attitudes towards the issues raised during this period about civil rights, the Viet Nam War, and ethnic studies prompted many persons to develop their own publications. In effect, these newspapers, pamphlets and magazines were the life-blood of the movement. Correspondingly, the participants in this new series of ethnic press mirrored the membership within the movement; the large majority were students.

Some of these student-initiated publications attempted to formulate a new "Asian American" perspective as opposed to any singular ethnic outlook on a wide variety of topics. Nonetheless, their contents often reflected a certain ethnicity, i.e., more Japanese American or Pilipino American news was reported depending on a particular newspaper, or analyses, while described as "Asian American," were often relevant to only a single Asian ethnic group. Perhaps as a result, more attention has recently focused in Asian American publications on the dynamics of class rather than race.

The publications also developed along the lines dictated by their institutional origins. *Amerasia Journal,* founded by a group of students at Yale, continues to be the only Asian American publication which encourages scholarly research on Asian Americans. *Gidra,* an Asian American newspaper founded in Los Angeles in 1969, had somewhat different beginnings and a different pattern of growth. Produced by a group of students who individually pooled together $100 each, *Gidra* covered an international area from a small office in the Crenshaw district in Los Angeles. Mike Murase, who was one of those original students, describes the paper's history as a reflection of the personalities and ambitions of its many members. Overall, about 200 individuals at one time or another participated in producing *Gidra* every month for nearly five years, making it a process of growth for its participants as well as an informative source for the community it served.

Gidra's current state of suspension is illustrative of the present status of organizations which sought to develop an alternative media. Many organizations have undergone significant changes, the most characteristic of which has been the turnover of membership. Others have permanently disbanded or re-defined the character or goals of their group. Simple economics often determined these modifications. Often, in order to survive, productions had to be performed which were not always politically desirable, grants had to be "hustled" from government institutions which were the very ones targeted for reform, or repertoires had to be widened to attract bigger audiences.

In another sense, economics places the greatest constraint on Asian Americans seeking social change through or within the media. Notwithstanding obfuscating statistical linguistics which place Asian American families "above the median income," even two working Asian American adults cannot purchase a television station or produce a nationally distributed newspaper or movie.

Although effectuating social change by direct protest and alternative media seems to have its limitations, technically speaking, relief is available through the legal system or government agencies such as the Federal Communications Commission. The Commission is empowered to issue licenses for broadcasting and to renew them based on a showing that the station has served the "public interest." It can also mandate "the right to reply" or "equal time" doctrines.

However, who gets to own broadcast licenses is who can pay for them. At the same time, legal or administrative actions by Asian Americans against renewal of licenses of offending stations are hampered by the fact that their community interest is not synonymous with the "public interest." Furthermore, attempts to expand the "right to reply" or "equal time" to specific minority groups as injured parties have not been recognized by the courts.[14] Finally, none of these potential remedies is available against printed communications, which can distort with impunity.

While this picture seemingly points the way to pessimistic politics for many Asian Americans, it has simply meant that changing the nature of media in the United States is not possible without concurrent wider social reform and deeper economic transformation. The articles selected for this section reveal only the bare outlines of this problem and just a small portion of the kinds of expanding consciousness which have responded to it. Certainly, the nature of media ownership and the enormous power which the media industry possesses should be more carefully analyzed. Also, the history of the media and its relation to Asian Americans, along with the history of how Asians expressed their concerns and life styles through their own press are topics which still need more study. At the same time that knowledge develops in these important areas, Asian Americans will have to continue generating vocal and organized protest and refining their approaches in alternative media.

The articles which were selected for this section are indicative of all the kinds of activity described above. They portray a participation which has spanned the last decade, a demonstration of the willingness and commitment of individuals to take part in a movement for change in America.

—Jesse Quinsaat

Notes

1. The ownership of media with its fancy interlocking directorates and financing schemes is a subject in itself. For a general survey of media ownership of the television networks see "Directory of the Networks," available from The Network Project, 104 Earl Hall, Columbia University, New York, New York 10027. Notebook Number 11, February, 1973 has pertinent information on network ownership.

2. In general, the pattern of ownership for all communications and news services has become increasingly monopolistic. Twenty-five newspaper groups control more than half of the daily newspapers in circulation in the United States. See Bob Litterman, "Who Owns the Media," *Pacific Research and World Empire Telegram,* 4C (Jan./Feb. 1973), 9-16.

3. Dan Caldwell, "The Negroization of the Chinese Stereotype in California," *Southern California Historical Quarterly,* 3: 2 (June 1971), 123.

4. Roger Daniels, *The Politics of Prejudice* (New York: Athenum Press, 1972), 70-78. Warner Oland, the Swede who starred in many Asian roles in early Hollywood cinema, played the part of a Japanese secret service agent in *Patria* as noted by Jacobus ten Broek, Edward N. Barnhart, and Floyd Matson in *Prejudice, War and the Constitution* (Berkeley: University of California Press, 1954), 29-32.

5. U.S. Congress, House, "A Bill to Exclude Certain Citizens of the Philippine Islands from the United States," H.R. 8708, 71st Congress, 2nd Session, 1930, p. 29.

6. Japanese American Curriculum Project, "Wartime Hysteria: The Role of the Press" (San Mateo, Ca., n.d.). This is a gathering of actual newspaper and magazine clippings from that period.

7. See the rich lore of Asian American writings in the "Literature" section of this anthology.

8. See articles in this volume by H. Mark Lai and Yuji Ichioka.

9. Stuart W. Hyde, "The Chinese Stereotype in American Melodrama," *California Historical Society Quarterly,* 34: 4 (Dec. 1955). Bret Harte, creator of the "Heathen Chinee" also wrote a play with similar Chinese character types.

10. One writer has pointed out that the physical traits and negative characteristics used to depict Chinese in the 1800s corresponded with their social disenfranchisement. Chinese were made to look progressively "black" in caricatures and described with terminology associated with blacks as racial prejudice against them intensified. See Caldwell.

11. Manuel Buaken, *I Have Lived with the American People* (Caldwell, Idaho: Caxton Printers, Ltd., 1968), 178-181. "Three hundred" was Buaken's own estimate. Christian-raised Manuel was not impressed by the defense of the story as "an attack on the social system in America—dance halls and taxi-dance dames."

12. Michio Kaku, "Racism in the Comics," *Bridge,* 3: 1 (Feb. 1974) 24.

13. Buck Wong, "The East/West Theatre Group," *Bridge,* 2: 5 (June 1973), 41.

14. Linda Matthews, "Why Do Poles Go to Supreme Court," *Los Angeles Times,* Oct. 25, 1975. An attempt by Polish people to halt ethnic jokes by demanding a right to respond was refused by the FCC and the U.S. Court of Appeals in Chicago.

"Westerns" may have been America's most versatile art form. For several generations of Americans, Westerns provided history lessons, entertainment and a general guide to the world. They created or recreated a flood of American heroes, filled popcorned weekends and overwhelmed untold imaginations. It's as difficult today to imagine movies without them as to think of a luncheonette without Coca Cola. In their folksy way, they intruded on our minds. Unobtrusively they lent us a hand in grinding a lens through which we could view the whole of the non-white world. Their images were powerful; their structure was satisfying; and at their heart lay one archetypal scene which went something like this:

White canvas-covered wagons roll forward in a column. White men, on their horses, ride easily up and down the lines of wagons. Their arms hang loosely near their guns. The walls of the buttes rise high on either side. Cakey streaks of yellow, rusty red, dried brown enclose the sun's heat boiling up on all sides. The dust settles on their nostrils, they gag and look apprehensively towards the heights, hostile and distant. Who's there? Sullenly, they ride on.

Beyond the buttes, the wagon train moves centrally into the flatlands, like a spear pointed at the sunset. The wagons circle. Fires are built; guards set. From within this warm and secure circle, at the center of the plains, the white-men (-cameras) stare out. There, in the enveloping darkness, on the peripheries of human existence, at dawn or dusk, hooting and screeching, from nowhere, like maggots, swarming, naked, painted, burning and killing, for no reason, like animals, they would come. The men touch their gun handles and circle the wagons. From this strategically central position, with good cover, and better machines, today or tomorrow, or the morning after, they will simply mow them down. Wipe them out. Nothing human is involved. It's a matter of self-defense, no more. Extermination can be the only answer.

There are countless variations on this scene. Often the encircled wagon train is replaced by the surrounded fort; yet only the shape of the object has changed. The fort, like the wagon train, is the focus of the film. Its residents are made known to us. Familiarly, we take in the hate/respect struggle between the civilian scout and the garrison commander; the love relations between the commander's daughter and the young first lieutenant who-has-yet-to-prove-himself; the comic routines of the general soldiery. From this central point in our consciousness, they sally forth to victory against unknown besiegers with inexplicable customs, irrational desires, and an incomprehensible language (a mixture of pig-latin and pidgen Hollywood).

What does this sort of paradigm do to us? Mostly, it forces us to flip history on its head. It makes the intruder exchange places in our eyes with the intruded upon. (Who ever heard of a movie in which the Indians wake up one morning to find that, at the periphery of their existences, in their own country, there are new and aggressive beings ready to make war on them, incomprehensible, unwilling to share, out to murder and kill, etc.) It is the Indians, in these films, who must invade, intrude, break in upon the circle—a circle which contains all those whom the film has already certified as "human." No wonder the viewer identifies with those in the circle, not with the Indians left to patrol enigmatically the bluffs overlooking humanity. In essence, the viewer is forced behind the barrel of a repeating rifle and it is from that position, through its gun sights, that he receives a picture history of Western colonialism and imperialism. Little wonder that he feels no sympathy for the enemy as they fall before his withering fire-- within this cinematic structure, the opportunity for such sympathy simply ceases to exist.

Such an approach not only transforms invasion into an act of self-defense; it also prepares its audiences for the acceptance of genocide. The theory is simple enough: We may not always be right (there are stupid commanders, etc.), but we are human. By any standards (offered in the film), "they" are not. What, then, are they? They are animate, thus they are, if not human, in some sense animals. And, for animals facing a human onslaught, the options are limited. Certain of the least menacing among them can be retained as pets. As a hunter trains his dog, these can be trained to be scouts, tracking down those of their kind who try to escape or resist, to be porters, to be servants. Those not needed as pets (who are nonetheless domesticable) can be maintained on preserves. The rest, fit neither for house

illustration by KEN MINAMIJI

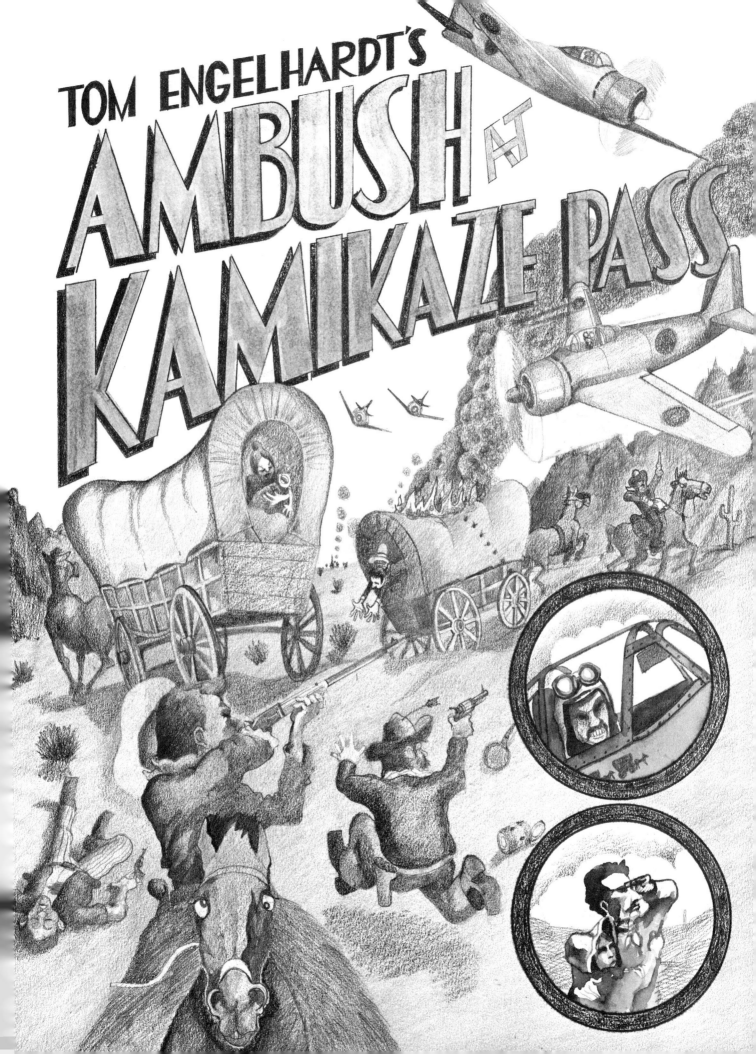

training nor for cages, must be wiped out.[1]

From the acceptance of such a framework flows the ability to accept as pleasurable, a relief, satisfying, the mass slaughter of the "non-human"—the killing, mowing down of the non-white, hundreds to a film and normally in the scene which barely precedes the positive resolution of the relationships among the whites. Anyone who thinks the body count is a creation of the recent Indochinese war should look at the movies he saw as a kid. It was the implicit rule of those films that no less than ten Indian (Japanese, Chinese. . . .) warriors should fall for each white, expendable secondary character.[2]

Just as the style and substance of the Indian wars was a prototype for many later American intrusions into the third world (particularly the campaigns in the Philippines and Indochina), so movies about those wars provided the prototype from which nearly every American movie about the third world derived. That these third world movies are pale reflections of the framework, outlook, and even conventions of the cowboy movie is easy enough to demonstrate. Just a few examples, chosen almost at random from the thirty or forty films I've caught on T.V. in the last few months. Pick your country: the Mexico of toothy Pancho Villan bandits, the North Africa of encircled Foreign Legionaires, the India of embattled British Lancers, or even South Africa. One would think treatment of South Africa might be rather special, have its own unique features. But Lo! We look up and already the Boers are trekking away, in (strange to say) wagons, and, yep, there's, no. . . let's see. . .Susan Hayward. Suddenly, from nowhere, the Zulus appear, hooting and howling, to surround the third-rate wagons of this third-rate movie. And here's that unique touch we've all been waiting for. It seems to be the singular quality of the Zulus that they have no horses and so must circle the wagon train on foot, yelling at the tops of their voices and brandishing their spears. . .but wait. . .from the distance. . .it's the Transvaal cavalry to the rescue. As they swoop down, one of the Boers leaps on a wagon seat, waving his hat with joy, and calls to his friend in the cavalry, "You've got 'em running, Paul. Keep 'em running, Paul! Run 'em off the end of the earth!"*(Untamed, 1955)

Or switch to the Pacific. In any one of a hundred World War II flicks, we see a subtle variation on the same encirclement imagery. From the deck of our flagship, amidst the fleet corraled off the Okinawa coast, we look through our binoculars. The horizon is empty; yet already the radar has picked them up. Somewhere beyond human sight, unidentified flying objects. The sirens are howling, the men pouring out of their bunks and helter-skelter into battle gear. At their guns, they look grimly towards the empty sky: the young ensign too eager for his first command, the swabby who got a date with that pretty Wave, the medic whose wife just sent him a "Dear John" letter

(he's slated to die heroically). A speck on the horizon, faces tense, jokes fall away, it's the Kamikaze! Half-man, half-machine, an incomprehensible human torpedo bearing down from the peripheries of fanatical animate existence to pierce the armored defenses of the forces of Western democracy. The result? Serious damage to several ships, close calls on more, several secondary characters dead, and an incredible number of Japanese planes obliterated from the sky.[3]

That there is no feeling of loss at the obliteration of human torpedoes is hardly surprising. Even in those brief moments when you "meet" the enemy, movies like this make it immaculately clear that he is not only strange, barbarous, hostile and dangerous, but has little regard for his own life. Throwing himself on the gatling guns of the British with only spear in hand, or on the ack-ack guns of the Americans with only bomb in portal, he is not acting out of any human emotion. It is not a desire to defend his home, his friends, or his freedom. It has no rational (i.e., "human") explanation. It is not even "bravery" as we in the West know it (though similar acts by whites are portrayed heroically). Rather, it is something innate, fanatical, perverse—an inexplicable desire for death, disorder and destruction.

When the enemy speaks a little English, he often explains this himself. Take, for instance, the captured Japanese officer in *Halls of Montezuma* (1950). The plot is already far advanced. On an island in the Pacific, hours before the big attack, Marines are pinned down by Japanese mortars whose position they cannot locate. Yet if they do not locate them, the attack will fail. The Japanese officer obstinately refuses to help them. Richard Widmark pleads with him, appealing to his life force, "You have a future—to rebuild Japan—to live for. . . ." But the officer replies: "Captain, you seem to have forgotten, my people for centuries have thought not of living well but dying well. Have you not studied our Judo, our science. . . . We always take the obvious and reverse it. Death is the basis of our strength." Suddenly a mortar shell explodes above the bunker. Everybody ducks. Rafters fall; dust billows; slowly the air clears; a shocked voice yells out: "My God, the Jap's committed Hari Kari!" Fortunately the idiot gave it all away. He reminded the Americans of the quirks in the non-white mind. As any schoolboy should have known, orientals think backwards. The Japs put their rockets on the front slope of the mountain, not the protected rear slopes as an American would have done. The attack, to the tune of the Marine Hymn, moves forward, preparing to wipe the Japs off the face of the island.

If, in print, such simple idiocy makes you laugh, it probably didn't when you saw the film; nor is it in any way atypical of four decades of action films about Asia. The overwhelmingly present theme of the non-humanness of the non-white prepares us to accept, without flinching, the extermination of our "enemies" (as John Wayne commented in *The Searchers*, 1956, there's "humans" and then there's "Comanches.") and just as surely it helped prepare the ideological way for the leveling and near-obliteration of three Asian areas in the course of three decades.

It is useful, in this light, to compare the cinematic treatment of the European front in World Wars I and II with that of the Pacific front. From *The Big Parade* (a silent film) on, a common and often moving convention of movies about the wars against Germany went something like this: The allied soldier finds himself caught in a foxhole (trench, farmhouse, etc.) with a wounded German soldier. He is about to shoot when the young, begrimed soldier holds up his hand in what is now the peace symbol, but at the time meant "Do you have a cigarette?" Though speaking different languages, they exchange family pictures and common memories.[4]

The scene is meant to attest to man's sense of humanity and brotherhood over and above war and national hatred. Until very recently, such a scene simply did not appear in movies about the Japanese front. Between the American and his non-white enemy, a bond transcending enmity was hardly even considered. Instead, an analagous scene went something like this: A group of Japanese, shot down in a withering crossfire, lie on the ground either dead or severely wounded. The American soldiers approach, less from humanitarian motives than because they hope to get prisoners and information.[5] One of the Japanese, however, is just playing possum. As the American reaches down to give him water (first aid, a helping hand), he suddenly pulls out a hand grenade (pistol, knife) and, with the look of a fanatic, tries to blow them all to smithereens. He is quickly dispatched (see, for instance, *In Love and War*, 1956).

The theme of alien intruders descending on embattled humans and being obliterated from an earth they clearly are not entitled to is most straightforwardly put in Science Fiction movies; for monsters turn out to be little more than the metaphysical wing of the third world. These movies represent historically events which have taken place only in the Western imagination. Thus, the themes of the cowboy (-third world) movie come through in a more primeval way. An overlay of fear replaces the suspense. Metaphorically, the world is the wagon train; the universe, the horizon. (Or, alternately, the earth space-ship is the wagon train; an alien planet, the horizon.) From that horizon, somewhere at the peripheries of human existence, from the Arctic icecap (*The Thing*, 1951), the desert (*Them*, 1954), the distant past (*The Beast from 20,000 Fathoms*, 1954), the sky (*War of the Worlds*, 1953), at dawn or dusk, hooting and beeping come the invaders. Enveloping whole armies, they smash through human defenses,

forcing the white representatives of the human race to fall back on their inner defense line (perhaps New York or Los Angeles). Imperiling the very heartland of civilized life, they provide only one option— destroy THEM before THEM can destroy us.

In this sort of a movie, the technical problems involved in presenting the extinction of a race for the enjoyment of an audience are simplified.[6] Who would even think about saving the Pod People? (*Invasion of the Body Snatchers*, 1956). Ordinarily the question of alternatives to elimination barely comes to mind. If it does, as in that prototype "modern" Sci-Fi film, *The Thing* (James Arness of Matt Dillon fame played the monster), usually the man who wants to save Them, "talk to Them," is the bad mad scientist as opposed to the good, absentminded scientist (who probably has the pretty daughter being wooed by the cub reporter).[7]

Unfortunately for American movie-makers, Asians and others could not simply be photographed with three heads, tentacles, and gelatinaceous bodies. Consequently, other conventions had to be developed (or appropriated) that would clearly differentiate them from "humanity" at large. The first of these was invisibility. In most movies about the third world, the non-whites provide nothing more than a backdrop for all-white drama—an element of exotic and unifying dread against which to play out the tensions and problems of the white world. Sometimes, even the locales seem none-too-distinguishable, not to speak of their black, brown, or yellow inhabitants. It is not surprising, for instance, that the Gable-Harlow movie *Red Dust* (1932), set on an Indochinese rubber plantation (Gable is the foreman), could be transported to Africa without loss two decades later as the Gable-Kelly *Mogambo*. It could as well have been set in Brazil on a coffee plantation, or in Nevada with Gable a rancher.

As George Orwell commented of North Africa in 1939,

> All people who work with their hands are partly invisible, and the more important the work they do, the less visible they are. Still, a white skin is always fairly conspicuous. In northern Europe, when you see a labourer ploughing a field, you probably give him a second glance. In a hot country, anywhere south of Gibraltar or east of Suez, the chances are that you don't even see him. I have noticed this again and again. In a tropical landscape one's eye takes in everything except the human beings. It takes in the dried-up soil, the prickly pear, the palm tree and the distant mountain, but it always misses the peasant hoeing at his patch. He is the same colour as the earth, and a great deal less interesting to look at. It is only because of this that the starved countries of Asia and Africa are accepted as tourist resorts.[8]

Theoretically, it should have been somethat more difficult since the Chinese and Vietnamese revolutions and other uprisings of the oppressed and non-white around the world, to ignore the people for the scenery. Yet we can't fault Hollywood for its valiant attempt. Generally, American films have hewed with unsurpassed tenacity to this framework—reproducing the white world in the Orient, with Asians skittering at the edges of sets as servants or scenic menace (as in the recent horrific extravaganza, *Krakatoa, East* [sic.] *of Java*, 1969, where a volcano takes over the Lassie role and the Asian female pearl divers go under in the final explosions.) This is even more true in films on Africa, where for generations whites have fought off natives and lions, not necessarily in that order.

A second convention of these films concerns the pecking order of white and non-white societies when they come into conflict. It is a "united front" among whites. Often the whites portrayed are the highly romanticized third-rate flotsam and jetsam of a mythologized American society—adventurers, prostitutes, opportunists, thieves (just as the films themselves, particularly when about Asia, tend to represent the brackish backwater of the American film industry). Yet no matter how low, no matter what their internal squabbles, no matter what their hostilities towards each other, in relation to the third world the whites stand as one: Missionary's daughter and drunken ferryboat captain ("I hate the Reds," he says to her, "because they closed a lot of Chinese ports where they have dames. Chinese, Eurasian, and White Russian. . . .Somebody pinned the bleeding heart of China on your sleeve but they never got around to me."/ *Blood Alley*, 1955); soldier of fortune and adventurer-journalist, natural enemies over The-Woman-They-Both-Love (They escape Canton together, avoiding the clutches of the Reds in a stolen boat / *Soldier of Fortune*, 1955); sheriff, deputies and captured outlaws (They are surrounded by Mexican bandits / *Bandalero*, 196?); or on a national level, the British, Americans and Russians (They must deal with "the chief enemy of the Western World," Mao Tse-tung / *The Chairman*, 1970). This theme is, of course, simply a variation on a more home-grown variety—the Confederates and Yankees who bury their sectional hatreds to unite against the Indians; the convicts on their way to prison who help the wagon train fight off the Sioux, bringing the women and children to safety etc. (See, for example, *Ambush at Cimarron Pass*, 1958, which combines everything in one laughable mess—a Yankee patrol and its prisoner team up with a Confederate rancher to fight off an Apache attack.)

The audience is expected to carry two racial lessons away from this sort of thing. The first is that the presence of the incomprehensible and non-human brings out what is "human" in every man. Individual dignity, equality, fraternity, all that on which the West theoretically places premium value, are brought sharply into focus at the expense of "alien" beings. The second is the implicit statement that, in a pinch, any white is a step up from the rest of the world.

They may be murderers, rapists, and mother-snatchers, but they're ours.

When the inhabitants of these countries emerge from the ferns or mottled huts, and try to climb to the edges of the spotlight, they find the possibilities limited indeed. In this cinematic pick-up-sides, the whites already have two hands on the bat handle before the contest begins. The set hierarchy of roles is structured something like this: All roles of positive authority are reserved for white characters. Among the whites, the men stand triumphantly at the top; their women cringe, sigh and faint below; and the Asians are left to scramble for what's left, like beggars at a refuse heap.

There is only one category in which a non-white is likely to come out top dog—villain. With their stock of fanatical speeches and their propensity for odd tortures, third world villains provided the American film-maker with a handy receptacle for his audience's inchoate fears of the unknown and inhuman. Only as the repository for Evil could the non-white "triumph" in films. However, this is no small thing; for wherever there is a third world country, American scriptwriters have created villain slots to be filled by otherwise unemployable actors (though often even these roles are monopolized by whites in yellowface). From area to area, like spirits, their forms change: the Mexican bandit chief with his toothy smile, hearty false laugh, sombrero and bushy eyebrows (see, f.i. the excellent *Treasure of the Sierra Madre*, 1948, or the awful *Bandalero*); the Oriental warlord with his droopy mustache and shaven head (see *The Left Hand of God*, 1955, *The General Died at Dawn*, 1936, *Shanghai Express*, 1932, *Seven Women*, 1965, etc. ad nauseum); the Indian "Khan" or prince with his little goatee and urbane manner (*Khyber Pass*, 1954, *Charge of the Light Brigade*, 1936). Yet their essence remains the same.

Set against their shiny pates or silken voices, their hard eyes and twitching mouths, no white could look anything but good. In *Left Hand of God*, Humphrey Bogart, the pilot-turned-opportunist-warlord-advisor-turned fraudulent priest becomes a literal saint under the leer of Lee J. Cobb's General Yang. Gregory Peck, an "uninvolved" scientist-CIA spy, becomes a boy wonder and living representative of humanity when faced with a ping-pong playing Mao Tse-tung in *The Chairman*. How can you lose when the guy you want to double-deal represents a nation which has discovered an enzyme allowing pineapples to grow in Tibet and winter wheat in Mongolia, yet (as one of the Russian agents puts it) is holding it so that the rest of the "underdeveloped" world, "90% poor, 90% peasant. . .will crawl on their hands and knees to Peking to get it." All in all, these non-white representatives of evil provide a backboard off which white Western values can bounce in, registering one more cinematic Score for Civilization.

The other group of roles open to non-whites are

roles of helplessness and dependence. At the dingy bottom of the scale of dependence crouch children. Non-white children have traditionally been a favorite for screenwriters and directors. Ingrid Bergman helped them across the mountains to safety (*The Inn of the Sixth Happiness*, 1958); Deborah Kerr taught them geography (*The King and I*, 1956); Humphrey Bogart helped them to memorize "My Old Kentucky Home" (*Left Hand of God*); Carrol Baker went with them on a great trek back to their homelands (*Cheyenne Autumn*, 1964); Richard Widmark took one (a little half-breed orphan girl—sort of the black, one-eyed Jew of the tiny tot's universe) back to the States with him (*55 Days at Peking*). And so on.

Essentially, non-white children fulfill the same function and have the same effect as non-white villains. They reflect to the white audience just another facet of their own humanity. Of course, if you ignore W.C. Fields, children have had a traditionally cloying place in American films; but in the third world movie they provide a particularly strong dose of knee-jerk sentiment, allowing the white leads to show the other side of Western civilization. It is their duty not just to exterminate the world's evil forces, but to give to those less capable (and more needy) than themselves. And who more closely fits such a description than the native child who may someday grow up to emulate us.

While it is children who demonstrate the natural impulses of the white authorities towards those who do not resist them, but are helpless before them or dependent upon them, it is women who prove the point. Even within the cinematic reflection of the white world, women have seldom held exalted positions. Normally they are daughters of missionaries, sweethearts of adventurers, daughters, nurses, daughters of missionaries, wives on safari, schoolmarms, daughters of missionaries, or prostitutes. (The exceptions usually being when women come under a "united front" ruling—that is, they confront Asian men, not white men. Then, as with Anna in *The King and I*, while their occupations may not change they face society on a somewhat different footing.) Several rungs down the social ladder, non-white women are left mainly with roles as bargirls, geishas, belly dancers, nurse's aids, missionary converts, harem girls, prostitutes. In such positions, their significance and status depends totally on the generosity (or lack of generosity) of those white men around whom the movies revolve.

However "well-intentioned" the moviemaker, the basic effect of this debased dependency is not changeable. Take that classic schmaltz of the 1950's, *The World of Suzie Wong*. William Holden, a dissatisfied architect-businessman, has taken a year's sabbatical in Hong Kong to find out if he can "make it" as an artist. (It could have been Los Angeles, but then the movie would have been a total zilch.) He meets ***Susie Wong***, a bargirl who is cute as a Walt Disney button and speaks English with an endearing "Chinese" accent. ("Fo' goo'niss sakes" she says over and over at inappropriate moments.) He wants her to be his model. She wants to be his "permanent girlfriend." Many traumas later, the moviemakers trundle out their good intentions towards the world's ill-treated masses. They allow Holden to choose Susie over Kay, the proper, American, upper class woman who is also chasing him. This attempt to put down the upper classes for their prejudices towards Chinese and bargirls, however, barely covers over the basic lesson of the movie: a helpless, charming Chinese bargirl *can* be saved by the right white man, purified by association with him, and elevated to dependency on him. (Her bastard child, conveniently brought out for his pity quotient, is also conveniently bumped off by a flash flood, avoiding further knotty problems for the already overtaxed sensibilities of the scriptwriters.) It all comes across as part act of God, part act of white America.

Moving upwards towards a peak of third world success and white condenscension, we discover the role of "sidekick." Indispensible to the sidekick is his uncanny ability to sacrifice his life for his white companion at just the right moment. In this, he must leave the audience feeling that he has repaid the white man something intangible that was owed to him. And, in this, we find the last major characteristic of third world roles—expendability. Several classic scenes come to mind. In this skill, the otherwise pitiful Gunga Din excelled (*Gunga Din,* 1939). Up there on a craggy ledge, already dying, yet blowing that bugle like crazy to save the British troops from ambush by the fanatic Kali-worshippers. Or, just to bring up another third world group, the death of the black trainer in *Body and Soul* 1947), preventing his white World Heavyweight Champion (John Garfield) from throwing the big fight.

The parts blend into each other: the Filipino guide to the American guerillas, the Indian pal of the white scout, that Mexican guy with the big gut and sly sense of humor. In the end, third world characters are considered expendable by both moviemakers and their audiences because they are no more a source of "light" than the moon at night. All are there but to reflect in differing mirrors aspects of white humanity.

While extermination, dependency and expendability have been the steady diet of these movies over the decades, American moviemakers have not remained totally stagnant in their treatment of the third world and its inhabitants. They have over the last forty years, emerged ponderously from a colonial world into a neo-colonial one. In the 1930's, the only decade when anything other than second-rate films were made about Asia, moviemakers had no heistation about expressing an outright contempt for subjugated and/or powerless Asians: nor did they feel self-conscious about proudly portraying the colonial style in which most Westerners in Asia lived. The train in

Shanghai Express (1932) is shown in all its "colonial" glory: the Chinese passengers crammed into crude compartments: the Westerners eating dinner in their spacious and elegant dining room. Here was the striking contrast between the rulers and the ruled and nobody saw any reason to hide it.

During this period, with the European imperial structure in Asia still unbroken, colonial paternalism abounded. No one blinked an eye when Shirley Temple asked her Grandfather, the British Colonel (*Wee Willie Winkie*, 1937), why he was mad at Khoda Khan, leader of the warlike tribes on India's northeast border; and he replied, "We're not mad at Khoda Khan. England wants to be friends with all her peoples. But if we don't shoot him, he'll shoot us. . . (they've been plundering for so many years) they don't realize they'd be better off planting crops." [a few poppy seeds maybe?] Nor were audiences taken aback when Clark Gable kicked his Indochinese workers out of a ditch (to save them from a storm, of course), calling them. . .names (*Red Dust*).

A decade later such scenes and lines would have been gaffes.[9] In the wake of the World War and its flock of anti-Japanese propaganda flicks (whose progeny were still alive in the early 1960's), the destruction of the British, French and Dutch empires, the success of the Communist revolution in China, the birth and death of dreaded "neutralism," and the rise of the United States to a position of preeminence in the world, new cinematic surfaces were developed to fit over old frames. In their new suits, during the decade of the 50's, cowboy-third world movies flourished as never before. A vast quantity of these low-budget (and not-so-low-budget) films burst from Hollywood to flood the country's theatres. In the more "progressive" of them, an India in chains was replaced by a struggling, almost "independent" country; the "regimental beastie" by a Nehru (—Ghandi) type "rebel" leader; the Kali-worshipping, loinclothed fanatic by Darvee, the Maoist revolutionary ("You cannot make omlettes without breaking eggs."). Yet this sort of exercise was no more than sleight of hand. The Nehru character looked just as ridiculously pompous and imitative as did Gunga Din when he practised his bugle; nor did the whites any less monopolize center stage (holding, naturally, the key military and police positions); nor could the half-breed woman (Ava Gardner) any less choose light (the British officer) over darkness (Darvee and his minions). Soon, all this comes to seem about as basic a change in older forms as was the "independence" granted to many former colonies in the real world (*Bhowani Junction*, 1956).

If any new elements were to enter these movies in the 1950's (and early 60's), it was in the form of changes in relations within the white world, not between the white and non-white worlds. These changes, heralded by the "adult westerns" of the late fifties, have yet to be fully felt in films on Asia; yet

a certain early (and somewhat aborted) move in this direction could be seen in some of the films that appeared about the Korean war (not a particularly popular subject, as might be imagined)—a certain tiredness ("Three world wars in one lifetime" / *Battle Circus*, 1953) and some doubts. The WWII flick's faith in the war against the "Japs," in a "civilian" army, and in "democracy" comes across tarnished and tired. The "professional" soldier (or flyer) takes center stage. ("We've gotta do a clean, professional job on those [North Korean] bridges." / *The Bridges at Toko-ri*, 1954). There is, for instance, no analogue in your WWII movies to the following conversation in *The Bridges at Toko-ri*. Mickey Rooney (a helicopter rescue pilot) and William Holden (a flyer) are trapped (shot down) behind the North Korean lines. Surrounded, they wait in a ditch for help to arrive. During a lull in the shooting, they begin to talk:

> Holden: "I'm a lawyer from Denver, Colorado, Mike. I probably couldn't hit a thing [with this gun]. . . ."
> Rooney: "Judas, how'd you ever get out here in a smelly ditch in Korea?"
> Holden: "That's just what I've been asking myself . . . the wrong war in the wrong place and that's the one you're stuck with. . . You fight simply because you are here."

Within minutes, they are both killed by the advancing Korean soldiers.

Yet though the white world might seem tarnished, its heroes bitter, tired and ridden with doubts, its relationship to the non-white world had scarcely changed. If anything, the introduction of massive air power to Asian warfare had only further reduced the tangential humanity of Asian peoples. For in a movie like *Toko-ri* (as at Danang today), you never even needed to see the enemy, only charred bodies.

This attempt, particularly in westerns, to introduce new attitudes in the white world, increasingly muddied the divisions between stock characters, brought to the fore the hero-as-cynic, and called into question the "humanity" of the whites vis-a-vis each other. Such adjustments in a relatively constant cinematic structure represented an attempt to update a form which the world's reality put in increasing danger of unbelievability. By the early 1960's, the "adult western" had reached a new stage—that of elegy (see, for instance, *The Man Who Shot Liberty Valence*, 1962). Superficially, such movies seem to be in a state of sentimental mourning for the closing of the frontier and the end of a mythical white frontier life. However, westerns as a form were originally created amidst industrial America partially to mourn just such a loss. The elegiac western of the 60's was, in fact, mourning the passing of itself. Today, this form has come to what may be its terminal fruition in America, the "hip" western—*Butch Cassidy and the*

Sundance Kid (1969), which is a parody not of the western, but of the elegiac western, since not even that can be taken totally straight any more.[10]

However, even in this extension of the western, one thing has not changed—attitudes towards the third world. When, for instance, Butch and Sundance cannot make a go of it in a hemmed in West, they naturally move on, "invading" Bolivia. In Bolivia, of course, it's the same old local color scene again, with one variation: instead of the two of them killing off hundreds of Bolivians in that old wagon train scene, hundreds of unidentified Bolivians band together to kill them. It all boils down to the same thing.

Whatever *Butch Cassidy* may be the end of, I think we stand at the edge of a not totally new, but nonetheless yawning abyss—the "sympathetic" film. The first of what I expect will be an onslaught of these are appearing now. They have at least pretensions towards changing how we see relationships not only within the white world itself, but between the white and Indian worlds. And what is appearing in westerns today may be the transmuted meat of Asian or African films within the next decade.

The recent *A Man Named Horse* (1970?) is a good example. It seems to have been a sincere and painstaking attempt to make a large-scale, commercially successful movie about the Sioux (before they were overrun by the whites), to show from an Indian point of view their way of life, their rituals (recreated from Catlin's paintings) and beliefs, their feelings and fears. Yet, at every turn, the film betrays the edges of older and more familiar frameworks.

It concerns an English Lord hunting in the American West early in the 19th century. Captured by a Sioux raiding party, he is brought back to their village (where the rest of the film takes place). There he becomes a slave (horse) for an Indian woman (Dame Judith Anderson). Already a white "hero" has been slipped into this movie about Indians, betraying an assumption that American audiences could not sustain interest in a film without whites. Given the way we look at these films, he immediately becomes the center of our attention; thus, in the end, you are forced to relate to the Sioux village through his eyes; and to relate to the Sioux as they relate to him (aiding him or mistreating him). Second, by following the travails of this Lord-turned-beast of burden as he assimilates to the tribe, the movie seems to prove that old adage, "put a white man among even the best of savages and you have a natural chief." (He kills enemy Indians, goes through the sun initiation ritual, marries the chief's daughter, teaches the tribe British infantry tactics, and, in the end, his wife and adopted mother being dead, he splits for the white world.)

His girlfriend has that Ali McGraw look which probably is supposed to allow the audience to "iden-

tify" better with the Indians, but looks about as fitting as it did among the Jews of New Jersey (*Goodby Columbus*). Even a stab at righting the wrongs westerns have done to language has a similarly dismal result. The movie's makers, reacting to the common use of pidgen-Hollywood by Indian characters in normal westerns, allow the Sioux in this movie to speak their own language. As all but two of the characters are Sioux, much of the movie is conducted in the Sioux language. If this were a French movie, there would naturally be subtitles; but as these are Sioux *au naturel,* and as there is already a conveniently English-speaking character, an alternate means is called upon. Another "prisoner" is created, an Indian who spent some time with the French and speaks broken English. At the behest of the English Lord, he translates what is necessary to his and our understanding. In this way, the Indians, while retaining the dignity of their own language, are perhaps slightly less able to express themselves comprehensibly in this picture than in a normal western. More important, just as if it were the normal wagon train scenario, it forces us to see everything through white eyes.[11]

And as long as the eyes through which we see the world do not change, so long as the old frameworks for movies about the third world are not thrown away, "intentions" go for little indeed. It is hard even to think of examples of films where sympathetic intentions are matched by deeds. Certainly one would have to venture beyond the bounds of the U.S. to find them—perhaps *The Battle of Algiers* (which, in reverse, does for the French colonizers what we were never willing to do for the Indians). Its view begins at least to accord with the brutal history of the third world; to tell a little what it means, from the colonized point of view, to resist, to fight back, to rebel against your occupiers.

American moviemakers, however, are at heart still in love with an era when people could accept the six year old Shirley Temple telling Khoda Khan not to make war on the British because "the Queen wants to protect her people and make them rich." Their main substitution in later movies being to replace the Queen with (American) technology—machine guns to mow 'em down, and band-aids to patch 'em up. This mood is best captured by Gene Tierney in *The Left Hand of God* when Humphrey Bogart says, "China's becoming a nightmare, Anne...What are we really doing here? ... We belong back in the States, marrying, raising a family." She replies, "...There's too much work to do here...the things we're doing here are what they need; whether medicine or grace. And we can give it to them..." Of course, the historical joke of this being uttered in China's Sinkiang province in 1947, a time when the unmentioned communist revolution is sweeping through the central provinces, passed the scriptwriters by. Yet, on the whole, just this distance between the film's "message" and Chinese reality about sums up the American approach to the third world. In the end, no matter where the moviemakers may think their sympathy lies, their films are usually no more than embroideries on a hagiography of "pacification."

Within such a context, there is no possibility for presenting resistance, rebellion, or revolution by the intruded upon in a way that could be even comprehensible, no less sympathetic. Quite the opposite, the moviemakers are usually hell-bent on glorifying those Asians (or other third worlders) who allied with the Western invaders, not those who at some point resisted either the invasion or its consequences. However, there is an insoluble contradiction here. The method for judging non-whites in these films is based on how dependent or independent they are of the white leads and the white world. To the degree to which they are dependent, they are seen as closer to humanity. To the degree to which they are independent (i.e., resist) they are seen as less liable to humanization or outrightly inhuman and thus open to extermination. ("Mitchell, we must stamp this out immediately." / *Gunga Din*). In other words, there is an inherent bias in these movies towards the glorification of those "natives" who have allied with us. Yet what makes the white hero so appealing is the audience's feeling that no matter how low he sinks, he retains some sense of human dignity. There is always that feeling (as Bogart and countless cowboy stars brought out so well) that despite appearances, *he is his own man.* Yet no movie Asians linked to the West can ever really be that. Though they can bask in the light of humanity, they can never be much more than imitation humans. In only one non-white role is this possibility open—that is the role of villain (he who refuses white help and actively opposes him). Only the villain, already placed outside the pale (sic) of humanity, can be his own man.

The result is a knotty problem. If those close to the whites are invariably dependent, they cannot but be viewed in some way with contempt, no matter how the movie makers go about trying to glorify them. On the other hand, if those most contemptible nonhumans, the villains, are the only Asians capable of "independence" in these films, they are also the only Asians who are the cinematic equivalents of the white leads. Thus, we cannot help but have a sneaking respect for those who oppose us and a sneaking contempt for those who side with us. (How similar this is to the attitudes of many American soldiers in Vietnam towards ARVN and towards the NLF forces.) No doubt this is at least partly responsible for the extremes American moviemakers have gone to in glorifying one and despoiling the other.

What Lewis and Clark's Indian guide Sacajawea was to American history high school texts, Gunga Din was to third world movies. He makes the classic sacrifice for the white world, and in death theoretically proves he is a "better man" than his British mentors. Yet how hollow this "triumph" is for the viewing audience. No one is fooled by the words. Doing his mimic marching shuffle, around the corner from the practicing British troops, what a pitiful imitation "human" he appears to be. And even his greatest hopes—to get one toe on the lowest rung of the white regimental ladder as company bugler—leave him second best to any white who comes along. On the other hand, the leader of the Kali worshippers (read: native resistance forces) is portrayed in a paroxysm of caricature ("Rise brothers and kill. . .kill for the love of Kali, kill for the love of killing, KILL, KILL, KILL!"). He is a mad murderer, a torturer, a loin-clothed savage, a megalomaniac with bulging eyes. Yet he is the only Indian in the film who has the real ability to "love his country" like a white man. "I can die as readily for my country and my fate as you for yours," he says and voluntarily jumps into the snake-pit, yelling "India farewell!"

This inability, despite pulling all the stops, to deny the enemy a certain dignity is not extraordinary. Even Mao Tse-tung, in the otherwise rabid *The Chairman* proves in some grim sense, irrepressible. On the other hand, no matter how charmingly portrayed, our allies' dependency cannot be totally overcome. They are always, in a way, trained spies in the camp of their own people.

American movies about the third world should not be given more credit than is their due. Despite the impression you might get in the theatre, American moviemakers did not invent the world, nor even the version of world history they present in their films. However, they must be given full credit for developing a highly successful and satisfying cinematic form to encapsulate an existing ideological message. With this form, they have been able to relegate the great horrors of Western expansion into the rest of the world, and present-day American hegemony over great hunks of it, to another universe of pleasure and enjoyment. They have successfully tied extermination of non-white peoples to laughable relief, and white racial superiority to the natural order of things. They have destroyed any possibility for explaining the various ways in which non-white (not to speak of white) people could resist invasion, colonization, exploitation, and even mass slaughter.

Cowboy (-third world) films are, in the end, a vast visual pacification program, ostensibly describing the rest of the world, but in fact aimed at the millions of people who for several generations have made up the American viewing audience. It's hardly a wonder that Vietnam did not sear the American consciousness. Why should it have? For years, Americans had been watching the whole scene on their screens: REV DEV, WHAM, endless My Lai's, body counts, killing of wounded enemy soldiers, aerial obliteration, etc. We had grown used to seeing it, and thrilling with pleasure while reaching for another handful of popcorn.

Such a "pacification" program is based on the inundation principle. It is not a matter of quality (probably there have been no good films on Asia since the 1930's), but quantity. So many cowboy-third world movies have rolled factory-style off the production line that the most minute change of plot is hailed as a great innovation. In the end, all the visual "choices" available to a viewer just emphasize the way in which America is strikingly a one-channel country. In fact, it might not be too far wrong to say that while pacification may have failed in Vietnam, its pilot project here in America has generally succeeded; that we are a pacified population, living unknowingly in an occupied country. ★

Notes

1. The men who historically advocated or pursued such a policy in the American West openly and unashamedly referred to it at the time as an "extermination" policy.

2. One must at least credit John Ford, the director, with keeping the carnage down in several of his films (for example, *She Wore a Yellow Ribbon,* 1949) and with allowing the Indians (*Fort Apache,* 1948) to emerge victorious, if no more comprehensible, from at least one movie in the history of the western film.

3. The land equivalent of the Kamikaze onslaught is the Banzai! charge (as in Fuller's *Merrill's Marauders,* 1962)

4. While somewhat harder to find in Nazi war flicks, see *The Enemy Below* (1957) for the World War II (and naval version) of the same scene. The last shot is of the opposing American and Nazi commanders who have disabled each other's ships and saved each other's lives, standing at the stern, sharing a cigarette and looking out together over the endless sea.

5. This is not to say that Americans are portrayed as lacking generosity. Quite the opposite, humanitarian gestures are second nature to them; however, those gestures tend to be directed towards humans. As in the scene where Merrill's Marauders, having smashed thru a mass of Japs, are confronted with a wounded comrade. "You wouldn't leave me?" he asks. "We never leave anybody," is the reply.

6. Extermination has, however, been spoken of quite bluntly in certain third world movies. This was particularly true of those movies made during the war against Japan. Take, for example, *The Purple Heart* (1944), about Japanese attempts to try the Doolittle flyers for "war crimes." At the trial, the leader of the American flyers tells the Japanese judge: "We'll come by night and we'll come by day. we'll blacken your skies and burn your cities to the ground until you get down on your knees and beg for mercy...This was your war. You asked for it. You started it...and now we won't stop until your crummy little empire is wiped off the face of the earth." The Japanese chief prosecutor immediately commits Hara-kiri because of loss of face in failing to break the American prisoners. Or again, *Objective Burma* (1945): The American journalist sees tortured and dead American prisoners. In anger, he says, "This was done in cold blood by a people who claim to be civilized...stinking little savages. Wipe 'em out. Wipe 'em off the face of the earth, I say. Wipe 'em off the face of the earth!"

7. Of all the forms discussed, only Science Fiction films exhibit certain themes which run against this grain. It seems to me there are two sources for this opening towards "deviation." First, in the particularly chilly years of the fifties, anti-nuclear, anti-military freaks flocked to this form whose very fantastical nature provided an allegorical legitimacy for their questionable messages. Thus, even the monster-eradication movies often hide a plea for "peace"/deliverance from incompetent military defenders and their nuclear disasters, whose by-products are sci-fi's ubiquitous radioactive creatures. Second, a traditional tie-in with the sky, heaven, and God led to a semireligious counter-theme of "divine intervention" and human (implicitly white) inferiority. This conception of wisdom descending from above to straighten out the stupid problems of blundering, incapable humanity is basic to *The Day the Earth Stood Still* (1951), in which "Klaatu" appears from space to tour Washington and plead for nuclear peace (and a fascist robot-police force to patrol the world); or *The Next Voice You Hear* (1950), in which God intervenes in person—via radio.

8. George Orwell, "Marrakech," in *Essays* (New York: Doubleday, 1954), pp. 189-190.

9. There were, of course, some holdovers from the 30's. Particularly junk like *Khyber Pass* (1954), in which British lancer Richard Egan, getting ready to capture rebel leaders in a village, tells a fellow officer: "I don't want any of those devils to escape us."

10. Even John Wayne, the last of the cowboy superstars still in the saddle, is forced to mourn his own passing in *True Grit* (1968?).

11. For another recent example, see *Tell Them Willie Boy is Coming* (1970); and I feel certain (though I have yet to see it) that *Soldier Blue* (1970) will fall in the same general category.
    As for the newness of "sympathetic" films—at least a couple of historical antecedents come to mind: first, *The General Died at Dawn* (1936) with Gary Cooper, and Akim Tamiroff as the warlord Yang (seems to have been a pretty popular name among warlord's mothers). This Clifford Odets script hangs heavy with the hand of the 30's Left. ("You ask me why I'm for oppressed people, because I have a background of oppression myself.") But despite its professed sympathy for the oppressed people of China, its protestations of Asian dignity and love for life, and its unbelievably murky politics, it is loaded with all the normal stuff: white-centeredness ("Mr. O'Hara, from the time you leave this room until you deliver the money, the fate of China is in your hands."); a Chinese superevil villain; and a mass suicide scene that only could have taken place among those for whom human life meant nothing at all (In the movie's climactic scene, General Yang—who is dying at dawn—has his troops line up in two facing lines several feet apart and shoot each other), to name just a few of the more salient points.
    For an example from the earlier 60's, see John Ford's "bow" to the tribulations of the Indians, *Cheyenne Autumn* (1964). Exactly the same sort of process occurs and a good book by Marie Sandoz, written from the viewpoint of the Cheyenne, is destroyed in the bargain. Even its historical ending is twisted to imply that Secretary of the Interior Schultz (Edward G. Robinson) allowed the remnants of the Cheyenne to return to their homeland—which he most definitely did not.

FAREWELL TO
A CASE OF

By Raymond Okamura

It is difficult to watch *Farewell to Manzanar*[1] without becoming emotionally involved. The drama is absorbing, the acting heartrending, and the scenes are near-perfect recreations of the World War II concentration camps for Japanese Americans. Television viewers are taken back in history, treated to two hours of emotion-draining euphoria, and released feeling good about themselves and America. But after the tears have been wiped away, a sober review of what this film accomplishes reveals a disturbing underlying theme.

Farewell to Manzanar is produced and directed by John Korty, and is based on the experiences of the Wakatsuki family as told in the book with the same title by Jeanne Wakatsuki and James D. Houston.[2] *Farewell* is remarkably similar to Korty's previous award-winning television production, *The Autobiography of Miss Jane Pittman:* both use the first-person narrative from the point of view of a minority woman; both use teary sentimentality combined with strong drama; and both show minorities overcoming injustices through patience and forbearance.

Farewell is not the first national television exposure to the Japanese American concentration camps: two documentaries shown before were: *Nisei: The Pride and the Shame* (CBS-TV, 1965, Walter Cronkite) and *Guilty by Reason of Race* (NBC-TV, 1972, Robert Northshield). *Farewell* is not as clumsy

bottom row photos by STEVEN MORI from the production of Farewell to Manzanar

MANZANAR:
SUBLIMINAL RACISM

in its racism as *Escape from Manzanar* (a 1945 serial about a Japanese espionage agent who escapes from Manzanar), nor as obvious in its patriotism as *Go For Broke* (a 1951 feature about the 442nd Regimental Combat Team), but it accomplishes identical objectives through more sophisticated techniques. The professed liberalism and apparent sympathetic treatment make it more comparable to *If Tomorrow Comes* (a 1971 ABC-TV *Romeo and Juliet* adaptation with a Japanese American backdrop), or the Chinese American equivalent, *Flower Drum Song* (a 1961 musical and movie about a San Francisco family).[3] While granting relief from the gross hate movies, *Farewell* opens a new trend toward subliminally racist films, which are ultimately more treacherous.

By most criteria, *Farewell* should have been a

good movie. All of the lead roles are played by outstanding Asian American actors and actresses; the Northern California Japanese American community groups participated by providing extras; and the film was made at appropriately grim locations (Tule Lake and Santa Rita Prison). But *Farewell* was controversial from the moment of its public announcement in June, 1975. The Manzanar Committee, joined by Asian Americans for Fair Media, Japanese American Community Services/Asian Involvement, Japanese American Citizens League Hollywood Chapter and Pacific Southwest District Ethnic Concerns Committee, promptly issued a statement declaring:

> We were greatly disappointed that community input was not sought earlier from the Southern California Japanese American community, 80% of whom were incarcerated at Manzanar, and whose

top row photos courtesy of VISUAL COMMUNICATIONS

emotional ties 33 years later are still as tenacious as ever. The script has some serious mistakes which lead to gross distortions of perspectives.[4]

A number of serious charges may be filed against *Farewell*: (1) it uses the unique story of one untypical family to distort the common experience and history of Japanese Americans; (2) it denies the role of white racism and absolves white Americans of accountability; (3) it destroys Japanese Americans as a people by robbing them of humanity, pride, language, and names; (4) it stifles legitimate protest and generates submissive behavior by minorities; (5) it protects the American egalitarian myth and thereby promotes white supremacy. A review of the screenplay will provide the evidence to support these indictments.

After a short prologue, the drama opens with a joyful integrated party at the Wakatsuki home. The good fellowship with white friends gives the impression Japanese Americans were well accepted in 1941. But that was not the actual case.[5] Much later in the screenplay, references are made to the father's inability to gain citizenship or own land, but the lesson is muted by being discussed out of context. The racial tensions could have been depicted through some name calling or hostile stares as in *If Tomorrow Comes*, but everyone is seen happy and friendly in *Farewell*, and the viewer is cleverly set-up for the next event.

The next scene is suddenly about the Pearl Harbor attack. This sequence leaves the viewer with no alternative but to conclude war hysteria resulting from Pearl Harbor was the cause for the Japanese American concentration camps. This illusion becomes the perfect white man's alibi: momentary panic or temporary irrationality can be excused; and the basic racist institutions are never brought under scrutiny. *Farewell* hides the sober, calculated, deliberate, and organized use of the war as a convenient pretext to accomplish the long-desired goals of white supremacists.[6]

Farewell manages to defuse the concentration camp issue by isolating it as a period piece. There is some purpose to all that 1940's nostalgia. Seen only in the World War II Japanese American context, the camps become a long-past aberration, and therefore irrelevant and non-threatening to other Americans at other times. A powerful statement could have been made by a brief mention of the similar expulsion, incarceration, and extermination of Native Americans, or the exclusion, segregation, and mass murder of Chinese Americans,[7] but such revelations would have blown the lid on the underlying white racism.

The stark face of white racism is never shown as direct and ugly as with the heckling white gang in *If Tomorrow Comes*. *Farewell* masks white racism through the techniques of unseen radio announcers and second-person discussions. Low ranking government agents, common soldiers, and ordinary guards are depicted as stupid robots, and thus blameless. But white persons in positions of authority are portrayed as kind and sympathetic. The camp commander becomes a super-patron, returning contraband to prisoners and making speeches about how well he understands their problems. Yet, the responsibility of this same camp commander for the deaths of two demonstrators is glossed over. Even the soldiers who did the shooting are shown horrified at their own misdeed, and are thus instantly pardoned. *Farewell* instills respect, trust, and gratitude for white authority. Meanwhile, white racism is allowed to permeate the whole camp as a nebulous and ghostly force. Japanese Americans cannot respond to a cosmic power; they cannot reach out and hit it like the Japanese American brothers could do with the hecklers in *If Tomorrow Comes*.

The love affair between a Wakatsuki brother and a white female nurse's aid takes place in a complete vacuum. Nothing is said about the existing anti-miscegenation laws and attitudes, and the Wakatsuki family and other Japanese Americans in the camp act as if nothing is out of the ordinary for a white woman to be intruding in their innermost circles. The forbidden love problem is solved in the usual fashion by the Japanese American partner being killed. This romantic interlude is interposed without context, and has no apparent meaning other than to reinforce the double standard. White male-Asian female love is acceptable (as evidenced by the happily married couple in the prologue and epilogue), but Asian male-white female love is taboo. The Japanese American man in *If Tomorrow Comes* also pays with his life for daring to love a white woman, but that ending was central to the Shakespearian tragedy.

Although the characters are based on real people, and the dialogue is patterned after actual speeches made at Manzanar, *Farewell* uses false names and omits Japanese American words. Stripped of their language and culture, Japanese Americans end up sounding like ventriloquist's dummies in a classical morality play.

The constant speech making and intellectual debate leave no time for the Japanese Americans to relate to each other as human beings: as husband and wife, mother and daughter, father and son, brother to brother, friend to friend, and as strangers and enemies caught in the same trap. There is just one fleeing moment of concentration camp camaraderie when the photographer encounters a boy at the woodpile. Japanese American humanity could have been salvaged through the children—after all, this story is supposed to be about the recollections of a person who was a child at the time. But there is nothing about young Jeanne missing her father, being curious about her brother's girlfriend, asking about a new baby in the family, being afraid of those huge soldiers, playing a game of "chicken" with the guards, or doing any of the innocent things of childhood.

Even the father's degradation into alcoholism is plasticized by not showing his former proud and vibrant self. The emotional distance prevents viewers from identifying too closely with his problems, or thinking too deeply about the causes for Ko Wakatsuki's destruction. Japanese Americans become a people without names, without language, without humanity, and without dignity, who might be pitied like animals in a zoo, but whose image can be quickly erased from the consciousness.

The one-sided treatment of the protest demonstration[8] and loyalty oath issue[9] makes the propaganda intent of *Farewell* abundantly clear. The people with legitimate grievances are pictured as malcontents and hoodlums who go around in gangs beating up people. For people helplessly incarcerated in a concentration camp, the loss of food is an extremely serious issue which jabs right at the survival instinct. But the film treats the stolen sugar as a trivial matter and makes the protesters look childish for crying about it. *Farewell* favors the collaborators by making their speeches sound more reasonable, and honors the *shikataganai* (it can't be helped) ethic by making inaction seem noble. The same line-up of antagonists face each other in the loyalty oath controversy, with the same result. The idea of demanding a loyalty oath from a group of people already judged disloyal and locked up is absurd, and can be considered the ultimate outrage and final insult. Yet this film transforms legitimate conflict into a mindless pro-America versus pro-Japan fight, and of course, the Red-White-and-Blue wins. The father pummels his arch rival, and the loyalist Wakatsuki brother finally converts his dissenter brother and they go riding off to war together. Naturally, the former hot-headed dissenter and lover atones for his indiscretions by dying in battle.

Playwright Frank Chin (*Year of the Dragon, Chickencoop Chinaman*) observed:

> Harry Ueno, Togo Tanaka, Joe Kurihara, Fred Tayama, and other Japanese Americans who were moved to heroic acts of will and greatness to maintain Japanese American integrity are real people. Villains or heroes of Manzanar depending on your point of view, but real and courageous. . .what they said and did at Manzanar are matters of public record and more, they are the substance of Japanese American courage in the most trying time in Japanese American history.[10]

As the end approaches and the camp prepares for closing, Ko Wakatsuki reminisces about his youth in Hiroshima. Suddenly, a blinding flash vaporizes the memories of Hiroshima. The viewer momentarily thinks he sees the ashes of Hiroshima, but quickly realizes he is back at the stark ruins of present-day Manzanar. If the movie had ended on that note, a

significant message could have been conveyed. But a postscript follows and reverses the effect: there is a flashback to the Wakatsuki family happily riding off into the plains, seemingly unaffected by years of deprivation, degradation, and death. That little sequence reversal lets the white folks off the hook. The American dream is fulfilled, white consciences are cleared, and Japanese Americans are still left holding the bag.

In conclusion, *Farewell* represents a skillful filmmaker's utilization of drama, sentimentality, and nostalgia to distort an important lesson from American history. By distracting from hard issues, and obscuring the root causes for the concentration camps, it succeeds in protecting, perpetuating, and promoting white racism. This film is all the more insidious because it achieves its goal under a facade of liberalism. The haunting afterimage left by *Farewell* is that of a Japanese American obediently kowtowing at the feet of the great white benevolent father-protector, and being told kindly to have patience, keep faith in America, and everything will turn out happy at the end. But unseen in the shadows is a faceless, white-hooded executioner, sword poised and ready to strike if the Japanese American dares to rise from the prostrate position. ★

Notes

1. First telecast by the National Broadcasting Company on March 11, 1976.

2. Jeanne Wakatsuki Houston and James D. Houston, *Farewell to Manzanar,* Boston: Houghton Mifflin, 1973.

3. Irvin Paik, "That Oriental Feeling," *Roots: An Asian American Reader,* Los Angeles: University of California, 1971, p. 30.

4. *New York Nichibei,* July 10, 1975. Also printed in *Hokubei Mainichi* and *Rafu Shimpo.*

5. Roger Daniels, *The Politics of Prejudice,* New York: Atheneum, 1967; Jacobus tenBroek, Edward N. Barnhart, Floyd W. Matson, *Prejudice, War and the Constitution,* Berkeley: University of California Press, 1954, 1968.

6. Morton M. Grodzins, *Americans Betrayed,* Chicago: University of Chicago Press, 1949.

7. Robert F. Heizer and Alan J. Almquist, *The Other Californians,* Berkeley: University of California Press, 1971; Paul Jacobs and Saul Landau with Eve Pell, *To Serve the Devil,* New York: Vintage Books, 1971, Volumes 1 and 2.

8. Arthur A. Hansen and David A. Hacker, "The Manzanar Riot: An Ethnic Perspective," *Amerasia Journal,* Volume 2, Number 2, page 112, Fall 1974; Arthur A. Hansen and Betty E. Mitson, *Voices Long Silent,* Fullerton: California State University, 1974.

9. Dorothy Swaine Thomas and Richard S. Nishimoto, *The Spoilage,* Berkeley: University of California Press, 1946; Michi Weglyn, *Years of Infamy,* New York: William Morrow, 1976.

10. "Open Letter to John Korty," *Hokubei Mainichi,* January 13, 1976. Also printed in *New York Nichibei* and *Rafu Shimpo.*

Anna May Wong

by Judy Chu

She was born in Los Angeles Chinatown in 1907, one of seven children of a Chinese laundryman. Her Chinese name was Wong Liu Tsong (frosted yellow Willow), and having gone to Chinese school she spoke Cantonese fluently. She attended Los Angeles High. Her friends there used to serve as extras in films for extra money.

Anna May was still in her teens when she entered the silent film world. There are several versions on how she got started. *Motion Picture Magazine,* (1931), says she always had a "craving to be a movie star. Most of her schooldays were spent playing hookey—either at the picture show or watching companies at work. She asked innumerable questions about how it was done, and was known to everybody, from the director to the propboy, as the Curious Chinese Child."

Anna May Wong's first exposure in films was as one of the 300 extras in Nazimoza's *The Red Lantern* (1919). It was an opportune time to get into the then-developing film industry. Hollywood was still a small town. New York theater-goers looked down on the film industry. It was not "real" acting. Theater was acting and filmmaking was making funny faces.

It was also a very opportune time to be an Asian. The orient was an exotic, foreign and moreover, comfortably distant culture. The 20's saw the oriental cultural influence in home, dress and artwork: Japanese and Chinese antiques became popular,

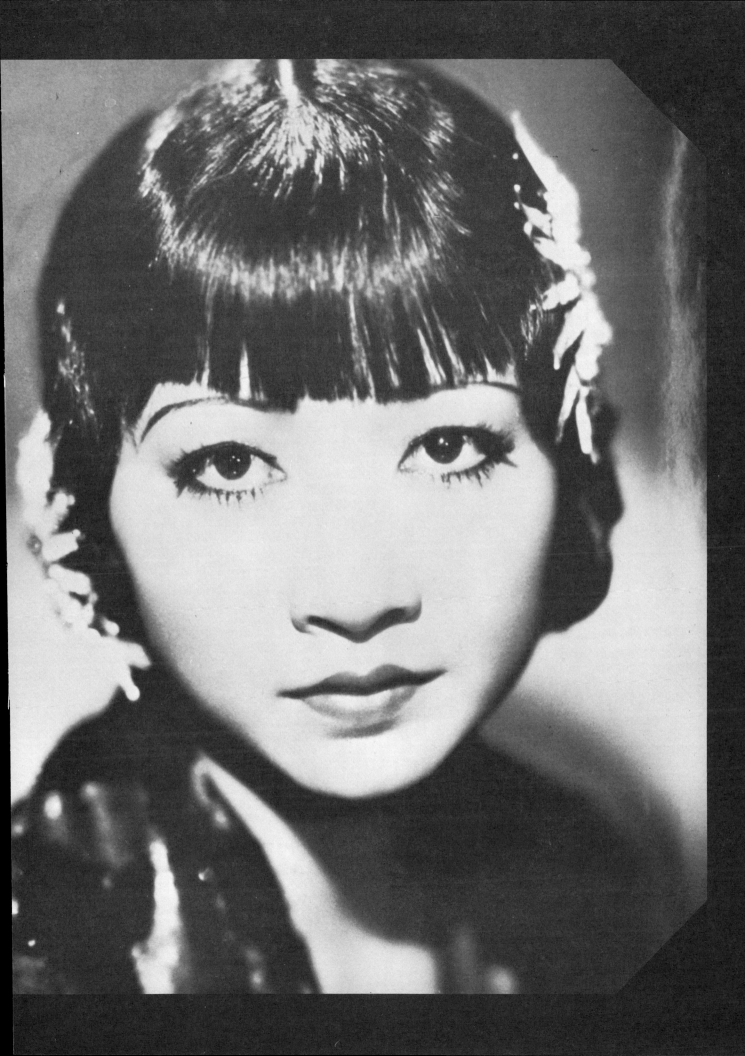

middle-aged housewives flew around in silk kimonos. At movie houses, there were films with scenes of opium dens, fierce sinister Fu Manchus with designs on white women and passive servile Asian women.

It was in this setting that Anna May landed a bit part as a handmaid to princess opposite Douglas Fairbanks Sr. The film was *The Thief of Baghdad* (1924), a landmark in film history because of its fantasy of costumes and sets. Anna May went on to become Hollywood's oriental.

When Anna May appeared on the screen, the American public was confronted with a different concept of the Asian woman. Anna May didn't play the passive straight Asian Geisha Girl role or the part of the peasant woman, and even her costume roles were always done in contemporary settings. To a public that could not quite grasp or accept the strange, often bewildering customs of the Orient, Anna May was a satisfactory blend. The first Asian in America to have wide exposure, she soon became known as the Chinese Flapper.

> From crown to sole, Anna May Wong is Chinese. Her black hair is of the texture that adorns the heads of the maidens who live beside the Yang-tse Kiang. Her deep brown eyes, while the slant is not pronounced, are typically oriental. These come from her Mongol father. But her Manchu mother has given her a height and a poise of figure that Chinese maids seldom have.
> She . . . was raised as other Chinese children. But something in her environment changed her mental trend. She was artistic, she loved beauty. In school she soon picked up the ways of the West. She lost her Chinese accent. She read American books. She was even a close student of the Bible.
> —*Photoplay*, June 1924

So started a career that would eventually include 100 films. She was a vamp in *Forty Winks,* the Indian princess Tiger Lily in *Peter Pan,* countless slave girls and "the other woman" committing suicide. In *Toll of the Sea* (1927), the first all technicolor film made, she played a Chinese girl married to a white in China. He dies and she comes to America with their baby to confront the family. The main theme of the movie lies in her affinity for the sea; there are shots of her walking along the sea coast, among rocks, surf pounding, longing for her homeland. In the end the Asian-white love affair cannot be consummated and she walks into the sea. The reviews say: "someone recognized the story needed something else, even with the acting of Anna May Wong which is exquisite without question."

Subsequent oriental film spectaculars, *Old San Francisco* (1927), *Mr. Wu* and *A Trip to Chinatown,* established her popularity not only in America but internationally. There was little difficulty at that time in the exchange of films; with silent films there was no dubbing problem. In 1929 Anna May left Hollywood for Europe for three years. She was

286

received very well. She starred in Alfred Hitchcock's *Picadilly* (1929), which was nominated as one of the top ten films in Europe. She also did some stagework in London with Laurence Olivier in *Circle of Chalk*. In Vienna, Anna May had three leading men for a Chinese operetta, *Hai Tang* in which she danced and sang the English, German and French versions. She became fluent in all three languages after spending five hours daily learning German and after taking 200 guineas worth of lessons to acquire an English accent.

> And she got her money's worth. Anna May begins her conversation with "Isay," ends them with "Well, cheerio!," says it's a jolly nuisance and calls her native land "Amuddicah."
> —*Motion Picture Magazine,* Oct. 1931

She returned to Hollywood, with a Paramount contract and leading men such as Phillip Ahn and the popular Warner Oland, a Swede who played Asian roles. With the other prominent Asian film star of the times, Sessue Hayakawa, she played the daughter of Dr. Fu Manchu in *Daughter of the Dragon* (1931). In this film, known today primarily as camp, Anna May slinks through in wild costumes and headdresses. This period was the peak of her career. Along with von Sternberg's *Shanghai Express* (1932) (a highlight in movie industry because of its excellent visuals and its Academy Award in cinematography) came *Limehouse Blues* (1934) and *Study in Scarlet* (1933).

The American public gave its approval to this special blend of an "oriental" who had been developed to suit American wants and needs.

> Sessue Hayakawa smokes Japanese cigarettes, has Japanese people around him, talks with a completely bewildering Japanese accent, looks oriental, and above all, thinks with the oriental attitude. "Never make plan," says Sessue with his difficult accent. "Never plan ahead." Anna May, with Western verbosity, is more explicit in expressing her philosophy.
> Anna May Wong has been away three years.
> In that time she has learned German and French and acquired an English accent.
> She has made three successful pictures in German, two in English, and one in French—and has been a sensation on the stages of the Continent, London and New York.
> She is glad to be back.
> She went away a Chinese flapper—and now many tell her that she no longer even looks Oriental.
> Sessue Hayakawa has been away twelve years.
> He went to London by way of New York, and was a success on the stage of both cities.
> He made a picture in France, and wrote a novel there.
> In one evening at Monte Carlo, he lost his entire fortune.
> He returned to Japan, broke a tradition of his native stage, and became Japan's greatest actor.
> He did not want to come back to Hollywood.
> He has remained completely Oriental.
> —*Motion Picture Magazine,* Oct. 1931

The niche that provided for Anna May Wong's rise to fame also served to isolate her. *Motion Picture* called her Hollywood's "stepchild." She was popular with the film colony but her "success as an actress left her partly estranged from the California Chinese community." (*Variety*, 1961) Still, the superficial image of the sexy erotic that propelled her at the same time gave to the American public an Asian in America with personality. Anna May's views became more widely known.

On her personal philosophy she states:

"I think it was my fatalism that made me able to start working out my seemingly impossible ambition. That, and the fact that I was very imaginative—it was possible for anything to happen, it seemed to me. I was so young when I began that I knew I would still have my youth if I failed so I determined to give myself ten years to succeed as an actress. Ten years is not long in the Chinese mind.

"People tell me I've changed so since my European experience, and that I don't look like a Chinese girl anymore. I believe the mind and spirit show through the features. My face has changed because my mind has changed. I look like the people of the West—except in some moments of despair and stress. Then I fall back on Oriental philosophy, which is to accept, not to resist. There's no use to struggle. That philosophy gets you through a lot of tight places."

—*Motion Picture Magazine*, 1931

One such place in which the philosophy may have been useful was in her encounter with race prejudice:

"That's one reason why I was so happy then. Of course it depends a lot on who you are. People who might ordinarily have racial feelings would make an exception in the case of a celebrity. But there, everyone was lovely to me."

That is not always true of America. "But what difference does it make?" asks Anna May. "People like that—who would be rude and unkind—you wouldn't wish to know anyway, so it doesn't matter."

—*Motion Picture Magazine*, 1931

During the 1930's Anna May is photographed in London and flies back and forth between Europe and Hollywood. But it was soon realized that her "homeland" had yet to be seen. In 1936, she went to China to "observe the Oriental culture for one year. Because I had been the villainess so often in pictures, it was thought I had not been true to my people. It took four hours one afternoon to convince the government this was not so. I couldn't give up my career because I feel it is really drawing China nearer and making it

better understood and liked." (*Hollywood Citizen News*, 1958)

In the late 30's and early 40's, Anna May's films became routine and easily forgettable. Gradually, the studios were using her chiefly as a coach or consultant when they made a picture about Orientals with occidental actors. With the outbreak of World War II, Anna May announced her retirement to work for the USO and United China relief, and in 1942 went on an entertainment tour of Alaska. She reports: "Many of the boys I met had fought the Japs in the Aleutians and in spite of the fact that they are terribly anxious to get home, they have an outspoken urge to take another shot at the enemy. They think of the Japs only in terms of extermination." (*Time*, 1944)

As the oriental mystery theme became exhausted, her roles became even more limited. Except for a comeback in the late 40's there was a long inactive period of minor television and film work for Anna May. Seventeen years after her announced retirement, she had a final comeback in the box office success *Portrait in Black* (1960), a woman's tear-jerker of a movie in which she played Lana Turner's maid.

A lone national and international Asian "name" plus thirty-seven years of experience in film culminated in a contract to play the part of the mother who sings "Chop Suey" in *The Flower Drum Song*. She died before she could do it. Newspapers report her death as caused by a heart attack.

Anna May Wong, 54, Los Angeles-born daughter of a local laundryman, who became a film star over her father's objections that "every time your picture is taken, you lose a part of your soul," died a thousand deaths as the screen's foremost Oriental villainess.

—*Time* (10 February 1961)

Her survivors were listed as her brothers and sisters, Anna May never married. Even on film, she was only allowed on occasion to have a love interest, and did not kiss until late in her career in the British film *Java Head* (1943).

The fantasy of film was extended into her reality. An Asian-white love affair was an impossibility for this daughter of the Chinese community. Anna May not only acted but lived the "oriental" image. Cruelly, even in the announcement of her death, she is remembered less for her accomplishments than for being the butt of another oriental joke about a "thousand deaths."

Conspicuously lying among movie-magazine

photos of Gloria Swanson, Sylvia Sidney and Greta Garbo, are those of Anna May Wong. Together, the photographs, some in exotic beads and headdresses, most in smart 30's clothes, represents a timeless "before and after" editorial on this Asian American woman whose dreams and ambitions were so much like any other woman growing up in the glittery 20's.

Now, thirteen years after her death, there is rising interest in her contributions to media. In January 1973, the Asian Fashion Designers conceived of the Anna May Wong Award. "We the Asian Fashion Designers, feel we can . . . look back to the past to Anna May Wong and relate to her as a symbol of fashion inspiration . . . for in her long film career (1920-60), she held her own with the image setters of the silver screen and the fashion world. With her unique looks and style, she moved from one fashion period to another—20's, 30's and the 40's and in each era maintained her individual style.

And Terry Tam Soon, one prominent Asian fashion designer looks in retrospect: "The thing with her is that they thought of her as a sex symbol; she was a pretty Asian woman that would play these superficial roles and if they needed an actress of depth, they would get a white actress and make her up . . . like Helen Hayes or Loretta Young.

"She had a definite influence on stereotyping. She was one of the first Asians to play an Asian. Previously, Asian women had been portrayed by Caucasian actresses who tended to play heavy costume pictures with beaded robes and heavy make-up, and relied on stories based on China and Japan prior to 1900. Anna came along; and here was a beautiful Asian woman who had a figure, a pretty face, who could be associated with the exotic, superficial and represent the glamorous. For me, my primary thing about Anna May Wong is to make the Asian people who are interested in theater and the younger generation aware of her contributions as a person—good or bad—to the overall image of Asians in America."

Anna May set a precedent not only for Asians in the media, but for all Asians, in making one step in breaking the chain of white stereotypes. A major figure in Asian American history, her story is one of struggle against contradictory standards. It is a story of alienation, of the isolation of a woman having to be both the symbol of everything Oriental to a white audience and the Asian-who-made-it to an Asian audience. Hers was a time of living as an American first, Chinese second; and being seen as Chinese first and American second by a larger white public. This situation was perhaps more magnified and fantasized in Hollywood, where white American "melting pot" mentality took blatant pride in her as a paragon of an individual who could overcome race prejudice.

If you ask an older person, white or Asian, to name outstanding Asian stars, they will name Sessue Hayakawa and Anna May Wong. People have different reasons for relating to her. Some see her as camp. Others see her as part of film history. And some Asians will say she was beautiful and glamorous and someone to identify with. David Jung, one former Chinatown resident who used to watch her at the movies, thinks back: "The Chinese people accepted second best, second best was looked on as a star. They accepted her saying, 'Well, somebody made it.' Anna May Wong was actually a star; outside of the Chinese community, she was just an actress but she was a star in our community. When we had those moon festivals and new year parades, she rode in those parades as our number one star. She probably despised the roles she was given. In white America she had to accept them. Today, people speak out but it wasn't like that then.

"She was the pioneer of Chinese actresses. Maybe she was the pioneer of why we get any action today. When Chinese people see her on the screen, they admire her cause they can identify readily. We know she had a miserable life. She was always somebody's China doll."

Just as saddening is to think of all the tired and vulnerable minds within the nation who have looked for an escape at the movies. Beneath the atmosphere of fun and relaxation can be found the stereotyping and degradation of ethnic people. Media has the power to indiscriminately reach the masses from the housewife in Illinois to the Asian in Chinatown. On the overwhelming professional screen in which Anna May played her inevitable role the housewife finds out what the Asian is, and the Asian finds out what she is supposed to be.

Anna May Wong was a puppet in a country that needed a sexual tantalizer, and a unique—but not too unique—experience. Whether she was willing or unwilling is immaterial considering her basic needs for economic survival and a positive self-image. Anna May was like so many other Asians who knew about co-optation and about being coopted, but saw few alternatives to that pat on the back for passivity.

The limitation of Anna May's role on screen is a concrete example of the limitation for roles for Asians in general. To see an Anna May Wong film is to see a potential for more depth and more feeling. It causes a mixture of frustration, sadness, admiration and anger for Anna May, and for all peoples whose expression has been stunted.

In the past Anna May symbolized everything from cheesecake sexiness to exotic assimilation to droll camp. But Anna May is not just an object of the past; she is a very contemporary comment on the imposed roles of Asians in America and on the sexist expectations still internalized and acted upon by Asian women. With knowledge of her history, one finds that beyond the charming exotic imagery emerges an understanding and somehow a closeness to the very real woman labeled the "lady of mystery." ★

KUNG-FU FAN KLUB
by Irvin Paik

"Kung Fu," an ABC Movie of the Week, aired in June, 1972. Warner Brothers was contracted to produce one sixty-minute show a month starting in September. By December they were making one sixty-minute show a week. Hong Kong-produced kung fu films flooded the country and the "kung fu kraze" was on. Movie fans paid millions to see backs broken and faces smashed with only bare hands and feet. It was a new, exciting and innovative way to kill, maim and cripple.

The main character of "Kung Fu" was "Kwai Chang Caine" who was played by David Carradine. Caine's mother was Chinese and his father white. When they were killed by bandits in China, he was accepted to the Shaolin Temple and survived the rigorous and deadly training. In avenging the death of his beloved Master Po, he kills an imperial prince and flees to America. Haunted by "wanted" posters and driven by a need to meet his half brother, Caine is a non-violent, non-materialistic superman who can virtually "walk through walls."

"Master Po," played by Keye Luke was identifiable by his opaque white contact lenses. He is the blind master who teaches Caine "to see." He is also full of wisdom, which never ceases to perplex young Caine. "Master Kan," the chief monk of the Shaolin Temple was played by Philip Ahn. He counsels Caine with pithy sayings and maxims.

A typical Kung Fu story finds Caine walking in a Southwest American locale. He witnesses something which triggers his memory. The scene dissolves slowly and the viewer is in China witnessing a bit of Caine's experience. Master Po or Master Kan are usually present. As the scene dissolves once more the viewer is back in America and the story continues, flashing back to China to comment on events in America.

The switch from one show a month to one show a week put Warner Brothers on an extremely tight schedule. The finished hour show went to New York for approval on a Monday and aired on Thursday. Creative decisions were dictated by the clock, the calendar and by panic.

The 1973-74 season began with a writers strike which set back production of twenty-three one hour segments about two months. Scripts were hurriedly written and changed and approved and additions made even after shooting had finished. The 74-75 season began normally but promptly slipped behind schedule. The ratings were awful. David Carradine's drunken antics didn't help. The show moved from Saturday at 9 p.m. to Friday at 8 p.m. back to Saturday at 8 p.m. (opposite "All in the Family") and was not picked up for the next season.

I worked on almost every show of the 73-74 season except the pilot. My job was in the department that replaces dialogue which was poorly recorded on location. I saw most of the shows before the effects and music were added. It was my intention in the following interview of Alex Beaton and Herman Miller, who were the co-producers of "Kung Fu," to find out about how producers perceive Asians and how they develop Asian themes and characters.

Alex Beaton started as an associate producer and was co-producer with Herman Miller for the last season. Jerry Thorpe, who also produced "Little People" remained as executive producer. Both were employed by Warner Brothers. Alex came up through the studio system from messenger. One of his film editing credits is "Tick Tick Tick." Herman Miller rewrote the original pilot script of Ed Spielman and the first three scripts of the series. He left to produce "Cannon" for Quinn Martin and came back for the end of 73-74 season and co-produced the 74-75 season.

Beaton and Miller are both young men who do not fit the stereotype of dried up movie moguls sitting behind huge desks pushing buttons and pinching thighs. The task of accounting for roughly a $200,000 per hour show kept them thin and active. When the television season started, around June and July, their lives became a four-ring circus. They were running between their offices, the shooting stage, the looping stage and the final re-recording stage. While one show was being prepared for airing, another was ready for effects and music, another was shooting, another was being cast and others were being written. There was no time for philosophical or sociological questions. That is a luxury available to television producers only before the shooting starts. Decisions after that were made by instinct. Because of the lack of other Asian representation in the media, they had *by default* become the spokesmen for Asians in America. They, more than anyone else, were shaping opinions and attitudes about Asians.

The following interview was conducted at the beginning of the last season.

The Burbank Studios, May 1, 1974, Alex Beaton's office.

Irvin: What is your concept of the show? What do you hope it will be next season?

Herman: Exciting entertainment with a touch of Oriental mysticism. We have a unique hero for American television. He is inwardly turned, looking for the way, for himself in tune with nature. He is unpredictable in anybody's terms. He is disciplined, has skills and talent, is peaceable, seeks non-violent solutions but is well equipped to take care of himself.

Alex: He is seeking that inner peace that anybody looks for. He is seeking to identify himself, his roots, who he is.

Herman: He is after all of mixed blood. Half his roots are in America, half in China.

Alex: If we have done our job correctly, you will not know what you are going to see when you tune in. If the three of us go into a town and see the town bully beating up on the town weakling, we will have three separate reactions. We will spend more time in *his* mind working with *his* imagination. We will examine the kinds of things that he has to be thinking about.

Irvin: What's Oriental mysticism?

Herman: I wish I knew. We play it as it comes along.

In western eyes, Zen and Buddhism have taken a large hold. It seems to have something vital to say to us or it wouldn't catch. I am not knowledgeable enough to know exactly what it has to say, but we do have writers who do come in here with ideas and tend to shape them in terms of some book wisdom, some modern feeling, some intuition. If you ask me to pin it down much past that I couldn't.

Irvin: What is the source of the philosophy spoken by Master Kan and Master Po?

Herman: It comes from some of the writer's own ideas, his readings, some of our ideas, our readings. We have some people who have delved into Zen. Lyn *(secretary)* has a list of some of the books we use. The story editor *(Ed Waters)* has some books and the writers have their own sources. We seem to attact writers who are interested in this and have done

photos by ED IKUTA

reading in this area which is natural.[1]

Alex: I think the philosophy evolved beyond this show. I think a lot of the attitudes of the people who follow Zen have gone through a process of evolution. Our show may have been involved a bit. We don't get philosophy into every show. By definition, a show called "The Gunman" is going to be 95% western.

Irvin: Why do you think people are watching your show?

Herman: I think we are successful in providing interesting entertainment. We have a unique character and the stories are unique. We fulfill some kind of psychic need or "spirituality" that westerners are looking for. People are interested in the whole East, India, not just China and Japan, the mystique of the East.

Alex: There is nothing else like our show. I think there has been a resurgence of anything Oriental which was triggered by Nixon's visit to Red China. Up to that time China had been closed to us for over twenty years. When we opened trade with the Orient, there were a lot of people interested. Also maybe some people are seeing a failure of the Western system and are looking for an answer in the East.

Irvin: How much does ABC guide you, or direct you, or force you?

Alex: I don't think they do any of those things in these areas. They generally accept what we do. They must feel that we know what we're doing. They want to know if it satisfies their "norm," which is action or a believable love interest.

Herman: They're generally more worried about content rather than philosophical idea, things such as excessive violence. It's one of their favorite shows and they're more likely to look at what's happening on it than on other shows.

Irvin: The period of the show is 1870-1880. What are your beliefs as to the standing of the Chinese in America during that period?

Herman: It was a period of considerable mistreatment. Some pretty harrowing things happened. We have a book in which some of the atrocities against the Chinese are recounted. They're appalling. It was a rough road as it was for any minority, the Irish for instance who had all gone to the mine fields. According to the information in the pilot, the Chinese were brought here for, I guess, mining and railroads and then went into things they felt more at home with like farming and everything else like store-keeping. They were contracted for in China and they

paid their passage out of their wages. The men came over with the intention of supporting a family and returning home when they had enough money. Some remained, many men went back and then women came. That comes to mind quickly. They were the traditional coolie and affectionately looked at like you might look on a beast of burden. They were no threat and they did the dirty work. They did not complain. Most of our scripts are pegged about the time when the Chinese are starting to spread out and get established in other vocations and thereby competing with the poor white man. We do use Chinese who had established themselves in stores or as merchants. I would say it's just prior to the time when the hatred of the Chinese was the strongest. There were a lot of sociological reasons why they were hated, they were imported for the lowest menial labor which put them at the bottom of the social scale, but mainly it was the cheap labor replacing local labor.

Alex: The Chinese were oppressed and they had that type of spirit that overcame the oppression of white dominance which took the form of prejudice and ill treatment. The Chinese were different, they were somebody to kick and these are the reasons that men have always held power over other men and those reasons never seem to change.

Irvin: Who determines the authenticity of props and costumes?

Alex: The research department here is very good. Herman and I try for what we feel is the most authentic look we can get. Writers come in with well researched ideas of what things should be. Our costume and prop men go through a lot of research. One of our prop men goes shopping for props after the day's shooting. I know because there's a letter on my desk asking for reimbursement for those hours. Right now we are looking for photography equipment for a show that will shoot in October. There is not as much research material available for China. Our research department has access to the downtown library (main Los Angeles Library) and other studios. I think our costume and prop men work harder than any other department in Hollywood. I don't know of any other show that has the kinds of problems we do. We generally accept their recommendations. Now ABC Program Practices and Broadcast Standards restrict us from the violence standpoint. We could not use a mace and chain although it was authentic to the period of "Cenotaph" our last show of the season. I've seen more violent things on ABC than on other networks. I have a feeling our show is curtailed perhaps more than other shows but maybe that's because I'm involved in it. It's difficult to say. I don't see that much television.

Herman: Now to the extent that westerns have become traditional morality plays that no longer reflect a reality, we are doing a western on television and we don't have the freedom to be honest totally. We accept many of the preconditions associated with the gunfighter and the hero. These are stock characters and we are not exempt from that. In areas where research is inadequate we compromise between what we can find out and what is possible to us. We don't have all the resources in the world.

Alex: For instance, the sculpture in "The Passion of Chen Yi" was not available in books. We manufactured it by looking at similar types of sculpture, tools available, materials available and styles at the time. We came up with what we thought was the most authentic.

Irvin: How do you arrive at authenticity in the fights?

Alex: Our technical advisor, Kam Yuen[2] who is an instructor in kung fu and studied in China, meets with us in the production meeting, the same one attended by the costume and prop people, and quite often he has ideas from a reading of the script, and we discuss with him what we want. Once on the set, he will make the final fight in coordination with the director, David Carradine and Greg Walker who is stunt coordinator and double for Carradine. They try to find a workable fight within the dramatic needs of the script that would be exciting and different and interesting to look at. We get something that falls within the restriction of the pure kung fu to the less pure kung fu. So that we have a fight that incorporates the basic movements and is different from the fight last week.

Irvin: How much do you know about the pure kung fu?

Herman: It's hard to know how to measure that.

Alex: Have I studied pure kung fu? No.

Herman: But the man who did the original pilot script, Ed Spielman, did. And it is this material that we began with. He included a lot of material that he had studied and indicated how long he had been at it, what he had seen himself with his own eyes and the studies he had made. Our main concern is that we're putting on a show for entertainment, for people, so we want something exciting and something with a visual look to it.

Irvin: Then you have the final word on authenticity?

Alex: I would say that's true. We will say "throw that axe out and put that one in." Certainly we have done that but we will rely heavily on the people who

function in these areas. It generally works because of the large percentage of the mail from people who comment on something they think was authentically done. Our experience increases with each show we do.

Herman: We get letters from all over the world.

Irvin: Does Kam try to accommodate you or does he try to hold out for more authenticity than in the past?

Alex: He tries tremendously hard.

Herman: He accommodates us by giving us authenticiy.

Alex: Yes.

Herman: That is the accommodation we ask for.

Alex: Obviously there are restrictions. Doing a full fight in this room is a restriction for a man like him.

Irvin: He is employed by you and he has to fight you.

Alex: Fight?

Irvin: That is he has to oppose you. He wants to do a certain type of fight and you want to do it in this room.

Alex: How does he handle it? We come to a meeting of the minds. If we can't do the fight he wants to do, we'll find another site which is very often what happens.

Herman: Everybody has to accommodate themselves to the medium, so must he. Nothing more than that.

Alex: We're all in the same boat. We have used many people who are studying martial arts and almost to a man they revere Kam.

Herman: Bruce Lee was in on this thing before it got off the ground. He would be one of the resource people we were talking to.

Irvin: He thought he was going to get the part.[3] Do you know why he didn't?

Herman: I was not in on the casting. I would imagine that many things would be involved. I would think that ABC would say they want somebody with kind of a marquee value.

Alex: I'm frowning a bit because I'm questioning your statement. Where did you hear such a thing?

Irvin: Nancy Kwan told me.

Alex: That sounds like something you picked up off a . . .

Irvin: He had done several roles and wanted to get into show business. He was teaching martial arts to Ted Ashley's wife (president of Warner Brothers).

Herman: That's perhaps where he got the idea, in private. I talked to him a little bit and got a little of that. I would imagine the practical realities of the medium had a lot to do with it since he was not a trained actor. A lot of money rides on a series as you know. They have to cover their risks as best they can, and they do that all the time with all the people including writers, actors and directors.

Irvin: Have you heard or do you believe that there are more Japanese actors available than Chinese actors?

Alex: I haven't heard it and I don't think so.

Irvin: Have you heard or do you believe that Japanese actors are better than Chinese actors?

Alex: That's an extraordinary question. No! And let me qualify that, I don't think the reverse either. Where does that question come from?

Herman: A man is a good actor or a bad actor.

Irvin: I've been told these things and I'm trying to find out how many people in positions like yourself believe them. Are you making any unusual efforts to involve Asians behind the cameras?

Herman: That's out of our area.

Alex: You mean guilds and unions? No. We are subject to I.A.T.S.E. *(union)* regulations. I wouldn't know what the union would say if I asked for an Asian cameraman because I've never asked. I would suspect they would say we have no Asian cameraman that by virtue of ability or time in grade or whatever the hell it's called.

Herman: They'll say: "This is the list of people available, take them or leave them." I would imagine that the same things are happening in all the minority groups, Black and so on. All these people are being trained so that they are moving up and soon they will become available to us. Up until very recently there were no Black cameramen.

Alex: Or Black writers or Black directors and now that's getting to be commonplace.

Herman: There are no women cameramen. But this has been in the past and hopefully these things are changing.

Irvin: So your answer is no, you're not really seeking?

Herman: Our answer is that this is not really our province, at this particular time. We will certainly be glad to see them become available.

Irvin: Do you feel a social responsibility to the Asian in America?

Herman: To the extent that we are working people yes. That is we don't take the burden of the world on our shoulders. We are after all working line producers. Sure, we're aware of it and take it into account. We wouldn't be successful as producers if we didn't.

Alex: I have a tremendous prejudice, but I happen to think that Herman and I do what we do regarding the Asian community with an inordinate respect and desire for their wishes. I think that's what makes us successful as producers.

Irvin: What kind of feedback do you get?

Alex: Almost without exception, there are no bummers, no bad mouthing, the show has something to say.

Herman: It appeals to young people, college kids, high school kids. When you're in a group and they know you've done *Kung Fu* you can feel their excitement, you can sense it.

Irvin: You mean you go out to speak to groups?

Herman: No, people at the beach, friends over to the house, their kids. No, I don't go out and ask people but there's no question that you are approached and this good feeling exists.

Irvin: Have you heard anything from the Asian community?

Herman: I know that actors have said to us: "Thank God for a chance for us to work."

Alex: That's our most constant source of communication with the Asian community, the actors.

Irvin: Do you think an Asian male can play a lead on a tv series?

Alex: Sure, yes in a flash. I think we've used two of the best actors in this town. And interestingly we've used one of them three times. Not two of the best Asian actors, two of the best actors.

Irvin: About three years ago a Warner Brothers vice president said an Asian male lead could not hold an audience longer than ten minutes. What do you think?

293

Herman: It may have been true three years ago or five years ago. Things have changed and are changing. Five years ago a Black man could not carry a series. Today there are a lot of Black leads.

Irvin: In the history of films there haven't been that many Asian characters available to you outside of Charlie Chan, Fu Manchu and this *Rashomon* type bandit which was a new Asian characterization about twenty years ago. Because writers haven't seen any other types of characters they just go with what they think is available. Is this the reason we see this *Rashomon* type bandit so often? For instance Jimmy Hong, Yuki Shimoda, Khigh Dhiegh and Stephan Gierasch.

Alex: I'm not so sure that we do cast that frequently. I do know that we've done shows that call for characters that are 180° from that. Since we're in the temple, the other people other than Keye Luke and Philip Ahn have got to be masters. Jimmy Hong also played an old man. And where to you they may be exhausted in the Asian community, that may not be true with a non-Asian community.

Herman: I'm not sure which roles you're talking about. One of the things we look for in our show is theatricality. And I suppose that the threatricality of these characters is one of the reasons we have them in the show.

Irvin: Do you think people believe David Carradine is in real life half Chinese?

Herman: It's hard to know what people think in, say, Nebraska. I know the college kids certainly know that he is not, and certainly anyone that is familiar with the Carradine family would not.

Irvin: Nancy Kwan was flown in from Hong Kong for "Cenotaph." Why did you cast Stephan Gierasch[4] as a Chinese?

Alex: Robert Ito *(Canadian born Japanese)* was cast but the 20th Century Fox Company he was working for in *Judge Dee* changed their schedule and he had to honor his committment to them first.[5] It was a Thursday evening, the camera was ready to roll on Monday. Agents close up on Friday afternoon and it is illegal for a producer to call an actor directly. That meant we had Friday morning to decide what to do. A number of Asian actors were discussed but were rejected or not available.

Herman: There was for us a certain promotional value in an actor who could show this versatility. Normally, it is something we wouldn't consider. But since he had played that first part we asked him.

Alex: This was not considered when we went after and cast Robert.

Irvin: Speaking of *Judge Dee,* what race do you think Khigh Dhiegh is?

Alex: He's Indian isn't he?

Irvin: He's a mystery. We don't know. I've heard he is a Black from Brooklyn and he's published as being Sudanese-Egyptian. Twentieth Century Fox claims the cast is all Oriental.

Herman: He seems like a man who is trading on an unidentifiable identity.

Irvin: But he's always played Chinese.

Alex: Do you think he's Chinese?

Irvin: No.

Alex: Are you Korean?

Irvin: Yes. I shouldn't have told you. I should have kept you guessing. ★

Notes

1. Some of the books referred to were: *The Analects of Confucius* by Arthur Waley, *A Primer of Soto Zen* by Reiho Masunaga, *The Wisdom of Buddhism* by Christmas Humphreys, *What the Buddha Taught* by Walpola Rahula.

2. Yuen was born in Hong Kong and has some training in Kung Fu. He also runs a school in Los Angeles. The title of technical advisor suggests expertise in an area which is actually more legend and folklore than fact.

3. The role of Caine, which was played by David Carradine. In 1974, Bruce Lee signed a two million dollar feature film contract with Warner Bros. shortly before his death at age 32.

4. Stephan Gierasch had been cast to play a Scottish eccentric who runs into Caine in Arizona. He also played a Chinese war lord in the flashback sequences complete with taped eyes and Fu Manchu mustache. He said he based his characterization on Akim Tamiroff as a Chinese General in the 1936 film *The General Died at Dawn.* He wanted to play the character very stiff and tight lipped because the make up was squeezing his head and he was wearing fifty pounds of armor plate. It was so heavy he lost his balance and fell off of his horse during a take. The director pushed him to follow the character of the Bandit in the play *Rashomon.*

5. Robert Ito was working on a CBS Movie of the Week "Fer-De-Lance" filmed at MGM.

MEDIA GUERRILLAS

by Ron Hirano

I. Introduction

Much of the concern of the Asian American community in recent years focused on the role and use of the "mass media". The term alternately included the press, radio, television, handbills and posters. The interest in the media was consistent with the goals of "self-determination" or "self-definition" espoused by groups and individuals within the community who saw the media as a powerful means of presenting issues and information. A number of groups have been active in the media and related fields. The Basement Workshop, Asians for Fair Media (both of New York), and the Chinese Media Committee in San Francisco are examples. Those who chose to work in or with the media generally divided their efforts between monitoring them, or attempted to develop an Asian American alternative. Although groups did not limit themselves exclusively to one or the other, Asian Americans for Fair Media in Los Angeles exemplified a group engaged in the former activity, and Visual Communications, a group in the latter. The purpose of this article was to examine a single group, Visual Communications, and place their experiences into the broader context of media in the United States.

The history of the development of Visual Communications, or VC as it is more commonly known, offers valuable insights to those interested in the impact of mass media on the Asian American community and the political and economic constraints they impose on community groups. Over a period of five years, the group moved from preparing posters and other visual material for community groups to developing curriculum materials and films on Asian Americans. VC also experimented with videotape as a medium for community organizations, and individuals in the group explored the possibilities of television and cable TV for the Asian community.

The progress and difficulties which VC experienced serve to illuminate the essential features of both mass media and public education in the United States. The three areas which VC explored will be used to demonstrate the effect of such structures for Asians in America: the educational system; television; and cable TV. The following article will trace the development of the group, its current status, and, ultimately, attempt to shed some light on the questions which its experiences raises.

II. The Development of the Group

As with many community organizations, the beginnings of Visual Communications coincide with the student unrest of the late 1960's. While the relationship between Asian community groups and the student movement was not always clear, in fact, it was often more than casual. In the case of Visual Communications, and the Asian American Studies Center at UCLA, both worked with common concerns and in overlapping areas. Both sought to provide new information and new perspectives about and by Asian Americans with a view toward generating social changes through a more socially conscious Asian community. The Center worked through its curriculum, research and other projects with students and community, and VC through its films and photographs. The work and existence of each proved to be mutually beneficial.

During the summer of 1969, a "community college" was organized in the Los Angeles Asian community. The curriculum was varied, the instructors were volunteers, and the tuition was free. One of the courses taught that summer was a photography workshop led by Robert Nakamura and Alan Ohashi. Nakamura was a photographer by training and background who had free-lanced, and was then working at a photographic lab, and the Country Museum of Natural History. Ohashi was an art student at UCLA. The two, with Gail Nakamura, Robert's wife, were to form the initial core for Visual Communications.

In the early spring of 1970, Nakamura called together a small group to discuss the possibility of producing some educational material on Japanese Americans utilizing photographs he had come across in his work with the Japanese American Citizens League (JACL). Although nothing specific was to come of the meeting, the discussion of educational needs and issues gave some impetus and direction to the group which was to become VC.

Nakamura had been introduced to JACL through Bob Suzuki who was active with the organization's "Repeal Title II Campaign."[1] The Title II Committee had a budget of $100.00 for its kick-off

295

dinner, and Suzuki had asked Nakamura to enlarge some photographs of the World War II concentration camps for Japanese Americans. Not satisfied with merely enlarging the photographs, Nakamura designed and constructed an elaborate exhibit in a manner which was to become characteristic of Visual Communications. The exhibit was an immediate success and the Nakamuras were adopted by JACL as a committee of their Pacific Southwest District.

By the summer of 1970, the committee had grown to a rather large, loosely affiliated group which came together on an *ad hoc* basis. The group was made up of people with two basic concerns: those who were interested in seeking out and filling the Asian American community's need to utilize the media; the others were those who recognized the potential of the first group and were willing to help if they could. A request for funds was made to JACL's National Council, and with the assistance of Bob Suzuki, a grant was given and the Nakamura family and Ohashi were elevated to the status of a National Committee.[2] The JACL money allowed the group to set up an office and a photographic lab in the Crenshaw community of Los Angeles. Much of

the early work revolved around a silk-screening operation that the Nakamuras, Ohashi and John Ito, a local Asian American artist, made available to community groups.

Posters were printed to publicize various events, issues and organizations. Visual Communications was basically a graphic arts service group at the time. It provided posters, photographs and some graphic arts training to interested individuals and groups.

Nakamura entered the Ethno-Communications Program at UCLA as a graduate student in the fall of 1970. The program consisted of the Department of Fine Arts' film curriculum directed to Third World people. An Asian American group formed within the program and included Nakamura, Eddie Wong and Duane Kubo. Eddie Wong was a student at UCLA and had been involved with Asian groups on campus. Kubo, also a UCLA student, had been involved with *Gidra*, a new community newspaper initially supported by the Asian American Studies Center. The membership of VC was not clearly defined during this time. The group worked closely with other community groups such as *Gidra* and the Amerasia Bookstore, and, at times, it was difficult to determine who was

illustration by STUART IWASAKI

implementing social change, with the implicit belief that this would be the result of a mass movement, led to some experimentation and investigation into wider applications of the media. As Wong and Kubo were to write, "We can't expect leaflets to do it forever. . . . the best guarantee of quality community service is an aroused, educated and organized public."[3] This experimentation led them to produce cinematic and photographic material. The development was an indeterminant mixture of conscious planning and exploiting opportunities as they became available.

Several Asian American films were finished in the first year of the Ethno-Communications Program. Among these first efforts were Nakamura's "Manzanar" and Wong's "Wong Sinsaang." "Manzanar" was Nakamura's recollection of his experience in one of America's WWII concentration camps for Japanese. Wong's film focused on that classic Asian stereotype, the Chinese laundryman. The central character of the film was Frank Wong, Eddie's father. The demand for the two films was immediate, and their distribution was an important service performed by VC at the time. Since a good deal of the demand for the films emanated from Asian American studies programs and public schools, it was natural that VC focus on the educational applications of their material.

Film was an expensive medium with which to work. Some documentary film budgets ran in excess of $1,500 per minute. Even at that, film-makers relied on tight scripts and a lot of experience. VC was lacking on both counts. An advantage that the group did have in producing Asian American materials was a familiarity with their subject.

One way to cut down costs was not to pay your crew. Another was to use still photographs in the film. VC utilized both to varying degrees. A proposal to develop their photographic archive was submitted to the National Endowment of the Humanities and approved. The grant allowed the group to expand and organize their collection. Eventually, the Dorthea Lange photographs of the camps, commissioned by the War Relocation Authority, were donated by Richard Conrat. Along with the photos taken by the VC staff, the collection represents one of the most comprehensive on Asian Americans.

During this same period of time, spring 1971, a small group within the Greater Pasadena Chapter of JACL had been trying to promote Asian American studies in the Pasadena schools. The group had convinced the schoool district to purchase VC films and photographs. Agnes Suzuki and Marion Sata of the JACL group secured a commitment to try an Asian American studies program at the primary school level. They also discussed the possibility with VC staff. By October, 1971, a grant was received to fund the work, and the project began. VC knew nothing about developing educational materials for third graders which put them on par with most publishers, and their background in Asian American studies gave

working for whom. Both Kubo and Wong joined the Nakamuras and Ohashi, and the group began to direct most of its effort to films.

One of the first endeavors of the Asian group in the Ethno Program was an attempt to put together a film on the "Issei," the first Japanese immigrants to the United States. The group was able to secure small grants from various community organizations including the Pioneer Project and the JACL. The Pioneer Project was a group of Japanese elderly who had organized with the assistance of younger elements in the Japanese community to provide assistance to the Isseis. Although the film proved to be too ambitious an undertaking at the time, it became the basis for the film, "Wataridori" which VC eventually produced five years later.

During the first three years, VC operated on a volunteer basis. Some clerical and administrative help was provided by Ron Hirano and Faye Matsuoka. The current staff characterizes this period by its close ties with other community groups and VC's responsiveness to their needs. Even though most of the participants perceived VC as a media service group, long range, they sought to implement more fundamental changes through media. Initially, the objective of them a slight edge.

In typical VC fashion, the group had underestimated the requirements of the work and the budget required. The group made the decision to forgo any personal compensation, and to put the money into the development of the materials. Meanwhile, the staff continued their full-time student status. The spirit of the times was characterized by the two new staff members added during this period, Patricia Lau Miller and Candace Murata. Pat Miller drove into Los Angeles three times a week from Newhall to volunteer her time, a round-trip of about 70 miles. Murata took over much of the administrative responsibilities of the group.

By the summer of 1972, VC had finished the Pasadena Project, the photographic collection, and had developed an idea for a film on the Issei. The idea for the Issei film was presented to JACL at its National Convention in July as a part of a larger Visual Communications package. At the same time, it was decided that other potential sources of funding would be explored. The timing of the request turned out to be bad. Most of the attention of the Convention delegates turned on the question of who was to succeed the retiring Masao Satow as National Director of the organization. The Convention majority decision to offer the position to David Ushio was interpreted by the minority as a turning away from the kind of community involvement and programs which had developed over the past couple of years. As a result, six of the staff resigned. VC supported the minority and withdrew from the organization.

The search for other sources of funds proved equally unproductive. A couple of days of walking the corridors of the Department of Health, Education and Welfare, knocking on doors and cornering middle-level bureaucrats in hallways initiated the VC staff to the realities of grantsmanship. Even with the help of Bob Suzuki who had taken a position as Assistant Dean of the School of Education at the University of Massachusetts, little was gained other than some information and cautious invitations to submit proposals.

The following months were anxious ones for VC. The JACL relationship had provided a stability that comes with the knowledge that the next month's rent and operating overhead were covered. Leads, however remote, which were uncovered during the Washington, D.C., trip were followed up with letters and/or proposals. Other possibilities were explored, but finally a new relationship was negotiated with JACL. JACL needed material which could be used by its local chapters in educating non-Japanese about Japanese American history and issues. VC was contracted to produce the workshop kits, but retained its organizational independence. In exchange for this *ad hoc* arrangement, VC was paid a sum of money and provided with office space in JACL's Reigonal Office in Los Angeles.

Nineteen seventy-three was a frenetic year. VC was subcontracted by JACL to produce a film on the Issei. Independently, a grant was received from the Office of Education (OE) as a part of its Emergency School Assistance Act (ESAA) Program to develop filmstrips on Asian Americans. VC was later able to persuade OE the project would be better done as film. Aardvark Books published a series of books with multi-cultural themes for which VC supplied the photographs and illustrations. The group also worked on some pamphlets for high school use in conjunction with the Asian American Studies Center at UCLA. The year was a landmark in another sense; it marked the first time that the staff was able to draw regular salaries. The grant made it possible to add two additional staff members, Joyce Okamoto, who took up the increased administrative work, and Don Miller, who became the group's production manager.

Over the next two years, VC produced a total of eight films and two filmstrips. Three new people joined the group: Alan Kondo, a film-maker from Canada; Dennis Kuba, formerly with the Asian Pride Program, California State University-Los Angeles[4]; and Rob Yamamoto who had been studying to be a disc jockey, and working as a gardener. A second grant was received from OE, and some thought was given to the possibilities of moving in the area of television and cable television. Members of the group had participated in some public service programming, and the results and conclusions of the investigation into cable TV were written up in an article by Duane Kubo and Eddie Wong in *Gidra*.[5] A proposal to develop some Asian American programs for the Los Angeles school district's educational TV station was submitted to OE and denied.

III. Current Status

During the summer and fall of 1975, Eddie Wong and Robert Nakamura decided to leave Visual Communications to work in other areas. Wong has been active with a group assessing the possibility of a publication focusing on the Asian American community and has directed much of his time to writing. Nakamura has taken a job as a photography instructor at San Diego City College. The remaining staff is working under contract to the Berkeley Asian Bilingual Center. The resultant curtailment of activity has meant a period of reorganization and planning. The group has attempted to reassess its work in light of its understanding of the socio-economic context of Asians in America. Their study has been directed toward the development of a clearer perspective and direction for their work. The group has consciously attempted to make the decision-making process more of a collective responsibility. New plans are being formulated, alternative directions discussed and the ultimate question of VC's future is being weighed.

Besides cleaning up the work from the last grant from OE, the Bilingual Center work constitutes the most immediate task for VC. As part of the curriculum being designed and produced by the Center, VC is providing series of study-prints (still photographs depicting Asian American themes) and illustrations for books. Other work on a contractual basis is also being considered.

Long range, the group would like to restrict its work to film. To this end, three proposals are being submitted to various funding agencies. One is a request for support for an expansion of the photographic collection which has been important to the films. The other two are requests for developmental grants for a major documentary on the Japanese in the United States, and a film of John Okada's *No-No Boy*. VC recently received a grant to develop a film treatment from the American Film Institute.

All in all, Visual Communication's performance has been mixed. The group has not been able to achieve the broad impact to which its members aspired. On the other hand, its films and other materials provide an alternative to mass media images of Asian Americans available for some, and VC materials are widely used in Asian American studies classes. VC has not achieved any significant degree of independence from outside funding agencies, and its existence is tenuous and subject to the whims of an evanescent political climate. In a word, the group has not achieved the institutional change it initially sought.

The next few months will tell whether the current curtailment of activity is a temporary lull or indicative of longer-range trends in the opportunities for Asians interested in the media. The questions of effectiveness and viability for community groups such as VC require some analysis of the organization itself, but more importantly, the institutional structure in which VC operates. Much of the value of studying the group's experience lies in the light it brings to these questions. Its successes and failures have mapped out the important features of the institutional constraints which shape its existence.

IV. Analysis and Conclusions

The experience of Visual Communications in moving from printing posters to media encompassing wider audiences raises important issues concerning the ability of community-based organizations to utilize public education and television to the benefit of the Asian American community. Since it is difficult to generalize from the history of a single group, the questions bear further scrutiny in the light of the experiences of other organizations. As far as Visual Communications is concerned, the analysis will include the organizational limitations which VC brought to its work, the nature of the media, and

the structural environment of public education and the electronic media in the United States.

Internally, VC suffered from all of the constraints familiar to volunteer community organizations. The individuals were always caught in between doing the work of the organization and doing those things necessary to earn a living. In VC's case the problem was compounded by the technical nature of the work which required its reliance on outside people and specialized equipment which had to be rented. The resultant scheduling problems led to an intense, frenetic style of work which almost precluded any outside activity—sometimes including even sleeping.

Most of the individuals in the group had to acquire the necessary skills for their work on the run. With the exception of Nakamura, who had freelanced as a photographer, and Alan Kondo, who had worked as a film editor, none of the individuals brought much in the way of professional experience. This inexperience increased production costs in time and money. It meant that the particular requirements of any specific project often necessitated the development of new skills. In fact, VC did not usually realize the requirements of their work until well into a project. Given these constraints, the group's considerable accomplishments constitute a minor miracle.

The group was fortunate to have acquired the services of Candace Murata relatively early. Murata, Ohashi and Kubo are now the senior members of the group. Because other members were primarily interested in production work, and because of a latent sexist tendency within VC, administrative work became a residual activity which meant it became Murata's responsibility. Even so, administrative problems and problems of consistent leadership and direction continued to trouble the group.

In spite of these internal problems, VC was able to generate materials which were innovative and useful. Their films, photographs and other classroom materials are currently used by community groups, in the educational system and in other media productions on Asian Americans. Over 250 copies of *Manzanar* and *Wong Sinsaang* have been purchased, the majority by school districts. Judging from the material on Asians developed by the so-called "professional film-makers" and large publishing houses, VC has not been as handicapped as it might first appear.

If its own limitations have not been the primary determinants of its impact, what other factors have contributed to VC's performance? Some variables which will be suggested and examined below are the organization of the educational system, the mass media and the role which various governmental agencies play in respect to these structures.

The public educational system in the United States has historically catered to the needs of its white population which is, of course, the majority.[6]

In California, schools are organized into several hundred districts, some of which have a majority of Third World students. These districts depend on the state to provide, at least in part, their classroom materials. Since the selection of textbooks is the responsibility of the State Board of Education, publishers submit volumes for consideration which appeal to the broadest base of people state-wide, the white population. The result is a series of innocuous books which are not well-suited to anyone's needs. The mention of any group becomes a function of their number or percentage of that group in the population. For Asian Americans, the numbers game translates as a paragraph or two at best. Often minority groups are treated as a homogeneous mass with some reference to a social problem which is also shared by "blacks, Mexican Americans and others," Asians, presumably, being included in the "others." Even if a publisher were receptive to putting in material on Asian Americans, it would mean risking exclusion from a multi-million dollar market, a big chance for a profit-motivated firm.

Although the public school system incorporates the overwhelming majority into its number, the opportunity to address the needs and history of any minority are minimized. In the single instance in which VC worked on a series of multi-cultural books, the submission was considered as supplementary material. In cases where district funds are available to purchase other than state-provided texts, there are opportunities for Asian American materials. Even in these situations, the curious nature of educational bureaucracies works against them. Such bureaucracies recognize individuals only when problems occur, which builds a conservative bias into the organization. Administrators tend to see themselves in maintenance or monitoring roles whose primary responsibility is to make sure that the day-to-day affairs of the district run without disruption, and that potential sources of conflict are minimized. Thus new materials on Asian Americans for which there is no precedent are subjected to endless bureaucratic scrutiny in the most minute detail to insure that they are "safe" for public consumption, i.e., innocuous enough.

An example from VC's experience will suffice.

At the completion of the first year of ESSA funding, VC had produced five films for classroom use. One of the films, *Tony Quon: To Be Me,* was a fictional account of an immigrant Chinese boy and his life in the Los Angeles Chinatown community. The film was amongst those previewed by the audio-visual section of the Los Angeles Unified School District. The only comment concerning *To Be Me* was that the scenes depicting the celebration of New Year's would have to be deleted since it showed firecrackers exploding, and firecrackers are illegal in Los Angeles County.

An analogous structure in the electronic media, radio and television, similarly limit the access of Asian Americans. Whereas access to the educational system is controlled by state or local boards, the Federal Communications Commission (FCC) is given the responsibility for regulating television and radio. The basic result is the same, access is justified in terms of numbers and percentages and profits. The influence of Asian Americans is washed out when networks are nationwide.

As noted above, VC's impact on television was limited to "public service programming," the typically low budget shows in obscure time slots which stations provide to qualify for FCC license renewals. The history of television's response to Asian Americans generally, and other minority groups has not differed significantly from that of public education. Depictions of Asians directed to wider audiences cater to popular stereotypes rather than any need within the Asian community. The factors which contribute to this behavior have their roots in the nature of broadcasting and the role of the Federal Communications Commission.

In a profit-motivated economy, the primary objective of the network is to make as much money as it can. Television stations accomplish this by providing programming which appeals to the widest segment of the population it can. This, in turn, enhances the value of the time the station sells to advertisers, its source of revenue. The consideration of Asian American needs may then be reduced again to a set of numbers. Table I shows the number of Chinese, Japanese and Pilipinos in the United States and in selected SMSA's.

Table I.[7]

	Los Angeles Long Beach (3,174,694)	New York (7,894,862)	San Francisco Oakland (1,077,235)	U.S. Totals
Chinese	41,500 (1.3%)	77,099 (1.0%)	88,402 (8.2%)	431,583 (0.21%)
Japanese	104,994 (3.3%)	16,630 (0.2%)	33,587 (3.1%)	588,324 (0.29%)
Pilipinos	32,018 (1.0%)	12,455 (0.2%)	44,326 (4.1%)	336,731 (0.16%)
Total	178,512 (5.6%)	106,184 (1.3%)	166,315 (15.4%)	1,356,638 (0.67%)

If one assumes that stations behave in such a way as to allow them to make as much money as possible, the percentages and figures would lead to the expectation that national networks would be less "responsive" than local stations. One would also anticipate that San Francisco/Oakland stations would be more amenable to Asian programming, particularly to that which is directed to the local Chinese community. No effort was made to empirically test the hypotheses, but the impressionistic evidence seems to be supportive. Community groups such as the Chinese Media Committee have been relatively successful in their efforts in the Bay Area.

The phenomenon of "public service" broadcasts may be understood by an examination of the structure and role of the FCC. Although regulation of the air waves predates the FCC by more than twenty years, it is currently the agency which has the responsibility for determining who will be granted broadcast licenses. The FCC's authority emanates from an act of Congress passed in 1934, which created the agency and required it to grant licenses where the "public interest, necessity or convenience would be served." The FCC bases its decisions on a determination of an applicant's citizenship, character, and financial, technical attributes. Judging from the Commission's past performance, the financial criterion must rank high. Licenses have been granted to the large networks and to relatively wealthy individuals or firms.

One immediate consequence of this process is that the FCC makes whomever it grants a license substantially wealthier. The license amounts to a subsidy to the corporate interests which receive them. Any one who harbors any doubt of this, need only imagine the consequence to the stock of a company holding such a license if it were suddenly taken away. In exchange for this gift, licensees are judged in their performance in:

(a)maintaining an overall program balance, (b) providing time for programs inappropriate for sponsorship, (c) providing time for programs serving particular minority tastes and interests, (d) providing time for non-profit organization—religious, civic, agricultural, labor, educational, etc., and (e) providing time for experiment and unfettered artistic self-expression.[8]

Public service broadcasts are stations' concessions to the above.

The implications to Asian groups such as VC are clear. If their programming is not directed to a numerically substantial portion of the population, it will be relegated to the unprofitable public service slots which tend to be the bastard children of the networks. Non-profit, community-supported television remains a possibility, but their chronic financial problems limit their ability to serve a wide range of interests. Another alternative would be that Asians be utilized to depict the "universal qualities of the human experience" (i.e., majority qualities). For community groups seeking to create an Asian American alternative, this appears to be self-defeating.

At first glance, the technical innovation of cable TV (or CATV, for community antenna television) appears to offer another alternative.[9] Because of the fact that specific geographic communities may be wired, it is possible to create programming for a particular group. As an example, the Chinese constitute 1.3% of the population of the Los Angeles/Long Beach SMSA, but they represent 43.0% of the four census tracts which comprise Los Angeles' Chinatown.[10] The implications of a cable TV franchise in the Chinatown area are enormous. However, at the moment it is the same FCC which has responsibility for the regulation of CATV except, in this case, it is the municipal government which grants the franchise. In spite of the fact that over-the-air television and CATV are vastly different media, it is not clear how their impact will differ if they are treated the same and subjected to the same regulations.

Visual Communications provides one example of a community group which has attempted to utilize public education and other media to meet the needs of the Asian American community. Long range goals aside, the group may continue to function as an important source of Asian American films and educational materials. While their experiences cannot be generalized to every situation, they suggest several areas which would benefit from additional study. VC's problems and limitation serve to point out the need for changes which would allow for the development of a viable Asian alternative to mass media stereotypes. They do serve, in addition, to point out that hard work and perseverance are not the only, nor even the most relevant criteria for success in America.

★

Notes

1. JACL's Title II effort was directed toward the repeal of Title II of the Internal Security Act of 1950. The Act, which was passed by Congress during the McCarthy era, allowed for the incarceration of people who were suspected of representing a "potential" threat to the internal security of the United States during times of declared national emergency. Although the legislation was never used, its very existence raised the specter of the WWII camps in which Japanese and Japanese Americans were interned. JACL's campaign was primarily educational, showing the injustice of the Japanese experience. Title II was finally repealed in late 1971.

2. Although for any given project, VC was much larger, the core group remained Ohashi and the Nakamuras. VC was very much a "family affair." Viewers of *Manzanar* will remember that the credits include Robert, Gail, Norman

and Janice Nakamura. Norman and Janice were Robert's brother and five-year-old daughter respectively. It should also be noted that *Manzanar* was not, in a strict sense, a VC project. As with the Kubo and Wong article cited below and other work, it is difficult to determine where the work of individuals ends and the group's work begins.

3. Duane Kubo and Eddie Wong, "Cable TV Meets the Community," *Gidra*, vol. 6, no. 4, April 1974, p. 69 ff.

4. "Asian Pride" was a subcomponent of California State University at Los Angeles' community education program. "Pride" developed a series of lessons on Asian Americans which was regularly presented in selected elementary schools.

5. Kubo and Wong.

6. See, as an example, Mike Murase's article on the history of ethnic studies in this volume.

7. Census of Population: 1970, *General Population Characteristics* Final Report PC(1)-B1 United States Summary, U.S. Government Printing Office, Washington, D.C., 1972.

8. U.S. Federal Communications Commission, *Public Service Responsibility of Broadcast Licensees,* (Washington, D.C., 1946), p. 55.

9. For a discussion of the nature of CATV see: Kubo and Wong, and also Richard Posner, "The Appropriate Scope of Regulation in the Cable Television Industry," *Bell Journal of Economics and Management Science,* vol. 3, no. 1, Spring 1972, pp. 98-128.

10. Lucie C. Hirata, "Toward a Political Economy of Chinese America: A Study of Property Ownership in Los Angeles Chinatown," *Amerasia Journal,* vol. 3, no. 1, Summer 1975, p. 80.

FILMS
(16 mm color, except where indicated)

Chinatown 2-Step
This documentary film examines the hopes and fears of a segment of the Chinese American middle-class, the Los Angeles Chinese Drum and Bugle Corps. Secondary level use. 17 minutes.

City City
An abstract depiction of the variety of life found in the contemporary city using sights and sounds to protray the multi-ethnic personality of society. Elementary level use. 12 minutes.

I Told You So
A portrait of an Asian American poet, Lawson Inada, which travels from his past as a child in Fresno, California, to his present day role as a professor of English at Southern Oregon University. The film examines the multicultural influences which have created a unique artist. (Black and white) Secondary level use. 18 minutes.

The Journey
An animated parable about a scientist who decides to leave his comfortable environment to explore the unknown world. Illustrated by Glen Akira Iwasaki. Elementary level use. 6½ minutes.

Kites and Other Tales
A profile of an Asian American kitemaker who tells an animated story of the origins and history of kites in Asia. Illustrated by Alan Takemoto. Elementary level use. 12 minutes.

Manzanar
A documentary by Robert Nakamura which depicts a Nisei's memories of boyhood spent in a U.S. concentration camp during World War II. Secondary level use. 16 minutes.

Pieces of a Dream
An overview of the struggles of Asian American farm laborers in the Sacramento River Delta. The film provides the necessary background to the understanding of the contemporary problems of Asians in California agriculture. Secondary level use. 30 minutes.

To Be Me: Tony Quon
An account of an active ten-year-old Chinese immigrant who is learning how to adjust as a non-English speaker in an American elementary school. Elementary level use. 10 minutes.

Wataridori: Birds of Passage
This film lends understanding to the history of Japanese immigration through the accounts of three surviving Issei, first generation Japanese Americans. Secondary level use. 37 minutes.

Wong Sinsaang
A documentary film by Edward Wong that examines the Chinese laundryman stereotype. It is a sensitive portrait of one man's resistance to a dehumanized role. (Black and white) Secondary level use. 12 minutes.

Cruisin' J-Town
A group of Sansei (third-generation Japanese Americans) musicians discuss their lack of cultural identity as members of a visible minority and their efforts to express their multicultural influences through music. Secondary level use. 30 minutes.

Other Materials

Asian American People and Places
A packaged set of nine human interest stories on personalities, events and places in Asian American communities which provides a basic introduction to contemporary Asian American lifestyles. Nine stories for grades 3 through 6. With teacher's manual.

East/West Activities Kit
This kit consists of four sheets of arts and crafts, games and lessons. Each activity is designed to encourage active participation as a means of developing awareness, familiarity and understanding of Asian Americans and Asian cultural roots. Twelve activities for grade 3 through 6. With teacher's manual.

The Asian American ABC's
A filmstrip aimed at encouraging a sense of self-identity and culture among young Asian Americans. It is a presentation of the alphabet using Asian cultural objects and Asian American children drawn from five Asian cultures (Chinese, Japanese, Pilipino, Korean and Samoan). Color filmstrip for preschool and primary use. 15 minutes. With teacher's manual.

Mr. Tani
A filmstrip portraying a Japanese immigrant's life in America as interpreted by children and the man himself. Beginning with his childhood in Japan, the filmstrip follows Mr. Tani as a tuna fisherman in California, a World War II relocation internee, and finally ends with his life today. Color filmstrip with cassette for elementary use. 8½ minutes.

World War II Evacuation Notice
A reprint of the now infamous Civilian Exclusion Order No. 33 which began the removal of all persons of Japanese ancestry from the West Coast during World War II. 14 X 23 inch poster size.

Manzanar Monument
A contemporary photograph of the memorial obelisk at the Manzanar Relocation Camp cemetery. 17 X 22 inch poster size.

Getting Beyond

Vol.1,No.1:

Asian American Periodicals

by Rockwell Chin

During the early 1970's, periodicals written by and for Asian Americans began to proliferate. Many of the early publications were student efforts, put out by Asian American student organizations being formed on campuses across the country. These campus newsletters and newspapers were unprofessional products, but they had in common a freshness, creativity, honesty and political perspective lacking in other student publications and the traditional ethnic press. From the pages of these publications, Asian American students communicated their new sense of identity and ethnic pride, and a growing awareness that the history of Asians in America—like the history of other oppressed national minorities in this country—was replete with exposures of the so-called "American Dream."

But if these new periodicals were creative in form and bold in political content, they also suffered from an absence of disciplined and stable staff, financial certainty, and any sense of political clarity regarding future direction. Like the movement of which these publications were a part, spontaneity and idealism characterized their content. Many of these publications never made it beyond Vol. 1, No. 1, and many of those that did have suspended publication to re-evaluate their direction.

All this reflects the ebb and flow of the Asian American movement on college campuses. How long the current ebb period on campus will last no one knows. What has become clearer to those activists who have come through this period from the late 1960's through the 1970's is a common understanding of the errors made in the past: spontaneously jumping from one demonstration or sit-in to another without any larger plan or strategy; neglecting and even downgrading systematic political study about imperialism, class oppression, political economy, sexual oppression, racism, and other political questions; adhering to ethnic narrowness which divides Third World people; and finally, not seeing the links and relationships between the Asian American Movement and the working class movement. As clarity and unity begin to develop around the analysis of these errors, Asian American student organizations and their publications will likewise grasp this understanding and use it to propel the movement, once again, forward.

Campus News Publications (partial listing)

Third World News, UC Davis, newspaper, covered campus and community news focussing on Third World students and issues.

The Asian Student, UC Berkeley, newspaper, campus and community news, particularly community projects in which students are participating.

Harmony, Chinese Students Council (New York City), one of the earliest newsletters to come out, covering campus, community but also social news.

Scooper Dooper, jointly published by Cal State Long Beach, Los Angeles, UCLA, magazine form, covers campus and community news and includes poetry, graphics, photographs.

Ta-Hsueh, Chinese Student Association at UC Berkeley, magazine, bilingual.

Other college newsletters: *AASA,* Cal State at Northridge; *Asian Expression,* Cal State at Dominguez Hills; *Spark,* South Asian Students Association at UC Berkeley; *Asian Horizon,* Laney College; *Asian Spotlight,* College of San Mateo; *Ichimi Doshin,* Stanford; *Asian Student Voice,* San Francisco State; *AASA,* Cornell; *Asian Student,* City College of New York; Oberlin, Yale, Brown, University of Southern California, and various joint efforts such as the *United Chinese Student Post* (LA) and the *Newsletter of the Union of Vietnamese in the United State.*

Community Newsletters

Community newsletters are published by community agencies, organizations, and campus-community projects. These special interest newsletters generally have limited distribution to members and serve to implement the principles of the sponsoring group.

Family Newsletter, Wei Min She, an anti-imperialist community organization working in San Francisco's Chinatown. This newsletter focussed on various health, housing, food, and educational needs of families which participated in programs sponsored and organized by Wei Min She.

Family Newsletter, Chinatown Education Project, distributed to families in Chinatown Los Angeles working with the project, trilingual.

Changes, Gardena, California Youth Agency publication, directed at Sansei (Third Generation Japanese Americans).

Eastern Wind, published to "create an awareness within the Asian American population of policies, structure and events of a harmful nature to Asians . . ." originally funded by the Youth Opportunity Services in Washington, D.C.

AACTION, Asian American Council of Greater Philadelphia newsletter.

Newsletter of Chinese for Affirmative Action, published in San Francisco in Chinese and English, covering civil rights issues, discrimination, racism in the media, affirmative action news, employment opportunities, and organizational news.

Pineapple Times, Asian American prisoners newsletter at Lompoc State Prison.

Newsletter of Asian American Legal Defense and Education Fund, circulated to membership of this civil rights and legal defense and education oriented organization, publishing address is Oakland, California.

Collage, Young Buddhists, NYC, newsletter which was published for several years under the direction of two talented Asian American artists, making *Collage* a very attractive newsletter.

Newsletter of the Asian Women's Center (Los Angeles) and the Asian Women's Collective (Berkeley), ran articles covering sexual oppression, health, Asian women and the law, and so forth.

Community Newspapers

The community newspapers surveyed here are not a representative sample of all the ethnic press in Asian communities. Those presented are either in English or bilingual. However, many young immigrant families and older members of the first generation do not read English, and do not subscribe to or buy the newspapers listed below. Rather, they subscribe to newspapers which are mailed directly from Hong Kong, Korea, or Japan, as the case may be. The bilingual press tends to court two types of readers.

Consequently, it varies the contents in each section, trying to please two sets of readers, but often failing to satisfy either. Often the English-speaking reader rejects the bilingual publication in favor of an all-English alternative. That reader argues that one half or more of the paper(s) he buys is useless, and hence the switch. The same type of argument can be made by the non-English speaking reader. Unfortunately, however, many of the foreign language press do not carry any local or national news, and continued reading of this press does not contribute to educating the immigrant to the workings of the American society.

The bilingual press listed below indeed walk a difficult path, but not only for the above reasons. For many Asians in America, the politics of the mother country are still fiercely debated. For China, Korea, Vietnam, the Philippines, and to a lesser extent, Japan, families and the community line up according to the support, or lack thereof, of the existing government—e.g. Marcos in the Philippines, Park in South Korea. Editors of the community papers are sooner or later forced to take some position on these critical issues, but with two sets of readers, the bilingual press often finds it necessary to adopt different perspectives in each section.

Whether bilingual or monolingual, all ethnic community press suffer from constant financial problems, limited staff, and limited resources for the staff to cover news stories. As a result, many of these newspapers rely on columnists and contributions from the readership. Although the future of the ethnic press may be in doubt, the need for a press which addresses the democratic rights of Asian Americans who suffer from discrimination and racial oppression is unquestionable.

Japanese Community Newspapers

Rafu-Shimpo, published daily in Los Angeles. This newspaper boasts one of the largest circulations of any Asian American newspaper printed in the United States. The *Rafu* has been in print since 1903. Available at 242 South San Pedro, Los Angeles, California, 90012.

Other Japanese-English newspapers but with smaller readership are:

Hokubei Mainichi, 1737 Sutter St., San Francisco, California, 94115.

Kashu Mainichi, 346 East First St., Los Angeles, California, 90012.

New York Nichibei, 250 W. Broadway, New York, New York, 10013.

Pacific Citizen, published weekly in English by the Japanese American Citizen's League (JACL) circulates to that organization's membership, communicating JACL news, policies as well as local, national and international news affecting the Japanese American community. Available at 125 Weller St., Los Angeles, California, 90012.

Cross Roads, the L.A. Nisei (2nd generation Japanese Americans) was discontinued August, 1971 after 23 years of publication.

In the seventies a number of new community newspapers were inaugurated: *Rodan, New Dawn, Taishu,* and *Come Unity.* The first three were published by Sansei (3rd generation Japanese Americans) working in the Japanese community of Nihonmachi of San Francisco. *Rodan,* named after the famous Japanese fictional monster, began publishing in 1971 but suspended operation after 3 years. It was designed to serve the northern California Japanese American community, but it came out only in English, thus limiting its readership. Of the three newspapers only *New Dawn* is still publishing. It is published by a political organization called the J-Town Collective. *New Dawn* covers local, national and international news from a progressive perspective. Recently it devoted attention to the struggles of Japanese residents of San Francisco's Nihonmachi who were adversely affected by redevelopment.

Chinese Community Newspapers

East-West, The Chinese American Journal comes out weekly in Chinese and English. It focuses primarily on news from the San Francisco Chinese community. Recently, however, this newspaper has broadened its news coverage and has made structural changes (a broader editorial board) to encourage more community input. *East-West* maintains a moderate political line in its editorials and covers local, national and international news. Typically, *East-West* suffers from an unstable financial base, small staff, and few correspondents. The English section, however, does contain a variety of news including feature articles, language lessons and recipes, making *East-West* more of a magazine than newspaper in form as well as content. Available at 758 Commercial St., San Francisco, California, 94108.

Getting Together, a bilingual newspaper published out of San Francisco Chinatown, was originally the political organ of I Wor Kuen (IWK), a Marxist political organization. It published local, national and international news. Recently, *Getting Together* suspended publication, stating that it was reexamining its direction.

Wei Min Bao, the newspaper of Wei Min She, an organization previously discussed, published for several years out of San Francisco. Recently, *Wei Min Bao* was merged with a newspaper called "The Worker," a political, tri-language newspaper of the Revolutionary Communist Party.

Chinese Awareness is a bilingual monthly published out of Los Angeles Chinatown since 1971. All of its staff are volunteers. *Chinese Awareness* has run workshops for Asian American youth during the summer. Available at P.O. Box 3044, Terminal Annex, Los Angeles, California, 90030.

Asian Americans for Equal Employment Newspaper is a relatively new bilingual newspaper which focuses on issues concerning Chinese, Third World, and working class people in New York City. This newspaper is published by AAFEE, a mass organization seeking to fight for the democratic rights of Asian Americans and other working class people.

Sampan, monthly bilingual (Chinese, English) newspaper. This newspaper seeks to provide information about community events in Boston Chinatown as well as serve the broader Chinese community in New England. It began as a bilingual newsletter published by the Chinese American Civic Association (CACA), and has been in print for several years. Available at CACA Multi-Service Center, 85A Tyler St., Boston, Mass., 02111.

Pilipino Community Newspapers

Philippine News, a weekly in English claims that it has "wider circulation and news coverage than the combined circulation and news coverage of all Filipino American newspapers in the U.S." Its international coverage of the Philippines reflects a clear anti-Marcos position. Recently, the *Philippine News* ran a series of articles on an apparent attempt by Marcos to undermine the financial support of the newspaper. Available at P.O. Box 410, San Francisco, Calif., 94101.

Fil-American Express publishes community news in Los Angeles and San Diego.

Balitaan is a small, newly published bi-monthly newspaper serving the Pilipino community of Los Angeles. Available at 450 S. Cochran, Los Angeles, Calif., 90036.

Ang Katipunan is the national newspaper of the Katipunan ang Demokratikong Pilipino organization (KDP). Formerly published as *Kalayaan,* it is a monthly periodical which reflects the politics of KDP a mass organization based in the U.S. and committed primarily to the struggle for basic and long term needs of the Pilipino people both in the Philippines and here in America. KDP has chapters in New York, Chicago, Philadelphia, Seattle, San Francisco-Oakland, Los Angeles, San Diego and Hawaii.

Available at P.O. Box 23644, Oakland, Calif., 94623.

Korean Community Newspapers

New Korea, weekly newspaper printed in Korean. Available at 1368 West Jefferson Blvd., Los Angeles, Calif., 90007.

Korean Herald, a daily newspaper printed in English by the Korean Information Services in South Korea. It reflects a very conservative pro-Park political position. Available through its Los Angeles bureau, 1212 N. Vermont Ave., Los Angeles, Calif., 90029.

Insight, a bi-monthly new magazine no longer in print. This periodical covered the growing awareness of Koreans in America as part of the Asian American movement. *Insight* took an anti-fascist (anti-Park) position.

Samoan Community Newspapers

Le Amerika Mail, a bilingual, monthly newspaper published its first issue early 1975. Available at 1286 E. Bankers Drive, Carson, Calif., 90746.

Hawaii Publications

Hawaii Observer, a bi-weekly publication which attempts to explore and explain issues of local politics and economy, particularly in regard to the mechanics of local government and the personalities of local legislators. In-depth articles also include book and art reviews as well as critical essays. The *Observer* is multi-ethnic in scope as well as staff. Address: 835 Keeaumoku St., Room 203, Honolulu, Hawaii, 96814.

Hawaii Pono Journal, published in 1971-72, was a short-lived attempt by Hawaii locals to present historical, analytical articles on the economic and political struggles of people in Hawaii.

Hoe Hana, published by the Labor Community Alliance in Hawaii in the early 70's featured coverage on key labor and land struggles in Hawaii. This newspaper was discontinued in 1975.

The Worker for Hawaii, an organ of the Revolutionary Communist Party in Hawaii, features articles on working class struggles in Hawaii as well as those on the mainland from a multi-national perspective.

Working Together, a newspaper published by Third Arm organization in English, Ilocano and Chinese on issues facing the Chinatown community, particularly regarding the urban renewal project which is scheduled to displace present residents and small businesses. Was a monthly until 1975;

publication temporarily suspended in 1976. Address: 121 N. Pauahi St., Honolulu, Hawaii, 96817.

Asian American Publications

Newspapers

Asian Family Affair, bi-monthly, Seattle, covers issues affecting Asian Americans in Seattle.

Gidra, founded in 1969, was the first and most widely circulated wholly Asian American publication. It focused on community affairs, ethnic studies, foreign policy, creative writing and political analysis. Presently in a state of suspended publication.

(Ed.'s note: see article by Mike Murase on the history of *Gidra* in this volume).

Magazines

Bridge: An Asian American Perspective, bi-monthly in English. This nationally circulated magazine began publication in July of 1971 and continues to come out, albeit irregularly. *Bridge* has covered such issues as Asians in the media and Asians in the law. Except for the printing, it is put together by non-professionals. *Bridge* receives nominal support from the funding sources of the Basement Workshop, a non-profit cultural organization for Asian Americans in New York City. Available at 22 Catherine Street, New York, New York, 10038.

Jade: The Asian American Magazine, a recently published quarterly magazine printed in English. It carries regular features on the best Asian restaurants, famous Asian Americans, sports, recipes and some news articles. Available at 8240 Beverly Boulevard, Los Angeles, Calif., 90048.

Journals

Amerasia Journal, bi-annual, Asian American Studies Center, UCLA, Los Angeles, California, 90024. *Amerasia* is the only national journal devoted exclusively to a critical examination of the experience of Asians in America. The form, while primarily academic, is open to occasional short stories, poetry and photography. *Amerasia Journal* has run a number of research articles covering such topics as bilingual education, community law collectives, Japanese American experiences in U.S. concentration camps, early Issei socialists, and Chinatown garment shops. It should assist in the development and publication of a rigorous, well-documented body of research on the history and current status of Asians in America. ★

TOWARD BAREFOOT JOURNALISM

By
Mike Murase

[Editor's Note: *Gidra* suspended publication after the Fifth Anniversary issue in April 1974. The following article originally appeared in the final issue of *Gidra*.]

This issue of *Gidra* will be the last issue of *Gidra,* at least for three months—probably longer and possibly forever.

It is difficult now to recall what happened during the five-year life of *Gidra,* to write down all that has transpired. Yet, an explanation of why we decided to suspend publication seems to be in order. As well, some reflections, predictions and random thoughts are unavoidable.

It should be noted at the outset that what follows is not the collective statement by the entire staff, but is only a part of what I feel and see personally. While we as a staff agree on many things, we are by no means singular in our outlook toward change, neither are we always united in the methods. The fact that no blanket conformity exists has been a strength, I think, but there is a need for struggle between ideas of different kinds. In the past we haven't always settled questions of an ideological nature or controversial issues by the democratic method of discussion, of criticism, of persuasion and education. We have yet to examine many of our shortcomings in a systematic fashion, and, worse, we have not always taken steps to correct those that we already recognize.

As it is said, dust will accumulate if a room is not cleaned regularly, and our faces will get dirty if they are not washed regularly. *Gidra,* the paper and the staff, may also collect dust, and also need sweeping and washing. And the collective dust of *Gidra* has a way of piling up, so much so that we must stop all else to sweep and wash. Problems have a way of being cumulative, so much so that only a comprehensive problem-solving approach can make a difference in what we do. It is time for self-appraisal and evaluation, not only as an organization, but for many of us, as individuals.

There is a shared feeling, a premonition if you will, that now is somehow a good time to sum up our experiences. We want to go on, continue publishing, but we need now to see how far we have come, so that we may be clear about where we are headed and how we will get there.

What is happening at *Gidra* is not unique to us alone. Many groups seem to be undergoing similar experiences. In Los Angeles, Yellow Brotherhood, a self-help group for youth on the Westside, and JACS-AI (Japanese American Community Services/Asian Involvement), a multi-service community office in Little Tokyo, both organized soon after the birth of *Gidra,* are now in the process of evaluating their programs and face critical periods in their development. Other organizations are confronted with pessimism and confusion within their own ranks.

For us at *Gidra,* what we face isn't a phenomenon that hit us broadside without warning. It is something we had lived with for at least three years, and something that was anticipated from the very beginning of our involvement. *Gidra* has never been without problems. Even in 1969, our first year of existence, we faced organizational problems with inequitable work distribution, not to speak of uneven political and personal development.

More recently, for several months now, the process of putting out the paper—the tedious routine of investigating, writing, editing, typesetting, layout, mailing—had become mechanical, individualized and alienating. Fewer people came to the office to do the work each month. Attendance at staff meetings became irregular. At one meeting not long ago, there were only four of us. With only a handful of people working long hours, deadlines passed. . . . The "press runs"(originally one week periods set aside each month for actual production of the paper) became longer and longer. Tasks began to consume more of our time and drain people of energy. Morale and discipline plummeted.

So, after this Fifth Anniversary Issue, we will concentrate our efforts on summing up and developing new approaches to creating a vehicle for communication/expression/education that will be relevant to and meaningful for people.

The staff will be meeting twice weekly in the months to come, and plan to get together with various community organizations to invite feedback and suggestions. We will also be thinking of ways to keep our subscribers informed of our progress during the evaluation and planning period.

There is still the possibility that *Gidra* will be revived. On the other hand, *Gidra* may never "hit the streets" again in its present format. Some alternatives to be discussed include weekly or bi-weekly newspaper with more emphasis on community events and issues; a series of educational pamphlets dealing with specific issues, concepts or themes; an anthology of literature relating to Asian Americans or a compendium of past *Gidra* articles and other works; and an Asian American Movement news service. The scope of each of these ideas may be local, state-wide or national. It may become truly Asian American in perspective or more decidedly Japanese American in focus. One thing has become clear: *Gidra* cannot go

on unchanged. It *will* change, but the direction and the ultimate quality of that change must be consciously and methodically discussed. And that change will depend on the future composition of the staff and that staff's perceptions about what people need.

A new staff may take shape in different ways, too. With the present staff as a nucleus, others interested in media/communication/propaganda may be recruited. The possibility of a merger between *Gidra* and another progressive media group or community newspaper cannot be ruled out. Or, *Gidra,* as an entity, may be dissolved, so that individuals from *Gidra* and others can have a new beginning, on an equal footing, in a totally different venture, including a new name, new structure and new format. In short, many things can be done, but hopefully, they will be accomplished by design rather than by default or accident.

Before we get too wrapped up in the prospects, I think it worthwhile to retrace briefly our five-year history.

On the campus of UCLA on the afternoon of February 5, 1969, five students—Dinora Gil, Laura Ho, Tracy Okida, Colin Watanabe and I—met with the administration of the school to discuss the possibility

of starting a community-oriented publication which would reflect the sentiments and ideas of the students and the communities from which we came. The rationale was simple: Like the rationale for ethnic studies, we argued that an institution of higher learning has the responsibility of teaching its students not only the ideas of the dominant society but the ideas of the many cultures and many histories that make up America. We explained to the administration that a forum for discussion of socially relevant topics as well as a vehicle for creative expression was urgently needed in the Asian American community. It was to be an educational experience, we said. The administration didn't buy it, but stood firm on its own proposal to publish a scholarly sociological journal to insure that a university-sponsored publication would not mar the delicate image of the university.

Later, as we sat and talked in the office at the Asian American Studies Center, someone suggested, "Why not start our own paper?" Good idea. But how do we do that? We decided that if each of us contributed $100, it would be more than enough to get started. So it was that five of us, students who had no practical experience in journalism, gave birth to the idea that was to become *Gidra*.

Tracy Okida, who had a penchant for being where he wasn't, dragged out the name *Gidra* from deep within his nepenthean cerebrum. He had a way of making most politicians look amateurish when it came to impromptu speeches. One day not long ago, he walked into the office and soliloquized:

> And that is how it probably happened for me, unless it happened the same way else-where. That is how I became involved with it and that is why I stayed. I'm glad you asked me this, because this is a very tricky question and one that is intimately connected with the answer in more ways than I can truthfully say I know about. After all, it started a long time ago and it's pretty hard to judge distances; it could be really close.

He paused for about four days, then continued:

> Now that I think about it, I would never have known *Gidra* if I were someone else instead of me, or even just someone else

with better ears too. I would even go so far as to say that I am positive that such would have been the case if it happened. And it did, which is better than nothing at all, and I think we all want something better with all the different kinds of ways we ask and search for it.

A very sensitive artist and poet, Tracy was at his best when he escaped the conventions of prose:

How sad Yellow Brother
    you must be,
    born so small and loving—
    tiny hands reaching. . .
Just to grasp. . .just to have a warmth
. . .just to hear, "I love you, you are mine."
And who will love you, sad Yellow Brother. . .
. . .sad little brother of mine.

How sad Yellow Sister
    you will be,
    to learn that you are mute—
    pretty voice longing. . .
Just to speak. . .just to sing a song
. . .just to say, "I love you, you are mine."
And who will love you, sad Yellow Sister. . .
. . .sad little sister of mine.

How sad my family
    we should be,
    to be so short in thinking
    young men dying. . .
Just to free. . .just to give us life
. . .just to prove, "I love you, you are mine."
And who will love them my Yellow Family. . .
. . .sad Yellow Family of mine.

How sad my people. . .
    we needn't be!
    be strong and join the marching
    we all are fighting. . .
Just to be. . .just to have our way
. . .just to be proud of our heritage
To be together and love all mankind—
And who will love you, my Yellow People
. . .sad Yellow People of mine. . .

Who will love you, my Yellow People?
"I love you, you are mine."

P.S. . . .but you piss me off one hell of a lot. . .!

More recently, Tracy has been working for a printing and graphics enterprise in Los Angeles.

Colin Watanabe recalls that day when we started Gidra, and the months he spent on the staff:

I've found that many people have

great ideas, but that's about all. When it comes down to acting out their convictions, something happens to them. Gidra, as a radical departure from what's been done by Asian American youth in the past, may help to break the mental hangups that prevent more people from doing the things they believe in. It's a tribute to the determination, not the ability, of people."

Within days of our decision, the Asian American Studies Center office, where all of us worked as volunteers, had been converted into a small production room for the first issue of Gidra. New members joined the staff—Seigo Hayashi, Carol Hatanaka, James Okazaki, Carol Mochizuki and others.

As articles filtered in, arguments arose as to how contributions should be edited, if at all. The conflict arose again in the selection of an appropriate editorial. These were the indications of a philosophical dispute that was to eventually result in a permanent split in the original group. However, work went on through days and nights despite classes, grades and ill health. And on the night of March 31, 1969, the maiden issue of Gidra rolled off the presses, a modest four-page tabloid that had consumed the full energies of ten people for over a week.

The following month, the number of pages doubled as we covered the JACL (Japanese American Citizens League) convention held at Disneyland. There was a demonstration by young Asian Americans in which we took part to renounce S.I. Hayakawa's assumed leadership of the Asian American people. In the convention, the keynote speaker Hayakawa denounced Gidra as "errant nonsense" and "the work of childish Sansei."

It was also during this time that the infant Gidra was being welcomed as a vital force by local ethnic vernaculars as reviews of our first issue were published in the Kashu Mainichi, the now-defunct Crossroads, and the JACL-sponsored Pacific Citizen.

Wimp Hiroto of Crossroads described Gidra as "self-expression, hope and action," and quoted our first editorial in his column, which read in part as follows:

Truth is not always pretty, not in this world. We try hard to keep from hearing about the feelings, concerns, and problems of fellow human beings when it disturbs us, when it makes us feel uneasy. And too often it is position and power that determines who is heard. This is why Gidra was created. Gidra is dedicated to truth. The honest expression of feelings or opinions, be it profound or profane, innocuous or insulting, from wretched or well-off—that is Gidra.

Kats Kunitsugu of the Kashu Mainichi welcomed

"the emergence of *Gidra*. . .and we appeal to those of our generation, their parents, to read it with close attention and an open mind. Don't be turned off by the excesses that come from youthful zeal or the four-letter words which make us uncomfortable or bravado that often rides roughshod over finer points." Of late, Kats and *Kashu* have been more critical of *Gidra,* perhaps forgetting the appeal she made to people of our parents' generation.

The incident described below serves to illustrate this point. Tracy had written a fictional short story about Vietnam under a pseudonym, Nam Am Songh. At the next staff meeting, we discussed the story and the use of a by-line that could mislead our readers into believing the author to be Vietnamese. So, in the following issue, Tracy wrote an apology, commenting that ". . .it is wrong for someone other than a Vietnamese, or a reporter in Vietnam, to write from the perspective I had. My sincere apology and pledge to continue to struggle with my incorrect ideas and ways."

Kats reacted through her column, "I read (the apology) with some horror—horror, because it seemed to illustrate the kind of thought control that Marxist-oriented organizations feel they have a right to exercise. The last phrase bothered me, because it sounded as though *she* were knuckling under to someone else telling *her* what were 'correct' and 'incorrect' ways of thinking." Kats also criticized staff writer Evelyn Yoshimura, alleging that Evelyn had written an article on Little Tokyo Redevelopment without investigation. The irony of this incident is that Kats also failed to investigate: Tracy is actually a male staff member who voluntarily wrote the apology.

Rafu Shimpo, the nation's largest Japanese American daily published in Los Angeles, and its English section editor Ellen Endo, was curiously silent until the third issue aroused her to recognize the existence of *Gidra.* And at that, the first official correspondence came from her attorney stating in part, "Please be advised of our representation of Miss Ellen Endo, in connection with her claim against you for libel and slander." The alleged libel appeared in the June, 1969 issue in our editorial about the press coverage of the month-long hearing concerning Los Angeles County Coroner Thomas T. Noguchi's dismissal by the Board of Supervisors for suspect reasons. Since we had attended the hearing ourselves, we became aware that *Rafu Shimpo* had been using wire services and other inaccurate accounts rather than in-person coverage. Ellen also implied in her column that those who support Noguchi, who subsequently was exonerated, would soon be "wiping eggs off their faces." And she asked, "How do you like your eggs—scrambled or poached?" Our editorial reply was that "we will take it scrambled, Ellen, just like your head." And in return we inquired, "What's the matter Ellen, is three blocks too far to walk for the truth?"

In another incident worth noting, the *Rafu*

accounts of anti-war activities that took place during the Nisei Week festivities in 1972 contained numerous inaccuracies and distortions.

Gidra (and I) have long been critical of the perspective Ellen Endo represented in her role as a journalist, especially with reference to reporting of community events. But there is another side to this story. In the past year or so, Ellen has transformed *Rafu Shimpo* (English section) into a socially relevant, reliable source of community news, and has brought to the public's attention many local and national issues of concern to all of us. Through her weekly columns, she also keeps us informed of concerns of segments of the community we often overlook. In some measure, I believe that what we set out to do with *Gidra* has partially been accomplished by Ellen and *Rafu Shimpo.*

Within months since the inception of the paper, we were to lose three key members of our staff. As the paper demanded more attention, some questioned whether it was becoming an end in itself. They argued that direct involvement and organizing were more important than the production of a newspaper. Others of us felt that through *Gidra,* we could organize and promote community involvement. The time came for a choice to be made, and the outcome was that Dinora, Laura and Suzi Wong, who had joined the staff in May, decided to work on organizing students at UCLA.

In the months that followed, the efforts of these three culminated in the formation of the Asian Radical Movement (ARM) at UCLA. In November, 1969, all three were arrested during a sit-in demonstration to back demands for the rehiring of a black cafeteria worker and for an improvement in the conditions of all campus workers. As a result of the arrests, and subsequent convictions, all three received suspended jail sentences and probationary status which prohibited them from participating in demonstrations and rallies. They have, for the most part, been politically dormant since then. Now, Laura is an assistant editor for ABC television and Dinora will be entering medical school at UC Davis in the fall, while Suzi is doing graduate work in comparative literature at the University of Indiana.

For those who remained with *Gidra,* there was much work to be done. New offices on Jefferson Boulevard on the Westside were rented and refurbished. *Gidra* was incorporated as a non-profit corporation. In this rebuilding period a number of others joined the staff. Warren Furutani, perhaps known for more significant contributions to the Movement, became our first regular columnist. Julia Aihara and Amy Murakami contributed by working long hours. Amy reorganized the subscription and mailing system that had perplexed us. They are both teachers now. Vivian Matsushige, who now works at the Asian American Studies Center, and Laura Shiozaki and Naomi Uyeda, former UCLA students, also contributed their time and energies.

Ivan Ohta and Danny Matsumura were the first staff members without college backgrounds. Ivan was a student at Roosevelt High on the Eastside where he was involved in a movement for students' rights. Danny, a former member of the Yellow Brotherhood and a high school dropout, brought with him a perspective "from the streets" which contributed to the milieu in a unique way. He shared with us his perceptions of things while he worked on tasks the rest of us were unwilling to undertake.

During the first year, Gidra gradually changed its focus from the campus to the community, from Asian identity to Asian unity, and from "what happened" to "what can we do." Despite our efforts to be informative and relevant, there were those who disagreed with the views and disregarded the value of Gidra.

A Chinese woman in Los Angeles called Gidra "atrocious," and intimated that the quality of the newspaper can only improve when "some of you staff members (who are) SDS members and gangsters depart."

And apparently, the paper circulated beyond the Asian community. We got a letter from "a happy white mother," which is exerpted below:

I don't no what is wrong with you poor minority groups. As a white mother Im awfully proud of it. Sorry you poor minority dont appreciate your color. Its a shame you have to feel so unsuperior.

I surely cant see for the like of me why you have to have such a thilthy mind. I can see why you are all in such a fix. Now take the black man why hasnt he been able to get anywhere on his own. He had a land of his own. His own black brothers sold them as slaves. Also China. Also Japan. Its only been in the last twenty years that they have been able to come out there ancient ways. Take the Mexican they have more resources then we do in America and yet they havent been able to do anything on there own.

You can use your nasty little four letter words if you want to. Because boy Im glad Im white I wouldnt want to be your color it must be awful to be what you are, that you have to go so low that you have to use nasty words to express your selfs your naughty nasty thilthy little people and I pity your kind.

Meanwhile, back at the office, while the structural problems were being attended to, the vitally important areas of interpersonal relationships and leadership development had been neglected. Seigo recounts, "The history of Gidra clearly shows a problem that plagues not just us but the entire Movement—a shortage of manpower. The blame for this problem is usually placed on people outside the Movement. They are too lazy or apathetic to get involved, so the argument runs."

There were definite indications that certain policies within the organization inhibited growth and development of people within it. The shortage of people power was just a manifestation of a deeper problem. Structurally, Gidra was gradually becoming more like traditional newspapers. Art Kunkin's answer to the same problem at the L.A. Free Press was to install a time clock and assign role titles to the staff, and that spelled the eventual qualitative downfall of the Freep. Seigo explained further that at Gidra "certain people had assumed decision-making powers and members of this informal hierarchy used various methods, consciously or unconsciously, to maintain their power that prevented the development of new leadership."

In May of 1970, in an effort to break down that hierarchy and to develop new leadership as well as social equality within the staff, it was decided that high-ranking members of the informal hierarchy would not participate in the decision-making process or the production of the May issue, a decision which, in retrospect, was a mechanical attempt to correct a serious problem. What emerged as a by-product of that decision was a new concept of Gidra as a visual experience.

Alan Ota, who had been on the staff for several months, assumed the responsibility of coordinating and almost single-handedly put out the paper with a new, well-integrated and creative format that added a new dimension to Gidra. The experiment to tear down the hierarchy was only qualifiedly successful, if you can call it that.

Alan, a veteran of many different colleges and an ex-president of the Nisei Trojan Club, settled at UCLA in the graduate school of theater arts for the next three years, but spent many of his waking hours at the Gidra office, editing, keeping books, and doing the wearisome but indispensable "shit work." The many organizational aspects of the paper demanded close scrutiny and undivided attention, and Alan was right there on top of things. Now Alan, at twenty-eight, is the oldest member of the staff.

Also, during the month of May, the Asian American Student Alliance (later called the Asian Strike Committee) at UCLA led a general student strike to protest the bombing of Cambodia and the chain of events that followed: The shooting of four students at Kent State, the killing of two students at Jackson State, and the "police riot" on the UCLA campus.

On Tuesday, May 5, 1970, many Asian students were on campus and witnessed first hand, some for the first time, the indiscriminate sweep of the campus, the arrests and the brutalities committed by the Los Angeles Police Department.

Jeanne Nishimura will never forget that day. "I was sitting on the cement watching people getting pushed into Dickson's lawn by the pigs. They were forced to go in that direction by the pigs. Then some people started running toward us. The pigs were rushing them, pushing people who didn't move out of their way. We had to run too, and hop a cement wall about six feet high. A fellow behind me was pushed head first by the pigs. His head started bleeding on the side and he couldn't get up. Pigs were rushing at people, chasing them like animals. It seemed to me that they had no reason to charge at people. Another incident. I saw a young guy who didn't do a thing to the pigs but a cop clubbed him on the neck."

Amy Murakami added, "I thought the police was supposed to serve and protect people, but they were picking out people and attacking them, and intimidating those who had already been handcuffed by beating them with sticks. After what I've seen today, I don't have any compunction about calling them pigs."

And Russell Kubota observed, "The thing that really bothers me, besides the beating I saw, is that I can't imagine what American soldiers in Vietnam are doing to the Vietnamese when I see policemen beat the shit out of us. At least we can run home, but the Vietnamese can't go anywhere."

On that day, Steve Tatsukawa, a junior at UCLA, was trapped and beaten by three officers, then handcuffed and dragged away at a run to a police van. And when Colin went to see about Steve's condition, he was grabbed and clubbed by four policemen who arrested him.

With the *Gidra* office serving as the community outpost, the Asian Strike Committee carried on community educationals and leafletting to inform our community about the events that took place at UCLA, Kent State and Jackson State and the issues related to the war in Indochina.

By late May, the *Gidra* staff was drained of energy after a hectic month. As a result, the June issue never came out, the only time in the five years that we failed to publish an issue. The following month, we came out with an issue and called it the June/July issue.

Soon after that, though, prospects for *Gidra* brightened considerably as many of the leaders from the Asian Strike Committee joined the staff, among them Duane Kubo, Russell Kubota, Steve Tatsukawa, Linda Fujikawa, Bruce Iwasaki, Jeff Furumura and Candi Ota.

But it was also a time when some people moved on to do other things. Colin, who had played a key role in almost every aspect of *Gidra*, dropped out and moved to Berkeley where he later became the director of Asian American studies.

Carol Hatanaka and Seigo Hayashi, who had provided stability and warmth in a conflict-laden environment, also moved on. Carol is now an active participant of the Joint Counseling Center and JACS-AI. She also teaches at the Juvenile Hall and the Creative Workshop. Seigo serves on the board of Asian Rehabilitation Services.

Carol recalls her experience with *Gidra*, "For me, *Gidra* was one method of trying to create a new world where poverty, hunger and racism are no longer permitted to exist, and where children, untouched by the ugliness of this world, can run free and beautiful. By writing about all that is happening, and by presenting a variety of opinions, some type of awareness has to emerge. I felt that, once confronted with what's really going on, people no longer would be able to ignore the conditions surrounding and engulfing us. I know I'm idealistic and I guess I always will be. . .I have to be."

The turnover of the staff was actually fast and furious by the end of 1970. Evelyn Yoshimura, formerly an instructor of Asian American studies at Cal State Long Beach and active in other community organizations, joined the staff. Doug Aihara, Jane Morimoto and Jeanne Nishimura joined soon after, and along with the rest of us formed a nucleus that built a cohesive staff over the next three years.

After a tumultuous two years—a period in which over two hundred preople came to *Gidra* to contribute their time and talents, and at the end of which most eventually moved on to do other things—the staff began to solidify, but many of the problems remained unresolved and many hardships were yet to come.

We concentrated on developing an awareness of our own history, a sensitivity and identification with our community, and an international perspective. Pat Sumi, who had traveled to North Korea, China, North Vietnam, and other parts of Asia, had a large impact on us as she taught us to become more aware of developments throughout the world. She challenged us, encouraged us, and defied us. I remember that we were sometimes in awe of her, sometimes angry at her, and sometimes just glad she was around. In retrospect, her presence was felt long after she moved up north. Now, Pat is teaching the Asian women's class at San Francisco State.

In 1971, we began publishing a series of issues focusing on specific themes beginning in January with the Women's Issue produced under the guidance of fifteen Asian women. Their editorial comment was clear and bold:

> We as Asian women have united in opposition to this society which has reduced women to economic and psychological servitude, and Third World women and men to racist, dehumanizing stereotypes.

They emphatically rejected notions prevalent among some circles of women that men are the oppressors and stated their intention to

> oppose the capitalist system, resist the racist images imposed on both ourselves and our brothers, and struggle with our brothers against male chauvinism (so that we can) join in constructing new definitions for self-determination in the revolutionary society.

Subsequent issues highlighted Street People, the Middle Generation, Youth and Children, just to name a few. The idea of focusing on a theme each month was later abandoned in order to have a wider coverage of events and personalities within each issue.

The Neighborhood Youth Corp (NYC) program was set up by the federal government after the 1965 Watts rebellion to keep the inner city youth occupied during the hot summer months. During the summer of 1971, *Gidra* "employed" three youths—Minako Kawahira, Glenn Oshima and Scott Nagatani—through the NYC program for $2.00 an hour. Meanwhile, top officials in NYC were pilfering a cool $2.7 million from program funds. High administrative costs.

And more people joined the staff too. Tom Okabe, Lloyd Tanaka, Kyoko Shibasaki, Teri Nitta and Tomo Hisamoto. Tomo, only fourteen at the time, wanted to be a *Ninja* (a spy during the samurai days in Japan who is said to have perfected the "art of invisibility") but he talked too loudly to be unnoticed and was too clumsy to be evasive. He dropped out of Dorsey High in the tenth grade, complaining that school was irrelevant. It wasn't that he resisted learning; he was always searching for new knowledge. He is still very inquisitive, and likes to talk, in fact some people say he talks too much. But he listens too, and asks questions. He is endowed with a wealth of knowledge on a wide range of things that most people know nothing about. One of the things Tomo did best was to remember where small but important items in the office were. Our office got pretty messy sometimes, and in the heat of the press run, we would misplace scissors, articles, checkbooks, and things like that, and Tomo would know where everything was. Most people talk about parts of his anatomy that are big: his mouth and his feet. But Tomo has a heart to match.

In July we took a major step to correct an internal problem that had perplexed us for two years. In order to break down that old hierarchy again, and so that we can develop leadership and organizational qualities among all, a system of rotating monthly "coordinators" was set up. The first two people to take on that responsibility were Doug Aihara and Jeff Furumura. They directed the entire operation of the staff and organized the contents of the July issue. We have worked with the system of coordinators ever since.

Along with structural changes, the purpose of

Gidra was reiterated in the July 1971 editorial:

> We of the *Gidra* staff firmly believe that an exchange of ideas among all segments of the Asian community as well as the community-at-large is essential to understanding the conditions that exist in our society. Further, we feel that communication of ideas and ideologies relevant to all people is the precursor to the resolution of problems and of social change.
>
> In the future, *Gidra* will reaffirm its goal of striving to bring people together by emphasizing issues of concern to all people. Also, *Gidra* will endeavor to report events, personalities, organizations, and social conditions interpretively and analytically.

We had faced a dilemma regarding the contents of the paper. Some of our readers, not insignificant in number or in the substance of their criticism, were saying that we were too one-sided—entirely too negative in our interpretation of history and altogether too subjective in our analysis of current conditions. These people expressed a desire to see articles with a more tolerant and hopeful outlook which serves as an affirmation of all that is good in people. They argued, "People can't relate to something that jumps out at you every month to remind you how messed up society is and how fucked up you are. Besides, what can they do about it?"

Partially in response to such criticisms, but mostly because we wanted to change ourselves, we consciously struggled to eliminate acrimonious rhetoric and to present constructive alternatives for our readers. What resulted in the ensuing months was a hodge-podge of do-it-yourself ideas that included recipes for ethnic foods, directions for a vegetable garden, tips on how to buy a used car, and instructions for sewing your own pants, and shirts, and hats. There were suggestions for pasting up protest posters and hints on how to get into contact with community groups. We even had a detailed description of how you can fix your own toilet.

Jeff Furumura, a soft-spoken teacher's aide, who spends long hours perfecting the art of Kung Fu, conveys very political ideas in his "down home" style:

> Let's imagine you come down with the flu. Alluvasudden, your temperature shoots up to 104, you can't climb out of bed, you begin babbling incoherent gibberish but between sentences, your mind flashes: '. . . better see a doctor. . .' So, there you are at the doctor's office, in the waiting room, seeing Dark Clouds. . . 'I've probably got a type of bronchial pneumonia, maybe with rheumatic fever. . .my hair is going to fall out soon, then my legs will give way, and

then I'll go deaf. If I'm lucky, they'll be able to save my eyesight...' In a quick minute, the examination is over—you await the diagnosis. "You have a cold. Drink a lot of water, some aspirin and stay in bed." "Oh." And before you're completely well, there's a $20.00 doctor bill sitting in your mailbox.

This happens a lot when your car makes funny noises, when the sink doesn't work right, or when we don't feel good. We rely to a sometimes ridiculous extent on professionalism. As a result, we oftentimes pay for simple adjustments, remedies, and repairs that we ourselves could have been capable of performing—if only we had known how to do it.

It's all part of building self-reliance, and in the process, creating our own alternatives. By breaking down those mystical exaggerations concerning who is able to fix this, who is qualified to operate that, we can learn to do a lot of those things ourselves.

Of course, in a highly technological society like ours we must rely on those with specialized skills for some things, but we tried to emphasize that there is an alternative to the price-gouging and profiteering that goes on. All the skills and knowledge within society ought to be shared for the benefit of people.

Not surprisingly, there were other readers who wanted *Gidra* to be more persuasive and more direct in explicating our "politics" and scowled at the "how-to-do" articles, labeling them "petty boojiwah" or "imitations of white hippie counterculture."

We tried to present the progressive viewpoint in a principled way, but our response was to publish a wide range of perspectives in a variety of styles, writing about many issues and activities. The paper's diversity of perspectives stems from our varied attempts at defining ourselves. We tried to extend the role *Gidra* plays in the ongoing revolution both through collective policy decisions and our personal interactions. Therefore there is much more freedom than consistency in our pages.

In the spring of 1972, *Gidra* learned of an opportunity to send a representative to the People's Republic of China. There were many enthusiastic volunteers, but after the excitement subsided we began to discuss not "who wanted to go" but "who should go" as our delegate. We wanted to select someone who would be able to absorb as much as possible about socialism in practice in a short period of time. The perceptions of one person, we knew, would be limited, but how a person interprets what she/he observes is largely determined by the experience and political development that that person has. More than being able to grow personally from such experience, as all of us can, the person had to be able to

transmit that experience to people upon return to our community. To convey the *total* experience of seeing, doing and feeling something so alien to us as revolutionary China, and to translate that experience to our situation in America would not be easy.

After hours of discussion, we selected Evelyn Yoshimura to represent us because of her many qualities. She is perceptive, tactful and articulate. She relates well with a variety of people, and she has the rare ability to break down abstractions into concrete, day-to-day terms.

Evelyn returned in the fall and gave presentations and informal talks on China with many community groups, and shared her experiences by writing articles about her trip. What we learned through her about China was an important element of our political development and understanding of socialism at work.

Through 1972, we were undergoing more changes, but the most significant was that we began a study group of our own. At our first meeting on April 7, we talked about what we wanted to learn from the study. Evelyn wanted the answer to the question, "How does *Gidra* fit into the overall Movement?" Bruce Iwasaki hungered for "facts—concrete knowledge of concepts like 'imperialism'—some kind of objective body of knowledge." Steve said that "our life-styles and behavioral patterns are expressions of our ideologies. I want to see how I fit into *Gidra* and the Movement." And so it went.

Doug Aihara, who grew up in Montebello and was an Eagle Scout in the 379 Koyasan troop, asked, "How do we move people to action?" Doug had often talked about wanting to make *Gidra* more accessible to people and about wanting to rid the Movement of its seeming exclusivity. He discussed new ideas and concepts with his mom, his boss and with practically anybody he could find to talk with. Tirelessly, he pursued the answers, and tried to get other people involved. When people came to visit the office, Doug would show them around, patiently explaining the procedures we go through each month. Now, he's getting into music more, but during the day he works at Naris Cosmetics.

Finally a study group was organized. We set up study for six week sessions, having a recess and evaluation after each session, and with rotating chairpersons, and a permanent meeting day, time and place. The study was divided into three parts:

(1) The Objective Conditions—Racism, Sexism, Capitalism, Imperialism... and alienation, inequality and irrationality...which engenders individualism, intolerance, irresponsibility, negative self-image and pessimism. We wanted to study Asian American and Third World histories, the War, the institutions in our society, the state of the Movement, etc.

(2) The Goals—Humanism, Socialism, Revolution. The examples of the Vietnamese, the People's Republic....collectivity, self-respect, self-reliance,

self-determination, self-discipline, self-defense.

(3) How to Get from One to the Other. Step by step. . ...

Naturally, it broke down into more manageable sub-categories but that's the rough idea. We read political pamphlets, newspapers, introductory readers, and some "classics." We used different techniques: discussion, investigation, role-playing, autobiographical histories, criticism/self-criticism.

During those days, there was a definite feeling that we were becoming a tighter group, but not all of that can be attributed to political study. As students, our hours were flexible. Most of us went to the office in the late afternoons and evenings, many times just to see our friends. We sat around in the office for hours, sometimes all night, working at a leisurely pace and talking and sharing and learning from each other. We used to go out to eat so often that it had become a custom that became known to friends who would drop by the office just to go out to eat with us late at night: Mago's, Lucy's, Tommy's, Leo's, Fatburger, Johnny's and Holiday Bowl. During more standard hours there were Walt's, Angelo's, Tenri, Bungo, Ho Sai Kai, and Chin's right across the street.

We learned to have fun together and enjoy each other's company. We shared in adversity and in joy. That's what kept the group together for so long. We supported each other and criticized each other. The difficult times that we endured together made us stronger. It seemed that for most of us, offering criticisms in a loving way was a difficult thing to do, and it was equally painful to freely accept them. This hesitation to give and accept criticism is an artificial by-product of a society that keeps people out of touch with their own feelings and afraid to communicate them to others. So many stones beside so many glass houses. Undoing this requires struggle, but too often we have chosen not to risk 'hurt feelings' or 'bad vibes' and settled for an unprincipled peace within the staff. In order to effectively accomplish the goal we have set for ourselves, there must *necessarily* be times when we question and criticize each other, *even* at the risk of creating tension and anxiety temporarily. A thorough and continuous ideological struggle is a prerequisite to building trust, understanding and love for one another as sisters and brothers.

Steve Tatsukawa, who made his mother very happy when he got perfect attendance at Henry Clay Junior High School, personifies someone who is able to relate to people. In the four years that he's been with *Gidra,* he has never demonstrated anger toward people, and is endowed with the ability to make people laugh and to make them feel good. Steve says that when people think of revolution, they conceive of it as being the equivalent of political upheaval. "In essence they are correct in their assumptions, for revolution does mean political upheaval or change or overthrow or substitution," he agrees, but adds, "but

it means much, much more." He explains further:

No revolution has ever succeeded unless it was carried through by people with total revolutionary intent. Today in America, this type of person is now emerging. The foundations of American culture have been rejected by many: the materialism, the profit-motive, the competition, the basis of western culture as we know it.

The importance of the situation lies in the fact that we are witnessing an old culture dying and a new culture being shaped. This is a rare occurrence in history. And we, the movement people, have the responsibility of shaping the new way of life. It will be shaped not by writing or talking or thinking about it. The new way of life will come about by living it. Live the Revolution!

The creative mind of Steve Tatsukawa has played a vital role in the growth of *Gidra.*

Again when summer rolled around, we had NYC youth work with us, only in 1972, we had *fifteen* high school students coming down to the office every afternoon and most evenings. Because the program was so hastily organized, we had set up limited training sessions. Many of the NYC people who had extra time worked with Yellow Brotherhood. They also led a group of two hundred youth to the streets of Little Tokyo during Nisei Week to demonstrate their opposition to the war in Vietnam under the banner of the Van Troi Anti-Imperialist Youth Brigade.

But not all youth in our communities were being politicized or given support as the editorial from that month attests:

Many *Gidra* articles have been written in strong opposition to war—to the waste of lives and resources, the atrocities, and the weaponry. We say that we want peace, and we say that we are willing to fight for it. Many of our articles have also reflected serious skepticism about the effectiveness of rallies and demonstrations, not only against the war, but also concerning other social/political injustices. Many of us have participated in these demonstrations, and at those times have stressed nonviolence although we have often felt the urge to take more militant actions. But most of the work done in the name of the Movement is aimed at positive alternatives, meaningful changes, and not alienating the community. We often confuse our understanding of the need for a "fighting spirit" to carry out a protracted struggle with our feelings of wanting quick

316

action and fast changes. We often feel frustrated and begin to have doubts about our effectiveness in bringing about the desired changes, or in reaching the community with our intentions.

Meanwhile, back in the streets, many sisters and brothers are busily, energetically, and resolutely going about fighting among themselves, or carrying on with some other forms of self-destruction. Beginning with negative self-images, sisters and brothers become apathetic and unproductive, drop reds and take other drugs, slash their own wrists, and attempt many other forms of suicide. If only the energy spent by these sisters and brothers could be turned from negative, self-destructive violence into a positive fighting spirit directed at the sources of common problems. . . .

What we see in the streets of our communities is often a grim reality seemingly unreached and unaffected by our Movement. When sisters and brothers get fucked up on drugs, fight each other, steal from each other, and slander each other uncaringly—all of this happening in an environment of community apathy—what we are seeing is community self-destruction. What we are seeing is a force, in and of itself, that is counter to the Movement, counter to the revolution; so are the problems and symptoms stemming from this society and its values which we oppose. This problem can no longer be shined on to be dealt with in reactionary fashions, or to be dealt with by the "humanism" of the Movement (our sensitivity, openness and warmth) when it is so often overshadowed by our frustrations and confusions. This problem requires heavy thought and courage to be solved within the framework of building the aims of the Movement."

A young Asian sister, Clara, was one of the more than 60 to die of drug overdose in our community within the last four years. The numbers reflect only the cases known to *Gidra;* there are probably many more. What could have prevented those deaths? How do we prevent future drug-related deaths? We still grope clumsily for answers, hoping that we are in some way filling a need and that what we are doing will bring all of us closer together as we begin to share very personal feelings and experiences through the paper.

Clara,
. . . Now, I sit and think quietly of you. Before, I sat and spoke loudly of you. Now, there is nobody there. I can just see you waiting for me at work. Even if I were depressed, I would look at your smile and it would make me feel good. I expect to see you there, but you won't be, and I'm sorry. I always thought of you as a lucky girl, no problems, just live life as it comes. I was wrong. I should have realized everybody has problems. Why did you have to do it? Why?

I wish I was there. I'm sorry I wasn't. Clara, don't you see? We loved you. I loved you. I cared about you. I wish you had more people to open up to. Maybe then some of it would have been all right. You had all of us, but it's too late. I wish you would have waited. . . Why Clara. . . .

Ivy

(May, 1972)

It was too late for Clara, but we hoped that this letter and other expressions of love can make a difference for future Claras.

In the pages of *Gidra*, we condemned the use of some drugs, not because they were drugs, but because they were killers of human beings. It is not unlike denouncing other killers of people—war, poverty and hunger. We are *not* against the users of drugs, we are against the conditions that force people to seek self-destructive alternatves. We are against manufacturers of drugs, like Eli Lilly Company, a multi-national corporation, that cannot account for the distribution of 40 percent of their seco-barbitols. We are against the black-marketeers who pour the drugs into our communities in order to pacify and kill us.

Drugs have been an integral part of the culture of America, and so has it been with those who want to change America. One drug is replaced by another. Many on the staff smoke marijuana, and some have tried other drugs, but we have had a policy of "no possession or use" in the office ever since we began. And that policy has been scowled at, ridiculed and sometimes violated by some. Some have argued that "to smoke (marijuana) or drink (beer) in the office seems to be an activity geared not to escape reality but, in fact, to be right in the center of reality."

At the end of 1972, we almost didn't make it. Two days before the scheduled press date for the December issue, when there were only a few articles turned in, we were seriously considering skipping that month. We decided, however, to go ahead because we felt a responsibility to our readers. It was two weeks late in getting out, but volume four was completed.

Early in 1973, artists David Monkawa, Dean Toji and Glen Iwasaki joined Alan "Batman" Takemoto (who had been on the staff since April 1972) to make up the most talented group of Asian American illustrators to be on any one staff. All of them had been serious artists in the traditional sense, but they struggled wth their former conceptions of Art and became a vital force within *Gidra* as they began writing and participating in other staff functions.

David talked about art in America, and what he is trying to accomplish:

> In America, popularized art in the media neutralizes and dulls the senses, instead of trying to sharpen them. Comic books are not meant for you to think too much because people might start getting too aware of what's really happening. Then the boat begins to rock. But the point is we shouldn't let ourselves be strayed by entertainment that deals with mysticism or takes you on supernatural trips. Or by entertainment that drains you of your mental energy by seducing you into watching unrealistic and romanticized movies about pseudo-revolutions, personal relationships or anything else.

> Sure, we like to entertain too, but we'd like to do much more than that. We want to free our minds at the same time you free yours by developing them through looking at comics, movies, books and television with a critical eye; that is, asking ourselves "how" the thing we're viewing is supposed to be judged. Is it trying to communicate a certain feeling, a political idea, a message about life or a depiction about how a particular person thinks? Whatever it's trying to communicate, does it do it in a way that shows care and thought or haphazardness? Is the medium in which the artist works the best medium for what he or she is trying to say.

Even in high school, David questioned the way all of us were conditioned by rituals that were imposed on us. As a Sunday school teacher at Centenary Methodist, he discussed with his eighth grade students the meaning of the Pledge of Allegiance. He was asked to leave by the church hierarchy.

When Dean first started coming down to the office, he was abrasive and autocratic. "Batman" protested, "Hey, you can't boss me around; I've been here longer than you have!" When Dean was little, he was very shy, and he never did much with groups. He once sent away to the Archie Fan Club to be a cub reporter, but they never wrote back. When he was in high school, he got into rock 'n roll and read a lot of books about total and all encompassing "ways of being," but his real passion in life was art. When Dean discovered *Gidra* he found a way of combining his love of art, search for a "way of being," and a chance to create changes in a society that had alienated him earlier.

Many personal changes were to take place during 1973 for many on the staff. The process and content of the paper were greatly influenced by those changes in our lives. Most of us were already involved with other community organizations and "work areas": Creative Workshop, Little Tokyo Anti-Eviction Task Force, Yellow Brotherhood, Joint Counseling Center, Asian Women's Center, Amerasia Bookstore, Asian Law Collective, just to name a few. Changes in personal relationships and living situations also had an impact. Many of us were forced to readjust priorities as we took on full-time "straight gigs." The three students: Bruce and I were studying law. Linda Fujikawa was becoming increasingly involved at UCLA's school of social welfare, and in the area of casework.

Linda, who was a cheerleader for the Gardena High Mohicans, is a pragmatic and dedicated person. Linda wanted to be effective in what she did, and not just adopt the superficial embellishments of a radical. She once commented:

> In the movement's revolutionary fervor to forge a new lifestyle free of materialistic hang-ups we often try very hard to discard any traces of our recent petty bourgeois existence. A good case in point is in the clothing we wear. In fact, we often find ourselves in contradiction when we buy jeans and work shirts rather than wear our now-dated but perfectly wearable pin-striped ivy league shirt or that hot pink princess line dress. Nevertheless, the movement among Asian American people is relatively recent and for that reason, although realizing clothes are not and should not be important, they still often are.

Another symptom of that "revolutionary fervor" was our unwillingness/inability to deal with the realities of our economic condition: the problem of money has been a constant source of concern and apprehension for the staff. When we were students, it was easier because we did not have to worry about many of the financial responsibilities that troubled others, but concerns about "paying our bills" and economically surviving soon became real enough.

In our five-year history, no one received a single payroll check from *Gidra*. We tried to think of ways in which "survival needs" and our work at *Gidra* could be integrated, but because we had to work at other places in the meantime, we weren't able to become financially self-sufficient, at least not enough to have salaries for the staff. A vicious cycle.

We owe a debt of gratitude to the many generous contributors who believed in us—our subscribers and advertisers, our friends and our parents—and the Asian American Studies Center at UCLA who, from time to time, subsidized us, and GCYP, who gave us a grant. But in the final analysis, we weren't able to meet the financial burden of rising costs, both in our own bills and *Gidra's*. Yet we know even now, that there is a way to build and sustain a self-sufficient progressive media, and that someday we will do it, as changes keep happening within us and around us.

The ever-changing conditions call for deeper analysis, new strategies and greater resolve. And we need to understand the present, not as a static and isolated instant, but as a flowing moment in history.

Bruce Iwasaki, a son of a produce man and a graduate of UCLA, is an avid reader and a prolific writer who once wanted to be the Asian American Shakespeare. Now, he is more concerned with change, and the lack of change. The displined in-house expert expert on Vietnam deliberated in his usual analytical and long-winded way:

> From my limited, absent-minded perspective (L.A. Japanese American, male, "student"), it's hard to say how the Asian movement has progressed except to be simply older, larger and different. It probably has less per capita macho trips than three years ago, less level chaos than two years ago, less tripping on and stumbling over new personal-political relationships than last year. Things seem to be condensing, settling (collectives, study groups) even as they are beginning (Women's Center) or restructuring (everybody). And though most individuals are less spread out—without, as one friend says, the urge to attend every movement meeting around—groups, projects, and organizations also get isolated. Even among friends, it's hard to keep abreast—if you're in different work areas. (*Gidra* hasn't always been much help on this I'm afraid, we all share in that blame). With this happening it is no wonder that coalitions so far have been precarious structures: either dissolving as they spread, coalescing no new minds, or never seeing day.
>
> Our hand-waving sort of communications is, I trust, temporary for now. Somehow I figure some structural networks will evolve to remedy that. What concerns me much more is the communication over time. I mean this: Many people who come into the movement now don't think of themselves as stepping into any historical train of events—any movement—at all. Programs, plaforms and people are givens. Proof that this occurs is demonstrated by people still having to go through any one of a variety of movement syndromes (macho, overextension, elitism, etc.). And on every hand there's still the rhetoric. Maybe all these rites of passage are necessary; I don't know. But with our expanding sense of numbers, consciousness,

and possibilities, comes an enlarged responsibility too. That is, the responsibility for preserving the movement's past, its sequence of ideas, its different experiences, its changing spirit. Many of us know as little about where we've come from in five years as we do about the Nisei Progressives in the '40s or the Issei socialist labor organizers of the '30s. We don't need scrapbooks. But we somehow need to institutionalize the lessons we learn. Allow for an expanding of consciousness instead of the diminution of consciousness which comes every political generation every eight months or so. I don't know what the mechanism will look like. I don't even know whether it's bound within our will or our karma. That such humble prerequisites seem like such lofty goals shows how far away is our political horizon. But without a sense of past how can we have a set of plans? And without plans how will we determine if that horizon heralds the New Day, or more neon?

The advances in political theory, as in other fields, belong to a long historical process whose links are connecting, adding up, molding and constantly perfecting themselves. We, therefore, need to interpret history, understand its dynamics, predict the future. Then the world must not only be analyzed, it must be transformed. In that light, *Gidra* becomes not only the chroniclers of events, but the makers of history as well.

During the last five years—a long time, yet really so short—we have learned slowly, and sometimes painfully, to do things that had been totally alien to us before, to become aware of ourselves and others, and to look at the conditions around us in ways very different from the traditional view. Often, we were called upon to do things that made us feel uncomfortable at first: participating in marches and demonstrations, speaking before large audiences, appearing on radio and television programs, selling the paper, and sharing with each other some of our deepest feelings and most private thoughts.

As we continue to struggle, what needs remembering now is the richness and vitality of this total experience called *Gidra,* which is much more than just a newspaper. It has been an experience in sharing—in giving and receiving—in a sisterly and brotherly atmosphere. It has meant a chance to actively work for something we really believe in. It has meant a chance to express ourselves in a variety of ways. It has been a lesson in humility and perseverance. It has meant working with people who care about people, and genuinely feeling the strength that can only come out of collective experience.

But, what a struggle! ★

Introduction

Asian Americans in the United States totaled only 1,800,000 persons in 1973[1] and comprised less than one per cent of the total population.[2] By any standards, they are numerically a "small minority." However, they have played a significant role in the history and development of the western United States from the mid-nineteenth century to the present. From the beginning, Asian workers have fulfilled the large mining, railroad, and agricultural interests' insatiable demand for unskilled, cheap labor. Working for low wages and under poor conditions, these "Oriental" laborers have helped to build the railroads and to harvest the crops of the American West since the 1850's. From the ordeal of the Asian contract laborer to the plight of the Chinatown garment worker, Asian Americans have endured and struggled against the exploitation of American capitalism. This section will attempt to examine various facets of this oppression and struggle.

The major stages of Asian immigration are the Chinese period from 1848 to 1882, the Japanese period from 1890 to 1924, and the Pilipino period from 1920 to 1935.[3] These three phases contain a similar historical pattern of exploitation and exclusion: "Just as all groups were utilized as a supply of cheap labor for the demand of the rapidly expanding western economy, so were all of the group [including Koreans] effectively excluded from the United States by law."[4] These Asians faced a violent "anti-Oriental

crusade" which eventually resulted in the legal exclusion of all Asian immigration to this country.[5] The Chinese was the first immigrant group to be barred from immigrating into this country in 1882.[6] Korean immigration was halted in 1905.[7] The Immigration Act of 1924 excluded all "Oriental" immigration into this country except for Pilipino and Hawaiian workers.[8] Finally, Pilipino immigration was limited to only a token quota of fifty people per year by the 1935 Tydings-McDuffie Immigration Act:[9] "What is significant is that all of these varied Asian groups, each representing a separate country and unique culture, encountered a similar or identical pattern of racial oppression and economic exploitation."[10]

Especially important to American capitalism was the use of Asian Americans as cheap labor.[11] Indeed, all the Asian immigrant groups—Chinese, Japanese, Korean, Pilipino, and East Indian—have entered this country as a cheap labor force for such large and dominant industries as railroads and agriculture.[12] In California, the big railroad companies such as Central Pacific and the Southern Pacific dominated the state's economic and political structure during the period from the late nineteenth century to the first quarter of the 20th century.[13] Controlled by a small group of landowners, agriculture became "factories in the field": "The land is operated by process which are essentially industrial in character, the 'farm hand'

LAND, LABOR, AND CAPITAL

... has been supplanted by agricultural proletariat indistinguishable from our industrial proletariat."[14] In Hawaii, the dominant sugar industry was dominated by five corporations.[15] These "Big Five"—American Factors; C. Brewer and Company, Ltd.; Alexander and Baldwin; Castle and Cook, Ltd.; and T.H. Davie and Company, Ltd.—control much of the land even today.[16] Lacking unskilled workers, these industries actively recruited Asian workers by sending recruiters and agents abroad to seek this source of labor.[17] The railroads in the late nineteenth century hired labor brokers to secure Chinese laborers for their use.[18] The sugar plantation owners of Hawaii formed the Hawaiian Sugar Planters Association to carry on the recruitment of Asian labor for their plantations.[19]

These Asian workers worked long hours in poor working conditions and for low wages. Chinese workers who worked on the building of the transcontinental railroad during 1865 to 1869 were paid only thirty dollars a month; some were paid as little as twelve dollars a month by Central Pacific Railroad.[20] In 1890, the Hawaiian sugar plantations were paying Japanese contract laborers nine dollars a month.[21] These workers lived in virtual servitude created by three to five-year contracts which controlled almost all aspects of the laborers' lives.[22] These plantations continued to oppress Asian workers, including Korean and Pilipino laborers, in the 20th

century.[23] During the 1920's and 1930's in California, Pilipino migrant farm workers were paid as low as $2.60 a day.[24] They were among the lowest paid agricultural workers in that period.[25]

Facing the racism and restrictions of the anti-Asian legislation discussed above, many Asian Americans were forced to live in urban "ethnic enclaves" such as Chinatowns, Little Tokyos, and Manilatowns, and to engage in certain "ethnic occupations" and businesses in these ghettoes. Gardening, laundry and restaurant work, and sewing were some of the most common occupations. Barber shops, grocery stores, art shops, laundries, restaurants, and garment shops were some of the typical businesses.[26] The majority of Chinese have dwelt in cities and small towns from 1850 to the present.[27] But especially after the passing of the Alien Land Laws in 1913 and 1920 and the Immigration Act of 1924, this trend grew to include other Asian groups who moved from rural areas to live in such urban areas as San Francisco and Los Angeles.[28] In 1929, for example, Asian American owned "fifty per cent more commercial establishments per capita than did the general population."[29] Historian Roger Daniels believed this development was a reaction to the severe harassment of Asian labor:

> By the early 20th century practically none [Asian Americans] were found in the growing western industrial sector and the statistical incidence of

small commercial proprietors among them become striking. . . . While this has been interpreted as indicating the great success in pursuing the American Dream my view is that this mostly represented a retreat from competition, a way of not assimilating rather than successful assimilation.[30]

In 1965, when immigration law reforms eliminated the almost total exclusion of Asian immigration to this country, a new period of Asian immigration began, creating a "new working class" who filled the need for cheap labor in the electronics and garment industries.[31] This development has especially occurred in the Chinese community, "which has reinvigorated Chinatown as a place of residence, a business center and a community."[32]

The Immigration Act of 1965 also increased the number of Korean and Pilipino immigrants entering into this country. From 1966 to 1971, 114,107 Pilipinos immigrated to the United States.[33] In the last five years, the Philippines has led all other nations except Mexico in the number of new immigrants entering this country.[34] Korean immigration from 1966 to 1973 totaled 74,000 in number.[35] Most of these Korean immigrants have settled in Los Angeles creating the growth of a new Korean community in the Olympic Boulevard area of Los Angeles.

This new wave of immigration differs in certain aspects from the earlier periods of immigration. First, unlike the earlier "sojourners" and "manongs," these new Asian Americans have entered the United States with their families. A high proportion of these immigrants are from the professional or technical worker class. This is especially true for the new Pilipino and Korean immigrants. It is not uncommon to find lawyers, pharmacists, and doctors working as clerks, janitors or factory workers: "the average Korean immigrant, regardless of his educational background and experience, must accept menial-type jobs such as laborers, warehousemen, nurse's aides, service station attendant, or helper-trainee to name a few. . . ..[36] In 1973, it was estimated that unemployment in the Korean community of Los Angeles reached the rate of 18 per cent of the work force. Professor Jovina Navarro of UC Davis comments on the exploitation of the recent Pilipino immigrants:

> Several thousand Pilipinos, most of them products of colonial education, left their native country to look for a better life in America. But like their brothers and sisters before them, they have encountered social and job discrimination. Employment problems have become more acute as immigration figures continue to rise. Major companies have remained insensitive to the problems of newly-arrived immigrants and have continued their discriminatory hiring practices; if they hire them, their remuneration has been far lower than what their job duties call for. Federally sponsored training programs designed to prepare them for the job market in America have negligible effects because slots allocated are so few.[37]

American capitalism's exploitation of Asian Americans continues in their communities. A recent example is the controversial struggle over housing and urban renewal in various Asian neighborhoods throughout the country. Los Angeles' Little Tokyo, Seattle's International District, Honolulu's Chinatown, and San Francisco's Nihonmachi (Japanesetown) are some of the many Asian communities facing this problem of redevelopment.

Urban renewal ostensibly attempts to solve a pressing problem in our society, the lack of adequate housing for its citizens. Unfortunately, in practice, the effect of urban renewal is to raze the buildings and to evict the residents of the area in question. Thus, ethnic districts face possible elimination as communities, replaced by luxury apartment buildings or clusters of high-rise office buildings and shopping centers. For example, the urban renewal program for Nihonmachi in San Francisco included the building of a Japan Trade Center and tourist hotels.[38] The program for Little Tokyo in Los Angeles proposed the building of tourist hotels and a shopping mall by the large Japanese construction corporation of Kajima International.[39]

An urban renewal project follows a fixed pattern.[40] First, the City Government chooses a district to be "redeveloped." A local agency uses the power of eminent domain to buy up the land and buildings within the chosen area paying prices based on appraised values determined by the existing state of the area. After the buildings are razed and the inhabitants are removed from the area, the agency then sells the land cheaply to developers who undertake to rebuild the area. The goal of this private developer is simply to maximize the return of his investment:

> Profits are not made by building sound, low-rent (or lowpriced) housing for low-income families. They can be made only from constructing and leasing or selling luxury apartment buildings, skyscrapers for commercial use, or private houses for middle- and upper-class residents. . ... The big renewal projects in residential areas have been called land grabs aided by government subsidies and the powerful privilege of eminent domain.[41]

Asian American communities are organizing to struggle against this threat. In the last four years, various community groups have been protesting the destruction and dispersal of their respective communities through demonstrations, publicity and educational campaigns, legal suits, tenant strikes, and sit-downs among other tactics.[42] In San Francisco, for example, Committee against Nihonmachi Eviction (CANE) is fighting to preserve Nihonmachi as a residential and small business community for the Japanese American residents of the area: "when the Japanese first came to this country, we were segregated, but we built a strong, viable residential community: now that the location of our community makes it valuable, outsiders want to take away our community and force the residents out."[43] The Little Tokyo Anti-Eviction Task Force is another community group—organizing and struggling against the threat of urban redevelopment to one of the most important Japanese American communities in Los Angeles:

> It is becoming increasingly clear that like so many other federal programs, the Little Tokyo Redevelopment Project, although touted to be aimed at improving the community for the community people, is geared so that the little man will be taken advantage of. Despite all the promises made, the built-in inequities of our present capitalist economic system are also built into the redevelopment program.[44]

This Land, Labor and Capital section consists of thirteen articles which focus on specific aspects of this relationship between capitalism and the exploitation of Asian American workers and communities. The editors have attempted to use, whenever possible, articles written by actual participants and observers of the events discussed. These articles can be divided into four subject groups: urban renewal, agriculture, ethnic businesses, Asian workers and their experiences, and Asian labor and strikes.

First, analyzing the controversial issue of urban redevelopment, Little Tokyo Anti-Eviction Task Force's "Redevelopment in Los Angeles' Little Tokyo" discusses the attempts of the Community Redevelopment Agency of Los Angeles to direct the redevelopment of Little Tokyo. This article delineates in detail the danger of this urban renewal project to the well-being and very existence of this community. It especially reveals the intrinsic exploitative nature of these projects which eliminate the very communities that they were supposed to save. Next, Hashiji Kakazu's "Forty-Four Years of Raising Avocadoes" relates the author's own account of his oppression as a tenant farmer on the island of Hawaii from the devious tactics of large farm-owners. Written when the author was eighty-one years old, the article describes his persistent and unyielding struggle against the exploitative tactics of his "bosses."

The next three articles deal with problems of Asian American small businesses and their "middle-man" role of being at the same time the oppressed as well as the oppressor. Buck Wong's "Growing Up in a Los Angeles Chinese Laundry" reveals the plight of the owners and workers of Chinese laundries who rely on this dying "ethnic business" for their livelihood. An excerpt from Victor and Brett Nees' *Longtime Californ'*, "Six in the Morning, Six at Night" relates an interview with Frank Eng, 33, who describes his difficult experiences growing up in his parents' Chinatown grocery store. Dean Lan's "Chinatown Sweatshops: Oppression and an Alternative" is one of the most informative articles on the garment industry in San Francisco's Chinatown. The author presents an historical background of the San Francisco garment shops as well as offering some alternatives (developing unions or workers' cooperatives) for alleviating the oppressive conditions of these "sweatshops."

The next group of articles depict the oppression of Asian American workers and their struggles against this subjugation. Emma Gee's "Issei Women" describes the experiences of the pioneer Issei women who worked alongside their husbands in the farm fields of the American West and who also raised families in a hostile land. Unlike the Chinese and the Pilipinos during the period from 1900 to 1920, Japanese immigrants were able to bring wives over from Japan to the United States. This fact had profound influence on the Japanese American worker: "The immigration of these women made possible and produced the second generation, the Nisei, marking the transition from a society of single, male sojourners to permanent immigrants."[45] Unfortunately, the Chinese and Pilipinos were unable to bring wives from their native countries over to the United States, thus creating the plight of the "manongs" and the "sojourners"—single male Pilipino and Chinese laborers.[46]

H. Brett Melendy's "California's Discrimination against Filipinos, 1927-1935" and Carey McWilliams' *Factories in the Field* include interesting historical accounts of the Pilipino labor activities, especially in the 1930's. However, Carlos Bulosan's autobiography, *America is in the Heart,* is the most eloquent and revealing book of that experience.[47] Entering the United States in 1930 at the age of seventeen, Bulosan worked in this country as a laborer, writer, and and union organizer until his death in 1957 in Seattle. We have included an excerpt from his book which describes Bulosan's experiences as a participant in the attempts of Pilipinos and left-wing political groups to organize independent Pilipino labor unions in California in 1934. His account is a revealing personal depiction of the social and economic oppression that he and other Pilipinos faced and their political struggle against it. It delineates the tragedy of the thousands of young, single Pilipino men who came to this country in the 1920's and 1930's with hopes of obtaining a better life and who turned into the endlessly wandering armies of Pilipino farmworkers, "manongs," moving without wives or families from one dusty labor camp to another:

> The white majority has never fully appreciated the contribution made to western agriculture's "factories in the fields" by Filipinos or other migrant workers. That same majority has not understood the dream that motivated the Filipinos to work long hard hours. Instead, the Filipinos have been the object of scorn and prejudice for some Americans. And for others, the Filipinos have been the prey of the unscrupulous and the unethical, who have fleeced them of their earnings.[48]

Sandy Maeshiro's "It Ain't All Smiles and Sukiyaki" describes her experience as a Japanese American female stuggling against sexism and poor working conditions and wages. The article relates Ms. Maeshiro's experience working in a Beverly Hills restaurant and depicts the plight of waitresses. It scrutinizes the increasingly common situation in which Japanese-owned businesses in this country exploit Asian American workers. Moreover, Maeshiro shows how workers are increasingly resisting this situation through union collective actions and how unionization is increasing in the restaurant industry.

Finally, Victor and Brett Nee's "Emergence of a New Working Class" describes and analyzes the effect of the increased immigration of Chinese workers on the economic and social structure of San Francisco's Chinatown. It especially focuses on American capitalism's familiar use of these immigrants as a new source of cheap labor. It also discusses the severe problems and hardships that this new working class of Chinatown faces and undergoes.

The last group of articles discusses the union and strike activities of Asian American workers in their struggle against capitalist exploitation. Throughout the history of Asians in this country, we have seen Asian American workers organize and either form or join unions in order to improve working conditions and to obtain higher wages. In the 20th century, many Chinese, Pilipinos and Japanese workers played leading roles in the union movement such as the Alaskan Cannery Workers Union, in the ILWU, and the California Japanese Agricultural Workers Union.[49] Karl Yoneda's "One Hundred Years of Japanese Labor History in the United States" describes the union activities of Japanese workers in this period.[50] The discontentment of Chinese Garment workers in San Francisco resulted in the National Dollar strike of 1938.[51]

In Hawaii, Asian American workers have engaged in over eighty years of union struggle especially against the powerful interests of Hawaii's Agribusiness. In the late 1800's, needing cheap labor, the Hawaiian sugar plantation owners recruited Chinese and Japanese contract workers. The recruitment of contract laborers under Government supervision ended in May, 1894.[52] All contract labor was ruled unconstitutional in 1900 when Hawaii became a territory of the United States.[53]

Soon after, the sugar workers began to organize and strike against the poor working conditions and low wages. From 1900 to 1946, the plantation labor movement was a history of conflicts and strikes. The workers mainly composed of Japanese, Chinese, and Pilipino attempted to form an unified multi-national union which would represent all the plantation workers in their struggles against the plantation owners and their organization, the Hawaiian Sugar Plantation Association. Not until the International Longshoremen and Worker's Union organized

Hawaii's agricultural workers did they win the first territory-wide strike in 1946. This event greatly improved the working conditions and rate of pay for these largely Asian American workers. The union states that the sugar industry "pays the highest year around agricultural wages in the world to their members."[54]

Koji Ariyoshi's "Plantation Struggles in Hawaii" describes this history of plantation labor conflicts from 1900 to 1946 culminating in the victory of ILWU. The author is a respected labor figure who participated in the struggles of the plantation workers and served as editor of the pro-labor Honolulu Record during the first twelve years of rapid social change in Hawaii after World War II.

In recent years, especially in New York and California, there has been a series of strikes and workers' struggles involving Asian Americans. Recent Asian immigration beginning in 1965 has created a new working class which becomes a source of cheap labor especially in the garment, restaurant, and electronics industries. The San Francisco area especially has been the site of much labor unrest. Strikes at the Mandarin and Kiku restaurants, Le Mah Electronics, and San Francisco Gold Garment Company have occurred since 1974.

The most controversial struggle in recent years was the Jung Sai strike in which Chinese immigrant garment workers picketed the Great Chinese-American Sewing Company, then the largest sewing factory in San Francisco's Chinatown. To improve their poor working conditions and low pay, the Jung Sai workers had decided overwhelmingly to join the International Ladies Garment Workers Union (ILGWU), Local 101. They walked out on July 15, 1974 to protest the unfair firing of Frankie Mah, a leader in the unionization drive.

Supported by community organizations and residents, for six months the workers first picketed the Jung Sai plant and, when it was closed, moved their picketing to the parent company, Esprit de Corps, owned by Douglas Tompkins. After much violence and police arrests on the picket line, Tompkins seemingly sold the Jung Sai plant to a former employee of Esprit de Corps, Mike Kozak, in October, 1974.[55] After negotiations, on January 13, 1975, the workers represented by ILGWU signed a union contract with Kozak, establishing Jung Sai as a union shop.[56] One of the longest strikes in the history of San Francisco's Chinatown, it was hailed as a victory for Chinese immigrant garment workers who have been long denied basic union rights.

Unfortunately, this proved not to be the case. Tompkins revealed three weeks later that he had never sold the plant to Kozak, and thus the union contract was not valid.[57] Tompkins then removed all the equipment from the Jung Sai plant and permanently closed it. ILGWU officers stated that they were "fooled" by Tompkins and that the National Labor

Relations Board would have to arbitrate the whole controversy.[58]

Seven months later, in December, 1975, the NLRB ordered the Great Chinese American Sewing Company to reopen the factory that it had shut down 17 months ago, to award back pay to the workers, and to bargain with the union for a contract. Judge David Heibrun stated that he found pervasive extensive violations of labor relations laws by the management: "Also, the company was found to have used illegal interrogations, threats to withhold paychecks, pay raises, and threats to close the plant in attempts to stop the union drive."[59] The company owner, Tompkins, announced that he will appeal the decision to the full National Labor Relations Board.[60]

Despite this favorable decision, the legal aspects of this controversy might take years to be settled. The Jung Sai workers still have not regained their jobs, and the plant remains closed. The workers and their supporters have criticized the actions of ILGWU, alleging that the union has not shown full support of the workers. Indeed, the strike has caused conflicts among various community organizations such as Wei Min She, I Wor Kuen, and the Asian Community Center. From July 1974 to December 1975, four community newspapers, *New Dawn*, *Getting Together*, *Wei Min*, and *East/West* have discussed extensively in their publications the events of the strike and its attendant conflicts. These articles reveal in detail the community involvement and struggles around the issues of this strike. We recommend to those who want to learn more about the Jung Sai strike to read the articles from the four community newspapers. While the final outcome is not yet determined, the strike is another stage in the growing struggle against the garment industry's exploitation of Chinese immigrant workers and its denial of their right to organize.

New York also has been the location for a great deal of labor and community struggles. On May 12, 1975, approximately 10,000 Chinese marched in protest of the arresting and beating of Peter Yew, an engineer from Brooklyn, by the New York Police. One of the organizers of this demonstration was Americans for Equal Employment, a community organization of workers, students, and community organizers who, in May of 1974, led the protest of the discriminatory hiring practices of the DeMatteus Construction Company which had begun work on Confucius Plaza, Chinatown's newest housing project. One of the leaders of AAFEE, R. Takashi Yanagida, describes and analyzes the Confucius Plaza struggle to have Chinese and other Asian American workers hired in the building and construction trades in New York in his article, "The AAFEE Story: Asian Americans for Equal Employment."

To better understand the relationship between capitalism and Asian Americans, much more analysis needs to be done. This section makes no pretense of trying to be a comprehensive, definitive treatment of this important subject. It has tried to present articles which introduce some of the more relevant and controversial issues concerning the subject of Land, Labor, and Capital.

—Megumi Dick Osumi

Notes

1. Roger Daniels, "American Historians and East Asian Immigrants," *Pacific Historical Review*, 42 (1974): 452.

2. Ibid.

3. Ibid., pp. 450-1

4. Lowell Chun-Hoon, "Teaching the Asian American Experience: Alternative to the Neglect and Racism in Textbooks," *Amerasia Journal*, 3, no. 1 (1975): 47.

5. Daniels, pp. 450-1.

6. Ibid.

7. Ibid.

8. Ibid.

9. Ibid.

10. Chun-Hoon, p. 47.

11. Carey McWilliams, *Factories in the Field*, (New York: Archon Books, 1969), p. 104.

12. Ibid.

13. McWilliams, *Factories in the Field*, p. 47.

14. Ibid., p. 48.

15. Andrew W. Lind, *Hawaii's People* (Honolulu: The University Press of Hawaii, 1971), p. 68.

16. Carey McWilliams, *Brothers Under the Skin* (Boston: Little, Brown and Company, 1964), p. 186.

17. McWilliams, *Factories in the Field*, pp. 103-4.

18. Alexander Saxton, *The Indispensable Enemy* (Berkeley: University of California Press, 1971), p. 65.

19. H. Brett Melendy, "Filipinos in the United States," (see Recent Immigration section).

20. Saxton, p. 63.

21. McWilliams, *Brothers Under the Skin*, p. 185.

22. Ibid.

23. Ibid.

24. Melendy, pp. 528-9.

25. Ibid.

26. Chun-Hoon, p. 48.

27. Roger Daniels, "Westerners from the East: Oriental Immigrants Reappraised," in *Racism in California*, ed. Roger Daniels and Spencer C. Olin, Jr., (New York: Macmillan Company, 1972), p. 62.

28. Stanford Lyman, "Strangers in the City: the Chinese in the Urban Frontier," in *Roots: An Asian American Reader,* ed. Amy Tachiki and Eddie Wong, (Asian American Studies Center: UCLA, 1971), p. 166.

29. Ibid.

30. Daniels, "Westerners from the East," p. 62.

31. Melendy, p. 520.

32. Victor and Brett Nee, *Longtime Californ'* (New York: Pantheon Press, 1972), pp. 17-18.

33. Melendy, p. 525.

34. Ibid.

35. U.S. Commission of Immigration and Naturalization, Annual Report, 1973, Washington, D.C., 1974, p. 60.

36. Cooke Sunoo, "Koreans in Los Angeles," n.p., p. 4.

37. Jovina Navarro, "The Plight of Newly-Arrived Immigrants," in *Diwang Pilipino,* ed. Jovina Navarro (U.C. Davis: Asian American Studies, 1974), p. 40.

38. Glenn Omatsu, "Redevelopment in San Francisco Nihonmachi," n.p., p. 5.

39. Ibid.

40. Paul M. Sweezy and Paul A. Baran, *Monopoly Capital* (New York: Modern Reader Paperbacks, 1966), pp. 294-5.

41. Ibid., p. 297.

42. Omatsu, p. 3.

43. Dr. Kazue Togasaki, quoted in Omatsu, p.6.

44. Evelyn Yoshimura, "Redevelopment or the Rape of Little Tokyo," *Gidra,* Feb. 1973, p. 10.

45. Emma Gee, "Issei: The First Women," in *Asian Women* (Berkeley: University of California, Berkeley, 1971), p. 9.

46. Nee, pp. 1-18.

47. Carlos Bulosan, *America is in the Heart,* (New York: Harcourt, Brace, and Company, Inc., 1946).

48. Melendy, p. 546.

49. Bulosan, p. vii.

50. Karl Yoneda, "One Hundred Years of Japanese Labor in the U.S.A.," in *Roots: An Asian American Reader,* ed. Amy Tachiki and Eddie Wong (Asian American Studies Center, UCLA, 1971), pp. 150-58.

51. Patricia M. Fong, "The 1938 National Dollar Store Strike," *Asian American Review,* 2 (1975):182-201.

52. McWilliams, *Brothers under the Skin,* p. 183.

53. Melendy, p. 543.

54. Ibid.

55. *Wei Min,* Feb.-Mar. 1975; *Getting Together,* Jan. 1975.

56. *New Dawn,* March 1975, Vol. IV, no. 7, p. 4.

57. Ibid., p. 1.

58. Ibid., p. 4.

59. *East/West,* December 17, 1975, Vol. 9, no. 50, p. 4.

60. Ibid.

REDEVELOPMENT

IN

LOS ANGELES' LITTLE TOKYO

BY LITTLE TOKYO ANTI-EVICTION TASK FORCE

The history of Little Tokyo in downtown Los Angeles has always been one of struggle. Its initial formation as a community during the early 1900's was a direct response of Japanese people struggling to survive and surmount all the barriers of discrimination and racism that was directed at them during that time. Little Tokyo then served as the focal point for the Japanese Americans in Southern California. While no longer the single center of Southern California Japanese Americans, this district is still a vital community for the people of other nationalities who live and work there, for the many Japanese residents who still live there, and for the Japanese Americans who visit Little Tokyo's shops, churches, temples, restaurants, and cultural and community service organizations.

But Little Tokyo is an old community badly in need of rebuilding and improvement for the people who live and work there. Walking through Little Tokyo, down First Street through Monline Alley to Second Street, one can see how badly Little Tokyo has aged. It needs housing of all kinds, housing for families and for single people of all ages. It needs low-cost housing that is well-built and safe with rents that people can afford. But the private economy is incap-

able of providing it. The community by itself lacks the funds to rebuild Little Tokyo. Thus, it was forced to turn to the government for assistance.

In Los Angeles, the Community Redevelopment Agency (CRA) is the municipal agency which directs federally funded urban redevelopment programs. These programs ostensibly are supposed to supply new housing and to improve the living and working conditions for the city's communities and citizens. Unfortunately, these projects have largely aided the construction of corporate office buildings, luxury hotels and shopping malls. It is against the problems of physical deterioration, the lack of new housing and the threat of urban renewal that the community continues its history of struggle against racism and for survival, equality, and democracy.

Why don't redevelopment projects help communities rebuild and improve the living and working conditions for their residents? The answer lies in the real goals and purposes of the government's urban redevelopment programs. In the United States starting from the 1930's and proceeding to the present, the major cities have become overcrowded with a resulting lack of adequate housing and transportation. The more affluent citizens have moved out

photos by ROY NAKANO

of the decaying inner cities and into the more fashionable suburbs. This exodus has left mainly the poor, elderly and minority citizens behind in the inner city. Thus, a significant number of inner city areas are now minority communities. For the major cities, this transition has become critical. With their downtown areas decaying into "slums," these cities have experienced dwindling tax revenues and increasing demand for social services.

Congressional action was called to help reverse the trend. Thus, the whole concept of urban renewal, or as it is now called, redevelopment, became a national program whose purpose was to "eliminate urban blight and slums" But this program came into existence not to meet the needs of the community or its residents. Instead it was developed principally to help urban bureaucracies rebuild their tax base by catering to the needs of big business. It is clear now that the real goal for CRA's Little Tokyo Project can be described in this manner: "Instead of being social uplift programs as sometimes depicted, the big renewal projects in residential areas have been called land grabs aided by government subsidies and the powerful privilege of eminent domain" (Paul M. Sweezy and Paul A. Baran, *Monopoly Capitalism,* p. 298).

In sharing the struggle of the Little Tokyo community, we hope that this article will reveal the real nature of redevelopment and encourage people to continue to struggle for their democratic rights. Therefore, this article will deal principally with (1) the CRA's constant efforts to aid large corporations in obtaining Little Tokyo's land and building luxury tourist hotels and office buildings and (2) the community's efforts to prevent this "land grab" and force the government agency (CRA) to meet its responsibility of improving the living conditions and of meeting the needs of the Little Tokyo people. We have divided our discussion into five major sections: 1) Redevelopment in Los Angeles; 2) History of Redevelopment in Little Tokyo; 3) CRA's Promises; 4) The Reality; and 5) Conclusion.

Redevelopment in Los Angeles

A look at the City of Los Angeles' master plan for redevelopment might further illuminate our situation. In 1965 the L.A. Master Plan was approved to redevelop the city around a financial and governmental center. One of its major features was the coordinated development of an "International Zone," which included Little Tokyo, Chinatown and Olvera Street. In 1972 the L.A. Central City Plan spelled out the role of Central City as being:

(1) A focal location for business, especially financial institutions and corporate headquarters. . .
(2) the major concentration of governmental administrative facilities, (3) the location of unique, one-of-a-kind, cultural, recreational and tourist

facilities, including the Music Center, the El Pueblo Historical Monument, the Convention Center, Pershing Square and Little Tokyo.

How has redevelopment affected Los Angeles' inner city communities? Of several projects, Bunker Hill typifies the effects of redevelopment. Located just west of the Civic Center, the Bunker Hill community was once a residential area for many low-income and elderly people. Now it holds several new high-rise office buildings, a luxury high-rise apartment complex (renting as high as $1650 a month) and an international trade center. The original residents were evicted and forced to scatter back into other remaining low income areas. Thus, redevelopment did not correct the problem, but merely moved it physically out of the area to benefit the city and the big businesses.

So, how does Little Tokyo fit into Los Angeles' plan: It is seen as a cultural amenity, a playground for tourists. The City Planning Department stated, "The relationship between the Central Business District and Little Tokyo is symbiotic. Little Tokyo relies on the district for tourist retail trade and the district relies on Little Tokyo for the added amenity value it provides to a rich and varied downtown." The city wants to redevelop Little Tokyo as a tourist area. In contrast, the Japanese American community wants redevelopment to provide new housing for Little Tokyo and its residents: "Redevelopment should mean rebuilding and improving a community for the people who live in that community, but this has not taken place in Little Tokyo." To better understand how this confusion developed, let us take a look at how redevelopment first began in Little Tokyo.

History of Little Tokyo Redevelopment

The history of Little Tokyo has been one of a

struggle for survival and democratic rights which dates back to its very inception. Thus, the community's desire to rebuild and improve the living conditions has encompassed many more years than just those under CRA redevelopment. Redevelopment is only the latest phase of this struggle.

The pioneer Issei created Little Tokyo in the first decade of the century. Because they were primarily looked upon as a source of cheap labor by big industrialists, they were therefore considered a threat to the existing labor force and faced severe hostilities from the surrounding society. This quote by James Phelan, Mayor of San Francisco in 1900, typified the attitude towards Asian immigrants at that time:

> The Japanese are starting the same tide of immigration we thought we had checked twenty years ago. . .The Chinese and Japanese are not bona fide citizens. They are not made of the stuff of which American citizens are made. . .Personally we have nothing against Japanese, but as they will not assimilate with us and their social life so different from ours let them keep at a respectful distance. (R. Daniels, *Politics of Prejudice,* p. 50).

To the immigrant the stories of America as the "Land of Opportunity" were proven to be false. Equality and democracy were not to be found. Thus, the Issei found it necessary to band together in their own ethnic communities for the things necessary for survival. To them this not only meant food, housing, and employment, but also friendly faces that would welcome them.

To many Nisei, in the 1930's and 40's, Little Tokyo was a neighborhood where a generation was born and raised in small white framed houses which stretched from as far north as First Street to as far south as Ninth. It was a haven from the hostile society, a place to shop, eat and meet friends. In every sense, Little Tokyo before World War II was the social, cultural and economic center of Japanese Americans in Los Angeles.

World War II, however, was a major turning point in the history of Little Tokyo just as it was for all Japanese Americans. Japanese Americans on the West Coast faced mass evictions and evacuation at the orders of the U.S. government.

After the war, fewer Japanese Americans returned to Little Tokyo than had lived there before the evacuation in 1942. Little Tokyo as a community has never regained its prewar prominence. Nevertheless, the people who did return to the area reestablished much of what was the central core of the community. Japanese American businesses reopened on First and San Pedro Streets, and many people reestablished residence in the old apartments and hotels. Many community organizations and cultural groups also returned to the area. Years later, in the 1970's, many Sansei, taking pride in the Japanese American community's long history of struggle, would come and develop in Little Tokyo such programs as Japanese American Community Services-Asian Involvement, Pioneer Center, and the Little Tokyo Anti-Eviction Task Force, among others. Thus, although greatly decreased in size and population, Little Tokyo presently remains a major center of activity for the Japanese American community.

Another major event which influenced the future of the community came in the 1950's. No sooner had the community resettled from the camp experience than the city took away part of the community to build Parker Center, the headquarters for the police department. Taken by surprise and perhaps still unsure of itself after the traumatic experience of the camps, the community residents stood by as the city condemned an entire block of Little Tokyo, evicting residents, small businesses and community groups before a strong resistance could be formed. This event meant the loss of more Little Tokyo residents and one-quarter of Little Tokyo's main commercial area along First Street. This was only the beginning of the city's plans for Little Tokyo.

In the early 1960's, it was discovered that the city meant to continue its expansion of the Civic Center (the largest concentration of local, state and federal buildings outside of Washington, D.C.) into the Little Tokyo community. The plans that came to light showed that the city planned to acquire the northside block of First Street, between San Pedro and Central Avenue for the further expansion of the police facilities, and to widen First Street, meaning the forced removal of another large section of the community. But this time the community was more able to respond.

Rallying together behind leaders like Rev. Howard Toriumi of Union Church, many of the small business people and other community-minded persons organized a group known as the Little Tokyo Redevelopment Association (LTRA), which sought to stave off the impending city encroachment by trying to rebuild the aging Little Tokyo area. The attempt to rebuild was necessary because the city was using the excuse that Little Tokyo was a blighted area to rationalize this government expansion.

The LTRA struggled for several years during the 1960's to encourage rebuilding in Little Tokyo. Successful in the sense that it was able to hold off Civic Center expansion for a number of years, in the final analysis, LTRA soon found that it was impossible for a community with limited financial resources to come up with the kind of money necessary to rebuild the entire area. Recognizing their time and energy was beginning to run out and without other options available, they requested assistance from the city and were referred to the Community Redevelopment Agency of Los Angeles (CRA). In keeping with the responsibilities of the CRA to redevelop the inner city, the CRA agreed to "assist" the community in its efforts to rebuild itself.

But even while the "assistance" was in the preliminary planning stages, the struggle to maintain the area continued. In 1969, the City Traffic Commission proposed the widening of Second Street into a major thoroughfare, in addition to the existing plans to widen First Street. Knowing that this would split the community in two, a community campaign was organized in opposition to the street widening. On December 29, 1969, the City Council was forced to concede to the community's demands, and Second Street was retained as a local street.

The Dream—The CRA's Promises

With the immediate danger averted, the community looked towards the future of Little Tokyo once again. People continued to work with the CRA, developing plans which the community felt would help solve the problems in Little Tokyo. The involvement of the CRA would eventually become one of Little Tokyo's biggest problems, but the agency's promises for a time masked its real intent.

The CRA made assurances that the redevelopment of Little Tokyo would reflect the needs of all the people in the community. The Little Tokyo Community Development Advisory Committee (LTCDAC) was formed to provide community input for the redevelopment project. The CRA claimed that no one would be forced to relocate outside of Little Tokyo, not even temporarily: an "action area" concept would be used, meaning that as one "action area" was developed, it would provide the relocation space and facilities for the next area to be developed. Furthermore, the Agency made these specific promises to the community:

For the residents: "The total number of dwelling units planned for Little Tokyo, including youth and family dwellings to be approximately 1,000." (CRA, *Little Tokyo Redevelopment Project Plan,* February 24, 1970)

For the cultural, community, and service groups: "Key elements of the plan include a cultural-community complex for group meetings, performances of the arts, social services, and other functions. (CRA, *Little Tokyo Fact Book,* January 1970).

For the merchants: The First Action Area Shopping Mall. "Recognizing the fact that the business occupants of Little Tokyo are ethnic and their survival in business is dependent upon remaining in the area, the project's operational concept and strategy are based upon keeping business people in Little Tokyo." (CRA, *Environment Impact Report for the Little Tokyo Project,* March 22, 1973).

For Asian American and minority workers: "To the greatest extent feasible opportunities for training and employment arising in connection with the construction in a redevelopment project area be given to members of racial or ethnic minorities in proportion to the numbers of such members residing in the project area." (CRA, *Resolution 759,* February 18, 1970).

In meeting after meeting, the CRA reassured the community that the Little Tokyo project is one which the local people will develop. It then would be urban renewal's great exception unlike Bunker Hill, Honolulu's Chinatown, and San Francisco's Nihonmachi. The community was told that this redevelopment would be a restoration, not a removal process, which would supply badly needed new housing and would meet the needs of the area's residents and organizations. But what has actually happened since then is another story.

The Reality

A major stumbling block to the implementation of this beautiful plan was the City Council's insistence that redevelopment projects begin paying for themselves through increased tax revenues. Since noncommercial development, such as housing projects, or community centers, contribute little to the city's revenues, the Little Tokyo project was under extreme pressure to ensure the development of large commercial ventures. The effect of these economic pressures was to place community developments in a secondary position and to shift the emphasis of the project towards big commercial development.

The construction of a high-rise luxury hotel was added to the Little Tokyo Redevelopment Plan by the CRA. The agency argued to the community that this addition was necessary because the project would need some type of economic base to ensure the development of its other areas.

In December, 1972, the CRA arrounced the selection of Kajima International as the developer of the hotel. Kajima is a giant Japan-based multinational corporation, the fourth-largest construction firm in the world. Richard Mitchell, the executive director of the CRA said, "This was a close choice. Two of the proposals were outstanding, but Kajima has had a great personal interest in Little Tokyo" (*The Rafu Shimpo,* January 4, 1973). The company's "interest" in the community so far had included the Kajima Building, which takes up most of a block in the middle of Little Tokyo. When it was built in the mid-sixties, it forced out a number of small shops

and a larger moderately priced hotel and replaced them with high-rent offices and storefronts. It now serves as the home of the Japanese Consul and Kajima International, Inc.

The CRA director also said that the company would encourage local residents to invest in the hotel project. But in October, 1973, the Little Tokyo Anti-Eviction Task Force disclosed who the real investors were: Kajima has formed a consortium of thirty of Japan's largest financial institutions to develop the New Otani Hotel, under the name of the East-West Development Corporation (*The Rafu Shimpo,* October 27, 1973). The task force also discovered a complicated land deal between Kajima and the CRA that would net Kajima nearly a quarter million dollars for merely manipulating papers. In the deal, Kajima would sell a parcel of land to the CRA for $407,000, buy it back for $179,000 and pocket the difference of $226,000. The CRA explained that this was "normal procedure."

The next month, a petition with over one thousand signatures was presented to the Los Angeles City Council. It asked the council to postpone the zoning changes needed for the hotel until adequate relocation plans for housing, business, and community facilities were guaranteed. The petition was rejected; and in September, 1974, the hotel was the first construction to be built in the redevelopment project.

These initial skirmishes over the Hotel Project were just a prelude of things to come. Because of the construction of the Hotel New Otani, all of the tenants on the Weller Street Triangle face eviction by the end of 1976. The evictees include the residents of three low-rent hotels, the operators of all the small businesses on Weller Street, and the occupants of the Sun Building which houses over half of all the cultural and community service organizations found in Little Tokyo. The CRA plans to clear the block of tenants in order to keep its promise to the hotel developers that its construction can go on without delay. But what about the promises to the Little Tokyo community? Let us look at these "promises" now, five years after they were made.

1. Housing

The first promise to the community was to provide new and improved housing. The original redevelopment plan promised 1,000 units, most of which was to be affordable by low income families and individuals. But after several years of redevelopment, only 300 units of senior citizen housing, the Little Tokyo Towers, has been built. The Towers was built only after a long, hard struggle. Today residents of Little Tokyo who are not senior citizens still have no place to go, and the CRA now admits that homes might never be built for them in Little Tokyo.

Tenants on the Weller Street Triangle face evictions to make way for the New Otani Hotel. The residents on the northside of First Street are still pressured by impending evictions by the expanding Civic Center. Those on the southside of Second Street are being asked to move out to make room for auxiliary parking for the hotel. Still the CRA has not attempted to meet its responsibility to find the evictees acceptable replacement housing. Thus, the CRA has refused to keep its word that no resident would be forced to move until relocation areas were built in Little Tokyo. Moreover, the agency has not met its legal obligations to the community.

2. Community Center

The construction of a new community center was an exciting idea for the entire Japanese American community. The CRA once described the Cultural-Community Center as the focus for the entire redevelopment project. It was to serve as the central point of activity for all the people in Little Tokyo. Thus it was to be the relocation place for all of Little Tokyo's community service and cultural arts organizations.

But since 1971, when the Japanese American Cultural Community Center (JACCC) was formed, only a little more than one-tenth of the money needed to build the center has been raised. Most of this money is in the form of pledges.

Whom the center would serve has also come into question. Will the center be for the community and meet the recreational and service needs of the people, or will it become a tourist and trade center, serving the needs of the Japanese corporations and the Japanese government? When the JACCC Board was formed, it included representatives of Kajima, Japan Air Lines, Honda, the Bank of Tokyo, Sumitomo Bank and other potential big donors. The rationale for their selection was that these people would be able to raise the large donations sought from other corporations and from the Japanese government. In July, 1975, the board voted to change the name of the center to the American Bicentennial Commemorative Japanese American Cultural Center. Supposedly, this action would "facilitate funding" from the United States government, and appeal to the Japanese government's desire to participate in the Bicentennial Celebration. The implications of the name change triggered off a community uproar. The new name had conspicuously dropped the word "community." Many felt that this was an indication of the community concept being forfeited in the interest of gaining funding and that the function of the center would shift to serve the interests of the Japanese corporations. Because of the adverse community reaction, the original name was quickly restored; but the question of the board's intent still remains. An excerpt from a leading Japanese business monthly reflects the prevailing Japanese corporate and government view of Little Tokyo:

Little Tokyo is conveniently situated, giving the Japanese tourists and *hakujin* visitors alike an easy access to Japanese goods. . .But it is an old shabby place with an atmosphere far from the modern mammoth Tokyo. . .It is, after all, almost like an exhibition place for Japan in America. Japanese corporations and the government ought to assist in redevelopment (*Keizai Saron*, May 1973).

3. Aid to Little Tokyo Business

In 1971, a group of small businesses organized the Little Tokyo Development Corporation to build a shopping mall in which all the local businesses forced to move by redevelopment could relocate. CRA hailed the group as an example of how the community could rebuild itself through redevelopment. In 1975, this community corporation had to fold, being unable to raise the necessary $5 million financing required for the shopping mall project. CRA's idea of assistance to Little Tokyo's local businesses consisted of reopening the first action area to the bids of new developers, who were all large multinational corporations.

The small businesses of Little Tokyo are left with little alternatives. Most of them face eventual redevelopment eviction. Like the residents these small business operators are being forced to give up their existing shops and offices. Most of them can't afford to move to the proposed high-rent, luxury shopping mall. These community people will be forced to move their businesses out of the Little Tokyo area. Some have stated that they are too old to start a new business in a new area and would instead close their businesses for good, if evicted from Little Tokyo.

4. Asian American and Minority Workers

The CRA promised that it would open up the construction trades for minorities, especially Asian Americans. Although Asians are 3.9 per cent of the city population, they make up less than 1/3 of one per cent of the workers in all but one of the several construction trades. The CRA said that it could struggle against the racist hiring practices of the industry by enforcing federal Affirmative Action laws.

Late in 1974, the community formed the Affirmative Action Task Force (AATF), when it was recognized that the CRA wasn't doing its job. The AATF soon discovered that only two Asians had been newly hired to work on the pre-fabricated housing parts for the Little Tokyo Towers. When the CRA and the contractor responsible were confronted over this, they said that the situation would be remedied. But when construction on the site began, community inspections found that hiring and training were also deficient there. The contractors were using unscrupulous tactics to make it appear like more Asians were working there than was actually the case. A number of Asian laborers were hired and fired in quick succession. In another instance, two Asian workers were simply transferred from the company's other worksites to work temporarily in Little Tokyo. Recently on the New Otani Hotel site, contractors have already been caught in violation of the hiring laws.

In the struggle against racist hiring practices of the construction industry, the AATF has tried not to take away jobs from those workers who are already in construction. Instead it has emphasized the hiring of Asians and other minorities for new job openings. Throughout this struggle, we have found that the CRA is incapable and unwilling to make sure that the Affirmative Action goals are met. The CRA originally set a goal of 70 per cent Asians on the Little Tokyo redevelopment workforce. But so far, Asians have only made up 18 per cent; and to date, only two Asian Americans have been able to enter the construction industry through the Little Tokyo Redevelopment Project.

Conclusion

The struggle over redevelopment has progressively revealed more and more about the forces in society that shape our lives. Like all other government agencies, the Community Redevelopment Agency (CRA) exists supposedly to serve the needs of the people and the community. But the CRA has actually worked for the interests of big business and the government bureacracies, ignoring and denying the rights and needs of the people. Initially the CRA was able to cloak the real intentions of redevelopment by making unattainable promises. The CRA has since tried to hide behind community efforts such as the senior citizens housing project in an attempt to surgarcoat the evictions of resident and small businesses. The CRA continues to justify as necessary the commercialization and selling of the Japanese American heritage and ignores the continuing discrimination against Asian Americans in construction. It has become clear that what began in many ways as a local community effort to rebuild Little Tokyo has developed into a more intense struggle to uphold the people's rights and defend Little Tokyo from the desires of big business and government officials.

But this struggle is not a new one. When looking more closely at these problems, we see that they are basically the same problems and forces that we have faced in the past. The history of Japanese Americans is a rich heritage of struggle against racism and for survival, equality, and democracy.

Our history is one which spans over three generations. From this history of struggle for equality and a better way of life, we can better understand today's conditions and our heritage as an oppressed minority. We should learn lessons and draw inspiration from this history. We must be able to cast away these negative and harmful aspects of the past and unite as people of different generations and nationalities.

In order to continue a strong struggle against oppression, it must be a unified struggle. We must unite as people of different nationalities. Racism, discrimination, and economic exploitation have affected not only Japanese Americans, but also other Asian Americans and Pacific peoples, Blacks, Chicanos, and Native Americans. History has shown that our struggles as Japanese Americans has been intertwined with these other struggles. We have learned from the similarities in these struggles for democracy and equality of oppressed nationalities in the United States and of oppressed nations around the world. These lessons have developed the concept and spirit of Third World unity. Furthermore, Third World and white workers have much in common as working people and have often united in struggle. This is especially true in the current fight against redevelopment.

In Little Tokyo's struggle it is important for the whole community to unite as people of different nationalities. While predominantly Japanese American, it is also the work place and home for people of other nationalities, for Latinos, Blacks, and whites. The struggle to improve the living and working conditions of the people in Little Tokyo is a common one for us all.

But the redevelopment of Little Tokyo will not only affect those who stand to lose their homes, jobs, and businesses, but other Japanese Americans as well. Little Tokyo's function as a center for the Japanese American community is imperiled. The commercialization of our culture is part of the dangerous practice of playing up the differences between people, makes curiosities and oddities of us, and helps to foster and continue racist stereotypes. This type of redevelopment will reflect neither the multi-ethnic composition of the local community nor the character of Japanese Americans.

What we must do to effectively continue our struggle is organize ourselves. Already, the people in the Sun Building, which houses offices, and cultural and community groups, have begun to meet together on a regular basis. Residents of the three hotels on the Weller Street Triangle block have begun to meet in recent months as well. Group discussion and collective action are indispensable in fighting for our rights. The community has had positive experiences in struggling against the widening of Second Street, and in confronting the CRA over job discrimination.

We must continue to unite as a whole community, representing the needs of residents, workers, small business, community groups and other ethnic minorities. As a community and as concerned individuals, we must come together to defend and support the rights of the people in Little Tokyo, as well as the rights of all people struggling against racism, injustice, and economic exploitation. ★

Forty-Four Years of Raising Avocados

By Hashiji Kakazu

How old am I? I am taken up with my work so much that I often forget my own age. That is why I put this question to myself once in a while, just to make sure I know how old I am. When I first came to Kona in 1926, I was thirty-six years old. I am eighty years old now. I had failed in sugar-cane farming at Waiakea-Uka and had put myself in debt of pretty close to five thousand dollars.

What should I do? What could I do? How could I pay the debt? After some wondering and still some uncertainty, I came to Kona to try my luck at coffee farming. As a young man I had tried various occupations and had failed. I could not afford to fail another time. I thought of raising avocados on the side so as not to depend solely on coffee farming. This is how I got started in avocado farming. My days thus far have been full of difficulties. Let me tell you about my forty-four years of avocado farming.

How did I come to Kona? One of my friends in the Hamakua District, Toyotaro Chibana, had gone to Kona two or three years ahead of me. One day I talked to him and got first-hand information about farming in Kona. He was raising coffee and so I wanted to move to Kona to try my hand at it too. In Chibana's neighborhood there was a farmer named Risaburo Ono who was old and suffering from hemophilia. He could not keep the farm so I bought his farm on the advice of Chibana-san and other farmers in the neighborhood.

In those days in Kona the farmers were accustomed to have their daily needs supplied by their neighborhood store on credit. At the time I bought Ono-san's farm, he owed Komo Store over one thousand dollars. I took over Ono's debt to the store, paying it up to Mr. Komo, himself, in cash. Thus, my close financial relationship with Komo Store began.

The store is now under the management of the younger generation of the family. I am in good credit with the store even to this day.

The Guava Bush:

Having bought the Ono farm and begun a coffee farm, I thought about Kamaroku Tamashiro, a friend of mine and about Kama Kakazu, one of my relatives, who were working for a sugar plantation at the time. They were not doing well there. I wanted to bring them over to Kona and help them become farmers. Right next to my coffee farm there was a thick guava bush. I was leased by Matsu Nakasone. He had his own coffee farm nearby and looked to me as though he'd not be able to clear the guava bush for farming. So, after talking things over through Chibana, I bought the lease from Nakasone for the sum of four hundred and fifty dollars.

The guava bush was a thirty-five acre piece. Of the thirty-five acres Nakasone had sub-leased fifteen acres to a man named Asato. So I paid two hundred and fifty dollars to Nakasone for his twenty-five acres and two hundred dollars to Asato for his fifteen acres.

When negotiations for the lease were about to be completed, Nakasone and I went to Mr. Ackerman, agent for Miss Ellen, the owner of the land. We told him about all circumstances of our transaction. I asked Mr. Ackerman to renew the lease in my name when the term of the current lease expired. "I will renew the lease as many times as you wish," Mr. Ackerman answered. At this meeting, I learned that Nakasone was not the original leasee. The lease was first made with an old man named Aoki who had transferred the lease to Nakasone.

With the guava bush acreage, I sub-leased twenty

illustration by GLEN IWASAKI

acres to Kama Kakazu and fifteen acres to Kamaroku Tamashiro. His children were still little, so he could not put much time into clearing the guava bush. I felt happy about having two good friends brought over to live in my neighborhood. Working together and helping each other, I dreamed of achieving success together.

However, looking back on those early days, I find how "green" and careless I was then. For myself, I could endure living in a tent for any number of years until I realized my aim. But the houses for Kakazu and Tamashiro were really too small for their big families. Possibly because of this difficulty, they bought coffee farms elsewhere and moved away from my neighborhood. Thus, I was forced to open up the guava bush by myself. At that time I went to report the matter to Mr. Ackerman. I told him that Kama Kakazu had left the place and that I intended to clear the bush myself. I told Mr. Ackerman that I wanted to go into "big-tree farming" with long range plans. For this reason I asked him to let me know before anybody else if and when the place should ever be put up for sale. Mr. Ackerman assured me at that time again, as he had on previous occasions, that I need not worry about the lease and about my priority in buying the place, if and when it should be put up for sale.

With that assurance and understanding, I took to clearing up the guava bush wholeheartedly. Now I was full of confidence. I wasn't afraid of working hard. I was young and aching for success. Within a few months, a big portion of the guava bush was cleared. About six months later, Mr. Ackerman came to see the place. He went away very pleased because he saw the big guava trees and various other trees had been dried up. Naturally he went back very pleased. The guava bush was first leased to Aoki-san who couldn't clear it up due to old age and illness. Nakasone bought the lease next but could not open up the guava bush. Then my relative Kama Kakazu tried his hand but also failed. Now Mr. Ackerman saw that the bush was really being cleared.

Mr. Ackerman seemed to have reported to Miss Ellen about the way I was working because she was very kind ever since then. She must have thought that it required much money and effort to clear the wild bushes. During the depression years, she lowered the lease price without my asking for it. She was a very kind landlady although I never had the chance of seeing her in person. I worked on her land as if it were my own property. I was not worried about the lease. I worked only to raise good avocados.

Notes of an Avocado Farmer:

In doing anything I have always wanted to be a few steps ahead of the others. I spent many, many hours thinking about avocado farming. Seeds from the same tree never produce the same kind of trees, with similar quality of fruit and time required for bearing. Each sapling is different from the others. A hundred saplings result in hundreds of different trees. A thousand saplings result in a thousand different trees. I found that in order to produce marketable avocados which are uniform in size, taste and handling, I must do a lot of grafting. By grafting the trees, I found a way to supply the market year-round with fruit of more or less uniform taste and size.

Today, if a farmer wants to learn about something, all he has to do is go to the Agricultural Experiment Station and ask for help. Mr. Fukunaga, the agent, is there to teach him. Sometimes there are even give-away plants ready just for the asking. Forty years ago, a famer could not do this. The Agricultural Experiment Station in those days was inadequate. I remember when there was just one avocado plant in the whole station.

I suffered from all sorts of difficulties. First, I was not good at grafting. If I made ten graftings, only two or three took. Sometimes all ten failed. But I did not give up. With patience I kept on trying. Quality of avocados was constantly being improved. People asked for better tasting, better keeping avocados. I had to improve the quality of my products to compete with the market. I made several graftings on my trees to improve the quality of fruit. Sometimes my efforts were labor lost for nonsense.

It took many years of patient waiting to check whether my grafting had really improved the quality of the fruits or not. This is because avocado trees take six or seven years to mature and bear fruit. I checked every tree on my farm and turned undesirable trees into desirable ones by grafting.

The Lease Expires:

Having a very good landlady like Miss Ellen, I never worried about my priority in renewing the lease of my property. I put all my efforts into improving the trees. I worked as though the property were my own. Then one day the owner of Komo Store who kept my lease-paper said, "Kakazu-san, the term of the lease expired. You'd better tell Mr. Ackerman about it, and have the paper rewritten for you." I was not worried about the lease paper except for relieving Komo-san of his concern. You see, Komo Store had advanced me over five thousand credits worth of merchandise on the credit of my lease-paper.

I went to Mr. Ackerman about having the lease renewed. He said, "I think so. The term should be up by now. I will renew the lease for you, but you wait for awhile. There are some other leases terminating. I will have your papers made when I have the papers made for the other people. I'll have all of the papers made at the same time."

I expressed my concern about the proposed procedure. But Mr. Ackerman said, "Don't worry. I will not lease your place to anybody without first consulting with you about it. In case the place were to be sold, I will first ask you to buy it. If you don't want to buy it, only then will I sell it to anybody else." Because of what Mr. Ackerman had done for me up to that time I was willing to take his word for it. I still think he meant what he said. So I left the matter up to his discretion, at the same time requesting him to sell the property to me in case it should ever be put up for sale.

As I was going to depend on this farm for my bread and butter, I thought about this matter for a long time after parting with Mr. Ackerman that day. This is why I thought about it: if I had my residence somewhere outside of this avocado farm and came daily to work on the farm, I must have the lease-paper all the time. But since I built my house on the property and lived many years and worked on the farm, would it not be to the disadvantage of the land-owner not having the lease-paper written? Why? Because by having a lease-paper, the land-owner could change the lease at the end of the term. If, on the other hand, a land-owner lets the leasee make his house on the property and agrees with him on engaging in long-range tree farming without a properly executed lease-paper, would this not make for a termless lease? One day I asked Komo-san for his opinion on the matter. Komo-san said, "I don't think you need to worry about getting the place leased to you again because Mr. Ackerman trusts you very much." So it was that the matter was left without any immediate action on it.

The Misfortune:

Man's way of life is full of uncertainties and difficulties. Working earnestly and honestly is not enough. Miss Ellen who had trusted me very much died. Then there came a wealthy man who tried to take away my avocado trees. The rich man's name was Mr. Grover. I do not think this is a personal problem. This is a case of social evil. I believe this is a problem of human society. I think American civil rights need better protection. For explanation of what I am to say, let me tell you about the law case between Mr. Grover, a business tycoon, and myself, Hashiji Kakazu, a little farmer.

As I told you before, I trusted Mr. Ackerman, and I left the matter of writing the lease-paper up to his discretion. In the meantime, Miss Ellen, the land owner died. She had always been understanding and sympathetic. I wanted a chance to meet her face-to-face to thank her for her kindness and understanding. However, for thirty years, I had never had the chance of meeting her. When I heard that she had passed away, I felt as though I had lost my own mother. I

would have done all I could to see her had I known of her failing health; but as it happened I was told of her death several months afterwards.

I was not worried about my lease-paper as yet because I entrusted that matter to Mr. Ackerman. I was waiting for his action on the matter when, out of the clear blue sky, misfortune fell on me. One day a young man known as Ahuna came with Fukunaga-san of the Agricultural Experiment Station to see me where I was working on the farm. After chatting for a while Ahuna said, "Kakazu, you like buy this place?" I answered him, "Yes, I have been asking Mr. Ackerman for this place right along all these years." Then Ahuna said, "If you want to buy, I'll give you priority." I answered him, "Eh, Ahuna, I have priority. It sounds funny for you to say that you are going to give me priority!" Ahuna said, "But we bought the place." I answered angrily, "Then I will pay you the lease money!"

Had Ahuna said something similar to "you like buy this place we will give you special consideration" or something of similar nature expressing human understanding, my attitude would have been different. Ahuna giving me priority! I could not take it. Look, I put thirty years of my labor into the development of this farm. It is a farm because I put thirty years of sweat and blood into the place. At the very modest estimate, I think the value of the property must have increased five times the value when it was a wild guava bush. I simply could not accept the idea of competing with others in buying the place. I clearly saw in my mind that here was somebody who was trying to take away the fruits of thirty years of my labor; that life-work was in danger of being stolen from me. I realized that I needed resolution and "guts" to defend my rights.

I suspect that the new owner of this property did not buy directly from Miss Ellen, but from someone who had inherited it after her death. He must have bought it from someone who did not know anything about the circumstances under which this farm had been developed. But I took this misfortune as God's test of my courage. I waited for the outcome with resolution to defend my rights as long as I lived.

Meeting Mr. Grover:

One day I received a message from Mr. Grover, the employer of Ahuna. He wanted to have a talk with me. He wanted me to come to see him at his office in Honolulu. So I went out to Honolulu. Jiro Kaneshiro, one of my friends in Honolulu, accompanied me to the meeting.

Mr. Grover was a man, smaller in stature than I had imagined. He did not arouse any feeling in me of a business tycoon. He was approachable. When I introduced myself, he said, "Oh, you're Mr. Kakazu," and he shook hands with me. He talked very clearly and at the time, understandingly, I thought. Mr. Grover said he had no intention of making matters hard for me. Mr. Grover proposed to have the matter between us arbitrated by three persons—one representative for each of us and a third party. He named his representative, a Mr. Nakahara of Kona. He told me to name my representative and my choice for the third party for the arbitrating team. Mr. Grover said, "I will follow their arbitration and you will do the same." When I heard him speak thus, I thought to myself, "Ah, Mr. Grover isn't a bad man. I, myself, would be a bad man if I couldn't cooperate with a fine man as he." And so I agreed with him saying, "That's all right with me, Mr. Grover. I name Mr. Ackerman as my representative. I suggest for the third party either Mr. Greenwell or Mr. Heine. Please take your choice." As soon as I got back to Kona, I told both Mr. Nakahara and Mr. Ackerman all about my meeting with Mr. Grover. I also told them that I had informed Mr. Grover that my representative would be Mr. Ackerman. For the third party I told them I had asked him to choose between Mr. Greenwell and Mr. Heine.

A few days later Mr. Ackerman told me that Mr. Greenwell, Mr. Nakahara and he—three persons— had agreed on the price of my farm at three hundred and fifty dollars per acre. I thought their valuation fair though I thought that Mr. Grover had probably bought the property at a way lower price. Nevertheless, I accepted the arbitration of the three gentlemen. Did Mr. Grover think the arbitrator's price too low? I could not tell but he refused to abide by their decision. It was Mr. Grover himself who had proposed to have our differences settled in this manner. It was he who said that he would accept the decision of the three arbitrators, and it was he who asked me to abide by the same. I did not like this betrayal of his own word. I got stubborn.

The Case Goes to Court:

This was a case between a well-known businessman, Mr. James Grover, and a little farmer, Hashiji Kakazu. Through this trial I found that the following shortcomings exist in American judicial practice:
   A) There are cases in which the presiding judge does not know what a judge should be doing in court.
   B) There are illogical laws even in this great country of America.
Let me explain what I mean when I say, "there are cases in which the presiding judge doesn't know what a judge should be doing in court." I think a judge in court should have a fatherly feeling toward each party, rich or poor, strong or weak. It is my belief that a judge's attitude in court should be that of the father in a family. He should encourage the weaker ones in the family to speak their grievances. If the weaker

ones hesitate to speak out for fear of offending the stronger, the judge should try to lead them out of hesitation and silence. I think you will readily understand why I thought the judge who ruled in our case did not really understand the callings of his own profession.

The judge asked me, "Kakazu, do you have the lease-paper?" I answered him, "Due to certain circumstances I do not have the lease-paper." The judge then declared, "No lease-paper, no right." But I have testimony of my residence on the farm more real than a piece of paper-lease. I have built a house on the farm. I have planted various fruit trees. I have lived on the farm for nearly thirty years. If the judge were one who really understood the callings of his own profession, he would have given me a chance to explain what I meant by "due to certain circumstances." But he did not give me the chance to explain myself. He only said, "No lease-paper, no right."

The reason I say "there are illogical laws even in this great country of America" is that I believe that in the trial involving our case, there was too much emphasis on paper rights and none on rights-in-fact. Where facts are lacking, paper evidences are shown to establish facts of a man's rights. I believe there is no evidence more real than facts. I spent nearly thirty years of my labor on that property. I built my house on it. I cleared the guava bush. I planted coffee-trees and avocado trees. These are some of the facts about my residence on the place. Why did the judge ignore these facts and declare, "No lease-paper, no rights"? Being a little farmer of Okinawan origin, I could not take the judge's ruling. I left the court expressing my dissatisfaction of the judgment.

Later Events:

That this sort of injustice could happen even in this great country, the United States of America, got into my mind. This should not be allowed to happen in America. Thinking this way, I resolved in my mind to defend my rights in this case as long as I lived. But due to lack of financial means, I could not take this case up to higher court. The only thing I could do was to resolve not to be taken away from the house that I had built and from the avocado trees which I had planted on the farm. I planned on a long fight with Mr. Grover. Just because the court ruled in his favor, Mr. Grover thought he had succeeded in taking away thirty years of my labor on the farm for nothing. He seemed as though he enjoyed visiting the farm and looking at the trees. He did not insist on my moving out of the house that I had built. He even tried to cajole me into working for him. Believing in my final victory, I did not resist Mr. Grover openly. My resolution stood: "I will never leave the house that I built on this farm." ★

LIFE IN A CHINESE LAUNDRY

•

INTERVIEW WITH JOHN GEE
BY BUCK WONG

Interviewer's Preface: A Perspective

Growing up and living in my parents' laundry, I did not fully understand how they worked and struggled. I would not stop to consider that my father immigrated to America as a teenager and could not go to high school because he had to work in a laundry to make money. Yet, he had learned to speak English well, and people were surprised when they discovered that he was not born in this country. Accordingly, watching my mother ironing hour after hour, I would forget

how laundry work limited her abilities. Anyone who saw her laboring over the ironing table would not know that she had received a fine education in China and had worked as a teacher. However, I always realized that they worked very hard. I saw that every day. Years later, I began to understand that my parents' struggles were not isolated from those of other Chinese. Now I view Chinese laundry work as an important part of the Chinese American experience and as a reflection of people's struggle against social and economic oppression.

Class oppression is dominant in America, where the capitalist class (those few who own the means of production) oppress the working class (the vast majority who produce the goods in society). The majority of Chinese immigrants have been working people and, as such, they have suffered class oppression. However, capitalism breeds racism and sexism, using them as the means to further exploit women and national minorities like Chinese. The following discussion illustrates some of the more important aspects of the laundry experience and the oppression that Chinese laundry people have encountered.

Why Do Chinese Work in Laundries?

When asked this question, one man who owns a laundry in West Los Angeles replied,

It was inherited from one generation to the other. After the railroad workers finished work, there was not much that they can do at the time so naturally they pick up what they can do. My grandfather and

338

my father both tried farming. But they didn't do too well. So sooner or later they found the laundry work.

Another person said of his father, a former laundry owner,

I guess he would probably agree with me that when they came here, it was probably the only avenue they could go to. Except for maybe the restaurant business. It was either the restaurant or laundry... And almost anybody knows how to iron clothes, and English is not a barrier when you work in a laundry.

These statements illustrate the hostility that Chinese faced in America in the late 1800's. Unwelcomed in many occupations, they found refuge in laundry and restaurant work. Working in laundries was not a matter of free choice. Instead, Chinese saw it as one of the few ways of survival when they first came to America. The 1920 US Census showed that out of 45,614 Chinese workers in the country, 12,559 were laundry workers and 11,438 were restaurant workers. Even in 1950, 430 of the 669 Chinese business enterprises in Chicago were laundries.

Working in a Laundry

General descriptions of laundry work are usually very similar to those made in the following statements:

You labor. You are always below anybody else price-wise. Although you make this up with your labor, you're at harder work and longer hour. That is the only way that you can catch up with the steam laundries. For us, the majority of the Chinese laundry community, they did not have any equipment to work with. That's what they call the Chinese hand laundry.

We used to work a lot; it would be over 10 hours a day. We used to live in the laundry. Everybody used to do that. The work would be as much as 60 to 70 hours a week.

I really hated going there to the laundry every morning. First of all, it was a very gloomy and dreary type of place. And then—we came in from the back door—once you open the door, and the sunlight shines in, you see all these roaches crawling through the floor back into the corner.

Chinese laundry people found themselves in an unfortunate position. They did not want to suffer the long hours, hard work, monotonous repetition, and loneliness of the laundry. But they had to take it. Outside the laundry, Chinese constantly faced the barriers of racism. Said one laundryperson about trying to buy a house, "They come right to your face and say 'I'm sorry. We can't sell you a house because you are Chinese.'" Another person remembered a place in Long Beach which used to allow dogs to enter but not Chinese.

Consequently, many felt like the man who said,

I am not an old man yet, but I feel old. How can a man feel good when he is forced into an occupation he doesn't like. But I get used to it. After you are at it for so many years, you have no more feeling but to stay on with it.

Chinese Laundries—Their Good Points

Later on, after the war, that was the booming period. Between '45 and '55, that was the best of the laundry business. For one thing, the laws had been changed; you could bring the family and wife in. So from then on, it was more like a family affair.

The one good thing that stands out in my mind is that it was a form of employment for the Chinese who probably would have had a hard time finding any other type because of the language barrier.

As a response to the racism in American society, laundries have provided one mechanism for Chinese to survive in a hostile world. The Chinese laundry was never the road to riches, but it gave one enough money to buy food and obtain shelter. Racist and sexist immigration laws made it even harder for Chinese women to emigrate. But for families that did settle in America, the laundry afforded them the means of making a living. This history of Chinese laundries shows that hard times can lead people to resolve to struggle and overcome hardships.

Chinese Laundry Associations

The struggle against oppressive conditions that created and sustained Chinese laundries occurred on a collective as well as individual basis. One such mechanism was the L.A. Chinese Laundry Association, founded in 1933 during the Depression. Working conditions were such that many people slept under their ironing tables. When the health department discovered these violations of the city codes, they put pressure on the laundries for compliance.

In response, the Laundry Association began. One L.A. laundry owner described it as a

business person's group. If they got trouble from anyone, then they can band together to fight back... if they had to go to City Hall, then the English secretary would have to help out. A lawyer used to be hired and served mostly as an advisor.

Supported by nominal dues, the association included about 3/4 of the Chinese laundries that existed. The association also helped the Chinese to get along by preventing two laundries from opening shops too close to each other.

New York City had an organization called the Chinese Hand Laundry Alliance. Also founded in 1933, it first united in protest against a city ordinance charging license fees on small laundries and forced a reduction in the fees. The CHLA had an active membership of over 3,200 in 1934 and was one of the more progressive political Chinese groups in the country. It got involved in some of the national politics of the New Deal era and gave strong vocal support to the Chinese Revolution. During the Korean War, it refused to join the anti-communist campaign of the Chinese Benevolent Association. Subsequently, immigration authorities and the FBA harassed CHLA members and caused a sharp decline in its membership.

The Decline of Chinese Laundries

While the stereotype of Chinese as laundry workers remains, the laundry is no longer a prevailing institution of Chinese American society. Those people who have lived laundry life have seen the decline occur. One Chinese woman in an L.A. laundry thought that the younger people have no desire to work in laundries and would rather go into something like the restaurant business. The son of a laundry owner remembers his parents' friends saying to him, "You had better study hard because you don't want to end up working in a laundry like us. Because it is a very very bad form of labor."

An even more crucial factor in this decline has been the changes occurring in the clothing industry. One person revealed this effect on laundries by saying that,

> If there is good business, then working in a laundry is good. If there is no business, it is bad. It used to be better because now they come out with these new types of material called "permapress" which do not need to be ironed. So that has cut down on the business of laundries.

The decline in the L.A. Chinese Laundry Association has been a clear indicator of the general demise. One person recalled: "The highest that we had was 385 members in the laundry association; now there is about 86 members." A Hollywood laundry owner stated that there were about 400 Chinese laundries in L.A. as late as 1965. Now there are only about 200. So it seems that more and more, Chinese laundries are becoming a legacy of the Chinese American experience.

The Present-Day Outlook

The story of Chinese who have struggled through laundry work illustrates the oppression that working people experience, particularly that of non-White ethnic groups. Many Chinese immigrants were forced into an unhappy life of toil and labor, isolated from the "Mountain of Gold" they wanted. Yet, there were strong people who survived hardships and would unite to fight against these obstacles.

The Chinese today need this same strong spirit more than ever. American-born Chinese continue to encounter economic oppression and racism, though often in subtler forms. Meanwhile, the great majority of the recent Chinese immigrants find that America is insensitive to their needs. The government refuses to help them overcome the language and cultural barriers and to provide adequate social services. Instead immigrants find themselves sewing for long hours and low wages to create gigantic profits for the clothing industry. They find themselves working for meager wages in restaurants, but sharing few of the luxuries of those who build thriving businesses on their labor. The barriers of oppression that created the institution of the Chinese laundry continue to plague Chinese Americans in different forms. Like the Chinese immigrants in the past, Chinese Americans today must see themselves as part of the larger struggle against all forms of oppression.

Hopefully, the following interview with John Gee will give the reader even more insight into particular facets of the Chinese laundry experience through one participant's personal response to this experience. John is a young Chinese American whose father was an immigrant who owned and worked in a Chinese laundry in Los Angeles. The interviewee's name has been changed to preserve his and his family's anonymity. While one example cannot provide a complete picture, the interview reveals clearly the day-to-day struggles that Chinese Americans have undergone in this country, the pride and tenacity they have shown in struggling, and the nature of national oppression in this country.

●

INTERVIEW WITH JOHN GEE

Wong: Since your father didn't want to be interviewed, I'm going to ask you as many questions as you can answer about him. Was he an immigrant, or was he American-born?

Gee: He was born in China; he is forty-two now. He came to the United States in 1951, about a year and a half after I was born. When he first came here, he went to San Francisco to stay for a while. Then he went to New Orleans. He worked in his father's laundry in New Orleans, and then he came here. Almost all his life here, he worked in a laundry, until recently. Now he works in a take-out restaurant as a cook. He worked for his uncle when he first came to Los Angeles and continued to work for him until about 1965. He worked as a general laborer there—ironing, pressing, and everything else. In 1965, he bought a small laundry on Temple near Rampart Boulevard. My father always had this dream—he always wanted to work for himself because he used to tell us that you can never make any money unless you work for yourself. When you work for somebody else, you never get the same wages, and there is no future in it. That's why he bought that small laundry. He worked in that until 1969 when he gave it to my uncle.

Wong: Was it sold over to your uncle?

Gee: No, it was just given to him. My uncle had just come back from Hong Kong.

Wong: Was that the uncle that he worked for before?

Gee: No, it was a different one. This one was on my mom's side. I should say that that laundry really drove my uncle kind of crazy. He later committed suicide. He had the same dreams as my dad; he wanted to make a lot of money. He wanted to work for himself, but he didn't have any type of business mind. He hired a girl to work for him and paid her wages. After he paid her wages, he only had about

$20 or $30 left for himself. Anyway, back to my dad. He had the Beacon Laundry for about four years, five years. He always wanted to improve it. He was a pretty good ironer, and he always wanted to do a good job, but about that time, the laundries were kind of dying out. So after a while he got frustrated and gave it to my uncle.

Wong: Jumping back a bit, when he came from China, could you tell me something about his family background. Where did he come from?

Gee: He came from a village. His father and mother were landlords. So during the war, they had to go to Hong Kong to escape persecution. When they went to Hong Kong, they were still fairly well off. So his father and mother are now in San Francisco, but he never did get along with them too well.

Wong: Did he stay in San Francisco very long when he first came? Did he work in a laundry there?

Gee: I think it was just a stop-over. He might have been there for just a few months. Not too long after he came here, he went to New Orleans where his father and mother worked.

Wong: They had a laundry?

Gee: They had a laundry. I think it was really terrible working in New Orleans in those days because they were treated very badly. I guess people are different here, working here is somewhat different from working in New Orleans.

Wong: Did he ever talk to you about how it was in New Orleans?

Gee: He talked to me, but it wasn't very much. What he told me about, I can't remember too much. He just told me that it was very bad; he had to sleep on the ironing tables.

Wong: It must have been a major change for his father and mother to have been landowners in China and then come over here to work in a laundry. Did he ever mention how that affected your grandparents?

Gee: Well, my grandmother—I think she stayed in China. But my grandfather—I think—came here to find the "Gold Mountain." I think he was here maybe right after he was born. I guess he made trips back to China. I think my grandmother tried to start some business here.

Wong: Also, he was here for a long time even though he was a landowner in China. So at the time of the war for liberation, he happened to be in China.

Gee: I think so.

Wong: Was your grandfather a laundryman in this country?

Gee: Yes, he also worked as a cook sometimes.

Wong: So it wasn't so much of a drastic change for him to have the laundry in New Orleans because he had done that kind of work before?

Gee: Yes, but I think it affected him somehow. He appears to me to be a strange type of person. He is still alive now. He's living in San Francisco. He never talked, and I think it was very hard to be a landowner in China even if it was handed down to you unless you had some type of business in mind. Now he doesn't talk unless you talk to him; it just seems like he is not paying attention to you very much.

Wong: What was your father's educational background?

Gee: I'm not quite sure, but I don't think he had very much. He might have had some tutors, and he might have gotten through the equivalent of junior high there. I don't think he ever got above that. He knows enough to read books (Chinese), but he's not literate in the sense of being very knowledgeable. My mom told me that my father never went to school here. He just tried to go to night school here for a week or so. Then he quit because he had to work in the laundry. The laundry must have been really bad because they worked from 7:30 to 8 or 9 at night, six days a week, although on Saturday they got out at 5:00.

Wong: Did your father keep pretty much those kinds of hours in all the laundries that he worked in?

Gee: He worked for my uncle for a good 10, 11, 12 years. He kept the same hours. When I was small, I never did think of how many hours he worked. He just went to work and came back, and that was that.

Wong: When your father came here, did he have any intentions of going back to Hong Kong?

Gee: I think when he came here—I think people have had intentions of going back to China, but I don't think too many had intentions of going back to Hong Kong—I think when he came here, he knew he was going to stay here. And make some money and bring us over.

Wong: But he came in '51, and that was after the revolution. So he probably couldn't feel that he could go back to China.

Gee: He just came here to make it.

Wong: From talking to your father or from what you observed, why do you think so many Chinese entered into the laundry business?

Gee: I don't remember my dad ever mentioning it. I guess he would probably agree with me that when they came here, it was probably the only avenue they could go to. Except for maybe the restaurant business. It was either the restaurant or laundry. First of all, to start, you don't have to be—there are no prerequisites for being very skilled in it. As soon as you worked, that is when you started getting skills. It's not that serious of a business where when you make a mistake it is a major one. And almost anybody knows how to iron clothes, and English is not a barrier when you work in a laundry.

Wong: From what you observed in Los Angeles, did you think most of the laundries were family-owned businesses, or were they larger laundries?

Gee: Most laundries are smaller laundries that are family-owned. Recently, a lot of the families have been going out of the laundry business, and that leaves the larger laundries. I think that there are still quite a few family-owned laundries. I think the amount is decreasing. The larger laundries—the ones that have made it—are building themselves up.

Wong: Was your father's laundry always a hand laundry, or did it ever have any machines in it?

Gee: It was a hand laundry. We sent the clothes out to be washed and pressed, and then when they were brought back, we would iron and package them. We didn't hand wash them, which is what hand laundry implies.

Wong: If you were to divide up the good vs. the bad points of the laundry business, what would you say would be the two or three major things that were good and bad?

Gee: The one good thing that stands out in my mind is that it was a form of employment for the Chinese who probably would have a hard time finding a job of any other type because of the language barrier. As for the other good points, right now I can't think of any except that maybe some families still live in the laundry—not too many I think—so that it is kind of convenient for them.

The bad points, I don't know whether it is that they were bad or not. If I looked at them, considering just the fact that I wouldn't want to work in a laundry, I might say they were bad. A lot of times—though it shouldn't be looked at in that way—people that work in it, they feel a little bit degraded. Maybe they shouldn't look at it that way. I remember when I was a kid, and my dad worked in the laundry. I filled out the card at school when I first went to junior high to check out books or anything, and they wanted you to write down your father's business. I wouldn't write down laundry; I was very much ashamed by it. I would write down cleaners, which to me was a little bit different: laundry, to me, being more Chinese; cleaners being more White work.

Wong: Did your father feel that way?

Gee: I think my father didn't feel so much degraded, but he felt that he wasn't successful—the main thing in his mind was to make money. I think that if he did feel degraded, he probably would have gotten out of there. I still think about times when I heard my dad talk to his friends, and a lot of them said, "We have to work in the laundry business; that is pretty much all we can do; we can make money anyway." Then they would come and talk to me and say, "You had better study hard because you don't want to end up working in a laundry like us. Because it is a very bad form of labor." So I think some of them did feel that they were on the lower end of the social ladder.

342

Wong: So it seems true that the parents always encouraged the kids to go on to something else.

Gee: Yes.

Wong: We've talked about this before, but what was the role of women and children in your family? For example, how much did you and your mother work in your laundry?

Gee: In my family, there were four of us; my mom, my dad, myself, and my brother Stewart. At the time we had the laundry, Stewart was too young to do any work so it was mainly me, my mom, and my dad. My mom, she did a lot of ironing and marking the clothes. She did just as much as my dad did. I went to school, but when I came back, all the pressed clothes would be back at the laundry and all the sheets would be back by about 5:00 or 5:30. After school, I would come back and I would have to iron and press clothes. And put the sheets in the right order and package them. So it was pretty much a family business for all of us.

Wong: You sorted out the clothes and folded them?

Gee: Yes. The shirts, we just folded them in the cardboard; we had to iron them first. My dad always wanted to make the shirt look good. And then my mom did other things in the laundry that you have to do such as washing the floor. So it was pretty much that you always had something to do. My mom made my brother study. If you have to study, you don't work. In some of the laundries of the other relatives such as my uncle, Uncle Stanley, all the kids had to work. All of the kids had to go back after school or after work to help out in the laundry. Fold the clothes and help press. They had pressing machines there, though they also sent the clothes out to be washed. All of them had to come back even though they had their separate jobs. Even in the larger laundries, like Tom's Laundry, his son and daughter would have to help out and wash, and the daughter would have to go around in a truck and collect money. And maybe sometimes help the driver put the clothes in and bring the dirty sheets to their own laundry to wash from the smaller laundries. Even the son had to help out and wash the clothes. So even in a larger laundry like that, the family still had to do some part in the work. You find that if the father was maybe a little conservative, and maybe wanted the kids to study, he wouldn't have them help out; but if the father was very "goo low" (old-fashioned), more likely than not he was going to make his son and daughter work. In some cases, there are even some who say that there is no future in education, so "I want you to work in the laundry, and then to take over the laundry after I retire." One example is my grandfather, who does that with his restaurant. He tells my uncles not to go to school,

but to take over the restaurant after he retires: "You make more money doing that than anything else."

Wong: But your father never told you that?

Gee: Funny thing with my father—I kind of thought he wanted me to study, but when it came to a decision of whether I should study for my test or help with the work, I always worked. I knew he wanted me to get a good education. But at that moment, he forgot about it. And also at one point, he wanted me to go into the military instead of going to school, so it was a very funny situation.

Wong: Was there ever a division, like in terms of the business end of the laundry, where even though the women worked just as much or more, the men took care of the business part?

Gee: I think that it was true in almost all the laundries that I know of. Sometimes actually the women do more than the men, but I don't think—I don't like to say this—but in some cases like my dad's, he figures he owns the business and that he's the boss. And sometimes the men have the habit of being a little lax at working, and they expect you to do a little bit more.

Wong: Was your father ever in the laundry association?

Gee: I don't think so. I think he probably knew about it; he must have known about it because he worked so long, but myself, I never heard about the laundry association. I think that a lot of the smaller laundries never even heard of it.

Wong: Did your father ever belong to any other organization like the family association?

Gee: Well, he belongs to the Family Association, but he never took much part in it. He just paid his dues, and that was it. He never went to the activities that they had.

Wong: Did you iron when you were in the laundry?

Gee: I ironed quite a bit.

Wong: How old were you when you finally stopped working?

Gee: I think I was about nineteen.

Wong: It wasn't a gradual thing where at first you started out doing a lot of bundling.

Gee: I think the first week or so he introduced me to ironing.

Wong: How old were you when you first started?

Gee: I started when I was about fifteen.

Wong: Could you ever keep track of how many hours of work you averaged in the laundry, while you were going to school as opposed to the summer?

Gee: When I first started working, I was going to junior high, so right after school I would go back and start working, which would be from about 3:15 or 3:30 till about 8:00 or 8:30 at night, when we went home. During the vacation, I spent my whole day there. My dad wouldn't let me out unless I had something important to do. Then in high school, I was on the track team, so when it was the track semester, I would get back about 5:00 or 5:30 and work until 8:00 or 8:30; and sometimes when there was a lot of clothes, my dad wanted us to finish ironing, and we would stay until 9:00 or 9:30. One time I think we stayed really late. So it varied, but let's put it this way—I spent more hours there than I wanted to.

Wong: Did you ever live in the laundry?

Gee: No, luckily, because I really hated going to the laundry. First of all, it was a very gloomy and dreary type of place. And then—we came in from the backdoor—once you open the door, and the sunlight shines in, you see all these roaches crawling through the floor back into the corner. When you see those roaches, you don't feel like eating. We ate breakfast there, and you wouldn't have any appetite. I could never see how my dad ate so many pancakes every morning.

Wong: Did you feel any better for having to do this because the work was at least your father, so you didn't feel oppressed let's say in the same way that a worker would? Working for the family, did you feel that you had a stake in the work, or did you feel that it was a real burden on you?

Gee: I thought that it was a real burden on me. At that time, I never really thought too much of how my parents felt. I was really happy when they gave it up. And frankly, I really hated the place. It was like a prison to me. But my dad always wanted to keep me in when I was there. I'd say that I wanted to go to the library; he always yelled at me. He would say, "Why do you have to go so much?" He would never let me out. I really hated the place, to be honest. I think I would rather have worked for somebody else because just being around my dad all the time, it just really teed me off. Especially the way he sometimes acted, and sometimes the way I acted teed him off. But I never got paid when I worked there. One time when my aunt came down, she talked to my father and said that he ought to

pay me at least $3 a week or so. So that week he gave me $3. Then after that first week when he paid me $3, I never heard about it again. I never had any spending money, except for my lunch money which I never spent for lunch. I saved it up. Sometimes I would sell a few papers. I got $3 for working all that time in the laundry. So I really hated working there, and I guess being personally selfish at the time, I really hated the place. I didn't get paid, so I didn't see the point. One time, I hated it so much—that was when we first got the laundry—I told my mom, "I'm going to burn this place down." But I guess it was just in a fit of anger.

Wong: What about friends of yours, your relatives, your cousins who worked in your uncle's laundry? Did they ever get paid?

Gee: I don't think so. They never had too much spending money. I think in most laundries, they don't get paid. I think in the family type of place the father usually feels that "if I brought you up, this is the least you can do for me."

Wong: Did your cousin feel the same way about working in the laundry as you did?

Gee: Yes, I know they didn't like working in a laundry. I really believe that working in my uncle's place has in a way damaged their whole mental growth. Because, after all this time, they still don't go out. They don't know how to go out and have fun. They usually stay home, and they can't interact with people, except for Esther, who I think is about twenty-four and works in an office. It's because of the way they were brought up in the laundry. Uncle Stanley is very hard on them. He's always bragging about how good his kids are. Other people will say that they are very good kids because they always stay home and help the family. But I really feel sorry for them because there is no way they can come out and have a well-adjusted type of life.

Wong: Did your father leave the laundry business because he just wanted to get into something else or because it had become unprofitable?

Gee: I think that there were two reasons that he left. One was that, first of all, he wasn't making that much money. The other was that he was really just getting sick of working in the laundry. He wanted to go to something else that had more future in it. And he knew that the laundries were going downhill. So he wanted to get into the restaurant business. The reason that he is working as a take-out now is that he wants to get the experience to open up his own restaurant, either a regular restaurant or a take-out. I think right now he wants to open up a take-out because you can really make a lot of money. I guess he's still trying to find the "Gold Mountain." ★

SIX IN THE MORNING, SIX AT NIGHT:

GROWING UP IN A CHINATOWN GROCERY STORE

By VICTOR G. and BRETT de BARY NEE

INTERVIEW WITH FRANK ENG, 33.

He works for the City Department of Parks and Recreation. Frank's father keeps the truck parked beside the sidewalk, he walks out and brings crates of pears into the store on and off during the day. In the back of the store, we can see the loft that he built below the ceiling, it's completely covered by a red cloth.

About eight winter melons are piled on top of each other in a huge stack next to the cash register. There doesn't seem to be any order to the arrangement of goods on the shelves. Boxes of sugar and Betty Crocker cake mix stand next to cans of chicken broth, bottles of soy sauce, and peanut oil. There's a plastic clock radio on the middle of the shelf above the counter. Beside a scale, a galvanized tub is full of rotting pears. His disordered tray of candies is set on a counter next to the soda cooler. Underneath bags of salted peanuts, we find the cloudy cellophane packages of shrunken persimmons, red dates, and translucent pieces of water chestnut and coconut, all coated in white crystalized sugar. The labels on the bags are made of inexpensive pulpy, off-white paper, purple letters from a rubber stamp give the name of the store, no price. Frank's father says he only makes the candy at Christmas now.

Well, my father makes Chinese candy, coconut candy and melon candy, and there's a lot of work in preparing that, so we ended up doing a lot of little things to help. We would help with the coconut, you have to boil it, cut it in half, peel it, then take the meat out of the shell and cut it in little strips. That's

all tedious work that has to be done by hand. There was no machinery, my father just used to saw the coconut in half, and then we used something like a potato peeler to peel the skins. In fact, he still does all this by hand, but now some of his relatives and other people come in, it's like a meeting place for them. You know how Chinese people are, the clan always had a place to get together. I think my dad's store is like that, so many of his old friends who are still around come over when they have nothing to do and help. Afterwards they have a couple of drinks. They don't get paid or anything but it's part of their life.

We lived in the store. I guess, looking at it now, you'd say it was one of these old mom-and-pop stores. Nobody really makes money but they're happy with it and they get by with it. He's never owned the property, you have to realize this. It's owned by somebody else. For all these years he's rented the place and it's very old. Never had hot running water, we had to boil the water to wash, so I guess they would say the health conditions were pretty poor. We lived in one big room when we were young, all ten of us, and then during the war when three of my brothers were in the military service we only had seven or eight. What they did, you see, was divide the whole room. There was a high ceiling and they just built another floor between the ceiling and the regular floor, and we lived on top. As I said, there were usually a lot of other people around, too, and I remember that they had mahjong tables, people used to come in and play mahjong and have a great time. I remember hearing them late at night, but I guess we got used to the mahjong rattling because it didn't seem to bother us, even when they played till early in the morning while we were sleeping upstairs.

My father was never very structured as far as business was concerned. I think he could have done better, could have made a little more money if he had more guidelines. He's in the fruit business, for instance, so he sells a lot of perishable items. There are some things he can buy, say he buys a crate of persimmons, they don't go, and after a week he has to throw them out. But then the next week he'll go and buy persimmons again, they still won't go, and he'll thow them out again. So he's losing money on all these items, but he continues to buy them.

He had the store before I was born. I guess there just wasn't anything else he could get into. He came from a farm in China and I think my mother was a laborer, picking fruits. There wasn't any other opportunity open to them. Probably opening a store was one of the few things that he could do other than opening a laundry. It had an advantage because it was a living quarters, too.

My father was always a disciplinarian. He always worked very hard. That has been his life, and I think the one other important thing to him was the family association. We belong to a very small one, but he's always been proud to be part of that, and he's served as local president several times. But primarily his life has been spent on the job. . .including Christmas and New Year's. For instance, Chinese New Year is a big holiday and most people are closed. He is closed as far as the sidewalk part if concerned, but the door is open. Anybody that wants to come in and buy anything, he's still sitting in the store waiting for them.

I'd say he puts in more than twelve hours a day and in the past he even worked longer than that. He would get up or leave the house about six in the morning and not close the store until almost nine at night. So what's that? Fifteen hours? Now it's a little less, because he's older. He gets up about six in the morning and he closes about six at night. He's about seventy-three now.

One of the things he does is he has this truck and he makes a lot of deliveries. He handles winter melon, the big squash-type vegetables Chinese use for soup, they're about twenty or thirty pounds apiece. When somebody phones to order, say, five winter melons, he takes them over. But it's physical work because he has to keep running up and down those stairs from the basement, you know, one trip for each melon. I've never seen anyone work as hard as he does for that long a period and not be tense. I guess he is, but he doesn't show it.

Then when he's not delivering he handles the selling. He sits in the back and maybe somebody walks in every fifteen minutes and buys something, or sometimes nobody comes in for half an hour or so. So it's not a booming business, and I think most of what he can make is from wholesaling. Winter melon throughout the year, fruits during the summer. Again, with the fruit it's hard work, because he picks up about a hundred boxes at a time from the farm. If no one helps him, he has to unload these hundred boxes by himself. And then the rice he sells at the store comes in 150-pound bags. He does all that lifting at his age. But, well, actually I think he's so used to physical labor that if he didn't do it it would be a big void in his life. It wouldn't be a complete day for him. He likes to drink, too, like most Chinese, like any Chinese, but I've never seen him unable to do a day's work. It just doesn't stop him.

One thing I've noticed is that he has lost a lot of weight in the past few years. And he has bad eyesight. That's been a problem for a long time and it's getting worse. I remember a few years back he needed glasses, so he just went to the five-and-ten and picked out the glasses that are on display there. I remember him buying glasses like that when I was young. I think that's what ruined his eyesight. But he has still never been in a hospital.

I wouldn't say we were "close" to my parents the way Americans use the word. I guess Chinese parents, well, my parents, don't like to show you their affection as such. They loved us, but they never really wanted to show it, you know. That was the way they lived. And I never had any qualms, I never wanted to change things, because that was just their way of expression. Maybe my mother was a little more sentimental, but even she always had to try to be very fair, you know, with ten kids in the family.

For instance, when we were younger, we all had a night to mind the store. We kind of worked it out together, one person would take Monday, then Tuesday, and so on, so we all wouldn't have to stay around every night. It got to be a sort of a hang-out for some of my friends, too, because the door was always open and they didn't have to worry about no one being home. We used to play cards in the back. But I remember my dad used to be stern about any of my friends coming. He used to tell us, "Don't fool around out front. This is still a store. If you want to do something, go to the back room and do it. This is a business establishment." Sometimes my friends and I used to stand around in the store and there would be boxes to unpack, tissues or napkins to stuff into containers. He would putter around for a while and then say, "Oh, well, I guess I might as well ask you boys for a hand." I think he would pick the nights when we were all together! Or he would have a package to deliver and he would come over to me and whisper, "Why don't you ask your friends?" But he's very cordial to them now they've all grown up. I don't think anybody has any gripes about how he was treated by my father. ★

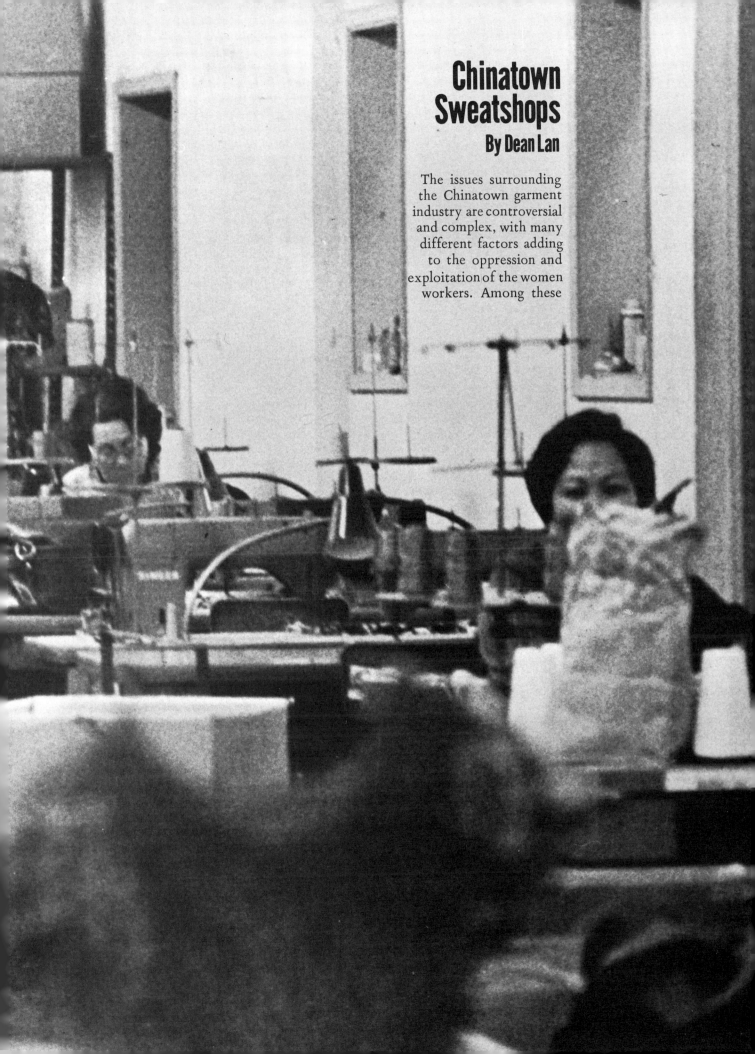

Chinatown Sweatshops
By Dean Lan

The issues surrounding
the Chinatown garment
industry are controversial
and complex, with many
different factors adding
to the oppression and
exploitation of the women
workers. Among these

factors are: the inherently exploitative nature of the apparel industry, the historical absence of self-determination for the Chinese garment workers, the dubious interests of local unions, and the socio-economic ghetto of Chinatown as an environment for the shops. Asian students and workers have recently helped establish an alternative model to the present system of sub-standard wages and conditions. This paper analyzes the San Francisco Chinatown sweat-shops from economic, historical, and cultural perspectives, while seeking to find alternative means of reorganizing them to alleviate their harsh conditions.

Currently, a worker receives $1.00 to $2.00 per dress, which the manufacturer will sell for $12.00-$15.00 to a retail outlet who will sell the dress for up to $25.00.[1] This exploitative and dehumanizing production system that was once the horror of every humane Occidental has now all but disappeared—except in Chinatown. In dealing with the problem of sweatshops, racism and oppression are only partial manifestation of the problem, a bigger part is economics. Trapped within the parameters of the larger economic system, these women must in some way deal with those constraints imposed by the larger society in order to achieve self-determination and personal freedom.

The Apparel Industry

The economic characteristics of the apparel industry, such as its inherent advantages for the manufacturer, are part of the oppressive conditions that encourage and perpetuate sweatshops in San Francisco. The apparel industry historically has been located in big cities like New York, Los Angeles, and San Francisco because of the prerequisites of the industry:

> In addition to a plentiful skilled labor supply are convenience of location to the markets for yard goods on the one hand, and to the markets for the sale of the finished products on the other . . . Proximity to other manufacturers and the opportunity to observe what the leading fashions are, (and to enable copying) . . . are some of the reasons for concentration of the apparel industry in large cities.[2]

photo on preceding page courtesy of VISUAL COMMUNICATIONS

Left, Cigar making. Chinese laborers by the 1880s took over both skilled and unskilled operations in this national market industry. *Above,* Shoe making. Chinese workers in a shoe factory in North Adams, Massachusetts, 1870.

Apparel production is generally a small, labor intensive operation with limited economies of scale.[3] Consequently, production can be oriented to local or regional markets. Other factors however, such as a trained labor force, and the development of style creation centers tend to draw these operations together.

The industry has historically been centered in New York City, but in recent years there has been some decentralization. The garment industry has followed textile centers which have relocated in the South and the West because of lower-cost labor, land, and power. This movement of industry to areas of low wages reinforces oppressive conditions. "Much of the relocation has been to southern states but activity has increased in California, too. The growing California market and the emergence of Los Angeles as a style center will likely result in most western U.S. production being centered there."[4]

The empirical picture of the apparel industry emerged when in 1964, the International Ladies Garment Workers Union and the employers' association hired a research team headed by economist Leon Keyserling, former chairman of the Council of Economic Advisors under Truman, to do a $100,000 study of the ladies' garment industry in New York. The Keyserling study found that in real terms (i.e., buying power after adjustment for inflation), weekly and annual earnings had actually declined over the preceding decade.[5] This despite an increase in real productivity (the average amount of goods produced per worker) of at least 15 per cent in the same period. When compared with other industries, the pay for garment workers has declined. In 1947, dress-making paid an average of 42 cents an hour more than steelworking; in 1966, it paid 95 cents an hour less. Dress-making also paid 33 cents an hour more than autoworking in 1947. Twenty years later, it paid $1.17 less. The study also showed the heavy reliance on unemployment insurance, which still is characteristic of the industry. At the time of the study, only 3.5 per cent of New York's workers were in the garment industry, yet they drew 24 per cent of all the unemployment benefits paid in that state.

Suppression of wage levels has been the active policy of the union. "The union attempts to keep the garment industry in New York City by maintaining low wages and minimal standards for the majority of the workers,"[6] according to Herbert Hill, labor secretary of the NAACP. It is the same dilemma that confronts San Francisco Chinatown: "Don't ask too much or it will go away and leave us with nothing."

The industry's mobile character and its threat to relocate in areas of lower wages maintains the onerous conditions and aggravates the problems of the community: "The average producer of clothing is comparatively free in choosing the location of his shop. In selecting the sites for clothing plants, local supply of skilled labor and special transportation facilities are less important than they are in other industries."[7] The biggest manufacturer in Chinatown, with some 40 to 50 shops, is Fritizi, one of those companies that has threatened to take its work to Texas. It is a producer that can establish its plants in almost any locality. The opportunity to get cheaper labor will largely influence a producer's choice:

> The clothing manufacturer does not need special transportation facilities. In fact, differences in transportation costs are less important than in many other industries; this applies to supply of raw materials as well as to shipping of the finished product. Both can be transported fast and at low cost by rail or truck. Also, it's not difficult or very expensive to move an average clothing plant from one locality to another, since machines used in manufacturing garments are relatively few and light.[8]

The apparel and textile industry is now a major employer in California. According to 1970 statistics from the California Department of Industrial Relations, there were 73,200 industry employees in the state, of which 56,100 were women.[9] Of this, 9,100 were in the San Francisco-Oakland metropolitan area. The garment industry in Chinatown thus has a major economic and social impact on the community. Some 3,500 women are employed in the Chinatown area.[10] Estimates of Chinatown's proportion of the total San Franciso apparel industry range from one-third of the production by the ILGWU's Cornelius Wall to one-half of the production by *The Report.* The estimated annual wholesale value exceeds $15,000,000, and the annual payroll totaled $6,000,000 according to the most recent statistics from the Chinese Garment Contractors Association.

The unique characteristics of the apparel industry itself which act to maintain oppressive conditions for workers are the small scale methods of production, the small size of establishments, the separation of functions at the manufacturing level, and the seasonal variation. The transitory nature of clothing styles themselves has made it impossible to have large-scale methods of production and the development of equipment for highly specialized process. "Fashion is fickle. It is constantly changing and cannot be governed by the rules of other businesses or the results

of other years of past performance. Constant change creates good business...."[11]

The industry has been described as difficult to mechanize and practically impossible to automate. While methods, equipment, and machinery have been modernized, the sewing room itself hasn't advanced much technologically.[12] This lack of important technological advantages for large plants with economies of scale that reduce costs (bigger size resulting in increased efficiency), has made the small firm predominant.[13] The small size is characteristic, especially in the shops in which the fashion element is relatively important. Such is the case in San Francisco's Chinatown. The huge plants found in most important American industries are completely absent in the garment trades. Occasionally, there are some factories which employ several hundred workers. But these are mostly branches of the industry which produce merchandise of a cheaper type in large quantities, in which style is less important and mass production methods are used (e.g., plants like Levi Strauss).

The economic structure of the women's garment industry is unlike most industries, where the manufacturing is closely related with distribution. Because of the importance of the merchandising function and its designing aspects, as distinguished from physical production, there is often a separation of functions, each handled by different businessmen. The manufacturer is the one who obtains the materials and determines the "what, when and where" of production. He may perform all the production in his own plant. But in most cases, as in San Francisco, the manufacturer acquires the materials, cuts the garments, and then contracts with a submanufacturer for physical production. Submanufacturers, also known as contractors, own the 156 shops in Chinatown. The contractor bids for work from the manufacturers and receives a certain amount for the production of the garments. The procurement of labor and the management of the shop are his concern. Thus, the manufacturer is relieved of the responsibilities in the physical and material sense.

The ease of entry into the contracting business, which requires little capital, results in a number of contractors competing among themselves; thus the manufacturers frequently find a substantial savings can be made by contracting.[14] Also, in an industry where manufacturing is subject to great fluctuations in volume, such a system transfers the burden of this instability to the contractor. A manufacturer finding himself with a "hit number" need only to add contractors rather than to undertake the expensive and prohibitively time consuming process of expanding his own plant to handle his temporarily increased volume. Through contractors, he has an almost unlimited supply of labor without the expense or responsibility of maintaining a labor force. More important, through this contracting system, the manufacturer is freed from the responsibility of factory management and permitted to figure production costs with complete disregard to labor costs. Prices paid for contract work are forced downward by pitting one contractor against another. The knowledge that there is always another competitor eager to snap up the order, remains a constant threat to the contractor.

The development of contracting was paralleled by the development of the sweatshop.[15] As has been pointed out, the contractor, in his attempts to compete successfully for the work, tried to decrease labor costs. Thus, wages were lowered; hours were increased. Homework has been another evil that grew out of decreased wages. Many workers found their meager earning insufficient to supply their families, so they added to their income by taking work home at the end of the day. "Not only are the workers paid less than market rates for their work, but in addition they have to bear the cost of rent for their working place, as well as light, power and heat which in a shop are paid by the owners."[16] They must also supply their own machines. Consequently, there is a further reduction in labor costs, which workers themselves must obviously bear.

Another facet of the contracting system is that the manufacturer avoids any responsibility for the maintenance of working standards or for the provision of seasonal unemployment. Seasonal variation requires that producers have available adequate facilities to handle peak loads, thus further encouraging the continuance of the contract system.[17] There are wide variations in the apparel industries, but the general trend in women's wear is one of two peak periods centering around March and October. The troughs are reached in December or January, and June or July. The fall peak is important for the heavier garments, such as coats, suits, and knitted wear, while the spring peak is important for dresses.

These then, are the characteristics of the apparel industry which maintain oppressive conditions. The mobility of the industry, the importance of fashion, the small firm, the contracting system, the resulting sweatshops and homework, and the season variation— these are the many advantages for the manufacturer. These are the parameters in which the San Francisco Chinatown garment industry operates.

History of the San Francisco Chinatown Garment Shops

The garment industry has been part of San Francisco's Chinatown scene for at least a century. There exist many parallels between the Chinatown garment industry of yesterday and today. The entry of Chinese firms into clothing manufacturing dated from the late 1860's. The gold rush and the subsequent development of the West provided a great demand for clothing and the existence of Chinese

guilds prevented low wages in the industry.

Chinese were already in the sewing trades in the late 1860's. In 1869, Reverend A. S. Loomis noted that, "Pantaloons, vests, shirts, drawers, and overalls are made extensively by Chinamen."[18] In 1873, it was reported by one paper:

> . . . Next, if not superior in importance to the Chinese cigar factories, are the Chinese clothing factories of which there are altogether 28, including 3 shirt factories. . . These factories employ from 50-100 men each and their employees number in the aggregate about 2000.[19]

By 1876, Chinese workers were a major force in the San Francisco garment shops. Following is the table showing the number of Chinese and other workers in the apparel industry that year:[20]

Employment	Men	Girls	Chinese
Embroidering	-	-	28
Lacemaking	-	32	20
Shirtmaking	30	246	239
Men's Clothing	558	884	620
Other Sewing Trades	163	1566	-
	751	2728	907

However, these figures are conservative because many Chinese working by the piece were not included. The number of Chinese employed in the San Francisco clothing industry was estimated as high as 3,250 and as low as 1,230 in 1876. In 1880, the total number of Chinese working in the industry appeared to be no more than 2,000.[22] Most of the ready-made clothing and nearly all underclothing made in San Francisco was manufactured by Chinese. Approximately 80 per cent of the shirtmakers were Chinese. With their lower wages, the Chinese workers reduced the importation of garments from the East.[23] Sweatshops were in their infancy in the 1870's. Like today's system, wholesalers hired Chinese to do piece work and supplied the workers with the materials.

No organized industry existed in San Francisco before 1880.[24] Even in the beginning, during the 1880's, the clothing industry became noted for "cut-throat" competition. As is true today, the garment industry was characterized by its highly seasonal nature of marketing and employment. The seasonal variations for the industry in California were 32 weeks of employment for ready-made and 24 weeks for custom-trade clothing manufacturing.

In the ready-made trade, Chinese firms and laborers dominated. Chinese laborers commonly felt a strong desire for self-employment. A Chinese would serve as apprentice and journeyman at $6.00 to $20.00 per month for a short period to acquire the necessary skill and capital to open his own shop, and then quit.[25] This would be repeated as soon as another Chinese learned his trade—he would fall sick and recommend another Chinese to take his place; it was a constant cycle.

The need soon arose for some type of organization to protect the workers' interest. Three guilds were established in San Francisco, corresponding to the three broad divisions of the sewing trades in Chinatown: the Tung Yip Tong (Hall of Common Occupation) comprising tailors, the Gwing Yee Hong (Guild of Bright Clothing), comprising workers on skirts, ladies' garments and undergarments, and the Gum Yee Hong (Guild of Brocaded Clothing), comprising workers on overalls. With the current interest in the organization of the Chinatown garment workers, some knowledge of these past guilds might provide a historical perspective.

Both Gwing Yee and the Gum Yee Hong were labor organizations which functioned in a similar way to craft unions. The latter was organized in the early 1880's. At the height of its power, it boasted a membership of more than 1,000 and was one of the most effective Chinese labor guilds. Guild membership was obligatory for all Chinese sewing machine operators. For a novice, this required a period of apprenticeship before he was admitted as a journeyman. But, once a worker was accpeted as a guild member, he was guaranteed certain basic employment rights because he could not be discharged by an employer unless his co-workers approved the action.

Like today's system, the work was on a piece-work basis. But a wage rate negotiated for any particular work was recorded and registered at guild headquarters; thus the same work done in another factory by Chinese operators must follow this standardized wage formula. Violation of this agreement was a serious offense in which the factory owner was subsequently boycotted and black-listed, while the "scabs" were fined and expelled from the guild.

The Gum Yee Hong, through its collective bargaining strength, was able to assure good wages for its membership for several decades. It is said that around 1910, when general wages in Chinatown ran around $40.00 monthly, many garment factory workers were making as much as $70.00 per month.

Women machine operators were introduced into the garment factories during the first few decades of this country. These women often worked to gain supplemental income for the family. There were many outside pressures, like immigration and language, which did not permit the women to fight for higher wages. This fact, added to the gradual attrition of the ranks of the male operators by death and old age, slowly eroded the strength of the guilds. The Gwing Yee Hong had disappeared by the early 1900's, but the Gum Yee Hong persisted a little longer. By the end of World War I, they were working in the overall and workers clothing factories also.[27]

By the 1920's, female operators dominated the Chinatown factories, and the power of the Gum Yee

Hong had been broken. By the thirties, the guild was impotent. In 1932 the 30 garment factories were dependent upon contract orders from major apparel manufacturers. The following conditions were observed of the shops then: "Garment workers . . . are not organized at all. Factories usually open from 7 A.M. to 10 P.M., and sometimes go till midnight."[28]

The female garment workers were not organized until 1937, when Jenny Matyas helped to organize the Chinese Ladies Garment Workers, an affiliate of the International Ladies Garment Workers Union. This new local had 80 charter members, and one of its first acts was to strike against the factory of the National Dollar Store. The 13-week strike was the longest in Chinatown history. Similar to the threat faced today, the factory, Chinatown's largest, closed rather than agree to the union's demands. (More recently, this happened again. The small Maguerite Rubel shop closed its doors in April of 1968, rather than negotiate with the union.)[29] Since those first days, the union has organized about 700 women in Chinatown.

Thus, the contracting system has remained; the piece-work pay has remained; the need for organization has remained; the substandard wages and sweatshop conditions have remained. Except for the introduction of female labor and the decline of the guilds, little has changed for the San Francisco Chinatown garment industry during the last one hundred years—if anything, conditions have worsened, and exploitation of cheap labor has increased.

Chinatown

The garment shops in Chinatown must be defined in the context of a ghetto, with its compounding myriad problems. In the 1960 census, the median personal income in Chinatown's core area (bounded by Mason, Pacific, Kearny, and California Streets), was $4,484, which was $2,200 below the citywide median. This sector also has the lowest educational achievement with a median of only two completed years of school. This compares with an overall city median of twelve school years. Consequently, male unemployment in Chinatown totaled almost 13 per cent in 1960 and was twice the city figure.

In 1967, it was estimated that 30,000 of the city's 48,000 Chinese lived in Chinatown.[30] With the liberalization of the immigration laws, there has been a tremendous influx of immigrants. The 1960 census revealed that the Chinese constitute almost ten per cent of San Francisco. By reason of language, custom, and economic necessity, most of the Chinese immigrants will seek housing and jobs in the already crowded ghetto. According to a survey of Chinatown's core conducted by the San Francisco Department of Social Services, the average monthly income per family of $311 was astonishingly low.[31] Sixty-three per cent had an annual income under $3,600. This shows a higher incidence of poverty that was reflected in the 1960 U.S. census which estimated an annual income of under $3,999 for only forty-one per cent of the families in the core area of Chinatown. Some more recent statistics add to the grim picture:

> The density rate is 885.1 people per acre, ten times the city's average.
>
> The suicide rate is three times the national average.
>
> Two-thirds of the adults have less than a seventh-grade education, and the last new school in the area was built in 1925.
>
> The rate of substandard housing is 67 per cent, versus 19 per cent for the rest of San Francisco.[32]

In addition, it has the nation's highest tuberculosis rate. These statistics help explain why and how the Chinatown garment shops persist with their substandard wages and conditions. To a lack of skills and mobility may be added the handicap of not knowing English. Sewing in the shops is the only way the women can make a living.

With these serious problems growing, it is remarkable that the Chinatown establishment, like the Chinese Six Companies and the family and district associations, have failed so dismally in taking steps to counteract these ills. The family and district associations are the most unusual feature of Chinese social structure in the United States. Chinese sojourners banded together for mutual help and self-protection into associations based on loyalties to clan or place of origin. Men with the same surnames formed the various "family" associations; the district associations allowed a broader membership from people originating from the same political district in South China. Sometime in the 1860's, the district associations federated into the Chung Wah Wui Kun, which later became known as the Chinese Consolidated Benevolent Association, or the Chinese Six Companies.[33] (The number of "companies"—district associations—actually varied from five to eight; seven district associations now make up the "Six Companies.")

The increasing mobility of Chinese in the postwar years and the emergence of a new Chinese middle class has spelled the decline of the Six Companies' historical power in Chinatown. But to the outside world, it has kept its reputation as the "Official Representative Association of Chinese in America." Yet, it is common knowledge that the Six Companies is generally considered the first stumbling block to any reform in the community. Always dominated by a merchant elite, the Six Companies' main function seems to be the preservation of the Chinatown image instead of dealing with the deteriorating social conditions.

When the *San Francisco Examiner* ran a series of articles about Chinatown's economic and social conditions,[34] the Chinese Six Companies vehemently denied the existence of problems. The August 14, 1969 issue of the *Examiner* described Chinatown as a serfdom for immigrants with suspicion, fear, and hostility—a place where men, women, and children work for pittances and live in the deepest deprivation. The community was said to be one where poverty, gambling, oppression, disease, crime, and fear ran wild, further aggravated by the influx of poor, uneducated, undernourished immigrants from Hong Kong.

On August 15th, the paper documented a variety of specific cases of deprivation: children less than a year old who had already contracted active tuberculosis, babies with all their primary teeth completely rotted away due to poor nutrition and over-crowding, inadequate and unsanitary conditions; families working for low pay whose properties are owned by the wealthy family and district organizations. Describing the sweatshops in August 16 and 17th, the *Examiner* observed that the shops were located in low-ceilinged basements and that they were poorly ventilated, improperly lighted, and unsanitary.

The Chinese Six Companies responded that these articles "brought forth considerable misunderstanding among the Chinese and Caucasian communities concerning the development and progress of San Francisco Chinatown when it has now become the mecca of tourism with thousands of tourists pouring in every day for sightseeing, enjoyment and pleasure."[35] It reviewed the historical progress of the Chinese people, "noted for their traditional heritage of morals, ethics, virtues, prudence and condolence." The Chinese, they maintained, are "peace loving like the Americans and are firm believers of freedom and democracy and anti-Communism."[36] "Low wages and long working hours," the Association dismissed as "a typical characteristic (that) is unique and family like."[37] "On the whole," the Six Companies concluded:

> The fascinating and virtuous charm of San Francisco Chinatown must not be hurt by the slanderous and erroneous statements. San Francisco Chinatown will continue to meet the problems which can be solved with proper understanding and guidance from public officials. This, in our opinion, is the proper solution.[38]

In distinct contrast to the powerfully complacent attitude of the Six Companies, sociologist Stanford Lyman has more accurately summarized the realities of the community as follows:

> The ghetto with its congregational inner spirit and its surrounding segregationist pressure, with its nationalistic fervor and its economic debilitation, with its powerful concentration and its political impotence, is a creature of modern racism whose perfection was first worked out with respect to the

Asian challenge to a modern industrial racist society.[39]

The Garment Shops

The continuing maintenance of a ghetto or entrapment of unskilled and semi-skilled people is essential in a society that demands cheap labor. The Chinatown garment shops serve as a pool of cheap labor in such a ghetto. Those who have not "made it" or those who are stranded in the ghettos become the victims of profit-minded Chinese businessmen who serve as go-between among workers in the ghetto and the big manufacturers and businessmen outside of the community.

For the women workers, the sewing shop is more than an economic institution and a place to work; it is a way of life. Its flexible hours and casualness distinguish it from a regular eight-hour job. A woman can take time off to shop, pick up children from school, or cook dinner for her family whenever she wants.

> In general, (the garment shop) is a manifestation of her culture, embodying all that is familiar. It is a home away from home. As such, it is a social institution, and this is what makes it different from a typical American place to work.[40]

However, the image favored by management of contented housewives helping out the family budget and taking care of the children at the same time by skipping off for a few hours each day to the nice little cottage industry around the corner is far from accurate. On the other hand, the version of the union's Mr. Wall is a grim one: cynical capitalists reaping huge profits at the expense of frightened women, many of them immigrants who don't speak English and who are forced to work in poorly lit, badly-ventilated firetraps for as little as 64 cents an hour.

The empirical situation of the Chinatown sweatshops emerged in a study conducted by Stanley Lim, a Human Rights Commission staff member.[41] From the interviewing of 45 workers, came the following data. All the women work six days a week with 40 per cent on the 9 A.M. to 7 P.M. shift, broken only by a short luncheon interval. Another 48 per cent said they also took garments home to work on them. Eighteen per cent said they worked 9 A.M. to 10 P.M. with lunch and dinner breaks (the latter averaging 75 minutes).

The median age of the workers was 47. Seventy-two per cent are "secondary wage earners," having husbands who also work. This does not imply income above necessity as would generally be the case in a middle class family, but the secondary income brings family income up to a rate that is still below poverty level. Eighty-six per cent said they used a time card but half of these said the employer filled in the time. The "time card" in this case was not the card-punch type. All women said there were cooking facilities available and were able to get up or go out of the shop for a while anytime they wanted to.

All reported that they were paid on a piece-rate basis, and earned $140.00 bi-weekly during peak seasons and $78.00 during slack times. Their annual salary for 1968 averaged $2,000.00. Forty-eight per cent, nearly one-half, said they held the job because "it is the only kind of work I can do."

In regards to the enforcement of the minimum wage laws, both the state and federal agencies have trouble obtaining accurate records. In an interview between Cornelius Wall, manager of the International Ladies Garment Workers Union, and the author in February, 1970, he stated:

> Neither the state or federal agencies have the manpower (to obtain accurate records). The State Division of Industrial Welfare has 40 agents for California and five agents for the Bay Area. (In comparison, the union has six business agents for San Francisco alone.)
>
> Secondly, the enforcement depends on who is head of the departments. If they take a positive view, a lot more could be done. The state's attitude is negative. I accuse the State Labor Commissioner of not doing his job. (The Division of Industrial Welfare is under the Commissioner.)

Under the manufacturer-contractor system described earlier, it is relatively easy for a man to go into business for himself, and the manufacturers encourage this. The result is—as was intended—keen competition among too large a number of contractors for relatively too small a volume of business. The business life of the contractors is highly insecure. But their workers' existence is even less secure, as witnessed by the closing of numerous garment shops.

The insecurity of the workers is best illustrated by Stanley Lim's study in which he discovered that twenty women workers of the Hoi Ming factory worked for months without pay, but did not complain for fear of losing their jobs.[42] This particular factory was closed by the Internal Revenue Service for non-payment of taxes. The total amount not paid by the Chinatown contractor was $7,500. The women were so intimidated and fearful of their jobs, that they dared not make complaints until after their employer went out of business.

This fear makes compliance with the minimum wage laws impossible, according to Kenneth Hedberg, regional director for the Labor Department's division of wages and hours. "Workers," he says, will not be candid with us to give us the statements we can use. Off the record, they tell us what conditions exist."[43] He revealed that among off-the-record disclosures are wages ranging down to 40, 50, 60 cents an hour.

These employees are among the most trapped. These women have no place to go if they lose their jobs, and they are not likely to retain a job in the industry in Chinatown, if they reveal their true situation. Willing to work for whatever wages they can get rather than no wages at all, they are limited to the community with little chance of escape and so they dare not complain.

The Rezoning Issue and the International Garment Workers Union

The Chinatown area is composed of residential and commercial district. Historically, zoning laws have discouraged the mixing of the two functions and prohibited factories from engaging in light manufacturing in residential area. This was the case in San Francisco until the late 1950's, when the rapidly expanding garment shops were violating the General Zoning Regulations of the City Planning Code (commonly referred to as the zoning ordinance) by engaging in light manufacturing in prohibited areas. When it was observed that the existence of garment shops in Chinatown constituted a zoning violation, James McCarthy, the director of Planning in the Department of City Planning, conducted a study of the issue. On October 23, 1958, in the report of the study addressed to Roger D. Lapham, president of the City Planning Commission, he concluded that:

1. The operation of garment factories in residential and commercial district in Chinatown constitutes a serious violation of the General Zoning Regulations of the City Planning Code.

2. The recent sharp increase in the number of garment factories has made it necessary to review the zoning regulations governing these Chinatown factories.

3. Continued toleration of substandard conditions associated with the violation in many instances is indefensible from the standpoint of the general welfare and sound city planning and zoning principles, and is contrary to San Francisco's announced policy as set forth in its Workable Program for Urban Renewal submitted to the U.S. Housing and Home Finance Agency as a basis for federal assistance.

4. Elimination of all garment factories from the entire Chinatown area through strict enforcement of the zoning regulations would impose an extreme hardship on many elements of the Chinatown community, and on the San Francisco garment industry.

5. The unusual social factors characteristics of the garment factories make it highly undesirable to force the removal of all of the small garment factories from the ethnic Chinatown community.

Among his recommendations was the suggestion that strict regulation of the small garment factories, rather than their relocation, would be desirable. He advised that the small garment factories—i.e., those which employ not more than 25 machines and do not engage in cutting and large-scale manufacturing—should become permitted, subject to appropriate regulations in a designated area within the commercial district of Chinatown.

As a result of the above report, most of the existing shops acquired legal status in 1960 upon enactment of Section 237 of the City Planning Code: "In order to provide for garment shops of limited size in a recognized area of the City, there shall be a Garment Shop Special Use District."

There are several reasons which encourage the establishment of special districts—special because they are exceptions to a district that is designated as residential, commercial, or industrial.

> The first of these is the growing understanding that since individual communities have unique characteristics, it may be necessary to establish a special and perhaps 'unconventional' district to meet a particular need... These zones grow out of the characteristics of the community and are designed to fit a special need.[44]

This was the situation of the Chinatown garment shops.

The Garment Shop Special Use District was re-enacted in 1968. However, a recent controversy in the status of the shops arose once again in October 1969. Conceding its failure to unionize the majority of the garment workers in Chinatown, manager Cornelius Wall of the International Ladies Garment Workers Union, proposed an amendment to the zoning ordinance "to provide that the Garment Special Use District shall terminate as of December 31, 1970, and that all garment shops and factories shall close and cease all operations within the district as of December 31, 1970."

Elimination of the garment shops from Chinatown would affect no less than 20,000 Chinese residents.[45] From the view of race relations and economic competition, the union's move, under the rhetoric of unionism, of humanitarianism, and of the need for the Chinese to integrate, is another attempt to exert its control and wipe out the industry that is the basic fabric of Chinatown's economy. The union assumes that if the garment shops are removed from the Chinatown environment to an area south of Market Street, the ILGWU will be able to enforce its contracts and thus have more control over the shop condition. It assumes that the workers will become much easier to organize in the new area. Of the ILGWU's 1,200 members, about 700 of Chinatown's 3,500 women are unionized.[46]

The union has been unsuccessful in organizing most of the women because of their traditional distrust and the women's concern for their jobs. One must remember that the ILGWU was not a "grassroots," rank and file type of organization. Instead, it was a "top-down" organization in which the workers, in one fell swoop, would become unionized. Thus, three ways to change the sweatshops: 1) organizing for and joining the present ILGWU,

2) organizing an all-Chinese union, 3) developing a workers' cooperative.

Organizing for the ILGWU would be unfeasible because of the Chinese women workers' suspicion of the union. The union's proposal to zone the sweat-shops out of Chinatown, as was discussed earlier, is an indication of the union's distance from the problems of Chinatown.

The second alternative of an all-Chinese union appears more promising, but unfortunately this currently would not be feasible. There would be a conflict between the existing union organization efforts of the ILGWU and the Teamsters. But more important, the solidarity and the support needed for the success of such a union does not now exist. Other factors include the unions' past racist actions toward the Chinese, the U.S. Government's intimidation of the Chinese through immigration laws, and right-wing forces within the Chinese community; these negative conditions make a community movement toward unionization impossible at the present time.

In any solution, the Chinese must provide the organization, the leadership, and the control. Chinatown should try and keep its own social relations based on Chinese traditions instead of assimilating into American society, thus losing its identity. This is an important assumption, as opposed to the opinion of the union's Mr. Wall, who wants to "bring the women into the mainstream of American life and become first-class citizens." The *San Francisco Chinese Community Citizens' Survey and Fact Finding Committee Report* distinguishes the Chinatown garment shops as a social institution—it is a manifestation of the working women's culture—and any solution must treat it as such.

The last alternative, a workers' cooperative meets the requirements of what is now needed in Chinatown. It should educate workers about their rights, provide English and administrative skills, provide workers with the opportunity to control the means of production and give them power to make their own decisions, controlling all phases of the business. One of the objectives is to develop among the women a co-op philosophy that would embody the concept of self-determination by decentralizing the decision-making process of the organization.

Politically, the co-op can mean no less than power to the working class; economically, it can mean nothing but collective ownership of the means of production and the end of exploitation in the sweatshops. The co-operative is a new type of relationship among women, a new order of priorities, a new model of life and culture. The needs are many: the need for a free and many-sided development of human faculties, the need for information, for communication, for fellowship, the need to be free—not only from oppression and alienation in work, but in leisure as well. The present San Francisco Chinatown Co-op has driven women on trips to the beach and other diversions for a change in the daily drudgery. Workers cook and eat together daily; some are learning English and teaching Chinese (to the students), and some are learning to drive.

The theory of capitalism, as outlined by Adam Smith, is that progress and production is best promoted, by entrepreneurs owning the means of production, whose activities are guided by the profit motive (which is reflected in the consumer's demand for various goods and services). Implicit in this goal is the view that labor is mainly an input, a factor of production, a means to an end. The end is usually not the development of human beings, but the development of output, thus ignoring the social consequences

The emphasis, values, and goals of a co-op are radically different. The decision making is in the workers' hands. They vote on all issues of concern; their co-op is a vertical organization (as opposed to the traditional horizontal one). The emphasis is on the development of human beings and encouraging the women to realize their manifold creative powers by fully participating and sharing in all aspects and responsibilities of their job. The co-op is thus trying to achieve an egalitarian development, one without dehumanization that involves and affects all its workers. Even Adam Smith himself once noted that labor specialization, while it may increase productivity, is often at the expense of the workers' general intelligence and understanding. "The man whose whole life is spent on performing a few simple operations," he wrote, ". . . generally becomes as stupid and ignorant as it is possible for a human creature to become."[48] A major aim of the co-operative is to avoid this kind of oppressive reductionism that often brutalizes workers in an industrialized, capitalistic system and prevents them from becoming full participants in the productive process.

This point was successfully illustrated by William A. Williams in his book *The Great Evasion*, a reinterpretation of Marx in an American context. Marx concluded (in Williams' interpretation) that one cause of alienation was the progressive use of machinery within capitalistic assumptions. Alienation resulted when it was beyond the power or ability of the individual to adapt to his own creativity: "A lathe, for example, does not in and of itself alienate a man. But a lathe used for purposes set by other men, and for only the repetitive performance of one of its many functions (i.e., the endless production of one inch wood screws), can lead to alienation."[49] Another cause of alienation was the exclusion of workers from any participating role in the system. Capitalism, declares Williams,

includes a good deal more than economics. It is a complex network of procedures, habits, customs, rules, laws, institutions and ideas. These elements modify—by reinforcing or limiting—the impact and effect of the economic factors. But since the system is based upon and operates through the economic marketplace, the individual occupies a key position in the marketplace. It defines the opprotunities open to him. Marx viewed proletarianization as the process, similar and related to alienation, whereby the individual was progressively excluded from full and effective participation in the political and social parts of the system as a result of his reduction to a wage laborer in the economic sphere. He is increasingly acted upon instead of participating in.[50]

The condition of the contemporary Chinese woman in the garment industry offers a striking example of alienation in advanced capitalism. Instead of working in a truly human and creative way in a cooperative, she sells her labor in the impersonal marketplace. There is a loss of any participating role in the primary decisions in the capitalistic marketplace.

Perhaps the most difficult concept the San Francisco Chinatown co-op tries to educate is that the factory belongs to those who work in it—it is not a place where one sells her labor eight hours a day. Instead, the co-op's success or failure is determined by the worker's commitment. The workers make the decisions, share the profits, keep the books, design, buy, cut, sew, press, and sell their products. Along with the increased participation comes the sharing of the problems. One co-op worker remarked that at her previous shop, she didn't care what happened after her day at work, but now she constantly worries and thinks about the co-op's situation.

Among some of the feelings of the workers are those of Mrs. Chow:

> I didn't understand what a co-op was at first. I thought the students were very good and really wanted to help the people in Chinatown. But I didn't think they understood the garment industry very well.
>
> I wasn't the first worker here. I came by here one day to watch them make clothes and I asked if I could have work. The students talked about what the co-op was. They said it was for the people and that all Asians should work together to help each other.
>
> It depends on the people in the co-op whether it works or not. We do the work, so the co-op belongs to all the people who work in it. We talk about how to improve our work. When we have meetings we speak our minds out.
>
> I talk to my friends about the co-op and they say, "If it works, let me know." They they will come here, too. They hadn't thought about a co-op before.[51]

Mrs. Chang remarked,

> Yes, I think the co-op is much better than other places. It's much freer. You don't have to worry about the boss and all. In the other garment factories I just worked for the boss.
>
> The pay isn't that much more here, but it's not for the money that we work here. The young

people are very nice. All the bosses want is dollars, but the students want what's good for the people.[52]

Because of the nature of the system that allows manufacturers to pay too little for work done, the co-op is not self-sufficient. Limited by the small size of the operation (seven to ten operators with nine machines), it cannot compete to buy fabrics at wholesale prices. There is a problem in finding retail outlets for the shop's clothing. Currently, subsidies derived from the showing of movies on the Berkeley campus are used to offset these difficulties. The long range goal however, is to make the co-op financially self-sufficient by establishing its own non-profit storefront for the Chinatown community. The Chinatown co-op is currently making Asian worker jackets which are being distributed in some cities across the nation.

The struggle against exploitation does not take on its full meaning until it becomes a conscious struggle against the social consequences of exploitation. To build a community with self-determination, we have to examine and deal with the basic problems of health, child care, housing, food, and other crucial questions. As there is a growing awareness of repression, oppression, and exploitation among Asians, there is a type of nationalism developing—perhaps a revolutionary one—revolutionary in the sense of rapid and fundamental development and reorganization in the community, leading to reform and progressive social change.

The small number of students will help steer the co-op garment factory in the beginning, but the only way the revolution will be truly realized is if the people, the community themselves, accept that direction. One of the goals of the garment co-operative is to work with the people towards changing the traditional structure of the system by mobilization, unification, and education of the working class.

As we have seen, conditions for the workers have declined and the relative proportion of exploitation has increased in the last century. A huge amount of work must be completed if there is to be a revolution in Chinatown. The San Francisco Chinatown Co-op is merely a beginning point, an alternative model to stimulate further criticism and new initiatives. Its goal is not revenge or suicide, but the building of a society in which human values will have primary consideration.

†

Acknowledgement

I am grateful to the many people, especially the San Francisco Chinatown co-operative, who have generously given of their time for interviews, assistance, comments, and criticism.

I would like to acknowledge Professors Frank

Levy, Lyn Lofland, and Paul Wong for assistance in earlier drafts and sections of this paper.

I alone, of course, am responsible for the errors and shortcomings of this article. ★

Notes

1. "Co-operative Garment Factory," *Rodan*, Northern California Asian-American Community Newspaper, May, 1971.

2. Paul H. Nystrom, *Economies of Fashion*¹ (New York: Ronald Press, 1928), p. 403.

3. Gerald B. Skutt, *A Brief Review of the Apparel and Textile Industries in the State of Washington* (Washington State Department of Commerce and Economic Development, 1966), p. 10.

4. *Ibid.*

5. Michael Myerson, "International Ladies Garment Workers Union: Fighting for Lower Wages," *Ramparts*, October, 1969, p. 51.

6. *Ibid.*, p. 52.

7. Kurt Braun, *Union-Management Co-operation, Experience in the Clothing Industry,* (Washington, D.C.: The Brookings Institute, 1947), pp. 66-67.

8. *Ibid.*

9. *California Labor Statistics Bulletin,* December, 1970.

10. *Report of the San Francisco Chinese Community Citizens' Survey and Fact Finding Committee* (Hereafter referred to as The Report) (San Francisco: H. J. Carle & Sons, 1969), p. 66.

11. Pauline Arnold, et. al., *Clothes and Cloth, America's Apparel Business* (New York: Holiday House, 1961), pp. 122-123.

12. *Ibid.*

13. Charles Goodman, *The Location of Fashion Industries; With A Special Reference to the California Apparel Market* (Ann Arbor: University of Michigan Press, 1948), p. 18.

14. Helen E. Meiklejohn, "Dresses—The Impact of Fashion on a Business," in Walter Hamilton, *Price and Price Policies* (New York and London: McGraw-Hill Book Company, Inc., 1948), p. 347.

15. Lazare Teper, *The Women's Garment Industry, An Economic Analysis* (New York: Abco Press, 1932), p. 15.

16. *Ibid.*, p. 12.

17. Goodman, p. 18.

18. Rev. A. S. Loomis, "How Our Chinamen Are Employed," *Overland Monthly,* vol. 2, 1869, pp. 231-240.

19. *San Francisco Morning Call,* 27 May 1873.

20. George F. Seward, *Chinese Immigration, Its Social and Economic Aspects* (New York, 1881), pp. 109-110.

21. Thomas W. Chinn, *A History of the Chinese in California* (San Francisco: Historical Society of America, 1969), p. 54.

22. Ping Chiu, *Chinese Labor in California, 1850-1880, An Economic Study* (Madison: University of Wisconsin Press, 1963), p. 98.

23. *Ibid.*, p. 101.

24. Hubert H. Bancroft, *History of California* (San Francisco, 1888), VII, p. 89.

25. Chiu, p. 95.

26. H. Mark Lai, "Chinatown Garment Industry Started A Hundred Years Ago," *East/West,* 3 December 1969, p. 7.

27. Chinn, p. 54.

28. Helen V. Cather, "History of San Francisco's Chinatown," (M.A. thesis in economics, University of California at Berkeley, 1932), p. 85.

29. Ken Wong, "Walkout Flops, Sewing Factory Closes Shop," *East/West,* 1 May 1968., p. 1.

30. *The Report,* p. 11.

31. Chinatown Information Campaign, San Francisco Department of Social Services, July, 1969.

32. Min Yee, "Chinatown in Crisis," *Newsweek,* February 23, 1970, p. 57.

33. George Chu, "Chinatown: Stereotypes and Myths Have Made this the Only Pocket of Poverty in the U.S. to be a Major Tourist Attraction," *San Francisco Magazine,* June, 1969, p. 23.

34. Jane E. Conant, "The Other Face of Chinatown," "Chinatown Tragedy, Widespread TB," "Unrest Stirs Chinatown Sweatshops," "The Seaming Side of Chinatown," "Coolie Labor Pours From Hong Kong," *San Francisco Examiner,* August 14, 15, 16, 17, 18, 1969.

35. Dr. Kalfred D. Lum, "A Refutation of Misunderstanding About San Francisco Chinatown," Chinese Consolidated Benevolent Association, mimeographed statement, 1969, p. 2.

36. *Ibid.*

37. *Ibid.*, p. 4.

38. *Ibid.*, p. 5.

39. Stanford M. Lyman, *The Asian in the West* (Reno, Nevada: Desert Research Institute, University of Nevada, 1970), p. 8.

40. *The Report,* p. 68.

41. Stanley Lim, *Analysis of Chinatown Garment Workers Survey Questionnaire,* A report submitted to the Employment Committee of the Human Rights Commission, October 23, 1969.

42. "Twenty Seamstresses Unpaid for Months," *East/West,* 17 December 1969.

43. Susan Almazol, "Sweatshops of Chinatown Hit," *San Francisco Examiner,* 9 October 1969, p. 28.

44. George B. McGimsey, "The Economic Rationale Behind Urban Zoning," M.A. thesis in economics, University of California at Berkeley, 1953, p. 49.

45. *East/West,* 20 August 1969, p. 1.

46. *The Report,* p. 27.

47. Myerson.

48. Adam Smith, *The Wealth of Nations,* Book V, Chapter 1, Part III.

49. William Appleman Williams, *The Great Evasion* (Chicago: Quadrangle Books, 1964), p. 102.

50. *Ibid.*, p. 114.

51. Victor and Brett Nee, *Long Time Californ'.*

52. *Ibid.*

Issei Women
by Emma Gee

The history of the Japanese immigrants in America, not to mention that of the Issei women in particular, has yet to be written. Existing historical works on the whole have treated the Issei as "objects" of the past exclusion movement. Emphasizing this aspect of Japanese immigrant history, hostile as well as sympathetic writers have been responsible for creating a one-sided picture in which the Issei are depicted as a nameless mass victimized by history rather than active human participants in the making of history.

In this sense, the Issei have been portrayed as devoid of human will, initiative, and ability. This sad state of affairs in our historical knowledge has led us at times to herald romantic notions or exaggerated horror stories about the Issei. The oppressive conditions under which the Issei were forced to live were very real, but Japanese immigrant history does not begin and end with them.

Rather than just asking what was done to the Issei, we should examine the human drama in their history by raising new questions. How did the Issei, for example, view themselves? How did they respond and adapt to the hostile, foreign land which was America? What kind of meaning did they derive from immigrant life? What accounted for their tremendous strength of character which enabled them to survive an unkind world of racial injustice, poverty, hard work, and loneliness with dignity and humor?

In short, we need to ask: what is *their* history? This article will not answer these questions. It will merely attempt to give a glimmer of the rich history of the Issei pioneer women by presenting excerpts from accounts of their own experiences written by a few of them, illustrating the human element in their history which had been neglected too long.

Background

Before presenting them, the general background to the immigration of Japanese women to America should be given. Like the Chinese pattern of immigration in the 19th century, very few Japanese women came to America in the early period of Japanese immigration during the late 1880's through the 1890's. Unlike the Chinese pattern, however, within a couple of decades many young adult Japanese males began to bring over wives. The turn of the century signalled the beginning of Japanese female immigration to America which continued until the Japanese government curtailed it in 1920.

In 1900 out of the total Japanese population of 24,326 in America, there were only 985 females, making for a sex ratio of approximately 24 males for every female. During the succeeding decades this ratio was significantly reduced with the arrival of additional females. In 1910 the number of females jumped to 9,087; by 1920 there were 38,303 out of the total population of 111,010.[1] The immigration of these women made the Japanese American family unit possible and produced the second-generation, marking the transition from a society of single, male sojourners to permanent immigrants.

This remarkable demographic change stemmed from the so-called "picture-bride" practice. For the Japanese males in America, there were a number of ways to secure a spouse. On the one hand, the problem was straightforward for those who had married prior to their emigration. Upon establishing themselves in this country, they simply summoned their wives to rejoin them, and so, properly speaking, these wives were not picture brides because they were married before their husbands had departed alone for America.

On the other hand, the problem was not as easily solved for the majority of Japanese males who were still single. If they had the opportunity, some married single Japanese women already here, but these cases had to be rare because of the small number of such women. Most single men resorted to one of two other ways to secure wives. Many returned to Japan to seek them, usually to their home villages, married while there, and then came back again to America with their new brides. Though widely practiced, this method was not the most common, reserved as it was for those who had the economic means, for not only did the return trip but also myriad of social festivities and responsibilities of marriage in Japan entailed onerous expenses. Hence the majority of the single Japanese males adopted the

last method, the often misunderstood and maligned practice of picture brides.

Picture Brides

Picture-bride marriages grew out of the *omiai-kekkon* or arranged marriage prevalent during late Meiji and Taisho times in Japan (and indeed still in practice down to the present). Since marriage was considered a family matter, not an individual affair, Japanese families exercised almost complete authority over it. Their control involved careful scrutiny of any prospective spouse and the spouse's family and their background. To insure an appropriate marriage, socio-economic factors, physical and hereditary traits, and

even political considerations were given their due attention by respective household heads.

An agreed upon go-between or go-betweens carried out the negotiations between families through-out the selection process, and the initial customary meeting or *omiai* between prospective brides and bridegrooms often was preceded by an exchange of photographs, especially in cases in which the families were separated by long distance. For a marriage to be legal in Japan, both parties did not have to be physically present for a wedding ceremony, though customarily, of course, they were. The crucial factor was the bridegroom's *koseki* or family register. The bride's name had to be entered officially in her husband's family register at the local government office, signifying that she had legally become a

360

member of his household.

Thus the picture-bride marriage, though conducted on either side of the Pacific Ocean separated by some four thousand miles, was essentially an extension of an established Japanese social custom. Since physical presence was not an absolute requirement, a proxy, usually a family representative, assumed the ceremonial role of the absent bridegroom. Apart from the fact that the partners to a union neither met during the course of negotiations nor were both present at the wedding ceremony, the picture-bride marriage satisfied all the recognized social conventions in regard to marriage in Japan.

Moreover, it became a legally recognized marriage as soon as the bride was entered in her new husband's register. To apply for a passport to America, the Japanese government required the bride to present a certified copy of her husband's family register with her name entered in it for at least six months which bore the registrar's official seal.

Anti-Japanese Movement

The coming of the picture bride added fuel to the anti-Japanese movement.[2] One of the chief arguments against the Japanese was their "non-assimilability." To the rabid exclusionists, the picture brides provided additional substantiation of this allegation, for they interpreted, and hence condemned, picture-bride marriages as an immoral social custom antithetical to American Christian ideals. That the Japanese engaged in such a degrading practice was evidence of their non-assimilability.

In their condemnation of picture brides, the exclusionists circulated exaggerated figures on Japanese fecundity, conjuring up the ominous specter of picture brides breeding like rats and producing even more unassimilable Japanese. They also charged that picture brides became laborers as soon as they set foot on American soil. Since the Japanese government had consented to curtail the emigration of laborers with the Gentlemen's Agreement of 1907-1908, the Japanese, according to the exclusionists, violated the spirit, if not the letter, of this agreement. Thus, immorality was linked to Japanese governmental treachery in the exclusionists' virulent attacks upon the picture brides.

Because of these attacks and U.S. government pressures, the Japanese government discontinued issuing passports to them in 1920 which, along with the subsequent 1924 Immigration Act, left 42.5% of the adult Japanese males still single in America with no hopes of getting married[3]—a cruel blow to a people who believed that "no matter what possessions a man may have, he is not a success unless he is married and has a family," because to "fail in this is to fail in life."[4] With this general background to the immigration of Japanese females in mind, let us now turn to the experiences of a few Issei women.

Pioneers

It is difficult for us today to imagine the experience of the Issei pioneer woman from the time of her marriage to her arrival and settlement in America. The following excerpts from accounts written by some of them will provide, hopefully, some insight into their experience.[5] To begin with, just how did she feel and think about her marriage and her future in America? One picture bride comments on her husband:

> I had but remote ties with him. Yet because of the talks between our close parents and my parents' approval and encouragement, I decided upon our picture-bride marriage.

The family in her specific case—indeed, in most marriages—had played the decisive role, and her decision was dependent upon it. But however the decision was arrived at, the prospects of coming to America must have been viewed with mixed emotions. On the one hand, there is the example of a wife whose husband had preceded her to America:

> I was bubbling over with great expectations. My young heart, 19 years and 8 months old, burned, not so much with the prospects of reuniting with my new husband, but with the thought of the New World.

Many women like her placed great store in America, and their glowing images of America accounted for their enthusiasm. This same person continues:

> My husband who had returned to Japan to seek a wife wore a Western style high-collar suit at our *omiai*. He told unusual stories about America which were like dreams to me. Being reared in the countryside, I listened intently with wide-opened eyes. Thus, I thought about how heavenly America was.

Attired in latest Western suits, Japanese males who returned to Japan naturally told tales which, while not necessarily fictional, were probably embroidered to impress prospective brides. After all, they were the "successful" individuals who had the economic means to return to Japan! Other women received similar impressions from letters and photographs from their husbands-to-be in America who were equally anxious to secure wives. An element of vanity no doubt was intermingled, especially with a captive audience eager for news about foreign lands, and the tendency was toward the hyperbole.

Still there were husbands who were candid. "My unknown husband had said," according to another picture bride, "'If you come with great expectations about living in an immigrant land, you will be disappointed.' I had received letters which said that if I intended to see things through without giving up, then I should come to America." And this particular woman, having this understanding clearly in mind, made the following resolution:

> On the way from Kobe to Yokohama, gazing upon the rising majestic Mount Fuji in a cloudless sky aboard the ship, I made a resolve. For a woman who was going to a strange society and relying upon an unknown husband whom she had married through photographs, my heart had to be as beautiful as Mount Fuji. I resolved that the heart of a Japanese woman had to be sublime, like that soaring majestic figure eternally constant through wind and rain, heat and cold. Thereafter, I never forgot that resolve on the ship, enabling me to overcome sadness and suffering.

The passage across the Pacific was a mixture of sadness at leaving Japan and apprehensions concerning the future. Having left families, relatives, and all that was familiar to them, now the women were actually enroute to meet and live with their husbands in an alien land. In this regard, a picture bride records:

> I left Yokohama on the *Minnesota*. Passengers from Yokohama were placed into rooms partitioned by canvas. Besides myself and two other married women returning to America, there was a couple. The two married women had left their children in Japan and would cry when they talked about them. I, too, broke out in tears when I thought of my father, who had passed away just before my departure.

Yet the passage was tolerable, for in most instances there was the companionship of other women who also were coming to America under similar circumstances, among whom the sadness, excitement, and uneasiness could be shared.

As the ship neared the port of debarkation, the excitement of the future prevailed over the sadness of leaving. Apprehensions also increased as the ship pulled alongside the pier. One of the most typical scene was the sight of the brides on board and the bridegrooms on the pier both trying to match the photographs in their hands with their respective partners. Since some individuals had forwarded old photographs of themselves, taken as much as ten to fifteen years ago, in such cases both sides had a difficult time of it.

And in other cases the photographs did not match with the actual person—the village "old maid" or the "ugly old man" may have sent someone else's picture out of a fear of rejection. One of the more fortunate picture brides who quickly recognized her husband describes her experience:

> I landed in Seattle in 1911 as a picture bride. I am a native of Yahatahama City in Ehime Prefecture, and my husband . . . was also from this city. I had no memory of him after he had gone to America, not only because he was 14 years older but because he had left when I was 13 years old. I searched for him by comparing his photographs with the people who had come out to meet us. Fortunately, my husband looked very much like his older brother in Japan, and so I recognized him immediately and said to myself, 'That's he!'

What a relief it must have been for her! And by the same token what a source of continued anxiety it must have been for those who could not match the photographs with their husbands.

Another trying experience was to run the gauntlet of immigration inspectors. Before being allowed to join their husbands, they first had to pass immigration officials who, no doubt, were officious and who, in any case, spoke a foreign tongue. The fear of being sent back to Japan was ever present. And since these officials had the power to prohibit debarkation, nervous questions haunted them. Were my documents in order? Would I be detained for trachoma, an eye disease for which the inspectors were on the look out? Would I have to speak to them in English? These were real anxieties which gripped these women as they prepared to go through the immigration process. Unlike the picture bride who recognized her husband much to her relief, another one was not as lucky:

> Upon disembarking at Seattle, I was detained for two weeks in the Immigration Center on suspicion of having trachoma. My husband had come from Spokane to meet me, but he returned alone because of my detention. On the first morning of my two-week detention, there was oatmeal for breakfast. In Japan the poor eat wheat, and I cried thinking that I would have only that to eat in America.

After two weeks she was finally released, and "traveled 350 miles alone without any knowledge of geography or English" to Spokane where her husband was.

As soon as they were able to debark, it was common for the husbands to whisk off their new brides to a clothing store. The Japanese were well aware that the Chinese had been excluded in 1882. Since the Chinese had not adopted Western-style clothing, according to the common belief among the Japanese, they had provided substance to the charge that they were non-assimilable. To avoid any recurrence of this accusation, Japanese husbands had their new brides fitted in a new set of Western clothing to replace the traditional Japanese kimono in which they had landed. A picture bride describes this event in the following manner:

> I was immediately outfitted with Western clothing at Hara's Clothing Store . . . At that time a suit of Western clothing cost from $25 to $27-28. Because I had to wear a tight corset around my chest, I could not bend forward. I had to have my husband tie my shoe laces. There were some women who fainted because it was too tight.

There are stories of women being carried to the hotel rooms by their husband who hurriedly untied the corset strings which were not joking matters. In my case, I wore a large hat, a high-necked blouse, a long skirt, a buckled belt around my waist, high-laced shoes, and, of course, for the first time in my life, a brassiere and hip pads.

For these women unaccustomed to wearing Western-style clothing, their new wardrobe was as strange as it was uncomfortable. This same woman goes on to say:

> What gave me trouble was the underwear. Japanese women used only a *koshimaki* (a sarong-like underskirt). Wearing Western-style underwear for the first time, I would forget to take it down when I went to the toilet. And I frequently committed the blunder.

Once the ordeal of landing and the initial encounter with America were over, their new life with their husbands began which was anything but easy. For not only did they have to adjust to an alien environment, they also had to establish a new household. On the lack of modern amenities, a woman writes:

> At the farm on Vashon Island to which I went, I had to draw water by bucket from a well. There was no *furo*. I boiled water and put it into a tub. There was no electricity. I used oil lamps. No matter how backward Japan may have been, this was life in the hinterland. Still I toiled in sweat alongside my husband.

In rural regions, especially in the remote areas to which the Japanese went, the living quarters were primitive:

> . . . I discovered that our house was a house in name only, a shack where hunters had lived located in the middle of the field. There was only one room with beds placed in three corners. My husband was living here with a younger boy and older person. Since he and I had no honeymoon period, a makeshift curtain was created by stretching a rope across the room and hanging clothes from it. It was unsuitable for us newlyweds to say the least! . . . The shack had been fashioned out of boards and leaked. There were no eaves to drain the rain. Sometimes we passed the night with raincoats over our beds.

Small hotel rooms were common quarters for those who settled down in the cities:

> Everyone lived in a hotel. We ate beside the beds. And since we had the minimum amount of eating utensils for two persons, if friends came during mealtime, we said 'just one minute please,' washed our bowls, and then had our friends use them. The room was about the size of six tatami with a coal stove which we used for cooking meals.

The room had only cold water.

Most Issei women immediately began to work alongside their husbands. Because of the need to eke out a living, they could not afford the luxury of a honeymoon. Besides doing the regular chores of cooking, washing, cleaning, and sewing, they also labored long hours in the fields or shops. A women recounts her early agricultural work:

> At the beginning I worked with my husband picking potatoes or onions and putting them in sacks. Working with rough-and-tumble men, I became weary to the bones; waking up in the mornings I could not bend over the wash basin. Sunlight came out about 4:00 a.m. during the summer in the Yakima Valley. I arose at 4:30. After cooking breakfast, I went out to the fields. There was no electric stove or gas like now. It took over one hour to cook, burning kindling wood. As soon as I came home, I first put on the fire, took off my hat, and then I washed my hands. After cooking both breakfast and lunch, I went to the fields.

Work was not less difficult nor shorter in the urban occupations. Take, for example, the case of a woman whose husband operated a laundry. After working the entire day, she records that:

> . . . I started at 5:00 p.m. to prepare supper for five to six persons, and then I began my evening work. The difficult ironing remained. Women's blouses in those days were made from silk or lace, with collars, and long sleeves and lots of frills. I could only finish two in one hour, ironing them with great care. Hence, I worked usually until 12:00 to 1:00 a.m. But it was not just me—all women who worked in the laundry business probably did the same thing.

Soon after these experiences with the harsh realities of life in America, Issei women began to bear children. In most rural areas where the Issei settled, doctors were not readily available. Even if they were, either the white doctors refused to treat them or the Japanese could not afford their services. Certainly no such institution as a prenatal clinic existed to which the Issei women could turn and prepare themselves for childbirth.

As a general rule, midwives substituted for doctors in the delivery of children. One woman whose inexperienced husband performed the role of a midwife for their first child writes about the advice which he received from a friend who had successfully delivered a child. She quotes this friend as stating:

> The cutting of the umbilical cord is what is important. First, you must firmly tie the cord near the navel with a string in two places. Then you cut in between the two knots with a scissor.

Following this advice, she reports that she and her husband gave birth to eight children in this manner.

"As a wife in a farming household there were many trying matters," another Issei woman states, "but the most difficult was giving birth." But unlike the first woman, working right up to the moment of childbirth, she notes:

> My bedside midwife was a man. He was quite knowledgeable. But hearing that cutting the umbilical cord was the most important, I did it myself. Since I gave birth ten times and was myself knowledgeable, I often served as midwife for others.

We can safely assume that not all Issei women were as stoic as these two incredible females. Think of the young women in remote isolated areas who did not have the benefit of advice and comfort, and who had no one with whom to share their anxieties. What courage it must have taken to bear their children alone! And what happened to the women who developed complications during pregnancy and in the act of giving birth? Until detailed studies are undertaken, we will have to rely upon our imagination to answer this question.

Problems of post-natal care and child-rearing naturally followed successful childbirth. In households where the women also performed crucial economic functions, especially in farming areas, a reasonable period of post-natal recuperation was considered a luxury which could not be afforded. Commenting on her experience, an Issei woman writes:

> Twenty-one days of post-natal rest was common even in Japan. Even busy housewives with household chores to do took this 21-day rest without doing anything. I, however, could not rest for more than three days.

Being a member of a farming household, she had to resume her agricultural work responsibilities after only three days of rest. Most Issei women had to raise their children by themselves because of the sharp sexual division of labor within the home. Even if they worked in the family economic unit, they still had to carry the entire burden of housekeeping and child-rearing. An Issei woman reveals:

> My husband was a Meiji man. He did not think of helping in the house or with the children. No matter how busy I may have been, he never changed the baby's diapers. Though it may not be right to say this ourselves, we Issei pioneer women from Japan worked solely for our husband. At mealtime, whenever there was not enough food, we served a lot to our husbands and took very little for ourselves.

Despite long, arduous hours of labor and the innumerable difficulties of childbirth and child-rearing, the Issei women persevered.

From the foregoing brief excerpts, it is clear that these were truly remarkable women. From their initial decision to come to America, whether as picture brides or not, through the Trans-Pacific voyage and ordeal of disembarkation, and finally to their adaptation to life in America, they had the physical stamina and moral courage to persist and survive. In spite of the primitive conditions, particularly in the rural areas, they worked unremittingly with a minimum of complaints. They never thought solely of their own welfare. They thought more about giving than taking. They labored beside their husbands and raised their children as best as they could within the framework of the beliefs and values they had been taught in late Meiji Japan. Their lives were not sensational. Possessed of an extraordinary strength of character derived from quiet fortitude, the Issei women found life meaningful.

Many Sansei today are decrying the image of the "Quiet American" with some measure of justification. Yet amid the clamor for social change, accompanied at times by loud political rhetoric, we should not disparage the quiet fortitude of these Issei women. In America, quietness and modesty tend to be equated with weakness, but with these Issei women, quietness and modesty are sure signs of strength.

Just how typical these women are of Issei women in general can be determined only by later historical studies. Still I venture to guess that they indeed are representative. By looking only for the dramatic and heroic moments in history, we tend to forget the small struggles and little victories of human beings. We are here today because our immigrant parents and grandparents—ordinary people—had the strength to survive. One way we can begin to value their struggle is by uncovering their buried history, for their history is in essence our history. ★

Notes

1. Dorothy Thomas, Charles Kikuchi, and James Sakoda, *The Salvage* (Berkeley and Los Angeles: University of California Press, 1952), p. 575. Almost 40% of the new arrivals in 1910-1920 were females, of which three-fourths were wives of residents. Thomas et al., p. 8.

2. For details see Yamato Ichihashi, *Japanese in the United States* (Stanford: Stanford University Press, 1932); Roger Daniels, *The Politics of Prejudice* (New York: Atheneum, 1967); and Thomas A. Bailey, *Theodore Roosevelt and Japan-American Crises* (Stanford: Stanford University Press, 1934).

3. Ichihashi, p. 92. Moreover, they could not marry whites due to state anti-miscegenation laws. See Ichihashi, pp. 216-219 and Milton R. Konvitz, *The Alien and the Asiatic in American Law* (Ithaca: Cornel University Press, 1946), pp. 231-232.

4. R. D. McKenzie, *Oriental Exclusion* (Chicago: University of Chicago Press, 1928), p. 79.

5. These examples have been translated from Kazuo Ito, *Hokubei Hyakunen Sakura* (Hundred-Year-Old Cherry Blossoms in North America) (Seattle, 1969), pp. 311-358. My thanks to Yuji Ichioka for his sensitive translations.

Organizing Pilipino Farmworkers in the 1930s

By CARLOS BULOSAN

The old world will die. . . .

This was the new dictum of my life. I did not exactly know what it meant, but it was enough that my brother Macario had expressed it. It was a stirring law that governed my life and thoughts. And it did not matter who was going to die; it was enough that something horrible was to perish from the earth.

The simple beginning of my intellectual awakening—the tragic death of Pascual and the imprisonment of Jose, the sudden change of Macario into a personality passionately reaching out for understanding, and my second encounter with Felix Razon—all these influences were enough to make my last few months of freedom useful and significant.

The first issue of *The New Tide* was with the printers; when it came out, Jose and I took a hundred copies and distributed them to some of the more literate farm workers. It did not create a sensation, but we did not expect anything spectacular. It was the first of its kind to be published by Filipinos in the United States, and it was fumbling and immature, but it promised to grow into something important in the history of Filipino social awakening.

The magazine was one of several publications that had arisen all over the nation, and had tried to grasp the social realities and to interpret them in terms of the needs of the decade. It sustained our lives, drowned our despair, and gave us hope. It broadened our scope and vision.

Then it went out of existence. Its founders tried to revive it. But like the other publications born overnight to rally behind a new social idea, it died a natural death. It was like a world that died. Felix Razon wanted to save it; he went to work in a hotel in Hollywood and lived in the basement in

order to save it. Nick found an apartment house in Beverly Hills; he worked seven days a week for twenty-five dollars a month. Macario went to work in a restaurant but, upon my advice—since there was no hope for the magazine—he went to New Mexico hoping to attend the University there.

However, the magnificent spirit behind it did not die. It was born again, in a more dynamic form, when I acquired enough knowledge to revive the high idealism behind it. But what awed me, in those early days, were the sacrifices of the founders. I would ask myself why three starving men were willing to give up their hard-earned money to make an obscure magazine live, denying themselves the simple necessities of food and shelter. They had surrounded the publication as though it were a little life about to die, or dying, or dead—and breathed life into it one after the other, looking desperate and lost when they realized that their efforts were futile. But it was an inspiring experience, watching these young men breathing life into a dead thing. Their efforts came to me again and again in the course of my struggle toward an intellectual clarification and a positive social attitude.

An old world literally died with the magazine. An old generation of writers died with it, too. A new generation was born with the same ideals, perhaps, but re-invigorated with new social attitudes. The labor movement was the paramount issue; it was winning the support of intellectuals and the advanced sections of the proletariat. Listening and watching attentively, I knew that it was the dawn of a new morning. I did not have to wait for the birth of a new world, because what I had been told to fight for was here with its brilliant promises.

How was I to understand? Could I help? I knew that the most forlorn man, in those rootless years, was he who knew that love was growing inside him but had no object on which to bestow it.

Upon my return to the Santa Maria Valley, I found that the Filipino Workers' Association, an independent union, was disintegrating. I rushed to join Jose in Lompoc, where he had gone with Gazamen to see if there was a possibility of establishing a workers' newspaper. The three of us decided to form a branch there and to make it the center of Filipino union activities in Central California.

Salinas was still the general headquarters of the Association, but it was fast losing its authority and prestige. There was a mad scramble for power in the Association among the national officers, and their bitter rivalries wrecked our chance toward the establishment of a more cogent labor organization. Actually, however, it was the birth of progressive leadership in the Filipino labor movement.

The membership of the Filipino Workers' Association was tremendous, considering the myriad difficulties it met in the campaign to spread throughout the agricultural areas of California. The vigilant Filipino workers—their whole-hearted support of the trade union movement, their hatred of low wages and other labor discriminations—were the direct causes that instigated the persecutions against them, sporadic at first and then concerted, but destructive to the nation's welfare.

In Salinas, for instance, the general headquarters were burned after a successful strike of lettuce workers, and the president of the association was thrown in jail. Upon his release, he moved to Guadalupe, in the south, and campaigned for the purchase of a new building. Always alert, the Filipino agricultural workers throughout the valley rallied behind the proposal, and after a few months a new national office was established. Again, striking for better wages, the Filipino lettuce cutters and packers succeeded, but lost the building and their right to build another in Guadalupe.

Finally, Jose and I made the office in Lompoc the temporary general headquarters. It was unconstitutional, of course, but the moment called for drastic action. Our move was without precedent, but we hoped to accomplish something, and we did.

It was during our membership campaign that I came in contact with fascism in California. The sugar beet season was in full swing in Oxnard, but the Mexican and Filipino workers were split. The companies would not recognize their separate demands, and although there were cultural and economic ties between them, they had not recognized one important point: that the beet companies conspired against their unity.

I contacted a Filipino farm-labor contractor and a prominent Mexican, and Jose, who joined us later, planned a meeting in the town park. I felt a little elated; harmony was in the offing. But in the

evening, when we were starting the program, deputy sheriffs came to the park and told us that our right to hold a meeting had been revoked. I did not know what to do. I was still a novice. An elderly Mexican told us that we could hold a meeting outside the city limit.

There was a large empty barn somewhere in the south end of Oxnard. A truck came and carried some of the men, but most of them walked with us on the highway. They were very serious. I glanced at Jose who was talking to three Filipinos ahead of me, and felt something powerful growing inside me. It was a new heroism: a feeling of growing with a huge life. I walked silently with the men, listening to their angry voices and to the magic of their marching feet.

I was frightened. But I felt brave, too. The Mexicans wanted a more inclusive union, but that would take time. We were debating the issue when I heard several cars drive into the yard. I signaled to the men to put out the lights and to take cover. They fanned out and broke through the four walls, escaping into the wide beet fields.

I rushed upon the improvised stage and grabbed Jose, whose wooden leg had become entangled in some ropes and wires.

"This is it!"

"Yeah!"

"Follow me!"

"Right!"

I jumped off the stage, Jose following me. Then there was the sudden patter of many feet outside, and shooting. I found a pile of dry horse manure in a corner of the barn. I told Jose to lie down; then I covered him with it, exposing only his nose. I lay beside him and covered myself with it, too. When I tried to talk, the manure went into my mouth and choked me. I lay still, waiting for the noise outside to subside.

A man with a flashlight came inside and stabbed the darkness with the steely light, butting swiftly from corner to corner. He came near the pile of manure, spat on it, and searched the ceiling. A piece of manure tickled my throat, and I held my breath, bringing tears to my eyes. The man went outside, joined his companions, and drove off to town.

I pushed the dung away and jumped to my feet. "Did you see his face?"

"No!"

"I saw it. He is a white man, all right."

"Let's run. There is still time."

I crept to the wall and crouched in the darkness. I wanted to be sure that every man had gone. The way was clear. Jose followed me outside. Then we were running across a beet field, our feet slapping against the broad leaves that got in our way. The moon came up and shone brightly in the night. As I ran, I looked up to see it sailing across the sky.

Then my fear was gone. I stopped running and sat down among the tall beets. Jose sat beside me There were no words to describe the feeling in our minds and hearts. There was only our closeness and the dark years ahead. There was only the dark future.

We walked across the beet fields to Camarillo, five miles south. The town was quiet and dark. It was surrounded by orange groves. We went into the local school building and slept on the floor. A teacher found us there in the morning. She threatened to call the police, and we rushed outside. We walked in the morning sun, smelling the orange blossoms and the clean air. I looked at the tall mountains on our right and stopped, remembering the mountains in my village.

"You like the landscape?" Jose asked.

"It's like my village," I said.

illustration by **FAUSTINO CAIGOY**

"Tell me about it."

"Well, it is hard to describe it to you. But the farther I go from it, the more vivid it becomes to me. Perhaps I am sentimental. But my village is not like any other village. There are mountains on one side, and there is the wide river on the other. A tongue of land extends into the river and on this land are hills that are covered with guava trees. Now is the time for the guavas to bloom. I used to go there when I was a child and the smell of the blossoms followed me down into the valley. Between the mountains and the river, in the center of the valley, is a papaya grove. Papayas are in bloom now. Did you ever smell papaya blossoms? There is nothing like it. Someday I will go back and climb these guavas again. Someday I will make a crown of papaya blossoms. Do you think I am sentimental?"

"No," Jose said. "I know what you mean. We will go back someday. I will climb those guavas with you. We will swim in the river. The papayas are in bloom now, you say?"

The journey to Ventura was shortened. We were following the state highway when a police patrol stopped us and took us to the city jail and held us on charges of vagrancy. When we were released, three days afterwards, we took a bus to Lompoc.

But another strike was in progress there. The lettuce workers had walked out three days before. I was informed that some of the men did not approve of the strike, but a white woman from Fresno had agitated them. Gazamen told me that she was staying at a local hotel. I asked Jose to go with me.

It was already one in the afternoon, but the hotel was very quiet. I knocked on the door. A short, stocky, ordinary-looking woman with dark hair stood before me.

"My name is Helen," she said, coming out with her overnight bag. "How is the strike this morning?"

"My name is Jose," Jose said. "We came to you to talk about it. I hope you don't mind our bothering you."

"Jose!" Helen was beaming. "You are the person I've been looking for in Lompoc. Mr. Magna in San Francisco recommended you—"

Jose's doubts vanished immediately. He knew Magna intimately. I walked eagerly with them to the office. But why did Helen talk as though this strike were a business? I was filled with doubts and premonitions.

Helen, realizing the importance of time, suggested that we proceed with the strike. Fired with a new impetus, Jose worked night and day. The strike spread to Solvang and Las Cruces, where the Lompoc farmers controlled the agricultural products. The strikers organized reconnaissance squads and guarded the highway and other exits from the valley.

It was exactly what Helen wanted. The trucks that carried the lettuce were driven by Japanese and white men to Las Cruces, where they were inspected by government officials before proceeding to Los Angeles. Helen wanted the hauling stopped. It was a dangerous move, because the job of taking out the crates from the fields was done by Japanese and Mexican workers under the surveillance of highway patrolmen.

I tried to argue with Helen against the use of firearms and violence in general, but gave up when some of the strikers became hysterical. The leaders of the squads wanted to install me as the new secretary of the local. I accepted it, not because I wanted it, but because the strike called for quick decision. Besides, I was beginning to understand the organized conspiracy against the agricultural workers in California.

The strike taught me that I was definitely a part of the labor movement. On the third day, the reconnaissance squads rushed to the main highway where the loaded trucks would pass. The men spread out and waited on both sides of the road, becoming tense when the trucks appeared in the distance. But the drivers were guarded by motorcycle patrolmen, three on either side, releasing their sirens whenever they approached the strikers.

When the first truck appeared in the bend of the road, the strikers came out and signaled to the driver to stop. The patrolmen rushed forward, clubbing the men who tried to climb into the trucks. About a dozen men turned over a truck, fighting their way out when the patrolmen turned around to beat them. The drivers leaped out and stayed away from the fight.

In a few minutes, finding resistance impossible, the strikers rushed to their cars and drove madly to the office. Three strikers were arrested on the spot, brought to town, and thrown in jail. In the afternoon a newspaper reporter from Santa Barbara came to our headquarters and reported that the strike was inspired by Communists. The next day, believing the newspaper story, some of the townspeople joined the Mexican and Japanese laborers in the fields.

The strike was completely broken. Great damage was done to organized Filipino labor. I was reluctant to believe that Helen had betrayed us, but when she disappeared at the termination of the strike, I suspected that she might be a professional strike-breaker.

Helen had shown me a subtle way of winning the rank and file. But she had also shown me a way of winning the leaders. In fact, she had shown me another way of abusing the trust and confidence of honest working men.

When the strike was broken in Lompoc, Jose followed Helen to Salinas, where she had gone to spread calamity. I knew that they were living together as husband and wife, in the Mexican section, and I intimated to Jose my suspicion. But he ignored my warning. Because he was the ablest organizer among Filipinos in California, Helen got her man.

She was paid to curtail the trend of agricultural workers toward the labor movement.

Then I heard that the Salinas strike had been defeated, or betrayed, and again Helen disappeared. A ranch house was burned by unidentified persons, and the blame was put on the strikers. It was the same old tactic, but still workable. Jose was arrested; but Helen, who was also arrested, was released immediately. It was evident that she was paid to create disunity among the strikers and to turn public opinion against them. When Jose was released by the International Labor Defense, which handled such cases, he went to San Francisco where he attended a workers' conference.

I went to Los Angeles hoping to persuade my brother Macario to go to Santa Maria with me, where the two of us could work together, because he was proficient in languages and was a forceful speaker. But he already had a job. He was more interested in the theoretical approach. I discovered with disappointment that his desire to go to college was fading. He was, however, reading extensively and acquiring books about world politics.

I wanted Macario to complete his education because, at that time, I still believed that it was the only course for him. I remembered how our family had sacrificed everything for him, and when I saw him losing interest, I thought of the years when I had been with my father on the farm in Mangusmana. I recalled that my most wonderful days were those centered around Macario—when he was away from Binalonan, when he was studying in Lingayen, and when he came back one vacation time to cut my hair.

I wrote to my brother Amado, in Phoenix, but when he received my letter he was already in San Francisco. He was living at the St. Francis Hotel with the man for whom he was working—a big-time racketeer lawyer from Los Angeles. I went to San Diego, where the Filipino pea pickers were on strike. When I returned to Los Angeles a letter from Amado was waiting for me. He was in Hollywood.

I went to see him immediately. He was staying in a luxurious room. But it was actually rented by the lawyer; they always lived together when they were traveling.

"In fact," Amado said proudly, "we sometimes sleep with the same woman."

I did not believe him. How was it that a successful lawyer would share a room with his servant? But Amado disappointed me; he was in a position to help Macario go to college but would not. It was the beginning of a long estrangement between Amado and me.

"I'm going into a new world, Carlos" Amado said. "Away from our people. I'm sorry it's this way."

I knew that he had deserted us—even his speech was rapidly becoming Americanized.

"I'm sorry, too," I said.

"Good-bye."

I walked out of his room and his life forever.

I lived with Macario in his little room on Flower Street, hoping to read some of his books and magazines. I went to the public library, fumbling for knowledge in the enormous building. One day Macario took a civil service examination, although he knew that he could not get the job.

"Why?" I asked.

"California doesn't employ Filipinos in civil service jobs," he said.

"Is there a law about it?"

"None. But it is a matter of personal interpretation of our status in the United States."

"Citizenship, then, is the basis of all this misunderstanding?"

"You can put it that way."

I was discovering things. Where should I begin? It was then that Helen came to Los Angeles. She saw me at a meeting of the Labor Relations Board and the workers' representatives at the post office. She grabbed me, pretending excitement and joy. I played my part, wanting to know what she was doing.

We went outside and walked in the autumn shower: the sky was dark and there was a cold wind. I took Helen with me to my brother's room; there was no place for us to go. Because my brother was beginning to integrate his beliefs, I warned him against Helen. But it was useless. She had found her next victim, but her method was more subtle. She was dealing with an intellectual, and used a different strategy.

She succeeded, living with Macario and despising me. I was dejected and lost. I could not believe it: the gods of yesterday were falling to pieces. They were made of clay. I had to make my own gods, create my own symbols, and worship in my own fashion. Yes, this is what I would do, now that all of yesterday was dying.

I was about to leave Los Angeles when Jose arrived. He had heard that Helen was in town. He wanted to stop her doing any more damage to the Filipinos. She was not only involved with powerful agricultural groups, but was also connected with certain self-styled patriotic organizations that considered it their duty to terrify the lives of minorities in the state.

Helen's suspicion that Macario was what she called a "professional agitator" revealed her stupidity. There was nothing in my brother's activities that would indicate his political connections; he was simply a man who had been awakened by a dynamic social idea. How to realize it was beyond him. Although he wanted a course of action, he was incapable of working it out to the end. He was by inclination an intellectual, a visionary, a dreamer. The turmoil in the agricultural areas of California were but reverberations of a greater social catastrophe.

When Jose, infuriated by Helen's lack of integrity, accused her of being an agent of anti-union interests, she retorted savagely:

"I hate the Filipinos as deeply as I hate unions! You are all savages and you have no right to stay in this country!"

I struck her in the face with a telephone receiver. Something fell from her mouth. Now let her speak arrogantly about the Filipinos! When Jose saw that I was going to hit her again, he charged suddenly and knocked me down. When I scrambled to my feet Helen was already running down the alley toward the street.

It was the end of Helen among Filipinos. But she had done enough damage. I had often wondered what became of her. I later heard unconfirmed reports that she had been beaten to death in Visalia.

The disappearance of Helen marked the end of the Filipino Workers' Association. Terrorism was loosed upon the agricultural workers and special committees were formed to lobby in the state legislature and in Congress to bring about the regimentation of migratory workers. The big farmers had gone so far as to curtail all civil liberties for farm laborers. They also designed to wreck unionism by instigating lurid campaigns among the urban population to teach them to fight union activities.

In this open conspiracy to undermine a democratic government, the farmers had miscalculated the reaction of the workers who led an urban life; for they succeeded only in epitomizing the fact that both urban and rural workers depend on each other's labor in the struggle for security and the right to organize and bargain collectively.

But not realizing that we were facing a powerful enemy, Jose and I and other labor leaders met in the house of a newspaper reporter, Millar, in San Francisco, and mapped out a plan to start a unified statewide union campaign. When we adjourned Ganzo, who was working with Pascual's wife on a new newspaper in San Francisco, went to Santa Maria where he was familiar with the workers. Jose and I wanted to work together in Central California, embracing, of course, all the agricultural towns in San Luis Obispo and Santa Barbara counties.

Felix Razon, toughened by the years, enthusiastically went to Imperial Valley, where the fascist elements worked more openly than in other parts of the state. Nick went to Los Angeles, where he could work with my brother Macario among the city laborers, but the orange counties and San Diego were also his territories. Millar remained in San Francisco, to work closely with a Filipino Communist in Sacramento, who went to Stockton afterward to help me organize a political steering committee.

Conrado Torres, who had worked with me in the fish canneries in Alaska several years before, went to Seattle and from there proceeded to Yakima Valley, leaving Maura Perez consolidate what he had started to organize. Gazamen went to Portland, where they were joined by Mariano—and the three started an aggressive, militant, and progressive committee. Jim Luna and I were the only members of our group who had no college education. But Jim had served in the navy for many years and had gained experience.

When we parted we were conscious of the tremendous task before us, that if we failed in ourselves we would also fail in its realization. From this day onward my life became one long conspiracy, working in the daytime and meeting other conspirators at night. I was so intensely fired by this dream of a better America that I had completely forgotten myself; but when I discovered myself again, I found that I was still a young man though broken in health. I was suffering from a disease that changed the whole course of my life, that halted my pursuit of the dream in a corner of the terrible years.

In Santa Maria, where I was working with Jose, I received a disturbing communication from Millar. Trouble was brewing in San Jose, forty miles south of San Francisco. Jose and I took the first bus, stopping a few hours in San Luis Obispo to see how Ganzo was progressing. In the early morning, after a lengthy deliberation with Ganzo in his cabin, we rushed to the station and slept in the bus until Salinas.

I still do not know why Jose and I never discussed unionism and politics when we were alone. It was only when we were with others, when we were in action, that we spoke aloud and acted according to our judgment. But I knew that I was coming to a way of thinking that would govern my life in the coming years. I surmised that the same evolution was taking place in Jose. But there was still no term for it. I believed then that agitating the agricultural workers was enough, but the next five years showed me that a definite political program was also needed.

Millar was not at our rendezvous in San Jose. I went to the lettuce fields and talked to the workers. The companies had drastically cut the wage scale: the year before it had been thirty cents an hour, but now it had been reduced to twenty cents. The Filipino workers struck, but the companies imported Mexican laborers.

"There should be a law against the importation of labor," I said. "It should be included in the interstate laws."

"The time will come," Jose said.

"Without it the workers will always be at the mercy of the employers."

"You are absolutely right, Carl," Jose said. "But we have a good president in Washington, so we will probably win some of our demands—if we use enough pressure."

I was not satisfied, but there was some hope. I went to the Mexican district and gathered together some of the Mexicans who had quit the fields that day. Jose, who spoke fluent Spanish, came and explained to them the importance of the strike. They were enthusiastic. A runner was sent to the fields to stop the Mexicans who were still working, and he came back to tell us that only fifty remained.

But we wanted an all-out strike, although we doubted that it would be possible. That night, when Jose and I were in the back room of a restaurant, preparing a leaflet to be circulated, five white men came suddenly into the room. I started to run to the door, but it was too late. Two big men, one wearing dark glasses, carried off Jose. The other man suddenly turned around and shot out the light bulbs.

I was kicked into the back seat of a big car. Jose was in the front seat, between the driver and the man with dark glasses. When the car started to move, I looked down and saw Millar bleeding on the floor. He looked up at me with frightened eyes, pleading, wanting to tell me that he had nothing to do with our arrest. I turned the other way, aching to hit him in the face.

I looked through the window hoping to find some escape. I was sure that if the car turned a corner, I could jump out. If I succeeded in jumping out—could I escape their guns? My heart almost stopped beating. It was better to die trying to escape than to wait for death.

But when the car came to a deserted country road, I knew that flight was impossible. I lost all hope. I glanced quickly at the wide, clear fields, catching a fleeting glimpse of the sky. Looking swiftly to the east, I saw the big moon and below it, soon to move away, a mass of clouds that looked like a mountain of cotton balls. Suddenly I remembered that as a child I used to watch snow-white clouds sailing in the bright summer skies of Mangusmana. The memory of my village made my mind whirl, longing for flight and freedom again.

I was helpless now. I watched my companions: they seemed to have given up all hope. There was only death at the end of the road. The white men were silent. Millar touched my legs when we passed in the shadows of trees. The driver turned off the road and crossed a wide beet field, heading for the woods not far away.

We entered the woods and in five minutes the car stopped. One of the men in front jumped out and came to our door.

"You have the rope, Jake?"

"Yeah!"

The man on my right side got out and pulled me violently after him, hitting me on the jaw. I fell on my knees but got up at once, trembling with rage. If only I had a gun! Or a knife! I could cut these bastards into little pieces! Blood came out of my mouth. I raised my hand to wipe it off, but my attacker hit me again. I staggered, fell on my face, and rolled on the grass.

"Up! Goddamn you! Up!"

Painfully I crawled to my feet, knelt on the grass, and got up slowly. I saw them kicking Millar in the grass. When they were through with him, they tore off Jose's clothes and tied him to a tree. One of them went to the car and came back with a can of tar and a sack of feathers. The man with the dark glasses ripped the sack open and white feathers fell out and sailed in the thin light that filtered between the trees.

Then I saw them pouring the tar on Jose's body. One of them lit a match and burned the delicate hair between his legs.

"Jesus, he's a well-hung son-of-a-bitch!"

"Yeah!"

"No wonder whores stick to them!"

"The other monkey ain't so hot!"

They looked in my direction. The man with the dark glasses started beating Millar. Then he came to me and kicked my left knee so violently that I fell on the grass, blinded with pain. Hardening my body, I wished I were strong enough to reach him. He spat in my face and left.

Another man, the one called Jake, tied me to a tree. Then he started beating me with his fists. Why were these men so brutal, so sadistic? A tooth fell out of my mouth, and blood trickled down my shirt. The man called Lester grabbed my testicles with his left hand and smashed them with his right fist. The pain was so swift and searing that it was as if there were no pain at all. There was only a stabbing heat that leaped into my head and stayed there for a moment.

"Shall we burn this yellow belly?"

"He's gone."

"I'd like a souvenir."

"Scalp him!"

"What about the other bastard?"

"He's gone, too."

They left me. On of them went to the car and took out a bottle of whisky. They started drinking, passing the bottle from hand to hand. Once in a while, when a bottle was emptied, one of them would come over and beat me. When they were drunk enough, I feared that they would burn Jose. Millar crawled painfully over to where I was lying.

"Knife in my left shoe," he whispered.

"Quiet." I rolled over and reached for the knife. Now I could cut the ropes that tied my legs. My hands were free! Then I was ready to run! I handed the knife back and whispered to Millar to roll away. I crawled in the grass slowly; when I reached the edge of the woods, I got up and tried to run. But I had almost no use of my left leg, so that most of the time I hopped through the beet fields like a kangaroo.

The night was clear and quiet. I was afraid they would see me. I heard their voices on the wind. Once a flashlight beamed from the edge of the woods. I lay flat on my stomach and watched it disappear among the trees. Then I got up and staggered toward San Jose. ★

It Ain't All Smiles and Sukiyaki

by
Sandy Maeshiro

When was the last time you went out to eat, a few hours ago, yesterday, last week? Today more and more people are eating out, not just for enjoyment but also for convenience. Because of this and the increasing ease and speed of travel, industrial food services is one of the fastest growing industries. It is also an industry that demands large numbers of unskilled laborers. In 1970, of approximately 1,000,000 waiters and waitresses, a vast majority were women. The nature of their work varies with the size and kind of food establishment, but basically the job is one of being servants to customers who are mainly male. This article will describe the oppression of waitresses by employers and customers in a high-priced Japanese restaurant where I worked.

First let me explain a few particularities about this restaurant. It is located in Beverly Hills and is considered one of the leading Japanese restaurants in the city. It prides itself on having won several awards. Most of the clientele are rich businessmen, movie stars, lawyers, and doctors who come to the restaurant for more than just a meal. Almost all of the workers are from Japan, and there were only two American-born waitresses when I worked there. Also, it is one of the few Japanese restaurants in the city that is unionized.

In the last few years there has been a sharp increase in the popularity of Japanese restaurants in Southern California. This is due in part to the overall popularity of Eastern culture in the U.S., the media image of Asia and its "charming and hospitable culture", the interest that white America has in "ethnic culture", the so-called friendship between East and West, and increasing Japanese capital in the U.S. With this rise in popularity, many Japanese and Japanese American businessmen are exploiting their culture by using it as a way to make a profit.

These restaurants symbolize places away from the hustle and bustle of the outside world. They offer comfort and escape to the customer where he is waited upon by "beautiful and charming" women who have been trained in the arts of waiting on others. The attire is a kimono and zoris, lovely to look at but highly uncomfortable and impractical. The kimono is a very confining garment, and zoris do not offer any support. This is especially important when you stop to consider that most waitresses are standing for their entire shift, which is anywhere from 6 to 8 hours. A waitress also has to be very careful of any movement she makes and never be caught in any "unladylike" positions. Thus, the waitress must take very small, careful steps (even if she's carrying a tray that weighs ten pounds and her customers want their food right away). She must make sure that her legs are covered at all times and

that when she sits she does so in a gracious manner.

Great emphasis is placed on a waitress' appearance. To insure this, daily inspections are made to check clean fingernails, clean hair, clean kimonos, and adequate make-up. Because the management is overly concerned with appearances, the women are encouraged to wear more make-up, don false eyelashes, wear wigs—in other words, become clean and inviting sexual objects.

Much of a particular restaurant's success depends on the atmosphere it sets. Waitresses are considered to be an integral part of upholding this atmosphere because of their close contact with the clientele. Therefore, waitresses in this situation are not only subjected to the regular pressures of being a waitress, but they are also expected to act out the stereotyped image of a Geisha girl.

Customers who come to these fancy Japanese restaurants are generally middle and upper-middle class people; most of them are usually white. They always ask questions like, "What part of Japan are you from?"; What does the *obi* signify?"; "Where did you learn to speak such beautiful English?" But, as soon as you begin to answer their questions, very often the customers start recounting their experiences in Japan, tell you that you are sweet and charming, and act as though they were experts on your culture. While these questions are being asked and answered,

the waitress is also suppose to remember everything that is ordered. I found that male customers often make very sexist and racist remarks, but since they are said with a smile and considered "complimentary," a waitress is supposed to respond with a smile or a blush. But, just forget something or make a human error, and you are no longer the sweet and charming Geisha, but an incompetent and irresponsible waitress.

The customers expect to be treated as though they were guest in your home, especially since part of the appeal of a Japanese restaurant lies in its emphasis on courtesy and hospitality. That is why, despite what a customer says or does to you, a waitress must keep smiling and never answer back. Remarks like, "Do you want to come home and cook for us?", are supposed to be met with humility. Never mind the racism or the degradation, you are a representative of the restaurant, and it is a part of the job to maintain a calm and relaxed atmosphere.

Working in a restaurant is like doing two jobs at the same time: one in the kitchen and bar and the other in the dining room. In the kitchen a waitress must be pushy and aggressive to be heard and get all of her orders in. She has to keep her eyes and ears open all the time. While her orders are being cooked, she also has to prepare many small dishes of tsukemono, daikon, and perhaps a raw egg: a

photos by ALAN KONDO

"hassle" during a rush hour, but considered vital part of Japanese dining.

Besides all the pressure and confusion, a waitress also has to contend with the cook and bartender who are almost always men. They too are underpaid, but instead of seeing who is causing their problems, they take out their frustrations on the waitress. They are also behind-the-scenes, so it is easy for them to be insensitive to a waitress. I often saw them release their tension, particularly on waitresses who are slow, older and losing their youth, not well liked, or women who were not willing to play games to build up their egos. A cook or bartender who does not like you can ruin your career as a waitress. This makes a waitress especially vulnerable, and the first lesson one learns is how to cope with these men in the hierarchy. If no rapport is established (that is, if you do not recognize their superiority), then a waitress will have a very hard time. Despite all the pressure of the kitchen, a waitress is expected to be calm and serve the food in a pleasing manner once she returns to the dining room.

Another unique aspect of working in a Japanese restaurant is cooking sukiyaki right at the table. During my training period, much time was spent in learning how to do this without letting my kimono sleeve slip into the pan, spilling any bean sprouts on the table or letting the tofu burn. This is one time when the customers' eyes are on you, and one must be extra careful not to make any mistakes.

The management is usually aware of some of the problems of waitressing, but because their primary concern is profits, they often use these job pressures as ways to further competition; for example, in the area of appearance, they generally do not want women who are older or who are unattractive. Knowing this and fearing the loss of their jobs, the women become very competitive, put each other down, and constantly try to outdo each other. All the while, the boss profits from their division.

In these restaurants, most of the workers speak very little English and are usually immigrants which makes it doubly hard finding other employment. Realizing this, the management makes the employee feel obligated and forever grateful, reminding him or her that employment is difficult to obtain for immigrants and that conditions in the United States are better than those in Japan. Therefore the management feels justified in taking the attitude that everyone must blindly follow their rules. This also makes it easy to keep things running smoothly, superficially, because the management can very easily intimidate the women by using various forms of harassment such as threatening to take them off the schedule for a few days to "teach them a lesson", delegate them to the poorer sections of the restaurant, singling them out as an example to the rest of the waitresses or having the cook foul up their orders. Faced with this oppressive situation, Japanese waitresses are forced

to comply with the most backward labor codes, especially in the area of ownership of gratuities (tips), length of work shifts, and union recognition.

During the time that I worked at this restaurant, there was a struggle taking place regarding the ownership of tips. To a waitress, a tip is the most direct way of letting her know whether or not she has been successful in playing the right roles throughout the hierarchy. It allows the owner to pay far below minimum wages because supposedly "tips" make up the difference. In some restaurants, particularly the one I worked in, the tips were used as a way to supplement the wages of other employees, the captains (head waitresses or waiters), bus boys and hostesses. Despite the fact that a waitress does most of the work for the tip, in the restaurant where I worked, it was common practice to seize them, take off so much for the other workers, and then re-divide them. It was precisely around this issue that we began to organize.

Section 15 of the Uniform Contract between the Restaurant-Hotel Employer's Council and the Los Angeles Joint Executive Board of the Hotel and Restaurant Employees and Bartenders' Union states:

> The gratuities shall be the property of the individual employee and shall not be deemed a part of the basic wage. No employee shall be required or permitted to contribute any part of his wages, tips or gratuities to the Captain, Headwaiter, Headwaitress. . .or anyone in charge. The Employer shall have no right to order the manner in which tips should be distributed among employees.

This particular section of our contract was being grossly violated everyday as we were forced to give 15% of our tips to the captains. We contacted the Union about this illegal practice, but it was hard to get them to enforce the contract because they knew that the management would resort to various means to single out the agitators and terminate them. The Union also wanted absolute proof and said that the only way to get action was if all the waitresses refused to comply with the management's rules, or if one waitress was willing to risk losing her job by filing a written complaint.

This was very difficult to mobilize around for several reasons: (1) waitressing, as presently organized, is an individualized occupation. Cooperation is desired, but difficult to achieve; (2) often tips are very good, so good that a waitress would hardly miss 15%; (3) most of the women were fearful of losing their job and did not want to jeopardize themselves by taking a stand; and (4) since the restaurant business fluctuates greatly, it is easier to organize during a slump. Nevertheless, we did make some progress and we were able to raise some issues. There were more than a few women involved in this struggle, and they began to see it not only as an economic problem, but also as a question of how much control they had over their jobs. In fact, one of the women's husband drafted an idea on the solution to the problem based on the principle of self-determination. The proposal first stated that the tips from customers belonged to the waitress; no one can interfere with the ownership. Secondly, it should be the waitresses who should decide how they were to distribute tips (whether they should be pooled, whether they would pay the bus boys, the amount, etc.). This proposal was supported by the women, but unfortunately we couldn't get enough cooperation from the union. In fact, I don't think that they were sensitized enough to the particular problems of Japanese restaurants.

Another resolution that was proposed was to elect a shop steward who would be the union representative at the restaurant. This way, the waitresses would have someone from their own ranks who could deal with grievances immediately. In Japanese restaurants this would be essential as there are no Asian business agents employed by the union, let alone anyone who could speak Japanese. The women did not readily agree to this proposal because they feared being singled out, due to the paranoid atmosphere. They preferred a more discreet way of dealing with the situation such as voting, a poll, or some other means. This particular struggle went on for over four months and was never fully resolved. In fact, the women often told me that they had tried before to change conditions but, after their defeat, things usually became worse. This was a constant obstacle that we faced. Nevertheless, we did learn many things through this struggle: that solidarity and trust are developed through struggle, that we each have a responsibility to each other and that the boss is not an emperor who could control our lives. We also learned more about the union we belonged to and found that even though it was not as strong as other unions, it at least offered some legal avenues for our grievances.

Waitresses have never been a militant or organized group of workers. There are many reasons for this, the most obvious being the individualized nature of the work and the constant turnover. Besides this, the tipping system discourages militancy because it gives a waitress the illusion that she can, on her own initiative, gain financial security by pleasing her customers and the boss. Despite all of these things, waitresses have gone on strike and won the right to union recognition and basic benefits. One of the most famous strikes of waitresses took place in Chicago in 1914. It lasted for approximately five months and is noted not only for the militancy of the women, but also for the horrifying brutality of the police and repressive manueverings of the legal system. The grievances expressed then are not unfamiliar to waitresses today as they revolved around conditions that continue to exist. The women were protesting the fact that they were forced to make payments to busy boys, that a dollar a day was deducted from their pay for laundry and that they were forced to pay for food which customers refused and sent back to the kitchen. This strike not only won massive support, but it also helped to pave the way for a stronger waitresses' union.

Waiters and waitresses belong to the Hotel and Restaurant Employees and Bartenders' International Union (AFL-CIO). This Union is broken down into the various crafts. Today there are no longer separate unions for waitresses or waiters. They have merged together to become a stronger collective voice in trade union activities. This merger is seen as a way to further protect the benefits and rights won by restaurant workers. It is also a way for women to obtain equal rights and pay with male workers. This action was long overdue, occurring only after State and National legislative bodies deemed it mandatory. The new union is the Dining Room and Cafeteria Union (Local 8 in Los Angeles). Since the merger was effective January 1, 1974, it is still hard to measure what effects it will have, but the leadership of the Local in Los Angeles has expressed confidence in this merging of efforts.

Despite some advancements and victories, the Union is still only a partial solution at this point. But for many restaurant workers, union recognition should be seen as the first step towards workers gaining control over their jobs. One recent significant event, particularly for Japanese restaurants, is the victory at the Nippon Club in New York City. It is the first Japanese restaurant to be organized in the history of that city and has spurred other locals into an extensive organizing campaign at other Japanese restaurants. Last year, in spite of an overwhelming National Labor Relations Board election victory by the 40 employees of the Club, the owner refused to bargain. New York Locals 1, 15, and 89 called a strike against the Club on November 9, 1973. It ended on January 10, 1974, when a three-year labor contract was signed by the Club and the three unions. This event demonstrates that it is possible to defeat the bosses by organizing and acting collectively.

The demands for more benefits and higher wages should also be coupled with challenges to the sexism and racism that waitresses face daily. Waitresses must consciously combat male supremacy and begin to see that they share a common sisterhood that could destroy the competition and rivalry that now exists. When waitresses and other restaurant workers (especially bus boys, dishwashers, bartenders and cooks) recognize that they share common problems as workers, they will be able to unite as a class to fight effectively the owners who exploit their labor, thereby fundamentally challenging a system that permits low wages, poor working conditions and racism. ★

By
Victor G.
and
Brett
de Bary
Nee

In the quiet decade of the fifties, that particular confluence of historic factors which had kept Chinatown in existence for a century seemed to dissolve. GIs who returned from the Pacific theater as American citizens found the restrictive covenant on real estate lifted in 1947, making possible for the first time the purchase of land by Chinese anywhere in the city or state. With the post-war boom in the economy, job opportunities multiplied, and college educated sons and daughters of Chinatown's small business families were absorbed in growing numbers into the expanding white collar and professional sector of American society. As these young civil service workers, accountants, engineers, doctors, and businessmen sought modest homes in the suburbs of San Francisco and cities up and down the peninsula, the dense population of Chinatown's core area began to decline. Older people remained: the owners of small groceries and laundry shops, the aging bachelors, a younger group of men who had entered Chinatown as "paper sons" during the forties, spoke no English, and depended for their living on employment in the restaurants, markets, and small factories which served the community. Businesses which catered to the specific needs of the Chinatown community, or to the tourist trade, continued to operate quietly, but there was a sense that Chinatown had outlived its usefulness and, like so many other ethnic communities at the time, was on the wane. Even the physical disintegration of the community was foreseen in the not too distant future. "It is difficult to make recommendations concerning the future of Chinatown," a San Francisco Community Renewal Program report stated in 1965, when extensive redevelopment plans were being carried out in San Francisco. "There is some evidence that this ethnic enclave is breaking up. Many younger Chinese are choosing to live away from Chinatown." All suggestions to construct new housing in Chinatown were rejected. For a decade, life went on within the static structure of the community, physically circumscribed by the same boundaries it had known for a hundred years.

In the mid-sixties, however, on the very eve of its decline, two events set in motion a process which has revitalized Chinatown in answer to a new need. On May 23, 1962, the signing of a Presidential Directive for refugees from mainland China by President John F. Kennedy broke through quota restrictions which since 1943 had held the number of Chinese immigrants to 105 a year. Three years later Lyndon Baines Johnson abolished permanently all laws limiting immigration on the basis of race or nationality, raising to 20,000 per year the quota for each Asian country, the same number set for Europe. For the first time in the history of the United States free immigration leading to the acquisition of citizenship through naturalization was possible for large numbers of Asian people. The two historic acts signaled the start of a new Chinese immigration to California on a

scale matched only by the nineteenth century flow preceding exclusion, which has reinvigorated Chinatown as a place of residence, a business center, and a community. A sharp difference in the nature of this immigration from that of the nineteenth century, however, coupled with the changed character of American society into which it has been absorbed, has placed the reborn Chinatown in a new confluence of factors from that which gave birth to the old. While the infusion of two to four thousand new residents per year has swelled the boundaries of Chinatown and reaffirmed its existence as a physical unit, the

376

The Emergence of a New Working Class

both in American society and in the lives of American Chinese. Most importantly, the liberalized immigration policy has meant that Chinese immigrants of the 1960s enter the United States as families, not, like the early laborers, as single men. They, therefore, lack the bond to China which weighed on the shoulders of men who had left their wives and children there, and confront American society as the permanent context for their lives. In addition, almost all immigrants who have entered under the 1965 Act have spent a considerable portion of their lives in Hong Kong. Fleeing the villages during the Sino-Japanese war or the period of revolutionary land reform, they have had to spend years or even decades in Hong Kong awaiting approval of their immigration. Exposure to the cosmopolitan culture of Hong Kong and the experience of working in factories, department stores, and large offices have provided a basic sense of familiarity with the workings of a big city as well as preparation for assuming some role in an urban economy. Finally, as recent Chinese immigrants have begun the process of assimilation, their transition has been further aided by the existence of nationwide movements for minority rights spawned by the black civil rights movement of the early sixties. Active struggles waged by younger, American-born Chinese have already achieved some degree of success in opening areas of employment previously closed to Chinese, thus reducing dependency on the Chinatown economy and the narrow range of occupations defined in the nineteenth century. All these factors guarantee that never again will a community of Chinese in America exist with the degree of isolation that characterized Chinatown in the past.

The high proportion of Chinese immigrants now entering the United States in a professional or technical status has been another striking distinction of the present immigration from the peasant-laborer immigration of the nineteenth century. In 1970, 3,715 Chinese professionals and technicians entered California, as compared with 2,098 service workers. In the American experience of these professional and technical immigrants, Chinatown has proved to be superfluous. Although those who have received their training and advanced degrees at Chinese institutions generally experience a brief period of downward mobility in their first few years in America, they are usually able to find jobs commensurate with their training. Other members of this group, immigrants from upper-class or professional families on the Chinese mainland who had received training and advanced degrees at American universities, have found the movement to professional positions even more smooth. In California, they have found satisfying positions in universities, laboratories, hospitals, or architectural and engineering firms and have settled in suburban homes and good residential districts. It is generally Chinese from these two groups who are the highly respected scientists, architects, scholars, or

predominance among these new residents of low income working-class families is rapidly changing the nature of Chinatown society itself and posing a severe challenge to the institutional continuity of the community. The future of Chinatown's century-old organizations, spawned by the bachelor society, adapted to the family society, and now confronting the needs and life style of this emerging working class, hangs in the balance.

Marked differences between the Chinese immigration of the 1960s and that of 1850-1880 have transformed the position and meaning of Chinatown

illustration by ROSEANNE LITZINGER

financiers well-known to American society today. While they may come to Chinatown from time to time to visit restaurants and buy food, nothing in their situation demands establishing direct ties with the community, and they do not identify with it. Of Chinese professionals now living in San Francisco only a small minority of graduate students, recruited as bilingual community workers by the anti-poverty agency, have become involved with Chinatown on a day to day basis. Indeed, as the number of Chinese who work and move freely in all areas of American society increases, Chinatown is slowly losing its significance as the center of American Chinese life.

Yet if Chinatown is no longer an inevitable necessity for all Chinese immigrants, its continuing existence is symbolic of the needs and difficulties of many of them. Despite the obvious improvement in the general situation of American Chinese over the nineteenth century, examination of the immigration of the sixties reveals that the ease of entrance into American society is still strongly affected by the social background of the immigrant. The relatively painless assimilation of recent, upper-class Chinese immigrants, thus, has not been duplicated by an equally large portion (nearly half) of Chinese who enter the United States in the status of service workers, machine operatives, craftsmen, and household workers. And what is the social background of these Chinese? By and large, they are the family members of older Chinatown laborers, separated for years and even decades by harsh immigration laws, they emigrated from Hong Kong, partly to reunite their families and partly in the hope of attaining a measure of economic improvement from increased occupational and educational opportunity in America. A long chain of circumstances, however, has determined that the realization of the dreams of this group will be slower and less certain than those of their professionally trained counterparts. As sons and daughters, or perhaps grandchildren, of Chinese overseas, most immigrants in this group grew up in families which were barely above poor peasant level in Kwangtung. Most began work when they were teenagers, as did their fathers, and never received more than a high school education.

During the Japanese occupation, World War II, or the Chinese civil war, they fled to Hong Kong with little or no savings, and found employment in sweater, jewelry, or plastics factories, and occasionally as white collar workers. In some cases, money sent in remittances from America allowed the family (because of a favorable exchange rate) a living standard which was somewhat higher than average in Hong Kong. But when the move to America at last came, all family possessions were sold and the savings of both father and children exhausted to cover transportation expenses. As they entered San Francisco—with no financial resources, with experience in manual labor but no professional skills, and with no ability to speak English—the welcome extended to this group of immigrants bore little resemblance to that experienced by the other half. The tight job market brought on by the economic recession of the late 1960s and residual discriminatory practices among many small trade, construction, and craft unions critically affected the nonprofessionally trained. Sensing insuperable language difficulties, many eventually rely on fathers or relatives (whose knowledge of English is often only slightly better) to find them jobs. Inevitably they are then thrown back, for both employment and living accommodations, on Chinatown. Within a few weeks or months of their arrival in America, they find themselves living side by side with the last of the bachelors in aging tenement houses in the old core area, and working next to the "paper sons" who came before the Second World War in the restaurants, markets, and small factories of Chinatown.

For such immigrants who find themselves forced back to Chinatown, the realization that they have entered a status in American society even lower than the one they had in Hong Kong comes as a blow. Perceiving English as the only way out of the vicious cycle of low-paying Chinatown jobs in which they have been trapped, they may enroll in night adult education courses or try to enter recently established, federally funded, English programs for Chinese. But the fact that they are already mature adults, lack academic training, must spend as much as sixty hours a week at their jobs, and study in small apartments where it is difficult to concentrate makes thorough mastery of English an unrealistic hope for most of them. All but a few eventually abandon the effort, and at that point the patterns and conditions of life which still prevail in Chinatown today—long hours of work, low pay, substandard living conditions and little expectation of change—slowly begin to make their lives bear greater and greater similarity to those of their fathers. Social workers who have watched the progress of the earlier immigrant families say that within a few years severe problems have arisen. Often they appear first in the adolescent children, who find themselves having little contact with their hard-working parents, encountering tremendous difficulties of adjustment in school, eventually dropping out and taking to the Chinatown streets. Within four or five years, when all the efforts of the parents to find better jobs and housing have failed, cases of divorce and even suicide may bring about the eventual disintegration of the family.

The continuous absorption of these new immigrants into skilled and unskilled manual positions (whether in Chinatown or outside) has transformed the nature of Chinatown's working class which previously had been made up almost exclusively of single men. Since the late 1960s this new working class made up of the families of recent immigrants plus those of middle-aged "paper sons," enabled by the new laws to bring in their wives, constitutes the majority of the population of Chinatown. In accordance with its life style and needs, it has changed the community to such a degree that those who knew it in the "quiet fifties" say they no longer recognize Chinatown today. Not only have the resurging density of population, the outcropping of scores of tiny stores piping Hong Kong popular music into the street, and a constant flux of faces in and out of Chinatown remolded the physical face of the community, the contours of its social structure itself are being subjected to intense pressure.

On a most fundamental level, the disruption of Chinatown's social fabric grows out of the qualitative difference in the life style of its new working class from that of the former small business family. In contrast to the close integration of business and family life which prevailed in Chinatown's small stores, alienation of work from family life characterizes its new working class. The severe limitation in employment opportunities for non-English-speaking immigrants, forcing both parents to take low-paying, long-hour jobs which require their absence from the home for the greater part of the day, has led to a tragic disintegration, among Chinatown's new working class, of the close and stable family life which had often in the past been seen as the basis of Chinatown's relative stability as a low-income ghetto. An explosion of juvenile delinquency which has rocked Chinatown since the sixties is the most conspicuous symptom of this. Covered sensationally by the San Francisco press, it has caught the attention of the public at large, giving rise to a sense of confusion and apprehension about the future of what had for so long been regarded as a "model ethnic community."

Simultaneous to dramatic changes in Chinatown family life has been a flaring up of age-old problems in the ghetto, now exacerbated under the pressure of unprecedented numbers of incoming residents. Basic demands for employment, housing, health, and education, which had formerly been met, in however makeshift a fashion, through Chinatown's institutions and tradition of collective responsibility, are now straining the community's resources to the breaking point. Unemployment, always high in American minority communities, was estimated at thirteen per cent for Chinatown in 1971, without taking into account the underemployment or parttime employment of hundreds of its population. Housing in the core area of Chinatown was in the most acute state of crisis of any ethnic ghetto in San Francisco. With the second highest population density rate in the nation, seventy-seven per cent of the housing in this area is sub-standard by city codes. Communal kitchens and communal bathrooms are still a way of life in the old tenement houses, where immigrant families often find themselves forced to crowd three or four people into barren 9 by 12 foot rooms built fifty years ago for single laborers. In the area of health care, as well, a crisis situation had developed by the late sixties. The old Chinese Hospital, built singlehandedly by the Chinese community during its period of severe isolation, offered sixty beds to a population which had swelled to over over forty thousand. In 1969, despite the fact that Chinatown had the highest suicide rate in the nation, there were only two Chinese-speaking psychiatrists in the city of San Francisco and an estimated twenty hours of direct psychiatric service available per week to the entire non-English-speaking, low-income population of the community. For the first time in their history, the institutions of Chinatown face a crisis the dimensions of which they lack even the physical resources to solve.

A final impact of the immigration which cannot be overlooked lies in a spiritual dimension. Despite the disruptions they have caused and the new sense of crisis in Chinatown life, the immigrants have infused a new energy and hope to a community long overshadowed by its history of defeat. In the majority of immigrant working families, this hope is expressed by a tenacious commitment to struggle on in the face of all the obstacles they are currently encountering. No matter how difficult their situation here, most say it represents an improvement over their hardships in China and later in Hong Kong. Since they have not yet encountered such a devastating force of discrimination in America as that which bore down on their fathers and the older men in Chinatown, they refuse to despair completely of someday overcoming their present difficulties. In their children who, at the very least, will receive in America the benefits of an education which they themselves could never obtain, they find hope and consolation.

The small group of immigrant professionals who have committed themselves to the Chinatown community have also contributed a new force for change. The addition of their strength to younger groups of American Chinese who are emerging as leaders of Chinatown will be a strong determinant of the new character of the community. Like the working-class immigrants, they have not had to grapple with a culture of defeat and their response to the American context has been bold and aggressive. Their education in the cosmopolitan society of Hong Kong has endowed them with valuable professional competence, fluency in English and Cantonese, and a sense of ease and familiarity in both Chinese and Western cultures. As children of refugees from mainland China, they witnessed the revolutionary transformation and emergence of modern China from universities in Hong Kong or America, and caught from it a sense of confidence, elan, and social vision. They have brought both a new self-confidence and a new perspective to the American Chinese situation as they have joined in the vigorous struggle of younger American-born Chinese for full equality and participation in American society. ★

PLANTATION STRUGGLES IN HAWAII

BY KOJI ARIYOSHI

The roots of plantation unionism in Hawaii go deep into the past—into more than 100 years of sugar workers' struggles—in the blood, sweat, tears, frustrations and hopes of thousands upon thousands.

When the sugar planters (who preceded the Big Five) trampled and inhumanely abused workers under the penal contract system prior to 1900, these roots kept growing. This was not remarkable but inevitable, for the contract laborers kept protesting, kept fighting back under a system of near slavery when planters owned them under three to five-year contracts.

Kahuku Workers Protest

Take the case of Japanese contract laborers at Kahuku plantation. On November 21-24, 1894, 150 of them marched into Honolulu, complaining of a brutal *luna* (supervisor) and miserable conditions. They were fined $5 each and marched back home, a distance of 90 miles all told. Their average monthly pay for 26 days was $12.50 and quarters.

Then again on January 4, 1895, 94 Kahuku laborers marched into Honolulu because of trouble with a *luna*. Again the fine was $5 each, and they were sent home.

As for conditions, here is a sampling: Japanese contract laborers at Paia, Maui, protested the beating of one of them in 1885. Each was fined $3. Shortly thereafter, three men dying on their feet from beriberi caused by inadequate food, refused to work. They were fined $5 each and were whipped along the 13-mile march to Wailuku. There one died in the hospital.

Early Japanese immigrant laborers waiting on the Honolulu docks. From here they were sent to various plantations throughout the islands.

Above - Japanese women gathering *kiawe* firewood for stoves and baths around the turn of the century in Hawaii.
Right - Harvesting sugar cane. Native Hawaiians carry portable tracks in right foreground while the Chinese carry and load cane in the background; a *luna* oversees on horseback.

All photos in this article are reprinted from the collection of the International Longshoremen's and Warehousemen's Union, and the Hawaii State Archives, courtesy of the Ethnic Studies Program, University of Hawaii.

Win New Freedom

The time came when in 1900 the contract system was outlawed, as islands were made a territory of the United States which itself had outlawed slavery in the 1860's, during the presidency of Abraham Lincoln.

The new freedom gave impetus to workers' struggles to win human dignity and a decent standard of living. The sugar barons and their puppets in government chopped down the workers' efforts by force and violence, economic reprisals and the use of the courts. But the roots of the movement kept growing.

Finally the workers became strong enough. In their inexperienced stage they received guidance and help from the outside. In time, they produced their own leaders who came up from the ranks. Unionism flowered. The roots became stronger, began breaking up the ground of feudalism upon which the outmoded plantation system thrived.

Unity Out of Segregation

This is a glorious history—a measure of the growth of democratic processes in Hawaii in the face of a ruthless colonial system of labor oppression by plantation management, which now clings to its weakened oligarchy and diminished special privilege.

In the march of labor on the plantations, there were Hawaiians, Chinese, Japanese, Puerto Ricans, Portuguese, Spaniards, Koreans, Russians from Siberia, Filipinos and about a dozen small groups.

Despite the plantations' divide and conquer policy of pitting workers of varying ethnic origins one against the other, they came together in the International Longshoremen's and Warehousemen's Union, whose constitution states as one of its objectives:

> To unite in one organization, regardless of religion, race, creed, color, political affiliation or nationality, all workers within the jurisdiction of this International.

With a yardstick of time and progress, measure back to 1908, when F.A. Schaefer, president of the Hawaiian Sugar Planters Association, said in his annual report:

> It is very desirable that such labor should not be too largely of one nationality as far as this can reasonably be carried out. The benefit (to the employers) of such diversity in the labor element, is too apparent to require any argument.

Or slide the yardstick back to 1894, when H.F. Glade and F.M. Swanzy stated for the Planters' Labor and Supply Company:

> ...when the planter is entirely restricted to Japanese for his labor, employing, as some do, on one estate, 800 to 1000 men, they become a menace

showing a disposition to get exacting and quarrelsome, and if disposed to make a "strike" could produce results very disastrous to the plantation. . .

    . . .a single nationality of labor on a plantation is objectionable.

First Strike at Koloa

Every immigrant labor group was brought here to be exploited, except the native Hawaiians. They were here.

The first known sugar strike took place at Koloa plantation in 1841. Hawaiian workers struck for 25 cents a day, demanding double their pay of 12½ cents. They lost after eight days.

More labor unrest of Hawaiian workers broke out in Koloa in 1850.

During this year the planters organized their first union, the Royal Hawaiian Agricultural Society (1850-56), to recruit and maintain a supply of cheaply-paid labor. It started bringing in Chinese on five-year contracts. The Chinese were called "coolies," and treated as such. Their pay was $36 a year for each laborer. The planters paid an estimated $48 for their food, housing and clothing.

R.C. Wyllie happily reported at the sixth annual meeting of the Royal Hawaiian Agricultural Society in 1856:

The wages of natives and coolies, including their

food does not exceed 33 cents a day, and that is cheaper than slave labor in the United States.

The cost of maintaining a slave on a Southern plantation was estimated at 37½ cents a day by Wyllie.

Forced to Recognize. . .

The Planters' Labor and Supply Co. was organized in 1882 to bring more workers to the islands. This was replaced by the Hawaiian Sugar Planters' Association (HSPA) in 1895.

From 1900, after the outlawing of the penal contract system, the HSPA wielded its club to destroy organizations of their demands and refused to even acknowledge their letters.

Then on July 16, 1943, the Hawaii Employers Council was formed. It became the bargaining agent for employers. In three years its representatives were to sit across the table from representatives of sugar workers to negotiate a Territory-wide contract.

Lynching of Goto

The recorded history of plantation labor struggles is far from complete. Here and there in old newspapers are brief accounts, written from the planters' point of view, generally with a planter's mentality. A few immigrants wrote their experiences, as for instance, in Japanese, but almost none of them have been translated into English. They give a picture of planter-labor relations.

Ryukichi Kihara writes in his "History of Japanese in Hawaii" about the lynching of Hiroshi Goto who came to Hawaii as a commercial observer in 1885 on the first ship that brought Japanese contract laborers. On October 29, 1889, in Honokaa, Hamakua plantation, Goto was hanged from a telephone pole with his hands and feet tied.

Goto was murdered by haoles connected with a plantation because he had learned English and fiercely championed the interests and rights of Japanese laborers. The murderers were arrested and sentenced, nine years being the maximum punishment. All managed to escape the Territory.

Vigilante Activities

Kihara gives another insight into labor relations of that period through an account about Keigoro Katsura, who played an important part in the arrest of Goto's murderers. Katsura, a lawyer in Yokohama who went to the U.S., came to Hawaii when he heard of mistreatment of Japanese on Hawaiian plantations.

Dressed in kimono and hakama (skirt) and carrying a long samurai sword, he visited the plantations on various islands, taking up the grievances of Japanese contract laborers with plantation owners. He was feared as well as hated by the white planters, and on a Big Island plantation he was beaten and locked up in a warehouse. The plantation owner complained of Katsura to Joji Nakayama, chief of the Hawaii Immigration Bureau and asked him to do something with Katsura. Nakayama made Katsura his advisor. Katsura later passed the bar examination and became the first Japanese lawyer to practice in Hawaii.

The vigilante hoodlums that lynched Goto and beat up Katsura became more organized as the years passed and labor unrest grew.

Organized Forces

In the country districts, white men were organized into a Citizens' Guard. L.M. Baldwin, sheriff of Maui, reported in 1897:

> The Guard is a useful organization and should be encouraged. Riots among our Japanese and Chinese labor are not uncommon occurrences and it is the presence of the Guard that gives assurance of security that otherwise would not prevail.

The Citizens Guards were the predecessors of the deputy sheriffs and police who were used to break strikes in recent times.

The adjutant of the Citizens' Guard wrote in 1899:

> The companies of Citizens' Guards in these outer districts are in good working order, and are in a position to be called upon at a moment's notice to check any trouble or uprising that may occur at any time amongst the ever-increasing number of Asiatics continually arriving in the Islands to supply needed labor...
>
> The moral effect upon the Asiatics of having a body of thirty or forty white men well-armed and commissioned as Special Police Officers ready at all times, has without doubt been the means of saving a great deal of trouble.

But where was the source of trouble, and who was responsible?

1890: When there were 7,612 contract laborers on sugar plantations, there were 5,706 arrests for deserting servitude and 5,387 convictions. Of the total arrests in the islands, one-third were for desertion of labor.

August 1891: 300 Chinese at Kohala rioted against planter L. Aseu, who they claimed had "shipped" them under false pretenses. Dispersed with bullock whips, 65 were arrested and dragged to jail by their queues. (This account was reprinted in the "Looking Backward" column of the *Honolulu Record*, August 10 and 17, 1950.)

December 27, 1893: 66 contract laborers struck at Paauhau because of the scarcity of water allowed them. They were fined $3.25 apiece. Their monthly pay was then $17.21 (*HR*, June 18, 1953).

January, 1894: Japanese at Koloa struck over the beating of a workman by a *luna*. The *luna* barely escaped with his life. (*HR*, June 18, 1953).

February, 1894: Japanese at Mana struck H.P. Faye's plantation after a *luna* brutally assaulted a laborer. Eighty-nine of the strikers were sent to Oahu Prison and put to work on the Pali Road (*HR*, June 18, 1953).

March 11, 1897: A group of Japanese at Spreckelsville chased and killed an interpreter who had been taking advantage of his own countrymen.

May, 1897: A riot at Lihue against head *luna* Zoller by Chinese workmen ended in Zoller's killing one man. A government investigation showed that Zoller used to swing laborers by their queues and dock them over one-third of their wages. He was fired, but several of the protestors were deported to China. The Chinese government representative said:

> The men are goaded to a point of desperation by the lunas and in the presence of the managers; then, when the Chinamen rebel at the inhuman treatment, they are battered with clubs, shot and put in prison, while the white men, who are responsible for the trouble, are allowed to go free. (*HR*, December 16, 1948; October 18, 1951)

November, 1897: 80 Japanese at Ewa started to march to Honolulu in protest against the breaking of a man's arm by a *luna*. They were arrested and fined. (*HR*, October 25, 1951)

November 1898: Galician (Ukrainian) laborers at Oahu Sugar Co. claimed that they had been brought to Hawaii under false promises. They struck for an eight-hour day. Forty of them were marched through

Honolulu "in prison garb and in regular chaingang." (*HR*, March 24, 1949; October 2, 1951)

Smallest Grievance!

Despite the planters' open control of government power, making the laws to suit their needs to exploit laborers, using vigilante outfits and the courts and the newspapers for whipping up feeling against any particular immigrant group that the planters wanted to "keep in their place," the struggle for human dignity went on ceaselessly.

The planters with a slaveholder's mentality wrote in the *Planter's Monthly* of 1894:

> Japanese and Chinese seized on the smallest grievance, of real or imaginary nature, to revolt and leave work, and it is a matter for regret that the facilities of free legal defense do much to promote appeals to law courts on frivolous pretexts.

Drawing from experience and from necessity, laborers tended to collective action. The *Report of the Bureau of Immigration*, Honolulu, said in 1899:

> Let some real or fancied grievance break the monotony and the scene changes. A tin pan is beaten noisily to alarm and summon the camp. The motley camp gathers, generally at night. The leaders harangue the followers and the mob, most of them ignorant of the real cause, rush off to demand redress or punish the offender. . . .
> The grievance is to the individual and the crowd makes it its own.

Here the immigration official expressed in his own way that laborers understood that "An injury to one is an injury to all," a slogan adopted by labor years later.

A State of Slavery

When Hawaii was annexed as a Territory to the U.S., the trade union experience here was meager. The first bona fide trade union was the Typographical Union No. 37 in Honolulu. It received its charter on August 9, 1884.

The AFL took an interest in labor conditions here. In its 19th annual convention it passed a resolution condemning contract labor as "a state of slavery," a "grave menace to the liberties of the American workers" and a violation of the U.S. Constitution since the islands had been annexed to the United States.

Contract labor was terminating, and the planters knew it. They planned for it and imported a large number of Japanese.

Congress had outlawed contract labor. It was terminated in Hawaii on June 14, 1900. The newly freed laborers began asserting their demands.

To beat down the Japanese, the planters in 1901 imported Puerto Ricans. Wages fell the following year. The wholesale importation of Japanese continued until 1907.

Today the Big Five and their propaganda fronts accuse the laborers of stirring up "racial hatred" and antagonism. They still have the monopoly on propaganda organs which are shrill in denying that they ever pitted one nationality against another.

This doesn't change history—the dilapidated shacks in the plantation areas still carry the names of Chinese Camp, Japanese Camp, Puerto Rican Camp, Spanish Camp, Filipino Camp and Portuguese Camp.

The segregation, the using of one to scab against the other, paying differential wages to national groups for performing the same work—all paid off for the boss-*haole* planters for decades until the workers realized what they were doing to themselves many years later.

Strike Won at Lahaina

At the turn of the century the quality of worker militancy changed. Before contract labor was terminated, field workers at Olaa struck in June 14, 1900, for the discharge of two *lunas*. Then 700 Olaa field hands struck again March 20-22. These strikes were lost.

The first successful strike in the history of plantation labor, April 9-14, 1900, involved 1,160 Japanese field workers at Pioneer Mill, Lahaina. Demands included wage increase, improved working conditions and industrial injury compensation. The strike was a complete victory.

Olaa field workers struck again June 6-16, involving 1,350. The workers won every demand, including increase of wages, except discharge of *lunas*.

On June 14, while the Olaa strike was on, the contract system was outlawed. A few strikes in 1900 made surrender of cancelled contracts a key issue. At Kilauea, 762 field workers lost their strike June 18-25 on this issue.

People Fight Together

In 1900 there were 25 recorded strikes, more strikes than in all the years prior to that time. These involved about 8,000 workers. Because of lack of organization, the strikes lasted but a few days.

All these strikes were a result of the ending of the contract labor system. Workers wanted to win higher wages and to gain assurance that they lost none of the benefits guaranteed them when they signed contracts.

Another new development, although isolated, was experienced in this growing labor movement. The first recorded instances of interracial cooperation of plantation laborers occurred at:

Puehuehu, June 22-24, where 188 Chinese and

Japanese field and mill workers fought together against retention of part of their wages. This strike was won.

Kilauea, November 23-December 3, where 43 Portuguese and Japanese female field workers organized to demand a raise from $8 to $10 a month. The workers won.

By 1906 the employers were using armed police intervention. Violence occurred as planters employed the "law" and tried to break strikes.

First Big Strike

A semi-union of plantation workers came to life in 1903. The Central Japanese League concerned itself with labor problems and its officials attempted to function as a conciliation board. It died after 1905.

The first plantation labor organization was formed in December 1908. It adopted the name of Higher Wage Consummation Association, more popularly known as the Higher Wage Association.

The Higher Wage Association rallied the workers for the 1909 strike, the first big strike on the Territory's sugar plantations.

"It is ironic that the first spark was struck by the *Nichi Nichi Shimbun,*" wrote Yasutaro Soga, editor of the *Nippu Jiji* for many decades, in his *Looking Backward 50 Years in Hawaii.*

The *Nichi Nichi* later became an anti-strike propaganda organ for the planters.

Newspaper Raised Demand

On August 25, 1908, the *Nichi Nichi* published an article that commented that while prices increased 20 per cent, monthly pay for the Japanese laborer was still $18 for 26 days.

Yokichi Tasaka of the *Nippu Jiji* quickly grasped this subject as the "burning issue" of the day. After wages for Japanese laborers had been increased from $16 to $18 in 1905, cost of living had gone up 23 per cent, he wrote. Furthermore, the planters paid Portuguese and Puerto Ricans $22.50 a month for doing the same work, gave them better housing and an acre of land to till.

Another paper, the *Hawaii Shimpo,* which also became the planters' mouth-piece during the strike, cautioned the Japanese workers to act with extreme prudence.

Nippu Fought. . .

The *Nippu Jiji,* alone of the Japanese newspapers, fought for the principal demand of the workers for equal pay for equal work. The Higher Wage Association demanded $1 a day or $8 a month increase, no racial differential, overtime after 10 hours, and double time on Sundays, improvement of

housing and a workers' committee to look into any discharge of Japanese employees.

The HSPA refused to bargain, an attitude it maintained for nearly 30 more years. Some Chinese went out on strike when the call went out but quickly returned to work under pressure of their consul. The Koreans stayed on the job. Hawaiians and Portuguese strikebreakers were recruited in Honolulu at $1.50 a day, almost double what the strikers had been getting.

Eviction and Jailing

The strike, which was restricted to Oahu, began May 9. Soga writes: "Aiea workers beat upon kerosene cans in an emergency summons, raising the first flame of this strike." The strike spread to Waipahu, Ewa, Waialua, Waianae, Kahuku and finally, to Waimanolo.

Eviction was a formidable weapon of the employers. Numerous arrests quickly followed the outbreak of the strike. Members of the association and storekeepers at Aiea and Waipahu—who had no connection with the strike—were arrested without warrants and held for several hours to several days in Oahu Jail (now Honolulu Jail).

Waipahu workers and their families under leadership of Masao Haneda left the plantation under eviction orders with a band leading them. Aiea workers also marched to Honolulu. From Kahuku, workers and their families marched to Honolulu, camping on the way. Waipahu and Aiea groups were met by Honolulu sympathizers with Japanese paper lanterns at Moanalua Gardens.

The Wage Association was formed and led by intellectuals in Honolulu. It was the beginning of a fledgling labor movement among alien Japanese workers and rank and file leadership which was to be forged into labor struggles.

Among the leaders of the Association were Soga; M. Yamashira, hotelkeeper; Fred Makino, a druggist; Motoyuki Negoro, who held a doctor-of-laws degree from the University of California; and other businessmen.

Use Conspiracy Charges

The planters directed their attack against these leaders, having them arrested on various "conspiracy" charges. On June 10, 1909, Soga, as well as his *Nippu Jiji* editorial, business and printing department staff, was arrested. The paper continued to come out, with outside sympathizers assisting with the company's work. The *Nippu* was the nerve center of the strikers' publicity.

Other leaders were also locked up. While they were in jail the police broke into their homes, taking their papers and valuables. At Makino's store, they blew open a safe to get at his valuables.

Leaders of the island-wide Oahu Sugar Plantation Strike of 1909, who were arrested and found guilty of third-degree conspiracy charges. *Clockwise from top left:* Motoyuki Negoro, a graduate of the University of California; Frederick Kinzaburo Makino, founder and editor of *Hawaii Hochi* in 1912; Yasutaro Soga, editor of the *Nippu Jiji*; and Yokichi Tasaka, small businessman and reporter.

The Association leaders could not engage any lawyers in Honolulu to defend them, for the lawyers were with the planters or were afraid. Only one capable attorney, J. Lightfoot, agreed to defend them at a reasonable fee.

The Territorial Attorney General appointed the law firm of Kinney, Ballou, Prosser & Anderson for the planters to handle the case arising out of the strike.

In and Out of Jail. . .

Makino, Soga and other strike leaders again were indicted and thrown in jail, and every time supporters bailed them out. Once they were bailed out in the morning and were back in Iwilei jail by nightfall on another trumped-up charge, only to be bailed out the following day.

They were charged with conspiring to boycott the anti-strike *Hawaii Shimpo* of Sometaro Sheba. Issues of the *Shimpo* piled up in post offices as workers refused to accept the copies. In this instance, bail was set at $1,200 each. Soga writes that he was indicted more than ten times.

Finally the prosecution tried four leaders for conspiracy to boycott Oahu Sugar Co. plantation business. The other charges were dropped. The trial went on in the summer of 1909, and on August 22 the four were found guilty of third degree conspiracy. They were sentenced to 10 months in jail and $300 fine. The Supreme Court upheld the lower court and denied appeal.

About this time the strike was broken. The planters had spent an estimated $2 million. The Higher Wage Association had collected $40,000 in contributions to carry on the strike and fight the court battles.

HSPA Pays Off

The Japanese workers had neither capital nor organization. Politically, they were "completely impotent" against the planters, Soga wrote later.

A Federal government report observed: "A strike conducted on exclusively national lines can hardly succeed in Hawaii. Employers are too well organized, disciplined and financed."

The first impetus for the higher wage movement had come from the Japanese newspapers, but only the *Nippu* agitated the workers and made them conscious of the need to make demands and fight for them.

The *Nichi Nichi*, which carried the first article on low wages and high cost of living "scratched the planters' palms" and received payoff money even before the strike. From February 1909 to March 1910, HSPA paid the newspaper at different times a total of $8300 in bribes.

The strike lasted from April to August 1909, but the HSPA paid off the *Nichi Nichi* through March 1910, the month the four strike leaders were jailed. All this information was revealed by Yoshigoro Kimura, reporter on the *Nichi Nichi,* to Reporter Tasaka of the *Nippu*. Editor Sometaro Sheba of the *Shimpo* is known to have received at least $100 a month from the HSPA.

387

Frameup Exposed

There was no question the plantation owners and the large business interests were behind the conspiracy frameup. To offset the Japanese militancy they imported Russians from Siberia and Portuguese. To the Russians, the planters paid $22.50 per month, a sum never before paid to new immigrants, plus daily necessities at cost and special money allowance during illness.

The frameup of the strike leaders was further exposed when J. B. Cooke, president of HSPA, gave the word to the acting governor of Hawaii to pardon the four Japanese after they had served three months in jail. Pressure came from *haole* and Japanese groups.

Again Papers Agitate

The 1909 strike brought gains, although the workers went back to their jobs in defeat. Three months after the strike the planters established a bonus system and a policy of no differentiation in ordinary laborers' wages. In 1911 the field workers' wages went up to $20 a month.

The war came, and prices soared. Sugar prices jumped from $60 to $200 a ton. A 100-pound sack of rice, which cost $3 before the war, sold for $15. *Miso* and *shoyu* prices were up. But wage rates remained the same.

From July 1917 the Japanese newspapers began agitating for higher wages. Finally, under the auspices of the Honolulu Japanese newspapers, the Plantation Laborer's Wage Increase Investigation Association was organized August 29, 1917.

The HSPA rejected wage increase proposals. Dr. Motoyuki Negoro, a leader of the 1909 strike, who was one of the four failed, wrote the HSPA for a pay raise for sugar workers in behalf of the Japanese Association of Hawaii. This proposal was rejected also.

Rank and File Moves

The voice of the rank and file was heard from the Hamakua Association of the Young Men's Association.

Takashi Tsutsumi, principal of the Japanese high school in Hilo and editor of *Hawaii Asahi Shinbun,* who became a guiding force of the 1920 sugar strike, wrote:

> Hitherto, all wage increase movements were sponsored and led by Japanese newspapers. Laborers had had nothing to do with them. The most remarkable thing about the Hamakua campaign was that these associations of young men, far removed from cities and towns, and uninfluenced by Japanese newspapers, voluntarily presented their own petition to the Planters' Association.

As usual the HSPA ignored the petition.

The rank and file movement grew. The Federated Young Men's Association of Hawaii on October 19, 1919, met in Hilo. It decided to make a collective demand to the HSPA, which could not ignore the petition.

For 8-Hour Day

Among the demands was one for an eight-hour day on plantations where field hands worked 20 hours and mill workers 12 hours.

Next, the Waialua Young Men's Buddhist Association called on all YMBA's on Oahu and in the Territory on October 25 to struggle for a wage increase.

The Japanese Association of Hawaii came forward to give leadership. Included among the leaders were newspaper editors and professional self-employed people. They formed the Plantation Laborers' Supporters Association, conducted speaking tours on the plantations for a month, and raised a strike fund and mobilized support for the wage demand. The Japanese Association was succeeded by the Federation of Labor, which carried on the strike struggle.

Tsutsumi writes in his *History of Hawaii Laborers' Movement* that the "so-called leaders of the past" attacked the leaders of 1920 who were young men who spoke both English and Japanese and thus could function independently of the past leaders. The Japanese newspapers began attacking the 1920 strike leaders. The *Nippu Jiji,* the strikers' organ of the 1909 strike, was not supportive of the leaders. Thus, the strikers took over the *Hawaii Shimpo* and put out their own paper.

Interracial Strike

The 1920 strike was the first major plantation strike which was interracial. Under the leadership of Pablo Manlapit, the Filipino Labor Union cooperated with the Japanese. Filipino workers struck first. A large segment soon went back to work, but a considerable number remained out on strike and received financial aid from the Federation of Labor. The strike was broken after six months on July 1, 1920. Over 12,000 people had been evicted from their plantation homes.

The planters spent $12 million to break the strike. The Federation had raised $600,000.

In this strike, the planters again used anti-Japanese propaganda, influencing large segments of the people that the Japanese workers wanted to take over Hawaii and overthrow the government. Despite this, the Japanese Consul General in 1920 as in 1909 took the planters' side.

Within the Japanese community a strong controversy continued after the strike. The Japanese consulate and many influential Japanese wanted to make the Federation of Labor an organization of the Japanese community.

Tsutsumi and many of those who gave leadership to the 1920 strike fought for the plan to make the Federation of Labor a Territory-wide, interracial labor oganization. A labor organization should not be used to proagate Japanism, Tsutsumi argued:

> Form a labor organization and admit all nationalities into its membership! The capitalists would not be able to raise a finger of opposition. If instead, an organization of Japanese alone is formed, the capitalists would take advantage of an excellent pretext, and would incite a racial disturbance, pitting one race against another.

Consulate's Views Prevail

The Japanese consulate and those in influence in the Japanese community had their way. Japanese plantation workers became inactive in the labor movement for about 20 years.

This was a period of diversion of alien Japanese. The strike leaders were arrested and jailed. This was a blow to labor. The Japanese school case was fought up through the U.S. Supreme Court and won. As aliens who were denied naturalization, the older Japanese were influenced in varying degrees by nationalism as Japan started on its path of aggression.

Anti-Japanese feeling increased during post World War I years. In the past the planters had whipped up this sentiment to intimidate Japanese workers and silence their demands. Now the anti-Oriental feeling on the West Coast overflowed, mixing with anti-German and anti-foreign sentiments. A result was the passage of the Japanese Exclusion Act of 1924.

These are some of the reasons that made the Japanese sugar workers withdraw from militant labor struggles.

It remained for the Filipino laborers, the last to arrive as immigrant workers, the lowest-paid and living under the worst housing conditions to carry on the plantation labor struggle.

HSPA Pays Off Ligot

The Higher Wage Movement of Filipino laborers was established in the fall of 1922. The key issue it raised was an increase in basic wage from $1 to $3 a day, without bonus. The majority of those receiving $1 a day for 10 hours of work were Filipinos.

A significant demand of the Filipinos was equal pay for men and women doing the same kind of work.

The HSPA continued to ignore the letters of the Higher Wage Movement for collective bargaining. The strike began April 1, 1924, and ended in defeat more than a year later. While Pablo Manlapit, Filipino labor leader, claimed that at the high point 12,400 were out, affecting 24 out of 45 plantations, this was, apparently, highly exaggerated.

Just as the Japanese consulate threw cold water on the strikers in 1909 and 1920, Cayetano Ligot, Philippines resident commissioner, did likewise. He actively worked hand in glove with the HSPA and was exposed for accepting money from the employers. Ligot, in an interview with the *Star-Bulletin* October 13, 1923, said the money was only a "loan."

The 1924 strike hit a new high in arrests and criminal prosecutions. Manlapit, a lawyer, and Cecilio Basan, an editor, were framed for subornation of perjury. Immediately after the trial the witnesses against Manlapit were rushed out of the Territory. One of them, Pantaleon Enayuda, chief prosecution witness, admitted in an affidavit taken at San Fernando, province of Cebu, that all the government witnesses were paid off by the HSPA. The conviction stood; a new trial was denied.

Manlapit served his minimum sentence and was forced to serve his parole in exile on the Mainland. He returned here in 1932 and with Epifanio Tack and Antonio Fagel formed the Filipino Labor Union on Maui. Manlapit left for the Philippines shortly after.

In the thirties the labor movement, nationally as well as locally, reached a new stage. Workers demanded a better deal; all people did during the depression. The political climate changed.

Last "Racial" Union

In 1937 the HSPA said:

> Since the inception of the maritime strike in 1934, we have had labor difficulties in varying degrees... The sporadic strikes have served to point out the need for closer relationship and understanding between employees and management.

The NLRA had come into effect, and seamen from the West Coast began to help organize the Hawaiian waterfront. By 1937, unionism had come to the Hilo and Honolulu docks.

On Maui, Antonio Fagel organized the last one-nationality union in the islands. On April 20, 1937, the Vibora Luviminda struck for higher wages, involving at the peak 3,500 workers. Japanese laborers provided some financial support. For the first time, outside unions gave aid, as did the militant CIO of that time.

HSPA Runs Prosecution

Fagel and nine others were arrested for kidnapping a scab. A government's prosecuting attorney was hired and paid for by the HSPA. The International Labor Defense on the Mainland sent an attorney to help the laborers.

The 1937 strike brought a turning point in collective bargaining in the sugar industry. The HSPA, which for decades had ignored representatives of

Above -Harry Bridges (left) and Jack Hall, leaders of the International Longshoremen's and Warehousemen's Union.
Left - Protesting the political persecution of their leaders during the 1950s, union members displayed floats like this all over Hawaii.

labor, finally met with them across the table.

The Vibora Luviminda strike was the first successful major strike in plantation history. The workers won a 15 per cent pay increase, the first ever to be obtained as a direct result of a plantation strike.

This was a period when the quality of labor leadership began to change rapidly through militant struggles. A few seamen interested in helping Hawaii workers assisted strikers on Maui. Among them was 23-year-old Jack W. Hall, who two years before, got off a ship in Honolulu. Years later he said:

> Well, I had been in and out of Honolulu many times on Matson and Dollar Line ships and knew the Territory needed organization. Everybody was scared to death, unemployment was terrific. The system of economic control was complete. There were blacklists and a system of espionage. . .The SUP business agent asked me to help. It looked like a good place to pitch in.

Here was a new type of labor leader who had come up from the ranks. Hall was not from the plantations, but he was a worker himself.

The days of intellectuals leading plantation labor struggles as during 1909, 1920 and 1924 strikes were over. The quality of labor movement on the plantations changed. In men like Hall and a few others who dedicated themselves to organizing sugar and other workers, the labor movement found continuity. Labor movements on the plantations no longer meant the raising of workers' demands, preparation for a strike and a strike—all conducted in a one-shot campaign fashion.

Voices of Experience

Plantation workers now heard the talk of union brotherhood, of the need of an interracial union, a one big union for all. Hall and his associates urged

Above - A "broom brigade" of haole housewives staging an anti-union demonstration.
Right - Militant workers demanding a better life in the post-World War II era.

this at Maui during the 1937 strike.

The seamen who came to Hawaii gave voice to the workers: first through the *Voice of Labor,* then the *Kauai Herald* and *The Herald.* Jack Hall was one of the editors of the *Voice,* and he edited the other two papers. Hall later became ILWU regional director. Robert McElrath, now ILWU public relations director, worked with Hall when he edited the *Kauai Herald* and *The Herald.*

These papers gave voice to the rank and file, listing their demands sharply and clearly and raising the understanding of the workers.

Here again was a new development—the publication of labor papers in the English language, giving the labor movement a continuing consciousness. Prior to this, the Oahu Japanese strikers of 1920 had put out their own paper. The *Hawaii Shimpo,* an HSPA tool in the 1909 strike, was bought by the 1920 strikers to strengthen their publicity.

History of Labor Papers

After the 1920 strike, the Kauai Labor Union of Japanese workers established the *Yoen Jiho* at Koloa on February 2, 1921. This weekly was read by alien Japanese and older AJA's [Japanese Americans] who were conversant with the language. Nearly 20 years later when the Hall edited the *Kauai Herald,* voice of the progressive league of Kauai, the new paper was published in the *Yoen Jiho* plant.

This English language labor paper had a much broader audience and a growing one. The English-speaking workers read it, including the second generation offspring of immigrant workers. Among them were AJA's whose parents had been quiet on the labor scene, since the 1920 strike. *The Voice,* the *Kauai Herald* and *The Herald* took up political issues and action and hammered away—something the alien press could not do.

ILWU Organizes

Hawaii's labor movement was no longer isolated. It was woven into the tapestry of the growing national industrial unionism.

In 1937 Hall applied for a charter for the UCAPAWA-CIO when Port Allen longshoremen whom he was aiding, led the movement to organize sugar workers on Kauai. The new movement stressed an interracial union, organizing among all types of racial groups and kinds of workers.

In August, 1941, a collective bargaining agreement, the first in the history of Hawaiian plantations, was signed with McBryde Plantation, with the union representing non-agricultural workers. This was a big milestone.

The ports in the islands were organized under the banner of the ILWU. In early 1944, the longshoremen began an organizing drive of plantation workers who were frozen to their jobs for as little as $1.50 a day when defense workers were earning $1.50 an hour.

Labor engaged in political action. In 1945 the "Little Wagner Act" was passed by the Territorial legislature.

Sugar workers who were getting a 43½-cent minimum per hour, demanded 65 cents plus perquisites, union shop, 44 instead of 48 hours per week. The employers resisted and on September 1, 1946, 28,000 sugar workers went out on strike, the first Territory-wide strike involving all nationalities. Thirty-two out of 34 plantations were struck for 79 days. The strike ended in victory for the workers, with a new minimum pay rate of 70½ cents an hour.

Rank and file laborers had come of age. In the early strikes the employers baited Japanese nationalism. By 1920 there was red-baiting, with Japanese-baiting continuing. In 1946 the employers whooped up the red scare in trying to isolate the membership from the leaders, especially from the ILWU international officers.

The object of the attack remained the same—to keep the working people down—the same as during the days when Soga, Makino, Negoro and Tasaka were prosecuted by HSPA attorneys with government titles, and when the courts were ruled by the big employers.

The facts remain the same today—the employers run the government.

In 1909, Soga and his associates were convicted by a "millionaire" jury for alleged conspiracy to disrupt plantation business.

In 1953 Jack Hall was convicted with six others for an alleged conspiracy to advocate and teach the forcible overthrow of the government.

Throughout the years the employers have sharpened and intensified political attacks on labor leaders and unions, obviously thinking it easier to confuse and divide the rank and file by such attacks.

Answer Political Attacks

But Hawaii's plantation workers and their sisters and brothers in allied unions of longshore, pineapple and miscellaneous industries, have seen through this smokescreen.

The political attacks of employers—un-American congressional hearings, public reports of the Territorial subversive committee, the red-baiting of the ILWU during strikes, the jailing of Bridges and the conviction of Hall—all have caused laborers to answer in kind. They see that economic and political struggles are tied together.

Thus, in 1950, when Bridges was jailed for speaking out against the Korean war and calling for peace, the first known political demonstration of laborers swept the plantations, setting an example for Mainland ILWU members in protesting the persecution of their leader.

Then in August 1951, when Hall was arrested under Smith Act charges, political demonstrations again swept the plantations and other industries where ILWU members work. Hall's conviction, with that of his six co-defendants, in June 1953, caused an unprecedented political protest of workers in the Territory, the like of which has never been experienced in the U.S. in this witch-hunt period and in the past few decades.

Progress. . .Progress. . .

In 1894, plantation contract laborers from Kahuku marched 45 miles to Honolulu to protest against the brutality of a *luna*. They were fined and marched back to Kahuku. Again they protested the following month and marched to Honolulu—still fighting for human dignity and a better life. Again they were fined and sent back to Kahuku.

Hawaii's labor history is written in blood, sweat, tears, hopes and laughter of people, thousands upon thousands of people—many are dead today, many have left these islands, many have left the working class to become small and medium businessmen. All have in one way or another, contributed in small and large portions, to making Hawaii a better place to live in, in the face of constant ruthlessness and scheming of employers to deprive the common people of the fruits of their labor. A few have fallen by the wayside and have sold out the workers, but the labor movement marches on.

And in the sweep and breadth and depth of their movement to uplift themselves and others along with them, plantation workers—a large segment of Hawaii's workers—have developed brotherhood and have fought discrimination. They have worked for decency instead of degradation, and a better life for working people in Hawaii. ★

THE AAFEE STORY:
Asian Americans for Equal Employment

By R. Takashi Yanagida

UNITE TO FIGHT DISCRIMINATION IN THE CONSTRUCTION INDUSTRY!

This is the story of the Confucius Plaza fight for construction jobs. It involves both new and traditional organizations in New York's Chinatown, and it portends important political changes in the Chinatown of the future. For this reason, the Confucius Plaza struggle is likely to become a watershed in the history of Chinatown and in the struggle of Asian Americans for equality everywhere.

Political movement in Chinatown in recent years, partially triggered by the sharpened conflicts of the civil rights, Black Power, and anti-war movements of the 1960's and 1970's, has been on the attack against institutions that deprive the community of adequate services and fail to advocate the civil rights of the predominantly working-class community. The rise of the People's Republic of China in world affairs undoubtedly has influenced the political temperament of the community as a whole. Thus, serious questions have been raised regarding the role of traditional community associations, in particular, the Chinese Consolidated Benevolent Associations.

The community forces pushing the Confucius Plaza issue at times drew temporary alliances with certain leaders of the CCBA and at times directly challenged the authority of the traditional institutions of the community and condemned the meddling role

that old-line officials assumed. The political support of hundreds of garment, restaurant, community office workers, and students must be seen in light of the burdening economic problems that the community faces. The conflict at the construction site and the significant political changes it portends for Chinatown can be traced through the history of one of the new organizations during this period.

Construction Industry

During the planning period for the Confucius Plaza project, the DeMatteis Construction Corporation, the developer and general contractor for the site, was concerned about acquiring special federal subsidies which required "contract compliance" approval regarding minority hiring. The company assured members of the area's Community Planning Board No. 3 and the sponsors, a group of prominent Chinese businessmen, that community workers (in particular Chinese workers) would be hired to build the complex.

Federal monies were approved to help "renew" this blighted area of southern Manhattan. The Chinese businessmen, who would eventually own the complex, many of whom are local slum landlords, were delighted and boasted of their new prominence. The city's Housing and Development Administration (HDA), the agency responsible for the site's development, looked at the project as another successful venture of big business, minority businessmen, and the government in solving the pressing housing needs of the city. And the DeMatteis Corporation itself chalked up a contract which promised $1.5 million in profits and fees plus other assorted side deals.

The $40 million required for the Plaza's complex of middle-income cooperative housing, school, stores and community service facilities is a drop in the bucket compared to the $4 billion annual New York City construction industry.

Over a decade ago, coalitions of minority community groups had initiated direct actions on construction sites throughout the city and focused attention on the blatantly racist hiring practices in the construction industry. New community groups, organizations of minority construction workers such as Harlem's Fight Back, emerged in the mid-1960's. The integrationist thrust of the Civil Rights Act of 1964 was extended through new laws and government programs to enforce "Equal Employment Opportunity" in the building trades, especially on government funded projects.

During this period, however, "contract compliance", by which construction companies agree to hire more minority workers and guarantee equal opportunity, remained unenforced "paper" commitments.

The growth of the economy created new demands for labor. The unions, restrictive and racist, continued to limit the labor pool, resulting in soaring wages for New York construction workers. The demand for minority jobs grew, however, and coupled with the month's long struggle on the streets at sites like Harlem Hospital and Boys' High School, more minority workers were finally put on the job, but in lower paying and less skilled crafts.

Mayor's Plan

In 1973, after pulling out of the infamous "New York Plan", an extremely limited minority training program, Mayor John Lindsay announced a bold new plan to break discrimination in the building trades. Executive Order 71, also known as the "Mayor's Plan", included "orientals" as a specified minority. The Plan proposed that within a few years, hundreds more Asian American workers would be hired in the higher paying and unionized construction industry. This gave community people hope that employment discrimination would end.

In early January, 1974, a group of concerned community workers and supporters approached the Equal Opportunity Office of New York City's Housing

and Development Administration with Executive Order 71 in mind. Representatives from the major local social service agencies and a new group, Asian Americans for Equal Employment (AAFEE), put forward proposals concerning the "contract compliance" of the contractors at Confucius Plaza and made known the exclusion that Asian communities sense when equal opportunity programs are implemented.

Despite repeated references by the office director, Laila Long, that granting equal employment rights to Asians would in effect take away jobs from other minorities and her threat to call out the police if protestors took actions on the site, the community workers, instead of relying on the "prestige" of social service agency directors and lawyers, continued to organize a base among people of the Chinese community.

Seventy workers attended an AAFEE Workers Committee meeting at Transfiguration Church on Mott Street in early February. A majority of the men had experience in construction work, mostly in Hong Kong; more than one-third had six or more years of experience. Also, a few had done some construction work in the U.S.

Two of the organizers, who were members of a construction local, explained the situation with hiring halls, construction sites and various programs. Other organizers explained that they had spoken with several of the project sponsors, who were members of the Chinese Chamber of Commerce and the Association for Chinatown Housing, with city agencies, with the Director of the New York Plan and the site superintendent.

All parties spoken to believed in "affirmative action" programs, whether they were real estate developers, equipment and supply companies, the unions, general contractors, subcontractors, government agencies, sponsors—but no new jobs developed.

AAFEE Emerges

In this chain of interrelated groups and interests in the mammoth construction industry, a chain which had effectively barred minority workers from fair participation in the industry, the general contractor at Confucius Plaza was seen as the link to break if Asian American workers were to make any headway. Based on this assessment, a group of Asian American construction workers, long denied their rightful opportunity in American industry, formed AAFEE to combat employment discrimination. They were joined by students and community workers in this endeavor.

That month several dozen construction workers, both unemployed and currently employed in substitute jobs entered the site. The heated argument with the site superintendent reported by the Chinese newspapers recalled the pattern of abusive job discrimination, and the coverage helped to stimulate a wave of sympathetic response from many sectors of the community.

As news spread, one of the sponsors took a more active role. Man Bun Lee, an officer of the Chinese Chamber of Commerce and the million dollar Lee Credit Union, a stock-holding board member of Confucius Plaza, was also the president-elect of the Chinese Consolidated Benevolent Association. While previous leaders of the CCBA had been vigorous proponents of Taiwan's Kuomintang involvement in American Chinatown politics, M. B. Lee preferred not to comment about Nationalists and Communists and talked only about the social problems of the community.

Several months later, Mr. Lee would steal the limelight from liberal Chinese professionals by testifying at a U.S. Civil Rights Commission hearing in New York, hitting hard at the "model minority myth" and explaining the severity of the under-employment problem, that Chinese workers must work "twice as hard to keep up" and when Asian Americans protest "we are told, you are too much of a minority!"

M. B. Lee is a new-styled liberal in Chinatown. As a self-assured businessman, he is palatable to the declining right-wing elements in the CCBA, and, by being as liberal in his rhetoric as any of the leaders of Chinatown's political clubs and social service agencies, he maintains the dominance of the CCBA in Chinatown's new politics.

M. B. Lee came to an AAFEE workers meeting in February, 1974, to make an appeal on behalf of all those wanting to see decent housing in Chinatown. DeMatteis was striving to seize ownership of the 44 story apartment tower complex, and because of certain legal clauses, the sponsors had difficulty in stopping him. The president of the powerful CCBA told the workers not to cause any controversy until the sponsorship problem was solved.

Education Campaign

AAFEE decided to mount a massive educational campaign in the community, seeing that certain interests in the community (that of the sponsors and other landlords) would try to divert the issue and confuse other workers in the community. The March, 1974, petition campaign collected 8,000 signatures, mostly from Chinatown residents, but included supporters from college campuses and other ethnic groups from the Lower East Side. The main demand of the petition was for immediate on-the-site hiring of Asian American workers. Seeing the growing interest in the issue, CCBA leaders made speeches supporting the effort, but instead of supporting demonstrations, announced that they would contact Mayor Beame to solve the controversy.

Since December, 1973, AAFEE's aim was to have a meeting with the general contractors and various subcontractors because an estimated 400 jobs would be made available during the two years of construction. According to the "Mayor's Plan", the contractors at the site were not in compliance with the law.

In April, 1974, AAFEE representatives finally had a meeting with Al DeMatteis, the President of the DeMatteis Corp., and prospects for jobs at Confucius Plaza were further dimmed. It was made clear that the Asian workers, as well as the Chinese sponsors, were seen as just little pawns in the developers' big-time game of urban redevelopment. Al DeMatteis was the man with (as he said) "big shoulders," but there was nothing more that he would do beyond attending this meeting.

On April 24, several hundred people, mostly unemployed minority construction workers, attended a rally at City Hall protesting the inaction of the new Mayor Beame's administration regarding minority employment in the building trades. Sponsored by a broad coalition of groups, the rally marked the first step of the minority workers' spring offensive on construction sites. An AAFEE speaker, Takashi Yanagida, spoke about the rich history of Asian American workers in this country and drew attention to the struggle in Chinatown.

A new coalition of six construction worker groups—including the Black Economic Survival, the Black and Puerto Rican Coalition of Construction Workers, Fight Back and AAFEE—was formed after the rally and all agreed to support AAFEE at Confucius Plaza, and a date was set for a rally.

May 16 Rally

The Chatham Square Rally was held on Thursday, May 16. Speakers from agencies such as the Chinatown Planning Council and Immigrant Social Services were heard, and there were messages from various public officials, ministers, and workers. It was then announced to the crowd of 250 that the first group of demonstrators had entered the site and that support was needed to picket the main gate. The entire crowd moved at once and marched up the Bowery.

Work stopped on various parts of the construction site as dozens of demonstrators converged on construction site. The demonstrators demanded the immediate hiring of forty Asian American workers, the inclusion of specific employment goals for increased numbers of Asian American workers in the industry, beginning with Confucius Plaza and the hiring of an investigator to monitor Confucius Plaza and other sites.

To stop the work and hit the contractors financially, demonstrators had to sit on cranes in the roads, persuade workers to stop, and argue with foremen. The police were mobilized, but with hundreds of demonstrators around the site, there was a standstill. Finally, at the end of the day, with most of the work stopped, the DeMatteis Corp. signed an arrest order, and the police arrested ten Asian American demonstrators. The war was on.

The community mobilized again the following day. Eleven were arrested, including the leaders of the Black Economic Survival Group and the Black and Puerto Rican Coalition. Site actions and picketing continued daily. But the DeMatteis Corp. refused to meet with AAFEE. Mediators from the Department of Justice, the U. S. Civil Rights Commission, and Police Headquarters tried to cool the possible "riot" situation.

Arrests

During two and a half weeks of major demonstrations, 57 arrests were made. Most counts were for criminal trespassing, though there were several charges for obstructing justice, assaulting an officer and resisting arrest. Hearings were held a month and a half later, and all charges were dismissed by the court.

Television audiences got to see skirmishes at the *Plaza* and images of a "not so quiet" Chinatown for six days. Community support swelled each day. Shops of garment workers came to maintain the picket lines, and one afternoon, garment workers at various factories donated $300 to AAFEE. The elderly of the Golden Age Club marched in every major demonstration. Signs of change were in the wind.

On May 27, AAFEE presented the issue to a meeting of the Board of Directors of the CCBA. The reactionary leaders, caught in a shifting political tide, issued a public statement supporting more jobs for Chinese, but barely veiled their actual denunciation of the demonstrations and participation of Black and Latin workers.

Chinatown's radio station, piped into most of the area's 200 garment factories, blared forth the position and told people not to attend any more demonstrations. Newspapers that previously published articles and editorials lauding the efforts of AAFEE supporters declaring that these modern day heroes were wiping away the decades of bitterness that Chinese people had faced, now refused to publish announcements from AAFEE.

Leaders of various social service agencies, many receiving funds to run employment referral programs, refused to openly support the issue any further. Social workers, who actively helped build the new organization, were pressured into taking other assignments. Meanwhile, representatives of the Housing and Development Administration (representing the City)

and various federal mediators met quietly with M. B. Lee to arrange a settlement with a "responsible" representative of the Chinese community.

Police officers spoke to leaders of other minority construction worker organizations attempting to paint a picture of tremendous chaos in the Chinese community to discourage their participation in the upcoming city-wide mobilization at Confucius Plaza.

Several low-paying trainee jobs were offered to the sponsors to help split up the community.

May 31 Demonstration

The call for a city-wide demonstration on May 31, 1974, resulted in the biggest display of public support for the struggle. 400 demonstrators joined marches throughout Chinatown and picketed the site. CCBA leaders were stunned as the issues gained wider notice and support.

The scene was rougher than previous demonstrations. The new York City Police Department deployed its full array of horses, scooters, special equipment trucks and 70 police. Hired thugs assaulted demonstrators. The clash was covered by all the major news media; yet, beyond the image of Chinatown residents kicking up some dust, few of the key issues were reported.

The first pre-trial hearing for two of the Confucius Plaza related arrests was held the following Thursday, June 6, 1974. An AAFEE volunteer, Jim Lee, operating the sound truck was stopped by a 5th Precinct police officer, and, along with an innocent middle-aged bystander, Mr. Kung, was knocked to the ground and assaulted by a policeman named Fisher. The policeman, who was known for his harrassment of youth in the community, brought the two to court on several charges, including assaulting an officer.

At the hearing, the Assistant District Attorney Hood alternately tried to impress upon the supporters in the audience that the policy of the District Attorney was to crack down heavily on disruptive demonstrations and then tried to impress on the judge that these arrests had nothing to do with the site demonstrations.

The original jailings and arraignments leading to the hearings stretched out over a two-month period. Excessive delays and undue harrassment led one of the lawyers to protest the "armed camp" atmosphere of officers lining up around the courtroom when Confucius Plaza demonstrators came for arraignment. During this period, demonstrations were held both inside and outside the Criminal Court building.

City Hall Meetings

In early June, 1974, a demonstration was held at City Hall to denounce the city government's "head-in-the sand" attitude towards the injustices at Confucius Plaza. A meeting was held at the City Council President's office on June 10, 1974, with Jane Ozeki, a representative of the President's office, Arthur Barnes and Basil Paterson of the Institute of Mediation and Conflict Resolution (the group selected by Mayor Beame to deal with construction industry disputes), AAFEE representatives, Fay Chew, Harold Lui and Takashi Yanagida and M. B. Lee, representing CCBA.

The Confucius controversy was clearly a political "hot potato" for interest groups such as the CCBA, HDA, DeMatteis Corp., and the Board of Urban Affairs. Two days later a meeting at City Hall was held with Deputy Mayor Paul Gibson and City Councilwoman Miriam Friedlander.

That week the *Village Voice,* and later the *New York Post,* exposed a corruption scandal in the Mayor's Bureau of Labor Services, the Bureau that is responsible for monitoring construction sites throughout the city. James Norton, the Director of the Bureau of Labor Services, had been caught taking taxpayers' money and using it for private vacations and paying off political cronies. Norton and seven Labor Service employees and investigators were dismissed within a week.

M. B. Lee, representing both conservative and liberal forces in the Chinatown community, was caught in a delicate situation. Norton had been in contact with the CCBA president up to the day he was fired. In an effort to appear as the responsible leader of Chinatown, Mr. Lee served to condone government corruption and divert the thrust of the protest, but he managed to emerge with his reputation relatively untarnished.

During this period, newsmedia attention was increasingly focused on the construction industry. Radio stations held special programs on Asian Americans for Equal Employment, a half-hour show appeared on WCBS and WPIX-FM broadcast editorials supporting AAFEE.

The DeMatteis Corp. and the Board of Urban Affairs held a press conference, condemning AAFEE as a "bunch of gangs" and looked forward to meeting any "responsible" representative of the Chinese community. The Consulate General of the Republic of China came forth as the "responsible" representative of the Chinese community.

The meddling of the Kuomintang Party in the local affairs of the Chinese community has for decades deadened the struggle of Chinese Americans for their rights in this country. But sweeping changes in U.S.–China relations have given the KMT regime little hope for survival.

Shifting Tides

A shifting tide has realigned certain aspects of the minority employment struggle in the construction industry in New York City. The Department of Labor issued a statement that approximately 25% minority workers be viewed as a compliance goal on New York City construction sites.

The groups that had been arranging a job settlement with AAFEE now pushed for a quick settlement. The Housing and Development Administration acknowledged that dozens of Asian workers whose names were submitted months previously, by dint of years of experience, were qualified as full-scale journeymen. Therefore, the three to five-year apprentice programs established for each trade were unnecessary. Twelve of these workers were placed on job sites by HDA, but *none* at Confucius Plaza.

Jobs at the site were a key issue to the minority worker organizations, who could exert a certain amount of political pressure when sites were located in their communities. In the absence of site monitoring, the community's ability to picket a site was the only assurance that workers once placed would have their rights upheld. Government adminstrators contended that if Asian Americans insisted that Asian Americans be hired at Confucius Plaza, then they could not work in Harlem or Bedford-Stuyvesant, since minority residents of those areas would claim the same for groups.

On Wednesday, July 10, 1974, a settlement was finally reached between the Board of Urban Affairs, the Housing and Development Administrations and AAFEE. The initial on-site immediate demand for 40 jobs for Asian Americans was exceeded, two months after the initial work stoppage and arrests. However, the site investigation program is weaker than ever. Federal Court Judge Morris Lasker, soon after the Confucius Plaza settlement, announced a ruling which was sharply critical of the Board of Urban Affairs' "New York Plan." The plan has served as the accepted, though flimsy legal guideline for the entire industry, and until this point, protected contractors from losing any government contracts, though they maintain blatantly discriminatory hiring practices.

AAFEE supporters set up a Columbus Park Rally in August, 1974, to celebrate the job victory and discuss other community issues such as inadequate schools and medical care.

If there is one point to mention about the significance of Confucius Plaza, it would have to be that once the idea of fighting against racial oppression was grasped by the community, sweeping changes and powerful forces were set in motion. The experience of oppression runs deep both in the history of Asian workers in America during the past century and in the imperialist exploits of Western powers in Asia. Where there is oppression, there is resistance. The example of Confucius Plaza in New York's Chinatown has certainly been no exception to this maxim. ★

Introduction

Past writings on Asian Americans have been predominantly on Chinese and Japanese immigrants and their descendants. The literature on other Asian immigrant groups is scanty, if not entirely lacking, at least until recent years. Apart from the national controversy aroused by Chinese and Japanese immigration, there are many reasons for this state of affairs.

The number of Korean and East Indian immigrants was miniscule in the early twentieth century, and the 1924 Immigration Act, prohibiting their entry as "aliens ineligible to citizenship," terminated this small immigration. In the case of the Koreans, moreover, they were not perceived as a distinct ethnic group. After Japan colonized Korea, unofficially in 1905 and officially in 1910, Korean emigration was sharply curtailed, and Koreans in America, against their wishes, were considered "subjects" of Japan and lumped together with Japanese immigrants by American authorities.

Numerically more than either Koreans or East Indians, early Pilipino immigrants were treated in a peculiar way. Arriving from an American colonial possession, they were considered "American nationals" on the one hand but "undesirables" on the other so that the limited literature relating to them deals with this so-called special status and the "undesirable" nature of Pilipino immigration. The fact that emigration from eastern Samoa is a post-World War II occurrence accounts for the dearth of writings about

Samoans in America. Like the early Pilipino immigrants, Samoans are classified as American nationals — neither citizen nor alien — owing to their status as subjects of an American island possession taken as a protectorate in 1889 and annexed in 1900.

To partially redress this imbalance, the selections of this section are devoted to Korean, Pilipino, East Indian, and Samoan immigrants. The elimination of the racially discriminatory quota system based on national origins, which regulated immigration from 1924 to 1965, has had a dramatic effect on the character of recent immigration, especially from South Korea and the Philippines. New Korean immigrants now constitute the third largest group of immigrants entering the United States. An original piece, the exploratory sociological essay by Edna Bonacich, Ivan Light, and Charles Choy Wong covers the growing Korean population of Los Angeles. Enumerating reasons for the prominence of Koreans in small business enterprises, they discuss the future prospects of these new arrivals in the American economy in which small business plays a diminished role.

The two historical essays on the East Indians and Pilipinos are reprints. Covering mainly the period from 1907 to 1926, Gary R. Hess traces the origins of East Indian immigration, the history of East Indian immigrants as agricultural and railroad construction laborers on the Pacific Coast, and the racism they experienced. The author also notes the participation

RECENT IMMIGRATION

of East Indian immigrants in nationalist activities to free their native country from British colonial rule, and concludes his essay with statistics on recent arrivals.

The Philippines ranks second behind Mexico as the country contributing the most immigrants to the United States since 1970. In fact, Pilipinos are expected to replace the Japanese as the most populous Asian American group by 1980.[1] In his essay, H. Brett Melendy provides a history of the old and new Pilipino immigration, comparing and contrasting the agricultural laborers of the 1920s and 1930s with the skilled professionals of the 1960s and 1970s. Discussing the motives for Pilipino immigration, Melendy also touches upon white American attitudes toward Pilipinos in America.[2]

Samoan immigration, or strictly speaking migration, began in 1951 after the closing of the American naval installation in Pago Pago on the major island of Tutuila. Many Samoans who had been employed on the naval base moved to Hawaii and a good number subsequently to the west coast. Twice as many Samoans are living now in the United States as those remaining in their native land.[3] This anomaly accounts for Samoans having one of the world's highest rates of emigration from their homeland (a situation, no doubt, shared by Puerto Ricans). Samoan communities are concentrated in areas adjoining American military establishments in Hawaii and on the west coast.[4] The largest California community is in the greater Los Angeles area centered in Carson City, Compton, and Wilmington,[5] while the second largest is in the San Francisco Bay Area. In her anthropological essay based on extensive field research in the late 1960s, Joan Ablon describes in rich detail the central role of the extended family and the Christian church in the Samoan community. These two institutions by and large facilitated the transition made by Samoans from a rural Samoa to an urban America and cohesively bind the community together. Her study suggests that the overlapping bonds of kinship, church, and ethnically-linked occupations, modified by the Samoans' new experience, contribute substantially to their survival in an urban setting.

These essays of course do not fully cover the past and present experience of these neglected Asian Americans and Pacific peoples. Much more research needs to be done. The Koreans and Pilipinos are major Asian American groups in terms of their current populations that will continue to grow barring any new nativist reactions. The East Indian and Samoan populations in all likelihood will increase, too.[6] In recent years, there has been an influx of Thais, Vietnamese, and Guamanians. While not as numerous as older, established Asian American groups, they are the newest Asian Americans who have yet to be studied at all. All of these Asian American groups, whether old or new, deserve more

399

scholarly attention than they have thus far received.

—Emma Gee

Notes

1. Tom Owan, "Asian Americans: A Case of Benighted Neglect" (unpublished Paper delivered at the National Conference of Social Welfare, San Francisco, 13 May 1975), p. 3. This paper is to be published by the Asian American Mental Health Research Center in San Diego.
2. For a recent anthology on Pilipino Americans largely from their perspective, see Jesse Quinsaat, ed., *Letters in Exile: An Introductory Reader on the History of Pilipinos in America* (Los Angeles: UCLA Asian American Studies Center, 1976).
3. Gordon R. Lethwaite et al., "From Polynesia to California: Samoan Migration and Its Sequel," *Journal of Pacific History,* 8 (1973), 133. For an annotated bibliography of the few existing works on Samoans in America, see Larry Potasi, "Bibliography on Samoans in America" (Los Angeles: UCLA Asian American Studies Center, Working Papers on Asian American Studies series, 1976).
4. California Advisory Committee to the United States Commission on Civil Rights, *Asian Americans and Pacific Peoples: A Case of Mistaken Identity* (Washington, D.C., 1975), 53. A recent report from the Office for Asian American Affairs, Department of Health, Education, and Welfare, suggests that half of the Samoan families in California are living in economic poverty (cited in Owan, 32).
5. "Samoan Community Needs," *Omai Faatasi Newsletter* (Carson City, Ca.), August 1974, p. 2.
6. In 1973, Asian Americans of Chinese, Japanese, Pilipino, and Korean descent totaled around 1,932,600 persons (see Table 14 on immigration of Asians since the 1970 Census in the appendix). According to the U.S. Immigration and Naturalization Service, 32,857 Pilipinos, 28,028 Koreans, and 22,685 Chinese in the fiscal year of 1973-1974 were classified as new immigrants. If we add these figures to the 1973 population, the total Asian American population increased to approximately 2,016,170 by the middle of 1974. In a staff paper prepared for the U.S. Social Security Administration, Tom Owan, incorporating the latest immigration figures, projects an Asian American and Pacific peoples population of over 3 million by 1980, a total which will be double the 1970 census figure of 1.5 million. (see Owan, 12). If this projected figure proves to be accurate, despite the dramatic increase in one decade, this segment of the American population will constitute just over 1 percent of the total population. Its miniscule size testifies to the effectiveness of over a century of countless anti-Asian acts, legal and extra-legal, committed to restrict severely the growth of this population. But for the various Asian American communities and the limited number of metropolitan areas in which they heavily concentrate (90% of all Asian Americans compared to 73% of the total population), these new and future arrivals will have a significant impact on reshaping the character of these communities.

The Social Organization of an Urban Samoan Community

By Joan Ablon

The definitions of the term "community" vary, but most include one or a combination of three characteristic elements: a shared geographic area; a shared culture, goals, common investments, or common destiny; a functional field of collective social action.[1] The anthropologist typically has worked with small relatively homogeneous territorial aggregates, where these and other characteristics are readily apparent. For him the term "community" has the special meaning of a close-knit social network of individuals and groups, overlapping and inter-relating in meaningful ways over a period of time.

In urban areas of the United States, one rarely finds the homogenous community familiar to the anthropologist. The nearest approximations are small ethnic or racial populations that have either chosen geographic self-segregation or have been forcibly rele-gated to a circumscribed geographic area or ghetto by poverty, language barriers, or social discrimination. The intrinsic historical significance of the geographic area often disappears with the emigration from rural farming, fishing, and hunting and gathering communi-ties. Yet, for many urban immigrants, long disenfran-chised from power or social and economic security, their urban area or "turf" may take on great symbolic importance, despite objective living conditions. The land then becomes again sacred and precious as the base of social interaction. Those who invade it in any sense may be open to attack.

Some urban anthropologists and sociologists have focused on aspects of network theory as concep-tual tools to aid them in their considerations of populations in the urban social matrix.[2] The exami-nation of personal, family, and group networks provides a flexible and realistic mode of analysis for the complex and individuated social interaction characteristic of urban life. "Community," then, might be broadly applicable to any set of social relationships as defined by specific criteria. Unless the

social field is a very small one, however, it can rarely constitute anything approaching a bounded popula-tion which shares overlapping personnel, social roles, or a functional *esprit de corps.*

A scrutiny of the social organization of ethnic populations in urban areas suggests that the concept of a functionally monolithic "little community" with a high congruence of roles and interaction as Redfield described so elegantly is not appropriate.[3] Likewise, the existence of a widely attenuated ethnicity does not necessarily provide a basis for common goals and a framework for social and political action.

Contemporary community service agencies and indigenous field workers whose interests fall under the broad rubric of community organization have faced the fact that their target populations in urban areas are exceedingly diverse. Urban dwellers are split into political, social, or religious factions and contain so few persons who know others well that developing a stable constituency for any kind of leadership or consensus for concerted action may be extremely difficult, if not impossible. In these communities, organization for hostile confrontations focused on loaded issues has proved pragmatically to be more successful and realistic than organization based on existing traditional social or political bonds. The West Coast Samoan community described here, while geographically dispersed, offers a remarkable contrast to the pattern.

This paper considers the social system of a Samoan adult population that has migrated to a West Coast city during the past two decades. The members of this population have retained a modified-traditional set of social and religious linkages, roles, and activities that makes possible the subordination of existing heterogeneity, personal disputes, and religious factions. The result is an incredibly active and viable community, readily identifiable, yet little known to the surrounding non-Samoan population of the area. The structural linkages that exist in the population are so pervasive as to constitute a func-tional little community within the city.

Migration to the Mainland

During the past two decades, an ever-increasing stream of immigrants has come to the West Coast cities from American Samoa. Some come to seek employment that will enable them to buy material

The field research on which this paper is based was carried on from 1968 to 1970. Some 75 families who represented as many of the diverse segments of the Samoan population as could be identified through on-going observation were interviewed. Contacts were made in Samoan churches, places of employment, and community agencies, although most interviews were conducted in private homes. The field research was supported by the National Institute of Mental Health, USPHS Grant No. MH-08375; General Research Support Grant No. FR-67-23 (Langley Porter Neuropsychiatric Institute), from the General Research Support Branch, Division of Research Facilities and Resources, National Institutes of Health; and Ford Foundation Grant No. 690-0231 (administered through the Urban Research and Public Service Program, University of California).

possessions which they could not afford in Samoa, even though their living standard there was comfortable. Many come because they want a mainland education for themselves or their children. Others come to investigate a larger world that will allow them to escape the restrictions of the traditional social structure, specifically the onus of immediate and constant responsibility to the family chiefs. Many persons say they wish to return to Samoa but find themselves trapped by bills and by their concern for securing the best possible educational opportunities for their children.

Sizeable emigration from American Samoa to Honolulu and the mainland cities began after 1951 when the Department of the Navy, which had administered the islands since 1900, closed the naval base at Pago Pago on the major island of Tutuila, and the administration of the territory was transferred to the Department of the Interior. Many Samoan naval personnel and their dependents were then moved to Honolulu and from there to the West Coast cities in the late 1950s. Many of these naval personnel have since retired and their families have remained in California. Other Samoans who are currently in the various branches of the service are based in California cities where their wives and children establish homes and reside during their tours of duty. The closing of the naval base in Pago Pago also reduced wage labor opportunities for civilians, and thus many more persons not directly involved in navy operations made a decision to emigrate.

An additional motivation for migration for some of the population described in this paper was active recruitment for farm labor. A California farmer transported several airplane loads of Samoans to the mainland to work in his fields in 1953. All of the men he recruited soon left this work and moved into the nearby metropolitan area. Those who had left their families in Samoa sent for them as soon as possible, and most of the single men married and settled in the area.

Some 15,000 to 20,000 Samoans now reside in San Diego, Oceanside, the greater Los Angeles area, and the San Francisco Bay area.[4] The Samoan population to be described is that residing in "Pacific City," a pseudonym for one of these urban areas, and numbers from 4,000 to 5,000 persons. These persons have adjusted with relative ease to an environment that could hardly be more different from that of their native islands. Most have little difficulty in getting and keeping jobs. A large proportion of the men work in shipyards or in heavy industry, and the women often are employed as nurses' aides in convalescent homes and hospitals. Many families are buying their own homes. They live comfortably, although not extravagantly. Samoans lead full and active lives centered about their families, their churches, and their jobs. Many live in a virtual Samoan world. They

are surrounded by extended family members. They speak Samoan most of the time, wear brightly colored Samoan attire, and eat traditional Samoan foods. Yet many of their instrumental values could be labeled "middle class." When asked why they seem to adjust rapidly to urban life, Samoans respond: "We work hard, and we help one another."

The Samoan social system, or the social network in the broadest sense, is characterized by the overlapping of personnel, social roles, and activities that are common to the small closed community, but supplemented and blended with many highly differentiated relationships with non-Samoans that are largely, although not entirely, impersonal and instrumental. This wedding of the traditional and the new, the affective and the instrumental, has resulted in a successful mode of urban adaptation.

Individuals and families in the mainland cities are functionally interrelated by traditional linkages of family and church. Because the Samoan population of Pacific City is so large, Samoans may only know relatives, friends, and persons attending their church. However, because of early village ties, schools attended in the islands, and wide affinal involvement, they *know of* other people. This general knowledge of individuals and families in Samoa springs from a relative homogeneity of culture in a small geographic area. The land mass of American Samoa comprises only 76 square miles, and the total population is only about 28,000. The great emphasis on family titles and the prestige and honor which adhere to them also tend to make family names widely known.

The following discussion focuses on the chief areas of Samoan social interaction in Pacific City: family, church, occupation, and neighborhood. The all-encompassing dimension of ethnicity is implicit in all of these.

The Extended Family

Mead provided a functional definition of the Samoan extended family that seems as appropriate to the Samoan family of California in 1970 as to that of Samoa of 1925:

> *Aiga* means relative by blood, marriage and adoption, and although no native actually confuses the three ways by which the *aiga* status is arrived at, nevertheless a blanket attitude is implied in the use of the word. An *aiga* is always one's ally against other groups, bound to give one food, shelter and assistance. An *aiga* may ask for any of one's possessions and refuse to take "no" for an answer; usually an *aiga* may take one's possessions without asking. . .No marriage is permitted with anyone termed *aiga* and all contemporary *aigas* are considered as brothers and sisters. Under the shadow of these far-flung recognized relationships children wander in safety, criminals find a haven, fleeing lovers take shelter, the traveler is housed, fed, and his failing resources reinforced. Property

is collected for a house building or a marriage; and a whole island is converted into a series of cities of refuge from poverty, embarrassment, or local retribution.[5]

The cohesiveness of the extended family strongly persists in the mainland cities. One indication is the prevalence of the extended family household. The average Samoan household numbers from 6 to 10 persons. Household composition is fluid, and various relatives come and go, the duration of their stays dependent on their reasons for being in the household and in the area. Of some 75 households spread throughout Pacific City that were contacted in the course of this research, almost all had at least one extended family member living in the home. While all categories of bilateral relatives were encountered, the more permanent relatives were frequently aging parents or unmarried siblings of one or both spouses. Temporary residents often are visitors from Samoa who may stay as long as a year on the mainland, moving through various households from city to city.

Younger relatives frequently come from Samoa to stay with married siblings, aunts, uncles, cousins, or even close family friends, for the purpose of attending school. A survey of some 17 Samoans in their late teens and early twenties revealed that only 6 were living in the homes of their parents. Mead observed that Samoan children who became dissatisfied in the household of their parents might easily move to any one of a number of other related households.[6] This access for young people desiring mainland educations remains open between households in Samoa and the mainland cities.

Young women frequently come to the mainland to serve as babysitters for relatives. Often, both the men and women in the household are employed, and even though they may ingeniously manage work shift arrangements so that adults overlap in being at home to take care of children, they desire babysitters. These young women share the economic fortunes of the family with whom they live. Most eventually go on to jobs outside of the household, frequently as nurses' aides in the same institutions where older women of their households work. Some single relatives live with a family as a cooperative endeavor to share living expenses. When single persons marry, they may continue to live with the parents or siblings of one spouse before moving to an apartment of their own. A married son may stay in the home of parents until he has several children of his own. This type of arrangement frequently occurs when the husband is a serviceman stationed out of the area, is in the merchant marine, or is employed by one of the shipping or passenger lines.

Almost every Samoan contacted in the course of this reasearch had a great variety of relatives living in separate households in the area and visited them frequently. Of some 50 adults who were queried concerning local relatives living in households other than their own, more than two-thirds had siblings in the city, and about one-half had aunts and uncles. Almost every respondent had many cousins, some as many as 5 to 10, in households of their own.

Aside from the sheer quantity of relatives, the frequency of contact between relatives was striking. Most stated they customarily see siblings more than once a week. The majority also reported they see most of their aunts, uncles, nephews, nieces, and some of their cousins at least once a week. There is a distinct correlation between attendance at Samoan churches and frequency of interaction with relatives. Most of the relatives that respondents reported seeing weekly or more than once a week attended the same church as the respondent. Those persons who said they see relatives only infrequently or on special occasions generally were those who attended small Samoan churches, non-Samoan churches, or who did not attend any church. Many Samoan churches offer a variety of activities throughout the week, providing an arena for family interaction and shared activities. The relatives whom the respondents reported seeing only once a month or less frequently were persons who attended other churches.

Every family contacted reported that they have close relatives living in the opposite end of the state; however, somewhat surprisingly in view of the frequency of local interaction, most stated that reciprocal visiting with these relatives occurs at the most once a year or not at all, unless a family crisis or special occasion necessitates such a visit.

Even with the great amount of interaction between relatives, most persons stated that they see at least some other Samoan friends or churchmates with more frequency than they see family members. It is no coincidence that the most mentioned use of free time and source of recreation was "visiting." The life style of the Samoan family and individual is a highly socially oriented one.

Most of the Samoan's kin ties can be classified as affective; they are relationships that are not only emotionally supportive but also instrumental in that they assist him in practical matters. Mead clearly described the prototypic mutual aid functions performed by members of the extended family in Samoa:

> A relative is regarded as someone upon whom one has a multitude of claims and to whom one owes a multitude of obligations. From a relative one may demand food, clothing, and shelter, or assistance in a feud. Refusal of such a demand brands one as stingy and lacking in human kindness, the virtue most esteemed among the Samoans.[7]

In Pacific City, the Samoan family and community function as a clearinghouse for information concerning employment and housing. Jobs usually are available in ship-building and ship-maintenance industries and in nursing, both familiar areas of employment in Samoa. Family and community cooperation may be a significant factor in finding jobs in these and other fields. The many small and large pockets of Samoans working together throughout the Pacific City metropolitan area attest to the effectiveness of family and community as agencies of employment.

The mutual aid function of the extended family is extremely important in times of crisis. The family may serve as an economic cushion while a person is job hunting or when he is laid off work temporarily. When family members are confronted by the expenses of a funeral or wedding, they expect to receive cash contributions of several thousand dollars, a sum always adequate to cover expenses, and money usually is left over for redistribution among kin.

Samoan informants have suggested that if a family is in chronic financial need, the relatives will contribute to pay for the trip home. The number of families receiving public welfare benefits appears to be very small in proportion to the size of the community.

Informants categorically state that no matter how infrequently they see any relative they would feel responsible for helping him with money or services at times of crisis or need. Obviously, personal attitudes toward individual relatives enter into the implementation of this idealized statement as well as the condition of the person's finances when asked to give. My own observations of behavior at the time of specific crisis situations that arose during the course of the research suggest that most relatives do indeed respond spontaneously with such aid when the need arises.[8]

Family Chiefs

Perhaps the most significant change in the social system that has occurred in the process of Samoan settlement in the mainland cities has been the diminution of the *matai* system, which defined the traditional leadership and authority structure of Samoan society. The *matai*, the family chief or title-holder, bears the responsibilities and privileges of leadership of the extended family.[9] The ranking of *matais* has traditionally structured the hierarchies of family, village, and island power. The power of *matais* in contemporary Samoa is still considerable. The *matai* of a family may dictate the daily activities of family members and may divide and distribute family resources as he sees fit. The scope and importance of the powers of the *matais* in the mainland cities have changed through the complex interaction of factors related to age and social status of migrants who first settled in California, the development of the Samoan churches, and the desires of some persons to escape the strictures that the traditional *matai* system places on their personal, social, and economic aspirations.

There are relatively few actual *matais* or family titleholders in Pacific City, and by no means one for each extended family, as in Samoa. The powers and prerogatives of the *matais* are most frequently recognized at certain circumscribed life cycle occasions, such as weddings or funerals, where they take care of business matters and serve as family spokesmen. Some changes in protocol concerning chiefly prerogatives have occurred in the absence of traditional controls imposed by the structural hierarchy in the islands and by a genuine shortage of *matais*. *Matais* who reside in the area are accorded special respect, and visiting *matais* may be honored during their presence in the area. Nonetheless, the feeling now widely exists that a family which works hard and lives well can "make it on their own" socially and economically, without a family title or titleholder.

404

The Churches

A prominent Samoan Mormon of Pacific City provided the following reminiscence:

> I have a beautiful memory from my childhood. Early on Sunday morning at 4 or 5 o'clock, the bells would ring. Not in just one village, but in every village over the whole island. All of the bells would ring, and then it would grow light slowly as the sun rose, and smoke would appear from the fires of every house. By 8 o'clock the smoke from the underground ovens would be gone because the fires would be all covered up. Then the bells would ring for church, and all the people came out. It was a vision of white, for the people came to church dressed all in white. Then after church they returned home and then the rest of Sunday was a relaxed day, a very lovely day. Samoans are a very religious people. Church going is very natural to them, but when they came here some of them got away from the church. They fell under the power of evil and worldly things.

A highly effective integration of the Christian religion with the traditional Samoan social structure has developed since the 1830's when the London Missionary Society and other Christian church groups first brought their message to the Samoan people. Students of Samoan life have clearly commented on the zealous acceptance of Christianity. Keesing observed:

> Product of a religious and philanthropic zeal that grew up in Europe and America coincident with the urge for economic and political expansion, the mission enterprise has played in Samoa an even more important role from the viewpoint of native life than either trading or political domination. In many villages today rise veritable cathedrals; every community has one church or more; a visitor may count on the largest and most handsome house in each village as belonging to the native pastor; as in medieval Europe the Bible, interpreted by those placed in authority, forms the basis of intellectual life, and the church is a center not only for religious exercises but also for social and recreational activities.[10]

The church remains the center of contemporary Samoan village life, and church attendance and household family prayer are routine. In the West Coast mainland cities, churches developed with the mushrooming of Samoan settlement to meet the needs of the new immigrants for religion and the fellowship of other Samoans. Here, too, the churches quickly became the centers of Samoan life, and stand as the perpetuators of *fa'a Samoa,* the Samoan custom. Likewise, in circular fashion, the continuing tradition reinforces the strength of Samoan Christianity in family life. There are at present 13 church groups in Pacific City: 4 Congregational, 3 Methodist, 3 Pentecostal, one Seventh Day Adventist, a Polynesian Ward of the Mormon Church, and a Catholic Benevolent Society made up of Samoan Catholics who attend various parish churches in the city.

The History of Church Development

The first Samoan church was established in Pacific City in 1957 by former members of the London Missionary Society (LMS) churches, and it ultimately affiliated with the United Churches of Christ of California. The following year a group left the church, desiring services more in the tradition of the Samoan LMS churches, and established a new congregation affiliated with the parent LMS churches in Samoa. This LMS congregation remains the most traditional church of the area as well as one of the largest. It, too, has experienced later breakaways by other groups. These two initial congregations rented facilities of other churches during their early years but since have erected impressive church structures of their own. In later years, two other Congregational church groups broke away, one maintaining an independent status connected with the Congregational Church of Jesus Christ in Samoa, a breakaway from the Samoan LMS churches, and the second affiliated with the Samoan LMS churches. The LMS churches are joined with other Samoan LMS-affiliated churches in various California cities and in Seattle. Representatives of these churches gather for meetings several times a year, and senior ministers and some deacons and other officials return to Samoa in May of each year for their annual LMS convention there. Almost all of the Samoan "Congregational" and LMS churches in the mainland cities cooperate for a variety of events throughout the year, such as church dedications.

The first Methodist church was established in the Pacific City area in 1958. Three Methodist groups now exist; they are composed of some persons who were from Methodist background in Samoa and of some who have broken away from the Congregationalist groups here. The Methodist churches are affiliated with the Samoan Methodist churches. All three are relatively small groups of 50 to 100 persons and use the church buildings of non-Samoan congregations (not necessarily Methodist) to hold their services.

In 1959, a small group left one of the LMS congregations and incorporated some Pentecostal beliefs within the LMS ritual. Two other groups eventually split away from this one. These three churches are basically Pentecostal, but they now display a range of fundamentalist belief and ritual. The smallest of these congregations, numbering about 50 members, exhibits the most emotionalism in their services, and speaking in tongues is common and expected. The tone of worship for this congregation has been set by several non-Samoan members, ardent street evangelists who were instrumental in organizing the church. While all the Pentecostal churches conduct at least some small parts of their services in English, contrary to the practice of other Samoan churches, the most fundamentalist of the Pentecostal groups conducts most of its services in English for the benefit of non-Samoan members. Standard American

began to meet with a Chinese group in a Chinese-Polynesian branch. The Polynesians formed their own branch in 1957, and the Polynesian Ward developed from this. Most of the Mormon families had been of this faith in Samoa, and many attended Mormon schools there.

Samoan Catholics in Pacific City belong to various parishes throughout the area. During the 1950's and early 1960's when many Samoans lived in one of the city's public housing projects, most Samoan Catholics belonged to the parish church nearest that project. During recent years, as families have moved to other parts of the city, they have joined other parishes. Many Catholics belong to a Samoan Catholic Benevolent Society that was established in 1959. This group meets monthly and spon-

Pentecostal hymns are sung in English or Samoan in the churches. Week-long revivals are held frequently in these churches by fundamentalist American itinerant evangelists or by visiting Samoan ministers. The Pentecostal churches are relative newcomers to Samoa; they began their activities in Samoa some 50 years ago and now have 6 churches in the islands.

A Samoan Seventh Day Adventist group began in Pacific City in 1958 as a small study group that met with a non-Samoan minister of that faith. The church developed through the years, and now holds its own Saturday religious school and church services in the church building of this minister. Another group of Samoan Seventh Day Adventists participates with the regular congregation of the church for some activities. Many Seventh Day Adventists, like the Pentecostals, tend to limit social interaction to others of their own religion. Likewise, the rigid moral stance and evangelistic mission of both groups sometimes alienates other Samoans.

There is a very active Samoan Mormon population numbering several hundred persons in Pacific City. This group comprises the majority of members of a Polynesian Ward. The history of the Ward dates from the mid-1950's when a few Samoan families

sors a number of social functions for its members throughout the year; it also staffs a choir that still returns to the original parish church mentioned above to sing during the noon mass on the last Sunday of each month.

The number of members of the Congregational and LMS churches almost equals that of all other churches combined. The two largest Congregationalist groups have memberships of more than three hundred persons. Other congregations vary from fifty to two hundred persons. There are perhaps some three hundred Mormons and probably two hundred Catholics.

Most Samoan ministers carry full-time employment in addition to their heavy church responsibilities. Only a minority receive a full salary from the church or even a meager monthly "love offering." About half of the ministers of the area are ordained; these may conduct the communion service and perform marriage and baptismal rites.

Most Samoans who migrate to the mainland cities continue to attend the church of the denomination in which they were raised or to which they were converted in the islands. A majority of the members of most churches frequently are relatives of the

photo courtesy of VISUAL COMMUNICATIONS

minister and/or of his wife. A correlated fact of church composition is that many members of a church may have emigrated from the same village or district. These facts of kinship and geography result in congregations where many members have long histories of mutual contact. Such persons may also constitute the active core members of a church. While others may be church members or attend services sporadically, they often are peripheral to the core membership in their interest and activity in church affairs.

Many persons change to another denomination if they marry a person of the other faith. Most personal conversions with strong emotional affect appear to occur in those persons swayed by the Pentecostal or Seventh Day Adventist churches. In these cases converts seek more personal communication with God or Jesus than the highly formal LMS or Methodist religions allow them. Many Samoan Pentecostals state that they have found relief from acute personal problems, such as drinking or marital discord, in their conversions. A relatively small number of Samoans attend non-Samoan churches.

The splitting-off of church members to form new congregations has a number of causes. The foremost are disagreements over religious doctrine, format of service, church administration, or management of finances. Some persons also become embroiled in personal quarrels with fellow members, or are dissatisfied with the actions or personality of their minister. Kinship appears to be a significant factor in determining church stability. When factional disputes occur, and a group breaks away from a church, those who leave are seldom close relatives of the minister or his wife. Extended family members and the affines of close relatives will often stay, despite their disenchantment with the situation.

The phenomenon of the splitting of established churches and the growth of new ones in the mainland cities is in large part owing to the absence of traditional village social structure, the functional context or matrix of the church as it has existed in Samoa. The village LMS church is integrated into the social and political structure of village life. The actions of the minister and the way he administers his church are both backed by the chiefs and villagers and subject to their approval. Likewise, church members are limited by village social structure in their actions and criticisms. Thus, stability in the performance of the pastor and the actions of the parishioners is worked out in a relationship controlled by the traditional power of the chiefs and concerted village public opinion. In the mainland cities there are no such threatening controls over the behavior or decisions of the minister. At the same time, when parishioners become upset with the actions of the minister or of fellow church members, they have other choices of Samoan churches in the area; and they usually are welcomed to any of these because churches always desire more members and more financial support.

When describing the events that led to the formation of a new church group, a minister of such a group usually relates how he was drafted or asked by a frequently disgruntled delegation of persons from his former or another church to assume leadership of a new congreagation. In such a situation, the man, often already a lay preacher, may refuse or may ask the parties to reconsider, to try to reconcile their differences with their minister, and to pray about this important matter for a period of time before deciding. If they repeatedly ask him, after taking all of these courses of action, he may yield to the wishes of the people and assume the responsibility of a new congregation.

On the other hand, many informants speak of personal ambition on the part of ministers and somewhat cynically comment on the bewildering number of churches that have developed in the past decade to serve this population of some 4,000 to 5,000 persons:

> When a man wants to be a minister, he gets a few people around him and he just starts a church. This is a problem here. In Samoa, the church is protected by the chief. But here, if people don't like what a minister does, or the minister doesn't like what the church does, they just pack up and go to another church.

And another:

> Everybody wants to be a minister. When a guy wants to be a minister, he just takes all his relatives and starts a new church. Every one of these churches is made up of people's relatives. Look at X's church. Between his family and his wife's family, they are practically all relatives except for just a few others that don't mess around that much in church business.
>
> (What if a man's relatives don't want to go with him to start a new church?)
>
> He evaluates the situation. He knows how many people will go with him and he won't start a new church unless he knows that he has enough relatives to go with him. The trouble with these Samoans is that one gets mad about something and they will say, "I'll go over there." But then, they will get mad at that church, so then they will go to another one. There are all these churches around, so they can always get mad and go to another one.
>
> When somebody gets mad and has just walked out of one church, people from the other church find out and they run to him and say, "Why don't you come to our church? Come to our church and help." Everybody is looking for more new members. Meanwhile, people are building more and more churches hoping to attract more people with the building. These churches are for several things. They are to praise God and also to build more buildings.

The Functions of the Samoan Church

As in Samoa, the churches here serve as the chief

centers of religious and social life for their members. They are also the custodians of the Samoan tradition and form the structure within which much of the cultural reorganization is taking place. Keesing commented on this function of the church in Samoa:

> In social life the church still forms the essential stabilizing, regulating, and integrating force: sanctioning the old kinship and *matai* systems together with traditional customs, providing new outlets in place of those passing or passed—opportunities for assembling and engaging in cooperative activities, means of self-expression and competition as in singing, giving, churchgoing, and the like—and making new adjustments and fusions between the old way and the new.[11]

A significant part of whatever facility in the Samoan language American-born Samoan children have frequently is developed in Sunday schools, although some Sunday schools that are less determined to maintain the language simply offer their classes in English for the benefit of the non-Samoan speaking children. In contrast, adult Sunday school classes and regular church services customarily are presented in Samoan.

Most churches offer a wide variety of activities that easily absorb a large proportion of the nonworking hours of church members. Sundays are full, beginning with Sunday school and morning, early afternoon, and/or evening services. The most traditional of the LMS churches begins Sunday with a predawn 4:30 prayer service according to the custom of some churches in Samoa. This group then meets continuously for a variety of other activities until late in the evening.

If a congregation meets in the building of another church, as is often the case, the main Sunday services cannot be held at the usual prime church hours. Some Samoan groups meet at 7:30 or 8:30 a.m. or at 1:00 or 3:30 p.m. A significant consideration in setting the time for services is the reconciliation of the work shifts of the majority of the members, many of whom work week-end days, afternoons, or nights.

A significant component of the Sunday routine of almost all Samoan church groups is the mid-day or afternoon fellowship meal, to which those who attend contribute food. While some families choose to return to their homes to eat, most stay for this sumptuous affair. Traditional Samoan foods are served: chicken, pork, ham, fish, taro, bananas, salt corned beef, salad, potato salad, a specialized dish called "chop suey" made with Chinese long rice, and other foods, supplemented by rich desserts. Bountiful display and consumption of food constitute highly important elements in Samoan social life.[12] Great quantities of food are served, and as on special occasions such as the dinners following weddings and funerals, diners often leave carrying extra food in boxes or cartons. Some groups retire to the home of the minister or to a special hall for this meal. Both men and women may exchange their very proper formal Sunday dress for colorful *lava lavas* or Samoan attire. Some groups prefer to be seated in traditional Samoan fashion on the floor. Elaborate protocol in serving usually is followed, and if there is a guest minister that day, he is properly honored with food and money. As is true of most Samoan social occasions, the spirit of the event is festive, and good-humored joking and conversation are typical of the interaction that takes place.

Many churches have Wednesday evening prayer sessions, and usually one evening a week is given to choir practice. Special church services are held for

photo courtesy of VISUAL COMMUNICATIONS

holidays, such as Thanksgiving, Christmas, New Year's Eve, and Easter, and for "White Sunday," a day in October honoring children and their accomplishments in the church. This holiday was introduced by the LMS churches and has been adopted by some other denominations. The Pentecostals and Mormons seem to arrange the busiest schedules for adult church members, and also to have a definite focus on the religious and moral education of their youth. Most churches have men's and women's service organizations that help plan and finance church activities.

All Samoan churches take great pride in their choirs. Most choirs represent their churches at various special occasions, often traveling to other cities for church dedications or special regional church meetings. The choirs also have a particular significance in the series of rites held at the time of a death.

Some churches sponsor picnics during holidays. In the past there were Samoan church softball teams, but such activites as now exist are organized by individuals and are not church-sponsored. A weekly cricket game that attracts as many as 50 or more Samoan men is held at one of the local parks. Membership of the two teams is decided by the geographic area of residence of the players.

Some churches sponsor annual fund raising *luaus* or *fiafias,* at which great quantities of food are served and a floor show of Polynesian dances is presented. Social dances are sponsored by churches for fund raising purposes. One of the several Samoan combos or rock groups of the area usually provides the music for these dances. Although the majority of persons attending such functions are Samoans, a small number of non-Samoan friends or workmates of church members usually attend also. Occasionally, several families will organize and sponsor a dance, turning over all profits to their church. An impressive amount of organization goes into all of these undertakings, reflecting both a hierarchically organized social system that carefully allocates responsibility and many years of experience with church activities.

Life Crisis or Personal Events Celebrated Within the Structure of the Church

The Samoan churches serve as the chief matrices of extra-familial social interaction in Pacific City. This is evidenced by the fact that most social activities involving more than one family are carried out within some dimension of church social structure or influence. Some families celebrate special occasions, such as birthdays, baptisms, housewarmings, school graduations, and such events as a patient's release from the hospital or a visitor's arrival from Samoa, with receptions at church or in the home. Relatives, friends, and churchmates are invited to these. The minister presents a short service, and a meal is served to the guests.

The two events of the life cycle celebrated most elaborately within the structure of the church are weddings and funerals. Both are carried out in a highly formal manner and display traditional Samoan custom modified in certain details to meet modern mainland expectations and the practical demands of the new urban area.

Most Samoan weddings take place during the spring and summer. A couple typically marries in the church of the bride's family. The church may be decorated with fine mats, which are traditional items of ritual and economic exchange in the islands,[13] and *tapa* cloth for the occasion. The wedding party ordinarily is composed of 8 or 10 attendants, formally attired in long dresses and tuxedos. The service is performed in Samoan. Weddings are held on Saturday in the late morning or at noon, and are followed by two receptions, one sponsored by the family of the bride and the other by the family of the groom. Various traditional goods such as *tapa,* sleeping or decorative mats, and fine mats are presented by the bride's family to that of the groom. His family reciprocates with the traditional gifts of money and a dress for the bride. The bride may appear at each occasion in a different formal gown. The families of both bride and groom may donate money, which is used to pay for the receptions that follow the wedding.[14]

The receptions may be held in a church social hall or in a banquet room of a large restaurant. If the groom or a parent of the bride or groom is in the service or retired from the service, the reception may be held at the local service club. The reception features an elaborate feast. Traditional speeches are presented by representatives of the newlyweds' families and by talking chiefs speaking in behalf of attendant guests. Frequently there is a floor show, and a local Samoan combo may play for dancing that continues into the evening. Cash gifts are publicly presented by a family spokesman to ministers or representatives of each of the Samoan churches of the area.

The occasion of a death calls forth a round of activities involving not only relatives, friends, and churchmates of the deceased but also at least some members of most of the Samoan churches of the area. The church attended by the deceased hosts a number of formal ceremonies prior to interment. There are often two evening religious services held in the mortuary or church. The first is a family service, attended primarily by family, close friends, and members of that church. The second service is held the evening or afternoon before the funeral. This is a public service attended by several hundred persons—family, friends, and representatives of the other Samoan churches of the area. A number of local Samoan ministers and members of the family of the deceased take part in the religious service, which constitutes the first part of the evening. Following this service, a series of hymn-singing presentations by choirs of the various local churches begins. The number of choirs varies from 7 to 12, depending on the social position of the deceased, his church affiliation, and the number of relatives and affines he has in the area, as well as the effectiveness of the communications network utilized by the family and the choir director. The director of each choir presents a gift of money to the family of the deceased before or following the choral presentation. The funeral service and burial are held the morning after the public service. Immediately following the burial, an elaborate dinner is held at the church or at a restaurant banquet hall. An exchange of traditional oratory by family spokesmen and representatives of the guests occurs during this meal.

While the series of formal services held at the time of death emphasizes relations between churches and families, a traditional ritual exchange of fine mats and gifts of money activates and places in high relief the network of relationships between members of the *aiga* and members of the Samoan community at large, all of whom may donate money to the immediate family. This money is used to pay the funeral and burial expenses, and the cost of food for visiting relatives and for the closing feast. Money that remains after all expenses are paid is distributed between the immediate family and the bilateral kin.

Collections of money are frequently organized along sibling lines or by representatives of various family and affinal groups. Relatives give fine mats and amounts of money proportionate to their closeness of relationship to the deceased and his family. The mats are later returned to their donors. By the analysis of activities involved in the donations, property exchanges, and attendance at funeral rites, significant affective relationships can be objectively mapped and weighed. I have described elsewhere, in detail, the complexities and cultural richness of these Samoan funeral rites.[15]

The Samoan Civic Association

Aside from the Samoan church congregations, the Samoan Civic Association is the only other formal Samoan social group. This group was organized in 1960 with some 200 members. The membership has decreased through the years to about half of the original number, with less than 20 persons regularly attending the monthly meetings. The Civic Association sponsors several fund raising events, usually dances or dinners, during the year. The Association offers employment assistance and gives financial help to Samoan families in times of crisis or acute need. During the early 1960's, the Association sponsored sports leagues, but these were discontinued after several years. Most of the members of the Civic Association are well established in the Samoan community and attend one or the other of the two largest Samoan Congregational churches of the area.

Occupational Settings

On-the-job contacts provide many Samoans with another dimension of social interaction with other known Samoans as well as an area for the recruitment of new Samoan or non-Samoan relationships.

Samoans work in a great variety of occupations in Pacific City. The majority of men work in the local shipyards or in heavy industry. Many others call Pacific City "home" but are away at sea much of the time with the Merchant Marine or with one of the shipping or passenger lines. Others are in one of the armed services, stationed at one of the surrounding bases. Some Samoans work in shipping and receiving areas or at ticket counters of the nearby international airport. Others are employed in service occupations. Some work in hospitals as X-ray or laboratory technicians. Others drive trucks or work in banks and small industries. A number of young Samoans are attending colleges of the area. Most Samoan women work as nurses' aides in hospitals, convalescent homes, and homes for the aged.

One of the significant economic functions of the Samoan extended family and community is to serve as a clearing house for information concerning employment opportunities. For example, three Samoans, two men and a woman, have together probably helped place more than 150 Samoans to whom they were related or who they knew would be good workers. These three Samoans are prominent in the Samoan community and are respected employees in three of the chief areas of employment mentioned above. As a result of this means of job recruitment, there are large and small pockets of

photo courtesy of VISUAL COMMUNICATIONS

Samoans working together throughout Pacific City. Many of a Samoan's workmates may be his relatives or churchmates, and these existing relationships are further reinforced by routine frequency of contact. One informant reported that among the 20 Samoan nurses' aides (of a total staff of 30 employees) at the convalescent home where she is employed, two are her sisters and two are sisters-in-law. These women live close to one another and can arrange car pools and cooperate in trading days off. Therefore, although this informant has considered higher-paying job offers, the conveniences of her present employment situation outweigh the lure of better pay. This situation is not uncommon.

On-the-job social interaction also serves as a context within which to form new friendships. Of some 50 Samoans queried as to friendships with non-Samoans, two-thirds stated that they had at least one non-Samoan friend, and most of these contacts were made at the places of employment or, in the case of those men in the Navy or Merchant Marine, with fellow servicemen.

Residential Areas

As was mentioned earlier, during the first decade of Samoan settlement in Pacific City, most of the population lived in a large low-rent public housing project. In the mid-and-late-1960's, many families bought their own homes or moved to single-unit rentals in other parts of the city. A few households still remain at the project, but most Samoans are now concentrated in several large working-class neighborhoods of the city, where families representing many ethnic groups reside, and in several adjoining suburban residential areas. The proximity of units at the housing project had allowed for more frequent casual contact between Samoan families than now is possible with the more dispersed patterns of residence. However, close relatives often live within a few minutes' automobile ride of one another, and, as mentioned above, contacts between relatives and friends are frequent.

Neighborhood does not appear to be a chief source of recruitment of new affective relationships. Very few Samoans stated that their non-Samoan friends are or had been neighbors. Relationships with non-Samoan neighbors appear to be guarded and formally cordial.

Relations with Non-Samoans

Samoans share the socially differentiated life of all city dwellers. While many significant social and even instrumental relationships can be maintained within the Samoan community, much of the daily business of city life cannot. Most Samoan families learn to cope with the complexities of urban life and to relate adequately with non-Samoans. Despite language problems that may cause some initial reticence when dealing with strangers, they customarily are outgoing and jovial. In relation to their employment, they are known to work hard and for long hours without complaint. When family obligations necessitate a Samoan's being excused from work (and this occurs frequently) or his not being able to pay his rent on time, he appears to find little difficulty in arranging for such exigencies with employer or landlord without penalty.

From their hierarchical social and political system of family and village chiefs, Samoans bring a prototypic pattern of showing respect for supervisors. For this reason many Samoans criticize current political, social, and racial protest activities as being "disrespectful," even though they may themselves be in sympathy with the cause that the protests support. I have discussed elsewhere some of the valued personality characteristics and the cultural and social factors that have facilitated the adjustment of Samoans as a group and as individuals to American life.[16]

Two-thirds of a sample of 50 Samoan adults queried about their friendships with non-Samoans stated they visited with or went places with non-Samoans. The majority of these non-Samoans were reported to be white Anglo-Americans with the remainder being Blacks, Spanish Americans, Orientals, Filipinos, and other Polynesians. By far the chief area of recruitment of these new relationships was on-the-job contact. Church events (primarily in the case of Pentecostals), neighborhood interaction, and sports activities were less frequently mentioned as areas for the development of new relationships.

Discussion

The major multi-dimensional network of Samoan kinship, church and occupational linkages in Pacific City constitutes a pervasive social system that has the potential for including almost every individual Samoan in the area. For example, one can trace the process of communication from Samoan to Samoan about a socially significant issue such as the death of a prominent local Samoan. The rapid dispersal of information concerning the death, time of funeral rites, and appropriate instructions about contributions of money, fine mats, or food can be timed and mapped.

Anthropologists are accustomed to observing the "grapevine" or system of rapid informal communication in the small community. Communication systems in the city assume more complicated forms. Funeral notices may not appear in the newspapers; nonetheless, those who need to know will find out. All Samoans have telephones, but customarily they do not list their numbers in the telephone directory. This holds true even in the case of prominent ministers. The essential point is that persons who need to know these numbers do know them or can obtain them. (The non-Samoan is the excluded party because he is largely non-essential to the Samoan social system.) Several hundred people representing all of the churches of the area can be contacted in the course of a day by telephone or face-to-face contacts at work or through home visits to recruit for emergency evening choir singing. Such a comprehensive coverage of the social field by social network extensions can be found in the small rural community but rarely in the urban situation.

The essential social frameworks in order of breadth, then, are those of ethnicity, church membership, kinship, and occupation. Ethnicity is all-encompassing. Individual village-of-origin lines do not appear significant enough to cause sub-groupings of the population. Particularly at times of crisis, Samoan identity establishes imperatives of responsibility to one's fellows simply because they are all Samoans in an alien land. Key traditional Samoan values such as hospitality, sharing, helping, and reciprocity are implemented over a field much broader than the traditional extended family or immediate church membership. Economic mobility does not appear to result in the abandonment of the Samoan social identity. Samoans who have achieved fame or prosperity in the terms of the larger non-Samoan population still relate primarily to the Samoan community, attend Samoan churches, and have not assumed a particularly ostentatious life style.

Church membership unites large numbers of people for ritual and social activities, in addition to the personal religious and moral significance of the Samoan Christian church for the individual and family. Within and overlapping church boundaries are the extended families, which maintain many of their traditional helping functions for the individual and have added new ones demanded by an environment characterized by complexities undreamed of by the Samoans whom Mead encountered in Manu'a 45 years ago. The many pockets of Samoans working together in shipyards, industry, service fields, and medical settings reflect the cohesiveness of family and community bonds, and reaffirm existing kinship and church relationships. They also reflect the interrelationship between traditional and new frameworks of social interaction. There is a surprising overlap in personnel in all of these settings, despite the immense and varied non-Samoan world in which these social networks are imbedded.

The urbanization experience of Samoans in Pacific City provides an unusual example of a non-Western village people who have adapted with relative ease to the demands of urban American life. A major factor contributing to their adaptation is the retention of a social system characterized by the traditional affective ties of the little community, modified to assist its members with the instrumental functions necessary for survival in the city. Ties of ethnicity, family, and church assist the individual in his search for employment and housing. They relieve the burden of finances at times of crisis, offer a many-faceted orientation for the new arrival, and provide an extraordinary social security in a complex and impersonal urban milieu. ★

Notes

1. For example, see Robert Redfield, *The Little Community* (Chicago: University of Chicago Press, 1955); Conrad M. Arensberg and Solon T. Kimball, *Culture and Community* (New York: Harcourt, Brace and World, 1965); Louisa Howe, "The Concept of Community: Some Implications for the Development of Community Psychiatry," in *Handbook of Community Psychiatry and Community,* ed. L. Bellak (New York and London, Gruhe and Stratton, 1964), pp. 16-46; and William J. Goode, "Community Within a Community: the Professions," in *The Concept of Community,* ed. D. Minar and S. Greer (Chicago: Aldine, 1969).

2. Elizabeth Bott, *Family and Social Networks: Roles, Norms and External Relationships in Ordinary Urban Families* (London: Tavistock, 1957); and Fred E. Katz, "Social Participation and Social Structure," *Social Forces,* 45 (1966), pp. 199-210.

3. Redfield.

4. There are no accurate census figures for the California Samoan population. The figures given here are estimates by Samoan ministers who travel widely between these cities.

5. Margaret Mead, *The Social Organization of Manu'a,* Bernice P. Bishop Museum, bulletin 76 (Honolulu: Bishop Museum Press, 1930), p. 40.

6. Margaret Mead, *Coming of Age in Samoa,* Laurel ed. (New York: Dell, 1961).

7. Ibid., p. 46.

8. Joan Ablon, "The Samoan Funeral in Urban America," *Ethnology,* 10 (1970), pp. 209-227.

9. Felix M. and Marie M. Keesing, *Elite Communication in Samoa, a Study of Leadership* (Stanford: Stanford University Press, 1956).

10. Felix M. Keesing, *Modern Samoa* (Stanford: Stanford University Press, 1934), p. 396.

11. Ibid., p. 412.

12. Keesing, *Elite Communication in Samoa,* pp. 78ff.

13. Fine mats are woven of the finest grade of pandanus and generally are about 4 feet by 5 feet in size. These mats assume much of their value from their age, the lineage of the weavers, and the various exchanges in which they have played a part. Fine mats are rarely woven now, and those in existence are considered precious possessions. They are circulated in a closed and traditional manner in the mainland cities. For a detailed discussion of the fine mat, see Mead, *Social Organization of Manu'a.*

14. For the details of the traditional wedding exchange, see ibid., pp. 74ff, 94ff.

15. Ablon, "Samoan Funeral."

16. Joan Ablon, "Retention of Cultural Values and Differential Urban Adaptation: Samoans and American Indians in a West Coast City," *Social Forces,* March 1971, pp. 385-393.

THE FORGOTTEN ASIAN AMERICANS:
The East Indian Community in the United States
By Gary R. Hess

Between 1820 and 1972, some 70,140 immigrants from India entered the United States. This immigration has been concentrated in two distinct phases. Between 1907 and 1920, approximately 6,400 Indians, mostly agricultural workers, were admitted and settled predominantly in California. Their modest numbers, by contrast with the Chinese and Japanese immigrants, did not protect the "Hindus," as immigrants from India were generally called, from the anti-Asian sentiment especially prevalent in California. Their Asian origin alone engendered fear of a "Hindu invasion" and demands for their exclusion and for reduction of their political and economic rights. Poorly educated, untrained in any skills, and ignorant of American society, the preponderance of these early East Indian immigrants were ill-equipped to cope with the situation they encountered in the United States. They quickly became and generally remained an alienated minority near the bottom of the socioeconomic scale.

During the period since World War II, and especially after the 1965 immigration law, a much larger wave of East Indians, nearly all easily assimilated professionals and their families, have migrated to the United States. Between 1946, when the American government modestly relaxed restrictions on Indian immigration, and 1965, nearly 6,000 immigrants settled in the United States. From 1966 to 1972, immigrants from India totaled 50,990, a number equivalent to more than seventy percent of all the East Indian immigrants over the last one hundred and fifty years.[1]

The East Indian community has not been fully studied. It is, of course, too early to examine very thoroughly the more recent arrivals, but even the earlier East Indian immigrants have been virtually ignored by both American and Indian scholars.[2] During the early twentieth century, the "Hindus" never approached the size of the Japanese and Chinese communities, and after 1920 they were outnumbered by the Filipinos as well. In California, the "Hindus" constituted a very small minority—both numerically and in terms of political influence—in a state of many minorities. Thus, studies of Asian Americans and of California's racial history have given scant, if any, attention to the East Indians. Scholars interested in Indian emigration have concentrated on the experiences of the more numerous overseas groups, especially those in Africa, Southeast Asia, the Pacific, and the Caribbean.[3]

By drawing on the available documents and the few studies of East Indians, it is possible to trace the history of this community in the United States. This paper will endeavor to examine not only the patterns of Indian emigration to the U.S., but also the East Indian political, social, and economic experiences, most of which proved similar to those of the other principal Asian American groups.

The early East Indian community was comprised mainly of unskilled agriculturists who arrived on the West Coast during the first decade of the twentieth century. From the beginning, however, a number of intellectuals, mostly students, also came to the United States and would later provide the leadership of the community. This migration to North America represented a very small fraction of the number of Indians who migrated overseas during the nineteenth and early twentieth centuries. Indian emigrants consisted principally of two groups: small entrepreneurs and unskilled laborers; the latter group included nearly all the emigrants to the United States and Canada. These emigrants came from the rural districts of the Punjab and, to a lesser extent, from Bengal, Gujarat, and the United Provinces (the present state of Uttar Pradesh). They were attracted by the propaganda of Canadian employers, notably railroad interests aided by steamship companies. These Canadian agents had their greatest success in northern India, especially among Sikhs. Some of the Indian immigrants had already worked overseas, usually for the British government in police and army stations in Singapore, Shanghai, and Hong Kong. Contacts with Westerners had acquainted these men, again almost all Sikhs, with the prospects for employment in America; those who had returned to India frequently experienced difficulties in adjusting to their homeland. Originating in these diverse areas, Indian emigration to Canada increased sharply; from forty-five arrivals in 1905 and 387 in 1906, the Indian immigrants in 1907 totalled 2,124 and, in the following year, they reached 2,623. In response to public pressures, the Canadian government in 1909 effectively ended Indian immigration through various means, including: (1) utilization of the "continuous voyage" provision of the Canadian immigration law, which permitted excluding immigrants who had failed to travel in a single, direct voyage from their native country; (2) a reprimand of the steamship companies for their misleading propaganda on economic opportunities available in Canada; (3) an increase in the amount of money required for immigrants to remain in the country. This Canadian policy caused much concern in the British colonial office in London, since Indians, as citizens of the British empire, had the right of migration. The effect of the exclusion policy of the Canadian government was to channel more East Indian immigrants to the United States.

Even before their exclusion from Canada, some Indians had migrated to the United States after either brief stays in British Columbia or denial of entry at Vancouver. The first relatively sizeable influx of East Indian immigrants into the United States occurred in 1907 when 1,072 entered; this represented more than the total number of arrivals from India (885) between 1899 and 1906. In 1908, an additional 1,710 Indians were admitted.[4]

Many of these immigrants sought work in the lumber industry of Washington, but they quickly encountered the resentment of white workers who feared the competition of cheap Asian laborers. On September 5, 1907, several hundred whites raided the living quarters of the "Hindu" workers in Bellingham. The mob forced about seven hundred East Indians to flee across the Canadian border. In early November, five hundred workers in Everett rounded up the "Hindus" and drove them from the city.[5] The East Indians who remained in Washington faced a worsen-

The author wishes to thank Joan M. Jensen for her suggestions and for permitting him to read her manuscript, "Outcasts in a Savage Land: The East Indian in North America," a detailed and thoughtful study of the East Indian experience.

Previous page and above - East Indians arriving in San Francisco, circa 1910.

ing economic situation. When employers increased their wages in order to avoid charges of relying on cheap labor, the public regarded the East Indians as overpaid in terms of their physical and intellectual capabilities. Such pressures, and the relative attractiveness of the California climate, prompted many Indians to move south and settle in California. The few hundred East Indians in Washington after 1910, although not posing any serious economic threat to the white workers, were still the victims of racial prejudice, which was especially manifest in residential segregation. For instance, when an Indian endeavored to purchase property in Port Angeles in 1913, real estate brokers entered into a covenant not to sell to "Hindoos or Negroes." The agreement, published in a local newspaper, rested on the premise that when "Hindoos and Negroes" settled in an area, they "have depreciated value of adjacent property and injured the reputation of the neighborhood, and are generally considered as undesirable."[6]

The incidents at Bellingham and Everett focused public attention for the first time on the latest group of Asian immigrants. Opponents of Asiatic immigration, most prominently the San Francisco-based Asiatic Exclusion League, took the initiative in warning of the East Indian "menace." In his first reports on the "Hindoo question," A. E. Yoell, secretary of the League, presented a stereotype of the East Indian as untrustworthy, immodest, unsanitary, insolent, and lustful. Responding to pressure from the

Exclusion League, immigration officials, beginning in late 1908, denied admission to many East Indians. Between 1908 and 1910, some 1,130 Indian arrivals were rejected, forty-one percent on the grounds that they would likely become public charges. Thus in 1909 only 377 East Indians entered the United States.

But in 1910, a demand for construction workers on the Western Pacific Railroad led to a relaxation of immigration restrictions. In that year, 1,782 East Indians were admitted, mostly at San Francisco. The 1910 census reported a total of 5,424 East Indian immigrants residing in the United States, with about half (2,742) in California.[7]

This influx of a few thousand East Indians into the California labor force made the "Hindus," for a brief period, the focus of anti-Oriental sentiment. On behalf of the Exclusion League, Yoell protested in December 1909 to officials in Washington against the "wholesale landings of large numbers of Hindoos," many of whom, he charged, suffered from diseases and all of whom competed against white labor. When Daniel J. Keefe, commissioner general of immigration, replied that the immigrants were not numerous and did not threaten the jobs of native Americans, Yoell recalled that Japanese immigration had started modestly only to increase by 2,000 percent in a decade. The League endorsed bills introduced in Congress to exclude immigrants ineligible for citizenship, but some believed that such legislation, designed to keep out all non-white as well as East Indians, might not be enough. They feared that the federal courts might accept "Hindus" as "white persons" eligible for citizenship. In a report of April 1910, the League reflected concern over any suggestion of racial affinity between "whites" and "Hindus":

> Students of ethnological subjects all agree that the Hindus are members of the same family that we are, and consequently all legislation based upon racial distinction might fail so far as keeping them out of the United States is concerned. As a matter of fact, we, the people of the United States, are cousins, far removed, of the Hindus of the northwest provinces, but our forefathers pressed to the west, in the everlasting march of conquest, progress, and civilization. The forefathers of the Hindus went east and became cnslaved, effeminate, caste-ridden and degraded, until today we have the spectacle of the Western Aryan, the "Lords of Creation," if we may use the simile, while on the other hand the East Aryans have become the "slaves of Creation" to carry the comparison to its logical conclusion.
>
> And now we the people of the United States are asked to receive these members of a degraded race on terms of equality. Or if they came under the law they may become citizens, and what would be the condition in California if this horde of fanatics should be received in our midst.[8]

The popular press augmented this campaign, frequently relying on the exaggerated reports of the Exclusion League. For instance, *Collier's* carried an article on the "Hindu invasion" based on the League's estimate of 10,000 East Indians in California. In October 1910, *Survey* told its readers that 5,000 "Hindus" had entered at San Francisco within the past year. In "The Tide of Turbans" published in *Forum*, Herman Scheffauer depicted the new immigrants as a "dark, mystic race," and warned that the "Hindoo invasion is yet in its infancy; only the head of the long procession has entered the Golden Gate."[9]

The primary thrust of the anti-Indian campaign was directed against the San Francisco commissioner of immigration, Hart H. North. In meetings with officials of the Exclusion League, North defended his relaxation of restrictions on the grounds that the East Indians could easily find employment in the San Francisco area. The League petitioned President William Howard Taft to remove North, accusing him of incompetence and personal gain from the employment of the cheap Indian labor. In 1910, the League's agitation encouraged a thorough examination of the East Indian community by H.A. Millis, superintendent of immigration commission investigations on the Pacific Coast. Millis' findings tended to support the League's position. While the East Indians were employed in railroad construction and in agricultural work, they were paid considerably less than other Asian laborers and were frequently employed for only brief periods. Employers, especially the railroad

companies, regarded them as the least efficient workers. On the basis of his observations and interviews, Millis concluded that no other group was so strongly opposed, and the demand for its exclusion was nearly unanimous.[10]

By 1911, the campaign to end Indian immigration had been effectively won. Washington officials encouraged North's resignation and immigration authorities at San Francisco began rejecting a majority of the East Indian arrivals. In 1911, some 517 were admitted and 861 were debarred. That trend continued during the next decade; less than 600 were admitted during the next five years before Congress virtually ended Indian immigration in 1917. Altogether, between 1911 and 1920, some 1,462 East Indians were admitted, while 1,782 were denied entry, most on the grounds that they would probably become public charges. The admissions did not equal East Indian departures; approximately 1,400 Indians voluntarily left the United States between 1911 and 1920 while an additional 235 were deported.[11]

Despite this trend toward a levelling of the East Indian population, pressures continued to formalize the exclusion policy. In Congress, Democratic Representative Denver S. Church of Fresno, California, waged a determined campaign for exclusionist legislation, but found little support. Nonetheless, his goal was accomplished as part of the 1917 immigration law which was intended to restrict immigration from southern and eastern Europe, but also provided for a "barred zone" by which laborers from nearly all of Asia, including India, were prohibited from entering the United States.[12]

The continual concern with the "Hindus," despite their numerical insignificance, underscored the pervasiveness of the anti-Oriental sentiment in California. As evidenced in the reports of the Exclusion League and the popular press, East Indians were commonly seen as but part of an Asiatic horde moving across the Pacific; they were not distinguished from the more numerous groups. Labor organizations accepted without question that Asians had to be excluded; as noted by one historian, anti-Orientalism had become an inherited and irrational act of faith. In this context, anti-Orientalism made for sound politics; thus California Progressives could couple legislation reflecting concern for the living conditions of European immigrants with other laws, for example, the 1913 Alien Land Law, showing enmity for Asians. And as recent studies have observed, California's racism reflected a national racist society. Except for its anti-Oriental emphasis, California was not unique; and its outlook toward Asians eventually gained national endorsement in the 1920s.[13]

In this atmosphere of marked hostility toward Asians, the few thousand East Indians gradually established themselves primarily in California and relied chiefly on agriculture as a means of livelihood. Typically the Indians sought work in groups with a leader serving as their agent in negotiating with employers. Owing in part to the desire of many farmers to break the Japanese monopoly on the labor supply in those areas, they had little difficulty finding employment in the Sacramento and San Joaquin valleys. Also, Indians moved into the Imperial Valley, another rapidly growing agricultural area. By 1920, many had become farm operators, leasing ranches on a share or cash basis for periods ranging from one to three years. In the vineyards and fruit orchards of the San Joaquin and Sacramento valleys, they operated farms averaging about forty acres; in 1920, Indians were operating some 85,000 acres in each of the valleys. In the Imperial Valley, they leased farms in the cotton and rice districts, and altogether were operating about 30,000 acres. Indebtedness was common, as the operators had to borrow heavily in order to meet pre-harvest rent payments. In addition, many other Indians worked, usually in groups, as itinerant farm laborers, who were often the victims of considerable seasonal unemployment.[14]

The social adjustment proved very difficult and accounted for most of the voluntary returnees to India. The 1909 Immigration Commission investigation of the East Indians suggested that they appeared the least assimilative of any immigrant group. Most of the Indians were illiterate and learned little English. They remained isolated, generally living in small groups on farms or on the fringes of towns. For all but a few, family life was unknown, at least during their first several years in America. Only a handful had managed to bring their wives from India. The possibilities for marriage in America were very restricted. The Indians regarded themselves as superior to Negroes, while whites were prejudiced against any dark-skinned people. The most acceptable and accessible mates were the Mexican women living in southern California, and, by 1920, a few East Indians had married Mexican women.[15]

The East Indians' isolation was enhanced by their retention of native customs and dress (especially the turban which was of religious significance to Sikhs). Modest Sikh temples were established, with one of the workers serving as part-time priest. At Stockton, a Sikh temple was constructed and became the headquarters of the Pacific Coast Khalsa Diwan Society. The Moslem Association of America, established at Sacramento, and the Hindustani Welfare and Reform Society of America, with its office at El Centro, sought to serve the needs of the non-Sikh population. Efforts of Christian groups to proselytize among the East Indians had negligible effect.[16]

On the political level, East Indians sought both immediate and distant objectives. Led by East Indian political refugees, they were active on behalf of their rights in America and for their native country's independence. During World War I, some nationalist leaders endeavored to mobilize the Indian immigrants for revolutionary activity against the British raj; this activity became popularly known by the British-inspired term, "Hindu conspiracy."

Political activity among the West Coast "Hindus" began as early as 1908 when Taraknath Das, a student at the University of Washington who had fled India to avoid imprisonment for his political agitation, began publishing *Free Hindustan.* In the next few years, several Indian revolutionaries sought asylum in America. Determined in their political goals, they frequently utilized the Sikh organizations as a vehicle for propagating among their fellow countrymen. In 1911 Har Dayal, who had resigned a scholarship at Oxford University as a protest against the British educational system in India, arrived in San Francisco and provided effective leadership for the West Coast political movement. He taught briefly at Stanford, but was dismissed for overplaying his university affiliation on behalf of political causes. Aided by Ram Chandra, Das, and others, Dayal organized the Ghadr (meaning "revolution" or "mutiny") party and published a weekly newspaper, *Ghadr,* and various revolutionary materials in English, Urdu, and other Indian languages. In his writings and speeches, Dayal urged his countrymen to return home for revolutionary work. In a speaking tour that brought him before gatherings of East Indians in California in 1913, he was greeted enthusiastically and secured considerable financial support. Following a speech before an anarchist rally in San Francisco, he was arrested as an undesirable alien and ordered deported, but he fled to Switzerland and then to Germany where he secured backing for Ghadr activities.[17] An immigration official in 1914 assessed the effectiveness of the revolutionary propaganda: "most of the Indian students. . .are infected with seditious ideas. Even Sikhs of the laboring class have not escaped their influence."[18]

After the outbreak of the First World War, Ghadr leaders believed that the time was now opportune to launch revolutionary projects in India. At meetings in Fresno, Sacramento, and Stockton, several hundred East Indian immigrants pledged to take part in revolutionary expeditions to India. In the fall of 1914, some four hundred East Indians left the United States in several Ghadr-organized revolutionary missions. The Ghadr party's projects to disrupt the British imperial system aborted, however, and they did so primarily because of poor planning, the effectiveness of British surveillance, and the lack of popular support in India.[19]

By 1917 the Ghadr movement in America had virtually collapsed. The British government pressured officials in Washington to curtail Ghadr activities. In early 1917, British agents helped the New York City police uncover the work of C.K. Chakravarty, who had been sent by the German government a year earlier to head the revolutionary work in the United States. Shortly afterward, the federal government indicted 105 persons on charges of conspiracy to violate the neutrality laws; only thirty-five, including seventeen East Indians, were brought to trial. At the conclusion of the well-publicized five month trial, Ram Chandra was assassinated by another Indian defendant who was immediately shot and killed by a U.S. marshal. The fourteen convicted "Hindu conspirators" received sentences ranging from four to twenty-two months.[20]

With the United States at war by the time of the trial, the "Hindus" were thus cast as traitors. It appears, however, that by the time of American intervention most East Indian workers had lost interest in the Ghadr party. The failure of the Ghadr leadership to sustain its following resulted from several factors. First, the party had virtually ignored the economic and social problems of the East Indian workers. Second, the majority of the East Indians were committed to remaining in the United States and found little appeal in the Ghadr's schemes. Once the United States had become a belligerent, the preponderance of the East Indians were loyal to the Allied cause. In this sense, the East Indian immigrants reflected the sentiment of the Indian people at home; the Indian National Congress, the Muslim League, and other political groups supported the British war effort. Finally, communalism and personal rivalries hindered efforts at cooperation in the Ghadr movement. By 1916, suspicions among the Sikhs, Muslims, and Hindus substantially weakened the Ghadr party. The "Hindu conspiracy" trial was marked by incessant bickering and disagreement among the East Indian defendants, culminating in the murder of Chandra.[21]

The moderate, but less-publicized, activities of Lala Lajpat Rai reflected more accurately the aspirations and plans of the majority of Indian nationalists at home and in America. Rai, who had long been active in the Indian National Congress, visited the United States in 1906 and returned in 1914, convinced that he could mobilize American opinion behind the nationalist cause. From his base in New York, he devoted the next five years to propagandizing the Congress party's commitment to self-government through constitutional means. He founded the India Home Rule League, lectured, and wrote extensively; his writings included the periodical, *Young India,* and a book, *England's Debt to India.* He cultivated the support of American politicians, especially those representing traditional anti-British constituencies, and liberal spokesmen, including Oswald Garrison Villard, George Kirchwey, Norman Thomas, J. G. Phelps Stokes, Roger Baldwin, Robert Morss Lovett, and John Hayes Holmes. J. T. Sunderland, a Unitarian minister who had twice visited India, lent enthusiastic backing to the Indian cause, including his book, *India in Bondage.* Yet Rai's intensive efforts were far removed from the majority of East Indians in the United States. The Home Rule League collapsed after Rai's departure in 1919, but

most subsequent nationalist activities in the United States followed the pattern set by Rai of relying for support on educated Indians and American liberals.[22]

After World War I, a resurgent anti-Orientalism adversely affected the status of East Indians and encouraged many to leave the United States. This agitation was not directed specifically at "Hindus"; rather it represented principally a renewal of the long-standing drive to exclude formally the Japanese. East Indians, however, suffered serious deprivations. With California Senator Hiram Johnson and V.S. McClatchy, retired editor of the *Sacramento Bee,* providing much of the leadership, a movement to legislate Japanese exclusion gained wide support. The Supreme Court, in the *Ozawa* decision of 1922, declared that Japanese were ineligible for citizenship; this facilitated the exclusionist campaign by enabling Congress to base the barring of the Japanese on the criterion that they were ineligible for citizenship.[23]

East Indian leaders initially welcomed the *Ozawa* decision, for it seemed to confirm their claim that persons of Indian origin were entitled to American citizenship. Since 1907 about seventy Indians had been granted citizenship, although the Justice Department had consistently contested the cases. The lower federal courts had adhered, however, to the precedent established in the 1910 *U.S. v. Balsara* and the 1913 *re Akhoy Jumar Mazumdar* decisions which held that Indians were Caucasians and thus entitled under the naturalization legislation of 1790 and 1875 to be considered "white persons" eligible for citizenship. The Supreme Court's position in the *Ozawa* case— that "white person" was synonymous with Caucasian —appeared to affirm the East Indians' right to citizenship. Although it was possible for East Indians to find support in the *Ozawa* decision, the Supreme Court justices were not concerned with the implications of their definition of "white persons" with respect to East Indians—a fact which became evident a year later.

In 1923 the Supreme Court, in the case of *U.S. v. Bhaghat Singh Thind,* relied on the "understanding of the common man" to rule that Indians were ineligible for naturalization. Thind, who had been granted citizenship by a federal court in Oregon, was a somewhat controversial figure owing to his friendship with some of the "Hindu conspirators" and his advocacy of Indian independence. In a unanimous decision, the Supreme Court held that the term "white person" in the naturalization statutes was not to be defined simply on the basis of race (as the *Ozawa* case suggested), but rather in accord with popular definition. Thus, it was argued that the Congress of 1790 associated "white persons" with immigrants from northern and western Europe, while the 1870 legislators assumed that "white persons" included immigrants from all parts of Europe. Moreover, the "barred zone" provision of the 1917 immigration law provided additional evidence that East

Indians were not regarded as fit for naturalization; in denying immigration privileges to East Indians, Congress was also expressing opposition to their naturalization. Through this reasoning, the Court concluded that the public and Congress never intended that East Indians be given naturalization privileges; "Hindus" and their children "would retain indefinitely the clear evidence of ancestry."[24]

Critics of the case frequently noted that Justice George Sutherland, who wrote the court's decision, had been born in England; perhaps, the *Modern Review* of Calcutta observed, Sutherland had been unable to overcome his prejudice against Indians.[25] It would be inaccurate, however, to hold one man responsible; the *Thind* decision represented but one phase of a widespread effort, backed by a popular consensus, to reduce non-Anglo-Saxon influences in America.

The ramifications of the *Thind* case extended beyond the establishment of a precedent for denying citizenship requests of East Indians. It provided as well a basis for annulling previous grants of citizenship. During the first three years following the *Thind* decision, federal authorities secured cancellations of the naturalizations of some fifty Indians; the courts consistently upheld the government's contention that the naturalization certificates had been illegally procured. Finally, in November 1926, the Ninth Circuit Court of Appeals, in the case of *U.S. v. Sakharam Ganesh Pandit,* denied a government request by upholding the argument of Pandit, a lawyer in California, that his naturalization in 1914 had been granted by a court fully empowered to act and hence had been procured legally. The *Pandit* decision slowed, but did not end the government's efforts to disallow Indian citizenship; as late as the mid-1930s, the government was still contesting the naturalization certificates of East Indians.[26]

In addition to its effect on the Indians' claim to citizenship, the *Thind* decision also subjected East Indians to the more restrictive provisions of the California Alien Land Law, which prohibited leasing or sale of land to aliens ineligible for citizenship. For several years prior to the *Thind* case, the Exclusion League and others had been calling attention to the rapid increase of agricultural land being leased or purchased by the "Hindus." It was especially for this reason that California newspapers, including the *Sacramento Bee,* the *San Francisco Chronicle,* and the *Fresno Morning Republican,* and various political leaders praised the *Thind* decision.[27]

In the face of these pressures, many East Indians left the United States. Between 1920 and 1940, some 3,000 returned to India; most left voluntarily, although a few hundred were deported. By 1930, the "Hindu" population had dropped to 3,130 and, in 1940, to 2,405. But during this same period, 3,000 East Indians, by conservative estimate, entered the United States illegally; they were mostly farm laborers who came via Mexico. Many of these men were apprehended and deported, but others, certainly at least several hundred, managed to remain and became absorbed in the East Indian community.[28] Although the preponderance (sixty percent) of the East Indians in 1940 still lived in California, their numbers in California had declined by forty-six percent since 1910 (from 2,742 to 1,476).

The status of the small community had not improved over the years. By 1940 only a handful (four percent) were professionals; nearly half were farm laborers, fifteen percent were farmers or farm managers, and an additional twenty percent were engaged in nonfarm labor. Of the 1,600 East Indians over age twenty-five, more than a third had not completed even a year of schooling. The median school years completed among East Indians were 3.7. This was lower than the educational accomplishment of any other racial and ethnic group reported in the 1940 census. (The Chinese were next at 5.5 median school years completed.) Moreover, the East Indians now constituted an aging community; fifty-six percent were over age forty, thirty-two percent over fifty, and nine percent over sixty.[29]

Indeed, it seemed to some observers that the East Indians were losing much of their cultural identity. Due to their small numbers and pattern of living in isolation, they had difficulty in forming a strong community. The strongest unifying force was religion, with East Indians from throughout California visiting the mosques and temples on holy days; the Sikh Temple at Stockton still served as the principal center of religious and social contacts. Occasionally, the rural East Indians found a sense of community among the Mexican Americans with whom they worked. Owing to similarities in physical appearance and socioeconomic status, the East Indians were frequently identified with the Mexicans. Generally, the Mexicans accepted the East Indians. Thus, some of the East Indians were assimilated within the Mexican-American culture, a process typically completed with marriage to Mexican women.[30]

During World War II, East Indian political activity in the United States intensified. The principal effort was to enlist American support for the Indian National Congress in its struggle to secure a British commitment to independence. The India League of America, led by the enterprising J. J. Singh and other Indian businessmen and intellectuals living in the eastern United States, attracted the support of the spokesmen of American liberalism, including those who had backed the India Home Rule League during World War I, as well as many labor groups and politicians. The writings, speeches, and other work of Anup Singh, Krishnalal Shridharani, Kumar Goshal, Taraknath Das, B. Shiva Rao, Syud Hossain, and Haridas Muzumdar helped to reinforce the American public's sympathy for the Indian cause. The India League, however, had difficulty sustaining public interest after the failure of the National Congress' "Quit India" movement in August 1952. Further, intensive British imperialist propaganda helped to reduce the pro-Indian sentiment in the United States. Generally, the India League made no effort to utilize the East Indian farmers and laborers in its political campaigns. The most notable exception occurred in early 1945 when Mrs. Vijayalakshmi Pandit, the sister of Jawaharlal Nehru, visited the United States and campaigned on behalf of the nationalist cause among East Indian audiences in California.[31]

This nationalist activity during the war sought a secondary objective which held important ramifications for the East Indian community. The India League of America and the India Welfare League, led by Mubarak Ali Khan and the American voice of the All-India Muslim League, won considerable sympathy, predominantly from American liberals, for granting Indians an immigration quota and extending naturalization privileges to East Indians. Overcoming the opposition of some congressional leaders and the problems caused by disagreements on strategy between the India Welfare League and the India League of America, champions of the Indian immigration-naturalization measure finally maneuvered a bill through Congress in early 1946 which President Harry S. Truman signed on July 2. It gave natives of India an annual quota of a hundred, thus ending nearly thirty years of virtual exclusion, and made Indians eligible for American citizenship, thus reversing the *Thind* decision of twenty-three years earlier.[32]

This liberalization of American immigration and naturalization policy facilitated an increase in the East Indian community and changes in its character. Between 1947 and 1965, nearly 6,000 immigrants from India were admitted to the United States. During the first few years after India's independence, the number of Indians returning to their homeland almost equalled the new immigrants, but by the early 1950s few Indians were leaving the United States. Moreover, the number of persons born in India and entering through other countries also increased. During this period, non-quota immigrants generally equalled or surpassed those admitted under the annual quota; most non-quota immigrants were husbands, wives, and children of American citizens. The largest number of the post-World War II immigrants were professional men and their families. The East Indians took advantage of the opportunity for American citizenship. Between 1948, when twenty-six East Indians were naturalized, and 1965, a total of 1,772 persons of former Indian allegiance acquired United States citizenship.[33]

The recent arrivals reinvigorated the older East Indian community. A 1954 study suggested that the agricultural workers in California were experiencing a "circuitous assimilation" into American culture through the Mexican-American subculture.[34] But that finding has been questioned by other more thorough investigations of the East Indians—a 1956 report based on extensive interviews and a 1968 survey of nine hundred East Indians residing in the Sutter County area of north central California.[35] Taken together these studies provide a comprehensive account of the development of the rural East Indians into a stronger and more unified community.

Several factors helped in this process. To begin with, the older East Indian men never lost their preference for East Indian wives. Although many intermarried, perhaps half the men chose to remain single. After it became possible to bring Indian women to America, some brought wives from India. The younger male immigrants from the Punjab married, almost without exception, East Indian women. Even the children of East Indian-Mexican marriages were not absorbed within the Mexican-American group; one sample of twenty-one marriage-age sons of such families showed that, while eight married Mexican-American girls, six found wives of mixed East Indian-Mexican parentage.

Economically and culturally, the rural East Indians have been notably strengthened. Aided by the virtual disappearance of overt anti-Orientalism and their characteristic thrift and hard work, the East Indians have increased their agricultural holdings and are, as a group, much more prosperous than thirty years ago. The Sikh heritage still provides the strongest cultural focus, with Sikhism represented in nearly all institutionalized activities. The political efforts of the early immigrants are not forgotten. Among the holidays celebrated by the East Indians is "Martyrdom Day," in recognition of the martyrs for Indian independence, and given special emphasis is the involvement of the East Indians in the Ghadr party. Other traditions and practices have been preserved, notably a continued preference for Indian food and the speaking of Indian languages at gatherings of East Indians.

As has generally occurred in overseas Indian communities, the caste system has had negligible influence. This has been especially true among Indian immigrants engaged in farm labor, which undermined traditional occupations, and where there was a shortage of Indian women, which served to weaken the demographic basis of caste by necessitating marriage between castes. An additional factor in the American scene was the predominance of Sikh immigrants, whose religion disavowed caste. There is, however, some evidence that among rural East Indians, caste affiliation has not been entirely forgotten, but serves more as an indication of status and prestige than of exclusiveness and privileges.

Although the members of the older East Indian community have adopted American material comforts, dress, and other features of American life, they have experienced only slight social integration and, as noted, retain important aspects of their own

420

culture. The acculturation of the rural East Indians thus remains limited.[36]

While the East Indians as a group never exerted much political influence, one immigrant, Dalip Singh Saund, did achieve political prominence. Saund, who in 1919 migrated from the Punjab to study at the University of California, became a prosperous farmer in the Imperial Valley. During the 1920s and 1930s, he was active politically, working on behalf of the rights of Indian immigrants and writing a book in response to Katherine Mayo's *Mother India*, a widely-read criticism of Indian culture. After being naturalized in 1949, he joined the Democratic party and was elected a county judge. In 1956 he won election to the United States Congress as representative of the district covering Imperial and Riverside counties. Saund served three terms in the House of Representatives. A massive stroke incapacitated him during his unsuccessful 1962 reelection campaign; he remained an invalid from then until his death in April 1973.[37]

Since the passage of the 1965 immigration law eliminating the quota system, East Indian immigration has increased dramatically. Between 1965 and 1970, immigrants born in India showed a higher percentage increase than newcomers from any other country. The overwhelming majority of the immigrants are professional men and their families; for instance, of the 10,114 persons born in India and admitted in 1970, some 5,171 were classified as holding professional occupations and 4,284 were housewives and children. These newer immigrants are predominantly young; of the 1970 arrivals, one out of seven was under ten years of age and more than three of five were under thirty years. Also there has been a sharp increase in naturalization; between 1966 and 1972, some 2,972 persons of former Indian allegiance were granted United States citizenship. Many more are anticipating naturalization; from 1970 to 1972, over 16,000 Indians were granted permanent resident status. It is, of course, too early to write definitively about this urban-centered, well-educated, affluent East Indian community, which already outnumbers the older, predominantly rural group. Certainly the newer arrivals can be more easily assimilated, but the evidence that they, like the older immigrants, prefer marriage to East Indians also suggests that a sense of Indian cultural identity will prevail.[38]

The East Indian experience in the United States has thus been largely shaped by the changes in American attitudes and policies toward Orientals. The older Indian community in California may still have little social and political integration with white Americans, nonetheless its relative prosperity and growth are not the target of any significant resentment. The "Hindu invasion" feared sixty years ago is occurring in the 1970s without any perceptible public concern. It is this group of new arrivals which will, in the next generation, contribute a fascinating new dimension to the history of Asian Americans. ★

Notes

1. U.S. Dept. of Justice, Immigration and Naturalization Service, *Annual Report, 1955* (Washington, D.C., 1955), 43-45; *Annual Report, 1960* (Washington, D.C., 1960), 43; *Annual Report, 1971* (Washington, D.C., 1971), 53; *Annual Report, 1972* (Washington, D.C., 1972), 34-36. Reference to the number of immigrants per year are to fiscal years ending June 30; this is the practice followed in the annual reports of the Immigration and Naturalization Service.

2. The principal studies of East Indians are Rajani Kanta Das, *Hindustani Workers on the Pacific Coast* (Berlin, 1923); Yusuf Dadabhay, "Circuitous Assimilation among Rural Hindustanis in California," *Social Forces*, XXXIII (1954), 138-141; Harold S. Jacoby, *A Half-Century Appraisal of East Indians in the United States* (Stockton, 1956); Lawrence A. Wenzel, "The Rural Punjabis of California: A Religio-Ethnic Group," *Phylon*, XXIX (1968), 245-256. Das based his book, a comprehensive examination of the early immigrants, on an investigation of East Indians which he made in 1921-1922 while working for the Labor Department. The works of Jacoby and Wenzel are based on thorough investigations and observations of the East Indians in California. Both Jacoby and Wenzel question the conclusions reached by Dadabhay.

3. C. Kondapi, *Indians Overseas, 1838-1949* (Bombay, 1951), 201-211, deals only with the legal status of East Indians in the U.S.; Barton M. Schwartz, ed., *Caste in Overseas Indian Communities* (San Francisco, 1967), draws some generalizations from the experience of other East Indian overseas communities which can be useful in understanding the East Indians in the United States.

4. Das, *Hindustani Workers*, 3-6; H.A. Millis, "East Indian Immigration to British Columbia and the Pacific Coast States," *American Economic Review*, I (1911), 72-76; S. Chandrasekhar, "Indian Immigration in America," *Far Eastern Survey*, XIII (1944), 138-141; Chandra Jayawardena, "Migration and Social Change: A Survey of East Indian Communities Overseas," *Geographical Review*, LVIII (1968), 426-428.

5. *Outlook*, LXXXVII (Sept. 14, 1907), 51-52; Werter D. Dodd, "Hindu in the Northwest," *World To-Day*, XIII (Nov., 1907), 1157-1160; Robert E. Wynne, "American Labor Leaders and the Vancouver Anti-Oriental Riot," *Pacific Northwest Quarterly*, LVII (1966), 174-177.

6. Joan M. Jensen, "Apartheid: Pacific Coast Style," *Pacific Historical Review*, XXXVIII (1969), 335-340.

7. *Proceedings of the Asiatic Exclusion League*, Feb., 1908, pp. 8-10; *ibid.*, Sept., 1908, pp. 11-12; *ibid.*, Jan., 1910, pp. 5-11; *ibid.*, March, 1910, pp. 7-10; Das, *Hindustani Workers*, 17-20; H.A. Millis, "East Indian Immigration to the Pacific Coast," *Survey*, XXVIII (June 1, 1912), 380-381.

8. *Proceedings of the Asiatic Exclusion League*, April, 1910, p. 8.

9. "Hindu Invasion," *Collier's*, XLV (March 26, 1910), 15; "The Hindu, the Newest Immigration Problem," *Survey*, XXV (Oct. 1, 1910), 2-3; Herman Scheffauer, "The Tide of Turbans," *Forum*, XLIII (June 1910), 616-618.

10. *Proceedings of the Asiatic Exclusion League*, Sept., 1910, pp. 45-52; *ibid.*, Oct., 1910, pp. 59-60; H.A. Millis, "East Indian Immigration to the Pacific Coast," *Survey*, XXVIII (June 1, 1912), 379-386.

11. *Cong. Rec.*, 64 Cong., 1 Sess. (1916), 4810; Gurdial Singh, "East Indians in the United States," *Sociology and*

Social Research, XXX (1946), 210-211; Das, *Hindustani Workers*, 12-16.

12. *Cong. Rec.*, 63 Cong., 2 Sess. (1914), Appendix, pp. 842-845; 64 Cong., 1 Sess. (1916), 724; 64 Cong., 2 Sess. (1917), 2452-2457, 2616-2629; *Biographical Directory of the American Congress, 1774-1961* (Washington, D.C., 1961), 691.

13. Roger Daniels and Spencer C. Olin, Jr., eds., *Racism in California: A Reader in the History of Oppression* (New York, 1972), v-viii; Roger Daniels, *The Politics of Prejudice: The Anti-Japanese Movement in California and the Struggle for Japanese Exclusion* (Berkeley, 1962), 65-91; Robert F. Heizer and Alan J. Almquist, *The Other Californians: Prejudice and Discrimination under Spain, Mexico, and the United States to 1920* (Berkeley, 1971), 178-200; Spencer C. Olin, Jr., "European Immigrant and Oriental Alien: Acceptance and Rejection by the California Legislature of 1913," *Pacific Historical Review*, XXX (1966), 303-315.

14. Das, *Hindustani Workers*, 22-26, 31-32, 49-50, 93-95; S. Chandrasekhar, "Indian Community in the United States," *Far Eastern Survey*, XIV (June 6, 1945), 147-149; Subhindra Bose, "Asian Immigration in the United States," *Modern Review* (Calcutta), XXV (May 1919), 524-526.

15. Das, *Hindustani Workers*, 77-80, 109-110; Millis, "East Indian Immigration to the Pacific Coast," 385-386.

16. Das, *Hindustani Workers*, 88-92; Lee M'Crae, "Self-Exiled in America: Something about the Hindus in California," *Missionary Review*, XXXIX (July 1916), 525-526.

17. Kalyan Kumar Banerjee, *Indian Freedom Movement Revolutionaries in America* (Calcutta, 1969), 7-13; L.P. Mathur, *Indian Revolutionary Movement in the United States of America* (Delhi, 1970), 18-25.

18. Mathur, *Indian Revolutionary Movement*, 30.

19. *Ibid.*, 26-29, 72-73; Banerjee, *Indian Freedom Movement*, 13-17; Jacoby, *Half-Century Appraisal of East Indians*, 25; Mark Naidis, "Propaganda of the Gadar Party," *Pacific Historical Review*, XX (1951), 252-253; Giles T. Brown, "The Hindu Conspiracy, 1914-1917," *ibid.*, XVII (1948), 299-300.

20. Banerjee, *Indian Freedom Movement*, 73; Don K. Dignan, "The Hindu Conspiracy in Anglo-American Relations during World War I," *Pacific Historical Review*, XL (1971), 57-76. The British government maintained an extensive surveillance of Indian nationalists, including the use of private detective and military intelligence agents. Joan M. Jensen, "Outcasts in a Savage Land: The East Indian in North America" (Unpublished manuscript), 488-572, details the British activities and their relation to the conspiracy trial.

21. Brown, "The Hindu Conspiracy," 307-309; Naidis, "Propaganda of the Gadar Party," 254-258; Mathur, *Indian Revolutionary Movement*, 155.

22. Haridas T. Muzumdar, *America's Contribution to India's Freedom* (Allahabad, 1962), 9-12; Naeen Gul Rathore, "Indian Nationalist Agitation in the United States: A Study of Lala Lajpat Rai and the Indian Home Rule League of America, 1914-1920" (Ph.D. dissertation, Columbia University, 1965), 284-293, *passim*; Diwaker Prasad Singh, "American Official Attitudes toward the Indian Nationalist Movement, 1905-1929" (Ph.D. dissertation, University of Hawaii, 1964), 235-264.

23. Daniels, *Politics of Prejudice*, 92-102.

24. *U.S. v. Bhagat Singh Thind*, 261 U.S. 204-215 (1923); *New York Times*, Feb. 20, 1923; Taraknath Das, "State-less Persons in U.S.A.," *Calcutta Review*, XVI (July 1925), 40-43.

25. *Modern Review* XXXIII (June 1923), 770.

26. Das, "Stateless Persons in U.S.A.," 43-44; Singh, "East Indians in the United States," 211; *New York Times*, Jan. 26, 1933; James W. Garner, "Denationalization of American Citizens," *American Journal of International Law*, XXI (Jan. 1927), 106-107.

27. *Literary Digest*, CXVII (March 10, 1923), 366-367.

28. U.S. Department of Commerce, Bureau of Census, *Fifteenth Census of the United States 1930*, Vol. II: *General Report, Statistics by Subjects* (Washington, D.C., 1933), 64; Jacoby, *Half-Century Appraisal of East Indians*, 7-9; Theodore Fieldbrave, "East Indians in the U.S.," *Missionary Review*, LVII (June 1934), 291-293; D. P. Pandia and Mme. Kamaldevi, "Justice for Hindus in America," *Christian Century*, LVII (March 13, 1940), 357.

29. U. S. Department of Commerce, Bureau of Census, *Sixteenth Census of the United States, 1940—Population: Characteristics of the Nonwhite Population by Race* (Washington, D.C., 1943), 2-7, 17, 34, 37.

30. Dadabhay, "Circuitous Assimilation Among Rural Hindustanis," 138-141.

31. Gary R. Hess, *America Encounters India, 1941-1947* (Baltimore, 1971), 16, 19, 85-90, 113-129, 151-155.

32. Gary R. Hess, "The 'Hindu' in America: Immigration and Naturalization Policies and India, 1917-1946," *Pacific Historical Review*, XXXVIII (1969), 71-77.

33. U.S. Department of Justice, Immigration and Naturalization Service, *Annual Report, 1949* (Washington, D.C., 1949), table 13; *Annual Report, 1950* (Washington, D.C., 1950), tables 6, 7, 13A; *Annual Report, 1955* (Washington, D.C., 1955), 45, 48, 50, 53, 55, 114-115; *Annual Report, 1960* (Washington, D.C., 1960), 23, 41, 78-80; *Annual Report, 1965* (Washington, 1965), 97.

34. Dadabhay, "Circuitous Assimilation Among Rural Hindustanis," 138-141.

35. Jacoby, *Half-Century Appraisal of East Indians*, 27-32; Wenzel, "The Rural Punjabis of California," 245-256.

36. Jacoby, *Half-Century Appraisal of East Indians*, 10-21, 26-32; Jayawardena, "Migration and Social Change," 441; Wenzel, "The Rural Punjabis of California," 245-256.

37. *New York Times*, April 25, 1973; *Biographical Directory of the American Congress, 1774-1961*, 1563.

38. U.S. Department of Justice, Immigration and Naturalization Service, *Annual Report, 1970* (Washington, D.C., 1970), 4-5, 49, 63-64, 110; *Annual Report, 1971* (Washington, D.C., 1971), 34, 38, 41, 47-50, 99-101; *Annual Report, 1972* (Washington, D.C., 1972), 32, 103. The above comments on recent East Indian immigration deal only with immigrants from India and does not include those from Pakistan. Until the last few years, the number of Pakistani immigrants was very small. After the partition of India in 1947, the United States gave Pakistan an annual quota of a hundred immigrants. The immigrants from Pakistan actually averaged about 150 per year, however, because some were admitted as non-quota immigrants. Between 1958 and 1965 the total Pakistani immigration was 1,224. Since 1966, the number of Pakistani immigrants has increased sharply; the total from 1966 to 1972 was 7,911. U. S. Department of Justice, Immigration and Naturalization Service, *Annual Report, 1967* (Washington, D. C., 1967), 62; *Annual Report, 1969* (Washington, D.C., 1969), 47; *Annual Report, 1972* (Washington, D.C., 1972), 34.

Filipinos in the United States

by H. Brett Melendy

For most of the twentieth century, Filipinos have been part of the flow of Asian newcomers to Hawaii and to the western shores of the continental United States. The migration has come largely as two distinct movements. The first influx during the 1920s consisted primarily of agricultural workers, while the second, occurring after 1965, was made up of people with a wider range of interests and skills. Since 1968, the Philippines have led all Asian countries in the number of new immigrants, and since 1970 it has led all other nations except Mexico.[1] The purpose of this paper is to review the two major periods of Filipino immigration to Hawaii and to the mainland United States, to discuss the motives of the immigrants, and to describe American attitudes towards the new-comers. Thus far, neither scholars nor the general public have paid much attention to Filipino Americans. Only during the 1930s, when this "third wave" of Asian immigrants who followed upon the heels of the Chinese and Japanese appeared to create problems for West Coast nativists, was any attention given to them or to their problems in becoming part of America's pluralistic society.[2] It is hoped that this paper will encourage a closer look at these much-neglected people.

For two decades following the annexation in 1898 of the Philippine Islands by the United States, those Filipinos migrating to the mainland came primarily as college and university students. United States citizens welcomed them as trainees in democracy who would eventually return to their islands, carrying the message of democracy to their own people.[3]

Though the students, few in number, pioneered the Pacific crossing, the first major influx experienced by the West Coast occurred during the 1920s. Filipino arrivals increased sharply after 1924 when a new immigration act excluded Japanese immigrants. With the elimination of Japanese labor, California farmers had to find other workers to perform the seasonal tasks in the fields and orchards. Workers were also sought by the salmon cannery industries of the Pacific Northwest and Alaska. Since white Americans were not available in sufficient supply, western employers turned to the Philippines and Mexico for relief. The use of labor from these countries proved temporary, however, for during the depression years of the 1930s the number of available white workers increased. In the face of declining employment opportunities and increasing racial prejudice, the number of Filipinos migrating to the West Coast dropped sharply during this decade.[4]

Filipino immigration to the Hawaiian Islands occurred at the same time as the movement to the West Coast, but it differed in some respects with that to the mainland. Immigration to Hawaii was tied to the fortunes of the islands' sugar companies. Following the 1907-1908 Gentlemen's Agreement, whereby Japan restricted the number of laborers migrating to the islands and to the mainland, the plantations faced a shortage of field and mill hands. From 1907 through 1919, the Hawaiian Sugar Planters' Association experimented with Filipino labor as a replacement for the Japanese. When the experiment proved successful, there followed for a decade after 1919 a heavy influx of workers from the Far East archipelago. During the decade of the 1930s, however, in the face of demand for exclusion and a labor surplus in Hawaii, the number of migrating Filipinos dropped to

a trickle. The one exception occurred in 1946 when, just prior to independence for the new Asian republic, some 7,361 Filipinos migrated to the Territory of Hawaii. Many came at that particular time because they expected easy access to Hawaii to end when the quota system went into effect following Philippine independence. Others came in response to a growing postwar need for labor on Hawaii's sugar plantations. Their arrival was encouraged by the Hawaiian Sugar Planters' Association, which requested the United States Department of Interior, under the terms of the Tydings-McDuffie Act of 1934, to arrange for Filipino immigrants to meet the sugar industry's labor shortage.[5]

The Philippines gained independence on July 4, 1946. Two days earlier, Congress made Filipinos eligible for naturalization in the United States. On July 4, President Harry Truman issued a proclamation fixing the annual quota at 100. This quota remained in effect for two decades.[6] On October 3, 1965, President Lyndon B. Johnson signed a law nullifying prior quotas and abolishing the long-standing national origins system. Under the new legislation, immigration was not based on ethnic considerations, but rather upon the occupational needs of the United States and whether or not a would-be immigrant had relatives in the United States.[7] The latter consideration, in particular, led to increased immigration from Asia, including, of course, the Philippines.

Those Filipinos coming in the wake of the 1965 legislation, as well as those arriving earlier, were representative of at least three different island cultures. Most immigrants, therefore, had to adjust to their own differing cultures as well as to an American culture. For many this intracultural adjustment did not come easily. The Visayan Islands, situated in and around the Visayan Sea, provided one distinct immigrant group with its own language. Those from the Manila area, with easy access to both immigration and transportation agents, formed another group. Their native language, Tagalog, is spoken by more Filipinos than is any of the other eighty or so dialects. The two northern provinces on the island of Luzon, Ilocos Norte and Ilocos Sur, have been and still are the source of most of the immigrants. Their native language is Ilocano. Two-thirds to three-fourths of all persons of Filipino descent or origin in the United States have come from one of these two Luzon provinces.[8]

Some additional statistics will help put Filipino immigration into sharper relief. By 1920, just prior to the earliest period of heavy immigration, there were more than four times as many Filipinos in Hawaii than on the mainland. They numbered 21,031, most of whom had been brought in on an experimental basis by the sugar growers. Those on the mainland numbered only about 5,600. Most immigrants of the 1920s were single males who were quite young, either in their teens or early twenties. Of those entering California between 1925 and 1929, some 22,767 were males and 1,356 were females. One-third of the males were between 16 and 21 years of age, while another 48 percent were in the 22-29 age range. In Hawaii, the sex imbalance was also present: 42,186 males, 1,468 females, and 750 listed as children.[9]

By 1930, as a result of the growing need for additional labor, the number of Filipinos in Hawaii rose to 63,052, an increase of nearly 66 percent, while the mainland's share during the same decade grew by 88 percent to a total of 45,208.[10] An indication of the rapidity of growth is shown in the figures for the last five years of the 1920s. During these years, 21,123 Filipinos entered through California ports, while some 44,404 entered through Honolulu.[11] With this large influx during the late 1920s, the Filipinos, when compared with other Asian groups, were a rapidly growing minority. In 1920 there were 85,146 Chinese and 220,284 Japanese in the United States and the Territory of Hawaii. Ten years later there were 102,133 Chinese and 278,645 Japanese.[12]

During the 1930s, the number of Filipinos on both Hawaii and the mainland remained at about the same level. By World War II, many of the older immigrants had returned home, while the younger Filipinos, who made up the vast majority of the immigrants, had decided to remain in the United States. Since World War II, each decade has seen a substantial increase in the number of immigrating Filipinos. Most of those who came to the mainland continued to settle in California, where, by 1970, 40 percent of the total Filipino population was located. Only 4 percent lived in New York, the mainland state with the second largest population, while Illinois and Washington had but 3.6 percent and 3.4 percent, respectively.[13]

With the diversification of California's industries during and after World War II, Filipinos congregated primarily where many of their fellows had lived during the 1920s and 1930s — in the San Francisco Bay area and Los Angeles. During the 1950s, Filipinos in California continued to shift, as did the

TABLE I
Filipinos in the United States

	1920	1930	1940	1950	1960	1970
Mainland	5,603[a]	45,208[b]	45,563[c]	61,636[d]	107,669[e]	241,051[g]
Hawaii[f]	21,031	63,052	52,659	61,062	68,641	95,680[g]
TOTAL	26,634	108,260	98,132	122,698	176,310	336,731
Mainland States: Subtotals						
California			31,408[c]	40,424[d]	65,459[e]	135,248[g]
New York			2,978	3,719	5,403	14,045
Illinois			—	—	3,587	12,355
Washington			2,222	4,224	7,110	11,488

[a]Lasker, *Filipino Immigration*, 349.
[b]Rojo, "Social Maladjustment Among Filipinos in the United States," 447.
[c]U.S. Bureau of the Census, *Nonwhite Population by Race, 1940* (Washington, D.C., 1943), 109.
[d]*Ibid., 1950* (Washington, D.C., 1953), 65.
[e]Calif. Dept. of Industrial Relations, *Californians of Japanese, Chinese, Filipino Ancestry*, 16.
[f]Hawaiian figures for 1920-1960 are from Lind, *Hawaii's People*, 28.
[g]U.S. Bureau of the Census, *Japanese, Chinese, and Filipinos in the United States, 1970* (Washington, D.C., 1973), 119.

TABLE II			
Filipino Immigration to the United States 1948-1971			
Year	Immigrants	Year	Immigrants
1948	1,122	1960	2,954
1949	1,068	1961	2,738
1950	595	1962	3,437
1951	760	1963	3,618
1952	1,066	1964	3,006
1953	1,160	1965	3,130
1954	1,633	1966	6,093
1955	1,784	1967	10,865
1956	1,873	1968	16,731
1957	1,996	1969	20,744
1958	2,236	1970	31,203
1959	2,633	1971	28,471
		1972	29,376

U.S. Immigration and Naturalization Service, *Annual Report, 1957* (Washington, D.C., 1958), 37; *Annual Report, 1961* (Washington, D.C., 1962), 43; *Annual Report, 1972* (Washington, D.C., 1973), 59.

TABLE III	
Number of Filipinos Residing in the City of Honolulu 1930-1970	
Year	Number
1930	4,776[a]
1940	6,887[b]
1950	17,372[c]
1960	21,807[d]
1970	29,481[e]

[a] U.S. Bureau of the Census, *Population (Second Series), 1940: Characteristics of the Population, Hawaii* (Washington, D.C., 1943), 5.
[b] *Ibid.*
[c] U.S. Bureau of the Census, *Characteristics of the Population, 1950*, II, Part 52, *Hawaii* (Washington, D.C., 1953), 22.
[d] U.S. Bureau of the Census, *Characteristics of the Population, 1960*, I, Part 13, *Hawaii* (Washington, D.C., 1963), 31.
[e] U.S. Bureau of the Census, *General Population Characteristics, 1970: Hawaii* (Washington, D.C., 1971), 27.

general population, from rural to urban areas — from 60 percent in the cities in 1950 to 80 percent in 1960.[14] By comparison, the shift in Hawaii was slight — only 2 percent.[15] Yet Honolulu possesses the largest Filipino population of any United States city. Other mainland cities, besides those in California, which have developed sizeable Filipino populations since the early 1950s are, in order of rank, Seattle, Chicago, New York, and Washington, D.C.[16]

In 1960, the Filipinos had the following statistical profile: Men in California and Hawaii were older than women. In California, the largest male age group (33 percent) was between the ages of 25 and 34. In Hawaii, 51 percent of the men were in the 45-64 age group, and 29 percent of the women were in the 25-34 age group. The change in the immigration law in 1965 had by 1970 produced a major impact on the age of Filipino immigrants. California's largest male group (62 percent) was under twenty-one years of age. The largest female group (56 percent) was also under twenty-one years of age. The same was true in Hawaii, where 58 percent of the males and 45 percent of the females were under twenty-one.[17]

The motivation for Filipino immigrants during the period of the first influx and after 1965 was the same. They came to the United States in response to economic factors in this country and because of local conditions in the islands. During the 1920s and 1930s, their life plan did not differ greatly from that of other Asians or most Europeans. Many Ilocanos, for example, left their homes for the United States or Hawaii in an effort to assist their families. The lure of comparatively high salaries attracted many who sought to improve their families' economic condition. A common pattern was for the family to mortgage a portion of its land in order to send one son to the United States. In turn he would send money home to pay off the mortgage or to assist a brother to obtain higher education.[18]

The young immigrant's persistent dream was to return home and reestablish his life in familiar surroundings. Any *Hawaiiano* who returned to Norte or Sur Ilocos to buy land became a person of prestige and economic prominence.[19] From 1920 through 1934, as young immigrants arrived at West Coast and Honolulu docks, others returned to their Filipino homes. The number leaving the United States in any one year during these fourteen years ranged from 16 percent to 50 percent of the arrivals for the same year.[20]

As with other immigrant groups, the dreams and hopes that motivated the Filipinos' ambitions frequently did not materialize. Wages, which appeared to be extraordinary when viewed from the Philippines, were quickly consumed by a much higher cost of living in the United States. Education often proved more difficult to obtain than had been anticipated by those seeking additional learning experiences. Young men, with a strong sense of pride, did not want to return home as acknowledged failures. While at first not too concerned about adjusting to their new environment, they found that they had to remain a longer time than they had originally planned in order to gain enough money to return home a success. But because they were "birds of passage," they had no inclination to become part of American society. As late as 1944, many Filipinos who had arrived before 1934 still clung to the hope that they would return home. J. C. Dionisio, a member of President Manuel Quezon's World War II exile government, explained the feelings held by those California Filipinos he had interviewed:

> The tragedy of our life in America . . . is that it has been predicated on wishful thinking — "I want to go home." We have been sentimental rather than realistic. "Why should I plan, why should I take life seriously here, when this is only an interlude in my life? I am going home. It is there where

426

I am going to take root."
Birds of passage, Mr. President, do not plan.
They drift aimlessly. [21]

California agriculture came to rely in large measure upon these men who were caught in a trap, partly of their own making. The state's major farming regions — the Imperial Valley, the San Joaquin Valley, the Delta Region, and the Salinas Valley — relied upon cheap migratory labor to produce a variety of crops. During the 1920s most Filipinos in the Delta area, near Stockton, worked in the asparagus fields. The Salinas Valley, another major Filipino center, has over the years provided seasonal work in the lettuce fields and packing sheds.

Because of the nature of the agricultural work, Filipinos migrated back and forth among farming regions and the larger cities in California and the Pacific Northwest. In his definitive study of the first period of Filipino immigration, Bruno Lasker noted that in 1931 Seattle's summer population of Filipinos consisted of only a few hundred. During the winter, however, some 3,500 of them moved into the city's ghettos. Stockton's Filipino summer population during the asparagus season of the same year was 6,000, while its winter population was only a thousand.[22] During the winter Stockton's temporary residents went to Los Angeles or San Francisco to seek other employment and to share with their fellow countrymen the varied experiences of urban living.

This shift from urban to rural to urban was a common way of life for these men, and it has been graphically described by Manuel Buaken, a former field hand. In 1927, after failing to find a city job, he left Los Angeles for Stockton's "Little Manila," the principal Filipino center on the West Coast. He found the city filled with other Filipinos searching for work, but he finally secured employment pulling celery seedlings and transplanting them. He also harvested onions, carrots, and potatoes. His first job paid $2.50 a day plus room and board for a six-day work week. At the end of the season, five months later, he had earned $500.[23] Nationally in 1927, farm workers were earning $2.28 for a ten-hour day, while factory workers made $5.52.[24] The average wage for Filipinos during the 1930 season, three years later, was $600. During the depression, wages sank to $300 a season.[25] It should be noted that "meaningful comparisons" between California farm labor wages and those in other occupations are difficult to make. Even a comparison between various agricultural segments and groups is hard to draw because of piecework payments in many crops.[26]

In general, Filipinos were among the lowest paid agricultural workers during the 1920s and 1930s. This situation is partially explained by racial considerations. Carey McWilliams, in *Factories in the Field*, reported that California farmers in 1937, and in earlier years, paid workers on the basis of race. A study by Harry Schwartz bears out this fact of racial

discrimination. His 1928 study showed that farmers employing both white and nonwhite workers paid higher wages to the white. At that time only Mexicans and blacks earned less than Filipinos. [27] Another factor causing the Filipinos to receive lower wages was their own actions. As had the Japanese earlier, they undercut other field labor, such as the Mexicans, by accepting lower wages. In 1935, for example, the Mexicans asked for $5 an acre to thin lettuce, but the Filipinos agreed to do the same work for $3.25 to $4.50. Once ensconced, however, they demanded higher pay.[28]

The Filipinos were used primarily as "stoop labor" — unskilled field hands. Usually the farmer needing labor arranged with a labor contractor to provide for a crew. The contractor arranged for transportation from a nearby town, supervised the work, and kept books. If room and board were furnished the worker, the contractor would deduct the cost from the men's wages. He also collected a service charge from each worker for any service he provided.[29]

Labor was the only commodity that the Filipino had to offer. The one way in which he could change his working conditions was to withhold his work at critical times. American farmers, always on the lookout for cheap labor, stiffly resisted the tactics that their new recruits used to improve wages and working conditions. Many Filipinos responded by adopting techniques — threats of strikes, strikes, and boycotts of hostile farmers — developed earlier by Japanese agricultural workers. The laborers would usually wait until it was time to pick a crop before making their wage demands. The farmer had to accede, obtain other workers, or lose his crop.[30] Not surprisingly, farmers became embittered with the Filipino "troublemakers." "The most unsatisfactory of any unskilled laborers we had ever hired," remembered one farmer. "They were the very essence of independence, taking every advantage to cause the employer trouble. . . ." In 1927, this farmer recalled, "the Filipinos evidently thinking we were in a tight place struck for higher wages. We were already paying a higher price per box than anyone else. . . . We refused to meet their exorbitant demands whereupon general rioting ensued. The Filipinos became enraged and began to destroy everything they could lay their hands on."[31]

Filipinos had become an important part of California agriculture by the 1920s and the early 1930s. But as noted earlier, new immigration declined as a consequence of the depression years. World War II further cut off immigration, and many of those already in the United States moved into industrial occupations. After the war, California farmers began to rely more heavily upon Mexican farm workers than they had in the past. This change to additional Mexican labor gave many farmers an opportunity to rationalize their dislike for the Filipinos. One com-

427

mon complaint was that the quality of work being performed by the Filipinos was below par. At the same time the Mexicans began to supplant the Filipinos in other ways too. In 1955 a study was made of the perceptions of some southern California high school students and farm owners in the Coachella Valley regarding the value of different minorities as agricultural workers. According to those questioned, the Mexican had replaced the Filipino as the least desirable worker.[32] Attitudes of West Coast agriculturalists toward minorities used as field laborers had not changed over the years. Decades earlier, Chinese and Japanese immigrants had experienced a similar contempt.

While Filipinos were readily employed in California agriculture, they also sought, with less success, employment in urban areas. During the 1920s and 1930s, they encountered the same kind of racial discrimination that had been faced by other Asians. While Filipinos could usually find employment as busboys, cooks, dishwashers, domestic help, and gardeners, opportunities in business and professional positions were restricted.[33] During and after World War II, as the industrial base expanded, they found jobs in factories, in some trades, and as wholesale and retail salesmen. They also were able to enter the professions. After 1965 more of them found employment open to them in the cities in unskilled, skilled, and semi-professional occupations. Nevertheless, union regulations and state licensing provisions have restricted opportunities for qualified Filipinos.

Even with the rural to urban move in California, agriculture in 1960 remained the largest employer of Filipinos with 3 percent classified as farmers and farm managers and with another 28 percent classified as farm laborers and foremen. In 1950, these percentages had been about 6 percent and 49 percent, respectively.[34] In Hawaii, Filipinos in 1960 provided the bulk of plantation labor. Forty percent of the gainfully employed males worked in agriculture, a decline of 12.5 percent from 1950. During the 1950s, they began to gain employment as craftsmen and factory workers.[35] According to a socio-economic study by the California Department of Industrial Relations, Filipinos in California, from 1934 to 1959, had not improved upon their earning power relative to other groups. By the end of the period studied, 1959, the median annual income for male Caucasians in California was $5,109; in Hawaii, it was $3,649. California Japanese males had a median income of $4,388, while Hawaiian Japanese averaged $4,302. Filipino males in California had a median income of $2,925, while in Hawaii their counterparts earned $3,071.[36]

The California Department of Industrial Relations 1965 study of the Japanese, Chinese, and Filipinos graphically showed that as late as 1960 the latter were still largely employed as unskilled laborers. The median annual income in 1959 for the Filipinos was the lowest of the three groups studied. In Hawaii they shared with other Pacific island people the dubious distinction of having the lowest median salary of all ethnic groups. As the "latest arrivals and least fortunately situated" of the immigrant groups, the Filipinos provided most of the unskilled plantation labor which was at the bottom of the wage scale. However, Hawaiian Filipinos have fared better than those in California, largely because the International Longshoremen's and Warehousemen's Union organized Hawaii's agricultural workers and gained wage increases for its members. The union boasts that the sugar industry "pays the highest year-round agricultural wages in the world."[37]

California's agribusiness, on the other hand, successfully resisted unionization of field workers until the 1960s. During most of the 1930s, the powerful Associated Farmers of California stayed all efforts to organize migratory farm workers. By the end of the decade, the Filipinos had achieved limited organizing success with their Filipino Agricultural Laborers Association. Created initially in response to a threatened wage cut in asparagus, the union had, by 1941, won several strikes and secured some wage increases and improved working conditions. The union disappeared as an effective force during World War II when most of its members joined the armed forces. The economic motivation for unionism disappeared as farm wages increased during the war years.[38] Following the war, agricultural workers called for improved working conditions and increased wages to meet inflation. California agriculture met this challenge during the 1940s and 1950s by utilizing strike breakers and court injunctions to hold at bay union activities.[39] But the situation changed dramatically during the 1960s. In 1959, the AFL-CIO formed the Agricultural Workers Organizing Committee (AWOC), and, at about the same time, César Chávez founded the National Farm Workers Association (NFWA). While both unions were racially integrated, the AWOC local, led by Larry Itliong, was predominantly Filipino. These new unions spent several years recruiting members. The climax to these activities came in 1965 over the pay scale of grape pickers in the lower San Joaquin Valley. On September 8, 1965, AWOC launched a strike against thirty-three grape growers near Delano in northern Kern County. Domestic agricultural laborers were being paid about $1.20 an hour, while braceros, under a U.S. Department of Labor ruling, received $1.40 for picking grapes. The domestic workers, including the Filipino Americans and Mexican Americans, demanded $1.40 an hour plus 20 cents a box. Chávez's NFWA joined AWOC's effort eight days later. After a lengthy strike of about seven months, which generated much public sympathy, Schenley Industries, owner of the largest vineyards, recognized NFWA as the sole bargaining agent. NFWA and AWOC continued to organize workers and pressure growers. Chávez's union became the stronger of the two. To end unnecessary conflict, the unions in August 1966 merged as the United Farm Workers Organizing Committee. This new organization became the bargaining agent for the workers of the Di Giorgio Corporation, another large Kern County vineyard owner.[40] The naming of a bargaining agent for the farm workers marked a turning point in labor relations in California agriculture.[41] The Filipinos and the Chicanos, working together in a common effort, were successful in improving wages and working conditions. They have, through the UFWOC, continued to struggle together against big agriculture.

Filipino immigrants from both periods of migration, in addition to the search for economic success, have sought to accommodate themselves in varying degrees to American society. In 1929, D. F. Gonzalo, a Filipino student at the University of Southern California, reflected upon the problems of social adjustment faced by recently arrived young Filipinos. For the first few months after arrival, the new immigrant was buoyed by a sense of exuberance and high anticipation of realizing his dream of success and financial achievement. The ability to send money home each month further increased his enthusiasm. He found ready employment as an unskilled worker in those jobs shunned by white labor, and he frequently upbraided his fellow countrymen who had been in the United States for several years and who appeared to have given up.

The newly arrived immigrant, Gonzalo reported, then moved to a second phase in his adjustment to the United States. Long hours of hard work soon dulled his outlook. The young man became lonesome and began to regret his decision to migrate. He also discovered that Americans in the United States were different from those he had met in the Philippines. He became conscious of his color and language, both different from those of the American majority. He became aware of acts of discrimination and prejudice aimed at him. Feeling cut off in an alien world, he sought to draw upon his own resources which frequently could not cope with those allurements aimed at capitalizing upon the lonely.[42] Many young men turned to prostitutes and to dance halls and gambling establishments run by Caucasians, Chinese, or other Filipinos. Many Filipinos have said their long hours in the field were really spent working for the "Chinaman" — their name for the gamester. Others noted that they had been through a comprehensive gaming course at the local "Chinese university."[43] Carey McWilliams, in his *Brothers Under the Skin*, estimated that in Stockton — "the Manila of the United States" — Filipinos spent some two million dollars annually on gambling and prostitution.[44] The *Philippine Free Press* of Manila wrote in 1929 of the ensnarement of the young Filipinos by gambling:

Those Filipinos who send money home are the "blanket boys." These have steady jobs on the farm.... The pastime of the "blanket boys" is playing cards. After a day's work they assemble around the improvised table and play cards till late at night. Poker and blackjack are the popular games. Their hard-earned money is easily lost. In the town or city the *Pinoys* may be found in the billiard rooms and pool halls from after breakfast till late at night.

There are many gambling houses, mostly managed and controlled by Chinese. They are popularly known as "sikoy-sikoys".... In Stockton there is one gambling house managed and controlled by white men. It is for Filipinos. It is one mile south from the heart of the city. Anyone who wants to go there gets a free ride back and forth. These hired automobiles are owned by Filipinos.

In Walnut Grove there are six "sikoy-sikoys"; in Isleton there are four; in Dinuba one; in Reedley four, and so on. All these gambling houses are patronized by Filipinos and a few Mexicans.

The gambling houses in Walnut Grove and Isleton serve free meals: breakfast at eight o'clock; a dinner at twelve; supper at five; coffee and bread at ten in the evening.[45]

Filipino gambling, although tolerated by native Americans, seemed to be an indication to them that the young immigrants lacked seriousness of purpose. But the sexual relationships of the young Filipino immigrants and white girls led to bitter animosity on the part of adult whites. Throughout California, Filipinos sought female companionship in the dance halls. To cater to the Filipino trade in Los Angeles during the 1930s, six taxi dance halls employed several hundred women. McWilliams opined that the taxi dance provided perhaps the most costly entertainment in the state. Each dance, lasting one minute, cost ten cents.[46]

There were mixed views about Filipinos and prostitution. In Stockton, Charles F. Crook, deputy labor commissioner of San Joaquin County, reflected an unfriendly attitude:

The Filipino never has a dime.... His money goes for cars, women, clothes and the like. The Filipino contractor furnishes some of these things. He brings women (white women) into the camp as well as booze and gives each laborer who cares to indulge a ticket. That is, he takes it out of wages.

I know of one taxi company in this city that makes $500 per month running prostitutes into the islands [the San Joaquin River Delta area]. These women must be white, weigh not over one hundred pounds, and be comparatively young — not over 24 or 25 years old.... They are worked through the islands and back down the coast toward the city. Then, they are worked back again.[47]

Manuel Buaken, one of the early immigrants, agreed in part with Crook, but he felt that prostitution was based upon the seduction of the Filipinos by white women. "Women professionals," he insisted, "fleeced the innocent Filipino of his money by pretending they loved and so managed to cheat and deceive him."[48]

The 1929 Gonzalo study noted that Filipino

immigrants moved through several phases as they attempted to cope with life in the United States. One undesirable aspect, as noted above, was the dependence of many upon gambling and prostitution. Gonzalo concluded that a large number of Filipinos, unable to adapt successfully, had to be classified as bewildered drifters who appeared to have no aim or purpose. The enthusiasm of former days had disappeared, leaving them bitter or resigned. Many who wanted to go home either lacked the money or feared the scorn likely to be meted out to failures. Consequently, they became entrapped in their new environment. From his study of his fellow Filipinos, Gonzalo concluded that they, like many other unskilled immigrants, did not have the background necessary for social adjustment in a country where every wage earner was a specialist of sorts.[49]

The problems noted by Gonzalo persisted for several decades. Aging Filipinos found themselves captive in what was to be their temporary home. Some of those who had migrated in the 1920s were still working in agriculture nearly fifty years later. In 1970, two students of Filipino ancestry, who wanted to understand better their own heritage, interviewed Filipino residents of a Salinas farm labor camp. Those interviewed portray vividly the hopes and frustrations of men who had become a permanent part of California's agricultural labor force. Even though the average age of the men was 65, they still dreamed of returning to the Philippines. Some were semi-retired, working only long enough to pay for their board and room at the camp. Others, too young to retire at the ages of 60-65, worked daily in the fields.[50]

The interviews of these Filipino agricultural workers point up their optimism — the dream of returning to their homeland remained a fond hope. The sadness of it all was that many had come to rely upon an external factor — the big win in gambling — to bring reality to the dream. Brief biographical sketches of three camp residents underscore the difficulties encountered by them and other aging Filipinos who had come to California in the 1920s.

Manong had migrated in 1924 from the Philippines to Hawaii where he had spent three years on sugar and pineapple plantations. Securing financial support from a relative in Stockton, he had then moved to California where he had worked in the potato and asparagus fields of the San Joaquin Delta. In 1938 he had moved to Salinas which became his permanent residence. Like many of his compatriots Manong did not seek citizenship because he always planned to return to his homeland. He claimed that he had an opportunity to return in 1938, but he could not pay for the ticket. Since that time, though he had made no effort to return to the Philippines, he maintained family ties. He sent money home, but that practice had become more difficult as retirement age approached.[51]

Nanding, another of the camp residents, arrived in San Francisco in 1925 with the idea of studying engineering. But his future was more or less determined at dockside when he and others were "greeted . . . by a man from an employment office in Stockton whose job was to pick up a truckload of men and transport them to Stockton." The driver, Nanding reported, made five dollars profit on each passenger by charging more than the normal fare. After his arrival in Stockton, Nanding worked as an agricultural worker. Once the harvest season had ended, he and several friends enrolled in the seventh grade, but he soon dropped out because he was nineteen and the white students were thirteen; he never went back to school. Nanding subsequently worked as an agricultural field worker, settling finally in the Salinas camp. Like Manong, he never applied for United States citizenship. He viewed that step as unnecessary, "for as soon as he 'makes it in Reno' he plans to return to the Philippines." Although he had never won enough money to cover his transportation costs, he had been able to send money home to support his relatives. Several of these had gained an education because of his financial aid.[52]

Benigno, the third Salinas camp resident, arrived in California in 1924. He began as a field laborer in the Delta region before moving to Salinas in 1935. There he worked in the lettuce fields until the start of World War II. Drafted into the army, he automatically became an American citizen. He was soon discharged because the Salinas agriculturalists needed his labor — the same reason that caused many other drafted Filipino farm workers to be released from military service. Despite the fact that he was now a citizen, Benigno still wanted to return to the Philippines. Like so many others, he was still "waiting for his big win in Reno" so that he could buy his ticket. Although he had never had much luck, his hopes remained high.[53]

As with other immigrant groups, the Filipinos have responded in many different ways to American life. Some were never able to adapt, while others contributed to the mainstream of American culture. One of the major themes in the history of Filipino immigration has been the difficult and continuing problem of racial prejudice and discrimination. A poignant expression of this was the lamentation uttered in 1937 by Carlos Bulosan, a Filipino immigrant who gained recognition through his writings about his countrymen:

> . . . . Western people are brought up to regard Orientals or colored people as inferior, but the mockery of it all is that Filipinos are taught to regard Americans as our equals. Adhering to American ideals, living American life, these are contributory to our feeling of equality. The terrible truth in America shatters the Filipino's dream of fraternity.
>
> I was completely disillusioned when I came to know this American attitude. If I had not been born in a lyrical world, grown up with honest

people and studied about American institutions and racial equality in the Philippines I should never have minded so much the horrible impact of white chauvinism. I shall never forget what I have suffered in this country because of racial prejudice.[54]

American attitudes towards Filipinos on the mainland and in Hawaii were shaped largely by the white reaction to immigrants of the 1920s. Prejudicial attitudes set at that time persisted for several decades. Emory Bogardus, a University of Southern California sociologist who spent years studying the Filipinos, believed that the general opinions held by white America during the late twenties could be divided into three categories: favorable attitudes, unfavorable attitudes, and the evaluation of an individual on the basis of that person's aims and evident merit. Favorable attitudes, largely paternalistic, developed, he held, from opinions growing out of American colonialism. The White Man's Burden created a sense of benevolent obligation to help Filipinos assimilate into American society. Bogardus believed this view resulted mostly from white contact with Filipinos on a superficial individual basis in hotels and restaurants where the latter held inferior positions.[55]

The more prevalent white view saw the Filipino as a savage, not far removed from the tribal stage. Some American missionaries, self-professed friends of the Filipinos, furthered public apprehension as they recounted the primitive conditions of some of the rural Filipino tribes.[56] The prejudicial attitude held by most Americans paralleled the outlook they had regarding other Asian minorities. Bogardus, in his study, noted that white workers exhibited hatred as Filipinos replaced them in the hotel-restaurant industry and in the maritime trade. White labor unions during the late 1920s and early 1930s were leaders in the opposition to Filipino immigration as they had been earlier against other Asian groups.[57]

In day to day living during the 1920s and 1930s, the Filipinos also found that their dark skin and their difficulty with the English language set them apart. On the West Coast, they were frequently refused service in restaurants and barbershops, barred from swimming pools, movies, and tennis courts. Californians, in particular, have a long record of discrimination against Asians in real estate and housing. Filipinos, seeking homes in white neighborhoods, were forced into slum areas. Often, because of lack of housing, fifteen or twenty were compelled to live in one room. They accepted these crowded conditions in an effort to save money for those at home, for transportation to the Philippines, or for the purchase of automobiles and American style clothing.[58] Most white Californians were unaware of the contradictions that their attitudes created. One segment of white society welcomed Filipinos to the state because they provided cheap labor. But prejudicial and discriminatory attitudes tended to keep them at a low level of existence. As a consequence, other Californians, critical of the Filipinos' substandard living conditions attacked them for creating health problems and lowering the American standard of living. Manuel Buaken, another spokesman for his people, cried out about the effect of this denial of adequate housing on the soul of a man:

> my personal pride was entirely subdued; I was wounded deeply in heart and soul for on that day I had tasted more pangs of life's bitterness and all the sordidness of this world than I [had] ever known before, and I learned what calamity and what tragic consequences race prejudice can inflict upon a man's life.[59]

The impact of prejudice shook the Filipinos who had had contact with the teachings of Christianity in the Philippines. Many were stunned by the double standards maintained by white Christians during the 1920s and 1930s. One Filipino reported:

> During my active membership in church, it always puzzled me to find that many members of the same church would converse with me congenially in the church but when I met them on the streets or in school or later on they acted as if ashamed to talk with me, even more so when they were with their friends. And sometimes when I would talk with them in spite of their being with their friends, they looked embarrassed and indicated that I should not appear to be knowing them.[60]

While subjected to covert economic and social discrimination, the Filipino was denied fewer civil and property rights than the immigrants from China and Japan. The only direct legislation aimed against the Filipinos involved mixed marriages.

White Californians had long been opposed to Asian males marrying their daughters. In 1901 Californians had enacted a law forbidding whites from marrying blacks, Mongolians, or mulattoes.[61] Although California Attorney General U. S. Webb believed that Filipinos were Mongolians, his opinion did not have the force of a judicial decision. Each county clerk could make his own interpretation as to the racial origin of Filipinos.[62] In 1931, the Los Angeles County clerk, accepting Webb's interpretation, denied a marriage license to Salvador Roldan, who then filed suit against the county. Claiming that the term, Mongolian, did not include Filipinos, Roldan was successful in both superior and appellate courts. In 1933 the county appealed to the California state supreme court which upheld the decisions of the two lower courts on the grounds that the state legislature had not specifically forbidden marriages between whites and Filipinos.[63] The California legislature quickly closed this loophole by amending the state's civil code in 1933 to include persons of the Malay race in the list of people whom whites could not marry. This action nullified the court decision,[64] and it was soon imitated by other state legislatures. By 1937, Nevada, Oregon, and Washington had enacted laws prohibiting marriages between Filipinos and whites.

California's miscegenation law was eventually ruled unconstitutional in 1948 in the case of *Perez* v. *Sharp*. The California supreme court held that legislation limiting the right of members of one race to marry members of another race was a violation of civil rights. Such laws, the court stated, had to be based upon more than "prejudice and must be free from oppressive discrimination."[65] During the year following the *Perez* decision, some 21,060 marriage license applications were taken out in Los Angeles County. Of these, 100 could be classified as interracial, and Filipinos comprised most of them — 40 males and 2 females.[66]

In addition to legal discrimination, there were incidents of violence against Filipinos. Hostility manifested itself in acts of individual violence as well as in riots in Washington and California between 1928 and 1930. The first of these hostilities, which occurred in Washington's Yakima Valley in 1928, grew out of white farm workers' fears that they would be replaced by Filipinos. On September 19, 1928, the white workers forced the Filipinos to leave the valley. A similar incident took place two days later at Wenatchee, Washington, where two hundred whites descended upon a camp of twenty Filipinos and forced them to flee.[67]

California's most violent discrimination came in the form of vigilante action. White motives were based in part upon the fear of economic competition from the Filipino and in part upon concerns about Filipino relationships with white women. The state's first serious riot occurred on October 24, 1929, when a Filipino stabbed a white man at a carnival in Exeter in the San Joaquin Valley. Prior to the stabbing, white farm workers had molested and shoved Filipinos off the town's sidewalks in an effort to intimidate them into leaving the region. At the carnival, whites threw objects at the Filipinos, particularly those who were escorting white women. This provoked the knifing. Following the stabbing, a mob, estimated at 300, rushed to the nearest ranch employing Filipinos and burned the barn. The Filipinos had fled the area before the mob arrived.[68]

The most explosive California vigilante incident occurred in January 1930 near Watsonville. This farm area, with many specialty crops, depended upon large numbers of transient farm workers. By the late 1920s, farmers had come to rely upon Filipino contract labor, which migrated to the region from other parts of the state to harvest the crops. This dependence upon alien labor laid the seeds for conflict in Watsonville, a town that was not prepared to accommodate such an influx. Soon the white inhabitants of the community were voicing a common complaint about the Filipino transients — they spent their money on flashy clothes and new cars in order to attract the attention of white women. The

growing resentment of the whites was perhaps best expressed by an anti-Filipino resolution adopted by the northern Monterey County chamber of commerce.

> Whereas, any foreign people coming to the United States of America whose customs, habits and standards of living prohibit them from assimilating and adopting our standard of living, are detrimental and dangerous to social conditions, and
> Whereas, the unrestricted immigration into the state of California of natives of the Philippines is viewed with alarm both from a moral and sanitary standpoint while constituting a menace to white labor, therefore be it
> Resolved, That we . . . petition . . . to prevent further immigration.[69]

Judge D. W. Rohrback, a leader of the chamber of commerce and a respected community leader, added to the growing hostility with his announcement that Filipinos "possessed unhealthy habits and were destructive to the living wage scale" of others. He also called them "little brown men attired like 'Solomon in all his glory,' strutting like peacocks and endeavoring to attract the eyes of young American and Mexican girls."[70]

At the same time that the Watsonville citizens were becoming highly agitated about the presence of the farm workers, a small Filipino group leased a dance hall in Palm Beach, a few miles west of Watsonville on Monterey Bay. About a dozen white women were engaged as professional dancing partners. The thought of white women dancing with Filipinos led to demonstrations by self-appointed white vigilantes which started on January 19 and lasted through January 23. On the 20th, about 200 armed men searched the streets for Filipinos, and, on the next night, they raided the dance hall. On the 22nd, a mob of 500 went to nearby farms and fired shots into the camp buildings. One Filipino was killed, several were beaten, and much property was destroyed. Following this violence, community leaders belatedly formed a law and order group to put down the vigilantes.[71]

Legislation and violence were two weapons often used by exclusionists in the past against Chinese and Japanese. Now fearing a third Oriental wave, the whites set out to eliminate Filipino immigration. Encouraged by such organizations as the American Legion, the California Federation of Labor, the Commonwealth Club of California, and the racist California Joint Immigration Committee, the California legislature in 1929 asked Congress to restrict the immigration of Filipinos because cheap labor "has had a tendency towards destruction of American ideals and American racial unity."[72] However, the exclusionists encountered a unique problem. Since the Philippine Islands were part of the United States overseas territory, the Filipinos had a status different from that of other Asian groups. The Filipinos who migrated to Hawaii and the mainland prior to 1946 were technically American nationals. This status was spelled out rather clearly in the 1924 immigration act, which specified that they were not aliens and were free to enter the United States. The 1924 proviso remained in force until May 1, 1934, when the Philippine legislature accepted the Tydings-McDuffie Independence Act, which limited the number of Filipino immigrants to an annual quota of fifty.[73] Prior to 1946, when the Philippines became independent, Filipinos travelling beyond the territorial limits of the United States or the Philippines carried United States passports, which gave them the apparent status of citizenship. However, in the Philippines the residents had only the fundamental rights of life, liberty, and property as set forth in the Insular Cases.[74]

The different status of the Filipinos did not daunt the exclusionists. At the federal level, Richard Welch, a San Francisco congressman, introduced exclusion and repatriation legislation. Nativist and humanitarian motives were entwined in the proposals. While there was an outright push to eliminate Filipino immigration, there was some concern about the plight of the immigrant farm workers in California. During the depression, Filipinos were among the first workers to be laid off. In 1931, the Philippine Society of California, comprised of recently arrived Filipino immigrants, urged the federal government to use army transports to take unemployed Filipinos home. The society found that thousands of Filipinos wanted to go home but did not have funds to purchase a ticket. Members of the society, who wanted to maintain the option of open access to the mainland for Filipinos, hoped that this voluntary return of the unemployed would reduce the clamor for complete exclusion.[75] But this hope dimmed as white racists continued to push for their goals.

Repatriation, another of the exclusionists' aims, was considered for several years by the House Committee on Immigration and Naturalization. Although cleared for House action by the committee in 1933, final passage of a repatriation bill did not come until 1935. The legislation provided that transportation would be provided at federal expense for those who wanted to return to the Philippines. Those who accepted this aid lost the right of immediate reentry. They could only return as part of the annual quota of fifty immigrants.[76] Repatriation, as an exclusionist tool, did not work. Only 2,190 of the 45,000 Filipinos resident in the United States took advantage of the federal legislation.[77]

Actually, the efforts of the exclusionists were largely unnecessary. With the collapse of the American economy in the early 1930s and the creation of a farm labor surplus, Filipinos stopped coming in any large numbers. The objective of exclusion was at the same time essentially achieved with the establishment of the small quota by the Tydings-McDuffie Independence Act.

While the mainland was concerned about immigration control during the 1930s, the Hawaiian Sugar Planters' Association worried about the lack of enough cheap laborers. Hawaii did not have ready access to the unemployed that California, Oregon, and Washington had. The planters lobbied successfully during the hearings on the Tydings-McDuffie bill against complete exclusion. Section 8 of the bill permitted unlimited Filipino immigration to the islands if a need could be demonstrated. Determination of a labor shortage and the approval to import additional Filipino laborers were vested with the Department of Interior.[78] Although section 8 represented a major victory for the planters, they found it necessary only once to invoke the provision. This occurred in 1946 when some 7,300 laborers were brought to Hawaii to meet an expected postwar manpower deficit.[79] Nonetheless, from 1946 to the present, Filipino labor has remained important to Hawaii's agriculture.

As noted earlier, Filipino immigration to Hawaii and the mainland increased significantly following the 1965 immigration act. An important study of this recent influx was made in 1971 by the University of Hawaii School of Social Work. Interviews were conducted with 503 Filipino families on the island of Oahu where most of the new immigrants settled. The study found that 474 (94 percent) of the families came from rural areas in the Philippines. Moving from a rural society to Hawaii's urban setting caused serious problems of adaptation for these new immigrants. Filipinos moving to West Coast cities experienced similar difficulties.[80] As with the earlier waves of Filipino migrants, most of the new arrivals were Ilocanos. Of those families interviewed, 461 (92 percent) came from the northern Luzon provinces, 20 came from the area around Manila, 14 came from the Visayan region, and 6 were from other locations.[81]

The university study also examined the occupational characteristics of the recent Filipino immigrants. Whereas the earlier arrivals were unskilled, those coming after 1965 possessed many different skills. Most of them had been farmers or fishermen (36 percent) in the Philippines; 10 percent had been in service occupations. These newer immigrants were better educated than had been the earlier ones. A significant number had completed high school (23 percent) or had earned a college degree (22 percent).[82]

This post-1965 wave of immigrants has been underemployed in Hawaii and on the mainland.[83] They have not been able to match up their former skills and training with jobs in the United States. Almost a fourth of those interviewed in Hawaii found employment as unskilled labor. Another 25 percent were in the service occupations. Only 15 of the 148 immigrants with technical or collegiate education found positions commensurate with their training.[84] Agricultural employment both in Hawaii and on the mainland still provided jobs for many of the new arrivals.

The white majority has never fully appreciated the contribution made to western agriculture's "factories in the fields" by Filipinos or other migrant workers. That same majority has not understood the dream that motivated the Filipinos to work long hard hours. Instead, the Filipinos have been the object of scorn and prejudice for some Americans. And for others, the Filipinos have been the prey of the unscrupulous and the unethical, who have fleeced them of their earnings. The same white majority during the 1930s, while using these people, also had turned upon them and sought to exclude them from the United States.

With the liberalization of immigration laws and an end to legalized exclusion, Filipinos have again seized the opportunity to migrate to the United States and to make a new life. Unlike the earlier immigrants, most of the recent arrivals wish to establish permanent homes, and this desire has added a new dimension to the history of the Filipinos in the United States.

Much more remains to be learned about the recent immigrants as well as the aging agricultural workers of earlier decades. There is an immediate need for trained oral historians to record more fully the experiences of the immigrants of the 1920s. Especially fruitful would be interviews with those still in the United States and those who have returned to the Philippines so that the experiences of these two groups could be compared. Another important area of investigation would be the involvement of the early Filipino immigrants in the Philippine independence movement and in World War II. The movement of Filipinos since 1965 would provide historians with an opportunity to examine recent adaptation in the United States — economic problems, social adaptation, and the response of the majority and other minorities to this new group. As indicated at the beginning of this paper, not much attention has been given to Filipino Americans, yet they have contributed, and continue to contribute, to the American experience. They merit the attention of scholars. ★

Notes

1. U.S. Commissioner of Immigration and Naturalization, *Annual Report, 1972* (Washington, D.C., 1973), 59.

2. Filipino immigration and settlement in the United States have not been the subject of intensive study; there is no comprehensive study of those Filipinos migrating since 1965. The major monograph for the first migration period is the work commissioned by the American Council on the Institute of Pacific Relations: Bruno Lasker, *Filipino Immigration to Continental United States and Hawaii* (Chicago, 1931). Other important monographs are John H. Burma, *Spanish-Speaking Groups in the United States* (Durham, N.C., 1954), and Carey McWilliams, *Brothers Under the Skin* (Rev. ed., Boston, 1964). Filipinos have written significant accounts of their immigration and adaptation experiences; see, for example, Manuel Buaken, *I Have Lived with the American People* (Caldwell, Idaho, 1948), and Maximo C. Manzon, *The Strange Case of the Filipinos in the United States* (New York, 1938). The journal, *Sociology and Social Research,* has published many analytical articles about these people.

3. Carlos P. Romulo, *I Walked with Heroes* (New York, 1961), 130-154.

4. Burma, *Spanish-Speaking Groups,* 138.

5. Sister Mary Dorita Clifford, "The Hawaiian Sugar Planters' Association and Filipino Exclusion," *The Filipino Exclusion Movement, 1927-1935* (Quezon City, Philippines Institute of Asian Studies, Occasional Papers No. 1, 1967), 14-28; Lasker, *Filipino Immigration,* 350-353; interview with James Misajon, chairman, Hawaii State Commission on Manpower and Full Employment, Dec. 18, 1972.

6. *U.S. Statutes at Large,* LX, 416, 1353.

7. *Ibid.,* LXXIX, 911-922; *New York Times,* Oct. 6, 1965, p. 1; U.S. Commissioner of Immigration and Naturalization, *Report, 1970* (Washington, D.C., 1971), 4.

8. Horacio Lava, *Levels of Living in the Ilocos Region* (University of the Philippines, College of Business Administration, Study No. 1, 1938); Henry T. Lewis, *Ilocano Rice Farmers* (Honolulu, 1971), 6.

9. Lasker, *Filipino Immigration,* 351; Calif. Dept. of Industrial Relations, *Facts about Filipino Immigration into California* (Sacramento, 1930), 37-38.

10. Andrew W. Lind, *Hawaii's People* (Honolulu, 1967), 28; Trinidad A. Rojo, "Social Maladjustment Among Filipinos in the United States," *Sociology and Social Research,* XXI (1937), 446-457.

11. Burma, *Spanish-Speaking Groups,* 141-145; Lasker, *Filipino Immigration,* 324-325; Manzon, *Strange Case of the Filipinos,* 7.

12. H. Brett Melendy, *The Oriental Americans* (New York, 1972), 183, 187.

13. U.S. Bureau of the Census, *Subject Reports: Japanese, Chinese and Filipinos in the United States, 1970* (Washington, D.C., 1973), 119.

14. Calif. Dept. of Industrial Relations, *Californians of. . .Filipino Ancestry,* 10; Burma, "The Background of the Current Situation of Filipino-Americans," *Social Forces,* XXX (1951), 42-47.

15. Lind, *Hawaii's People,* 28, 50.

16. Francis J. Brown and Joseph S. Roucek, ed., *One America* (3rd ed., New York, 1952), 361-372.

17. U.S. Bureau of Census, *Nonwhite Population, 1960* (Washington, D.C., 1963), 88; U.S. Bureau of the Census, *Japanese, Chinese, and Filipinos in the United States, 1970,* 123-124.

18. Lewis, *Ilocano Rice Farmers,* 92.

19. *Ibid.,* 26.

20. Burma, *Spanish-Speaking Groups,* 138.

21. J. C. Dionisio to Manuel Quezon, March 7, 1944, Manuel L. Quezon Papers, National Library of the Philippines, Ermiita, Manila.

22. Lasker, *Filipino Immigration,* 21.

23. Buaken, *I Have Lived with the American People,* 59-64.

24. Harry Schwartz, *Seasonal Farm Labor in the United States* (New York, 1945), 154.

25. Lillian Galedo, Laurena Cabanero, and Brian Tom, *Road-*

blocks to Community Building: A Case Study of the Stockton Community Center Project (Davis, Calif.: University of California Asian American Research Project Working Publication No. 4, 1970, mimeographed), 8.

26. Lloyd H. Fisher, *The Harvest Labor Market in California* (Cambridge, Mass., 1953), 11.

27. Carey McWilliams, *Factories in the Field* (Boston, 1939), 118; Schwartz, *Seasonal Farm Labor*, 83.

28. Fisher, *Harvest Labor Market*, 39-40.

29. *Ibid.*, 38; Benicio Catapusan, "The Filipino Labor Cycle in the United States," *Sociology and Social Research*, XIX (1934), 61-63.

30. Schwartz, *Seasonal Farm Labor*, 92-93; Fisher, *Harvest Labor Market*, 29.

31. Emory S. Bogardus, "American Attitudes Towards Filipinos," *Sociology and Social Research*, XIV (1929), 59-69.

32. Edward C. McDonagh, "Attitudes Toward Ethnic Farm Workers in Coachella Valley," *Sociology and Social Research*, XL (1955), 10-18.

33. Burma, *Spanish-Speaking Groups*, 141-145.

34. Calif. Dept. of Industrial Relations, *Californians of. . .Filipino Ancestry*, 12.

35. Lind, *Hawaii's People*, 75, 77.

36. *Ibid.*, 100; Calif. Dept. of Industrial Relations, *Californians of. . .Filipino Ancestry*, 14.

37. Lind, *Hawaii's People*, 76, 78.

38. Schwartz, *Seasonal Farm Labor*, 100-101.

39. Mark Day, *Forty Acres, Cesar Chavez and the Farm Workers* (New York, 1971), 36-37; John Dunne, *Delano* (New York, 1971), 77-83.

40. *Ibid.*, 39-43.

41. Walton Bean, *California, An Interpretative History* (2nd ed., New York, 1973), 496-498, 501-505.

42. D. F. Gonzalo, "Social Adjustments of Filipinos in America," *Sociology and Social Research*, XIV (1929), 167-169.

43. Lillian Galedo and Theresa Q. Mar, "Filipinos in a Farm Labor Camp," in *Asians in America* (Davis, Calif.: University of California Asian American Research Project Working Publication No. 3, 1970, mimeographed), 58; Galedo, Cabanero, and Tom, *Roadblocks to Community Building*, 10.

44. McWilliams, *Brothers Under the Skin*, 238.

45. Quoted in Lasker, *Filipino Immigration*, 133-134.

46. McWilliams, *Brothers Under the Skin*, 238-239.

47. Interview with Charles F. Crook, Feb. 1930, James Earl Wood Papers, Bancroft Library, University of California, Berkeley.

48. Buaken, *I Have Lived with the American People*, 178.

49. Gonzalo, "Social Adjustments of Filipinos," 173.

50. Galedo and Mar, "Filipinos in a Farm Labor Camp," 53-56.

51. *Ibid.*, 56-57.

52. *Ibid.*, 57.

53. *Ibid.*, 58.

54. Carlos Bulosan to Dorothy Babb, Dec. 12, 1937, in Carlos Bulosan, *Sound of Falling Light: Letters in Exile*, Dolores S. Feria, ed. (Quezon City, 1960), 191-192.

55. Bogardus, "American Attitudes," 59-60.

56. *Ibid.*, 63-64.

57. House Committee on Immigration and Naturalization, "Hearings on Exclusion of Immigration from the Philippine Islands," 71 Cong., 2 sess. (1931), 42-46.

58. Burma, *Spanish-Speaking Groups*, 144; House Committee on Immigration and Naturalization, "Hearings on to Provide for the Return to the Philippine Islands of Unemployed Filipinos Resident in the Continental United States," 72 Cong., 2 sess. (1933), 8-9.

59. Buaken, *I Have Lived with the American People*, 70.

60. Emory S. Bogardus, "Filipino Immigrant Attitudes," *Sociology and Social Research*, XIV (1930), 469-479.

61. *California Statutes*, 34th Sess. (1901), 335.

62. Nellie Foster, "Legal Status of Filipino Intermarriage in California," *Sociology and Social Research*, XVI (1932), 447-452.

63. *Roldan v. Los Angeles County*, 129 Calif. 267 (1933); *San Francisco Chronicle*, March 30, 1933, p. 1.

64. *California Statutes*, 50th Sess. (1933), 561.

65. *Perez v. Sharp*, Calif. Reports, 2nd Series, 711 (1948).

66. Randall Risdon, "A Study of Interracial Marriages Based on Data for Los Angeles County," *Sociology and Social Research*, XXXIX (1954), 92-95.

67. Buaken, *I Have Lived with the American People*, 94-97; Burma, *Spanish-Speaking Groups*, 152-153.

68. Calif. Dept. of Industrial Relations, *Facts About Filipino Immigration*, 73-74.

69. Quoted in Buaken, *I Have Lived with the American People*, 169.

70. *Ibid.*, 169-170.

71. *Ibid.*, 75; Buaken, *I Have Lived with the American People*, 97-105; *San Jose Mercury*, Jan. 11-23, 1930.

72. Commonwealth Club of California, *Transactions*, XXIV (1929), 320; Lasker, *Filipino Immigration*, v; California, *Senate Journal*, 48th Sess. (1929), 2690.

73. *U.S. Statutes at Large*, XLIII, 168; Garel A. Grunder and William E. Livezey, *The Philippines and the United States* (Norman, Okla., 1951), 205-233.

74. Manzon, *Strange Case of Filipinos*, 5-6; McWilliams, *Brothers Under the Skin*, 243.

75. *San Francisco Chronicle*, Jan. 30, 1931, p. 41.

76. *U.S. Statutes at Large*, XLIX, 478-479; H. Brett Melendy, "California's Discrimination Against Filipinos, 1927-1935," in *The Filipino Exclusion Movement, 1927-1935* (Quezon City, Philippines Institute of Asian Studies, Occasional Paper No. 1, 1967), 10.

77. McWilliams, *Brothers Under the Skin*, 243.

78. Clifford, "Hawaiian Sugar Planters' Association and Filipino Exclusion," 25-26.

79. *Ibid.*, 26-28.

80. Hawaii, Commission on Manpower and Full Employment, *Report of the State Immigration Service Center* (Honolulu, Jan. 1972), 46-47; interview with James Misajon, 1972.

81. Hawaii, *Report. . .Immigration Service Center*, 46.

82. *Ibid.*, 47.

83. Interview with James Misajon, Dec. 18, 1972.

84. Hawaii, *Report. . .Immigration Service Center*, 48.

SMALL BUSINESS AMONG KOREANS IN LOS ANGELES

By Edna Bonacich, Ivan Light, and Charles Choy Wong

Anyone familiar with the city of Los Angeles who has not driven through the downtown area in the last two or three years would be astonished at the transformation of the Olympic Boulevard area between Crenshaw and Hoover. The change has been dramatic enough to attract the attention of a national news magazine:

> It's called Koreatown, a 2-mile stretch along Los Angeles's busy Olympic Boulevard, where 45,000 Korean immigrants have settled into new lives during the last five years. What used to be Mexican-American, Japanese and Jewish stores and businesses are now mostly Korean, with giant Oriental letters spread across their low-slung storefronts.[1]

Small business is flowering among the Koreans in Los Angeles.

This paper is a tentative first statement of some of our early findings and ideas regarding Korean small business. We plan to pursue the study further, testing some of the hypotheses developed here. It should be noted that there are aspects of the Korean community other than small business which are worthy of attention. The immigrants face numerous problems, such as language difficulties and discrimination in the labor market.[2] It is not our intent to minimize these

An earlier version of this paper was presented at the American Sociological Association meeting in New York, 1976.

problems; they are simply not the subject of this particular paper.

BACKGROUND

The Korean community in the United States in general, and Los Angeles in particular, is mainly a new one, a product of the change in U.S. immigration laws in 1965. However, a small community had been established prior to this. The first Koreans who came to the U.S., starting in 1883, were diplomats, political refugees, students, and merchants.[3] Emigrants began coming in 1899,[4] arriving in any numbers only after 1903.[5] Between 1903 and 1905 over 7,000 Korean emigrants went to Hawaii,[6] and another 1,000 to the American mainland.[7] Many of the Hawaiian settlers moved on to the mainland.[8]

The immigration was rapidly curtailed by the establishment of Korea as a Japanese protectorate in 1905 and eventual annexation in 1910. On the emigration side, Japan restricted the issuance of passports to Koreans wishing to move to the U.S.,[9] while Koreans treated as Japanese in America, much against their will, were subjected to all of the anti-Japanese agitation. Thus the Asiatic Exclusion League, founded in 1905, was first known as the Japanese and Korean Exclusion League.[10] The presidential order of 1907 cutting off indirect immigration from Hawaii to the mainland, the Gentlemen's Agreement of 1907-08, and the Exclusion Act of 1924, all aimed primarily at the Japanese, adversely affected Korean rights to immigration.

As a result, the number of Koreans in this country was always exceedingly small. According to the 1930 census, there were 462 Koreans in the U.S. in 1910, 1,224 in 1920, and 1,860 in 1930. Most of these were in California: 304 in 1910, 772 in 1920, and 1,097 in 1930.[11] Givens estimated the Los Angeles Korean population at 650 in 1939, noting that this was the largest concentration in America.[12] By 1960 the South Korean Vice-Consul estimated that Los Angeles had about 7,000 Koreans, including immigrants, permanent residents, and non-immigrants.[13] Compared to a census count of 82,261 Japanese in Los Angeles in 1960,[14] the Koreans were a very small ethnic minority.

The early community is noteworthy for its affiliation to Christianity and its political concern with Korean independence from Japan.[15] Signs of small business concentration are evident even at this stage. Givens enumerated 73 small businesses, 33 of which were fruit and vegetable stands.[16] And Kim reports:

When Korean immigrants managed to gather some capital, they began to operate individual enterprises. . . . By the end of the Japanese occupation of Korea [1945] most of them became self-sufficient and often well-to-do.[17]

The Immigration and Naturalization Act of 1965 abolished discriminatory quotas based on national origins and set an overall annual limit of 170,000 from the Eastern hemisphere (territories outside of the Americas). Each country is now restricted to a maximum of 20,000 per annum. Both limits exempt immediate relatives of American citizens, including minor children, spouses, and parents.[18] Within these limits, preference is given to other relatives and workers with skills deemed necessary to the American economy.[19]

An unanticipated consequence of the new laws has been a sharp rise in immigration from Asia.[20] After a three-year phase-out of the old system, Asian immigration jumped to over 20 percent of the total (75,679 of 358,574) in 1969, and by 1974 comprised one-third (130,662 of 394,861) of all entering immigrants.[21] The total number of Asian immigrants to enter the country in the ten year period was 832,453.[22]

The Korean proportion of this immigration has gradually been rising to the point where Koreans make up over one-fifth of Asian immigrants.[23] As of 1974 they were the third largest group entering the U.S., less only than Mexicans and Pilipinos. Between 1965 and 1974 a total of 111,914 Korean immigrants entered the U.S.,[24] along with 145,459 non-immigrants,[25] some of whom adjust their status to immigrant after a while and then are enumerated with the newly-arrived immigrants, while unknown numbers remain illegally. Among students, for example, a survey conducted by the Korean Ministry of Education in 1967 estimated that 90 percent of Korean students in the United States do not return to Korea.[26] Of course, this figure may no longer hold true.

The 1970 census found 70,598 Koreans in the United States, 9,395 of whom lived in the Los Angeles/Long Beach SMSA.[27] This is widely believed to have been an undercount, the national figure at that time probably exceeding 100,000.[28] Reasons for the undercount include inability to read English language forms, suspicion concerning the goals of information gatherers, and classification practices of the census in ambiguous cases.[29] Recent immigration has raised the national estimate to 200,000 in 1975.

Although on entry less than ten percent declare Los Angeles as the place where they plan to reside,[30] there is good reason to suspect these statistics.[31] Leaders in the community invariably describe Los Angeles as the major center of Korean American settlement. Lee, for example, states that "the greatest concentration [of new Korean immigrants] is in Los Angeles, which now has become the center of Korean American activities in the United States."[32] In 1975 estimates of the Los Angeles community ranged from 60,000 to 75,000 and growing. Evidence supporting these estimates comes from a 1975 community directory put out by the Korean Association of Southern California. Generally recognized as incomplete, the directory lists 11,227 families. This would indicate close to 50,000 people if we adopt the 1970 census estimate of 4.4 Koreans per household.

THE PROBLEM

Immigrants who came to the United States from Asia before 1924, when immigration was effectively cut off, started small businesses in disproportionate numbers. Light found that, in California in 1929, Chinese and Japanese owned 31 percent more retail stores than one would expect from their numbers.[33] In a study of the Japanese in Seattle before World War II, Miyamoto points to "the overwhelming dominance in their lives of the 'small shop.' "[34]

The new immigration from Asia, of which Koreans are one example, is very different from the old in two important ways. First, the immigrants themselves are no longer a largely uneducated peasantry. This is partly a function of developments in the countries of emigration, where universal education has become commonplace, and partly a product of U.S. immigration policy which selects for skill and education. In eight out of the ten years from 1965 to 1974 over 50 percent of entering Koreans who declared an occupation other than housewife were professionals.[35] The net effect is that the Korean minority is a highly educated one. According to the 1970 census, the median school years completed for all Los Angeles/Long Beach residents is 12.4 years compared to 14.3 years for Koreans.[36]

The second change has occurred, not among the immigrants, but in the context into which they are moving. The U.S. economy has been transformed since 1924 from one in which there was considerable small business and self-employment, to a highly centralized economy with a small number of owners of large amounts of capital. The vast majority of the population have become wage earners.[37] Centralization has been accompanied by increased efficiency; technology has been introduced in many phases of production and distribution, increasing speed and reducing error. Scientific management has led to greater control over the work process.[38] Vertical integration, linking the production and distribution process under one corporate umbrella, has increased

reliability of supply and eliminated the middleman. As a result, the number of small businesses has been declining.

These shifts in the economy have a direct impact on traditional areas of Asian concentration. For example, many early Japanese immigrants entered truck-farming on a small scale. Today, large-scale mechanized agribusiness dominates the produce industry. The Japanese used to be active in the wholesaling and retailing of produce. Now chain stores, such as Safeway, link production to distribution, curtailing the need for wholesaling. Small grocery stores must face competition from supermarkets which need less labor in proportion to sales. Laundromats have undercut the traditional Chinese hand laundry. Small gift shops must compete with large department stores. Fast food chains, such as MacDonalds and Colonel Sanders, threaten the smaller ethnic restaurant. Centralization and capital intensity would seem to toll the knell of Asian entrepreneurship.

Despite these forces, Korean immigrants show a marked movement into small business. Our problem is to understand how and why this happens in an economy which is clearly moving in the opposite direction.

THE NATURE OF KOREAN BUSINESS

Extent of Business

The 1975 Directory of the Korean Association of Southern California lists over 1,300 "firms" in its yellow pages. Some of these (47 alumni associations, 72 churches, and 100 non-profit associations) are not, strictly speaking, businesses, though in some cases, as in the minister of an independent church, the person in charge may be virtually self-employed. Even if we eliminate these marginal cases, the directory lists over 1,000 businesses, and it is acknowledged to be incomplete. Indeed the Korean Association plans to put out a new, more complete, directory in 1976, which will include another 1,000 businesses. Many Koreans are not participating in the directory and a more accurate estimate of the number of businesses is 4,000.[39] The newspapers typically announce at least one opening per issue. One source reports:

> Hardly a week goes by without the 'grand opening' of a new store-front with hangul (Korean alphabet) signs proclaiming grocery stores, restaurants, barbers, hamburger stands, gas stations, or other small business.[40]

Whatever the precise figure, it constantly must be revised upward.

While there are clearly "many" Korean businesses in Los Angeles, are Koreans more likely than others to enter small business? Assuming the popula-

tion is 70,000 and household size is 4.4, the number of households in the community would be about 16,000. Taking the estimate of 4,000 businesses as accurate, about 25 percent of Korean families in Los Angeles are currently in business for themselves. For the U.S. as a whole, in 1973, eight percent of males 16 years or over who were not engaged in agriculture, and who may be seen to represent families (since we are mainly talking of "family businesses"), were self-employed.[41]

Business Lines

Korean business tends to be concentrated in certain lines. They are likely to be in wholesaling and retailing, in service "shops" such as barber shops and restaurants, and in the independent professions. They tend to concentrate in "middleman" occupations, mobilizing resources to provide a service to a client which the client might have provided directly for him or herself. For example, Korean maintenance companies provide janitorial services to large office buildings, not unlike labor contractors of old. Or real estate agents specialize in locating businesses around the city for Koreans to purchase. There is some light manufacturing, i.e., garment industry sub-contracting, in which the enterprise takes on one small part of the production process, such as sewing, and which, from the entrepreneur's point of view, again resembles labor contracting. One the whole, however, Korean businesses tend to avoid manufacturing or heavy industry or concerns which tie up large amounts of capital. They prefer more liquidable lines, perhaps because of the absence of large sums of capital among the immigrants.

The single most popular line is the wig business. One hundred and forty are listed in the directory and we were told by community sources the real figure is more like 200, about 50 of which are importers and wholesalers to Korean retailers. As of mid-1975, 90 to 95 percent of all wig shops in the city were owned by Koreans. The group "monopoly" of wig shops rests, in part, on the fact that, since wig production shifted from relying mainly on natural hair to synthetics, Korea has come to produce 70 percent of the world's wigs. Other popular businesses include gas stations (134 listed in the directory), grocery stores (107), restaurants (78), and liquor stores (22, but believed to be considerably undercounted).

It should be noted that, despite self-employment, Korean businesses are not all independent. A number, such as gas stations and some restaurants (e.g., hamburger stands) are franchised from larger corporations. Similarly, insurance agencies (32 listed) may be branches of larger operations.

Size of Businesses

In 1972, a study of businesses was conducted by the census bureau. It found 1,201 Korean businesses in the United States and 398 in Los Angeles,[42] obviously an undercount. The mean gross income for Korean businesses was $54,820 per annum. Only 21 percent had any paid employees and of these the average number of employees was six.

In a study of 278 Korean businesses in the Olympic area, David Kim found that about 70 percent were what he describes as "small scale."[43] In particular, 93 percent had ten employees or less, 68 percent had total assets of less than $50,000, and 47 percent, less than $20,000.[44] It seems safe to conclude that Korean business is mainly small.[45] There are, however, exceptions especially among trading companies, import-export establishments, and whole-

sale firms, e.g., Kim found two such firms with assets over $1,000,000.[46] Even so, the operation itself can still be small. We interviewed one clothing importer who had received over $3,000,000 in loans from a bank and admitted to an annual sales volume of $10,000,000. Yet his offices are small and he employs directly no more than two or three people. He acts as a middleman between producers in Korea, who may employ thousands, and large retailers here who may also employ an army of workers. But his own operation can still be characterized as a type of "small business."

Clientele

Koreans make up a significant portion of the clientele of Korean businesses. Kim estimates that slightly over half of the customers of Korean businesses in the Olympic area are Korean.[47] This is not surprising given that the Olympic area is the center of Korean residence. One would expect that businesses located elsewhere in the city would rely much less on a Korean clientele.

There is some variation in clientele by line of business. Restaurants and grocery stores cater more to Koreans, gas stations, liquor stores, and wig shops to non-Koreans. Entrepreneurs may change the ethnicity of their clients during the course of their careers as they move, for example, from gas stations to grocery stores, or from grocery stores to liquor stores. These shifts occur fairly frequently, suggesting that a Korean clientele is not an essential feature of their business.

It is possible that Korean businesses which do not cater to other Koreans tend to have a disproportionately large low-income minority clientele. At least we have been told that wig stores and liquor stores tend to be concentrated in the ghettos and barrios of the city. Even the Olympic area itself has significant proportions of minority residents who are likely frequenters of Korean shops.[48] Having a black, Latin and Chicano (and perhaps poor white) clientele suggests that Koreans may be playing a "middleman minority" role, acting as a commercial and service class to the poorer strata of society and bearing the brunt of their hostility.

In sum, Korean entrepreneurs concentrate heavily in trade and service, rather than in the production of commodities. Their businesses are small and rely little on wage labor. And their clientele is not confined to the ethnic community. These characteristics suggest that the Koreans are becoming a "middle-man minority."[49] Such groups are commonly found in economies where most people are producing for consumption, and where an alien group comes in and gains a disproportionate share of what little trade there is. That a similar group concentration in trade should arise in an advanced capitalist society is puzzling indeed.

HOW KOREAN BUSINESS IS ESTABLISHED

The new Korean immigrants, for the most part, come without prior small business experience. In this way, despite their higher levels of education, they are similar to the pre-1924 Asian immigrants, who were mainly laborers. The old immigrants relied on two major mechanisms for advancement into business: thrift and the efficient utilization of community resources. The Koreans use both of these means plus some new ones. We shall consider four factors which aid in the movement to entrepreneurship: thrift, the use of communal resources, the use of public resources, and the role of the South Korean government.

Thrift

Koreans are thrifty in two important ways. They amass capital by saving their earnings, and they and their families work long hours for little immediate remuneration.

Regarding capital, despite government restrictions on the amount one can take out (the upper limit is $1,400), some Koreans do come with capital in hand. Apart from smuggling it out illegally, an important segment of the Los Angeles community came indirectly, working in Germany and Vietnam as coal miners, nurses, and engineers,[50] and may have collected some capital there. The most common pattern, however, is to come with little and work hard for two or three years until one has saved about $20,000 to invest in a business. The wife typically works in a garment factory[51] and the husband may carry two jobs, perhaps working as a janitor or gas station attendant. Wages in these jobs are low, making it difficult to save, and the aspiring entrepreneur must sacrifice living standards for a while.

Korean thrift is shown not only in lack of spending, but also in hard work. A Korean family puts in more time than the average American family before they acquire a business of their own, and the pattern continues after the goal is reached. Korean businesses stay open longer hours and on weekends and holidays. They make use of unpaid family labor. In addition, the business may receive unpaid outside support in the form of babysitting by a grandmother either here or in Korea. The immigrants work so hard that their health suffers.

> According to a report made by the Korean Doctor's Association in Southern California, most of the immigrants are neglecting their health in the midst of struggle for survival in the new land.[52]

Communal Resources

The Koreans form a highly organized community. There are numerous associations which form hierarchies and overlap. According to one source, there are between 500 and 600 associations, and nine out of ten Koreans in Los Angeles belong to at least one, and most to more than one.[53] At the pinnacle is the Korean Association of Southern California, founded in 1961. It has a membership of about 5,000 families and coordinates roughly fifty constituent organizations. Especially important from the point of view of business development are occupational and trade associations. There are at least twenty-two of these, including such organizations as the Korea Hair Product Association of America or the Korean Food Association of Southern California.

Community organization is important for business development. Associations aid in the efficient distribution of resources through the community. Even those which do not have an overt economic purpose, such as alumni associations or churches, may serve this function by bringing people together and providing chains of communication. A number of resources are communally generated and distributed, including capital, labor and jobs, clients, and information.

Among early Chinese and Japanese immigrants, the pooling of capital, especially through rotating credit associations, was an important advantage in gaining a foothold in business.[54] Rotating credit is found among the Koreans, and is called *gae*.[55] A group of friends or members of an organization pool money and give it to one member, on a regular basis, shifting the recipient until everyone has had a turn. The system provides interest-free capital. Typically in Los Angeles a *gae* will collect about $500, the highest reportedly reaching $3,000. Such a system depends on trust and honor of participants in continuing to contribute after they have benefited. The high degree of community organization encourages honor since a person is visible in many roles and is dependent on others in many contexts. Despite this, people do occasionally default on a *gae*.

The early Asian immigrants developed a system of labor paternalism which is still evident among the Koreans. Preference is given to a member of the ethnic group in hiring, but work conditions are poor, the hours long, pay low and irregular, and membership in unions not contemplated. Apart from the guarantee of a job, the worker receives paternalistic treatment, including on-the-job training with a view to setting up a business of his own. In exchange, the employer obtains a reliable, loyal, and cheap worker.

Another feature of old Asian enterprises was a special relationship with ethnic community clientele. Fellow Asians would patronize Asian stores when they could, and would in turn get a special price or better credit arrangement. Among Koreans this does not occur overtly; if a Korean and non-Korean walked into a Korean store they would pay the same price for the same item. However, Korean clients do receive preferential treatment through indirect channels, by "specials" advertised in the vernacular press, and by referrals coupled with a discount through community organizations.

Information and training are important resources which the community can effectively mobilize. The ethnic press plays an important role in the process. In Los Angeles there are four Korean dailies, two weeklies, and two television stations each broadcasting a two-hour weekly program. Through these channels Koreans are given up-to-date information on business trends, and can read articles on how to manage a business. Community organizations help disseminate information by running lecture series and classes, or by operating a telephone Hotline which, among other things, offered aid in 71 cases of business and job counseling in 1974.[56] And some private Korean concerns (e.g., a real estate agency that locates small businesses being sold around the city) specialize in providing information as a service.

Needless to say, there are businesses (such as law firms) outside of the Korean community which specialize in information too. The point is that, by focusing on a specific ethnic group, the amount of business-related information generated in the Korean community far exceeds that available to the average Los Angeleno. As one source puts it:

> One of the ironies of our system is that for all our verbal commitment to the American Dream we seldom teach our youth the basic knowledge that anyone would need who wanted to go into business for himself....Knowledge about self-employment in this country is quite a well-kept secret.[57]

Not so for the Koreans.

The ability of the Korean community to mobilize its own resources in establishing businesses is impressive. However there is another, less rosey, side to the picture. Not only does the community "help its own;" it "exploits" them. There is a flowering of "middleman" firms, such as business consultants or immigration experts, which depend on the problems and aspirations of the new immigrants for their own success. One woman, for example, made a forturne selling real estate to other Koreans. There is a tendency to charge fees for all services. The labor contractor is another occupation which takes advantage of the difficult circumstances of new immigrants to turn a good profit. Indeed the use of non-union low-wage workers or even unpaid family labor which works long hours for little immediate return, can be seen as a form of exploitation. In general, there is a tendency for the older immigrants to climb the economic ladder on the backs of newer immigrants, a prevalent practice among pre-1924 European immigrants in the east. It is a system that works to everyone's advantage so long as immigration continues. Should the influx from Korea suddenly be curtailed, however, the latest arrivals could be trapped at the bottom of the economic ladder.

Non-Communal Resources

Unlike earlier Asian immigrants, the Koreans are determined to make use of all resources. They want to get full value for their tax dollar, and are not reluctant to use political means to get it, perhaps because they are more eduated than the old immigrants and the "system" more susceptible to minority demands. For example, aspiring businessmen do not only rely on their own or friends' savings for financing. Many turn to American banks or the Small Business Administration. Kim used data provided by the SBA showing that between 1971 and 1974 Koreans received 101 SBA loans totaling $10,328,750.[58]

The community helps members tap non-communal resources. Community organizations and the press will direct people to public agencies, such as the Office of Minority Business Enterprise (OMBE), the Asian American National Business Alliance (AANBA), and the Interracial Council for Business Opportunity (ICBO), which provide business assistance.

The community tries to gain access to government officials to make sure their needs are met. They pressured the Los Angeles Police Department into doubling the police protection in the Olympic area. They pressured the Mayor's office into appointing a Korean aide.[59] The ethnic press urges Koreans to be good citizens, at the same time encouraging them to exercise the rights of citizenship. An article will suggest, for example, that if a Korean should take a trip to Washington, D.C., he should visit his Congressman.

South Korean Government

Another resource which Korean immigrants can use which was not available to earlier Asian immigrants is aid from their home government. The South Korean government encourages emigration, its philosophy being to send overseas the less wealthy elements of the population (there is a ceiling on the amount of property one can own to emigrate), and to help them get rich there. They will either come home, or send back some of their wealth, enriching Korea either way.

The South Korean government helps local businesses in at least two ways. First, it aids in training and information; some of the classes in entrepreneurship run by the Korean Association are taught by visiting dignitaries. Second, and more important, it helps to provide capital. There are now two Korean banks in Los Angeles: the Korea Exchange Bank (specializing in international trade) and the Korea Exchange Bank of California (which is more concerned with local-oriented business).

Korea benefits from the development of local

business because it helps to establish export outlets. The Korean Exchange Bank, which deals mainly with local importers of Korean products, has an annual loan volume of $100,000,000. Two lines of export are of especial importance: hair products and clothing. As we have seen, Korea produces most of the world's wigs. Their dominant position depends on the use of cheap female labor which is paid about 50,000 won ($100) per month. "Vertical integration" is prevalent in that Korean importers use local Korean small businesses as their chief retail outlets.

Importing clothing is of a much larger scale and of far greater importance. According to a number of sources, the Los Angeles garment industry is now controlled by Jews, but the Koreans are starting to make a crack in the edifice. Although there is some local manufacture, the Jews depend on importing from "cheap labor" countries such as Brazil and Taiwan. They do not as yet import from Korea, leaving that trade to Koreans. About 20 percent of the clothing imported to the U.S. now comes from Korea. Unlike the wig business, the major outlets are not Korean small businesses, but large volume, Jewish-owned, retailers with annual sales of around $30,000,000.

The local Korean press plays a role in Korea's efforts to establish exports. Three of the local papers are versions of Seoul newspapers, with a section changed to provide local news and advertising. In turn the Seoul papers are sponsored by major corporations and conglomerates in Korea. The Los Angeles versions are shipped back and distributed to the corporate executives, who thereby learn of commercial possibilities here. The local press plays the role of "an eye on the U.S. economy."

Another benefit to Korea in aiding local business is the sending back of remittances to families in the homeland. The Korean Exchange Bank handles most of these, and reports that for the past few years it has been sending back about $5,000,000 per annum.

It should be noted that the South Korean government's activities in the local community are not all viewed in a positive light. There is considerable negative sentiment towards the Park regime. Some of the newspapers are vociferously anti-Park, which is not surprising given that a number of local Koreans emigrated for political reasons. Thus the community is divided over the government's intrusion.

WHY KOREANS ENGAGE IN SMALL BUSINESS

The reasons why Koreans enter small business in an economy which is becoming increasingly centralized in ever larger economic units can be discussed under two headings: the immediate reasons as experienced and articulated by the Koreans themselves, and the larger forces in the social system which the participants may not be aware of. The following discussion presents possibilities, not conclusions.

Immediate Reasons

One of the most frequent reasons given for entering small business is the lack of adequate alternatives. Koreans face discrimination in the job market, e.g., trained professionals are unable to get licenses,[60] and suffer a language handicap.[61] They are forced to work as gas station attendants, janitors, sewing machine operators, nurses aides, and lab technicians. In the face of such unattractive alternatives, self-employment becomes appealing.

A second commonly articulated reason concerns the immigration process itself. Establishing a small business is one way for someone on a temporary visa to become a permanent resident. The Immigration and Naturalization Service will adjust the status of persons who are self-employed on the assumption they will contribute to the American economy.[62] Once established, the business can be used for sponsoring other relatives, since assurance can be provided that they will be employed.

Both of the above reasons imply that Koreans enter small business against their will, or at best are so constrained that they have little choice. We question this, believing that many Koreans would enter small business even if they had better job opportunities and were not faced with immigration problems. This brings us to a third frequently mentioned reason: to provide education for their children. This suggests that Koreans view entrepreneurship as a way to make money. Education for one's children is one of the goals which can be achieved with wealth. This viewpoint is supported by anomalous stories of well-established professionals in Korea, with a secure reputation and large clientele, throwing over their practice to come to America to open a restaurant. Or we spoke to a Korean student in engineering at UCLA, who would not face language or licensing problems in getting a job, yet plans to enter small business rather than engineering. Why? Because he sees a definite limit on the life-time earnings of an engineer, while opportunities appear limitless in small business. It seems the Koreans see this country as a land of economic opportunity. They have bought the "American dream" while, paradoxically, most Americans have given up on it (at least judging from the low and decreasing level of self-employment). It is puzzling that immigrants see, more than the natives, opportunities for self-employment. Perhaps the answer lies in the larger social system.

Larger Reasons

Unarticulated reasons for concentrating in small business can be divided into two types: those which come from the Koreans themselves (internal factors),

and those which come from the American social system. One internal factor concerns the level of economic development in Korea. Koreans come from an economy where small business is still very much alive. That they aspire to enter it is, therefore, not at all surprising. The fact that Korea is a poorer country than the U.S. also encourages Koreans to be thrifty. They may be willing to live for a while on a level that an American would consider very low, but does not compare unfavorably with the Korean level of living.

We believe there is truth to this explanation, yet a puzzle remains. Given that the Korean immigrant approach of thrift and self-denial works and proves there are still opportunities for small business within American advanced capitalism, why do not her natives pursue the same path? The answer, we hypothesize, lies in a subtle issue of consciousness. Monopoly capitalism has made the American people into an army of wage and salary workers who have essentially given up the American dream of making it in small business. The reasons for this are not just resignation; they are unwilling to pay the costs of small business. How many Americans would be willing to keep a shop open seven days a week, fifteen hours a day? The fact is, the American working class has fought long and hard for a comfortable and secure life. They value leisure time and the right not to have to work too hard for long hours. They value job security and the comfort of not having to worry about the job folding. Needless to say, not all American workers have attained these goals, but we would contend that even the unemployed in the ghetto share this new consciousness,[63] preferring an eight-hour-a-day job with reasonable pay and fringe benefits, to the risky and hard-working life of the small entrepreneur. For Koreans, in contrast, hard work, long hours, thrift, taking economic risks (admittedly minimized by communal support) are not yet alien, since Korea has not yet experienced a labor movement on a scale remotely approaching the American.

But apart from internal factors, are there any forces within American monopoly capitalism which encourage Korean immigrants to enter small business? We shall consider three possibilities. The first is that the "system" helps to create Korean small business. It uses Korean immigrants as a middleman minority to deal with the masses, especially low-income minorities, helping to distribute corporate products, and bearing the brunt of hostility, crime, and low profits accruing to retailers in poor areas.[64] A number of points support this interpretation. The policies of the Immigration and Naturalization Service, as we have seen, help to push Koreans into small business, and the SBA provides some of the wherewithal. The largest number of SBA loans to Koreans were given to liquor stores (33 out of 101)[65] which are quite likely to operate in the ghetto or barrio.

Against this interpretation is the fact that

Koreans help to distribute not only American, but also Korean corporate products. In the wig, garment, and some food products industries, they are at odds with local big business. Also, American financial institions do not unambiguously support middleman-type firms. Despite the large number of SBA loans to liquor stores, Korean garment manufacturers received much larger loans, averaging $450,000 compared to $86,000 for a liquor store.[66] Similarly, private banks seem to favor manufacturing,[67] suggesting that the middleman role is less than encouraged by big business.

The second approach is to see monopoly capitalism as less active in the development of Korean business. The large corporations leave gaps in the economy which prove inefficient for them to fill. The corner grocery store between two shopping centers, satisfying the demand for the occasional few items needed between weekly shoppings or at odd hours, is a case in point. Similarly, the ghetto and barrio, with high crime rates and credit problems, may be deserted by the corporations for more profitable locations. In other words, the edifice of monopoly capitalism may be somewhat porous, leaving niches which the enterprising small businessman can take advantage of. This view fits with "dual labor market theory,"[68] which sees the economy as divided into core and peripheral industries. Korean business tends to fall in the latter category.

Whether the "gaps" in corporate domination will remain is another question. Some would argue that they are technologically determined so that it will never be efficient for big capital to take them over. We are inclined to believe the gaps are signs of uneven development, and will inevitably fall prey to centralizing pressures. The service industries tend to be newer and are therefore less "advanced" in their organization, but sooner or later a few large corporations will dominate these too. Meanwhile, Koreans help to fill the gaps with small businesses which are able to run fairly efficiently. Korean enterprise can be seen as a retarding influence on the total "monopolization" of the economy.[69]

A third interpretation is that Koreans actively create small business niches within monopoly capitalism, and are a positive decentralizing force, able, in some cases, to compete (in a sense) with the corporations. This seems to be the case in a few lines, namely, garment industry subcontracting and maintenance companies. In the garment industry, for example, sewing could obviously be done in large factories under assembly-line conditions. That it is subcontracted to small sweatshops, of which Korean shops are only one example, suggests they are able to produce the goods for less. Of course the "competition" is very limited since the sweatshop has virtually no control over most of the production process.

Unlike retailing and service shops, the garment factory and maintenance business have the character-

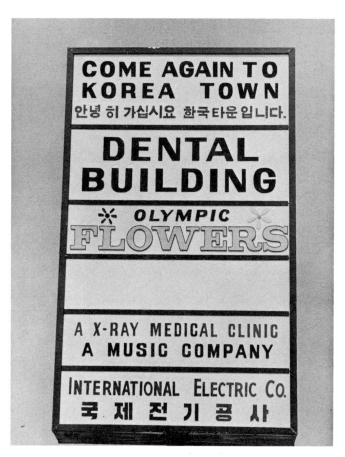

COME AGAIN TO
KOREA TOWN
안녕히 가십시요 한국타운 입니다.
DENTAL
BUILDING
✳ OLYMPIC ✳
FLOWERS

A X-RAY MEDICAL CLINIC
A MUSIC COMPANY

INTERNATIONAL ELECTRIC CO.
국 제 전 기 공 사

istic of using large labor pools. The firm owners are almost in the business of labor contracting to the large corporations, except that they retain some control over the labor process. The role of the Korean entrepreneur, then, is to help the corporations exploit cheap immigrant labor, which, through paternalism and community ties, is kept docile and non-unionized.

Of the three interpretations, we believe the second has most cogency, i.e., that the monopolization of the economy is incomplete, allowing enterprising Koreans to take advantage of the less developed areas. The third interpretation also appears to have some validity but is restricted to only a few types of enterprise. So far, we find little support for the idea that the big corporations encourage the Koreans to play middleman in minority areas. Their role seems more passive; they find the poorer areas to be less profitable and leave them to immigrants who are willing (or forced through lack of alternatives) to accept the reduced profit margins and higher crime rate.

CONCLUSION

Two questions relating to the future remain. First, what will happen to Korean entrepreneurship if, as we predict, monopoly capitalism continues to extend its influence into all branches of the economy? One possibility is that the process will never be complete, as new competitive industries will always be emerging. Another is that Koreans will adapt by running semi-independent shops, such as franchises.

The second question concerns the issue of race relations. Middleman minorities have notoriously been ill-received by the communities in which they reside. They face antagonism from their clientele, business competitors, and organized labor.[70] It is not impossible that Koreans may face some of this, especially if their businesses continue to expand at the current rate and to spread all over the city. At the moment the Koreans are not all that visible, but the day may come when a new anti-Asian agitation surfaces in Southern California. ★

Notes

1. *Newsweek,* 26 May 1975, p. 10.

2. California Advisory Committee to U.S. Commission on Civil Rights, *Asian American and Pacific Peoples: A Case of Mistaken Identity* (Washington, D.C.: U.S. Commission on Civil Rights, 1975).

3. Warren Y. Kim, *Koreans in America* (Los Angeles: Po Chin Chai, 1971), pp. 3-4; Hyung-chan Kim and Wayne Patterson, eds., *The Koreans in America, 1882-1974* (Dobbs Ferry, New York: Oceana, 1974), pp. v-2.

4. Hyung-chan Kim, "Some Aspects of Social Demography of Korean Americans," *International Migration Review,* 8 (Spring, 1974), pp. 23-42.

5. Lee Houchins and Chang-su Houchins, "The Korean Experience in America, 1903-1924," *Pacific Historical Review* 43 (Nov. 1974), pp. 553-54; Warren Kim, p. 4; Linda Shin, "Koreans in America, 1903-1945," in *Roots: An Asian American Reader* edited by Amy Tachiki, Eddie Wong, and Franklin Odo (Los Angeles: UCLA Asian American Studies Center, 1971), p. 200.

6. Kim and Patterson, p. v.

7. Kyung Lee, "Settlement Patterns of Los Angeles Koreans" (Master's thesis in Geography, UCLA, 1969), p. 18.

8. Shin, p. 201.

9. Warren Kim, p. 4.

10. Roger Daniels, *The Politics of Prejudice* (Gloucester, Massachusetts: Peter Smith, 1966), pp. 27, 126.

11. Cited in Kyung Lee, p. 69.

12. Helen Givens, "The Korean Community in Los Angeles County" (Master's thesis in Sociology, University of Southern California, 1939), p. 31.

13. Lee, p. 19.

14. U.S. Bureau of Census, *U.S. Census of Population: 1960. Subject Reports. Non-white Population by Race. Final Report PC(2)-1C* (Washington, D.C.: U.S. Government Printing Office, 1963), p. 214.

15. Houchins and Houchins; Warren Kim; Kim and Patterson; and Shin.

16. Givens, p. 48.

17. Warren Kim, p. 5.

18. Elliott Abrams and Franklin S. Abrams, "Immigration Policy—Who Gets In and Why?" *Public Interest,* 38 (Winter, 1975), p. 4.

19. How the preference system operates, and fails in some of its goals, is thoroughly discussed by David S. North, *Alien Workers: A Study of the Labor Certification Program* (Washington, D.C.: TransCentury Corporation, 1971; and David S. North and William G. Weissert, *Immigrants and the American Labor Market* (Washington, D.C.: Trans-Century Corporation, 1973).

20. Monica Boyd, "The Changing Nature of Central and Southeast Asian Immigration to the United States: 1961-1972," *International Migration Review,* 8 (Winter, 1974), 507-519.

21. U.S. Department of Justice, Immigration and Naturalization Service, *Annual Report 1974* (Washington, D.C.: U.S. Government Printing Office, 1975), Table 14.

22. Ibid.

23. Ibid., Table 14.

24. Ibid.

25. Ibid., Table 15.

26. James Alsop Thames, "Korean Students in Southern California: Factors Influencing Their Plans Towards Returning Home" (Ph.D. dissertation in Education, University of Southern California, 1971), pp. 4-5.

27. U.S. Bureau of Census, *Census of Population: 1970. Subject Reports. Final Report PC(2)-1G. Japanese, Chinese, and Filipinos in the United States* (Washington, D.C.: U.S. Government Printing Office, 1973), Tables 48 and 49.

28. Eui-Young Yu, "A Comment on the Number of Koreans in the 1970 U.S. Census of Population," *Korean Student Association of Southern California* (No. 5, 1974), p. 35.

29. California Advisory Committee, pp. 16-18; Yu, p. 35.

30. U.S. Department of Justice, Tables 12A and 12B.

31. Subcommittee on Equal Opportunities, "Koreans in Los Angeles: Employment and Education," Hearing on H.R. 9895, a Bill to Provide Federal Programs of Education, Employment, and Other Assistance to Areas with Heavy Concentrations of Foreign Born Persons. Committee on Education and Labor, House of Representatives, 93rd Congress, 1974, p. 182.

32. David Y. Lee, "Organizational Activities of the Korean Community" (Master's thesis in Social Welfare, UCLA, 1974), p. 8.

33. Ivan Light, *Ethnic Enterprise in America* (Berkeley: University of California Press, 1972), p. 16.

34. Shotaro Frank Miyamoto, "Social Solidarity among the Japanese in Seattle," *University of Washington Publications in the Social Sciences,* 11 (Dec. 1939), p. 70.

35. U.S. Department of Justice, Immigration and Naturalization Service, *Annual Reports, 1965-1974* (Washington, D.C.: U.S. Government Printing Office), Table 8.

36. U.S. Bureau of Census, *Census of Population: 1970. General Social and Economic Characteristics, California* (Washington, D.C.: U.S. Government Printing Office, 1972), p. 462. See also U.S. Department of Health, Education, and Welfare, *A Study of Selected Socio-Economic Characteristics of Ethnic Minorities Based on the 1970 Census. Volume II. Asian Americans* (Washington, D.C.: HEW Publication No. (05)75-121, July, 1974), p. 138.

37. Special Task Force to the Secretary of Health, Education, and Welfare, *Work in America* (Cambridge, Massachusetts: MIT Press, 1973), p. 21.

38. Harry Braverman, *Labor and Monopoly Capital* (New York: Monthly Review Press, 1974).

39. *Dong-a Ilbo,* 28 October 1975.

40. Subcommittee on Equal Opportunities, p. 183.

41. U.S. Bureau of Census, *Statistical Abstract of the United States: 1974,* 95th ed. (Washington, D.C.: U.S. Government Printing Office, 1974), Table 567.

42. U.S. Bureau of Census, *Minority-Owned Businesses—Asian Americans, American Indians, and Others. MB72* (Washington, D.C.: U.S. Government Printing Office, 1972), Tables 2 and 4.

43. David Kim, "Business Development in Koreatown, U.S.A." (Unpublished paper in Architecture and Urban Planning, UCLA, 1975), pp. 22-23.

44. Ibid., p. 40.

45. Subcommittee on Equal Opportunities, p. 183.

46. David Kim, p. 36.

47. Ibid., pp. 30-31.

48. Subcommittee on Equal Opportunities, pp. 183-84.

49. Edna Bonacich, "A Theory of Middleman Minorities," *American Sociological Review,* 38 (Oct. 1973), 583-594.

50. L. Clay Terry and Valiant R. Stull, "An Independent Study of the Los Angeles Korean Community and its People" (Unpublished student paper, California State University at Los Angeles, 1975), pp. 31-32.

51. Subcommittee on Equal Opportunities, p. 185.

52. *The New Korea,* 6 March 1975.

53. Terry and Stull, pp. 34-35.

54. Ivan Light.

55. Terry and Stull, pp. 37-39.

56. *The New Korea,* 26 December 1974.

57. Special Task Force, p. 147.

58. David Kim, p. 42.

59. *The New Korea,* 22 May 1975.

60. California Advisory Committee to U.S. Commission on Civil Rights, *A Dream Unfulfilled: Korean and Pilipino Health Professionals in California* (Washington, D.C.: U.S. Commission on Civil Rights, 1975).

61. Subcommittee on Equal Opportunities, p. 185.

62. Terry and Stull, pp. 33-34.

63. See Edna Bonacich, "Advanced Capitalism and Black/White Race Relations: A Split Labor Market Interpretation," *American Sociological Review,* 41 (Feb. 1976), 34-51, for the evolution of this consciousness among black workers.

64. E.g., Hubert M. Blalock, Jr., *Towards a Theory of Minority Group Relations* (New York: John Wiley, 1967), pp. 79-84.

65. David Kim, p. 42.

66. Ibid., pp. 42-43.

67. *The New Korea,* 16 January 1975.

68. David M. Gordon, *Theories of Poverty and Underemployment* (Lexington, Massachusetts: D.C. Heath, 1972).

69. This interpretation is not inconsistent with the fact that INS and SBA support Korean entrepreneurship, since the U.S. government reflects the interests not only of the corporations, but of those who would contain their power. The very existence of the SBA suggests this.

70. Bonacich, "A Theory of Middleman Minorities."

LITERATURE

Introduction

Fred:

. . . .

I just have a few words and they come at me. "Be
Chinese, Charlie Chan, or a nobody" to the whites
and a mad dog to the Chinamans . . . for what? To
die and be discovered by some punk in the next
generation and published in mimeograph by some
college ethnic studies department, forget it.

Year of the Dragon, Frank Chin, Act 2, Sc. 2. Reprinted
with author's permission.

Why is this section on Literature in here?

Invention is the mother of necessity. Necessity
because so many publishers, professors and critics
have tried to cut and deal the American literary
experience in their own image. By ignoring Asian
American writing, the cultural cop/pushers implicitly
determine that a bourgeois Anglo American literary
tradition provides the mainline fix for legitimate
statements on our society's life and times. There's a
lot more moving than what's sold at the white front
English department store.

To remain illiterate in a vital aspect of Third
World literary practice imposes a lie. An invention.
This notion is wrong more than in degree. Like other
Third World literary experiences, Asian American
works imply dimensions beyond simply rounding out,
or adding color to an otherwise okay show. Third
World writing provides a critique of America from

people who are uniquely prepared to provide one,
discouraged from doing so, and able to illuminate
how these two conditions are related. In part, this
section on Asian American literature is here because
of the necessity to set some things straight. But as we
will see, the writing also shakes out fistfuls of other
questions.

The first thing noticed about the literary output
of Chinese, Japanese and Pilipino America is how
little has been published. This relative lack confers
importance on there that is. On this level, the indifference accorded most of our writing says almost as
much about the Asian experience in America as the
writing itself. Writing ignored has the same impact as
writing suppressed. But one can overdo this rather
sociological view. Because the second fact which
strikes you about Asian American literature is its
range—its variety of form, voice, subject, consciousness, theme. Lots of stuff happening.

Asian American literature represents, I think,
the suds, the above surface manifestation of the
churning psycho-cultural frictions and social-political
conflicts which Asian communities take part in, in
the process of being Asian America. The experience
of struggle in the broadest sense is the basis; literature
is part of the expression of that.

An Asian American literary tradition exists
which involves more than the chance ethnicity of a
bunch of otherwise unrelated literary happenings.

452

LITERATURE

But given this: What are the components of this tradition? What is the writer's stance before it? What is the community's stake in it? And what are the writer's duties, if any, to this community—i.e. to express, reflect, lead, follow, serve or what? What are the issues of audience, language, style and politics?

Many different answers here, including no answer. Not all the writers explicitly state the problem. There are disgreements. The point is that Asian American literature is real. It's not the invention of hack opportunists like Wang dang doodle David Wand (who as critic prints and praises the poetry of his pseudonym David Wang). It's not a foregone impossibility as the shrug of the shoulder musings of Dan Okimoto suggest. Asian American writing's got as much speed, spins, angles and deft, soft clicks as any other ball on the table—and it'll stay on.

This genre generalizing does not suggest that the Writer is or should be some kind of inert barometer. The writer views the Situation from the historical perspective of the moment. He or she makes propositions about this condition, and mustering up all the honest insight available, strives to make them useful, valid, interesting, and maybe even pretty. The writer's definition of the scope, causes and consequences of our hour's follies, prospects, terrors and charms influence the extent to which the reader is engaged with this outlook. The degree to which the writer forces the activity of struggling with new/old ideas and emotions—to bolt up out of the chair a few times—is one way to judge the worthiness of the work's intent and execution.

Thus I impose upon the writer an active duty to know his or her time—which duty implies social choices one can simply not evade. The critic's duty is the same. Neither choosing among the various partisanships, nor explicating them is simplistic.

To put some of these twisty abstractions in context, we should check out the critical reception Asian American writers have received through the decades.

The place one often starts is William Saroyan's introduction to Toshio Mori's collection, *Yokohama, California* (Caxton, 1949):

> Of the thousands of unpublished writers in America there are probably no more than three who cannot write better English than Toshio Mori. His stories are full of grammatical errors. His use of English especially when he is most eager to say something very good, is very bad. Any high school teacher of English would flunk him in grammar and punctuation.

Something about Asian American literature affects many critics—white and Asian—even sympathetic ones, like some kind of reverse kryptonite acid. Orange sunset. When a critic reads our stuff, instead of expanding consciousness, the effect on some is to diminish consciousness. Further, it induces the delusion in them of having seen it all before, know what it's going to say, and how it's supposed to be said. And if it pops up different than what they know to be proper: they pull out the chalk and give a grammar lesson. They don't try to understand the writing or the people; they pencil a note in a grade book. Asian American literature finds the reviewers experts on the subject before they even read it.

Or else they assume our literature is not important. Or not possible. It's especially discouraging when Asian Americans who put out print say that. Something more than pessimism is working when Daniel Okimoto writes in *American in Disguise,* (Weatherhill, 1971):

> Though of course the possibility cannot be ruled out, it appears unlikely that literary figures of comparable stature to those of minorities like the Jews and blacks will emerge to articulate the nisei soul. Japanese Americans will be forced to borrow the voices of James Michener, Jerome Charyn, and other sympathetic novelists to distill their own experience. Even if a nisei of Bernard Malamud's or James Baldwin's talents did appear, he would no doubt have little to say that John O'Hara has not already said. (p. 150)

Behind Okimoto's impression is not merely the view that an Asian American, or here, a Japanese American literature is impossible, but that a Japanese America is impossible. Just before he writes that there's almost no hope for original writers from us, he says that there will always be, among others, successful nisei pharmacists. Fine, but Okimoto's been in the lab too. His book is a dilute elixer of the old half and half formula: Half Japan, half white, never original. He even has a chapter titled "Dual Identity." Bad medicine.

Bad history and bad prophecy too.

There were dozens of Nisei writers before the war. Check out the old newspapers. There was so much happening that columns held hot disputes among the critics and authors. And as far as having nothing new to say—except as dentists, pharmacists, businessmen and engineers—one column in the early 1940s declared:

> ". . . .the tuna fishers of the coast ports, the truck drivers, the swampers in the wholesale produce terminals, the underpaid clerks in the art goods stores, the small farmers, the cannery workers, the laborers in the pineapple plantations of Hawaii and the longshoremen and the girl barbers of Honolulu, these are the real prototypes of the U.S. Japanese. This is the world he [the Nisei writer] can present to America.
> (Iwao Kawakami, October 7, 1940)

Writers had things to say and they spun them out. The fact that even a Princeton boy like Okimoto never heard of them tells us that the racism that penned Japanese Americans into the camps still works through guardians with new pens, just as restricting. A link with the most perceptive, articulate voices of our people has been cut and forgotten.

I've never read a word from the novelist George Furiya. I've never seen a copy of *Reimei,* the "first and foremost of the Nisei magazines." You may have heard of five or six (the journalists probably) of the following writers who were publishing prior to World War Two, but the rest? Known then for their fiction and journalism were: Toshio Mori, Haru Matsui, Yasuo Sasaki, Eddie Shimano, Jimmy Shinkai, Tsuguya Okagaki, Roku Sugahara, Bill Hosokawa, Welly Shibata, Tosuke Yamasaki, John Fujii, Kay Nishida, Bob Tsuda, Tad Kimura, Carl Kondo, Yoshi Okubo, Iwao Kawakami, Joe Oyama, Mary Oyama, Dyke Miyagawa, Kenny Murase, Ayako Noguchi, Vince Tajiri, Joseph X. Shinoda, George Nakamoto, Togo Tanaka, Roy Takeno, Henry Shimanouchi, Goro Murata, Jimmy Omura and "a host of others." And poets: Toyo Suyemoto, Chiye Mori, Taro Katayama, Teru Izumida, Yasuo Sasaki, Ambrose Uchiyamada.

Even in the camps there was a fantastic output in publications like *Trek* (Topaz) and the *Manzanar Free Press.* There were poems, short stories, drawings, and commentary on generational conflicts, interracial relations, resettlement. Vigorous, lively, literary discussion. Things were different, before the war.

Now instead of getting recognition in the vernacular press, writers get shot at. Lawson Inada was the first Asian American to publish a book of poetry; his title recognized the importance of chronology on psychology: *Before the War,* (Morrow, 1971). It is a mean, lean book, comfortable in the rhythms both of jazz and Japanese American speech. There are times Lawson strips his character bare, twists it inside out and forces us to see parts of ourselves. When this historic literary event took place, the JACL's paper *Pacific Citizen* unleashed its most obtuse white racist reviewer, Allen Beekman, who called Inada's collection "outhouse poetry."

Oxford educated Warren Iwasa was also left out back when he reviewed *Aiiieeeee! An Anthology of Asian American Writers* (Howard, 1974) in the *Hawaii Observer.* Those mischievous editors of *Aiiieeeee!* slam the dual personality theory of Asian American identity, which makes Iwasa scratch his head. They rejected the view, which sometimes appears in our literature, that sees Asian Americans either as Asians in Asia or white America or a combination plate. Chin, Chan, Inada and Wong say that Asian America is unique, as black America is distinct from west Africa and Peoria. Iwasa: "I don't understand them very well if they are saying at the same time that they, as Americans, are not Americans." How does Iwasa picture America but as equivalent to white? Weird Hawaiian, he. He proposes that the editors of *Aiiieeeee!* come to grips with the fact that their natural medium is English and lists Dickens, Johnson, Swift, Dryden, Graham Greene, Kingsley Amis, Saul Bellow, John Barth, Phillip Roth,

Mary McCarthy and others as their linguistic comrades, throwing in Claude Brown and James Baldwin as if that proved his point.

Shawn Wong, one of the editors of *Aiiieeeee!* received this from a publisher who reviewed the manuscript for that book:

> It isn't enough to celebrate it [the writing] merely because it is by Asian American writers. . . The suggestion here is that you take a much harder look at the kind of anthology you want. . . . In the present collection the least ethnic pieces are the best. In other words, you as editors must assume a great more responsibility than you have in the collection you have given me. My interest goes on, but I think for your maiden voyage, this book must be more commanding and have more to say than it presently does.

Shawn shakes his head. "I was irresponsible. He graded my book and said that Chinese- Japanese- and Filipino-American writers flunked because we are supposed to say more than we presently do. After seven generations of our being here in this country, Asian American writers were still on a 'maiden voyage.' "

One of the publishers who originally rejected the manuscript, Doubleday, bought the paperback rights to *Aiiieeeee!* after it went through two $8.00 hard cover printings with Howard University Press.

Almost all the white reviewers of Frank Chin's play *Year of the Dragon,* even those who liked it, saw it as expressing the conflict between old and new, or Chinese and American culture, or between tradition and assimilation. They didn't see it as expressing a Chinese American—Chin's term: "Chinaman sensibility." Clive Barnes, the country's most powerful critic, couldn't resist framing the question: "How Chinese or how American is the Chinese-American? And you don't get the answer in a fortune cookie."

Fortune cookie. Then he says, ". . . a Chinese writer might well believe even his plays should come with an eggroll." *Newsweek's* favorable review of *Dragon* was titled "Sweet and Sour." The *Washington Star's* unfavorable critic said, "In a lot less than two hours you're still hungry."

Lot of malnourished critics skim over the writing like they do a menu. Yet when they don't understand, they're not even honest enough to ask the cook what's what. They complain when the bowl of noodles doesn't taste like spaghetti.

This exhibits the attitude that Asian Americans need only be understood superficially, that our works are unworthy of study and understanding. Instead of trying to grasp the historical and social context for our literature—a task requiring some homework—ignorant readers impose old line conventions. Cecil Smith, L.A. *Times* on *Dragon:* "Odetsian mishmash of colliding cultures. . . . [Y]ou've seen it many times before."

But where did Smith see it? Not in other Chinese American plays betcha. No, Mr. Smith is talking about something grander, more universal. The great themes of All Mankind. Literature, it is held, sits weightlessly (reclines genteely; stands majestically) *above it all.* Above race, above class, above politics, above and beyond the collective divisions of society and the frictions and struggles arising therefrom.

That's jive. Literature—literary form, creation and character—reflect, more than passively, the world, and the vision and vistas of the writer before it. Later for that. Focus for now on but one example: Cecil Smith's assumption about Chin's *Dragon.* The stresses of a Chinatown family falling apart just when they thought they were coming back together has not been seen on stage before. The seen-it-all-before tourist-critic is numb or lazy—in either case ignorant. And this particular ignorance is, there's no other name, racism.

The existence of honest Asian American writing in the teeth of these arrogant exclusion acts challenges this racism. The challenge may be neither conscious nor direct, but it works because the more the reader/viewer is forced to confront a hitherto unknown streak of self-ignorance, the better. For reality's sake.

White critics (and I include there the Wangs, the Okimotos) should not be deprived of the warm and reassuring knowledge that whites, as a race, have a particularized value laden sensibility. Not universal essence of humankind. They could then share something. For Third World people, oppression is among other things, never taking leave of the sense of being racial or ethnic minorities. For a long time the effect was us believing that People were whites, that we were variations. Supplements. One attack on white racism (superstructure level) is for whites to see that they are whites. This new found consciousness would be helpful all the way around; it's not imposing anything bizarre, just recognizing reality. The usual analysis when a majority culture suppresses or sanitizes the culture of the oppressed is the colonization, ghettoization—cultural genocide—of the oppressed. That happens and that is primary. But to the extent the cultural guardians have imposed a mental racelessness on whites we also have another form. Faking whites like Smith into thinking that their values were above their backgrounds is intellectually wiping out that race. Genocide again. If Third World people have been deprived access, white people are the ones with the deprived, retarded, consciousness of American life. "No more genocide" is a slogan anyone can get behind.

Yet one more turn of the screw. Not everyone plops Asian Americans into the same over potatoed riceless melting pot. Some feel there's nothing that *should* distinguish Asian American literature from John O'Hara. That is, instead of saying there is no difference (Asian American literature is impossible), they say there is a difference and such a pity, (Asian American literature is unnecessary): the difference is

455

bad. These folks get irritated by the ethnicity they recognize in the writing. ("The least ethnic are the best.") More of the yellow reviewers get offended by this. They think Asian Americaness detracts from the quality, or the work succeeds in spite of it. Again it's the fallacy of believing one sensibility represents an ideal and the rest is deviation. I think Asian American writers, in the whole of American literature, are no more specifically ethnic in values and style than any other writers fully reflecting their environment and education. This ethnicity and the consciousness of it is no more a handicap to the quality of the writing than Jewish, black, or Anglo American ethnicity are to those literatures.

Summing up so far. Asian American literature—by its existence—sets some things straight. By its reading, it does that too. First: it can't be read like "all literature" because there are no such people—and when that's proposed (Dryden!) it's usually just those whites (or white yellows) who forget that a particular literature reflects merely a particular race/class value cluster and not a norm/ideal.

Second: that the specificity of the literature is no more provincial than anybody else's stuff, since no literature is abstractly universal, but a reflection of specifics in historical context and social outlook. Finally, to understand the specifics of Asian American literature takes some work in getting to know Asian America.

So, if I'm right, most of the commentators are missing something. What's so interesting, unique, hot stuff about this literature? I'll try to discuss some of the writing, although I can't cover everyone, even in this selection, let alone a really decent sample.

First obvious problem: Asian America is a fiction. One should probably examine the Chinese-, Japanese-, Pilipino- American experiences separately. Then check out urban/rural, different generations, N.Y., Seattle, S.F., experiences, all that. Generalities are subject to many qualifications. There have also been different literary patterns in the production of the writing. For example, Japanese Americans started writing and publishing sooner, circulated literary magazines in the 1930s, and had creative writing in newspapers.

If these are limitations on broad propositions, still, literature adds a nonquantifiable way of feeling about Asian America. It supplements what the scholarly studies in the rest of this book can provide. On the other hand, maybe it's the opposite: Anybody can see that you learn more about identity from Lawson Inada than Harry Kitano. Hmmmm. Then again, maybe there's no comparison. I like Chin's quote on top: none of these writers did any of their work so it could get squashed into a college reader on Asian American Studies. Literature, in its expression of the subtleties of human relationships, may simply hold the only way to get some things said.

Sometimes what's more important is what is unsaid. The silences, the chasms of noncommunication among characters often grow and envelope the whole landscape, snaring all the actors—and the reader. We know mostly what's going on, but is no one talking about it from fear, habit, or resignation? Or because there's no need to?

Toshio Mori raises these questions in his short story, "The Chessmen."

The older worker Nakagawa-san has been teaching eager young George Murai all about nursery work. The Japanese owner says he'll have to let George go at the end of the season; he can only afford one worker. The heavy work of transplanting new carnations has begun.

> It was obvious that George being young and strong could hold a stiff pace; and that he was aware that he would be laid off when the heavy work was finished. With the last opportunity to impress the boss George did his stuff.
> . . .
> Two men were needed to lift the boxes with the old soil and toss it deftly onto the pile so that no clump of dirt would be left sticking to the boxes. Two men were needed to carefully lift the boxes with the new plants and haul them into the greenhouses. The pace which one of the men worked up could show up the weaker and the slower partner. A man could break another man with a burst of speed maintained for several days.
> One would be certain to break down first. When a young man set up a fast pace and held it day after day it was something for a middle-aged man to think about.

The story teller is witness to, "the struggle that knew no friendship, the deep stamp of self-preservation in human nature. Here was no flowery gesture; here were no words." "Flowery gesture" seems out of place, awkward at first. It's no pun. It's the in-close, personal, stammering description by a narrator whose hands know the soil as well as the people he's describing.

In this story Mori shows us more than he tells. The characters' eyes avoid the readers, yet even from a distance we understand. We are not *told* what Nakagawa knows, yet we're sure he feels his fate the way he feels his back and arms, hardly movable, shot with pain.

Instead of words breaking the silence, the silence spreads and stifles communication. It brakes the word. This isn't silence from passivity, but silence born from emotions which elude the container of words and then swell up, humid, claustrophobic, like steam around a sick bed. (Check out Wakako Yamauchi's story for this effect. The comparison is explicit.)

This intangible trap lies at the center of Hisàye Yamamoto's stories, especially the strong, sensitive women protagonists when they're most in need of communicating. Read her brilliant "Yoneko's Earthquake" in *Aiiieeeee!* or "The Brown House" in *Asian*

American Authors or in *Yardbird Reader/3*. Between husband and wife, one of her figures will, perhaps unknowingly, draw some sort of moral line. Beyond this line, communication ends—only physical violence, painful lessons and more silence.

Often a child focus-character innocently and ironically reflects the real action. We get the girl's sense of vivid collateral details, and very important, the ambivalent shifting of sympathies. Through her comes a barely comprehended picture of a rural Japanese husband and wife, grown apart without knowing, and beyond each other's telling. The violence alive just beneath the layer of frustrated noncommunication, as in "Seventeen Syllables" appearing herein, is terrifying.

This theme of grappling with the Unsaid as a material force affects the relationships in John Okada's *No-No Boy*. This novel, published in 1957, was the first novel Japanese America produced. Its mere existence should have been celebrated; its characterizations and wondrous capturing of Nisei speech, plant its achievement on more solid ground.

The central character, Ichiro, after being thrown into a concentration camp during World War II by the U.S. government, refused to swear allegiance to that government. He served two years in prison and returns home to Seattle. The first friend he meets spits on him for being a no-no boy. Ichiro returns to find a younger brother who wants to enlist in the Army, a mother who believes Japan has won, a weak father clutching onto the remains of his life by the neck of a bottle. Through the book, Ichiro tries to resolve who he is by exploring and rejecting who he is not. By this he answers future Oxford Sanseis who'd recommend the dry den of borrowed sensibilities. "I am not your son and I am not Japanese and I am not American." Okada takes this as a premise, a place to begin Ichiro's journey; he was ahead of those who have still to reach this conclusion.

Okada's characters can't understand each other or are too messed up to make the attempt; the core of unity, of common assumptions, was shattered by the war and the camps. Ichiro is a character emerging from those ruins, bewildered, blinking in the new day. Among other things, *No-No Boy* asks what price the adjustment to survive as a community has been. It was seemingly too hard for Japanese Americans in the 1950s to face this anxious, unsure self-portrait stark on paper. Okada understood and tried to delve beneath the pain the community struggled to forget, and which its virtual rejection of his book proved.

While much of the literature involves characters unable to communicate and the result/cause of splitting families, there is a countervailing strain as well. Its scope is more consciously historical. These pieces invoke images and myths from the Asian American past to explain and make whole—make comprehendable and comprehensive—the present situation.

Shawn Wong's excerpt from his novel *Night Driver* is explicitly myth seeking and myth making. This chapter utilizes a twist on the archetype romance form: the Journey where one gets lost enough to find oneself. Though the terrain, maiden, steed and grail are different, sought on this quest is to "be whole again beyond confusion."

Wong says that whereas a common thread in American literature pits the son rebelling against the father, here the father and the son are the same person. Shawn's story is one of dreams, changes of identity, ritual and magic. It also has a tough sense of history and the eye of a son who knows "more about the love of my father for my mother than most sons know."

Shawn's myths flip in and out of time, the movies, the other side of the planet, on the road. Myths aren't lies; they often have more power than the "truth." The stories and aspirations of ordinary people talking their love, hope and hate are expressed and crystalized in myth. They give structure, they organize a people's disparate experiences within the collective consciousness. They are a highly democratic form of literature. Myths are a source.

Our own Asian American myths have been stolen. (If they hadn't been there'd be no need to *introduce* any of these writers; they'd be well known, legendary. Toshio Mori was written up in the Japanese American press as "the famous writer, Toshio Mori." In 1949, *Nisei Vue* called him "one of the most widely discussed young writers in the country today.") Wong shows the need for new metaphors, models—myths—to replace the old and new stereotypes. In this excerpt, the maiden and leviathan are the same, the destination and the journey are one place, for all: America. The battlefield *and* the foe. As an expression of Asian America, that's new. For those of us concerned about the relevance of literature, in this particular journey into the self, literature is no mimesis, no formalized representation of experience: literature and experience become the same thing.

Also acutely conscious of history, not as a dry abstraction, but as vividly felt humanity is Wing Tek Lum. I made inexcusably sloppy, wrongheaded generalizations about Wing's poetry in my article in *Roots* in 1971. Far more than apologies are in order for that. But as Wing says, his poems should be allowed to speak for themselves. They do, well. Wing Tek Lum produces fine shadings even on a very large canvas, and confronts the ironies in the dialectic of sacrifice and privilege. I had been stupidly in error. Wing Tek Lum writes deft, intelligent, politically astute poems. In *To Li Po* he asks what all should expect every poet to ask. "How can I, in times like this, continue with this poem?"

Hey. I sense I'm losing some detachment here, some objectivity. I am. The work I'm talking about, I feel, is first rate. But one may damn with tainted phrase. You may be skeptical if you never read any of this stuff; you'd think my selecting these pieces may invalidate my judgments of them. A proper concern. First I say: you're deprived for not having read it. You owe it to yourself—for the sake of massaging a flow of warm blood to new found corner of your consciousness—to read it no matter what I say here. Second, if you insist, very well: what do I mean when I happen to praise the historical consciousness in these poems? Some young poets dredge up red letter day incidents, or spill guilt or sentimentality along with ink when they talk about their grandparents. Maybe this is too harsh. I chose not to print examples. Obviously neither Wing Tek Lum nor Mei Berssenbrugge (infra) do this. History is not an artifact to place on one's shelf. For them history are roots in the soil, tangled up, some not seen, deep, but organically part of oneself. To uncover without doing violence to those tender subterranean threads is a delicate operation. I guess evaluating how deep, revealing and careful this operation is provides one measure of merit.

Wait a minute, one more gratuitous item. Compare Wing's ambivalence about Li Po to the sales pitch David Rafael Wang writes for himself. "A direct descendent of Wang Wei (706-761), major T'ang dynasty poet and painter. . . ." If you are a tolerant person you are saddened by the spectacle of this aging literary eunuch groping to bask in the reflection of borrowed glory. If you are like me you want to throw up. David Rafael Wang is listed as a "prominent writer" on the back cover of *Asian American Heritage,* a paperback anthology by David Hsin-Fu Wand. Same silk smirk cluck. Here the dual personality number goes beyond goofiness almost to the level of trans-vestism. The book is an ugly rip off of our people and authors. So ignorant is Wan( ) of Asian America that he includes select English translations of Polynesian oral poetry. There are however several very good pieces by Asian American writers who will be remembered for their merit and not their opportunism. Wan( ) is a withered example of false historical consciousness.

"Chronicle" and "History" are two of my favorite poems by Mei Berssenbrugge; they are also the most historically narrative. I don't want to seem dogmatic, so I'll be thinking about the third one printed here, "The Suspension Bridge."

Her works are surgically precise, wildly imaginative, compressed whispers. Very personal, she can write anywhere: New York subways, New Mexico deserts, Nepal. Mei has a recurring image of smooth bones and skulls. My guess is that this is partly from a concern for the emotional analogue to the physical skeleton. Questions: What, in the social world, structures and supports us, and is supported in turn? What holds us together as one, as several? Are there parallel limitations on our capacity to feel for others the way bone shatters, muscles weaken, skin intervenes? The text: what suspends the bridge—holds it

up; and what suspends the bridge—makes it end. Mei Berssenbrugge is exploring the potentialities of human will.

A fundamental problem for political radicals has always been the showdown between fate and will. Carlos Bulosan, one of the great proletarian writers of America, examines the interaction between consciousness and the external world in *America is in the Heart.* An excerpt from this rich, visceral novel/autobiography also appears in this volume under the "Land, Labor, and Capital" section. The book, first published in 1946, has been issued in paperback by the University of Washington Press.

Bulosan wrote several volumes of fiction and poetry, and consistently took the outlook of the Pilipino peasant-worker. His depictions of racism and class oppression came from personal experiences. During the 1930s Bulosan was a labor organizer in the canneries and fields of the West Coast; this activity made him a visible target for insults and violence. In 1936 Bulosan began a two-year confinement in Los Angeles County Hospital where after thirteen operations he lost the ribs of one side of his body and the use of one lung. Even that did not halt Bulosan's lifetime fight for revolution.

Rather than a journey of reunion with the self, we have a journey—actually more a flight—of self-creation. This is no idealist conception of universal humanity, hovering above the historical condition. Bulosan realized that man is always a particular man. His interest was in the fullest aspirations of humanity realizable in the concrete situation of a particular time and place. A work of art—and its critique—is rooted in temporal and material circumstance. On the gap between will and world, as mediated by the word, the book's thematic focus is "the development of character within the objective historical process of society." (E. San Juan, Jr., *Carlos Bulosan and the Imagination of the Class Struggle,* Quezon City: 1972, p. 94.) Bulosan held that once people understood how their beliefs were dependent on material conditions, then the foundation was laid for remaking both character and destiny by collective action. The dialectic: Culture is basically an expression of objective social relations; it is also (but usually only secondarily) an influence upon these relations. Here Bulosan puts flesh on what are typically dry bones: the objective and subjective elements of social process and political change.

In Chapter Fourteen, reproduced here, Bulosan begins seeing the Pilipino workers' situation beyond an individual to a collective viewpoint. In a later chapter Bulosan writes:

> I put the blame on certain Filipinos who had behaved badly in America, who had instigated hate and discontent among their friends and followers. This misconception was generated by a confused personal reaction to dynamic social forces, but my hunger for the truth had inevitably led me to take

an historical attitude. I was to understand and interpret this chaos from a collective point of view, because it was pervasive and universal. (p. 143-144)

The episode also shows the class aspect to oppression; it is the Pilipino labor contractor who is the most immediate exploiter. Finally, despite the viciously brutal oppression Bulosan has seen and felt, and despite the easy avenues of cynicism and despair, there emerges the will for freedom. "Yet no matter what bestiality encompassed my life, I felt sure that somewhere, sometime, I would break free."

Important in reading Bulosan is the extent he exemplified Mao Tse Tung's dictum that the primary task for writers and artists is "to understand people and know them well." Bulosan knew from inside. A week before his death he said,

> I want to interpret the soul of the Filipinos in this country. What really compelled me to write was to try to understand this country to find a place in it not only for myself but my people.

Of course, good politics alone do not a poem make. I'm not sure what does. All I know is that what a poem has to say, and what one may say about it, cannot be printed on a picket sign or shouted on the street. There is ambivalence and complexity one cannot minimize by this incomplete wave-of-the-hand preface. For example, I mostly agree with Ron Tanaka's politics. He thinks about history and the duty of the Sansei artist to regain a true past as much as anyone. He understands that capitalism tends to corrupt the artistic process, rendering the product a commodity and the artist a pawn. Tanaka therefore, prefers not to make that scene. As compared, say, to Frank Chin, whose work I admire, but some of whose politics I think are in error, I think Tanaka is basically correct. But I think he's crazy. The overwhelming feeling I get from much of his poetry is nagging irritation. That's intentional; it's part of the message. He is saying you are irritated because you are afraid or ashamed to face the truth therein revealed. Maybe so. But it is also studied, smug and obsessive. Simple perceptions are pounded in as the ultimate profundities. Still, Tanaka is no dummy. He hasn't published much, but he's written a number of poems and essays which ought to be considered in any debate on culture and the community.

For a while here I've been carrying on about historical consciousness. We've seen it superimposing the self upon the person-past, in recognizing the living links to prior generations, and in seeing the specifics of history as a guide for analysis and change. Tanaka is concerned with all of this too. "To destroy a people's poetry," he says, "is to take away its past and future, to condemn it to being a parasite of the continuous present." Part of his thesis is that the Asian American movement, and specifically Sanseis, have reconceptualized themselves into white or Third World models and broken continuity with the Japanese past. This he feels is a kind of outside cultural control, thence community control through self-hatred. Meaning for Sansei, being ashamed of being Japanese.

There are probably some points there worth exploring. They make for interesting essays, although I think the cracks get more visible when Tanaka tries to apply the ideas in his poetry. On the whole though I feel Tanaka's sense of tradition is not objectively historical so much as romantic, idealized, sentimental. When I say he's crazy I mean morbidly, obsessively, self-consciously, guilty about his elders and their value system. What I like about him is that he anticipates these charges. He's already written the rebuttal to that:

> One of the implications of this analysis is that the continuation of some kind of system integrity in terms of the J-A community depends on the continued transmission of formal and informal Japanese concepts. The issue is . . . . one of preserving and synthesizing styles and conceptual frameworks. But of course the accusation that keeps being made when one talks of the continuation and synthesis of Japanese culture is that it is "unnatural," "artificial," "reactionary," "irrelevant" or simply too late when applied to Sansei. (One can see how effective conceptual oppression has been in respect to JAs.) *Culture, Communication and the Asian Movement in Retrospect,* p. 6.

This is a system without an outside to it; it is impossible to prove wrong. Criticism is taken as proof of the initial proposition (the mentality of Ichiro's mother in *No-No Boy*). A hypothesis which cannot be negated is a false one. It's like a Ptolemaic cosmology, the Old Left, or the Old Time religion. Religious systems stand impervious to rational arguments from outside; once within, all attacks can be absorbed. Perhaps that accounts for the selfless sweat on the upper lip evangelism in some of Tanaka's writing.

Since I have not printed Tanaka's essays these comments may be unfair. I will try to cover by including an excerpt from a long poem, *Contexts.* Tanaka doesn't cheat; he puts some good, if rather shrill arguments in the mouth of his opponent.

. . . .
"first of all, let me
tell you that you have
no concern for the real
issues which are racism
and imperialism. from
what i can see, you're
so busy being sentimental
about a bunch of half-
assed middle class . . ."

"o.k., you don't have to
insult my friends. just . . ."

"like why didn't

459

you come to asian
health day. don't
you care about whether
the issei ladies get
enough medical care?"

"yes, i do. but just
because you have an . . ."

"o.k. what've you done
for the issei? name one thing."

well, i can't give him an
answer. life isn't so simple.

"yeah, well, i didn't
think you would. so now
that we understand each
other, listen while i
read you this stuff, o.k.?"

"i'm listening."

"As subnations acculturate in some respects, they
thereby attain the status and the self-confidence to
maintain or reassert their independence in other
respects." . . . There are "manifestations among
Sansei of third-generation nativism in line with
Hansen's thesis."

"so?"

"so this means that what you
are doing or think you're
doing is completely and
absolutely predictable by
sociological laws. also,
it's not inspite of the
fact that you are middle
class, it's because you
are middle-class that you
can go around complaining."

"yeah, o.k., i agree."

. . . .

"yeah, but can't you
see. we aren't japanese.
learning about japan
and stuff will only
give a false sense of
hope to people who
can't make it here.
have you ever been
there? do you think
japan is any . . ."

"look, i never said that
going to japan would solve
anyone's problems, hunh?"

"yeah, o.k., but you
think that learning about
that stuff will fill in
some blank spaces in our
psychology, don't you?"

"well, not the way you
put it. no, i don't."

"shit, don't try to
back down now. i
heard you go to those
movies, do kendo,
like obonodori and
are learning all those
children's songs and
stuff. listen to this."

"Like the third generation of many nationalities,
Sansei are seeing their roots in the culture of their
grandparents homeland. . . . Japanese movies are
well attended by young people, most of whom can
barely understand a word of the dialogue. Among
a minority, a vogue has developed for such refined
pastimes as flower arrangement or the tea
ceremony."

"o.k., so what's your point?"

"do you know what
he calls all of
this? 'sentiment.'
you're just a bunch of
middle-class american kids
being sentimental about your
homeland, hah, hah, hah."

"yeah, so?"

"so this means that it's
all over for you."

"meaning what?"

"you're dead.
nothing you believe
in can live.
in fact, the only
reason you can jump
on the bandwagon
is because
these rich japanese
want to find something
better to do with
their time."

"what?"

"i mean that japanese
culture in america
represents the values
of the upper classes
and is used to oppress
the poor and exploited."

"yeah, o.k."

"so that by having
sansei think of the
race issue as being
cultural rather than
political and economic,
you're making them
identify with the
pig establishment."

"yeah, o.k."

"if change is going
to be made, it must
be a third world coalition.
whites, blacks, browns.
. . ."

"yeah, o.k. i've heard
that before. you through?"

he's smiling now. i guess
i've made him happy. when
i go fishing alone along
the sloughs, i'm always
afraid. there is the smell
and things floating in
the water. it all reminds
you of death. even the old
shoes, clothes, bedsprings.
all the time you read of

people shot down for no
reason or found buried there,
heads ripped open. i tell
myself that it's crazy to
go into a nothing world
where the slightest sound
makes your nerves tighten.

"say, jerry, you ever
gone fishing at a slough?"

"hunh? no, never go fishing.
don't have time for . . ."

"ever been scared out of
your mind before?"

"no, i'm not afraid of
anything. i know what's
happening, man, like . . ."

"well what about being
afraid of being alone?"

"what are you talking about?
alienation is for middle class . . ."

"i'm not talking about
alienation, . . ."

"look, ron, i gotta
go, o.k. just think
about love for a while."

"love?"

"yeah, radical love,
revolutionary love
like what malcolm had
and george jackson.
that's what we have."

"yeah, o.k., love."

i wanted to tell jerry
something but my heart
told me that he wouldn't
care. maybe that's what
love is about after all.

iv

"hey, ron, wanna cup
of coffee?"

"yeah, sure."

"hey, just ran into
one of your students,
jerry, i think his . . ."

"yeah, what about him?"

"he thinks you're
a fanatic or . . ."

"fanatic?"

"yeah, what you been
saying to him anyway?"
. . . .

In the end all we have is a sigh. Of course, that's
not the end, and one day I may get set straight on all
this. I agree when Tanaka says we need to understand
our past before we can have a realistic sense of the
future. But one doesn't come to this understanding
by an inventory of the historical warehouse. One
must make discriminations. There is a valid difference
between depicting those aspects that represent the
essence of our situation and the spurious fullness

derived from placing the essential and secondary on
the same plane. What criteria determine this difference
is of course the point of controversy.

It sometimes seems like the poems that tell the
most of what Tanaka is about are the clumsiest, the
most whining and guilt ridden. In my view, "Sansei
Farm Boys" is an example. A lot of complex questions
are raised and some evocative mood comes through,
but the resolution is Sunday school. (On the other
hand, "Congratulations" succinctly pins the brand
name effects of psycolonization. Cooler, it spits out
the message before you can blink.) Tanaka has some
things to say, but makes me think that a writer should
grasp his or her responsibilities to a community
without measuring insight by the agonies of self-
inflicted guilt.

Bienvenido Santos is right next to his characters;
they are ancient childhood friends. He knows their
rooms, speech, food, dreams. Santos may not be a
purposefully proletarian writer like his countryman
Bulosan, but "The Day the Dancers Came" shows
how precisely he knows the condition and consciousness of an aging *manong*.

In both Santos' story and some of Tanaka's
poems, there is an almost reverent love for the ethnic
foods. Both have a sense for how much meaning there
is in a familiar mouthful when you're away and alone.
But Santos merely begins there, he doesn't trip on
it; we are engaged with the emotions running through
his story, not embarrassed by them. With him we don't
worry about getting ourselves tugged through someone's sad eye lowlands wondering what the fuss is all
about. Santos gives us a story about a bashful-eager
Pilipino man, Fil, on an emotional occasion, taking us
right into his lonely bedroom—all with deep feeling,
all without an ounce of sentiment.

Santos reveals a struggle to transcend a culture
of deprivation. Fil's thoughts are all fantasies; even a
simple tape recorder becomes a "magic sound mirror."
This fantasy is both an expression of, and an escape
from, a lifetime of hard work in America, while also
preventing changing this condition. Fil wants to work
an exchange in the traditional culture of his homeland
with the touring Pilipino dancers, but finds the bond
has been severed, the common mode of communication is gone. He must resort to mechanical means to
preserve the art and life of the Philippines as he
remembers it. But just as memory is a "betrayer,"
art cannot be possessed, and Fil's life here has changed
him. Some things are erased—tragically perhaps—but
irrevocably.

Frank Chin does not leave you neutral. I'll not
write much here since he explains for himself; that's
why "Backtalk" is in. Read also his "Chinatown
Cowboy" in *Bulletin of Concerned Asian Scholars*,
vol. 4, no. 3, Fall 1972, and the *Aiiieeeee!* introduction. Chin's concern for an Asian American sensibility
and language has stimulated and informed many. To a
degree, if he weren't such a pushy madman hustler,

we might still believe Dan Okimoto and be content with Lin Yutang. Instead we gotta deal with him.

One day his work will be collected and annotated. Then more people will pick up on the levels of meaning in his references to Chinese cookbooks as literature, food talk, Helen Keller, Charlie Chan, trains, the Lone Ranger, racist love, talking in multiple tongues. Chin's words are real weapons and he's in no apparent fear–or danger–of running out of ammunition. Sometimes his talk zips by too fast– it's whisked across the page/stage quicker than eyeballs move in sockets, then comes bouncing back hard with just enough time to duck. I've sat in audiences where no one knows what's going on at the beginning of *Chickencoop Chinaman* or the end of *Year of the Dragon*. In *Dragon* Fred Eng tells his sister: "Food's our only common language." Chin serves it up hot and if you're not ready, it's slung way down the counter, and you only get a scent.

At least, that goes for the plays and other recent work. As his newest, they're what I would have liked to print here. But "The Only Real Day" is different. It is earlier, slower, more rambling, and at first I lost patience in parts. There are soft spots here and there and some too formal words throw off the rhythm. But in "Day" Chin is more richly, realistically close to the old bachelor's Chinatown than in anything since. It also gives insight into what Tampax Lum might have lived through before he became the Chickencoop Chinaman. The plays are about the concept of Chinese America and a Chinaman word-view. Quick shifts in dialogue and the spotlight dream scenes make ideas jump, bump and keep running. In this story however the theories aren't worked out, the layers of metaphor and laughs aren't constructed. There's not yet enough complexity to sustain a play. Yet the basic material, the situation and psychology of a Chinese dishwasher is right in focus. Some people will be surprised. Chin hasn't shaped up his scheme of bad mouth, myth and metaphor out of the air. Not out of the library either. When Chin wrote this story in his late teens, he'd had his eyes open for a while.

In a letter he writes:

> I like *Day* for Roots II cuz it represents my best work, and is my best work between 18 and 25, in terms of skill, voice, shape and texture. I don't consider myself an extraordinarily gifted writer, a genius of the pen, or word magician. I believe that any yellow writer should be writing at least as well as I did at a certain age. With this story in Roots I'm encouraging yellows to be a little more ruthless in their criticism and analysis of *Day* and all the stories of that period.

Excerpts from some of the off white reviews of Chin's *Dragon* on stage and public TV were reprinted above. In the face of that kind of ignorance it's natural to say, as Chin does, that instead of demanding a rewrite to satisfy their own racist conceptions, the critics should deal with the work according to its own aspirations. Okay as far as that goes, but it's just the start and leads to a trap. I'll let Chin speak one more time before I, armed with quotes I like, lunge in. Then I'll be done. (The point here is not to dump on Frank–the problems of evaluation and audience are complicated–but to facilitate some feverish ideas.)

In remarks prefacing publication of *The Year of the Dragon*, he wrote:

> The political hard hats would program art according to their own clubby notion of what was good for the "people." Art as I see it is not a service to the people or even a representation of the people. It's an expression of the people.

Sure. Art is no serve the people program. "Politics cannot be equated with art, nor can a general world outlook be equated with a method of artistic creation and criticism." Mao Tse Tung said that. And it shouldn't be programmed. "There is no doubt that literature is the last thing in the world to lend itself to mechanical levelling and uniformity, to the subjection of the minority by the majority. There is no doubt that in this field great freedom must be assured to individual initiative and personal inclinations, great freedom of thought and fantasy, form and content . . ." Lenin said that.

But. There are problems studying literature by taking it *strictly* on "its own terms." It leads to looking at writing,

> as a privately created world independent of the social and political context within which it developed. To complete the exaltation of the literary work, one must hold that its social, political and moral effects have nothing whatsoever to do with its value. That is, either the work doesn't influence behavior at all, or if it does, that behavior casts no reflection back on the work itself. The effects are merely incidental.
>
> Bruce Franklin, "The Teaching of Literature in the Highest Academies of the Empire," *The Politics of Literature*, ed. Louis Kampf and Paul Lauter (New York: Pantheon, 1972), p. 103.

Taking the writing on its own terms works only if those terms reflect truth. But to judge *that*, you need to evaluate from some outside reference. One at that vantage point must certainly be familiar with, literate in, what the writer is trying to do, but must also evaluate the writer's intentions, not just the execution, a unity of (Mao again) motive and effect. How else do you go after Okimoto, Jade Snow Wong, Virginia Lee, than by saying that their *politics* are wrong–their whole grasp of historical process on the situation of our people. Critics didn't dislike Chin's play for its pace or structure; they didn't understand the premises. They will be incapable of taking the play on its own terms until they understand something about the social history and literary contexts for Chinese America, and the fact that they have not been able to do so is less primarily a failing in their aesthetic astuteness as a political fact of the racism they have adopted.

To begin and *end* a critique by judging a work in its terms alone becomes a trap because it fosters the mistake that literature exists separate from social relations. This prevents seeing why whites or anyone else are never "just people"—a meaningless abstraction—but particular people of a place and time. Which is the premise of Chin's play the critics don't get.

> . . . all classes in all class societies invariably put the political criterion first and the artistic criterion second. The bourgeoisie always shuts out proletarian literature and art, however great their artistic merit. Mao Tse Tung.

I laid out all these wild cards on the table at the beginning, and if the intervening discussion has not made my bets clear, then I might as well finish here anyway:

Artistic productions reflect social conflict. They are mediated by the artist and the artist's courage and understanding of the experiences of his or her people. The artist unifies these experiences to and through symbols seized for that purpose. This is the development of a sensibility.

For Asian Americans there has been lots of conflict. As yet, not enough literature, though more than most think. I was surprised: Look at how many stories and poems here have at their core the thoughts and dignity of the working people we've always been. Thinkers, dreamers, fighters. Fascinating people: special, but not supernatural; heroic, but not heroes; not rabbits or seagulls, but human beings you want to get to know. Not dead: not marginal men, or people with dual personalities, or middleman minorities.

The literary imagination militates against those false abstractions, those formularized reductions. Art, the Chairman says, must move life to a higher, more concentrated, more typical level. To codify and assimilate a people's experience through a people's symbols is to shape a sensibility. The aggregate of commonly rooted—and routed—sensibilities in print make a literary tradition; we are just beginning to discover ours. I say we need this tradition. Not for its own sake, but for sake of our history and our future. The more revolutionary the artist, the greater the need for a tradition by which his or her originality can become meaningful. That's why this section is here.

—Bruce Iwasaki

The selections are in no particular order except that they seem to sit well among their closest neighbors. Too many writers were left out with regret. Several more anthologies could be filled with works by the writers below. Here are other collections you should inspect:

Aiiieeeee! An Anthology of Asian American Writers.
Frank Chin, Jeffery Paul Chan, Lawson Fusao Inada, and Shawn Hsu Wong, eds.
Washington, D.C.: Howard Univ. Press, 1974. *lxiii,* 200 pp. $7.95
Garden City: Doubleday, 1975. *xx,* 295 pp. $3.95 (paper)

Asian-American Authors.
Kai-yu Hsu and Helen Palubinskas, eds.
Boston: Houghton Mifflin Co., 1972. 184 pp.

Asian-American Heritage: An Anthology of Prose and Poetry.
David Hsin-Fu Wand, ed.
New York: Pocket Books, Simon & Schuster, Inc., 1974.
xii, 308 pp. $1.95

Time to Greez! Incantations from the Third World.
Janice Mirikitani, Luis Syquia, Jr., et al.
Glide/Third World Communications, 1975
330 Ellis St., San Francisco, California 94102.

Yardbird Reader, Volume 3.
Shawn Wong, Frank Chin, guest eds.
Yardbird Publishing Inc., 1974
Box 2370, Station A, Berkeley, California 94701
xvi, 294 pp. $4.95

Speaking for Ourselves: American Ethnic Writing.
Lillian Faderman and Barbara Bradshaw, eds.
Glenview, Ill.: Scott, Foresman and Co., second ed., 1975.
ix, 625 pp.

Amerasia Journal
various numbers, esp. vol. 3, no. 2. Asian American Studies Center, 3232 Campbell Hall, University of California, Los Angeles. L.A., 90024

Japanese American Anthology Committee, forthcoming volume. P.O. Box 5024, San Francisco, Cal. 94101

Partial list of writers whose work could not be included here:

Manuel Buaken	Ernest Imura	David Oyama
Faustino Caigoy	Iwao Kawakami	N.E. Ozawa
Jeffery Paul Chan	Kichung Kim	Lourdes Pammit
Diana Chang	Tsui Kit-fan	John Saka
Henri Chang	Alexander Kuo	Tomas Santos
Irene Chang	Geraldine Kutaka	Bill Shinkai
George T. Chew	Alan Chong Lau	Jon Shirota
Fay Chiang	Teri Lee	Monica Sone
Lois Chin	Joaquin Legaspi	Paul Suarez, Jr.
Curtis Choy	George Leong	Brenda Paik Sunoo
John Chu	Jeff Leong	Toyo Suyemoto
Louis Chu	Russell Leong	Ferris Takahashi
Frances Chung	Paul Stephen Lim	Steve Tatsukawa
J.C. Dionisio	Wally Lim	Carole Tokeshi
Pamela Eguchi	Stephen S.N. Liu	Philip Vera Cruz
Ben Fee	Alice Look	Stella Wong
Bob Fong	Juanita Lott	Robert Wu
David Fong	Ray Lou	Kay Yamada
N.V.M. Gonzales	Bayani Mariano	Amy Yamamoto
Jessica	Diane Mark	Doug Yamamoto
Tarahata Hagedorn	Wong May	Karen Yamashita
Thanh Hai	Deng Ming-dao	Eileen Yip
Larry Hama	Kazuo Miyamoto	Richard Young
Dennis Hirota	Nobuko Miyamoto	Connie Young Yu
Larry Hom	Paul Motoyoshi, Jr.	Cyn Zarco
Garrett Hongo	Milton Murayama	
Fred Wei-han Houn	Francis Naohiko Oka	
Veronica Huang	Tomi Tanaka Ohta	
Chris Iijima	Alan Ota	

GOOD LUCK, HAPPINESS, AND LONG LIFE

BY SHAWN HSU WONG

I was hiking on the 180 mile trail from Lake Tahoe to Yosemite Valley with a girl so much younger than myself we offended people. She was the dream-girl, the Lolita of Chinese-America, a patronizing blond-haired girl of fifteen. And in the dream about me I'm middle-aged, hiking with her alone, making up for those restless years, the lonely years of my grandfathers. She is the Lolita of Mr. Chinaman's Chance and we make love on the warm granite rock next to a river. And in the morning there is a scout troop camped across the river and the scoutmaster sees us, sees how close she sleeps to me, and he is offended. I'm fiercely loyal to her. We're on the run through America.

And in the dreams about me I'm in Australia visiting Father's lover and she is as young as she was then. I am my father. We are driving north from Sydney on the New England Highway past places

called Wollombi, Murrurundi, Wallabadah, Goonoo Goonoo, and Gunnedah. We are out on the Breeza Plains watching the clouds graze the surface of the dry plains. And when I tell my patronizing blond-haired girl of fifteen about Australia, about places I've been to, places where my father walked, she thinks I'm talking Chinese. Nobody goes to Australia to fall in love, it's the place you write about in grammar school, carefully listing in your report to the class, its industries, its population, its natural resources, its kangaroos. And when I was going to grammar school in Berkeley, kids would ask me where I was from, and I would say Australia when they were thinking China. I was lost in the Northern Territory, dropped out of a wagon when my parents were immigrating from China to the south, and I was raised by a herd of wild kangaroos. When I was in college, kids would ask where I was from and I would

illustration by ALAN TAKEMOTO

answer Jackson Hole, Wyoming, when they were thinking Hong Kong. Raised by a song about buffalo and antelope, by a song about a home on the range. I was brought up in the shade of that giant redwood tunnel tree at Mariposa Grove, Big Trees, Yosemite National Park, by my father who was a man of journeys.

What matters about a time in Hilo, Hawaii is what happened before that time. The day before my mother and I flew out of Guam, out of the humid morning, to begin the journey home to follow Father's hospital plane home, I remember my childhood from that time on rooted in a moment with Father in the hospital when all journeys end without speech. We arrived in Hilo in the middle of the night on a stop-over rest sometime in early spring 1957. I woke up when the vibration of the props died, and I felt the bump of the wheels touch down. And when I'm driving at night now, I think of that time when that giant Pan American Globemaster touched down on Hilo, and of my mother pacing in the hotel room all night long while I slept. I was tired of traveling at the age of seven, and Hilo was the last stop before home. And that night in Hilo was the longest night she would experience as my mother. Father was already at Oak Knoll and we were following him home. Because of the resignation to waiting in that hotel room, the last day of the last journey home was worse than her own sickness eight years later. To only hope and wait was a sign of weakness for her, hoping was a sign of impatience. And when father died, hope was gone, but patience was her only energy then. And in the eight years before her own death I saw no resignation to hope, no more midnight landings in Hilo.

I take my bride of fifteen now into the whole flux of life; she patronizes her way into my future, I have explained my past, sought it out, told about the Tumon Beach time, the Mariposa Grove time, the Hilo time, Wyoming, the Orote house before Spring, 1957. And now in America I say to her that I am still too much in the flux of my life to be a father myself. I have no place in America, after four generations there is nothing except what America tells me about the pride of being foreign, a visitor from China I've never seen, never been to, never dream about, and never care about. Or, at best, here in my country I am still living at the fringe, the edge of China. So now I take this fifteen year old blond-haired body with me on the road. She is the shadow, the white ghost of all my love life; she is the true dream of my capture of America. She buys me breakfast at six in the morning in Elko, Nevada. She is wearing a white T-shirt and white hot pants with no underwear, her blond hair shines in the desert sun, falling in baby curls on her neck. Her perfect breasts bounce, making the T-shirt move in waves, her fifteen year-old ass peeks out underneath the cuff of the shorts; she has no shoes on. And as we walk through the casino in Elko looking for breakfast, the gamblers ignore her and stare at me like I'm crazy. This is Chinese-America in Elko. I have steak and eggs for breakfast, she has a milk shake and fries. In the car she takes off her T-shirt because it is too hot, and I let her drive my snow-white Porsche in her snow-white hot pants across the desert at a hundred.

The road crews and truck drivers get a fleeting glance of her tanned breasts, her steady gaze on the highway ahead, and a Chinaman beside her yelling out the window, "I taught her how to drive!"

We take our Chinese-American road show to Idaho, to the Jerome County Fair just outside of Twin Falls. I'm sitting on the roof of the Porsche talking to the farmers about Chinese-America, while my bride has taken off her hot pants and is now wearing an extra long T-shirt to cover her bare ass. She is polishing my car, bending, kneeling, stretching up on her toes, while I'm giving my speech next to the cow barn and art show. They're all looking at me, some kids are talking in hushed tones about the Porsche engine.

". . . There are more like me." I say, "I'm not the most outrageous Chinese-American in this country. I am the least radical, the least offensive . . ." They're shaking their heads now, talking to one another like I'm showing them a Siamese twin, a man that is half a horse, a two-headed gorilla. "I am not a foreigner in this country I've been here for four generations. Some have been here for eight, folks." Mrs. Chinese-America is now bending over and washing the wheels, getting the front of her T-shirt wet. "I don't even know how to speak Chinese." They're muttering now, starting to shake their heads. I enter myself in the local spelling bee. My baby is out in the car keeping the engine running as I wind up the day in Jerome, Idaho. I win the spelling bee and flee from the tar and feathers.

My patronizing blond-haired, whining, pouting bride of fifteen, known to me as "The Body," is my whole responsibility to America. She is America. She tells me things about me that I am not. America patronizes me and loves me and tells me that I am the product of the richest and oldest culture in the history of the world. She credits me with all the inventions of modern life, when in fact I have nothing of my own in America. But I stay with her to get what I can out of her.

I do not like to linger on the summits of mountains. I do not take pride in standing on the summits of mountains, there is no dignity achieved by it. Had I climbed only one mountain in my life, I might have taken some pride in that as an accomplishment. It is an exercise of faith, of the heart, and once you've achieved that goal you have nothing to work for; it is a kind of disappointment to meet that goal. I do not consider death simply as tragedy, but rather the affirmation of life. When my father and mother died I considered myself at the summit of a mountain and out of all the advice I received in my youth I gave my spirit over to a woman who must have been a mountaineer in her own youth, and who said, "There is no time left for pride, for dignity, only to turn, without grieving, and to go."

And now when I dwell on my own grief for an instant, I like to think I'm on the road heading out to Wisconsin where I loved a woman, where she now lives. Her own grandfather lit out from China, sailed over the Pacific, and fled from the West Coast to Wisconsin and set roots there. She gave me part of her life back there one early summer when I was still dreaming about grandfathers, trying to pull all of my past together. She sends me pressed roses and lilies of the valley. And when I'm on the road at night, I am all of the romantic that I am, she plays the elusive spirit of my loving, she is the fresh smell of rain falling on the Wisconsin marsh lands in summer. She tells me that it is bitingly cold in Wisconsin in the winter time, but I know her only in early summer. When I'm on the road at night, she is that Wisconsin time when I held her close to me, hugging her in the sudden downpour, she is that Wisconsin time when I held her by that marsh bordering the green hidden lake and the rain came down into the thick forest growth. The air around us was claustrophobic. Small drops of water trickled down off her hair, off her face, wetted down her blouse against her skin. I saw her breathing the sweet air around us. It was the calm rain after the thunder, the rain comes straight down. But she is only the myth of the perfect day until I do get back to her home, she is the summit I must turn to in the end.

In the dream about me I do not go back to her. But it will be sometime before I get up there. I've got this thing going with my Lolita to straighten out America. Except now she does all the speaking and people listen to her when she's dressed the way she dresses. I've trained her to speak exactly like me, told her all my stories, all my dreams about my grandfathers, my father and mother. My whole life story became her life story. She swears like I do, she names names like I do. She was the pilot that took over the controls when the real pilot keeled over and died in the movies. I gave her instructions from the ground. Talked her into a perfect landing. She was driving a white Porsche named the "Enola Gay."

On the West Coast people didn't put too much stock in simply the two of us hanging around each other. People out here just looked at her when she was wearing that T-shirt. So we had to be more subtle. We opened a Chinese restaurant called the Seven Lanterns, complete with hanging lanterns, the waiters wore Chinese jackets, and I made up my bride to look Chinese, dressed her up in a *cheong-sam* just like in the movies. When a customer came in I taught her to say, "Wollombi Murrundi Wallabadah Goonoo Goonoo Gunnedah," without taking a breath and while bowing. On the cover of the menu were Chinese characters signifying, "Good Luck," "Happiness," and "Long Life," and inside the menu were the names of the finest Mexican food this side of the border.

In the dream about us, we had the most fun when we were on the road, except we ran into problems in Northern California and the Southwest. We weren't giving speeches then, we were just observing. People kept thinking I was an Indian and somehow this beautiful, sexy white girl who looked like everyone's daughter was in trouble, had probably fallen into my rapist hands. So I had to get out the make-up kit and make myself look more Chinese. She always had fun putting on my make-up in the morning, laughing at me as she made my eyes slanted.

In the dream about her body, I remember she always wore her bikini bottom around the motel room as a robe and nothing else when we were touring the Southwest. My bride came out of the bathroom in her "robe" one day just as the biggest sheriff I had ever seen broke down the door. She cradled her breasts in her arms in fright. I had my make-up on.

The sheriff had seen and took off his hat and sunglasses and said, "Pardon me, miss, but we got a call saying a young girl of your description was in trouble and," he looked at me, ". . . was kidnapped by an Indian." He looked at me again, ". . . but I see you are in no danger." I bowed. He bowed.

After that she wore the make-up too and that started even more trouble. Guys kept pushing by me and talking to her about the time they were on R and R in Hong Kong. So I only wore the make-up on our way home, nobody tried to save her from an Indian, nobody talked to her about R and R in Hong Kong. They just gave her the hotel room key, and the bellboy let me carry the bags, and he led her to the room. At restaurants they gave us one menu—for her. And one day when we were in a cafe some place I'd never been to before she was playing the game, reading the menu in Australian, perched on the seat with her legs folded under her. She was wearing a real short dress that looked more like a long shirt with nothing on underneath. The busboy kept dropping forks and bending down to peek up at her bare ass, kept bringing us water to look down the front of her dress at her magnificent loose breasts. I was getting tired of our game so I asked her for the menu, she looked at me with those pale blue eyes and sucked on the tip of her little finger mumbling out Australian towns until I yelled, "Give me the goddamned menu, you bitch!" The busboy stopped dropping forks. The cook lifted a noisy piece of ham off the grill. She started crying, and I hustled her out of the cafe, into the car, and out of the parking lot at eighty miles an hour. At one hundred forty she stopped crying so I slowed down; at ninety miles an hour she pouted. That was the end of the honeymoon. After that it was: "Why are you so sensitive? You shouldn't raise your voice at me. You don't have a healthy attitude towards me." And that was the end of the marriage.

She said she loved me. I didn't want her love. She said I saw her only from my point of view. She was right. In desperation she said, "You people are not polite, you should be more like . . ." She never finished the statement. She couldn't figure out whom we should be more like. Finally she said, "Just go back home." I gave her the car. I was already at home.

I knew America by living away from it. I caught glimpses of it from Guam, that tropical white sandy piece of America. I lived it everyday, every minute of the day. I saw what other boys in America saw, and I saw things they only imagined. The bombers, the fighters, the aircraft carriers, the submarines and everytime a ship or the air base had an open house my father took me.

My parents and I were invited as guests of the commander aboard a Chinese destroyer from Taiwan. When we got to where the ship was docked, I looked in horror at the slim gray destroyer and said, "That's not a Chinese destroyer. It looks just like one of ours."

We had lunch with the commander and officers and after lunch the sailors took me around the ship, gesturing in sign language when I knew what all the stuff was. They showed me the engine room, the depth charge rack, the bridge. They showed me the inside of a big gun turret and kept saying, "Boom! Boom!" and I kept saying, "I know. I know." I had a great time and they didn't even have to speak or understand English. We saw a movie with the crew called "The Long, Long Trailer." It was in English, but it must have been the funniest movie they ever saw because they laughed all the way through it.

These guys were Chinese and I knew then I wasn't one of them. It didn't bother me when I was a kid and the other kids called me Chinese, but occasionally I was called a Chinaman. The way they said it I knew they knew something I didn't know. The Chinaman was something right out of science fiction for me. When you called someone a Chinaman it didn't mean Chinese. It was a mutant name dragged up out of America's need to name names. When the Chinese came here they were no longer just Chinese because they threatened the white labor force, a way of life. They wanted something out of America, a way of life of their own. A "Chinaman" threatened history, culture, and language the way a "Jap" loosed chaos on the world. Being Chinese meant you kept to your history, your culture, your language from a country you've never been to. In the dream about me, I know my name.

In the dream about me they give me my bride back. I tell her about the real America where I saw it when I was six and seven. I tell her about a kid on Guam, how he used to go to the outdoor movies with his parents and sit with all the sailors on benches out in the warm night, how he didn't see a TV until 1957 when he came home. He grew up on Jerry Lewis movies, and Francis the Talking Mule movies. Out there in the warm night, I tell her about how I looked for fireflies in the night.

In the dream about me I get the girl I wanted when I was fifteen. She is the patronizing, slim, long-legged, blond-haired, full-breasted, wholesome, innocent, fifteen year old high school, whining, teaser of a cheer leader. She is pouting, telling me about how mad she is at her parents, how they try and make her live the life they lived. I tell her she can live the life I've lived. I tell her about a kid on Guam whose father brings home a tattered Charlie McCarthy puppet. He tells his father, "I don't play with dolls."

"But this is not a doll. His name is Charlie McCarthy and he talks." His father puts his hand through the back of the puppet, spins the head around, and pulls the string that moves the mouth.

"Hi, my name is Charlie McCarthy. I'm glad to meet you." The mouth claps open and shut. The arm pushes out to shake hands. The head spins all the way around. The kid shakes his hand. His mother comes over and sits in front of Charlie McCarthy and Charlie says, "Hi baby. What's for dinner? I'm hungry."

She says in Chinese, "Broccoli with beef, steamed fish, soup and rice." She winks at Charlie.

Charlie says, "*Ngoh m'sick gong tong hua.* Or in other words, sweetheart, I don't speak no Chinese. I don't care no how what's on the table just take me to it. Time to chow down, kid. Let's go wash our hands."

I named my Charlie McCarthy doll "Freddy." Other kids were going around telling me I couldn't name him Freddy because his name was already Charlie McCarthy. So I told them I called him Freddy for short. It was his Chinese name. I got pretty good at talking with my teeth clamped down into a pasted grin on my face. My mother made him a new suit out of pieces of left over Chinese silk from one of her dresses. Man, he looked sharp in a red silk suit, white shirt, and a tie my father had won with a map of Guam on it. And Freddy was how I learned a few words of Chinese. Nobody had a Charlie McCarthy doll on the island that could speak Chinese. My mother taught me Chinese by telling the words to Freddy, and Freddy would say them to me and I would say them back to my mother in English and Chinese.

We had lessons in the kitchen while my mother was fixing dinner. Between walking from the refrigerator to the stove she'd cast a glance at Freddy and teach the numbers to him from one to ten.

"*Yi*." said Mother.

"*Yi*." said Freddy.

"One. *Yi!*" I said.

"*Er*."

"Ergh." It came up through the teeth from the throat, like a cough.

"Two. *Er,*" I said. Freddy nodded.

"*San*."

"*San*," Freddy said when the tip of my tongue hit the roof of my mouth.

"Three. *San*."

"*Sz*."

"*Sz*." *Sz* was like spitting water between your two front teeth.

"Four. *Sz*," I said swallowing and licking my dry lips from so much air passing through the teeth.

"*Wu*."

"*Wu*," Freddy said, curling up the sides of my tongue.

"Five. *Wu*."

"*Lyou*."

"*Lyou*," Freddy said, making my tongue flap through the one syllable like a wave in the bottle of my mouth.

"Six. *Lyou*." I said as Freddy started to snore.

"Wake up, Freddy. It's time for *chi*."

"Eeegads. Chee! Take it away, kid," he said, his mouth clapping like the hooves of horses.

"Seven. *Chi*," I said relaxing the muscles of my jaw.

"*Ba*." My mother smiled at this one, because Freddy couldn't say *ba* without closing the lips of my mouth.

Freddy looked at me with his mouth open, "Are you ready for this one, kid? Here goes, *ba*." I couldn't do it without bringing my lips together. If I said *ba* while smiling it sounded like what a soldier says when he's been shot.

"Eight. *Ba*." I said.

"That was real nice," Freddy said.

"Thanks, buddy."

"Only two more to go, boys." she said and continued with, "*jyou*."

"*Jyou*."

"Nine. *Jyou*." I said as I flexed the muscles of my jaw.

"*Shr*."

"*Shr*." The air whistles through my bottom row of teeth.

"Ten. *Shr*."

"Okay, Freddy, say them all at once," she said while stopping all her work, because this was what she enjoyed about the lesson above all else. When Freddy said all the numbers it sounded like the soundtrack to the landing on the beaches of Iwo Jima.

After that, learning Chinese was really a challenge. My mother told me I had to learn a few

words of Chinese because we were going to visit my grandmother in Hong Kong for a few weeks. So me and Freddy learned all the necessary words to get by, including *ngoh m'sick gong tong hua*. When we got there it took me a long time before I could say any Chinese words without my teeth freezing into that plastered grin. It was the way I learned Chinese from that Chinaman, Charlie McCarthy. I knew I had hit something right because in all those war movies showing the bad Japs tearing up the Pacific Islands, screaming down out of the skies as Kamikazes, yelling banzai in the jungles of each Pacific tropical island, they, in all of those movies whispered, ordered, yelled, shouted, screamed, made speeches in English and Japanese with their teeth clamped into that grin I knew so well.

She sits in a chair in front of me in a position most girls by the age of eighteen lose; one foot is up on the seat of the chair while the other stays on the floor, her chin is resting on the knee of the raised leg. She is wearing her white blouse from gym class, a plaid Catholic school pleated skirt, white socks, and saddle shoes. She has been listening to my story. She is seated in front of me like that, wearing chartreuse panties. She is named after an American doll. She's got a name like Becky or Nancy Ann. She laughs at my story and says, "Who's Charlie McCarthy?" Things with us haven't been the same since I called her a bitch in that cafe. I've become more impatient. She is beginning to waste my time. I say let's go and park somwhere.

"What's an Enola Gay? How come our car is named the Enola Gay?"

"It's the name of someone's mother."

"Whose?"

"I don't know. He was an airplane pilot."

"What kind of name is Enola Gay? That ain't even a nice name for a boat."

"No, it ain't."

"I get to drive, don't I?"

"Yeah."

"How come you never look at me when I talk to you? You think I'm just a dumb girl, don't you, 'cause you're real smart."

"Take us somewhere dark and lonely."

"You just want to *see me* and *feel* these, huh?"

"I've *seen* you already and felt *them* and *it*."

"What kind of plane was the Enola Gay?"

It was a dark night in America when my mother and I flew home, touch down in San Francisco, came home from Guam.

We fly home on one engine, making a perfect crash landing. "Don't ever let me down Rita!" he says. He looks over at me, "Yeah, outlaw we'll make it. It's a clear day, and there ain't nothing to run into out here over the ocean."

It was dawn when we turned up the fur collars on our jackets and slipped down into the frosted seats of the cockpit, strapped on the radio and ear phones, buckled up and ran the check. Bobby was the best there was. Squadron leader. We had a tail gunner that always got sick from facing backwards. We had a bombardier who used to build shooting galleries. I was still reading the check list with the flashlight stuck under my arm, and blowing warm air in my hands, when Bobby pushed the starter for engine one. Heard it cough once and start. He smiled at me and said, "Good ol' faithful. That's Rita's best one. That's the one that'll get us through the clutch some day."

In another instant I had my gloves on. Then his thumbs-up signal to me. A glance amid the drone of the engines. The plane was shaking, straining to move forward, the wings flexing. I slid back my window and looked out at the engines. Said to him, "Let's get Rita up there! Go!" We lead off a line of B-17's named The Lady's Aces, Buttercup, Sylvia, Las Vegas, Baby Doll, The Dancer, and The King of Hearts.

"Okay. Take over, outlaw. Time for coffee. Keep them tight." We circle back around the island and head out to sea.

Yes, out there on Guam was where I stuck my head down into the cockpit of that crashed fighter behind our house at Orote. Looked down into the stale air of ghosts, afraid of seeing bad blood, afraid of seeing a piece of bone on a lever still guiding the plane up for more altitude. The dials and needles pointed to zero. They pointed their way home. The piece of wing I was standing on moaned when I lifted myself off it and eased myself down into the seat, brushing away the dust and broken glass. I kneeled down on the seat, grasped the bent and charred lever in front of me, heard my heart beating as I flicked one of the toggle switches. Breathed out, held it out, and, with no oxygen in my lungs moved another switch on. Took another breath. I heard the scream of my imagination catching the branches of the trees in front of me, heard the wings tearing off into the blaze of trees, felt myself slammed into the explosion of trees breaking open. I said to someone, "Can I get out now? Can I get out now?" There's a faded yellow sign on the wing that says, "Step Here."

Rita was going down, sending out a stream of black smoke behind her, Bobby said, "Jump." Everybody went out and we were losing altitude and he told me to jump and he'd be right behind me, but of course he wasn't. When we touched down in San Francisco that was the beginning of life with mother. I had to seek out friends to keep the imagination running at full pace. After a cousin and I saw "Pork Chop Hill" we played "Pork Chop Hill" all day long for a week. I wore a pair of Colt 45's, a Winchester slung over my back, a bow slung over the other shoulder, three plastic hand grenades stuck in the bottom holes of my shirt, two Jolly Roger Buccaneer rubber knives stuck in my belt, and a sailor's hat on my head. My cousin carried a

submachine gun, a .38 that shot suction cup darts, a Pancho Villa bullet belt slung over his shoulder, the suction cupped arrows to my bow, and a fire chief's helmet on his head.

There was a time in the Sierras when I was skiing over them in spring. I camped at the edge of a wide meadow and heard a plane in the night laboring over the mountains, heard it come down low, droning out an echo through this meadow surrounded by mountains, heard it in my dreams first as a touch of a melodious note in this cathedral of snows. I sat up in the cold freezing night and saw the wing lights of that plane come down low over the meadow, then lean out into a gradual turn to the west towards some city. The moon was covering the snows of the deep meadow. The plane's distant throbbing was absorbed into the powdery surface of the mountains.

There were sheets of ice clinging to the wings. One engine was sputtering. My teeth were chattering. All the crew had come forward and were huddled in the cockpit behind us for warmth, stamping their feet, clapping their gloved hands together. Icicles hung from my fur collar. We needed another 300 feet to clear the range and with one engine that would be difficult. The engine coughed, sputtered.

"Don't let it die, outlaw, keep it going!"

"It's dead. Frozen," I said.

"Okay boys, time for exercise! Unload everything heavy! We gotta get up, otherwise we're going through!"

The mountains got bigger and bigger. Bobby said look for a dip in the range so we can sneak by one of the peaks, fly down range and slip through another gap, and bring the bomber down to warm air, let the engine unfreeze. When the plane got so close you could make out large boulders and gapping crevasses in the glaciers, and when it was still not enough altitude, we were told we didn't have a "Chinaman's Chance" in hell of getting through. Bobby found a way to get through and down into the fertile farmlands of Europe. We were cheering all the way, hugging each other, then looked for landmarks for the way home. They made Rita into a weather plane after the war, painted the tail orange, and gave her to the Navy.

It was that dark night in 1952 when my father and I were walking down the brick streets of Chinatown looking for a place to eat. At two in the morning there were a few old men walking along the streets in heavy dark overcoats, and most of the stores were lighted. These streets and alleys smell of discarded food in the gutters, smell of fish scales washed out across the sidewalk into the gutters, and in the dark night this town smells wet, damp, penetrating. You walk carefully through this town at night, looking for a place to eat. There is a pulse at night, when the neon lights shine in the scales of the street. You never drive through this town, only walk.

"Can we go there sometime?" my bride had

said. She was adjusting the mixture in the carburetors on the "Enola Gay" dressed in her bikini, getting oil and grease on her legs and arms. In between engine revs she spoke. "Will you take me there for lunch sometime? Coffee? Anything."

"They make terrible coffee there." I was standing above her, looking down.

"I don't care what we have. I just want to see it."

"What do you want to see?"

"Just see Chinatown."

"Okay. We'll drive through sometime."

She pulled the carburetor linkage and the engine revved higher, she held out the linkage for a few seconds and let go. "My brother used to be a gas station mechanic."

"So did I."

"You ought to meet him sometime. He's a nice guy. He's done a lot of things. I used to try and be like him."

"So did I."

She laughed, "You don't even know him." She brushed her hair back with the clean little finger of her greasy hand and picked up a screwdriver. "I used to follow him on his paper route."

"A girl in my class named Katie who was the daughter of a famous writer used to follow me on mine when I was nine."

"My brother used to be a Boy Scout."

"I was too. And a Cub Scout."

"He played little league baseball."

"So did I."

"He was on the high school football team."

"I was on the water polo and swimming team."

"He has a letterman's jacket."

"So do I."

"He lettered three times."

"I lettered five times and was voted most valuable player."

". . . at a Chinese high school?"

"Your brother went to a Chinese high school?"

"No, stupid. Did you go to a Chinese high school?"

"What's a *Chi-neese* high school?"

"You know what I mean. A high school in Chinatown."

"I was the only Chinaman at an all white high school and I never tell anyone about those years."

"How come you were so athletic? You don't look athletic."

"I was a poor sport."

She shut off the engine and was cleaning the grease off her hands with some gasoline, "Can we go there today?"

"Where? A Chinese high school?"

"Chinatown. I'll wear that dress you like so much."

"Wear pants."

In the dream about me when I was staring into the darkness of my aunt's children's shop, I saw the reflection of the old trolley cars that rolled up and down the main street of Berkeley, I saw our old house down there on Bancroft Way where my father popped popcorn for me without the top on the pan. And I saw my bride sitting in the car waiting for me to start traveling, start moving out on the road.

When my mother died she left me in pursuit of myself at fifteen, left me without humility. There is everything at fifteen. When she died I knew my own violence, my anger, my desires, my own force to compete. I grew up away from Chinatown, away from relatives, away from America, yet in it all the time. I had only the two of them to keep pace with me. In the dream about me at Tumon Beach, at six years old I commit outrageous acts of heroism, at ten in little league I am the boy wonder in the major leagues, at eleven in the Boy Scouts I save the lives of girls from the grip of death, at fifteen I am violent, arrogant because I know what I want out of life. I want to pursue life, I want life to be difficult for me. I want to test myself. I want to feel like I'm being chased on the road at night. There is the glare of headlights at the back of my head, the rear view mirror casts a strip of light across my eyes.

You are more alone at fifteen than any other age. No lovers. Without a father, mother, brother, sister, there is nothing except your own energy that keeps loneliness and pity at arm's length. And everyday after school I swam dozens of laps, played water polo to exhaustion. I kept my appetite at a peak, I slept soundly all night long, I never let up a single day. After a water polo game, I pulled myself out of the pool by my limp arms, my back, neck and face red from sweating in the water. When I am awarded the Most Valuable Player trophy a year after my mother's death, my coach says to a crowd of athletes, parents and teachers, that I am the first Chinese in the history of this high school to receive this award in any sport, and they applaud. My heart is beating fast, I am short of breath, I begin my steps up to the platform where he is speaking. "This boy has more drive and more determination than any member of the team. . ." he says in a hollow voice that I do not recognize. I am still walking through the auditorium, I am sweating, my shirt sticks to my back like the hot humid days on Guam, my feet are soaking with sweat in my hot shoes. ". . . this is an award for more than doing your best, to pull a team together. . ." I say, I whisper, I do not want this award, I don't need it, I need to keep running. ". . . he is a credit to the team, to this school, to his race. . ." I am there, finally, everybody is applauding, and I am dizzy from the heat, on the stage, in the spotlights I need air, I take the award, I shake my coach's hand, I nod into the stage's spotlights at the darkened audience. ". . . I can say that I am proud of you, and I know the school and your family is proud of you. . ." I will never admit it. ★

MEI BERSSENBRUGGE

Chronicle

I was born the year of the loon
in a great commotion. My mother--
who used to pack $500 cash
in the shoulders of her fur gambling coat,
who had always considered herself
the family's "First Son"--
took one look at me
and lit out again
on a vacation to Sumatra.
Her brother purchased my baby clothes;
I've seen them, little clown suits
of silk and color.

Each day
my Chinese grandmother bathed me
with elaboration in an iron tub;
amahs waiting in line
with sterilized water and towels
clucked and smiled
and rushed about the tall stone room
in tiny slippers.

After my grandfather
accustomed himself
to this betrayal by First Son,
he would take me in his arms,
walk with me
by the plum trees, cherries, persimmons;
he showed me the stiff robes
of my ancestors and their drafty hall,
the long beards of his learned friends,
and his crickets.

Grandfather talked to me, taught me.
At two months, my mother tells me,
I could sniff for flowers,
stab my small hand upwards to moon.
Even today I get proud
when I remember
this all took place in Chinese.

The Suspension Bridge

You say all of us
even if we fail become lights
along the awesome bones. Separated
by darkness, humming through wires
on windy nights, bellying out,
you're so sure the current is personal.

Not like the firefly
that lives for a month
jolted at random by a blank force,
that never knows the brightness
of its shocked body,
even on cool nights above the grasses
when it loves, victim to victim?

History

My great grandfather dozed while drinking
hot liquor in his dark room full of books.
When she entered to wake him without knocking
as she did every night being the first grandchild
he was dead. One fur sleeve touched the floor.
Once he carried her in his big sleeve through
stone halls to the kitchen where they were burning
straw. His daughter took her smelling of wormwood
behind the fireplace to feed. It wasn't the same robe
he died in but the same color and cloth. My mother
really can't remember the smell of lynx and herbs
against moths, nor the slowness of his step,
which must have been told.

INTERVIEW WITH

Asians in America today are experiencing a literary renaissance. For Japanese Americans, young Sansei artists such as Chris Iijima, Momoko Iko, Lawson Inada, Janice Mirikitani, and Joanne Miyamoto, among others, are writing about their communities and are integrating the collective experiences of their people into their works. As this movement has developed, these writers are discovering that they are part of a hidden Asian American literary tradition. In January of 1975, a Nisei Writers' Symposium was held in San Francisco, featuring four Nisei authors—Hiroshi Kashiwagi, Iwao Kawakami, Toshio Mori, and Yoshiko Uchida. Other seminars and conferences as well are beginning to recognize the roots of Japanese American literature—Nisei writers.

For the majority of Nisei writers, this tradition has meant expression not only as individuals, but more importantly as members of an ethnic minority group in America. Through writing, they were able to understand the experiences of Japanese Americans and to give artistic expression to this experience. Author of *Yokohama, California*, Toshio Mori is a literary craftsman of great skill and sensitivity. Yet, his only published book has been out of print for many years, and even readers of *Counterpoint* may be asking, "Who is Toshio Mori?" and "What is his significance as an author?"

Born in Oakland in 1910, Mori was interested in art during his early years; and influenced by one of his teachers, he turned to writing as an art form. He spent most of his time during his teens in second-hand bookstores and in the public library, where he read the works of such authors as Sherwood Anderson, Theodore Dreiser, and William Saroyan.

Mori viewed himself as a "serious" as opposed to "commercial" writer and knew that he could not survive solely upon his earnings as a writer. He had to work an average of *twelve to sixteen hours each day* as a nurseryman, then wrote in his "spare time." Yet, he felt the need to accurately present the day-to-day experiences of Japanese and Japanese Americans in the setting of their own communities. From the people in his community in Oakland he developed his characters—very human and complex, rather than the wooden stereotypes portrayed in the novels of Peter B. Kyne *(The Pride of the Palomar)* and Wallace Irwin *(Seed of the Sun)*. In this sense, Mori's works have historical as well as literary value, for they reflect the feelings, emotions, and conflicts of the Issei and Nisei of the 1930's and 1940's.

Today, Toshio Mori's works are still unavailable. Many of Mori's writings, which include several hundred short stories and six novels, remain unpublished, and *Yokohama, California* has been long out of print. In response to an inquiry, the publisher stated it could not bring out a paperback edition of the novel unless sales of 10,000 copies could be guaranteed. This illustrates one of the difficulties which Asian American writers experience, and points out the need for Asian Americans to support their writers and help them find ways to publish, if we are to have a literature—which speaks for us and to us.

Because of the importance of his writings, Asians in America need to know more about Toshio Mori. In the following interview, a composite of interviews occurring between March 1973 and July 1974, he talks about his book, himself, and his situation as a writer.

The Author

Horikoshi: How did your parents respond to your aspirations to become a writer?

Mori: One of my main boosters was my mother, who encouraged me to write. I used to confide in her about some of the problems of a writer, and largely

TOSHIO MORI

BY

PETER HORIKOSHI

due to her influence I was able to continue on the side. I did not originally set out to become a writer. I believe I was more of an artist when I was in school and I was trying to become a better artist. Meanwhile through the influence of one of my teachers, I became interested in books as an art, so I started to take a side path towards books and writing. I started out by reading cheap novels, what they used to call "dime novels," because they were ten cents. Since I didn't have much money to spend on books, I used to visit all the bookstores, the second-hand bookstores, and stayed there for hours.

Horikoshi: Did you notice that you had to develop a specific kind of self-discipline when you started to seriously consider writing as a career?

Mori: Yes. When I was first seriously interested in trying to become a writer instead of some other field, I began to keep a strict schedule. I used to work during the day at the nursery, so daytime was out, but during the evening, I used to keep a schedule. From 10 p.m. to about 2 or 3 a.m. in the morning, I'd spend at least four hours every night, trying to write. Even without anything to write on or a subject, I used to sit at the table until I got something written.

Horikoshi: So you worked from twelve to sixteen hours a day?

Mori: Yes, in a nursery in those days. This was in

the depression period, so we had to work about fourteen, sixteen hours a day. We used to eat, have supper about nine, and then by the time we finished supper it was ten, so I used to keep a strict schedule open for writing from about ten to about two o'clock. Then in the morning we had to get up at least by seven, so it was a pretty tight schedule. But I noticed that a person with a tight schedule is apt to work more than when one has more time.

Horikoshi: Did the Nisei of your generation take any active interest in writing or literature, among your friends in particular?

Mori: Yes, there were several West Coast Japanese American newspapers which encouraged readers and writers to contribute stories, essays and poems. That was one of the reasons why there were some Nisei who became journalists and some who attempted to create Japanese American stories.

Horikoshi: Do you think that the noticeable lack of these kinds of papers and journals might be one reason why there's very few Japanese American authors today and why people aren't more encouraged to write?

Mori: Yes, I think there should be more encouragement for the Japanese American hopefuls to see their

The interviewer gratefully acknowledges the contributions of the following people: Michael Omi, Shingo Kamada, Ron Takaki, and of course, Toshio Mori.

[Editor's Note: Some of the stories mentioned in this interview appeared in anthologies. "Say it with Flowers" is in *Asian American Heritage: An Anthology of Prose and Poetry,* David Hsin-Fu Wand, ed. Pocket Books, Simon & Schuster, Inc., 1974. $1.95. "The Eggs of the World" is in *Asian-American Authors,* Kai-yu Hsu and Helen Palubinskas, eds., Houghton Mifflin Co., 1972. "The Chessmen" appears in this volume.]

work in print. Probably if the Nisei or Sansei of today reach the college level, they might be able to find their things printed, but I believe there should be some independent Nisei journals or periodicals that would encourage creative writing, which will not only be good for the writers, but also for the community.

Horikoshi: You make a distinction between commercial writing and serious writing. When you first started out, your first thing was geared towards commercial writing, like writing detective stories. Does the novel *Yokohama, California* reflect that you weren't concerned with the salability of your book, but you really wanted to write something that you considered serious writing?

Mori: I tried to present some of the life patterns of a Japanese Issei and Nisei of a community to reveal to the people in general some of the small details of living that would appeal to the reader of any nationality, so I tried to stay true to the characters that I believe were some of the typical Nisei and Issei people within our limited circle.

Horikoshi: During the period that you were writing *Yokohama, California,* you must have been aware of a lot of stereotypic perceptions on the part of white Americans about Japanese Americans. In some way, was the writing of your novel trying to combat that sort of image of the Japanese?

Mori: Yes, I believe at the time, there were several types of stereotypes of Japanese. For instance, Mr. Moto and the detective, (Hashimoto) Togo. They used to write (about) the so-called comical Japanese. I believe that it was one interpretation of a Japanese character. I believe that some of the Japanese that we have truly in the community would offset some of the so-called typical Japanese characters in the books, so I tried to stay as close as possible to the day-to-day, as-is Japanese.

Horikoshi: Do you think it takes a Japanese American to really write accurately about a community like the Japanese American community, about the people in the community?

Mori: No doubt of that. I believe no matter how great a writer or artist is, it's almost impossible to truly get into another person's skin and try to interpret. In fact, if a person has actually experienced some problems, that person is more of an authority than a person who could write it with imagination and create fantasies afterwards. So, I believe a good evacuation novel will come through the eyes that did experience it. I believe that it's a great shame that some of the Issei experiences are lost now due to the lack of writing opportunities of the Issei, and loss of some of the records during the evacuation. I believe some of the potent diaries and journals are lost although some of the superficial journals are probably remaining.

Horikoshi: We noticed that in your book, *Yokohama, California,* that you go up to the war. You stop there, and I was wondering if you've ever considered writing a novel of the evacuation experience.

Mori: Oh, I have a book based on the evacuation itself, which was written during the forties. It was almost accepted but it's still unpublished. That title was *Send These the Homeless.* Then I have another novel which I believe might be the next which I'd like to see printed, *A Woman from Hiroshima.* It's almost like an autobiography of an Issei woman, coming from Hiroshima as an immigrant and spending the rest of her life in America. That covers evacuation, through the camp life, and to the end of World War II.

Horikoshi: How do you as a Nisei male author attempt to get under the skin of an Issei woman? Did you base the character on any type of person that you personally. . . ..

Mori: . . .yes, I did have a main character background as my mother. (She) probably was the main character, although some of the features and some of the experiences might be consolidated as a typical Issei woman; but I had several influences of an Issei woman through my mother, which I collected together as a typical Japanese woman immigrant. Speaking of Issei, I was able to associate with some of the Issei whose experiences I collected, although it isn't as yet written. But I have a collection of Issei stories which I believe would be some revelation towards the Issei characters. I have several men Issei friends whose experiences were good enough to be printed as they spoke, but sadly these Issei who did have unusual experiences are practically gone today.

Horikoshi: Are you planning on publishing these?

Mori: If I could find a publisher, I'll be glad to publish. So far, I don't seem to have much luck there. I had some agents who told me that the sale or commercial value (of my stories) is nonexistent. From 1942 to the 1960's I wrote those books, so I haven't really written anything new since 1965, I guess. But now I'm thinking of going back to writing again. I took time out during a ten-year period, free-lanced and wrote those books hoping that I could sell some, or get interest in some publisher. After I finished that, I started going back to work. Now I'm just resting up and deciding which way to go. I'm pretty sure I'll start writing.

Horikoshi: Have you met a lot of young Asian Americans? You were telling me that you met Lawson Inada.

Mori: That's within a space of two years or so. The

474

reason why I started that must have been about two years ago when San Francisco State through Jeffrey Chan and a few others invited me to attend Lawson's poetry reading. I accepted it and through that meeting, I met Professor (Kai-yu) Hsu, Frank Chin and others, and found that they were interested in my stories which I wrote a long time ago. But I realize that the movement for Asian American identity encouraged me to associate with the younger group. That was my first beginning, the students that I have come close with are all recent.

I believe the younger generation has developed a deeper interest within themselves and their problems than the older generation. They seem to probe deeper into their circumstances, conflicts, and background historic-wise too. I believe that first generation was limited through lack of English knowledge, and purely manual labor was their primary purpose to exist. Then the second generation, through the influence of their parents, were education minded, but except for the Japanese community, their job and business opportunities were limited. In fact, it was a rarity for a white corporation or any civil service jobs or public officers to find a second generation accepted. Second generation was limited not by education but livelihood. Most jobs were found within a limited Japanese town, and the surrounding businesses, and in nurseries and farms, or by accepting the lower forms of manual labor. I believe that World War II broke that pattern. When the relocation camps encouraged movement towards the East and the Nisei world which was usually concentrated in California and some in Oregon and Washington found that there were more job opportunities back East and within their own choice. That probably broke the pattern of Japanese limitations.

Horikoshi: But then not that many Japanese moved back East.

Mori: No, no. But gradually California, which was the hotbed of anti-Japanese previous to World War II and during the war began to open up in all ranges of fields both public and private started to accept not only Japanese but Asian Americans which actually revolutionized the job opportunities that the Japanese had before the war. I believe the movement and the influence of the blacks coming into California also helped the change. You know, before the war it was rare to find a Nisei accepted even in the average union. There were probably one or two at the most, even in the big unions. Now it's so unimaginable. I used to have friends who had engineering degrees accepting import or dry good, Grant Avenue import clerk jobs. . .and I guess the Nisei at that time were usually thinking in terms of achievement as being equal or better than hakujin. If you become equal or better than hakujin, you're pretty good in that field. But there wasn't any so-called Asian writing as the Sansei have now. They're trying to start something

as a group which is much more substantial because it will help preserve some of the writing efforts, I think, of today.

Horikoshi: We can just continue talking about that area then; so you're talking about (how) it's difficult to pinpoint just the situation of a writer as a commercial writer or as a serious writer.

Mori: I believe that Sansei today, as you say; they're more on the serious side of writing, and that's a good thing. And also, there's a necessity for it, I think. Although it's limited, there's a certain amount of interest created by the present situation. It's just filling the need of today.

Horikoshi: Why do you think it's so necessary to have this kind of serious writing, maybe about identity or history that seems to be going on today? Is there anything that you can pinpoint?

Mori: By that, do you mean, say, value to it?

Horikoshi: Well, you said that you felt it was a necessity now, or at least important.

Mori: I believe each period, there's something that could be worthwhile enough to be a contribution to American writing. It seems like today there's an ethnic field which is probably a new field that hasn't been explored too deeply in America. That's a good field, especially for the ethnic people because they're the ones who have to originate the new field and explore it rather than so-called outside writers trying to interpret and understand it and represent the specialized field. And that, I believe, the minority writers can contribute much more effectively.

Previously to this, especially in the Nisei field, there wasn't any demand for it. A person just volunteered or was individually interested in that field. He just explored on his own. There was no background, nor any encouragement to attempt anything in the minority field. So it was largely up to the individual to find interest enough to explore and continue. A lot of times the economics will deter the ambitious urge of many students.

Horikoshi: How would you place yourself in this type of writing? It seems that at the time you wrote, in the 1930's, you could have basically written about anything if you were interested in commercial writing. But the book *Yokohama, California* shows that you wrote from a Japanese American viewpoint.

Mori: It's difficult to say what influenced me to turn towards Japanese American writing other than that some of the serious writers of the previous period were an encouragement to try something new. At least that was new to me. For example, in American literature there would be writers such as Sherwood Anderson, who wrote *Winesburg, Ohio,* portraying small-town American Midwest people living out their lives and that sort of influenced my vision towards Japanese American colonies. Another influence was Anton Checkov, the Russian short story writer who wrote especially of the small lives of average townfolk and the country people. That was another. . .

Horikoshi: model for you to use?

Mori: Yes, another model, I guess you could say. There were a few French writers who wrote of another generation, say fifty to seventy-five years before that which seems to be interrelated with the present characters and also the problems, they seem to repeat themselves in the lives of representative people, portrayed in fiction. That made me realize that there are quite a few interesting characters and individuals among the small Issei-Nisei world.

Horikoshi: Were you conscious that you were writing specifically about Japanese Americans or say, using the model these other people wrote about, just people that they knew. Was it in your case more that these were just the people that you normally came into contact with, or did you want to write specifically about Japanese Americans?

Mori: They were particularly Japanese to begin with because when I did create a character in my fiction, the character usually consisted of several individuals which I combined and by combining their characteristics they represented Japanese characters of my community, typifying their conduct, morals and hope.

Horikoshi: So you were fairly conscious that you were writing as a Japanese American author, rather than just, "Well, I'm a writer writing about the people in my community."

Mori: I was concentrating on the Japanese characters because I felt that the Japanese characters can be portrayed so that they will be interesting to the white readers. Only thing is, there was hardly any market for it among the general audience for anything of minority characters. That made it difficult to be a commercial success.

Horikoshi: So it was really a case of more serious writing in the case of *Yokohama, California.*

Mori: Yes, I guess you could call it serious because it didn't sell.

Horikoshi: Maybe non-commercial would be a better word. So would you say then that your situation as a Japanese American author in the 1930's really affected your writing style because you wanted

476

to write about Japanese Americans specifically?

Mori: Yes, that's true because when you write about Nisei or Issei, the language is a little bit different and in order for the Nisei of that time to understand, you have to write in the style that Nisei and Issei were used to. So as a person starts as a minority writer he has a tendency to follow the street language or the language that's most commonly used among the minority. That becomes the familiar dialogue and style.

Horikoshi: Did you notice whether your style had changed at the time of the camps? We know what your style basically was when you wrote *Yokohama, California,* but the situation of the camps was a very significant event in most Japanese Americans' lives.

Mori: To me, the style, I fear, didn't change. The only thing, the experiences changed. Probably some of the thinking of those characters I started with might react a little differently, but my own writing style hasn't changed. To me, it was just a continuation of experiences that an immigrant and his family have, trying to find their home in America.

Horikoshi: Can you evaluate yourself, Toshio, now as an Asian American author? You've been talking about the significance of a Japanese American author talking about his community. Do you see yourself in that light as how it relates to the so-called Asian American movement today?

Mori: Well, when I started as one of the Nisei thinking he could write, I was just writing for myself, hoping that it will interest some other readers. I didn't put too much value unless it was recognized by the American white people reading it. I didn't place much value to my contribution.

Horikoshi: Would you say today that if Asian Americans are interested, as they are in your literature; do you think that's significant enough?

Mori: Oh yes, if I had a little more audience interest, I probably would have had more to say and more to write. Since I had a limited time to write I believe I was more or less handicapped by the economics. A person has to survive and when you write just for serious writing with hardly any financial returns, then it becomes difficult to continue and try to contribute something worthwhile.

Horikoshi: Do you think that this kind of monetary situation or financial situation helps a writer's style or his determination to write? You had to write under very trying circumstances. But what you came out with is very interesting, and has a lot of significance today. Do you think that if you had more time, would you have written more or would you have maybe written even less?

Mori: Well, that's hard to say, because sometimes a good writer has to starve to write good stories, and if a person has too much time, a lot of the extra time is wasted. The limited time usually becomes more valuable, as well as being progressive in accomplishments. I think a writer has to learn to condition himself, just as in sports, he has to train himself so that he will be able to withstand the pressure, the mental pressure and the physical stamina. Without those two, a writer probably will have a breakdown or fail physically through bad health.

Horikoshi: So then you would say to striving Asian American authors today that self-discipline and stamina are two of the more important things to consider.

Mori: Writing is a very personal thing, and a writer goes through life with trials and errors just as others do. But when a writer sits down to try to express it, he has to review the experiences that he's had, the hardships; usually it's the crisis or the problems that become the most interesting subjects for a writer. So he has to go back and review what made him as he is today and try to find a solution to his problems and to his destiny. He usually has to be in good condition so that he can go back and review and relive the hardships. It's like going back again and getting the same emotional response and tragedy of life where suffering is the beginning of all the problems that arise in an individual.

Horikoshi: Toshio, in assessing your written work, what do you think has been the main goals of your writing? What kind of perspective did you have about writing, and what were you specifically attempting to address to your readers?

Mori: Originally, when I did start writing, I was hoping to introduce the Japanese characters to the white Americans as a whole and so by that I tried to stick to the familiar characters that I knew in my circle. It's just that recently when there was renewed interest in my stories, especially among the Sansei or the third generation, that I feel gratified to see that there's some interest among the Japanese community. I would like to see more contributions by the Sansei in the way of Japanese American literature and explore into many channels that still haven't been touched upon through historical narratives or fiction, or through scholarly research. There's an untapped wealth of materials that should interest the American people as a whole.

Yokohama, California

Horikoshi: Can you talk about the background of your book?

Mori: Mostly the characters are based in the city of Oakland, California. The characters are fictional, but they're a composite of various characters I knew previously, when I was associated with Oakland surroundings. Whatever conflicts or actions happened, happened at that time. I still have some more characters of that period that are not in the book, so there are quite a few characters for *Yokohama, California,* mainly from about the early 1900's. I tried to write from a Nisei, second generation, viewpoint, and so, much of the first generation lives were kept out.

Horikoshi: When you wrote your book, it seems that it was a collection of short stories written here and there and then put together. Is there a special reason that you wanted to write the book?

Mori: Well, I always wanted to publish a book, but it took a long time for me. Originally, it was like a hobby for me; reading was like a hobby, writing was like a hobby, so I wasn't serious about writing until the age of 22 (in 1932). Then from 22, I decided I really wanted to see if I could do something, so I quit everything. I had some examples before me: (Ernest) Hemingway got published at the age of 25, (William) Saroyan at 24, and Thomas Wolfe at 28. But one of the most influential writers on me was Sherwood Anderson, and he happened to quit his business and become a serious writer at the age of 40, so I still had a chance. At the age of 28, I was finally able to sell a story. I got many rejections—thousands upon thousands of rejections. But still, if I were young, I believe I would still go through it again. Although monetary wise it hasn't been rewarding, the adventure of writing is fascinating.

Of course, these stories were written around the middle thirties, so I'll try to recall as much as I can of the characters I created then. Are there any special characters that you want me to start on?

Horikoshi: Well, we were interested in the story, "The Eggs of the World."

Mori: That must have been Sessue Matoi, wasn't it? I created that character from a composite of different persons I knew. Different characters contributed one or two aspects of Sessue Matoi. One was a person who constantly wished to bring forth the unknown value of his message to the public, small or large; and his usual failure to receive any attention. Another character was a person who after drinking several bottles of sake, would become indulgent and loose of tongue and start to philosophize his version of living. Another character had a ministry background who constantly had to fight for existence due to poor attendance and financial backing, and usually had only a few followers in each church that he was assigned to. Another character that I believe contributed part of the character was a laundryman, an Issei who worked as a laundryman at a wealthy Piedmont family, and I believe those are the different types of contributors to the character of Matoi. As far as the character, that was the beginning, that was the start: four or five personalities, combined together to become Sessue Matoi. And the story itself arose from the combination of those personalities I knew, back in my early twenties, usually seen from the eyes of a youth, searching for some answer to life.

"The Eggs of the World"

Mori: As far as I could remember, I think I wrote with the intention of revealing that the eggs of the world are individual beings encased within a shell, and each individual must break their shells or enclosed worlds of their own and come out into the world, as a rebirth character or as a personality. And to do that, they must find a solution, how to crack their own shell. And that's through self-identity and self-education. Once out of the egg, each individual has some form of expression; no matter what type of action it is, they're expressing their own flavor of sake, which is a symbol, a taste of life, and when one is concentrated, in his expression or self-expression, he would contribute a flavor of his own, which is individual and original. I didn't express it well, but I believe that's what I intended to reveal in the story.

Horikoshi: I noticed that at the end of the story, Mr. Hasegawa doesn't seem to really understand what his egg is.

Mori: No, no, I believe that was right, yes, his friend wasn't able to grasp it, and that's one of the sorrows of a person trying to express and help others along. When there's a lack of communication, sometimes there's friction, also misunderstanding and sometimes a loss of great vision. The character, Mr. Hasegawa, since you mentioned that he was unable to grasp the message of Sessue Matoi, is earnestly trying to grasp or understand his friend's message. I believe Mr. Hasegawa, within his present period, will probably never understand his friend.

Horikoshi: It seems that the message in this story is similar to the message in "The Trees."

"The Trees"

Mori: Recalling the characters in "The Trees," the Hashimoto of the story had a hobby in Bonsai, and he was one of the earliest Bonsai hobbyists. Hashimoto was an Issei whose interest in Bonsai, dwarf trees, originated in Japan, and when he was here in America, he used to go to the Sierras and had a permit to dig up some of the dwarf trees by the snow

pack. He used to collect trees during the summer and bring them back and nourish them by transplanting them into planters. However, more than half of them did not survive. Half of the pine trees that he collected weren't able to survive and died. But the few that he did have became representative Bonsai trees. He prized them so much that he didn't sell them to visitors who came from surrounding cities. Hashimoto was originally a real person who understood the art of Bonsai, the life of a tree in the natural form. His friend, Fukushima, was another character who had interest originally in Bonsai, but his person was a little bit shallower, and through his friend Hashimoto was seeking some shortcut to moneymaking, to find some immediate answer to growing in quantity rather than quality. And that was what started the story. So these two characters were real, taken almost by a single personality.

Horikoshi: So the messages of the stories were. . .

Mori: . . .similar, but the characters were more narrowed. "The Trees" was almost straight from life, from actual living persons, whereas in "The Eggs of the World" each character had composite lives that I centered in one character, Sessue Matoi and Hasegawa, I believe. The effects of the stories were similar.

"Say It with Flowers"

Horikoshi: "Say It with Flowers" had kind of a surprise ending to it because I thought the person would end up selling flowers like the rest of them. But he broke out of his egg, it seems.

Mori: Yes, "Say It with Flowers"—I had some experience helping out with flowers at my brother's flower shop and I accepted the locale as part of that story. Some of it is personal experience which I expanded. I started to dislike business as a livelihood, which probably influenced the ending. It was part of the outside world, working for a livelihood that you must accept the bad and the good of business aspects, of trying to keep your head or yourself out of financial difficulties. In a way, it showed the powerful influence of money dominating each individual whether young or old. Money plays a big part whether that person will get his opportunity or he will sink before his opportunity comes. Some young minds will never be able to get a foothold or start, which is a sad thing about life. In life there's always a dirty part trying to make an existence. And in business especially you must fabricate or tell lies in order to keep your position or your profit or your very existence. That's a shame, but it's probably a necessary evil of business and that was a part of the self-expression that I included in "Say It with Flowers."

Horikoshi: But it seems that at the end of the story,

the person rejected business, and so you wonder about whether or not he'll survive.

Mori: I guess this youth Teruo was a strong independent who wished to seek other means for existence and was still young enough to rebel and look for more suitable work that would at least maintain his feeling for the ideas that he has. The ending, as you say, is more abrupt with just the youth leaving the job and with the confidence that he'll find something better. The character itself and his solution was not solved in a short time, but the story itself was feeling that he refused to buckle under the conflict of losing himself as a good man or as a good youth. I don't remember whether I continued in another story of that youth maintaining his philosophy, but that's another story.

You see, I wrote quite a few stories and the stories in *Yokohama, California* were edited by the publisher to reach a certain portion of the audience, especially the library audience, and so it is not complete. Some short stories are complete or maybe resumed again in another story which is still probably unpublished, but it's so long ago that I can't recall some of the characters of the aftermath.

Horikoshi: So this actually is incomplete as. . .

Mori: . . .it's part of life, it's an expression of a part of my life in a set period.

Horikoshi: When you had the final manuscript, you had more in it than this.

Mori: Oh yes, they weeded out from about sixty stories and they weeded out the sordid, the rough side of life. There must have been about twenty stories left.

Horikoshi: So this *(Yokohama, California)* as a book was a little short of your expectations of what you wanted people to read?

Mori: Yes, I would have, if it were possible, wanted to get some other conflicts that were portrayed at the same time.

Horikoshi: If you were to have this reprinted, would you want to include the other stories?

Mori: Well, as a book it probably did its part for me. If there are any other worthwhile stories to be published I would like that to happen. With the remaining stories, most were written about the early twenties. Some of the Issei were around the World War I period, including the twenties, thirties, and forties, but it ends around the forties. I think that period to me personally is a young man's book. Since then I've matured a little more, but I don't know quality-wise . . .I gained some more experiences with the years.

"The Chessmen"

Horikoshi: Would you care to comment on the story "The Chessmen"?

Mori: "The Chessmen"? Okay. Offhand, I believe that's about nursery workers. The setting is in the 1930s when the depression was in progress and the two nursery workers were competing for one actual job. They knew that one of them might have to go, because there wasn't that much to do, the profit was low and it was before the time of social security or retirement funds. So, the workers themselves were quite concerned about their health, their capability of holding the job, and especially single men without families in that period went from job to job which lasted from half a year to ten or twenty years. Sooner or later, each worker, including nursery workers, realized that a bachelor or single man will find himself without a job, and with ill health or physically unable to work for existence. I tried to reveal that these two young men were still physically able to compete for one job. They knew within themselves that there will come a time when they will no longer be useful to society.

I felt the loneliness and sadness of a worker in such a situation. I haven't read that story recently, but offhand that's what I believe I had in mind. I don't remember the ending, but manual labor comes in. A natural process also occurs where the old is replaced by the young in each generation.

Horikoshi: I think a lot of Issei who didn't marry felt that way.

Mori: There are quite a few, especially among the farm hands. They did pass on a lonely life, and as soon as their usefulness is gone, they're probably nameless. Well, within this story, I tried to show that the Japanese as part of the Asians have a fatalistic attitude, or accepting life as is, much more as reality than the so-called typical American outlook. But as the generations go on, we'll adapt ourselves more closely to America. American opportunities arise, I believe that Asian Americans have the adaptability to change there.

Horikoshi: Are there any other stories that you would like to discuss here? Or a representative story of the whole book?

Mori: I can't truthfully say that I could select a typical story to express the whole of the book. But I'd like to mention that in life, to exist, human beings have to learn to have humor. Without humor man might lose his sanity. In some grievous circumstances, with humor sometimes, which is the most difficult to grasp, humor in the individual may be the saving grace. ★

THE CHESSMEN

Perhaps I would have heard the news in time, but if I hadn't met the third party of the three principals at the beginning it wouldn't have been the same to me. By luck that day, while I was leaning on the fence resting after a hot day's work, a young Japanese came up to me. "Hello. Where's Hatayama's nursery?" he asked me. "I was told the place was somewhere around here."

"It's half a mile farther down," I said. I pointed out the road and told him to go until he reached the greenhouses. That was Hatayama Nursery. The young Japanese thanked me and went away.

At Hatayama Nursery I knew two men, Hatayama-san and Nakagawa-san. They were the only men there the year around. The boss and his help. The two managed the three greenhouses of carnations quite capably. Only in the summer months when the carnation boxes must be lined up and filled with new soil and the plants for the next year planted, Hatayama-san hired additional men. Hatayama-Nakagawa combination worked beautifully. For seven years the two men never quarreled and seldom argued with each other. While Hatayama-san was at the flower market selling

flowers to the florists Nakagawa-san carried on at the nursery. He was wise on everything. He attended the boiler, watered the plants, made cuttings, cut flowers and tackled the rest of the nursery work.

Every once in awhile I used to visit the place and talk to these middle-aged men. Perhaps Nakagawa-san was older than his boss. I don't know. "Listen to him, Takeo," Hatayama-san used to tell me. "If you want to become a good carnation grower listen to this man. He's got something. He has many years of experience and a young man like you will learn plenty by listening to him."

Nakagawa-san used to smile with these words. He talked very little. "I don't know much," he would say. "I know very little."

One of the strange things about Nakagawa-san was his family life. I used to visit him only on the weekdays. On Saturday nights and Sundays he was in Oakland to see his family. I used to wonder how he could stand it. His wife and three grown children lived in the city while he worked alone in the nursery. He made his bed, washed his work clothes, swept and mopped his bunkhouse after work hours. The only

480

illustration by DAVID MONKAWA

domestic work he didn't do was cook. He ate with the Hatayamas.

When I'd sit and talk with him he'd talk about his family and his week-end visits.

"My youngest boy is now out of high school," he would tell me. "He's a smart boy but I can't send him to college."

"That's too bad for him," I would say. "But you're sending Tom to Cal. That's plenty."

"Yes," he would proudly say. "I hope he'll amount to something."

Nakagawa-san's only daughter worked as a domestic in an American home and helped with the upkeep of her parents' home. Often he would tell me of his children and his eyes woul shine with a far-away look.

"Why don't you stay with the family all the time, Nakagawa-san?" I'd ask him. "Why can't you get a job in Oakland and live with your family?"

He would smile. "Ah, I wish I could," he'd say. "But what could an old nursery worker do in a city? I'm too old to find other jobs. No, I must remain here."

"It's a shame," I'd tell him.

"I guess we can't have everything," he'd say and smile. "I'm lucky to have this job so long."

Several weeks after the young man had asked about Hatayama Nursery he came to see me one night. He said his name was George Murai. "I get very lonely here," he explained to me. "I never knew a nursery could be so lonely."

"You're from the city, aren't you?" I asked.

"Oakland," he said.

He was a pleasant fellow. He talked a lot and was eager. "Whenever I have the time I'm going to drop in and see you. That's if you don't mind," he said. "Over at Hatayama's I don't see any young people. I'll go crazy if I don't see somebody. In Oakland I have lots of friends."

I brought out beer and shredded shrimp. George could take beer.

"How do you like the work?" I asked him.

"Fine," he said. "I like it. Someday I'd like to have a nursery of my own. Only I hope I get over being lonely."

"You'll be all right after you get used to it." I said.

"If I don't give up at the start I'll be all right," George said. "I don't think I'll quit. I have a girl, you see."

He pulled out of his wallet a candid shot of a young girl. "That's Lorraine Sakoda of Berkeley," he said. "Do you know her?"

I shook my head.

"We're crazy about each other," George said. "As soon as I find a steady job we're going to get married."

Before the evening was over I knew George pretty well. Several times when we mentioned friends we found them mutual. That made us feel pretty good.

After the first visit George Murai came often. He would tell me how the work progressed at Hatayama Nursery. It was getting busy. The carnation boxes had to be laid out evenly on the tracks. The soil had to be worked and shoveled in. The little carnation plants must be transplanted from the ground to the boxes. It was interesting to George.

"I'm learning everything, Takeo," he said. "Some day I'll get a nursery for myself and Lorraine."

When I went over to Hatayamas to see the boss as well as Nakagawa-san and George Murai, I would catch a glimpse of a new liveliness on the place. The eagerness of George Murai was something of a charm to watch. He would trot from one work to another as if he were eagerly playing a game. His shouts and laughter filled the nursery and the two men whose capering days were over would look at each other and smile. George's singing ability pleased Hatayama-san. After supper he'd ask George to sing. George knew only the modern popular songs.

Sometimes Nakagawa-san, George and I got together in the little house. Nakagawa-san shared the place with George. At such times George would ask question after question about carnation growing. He would ask how to get rid of red spiders; how such things as rust and spots, the menaces of the plants, could be controlled. He would press for an answer on how to take the crops at a specific period, how to avoid stem rot and root rot, what fertilizers to mix, how to take care of the cuttings. I would sit aside and listen to Nakagawa-san answer each problem patiently and thoroughly.

Sometime the talk swung to Oakland. The three of us were attached to Oakland one way or another.

"I know your son Tom pretty well," George Murai told Nakagawa-san one night.

"Do you? Do you know Tom?" Nakagawa-san asked eagerly.

"Sure. Tom and I used to go to Tech High together," George said. "He's going to college now."

"Sure! Sure!" Nakagawa-san said.

"I know your daughter Haruyo," George said. "But I don't know Tetsuo so well."

Nakagawa-san nodded his head vigorously. "He's a smart boy but I can't send him to college like Tom."

It wasn't until I was alone with Hatayama-san one day that I began to see a change on the place. In the latter part of August Hatayama-san was usually busy hunting around for two husky men to work on the boxes. It was the time when the old plants in the greenhouses were rooted out and the boxes filled with the old soil hauled away. Then the boxes with the new carnation plants were to be hauled in. It was the beginning of heavy work in a nursery.

This year Hatayama-san said, "I can't afford to hire more men. Flower business has been bad. We'll have no flowers to sell until November. That's a long way off. After the new boxes are in I'll have to lay off Murai boy."

"Who's going to work the boxes this year?" I asked.

"Murai and Nakagawa," Hatayama-san said. "They'll have to do it."

When the heavy work at Hatayama Nursery actually started George Murai stopped coming to see me. One afternoon when I got off early and went over there they were still out on the field. It was then I saw the struggle that knew no friendship, the deep stamp of self-preservation in human nature. Here was no flowery gesture; here were no words.

I stood and watched Nakagawa-san and George Murai push the truckloads of carnation boxes one after another without resting. In the late afternoon their sweat dried and the cool wind made the going easier. It was obvious that George being young and strong could hold a stiff pace; and that he was aware that he would be laid off when the heavy work was finished. With the last opportunity to impress the boss George did his stuff.

I was certain that Nakagawa-san sensed the young man's purpose. He stuck grimly to the pace. All this was old stuff to him. He had been through it many times. Two men were needed to lift the boxes with the old soil and toss it deftly onto the pile so that no clump of dirt would be left sticking to the boxes. Two men were needed to carefully lift the boxes with the new plants and haul them into the greenhouses. The pace which one of the men worked up could show up the weaker and the slower partner. A man could break another man with a burst of speed maintained for several days. One would be certain to break down first. When a young man set up a fast pace and held it day after day it was something for a middle-aged man to think about.

Nakagawa-san straightened as if his back ached, but he was trying to conceal it. His forearms must have been shot with needle-like pains but he worked silently.

As I watched Nakagawa-san and George Murai heaving and pushing with all their might I lost sight of the fact that they were the friends I knew. They were like strangers on a lonely road coming face to face with fear. They looked like men with no personal lives; no interests in family life, in Oakland, in Lorraine Sakoda, in the art of plant-growing, in friendship. But there it was in front of my eyes.

I turned back and went home. I wondered how they could share the little shack after what was happening on the field.

I went over several times but each night they were so worn out with the strain of their pace they slept early. I saw them less and less. Their house was often dark and I knew they were asleep. I would then go over to see Hatayama-san.

"Come in, come in," he would greet me.

By the manner in which he talked about Nakagawa-san and George it was plain that he too had seen the struggle on the field. He would tell me how strong and fast George was. At the rate they were going they would be finished a week ahead of the last year's schedule.

"Nakagawa is getting old," he would tell me of his friend. "He's getting too old for a worker."

"He's experienced," I would reply.

"Yes," he'd say, "but George is learning fast. Already he knows very much. He's been reading about the modern method of plant growing. I've already put in an electric hotbed through George's suggestion."

Then I knew George Murai was not so close to being fired. "Are you going to keep both of them this winter?" I asked.

Hatayama-san shook his head. "No. Can't afford it. I've got to let one of them go."

Several nights later I saw lights in their little shack and went over. George was up. He was at the sink filling the kettle with water. Nakagawa-san was in bed.

"What's happened, George?" I said. "Is Nakagawa-san sick?"

"No," George said. "He's just tired. His back aches so I'm warming it with hot water and mustard."

"I'll be all right tomorrow," Nakagawa-san said.

"You're working too hard these days, Nakagawa-san," I said. "You're straining yourself."

Nakagawa-san and George were silent. They looked at me as if I had accused them in one way or another.

Soon Nakagawa-san was back on the field. However, when I went to see how he was getting along I saw Hatayama-san out on the field with George. By the time I reached them they had pushed the truckloads of carnation boxes in and out of the greenhouses several times. George whistled when he saw me. Hatayama-san nodded his head and grinned. Something had happened to Nakagawa-san.

"I knew it was going to happen," Hatayama-san told me. "Nakagawa's getting too old for nursery work. His back troubles him again."

In the morning Nakagawa-san had stuck grimly to the work. At noon when he sat down for lunch he couldn't get up afterwards. He had to be carried to the little shack. Mrs. Hatayama applied a new plaster to his back.

"I've been on the job for two days. We'll finish on time," Hatayama-san said. "George's been a big help to me."

George looked at me and grinned.

When the pair resumed carting the boxes I went to see Nakagawa-san. As I entered the room he opened his eyes and smiled at me. He looked very tired. His repeated attempts to smile reminded me of his family and his pride for his sons.

"I'll be all right in a few days," he said eagerly. "When my back's healed I'll be like new again."

"Sure," I said. "You'll be all right."

He read to me a letter from his wife. It was filled with domestic details and his boys' activities at school. They wanted to see him soon. They missed him over the week end. They reasoned it was due to the work at the place. They missed the money too. They wanted him to be sure and bring the money for the house rent and the gas bill.

When I came away in the late afternoon Hatayama-san and George were washing their faces and hands back of the woodshed.

"How's he getting along?" Hatayama-san asked me.

"He says he's all right," I said.

"I'll go and see if he wants anything before I eat," George said.

George trotted off to the little shack. Hatayama-san motioned me toward the house. "At the end of this month I'm going to drop Nakagawa. I hate to see him go but I must do it," he said. "Nursery is too much for him now. I hate to see him go."

"Are you really going to let him go?" I asked.

"I'm serious. He goes." He took my arm and we went inside the house. I stayed for dinner. During the courses George talked. "Someday I want to bring my girl here and introduce her," he told Hatayama-san and me. "You'll both like her."

Hatayama-san chuckled. "When will you get married, my boy?"

George smiled. "I think I can get married right away," he said.

Afterwards we listened to a few Japanese records. George got out Guy Lombardo's records and we listened to them. Mrs. Hatayama brought hot tea and Japanese teacakes. When I left George accompanied me to the road. He was in a merry mood. He whistled "I Can't Give You Anything But Love."

We said, "So long."

"Be sure to come again," he said. As I walked down the road I heard his whistling for quite a distance. When the whistling stopped the chants of the crickets in the fields became loud. Across the lot from the greenhouses I saw the little shack lit by a single light, and I knew that Nakagawa-san was not yet asleep. ★

SERAFIN SYQUIA

A Photograph

Gathered
posed
for the flash
making us
immortal

no negative
only a fading
print of us
gathered
for a birthday or
graduation
was it

close
togethersqueezed
to fit the frame

brothers sisters cousins friends

everyone
was a relative
then tito tita
tito tita
ninong ninang
they came from islands
delano watsonville stockton
and we called them tito tita
tito tita

second generation
flips
gone to produce
the next

SAM TAGATAC

A Letter

dear francisco
no agbandoria
ni manong frank

ai

i still cannot cry
hear the swell
beating of Luzon's typhoon
sea against rice fields
norberta's wild black hair . . .

only glazing
white grass
round hills
eternal oaks
each morning
frozen now under
each turn of our
sharp steel plows.

AMERICA
IS IN THE
HEART

Carlos Bulosan

When I landed in Seattle for the second time, I expected a fair amount of money from the company. But the contractor, Max Feuga, came into the play room and handed us slips of paper. I looked at mine and was amazed at the neatly itemized expenditures that I was supposed to have incurred during the season. Twenty-five dollars for withdrawals, one hundred for board and room, twenty for bedding, and another twenty for something I do not now remember. At the bottom was the actual amount I was to receive after all the deductions: *thirteen dollars!*

I could do nothing. I did not even go to the hotel where I had left my suitcase. I went to a Japanese dry goods store on Jackson Street and bought a pair of corduroy pants and a blue shirt. It was already twilight and the cannery workers were in the crowded Chinese gambling houses, losing their season's earnings and drinking bootleg whiskey. They became quarrelsome and abusive to their own people when they lost, and subservient to the Chinese gambling lords and marijuana peddlers. They pawed at the semi-nude whores with their dirty hands and made suggestive gestures, running out into the night when they were rebuffed for lack of money.

I was already in America, and I felt good and safe. I did not understand why. The gamblers, prostitutes and Chinese opium smokers did not excite me, but they aroused in me a feeling of flight. I knew that I must run away from them, but it was not that I was afraid of contamination. I wanted to see other aspects of American life, for surely these destitute and vicious people were merely a small part of it. Where would I begin this pilgrimage, this search for a door into America?

I went outside and walked around looking into the faces of my countrymen, wondering if I would see someone I had known in the Philippines. I came to a building which brightly dressed white women were entering, lifting their diaphanous gowns as they climbed the stairs. I looked up and saw the huge sign:

MANILA DANCE HALL

The orchestra upstairs was playing; Filipinos were entering. I put my hands in my pockets and followed them, beginning to feel lonely for the sound of home.

The dance hall was crowded with Filipino cannery workers and domestic servants. But the girls were very few, and the Filipinos fought over them. When a boy liked a girl he bought a roll of tickets from the hawker on the floor and kept dancing with her. But the other boys who also liked the same girl shouted at him to stop, cursing him in the dialects and sometimes throwing rolled wet papers at him. At the bar the glasses were tinkling, the bottles popping loudly, and the girls in the back room were smoking marijuana. It was almost impossible to breathe.

Then I saw Marcelo's familiar back. He was dancing with a tall blonde in a green dress, a girl so tall that Marcelo looked like a dwarf climbing a tree. But the girl was pretty and her body was nicely curved and graceful, and she had a way of swaying that aroused confused sensations in me. It was evident that many of the boys wanted to dance with her; they were shouting maliciously at Marcelo. The way the blonde waved to them made me think that she knew most of them. They were nearly all oldtimers and strangers to Marcelo. They were probably gamblers and pimps, because they had fat rolls of money and expensive clothing.

But Marcelo was learning very fast. He requested one of his friends to buy another roll of tickets for him. The girl was supposed to tear off one ticket every three minutes, but I noticed that she tore off a ticket for every minute. That was ten cents a minute. Marcelo was unaware of what she was doing; he was spending his whole season's earnings on his first day in America. It was only when one of his friends shouted to him in the dialect that he became angry at the girl. Marcelo was not tough, but his friend was an oldtimer. Marcelo pushed the girl toward the gaping bystanders. His friend opened a knife and gave it to him.

Then something happened that made my heart leap. One of the blonde girl's admirers came from behind and struck Marcelo with a piece of lead pipe. Marcelo's friend whipped out a pistol and fired. Marcelo and the boy with the lead pipe fell on the floor simultaneously, one on top of the other, but the blonde girl ran into the crowd screaming frantically. Several guns banged at once, and the lights went out. I saw Marcelo's friend crumple in the fading light.

At once the crowd seemed to flow out of the windows. I went to a side window and saw three heavy electric wires strung from the top of the building to the ground. I reached for them and slid to the ground. My palms were burning when I came out of the alley. Then I heard the sirens of police cars screaming infernally toward the place. I put my cap in my pocket and ran as fast as I could in the direction of a neon sign two blocks down the street.

It was a small church where Filipino farm workers were packing their suitcases and bundles. I found out later that Filipino immigrants used their churches as rest houses while they were waiting for work. There were two large trucks outside. I went to one of them and sat on the running board, holding my hands over my heart for fear it would beat too fast. The lights in the church went out and the workers came into the street. The driver of the truck in which I was sitting pointed a strong flashlight at me.

"Hey, you, are you looking for a job?" he asked.

"Yes, sir," I said.

"Get in the truck," he said, jumping into the cab. "Let's go, Flo!" he shouted to the other driver.

I was still trembling with excitement. But I was glad to get out of Seattle—to anywhere else in America. I did not care where as long as it was in America. I found a corner and sat down heavily. The drivers shouted to each other. Then we were off to work.

It was already midnight and the lights in the city of Seattle were beginning to fade. I could see the reflections on the bright lake in Bremerton. I was reminded of Baguio. Then some of the men began singing. The driver and two men were arguing over money. A boy in the other truck was playing a violin. We were on the highway to Yakima Valley.

After a day and a night of driving we arrived in a little town called Moxee City. The apple trees were heavy with fruit and the branches drooped to the ground. It was late afternoon when we passed through the town; the hard light of the sun punctuated the ugliness of the buildings. I was struck dumb by its isolation and the dry air that hung oppressively over the place. The heart-shaped valley was walled by high treeless mountains, and the hot breeze that blew in from a distant sea was injurious to the apple trees.

The leader of our crew was called Cornelio Paez; but most of the oldtimers suspected that it was not his real name. There was something shifty about him, and his so-called bookkeeper, a pockmarked man we simply called Pinoy (which is a term generally applied to all Filipino immigrant workers), had a strange trick of squinting sideways when he looked at you. There seemed to be an old animosity between Paez and his bookkeeper.

But we were drawn together because the white people of Yakima Valley were suspicious of us. Years before, in the town of Toppenish, two Filipino apple pickers had been found murdered on the road to Sunnyside. At that time, there was ruthless persecution of the Filipinos throughout the Pacific Coast, instigated by orchardists who feared the unity of white and Filipino workers. A small farmer in Wapato who had tried to protect his Filipino workers had had his house burned. So however much we distrusted each other under Paez, we knew that beyond the walls of our bunkhouse were our real enemies, waiting to drive us out of Yakima Valley.

I had become acquainted with an oldtimer who had had considerable experience in the United States. His name was Julio, and it seemed that he was hiding from some trouble in Chicago. At night, when the men gambled in the kitchen, I would stand silently behind him and watch him cheat the other players. He was very deft, and his eyes were sharp and trained. Sometimes when there was no game, Julio would teach me tricks.

Mr. Malraux, our employer, had three daughters who used to work with us after school hours. He was a Frenchman who had gone to Moxee City when it consisted of only a few houses. At that time the valley was still a haven for Indians, but they had been gradually driven out when farming had been started on a large scale. Malraux had married an American woman in Spokane and begun farming; the girls came one by one, helping him on the farm as they grew. When I arrived in Moxee City they were already in their teens.

The oldest girl was called Estelle; she had just finished high school. She had a delightful disposition and her industry was something that men talked about with approval. The other girls, Maria and Diane, were still too young to be going about so freely; but whenever Estelle came to our bunkhouse they were always with her.

It was now the end of summer and there was a bright moon in the sky. Not far from Moxee City was a wide grassland where cottontails and jack rabbits roamed at night. Estelle used to drive her father's old car and would pick up some of us at the bunkhouse; then we would go hunting with their dogs and a few antiquated shotguns.

When we came back from hunting we would go to the Malraux house with some of the men who had musical instruments. We would sit on the lawn for hours singing American songs. But when they started singing Philippine songs their voices were so sad, so full of yesterday and the haunting presence of familiar seas, as if they had reached the end of creation, that life seemed ended and no bright spark was left in the world.

But one afternoon toward the end of the season, Paez went to the bank to get our paychecks and did not come back. The pockmarked bookkeeper was furious.

"I'll get him this time!" he said, running up and down the house. "He did that last year in California and I didn't get a cent. I know where to find the bastard!"

Julio grabbed him by the neck. "You'd better tell me where to find him if you know what is good for you," he said angrily, pushing the frightened bookkeeper toward the stove.

"Let me alone!" he shouted.

Julio hit him between the eyes, and the book-keeper struggled violently. Julio hit him again. The bookkeeper rolled on the floor like a baby. Julio picked him up and threw him outside the house. I thought he was dead, but his legs began to move. Then he opened his eyes and got up quickly, staggering like a drunken stevedore toward the highway. Julio came out of the house with brass knuckles, but the bookkeeper was already disappearing behind the apple orchard. Julio came back and began hitting the door of the kitchen with all his force, in futile anger.

I had not seen this sort of brutality in the Philippines, but my first contact with it in America made me brave. My bravery was still nameless, and waiting to express itself. I was not shocked when I saw that my countrymen had become ruthless toward one another, and this sudden impact of cruelty made me insensate to pain and kindness, so that it took me a long time to wholly trust other men. As time went by I became as ruthless as the worst of them, and I became afraid that I would never feel like a human being again. Yet no matter what bestiality encompassed my life, I felt sure that somewhere, sometime, I would break free. This faith kept me from completely succumbing to the degradation into which many of my countrymen had fallen. It finally paved my way out of our small, harsh life, painfully but cleanly, into a world of strange intellectual adventures and self-fulfillment.

The apples were nearly picked when Paez disappeared with our money. We lost interest in our work. We sat on the lawn of the Malraux's and sang. They came out of the house and joined us. The moonlight shimmered like a large diamond on the land around the farm. The men in the bunkhouse came with their violins and guitars. Julio grabbed Diane and started dancing with her; then the two younger girls were grabbed by other men.

It was while Estelle was singing that we heard a gun crack from the dirt road not far from the house. Malraux saw them first, saw the clubs and the iron bars in their hands, and yelled at us in warning. But it was too late. They had taken us by surprise.

I saw Malraux run into the house for his gun. I jumped to the nearest apple tree. I wanted a weapon—anything to hit back at these white men who had leaped upon us from the dark. Three or four guns banged all at once, and I turned to see Maria falling to the ground. A streak of red light flashed from the window into the crowd. Estelle was screaming and shouting to her father. Diane was already climbing the stairs, her long black hair shining in the moonlight.

I saw Julio motioning to me to follow him. Run away from our friends and companions? No! *Goddamn you, Julio!* I jumped into the thick of fight, dark with fury. Then I felt Julio's hands pulling me away, screaming into my ears:

"Come on, you crazy punk! Come on before I kill you myself!"

He was hurting me. Blinded with anger and tears, I ran after him toward our bunkhouse. We stopped behind a pear tree when we saw that our house was burning. Julio whispered to me to follow him.

We groped our way through the pear trees and came out, after what seemed like hours of running, on a wide grass plain traversed by a roaring irrigation ditch. Once when we thought we were being followed, we jumped into the water and waited. The night was silent and the stars in the sky were as far away as home. Was there peace somewhere in the world? The silence was broken only by the rushing water and the startled cry of little birds that stirred in the night.

Julio led the way. We came to a dirt road that led to some farmhouses. We decided to stay away from it. We turned off the road and walked silently between the trees. Then we came to a wide desert land. We followed a narrow footpath and, to our surprise, came to the low, uninhabited, wide desert of the Rattlesnake Mountains. The stars were our only guide.

We walked on and on. Toward dawn, when a strong wind came, we jumped into the dunes and covered our heads with dry bushes until it had passed by. We were no longer afraid of pursuit. We were in another land, on another planet. The desert was wide and flat. There were rabbits in the bushes, and once we came upon a herd of small deer. We ran after them with a burning bush, but they just stood nonchalantly and waited for us. When we were near enough for them to recognize our scent, they turned about and galloped down the sand dunes.

When morning came we were still in the desert. We walked until about noon. Then we came to a narrow grassland. We stood on a rise and looked around to see the edge of the desert. Julio started running crazily and jumping into the air. I ran after him. At last we came to the beginning of a wide plain.

The town of Toppenish was behind us now, and the cool wind from the valley swept the plain. We rested under a tree. Julio was different from other oldtimers; he did not talk much. I felt that he had many stories within him, and I longed to know America through him. His patience and nameless kindness had led me away from Moxee City into a new life.

After a while we crossed the plain again, hiding behind the trees whenever we saw anyone approaching us. I was too exhausted to continue when we reached Zillah, where some children stoned

us. We hid in an orange grove and rested. At sunset we started again. When we were nearing the town of Granger, I heard the sudden tumult of the Yakima River. Julio started running again, and I followed him. Suddenly we saw the clear, cool water of the river. We sat in the tall grass, cooling our tired bodies beside the bright stream.

I was the first to enter the water. I washed my shirt and spread it to dry on the grass. Sunnyside was not far off. I could hear the loud whistle of trains running seaward.

"This is the beginning of your life in America," Julio said. "We'll take a freight train from Sunnyside and go to nowhere."

"I would like to go to California," I said. "I have two brothers there—but I don't know if I could find them."

"All roads go to California and all travelers wind up in Los Angeles," Julio said. "But not this traveler. I have lived there too long. I know that state too damn well . . . ."

"What do you mean?" I asked.

Suddenly he became sad and said: "It is hard to be a Filipino in California."

Not comprehending what he meant, I began to dream of going to California. Then we started for Sunnyside, listening eagerly to the train whistle piercing the summer sky. It was nearly ten in the evening when we reached Sunnyside. We circled the town, and then we saw the trains—every car bursting with fruit—screaming fiercely and chugging like beetles up and down the tracks. The voices of the trainmen came clearly through the night.

We stopped in the shadow of a water tower. Julio disappeared for a moment and came back.

"Our train leaves in an hour," he said. "I'll go around for something to eat. Wait for me here."

I waited for him to come back for several hours. The train left. Then I began to worry. I went to town and walked in the shadows, looking into the darkened windows of wooden houses. Julio had disappeared like a wind.

I returned to our rendezvous and waited all night. Early the next morning another train was ready to go; I ran behind the boxcars and climbed inside one. When the train began to move, I opened the door and looked sadly toward Sunnyside. Julio was there somewhere, friendless and alone in a strange town.

"Good-bye, Julio," I said. "And thanks for everything, Julio. I hope I will meet you again somewhere in America."

Then the train screamed and the thought of Julio hurt me. I stood peering outside and listening to the monotonous chugging of the engine. I knew that I could never be unkind to any Filipino, because Julio had left me a token of friendship, a seed of trust, that ached to grow to fruition as I rushed toward another city. ★

ALFRED ROBLES

traveled north to the woods humboldt to oregon-washington, northwestern cascades

sharp jagged peaks
                    stretches high
pushes up to the sky
mountains rise strong
and tall in the morning
bends and sleeps all night
                    long
rocky green hills
                    twist and turn
disappears in the fog
no wandering chinese hermits
wind-stomping around here
no wild tongue flapping taoist sages
shooting fire out of their fingers
tread in these winter snow parts
no sign of raging buddhist nuns
urinating plum blossoms in the cold stream
not even even tao chie'n is here
laughing up the dead spirits
dangling his dirty feet
in a wooden tub of cow dung wine

black-brown mountains
spread far south
roads whip around narrow cliffs

snow on mountain tops
slowly breaks up
stop to watch
the water flow
                    down the mountainside
        into skagit river
                    skagit river
        fresh winter cold

where are the indians?
        dead in the ground?
no blacks seen around here
licking white cotton
no chicanos or pilipinos
in the valleys or fields
not even one chinaman drying
sea-weed or catching fish
not even one japanese farmer
seen turning the soil

carlos bulosan pilipino poet

carlos bulosan
pilipino poet

the manong's held you
down to the old cot

unbuckled
your leather belt

that kept
your thin tb body

together

yanked off your pantalon
and then retreated

in the background
of music and card playing

left your naked body
lying there alone

trembling with a woman

you kept
the cries down

for only a moment

wiping the pain away
releasing the milky sap

in pure savage-brown ecstasy

but lasting no more

than a split second

SEVENTEEN SYLLABLES

by

HISAYE YAMAMOTO

The first Rosie knew that her mother had taken to writing poems was one evening when she finished one and read it aloud for her daughter's approval. It was about cats, and Rosie pretended to understand it thoroughly and appreciate it no end, partly because she hesitated to disillusion her mother about the quantity and quality of Japanese she had learned in all the years now that she had been going to Japanese school every Saturday (and Wednesday, too, in the Summer). Even so, her mother must have been skeptical about the depth of Rosie's understanding, because she explained afterwards about the kind of poem she was trying to write.

See, Rosie, she said, it was a *haiku*, a poem in which she must pack all her meaning into seventeen syllables only, which were divided into three lines of five, seven, and five syllables. In the one she had just read, she had tried to capture the charm of a kitten, as well as comment on the superstition that owning a cat of three colors meant good luck.

"Yes, yes, I understand. How utterly lovely," Rosie said, and her mother, either satisfied or seeing through the deception and resigned, went back to composing.

photo by ED IKUTA

The truth was that Rosie was lazy; English lay ready on the tongue but Japanese had to be searched for and examined, and even then put forth tentatively (probably to meet with laughter). It was so much easier to say yes, yes, even when one meant no, no. Besides, this was what was in her mind to say: I was looking through one of your magazines from Japan last night, Mother, and towards the back I found some *haiku* in English that delighted me. There was one that made me giggle off and on until I fell asleep—

> *It is morning, and lo!*
> *I lie awake, comme il faut,*
> *sighing for some dough.*

Now, how to reach her mother, how to communicate the melancholy song? Rosie knew formal Japanese by fits and starts, her mother had even less English, no French. It was much more possible to say yes, yes.

It developed that her mother was writing the *haiku* for a daily newspaper, the *Mainichi Shinbun*, that was published in San Francisco. Los Angeles, to be sure, was closer to the farming community in which the Hayashi family lived and several Japanese vernaculars were printed there, but Rosie's parents said they preferred the tone of the northern paper. Once a week, the *Mainichi* would have a section devoted to *haiku,* and her mother became an extravagant contributor, taking for herself the blossoming pen name, Ume Hanazono.

So Rosie and her father lived for awhile with two women, her mother and Ume Hanazono. Her mother (Tome Hayashi by name) kept house, cooked, washed, and, along with her husband and the Carrascos, the Mexican family hired for the harvest, did her ample share of picking tomatoes out in the sweltering fields and boxing them in tidy strata in the cool packing shed. Ume Hanazono, who came to life after the dinner dishes were done, was an earnest, muttering stranger who often neglected speaking when spoken to and stayed busy at the parlor table as late as midnight scribbling with pencil on scratch paper or carefully copying characters on good paper with her fat, pale green Parker.

The new interest had some repercussions on the household routine. Before, Rosie had been accustomed to her parents and herself taking their hot baths early and going to bed almost immediately afterwards, unless her parents challenged each other to a game of flower cards or unless company dropped in. Now, if her father wanted to play cards, he had to resort to solitaire (at which he always cheated fearlessly), and if a group of friends came over, it was bound to contain someone who was also writing *haiku,* and the small assemblage would be split in two, her father entertaining the non-literary members and her mother comparing ecstatic notes with the visiting poet.

If they went out, it was more of the same thing. But Ume Hanazono's life span, even for a poet's, was very brief—perhaps three months at most.

One night they went over to see the Hayano family in the neighboring town to the west, an adventure both painful and attractive to Rosie. It was attractive because there were four Hayano girls, all lovely and each one named after a season of the year (Haru, Natsu, Aki, Fuyu), painful because something had been wrong with Mrs. Hayano ever since the birth of her first child. Rosie would sometimes watch Mrs. Hayano, reputed to have been the belle of her native village, making her way about a room, stooped, slowly shuffling, violently trembling (*always* trembling), and she would be reminded that this woman, in this same condition, had carried and given issue to three babies. She would look wonderingly at Mr. Hayano, handsome, tall, and strong, and she would look at her four pretty friends. But it was not a matter she could come to any decision about.

On this visit, however, Mrs. Hayano sat all evening in the rocker, as motionless and unobtrusive as it was possible for her to be, and Rosie found the greater part of the evening practically anaesthetic. Too, Rosie spent most of it in the girls' room, because Haru, the garrulous one, said almost as soon as the bows and other greetings were over, "Oh, you must see my new coat!"

It was a pale plaid of grey, sand, and blue, with an enormous collar, and Rosie, seeing nothing special in it, said, "Gee, how nice."

"Nice? said Haru, indignantly. "Is that all you can say about it? It's gorgeous! And so cheap, too. Only seventeen-ninety-eight, because it was a sale. The saleslady said it was twenty-five dollars regular."

"Gee," said Rosie. Natsu, who never said much and when she said anything said it shyly, fingered the coat covetously and Haru pulled it away.

"Mine," she said, putting it on. She minced in the aisle between the two large beds and smiled happily. "Let's see how your mother likes it."

She broke into the front room and the adult conversation, and went to stand in front of Rosie's mother, while the rest watched from the door. Rosie's mother was properly envious. "May I inherit it when you're through with it?"

Haru, pleased, giggled and said yes, she could, but Natsu reminded gravely from the door, "You promised me, Haru."

Everyone laughed but Natsu, who shamefacedly retreated into the bedroom. Haru came in laughing, taking off the coat. "We were only kidding, Natsu," she said. "Here, you try it on now."

After Natsu buttoned herself into the coat, inspected herself solemnly in the bureau mirror, and reluctantly shed it, Rosie, Aki, and Fuyu got their turns, and Fuyu, who was eight, drowned in it while her sisters and Rosie doubled up in amusement. They all went into the front room later, because Haru's mother quaveringly called to her to fix the tea and rice cakes and open a can of sliced peaches for everybody. Rosie noticed that her mother and Mr. Hayano were talking together at the little table—they were discussing a *haiku* that Mr. Hayano was planning to send to the *Mainichi*, while her father was sitting at one end of the sofa looking through a copy of *Life*, the new picture magazine. Occasionally, her father would comment on a photograph, holding it toward Mrs. Hayano and speaking to her as he always did—loudly, as though he thought someone such as she must surely be at least a trifle deaf also.

The five girls had their refreshments at the kitchen table, and it was while Rosie was showing the sisters her trick of swallowing peach slices without chewing (she chased each slippery crescent down with a swig of tea) that her father brought his empty teacup and untouched saucer to the sink and said, "Come on, Rosie, we're going home now."

"Already?" asked Rosie.

"Work tomorrow," he said.

He sounded irritated, and Rosie, puzzled, gulped one last yellow slice and stood up to go, while the sisters began protesting, as was their wont.

"We have to get up at five-thirty," he told them, going into the front room quickly, so that they did not have their usual chance to hang onto his hands and plead for an extension of time.

Rosie, following, saw that her mother and Mr. Hayano were sipping tea and still talking together, while Mrs. Hayano concentrated, quivering, on raising the handleless Japanese cup to her lips with both her hands and lowering it back to her lap. Her father, saying nothing, went out the door, onto the bright porch, and down the steps. Her mother looked up and asked, "Where is he going?"

"Where is he going?" Rosie said. "He said we were going home now."

"Going home?" Her mother looked with embarrassment at Mr. Hayano and his absorbed wife and then forced a smile. "He must be tired," she said.

Haru was not giving up yet. "May Rosie stay overnight?" she asked, and Natsu, Aki, and Fuyu came to reinforce their sister's plea by helping her make a circle around Rosie's mother. Rosie, for once, having no desire to stay, was relieved when her mother, apologizing to the perturbed Mr. and Mrs. Hayano for her father's abruptness at the same time, managed to shake her head no at the quartet, kindly but adamant, so that they broke their circle to let her go.

Rosie's father looked ahead into the windshield as the two joined him. "I'm sorry," her mother said. "You must be tired." Her father, stepping on the starter, said nothing. "You know how I get when it's *haiku*," she continued, "I forget what time it is." He only grunted.

492

As they rode homeward, silently, Rosie sitting between, felt a rush of hate for both, for her mother for begging, for her father for denying her mother. *I wish this old Ford would crash, right now,* she thought, then immediately, no, no, *I wish my father would laugh,* but it was too late: already the vision had passed through her mind of the green pick-up crumpled in the dark against one of the mighty eucalyptus trees they were just riding past, of the three contorted, bleeding bodies, one of them hers.

Rosie ran between two patches of tomatoes, her heart working more rambunctiously than she had ever known it to. How lucky it was that Aunt Taka and Uncle Gimpachi had come tonight, though, how very lucky. Otherwise, she might not have really kept her half-promise to meet Jesus Carrasco. Jesus, who was going to be a senior in September at the same school she went to, and his parents were the ones helping with the tomatoes this year. She and Jesus, who hardly remembered seeing each other at Cleveland high, where there were so many other people and two whole grades between them, had become great friends this Summer—he always had a joke for her when he periodically drove the loaded pick-up up from the fields to the shed where she was usually sorting while her mother and father did the packing, and they laughed a great deal together over infinitesimal repartee during the afternoon break for chilled watermelon or ice cream in the shade of the shed.

What she enjoyed most was racing him to see which could finish picking a double row first. He, who could work faster, would tease her by slowing down until she thought she would surely pass him this time, then speeding up furiously to leave her several sprawling vines behind. Once he had made her screech hideously by crossing over, while her back was turned, to place atop the tomatoes in her green-stained bucket a truly monstrous, pale green worm (it had looked more like an infant snake). And it was when they had finished a contest this morning, after she had pantingly pointed a green finger at the immature tomatoes evident in the lugs at the end of his row and he had returned the accusation (with justice), that he had startlingly brought up the matter of their possibly meeting outside the range of both their parents' dubious eyes.

"What for?" she had asked.

"I've got a secret I want to tell you," he said.

"Tell me now." she demanded.

"It won't be ready till tonight," he said.

She laughed. "Tell me tomorrow then."

"It'll be gone tomorrow," he threatened.

"Well, for seven hakes, what is it?" she had asked, more than twice, and when he had suggested that the packing shed would be an appropriate place to find out, she had cautiously answered maybe. She had not been certain she was going to keep the appointment until the arrival of her mother's sister and her husband. Their coming seemed a sort of signal of permission, of grace, and she had definitely made up her mind to lie and leave as she was bowing them welcome.

So, as soon as everyone appeared settled back for the evening, she announced loudly that she was going to the privy outside, "I'm going to the *benjo!*" and slipped out the door. And now that she was actually on her way, her heart pumped in such an undisciplined way that she could hear it with her ears. It's because I'm running, she told herself, slowing to a walk. The shed was up ahead, one more patch away, in the middle of the fields. Its bulk, looming in the dimness, took on a sinisterness that was funny when Rosie reminded herself that it was only a wooden frame with a canvas roof and three canvas walls that made a slapping noise on breezy days.

Jesus was sitting on the narrow plank that was the sorting platform and she went around to the other side and jumped backwards to seat herself on the rim of a packing stand. "Well, tell me," she said, without greeting, thinking her voice sounded reassuringly familiar.

"I saw you coming out the door," Jesus said. "I heard you running part of the way, too."

"Uh-huh," Rosie said. "Now tell me the secret."

"I was afraid you wouldn't come," he said.

Rosie delved around on the chicken-wire bottom of the stall for number two tomatoes, ripe, which she was sitting beside, and came up with a left-over that felt edible. She bit into it and began sucking out the pulp and seeds. "I'm here," she pointed out.

"Rosie, are you sorry you came?"

"Sorry? What for?" she said. "You said you were going to tell me something."

"I will, I will," Jesus said, but his voice contained disappointment, and Rosie, fleetingly, felt the older of the two, realizing a brand-new power which vanished without category under her recognition.

"I have to go back in a minute," she said. "My aunt and uncle are here from Wintersburg. I told them I was going to the privy."

Jesus laughed. "You funny thing," he said. "You slay me!"

"Just because you have a bathroom *inside*," Rosie said. "Come on, tell me."

Chuckling, Jesus came around to lean on the stand facing her. They still could not see each other very clearly, but Rosie noticed that Jesus became very sober again as he took the hollow tomato from her hand and dropped it back into the stall. When he took hold of her empty hand, she could find no words to protest; her vocabulary had become distressingly constricted and she thought desperately that all that remained intact now was yes and no and

oh, and even these few sounds would not easily out. Thus, kissed by Jesus, Rosie fell, for the first time, entirely victim to a helplessness delectable beyond speech. But the terrible, beautiful sensation lasted no more than a second, and the reality of Jesus' lips and tongue and teeth and hands made her pull away with such strength that she nearly tumbled.

Rosie stopped running as she approached the lights from the windows of home. How long since she had left? She could not guess, but gasping yet, she went to the privy in back and locked herself in.

Her own breathing deafened her in the dark, close space, and she sat and waited until she could hear at last the nightly calling of the frogs and crickets. Even then, all she could think to say was oh, my, and the pressure of Jesus' face against her face would not leave.

No one had missed her in the parlor, however, and Rosie walked in and through quickly, announcing that she was next going to take a bath. "Your father's in the bathhouse," her mother said, and Rosie, in her room, recalled that she had not seen him when she entered. There had been only Aunt Taka and Uncle Gimpachi with her mother at the table, drinking tea. She got her robe and straw sandals and crossed the parlor again to go outside. Her mother was telling them about the *haiku* competition in the *Mainichi* and the poem she had entered.

Rosie met her father coming out of the bathhouse. "Are you through, Father?" she asked. "I was going to ask you to scrub my back."

"Scrub your own back," he said shortly, going toward the main house.

"What have I done now?" she yelled after him. She suddenly felt like doing a lot of yelling. But he did not answer, and she went into the bathhouse. Turning on the dangling light, she removed her denims and T-shirt and threw them in the big carton for dirty clothes standing next to the washing machine. Her other things she took with her into the bath compartment to wash after her bath. After she had scooped a basin of hot water from the square wooden tub, she sat on the grey cement of the floor and soaped herself at exaggerated leisure, singing, "Red Sails in the Sunset" at the top of her voice and using da-da-da where she suspected her words. Then, standing, still singing, for she was possessed by the notion that any attempt now to analyze would result in spoilage and she believed that the larger her volume the less she would be able to hear herself think, she obtained more hot water and poured it on until she was free of lather. Only then did she allow herself to step into the steaming vat, one leg first, then the remainder of her body inch by inch until the water no longer stung and she could move around at will.

She took a long time soaking, afterwards remembering to go around outside to stoke the embers of the tin-lined fireplace beneath the tub and to throw on a few more sticks so that the water might keep its heat for her mother, and when she finally returned to the parlor, she found her mother still talking *haiku* with her aunt and uncle, the three of them on another round of tea. Her father was nowhere in sight.

At Japanese school the next day (Wednesday, it was), Rosie was grave and giddy by turns. Preoccupied at her desk in the row for students on Book Eight, she made up for it at recess by performing wild mimicry for the benefit of her friend Chizuko. She held her nose and whined a witticism or two in what she considered was the manner of Fred Allen; she assumed intoxication and a British accent to go over the climax of the Rudy Vallee recording of the pub conversation about William Ewart Gladstone; she was the child Shirley Temple piping, "On the Good Ship Lollipop"; she was the gentleman soprano of the Four Inkspots trilling, "If I Didn't Care." And she felt reasonably satisfied when Chizuko wept and gasped, "Oh, Rosie, you ought to be in the movies!"

Her father came after her at noon, bringing her sandwiches of minced ham and two nectarines to eat while she rode, so that she could pitch right into the sorting when they got home. The lugs were piling up, he said, and the ripe tomatoes in them would probably have to be taken to the cannery tomorrow if they were not ready for the produce haulers tonight. "This heat's not doing them any good. And we've got no time for a break today."

It *was* hot, probably the hottest day of the year, and Rosie's blouse stuck damply to her back even under the protection of the canvas. But she worked as efficiently as a flawless machine and kept the stalls heaped, with one part of her mind listening in to the parental murmuring about the heat and the tomatoes and with another part planning the exact words she would say to Jesus when he drove up with the first load of the afternoon. But when at last she saw that the pick-up was coming, her hands went berserk and the tomatoes started falling in the wrong stalls, and her father said, "Hey, hey! Rosie, watch what you're doing!"

"Well, I have to go to the *benjo*," she said, hiding panic.

"Go in the weeds over there," he said, only half-joking.

"Oh, Father!" she protested.

"Oh, go on home," her mother said. "We'll make out for awhile."

In the privy, Rosie peered through a knothole toward the fields, watching as much as she could of Jesus. Happily she thought she saw him look in the direction of the house from time to time before he

finished unloading and went back toward the patch where his mother and father worked. As she was heading for the shed, a very presentable black car purred up the dirt driveway to the house and its driver motioned to her. Was this the Hayashi home, he wanted to know. She nodded. Was she a Hayashi? Yes, she said, thinking that he was a good-looking man. He got out of the car with a huge, flat package and she saw that he warmly wore a business suit. "I have something here for your mother then," he said, in a more elegant Japanese than she was used to.

She told him where her mother was and he came along with her, patting his face with an immaculate white handkerchief and saying something about the coolness of San Francisco. To her surprised mother and father, he bowed and introduced himself as, among other things, the *haiku* editor of the *Mainichi Shinbun*, saying that since he had been coming as far as Los Angeles anyway, he had decided to bring her the first prize she had won in the recent contest.

"First prize?" her mother echoed, believing and not believing, pleased and overwhelmed. Handed the package with a bow, she bobbed her head up and down numerous times to express her utter gratitude.

"It is nothing much," he added, "but I hope it will serve as a token of our great appreciation for your contributions and our great admiration of your considerable talent."

"I am not worthy," she said, falling easily into his style. "It is I who should make some sign of my humble thanks for being permitted to contribute."

"No, no, to the contrary," he said, bowing again.

But Rosie's mother insisted, and then saying that she knew she was being unorthodox, she asked if she might open the package because her curiosity was so great. Certainly she might. In fact, he would like her reaction to it, for personally, it was one of his favorite *Hiroshiges*.

Rosie thought it was a pleasant picture, which looked to have been sketched with delicate quickness. There were pink clouds, containing some graceful calligraphy, and a sea, that was a pale blue except at the edges, containing four sampans with indications of people in them. Pines edged the water and on the far-off beach there was a cluster of thatched huts towered over by pine-dotted mountains of grey and blue. The frame was scalloped and gilt.

After Rosie's mother pronounced it without peer and somewhat prodded her father into nodding agreement, she said Mr. Kuroda must at least have a cup of tea, after coming all this way, and although Mr. Kuroda did not want to impose, he soon agreed that a cup of tea would be refreshing and went along with her to the house, carrying the picture for her.

"Ha, your mother's crazy!" Rosie's father said, and Rosie laughed uneasily as she resumed judgment on the tomatoes. She had emptied six lugs when he broke into an imaginary conversation with Jesus to tell her to go and remind her mother of the tomatoes, and she went slowly.

Mr. Kuroda was in his shirtsleeves expounding some *haiku* theory as he munched a rice cake, and her mother was rapt. Abashed in the great man's presence, Rosie stood next to her mother's chair until her mother looked up inquiringly, and then she started to whisper the message, but her mother pushed her gently away and reproached, "You are not being very polite to our guest."

"Father says the tomatoes . . ." Rosie said aloud, smiling foolishly.

"Tell him I shall only be a minute," her mother said, speaking the language of Mr. Kuroda.

When Rosie carried the reply to her father, he did not seem to hear and she said again, "Mother says she'll be back in a minute."

"All right, all right," he nodded, and they worked again in silence. But suddenly, her father uttered an incredible noise, exactly like the cork of a bottle popping, and the next Rosie knew, he was stalking angrily toward the house, almost running, in fact, and she chased after him crying, "Father! Father! What are you going to do?"

He stopped long enough to order her back to the shed. "Never mind!" he shouted. "Get on with the sorting!"

And from the place in the fields where she stood, frightened and vacillating, Rosie saw her father enter the house. Soon Mr. Kuroda came out alone, putting on his coat. Mr. Kuroda got into his car and backed out down the driveway, onto the highway. Next her father emerged, also alone, something in his arms (it was the picture, she realized), and, going over to the bathhouse woodpile, he threw the picture on the ground and picked up the axe. Smashing the picture, glass and all (she heard the explosion faintly), he reached over the kerosene that was used to encourage the bath fire and poured it over the wreckage. I am dreaming, Rosie said to herself, I am dreaming, but her father, having made sure that his act of cremation was irrevocable, was even then returning to the fields.

Rosie ran past him and toward the house. What had become of her mother? She burst into the parlor and found her mother at the back window, watching the dying fire. They watched together until there remained only a feeble smoke under the blazing sun. Her mother was very calm.

"Do you know why I married your father?" she said, without turning.

"No," said Rosie. It was the most frightening question she had ever been called upon to answer. Don't tell me now, she wanted to say, tell me tomorrow, tell me next week, don't tell me today. But she knew she would be told now, that the telling would combine with the other violence of the hot afternoon to level her life, her world (so various, so beautiful, so new?) to the very ground.

It was like a story out of the magazines, illustrated in sepia, which she had consumed so greedily for a period until the information had somehow reached her that those wretchedly unhappy autobiographies, offered to her as the testimonials of living men and women, were largely inventions: Her mother, at nineteen, had come to America and married her father as an alternative to suicide.

At eighteen, she had been in love with the first son of one of the well-to-do families in her village. The two had met whenever and wherever they could, secretly, because it would not have done for his family to see him favor her—her father had no money; he was a drunkard and a gambler besides. She had learned she was with child; an excellent match had already been arranged for her lover. Despised by her family, she had given premature birth to a stillborn son, who would be seventeen now. Her family did not turn her out, but she could no longer project herself in any direction without refreshing in them the memory of her indiscretion. She wrote to Aunt Taka, her favorite sister, in America, threatening to kill herself if Aunt Taka would not send for her. Aunt Taka hastily arranged a marriage with a young man, but lately arrived from Japan, of whom she knew, a young man of simple mind, it was said, but of kindly heart. The young man was never told why his unseen betrothed was so eager to hasten the day of meeting.

The story was told perfectly, with neither groping for words nor untoward passion. It was as though her mother had memorized it by heart, reciting it to herself so many times over that its nagging vileness had long since gone.

"I had a brother then?" Rosie asked, for this was what seemed to matter now; she would think about the other later, she assured herself, pushing back the illumination which threatened all that darkness that had hitherto been merely mysterious or even glamourous. "A half-brother?"

"Yes."

"I would have liked a brother," she said.

Suddenly, her mother knelt on the floor and took her by the wrists. "Rosie," she said urgently, "Promise me you will never marry!" Shocked more by the request than the revelation, Rosie stared at her mother's face. Jesus, Jesus, she called silently, not certain whether she was invoking the help of the son of the Carrascos or of God, until there returned sweetly the memory of Jesus' hand, how it had touched her and where. Still her mother waited for an answer, holding her wrists so tightly that her hands were going numb. She tried to pull free. Promise, her mother whispered fiercely, promise. Yes, yes, I promise, Rosie said. But for an instant she turned away, and her mother, hearing the familiar glib agreement, released her, Oh, you, you, you, her eyes and twisted mouth said, you fool. Rosie, covering her face, began at last to cry, and the embrace and consoling hand came much later than she expected. ★

WING TEK LUM

Juk

was what I used to eat
a lot of—like everyday
I'd cross the street to Hong Wah's
for a take-out. On seeing me
the owner by the register
would try to outguess me.
"Wat Gai Juk," she'd bellow
in a knowing way,
as if it were my name.

It was a game we played.
Depending on my whim
I'd simply nod my head, assenting,
or correct her, smiling:
"For Op"—to which she'd call
the order out again,
so that the waiter down the aisle
could write it for the kitchen.

Later, if she got a chance,
she'd go back personally.
You could see her through the open door:
first, with a ladle scooping
the soup, a light sprinkle
of scallions, and then the quick plop
of a handful of duck, chopped
in chunks, covered
I knew with lots of skin.

She would fill out a few orders
like this: soup
in the red containers, the dishes
of rice and of noodles
into white boxes. In turn,
they would all be dropped
into bags, which she'd carry
—maybe three to an arm—
as she rushed, waddling,
up to the front.
                Sometimes
I wondered if the hectic pace
would kill her in a year.
At other times I felt:
she's probably now a millionaire.
No one has made as good
a juk since then. I hope it tasted
as good to her
                as it did to me.

To Li Po

I liked that poem
—the one about getting drunk,
three hundred gold cups of wine,
to drown away the sorrows
of generations.
                In those days
for every poem you wrote
a million Chinamen suffered to die.

           pen from bone
           brush from hair
           ink from blood

They were illiterate, you knew.
Better than words,
the liquor was solace enough for them.

To My Father

In our store that day
they gathered together
my grandfather among them
each in his turn
cut off their queues:
the end of subservience.
They could have returned
the Republic soon established
or, on the safe side,
waited a year
to grow back that braid.
No matter, they stayed.
Your father was young
and shrewd: the store flourished,
then the crops, the lands.

Out of your share
you sent us to the best schools;
we were to follow the dynasty
set by the Old Man.
But he had died
before I was born, his grave
all I could pay homage to.
I was freed from those old ways.
Today, unbraided,
my hair has grown long
because and
in spite of your haircuts.

OSCAR PEÑARANDA

Birthday Child / Innercity Queen

My dad
he bad

he's been around
and still found the time
to be around me

and my baby brother
and my two older sisters
and my mama too
when she was alive

I know
don't have to tell me nothing
I've looked into his eyes
those puddles of quiet hurt I know
he's been around. My dad
he bad

He's about like a gas station popping
out of nowhere in the middle of a
blizzard and

he don't talk much—he don't talk
right, I guess, for most people

but not for me
he don't need talking for me
sometimes I like it better
then he can hold me
and make me feel warm
inside
and cuddly all over and
I can smell him
smell the beer from his mouth
the rubbish cans and dustpans
he's been working with all day, everyday

my dad, that's him

He's about like a fairy tale
comes from the forests, he's like magic
when I first learned to read
he fix everything, anything.
My dolls, braid my hair, tie my ribbons,
button my dress and fix my toys
everything.

He's brown too
and funny-looking
and funny-talking and funny-walking

But he don't care, he laughs even
Especially when I run to him
when he comes home
from a long trip
like Alaska or Delano or jail
and I laugh also, and cry a little
sometimes
because of his hard time bending
of the break in his voice
and I forget all about the stuff
he'd just brought me from faraway

he's that bad
my dad

He eats with his hands
and slurps too
and I try to do the same
to make him laugh

they say I'm pretty—
you prety gerl, they say

only feel it when he's around
but they don't know this, cuz I don't tell 'em

And them bill collectors be
calling on him
and his P.O. and the social worker
people be trying to take
my brother and me away

they're saying he's gotta pay
his debts
some people don't know nothing, I guess

not even the damn preachers
got nothing on him
cause he's clean

they can't touch him
got nothing on him

He's like the good times
on monday mornings—
they're around but you gotta try hard
to find them,

But they found him lying
face down on the gutter
one day, throat slit open.
So they told me.

He had a hard time trying
to look for them candles for
my birthday, I bet. That's

my dad
he bad

497

from John Okada's
NO-NO BOY

66 **I**chiro."

He propped himself up on an elbow and looked at her. She had hardly changed. Surely, there must have been a time when she could smile and, yet, he could not remember.

"Yeah?"

"Lunch is on the table."

As he pushed himself off the bed and walked past her to the kitchen, she took broom and dustpan and swept up the mess he had made.

There were eggs, fried with soy sauce, sliced cold meat, boiled cabbage, and tea and rice. They all ate in silence, not even disturbed once by the tinkling of the bell. The father cleared the table after they had finished and dutifully retired to watch the store. Ichiro had smoked three cigarettes before his mother ended the silence.

"You must go back to school."

He had almost forgotten that there had been a time before the war when he had actually gone to college for two years and studiously applied himself to courses in the engineering school. The statement staggered him. Was that all there was to it? Did she mean to sit there and imply that the four intervening years were to be casually forgotten and life resumed as if there had been no four years and no war and no Eto who had spit on him because of the thing he had done?

"I don't feel much like going to school."

"What will you do?"

"I don't know."

"With an education, your opportunities in Japan will be unlimited. You must go and complete your studies."

"Ma," he said slowly, "Ma, I'm not going to Japan. Nobody's going to Japan. The war is over. Japan lost. Do you hear? Japan lost."

"You believe that?" It was said in the tone of an adult asking a child who is no longer a child if he really believed that Santa Claus was real.

"Yes, I believe it. I know it. America is still here. Do you see the great Japanese army walking down the streets? No. There is no Japanese army any more."

"The boat is coming and we must be ready."

"The boat?"

"Yes." She reached into her pocket and drew out a worn envelope.

The letter had been mailed from Sao Paulo, Brazil, and was addressed to a name that he did not recognize. Inside the envelope was a single sheet of flimsy, rice paper covered with intricate flourishes of Japanese characters.

"What does it say?"

She did not bother to pick up the letter. "To you who are a loyal and honorable Japanese, it is with humble and heartfelt joy that I relay this momentous message. Word has been brought to us that the victorious Japanese government is presently making preparations to send ships which will return to Japan those residents in foreign countries who have steadfastly maintained their faith and loyalty to our Emperor. The Japanese government regrets

that the responsibilities arising from the victory compels them to delay in the sending of the vessels. To be among the few who remain to receive his honor is a gratifying tribute. Heed not the propaganda of the radio and newspapers which endeavor to convince people with lies about the allied victory. Especially, heed not the lies of your traitorous countrymen who have turned their backs on the country of their birth and who will suffer for their treasonous acts. The day of glory is close at hand. The rewards will be beyond our greatest expectations. What we have done, we have done only as Japanese, but the government is grateful. Hold your heads high and make ready for the journey, for the ships are coming."

"Who wrote that?" he asked incredulously. It was like a weird nightmare. It was like finding out that an incurable strain of insanity pervaded the family, an intangible horror that swayed and taunted beyond the grasp of reaching fingers.

"A friend in South America. We are not alone."

"We *are* alone," he said vehemently. "This whole thing is crazy. You're crazy. I'm crazy. All right, so we made a mistake. Let's admit it."

"There has been no mistake. The letter confirms."

"Sure it does. It proves there's crazy people in the world besides us. If Japan won the war, what the hell are we doing here? What are you doing running a grocery store? It doesn't figure. It doesn't figure because we're all wrong. The minute we admit that, everything is fine. I've had a lot of time to think about all this. I've thought about nothing else. Two years I've thought about it. and every time the answer

comes out the same. You can't tell me different any more."

She sighed ever so slightly. "We will talk later when you are feeling better." Carefully folding the letter and placing it back in the envelope, she returned it to her pocket. "It is not I who tell you that the ship is coming. It is in the letter. If you have come to doubt your mother—and I'm sure you do not mean it even if you speak in weakness—it is to be regretted. Rest a few days. Think more deeply and your doubts will disappear. You are my son, Ichiro."

No, he said to himself as he watched her part the curtains and start into the store. There was a time when I was your son. There was a time that I no longer remember when you used to smile a mother's smile and tell me stories about gallant and fierce warriors who protected their lords with blades of shining steel and about the old woman who found a peach in the stream and took it home and, when her husband split it in half, a husky little boy tumbled out to fill their hearts with boundless joy. I was that boy in the peach and you were the old woman and we were Japanese with Japanese feelings and Japanese pride and Japanese thoughts because it was all right then to be Japanese and feel and think all the things that Japanese do even if we lived in America. Then there came a time when I was only half Japanese because one is not born in America and raised in America and taught in America and one does not speak and swear and drink and smoke and play and fight and see and hear in America among Americans in American streets and houses

illustration by ALAN TAKEMOTO

without becoming American and loving it. But I did not love enough, for you were still half my mother and I was thereby still half Japanese and when the war came and they told me to fight for America, I was not strong enough to fight you and I was not strong enough to fight the bitterness which made the half of me which was you bigger than the half of me which was America and really the whole of me that I could not see or feel. Now that I know the truth when it is too late and the half of me which was you is no longer there, I am only half of me and the half that remains is American by law because the government was wise and strong enough to know why it was that I could not fight for America and did not strip me of my birthright. But it is not enough to be American only in the eyes of the law and it is not enough to be only half an American and know that it is an empty half. I am not your son and I am not Japanese and I am not American. I can go some-place and tell people that I've got an inverted stomach and that I am an American, true and blue and Hail Columbia, but the army wouldn't have me because of the stomach. That's easy and I would do it, only I've got to convince myself first and that I cannot do. I wish with all my heart that I were Japanese or that I were American. I am neither and I blame you and I blame myself and I blame the world which is made up of many countries which fight with each other and kill and hate and destroy but not enough, so that they must kill and hate and destroy again and again and again. It is so easy and simple that I cannot understand it at all. And the reason I do not understand it is because I do not understand you who were the half of me that is no more and because I do not understand what it was about that half that made me destroy the half of me which was American and the half which might have become the whole of me if I had said yes I will go and fight in your army because that is what I believe and want and cherish and love . . .

Defeatedly, he crushed the stub of a cigarette into an ash tray filled with many other stubs and reached for the package to get another. It was empty and he did not want to go into the store for more because he did not feel much like seeing either his father or mother. He went into the bedroom and tossed and groaned and half slept.

* * * *

For Ichiro, there was no intervening span of death to still his great unrest through the darkness of night. It was nine o'clock when he woke up and the bitterness and profanity and hatred and fear did not have to be reawakened. He did not have to ask himself where he was or why because it did not matter. He was Ichiro who had said no to the judge and had thereby turned his back on the army and the country and the world and his own self. He thought only that he had felt no differently after spending his first night in prison. On that morning, when he woke up and saw the bars, it had not mattered at all that the bars were there. This morning, for the first time in two years, there were no bars, but the fact left him equally unimpressed. The prison which he had carved out of his own stupidity granted no paroles or pardons. It was a prison of forever.

"Ahhhhhh." Out of the filth of his anguished soul, the madness welled forth in a sick and crazy scream, loud enough to be heard in the next room.

"What is it, Ichiro, what is it?" His father hovered hesitantly in the doorway, peering into the blind-drawn gloom of the bedroom with startled eyes.

"Nothing." He felt like crying.

"You are not ill?"

"No."

"Not sick someplace for sure?"

"No, goddammit, I'm fine, Pa, fine."

"That is all right then. I thought something was wrong."

Poor, miserable old fool, he thought. How in the world could he understand? "I'm okay, Pa," he said kindly, "hungry, that's all, hungry and . . . and glad to be home."

"Ya, you get used to it. I cook right away." He smiled, relief flowing to his face, and turned back hastily into the kitchen.

When he dressed and went through the kitchen to the bathroom, it was his father who stood beside the stove with frying pan in hand. When he came back out and sat at the table, his mother was there.

"Good morning, Ichiro. You slept well?" She sounded cheerful.

The eggs were done the way he liked them, sunny side up with the edges slightly browned. He felt grateful to his father for remembering. "Yeah, I slept pretty good," he answered as he broke the yolks.

"You are pleased to be at home and I am pleased that you are here."

"Sure. I feel like singing."

She sat rigidly with hands palms-down on her lap. "I did not tell you about Kumasaka-san's boy because it was not important."

"Yes, I know."

"Then you understand. It is well."

"No, I don't understand, but it doesn't matter."

"Oh?" Her mouth pressed into a tight little frown. "What is it you do not understand?"

"A lot of things, a whole lot of things."

"I will tell you. The Germans did not kill Kumasaka-san's boy. It was not he who went to war with a gun and it was not he who was shot by the Germans—"

"Of course not. You heard last night when the fellow told about it. It was an accident."

Patiently, she waited until he had spoken. "Germans, Americans, accident, those things are

500

not important. It was not the boy but the mother who is also the son and it is she who is to blame and it is she who is dead because the son did not know."

"I just know that Bob is dead."

"No, the mother. It is she who is dead because she did not conduct herself as a Japanese and, no longer being Japanese, she is dead."

"And the father? What about Mr. Kumasaka?"

"Yes, dead also."

"And you, Ma? What about you and Pa?"

"We are Japanese as always."

"And me?"

"You are my son who is also Japanese."

"That makes everything all right, does it? That makes it all right that Bob is dead, that the war was fought and hundreds of thousands killed and maimed, and that I was two years in prison and am still Japanese?"

"Yes."

"What happens when I'm no longer Japanese?"

"How so?"

"Like Bob, I mean. What happens if I sign up and get shot up like him?"

"Then I will be dead too."

"Dead like me?"

"Yes, I will be dead when you go into the army of the Americans. I will be dead when you *decide* to go into the army of the Americans. I will be dead when you begin to cease to be Japanese and entertain those ideas which will lead you to your decision which will make you go into the army of the Americans. I will be dead long before the bullet strikes you. But you will not go, for you are my son."

"You're crazy." He said it softly and deliberately, for he wanted her to know that he meant it with all the hatred in his soul.

Underneath the table her hands stiffened and jerked a few inches above her lap. Her face revealed only the same little tight frown that he had seen many times before. He waited, hoping that she would scream and rant and cry and denounce him, tearing asunder with fury the slender bond that held them together still, and set him free.

"Ah, Ichiro. I thought for a moment that you meant it."

"I do. I do."

She shrugged without actually moving. "That is what they all say. They who claim to be Japanese. I see it in their faces and I feel it on their lips. They say I am crazy, but they do not mean it. They say it because they are frightened and because they envy my strength, which is truly the strength of Japan. They say it with the weakness which destroyed them and their sons in a traitorous cause and they say it because they see my strength which was vast enough to be your strength and they did not have enough for themselves and so not enough for their sons."

"Balls!" He leaned across the table, letting the ugliness twist his lips and fill his voice with viciousness. "Balls! Balls!" he shrieked, his face advancing steadily upon hers.

A flicker of surprise, then fear. Yes, he saw it in her eyes in the fraction of an instant before her hands covered them. To the hands which had come forever between them he continued to shriek: "Not your strength, crazy woman, crazy mother of mine. Not your strength, but your madness which I have taken. Look at me!" He gripped her wrists and wrenched them away from her face. "I'm as crazy as you are. See in the mirror the madness of the mother which is the madness of the son. See. See!"

He was halfway to the bathroom door with her when the father rushed in to intervene. "Ichiro, Ichiro," he gasped excitedly as he extended a feeble hand.

With his fury at a sickening peak, Ichiro released the skinny wrists and arced his arm in a wild swing at his father. The mother collapsed limply to the floor and the father, propelled by the painful blow, collided against the wall.

For long moments he stood between them as the anger drained out of his body. He watched his mother rise and go out to the store, her face once again calm and guileless.

"Pa. I'm sorry, Pa." He put his arm around his father, wanting to hug him like a baby.

"Ya, Ichiro," the old man uttered shakily, "I am sorry too."

"Lost my head, Pa."

"Ya, ya. I know." He got a bottle from the cupboard and drank greedily. Then he sat down and offered the bottle to Ichiro.

The whisky was ugly tasting but it helped to relax him. He looked at his father, who seemed about to cry. "Ah, Pa, Pa. Forget it, won't you? I'm sorry. It just happened."

"Ya, sure." He smiled.

Ichiro felt better. "I've got to do something, Pa. I'll go nuts sitting around."

"Whatever you wish, Ichiro. It will take time. I know."

"Where's Freddie?"

"Freddie?"

"Yeah, Akimoto-san's boy. Where do they live?"

"Oh. Freddie. He was . . . yes. On Nineteenth. Small, yellow apartment house on the south side."

"I'll go see him. I can talk to him."

"Here, Ichiro," said his father, placing a twenty-dollar bill on the table.

"But that's a lot of money, Pa. I won't need all that."

"Take. Take. Go to a movie with Freddie. Eat someplace nice. Have a good time."

"Okay, Pa. Thanks." He pocketed the money and went through the store and on out without looking at his mother. ★

501

As soon as Fil woke up, he noticed a whiteness outside, quite unusual for the November mornings they had been having. That fall, Chicago was sandman's town, sleepy valley, drowsy gray, slumbrous mistiness from sunup till noon when the clouds drifted away in cauliflower clusters and suddenly it was evening. The lights shone on the avenues like soiled lamps centuries old and the skyscrapers became monsters with a thousand sore eyes. Now there was a brightness in the air and Fil knew what it was and he shouted, "Snow! It's snowing!"

Tony, who slept in the adjoining room, was awakened.

"What's that?" he asked.

"It's snowing," Fil said, smiling to himself as if he had ordered this and was satisfied with the prompt delivery. "Oh, they'll love this, they'll love this."

"Who'll love that?" Tony asked, his voice raised in annoyance.

"The dancers, of course," Fil answered.

"They're arriving today. Maybe they've already arrived. They'll walk in the snow and love it. Their first snow, I'm sure."

"How do you know it wasn't snowing in New York while they were there?" Tony asked.

"Snow in New York in early November?" Fil said. "Are you crazy?"

"Who's crazy?" Tony replied. "Ever since you heard of those dancers from the Philippines, you've been acting nuts. Loco. As if they're coming here just for you."

Tony chuckled. Hearing him, Fil blushed, realizing that he had, indeed, been acting too eager, but Tony had said it. It felt that way—as if the dancers were coming here only for him.

Filemon Acayan, Filipino, was fifty, a U.S. citizen. He was a corporal in the U.S. Army, training at San Luis Obispo, on the day he was discharged honorably, in 1945. A few months later, he got his citizenship papers. Thousands of them, smart and small in their uniforms, stood at attention in drill

by Bienvenido N. Santos

formation, in the scalding sun, and pledged allegiance to the flag and the republic for which it stands. Soon after he got back to work. To a new citizen, work meant many places and many ways: factories and hotels, waiter and cook. A timeless drifting: once he tended a rose garden and took care of a hundred-year old veteran of a border war. As a menial in a hospital in Cook County, all day he handled filth and gore. He came home smelling of surgical soap and disinfectant. In the hospital, he took charge of a row of bottles on a shelf, each bottle containing a stage of the human embryo in preservatives, from the lizard-like foetus of a few days, through the newly born infant, with its position unchanged, cold and cowering and afraid. He had nightmares through the years of himself inside a bottle. That was long ago. Now he had a more pleasant job as a special policeman in the post office.

He was a few years younger than Tony—Antonio Bataller, a retired Pullman porter—but he looked older in spite of the fact that Tony had been

bedridden most of the time for the last two years, suffering from a kind of wasting disease that had frustrated doctors. All over Tony's body, a gradual peeling was taking place. At first, he thought it was merely *tinia flava,* a skin disease common among adolescents in the Philippines. It had started around the neck and had spread to his extremities. His face looked as if it was healing from severe burns. Nevertheless, it was a young face, much younger than Fil's, which had never looked young.

"I'm becoming a white man," Tony had said once, chuckling softly.

It was the same chuckle Fil seemed to have heard now, only this time it sounded derisive, insulting.

Fil said, "I know who's nuts. It's the sick guy with the sick thoughts. You don't care for nothing but your pain, your imaginary pain."

"You're the imagining fellow. I got the real thing," Tony shouted from the room. He believed he had something worse then the whiteness spreading on his skin. There was a pain in his insides, like dull scissors scraping his intestines. Angrily, he added, "What for I got retired?"

"You're old, man, that's what, and sick, yes, but not cancer," Fil said turning towards the snow-filled sky. He pressed his face against the glass window. There's about an inch now on the ground, he thought, maybe more.

Tony came out of his room looking as if he had not slept all night. "I know what I got," he said, as if it were an honor and privilege to die of cancer and Fil was trying to deprive him of it. "Never a pain like this. One day, I'm just gonna die."

"Naturally. Who says you won't?" Fil argued, thinking how wonderful it would be if he could join the company of dancers from the Philippines, show them around, walk with them in the snow, watch their eyes as they stared about them, answer their questions, tell them everything they wanted to know about the changing seasons in this strange land. They would pick up fistfuls of snow, crunch it in their fingers or shove it into their mouths. He had done just that the first time, long, long ago, and it had reminded him of the grated ice the Chinese sold near the town plaza where he had played *tatching* with an older brother who later drowned in a squall. How his mother had grieved over that death, she who had not cried too much when his father died, a broken man. Now they were all gone, quick death after a storm, or lingeringly, in a season of drought, all, all of them he had loved.

He continued, "All of us will die. One day. A medium bomb marked Chicago and this whole dump is *tapus,* finished. Who'll escape then?"

"Maybe your dancers will," Tony answered, now watching the snow himself.

"Of course, they will." Fil retorted, his voice sounding like a big assurance that all the dancers would be safe in his care. "The bombs won't be falling on this night. And when the dancers are back in the Philippines..."

He paused, as if he was no longer sure of what he was going to say. "But maybe, even in the Philippines the bombs gonna fall, no?" he said, gazing sadly at the falling snow.

"What's that to you?" Tony replied. "You got no more folks ove'der, right? I know it's nothing to me. I'll be dead before that."

"Let's talk about something nice," Fil said, the sadness spreading on his face as he tried to smile. "Tell me, how will I talk, how am I gonna introduce myself?"

He would go ahead with his plans, introduce himself to the dancers and volunteer to take them sight-seeing. His car was clean and ready for his guests. He had soaped the ashtrays, dusted off the floor boards and thrown away the old mats, replacing them with new plastic throw rugs. He had got him-

self soaking wet while spraying the car, humming, as he worked, faintly-remembered tunes from the old country.

Fil shook his head as he waited for Tony to say something. "Gosh, I wish I had your looks, even with those white spots, then I could face everyone of them," he said, "but this mug.."

"That's the important thing, your mug. It's your calling card. It says, Filipino. Countryman," Tony said.

"You're not fooling me, friend," Fil said. "This mug says, Ugly Filipino. It says, old-timer, *muchacho.* It says Pinoy, *bejo.*"

For Fil, time was the villain. In the beginning, the words he often heard were: too young, too young; but all of a sudden, too young became too old, too late. What had happened in between? A weariness, a mist covering all things. You don't have to look at your face in a mirror to know that you are old, suddenly old, grown useless for a lot of things and too late for all the dreams you had wrapped up well against a day of need.

"It also says sucker," Tony said. "What for you want to invite them? Here? Aren't you ashamed of this hole?"

"It's not a palace, I know," Fil answered, "but who wants a palace when they can have the most delicious *adobo* here and the best stuffed chicken... yum...yum..."

Tony was angry. "Yum, yum, you're nuts," he said, "plain and simple loco. What for you want to spend? You've been living on loose change all your life and now on a treasury warrant so small and full of holes, still you want to spend for these dancing kids who don't know you and won't even send you a card afterwards."

"Never mind the cards," Fil answered. "Who wants cards? But don't you see they'll be happy; and then, you know what? I'm going to keep their voices, their words and their singing and their laughter in my magic sound mirror."

He had a portable tape recorder and a stack of recordings, patiently labelled, songs and speeches. The songs were in English, but most of the speeches were in the dialect, debates between him and Tony. It was evident Tony was the better speaker of the two in English, but in the dialect, Fil showed greater mastery. His style, however, was florid, sentimental, poetic.

Without telling Tony, he had experimented on recording sounds, like the way a bed creaked, doors opening and closing, rain or sleet tapping on the window panes, footsteps through the corridor. He played all the sounds back and tried to recall how it was on the day or night the sounds had been recorded. Did they bring back the moment? He was beginning to think that they did. He was learning to identify each of the sounds with a particular mood or fact. Sometimes, like today, he wished that there was a way of keeping a record of silence because it was to him the richest sound, like snow falling. He wondered as he watched the snow blowing in the wind, what took care of that moment if memory didn't. Like time, memory was often a villain, a betrayer.

"Fall, snow, fall," he murmured and, turning to Tony, said, "As soon as they accept my invitation, I'll call you up. No, you don't have to do anything, but I'd want you to be here to meet them."

"I'm going out myself." Tony said. "And I don't know what time I'll be back." Then he added, "You're not working today. Are you on leave?"

"For two days. While the dancers are here," Fil said.

"It still don't make sense to me," Tony said. "But good luck, any way."

"Aren't you going to see them tonight? Our reserved seats are right out in front, you know."

"I know. But I'm not sure I can come."

"What? You're not sure?"

Fil could not believe it. Tony was indifferent. Something must be wrong with him. He looked at him closely, saying nothing.

"I want to, but I'm sick, Fil. I tell you, I'm not feeling so good. My doctor will know today. He'll tell me," Tony said.

"What will he tell you?"

"How do I know?"

"I mean, what's he trying to find out?"

"If it's cancer," Tony said. Without saying another word, he went straight back to his room.

Fil remembered those times at night, when Tony kept him awake with his moaning. When he called out to him, asking, "Tony, what's the matter?" his sighs ceased for a while, but afterwards, Tony screamed, deadening his cries with a pillow against his mouth. When Fil rushed to his side, Tony drove him away. Or he curled up in the bedsheets like a big infant suddenly hushed in its crying. The next day, he would look all right. When Fil asked him about the previous night, he would reply, "I was dying," but it sounded more like disgust over a nameless annoyance.

Fil had misgivings, too, about the whiteness spreading on Tony's skin. He had heard of leprosy. Every time he thought of that dreaded disease, he felt tears in his eyes. In all the years he had been in America, he had not had a friend until he met Tony whom he liked immediately and, in a way, worshipped, for all the things the man had which Fil knew he himself lacked.

They had shared a lot together. They made merry on Christmas, sometimes got drunk and became loud. Fil recited poems in the dialect and praised himself. Tony fell to giggling and cursed all the railroad companies of America. But last Christmas, they hadn't gotten drunk. They hadn't

even talked to each other on Christmas day. Soon, it would be Christmas again.

The snow was still falling.

"Well, I'll be seeing you," Fil said, getting ready to leave. "Try to be home on time. I shall invite the dancers for luncheon or dinner maybe, tomorrow. But tonight, let's go to the theater together, ha?"

"I'll try," Tony answered, adding after a pause, "Oh, Fil, I can't find my boots. May I wear yours?" His voice sounded strong and healthy.

"Sure, sure!" Fil answered. He didn't need boots. He loved to walk in the snow.

The air outside felt good. Fil lifted his face to the sky and closed his eyes on the snow and a wet wind drenched his face. He stood that way for some time, crying, more, more! to himself, drunk with snow and coolness. His car was parked a block away. As he walked towards it, he plowed into the snow with one foot and studied the scar he made, a hideous shape among perfect footmarks. He felt strong as his lungs filled with the cold air, as if just now it did not matter too much that he was the way he looked and his English way the way it was. But perhaps, he could talk to the dancers in his dialect. Why not?

A heavy frosting of snow covered his car and as he wiped it off with his bare hands, he felt light and young, like a child at play, and once again, he raised his face to the sky and licked the flakes, cold and tasteless on his tongue.

When Fil arrived at the Hamilton, it seemed to him the Philippine dancers had taken over the hotel. They were all over the lobby on the mezzanine, talking in groups animatedly, their teeth sparkling as they laughed, their eyes disappearing in mere slits of light. Some of the girls wore their black hair long. For a moment, the sight seemed too much for him who had but all forgotten how beautiful Philippine girls were. He wanted to look away, but their loveliness held him. He must do something, close his eyes perhaps. As he did so, their laughter came to him like a breeze murmurous with sounds native to his land.

Later, he tried to relax, to appear inconspicuous. True, they were all young, but there were a few elderly men and women who must have been their chaperons or well-wishers like him. He would smile at everyone who happened to look his way. Most of them smiled back, or rather, seemed to smile, but it was quick, without recognition, and might not have been for him but for someone else near or behind him.

His lips formed the words he was trying to phrase in his mind: *Ilocano ka? Bicol? Ano na, paisano? Comusta?* Or should he introduce himself? How? For what he wanted to say, the words didn't come too easily, they were unfamiliar, they stumbled and broke on his lips into a jumble of coherence.

Suddenly, he felt as if he was in the center of a

group where he was not welcome. All the things he had been trying to hide now showed: the age in his face, his horny hands. He knew it the instant he wanted to shake hands with the first boy who had drawn close to him, smiling and friendly. Fil put his hands in his pocket.

Now he wished Tony had been with him. Tony would know what to do. He would charm these young people with his smile and his learned words. Fil wanted to leave, but he seemed caught up in the tangle of moving bodies that merged and broke in a fluid strangle hold. Everybody was talking, mostly in English. Once in a while he heard exclamations in the dialect right out of the past, conjuring up playtime, long shadows of evening on the plaza, barrio fiestas, *misa de gallo.*

Time was passing and he had yet to talk to someone. Suppose he stood on a chair and addressed them in the manner of his flamboyant speeches recorded in his magic sound mirror?

"Beloved countrymen, lovely children of the Pearl of the Orient Seas, listen to me. I'm Fil Acayan. I've come to volunteer my services. I'm yours to command. Your servant. Tell me where you wish to go, what you want to see in Chicago. I know every foot of the lakeshore drive, all the gardens and the parks, the museums, the huge department stores, the planetarium. Let me be your guide. That's what I'm offering you, a free tour of Chicago, and finally, dinner at my apartment on West Sheridan Road—pork *adobo* and chicken *relleno,* name your dish. How about it, *paisanos?*"

No. That would be a foolish thing to do. They would laugh at him. He felt a dryness in his throat. He was sweating. As he wiped his face with a handkerchief, he bumped against a slim, short girl who quite gracefully, stepped aside, and for a moment he thought he would swoon in the perfume that enveloped him. It was fragrance long forgotten, essence of *camia,* of *ilang-ilang,* and *dama de noche.*

Two boys with sleek, pomaded hair were sitting near an empty chair. He sat down and said in the dialect, "May I invite you to my apartment?" The boys stood up, saying, "Excuse us, please," and walked away. He mopped his brow, but instead of getting discouraged, he grew bolder as though he had moved one step beyond shame. Approaching another group, he repeated his invitation, and a girl with a mole on her upper lip, said, "Thank you, but we have no time." As he turned towards another group, he felt their eyes on his back. Another boy drifted towards him, but as soon as he began to speak, the boy said, "Pardon, please," and moved away.

They were always moving away. As if by common consent, they had decided to avoid him, ignore his presence. Perhaps it was not their fault. They must have been instructed to do so. Or was it his looks that kept them away? The thought was a

sharpness inside him.

After a while, as he wandered about the mezzanine, among the dancers, but alone, he noticed that they had begun to leave. Some had crowded noisily into the two elevators. He followed the others going down the stairs. Through the glass doors, he saw them getting into a bus parked beside the subway entrance on Dearborn.

The snow had stopped falling; it was melting fast in the sun and turning into slush.

As he moved about aimlessly, he felt someone touch him on the sleeve. It was one of the dancers, a mere boy, tall and thin, who was saying, "Excuse, please." Fil realized he was in the way between another boy with a camera and a group posing in front of the hotel.

"Sorry," Fil said, jumping away awkwardly.

The crowd burst out laughing.

Then everything became a blur in his eyes, a moving picture out of focus, but gradually, the figures cleared, there was mud on the pavement on which the dancers stood posing, and the sun threw shadows at their feet.

Let them have fun, he said to himself, they're young and away from home. I have no business messing up their schedule, forcing my company on them.

He watched the dancers till the last of them was on the bus. The voices came to him, above the traffic sounds. They waved their hands and smiled towards him as the bus started. Fil raised his hand to wave back, but stopped quickly, aborting the gesture. He turned to look behind him at whomever the dancers were waving their hands to. There was no one there except his own reflection in the glass door, a double exposure of himself and a giant plant with its thorny branches around him like arms in a loving embrace.

Even before he opened the door to their apartment, Fil knew that Tony had not yet arrived. There were no boots outside on the landing. Somehow he felt relieved, for until then he did not know how he was going to explain his failure.

From the hotel, he had driven around, cruised by the lakeshore drive, hoping he would see the dancers somewhere, in a park perhaps, taking pictures of the mist over the lake and the last gold on the trees now wet with melted snow, or on some picnic grounds, near a bubbling fountain. Still taking pictures of themselves against a background of Chicago's gray and dirty skyscrapers. He slowed down every time he saw a crowd, but the dancers were nowhere along his way. Perhaps they had gone to the theater to rehearse. He turned back before reaching Evanston.

He felt weak, not hungry. Just the same, he ate, warming up some left-over food. The rice was cold, but the soup was hot and tasty. While he ate, he listened for footfalls.

Afterwards, he lay down on the sofa and a weariness came over him, but he tried hard not to sleep. As he stared at the ceiling, he felt like floating away, but he kept his eyes open, willing himself hard to remain awake. He wanted to explain everything to Tony when he arrived. But soon his eyes closed against a weary will too tired and weak to fight back sleep—and then there were voices. Tony was in the room, eager to tell his own bit of news.

"I've discovered a new way of keeping afloat," he was saying.

"Who wants to keep afloat?" Fil asked.

"Just in case. In a shipwreck, for example," Tony said.

"Never mind shipwrecks. I must tell you about the dancers," Fil said.

"But this is important," Tony insisted. "This way, you can keep floating indefinitely."

"What for indefinitely?" Fil asked.

"Say in a ship . . . I mean, in an emergency, you're stranded without help in the middle of the Pacific or the Atlantic, you must keep floating till help comes..." Tony explained.

"More better," Fil said, "find a way to reach shore before the sharks smells you. You discover that."

"I will," Tony said, without eagerness, as though certain that there was no such way, that, after all, his discovery was worthless.

"Now you listen to me," Fil said, sitting up abruptly. As he talked in the dialect, Tony listened with increasing apathy.

"There they were," Fil began, his tone taking on the orator's pitch, "who could have been my children if I had not left home—or yours, Tony. They gazed around them with wonder, smiling at me, answering my questions, but grudgingly, edging away as if to be near me were wrong, a violation in their rule book. But it could be that every time I opened my mouth, I gave myself away. I talked in the dialect, Ilocano, Tagalog, Bicol, but no one listened. They avoided me. They had been briefed too well: Do not talk to strangers. Ignore their invitations. Be extra careful in the big cities like New York and Chicago, beware of the old-timers, the Pinoys. Most of them are bums. Keep away from them. Be on the safe side—stick together, entertain only those who have been introduced to you properly.

"I'm sure they had such instructions, safety measures, they must have called them. What then could I have done, scream out my good intentions, prove my harmlessness and my love for them by beating my breast? Oh, but I loved them. You see, I was like them once. I, too, was nimble with my feet, graceful with my hands; and I had the tongue of a poet. Ask the village girls and the envious boys from the city—but first you have to find them. After these many years, it won't be easy. You'll have to search every suffering face in the village gloom for a

hint of youth and beauty or go where the graveyards are and the tombs under the lime trees. One such face . . . oh, God, what am I saying?

"All I wanted was to talk to them, guide them around Chicago, spend money on them so that they would have something special to remember about us here when they return to our country. They would tell their folks: We met a kind, old man, who took us to his apartment. It was not much of a place. It was old—like him. When we sat on the sofa in the living room, the bottom sank heavily, the broken springs touching the floor. But what a cook that man was! And how kind! We never thought that rice and *adobo* could be that delicious. And the chicken *relleno!* When someone asked what the stuffing was —we had never tasted anything like it—he smiled saying, 'From heaven's supermarket' touching his head and pressing his heart like a clown as if heaven were there. He had his tape recorder which he called a magic sound mirror, and he had all of us record our voices. Say anything in the dialect, sing, if you please, our *kundiman,* please, he said, his eyes pleading, too. Oh, we had fun listening to the playback. When you're gone, the old man said, I shall listen to your voices with my eyes closed and you'll be here again and I won't ever be alone, no, not anymore, after this. We wanted to cry, but he looked very funny, so we laughed and he laughed with us.

"But, Tony, they would not come. They thanked me, but they said they had no time. Others said nothing. They looked through me. I didn't exist. Or worse, I was unclean. *Basura.* Garbage. They were ashamed of me. How could I be Filipino?"

The memory, distinctly recalled, was a rock on his breast. He gasped for breath.

"Now, let me teach you how to keep afloat," Tony said, but it was not Tony's voice.

Fil was alone and gasping for air. His eyes opened slowly till he began to breathe more easily. The sky outside was gray. He looked at his watch—a quarter past five. The show would begin at eight. There was time. Perhaps Tony would be home soon.

The apartment was warming up. The radiators sounded full of scampering rats. He had a recording of that in his sound mirror.

Fil smiled. He had an idea. He would take the sound mirror to the theater, take his seat close to the stage, and make tape recordings of the singing and the dances.

Now he was wide-awake and somehow pleased with himself. The more he thought of the idea, the better he felt. If Tony showed up now . . . He sat up, listening. The radiators were quiet. There were no footfalls, no sound of a key turning.

Late that night, back from the theater, Fil knew at once that Tony was back. The boots were outside

507

the door. He, too, must be tired, and should not be disturbed.

He was careful not to make any noise. As he turned on the floor lamp, he thought that perhaps Tony was awake and waiting for him. They would listen together to a playback of the dances and the songs Tony had missed. Then he would tell Tony what happened that day, repeating part of the dream.

From Tony's bedroom came the regular breathing of a man sound asleep. To be sure, he looked into the room and in the half-darkness, Tony's head showed darkly, deep in a pillow, on its side, his knees bent, almost touching the clasped hands under his chin, an oversized foetus in the last bottle. Fil shut the door between them and went over to the portable. Now. He turned it on to low. At first nothing but static and odd sounds came through, but soon after there was the patter of feet to the rhythm of a familiar melody.

All the beautiful boys and girls were in the room now, dancing and singing. A boy and a girl sat on the floor holding two bamboo poles by their ends flat on the floor, clapping them together, then apart, and pounding them on the boards, while dancers swayed and balanced their lithe forms, dipping their bare brown legs in and out of the clapping bamboos, the pace gradually increasing into a fury of wood on wood in a counterpoint of panic among the dancers and in a harmonious flurry of toes and ankles escaping certain pain—crushed bones, and bruised flesh, and humiliation. Other dances followed, accompanied by songs and live with the sounds of life and death in the old country; Igorot natives in G-strings walking down a mountainside; peasants climbing up a hill on a rainy day; neighbors moving a house, their sturdy legs showing under a moving roof; lovers at Lent hiding their passion among wild hedges, far from the crowded chapel; a distant gong sounding off a summons either to a feast or a wake. And finally, prolonged ovation, thunderous, wave upon wave . . .

"Turn that thing off!" Tony's voice was sharp above the echoes of the gongs and the applause settling into silence.

Fil switched off the dial and in the sudden stillness, the voices turned into faces, familiar and near, like gesture and touch that stayed on even as the memory withdrew, bowing out, as it were, in a graceful exit, saying, thank you, thank you, before a ghostly audience that clapped hands in silence and stomped their feet in a sucking emptiness. He wanted to join the finale, such as it was, pretend that the curtain call included him, and attempt a shamefaced imitation of a graceful adieu, but he said, thank you, thank you, his voice sincere and contrite, grateful for the other voices and the sound of singing and the memory.

"Oh, my God . . ." the man in the other room cried, followed by a moan of such anguish that Fil fell on his knees, covering the sound mirror with his hands to muffle the sounds that had started again, it seemed to him, even after he had turned it off.

Then he remembered.

"Tony, what did the doctor say? What did he say?" he shouted and listened, holding his breath, no longer able to tell at the moment who had truly waited all day for the final sentence.

There was no answer. Meanwhile, under his hands, there was a flutter of wings, a shudder of gongs. What was Tony saying? That was his voice, no? Fil wanted to hear, he must know. He switched dials on and off, again and again, pressing buttons. Suddenly, he didn't know what to do. The spools were live, they kept turning. His arms went around the machine, his chest pressing down on the spools. In the quick silence, Tony's voice came clear.

"So they didn't come after all?"

"Tony, what did the doctor say?" Fil asked, straining hard to hear.

"I knew they wouldn't come. But that's okay. The apartment is old anyhow. And it smells of death."

"How you talk. In this country, there's a cure for everything."

"I guess we can't complain. We had it good here all the time. Most of the time, anyway."

"I wish, though, they had come. I could. . ."

"Yes, they could have. They didn't have to see me, but I could have seen them. I have seen their pictures, but what do they really look like?"

"Tony, they're beautiful, all of them, but especially the girls. Their complexion, their grace, their eyes, they were what we call talking eyes, they say things to you. And the scent of them!"

There was a sigh from the room, soft, hardly like a sigh. A louder, grating sound, almost under his hands that had relaxed their hold, called his attention. The sound mirror had kept going, the tape was fast unravelling.

"Oh, no!" he screamed, noticing that somehow, he had pushed the eraser.

Frantically, he tried to rewind and play back the sounds and the music, but there was nothing now but the full creaking of the tape on the spool and meaningless sounds that somehow had not been erased, the thud of dancing feet, a quick clapping of hands, alien voices and words: *in this country . . . everything . . . all of them . . . talking eyes . . . and the scent* . . . a fading away into nothingness, till about the end when there was a screaming, senseless kind of finale detached from the body of a song in the background, drums and sticks and the tolling of a bell.

"Tony! Tony!" Fil cried, looking towards the sick man's room. "I've lost them all."

Biting his lips, Fil turned towards the window, startled by the first light of dawn. He hadn't realized till then the long night was over. ★

JANICE MIRIKITANI

Hospitals are To Die In

They finally
had to take obachan
she was dying

      hospitals
      takai
          takai

     she whispered

but she is dying

when they carried her
body
barely breathing,
they were carrying my soul
wrapped in the thin sheath
of her skin

the ambulance attendants
rushed from their
coffee break
irritated
dropped her on the
stretcher
and bumped her
against the door
violating her sleep

she wanted to stay
die in the house
that was like a body
wrapping her
in smells she knew
breathing memories
for her

in the corners
of her closed eyes
silent tears brimming
protesting
not the hospital

      cold
      white
      expensive

the attendants swore
as they slung
the stretcher

complaining
about the high cost of living.

One said
he had to buy a
side of beef
to hang in his freezer.

     it's cheaper that way.

The Only Real Day

by Frank Chin

The men played mah jong or passed the water-pipe, their voices low under the sound of the fish pumps thudding into the room from the tropical fish store. Voices became louder over the voices of each other with the thickening heat. And Yuen was with his friends now, where he was always happy and loud every Tuesday night. All the faces shone of skin oily from the heat and laughter, the same as last week, the same men and room and waterpipe, Yuen knew them. Here it was comfortable after the cripple in Oakland. He hated the sight of cripples and one had spoken to him tonight.

"That's impossible," Huie said to Yuen.

Yuen grinned at his friend and said, "It's true. You don't know because you were born here, but I remember that morning. I awoke with my father and my son, and we walked out of our house to the field, as we did every morning, and we walked to the peach tree and stood in a circle around it, as we did every morning, you see, huh? And we dropped our trousers about our legs and pissed at the base of the peach tree, making bubbles in the earth and mud over the roots, wetting the bark. And we stood watching the urine sink into the dirt, and the bubbles burst . . . as we always did after fertilizing our peach tree. And then I said I was going to Hong Kong the next day with my wife and son, and that I was leaving my father and mother, and I did. I left; then I left Hong Kong and left my family there, and came to America to make money."

"And did you?" Huie said.

"Make money?"

"Yes, did you make money?"

"I'm still here, my wife is dead . . . but my son is still in Hong Kong, and I send him what I can." Yuen looked up to the light bulb and blinked. "It's good to get away from all those American women that work in the restaurant," he said, not wanting to speak of his son or China. All the men were speaking loudly, shouting when they laughed, throwing the sound of their voices against the close walls of the room. Yuen enjoyed the room when it was loud; the noise of the voices of friends was exciting after a week of privacy in a kitchen; 'The boy should come sometime,' he thought.

"Perhaps you could," Huie said, laughing, "Perhaps you could make love to them, Yuen older brother." The men laughed, showing gold and age-yellowed teeth. Yuen snorted against the friendly laugh. "Not me," he said. He lifted the punk from the tobacco, then shot off the ash with a squirt of water through the stem. "I won't speak their language. I don't like them working in the same place as me. They don't think I'm anything anyway. They

illustration by RON BATTLE

511

change their clothes and smoke in their slips right outside my door in the hallway." His head lifted to face his friends, and his nostrils opened, one larger than the other as he spoke faster. "And anyway, they don't care that I come out of my room and see them standing half naked in the hall. They're ugly; they all have wrinkles and you can see all the dirt on their skins and they shave their armpits, and their powder turns brown in their wrinkles. They're not like Chinese women at all." Yuen chuckled, making it all a joke for his friends.

"I've always wanted to see a real naked American woman. There's something about the . . ." Huie said. "Ahhh, I know." He laughed and stuck out his tongue. "They've got bigger breasts than Chinese women, and their teats are prettier." He grunted and put his hands inside his jacket and hefted invisible breasts, "Like those so pink and pretty on the calendars!"

"I don't know. All the ones at my place are old . . . and you can't tell about pictures . . ." Yuen pulled at the deep smoke of the waterpipe. The water inside gurgled loudly, and singed tobacco ash jumped when Yuen blew back into the tube. He lifted his head and licked the edges of his teeth. He always licked the edges of his teeth before speaking. He did not think it a sign of old age. Before he broke the first word over his licked teeth, Huie raised his hand. "Jimmy Chan goes out with Americans; blonde ones with blue eyelids too, And he smokes cigars," Huie said.

"That's because he has money. If Chinese have money, everybody likes them" Yuen said. "Blue teats . . . pink eyelids, everybody."

"Not the Jews."

"Not the Jews," Yuen said, "I saw a crippled Jew . . . he looked like a Jew . . ." Yuen stopped, not wanting to talk about the cripple with his friends.

"The Jews don't like anybody," Huie said.

"The Jews don't like anybody," Yuen said and smiled.

"Nobody likes the Jews!" Huie said. He pulled the tip of his nose down with his fingers. "Do I look like a Jew?" The men sitting at the mah jong laughed and shook the table with their hands. Over their laughter, Yuen spoke loudly, licking the edges of his teeth, smiling and saying, "What do you want to look like a Jew for? You're Chinese!" And the roomful of close men was loud with the sound of tables slapped with night pale hands and bellyfulls of laughter shrinking into wheezes and silent empty mouths, breathless and drooling. "We have a Jew at the hotel my restaurant is in, Jews and Americans," Yuen said, and touched the glowing punk to the tobacco and inhaled through his mouth, gurgling the water. He let the smoke drop from his nostrils and laughed smoke out between his teeth, and leaned back into the small spaces of smoke between the men and enjoyed the whole roomful.

Yuen was a man of neat habits, but always seemed disheveled with his moist mouth, open with the lower lip shining and dangling below yellow teeth. Even today, dressed in his dayoff suit that he kept hung in his closet with butcher paper over it, and a hat he kept in a box, he had seen people watching him and laughing behind their hands at his pulling at the shoulders of the jacket and lifting the brim of his hat from his eyes. He had gathered himself into his own arms and leaned back into his seat to think about the room in San Francisco; then he slept and was ignorant of the people, the conductor, and all the people he had seen before, watching him and snickering, and who might have been, he thought, jealous of him for being tall for Chinese, or his long fingers, exactly what, he did not know or worry about in this half stupor between wakefulness and sleep with his body against the side of the train, the sounds of the steel wheels, and the train pitching side to side, all amazingly loud and echoing in his ears, through his body before sleep.

Tuesday evenings Yuen took the "A" train from Oakland to San Francisco. He walked to the train stop right after work at the restaurant and stood, always watching to the end of the street for the train's coming, dim out of the darkness from San Francisco. The train came, its cars swaying side to side and looking like a short snake with a lit stripe of lights squirming past him, or like the long dragon that stretched and jumped over the feet of boys carrying it. He hated the dragon here, but saw it when it ran, for the boys' sake. The train looked like that, the glittering dragon that moved quickly like the sound of drum rolls and dangled its staring eyes out of its head with a flurry of beard; the screaming bird's voice of the train exciting in him a child's impulse to run to grab, to destroy.

Then he stood and listened to the sound of the train's steel wheels, the sound of an invisible crowd being sucked after the lights of the train toward the end of the line, leaving the quiet street more quiet and Yuen almost superstitiously anxious.

He was always grateful for the Tuesdays Freddy walked him to the train stop. They left early on these nights and walked past drugstores, bought comic books, looked into the windows of closed shops, looked at shoes or suits. "How much is that?" Yuen would ask.

"I don't know what you're talking," Freddy would say when he could not answer in Chinese.

"What a stupid boy you are; can't even talk Chinese," Yuen would say, and "too moochie shiyet," adding his only American phrase. "Come on, I have a train to catch." They would laugh at each other and walk slowly, the old man lifting his shoulders and leaning his head far back on his neck, walking straight, when he remembered.

A look back to Freddy as he boarded the train,

a smile a wave, the boy through the window a silent thing in the noise of engines. He would shrug and settle himself against the back of the seat, and still watch Freddy, who would be walking now, back toward the restaurant. Tonight, he realized again, how young Freddy was to be walking home alone at night through the city back to the restaurant. He saw Freddy not walking the same way home, but running next to the moving train then turning the corner to walk up a street with more lights and people. Yuen turned, thinking he might shout out the door for Freddy to walk home the same way they came, but the train was moving; Yuen had forgotten, the train was moving. And he had no right. Freddy had heard his mother say Yuen had no right so many times that Freddy could say it too. In Chinese. That he was not Yuen's son. That this was not China. Knowing the boy could say such things made Yuen's need to shout and scold more urgent, his silence in front of the child more humiliating. Yuen was still and worked himself out of his confusion; the beginning of his day off was bad; nothing about it right or usual; all of it bad, no good, wrong. Yuen thought it out of his mind until it was funny, then relaxed.

"Jimmy Chan has a small Mexican dog too, that he keeps in his pocket," Huie was saying, "It's lined with rubber."

"The little dog?" Yuen asked. And the men laughed.

"The dog . . ." Huie said and chuckled out of his chinless face, "No, his pocket, so if the dog urinates . . ." He shrugged, "You know."

"Then how can he make love to his blonde American with blue whatever, if his pocket is full of the dog?"

"He takes off his coat!" The men laughed with their faces up into the falling smoke. The men seemed very close to Yuen, as if with the heat and smoke, they swelled to crowding against the walls, and Yuen swelled and was hot with them, feeling close and friendly, friendlier, until he was dizzy with friendship and forgot names. "A Chinese can do anything with Americans if he has money," Yuen said.

"Like too moochie shiyet, he can," Huie shouted, almost falling off his seat, "He can't make himself white!" Huie jabbed his finger at Yuen and stared. The men at the table stopped. The noise of the mah jong and voices stopped to the sound of rumps shifting over chairs and creaks of table legs. Heavy arms were leaned onto the tabletops. Yuen was not sure whether he was arguing with his friend or not. He did not want to argue on his day off, yet he was constrained to say something. He knew that whatever he said would sound more important than he meant it. He licked his teeth and said, "Who wants to be white when they can have money?" He grinned. The man nodded and sat quiet a moment, listening to the sound of boys shouting at

cars to come park in their lots. "Yuen always knows the right thing to say." "You're your mother's ass, play!" And the men laughed and quietly returned to their game.

The back room was separated from the tropical fish store by a long window shade drawn over the doorway. Calendars with pictures of Chinese women holding peaches the size of heads, calendars with pictures of nude white women with large breasts, and a picture that someone thought was funny, showing a man with the breasts of a woman were tacked to the walls. The men sat on boxes, in chairs, at counters with walls of drawers full of herbs, or at tables against walls under calendars. They sat and passed the waterpipe and tea and played mah jong or talked. Every night the waterpipe, the tea, the mah jong, the talk.

"Wei, hey, Yuen, older brother," a faceless voice shouted through the smoke, "Why're you so quiet tonight?"

"I thought I was being noisy . . ." Yuen said, "Perhaps it's because my employer's son might be sick again."

"The boy?" Huie said.

Yuen stood and removed his jacket, brushed it and hung it on a nail. "He has this trouble with his stomach . . . makes him bend up and he cries and won't move. It comes and goes," he said.

"Bring him over to me, and I'll give him some herbs, make him well in a hurry."

"His mother, my employer, is one of these new-fashioned people, giving up the old ways. She speaks American talk and has American women working for her at her restaurant. She laughs at me when I tell her about herbs making her son well."

"Herbs make me well when I'm sick."

"They can make any sickness well," Yuen said.

"They made my brother well, but he died anyway," Huie said. He took off his glasses and licked the lenses.

"Because he wanted to."

"He shot himself."

"Yes, I remember," Yuen said. He scratched his Adams's apple noisily a moment. "He used to come into the restaurant in the mornings, and I'd fix him scrambled eggs. He used to always speak to me with bits of egg on his lips and shake his fork and tell me that if I could speak American talk, I could be cook at the restaurant. I could too, but the cook there is Chinese anyway and buys good meat."

Huie sighed, said "Good meat is important I suppose." Then put his mouth to the mouth of the waterpipe.

"What?" Yuen asked absently at Huie's sigh. He allowed his eyes to unfocus on the room now, tried to remember Huie's brother's face with bits of egg on the lips and was angry. Suddenly an angry old man wanting to be alone, screaming. He wiped his own lips with his knuckles and looked back to Huie.

513

Yuen did not want to talk about Huie's brother. He wanted to listen to music, or jokes, or breaking bones, something happy or terrible.

"His fine American talk," Huie said. "He used to go to the Oakland High School at night to learn."

"My employer wants me to go there, too," Yuen said. "You should only talk American if you have money to talk to them with . . . I mean, only fools talk American when they don't have money. If you talk to them without money, all you'll hear is what they say behind your back, and you don't want to listen to that."

"I don't."

"No."

"He received a letter one day, did he tell you that? He received a letter from the American police, and he took the letter to Jimmy Chan who reads American well . . . and Jimmy said that the Immigration Board wanted to know how he came into the country, and wanted to know if he was sending money to Communists or not." Huie smiled wanly and stared between his legs. Yuen watched Huie sitting on the box; he had passed the pipe and now sat with his short legs spread slightly apart. He held his hands together between his legs and his head was down now, his eyes just visible to Yuen. Huie's slumped body looked relaxed, only the muscles of his hands and wrists were tight and working. To Yuen, Huie this moment looked as calm as if he were sitting at stool. Yuen smiled and tried to save the pleasure of his day off visit that was being lost in morbid talk. "Did he have his dog with him?" he asked.

"His dog? How do you talk about a dog when I'm talking about the death of my brother?"

"Perhaps the concern for the boy," Yuen said, "I shouldn't have let him wait for the train with me tonight."

"Was he sick?"

"That too maybe . . ." Yuen said; he did not want to talk about the cripple in the magazine store. It would not be funny to talk about, and Yuen wanted to laugh.

"Bring the boy to me next week, and I'll fix him up," Huie said quickly, and put his glasses on again. Yuen, out of his day off, loud, cheerful mood, angrily and ashamed of his anger, listened to Huie, "My brother was very old, you remember? He was here during the fire and earthquake, and he told this to Jimmy Chan." Huie stopped speaking and patted Yuen's knee. "Yes, he did have his little dog in his pocket . . ." The men looked across to each other, and Yuen nodded. They were friends, had always been friends. They were friends now. "And my brother told Jimmy that all his papers had been burned in the fire, and told about how he came across the bay in a sailboat that was so full that his elbows, just over the side of the boat could feel the water, and about the women crying and the men

shouting, and that no one thought of papers, and some not even of their gold."

"Yes, I know."

"And Jimmy Chan laughed at my brother and told him that there was nothing he could do, and that my brother would have to wait and see if he would be sent back to China or not. So . . ." Huie put his hands on his knees and rocked himself forward, lifting and setting his thin rump onto the wooden box, sighed and swallowed, "My brother shot himself." Huie looked up to Yuen; they licked their lips at the same moment, watching each other's tongue. "He died very messy," Huie said, and Yuen had heard it through again, for his friend, as he had a hundred times before. But tonight it made him sick.

The talk about death and the insides of a head spread, wet all over the floor, the head of someone he knew, the talk was not relaxing; it was incongruous to the room of undershirted men playing mah jong, and the men, quieter since the shout, were out of place in their undershirts. Yuen wanted to relax, but everything was frantic that should not be; perhaps he was too sensitive, Yuen thought, and wanted to be numb. "You don't have to talk about it if it bothers you," Yuen said to his friend.

"He looked messy, for me that was enough . . . and enough of Jimmy Chan for me too. He could've written and said my brother was a good citizen or something . . ." Huie stopped and flicked at his ear with his fingertips. "You don't want to talk any more about it?"

"No," Yuen said.

"How did we come to talk of my brother's death anyhow?"

"Jimmy Chan and his Mexican dog."

"I don't want to talk about that any more, either."

"How soon is Chinese New Year's?"

"I don't think I want to talk about anything any more," Huie said, "New Year's a long ways off."

"Yes, I know that."

"I don't want to talk about it," Huie said. Each man sat now, staring toward, past each other without moving their eyes, as if moving their eyes would break their friendship. He knew that whatever had happened had been his fault; perhaps tonight would have been more congenial if he had not taken Freddy to the magazine store, or if the cripple had fallen just once, or had not been there. Yuen could still see the cripple falling, falling and stumbling up and falling again faster than people could push him, falling as if he expected to be pushed, and how Yuen had wanted to push that obscene man down crashing into the cement. The joy it would have given him was embarrassing, new, unaccountable.

"Would you like a cigar, Yuen, older brother?" Huie asked, using the courtesy.

"No, I prefer the waterpipe." He watched Huie

514

spit the end of the cigar onto the floor.

"You remind me of my brother, Yuen."

"How so?"

"Shaking your head, always shaking your head . . . you do too much thinking. You have to shake the thinking out to stop, eh?"

"And I rattle my eyes, too." Yuen laughed a moment. "But what else am I to do here?"

"I don't know," Huie said and looked around, "Mah jong?"

"No."

"Are you unhappy?"

"I have my friends, right? But sometimes I have a melancholy feeling."

"Just like my brother . . . too much thinking, and thinking becomes worry. You should smoke cigars and get drunk and go help one of your American waitresses shave her armpits and put your head inside them and tickle her with your tongue until she's silly. I'd like to put my face in the armpit of some big American woman . . . with a big armpit!"

"But I'm not like your brother," Yuen said, "I don't shoot the back of my head off with guns."

"You only have to do that once."

Yuen waited a moment, then stood. "I should be leaving now," he said. Tonight had been very slow but over quickly. He did not like being compared to an old man who had shot himself.

Huie stood and shook Yuen's hand, held Yuen's elbow and squeezed Yuen's hand hard. "I didn't mean to shout at you, older brother."

Yuen smiled his wet smile. Huie held onto Yuen's hand and stood as if he was about to sit again. He had an embarrassingly sad smile. Yuen did not mean to twist his friend's face into its muscular contortion; he had marred Huie's happy evening of hoarse laughter and alcoholic wheezings. "I shouted too," Yuen said finally.

"You always know the right things to say, older brother," Huie squeezed Yuen's hand and said, "Goodnight, older brother."

And Yuen was walking, and was out into the tropical fish store. He opened the door to the alley and removed his glasses, for the sudden cold air outside fogged them.

For a long time he walked the always damp alley, between glittering streets of Chinatown. Women with black coats walked with young children. This Chinatown was taller than Oakland's, had more fire escapes and lights, more music coming from street vents. He usually enjoyed walking at this hour every Wednesday of every week. But this was Tuesday evening, and already he had left his friends, yet it looked like Wednesday with the same paper vendors coming up the hills, carrying bundles of freshly printed Chinese papers. He walked down the hill to Portsmouth Square on Kearney Street to sit in the park and read the paper. He sat on a

wooden bench and looked up the trunk of a palm tree, looking toward the sounds of pigeons. He could hear the fat birds cooing over the sound of the streets, and could hear the grass snap when their droppings dropped fresh. He looked up and down the park once, then moved to the other side of the tree, out of the wind, and sat to read the paper by the streetlight before walking. Tonight he was glad to be tired; to Yuen tiredness was the only explanation for his nervousness. He would go home early; there was nothing else to do here, and he would sleep through his day off, or at least, late into the morning.

****

He entered the kitchen and snorted a breath through his nose. He was home to the smell of cooking and greasy sweat of waitresses. His employer wiped her forehead with the back of her arm and asked him why he had come back so early; she did not expect him back until dinnertime tomorrow and was he sick? He answered, "Yes," lying to avoid conversation. He asked her where Freddy, her son, was, and she said that he was upstairs sleeping. Yuen nodded, "Of course, it's late isn't it," he said, avoiding the stare of her greasy eyes, and went upstairs. He looked once around the kitchen before turning at the first landing. He saw the large refrigerators and the steam table, being objects that made work for him, and he realized that he was truly tired now, and sighed the atmosphere of his day off out of his body. "You're trying to walk too straight, anyway, Yuen," his employer said from the bottom of the stairs. He did not understand her and went on up the stairs.

At the top of the stairs he turned and walked down the hall past the room of his employer and her husband, and past Freddy's room, toward his own room next to the lavatory. Facing the door, on the other side of the hall was a standup wardrobe, a box with two doors and rack inside for clothes, where waitresses kept their white and black uniforms and changed their clothes. A redheaded waitress was sitting inside the wardrobe smoking a cigarette. She sat between hanging clothes with her back against the back of the wardrobe, her legs crossed and stretching out of the box. One naked heel turned on the floor, back and forth, making her legs jump to the rhythm of her nervous breathing.

Yuen walked slowly down the hall, his head down, and his fingers feeling the edges of his long hair that tickled the tops of his ears. He looked down to the floor but could not still see the bare legs jutting from out of the box, the long muscles under the thighs shaking to the turning heel. He knew she was ugly. He snorted and walked close to the far wall; he would walk past her and not look at her. She

515

did not move her legs. He stopped and leaned against the wall and stepped one foot high over her legs, then lifted his other foot and gingerly swung it over the waitress' ankles. As the foot was over her ankles he glanced into the box and saw her pull a strap over her shoulder and giggle. He hopped to keep his balance and she kicked his ankle as she said, "Hiya, Yuen." The old man tripped, stepped down quickly and stumbled. He felt his shoe scrape the waitress' leg to blood and heard her short squeal. He turned in his fall and threw an arm toward her and kept falling with his legs tangled with hers. The waitress' legs twisted against his and she turned over to look for her cigarette inside the box. The nylon slip made her rump gleam as it swung up and down in front of Yuen's face, and he sat on the floor far from his face, far away from anywhere, confused and dazed from his fall as he watched her rump jiggle against her slip and heard her shouting and pounding after her cigarette inside the box. Huie had wanted to stuff his head into an American woman's armpit, and Yuen looked but did not know where her armpits were. He began to feel the jabs of her toes paining into him as she crawled deeper into the box. He rolled over onto his belly and grunted himself up to his hands and knees. He had dropped his hat and could not find it. He was pure unembarrassed angry now and slapped at the waitress' feet each time she jabbed him. He could not find his hat. He looked under the waitress.

The waitress stood from out of the wardrobe and pulled her slip straight around her belly. She looked down to Yuen, his head nodding, dangling on his neck. He looked like a large bird feeding on something dead, and the waitress laughed. "Come on there, Yuen," the waitress said, "I was just playing," and bent to help the man up. She took his shoulders with her hands and began pulling gently. The door to the bathroom was open and the light through the doorway shone white on the front of her powdered face. Yuen saw her face looking very white with flecks of powder falling from light hairs over her grin, a very white face on a grey wrinkled neck and a chest warped with wrinkled skin veined like blue cheese and thin muscles. He did not like her smiling and chuckling and breathing into his face.

"Are you all right now, Yuen?" she asked. He did not understand. He felt her holding him and saw her smiling and saw her old breasts quiver against her hanging slip and the skin of her chest stretch across her ribs, not at all like the women in calendars and magazines, Yuen thought. He took his shoulders closer to his body and she still held him, squeezing the muscle of his arm with strong hands, and pulled him towards her and muttered something in her rotten throated voice. He leaned away from her and patted his head to show that he was looking for his hat. He chanced a grin.

She looked at his head and moved her fingers through his hair. "I don't see a bump, honey. Where does it hurt?"

He felt her body close to his face. The smell of her slip hung into his breathing. He was angry because he felt that she thought he was stupid. "My hat! My hat!" he shouted in Chinese. He took an invisible hat and put it on his head and tapped the brim with his hands.

The waitress, also on her knees now, moved toward him and felt his head. "Where does it hurt?" she said. "I don't feel nothin' but your head."

He stood quickly and leaned against the wall and glared stupidly at her.

"I was just trying to see if you're hurt, Yuen," the waitress said. "Did I touch your sore or something?" She held her arms out and stood. A strap fell from her shoulder; she ignored it and stretched her neck and reached toward him with her fingers. "I was just joking when I kicked you, honey. I thought it was funny, the way you was stepping over me, see?" All Yuen could hear were whines and giggles in her voice. He shook his head. He held his coat closed with his hands and shoved at her with his head, "Go away, Hui Yah!"

A door opened and Freddy stepped into the hall in his underwear. "What'sa wrong?" he asked. The waitress turned then, fixed her slip and brushed her dry hair out of her face. "Make him understand, will you?" she said, pointing to Yuen. She jabbed her arm at Yuen again. "Him, he's . . ." she crossed her eyes and pointed at her head.

"She's drunk!" Yuen said, "Tell her to go away."

"I was joking, tell him. I didn't mean to hurt his old head."

"Don't let her touch you, she's crazy tonight."

"Do something! I can't."

"What? What?" Freddy said, "What? I don't know what you're talking."

The waitress was in front of the boy now and trying to explain. Yuen stepped quickly down the hall and pushed the boy into his room and closed the door. "Go to sleep . . . your stomach will hurt," he said.

"What'd you push me for?" the boy asked in English. He kicked the door and tried to open it, but Yuen held the knob. The boy shouted and began to cry.

"Coffee," Yuen said to the waitress and pointed to her, meaning that she should go have coffee. The waitress nodded quickly and took a robe from the wardrobe and went downstairs.

Yuen went to his room without looking for his hat. The boy opened his door and followed Yuen and stood in the doorway and watched Yuen hang his overcoat in his closet. Yuen did not notice the boy and locked the door in his face.

The old man put a hand under his shirt and rubbed the sweat under his armpit. He loosened his belt and flapped the waist of his underwear before lying on top of his bed. He felt under his pillow for his revolver; it was big in his hand. Then he swallowed to slow his breath and sat up to untie his shoes.

He saw the dark stain of blood on the heel of his right shoe and dropped it onto the floor. 'I guess I can't tell,' he thought, 'She'll say I kicked her.' He rapped the wall to speak to Freddy. "*Wei*, Freddy, don't tell, all right?"

"I don't know what you're talking. You . . ." Yuen heard nothing through the wall a moment. He wished that Freddy knew Chinese better than he did. "You hit me in the face," Freddy said.

"I didn't."

"You did, and it hurt."

"I'm sorry then. Does your stomach hurt?"

"You hit me in the face."

"Uhhh," Yuen groaned, and rolled away from the wall. He would buy Freddy a funnybook in the morning; he would buy Freddy a dozen funnybooks and a candy bar in the morning. He leaned back into bed and began unbuttoning his shirt.

He stopped and blinked a moment; someone knocked at his door again. He felt for his revolver.

"I got some coffee, Yuen bak, old uncle, are you all right; Anna says you hurt your head," he heard Freddy's mother say.

"Go away."

"But Anna says you want coffee. Have you been drinking?"

"I don't want coffee."

"Since you're here, I told the colored boy not to come in tomorrow morning . . . What's your hat doing in the bathroom?"

"Leave it," Yuen said, "Just leave it, I'll get it in the morning." He coughed and rolled over on the bed and coughed once into his pillow.

"You got a letter today . . . with your American name on it, Nelson Yuen Fong . . . your name looks nice," the voice outside said.

"What?" Yuen mumbled.

"Nothing. I'll keep it until tomorrow for you."

He coughed phlegm up from his chest, held it in his mouth, then swallowed it. His face was warm in his own breath against the pillow; he relaxed the tightness of his closed eyes for sleep . . . 'My hat's probably all dirty if it's in the bathroom . . .' and did not get up to shut the light.

The hallway outside was quiet now. He felt his eyes smarting and feeling dirty. He was not sure whether or not he was asleep. It was late; the night was wider, higher without lights on the horizon or lengths of sound filling the streets. The air was not silent but excited without noise. Yuen could hear sounds on the edge of hearing, and, listening for them, the small sounds of almost voices and cars somewhere, he occasionally heard nothing. Perhaps he was sleeping when he heard nothing, he thought.

If he opened his eyes now, he would know . . . but he could not open his eyes now, for he decided that he was asleep, sleeping, finally.

'How was it when we met?' he thought. He flexed his shoulders and put his arms about himself and lay on his side, his legs crossed, and he remembered himself, then, coming up the stairs one day with hot smoke from his waterpipe thickening and pleasant in his lungs. He had stopped in his doorway to see a small boy with large potato chip ears holding his revolver. He had thought it was his son at seeing the boy's knees. That was funny. That was laughable now.

Tomorrow he would buy Freddy a dozen funnybooks and a big candy bar, even if he was not angry any more.

And now truly asleep he was sitting at a table with this boy, but the boy's head was that of his own son, then the head of Huie's dead brother with scrambled eggs flecking the lips. It was a huge head with all the flesh looking soft as if it had been boiled for soup. Yuen wiped the boy's lip but more egg came up where he had wiped the egg until the lips were gone. And the boy laughed and took Yuen's hand and pulled him up. They walked from the table and were in a field with a birdless sky above them, smooth as skin and blue as veins. The boy pointed, and there, on the edge of the world was the peach tree, and they dropped their trousers about their legs together, and urinated the long distance to the tree and watched the streams of their yellow liquid gleaming under the bright sky. They urinated a very long time, and Yuen was surprised. He squinted to see if he was reaching the tree. The boy was laughing and urinating at Yuen's feet now, making mud and spattering piss onto the man's legs. "What are you doing?" he asked.

"Coffee," the boy answered in the waitress' voice and laughed. Birds, small black, with long wings were flying from the horizon now, coming low and fast from behind the boy.

"Was it that I didn't pray?"

"Coffee!" the boy answered.

Yuen was sinking; he could feel the lips of mud clinging to his ankles now. And the birds, silent except for the sound of wings, dived on him. "I'm going to die. Too moochie shiyet, I'm going to die," he said, still fertilizing the peach tree on the horizon. He was not shouting. "It's true!" He awoke to his own voice and the sound of curtains in the wind. His eyes were staring straight up with thick moisture over them. He felt under the sheets around his ankles to see if there was any wet. There was not. He got up and spat into the wash basin, then turned out the light, listened to the silence a moment for the sound of waitresses in the hall, then returned to sleep.

He bathed with his underwear on this morning and plugged the keyhole with toilet paper. He combed his hair then returned to his room. He had found his hat on the lid of the toilet. He did not like the hat any longer; it was too big and the band was dirty. The dream had left him by the time he went downstairs for breakfast, but he knew he had dreamed.

He sat down at a table at the end of the long steam table. He could hear a waitress laughing shrilly outside in the dining room, not the same waitress as last night, he knew, for the breakfast waitresses were different from the ones at dinner. He took a toothpick from a tin can nailed to the end of the steam table and put it in his mouth and sucked the taste of wood and read his Chinese paper. He did not greet his employer; she was younger than he was and should be the first to give greetings, out of respect. But, she was his employer; he did not think of that very long. He was reading about Chiang Kai-shek making a speech to his army again; he liked Chiang Kai-shek, he decided. Every morning, reading the paper, he decided he liked Chiang Kai-shek; it was a familiar and pleasant thing in his life, and he enjoyed it. "He made a speech to his army again," Yuen said.

Freddy was sitting at the table and said, "He made one last week to the army."

'He's forgotten last night,' Yuen thought, and answered, "That was to the farmers. This time it's to the Army. Next week to everybody." This was part of every morning also.

Margie wiped her hands on her apron and sat down next to Yuen. She took an envelope from her pocket and unfolded it. Before removing the letter, she turned to Freddy and said, "Go upstairs and change your pants. And comb your hair."

"I'll be late for school. I gotta eat breakfast."

"Go upstairs, huh? I don't have time to argue!" Margie said.

"Can I use your comb, Yuen bak?"

"You got a comb. Don't bother people. I wanta talk to him."

Yuen gave Freddy his comb, which he kept in a case. Margie watched the boy go past the first landing and out of sight and then took the letter out of the envelope. "I read this letter of yours," she said. She looked straight at Yuen as she spoke, and Yuen resented her look and the way she held his letter. "Who said you could?" he asked, "It might have been from my son; what do you want to read my mail for, when you don't care what else I do?"

"Now you know that's not so," Margie said, "Anyway, it had your American name on it."

"Well . . . What did Anna tell you about last night? You know what she was really trying to do, don't you? I'll tell you, don't believe what she says. She eats scraps, too."

"Oh, Yuen bak, you're so old, she was trying to see if you had a cut or a hurt on your head was all."

"I don't like her anyway," Yuen said. He went to the steam table and ladled cream of wheat into a bowl and sat down to eat it. "What are you looking at? You never see me eat before?"

"Don't you use milk?" Margie asked.

"No, you should know that."

"But your letter, Yuen bak, you're in trouble."

"What for?"

"It's from the immigrators. They want to know if you came into this country legally."

Yuen looked up from his cereal to the powder and rouge of her face, and oil from her Chinese skin had soaked through the mess. She smiled with her lips shut and cheeks pulled in as if sucking something in her mouth. He did not like Margie because she treated him with disdain and made bad jokes, and thought she was beautiful behind the steam table with an apron and earrings. And now she did not seem natural, to Yuen, being kind and trying to soften a harsh voice. "That's a bad joke," Yuen said.

"I'm not joking. Do I look like I'm joking, old uncle?" Here you can read it yourself if you don't believe me." She shoved the letter to him. He pushed his cereal bowl aside and flattened the letter on the table. He put his glasses on, then without touching the letter, bent over it and stared. He saw a printed seal with an eagle. The paper was very white, he noticed, and had a watermark that made another eagle. He removed his glasses and licked his teeth.

"You know I don't read American," he said.

"I know," Margie said, "Why don't you eat your breakfast and I'll tell you what the letter means; then you can get the dishes done."

Yuen nodded and did as she said. She wiped her hands on her apron and told him that the letter said that the immigrators wanted to know if he had any police record in the City of Oakland and that he was to go to the police and have his fingerprints taken. She folded the letter and ran her thumb along the creases, leaving grey marks where her fingers had touched. Yuen took the letter and unfolded it again and put on his glasses again and stared down at the piece of paper. He took a pencil and copied something he saw in the letter on a napkin. "What's this?" he asked, pointing at the napkin.

"That's a 'T'," Margie said.

"What's it mean?"

"It doesn't mean anything; it's just a 'T'."

"Did I make it right?" Yuen asked and saw Margie nod. He lost interest in his 'T' and wiped his face with the napkin. Margie was not his friend, he decided. He sighed and straightened in his seat; he was very conscious of the noises inside him, like the sounds of the night on the edge of hearing, only now, he could feel the noises, in his throat, in the muscles creaking over his shoulder blades. It ached his body to sit straight, to stretch the old skin of his shriveled neck firm and tight as he raised his head to see where he was. He had to sit straight to feel strength in his muscles now; aching slightly assuaged his fright. He thought about aching and wanting to ache. Every white muscle in his body felt raw and tender with soreness, at the base of his spine, and the muscles from his neck down to his shoulders and the hard muscles behind his armpit; he was conscious of every corner and bend in his body, and all this was inside him, private, the only form of relaxation he had. He wanted to sit back and enjoy himself, ignore the letter for a short moment. He looked to Margie. She looked away and he realized that she knew that he was frightened. He did not want her pity, her face to smile kindly for his sake, for he had always pitied her, and now he hated her and was frightened of her also because he needed her help.

She patted Yuen's shoulder and stood up and went to the foot of the stairs and called for Freddy, "You'll be late for school!" Then to the old man, "I'm going to have to tell him later, you know."

"Freddy," Yuen said, as if beginning a story-reading with the boy.

"Everyone will know sooner or later. They come and ask people questions, the immigrators," Margie said. They could hear Freddy stamping on the floor above them.

Yuen put the letter in his shirt pocket and removed his glasses and put them and the case in the tin can with the toothpicks. He went around the steam table to the dishwashing area, lit the fires under the three sinksful of water and started the electric dishwashing machine.

He put a teaspoonful of disinfectant into the washwater, then a cup of soap powder. He watched the yellow soap turn the water green and look like smoke as the green rose to the top of the water. He turned and saw Freddy sitting at the table again. "Wei, good morning, kid," he shouted, over the noise of the dishwashing machine. He waved a hand and smiled at the boy. Freddy looked up and waved back, then looked back at the breakfast his mother had just set in front of him. "Come here, Freddy, I got some money for funnybooks for you!" Yuen switched off the machine and repeated what he had said in a lower voice.

"Freddy's late for school; he has to eat and run," Margie said. She turned to Freddy and said, "Be sure you come right home from school; don't go to Chinese school today, hear?" She leaned through a space between a shelf and the steam table to see the boy, and steam bloomed up her face and looked like a beard.

"Oh boy!" Freddy said, and Yuen saw that the boy was happy.

"What did you tell him?" he asked Margie.

"That he didn't have to go to Chinese school today."

"Why? Don't you want him to be able to talk Chinese?"

"I want him to take you to the city hall this afternoon and do what that letter says," Margie said. She lifted her head back on her neck to face Yuen, and Yuen looking at her without his glasses on saw her face sitting atop the rising steam.

"I don't want a little boy to help me," he said. "You think I'm a baby? I'll call Jimmy Chan and ask him to help me. Freddy's too young to do anything for me."

Margie flickered a smile then twisted herself out from between the shelf and the steam table. "You've been watching too much television, old uncle, Chinatown's not like that any more. You can't hide there like you used to. Everything's orderly and businesslike now."

"How do you know Chinatown? I don't watch the television. And I know Chinatown. Not everybody is quitting the Chinese ways like you, you know."

"Ham and!" a waitress shouted through the door.

"Ham and!" Margie repeated. "I'm just as much Chinese as you, old uncle, but this is America!"

"What?" the waitress said, jutting her head through the kitchen door again.

"How're the eggs done?" Margie asked.

"Oh, scram'led!"

"Scram'led," Margie said and broke two eggs into a saucepan and began beating them with a large fork. "Listen, Yuen bak, I don't want to get in trouble because of you. I worked hard for this restaurant, and I gave you a job. Who else do you think would give you a job? You're too old to work anywhere else, and you'd have to join the union and learn American talk. You don't want to learn American talk? That's your business, but if you get in trouble here, I'm in trouble too. Now just do what the letter says . . ." she whipped the eggs faster, ". . . and just do what the letter says and don't make any trouble for me." She poured the eggs onto the griddle and turned her back on Yuen to fold the eggs with a spatula.

Yuen jerked his head up and straightened his back, his eyes flicking glances off and on Margie like any angry rooster. "Make trouble for you? I am in trouble!"

"And I'm trying to help you the best way I can. Now let me alone and go back to your dishes. Can't you see I'm nervous? Take the day off. I'll call the colored boy; leave me alone, will you?"

"I'm sorry," Yuen said, "I'll wash the dishes."

"I said take the day off." She quickly slid the spatula under the eggs and slapped them onto a plate. She had forgotten the bacon.

"The bacon," Yuen said.

"Freddy," Margie said, "You don't have time for your breakfast. Go take that little pie in the icebox for your teacher and go to school now."

Freddy looked to Yuen. "I'll walk you to

school," Yuen said. "Be back in time for the dinner dishes," Margie said after Yuen.

Looking down the street, they could see a shattered image of the morning sun on the lake. The grass on the shore was covered with black coots and staggering seagulls. Yuen had his glasses on and could see the trees on the other side of the lake and sailors walking with girls, and he could smell the stagnant water as he walked the other way with Freddy.

The boy watched the ground and stayed inside Yuen's shadow as they walked. Yuen glanced at the boy and saw him playing his game and knew that Freddy had forgotten last night, the waitress and the cripple. They were beyond the smell of the lake now and in the smell of water drying off the sides of washed brick buildings, and Yuen's morning was complete and almost gone. "What are you carrying?" Yuen asked.

"A pie for teacher," Freddy said.

Yuen smiled his wet smile. They stopped at the street that had the train tracks in the center. "Mommy said your hat was in the toilet."

"Do you want to go to San Francisco with me?"

"I can't. I have to go home after school."

"I mean right now. Would you like to go to San Francisco on the train right now?"

"I have to go to school."

"I'll take you to some friends and they'll give you some herbs for your stomach."

"But it doesn't hurt."

"For when it does hurt. They'll give you herbs that will make your stomach stop hurting again." Yuen put a hand on the boy's shoulder and stood in front of him. "I'll buy you a lot of funnybooks and a candy bar . . ."

There were more people on the train now than at night, and the train was dirtier in the day. They caught the train at the end of the line, near Freddy's school. As the train started, it rang its electric bell that sounded like a thousand screaming birds; they were moving noisily across Oakland towards San Francisco. Freddy had to adjust his hold of the pie when Yuen put his arm around the boy's shoulders. He was glad to have the boy with him; he was young and did not have to know what the man was doing, and he enjoyed being with the boy; that was something that he could still enjoy.

The train moved quickly, swaying its cars side to side over the tracks, and Yuen looked only once out of the window to the street full of people. He had been in Oakland for twenty years now, and he still felt uncomfortable in the streets. On the train he could sit and did not have to walk with the people. At night he did not see as many of them. He moved past quickly, out of the shadows of the tall buildings, and was moving down a street lined with low wooden houses now. He could see Negro women with scarves around their big heads, elephant hipped women with

fat legs walking slowly down the street; the train passed them, and now there were no more houses. They were in the train yards, and the train screamed its electric bell toward the bridge.

They passed broken streetcars and empty trains in the yards, and saw bits of grass growing up between the railroad ties; beyond the yards they could see the flat bay and the brown dung floating next to the shore. And they could smell the bay, dirty and thick smelling. Last night he had slept past this part of the route. "Shiyet," he said for the boy to smile, and the boy smiled. Yuen realized now what he was doing. He was trying to be brave, and knew he would fail. He felt the letter in his coat pocket without touching the letter and thought of how he would take the letter from his pocket to show Jimmy Chan.

The sounds of the wheels on the rails changed in pitch and they were on the bridge now, with shadows of steelwork skipping over their faces. They were above the bay and could see the backs of seagulls gliding parallel to them, their beaks split in answer to the electric bell. Yuen could see the birds stop and hang on the air with their wings stiff, then fall and keep falling until the bridge blocked his vision, and in his mind he counted the splashes on the bay that the seagulls made. He looked down to Freddy again and took Freddy's face in his hands and saw pie on the boy's lips. Freddy took his hand out of the paper bag and grinned. "That's bad for your stomach," Yuen said; he was too nervous to smile, he thought, then, 'No, not nervous, numb.' And suddenly, calmly, he was numb, and that was all he was; it was not pleasant or aggravating, not even lonely. The electric bell sounded and they were moving in a slow curve toward the terminal at the San Francisco end of the line.

Chinatown was very warm and the streets smelled of vegetables and snails set out in front of the shops. Among the shopping Chinese women, Yuen saw small groups of Americans with bright neckties and cameras pointing into windows and playing with flutes or toy dragons inside souvenir shops. Yuen bought Freddy some funnybooks and a small cap pistol and took him to Jimmy Chan's restaurant.

The dining room was dark with chairs stacked on top of the tables. A white jacketed busboy led them between the tables toward the office. Yuen left Freddy outside to read his funnybooks, then went inside after removing his hat.

Jimmy Chan's bow tie was very small against his thick neck, and the tie wriggled like wings when he spoke. Jimmy Chan's dog was walking all over his desk and Jimmy laughed at it when Yuen came in. "It's a chee-wah-wah," he said and asked Yuen to sit.

"How are you?" Yuen asked, "You haven't been to visit me," he said, beginning with courtesies.

"I'm busy. Going bankrupt to hell and damn."

Yuen nodded, then quickly put his hand into his coat pocket. "I got a letter from the United States," Yuen said.

"I can't help with letters from the government. I can't tamper with the government. I'm going to be naturalized next year, but people think I'm a Communist already because I got a big restaurant. I'm going bankrupt. People think I'm a smuggler. I'm not a goddamn all to hell smuggler!" All of his swearing was in English and sounded more obscene breaking the rhythm of his Chinese.

"Maybe you could read the letter?" Yuen held the letter out, and Jimmy Chan put a cigar into his mouth and took the letter. The dog walked over to Jimmy Chan's hands and sniffed, then sniffed at the letter. Yuen said, "Don't let your dog dirty the letter."

"It's a chee-wah-wah. You think I'd let my chee-wah-wah walk on my desk if it was going to dirty things up? . . . I'm sorry if I seemed short-tempered just then, uncle, but you asked with such force. You see, men with letters like this have come in before, and never, never, have they ordered me or asked me anything straight out. I was surprised. You should be in business. You should be a general!" He turned and held the letter up to the light and stared at the watermark. "Fine paper they use," he said, and patted the dog.

"I thought you could give me some advice."

"You don't want advice," Jimmy Chan said, "You want me to help you. Perform a miracle. But you said advice. I'll take you on your word and give you advice. There is no advice I can give you. Just do what the letter says. Want me to translate it? It says go to the police. Get your fingerprints made. Get your record of arrests and have the police send a copy to the government. It says it's only routine. Right here, just like this, 'I am routine.'"

"They might send me back to China."

"Not if you're all legal."

"Well, still . . ."

"Uncle, my sympathy is free. My advice too. I sympathize with you. You can't hide from them. They even have Chinese working for them; so you can't hide. I sympathize with you, but the only Chinese that get ahead are those that are professional Chinese. You didn't know that when you came here, and now you're just another Chinese person that's just stoically all Chinese and in trouble. I can't help you."

"You could write a letter for me telling them I'm all right," Yuen said. He leaned back as Jimmy Chan pushed papers to both sides with his hands and elbows.

"Uncle. I don't know you're all right. And I don't want to know. I'd like to help you; I'm grateful to your generation, but you're all anachronisms. You could have avoided all your trouble if you had realized that Americans like Chinese as novelties. Look at me. I'm happy; I like Americans. I'm becoming an American citizen, not because I want to be like Americans, but because it's good business; it makes Americans happy to think that I belong to them. Look! They like Chinese better than Negroes because we're not black; they don't like us as much as Germans or Norwegians because we're not white. They like us better than Jews because we're smaller. But! They don't like chauvinist Chinese because they remind them of the Indians. So . . ." he clapped his hands together and spread them and glanced around at his office, then adjusted his bow tie and grinned. "This is being a professional Chinese!"

"I don't like Indians," was all Yuen could say.

"But helping you would be bad for me. So I write a letter for you. I'm investigated, and then I get a letter. I don't become a citizen. Nobody likes me. Your people don't like me any more because I'm nobody and you'll say I stepped on you by trying to become a citizen and a professional Chinese. I have no friends. You see? I'm in more trouble than you."

"I'm going then, thank you," Yuen said and stood. There was no anger in his voice, and, looking at Jimmy Chan, Yuen could see that Jimmy recognized this reaction in him also.

"Listen, uncle," Jimmy said from his seat, "Don't do anything goddamn silly, if I can help with anything else, I'll be happy to do it. Want a job?"

"No," Yuen said and started to leave.

"Uncle, I trust you. I know you have a job and all that. You're respected here; I know that too." Jimmy stood and took a long time to walk around his desk to Yuen's side. He put an arm around his shoulders. "You are a wise man . . . if you die; die of old age. I feel bad when I can't help, and I feel real bad when men die." He grinned and opened the door for the old man, "But you're a wise man."

"Didn't even offer a drink," Yuen said outside with the boy.

Pigeons dropped from the sky to walk between the feet of people, and ate grains dropped from the cages of squabs and chickens in front of poultry shops. "Stupid birds," Yuen said, "Someone will catch one and eat it." He laughed and the boy laughed.

"I'm hungry," Freddy said. Yuen nodded and pointed at the pie still in Freddy's hands, then shrugged and went to eat.

As they left the restaurant, Yuen walked quickly. He held Freddy's hand and pulled him down the streets and pointed at fire escapes and told him what Tongs were there and what he had seen when he had been at parties there, and he walked over iron gratings in the sidewalk and pointed down inside and told Freddy that at night music could be heard down there; they passed men sitting next to magazine stands and shook hands. Then Yuen went to the bank and withdrew all his money in the form of a money order and borrowed a sheet of paper and an envelope, and in Chinese, wrote his son: "This is all the money I have. You will not get any more. I'm dead. Your father." He put the letter and money order in the envelope, addressed it, then went to the post office branch and mailed it. San Francisco was nothing to him now. He had said goodbye to his friends and seen the places he used to visit. They were all dirty in this daylight. The value of his death, to himself, was that nothing in his life was important; he had finished with his son and his friends and San Francisco, now he was going home. The tops of the buildings were shiny with their white tile and flags, Yuen saw. 'Jimmy Chan was wrong,' he thought, 'but he helped me start the finish. I'm a very lucky man to know when all I am to do in life is done and it's time to die. Jimmy Chan is too mercenary to know that. He doesn't know the difference between me and Huie's dead brother; that's unfortunate.' But Yuen knew himself well enough not to have to cringe or make excuses. He walked quickly down the hill, believing himself to the bus stop. Freddy had to run to keep up with him.

"What'd you take him to San Francisco for? And why'd you go, anyway? Do you know I had to wash all the dishes and cook too; that colored boy wasn't home, you know," Margie said, "You think I'm a machine or something."

"No, I'm sorry," Yuen said. Margie would not understand if he explained that he was all right now, he thought, so he did not try to explain. He smiled.

"Well, you have to hurry if you're going to get back in time for the dinner dishes. I'm sorry, ah bak, old uncle, but I'm all worried. All right?" She put a hand on his shoulder.

"All right."

Margie took the letter from Yuen's pocket and sat down at the kitchen table and looked at the letter. Yuen sat down next to her and put a toothpick in his mouth. Margie stared down at the letter and began scratching a slow circle around a breast. She talked to Freddy without looking at him. "Uncle's in trouble . . . Freddy, I mean uncle's got to go to the police and get his pictures taken. And you have to take him and help him answer questions police will ask in this letter."

"I been walk all day, mommy. I don't wanta walk no more," Freddy said, "Why don't you go?"

"What do you mean?" Her voice lifted shrill, startling Yuen. "How can I go?"

"You got a car," Freddy said, stepping backwards. "Listen," Margie said, "You take this letter . . ." she lifted the letter and pinned it with a safety pin inside Freddy's coat. "And you go to where the fingerprint place is and you tell them to read it, that the United States Immigrators want

them to read it, and that everybody like Yuen bak, huh? And you take him." She gave the boy some crackers to eat on the way and helped Yuen stand.

"Do you know how to get there?" Yuen asked at every corner. They walked streets full of rush hour traffic, walked past parking meters, a gymnasium, and Yuen put an arm about Freddy and held him. "Where are we in all this?" Yuen asked and pushed Freddy toward the edge of the sidewalk with each word.

"We got to go fast now, Yuen bak, or the police will close," the boy said.

The streets were not crowded, but everywhere on the sidewalks, along the sides of buildings Yuen saw people walking, all of their eyes staring somewhere beyond him, the pads of fat next to their stiff mouths trembling with their step. They all moved past him easily, without actually avoiding him. Yuen held the boy's hand and walked, numbing himself to the people.

The long corridor of the city hall was full of the sound of feet and shaking keys against leather-belted hips, and waxed reflections of the outside light through the door at the corridor's end, shrunk and twisted on the floor, as they walked further down, past briefcased, hatted men, nose-picking policemen, newspaper vendors with aprons. "Where do we go?" Yuen asked.

"I don't know," Freddy said, "I can't read all the doors."

In a low voice, almost as smooth as a woman's, Yuen said, "Do you see any Chinese around? Ask one, he'll help us." His hand rested on the back of Freddy's neck, and was very still there as they walked.

"Excuse me. . ." a large man said, walking into them, and they were trying to walk through each other a moment, then they were falling with the large man holding Freddy's head and shouting a grunt of excuse me's; their legs all tangled, they fell together into a soft crash. The man stood and brushed himself and said, "I'm sorry, coming out of my office, lot on my mind; you all right? Your father looks sick . . ."

"I have a letter," Freddy said and opened his jacket to show the letter pinned to the inside of the collar.

"What's this?" the man asked, bending again. "A safety pin. All you people are safety pinning each other, my god," he muttered. He took the letter and took a long grunt to stand up. Freddy turned and helped Yuen, who was still on the floor, waiting, and staring with drool over his lips up to the man. Yuen lifted himself to a crouch, rested, then stood and held Freddy.

"Immigration people want him fingerprinted," the man said, "You poor kid. Do you live under the freeway project?" He brushed his hair under his hat as he spoke. "I'll take you there. It's upstairs.

Don't worry, if things go bad, you can call me, Councilman Papagannis. I'll find you a nice foster home. Conditions must be very bad for you people under the freeway project." He adjusted his hat with his fat fingertips and walked quickly upstairs, swinging his arms after them with each step. They walked into a narrow hall with benches, and at a desk, sitting on a high stool, in front of a typewriter, his sleeves rolled sloppily over his elbows, was a police sergeant, typing. "You can wash that ink stuff off your fingers in there, through that office, you see?" he was saying as they walked up to his desk. "What do you want? You'll have to wait in line. All these men here are in a hurry to get fingerprinted, too."

"But I got a letter and supposed to tell you how people like Yuen bak, him." Freddy pulled Yuen to the desk.

"What?" the police sergeant said.

"Immigration people want him fingerprinted and photographed," Councilman Papagannis said. "Here's the letter. I'm Councilman Papagannis. I'd like to see them out of here in a hurry, you know, for the boy's sake." The Councilman shook his head and removed his tight-fitting hat.

"Says here they want a copy of his record, too," the police sergeant said.

"Well, do it!" the councilman said, stuffing himself between Yuen and the boy. The police sergeant took out a form sheet and put it in the typewriter; then he picked up the telephone and asked for the city's record on Nelson Yuen Fong. He put the telephone down and looked up to the councilman. "Never heard of him." he said.

"Nefarious," the councilman said.

The police sergeant removed Yuen's hat with a short motion of his arm, "Hair color, grey," he said and began typing. He dropped the hat onto Yuen's head.

Yuen took the hat from his head and looked inside the brim. "What for?" he asked.

"Nothing," Freddy said and took the hat and held it. Yuen watched now, his eyes wide with the lids almost folding over. This was all a fine joke for Yuen now. They were all so somber for his sake, and he had finished already. He could say anything and they would not understand, but Freddy might understand a little, and Freddy was too young to see the humor of the situation. 'Freddy should not be here,' Yuen thought, 'I'll buy him some funnybooks when we leave; he'll like that and won't feel so bad.'

Freddy yanked Yuen up to the edge of the police sergeant's desk and held his sleeve tightly. "How much do you weigh?" the police sergeant asked.

"He don't talk American," Freddy said.

"What is he?"

"He's alien," Freddy said.

"I mean, is he Filipino, Japanese, Hawaiian?"

"He's Chinese."

"Fine," the police sergeant said and typed, "Now ask him how much he weighs."

Freddy pulled at Yuen's coat until the man half knelt. Freddy's first word was in English, and Yuen frowned, then smiled. The boy stamped his foot and glared from the police sergeant to Yuen. He never knew the boy would ever hate him for not being able to speak American.

"You are how heavy?"

"What do you mean?" Yuen asked, "I can't understand you."

"You are how many pounds?"

"What's your old man say, boy?"

"We don't talk good together yet," Freddy said in English, and in slow Chinese, "You are HOW MANY POUNDS?" The boy stood straight and shouted, "How heavy the pounds?"

"Oh, how many pounds do I weigh?" Yuen grinned and nodded to the police sergeant. The police sergeant nodded and pointed at Yuen's stomach then patted his own belly. "Hundred and thirty pounds heavy," Yuen said.

"Hundred and thirty pounds," Freddy said. The police sergeant typed.

After the questions, the police sergeant stepped down from his high stool and held Yuen's arms. "Tell him we're going to take his picture now, boy." Freddy told Yuen, and Yuen asked Freddy to ask the police sergeant if he could comb his hair before being photographed. The men laughed when Freddy asked.

Freddy stepped away from Yuen and held the light blue stripe of the police sergeant's trousers. Yuen turned his head and combed his hair.

The police sergeant kicked a lever that turned Yuen's seat around. The police sergeant snapped a picture. Yuen yelled once and stared at Freddy. "Atta boy, Nelson," the police sergeant said, "Now for fingerprints." He took the frames from the camera and tapped Freddy next to the ear. "Tell him to get down now."

"Yuen bak, get down now."

They walked home with the first blue of the dark night coming. Yuen patted the boy's shoulder and kept asking him to stop and buy some funnybooks, but the boy pulled Yuen's sleeve and walked quickly, saying that he was hungry. "Come on, Yuen bak, I'm hungry," Freddy would say when the old man stopped to sit on garbage cans and nod his head at street corners. He sat as if he would sit forever, without moving his body or fixing grey hairs that the wind loosened, his head nodding slowly like a sleeping pigeon's. "Are you mad at me?"

"No," the boy said quickly.

"Your mother's waiting for us, isn't she?" he said, then stood and walked further and said, "You're a funny son. . ."

He touched the boy as he walked and muttered to himself louder as they neared the hotel restaurant.

All his old age shook in his thick-veined hands as he tried to gently touch Freddy's nose or his ears or to poke the soft of the boy's cheeks. "You're almost as tall as me. . . did you see the policeman's face when he saw me?" He stopped to look at the boy. In his slouch walk they were very close to the same height. Before he would have been disturbed to be the same height as a young boy. He took a breath and tried to straighten, then sighed; he was too tired, but that was not important. "And that chair . . ."

He walked slower as they came to the back door of the restaurant. He looked up to the light over the door with pigeon droppings on the hood. That light had gone out only once while he was here, and he had changed the light bulb himself, he remembered, and had polished the hood and wiped the bulb. It was his favorite light in the whole restaurant, perhaps because it was the light that had helped him open the door when he returned from San Francisco, or perhaps because it was the only light outside. 'It's stupid to think about a lightbulb,' he thought, but he could enjoy stupidity now, after all this time of trying to be smart.

He could hear Margie shouting the names of foods back to waitresses as if she was swearing, and could hear the sound of cold meat touching the grill, of running water, the heavy door of the tall icebox slamming. He waited to open the door and held Freddy's wrists together with one hand; then both hands were twisting Freddy's wrists. He shuddered and closed his eyes. "Help me upstairs," he said, "I don't feel well."

He leaned heavily on the boy, pushed him against the wall as they walked; the boy pushing at Yuen each stair up to his room.

In his room, Yuen sighed and fell backwards to his bed. He stared a moment to the ceiling. The boy did not leave the room. Yuen closed his eyes and pulled at his nose and wiped it with his fingers and smiled to the boy as he raised his face to stare at Freddy. He saw the boy clearly now, and the smile on his face closed, but his mouth remained open to loud breath. It no longer felt like a face, no part of him, his skin, his fingers, nothing felt like anything of his now; it all felt old and very dry and hot. "I have an idea," he said slowly, and took the gun from under his pillow. "We used to try to swallow our tongues to choke ourselves when we were scared, but we always spit them out, or couldn't get them down . . . I want you to watch so you can tell them I wanted to."

"I don't know what you're talking," the boy said, staring at the gun.

"I'm going to die myself," Yuen said in Chinese the boy would understand.

The boy stared and moved his face without speaking for a long time. "Who? You . . . what are you doing?"

"Your mother can find a dishwasher. She's a good businesswoman."

"Who'll buy books?"

Yuen pointed the gun at one ear, then switched hands and pointed the gun at the other ear. He looked at the gun and held it with both hands and pointed it at his mouth, aiming it into the mouth, toward the bulge at the back of his head. "Is that all I am to you?" He was angry at the boy now, even though he knew the boy did not know anything to say. The boy hit himself with a fist and shouted, "Yuen bak!" Freddy leaned and fell backwards, stepped once toward the old man before stopping against the towel rack. Then Freddy was weeping and groaning, holding a pain in his shoulder where he had hit.

Yuen looked over the gun and watched the boy's rhythmless stumblings in the close room. He released the hammer to safe and sighed a longer sigh than he had breath. "Can't do nothing . . ." he muttered. He went to the boy and pulled him to the bed and wiped over the boy's head with his hand. "It's all right, Freddy," Yuen worked for enough breath to speak. He bent to untie his shoes, dropping the gun to the floor when his fingers could not work the shoelaces. "Will you help me bathe? I feel . . . very weak." 'I've failed,' Yuen thought, but he had known he would, had expected it.

"Yes."

"I have soap; you can have some, if you like."

"I have soap too."

He patted the boy's shoulders with his hands and clutched into them with fingers as he pulled himself to standing. "You're a funny son," he said before turning to undress. "Help me with this."

Freddy held a towel about Yuen's pale waist as he took him out of his room to the bathroom and helped him into the tub. Freddy plugged the tub and turned on the water. Yuen eased himself lower into the water and did not complain about the temperature. He leaned forward and asked the boy to scrub his back. His body was loose over his bones, and the same color as his colorless wrists, with thick veins through the skin. He took the boy's hand and looked onto his face with eyes covered with thick moisture like the white of an egg. "You didn't write me," he said clearly, and, his body quivering, rippling water away from his waist, Yuen died. He closed his eyes with his mouth opening to the shape of a sigh, and at the end of the sigh, his chest low into the shapes of ribs, he was dead. There was no more for him; he had finished it.

Freddy took his hands from the water and put his cheek on the edge of the tub. His death had seemed so impersonal, as if he had given up the boy also. The boy tried to work his face to tears once more, as he felt he should, tears not all for Yuen, but for himself now because Yuen had been *his*.

Margie came up the stairs and walked down the hall noisily, saying, "Well, how did it go, you two?" before she leaned her head into the bathroom. ★

LUIS SYQUIA

piano lessons

my godfather
my *ninong*
professor calixto llamas
my piano teacher
quick-stoppin' ballroom
dancer - still whirling
the young & not-so-young
ladies around and around
still teaches them
new steps to keep time
and to dazzle
the eye

tito calixto
the man i used to fear
in my youth
i remember his boney
knuckles rapping
discipline into my skull
on wednesdays or saturdays
my sisters & cousins & i
would expectantly fearfully
wait for him to come
whoever was the first
brave or foolish
to take piano lessons
would report back to us
waiting/telling us
whether he was in a good
or bad mood

he looks more fragile now
like a delicate piece
of wrinkled jade
his step is still nimble
but the insistence of age
has made it slower
i see him sometimes
grippin a brown shopping bag
full of discount groceries
thin white hair
wizened eyes
cackling laugh
his back starting
to stoop like a comma

he's a smart old man, though
saved up enough coin to go
round the world again -whirling
whirling around and around

unmarried
my mom said that his
sweetheart broke his heart
long time ago back
in the islands
still he plays piano, travels
dances
laughing laughing

tito calixto
eighty-four yrs. old
my mom told me the
other day tito calixto
just became a u.s. citizen
—and got mugged
on his way home

SECOND CITY FLAT

BY MOMOKO IKO

*Radio, olive oil, vanilla, cigarettes, radio, olive oil, vanilla, shades.....*Outside the bathroom in the hall about to enter and cut across the living room to the closet kitchen or about to return to the bathroom to drape a towel around her naked body first, Mazie Murakami stood, a picture of indecisiveness. Her decision, taken, sent her into a rhapsody of efficiency.

In the kitchen, she grabbed bottles of oil and vanilla. In the living room, crouching along the wall and rising suddenly to pull down the shades, she managed to check the ashtrays for all dead butts and grab cigarettes, matches, turn up the radio and run back to the bathroom. *What do I need a towel for? It would have just gotten in the way, slipping down all the time.*

She closed the door behind her. Overpowered by the fumes of cheap paint coming off the sweaty walls and trapped in the steam cloud which was the room, she sat down on the floor, examined her dirty toe, and talked herself into a first-rate pedicure. *One of these days.* She opened the door a crack and feeling no change in the atmosphere, swung it wide open and scooted her ass over the door hump onto the rug in the hall. She put her hands under her breasts and felt the light weight of them against her palms and shrugged in disgust and what she considered Oriental stoic resignation. Her wandering around the apartment naked was not immodest, she thought, but practical. As she had no breasts to speak of, it was ridiculous to try to hang a towel off them. *Hitch it up. Hitch it up.* She stuck her head into the bathroom and retrieved her cigarettes. Deciding that she would rather listen to a record, she went into the living room and scanned the aluminum stand's listings. Jefferson Airplane, Miles Davis and Segovia. Taken singly, she didn't want to listen to any of them but together, the thought of them soothed her. She arranged them on the turnstile and

turning up the volume, switched off the radio and went back into the bathroom. The steam had settled into the walls or evaporated. At any rate, gone. She began to prepare her tub.

Small globs of oil fanning out into round flat slicks laced with a spiral-drop of faint brown. The penetrating intoxication of the vanilla hits the sinuses, each addition to the water carefully placed and watched for effect.

Holding the sides of the tub, she slid her body slowly into the pricking of sudden heat. Deep in the water, her head and hands and arms buoying on top of the water, already her mind began to swoon. Remembering other times when the fumes and hot water made her pass out, she looked toward the door and seeing it open, began to cry. Then, there was always someone around to pull her out. Her mind, the headless chicken, squawked and ran in circles looking for its head. *We're softer than them.* She meant the Japanese. *Passing out from hot baths. That's stupid. In Japan, Japan changes; in America, it remains the same. We're tougher than they are. Still.....there's no one around. Scurrying . . . scurry, scurry chick find your head.....first you see small*

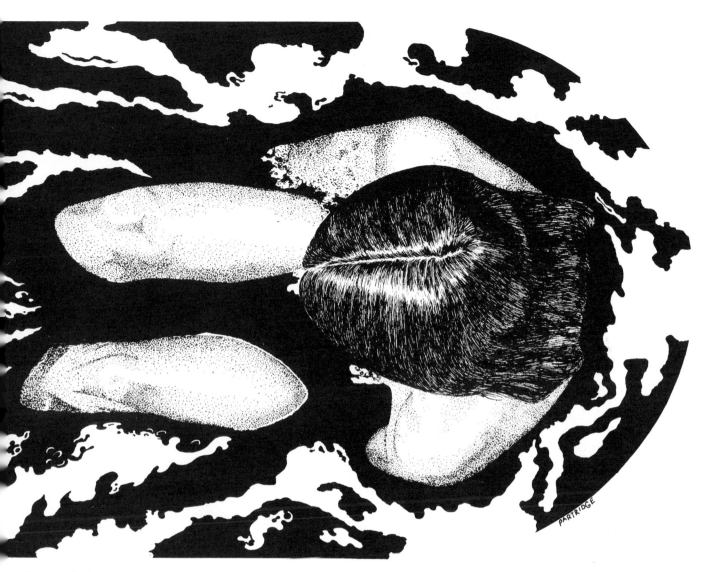

glowing lights and then pretty soon the lights begin to flash, off on off on in slow motion, then in colors, first black and then dull gold and then both colors glowing out from the other, luminous around the edges and then you have to get out fast and not have to fumble with a locked door and get out fast before you pass out and drown. She took precautions. She left the door wide open.

She leaned back against the slope of the tub and putting the washcloth on her breast dipped further into the water and watched it flow away. She got out of the tub and tying a towel around her body, went to the living room and opened all the windows and pulled down the shades again and returned to the tub, leaving wet high-arched tracks and a steady drip line. In the tub, she shivered against the goose-bumps and the awake mind. Now she could think, which was what the entire preparation was for, *wasn't it.* What was a ritualized bath but a clean start to begin thinking from the beginning of something instead of from the middle of some muddle which was where she was at before the bath.

Furo. Furo: a bath. Furo: perpetual youth.

Furo: wandering, vagrancy. Furo: wind and waves. Furo: sealing wax. Hot soaking baths served Mazie Murakami somewhat like churches or drugs served others and she used them as badly. She never managed any thinking in them, but she thought she did, she had such fine intentions, but once in the lulling half-dream world of steam and pungent smell, she was sedated not cleansed. Although she was no better able to think clearly, the sedation did have its effect, she wasn't quite as upset that her possible pregnancy would blow the totality of her cover; that is, her illusions about herself. She did a stupid thing. *Stupid!* She got lonely one night and went out to do something about her loneliness. She should have stayed home and read a book like her mother would have done. *What do you do when you get lonely ma? Read a book. Think. Think. Damn it, think!*

"DAMN IT! THINK!" she yelled at the walls, angry at the walls for sweating, angry at the walls for their odor of cheap paint, angry at the room for making the paint, olive oil and vanilla smell suddenly nauseating.

She had gone to the bar she liked and was sitting

illustration by SUZANNE PARTRIDGE   527

there drinking her second brandy and beginning to feel better with the liquid, such exquisite dark topaz warmth trailing down her body in such nice slow wavy lines, and looking around at the other customers talking soft and making the small room close and friendly when she noticed this misplaced white guy making an ass out of himself because he felt so misplaced. He started mumbling and grumbling and the people around him politely pulled away from him which made him mutter some more and she didn't like him ruining her nice night.

She said: Either talk real loud or shut up! That way no one will notice you.

And he was grateful. He was young and had been trying to get her attention because she was the only other young person in the place, the only one he was sure had even a chance at understanding him. That was how lonely she was, she didn't even laugh when he made his statement.

That's how it is, isn't it? You feel mean and so you talk mean and someone gets grateful and then you, guilty or embarrassed, give an inch.....and He came up to the bar and began talking, spilling out the edges of his problem and she went back to the booth with him and found out how very much they had in common. Neither of them could succeed at something important. A bond. His trouble he said was that he was a North Shore boy who lived in Old Town trying hard not to be a North Shore boy and getting fucked up in the process. Not succeeding at all. And tonight he had been not succeeding so badly that he jumped into his Morgan and started driving and landed up in this bar in Chinatown where they found each other. They had a bond, almost a divine revelation. And now she might be pregnant by that son of a bitch. She went back to his apartment and got stoned and made out. Or made out and got stoned. Soon and sudden, she woke up. It was daylight and you could hear people moving on the other side of those high windows. She looked at the expensive mess around her, the expensive mess of tape deck, stereo, signs: Mother Goose is a Racist/ Snow White Sucks / Take a Pig to Lunch / Better Yet, Eat him! / Caution! You Are What You eat! / masonry, objects of foreign cultures sticking off shelves, standing on benches, hanging off the ceiling, embedded in niches and she got sick. She looked at the young man whose face already had the markings of an old wrinkled petulant baby and got sicker. She looked in the mirror at her own face and got the sickest. And scared. Scared for herself. She left him asleep and swore and muttered at the C.T.A. bus driver: Drive! Drive, will ya, and felt shivery all the way home. The she didn't think about it anymore until today when right out of the blue, Chicken Little's piece of sky, she thought, Jesus, could I be pregnant?

The thought was so funny that she laughed loud and unabashed until she realized that pregnancy,

having nothing to do with your feelings, was possible. Then she got depressed and made preparations for the hot tub because friends or nice chats with yourself. *When did I get my last one? Why can't you be regular?* didn't help.

She watched the pubic hair washing against the current of hand movements. *Jesus, do you have to have a timetable even for the monthly crud. When it comes, it comes. You're so dumb. Even now. I was so lonely.* And she cried for herself. Her lack of organization angered her. *Mama was disorganized too. Who said the older a girl gets the more she becomes her mother. Who said that stupid thing! Now that you're dead, you're winning every battle. Who can fight the dead. One good thing about crying in the tub is you can't tell the tears from the washwater and it all goes down the drain.*

The air in the room stung her nostrils. She opened her mouth like a fish and grabbed gulps of air. She felt dizzy. She got out of the tub and sat on the floor resting her head against her ankles and when the lightheadness steadied, she returned to the tub. Her tenseness was still, so to speak, secured and if it didn't go away she could see herself in the morning baking cakes and brownies and tubs of spaghetti sauce, beans in a frenzy of controlled nerves. *Beans: red beans, pinto beans, navy beans, great northern white beans, black-eyed peas. Didn't even know dry beans existed until . . . Did everything start with that now?*

One Sunday evening, two Japanese films, one papa and one mama catch a late empty No. 36 Broadway Bus and get off and start to cross the street and then: Dead. They are dead. A car driven by a drunk. Just like that. Her father killed outright, her mother in a three-bed hospital room. You go and you don't even know you're in shock and you tell yourself to be brave because you're in shock and you don't quite grasp that one is dead and the other is dying. And you try to be brave because you are absolutely certain that their lives depend on your bravery and you don't even understand what "one already dead and one dying" means.

I could make some stroghanoff. How much hamburger do I have? They wouldn't let me run on like this. Read a book, go to sleep, take a walk, cry.

But they are dead. And she is free. What she always wanted. *Marvelous!*

Instead a hand holds you around the neck and it grabs tighter and harder but never tight enough and you suddenly realize that you are the one who is being comforted, that your life depends on someone else's bravery. You are the one someone is trying to keep alive, *Maeko. Maeko, Maeko, Maeko, Maechan, Maechan,* and the thought you have: Why can't she think of something else to say. A faint and loud and wavering name chanted until its meaning is gone and a hand that no longer can grasp or hold anything tightly must take the place of everything.

EVERYTHING.

Her mother's hands were soft and fat and flaccid and strong and her mother's arms were strong and it seemed to Mazie then that her mother through that one arm and hand and fingers was trying to transfer to her all the strength the rest of the useless body still stored and that she was doing this because she feared that her daughter, too much the lazy day-dreamer, lacked the *"gaman"* necessary to survive intact. She thought that then but now she wasn't sure. Maybe her mother, dying, decided for once to think about herself first and was holding on the closest life near her. And before her brother vacationing in New York or her sister in Washington could get to Chicago, Mama was dead too. *And Mazie was free: Don't cry Mazie. I'm not crying. Water, that junk is just water. And fight them back: Cry Mazie. It's better to cry. Get it over with. But you don't cry brother. We can't all be crying at the same time.*

Mazie's sister who came from the farm to the city and learned like the whole family to love tall buildings and the high beating pulse of streets and adult pleasures married a farmer and went back to the farm. Once she told Mazie: Get cultured, Maz, then if you're lucky, you'll marry a farmer. Now she came back to the city to bury a mother and a father. She saw two bodies encased in swirls of stiffened white satin, the heads propped on hard quilted pillows, the faces, last personal and touchable but hard to touch, reminders of two lives and she screamed and swore up and down that those people were not her mother and father and Mazie wanted to hit her. Hit her hard so that she would shut up. But she didn't.

Gaman Mama? See what you can teach me dead you couldn't teach me alive. And who needs it?

A woman who said once, if we didn't go into camp, we'd still be living on the horrible farm, needed it. The eternal fatalistic Oriental needed it, but not Mazie. Still she didn't hit her sister and felt herself being brave and experienced the light touch of ruthlessness that goes along with being brave. The heat of the volcano was contained and the churn denied, and that took ruthlessness.

"That is mama and that is papa and nothing you say will change that. Look at them! See. Mama, and she's dead. He's dead too. See him. He's dead too. Do you understand, dead!" Her sister seemed to understand and calmed down but Mazie didn't understand at all. What she could say and what she understood being so different. Still she told herself the same things: Those things there in those coffins there with aluminum bronze-painted flowers and on those hard pillows there, those things there with their powdered leather faces are Mama and Papa and they are dead. But she didn't understand. She was being the daughter her mother would have wanted, dutiful, sad but dutiful but she couldn't really accept. This is all stupid, making that sneak, Death, look dignified.

Still the faces looked serene and she couldn't give all the credit to the mortician and she put her arm around her sister and held her tight and was held tight and held on tight and they cried together. And there was comfort in that. Mazie didn't believe there could be any until then.

"You're right. That's not them. I don't know what's them anymore but that's not them. That's just some mortician's trick." And it didn't matter any more that the two of them cried for different reasons.

Most of the time, their brother stood around being a man and oddly there was nothing ludicrous about the stance. Mazie and her sister wanted to comfort him but they didn't know how. Being the oldest and the brother, what he gained in respect, he lost in the openness of affection and feeling shown by him. They didn't know how to show him their care without embarrassing him and they couldn't embarrass him. He wouldn't like that. He stood there, being the anchor to a flimsy family boat whose sails were wind-bitten and whose hull floated dreamless on the water.

Still crisis sometimes does destroy the long weaved fabric of day to day existence so that before the visitation began, before the undertaker put out cookies and tea and coffee, her brother pulled each of them into his arms and hugged them tight and although nothing was said, the three managed to be merrier than the other mourners. None of them fell apart; the hug demanded and confirmed their collective self-possession.

And the visitation went smoothly.

Mazie was surprised. People cried and talked about the Cubs and work, and church affairs and after three cups of coffee, their stomachs growled and they excused themselves and went home or to the bathroom and none of it bothered her. All of it made it easier. Mourning could be both a public and yet very private act. She spent most of her time checking the supply of cream and sugar and coffee and tea and cookies and napkins and folding chairs and tried not to talk to anyone and when she saw someone about to cry, she ran away and brought them a cup of tea or a cookie. She realized that the visitation was supposed to be like church, a reason for people getting together and found that she didn't resent it at all. Which surprised her. She found herself drinking coffee and found out that drinking coffee was a wonderful way to deny the terrible voids. Voids weren't, as she once thought, the one frightening lure that made you take the big plunge into dark fear in spite of yourself; voids were neuters and only pleasantries and coffee, tea and cookies erased them. The dark was real but voids were, voids.

Once she wished she were Irish. Liquor would be even better than coffee, tea or cookies, you could let go and deny everything the next morning.

Either you came together and laid out the dead on clean sheets in their own beds and keened for your loss or you kept everyone from you and kept yourself intact for the terrifying private moment. With the first impossible without forewarning and planning, the second worked best if you were numb.

Mazie was lucky, she was numb. She didn't feel grief, and displays of it neither upset her nor comforted her; sometimes she felt irritation. Only when she saw her brother or sister in the crowd talking to a friend and then suddenly take on the sudden posture that meant they were about to break down momentarily did she become aware of her own pain, of her own bitter anger. Only then did she try to comfort, but then the pain, so nebulous and unrooted, vanished and with it, her care for the pain of others.

And there her brother stood, forgetting he was the anchor and becoming a floating dreaming boat all alone in the ocean.

Mazie's sister did well throughout the visitation. Nobody there knew that she could scream. She smiled when friends smiled, cried when they got maudlin, gossiped and complained about the yield of the crops and price on a ton of sugar beets and drank coffee and smoked cigarettes and ate cookies and never let on in the slightest how well she could scream. Going to the visitation, her brother asked her sister if she could control herself and her sister told her brother that she wouldn't know until they got there and the people started coming but she did beautifully. Mazie was very proud of her sister and luckier, because she couldn't feel anything.

When the last of the viewers left, Mazie's brother and sister stood at the coffins and after awhile, she said to him: Did I do all right? and he said to her: You didn't do too bad and then they put their arms around each other's waist. Mazie loved them then and she envied them their ease with each other. She saw them clearly then as she had never seen them. He was once a minor god turned into a salted pillar for a minor infraction of law and now was lucky not to be blown or washed away and she was the green willow, however human her form, displaying now the tenacity of any well-rooted life. Side by side, making their own private peace with the eruption that would change their lives; even in their pain, for that moment, they were at ease with the world. It was as if they were taking communion with the spirits of the bodies lying in front of them and household gods surrounded and gave to them an aura of gentle touch and soft peace and as she saw that, she was released from her envy of them. For what comforted them could not comfort her. And she understood that.

The funeral was short and went off even better than the visitation. It was anticlimatic. Numb at the visitation, she steeled herself for the funeral and discovered that there was no necessity. She stared at the two closed coffins and listened to the latecomers fill up the pews as quietly as possible and knowing that some irreducible life was confined in the metal boxes, the entire time she watched as if for some magician's trick that would allow the coffins to open and her parent to sit up, chagrined and puzzled by the proceedings, step out of and down from hard quilted pillows and trudge up the aisle, bowing shyly and hesitantly to their guests and out on the street, making their way through the baseball crowds and cars and trucks and buses and bikes, say to each other: What do you think that was all about? They would shrug and talk about doing something about the roaches, and as they pottered down the street under the faint glow of dying sun, think of dinner. Mazie listened to the lilt and drone of a foreign language and found it most real of the two in the caskets, who had wanted their American dream but didn't know how to go about getting it and not knowing, their ignorance an island of safety, were able to the end to believe in it. The service went on: Ecclesiastes 3: 1-8. More acceptance.

Two days later, it was all over. Before cremation, each mourner in the small chapel got up, took the blossom given him by the mortician, a mum bud or a rose and placed it somewhere on one of the corpses. The members of the family were given two blooms each. Death was paid off with sweet smells and faces were haloed with flowers and short prayers and silence were given for the living.

Mazie's sister went back to the farm. Her brother, the wild freedom shriveled by concentration camp and castration of father and fear of his own unmanned future, left Chicago and went further East to New York. 37 and free of the past, unmarried and free of the past, no obligation or duty or shame, finally an American, he ran East out of despair, a freedom come too late and unwanted, already shaping a more devastating prison.

And Mazie moved to Chinatown. *Remember mama that nice new kitchen I was going to buy for you. Your dream. Remember how you said: My dream is a nice new kitchen without any roaches and you getting yourself a good future with a good husband and I will die happy. Didn't die happy, did you ma? You want to die miserable, go ahead! You've got to give me time. It isn't fair otherwise. Don't die. Please don't die. Live! Damn it, live! The smell of the singed dead meat is contained in a hot tunnel and all you are supposed to remember are the flowers and a nimbus about the face while the body yields to high licking flames like the submissive wife, wooden and dead and soon only the bones and if you believe in them, the household gods, remain. It's a clean death if you can accept it.*

The knocking on the door went on a long time before Mazie heard it. ★

The Boatmen
on
Toneh River

WAKAKO YAMAUCHI

Kimi Sumida knew the end was near. The bed she'd lived in for many months now ceased to resist the bony protuberances of her body and prolonged attitudes of discomfort reached a stage of stone-like numbness. The cancer that ate at her lungs had no more on which to feed.

Where once the long day steadily, slowly, inexorably moved into night, now darkness descended without warning—dark and light, dark and light, and dreams, always dreams. Sometimes daylight and reality seemed just beyond a door of pain—now near, now distant—on the other side of pain. "Mari, do I have to remind a 7-year-old every day to brush her teeth? What will your teacher say?" "Give me time, Daddy, you never give me enough time." "Shshsh. Not so loud." "Mommy still sleeping?" "Shshsh . . ." Like a stone at the bottom of the sea, Kimi lay on the ocean floor and the tide flowed over her. "Ryo! Mari! Me: wife and mother! Do you not need me?" Did she cry out?

The door opened and a thin light poured into the room with Ryo. A warped sandwich on the night stand indicated to Kimi it was still day—late afternoon.

"How do you feel now, dear?"

Did I feel worse before? How long before? His mien is one of enormous cheer: he has on his cheer face. What happened to your other face, Ryo, the one that mirrors your heart? Did you discard it along with hope for my recovery? Honor me with a little honesty, the reality of my disease. Despair a little; feel free to despair a little with me. This is the time to be yourself. I hear the things you tell Mari: that I am going away; that we will all meet again some day; that this is not the time of sorrow; that flowers are sometimes broken in the bud, or plucked in bloom, or sometimes mature to seed and fruition and seed again. Are these words to take the edge off the rawness of death, or do you really believe, or do you only wish to believe. But you haven't known this desperate reluctance to leave life—you don't know the terror of the things I face. You don't even see me any more; you turn your back while the doctor presses, turns, and probes me like a vegetable, and mutters, "Comatose; can't see what keeps her here."

Once you looked at me with eyes soft and tender; eyes dull with desire. Now only this cheer. You won't acknowledge me. I'm the woman who moved you through many dark streets hurrying, rushing to meet me; the woman who brought words and unspoken dreams from your lips; I'm the woman who brought the fire to your loins. I'm the one! Wasted now; my hair is too black against the fearful pallor of my skin. Do I frighten you? Do you drop your cheerful mask in alarm when you close my door? Do you keep my Mari from me to protect her from the horror of seeing me? Are you afraid I will sear the color from her warm lips, sow seeds of my disease in her tender body? But she's mine. Mine. And I have the right to insist she share my experience, just as, yes, just as my mother had shared hers with me. And she will no doubt travel the lonely channels I've charted; paths like the narrow canals on my cracked ceiling that angle off here, stop abruptly there, by-ways I've come to know as well as I know the palm of my hand. I'm at one of those dead ends now.

The door closed but the light remained and turned blood-red with pain. Slowly the red tide subsided and throbbing with the beat of her pulse, Kimi heard her own mother's voice call: "Kimi, Kimi . . ." Warm, a mother's voice. She opened her eyes.

This is the country kitchen of my childhood: furniture of raw unfinished wood, bare floors, sweaters on pegs, grey dishcloths drying on the sink rim, cosmic dust slowly sifting. And beyond the windows, the stretch of desert, broken nearby with rows of furrowed earth. All there. Am I mother or am I the child; am I the caller or the called?

"Kimi, go fix the bath for Father. He'll be back from the fields and will want his bath."

"Not now, Mother, I'll be back soon, and I will do it then."

"Now. Now. Every evening you go off when I need you. What's in this compulsion to commune with this nothing land. I need your help here; do you think this wild desert changes a whit for your walking through a piece of it? Stay here and use the strength God gave you where it'd do some good. Make the bath."

My Kimi, where do you go; what do you dream? Fancy clothes? Glittering lights? Love? There're none of these here. I was seventeen, the caress of my mother's fingers still warm in my hair, when they married me to a stranger from the next province. He must have a young healthy woman to help him in America, they said; and soon I would return, a rich, proud, honored lady. I looked forward to this promise in dewy-eyed innocence—unaware, unaware of even the conjugal night that lay before me. The years have devoured me with work and poverty and anxieties: early frost, fluctuating market, price of rice—what chance had love? They told me with this black mole on my ear lobe, I couldn't fail, a black mole on the ear lobe is a sure sign of fame and fortune, they said. I waited for this fortune; worked and waited and when finally my time was up, I counted my fortune. Fifty years of living and what was there to show? The worn-out place in my mattress, the tear stains on my pillow. Ten thousand nights I lay there remembering my Japan; clear lakes, lonely shrines, the lyric of flowering cherry trees, street vendors' calls, plaintive and sweet as a mother's lullabyes, the sound of a flute on a summer evening. I spent a lifetime waiting to return to these. I thought my happiness was bound to these. I reached too far for what was always here, in the dust, in the sunrise, in the sunset, in you.

"Kimi, make the bath."

"Yes, I'll do it now."

I'm going now to heat the bath with sage that you and I gathered and spread out to dry in early summer. It will shoot up in crackling flames and tiny sparks and I'll think of your fireflies in Japan. Though you may not believe it, I've found something here in this arid desert that is gentle and sweet too. I want to ask you about it, but to put it to words or

illustration by GLEN IWASAKI

to your critical eye may be to profane it. And now the tall summer reeds bend in the wind, cicadas hum, shadows lengthen, cottonwood leaves catch the last flutter of sunlight, and the lad who peddles down the warm dusty road each evening at this time is passing by, and I am not there. I shall not see the wind move through his black hair, and touch his smooth brown cheeks and fill his blouse with air. I want to be as close to him as that wind. Where he comes from, where he peddles to, I don't know; but when I watch him, I see west winds in the sage, I see tumbleweeds lope across the prairie, and primrose petals fall, and I am moved. From my hiding place in the reeds, I watch him scan the horizon, and I wonder if he looks for me. Does he watch for me? Does he yearn for me?

Kimi, how extravangantly you dream; what disenchantment you court. What loneliness you will know.

The room was dark and cold. Night had come; the sandwich on the night stand had been removed and a covered tray replaced it. This is Ryo's acknowledgement of me, Kimi thought; ashes of dreams he prepares for me. I am still here.

"Still here! Kimi, drat it! I tell you, put the dog out. He's still here!"

Three days of steady rain now; one more day and the tiny seedlings that last week pushed their tender shoots from the over-worked earth will rot. The kitchen is dank and murky with smoke from Bull Durhams and the smell of *sake* warming on the coal-oil stove. The patriarch sits at the table with Mr. Nagata, one of a legion of shifting rootless men who follows crops along the length of California. They sip the warm rice wine and talk, tugging exaggeratedly at one another's sleeve. They laugh; they sing half-remembered songs.

"Kimi, I tell you, put the dog out! If there's anything that annoys me, it's the smell of a wet dog. I've got troubles enough without that. The stench comes from the floor like something stepped on in the dark. Eh *Nagata-kun?* Heh, heh. What a life, eh? Heh, heh.

Yah, those seedlings. A month's work destroyed. You sow one more row before sundown, pull one more weed before nightfall, for what? Rain, more seeding, more weeding. Don't look at me like that, Kimi; I didn't order this rain. I didn't ask for this kind of life. What would you have me do? Run out and stop the rain with my bare hands? I can't change the shape of fate. I know. I tried. I left my native shore to tread these "gold-paved" streets, heh, heh; to live and die, unseen, among aliens. And I've found when it rains there's nothing to do but jump into bed and pull the covers over your head, or find a friend and drink a little wine, sing a few songs, and explore those feelings you've forgotten you'd had; so remote, so beautiful, so fragile they are. And then you can pull out your *koto* (chin-chiri-rin) and

close your eyes and leave this soggy life-style. Heh, heh. What would you have me do?

The smell of a wet dog isn't bad. There's hardly any smell sadder than the smell of *sake* and rain together. I read in school books where fathers return from work and kiss their wives and toss their children in the air, their pockets bulging with candies and balloons, and the smell of supper cooking on the range permeates the air. I'd like that. Warm smells and good sounds. Here rain drums on the tar-paper roof, and you and your crony sit and drink and you close your eyes and with this expression of tender sorrow, you pluck your imaginary *koto*, brown hands moving on the air; thick fingers touching phantom strings (chin-chiri-rin).

I am a dying reed by the river bed
As thou, a drying dying reed
Alas, our lives together lie,
Blossomless, on the river bed.

Whether we live, or whether we die
Tides will ebb and flow
Come then, thou with me, to dwell
As boatmen Toneh River.

Now you come to me. You come to haunt me as I had never permitted you to do when I was stronger. Sly old man. You waited until there was only a membrane between you and me. Is there still unfinished business? What do you want to tell me? That you are me and I am you and today is the same as yesterday, and tomorrow will be the same as today? I thought I could change the pattern of my life; I thought I could deny your existence, deny our lonely past together, but alas, I had preserved it carefully and when all the frills and furbelows are stripped away, you are here, the backbone of my life, the bleached hull of my shipwreck. And here between yesterday and today, I sing the same lonely song as you. I should not have denied you; I should have woven my life within the framework of our past. I should have loved you. Now my guilt comes home to me.

It's all right, Kimi. The pattern doesn't change, and the guilt doesn't change. It's too late now; too late for might-have-been and would-have-liked. Give yourself to the tide, give yourself to the river; the sun is setting, the desert is cooling. . . .

Kimi.

A nebulous anticipation filled Kimi's bowels as she drifted to a cold dimension. She surrendered to the chill that enveloped her, her lips twisted in a pain akin to joy as she moved with a wind that carried her out, back to the country road, and against the smooth brown cheeks of a lad on a bicycle, and into the blouse that billowed behind him. ★

533

LIN JOHN

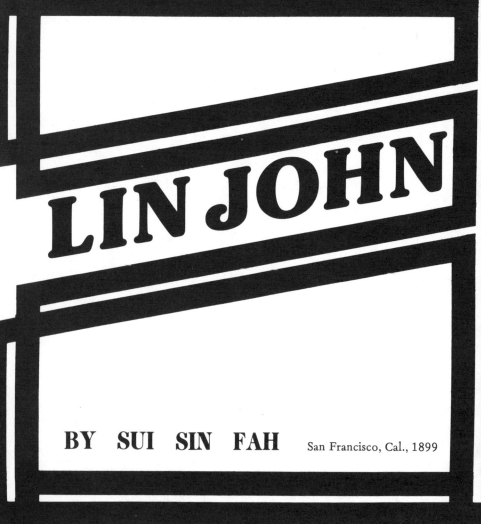

BY SUI SIN FAH   San Francisco, Cal., 1899

It was New Year's eve. Lin John mused over the brightly burning fire. Through the beams of the roof the stars shone; far away in the deep night sky they shone down upon him, and he felt their beauty, though he had no words for it. The long braid which was wound around his head lazily uncoiled and fell down his back; his smooth young face was placid and content. Lin John was at peace with the world. Within one of his blouse sleeves lay a small bag of gold, the accumulated earnings of three years; and that gold was to release his only sister from a humiliating and secret bondage. A sense of duty done led him to dream of the To-Come. What a fortunate fellow he was to have been able to obtain profitable work, and within three years to have saved four hundred dollars! In the next three years, he might be able to establish a little business and send his sister to their parents in China, to live like an honest woman. The sharp edges of his life were forgotten in the drowsy warmth and the world faded into dreamland.

The latch was softly lifted; with stealthy step a woman approached the boy and knelt beside him. By the flickering gleam of the dying fire she found that

for which she searched, and hiding it in her breast swiftly and noiselessly withdrew.

Lin John arose. His spirits were light—and so were his sleeves. He reached for his bowl of rice, then set it down, and suddenly his chopsticks clattered on the floor. With hands thrust into his blouse he felt for what was not there. He uttered a low cry and his face became old and grey.

A large apartment richly carpeted, furniture of dark and valuable wood artistically carved, ceiling decorated with beautiful Chinese ornaments and gold incense-burners; walls hung from top to bottom with long bamboo panels covered with silk, on which were printed Chinese characters; tropical plants, on stands; heavy curtains draped over windows. This, in the heart of Chinatown. And in the midst of these surroundings, a girl dressed in a robe of dark blue silk worn over a full skirt richly embroidered. The sleeves fell over hands glittering with rings, and shoes of light silk were on her feet. Her hair was ornamented with flowers made of jewels; she wore three or four pair of bracelets; her earrings were over an inch long,

enormous things of gold and three gaudy stones.

The girl was fair to see, in that her face was smooth and plump, eyes large and dark, mouth small and round, hair of jetty hue and figure petite and graceful.

Hanging over a chair by her side was a sealskin sacque, such as is worn by fashionable American ladies. The girl eyed it admiringly and every few minutes stroked the soft hair with caressing fingers.

"E-Sang," she called. A curtain was pushed aside and a short, heavy Chinese woman in blue cotton blouse and trousers stood revealed.

"Look," said the beauty. "I have a cloak like the American ladies. Is it not fine?"

E-Sang nodded. "I wonder at Moy Loy," said she. "He is not in favor with the Gambling Cash Tiger and is losing money."

"Moy Loy did not give it to me. I bought it myself."

"But from whom did you get the money?"

"If I let out a secret, will you lock it up?"

E-Sang smiled grimly and her companion sidling closer to her, said: "I took the money from my brother—it was my money; for years he has been working to make it for me, and last week he told me that he had saved four hundred dollars to pay it to Moy Loy, so that I might be free from him. Now, what do I want to be free for? To be poor; to have no one to buy me good dinners and pretty things—to be gay no more? Lin John meant well, but he knows little. As to me, I wanted a sealskin sacque like the fine American ladies. So two moons gone by I stole away to the country and found him asleep. I did not awaken him—and for the first day of the New Year I had this cloak. See?"

"Heaven frowns on me," said Lin John sadly, speaking to Moy Loy; "I made the money with which to redeem my sister and I have lost it. I grieve, and I would have you say to her that, for her sake, I will engage myself laboriously and conform to virtue till three more New Years have grown old, and that though I merit blame for my carelessness, yet I am faithful unto her."

And with his spade over his shoulder he shuffled away from a house, from an upper window of which a woman looked down and under her breath called "Fool!" ★

illustration by GLEN IWASAKI

EMILY CACHAPERO

miss philippine islands

miss PI at the miss universe contest
has highways across
her body
everyone at the show
has a map
and those men
un-fresh from nam
know the map
by heart
wearing their navy caps
at the same slanted angle
as an asian cunt
is supposed to be
waiting for miss PI
to parade
in a thigh high slitted
cheong-sam
even though
she's not chinese
waiting for a peek
she has highways
across her body
but bypasses isabella
she hides it
under that still ratted hair
trying to muffle the sound
of ating tao
cebu and leyte
her breasts
surrender time and time again
to the slightest touch
just like in the war
she has highways across her body
and mindanao
muslim land
moro land
is under the fold in her belly
it's a secret
kept between the thighs
miss PI at the miss universe contest
knows who the winner is
even though she doesn't like
the answer
because the winner is
the winner is
the winner is
the loser.

LAURA TOKUNAGA

Geography

it doesn't matter
what I hear inside
  that ocean sound
  is traffic.

when I close my eyes
I see dinosaurs
feathered serpents
burning in the air.
they scorch my ribcage black
  bones crumbling
  into ash
and I feel no pain.
smoke twists round my heart
floating in darkness
mingles
  white dust
  the moon
giant lizards.

here inside
that traffic sound
could be the ocean.

when I open my eyes
I see all the things
our hands have made
and unmade.
  buildings with mirror faces
  and windows you can't open
  or close
  broken bottles
  kicked into dry weeds
  around parking meters
  shining like dinosaur eyes
  in the sun.
the sky is blue
it's always noon

I can see we're held together
with telephone wire
and postage stamps.
impossible to pretend no distance
between inside and outside
much less
inside and inside.

stretch out your arms
  try to trace blue rivers
  from source to finish.
if you can
you do better than
  I
    never could say
    where they begin or end
  where they meet as one.

Tiger Year

new moon,
  you lie
in shadow--
traveling over the face
of silent water

as planets circle in the gathering dark
like pale insects
around the opened throats of flowers.

see how the stars are blossoming
one by one:
as if merely to breathe.

they blossom for you,
defining your way
through the clear night air
with hands as pure and bright as clouds.

will you hurry to my season?
it is time:
you bring the light.

LONNY KANEKO

Rooms

I

The old woman lay on an elevated shelf
and held court between my father
and herself. Her mother-tongued syllabic
nonsense overfilled that room stuffed already with
packing cases, stiff chairs, and steamer trunks,
and echoes even now between my ears.

I was caught in her maze of incense,
unwashed sheets, and mildewed age, hung
like a pendulum above streets
thirsting with sweating Eskimos.

II

I brace against the August wind;
movements forward come roaring back:
the hollow horsemen, their drawn swords
gleaming like black hair flowing in the wind,
their teeth yellow in the light of deep alleys.

They ride the crossroads of conception and sixty
and raise an incensed silken air
that settles into my clothes.

III

My father hangs between dignity and dust,
a rice paper collage of canneries and saloons
in Juneau and Ketchican,
and laundries of Peking and Yokohama,
the barbed wire of Minidoka,
The boredom of nights spent in lobbies of decrepit hotels.

I saw him wrinkle in fields alive with chrysanthemums.
In his dreams he still hangs on lines of conveyor belts
in rooms steaming with feathers and heads.
He is ragged at the edges, tearing apart at the seams.

IV

Dignity can rise from dust,
but not of its own accord.

The caterpillar cries for its own crooked flight.
The struggle outward weaves
its mottled shadow.
Moth dust clings to shattered glass.

The old woman is dead now ten years.
Park grass replaces the sagging duplex.
The wooden school stands empty as a skull.
Urban renewal and concrete slab
retirement homes line our treeless streets.

We steady ourselves
beneath a swinging, syllabic sun.
Our smiles cloak
the cubicles we live our lives in,
rooms in which
the rocks of our contentment rock.

RONALD TANAKA

Boku no Michi

A Recitation to be accompanied
by shamisen and Japanese dance.

i   *niwa no sanshu no ki*
      naru suzu kakete yo hoi!

      wait for me by the bridge
      with the green water
      that you love. tell them
      you've gone to feed the
      fishes and to weep.

      when you throw bread
      upon the water,
      they dance like fire.
      this is what it means
      to be poor and suffer.

      listen! the only sound
      is the wind. so teach
      them that every debt
      must be paid in blood.

      suzu no naru to kya
      dete ojyare yo.

ii   here,

      a handful of pebbles.
      throw them into the
      wind, the pool, into
      the spaces between
      the shadows and the
      leaves. now, as you

           dance, only
           your feet
           make music.

iii   *suzu no naru to kya*
      nanto yute demasho yo hoi!

         anata, misoshiru iru no?

         yes, sukoshi.

         kore de ii no?

         yes, ii yo.

      koma ni mizu kuryo to
      yute demasho yo.

iv   father   (fresno)
       mother   (los angeles)
       ronald   (poston)
       mark   (san lorenzo)
       debbie   (san lorenzo)

       becky   (fowler)

           (madera)

       (claremont)

            (berkeley)

         (vancouver)

       (sacramento)

           (tokyo)
           (tsuchiura)
           (yokohama)

        (sacramento)

       hardly worth a life,
       or a death.

v   *alas, my love, you do me wrong,*
      to cast me off so discourteously.

      do you know why
      spenser, spenser, spenser?

            sidney, please!
            flee from me now!

      sleepest thou?
      (yes, i sleep.)

            come, my love,
            and let us prove

      you are the very model
      of a modern major-general!

            (buddha wa
            unko da yo!)

      amazing grace,
      how sweet the sound.

            tell me, children,
            why is beethoven
            considered deep?

            (cheep! cheep!)

            quick! quick!
            cried
            the bird.

i see. a
grammatical joke,
i suppose.

oh yes,
you must.
you must.

wittgenstein
could be pleased.

and mendelssohn?

(ah, mendelssohn!)

i am ELIJAH.   and

you, the many
prophets of baal!

(cheep! cheep!)

sa!
ore to kite
asobe yo . . .

o come, o come emanuel,
and ransom captive israel.

vi   when i was a boy in fowler,
jii-chan would mystify me.

on sundays, he dressed in a black
suit and preached to his people.

but on saturday, i would peek
into the church and see him

on his hands and knees,
scrubbing the floors alone.

shigekawa sensei, jii-chan,
you are my only teacher.

i once was lost,
but now am found,
twas blind, but
now i see.

vii   to have dreamed of
a mountain,
mont-st. michel,
milton's room, monk on
fifty-second street,
cordelia now, or
felix randal, poor
felix randal, ah, to
have dreamed still.

but you entered

then
without knocking.

chikai ma!
chikai ma!
you whisper.

and bright blood
splatters
mindlessly
against the
frail white walls

until my guts ooze
to mingle with yours.

kore de ii no?

yes, ii yo.

(ii no?)
(ii yo)

viii   *mori mo iyagaru*
bon kara sakinya
white cranes rise
from winter tanbo,
and the wind comes
to comfort me now.

i walk through this
land, carrying my
bento and a book
of english poems.

when i come to a
place, we kneel and
sing, *itsuki no*
komoriuta,
hietsuki bushi.

this is how we
study
yeats, or the blues.

white bird,
my friend,
fly . . .

ix   *koko no yama no*
kari boshia sunda yo.

i have heard the
mud-covered women.

i have felt
their hands
turning past
my face
as i danced
the *sado okesa*
upon the sand.

540

at dawn, i run
to kiss the sun
    and their
    sightless eyes
come to me,
saying,
what a silly boy
    i am.

Sa! koi! lie with me
here, along the cold,
bright edge of time,

    and laugh,
    and laugh,
    and laugh.

x   the tea stops
    its turning
    in the bowl (oh, wait!)

        as the black
        crow cries:

        kocha e! kocha e!

xi   obon has come
    to the mountain.

        listen!

        the drum
        the drum

please,
walk softly
lest the
red dragon-fly
should go
away.

xii   and when the joy has gone
    and all you have left
    is a poem, you don't
    know whether to laugh
    or cry. was this the
    beginning or the end?

well, they used to
say i just know
a few more ways
to be selfish.

        anyway
        anyway

        ogenki de

xiii   *naite matsu yori*
no ni dete ojyare yo hoi.

when i
must go,

        let us eat
        a simple meal
        with all our
        spirits
        living and dead.

        let them dance
        around the fire

        and hang
        lanterns
        along the path
        where i walk.

as it gets dark,
if you could leave
a small light on,

and wait for me
by the bridge
with the green
water that
you love, and

tell them
you've gone to
feed the fishes
and to weep.

        no ni wa nogiku no
        hana zakari yo.

Furusato no Fruit

i

we weren't farmers,
        but in fowler,
        and even madera,
        we always had
        a fruit tree
        or two. and

we worked in
the berries
and peaches
and grapes,
        always eating
        what we picked
        or packed or
        pruned. and

once you
get the taste
        of a green apricot
        or a tree ripe
        plum, nothin' else
        tastes the same yo.

ii

when i was in
vancouver,
i'd find myself
        going to those
        small chinese markets
        they have on
        every corner

just to see
the fruit
boxes with names
        like

        selma,
        reedley,
        clovis,
        fresno,
        dinuba
        and
        even
        parlier.

then i'd pay
a quarter for
a peach and

hold it
for a moment.
the first
bite would
always bring
tears to
my eyes.

"oh, you're a
long ways from home."
i'd say to myself.

        "nande ron tanaka
        kuni o uru?"

iii

i gave richard
some plums,
and he just
ate them. well,

        richard,
        you know,
        he's from
        new york.

Congratulations

hey, remember when
        dickie sato
        celebrated
        getting a
        new
        lotus europa

by having
barbra
        give him
        a
        permanent?

LAWSON FUSAO INADA

Pumice, and Obsidian

(Dance With Janet)

I come to you holding candles
          Asking you to dance

It is the simplest rhythm

          frog
          fern
          green
          extras

become a broken line of ants
scattered, going
who knows where but
what happens, words linked elbows and running after song.

Listen. The quickness
that follows, slowly,
the silences.

        The way I place my
        jagged accents.

It is the simplest ritual,
holding candles for you to blow on as we dance,
each swift swirl
extinguishing what is
more for you, illuminating, until

I am left here
with you, for you, us,
falling from my feet, the rippled edges,

or, twirling my mustache at the murky bottom,
having come all this way, sleek and survived, in the elegant
slime of glint and bright-eyed

wisdom and surprise.

Yes, these that I am,
I am, proud and postured in my region
of need and exigencies.
These that I am, I am.

And above all, at bottom,
I want to be
          ingested, whole.

Listen. Look at me, will you.

I come to you
          lit and inquisitive,
asking you to dance.

Move with me.

Come, Sweet One,
where the music

wets and quickens from within.

Come. Dance.

II.

(For Frank Chin and Mako)

". . . drrr-unk as mothers
on our own
welfare 'n A-Mer-i-ca,
had rode
rails inta jails
'n come out
truckin, brother,
wide open
throttles 'n spaces
with dee-vor-cees
ringleting in their kitchens . . ."

        Which is how it was,
        and wasn't; each of us
        with our own sense
        of country
                history.

            (Which is how it was.
            Young, and Asian,
            never young at all.)

For me, it was the Frrr-ezzz-noh

              County Clink

early Sunday, I suppose,
some fanatic screaming sermon
gone the way of damn

        nation and uncapitalized
        french toast, the inedible
        way it was,

all of us brought to life
by radio and the light bulb.

            (Hit twere a true
             commune, mutual
             floor and john
             to show you
             what you was.)

And this pilgrim ghost what shoulda been called Dust Bowl
and was, well, he rosed up in his stumbly stubble,
yawned his dusty dust, shifted his shifty soil,
grinned his toothless tooth which said:

            "Yessirreee.
            Hits Sundee.
            And ah'm happeee
            as a lark."

And this other old dude, truthfully named Blue
but wasn't, none of my fault, shoot, I wasn't
no poet, blued out through his bruises:

            "No you ain't, buddy.
            You sad as a
            broke-dick-dawg!"

Laughter, as it happens,
was, the gathering

of wits and matchsticks to be bartered over cards.

"How 'bout chu, China?
Wanna play?"

"I just might, White."

"Aw, hey, come on, man,
move on over."

"Yeah. O.K."

            A show of hands. Man
            ipulations. Patterns.
            Passages through space
            in a span of cards . . .

III.

smell of mud
blood bones
tapping
blood mud bones
smell of mud
blood bones
tapping
blood mud bones

It takes a hole, first,
the conception
of something to be filled,
a displacement
of the will,

burrowing your
self in through
the scented depths

to tap root
tapping rhythm

in the sheer
exuberant exertion
of digging your
self in, burying your
self in
earth and over

as the senses
sense we need to

do this, over
and over, to keep from
deteriorating
that way,

emanating
from our sub
stance to the earth
and back,

extended
from a few
strong strands
of song,

breathing
that way,
releasing

a lone white butterfly
through the puffs of pine,
a flowing
substance more a hush
than sound.

Yes, I feel
now, that I can be
alone.

(left hand)

(left hand)

(pivotal/emanating)

Who says "left" is
"East" of what, "oriented"
to where you are always
center to start from,
lined up with, linked to
catamarans and caribou
in the tundraed slopes,
solsticed, in the swoop
of streets,

pivotal (left hand), to span
from, re-
gather forces
spun again into distances
(span/left hand)

and in this fashion
seek a life of love (emanating)

sufficient
more than to one's
self (left hand),

a succession of (left hand/span)
winds and relevances, pairs
on the vine (left hand),

red corona
            round the
            (mud blood bones)
            (left hand)

red corona
            round the
            (mud blood bones)
            (left hand)

red corona
            round the

            SUN

IV.

Clouds. Treed
in equinox.

There is an implied faith,
the way we live, a blind
trust riding six guns
coming around corners

I don't want to threaten
anyone, don't want to take
nobody's life

I say this, coming to life
with relied hatred, glib with it,
reminded on corners
of epaulets and statuary,
defined in passing,
passing elderly
embassies of peaches and pie

Our whole lives are portions
stuffed with our selves, proportioned
against what, vessels, vehicles
for the wind of breathing

(pine cones)

My light lays a road
My darkness takes it up again

(pine) (cones)

Who follows
And with what eyes

(cones) (pine)

It's not a hard thing
to get to Alturas

(cones) (cones)

listening at night to my own
breathing, how it shines

(pine) (pine)

if I listen quiet enough

(pine CONES)

waking with the expiration
of a phrase raised upward: (   )

of a phrase raised upward: (   )

(pine CONES)

the lilt and lift of what no one
has ever heard, except for forests

(cones cones) (PINE)

Then I feel (pine cones)
I am a good man

(cone pines) (soft moss)

much (soft moss)

about the size of wind

(moss) (soft)

luminous, light, long
things to figure out

(pine cones) (soft moss)

brushes, cinders and membrane

(soft)

the twists and winnowings

(soft) (pine)

twined

(soft cones) (moss pine)

Rivers opening to embouchures

With your song to sing

V.

(shrill and falsetto)
(taken at full)
(gallop, full)
(sway, birds reduced to walking)
(structures)

I've been to those places
where creatures cut their carapace
flat at the crown, to fit
philosophies and landscapes
where nothing justifies
as it always was,
as they say it was, carcasses
strung over rooves
of remote reception, signals
over borders, betrayals, where a mouth
of water is an act of mercy, of
gratitude to get you on your way
to the edge of where you
could go on and die
forever, or live to become
rain of your own resources,
snow, sleet, the society and heat
of alcoves and conifers
within you, yes, the eyes
narrowed to forgotten sunsets
low at the lid
and close together, closed
to but the one obsession
and what to do
till the sun rise, and
what to do again, your grace,
your bluster, your
dramatic sense of fashion and history
out to pasture,
postured and billowing in the cindered wind
with rifts of longing
over water
lost on some wide short somewhere
in the fog and coming of winter.
I've been there.

VI.

Driving a back
road full of sons

dozing, going
this way and that

to each wake I make.

Land, laid out with lakes.
Lakes, laid out with land.
A vocabulary
to these cycles,

come all this way
scraping
oceans and cattleguards,

molten on the mind
of an old range bull
drooling and dozing,
snorting and sucking
in the sinister dust

of the stance he takes.

Land, laid out with lakes.

Who are you, then,
among vistas?

The sweep
of wings and waves
in the face of night.

A ring of keys.

A piece of the galaxies
flames in the dusk
and dies.

Who are you, then,
among vistas?

What song
will you sing?

(continued)

VI. (continued)

And somewhere inside
rises the fugitive,
to the throat,

sons and daughters
of those
who hid us away
until the time seemed right,

saying eat shit
instead of forests
because someone way
down in a time of torment
said so, deemed it right

until they find you
backed into corners
of the quick and bone,
biting bullets
down to the last
ounce of borders

as they tell you
you are the ruler
of fools
and you better

eat shit
and how it goes,

and from somewhere
rises the fugitive,
in the bone,

who has always
been there
and more powerful,

breaking through borders
with the blood
of license, of orders,

sons and daughters
of all of us
who we are,

who died in the false
light of wars,
the wrong
songs of orbits

calculated
by the cause and course
of hatred and starvation
that takes
you from my arms,
as I take

you *in* my arms
in the war
of never hurting anyone
in the peace
of freedom and salvation.

Come all this way.
Come all this way.

Come all,
this way.
Come all,
this way.

I say this
over and over
to my self
in orbit,
in the song
of keys.

Fall. The thick way
sound hovers.

Driving a forward
road full of sons.

I pull them toward
me
in golden dominoes.

Moon through the trees
wherever we go.

VII.

like pain
like road
like wood
like rope

like pain
like fear
like hate
like hope

like pain
like word
like warm
like cold

like pain
like food
like time
like hold

like pain
like pain
like pain
like pain

like pain
like yes
like pain
like no

like pain
like pain
like pain
like pain

like pain
like hate
like pain
like hope

like pain

548

VIII.

We find another
                on the trail
nothing round but moonlight

we heard each other coming
bout the time we turned on
                        our lights

stopping, talking about
                    coming and going

leaning on legs, stances,
                        flicking
light among underbrush
for sly
            sideways glances
of response and recognition

We laugh about lights, the far
mysterious one
moving off and on
                course without sound

Of course, there is a light
lift of moonshadow
to her smooth and slopes

She doesn't know
                I'm Japanese
                of course

How can she
            even if she has
            a thing for accents

It's a pity
            what she's missing

But she digs me all the same

I can tell
of course
how much
she stays
on course
how much
her teeth
are breathing

But these kinds of things
aren't supposed to
            . .   effect you out here

a man, a woman
with juniper and moon

as she sings of like jupiter and abalone
with a slightly

some kind of accent (of course)

because by now, of course,
we're talking that, ahem, cavernous
cool air following us
through the course of pre-
history

as we deliberately
give the light
to our faces
in a slow ceremony

as we sing the soft
song of wrong
                compasses,
                of course,
                which goes:

                        "Turn out the lights.
                        Let's get lost."

IX.

I place my bass
in the bed of a stream,
peg extended through
softest sand and gravel
to surest bottom
responding, holding
firm in place
bodies wet and whirled
in eddied flow.

And in this way
do my fingers move,
quick and rippling
slightest scalloped
light and water,
interplay of naked
skin and wind.

And in this way
does my spirit move,
booming through
rooted depths to
sound become truest
music as much

as oak and ponderosa
muse among willows
and bass takes
keel to float
downstreams to feel

music at bottom,
throbbed and strummed,
hummed in trust
of thrust and flow
of fluid motion

become firmest
substance
become purest
music

become become become

become you.

X.

That area of resonance
come to fore, everything
frontal in the pendulum, nothing

with backs, even the most
backwater memory burnished
glow and lilt and tint

as love is grand, lyrical
hillsides and horses
promenading around water,

and slowly, slowly, slowly,
does night become day,
brimmed to the blur,

filled to the fore this way
of lightness and grace
as all our waves move

foreward in graceful promenade.

550

XI.

We meet in a corridor.

I had heard of her before,
about how strong she is, and how
she used to be
                    so beautiful.

She comes in dragged behind a handler,
a guide, an attendant, a trainer,
eyes out of line, slanted
and sloped lower than another,
looking at another, how

each broken part of body does,
parted, gnarled, gnashed and puckered,
splintered, shrunken, punctured,
going off in their own directions.

I am awed and shocked.
I would have preferred
the cafeteria, a dining table
on those terms and not
this sudden corridor
I was only moving through.

We are introduced.

"Hey, hey now. How's it going?"

"Oh, O.K., I guess. All right."

"Yeah, well, uh, glad to meet you, gal . . ."
as she is gone with her handler.

Later, she is telling me
how it was. I am not sure
if it was
war, or peace on those terms, except
something official and industrial
did this to her. For what, I am sure
they are not
except she is certainly and purely
Asian in the history of these wasted elements

and she dared to say it, to their wasted face
and broken moments, out
spoken to the core which fills with action,
blind with pain and outrage
of continual war, insidious

as those who came
and taken her beauty (in those terms),
leaving her to move her food
with the feet of a crane, cruel and mechanical,
her textured frame jerking
jerkily, with cabled attachments,

as shapes and shadows
doom through the corridors
of this institution.

Yes, I know she was beautiful,
revered now for what she was,
tolerated in the tension of those terms

that make it easier
to talk with her younger sister
to whom I have nothing to prove,
who thinks I am
muscular and beautiful
and will change the world.

She would follow me that way,
cute and approving,
dancing my waist
around fountains.

But I am thinking of her sister,
her sister,
who would die for me
and has, in those terms,
slow and impacted

small deaths out of love,
and huge love
that prompted her to action.

We meet in a corridor.

The agents are
always impending.

My Sister
rushes to fight them,
at the door.

My Sister, My Daughter, My Mother,
My Beautiful Crane

of Power and Flight

who I always love,
always, as ever before.

XII.

Everything threatens me.

You, over my shoulder,
what you've done.
Do. You.

What you don't do.
You.

It is the time without reason,
threats that take me
back of the mind and alleys, creating

    special occasions
    where we are free
    to do as always

    with gratuitous ease

    because I want to,
    because we need to
    partake of pain
    that breeds authority
    in its own sick way
    we never say,

    paid for through
    the nose of pockets,
    pressures of legs,
    the way we walk

    groping for wishes
    that never seem to
    happen, but can,
    if we let them

    come clean to
    understanding

    and the grief
    of bitches, bastards,
    whatever we call
    our selves, children,

    adultery and infantry
    our first concern.

    Is it any wonder then
    I push a pencil
    through your breast
    or penis the slow
    hard way of grim resolve

    watching for reaction,
    the hideous screech

    that comes groveling,
    the angered anguish
    that sends me

cowering into alleyways
to feed the dog.

The chase. The stabbing.
The frightful living
and existence to do.

But then I meet you,
fumbling and articulating
loose ends in alleys,

improvising easily again
without gist or reason
but what moves through me
like the natural instrument
commanding I am
what happens with skin and wind
    (perhaps you are not here yet, again)

as I dance
with your lovely cousins
and then your entire
holding family
at the festival

by the time you appear,
which rarely
and never
happens,

but with that feel and vision
I can go off through
the cruelest landscapes,

laughing, looking for you.

XIII.

If I count the bruises on you
there is little else
to cherish in the flesh.

What I have thrown at you
and all else. And what do
the bruises tell me, the welts?

Fissures and reasons.
Regions where the flesh
goes blue in black orgasms.

What we could have a life
without, down at the mouth
and brow all over the body.

Fissures and reasons
inhabit me, are not enough.

You have no reason
to dance with me but love.

XIV.

This pumice, I bring to you.
Obsidian I also bring.

Both from the same source,
soft and hard, as all of us.

Pumice came to my feet,
all bright and brilliant,
bubbling on a stream of wind.

Obsidian had to be
sought after, caught
cutting up a bighorn bluff
of so much heat and snow.

Someone like our selves
in their shine,
if we had sides.

Intermingled, I come to you,
both our bloods
twined in sunrise and our sons.

And what we have
is what we bring and give,
as giving is much
receiving, bringing forth
what gives is gift itself
in worth of asking

as I ask for
who you are,
soft and hard
pumice, and obsidian

raised upward and upward
and upward into rain.

XV.

"Come on, let's call this The Octopus Stomach."

"Ok. Hey, I wonder if we'll come out to the future?"

"Don't you like to go exploring?"

"Somebody's already been here."

"Well, exploring is the first time *we* ever been here."

And so we descend
further into darkness and the earth.

Cold, slipping on ice, even,
with only the senses
to get by on.

Falling and crawling, bringing
up the rear
all too high to get by on,
stiff and sore
from so much
upward arbitration, negotiation
straight through life,
cutting and scraping
the lofty
knuckles of the brain
all too high to get by on.

You can go that way
if you want,
says the mica.

We've been waiting
and we haven't.
It makes no difference to us.

Look up, around,
if you have the can and time.

Somewhere, beyond, are stars,
they tell us,
as *they* are,
as *we* are,

each of us
with our own high shine.
You can feel it, the eyes
open or closed.

And so we *do*
emerge into the future,
my sons grown
stronger and surer
with their own size and light

as I follow, out of the past and on to the road.

XVI.

blue bird
moon in its mouth

red ants
huge among lava

juniper planets
web in the branches

warm dry morning
of answers and warning

It is not the knowledge,
the need for sweep
of insights covered with dew
of famous money, brilliant solutions
leading into horizons.

It is not what you say
but do.

No matter how beautiful
the numbering, the alluring phrases
equationed off the curling tongue,
it comes back to you.

It is not the knowledge
but the tongue itself,
the surety of how it moves
without saying anything, curled
to itself in the full
mouth of integrity,
responding and responsible,
integral to its whole.

No one dances
without dancing
alone.

I want to give you a life
of laughter and fancy.

I come to my self holding candles
                    Asking me to dance

XVII.

And so I come to the end of all my crossings.
Nothing pushes past me to another shore.
Pumice, and obsidian rise to root and soil.
Who loves me, loves me all.

And so I come to the end of all my preparations.
Readied, in the center, for whatever will.
It is the courage gets us here, the conviction.
Gathered into the moment of calm.

And if I lose you, where would I be?
What of readiness for what may never come?
It is the courage gets us here, the conviction.
Gathered into the grandeur of calm.

And so I come to the end of all my crossings.
Readied, in the center, for whatever comes.
It is the courage gets us here, the conviction.
Pumice, and obsidian resume what has always begun.

XVIII.

I come to you holding candles
          Asking you to dance

It is the simplest rhythm

        frog
        fern
        green
        extras

        become
        nothing extraneous
        filled with rhythm

It is the simplest ritual

Yes, and there is no light

        lucid
        articulate
        scripture

                without substance
                without motion

        of what so ever
        moves
        within us now

                as what so ever
                shines
                within us now

                moving through the molten
                of the soul

And in the flow and chant

                of pumice pumice pumice
                and obsidian

I come to you asking you

                Asking you Asking you Asking you
                Asking

                YOU

                To Dance

FRANK CHIN: BACK-TALK

In virtually every article, story, movie, and television program that has appeared recently on Asian Americans, from pop to scholarly, from Tom Wolfe in the national slicks to the ABC movie of the week—*If Tomorrow Comes, Kung Fu*—to *Farewell to Manzanar,* the Asian-American has been portrayed as implicitly a believer in white supremacy, as anti-black, as living in a self-imposed exile from American culture, art, society, and politics. This white supremacist stereotype is expressed in the form of praise for the Chinese or Japanese-American for "not regarding themselves as a minority in the aggrieved sense of the word," for "preserving" their behavior and personality. The assumption is that white racism is a thing of the past. To any Asian-American who watches the Command commercial which features an Asian ping pong player who sweats and has floppy hair because he does not use Command beating the white blond (who does use Command and therefore has lovely hair and no sweat) but still losing the beautiful Asian girl even though he won the game, it is clear that our acceptability, the affection and reknown we supposedly enjoy, is not based on any actual achievements or contributions we have made, but on what we have not done. We have not been black. We have not caused trouble. We have not been men.

The Asian culture we are supposedly preserving is uniquely without masculinity; we are characterised as lacking daring, originality, aggressiveness, assertiveness, vitality, and living art and culture. What art and culture we do enjoy is passive in the popular mind—we don't practice it, we preserve it and are sustained by it. And our lack of cultural achievement and expression in America is explained by the fact that we are sustaining a foreign culture.

The cultural achievements and identity of blacks is suffused throughout the whole of modern American culture, on all levels, and this influence on the American past is being sought and discovered. But America has no awareness, much less any apprecia-tion, of organic Chinese-American or Japanese-American culture, literature, or art that is neither Asian or white American in sensibility. The black man's pride in his African heritage is not a way of excluding the influence of blackness in American culture; rather, it enhances and informs his American voice and achievement. African identity is not a substitute for American identity.

However, our supposed Asian identity is used to exclude us from American culture, and is imposed upon us as a substitute for participation in American culture. This has led to the popularization of the notion among us that, in America, culture, success, and money are white. Such a notion is fraught with self-contempt. It implies that to pick up a pen or brush, to move outside of "Chinatown" in body or field of interest, or to amass a small fortune carries with it the onus of rejecting our people. It also encourages us to 1) look on our success as Americans in terms of the degree to which we have been accepted by Americans and 2) to measure our degree of acceptance in terms of the degree to which the whiteman has rejected other minorities.

Our compulsion to gamble with our lives, and our self-esteem, in the Acceptance Sweepstakes has its roots in the knowledge that we are a small minority, less than one percent of the population, and that our history is a history of living in response to white racism. The popular belief is that Asians came over to America as sojourners, with no intention of settling. This is false. Like pioneers in any country, including America, the explorers of the unknown—seekers after gold, the big break, the new country—were the men of the family venturing away from home. In 1850, twenty Chinese men for every Chinese woman entered the country legally. In 1860, the figure was 17 to 1. We were taking our lives and the lives of our families seriously. We began settling heavily, looking for permanence on the Golden Mountain. By 1870, the figure was down to 12 to 1. Then, in the 1880's, came the Chinese Exclusion Act that forbade the naturalization of Chinese and the further entry of Chinese women. In 1924 the Exclusion Act was capped with a set of laws that convinced all Chinese and Chinese-Americans that America was deadset on driving them into extinction or out of the country. An American-born Chinese-American woman lost her citizenship and was subject to immediate deportation if she married a man from China. No more Chinese women were entering the country and marriage to a Chinese-American woman was impossible: according to the law, she was fit only to marry God or a whiteman. Chinese men saw themselves as the end of family lines. They lived with the conviction, they knew, that someday America would deport all of them, American born or not. So, like NASA preparing Americans to be citizens of the moon, we prepared for the big trip. When America orbited us and our children to planet China, we would be ready.

556

In the meantime, we devoted our minds, and our lives, to not angering the beast at the switch. Life here became a day to day exercise in forestalling the Great Deportation. We laid low (self-effacing, humble) and passed on the psychology of laying low to succeeding generations, but without passing on the roots of the culture—the less we knew about it the better. New York's Chinatown is a product of that psychology. We came here to get as far away from San Francisco as we could. In the '20's and '30's, we came here knowing that here "Negroes were the Chinks."

In 1943, the Exclusion Act was repealed in deference to the fact that China was America's ally against the Japanese, and the term Chinese-American came into currency, compounding our schizophrenic sense of identity rather than relieving it. The term contains the "concept of dual personality" that encourages us both to be Chinese and American, and to define every aspect of our behavior and appearance either in terms of China or white America. Chinese-American college students were once asked to divide a sheet of paper in half: on one half of the sheet they were to list the "Chinese" facets of their character; on the other half, the American. They did this after they had all agreed that they could, in fact, separate the "Chinese" from the American parts of their characters. Invariably, everything "old fashioned, inhibiting, dull, and cowardly" was Chinese. Their interest in "sex, fun, art, adventure, boldness," was American. To me, this implies that the standard English and American education is inadequate to the development of a healthy and accurate articulation of the Chinese-American sensibility—that the language itself is white supremacist in nature.

The term "Chinese-American," with or without the hyphen, encourages an either/or mentality. One version of this either/or cartoon goofy wired into us goes: "either we're Chinese or we're American." Another: "When I am with Americans, I am Chinese, When I am with Chinese, I am an American." Unaware of the suicide she is committing, a New York junior high school teacher, born here, stays together only by destroying a part of herself when she says: "I am Chinese first, American second." She arrived at this conception of herself because whites looked on her first as "Chinese," meaning foreign.

In terms of the use of language, especially descriptive language applied to Asian-Americans, the possibilities of offending the Asian-American sensibility or contributing to the deeply ingrown self-contempt that plagues us all is infinite. Our condition is more delicate than that of the blacks because, unlike the blacks, we have neither an articulated, organic sense of our American identity nor the verbal confidence and self-esteem to talk one up from our experience. As a people, we are pre-verbal, —afraid of language as the instrument through which

the monster takes possession of us. For us American-born, both the Asian languages and the English language are foreign. We are a people without a native tongue. To whites, we're all foreigners, still learning English, despite the fact that I am fifth generation Chinatown. And to Asians born to Asian culture—Asian by birth and experience and American by choice—our Chinese and Japanese is a fake.

I don't think that the phenomenon of a people born without a native tongue has been explored. One of the consequences of having no language, at least among us, is an inability to distinguish between fiction and non-fiction in reading. This inability exists among our college educated: We don't read, we memorize. Like ventriloquists' dummies, we are the tools of other men's language. Strange words organize our experience and make us the realities, the embodiments, of the words we don't understand. Language should be a tool for organizing experience and reality, not vice-versa.

We have no street tongue to flaunt and strut the way the blacks and Chicanos do. They have a positive, self-defined linguistic identity that can be offended and wronged. We don't. With us, it's dangerous to say anything, dangerous to talk because every time you open your mouth you run the risk of being corrected. The tongue-tying notion that everything out of your mouths is mimickry has been built into our psychology in our seven generations here. And if our basic means of expression is mimickry and ventriloquism, then our art and culture is mimickry and ventriloquism too. Such is our self-contempt. Chinatown rejects its writers because writing is an "American" thing. Also, standing outside the confines of the stereotype might bring the white man down hard on us and get our asses all deported. We grow up with that too. White America, likewise, has rejected every Asian-American writer who hasn't mouthed the cliches of the goofy stereotype. Asian-American writers—John Okada, Louis Chu, Lawson Inada, Toshio Mori, Hisaye Yamamoto....forty years of writing have taken the schizophrenic yakity yak we talk and made it a backtalking, muscular, singing stomping full blooded language loaded with nothing but our truth. No college course in American lit acknowledges them. Whites prefer to call us nuts, and ask us to put up the proof of a uniquely non-Asian, non-white Asian American sensibility, as if there's none.

There's plenty. Whites have suppressed us. The worst aspect of this suppression is that Asian-Americans going through white schools grow up with white assumptions about themselves. Racist assumptions. That this play [Chickencoop Chinaman] is the first play by an Asian-American to, in any sense, make it, that people should be surprised at our existence, is proof of the great success white racism has had with us. America might love us. But America's love is no good. It's racist love. I don't want it. ★

557

APPENDICES

A NOTE ON THE 1970 CENSUS

The 1970 Census is an important source of statistical information on Asian Americans. It is the most comprehensive and reliable data currently available on a nation-wide basis. It provides detailed information on five Asian American groups, Japanese, Chinese, Pilipinos, Koreans and Hawaiians. However, users should recognize the constraints on its application and the limits of its utility. They include problems of underenumeration, changes in population, interpretation and definitions.

The U.S. Bureau of the Census estimates that there is a 6.9% underenumeration of minority communities compared to 1.9% of white communities. Much of this underenumeration occurs within high-density urban areas. This is particularly important for Asian Americans, of whom 90% in 1970 resided in urban areas compared to the national average of 73 percent. Numerous community sources consider the 6.9% underenumeration to be a conservative estimate. Some of the reasons for the under-enumeration of Asian Americans are:

(1) Census forms were written in English, with the exception of New York and San Francisco where forms were translated into Chinese. Consequently, non-English speaking persons may have completed the forms improperly or not at all. Assuming some relationship between English-language fluency and income for non-English speaking persons, a bias toward high income individuals would result. The same bias might occur in other statistics as well.

(2) The forms were mailed to residents listed in the U.S. Post Office address registry. Thus, the probability that transient persons, particularly those residing in low income areas, did not receive Census forms is high.

(3) An arbitrary situation also occurs in the case of children of mixed parentage. In cases of ambiguity, children are classified according to the ethnicity of their father. For example, the out-group marriage rate for Japanese demonstrates the significance of this Census classification. Almost 1/3 of Japanese women are married to non-Asian men. If all the children of these marriages were classified by the ethnicity of the mother, a significant increase in the number of Asians enumerated would result. Since the 1970 Census, this has proven to be the case for the Spanish-speaking population. When the Census Bureau used the mother's ethnicity instead of the father's ethnicity to reclassify children the size of the Spanish-speaking population increased significantly.

Another important consideration is Asian immigration figures since 1970. Immigration from Asian countries is larger than immigration from any other country under the Immigration and Naturaliza-tion Service quotas. Since 1970, population increases from immigration alone were 14% for Chinese, 26%

APPENDICES

for Pilipinos and 80% for Koreans. These figures represent gross changes and do not take into account deaths, births or returns amongst immigrants. This population increase affects demographic characteristics of the Asian American community. The information provided by the 1970 Census on the Korean community in particular should be used with caution. Since the 1970 Census data are now several years old, adjustments are needed to account for other changing dynamics in the Asian American population.

Comparison between one specific ethnic group and the national average is common practice. The problem with this practice is that the figures on minority groups have been incorporated in the national totals. For example in the following table when comparisons are made between Japanese and the U.S. total and Japanese and Whites a major difference occurs:

1970 Median Income of All Workers 16 Years and Older [1]

	Men	Women
U.S. Total	$7,609	$3,649
Whites	7,875	3,738
Chinese	5,223	2,686
Japanese	7,574	3,236
Pilipino	5,019	3,513

Interpretation of national data on specific ethnic groups should also be used cautiously. National aggregates are not always representative of the group. To cite one example:

> The occupations held by the Pilipino women vary markedly from area to area. In Hawaii 55% of the women are employed as semi-skilled operatives, laborers or service workers. In California 42% are employed as clerical and sales workers while 21% are professionals. In areas outside Hawaii and California, 55% are employed as professionals. [2]

In addition to national aggregates some local data are provided in the Subject Report published by the Bureau of the Census, *PC(2)-1G Japanese, Chinese and Filipinos in the United States*. This data is enumerated by state and Standard Metropolitan Statistical Area (SMSA). Thus far, only limited information is available for specific census tracts by ethnicity. This represents a severe constraint on the data's usefulness to particular communities.

It will be important in most instances to be aware of Census Bureau definitions. In all likelihood Census categories will not conform exactly to any particular user's needs. For example, researchers interested in data on Japanese will note the Bureau's peculiar definition of this group.

> The category "Japanese" includes persons who indicated their race as Japanese, as well as

persons who did not classify themselves in one of the specific race categories on the questionnaire but who had such entries as Japanese-American, Nipponese or Oriental.[3]

Conclusion

Although the Census is the single most important demographic source, it does not reduce the need for primary research. The 1970 Census provides a general demographic profile. However, because of problems of underenumeration, population changes, interpretation and definitions the data must be used carefully. Although it provides valuable background information, the Census by its very nature is a poor indicator of particular social problems and needs.

Since the last Census was taken, DHEW contracted a special study to provide additional data on Asian Americans. This study, the Asian American Field Study, was designed to focus on low-income Asian Americans. The populations sampled were the Chinese in New York, the Japanese in Los Angeles,

the Koreans in Los Angeles, the Pilipinos in San Francisco and the Samoans in Los Angeles. The findings of this study will be available in late 1976. ★

—Irene Hirano

Notes

1. U.S. Bureau of the Census, *1970 Census of Population, Detailed Characteristics, United States Summary PC(1)-C1; Subject Reports: Japanese, Chinese and Filipinos in the United States, PC(2)-1G;* and *U.S. Summary of Part C: General, Social and Economic Characteristics, 1970 Census.* Statistics used in this article are from these two sources.

2. Department of Health, Education and Welfare, Office of the Secretary. *A Study of Selected Socio-Economic Characteristics of Ethnic Minorities Based on the 1970 Census. Volume II: Asian Americans.* July 1974.

3. U.S. Bureau of the Census. *1970 Census of Population, Subject Reports: Japanese, Chinese and Filipinos in the United States, PC(2)-1G.* Page X.

ASIAN AMERICAN CENSUS HIGHLIGHTS

Source: *A Study of Selected Socio-Economic Characteristics of Ethnic Minorities Based on the 1970 Census, Vol. II: Asian Americans,* Department of Health, Education and Welfare, Office of Special Concerns, HEW Publication No. (OS) 75-121, Washington, D.C., 1974.

Chinese American

Immigration and Population

The Chinese are the second largest Asian American subgroup with a 1970 population of 435,000 persons as reported by the Census. Over half of the Chinese population live in the western states; 39% in California alone with another 12% in Hawaii. Additionally, 27% of all Chinese live in the Northeast—with almost 20% in the State of New York.

During the decade between 1960 and 1970, the Chinese population in the United States increased by 84%. At least two-thirds of the additional people added to the population are new immigrants. Chinese immigration to the U.S. has averaged 19,000 persons per year in the last 6 years.

Few of the recent Chinese immigrants have settled in Hawaii, where only 11% of the Chinese population are foreign-born. High proportions of recent immigrants are concentrated in cities in California and New York; 52% of the Chinese in San Francisco, 54% of the Chinese in Los Angeles, and 67% of the Chinese in New York City are foreign-born.

The Chinese population has been historically an urban one, and the proportion of their population living in urban areas (97%) has not changed over the past 10 years.

Since the beginning of the century, the Chinese population in the United States has been predominantly male. Over the past decade, the differential between males and females, however, has decreased from 14% to 6%. Among the elderly, males are still 57% of the population and females only 43% of the population.

In 1970, the percent of Chinese under 18 was 32%, just under the U.S. average of 34%. Because the influx of new immigrants has not brought with it large numbers of elderly, the percent of elderly among the Chinese (9% of the 18 and over population) is lower than the U.S. total (15%).

Family Characteristics

Of all the ethnic subgroups, the Chinese have the highest proportion of husband/wife families (89%).

Of all Chinese husband/wife families, 66% have children under 18 (56% for the total U.S.) and 33% have children under 6 (27% for the U.S.). One reason for the higher percentage of families with children is the recent influx of young Chinese families of child bearing age.

The overall rate of marriage by Chinese to a spouse of the same subgroup is higher than that of other Asian groups. 87% of all Chinese men and 88% of Chinese women have married within their group. However, broken down by age, the data show that inter-marriages have increased markedly among the younger Chinese population.

Chinese families tend to be larger than families in the U.S. in general. 35% of Chinese families have five or more members compared to 25% of all families in the U.S. The average Chinese family has 4.0 persons compared to 3.5 persons among white families.

In 1970, 18% of all Chinese families were extended families, 1-1/2 times more than the total U.S. population (12%). 11% of all Chinese families have 3 or more generations—4% more than the total U.S. population.

Educational Characteristics

The Chinese present an unbalanced picture of an

extraordinarily high education at one end with a disproportionately large uneducated population at the other.

The percentage of Chinese American men who have not gone beyond elementary school (23%) is lower than the U.S. average (27%). Fully a quarter of Chinese males, 16 years old or older, have obtained their college degrees—double the U.S. average (13%); the highest proportion for any group in the U.S.

28% of Chinese females did not go beyond elementary school—3% greater than in the total U.S. female population.

The median years of schooling for foreign-born elderly Chinese men is 6.2 years and is less than 1 year (0.9 year) for such women. These statistics reveal the high incidence of illiteracy among elderly Chinese.

24% of all Chinese children, 3-4 years old, are enrolled in some type of preschool program—10% more than in the total U.S. population. The higher rate reflects the high labor force participation rate for Chinese women (16 years old and over), 50% of whom are in the labor force compared to 41% of women in the total U.S. population.

The enrollment figures for college-aged Chinese are about double the enrollment rates for college-aged young people in the total population. 71% of Chinese males, 18-24 years old, are enrolled in school compared to only 37% of males of the same age in the total population. 58% of Chinese females, 18-24 years old, are enrolled in school while are only 27% of females of the same age in the total population.

Among Chinese children under 14 years of age, 96% of the foreign-born and 70% of the second generation speak Chinese in their homes.

Employment Characteristics

The labor force participation rate of Chinese males 16 years old and over (73%) is 4% below the rate for men in the total population and almost 7% below the rate for men in other Asian groups, which reflect the higher school enrollment rates of young Chinese men.

With the higher proportion of college educated men in the population, professional occupations are the largest category of employment (29%) for Chinese men.

Another 11% of employed Chinese males are managerial workers, the same proportion as the total U.S. population. Those Chinese who are managers,

however, are largely self-employed owners and proprietors of small retail stores and restaurants.

Nearly a quarter (24%) of all Chinese men are employed as service workers, many of them in Chinese restaurants and laundries. The proportion is 3 times that of the total U.S. male population.

Between 1960 and 1970, the labor force participation rate of Chinese women increased from 44% to 50%. The greatest increase occurred in the working patterns of married women. Only 13% of all Chinese wives worked in 1960, but 48% did in 1970. The labor force participation rates of foreign-born and U.S.-born Chinese women are about the same although the occupations that they hold differ markedly.

Over half of all employed U.S.-born Chinese women are employed as typists, secretaries, sales clerks and other low status white-collar workers. Less than a quarter of employed foreign-born Chinese women are found in these occupations. 37% of the foreign-born Chinese women are working in factory-related blue-collar jobs (most of them as semi-skilled operatives). A mere 9% of the U.S.-born Chinese women are employed in such occupations.

There is evidence that many recent Chinese immigrants who were formerly highly trained professional and managerial workers have been forced to shift to less skilled occupations in the U.S. 46% of all Chinese immigrants, who immigrated between 1965 and 1970, were employed in their native countries as professional, technical, or managerial workers. By 1970, however, only 32% of the employed Chinese immigrating between 1965 and 1970 found employment as professional, technical and managerial workers—a 14% drop.

Income Characteristics

Of all Chinese men, 41% earn an annual income of less than $4,000—a much larger percentage of men with low income than the average for the country (31%), reflecting the very serious problem among both older Chinese men and the newly immigrated Chinese men, who are employed in low-paying, low-skilled jobs.

The proportion of Chinese men earning an income of $10,000 or more (24%) is just under the proportion for men in the total U.S. population.

Although the proportion of Chinese males in professional and managerial occupations is higher than any other population group, income levels of Chinese men are not commensurate.

About half the wives (48%) in Chinese husband/wife families are employed, compared to only 39% in the total population. 65% of these and other employed Chinese women earn less than $4,000 a year—close to the proportion for women in the total U.S. population (68%).

About 60% of all Chinese families have more than one earner, while only 51% of all U.S. families have more than one earner. The impact of these additional Chinese earners is to raise the overall income of a family and to obscure the large percentage of individuals earning very low incomes. As a result, although individual income is below the U.S. average, the median Chinese family income in 1970 was $1,000 higher than the U.S. average.

The median incomes of Chinese families whose heads immigrated to the U.S. before 1925 ($7,426) and after 1965 ($7,372) are far lower. These figures are an indication of the greater economic problems faced by both elderly Chinese and recent immigrants.

Poverty Characteristics and Sources of Income

Proportionally fewer Chinese American families are receiving Social Security benefits than the rest of the population (14% compared to 20%). Moreover, the average amount of Social Security income that Chinese families receive is lower than that of families in the total population.

There are 2.8 Chinese families in poverty for every one that is on welfare, compared to only 2.1 families in poverty for every one receiving public assistance in the entire United States. Ratios of families in poverty to families receiving public assistance among Chinese are particularly imbalanced in urban New York State, where there are four families in poverty for every one that is receiving welfare.

The national rate of poverty among Chinese families (10%) is close to the rate for the total U.S. (11%). In New York City, the rate of poverty for Chinese is much higher (15%).

Nationally, 28% of all the Chinese elderly are poor. In San Francisco, 31% are poor and in New York City the rate is a very high 40%. Well over half (58%) of the Chinese elderly poor live alone. Most of these persons are males who were consigned to an unmarried, childless status due to immigration restrictions.

A fifth of all Chinese housing in the United States is regarded as overcrowded. The conditions for the Chinese are worse in New York City where a third of all housing units are overcrowded. Additionally, a fifth of all Chinese housing in New York and San Francisco is without adequate plumbing.

Japanese American

Immigration and Population

The Japanese are the largest Asian-American subgroup with a 1970 population of 591,000 persons. 72% of all Japanese Americans live in Hawaii and California.

Between 1960 and 1970, the Japanese population in the United States increased by 27%. Since 1970, the rate of Japanese immigration to the United States has remained low, averaging 5,000 persons per year. About two-thirds of the additional persons added to the population since 1960 were attributed to births while the remaining one-third were new immigrants.

There has been a shift of the Japanese population from one that is predominantly male to one that is predominantly female and the gap is widening. Two factors are involved: first, there is a higher percentage of Japanese female immigrants and secondly, women tend to outlive men. Males are now only 46% of the Japanese population and, among the elderly, only 43%.

Japanese have a smaller percentage of young people under 18 in their population than does the U.S. population as a whole (29% compared to 34%). Part of this may be due to a lower birth rate among Japanese. Another factor is a relatively high intermarriage rate between Japanese and non-Japanese. The children and grandchildren of these parents may no longer be enumerated as Japanese by the Census.

The percentage of all Japanese adults who are elderly (11% of persons 18 and over) is lower than the U.S. average (15%). In rural areas, the concentration of elderly Japanese is higher (16% of persons 18 and over).

Of the Japanese in Hawaii, only 10% are foreign-born. In California, 21% are foreign-born while outside Hawaii and California 36% of the Japanese population are foreign-born.

Among all immigrants who came to the United States prior to 1925, 91% have become U.S. citizens. But only 46% of all Japanese who immigrated this early have become citizens. Victims of laws prohibiting the granting of citizenship to Asians, which were in effect throughout most of the first half of the century, these persons continue to be at a disadvantage due to their non-citizenship status.

Family Characteristics

86% of Japanese families have both husband and wife, the same rate as that of the country as a whole. Of such families, the percentage with children under 18 (61%) is higher than in the country as a whole (56%) while the percentage with children under six (27%) is just at the national rate, suggesting perhaps a lower birth rate among younger Japanese.

One-third of all married Japanese women have married outside of their ethnic group. 43% of the women, 25-44 years old, and 46% of the women, 16-24 years old, are married to non-Japanese. Many of these women are post-World War II Japanese wives of former American servicemen.

Among Japanese primary individuals (persons who live alone) the ratio of males to females is almost equal. Two-thirds of all elderly Japanese primary individuals, however, are women. As in the total population, many Japanese women who have outlived their husbands are left on their own in their old age.

Japanese families are slightly larger than families in the total U.S. population. The average white family in the United States has 3.5 persons while the average Japanese family has 3.7 persons. The Japanese family tends to be larger than the average U.S. family owing to extended family relationships with the presence of adult relatives such as grandparents, aunts, uncles, etc. While 12% of all families are extended families, among the Japanese, 16% are.

Educational Characteristics

In 1970, 62% of all Japanese in the United States had a mother tongue of Japanese. Over a quarter of those who had resided in the United States for three or more generations still had a mother tongue of Japanese.

Of all Japanese males 16 and above, 70% have finished high school and 19% have completed college—figures well above the U.S. averages of 54% and 13%.

As with the men, the percentage of Japanese women who have completed high school (67%) is greater than the U.S. female norm (55%). The difference between the Japanese and the total population is not as great for women as for men. The percentage of Japanese women who have completed college (11%) is greater than the percentage of all women in the U.S. (8%). The percentage, however, is lower than the percentage among women in the other Asian subgroups.

The educational attainment of the elderly Japanese is much lower. Japanese males 65 years old and over have had a median of 8.5 years of education and elderly Japanese females have had 7.9 years.

Over 30% of Japanese children, 3-4 years old, are in some type of preschool program. This is more than double the participation rate for the U.S. (14%). Among the factors creating this higher enrollment rate is the very high labor force participation rate of Japanese women (nearly 50%).

The college enrollment for young Japanese adults, 18-24 years old (56% of males and 48% of females enrolled), is higher than any other group except for the Chinese.

Employment Characteristics

Over the decade the proportion of Japanese women in the labor force increased from 44% to nearly 50%. The biggest change occurred in the proportion of married women in the work force. In 1960, only 12% of all Japanese wives were working while in 1970, 51% were.

The labor force participation rate of Japanese men (79%) is 2% higher than the rate for males in the total population (77%).

Considerable differences exist between occupational distribution of Japanese born in the United States and those born in Japan. 45% of all employed foreign-born Japanese men are in the so-called upper status white-collar occupations as professionals and managerial workers. Less than a third of the U.S.-born Japanese men, however, are in these occupations. On the other hand, fully a third of all U.S.-born men are in skilled and semi-skilled blue-collar jobs while only 13% of the foreign-born Japanese males are so employed.

68% of all U.S.-born Japanese women are in white-collar occupations chiefly as clerical workers; on the other hand, 68% of the foreign-born women are in blue-collar jobs.

While most of the foreign-born Japanese males immigrated as professionals or as students, sizeable proportions of the foreign-born Japanese females are elderly or war brides. Hence the distribution of jobs of foreign-born males and foreign-born females differs sharply.

There is clear evidence that many members of the Japanese population in the United States are under-employed. The proportion working in higher status white-collar jobs has not kept up with the proportion who are college educated. The gap is greatest among Japanese of foreign birth. There are only 0.9 foreign-born Japanese men in the higher status jobs for every one who is college educated while there is 1.5 men in the total U.S. population employed in the higher status jobs for every college educated male.

About 5% of all Japanese males are employed on farms, the same percentage as for men in the total population. Among the employed elderly, however, 15% are on farms. Another 22% of these elderly Japanese males are working as non-farm laborers.

Income

Almost a third (30%) of Japanese men, 16 and over, earn less than $4,000 a year (almost the same as the national rate 31%) while another third (33%) of the Japanese males earn over $10,000 a year. Although one-third are among the upper income groups, about 37% earn between $4,000 to $10,000, and the remaining one-third are among the lowest income groups in the U.S.

Only 51% of all U.S. families have more than one earner. In over half of all Japanese families, both husbands and wives work, compared to only 39% of the husbands and wives in the total population. Another factor is that over a third of all Japanese live in Hawaii where the cost of living is at least 25% higher than the rest of the U.S.

58% of all employed Japanese women are earning less than $4,000 a year. This percentage is smaller than the proportion of women in the total population (68%) who earn as little but far higher than the proportion found among men in any ethnic group.

Except in Hawaii, the income levels of Japanese families with a female head are similarly low. Only 18% of such families in Hawaii, but nearly a third (31%) of such families in California, and a very high 47% of such families in areas outside of Hawaii and California survive on less than $4,000 a year.

Poverty Characteristics & Sources of Income

20% of all Japanese families are receiving Social Security which is the same proportion as the rest of the population. The average amount of Social Security income that Japanese families are receiving, however, is lower than the average amount received by families in the total population.

There is an average of 2.1 families in poverty for every one family receiving public assistance in the United States; the ratio for Japanese families is 2.2 to one. The ratio is most imbalanced in states outside Hawaii and California where there are 3.8 Japanese families with incomes below poverty for every one family on welfare.

Nationally, the rate of poverty among Japanese families (6%) is lower than the U.S. average (11%). Of all Japanese families outside of Hawaii and California, however, the rate of poverty is up to 11%—equal to the U.S. average. Of all foreign-born Japanese families, 17% had incomes under the poverty level in 1970. Of all Japanese families in poverty, two-fifths are female-headed.

A fifth of all Japanese, 65 years old and over, are poor. Over half (58%) of them live alone. Among Japanese, a majority of the elderly poor who live alone are women, many of them widows.

Pilipino American

Immigration and Population

The Pilipinos according to the Census are the third largest of Asian American subgroups with a 1970 population of 343,000 persons. During the decade between 1960 and 1970, the Pilipino population of the United States nearly doubled. Two-thirds of the additional population were new immigrants while the remaining third were due to new births of Pilipinos in the U.S.

Pilipinos are now the largest of Asian groups immigrating to the United States and the second largest of all national groups to immigrate. Since the 1970 Census, an additional 90,000 Pilipinos from 1971 to 1974 have immigrated, representing an increase of about 25% over the 1970 figure. If the current rates of Pilipino immigration continue throughout the 70's, Pilipinos will outnumber both Japanese and Chinese in the United States.

Over two-thirds of the Pilipinos live on the West Coast, 40% in California alone and another 28% in Hawaii. A majority of the older Pilipinos who immigrated earlier in the century and their descendants live in these two states. The more recent immigrants are found concentrated in urban areas throughout the United States, particularly in the urban areas of California.

In 1960, 26% of all Pilipinos in the United States lived in rural areas. By 1970, however, that percentage had shrunk to 14%, though 22% of all elderly Pilipinos still live in rural areas.

In Hawaii, over a third of the Pilipinos (35%) are foreign-born. In California, 58% are foreign-born, while outside California and Hawaii are 63%.

In 1960 there were almost two Pilipino males for every Pilipino female in the United States. Since then, more Pilipino women have been immigrating and the ratio of males to females is becoming more balanced. By 1970, the proportion of males in the Pilipino population was only 10% higher than the proportion of females. Among the elderly, however, the imbalance is still very marked. Among Pilipinos 65 years old and over, there are 4.5 times more males than females.

Children, 18 and under, comprise 36% of the Pilipino population, slightly above the U.S. average of 34%. In Hawaii, the 18 and under population is up to 42% of the total population, while in the urban areas outside Hawaii and California, the proportion is down to 31% of the total.

Only 10% of all Pilipinos 18 years old and over are elderly while the proportion for the U.S. is 15%. In areas outside Hawaii and California, young adult immigrants far outnumber the elderly and only 7% of the Pilipino adult population are 65 years old or over. In the rural areas, however, where older Pilipino farm workers have tended to remain, the percentage of all persons over 18 who are elderly is up to the U.S. average of 15%.

Family Characteristics

The percentage of Pilipino husband/wife families is the same as that of the U.S. However, the percentage of such families with children under 18 (69%) and under 6 (42%) are far higher than among families in the total population (56% and 27%).

Pilipino families with a female head are relatively young, as are most Pilipino families. Of the female-headed families, 69% have children under 18 and 39% have children under 6. This high incidence is

in large part due to the growing number of young widows who married and bore the children of elderly first-generation immigrants.

The rate of interracial marriages involving Pilipinos is quite high with 33% of the males and 28% of the females married to a spouse of a different ethnic/racial group. Among the men, the Pilipinos have the highest rate of intermarriage for any Asian group.

Until immigration laws loosened, there were few Pilipino women in the United States. Many older Pilipino males who did not marry live alone as primary individuals. The largely male primary individual population is particularly visible in Hawaii and the rural U.S. where males living alone outnumber females living alone nine to one. Most of these persons are middle-aged and elderly; 83% of the Pilipino primary individuals in Hawaii and 90% in rural U.S. are 45 years old and over.

Of families in the three major Asian subgroups, Pilipino families are the largest. 38% of all Pilipino families have five or more members.

23% of all Pilipino families are extended families, nearly twice the proportion for the total U.S. population and a far higher percentage than in either the Japanese or Chinese population.

Educational Characteristics

Less than half of all Pilipino men (49%) have completed high school—a rate 5% lower than the rate for men in the total U.S. population.

Many of the older Pilipino males have had very little formal schooling; the median years of schooling completed by Pilipino males 65 years old and over is only 5.4 years.

Nationally, the percentage of Pilipino men who have completed college (15%) is slightly above the U.S. average for men (13%) despite the large number of older uneducated males in the population. This results from the impact of the large number of educated Pilipino male professionals who have immigrated to the United States.

A large proportion of the recent female immigrants are, like the males, educated professionals and they greatly outnumber the few elderly, less educated women in the Pilipino population. In general the Pilipino female population is much better educated than the Pilipino male population.

Of the Pilipino women, 64% have completed high

568

school—one of the highest rates of women in any subgroup and far higher than the 49% of Pilipino males who have completed high school. The proportion of Pilipino women with a college education (27%) is the highest for any population groups, male or female.

Despite the high percentage of educated Pilipinos who have already completed college, younger Pilipinos are not enrolled in school today at a rate adequate to continue this high educational level.

The rate of 3-4 years old Pilipino enrollment in school (15%) is at about the U.S. level but is much lower than the other two Asian subgroups. Yet, the labor force participation rate of Pilipino women is higher than for any other female population group, suggesting that 3-4 years old Pilipinos need more preschool enrollment opportunities.

The enrollment rates of college-aged Pilipinos 18 to 24 years old are below U.S. averages. Only 28% of Pilipino males and 23% of Pilipino females in that age group are in school, while the U.S. total rates are 37% and 27% for males and females. Pilipino young people, many of whom are second and third generation, are not getting as much advanced education as the rest of the country.

Employment Characteristics

79% of all Pilipino males 16 years old and over are in the labor force—2% higher than the participation rate of the total U.S. male population.

Some 40% of all the employed Pilipino men in the U.S. are working in low-skilled, low-paying jobs, such as laborers (including farm labor) and service workers. This is twice the proportion for men in the total population (19%).

12% of the employed Pilipino men are farm workers compared to only 5% of all employed U.S. men. In rural areas, 43% of the Pilipino men are farm workers. By far the majority of the farm workers are middle-aged or elderly. In California, 80% of all Pilipino farm workers are 45 years old or over. In Hawaii, 70% of all Pilipinos working on farms are as old.

Between 1960 and 1970, the labor force participation rate of Pilipino women underwent a phenomenal increase, from 36% to 55%. The participation rate of Pilipino women is now the highest nationally for any group of women. In 1960 only 9% of all married Pilipino women were in the labor force and by 1970 46% were.

The occupations held by the Pilipino women vary markedly from area to area. In Hawaii 55% of the women are employed as semi-skilled operatives, laborers, or service workers.

In California 42% are employed as clerical and sales workers while 21% are professionals. In areas outside Hawaii and California, 55% are employed as professionals.

With the immigration of large numbers of highly trained Pilipinos their numbers in higher level jobs in the United States have increased greatly. The proportion of Pilipino males who are professionals has tripled since 1960. On the other hand, despite the increase of highly skilled persons, the proportion of Pilipinos employed as laborers and in service occupations has remained about the same over the decade.

Income Characteristics

The income levels of Pilipino men are lower than for men in the total population. Of all Pilipino men, 40% earn less than $4,000 a year (the U.S. average is 31%) and only 12% earn over $10,000 (half the U.S. rate of 25%).

Income levels of Pilipino men have not kept up with their level of education. Of all men 25-34 years old in the U.S., 2.4 earn $10,000 or more for every one that is a college graduate. Among Pilipino men of that age, only 0.9 earn $10,000 or more for every one that is a college graduate.

More Pilipino women are in the labor force (55%) and their level of education (27% are college graduates) is higher than women in any other group. Despite these characteristics, however, the median income levels of Pilipino women are only slightly higher than those of other women. Of all Pilipino women, 56% have an income less than $4,000, a very high percentage of low-income earners.

The income levels of Pilipino families tend to be lower than for Chinese and Japanese families and at about the level of the U.S. average. The level should be higher, however, because 61% of all Pilipino families have more than one earner compared to only 51% of all U.S. families, and 46% of all Pilipino wives in husband/wife families work compared to only 39% of all U.S. wives.

46% of Pilipino female-headed families have incomes less than $4,000. The Pilipino female head is relatively young and thus is less likely to have grown children who could help support the family. Indeed, 39% of the Pilipino female heads have young children under 6. For these women, child care would be an additional income drain.

Poverty Characteristics and Sources of Income

Pilipino families in the U.S. are receiving Social Security at a rate far lower than that of families in the total population (14% compared to 20%) and the amount they receive is less. Elderly Pilipino household heads in both San Francisco and Los Angeles are receiving Social Security benefits at rates below the total population in those cities. This situation is duplicated throughout the country.

Pilipino families nationally are receiving welfare at a ratio equal to the U.S. national level (2.1 families in poverty for every one receiving public assistance). In selected local areas, however, there is a serious imbalance. In urban areas outside Hawaii and California, there are 3.5 families in poverty to every one on welfare. In San Francisco, while 31% of all poverty families are on welfare, only 19% of Pilipino families in poverty are.

25% of all Pilipino elderly are poor. 63% of the Pilipino elderly who are poor live alone; most are men.

28% of all Pilipino households in the United States live in overcrowded conditions, but 40% of all Pilipino families in Honolulu and 30% in San San Francisco live under such substandard conditions.

Korean American

Immigration and Population

The 1970 Census for the first time enumerated Koreans as a distinct ethnic group. In that year, 70,000 were reported, making them the fifth largest Asian subgroup in the United States (the Hawaiians being the fourth largest).

Currently, Koreans are the second largest Asian group immigrating to the United States. Since the 1970 Census, from 1971 to 1974, another 56,100 Koreans immigrated to the U.S. representing an 80% increase over the 1970 population. By 1980, the Korean population is likely to be more than the Hawaiian.

The Koreans in the U.S. are a more dispersed population than other Asians. In 1970, 44% of all Koreans were living in the West, 20% in the Northeast, 19% in the Midwest, and 17% in the South.

Among Koreans immigrating between 1965 and 1973, less than a third went to states in the West. The remaining immigrants have settled in all the other regions of the country in equal distribution—a pattern unlike that of the other Asian immigrant populations.

Family Characteristics

The proportion of Korean families in the U.S. headed by females (15%) is higher than the proportion nationally (11%).

The proportion of these female-headed families with children is also high. A quarter of the female-headed families in Honolulu, Los Angeles, and New York City have children under six; outside these three cities, 47% of the female-headed families.

A great many of the Korean children in the U.S. were born in Korea. Over a third (36%) of all Koreans immigrating since 1970 were under 20 years of age when they arrived; most of them were under 10.

Educational Characteristics

In the country as a whole, 55% of all adults have completed high school. Among Koreans, 71% (over 80% in Los Angeles and New York City). Nationally, over one-third of their population (36%) have a college education, more than triple the proportion in the country as a whole (11%).

English-language facility is a major problem for all Koreans, hampering the ability of adults to obtain a job commensurate with their education as well as the performance of children in school. In 1970, 58% of the native-born Koreans and 91% of the foreign-born Koreans listed Korean as their mother tongue.

Employment Characteristics

The labor force participation rate of Koreans, nationally, is close to the level for the total population. 76% of all Korean men are in the labor force compared to 77% of all U.S. men. 42% of Korean women are in the labor force compared to 41% of all women in the country. (This participation rate of Korean women is much lower, however, than comparable levels for women in other Asian sub-groups).

About three-fourths (72%) of those Koreans who reported an occupation when they immigrated to the U.S. indicated highly skilled backgrounds in professional, technical and managerial occupations. Data from the Census on the jobs Koreans obtained after they entered the U.S. are lacking, however.

Income Characteristics

In 1970, the income levels of Korean males and females were close to national levels. However, proportionate to the number of Korean college graduates the income of Korean workers lags behind that of the rest of the population.

Hawaiian

Population

In 1970, there were nearly 100,000 Hawaiians in the United States, 72,000 in the State of Hawaii itself, 14,000 in California and another 13,000 elsewhere.

Two thirds of the Hawaiians in the State of Hawaii live in the greater Honolulu area, and almost all of them were born in that state. Three-quarters of Hawaiians now living in California were born in Hawaii.

The birth rate of Hawaiians is higher than for most Asian populations in America—an average 4.5 children per woman 35-44 years old. Owing to this high birth rate, the proportion of young people in the Hawaiian population is high. Of their population nationally, 42% are under 18 (45% in Hawaii).

About 40% of Hawaiian men and women are married to non-Hawaiians.

The percentage of persons 65 and over in the population 18 years of age and over (7%) is less than half the proportion in the overall U.S. population (15%).

Educational Characteristics

The level of education of Hawaiians is comparable to that of the total U.S. population. A breakdown by states shows that the Hawaiians in California are doing somewhat better, and the Hawaiians in Hawaii are doing somewhat worse.

The rate of college enrollment of Hawaiians 18 to 24 years old is lower than the rate for the country as a whole. One-third of all 18-24 years old in the U.S. are enrolled in school, but less than one-quarter of the Hawaiians are.

Employment Characteristics

The rate of labor force participation by Hawaiian males in Hawaii (76%) is close to the rate for all males in the country (77%) and, for women, higher than all women (48% compared to 41%). In California, rates of labor force participation by Hawaiians are higher still: 84% for males and 51% for females.

Income Characteristics

Comparisons of incomes between persons living in Hawaii and persons living elsewhere in the United States must take into consideration the fact that the cost of living on the Islands is about 25% higher than elsewhere. Since 72% of all Hawaiians live in Hawaii, more accurate comparisons would be between the Hawaiians and other ethnic populations in that state.

The median income for Hawaiian men in Hawaii ($6,485) is lower than for Japanese or Chinese men in Hawaii, but higher than for Pilipino men in that state. The median income for Hawaiian women repeats the same pattern. But at $2,931, this income is very low considering the high cost of living in Hawaii.

Table 1   Population Characteristics of the U.S. Total and Asian American Populations, 1970

	U.S. Total	Japanese				Chinese					Pilipinos					Koreans			
		United States	Hawaii	California	Other	United States	Hawaii	California	San Francisco	New York City	United States	Hawaii	California	Rural	Urban*	United States	Hawaii	Los Angeles	New York City
Total Population of Subgroup (000's)**	203,212	588.3	217.2	213.3	157.9	431.6	52.6	170.4	59.1	70.2	336.7	95.7	135.2	48.4	97.1	70.0	9.0	9.3	4.7
% of Total Subgroup Population		100%	36%	36%	28%	100%	12%	39%	13%	16%	100%	28%	40%	14%	28%	100%	13%	13%	7%
Urban/Rural Distribution: % Urban	73	89	86	94	88	97	93	97	NA	NA	86	68	93	0	100	NA	NA	NA	NA
% Rural	27	11	14	6	12	3	7	3	NA	NA	14	32	7	100	0	NA	NA	NA	NA
% American Born	95	79	90	79	64	53	89	54	48	34	47	65	42	55	37	46	79	38	37
% Foreign Born	5	21	10	21	36	47	11	46	52	67	53	35	58	45	63	54	21	62	63
Age Distribution: % Under 18 Years	34	29	31	30	25	32	35	32	31	31	36	42	36	37	31	35	37	32	32
% 65 Years & Over	10	8	8	7	9	6	8	6	9	7	6	7	7	10	5	3	7	3	3
Median Age: Male (years)	26.8	29.6	30.5	29.2	28.8	27.8	28.1	27.1	27.1	30.9	28.3	28.2	29.3	34.2	28.2	NA	NA	NA	NA
Female (years)	29.3	34.3	32.9	32.9	37.8	25.8	28.8	25.8	25.9	26.7	24.5	20.2	24.4	21.5	25.1	NA	NA	NA	NA

*Except urban California and urban Hawaii.

**Totals for populations do not agree with data contained elsewhere in this report due to sampling error.

Source: U.S. Bureau of the Census, 1970 Census of Population
General Social and Economic Characteristics, United States Summary, PC(1)-C1
General Population Characteristics, United States Summary, PC(1)-B1
Detailed Characteristics, United States Summary, PC(1)-D1
Subject Reports: Japanese, Chinese, and Filipinos in the United States, PC(2)-1G

572

Table 2 Family Characteristics of the U.S. Total and Asian American Populations, 1970

	United States Total	Japanese United States	Japanese Hawaii	Japanese California	Japanese Other	Chinese United States	Chinese Hawaii	Chinese California	Chinese San Francisco	Chinese New York City	Pilipino United States	Pilipino Hawaii	Pilipino California	Pilipino Rural	Pilipino Urban***
% Husband-Wife Families	86%	86%	87%	86%	83%	89%	85%	88%	87%	89%	86%	86%	86%	88%	86%
% With Children Under 18	56	61	61	63	57	66	64	66	61	62	69	72	69	65	68
% With Children Under 6	27	27	25	28	28	33	28	32	26	31	42	40	39	34	49
% Female-Headed Families	11	10	9	10	14	7	10	8	9	5	9	6	9	4	10
% With Children Under 18	55	56	44	58	66	49	39	50	48	46	69	73	73	72	60
% With Children Under 6	21	15	10	18	18	13	12	9	7	10	39	38	40	35	39
% Primary Individuals	20	21	14	22	29	22	12	23	27	23	21	19	21	24	23
% Male	37	48	48	51	46	69	54	66	65	74	70	89	75	90	51
% Female	63	52	52	49	54	31	46	34	35	26	30	11	25	10	49
% Families with 3 or More Own Children Under 18	20	18	18	18	16	23	24	23	23*	22**	28	33	27	33	24
% Families with 5 or More Persons	25	27	31	26	19	35	38	37	37*	35**	38	49	37	44	30

*California, urban

**New York State, urban

***Except urban California and urban Hawaii

Source: U.S. Bureau of the Census, *1970 Census of Population*
General Social and Economic Characteristics, United States Summary, PC(1)-C1
Detailed Characteristics, United States Summary, PC(1)-D1
Subject Reports: Japanese, Chinese, and Filipinos in the United States, PC(2)-1G

Table 3

MARRIAGE WITHIN OWN SUBGROUP
BY SEX, 1970

Percent of all Married Persons with a Spouse of Same Ethnic/Racial Group		Asian Americans			
		U.S. Total	Japanese	Chinese	Pilipinos
Total 16 & Over:	Male	99%	88%	87%	67%
	Female	99	67	88	72
16-24 Yrs:	Male	NA	62	59	51
	Female	NA	54	72	50
25-44 Yrs:	Male	NA	84	84	72
	Female	NA	57	87	72
45 Years & Over:	Male	NA	93	90	63
	Female	NA	84	93	88

Table 4

MARRIAGE OUTSIDE OWN SUBGROUP
BY ORIGIN OF SPOUSE, 1970

	Origin of Spouse				
	% Other Asian	% White	% Spanish Origin	% Black	% Other*
Origin of Wife					
Japanese	8%	81%	4%	3%	4%
Chinese	18	59	8	3	13
Pilipino	7	54	22	7	9
Origin of Husband					
Japanese	14%	65%	8%	1%	12%
Chinese	25	49	12	3	11
Pilipino	12	42	30	3	12

*Includes Asian who are not Japanese, Chinese or Pilipinos; American Indians, etc.

Source: U.S. Bureau of the Census, *1970 Census of Population;*
Detailed Characteristics, United States Summary, PC(1)-D1;
Subject Reports: *Japanese, Chinese, and Filipinos in the*
United States, PC(2)-1G; *Subject Report: Marital Status,* PC(2)-4C.

EDUCATIONAL CHARACTERISTICS OF THE U.S. TOTAL AND ASIAN AMERICAN POPULATIONS, 1970
(16 years of age or older)

Chart 1

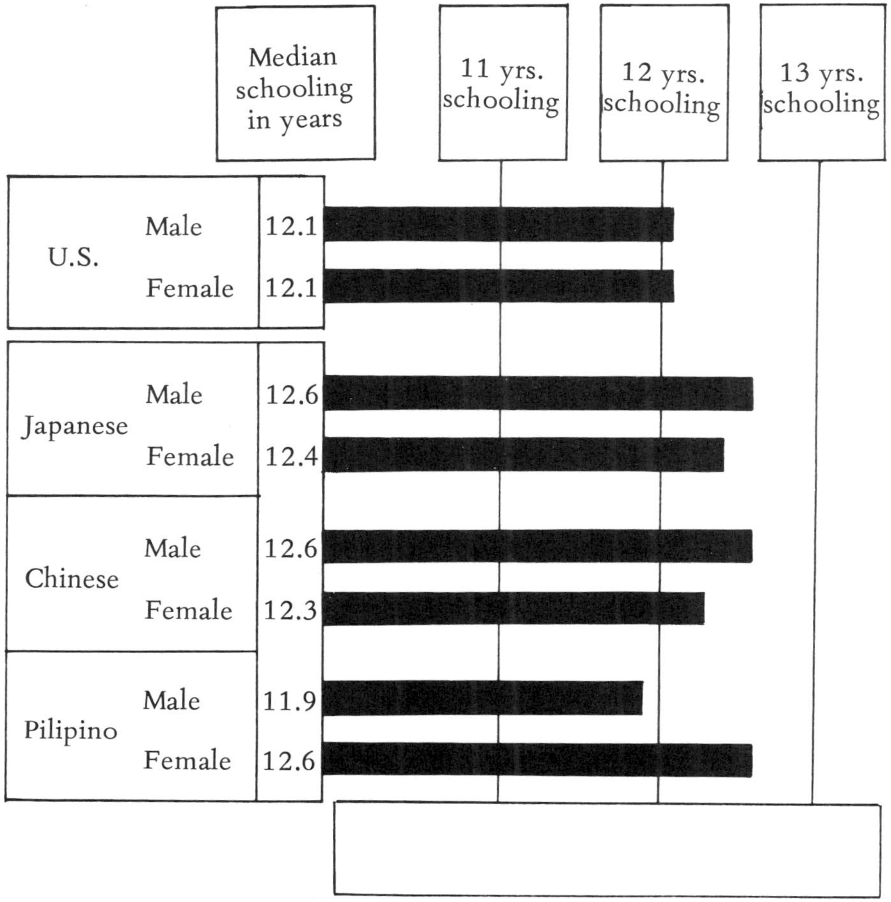

	Median schooling in years	11 yrs. schooling	12 yrs. schooling	13 yrs. schooling
U.S. Male	12.1			
U.S. Female	12.1			
Japanese Male	12.6			
Japanese Female	12.4			
Chinese Male	12.6			
Chinese Female	12.3			
Pilipino Male	11.9			
Pilipino Female	12.6			

Table 5

Schooling Completed	% of 8 yrs. or less	% of high school graduates	% of 4 yrs. of college or more
U.S. Male	27	54	13
U.S. Female	25	55	8
Japanese Male	15	70	19
Japanese Female	17	67	11
Chinese Male	23	62	25
Chinese Female	28	58	17
Pilipino Male	32	49	15
Pilipino Female	20	64	27
Korean*	19	71	36

Figures for other Asian groups not available.

*Census figures on Koreans are not tabulated by sex.

Source: U.S. Bureau of the Census, *1970 Census of Population Subject Reports: Japanese, Chinese, and Filipinos in the United States*, PC(2)-1G.

575

Table 6 EMPLOYMENT CHARACTERISTICS OF THE U.S. TOTAL AND ASIAN AMERICAN POPULATIONS, 1970

EMPLOYMENT STATUS (16 years and over)

		U.S. Total	JAPANESE United States	JAPANESE Hawaii	JAPANESE California	JAPANESE Other	CHINESE United States	CHINESE Hawaii	CHINESE California	CHINESE San Francisco	CHINESE New York City	PILIPINOS United States	PILIPINOS Hawaii	PILIPINOS California	PILIPINOS Rural	PILIPINOS Urban
% in Labor Force	Male	76.6	79.3	79.7	80.9	76.3	73.2	76.1	73.5	70.4	70.9	79.0	76.1	78.0	75.2	83.1*
	Female	41.4	49.4	57.2	49.6	40.4	49.5	54.2	51.0	55.7	50.5	55.2	47.8	55.4	43.1	61.0
% Unemployed	Male	3.9	2.0	1.4	2.4	2.5	3.0	2.1	4.0	4.9	2.5	4.7	2.8	6.2	3.7	4.7
	Female	5.1	3.0	2.1	2.8	4.6	3.7	1.8	4.7	3.8	2.9	4.7	4.8	5.9	8.5	3.2

MAJOR OCCUPATIONS

		U.S. Total	JAPANESE United States	JAPANESE Hawaii	JAPANESE California	JAPANESE Other	CHINESE United States	CHINESE Hawaii	CHINESE California	CHINESE San Francisco	CHINESE New York City	PILIPINOS United States	PILIPINOS Hawaii	PILIPINOS California	PILIPINOS Rural	PILIPINOS Urban
Professional & Tech. Workers	Male	14.3	21.3	14.0	24.0	30.4	28.9	21.7	25.8	15.0	16.9	18.1	4.6	12.6	5.9	41.9**
	Female	15.7	15.9	15.9	15.3	16.7	19.4	19.1	15.2	8.0	12.6	31.8	7.9	20.9	13.1	54.5
Managers & Administrators	Male	11.2	11.7	12.4	10.4	12.8	11.4	14.1	11.3	9.5	9.5	3.1	2.9	3.2	1.6	3.1
	Female	3.6	3.8	4.3	3.2	3.8	3.8	5.5	3.5	3.1	3.4	1.7	2.1	1.8	2.3	1.4
Sales Workers	Male	6.9	6.0	6.0	5.9	6.2	4.4	6.5	5.4	5.9	4.5	2.1	2.0	2.2	1.1	1.9
	Female	7.4	6.9	9.1	5.3	5.7	5.1	9.1	5.5	5.3	3.4	3.7	8.0	3.3	5.8	2.0
Clerical Workers	Male	7.6	9.0	9.7	8.8	8.3	9.4	11.3	12.2	15.8	8.5	9.2	4.8	12.1	2.9	10.1
	Female	34.9	34.3	34.6	38.1	28.5	31.8	37.1	36.6	37.3	24.8	29.1	25.0	38.9	16.9	21.7
Craftsmen, Foremen & Kindred Workers	Male	21.2	19.7	30.2	12.7	13.1	7.3	19.5	7.8	9.2	4.5	13.1	22.3	9.2	12.7	8.3
	Female	1.8	1.8	1.8	1.6	2.2	1.2	1.9	1.2	1.6	1.5	1.1	1.9	1.0	1.9	0.8
Operatives	Male	19.5	10.3	11.4	9.2	10.1	10.5	9.2	11.2	12.6	16.1	14.3	20.2	12.1	15.8	10.6
	Female	14.3	13.5	9.9	14.0	18.4	22.5	8.0	23.0	30.8	46.2	10.8	14.5	12.7	11.8	7.0
Laborers, Except Farm	Male	6.6	9.9	6.4	16.4	5.3	3.3	5.2	4.0	3.5	1.8	8.2	14.0	6.1	7.9	4.6
	Female	1.0	0.8	0.7	1.1	0.8	0.9	1.0	0.7	0.3	0.8	0.7	1.6	0.6	2.3	0.4
Farm Managers & Laborers	Male	4.5	5.2	3.1	7.0	6.1	0.7	1.1	1.1	0.3	0.1	11.7	14.2	16.1	43.3	2.4
	Female	0.8	2.1	2.0	2.9	2.5	0.5	0.6	0.9	0.3	0.0	1.9	5.3	1.5	14.0	0.5
Service Workers	Male	8.1	6.6	6.7	5.6	7.8	24.0	11.4	21.1	28.2	38.1	20.3	15.1	26.5	8.9	16.9
	Female	20.4	20.8	21.9	18.4	22.4	14.8	17.8	13.6	13.2	7.2	19.2	33.8	19.3	32.1	11.6

*Except urban Hawaii and urban California
**U.S. Total minus urban and rural California and urban and rural Hawaii

Table 7

Occupations of Japanese and Chinese* By Sex and Nativity: 1970

Occupations:	Japanese Males U.S. Born	Japanese Males Foreign Born	Japanese Females U.S. Born	Japanese Females Foreign Born	Chinese Males U.S. Born	Chinese Males Foreign Born	Chinese Females U.S. Born	Chinese Females Foreign Born
Occupations:	100%	100%	100%	100%	100%	100%	100%	100%
Professional, Technical and Managerial	31	45	21	13	38	42	24	22
Clerical and Sales Workers	15	13	47	19	18	10	51	24
Craftsmen and Operatives	33	13	11	31	22	15	9	37
Laborers, Non-Farm	9	13	1	1	5	2	1	1
Service Workers Including Domestics	4	9	18	33	16	30	14	15
Farm-Related Managers and Workers	10	7	2	3	1	1	1	1

*Comparable data on Pilipinos and Koreans are not available.

Table 8

Percent Japanese and Chinese Women in the Labor Force by Nativity and Age**

	All Women	Japanese Women U.S. Born*	Japanese Women Foreign Born	Chinese Women U.S. Born*	Chinese Women Foreign Born
Total (16 and Over)	41%	57%	32%	51%	48%
16-24 Yrs. Old	46	51	33	46	46
25-44 Yrs. Old	47	63	37	55	52
45-64 Yrs. Old	48	65	48	60	57
65 and Over	10	13	11	15	13

*Second generation only.
**Data on Pilipino women are not available.

Source: U.S. Bureau of the Census, 1970 Census of Population, Subject Reports: National Origin and Language PC (2)-1A.

Source: U.S. Bureau of the Census, 1970 Census of Population, Subject Report: National Origin and Language, Subject Reports: Japanese, Chinese and Filipinos in the United States.

Table 9 INCOME CHARACTERISTICS OF THE U.S. TOTAL POPULATION AND ASIAN AMERICANS, 1970

	U.S. Total	Japanese				Chinese					Pilipinos					Koreans			
		United States	Hawaii	California	Other	United States	Hawaii	California	San Francisco	New York City	United States	Hawaii	California	Rural	Urban	United States	Honolulu	Los Angeles	New York City
Income of Persons 16 and Over																			
% Under $4,000 Male	31	30	26	29	36	41	27	40	44	47	40	36	43	47	39**	34	26	31	24
Female	68	58	54	58	65	65	54	67	68	61	56	69	56	74	47	69	55	55	46
% $10,000 & Over Male	25	33	33	32	31	24	36	25	15	12	12	11	11	6	17	25	39	23	35
Female	3	5	5	3	4	5	7	4	3	3	5	2	3	2	8	3	7	4	3
Income of Families																			
% Under $4,000	15	10	6	9	16	13	7	13	16	16	14	12	15	16	15*	NA	NA	NA	NA
% $10,000 & Over	47	65	71	65	54	54	71	56	49	35	46	45	44	35	48	NA	NA	NA	NA
Median Income (dollars)	9,590	12,515	13,542	12,393	11,034	10,610	14,936	10,916	9,879	7,809	9,318	9,289	9,124	7,475	9,690	NA	NA	NA	NA
Income of Families with Female Heads																			
% Under $4,000	41	32	18	31	47	28	21	28	28†	26††	46	45	48	48	43	NA	NA	NA	NA
% $10,000 & Over	18	29	39	29	19	28	40	27	27	25	20	18	16	18	26	NA	NA	NA	NA
Median Income (dollars)	4,962	6,467	8,112	6,689	4,636	6,627	8,256	6,369	6,359	6,716	4,708	4,574	4,341	4,348	5,254	NA	NA	NA	NA

*Urban U.S. except urban Hawaii and urban California.
**Total U.S. except Hawaii and California.
†Urban California.
††Urban New York.

Source: U.S. Bureau of the Census, 1970 Census of Population
General Social and Economic Characteristics, United States Summary, PC(1)-C1
Detailed Characteristics, United States Summary, PC(1)-D1
Subject Reports: Japanese, Chinese, and Filipinos in the United States, PC(2)-1G

CHART 2: ASIAN AMERICAN INCOMES UNDER $4,000 AND $10,000 AND OVER

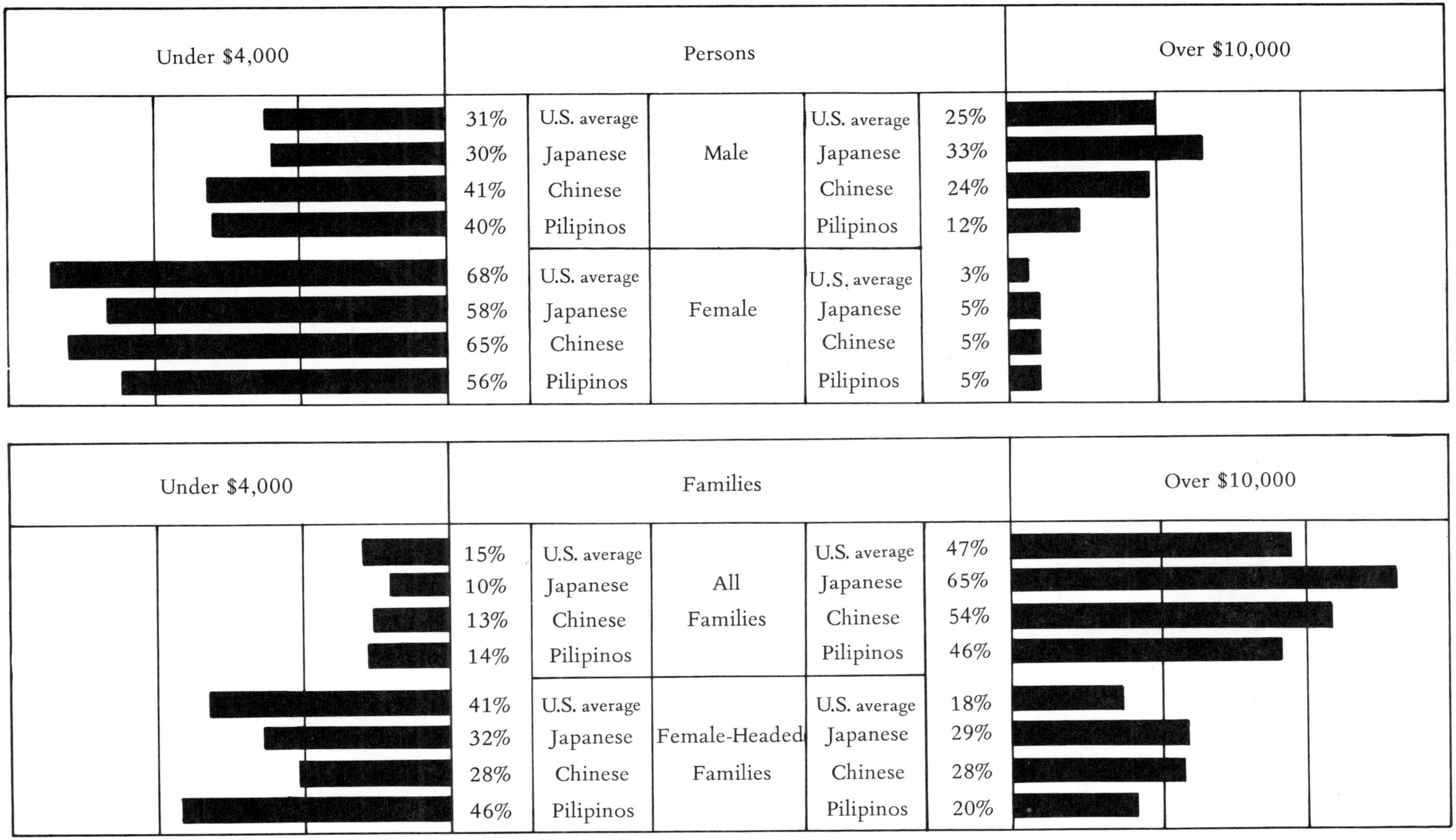

Persons

	Under $4,000	Over $10,000
Male		
U.S. average	31%	25%
Japanese	30%	33%
Chinese	41%	24%
Pilipinos	40%	12%
Female		
U.S. average	68%	3%
Japanese	58%	5%
Chinese	65%	5%
Pilipinos	56%	5%

Families

	Under $4,000	Over $10,000
All Families		
U.S. average	15%	47%
Japanese	10%	65%
Chinese	13%	54%
Pilipinos	14%	46%
Female-Headed Families		
U.S. average	41%	18%
Japanese	32%	29%
Chinese	28%	28%
Pilipinos	46%	20%

Source: U.S. Bureau of the Census, *1970 Census of Population, Detailed Characteristics, United States Summary*, PC(1)-D-1

Table 10

Ratios of Income to Persons in Professional, Technical and Managerial Occupations: 1970*

Ratios of Persons Earning $10,000 or More to Persons in Professional, Technical and Managerial Occupations

	Males			Females		
	25-34	35-44	45-64	25-34	35-44	45-64
U.S. Total	1.1	1.5	1.6	0.2	0.3	0.4
Chinese	0.6	1.0	1.0	0.2	0.4	0.5
Japanese	0.8	1.3	1.7	0.2	0.4	0.5
Pilipinos	0.6	1.0	1.9	0.1	0.3	0.4

Table 11

Ratios of Income to Education and Occupation for Asian Americans: 1970

Ratios of Persons Earning $10,000 or More to Persons With 4 Years College or More

	Males			Females			Males and Females 16 & over
	25-34	35-44	45-64	25-34	35-44	45-64	
U.S. Total	1.5	2.4	3.1	0.1	0.3	0.5	1.4
Chinese	0.5	1.1	1.5	0.1	0.3	0.4	0.7
Japanese	0.9	1.8	3.4	0.1	0.4	0.8	1.2
Pilipinos	0.5	0.9	2.2	0.1	0.3	0.3	0.4
Koreans	NA	NA	NA	NA	NA	NA	0.4

Source: U.S. Bureau of the Census, *1970 Census of Population, Detailed Characteristics, U.S. Summary*, PC-D1; *Subject Reports: Japanese, Chinese, and Filipinos in the United States*, PC(2)-1G

* This category of occupations includes self-employed owners and proprietors of small retail and service businesses (such as family-run grocery stores, restaurants, laundries, service stations). A sizeable number of Asian Americans are in these occupations.

ASIAN AMERICAN POPULATIONS, 1970

		Japanese				Chinese					Pilipinos				
	U.S. Total	United States	Hawaii	California	Other	United States	Hawaii	California	San Francisco	New York City	United States	Hawaii	California	Rural	Urban**
Type of Income															
% of Families Receiving Social Security	20%	20%	22%	17%	20%	14%	20%	16%	15%[1]	14%[2]	14%	17%	15%	21%	11%
% of Families Receiving Public Assistance	5.3	2.7	1.8	3.6	2.9	3.6	2.7	5.2	5.9[1]	3.4[2]	5.7	6.3	7.5	6.5	3.1
Incidence of Poverty*															
% of All Families	11	6	3.9	6.3	11	10	5.5	10	12	15	12	11	12	14	11
% Female Headed	33	40	28	28	48	13	31	15	11	7	29	24	31	15	32
% Female Headed Families in Poverty	32	25	13	24	37	20	18	19	16	20	40	43	41	48	36
% of All Persons	14	8	5	8	11	13	7	13	15	17	14	12	14	15	14
% Who are 65 & Over	19	21	26	16	22	13	19	13	18	17	12	19	11	20	8
% of 65 & Over in Poverty	26	19	15	17	26	28	16	27	31	40	25	33	20	31	24
% Unrelated Individuals in Poverty	37	34	34	31	37	40	38	40	37	36	30	33	30	28	31

[1] Urban California
[2] Urban New York State

*Per definition used by U.S. Census
**Except urban Hawaii and urban California

Source: U.S. Bureau of the Census, 1970 Census of Population
General Social and Economic Characteristics, United States Summary, PC(1)-C1
Detailed Characteristics, United States Summary, PC(1)-D1
Subject Reports: Japanese, Chinese, and Filipinos in the United States, PC(2)-1G

CHART 3 ASIAN AMERICAN POVERTY AND WELFARE DATA FOR SELECTED AREAS

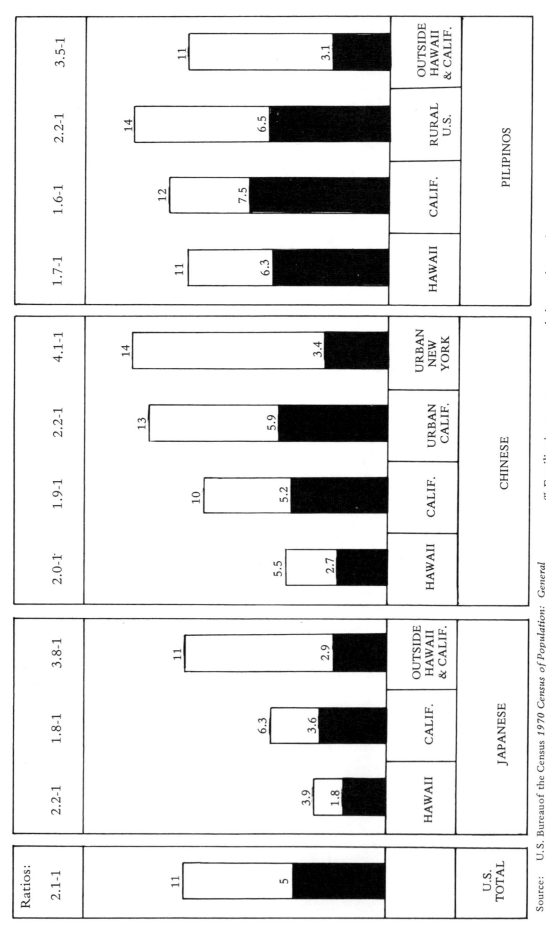

Source: U.S. Bureau of the Census 1970 *Census of Population: General Social and Economic Characteristics, United States Summary,* PC(1)-C1 *Subject Reports: Japanese, Chinese, and Pilipinos in the United States* PC(2)-1C

% Families in poverty represented above white columns.
% Families receiving welfare represented above black columns.

Table 13   Substandard Housing Among Asian Americans in Selected Areas

		U.S. Total	Japanese		Chinese		Pilipinos	
			Total	Poverty	Total	Poverty	Total	Poverty
Total U.S.	% overcrowded (1.01 or more persons per room)	8	9	NA	20	NA	28	NA
	% units without complete plumbing	7	4	NA	10	NA	9	NA
Los Angeles, Calif.	% overcrowded (1.01 or more persons per room)	8	7	9	23	23	27	31
	% units without complete plumbing	2	3	8	5	5	4	3
San Francisco, Calif.	% overcrowded (1.01 or more persons per room)	6	5	7	24	28	30	24
	% units without complete plumbing	8	5	5	20	41	11	28
New York, New York	% overcrowded (1.01 or more persons per room)	10	12	NA	30	37*	23	NA
	% units without complete plumbing	3	7	NA	22	NA	7	NA
Honolulu, Hawaii	% overcrowded (1.01 or more persons per room)	18	18	NA	19	NA	40	NA
	% units without complete plumbing	4	2	NA	4	NA	17	NA

*Data for area in and near New York City's Chinatown, all income levels included.

Source: U.S. Bureau of the Census, 1970 Census of Population, Subject Reports: Japanese, Chinese and Pilipinos in the United States PC(2)-1G; "Operation Leap" Tabulations (unpublished); Housing Characteristics, U.S. Summary HC(1)-A1.

Table 15

Occupational Distribution of Asian Immigrants: 1965-1973
At Time of Entry

	Country of Birth			
	Japan	China, Taiwan & Hong Kong	Philippines	Korea
All Immigrants Reporting an Occupation	100%	100%	100%	100%
Professional, Technical and Managerial Workers	53	50	69	72
Clerical and Sales Workers	17	11	8	7
Craftsmen and Operatives	8	16	6	12
Laborers, Nonfarm	2	2	2	1*
Service Workers Including Domestic	17	2	9	8
Farm-Related Managers and Workers	3	0.2	6	NA
% of All Immigrants with no Occupations or not Reporting an Occupation (includes housewives & children)	75	63	55	73

* Laborers, Farm and Nonfarm

Source: U.S. Immigration and Naturalization Service *Annual Reports*, 1965-1973.

Table 14

Immigration of Asians Since the 1970 Census

Place of Birth	China, Taiwan & Hong Kong	Japan	Philippines	Korea	Other Asia*	Total
Population 1970 Census	435,000	591,000	343,000	70,000	224,000	1,663,000
Immigration Since 1970 Census						
1971	17,600	4,500	28,500	14,300	14,000	78,900
1972	21,700	4,800	29,400	18,900	19,400	94,200
1973	21,700	5,500	30,800	22,900	15,600	96,500
Total as of 1974	496,000	605,800	431,700	126,100	273,000	1,932,600
Percent Increase:**	14%	3%	26%	80%	22%	16%

* Includes Southeast Asia—such as Burma,— Indonesia, Thailand, Vietnam; East Asia—such as Ryukyu Islands, Tibet, Mongolia; Oceania—Hawaii, Western Samoa, Fiji, Pacific Islands. Does not include Western Asia (the Middle East), South Asia, Australia or New Zealand. (Editor's note: The definition of "other Asia" by the Census is puzzling. For example, Ryukyu Islands are a part of Japan, Tibet a part of China, and Hawaii a part of the U.S.)

** Percent Increase can only be taken as low estimate as Immigration data do not take into consideration Asian aliens residing in the U.S. whose visa status is that of Non-Immigrant, but subject to change.

Source: U.S. Bureau of the Census, *1970 Census of Population: Detailed Characteristics, United States Summary* PC(1)-C1; *Subject Reports: Japanese, Chinese, and Filipinos in the United States,* PC(2)-1G
U.S. Dept. of Justice, Immigration and Naturalization Service, *1973 Annual Report,* Table 14

SOURCES ON ASIAN AMERICANS
Compiled by Carolyn Yee

Bibliographies

Alcantara, Ruben R., et al. *The Filipinos in Hawaii: An Annotated Bibliography*. Working Paper. Honolulu: University of Hawaii, Social Science Research Institute, March 1972.

Asian Women. Berkeley: University of California, Asian Women's Journal Staff, 1971. (See "Annotated Bibliography on Asian Women," pp. 132-43.)

Barnhart, Edward N. *Japanese American Evacuation and Resettlement*. Berkeley: University of California, General Library, 1958.

Chinn, Thomas W., ed. *A History of the Chinese in California: A Syllabus*. San Francisco: Chinese Historical Society of America, 1969. (See bibliography, pp. 79-80.)

Cowan, Robert E. and Dunlap, Boutwell. *Bibliography of the Chinese Question in the United States*. San Francisco: A.M. Robertson, 1909.

Daniels, Roger. "American Historians and East Asian Immigrants." *Pacific Historical Review*, Vol. XLIII No. 4, November 1974, pp. 449-472.

Dickson, Diane. *World Catalogue of Theses on the Pacific Islands*. Honolulu: University of Hawaii Press, 1970.

Engelberg, Linda and Hori, Joan. *Ethnic Groups in the United States: A Bibliography of Books and Articles of Groups in Hawaii and on the Mainland*. Revised ed. includes supplements. Honolulu: University of Hawaii, Sinclair Undergraduate Library, 1973.

Fujimoto, Isao, et al. *Asians in America: A Selected Bibliography*. Asian American Research Project, Working Publ. no. 5. Davis: University of California, 1971.

Gardner, Arthur L. *The Koreans in Hawaii: An Annotated Bibliography*. Hawaii Series no. 2. Honolulu: University of Hawaii, Social Science Research Inst., 1970.

Hansen, Gladys C. *The Chinese in California: A Brief Bibliographic History*. Annotated by William F. Heintz. Portland: Richard Abel & Co., Inc., 1970.

Ichioka, Yuji, et al. *A Buried Past: An Annotated Bibliography of the Japanese American Research Project Collection*. Berkeley and Los Angeles: University of California Press, 1974.

Imamura, Mari and Lum, William W. *Asians in America: A Bibliography Supplement (II)*. Davis: University of California, 1970.

Kim, Christopher. "Annotated Bibliographies on Koreans in America." Working Papers series. Los Angeles: University of California, Asian American Studies Center, 1976.

Kim, Hyung-chan and Patterson, Wayne, ed. *The Koreans in America, 1882-1974*. Ethnic Chronology Series, No. 16. Dobbs Ferry: Oceania Publications, 1974. (See "Bibliography of Selected References," p. 141.)

Kitano, Harry L., et al. "Asian Americans: An Annotated Bibliography." Los Angeles: University of California, Asian American Studies Center, 1971.

Lin, Che-Hwei. "Preliminary Checklist of M.A. Theses and Ph.D. Dissertations Related to Asian Americans in the UCLA Library." Los Angeles: University of California, Asian American Studies Center, 1972.

Lowe, C.[huan] H.[ua]. *The Chinese in Hawaii: A Bibliographic Survey*. Taiwan: China Printing, Ltd., 1972.

Lum, William W. *Asians in America: A Bibliography*. Davis: University of California, 1969.

—————. *Asians in America: A Bibliography of Master's Theses and Dissertations*. Asian American Research Project, Working Publ. no. 2. Davis: University of California, 1970.

Lum, William W. and Ong, Paul M. *Theses and Dissertations on Asians in the U.S. with Selected References to Other Overseas Asians*. Davis: University of California, Asian American Studies, 1974.

Lyman, Stanford M. *Chinese Americans*. New York: Random House, 1974. (See Bibliography at pp. 192-206.

Macadangdang, Fortunato U. "A Selective Bibliography of Filipino Experiences in America." San Jose State Library, 1973.

Matsuda, Mitsugu. *The Japanese in Hawaii, 1868-1967: A Bibliography of the First Hundred Years*. Hawaii Series no. 1. Honolulu: University of Hawaii, Social Science Research Inst., 1968. (Parts II and III: English materials.)

————. *The Japanese in Hawaii: An Annotated Bibliography of Japanese Americans.* Hawaii Series no. 5. Rev. by Dennis M. Ogawa with Jerry Y. Fujioka. Honolulu: University of Hawaii, Social Sciences and Linguistics Inst., 1975.

Ng, Pearl. *Writings on the Chinese in California.* University of California, 1939. (See Part II: Bibliography.)

Potasi, Larry. "Bibliography for Samoans in America." Working Papers Series. Los Angeles: University of California, Asian American Studies Center, 1976.

Quinsaat, Jesse, ed. *Letters in Exile: An Introductory Reader on the History of Pilipinos in America.* Los Angeles: University of California, Asian American Studies Center, 1976. (See Bibliography.)

Rubano, Judith. *Culture and Behavior in Hawaii: An Annotated Bibliography.* Hawaii Series no. 3. Honolulu: University of Hawaii, Social Science Research Inst., 1971.

Saxton, Alexander. *The Indispensable Enemy: Labor and the Anti-Chinese Movement in California.* Berkeley and Los Angeles: University of California Press, 1971. (See "Bibliographic Note.")

Strona, Proserfina A., comp. "Filipinos in Hawaii: A Bibliography." Honolulu, Hawaii and Pacific Unit, State Library Branch, 1974.

Sung, Betty Lee. *Chinese American Manpower and Employment.* Report to Manpower Administration, U.S. Dept. of Labor. New York: Dept. of Asian American Studies, City College of New York, 1975. (See "Bibliography" at p. 357.)

Whitney, Philip B. "Forgotten Minority, Filipinos in the United States." *Bulletin of Bibliography,* Vol. 29, no. 3 (July-Sept. 1972), pp. 73-83.

Young, Nancy Foon. *The Chinese in Hawaii: An Annotated Bibliography.* Hawaii Series no. 4. Honolulu: University of Hawaii, Social Science Research Inst., 1973.

Government Publications

California Dept. of Industrial Relations. *Californians of Japanese, Chinese, and Filipino Ancestry: Population, Education, Employment, Income.* San Francisco: Div. of Labor Statistics and Research, 1965.

Cummings, Orpha and Hennefrund, Helen E. *Bibliography on the Japanese in American Agriculture.* U.S. Dept. of Agriculture Biblio. Bull. no. 3. Washington, D.C.: U.S. Government Printing Office, 1943.

U.S. Bureau of the Census. *Reports on the 1970 Census of Population.* Washington, D.C.: U.S. Government Printing Office.

————. *Subject Reports: Japanese, Chinese and Filipinos in the United States.* PC(2)-1G. (Also contains data on Koreans and Hawaiians.)

————. *Subject Reports: National Origin and Language.* PC(2)-1A. (Data primarily on first and second generation persons of Japanese and Chinese origin.)

————. General Population Characteristics. PC(1)-B Series. *U.S. Summary.* (Number of Japanese, Chinese and Pilipinos in areas of 50,000 or more.) See also reports by individual states. (Total population count for Japanese, Chinese and Pilipinos by state and county.)

————. *Detailed Characteristics.* PC(1)-D Series. *U.S. Summary.* See also reports by individual states. (Number of Japanese, Chinese, Pilipinos and Koreans by sex, age, and nativity; also, mother tongue for Japanese and Chinese.)

————. *Subject Reports: Low Income Areas.* PC(2)-9B. (Number and percent of Japanese, Chinese and Pilipinos in poverty in 50 major cities.)

————. *Subject Reports: Family Composition.* PC(2)-4A.

————. *Subject Reports: Marital Status.* PC(2)-4C.

————. *"Operation Leap" Tabulations (Unpublished).* (Special tabulations of 1970 census data generated by the U.S. Bureau of the Census for the U.S. Office of Economic Opportunity. Data for metropolitan areas in California have been run separately on Japanese, Chinese, and Pilipinos. Data on non-whites and non-Blacks in one low income neighborhood in New York City is 98% Chinese.)

————. *Reports on the 1960 Census of Population.* Washington, D.C.: U.S. Government Printing Office.

————. *Subject Reports: Nonwhite Population by Race.* PC(2)-1C. (Social and economic statistics for Japanese, Chinese and Pilipinos.)

————. *Special Report: 1972 Survey of Minority-Owned Business Enterprises: Minority-Owned Business—Asian Americans, American Indians and others.* MB 72-3. Washington, D.C.: U.S. Government Printing Office.

U.S. Dept. of Health, Education and Welfare. *A Study of Selected Socio-Economic Characteristics of Ethnic Minorities Based on the 1970 Census. Vol. IV: HEW Regional Data.* HEW Pub. No. (OS) 75-123. Washington, D.C.: U.S. Government Printing Office, 1974.

586

————. *A Study of Selected Socio-Economic Characteristics of Ethnic Minorities Based on the 1970 Census. Vol. II: Asian Americans.* HEW Pub. No. (OS)75-121. Washington, D.C.: U.S. Government Printing Office, 1974.

U.S. Equal Employment Opportunity Commission. *Equal Employment Opportunity Report, 1973: Job Patterns for Minorities and Women in Private Industry.* Vols. 1-10, January 1975. (Vol. 1 United States; Vols. 2-10 by regions.)

U.S. Library of Congress, General Reference and Bibliography Division. *Japanese in the United States: A Selected List of References.* Washington, D.C.: U.S. Government Printing Office, 1946.

U.S. National Archives. *Preliminary Inventories, No. 77: Records of War Relocation Authority.* Washington, D.C.: U.S. Government Printing Office, 1955.

U.S. War Relocation Authority. *Bibliography of Japanese in America.* 3 vols. Washington, D.C.: U.S. War Relocation Authority, 1942-43.

————. *Bibliography on War Relocation Authority: Japanese and Japanese-Americans.* Washington, D.C.: U.S. War Relocation Authority, 1945.

CONTRIBUTORS

Joan Ablon, Ph.D., is associate professor of medical anthropology in residence at the University of California Medical Center and anthropology consultant at Langley Porter Neuropsychiatric Institute, San Francisco, California. Her publications include "The Samoan Funeral in Urban America," *Ethnology*, 9:3 (July 1970).

Koji Ariyoshi was born and reared on a tenant coffee farm in Kona, Hawaii. His immigrant parents came to Hawaii as plantation contract laborers. He has been a leading labor figure in Hawaii since the 1930s. Mr. Ariyoshi was editor and publisher of the pro-labor *Honolulu Record* for ten years. He is presently an occasional lecturer at the University of Hawaii in ethnic studies, president of the US-China Peoples Friendship Association of Hawaii, member of the National Steering Committee of the US-China Peoples Friendship Association, and a frequent visitor to the People's Republic of China.

Mei Berssenbrugge was born in 1947 in Peking, China. She grew up in New England, went to Reed College and earned an M.F.A. at the Columbia University School of Fine Arts. She has two books of poetry, *Fish Souls* and *Summits Move With the Tide* (Greenfield Review Press, 1974). Her work has appeared in various magazines and anthologies. Ms. Berssenbrugge now lives in the remote town of El Rito, Rio Arriba County, Northern New Mexico.

Edna Bonacich is associate professor of sociology at the University of California, Riverside, and received her Ph.D. from Harvard. Author of articles on "split labor market" theory, she is currently working on two research projects. One is on U.S. capitalism and Asian American labor before World War II and the other, with Ivan Light and Charles Choy Wong, on recent Asian immigrants in Los Angeles, a study of Chinese, Pilipino and Korean communities.

Carlos Bulosan was born in 1913 in the Philippines and came to America when he was seventeen. He worked as a fruit picker and labor organizer, riding the rails up and down the West Coast. A consequence of his activities was confinement in Los Angeles County Hospital for two years; he left with no ribs on his right side. It was during his long stay in the hospital that Mr. Bulosan began his voracious reading and meticulous writing. Mr. Bulosan authored several collections of poetry and stories including *Letter From America* (1942) and *The Laughter of My Father* (1944). The story of his life is chronicled in *America Is In the Heart* (1946), excerpted here. It is a dazzling, passionate work—a classic. The author seems to have led a dozen lives in a story which captures the scope of struggle of the first Pilipinos in America. Mr. Bulosan died in 1956.

Emily Cachapero, born 1953 in San Francisco, graduated from San Francisco State University in 1974. "My philosophy of art is such that my art *must* be community-oriented and that the artist must constantly be in contact with people. As a Pilipino-American artist my work reflects my roots. Also, I do not feel limited to the craft of poetry and have been performing with the Bagong Diwa Dance Co., Inc. (New Soul) for two years." Her work has appeared in *American Poetry Review, Bridge* magazine, *Third World Women's Book* (Third World Communications, 1971), *Flips*, an anthology of Pilipino-American writing (1971), *Time to Greez!* (Third World Communications, 1975), and *Liwanag*, a forthcoming anthology of Pilipino writing and artwork.

May Ying Chen, born 1948 in Boston, Massachusetts, participated in teaching classes on Asian American women at UCLA. She is currently a teacher in the Los Angeles City Unified School District.

Frank Chin was born in Berkeley in 1940, grew up in Oakland, then went to the University of California and Iowa State's creative writing program. He now lives in San Francisco and is always up to something. His first play, *The Chickencoop Chinaman*, was one of the first by an Asian American to hit the stage. Since then he has written and had performed *Gee Pop* and *The Year of the Dragon*, the latter on public television. Mr. Chin co-edited *Aiiieeeee!* and *Yardbird Reader*, Vol. 3, and his novel, "Charlie Chan in Maui," is in the works. He plays a loud Spanish guitar, usually with a menacing toothpick in his mouth.

Rockwell Chin is an attorney and member of the Asian Law Collective in Los Angeles. His articles have been published in *Amerasia Journal* and *Bridge* magazine.

Judy May Chu, a graduate student in clinical psychology at the California School of Professional Psychology, is a community worker with Asian American prison groups at various institutions and a consultant at Asian Joint Communications, a therapeutic community in Los Angeles geared for Asian drug addicts. She is also active in issues involving Asian women and Asian American mental health.

Tom Engelhardt, a free-lance writer living in San Francisco, is author of *Beyond Our Control: America* *in the Mid-Seventies,* to be published in May 1976 by Riverrun Press in San Francisco.

Sui Sin Fah published stories with Asian American characters in the late nineteenth century. Many of them were published in a California magazine called *Land of Sunshine.* Her real name was Edith Eaton. Her mother was Japanese; her father was an Englishman who lived in Japan and China. Edith Eaton had a sister, Winnifred, who also wrote and published under the name Onoto Watanna. This information comes from David Lambert.

Gary R. Hess is professor of history at Bowling Green State University. He received his Ph.D. from the University of Virginia in 1965. His principal interest is in the American diplomatic experience in South and Southeast Asia. Among his many publications are *America Encounters India, 1941-1947* (Baltimore, 1972) and "The 'Hindu' in America: Immigration and Naturalization Policies and India, 1917-1946," *Pacific Historical Review,* 38 (1969). At present he is working on a study of American policy in Southeast Asia from 1940 to 1954.

Irene Hirano is currently director of T.H.E. Clinic for Women in Los Angeles and serving on the California State Commission on the Status of Women and the California State Board of Education Health Curriculum Commission. She was associate director of the Asian Women's Center in Los Angeles and the former Japanese Site Supervisor and National Assistant Coordinator for the National Asian American Field Study funded by the U.S. Department of Health, Education, and Welfare.

Ron Hirano is coordinator of UCLA Asian American Studies Center. A former board member of Visual Communications, he was previously a Ford Foundation teaching fellow at UCLA.

Lucie Cheng Hirata is associate professor of sociology and director of the Asian American Studies Center at the University of California, Los Angeles. She received her Ph.D. from the University of Hawaii in 1970. Among her publications are "Leadership in China's Minority Nationalities Autonomous Regions — Continuity and Change," *Journal of Asian Affairs,* 1 (Spr. 1976) and "Mental Illness Among the Chinese, Myth or Reality?" *Journal of Social Issues,* 3 (Summer 1975). She is currently working on a book concerning women and the socialist revolution in China and directing a research project on U.S. capitalism and Asian American labor before World War II.

Peter Y. Horikoshi was born in Cambridge, Massachusetts in 1952 because his parents moved eastward from the Heart Mountain, Wyoming concentration camp after World War II. A graduate of the University of California, Berkeley in 1973 with an individual major in Asian American studies, he is a member of San Francisco's Japanese American Anthology Committee, and Yokohama, California, a group of Asian American musicians striving to represent the community life of Asian America today.

Yuji Ichioka is currently doing primary research on the history of Japanese immigrant society in America before World War II using Japanese-language sources. He has taught at the University of California, Berkeley and Los Angeles. His two latest works, one on Japanese prostitutes in America, the other on Japanese Associations in America, will appear in the forthcoming issues of *Amerasia Journal* and *Pacific Historical Review.*

Momoko Iko lives in Chicago where she is a teacher. She graduated from the University of Illinois in 1961 and the Writer's Workshop at the University of Iowa in 1966. In 1975 she was Issei Gerontology Project Director, Japanese American Service Committee. Her plays, *Gold Watch* and *When We Were Young,* have been performed by the East-West Players, Los Angeles. She has twice won the East-West Players Playwriting Contest and in 1976 received a Rockefeller Grant for Playwriting.

Lawson Fusao Inada was born in Fresno, California in 1938 and grew up a Westside Fresno loco. He went to college there and in Berkeley, Iowa, and Oregon. He is now associate professor of English at Southern Oregon College. Mr. Inada's *Before the War* (Morrow, 1971) was the first poetry collection by an Asian American to be published by a major firm. He co-edited *Aiiieeeee!* and has appeared in lots of anthologies and literary journals, including *Three Northwest Poets, Down At the Santa Fe Depot, New Directions 21, Asian-American Authors, Speaking for Ourselves, The American Poetry Anthology, Modern Poetry of Western America,* and *At the Stronghold.* Mr. Inada finished "Pumice" on Christmas just to meet the deadline. "Damn, man, knowing Lawson is like having a subscription."

Hashiji Kakazu, an 86-year-old avocado farmer, has worked most of his life as a farmer in Hawaii. In his article "Forty-Four Years of Raising Avocados," he relates his struggles as a poor tenant farmer resisting eviction from his land.

Lonny Kaneko was born in Seattle in 1939; his pre-school years were spent in "camp." Returning to Seattle, he attended the University of Washington; currently he is instructor of writing and literature and chairman of Humanities Division, Highline Community College. His works have been published in *Puget Soundings, Playboy, Kashu Mainichi, Amerasia Journal, Kansas Quarterly,* and *Yardbird #5.* A short story "Jawbone" will appear in *Niagara.* "I write to find out where I've been, who I am, and how many ways the future may lie."

Woon-Ha Kim, born in Masan, Korea, is editor and publisher of *The New Korea* in Los Angeles. Prior to coming to the United States in 1972, he headed the first movement for freedom of the press in South Korea to protest the efforts of the Park Chung-hee government to control the press. He was acting president of the Journalist Association of Korea, and a member of the Board of Directors of the Korea Press

Center. After Park declared his presidential emergency in 1972, Kim, reporter and associate city editor of *Chosun Ilbo* (Korea Daily News) for ten years, came to Los Angeles as its special correspondent. In August 1974 he took over *The New Korea*.

H. Mark Lai, born and raised in San Francisco Chinatown, is one of the leading authorities on Chinese American history. Currently, he is president of the Chinese Historical Society of America and a director of the Chinese Cultural Foundation of San Francisco. He has taught at California State University, San Francisco and has written many articles on Chinese Americans. Among his publications are *A History of the Chinese in California: A Syllabus* and *Outlines, History of the Chinese in California*. He was chairman of the Chinese American Youth Club (Min Qing) of San Francisco in the 1950s. He works as an engineer.

Dean Lan, born 1949 in Shanghai, China, grew up in San Francisco Chinatown and is a doctoral candidate in sociology at the University of California, Davis and author of *Prestige With Limitations: Realities of the Chinese American Elite*. He is currently employed with the Office of Civil Rights, State Department of Health in Sacramento.

Ivan Light is associate professor in sociology at UCLA. He received his Ph.D. from the University of California, Berkeley and is author of *Ethnic Enterprise in America* and several articles on Chinatown in the U.S.

John Liu, a Ford Foundation teaching fellow for two years, is presently working for his doctoral degree in sociology at UCLA. His current interest is to develop a theoretical approach to inter-racial relations in the U.S. He is a resource person in ethnic studies for the Los Angeles School District.

Wing Tek Lum was born in 1946. He studied at Brown University and Union Theological Seminary. He is presently teaching in Hong Kong. Mr. Lum's poems have appeared in *East West, New York Quarterly, PEN, Amerasia Journal*, and other publications.

Kingsley K. Lyu (1904-1976) was the bilingual editor of the *Korean Pacific Weekly* in Honolulu from February 1944 to January 1946. Active in the Korean independence movement in America, he served as treasurer of the Korean government delegation to the first United Nations Conference in San Francisco. Lyu studied at Syracuse University (B.A., M.A.), Duke University, University of Hawaii, and University of Washington. For a number of years he worked for the Library of Congress.

Sandy Maeshiro, born January 7, 1949, Honolulu, Hawaii, works for the Los Angeles City Unified School District as a substitute day care teacher and is active in United Teachers, Los Angeles.

H. Brett Melendy is professor of history at the University of Hawaii. He received his Ph.D. from Stanford University. He has written several articles

dealing with California politics and two articles on Pilipino immigration. Co-author of *The Governors of California* and author of *The Oriental Americans*, his current research interests continue to be Asian immigration to the United States. He has in press a new book on Pilipinos, Koreans, and East Indians in America.

Janice Mirikitani, born in Stockton, raised in a concentration camp, and a graduate of UCLA, writes and works among Third World street people in San Francisco. Her writing has appeared in several anthologies, including *Aion* and *Third World Women*. She co-edited *Time to Greez!*

Toshio Mori, born in 1910 in Oakland, California, is the first Japanese-American writer to publish a book of short stories, *Yokohama, California* in 1949. *Yokohama, California* (Caxton Printers) is a collection of stories written about the pre-World War II San Leandro, California community. His work has appeared in such periodicals as *Pacific Citizen, Common Ground, The Coast, Writer's Forum, Current Life, Clipper, Matrix* and in such anthologies as *New Directions, Best American Short Stories of 1943, Aiiieeeee!, Asian-American Heritage*, and *Asian-American Authors*.

Alan T. Moriyama, born in Honolulu, is currently studying at Tokyo University on a fellowship from the Japanese Ministry of Education. A graduate student specializing in Japanese American history at UCLA, he has taught Asian American studies classes there. He graduated from the University of Chicago and took an M.A. from the University of Michigan.

Don Nakanishi, born August 14, 1949, Los Angeles, California, is acting assistant professor of political science at UCLA. A co-founder of *Amerasia Journal* in 1971, he will receive his Ph.D. from Harvard University in 1976.

Brett de Bary Nee, born in Brooklyn, New York, received her Ph.D. in Japanese literature from Harvard University and also studied in Peking, China. She has co-authored with her husband, Victor, the influential book on San Francisco's Chinatown, *Longtime Californ'* (Pantheon Books, 1972). She will be teaching Japanese literature at Cornell University in the 1976-1977 academic year.

Victor Nee, born 1945 in Foochow, China, received his Ph.D. in sociology from Harvard University and has written *Longtime Californ'* with his wife, Brett. His other publications include *The Cultural Revolution at Peking University* (Monthly Review Press, 1969) and *Uninterrupted Revolution* (Pantheon Books, 1976), co-edited with James Peck.

John Okada was born in 1923 in Seattle. He attended the University of Washington and Columbia University where he received a master's degree in English. Mr. Okada served in the U.S. Air Force during World War II, published *No-No Boy* in 1957, and died in literary obscurity in 1971. *No-No Boy* is now being reissued by the Combined Asian American

Resources Project. For more information, write CARP Publishing Co., P. O. Box 3828, Rincon Annex, San Francisco, California 94119.

Raymond Okamura, former prisoner, Gila River, Arizona Concentration Camp, 1942-1945.

Irvin Paik has been in the motion picture and television industry for over ten years as a film editor, cameraman, actor, props and sound, and production manager with Warner Brothers, Universal, and Paramount. A member of the Board of Directors of East-West Players, he has written television scripts and articles on the Asian American experience.

Oscar Peñaranda was born in 1944, in Barugo, Leyte, the Philippines. "Went to Canada, September, 1956; came to San Francisco, August, 1961." His work has been anthologized in *Asian-American Authors, Aiiieeeee!, Time to Greez!* and others.

Alfred Robles was born in San Francisco. His work has appeared in *Time to Greez!, San Francisco City Magazine, Bridge* magazine, and *Literary Arts of Japan, 1 & 2,* 1966-1969. "Presently I am working on 'Oral History: Documentation of Manongs in America,' connected with Asian American Writers Workshop, San Francisco."

E. San Juan, Jr., born December 29, 1938 in Manila, the Philippines, studied at the University of the Philippines (A.B., magna cum laude) and Harvard University (M.A. & Ph.D.). Author of *Carlos Bulosan and the Imagination of the Class Struggle, The Radical Tradition in Philippine Literature,* and volumes of poetry in English and in Pilipino, he is currently completing a book on Amado V. Hernandez and the struggle for national democracy in the Philippines.

Bienvenido N. Santos is distinguished writer-in-residence at Wichita State University. He will not go back to the Philippines, his homeland, until — or unless — the repressive martial regime there comes to an end. In the Pilipino portion of his life, Ben Santos rose from high school teacher to college president; in the United States he has been a Philippine Embassy official, Rockefeller fellow, and Guggenheim fellow, and finally a teacher of creative writing. Currently, Santos is at work on his fifth novel tentatively entitled "What the Hell for Did You Leave Your Heart in San Francisco?" Like his other novels and collections of short stories, it is inhabited by Pilipino-Americans seeking to find their identity in their new land. Among his books are: *The Wounded Stag* (poems), *You Lovely People* (stories), *Brother My Brother* (stories), *The Day the Dancers Came* (prose works), *Villa Magdalena* (novel); and *The Volcano* (novel).

Alexander Saxton is professor of history at the University of California, Los Angeles. Previously a seaman, construction worker, and novelist, his experience in organized labor enhances his lucid writings on American labor history and racial minorities. He is currently chairperson of the Faculty Advisory Committee of the UCLA Asian American Studies Center.

Linda Shin is associate professor of Chinese history at California State College, Dominguez Hills. She previously taught Chinese history and ethnic studies courses at California State University, Fullerton and University of California, Los Angeles. She has written on Koreans in America, Wu T'ing-fang, and is currently researching social issues involving women and children in modern Chinese history.

Jerry Surh is currently completing a Ph.D. degree in history at the University of California, Berkeley. He has taught Asian American studies at the University of California, Berkeley and Santa Cruz.

Luis Syquia was born in San Francisco in 1949. He co-edited *Time to Greez!* and has been published in various anthologies. He is co-editor of the forthcoming anthology, *Liwanag*.

Serafin Malay Syquia, born January 3, 1943 in Manila, Philippines, came to America in 1948. He received a B.A. in 1967 and posthumously an M.A. in English in 1973 from San Francisco State. Serf, as he was called by his friends, was a working poet. During the summer months from 1963-1973, he worked in the salmon canneries of Alaska. His poems have appeared in many anthologies including *Time to Greez!* and *Liwanag*, a forthcoming anthology dedicated to him. Editor of *Flips*, the first anthology of Pilipino poets, he also co-authored the introduction to Pilipino-American literature in *Aiiieeeee!* At the age of thirty, he died of a brain tumor on June 7, 1973 in San Francisco.

Sam Tagatac was born in 1939 in the Philippines. Besides being a poet and short story writer, he is a filmmaker active in the Pilipino community. His work has appeared in numerous anthologies, including *Asian-American Authors, Aiiieeeee!,* and *Time to Greez!* He now lives in Santa Barbara.

Ronald Tanaka, born 1944 in Poston, Arizona, attended the University of California, Berkeley where he took a doctorate in 17th century British literature and literary theory in 1971. Currently teaching literary theory and Japanese American literature at California State University, Sacramento, he has published several papers on literary theory and has written essays, poems and stories dealing with Japanese Americans. For him, "the primary purpose of writing poetry is so that the poet can learn how to die."

Laura Tokunaga was born in Hawaii in 1950 and was raised in Los Angeles. She majored in pharmacology at the University of Hawaii, supporting herself while in school by volunteering as a subject for pharmacological studies. After traveling extensively in South America, she settled in L.A. and worked as a topless shoeshine girl while maintaining interests in music appreciation, doppelgangers and weight control. She is currently engaged in building popular support for a future presidential candidacy.

592

Le Anh Tu, a Thai-born Vietnamese woman, is currently a researcher at NARMIC (National Action/ Research on the Military Industrial Complex), a project of the American Friends Service Committee, and co-author of *Aid to Thieu* and *The Third Force in South Vietnam*. She has written extensively on various aspects on U.S. involvement in the Vietnam War.

L. Ling-chi Wang, lecturer in Asian Studies at the University of California, Berkeley, has been a longtime proponent of bilingual education and other community interests. A consultant on bilingual education to the U.S. Secretary of Health, Education, and Welfare, he serves in an advisory capacity on several national projects on research and evaluation of bilingual education. He was active in initiating the U.S. Supreme Court case of *Lau v. Nichols*. A linguist in a dozen languages, Wang has published articles on bilingual education and on Chinese Americans in various publications. He is currently president of the Chinese American Democratic Club, and a founder and a director of Chinese for Affirmative Action.

Linda Wing, born 1947 in Berkeley, California, is director of Asian American Bilingual Center, National Network of Bilingual Education Centers in Berkeley. After a community group of Asian American parents, students, and teachers applied pressure on the Berkeley Board of Education to establish Asian American studies in the public schools, she was hired to teach at Berkeley high school. From 1974-1975, she was coordinator of Asian American studies, Berkeley Unified School District.

Buck Wong, a second generation Chinese American, is currently a teacher of Asian American history classes at East Los Angeles College and a former research associate at UCLA's Asian American Studies Center. He is an associate editor of *Roots: An Asian American Reader,* published by UCLA Asian American Studies Center.

Charles Choy Wong is a graduate student in sociology at UCLA. He has authored a number of articles on Chinese Americans.

Shawn Hsu Wong was born in Oakland, California in 1949. He is co-editor of *Aiiieeeee!* and *Yardbird Reader,* Vol. 3. Presently, he is teaching in the Asian American Studies Department and Creative Writing Department at San Francisco State University and the Ethnic Studies Department at Mills College. Shawn Wong has just completed a novel and is waiting for a publisher to come and get it. He is currently at work co-editing a sequel to *Aiiieeeee!* of Asian American poetry and building a hot rod to cruise in.

Hisaye Yamamoto was born in 1921 in Redondo Beach, California. She studied English, Spanish, French, German and Latin at Compton Junior College, and Japanese at Japanese-language schools. Ms. Yamamoto won a John Hay Whitney Foundation Opportunity Fellowship for creative writing, 1950-1951. Her short stories have been published in *Partisan Review, Kenyon Review, Harper's Bazaar, Carleton Miscellany, Furioso, Arizona Quarterly,* and reprinted in various anthologies in recent years. She has had yearly contributions of either essays or poems to the *Rafu Shimpo* for the last 25 years. "Evacuated" from Oceanside to Poston, she was "relocated" to Springfield, Massachusetts. Later she worked for the *Los Angeles Tribune*, a black weekly, 1945-48. She is married to Anthony DeSoto and has five children and two grandchildren.

Wakako Yamauchi was born in 1924 in Westmorland, California. Her work has appeared in *Aiiieeeee! Yardbird Reader,* Vol. 3, *Amerasia Journal,* and *Rafu Shimpo*. She is currently occupied with writing a play. "Future projects: I'm looking, I'm looking. Philosophy: Hang loose."

R. Takashi Yanagida born 1948 in New York City, is a member of Asian Americans for Equal Employment. He was director of the Basement Workshop in New York's Chinatown and a leader in the minority workers' struggle at Confucius Plaza.

Carolyn Yee, a graduate of Boalt Hall law school, University of California, Berkeley, is co-editor of *Amerasia Journal* and coordinator of resource development and publications at UCLA Asian American Studies Center.

PHOTOGRAPHERS

Yumi Oshima Chuman
Ed Ikuta
Glen Iwasaki
Alan Kondo
H. Mark Lai
Steven Mori
Bob Nakamura
Roy Nakano
Alan Ohashi
Eddie Wong

ILLUSTRATORS

Karen Akamine
Ron Battle
Kevin Burton
Faustino Caigoy
Betty Chen
Anthony Cox
Glen Iwasaki
Stuart Iwasaki
Tony Lee
Roseanne Litzinger
Ken Minamiji
David Kiyoshi Monkawa
Mine Okubo
Suzanne Partridge
Alan Takemoto
Dean Toji
Qris Yamashita

SPECIAL THANKS

Asian American Resource Center
Ben Befu
Bridge
Aurelio Bulosan
California State Library, Sacramento
Judy Chu
Sue Embrey
Gordon Gilliam
Constance Hayashi
Chris Kim
Woon-Ha Kim
Young Ha Kim
Dennis Kuba
Li Min Cultural Center
Library of Congress
Che-hwei Lin
Gail Miyasaki
Royal Morales
Toshio Mori
Claudia Morimoto
Gail Nakatsu
The New Korea
Henry Ng
Office for Asian American Affairs, DHEW
Alan Ohashi
Carol Hatanaka Ono
Tom Ono

Janice Osumi
Candice Ota
Larry Potasi
P. C. Ramamorthy
Al Santos
Frank Shimazu
Janice Spencer
Jerry Surh
Tom Surh
Janice Tanaka
Chad Taniguchi
Steve Tatsukawa
Jamie Totsubo
Ann Umemoto
University of California, Berkeley
    Bancroft Library,
University of California, Los Angeles
    Publication Services
    University Research Library
        Oriental Library
        Special Collections
University of California Press
University of Washington Library
Dan Watanabe
Eddie Wong
Qris Yamashita
Sun Bin Yim
Danny Yung

STAFF

Emma Gee, editor, previously taught in the Asian Studies division at the University of California, Berkeley.

Bruce Iwasaki, who edited the Literature section, was born in Los Angeles in 1951, grew up on the Westside, and has not strayed. He graduated from UCLA in psychology and English in 1972, and then, ironically, the UCLA School of Law in 1976. This latter experience wrecked his ear for language; he's through with literature. Iwasaki has worked on *Gidra*, does work with the Asian Law Collective, and will teach occasional Asian American studies classes somewhere.

Glen Iwasaki, art director, is a free-lance illustrator/designer living and working in the Los Angeles area.

June Okida Kuramoto, assistant editor, is a classical kotoist and a member of the Asian American band, Hiroshima.

Mike Murase, associate editor, is a member of the Asian Law Collective of Los Angeles. A founding staff member of *Gidra*, an Asian American community newspaper published in Los Angeles from 1969-1974, he has taught Asian American studies at the University of Southern California and California State University, Long Beach.

Megumi Dick Osumi, who edited the Land, Labor, and Capital section, is co-editor of *Amerasia Journal*. A doctoral candidate in English, he is a 1976 graduate of UCLA law school. He has participated in the Joint Counseling Center in Little Tokyo, Los Angeles.

Jesse Quinsaat, associate editor, is a third-year law student at UCLA and editor of *Letters in Exile: An Introductory Reader on the History of Pilipinos in America* (Los Angeles: UCLA Asian American Studies Center, 1976).

Dean Seiki Toji, art director, was born in 1950 in Los Angeles. An artist and writer, he studied painting at Chouinard/Cal Arts, worked on *Gidra*, attended Columbia University Graduate School of Journalism, and worked in News and Public Affairs in Public Television.